Fodor's New South America

REVISED EDITION

D1240080

Fodor's Travel Publications, Inc.
New York • Toronto • London • Sydney • Auckland

Fodor's South America

Editors: Paula Rackow, Scott McNeely, Elaine Robbins
Editorial Contributors: Michael Adams, Robert Blake, Hannah Borgeson, David Brown, Karen Cure, Philip Eade, Andrea Fernandez Giardino, Catherine Healy, Carla Hunt, Richard Jarvie, Kurt Kutay, Nicolás Lynch, Sarah Lythe, Julia Michaels, Jane Onstott, Mariana Paiva Leite, Parker Pascua, Chris Philipsborn, Marcy Pritchard, Tom Quinn, Lake Sagaris, Corinne Schmidt-Lynch, Ed Shaw, George Soules, Edwin Taylor
Researcher: Mary Ellen Schultz
Creative Director: Fabrizio LaRocca
Cartographers: David Lindroth; Eureka Cartography
Illustrator: Karl Tanner
Cover Photograph: Gunter Ziesler/Peter Arnold

Design: Vignelli Associates

Special Sales

Fodor's Travel Publications are available at special discounts for bulk purchases for sales promotions or premiums. Special editions, including personalized covers, excerpts of existing guides, and corporate imprints, can be created in large quantities for special needs. For more information, contact your local bookseller or write to Special Markets, Fodor's Travel Publications, 201 E. 50th Street, New York, NY 10022. Inquiries from Canada should be directed to your local Canadian bookseller or sent to Random House of Canada, Ltd., Marketing Dept., 1265 Aerowood Drive, Mississauga, Ontario L4W 1B9. Inquiries from the United Kingdom should be sent to Fodor's Travel Publications, 20 Vauxhall Bridge Road, London, England SW1V 2SA.

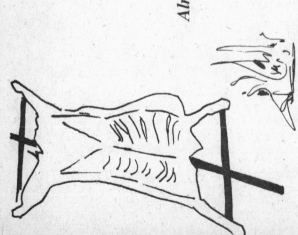

Contents

Maps

Contents

Foreword

We wish to express our gratitude to those who helped in the preparation of this guide:

Argentina: Francisco López Bustos; Ema Jatib; Miguel Angel Miranda of Nievemar Tours in Patagonia; and Samantha Warwick. **Bolivia:** the Bolivian Consulate in New York; Lloyd Aero Boliviano (LAB); Montaña Tours; and Mark Mooradian. **Brazil:** Maureen Callanan and the staff of Varig Brazilian Airlines; J. R. Francé; Sonia Maria M. Baraúna; Ray Noble and the staff of Avis Rent A Car; Carol Poister of the Leading Hotels of the World; Sidney Alonso; Helena Da Silva of Detur in Brasília; Susie Padovano; Deborah Gentio; the staffs of Bahiatursa, Portur, Tur Minas, Secretaria de Esportes e Turismo do Estado de São Paulo, and Anhembi Turismo e Eventos da Cidade de São Paulo; Tatu Tours in Salvador; and Felipe Chabert. **Chile:** Rodolfo González; Patricio Lanfranco; the staff of Hostería Pehoe in Torres del Paine National Park; and Carlos Vega, Elsa Barría, Expediciones Arka, and Andes Patagonico in Punta Arenas. **Colombia:** Avianca; Colombian Government Tourist Office; David and Greg Hélpor; Juan Gelbréro; and the BBC World Service. **Ecuador:** the Ecuador Tourism Office; La Selva Tours; Wildland Adventures. **Paraguay:** the staff of the Paraguayan Tourist Board in Asunción. **Peru:** Ana María Arrarte de Aliaga of Lima Tours; Pablo López de Romaña of the Peruvian Ministry of Industry and Tourism; Joy Koechlin of Cámara Nacional de Turismo; Adriana von Hagen; Peter Jensen; Charlie Munn; Janet Trabajal in Puno; Carmen Melly in Trujillo; Cecilia Kamiche in Chiclayo; Eduardo Ronalds in Ica; Carlos Mila and Marco Ugarte in Cuzco; and José Pardo Mesones of Faucett Airlines. **Venezuela:** José Donoso Davila of Cormetur; the Mérida National Tourist Office; the Corporación de Turismo de Venezuela; CORPTUR Mérida; Montaña Tours, especially Jerome Keeton, Scott Swanson, and Janet Thomas; Alpi Tour; VIASA; and Claire DiBoff and the Venezuelan Consulate General in New York.

While every care has been taken to ensure the accuracy of the information in this guide, the passage of time will always bring change, and consequently the publisher cannot accept responsibility for errors that may occur.

All prices and opening times quoted here are based on information supplied to us at press time. Hours and admission fees may change, however, and the prudent traveler will avoid inconvenience by calling ahead.

Fodor's wants to hear about your travel experiences, both pleasant and unpleasant. When a hotel or restaurant fails to live up to its billing, let us know and we will investigate the complaint and revise our entries where the facts warrant it.

Send your letters to the editors of Fodor's Travel Publications, 201 E. 50th Street, New York, NY 10022.

Highlights and Fodor's Choice

Highlights

Argentina Argentina is a country in transition. Nineteen ninety-four is a crucial year in that many of the changes will be felt for the first time, even by tourists. The population of Argentina is adjusting to the long-forgotten demands of economic and financial stability. President Carlos Menem's massive privatization program has included selling off the airlines and the railways. Aerolineas Argentinas and Austral airlines have been bought by an international consortium led by Iberia, the Spanish national airline. By late 1993, this arrangement has done little to improve service, and the cost of local flights is the world's highest. The railways, which operated at a $1 million a day loss to the government, have been privatized, and long-distance passenger service has been discontinued. Hopefully, service to Bariloche, Córdoba and Posadas, the nearest city to Iguazú Falls, will resume in 1994.

The state telephone, electric, gas, and water monopolies have all to a large degree been privatized as well, and the new owners have energetically ripped up streets and sidewalks all over Buenos Aires to install new lines and pipes. This temporary inconvenience should provide better phone service and ensure the continuity of other utilities, which had begun to deteriorate to a disturbing degree. Periodic power cuts and occasional gas and water shortages frayed tempers on blistering summer or freezing winter days. The perils of post-privatization, until the process is able to revert half a century of state negligence, will be part of life in Argentina in 1994.

Bolivia Despite its relatively strong economy and stable political climate, Bolivia continues to suffer from underexposure. Tourism remains a weak sector of the economy, and plans to build two four-star, internationally financed hotels in La Paz have been postponed indefinitely. Despite such setbacks, the Hotel La Paz (formerly a Sheraton property) is scheduled to reopen late in 1994 once renovations are completed.

Beyond the annual celebration of Carnaval and Gran Poder—the former around Ash Wednesday, the latter in late May—La Paz's cultural calendar remains uncluttered. Nonetheless, if and when Bolivia's soccer team qualifies for the 1994 World Cup, to be held in stadiums across the United States, you can bet that La Paz will host spontaneous celebrations of every sort—from raucous street parties to government-sponsored festivities. (According to sport analysts around the globe, Bolivia will almost certainly qualify.)

Brazil Brazilian travel authorities are hoping that 1994 will mark the beginning of the nation's comeback as an international destination. Tourism has been hurt in recent years by the country's increasingly negative image, particularly due to a rise in urban crime, especially in Rio de Janeiro.

In a drive to reverse that image, the city is establishing the **Rio de Janeiro Tourist Police,** who will begin patroling the beach areas and assisting foreign tourists in summer 1994. Similar initiatives in the past proved unsuccessful because the police did not speak any foreign languages.

For Brazil, 1994 promises to be a critical year as the country struggles to emerge from a decade of economic decline and political turmoil. Since 1980, Brazil has experienced a combination of runaway inflation (the highest rate in the Americas, topping 1,700% in 1993), sluggish to stagnant economic growth, and intermittent political crises, culminating in the 1992 impeachment of President Fernando Collor de Mello.

In October 1993, the Brazilian congress was scheduled to undertake a review of the 1987 constitution. This review could produce some changes in the constitution that would give freer reign to the federal government to clean up its finances and bring down inflation. If this happens, early 1994 may see new economic measures to stabilize the economy, such as a wage and price freeze. President Itamar Franco will be pressed to produce impressive results in this area, with an eye toward his own interest in the **elections** scheduled for November 1994.

Partly with the elections in mind, Bahia governor Antônio Carlos Magalhães last year completed the **renovation** of **Salvador's Castro Alves theater,** the **convention center,** and many museums, plus the restoration of the city's historic **Pelourinho district** and the building of new quarters for the handicrafts kiosks at the Lagôa de Abaeté. The Pelourinho restoration was expected to spur the opening of a spate of new restaurants and night spots in the area, beginning in late 1993 and continuing into 1994. In the same district, the brothers of the **Carmo monastery** hoped at press time to close a deal with local hoteliers to reopen their unusual inn, thereby preserving the building.

The Bahia state government at press time was also building a paved coastal road north from Praia do Forte to the village of Itanhi at the border with the state of Sergipe. Set for completion in late 1993 or early 1994, the **Linha Verde,** or Green Line, will include paved access roads to many pristine beaches along the way, plus a cobblestone access route to Praia do Forte, formerly reached by a short stretch of dirt road.

In 1994, the **São Paulo** municipal tourism board plans new investments in cultural events and holiday celebrations, parks and ecological preserves, maps, calendars and guides, and publicity. The city also intends to finish painting the bridges crossing the Tietê and Pinheiros beltways and rivers in a rainbow of colors in 1994, and may widen the Fernão Dias, Dutra, and Imigrantes highways.

Brazil lags far behind other South American countries in the regional trend toward **privatization** of public services, but this process could speed up in 1994, making more modern technology available to residents and visitors alike. At press time plans were afoot to privatize the municipal **CMTC bus system** in 1994 and replace the city's 23,000 fare collectors (*cobradores*) with an electronic ticket system.

Chile Chile is continuing a major campaign to increase tourism from abroad, with special projects for providing more information to foreign tourists. The number of hotel rooms and restaurants in Santiago and other important resort areas continues to grow. A special program for small and medium-size tourist companies will provide financing to enable them to upgrade their services. Major public works spending will turn most of the Pan-American Highway, which runs through Chile from north to south as far as Puerto Montt, into a divided roadway.

The Santiago airport's new international terminal is expected to greatly simplify flying to and from Santiago. The new four-story building adds additional gates and more parking, as well as restaurants, stores, and an observation terrace. The old terminal building will be used exclusively for national flights. The airport will eventually be expanded to include five interconnected buildings capable of receiving 9 million passengers a year.

Pollution continues to be a problem, although some towns are attempting to clean up their act. Generally speaking, the more quiet and isolated a place is, the cleaner the beaches and the more suitable the ocean or lakes are for bathing.

Chilean authorities and entrepreneurs will be working hard to open the more isolated areas south of Puerto Montt, along the Austral Highway. The spectacular stands of the world's oldest trees, Chilean Alerces, hot springs, narrow fjords, and majestic volcanoes have remained untouched over time, because the region in which they are located is virtually inaccessible.

Tours to Antarctica, which often depart from the world's southernmost city, Punta Arenas, continue to be controversial. With the advent of the Canadian Blyth & Company (Canada), cruise prices have dropped by as much as half.

Colombia Each year, Holy Week celebrations bring thousands of visitors to Popayán and Mompós to witness costumed penitents parade through the streets by candlelight. In 1994, Colombia will also host an **Arts Week,** with displays of contemporary national and international work in galleries throughout Bogotá. Scheduled for December, the week-long event will then travel in January, 1995, to the Caribbean Coast town of Cartagena. Also in early 1995, Bogotá's Museo de Arte Colonial plans to sponsor a special exhibit of colonial metalwork and religious engravings; already, the exhibit is being hyped as the largest of its kind ever to be mounted.

Colombia's adventure-tourism industry has suffered from the country's recent political upheavals, and tour operatrors are only slowly beginning to resume treks in the Andean highlands and western coastal areas. Still, operators based in Cartagena and Santa Marta, both on the Caribbean Coast, have expanded service to a variety of sites, including the impressive La Cuidad Perdida, the "Lost City" discovered in 1975 by hapless treasure hunters.

Ecuador The **Banco Centro del Ecuador** (Central Bank of Ecuador), which provides funding for archaeological digs and research throughout the country, is renovating its archaeology museums in Quito and Cuenca. Both are scheduled to reopen in late 1994.

Idaho-based **River Odysseys West** (Box 579, Coeur D'Alene 83814, tel. 208/765–0841 or 800/451–6034) is beginning to organize white- water rafting trips throughout Ecuador. The operation should be in full swing early in 1994. **Tuntiak Expeditions** (+ +tel+ +), based in Cuenca, plans to offer a shamanism tour to learn traditional healing methods of *curranderos* (medicine men).

Paraguay **Ansunción's** municipal government is renovating the former mid- 19th-century government building known as the **Casa Viola.** Slated to open in in late 1993 or early 1994, the building will house galleries for art exhibitions, both permanent and temporary, and auditoriums for lectures, readings, and concerts.

After having been closed for a complete renovation, the 136-room **Hotel Casino Casino Itá Enramada** should be operational by January 1994. Set amid 180 acres of landscaped gardens and park, this resort and conference center, on the banks of the Paraguay River 7 kilometers southeast of Asuncion, promises jet-skiing, water-skiing, and fishing.

The locks on the **Yacyretá hydroelectric dam** on the Paraná River are due to be closed in early 1994, flooding an area of 4 million acres, including the older part of the colonial city of **Encarnación.** Local wildlife organizations will launch an operation to rescue animals threatened by the flooding. A public highway linking Paraguay with Argentina is planned to run across the top of the 54-mile-long dam.

Peru The future is still somewhat uncertain for Peru, but 1994 will probably see an improvement in **security** for both Peruvians and foreign visitors. One armed underground organization known as the **MRTA** is likely to disappear completely as hundreds of guerrillas receive amnesty and turn in their weapons while their leaders face long prison terms. The more frightening and violent subversive group, the **Shining Path,** continues to suffer blows by government security forces. But despite its struggle to reconstruct its command structure, devastated by the capture of its top leaders in 1992 and 1993, the Shining Path is unlikely to disappear entirely, and in some parts of the jungle and highlands is expected to wreak periodic destruction in an effort to show the world that it is still a force to be reckoned with. Areas listed in this guide as safe for travelers are likely to remain so, while many listed as dangerous may improve. **Ayacucho,** the cradle of the Shining Path, is now largely pacified, and both Peruvian and foreign tourists are beginning to return to this colonial city, site of a famous market and religious processions. Still, the tourism industry there remains in shambles, and because the Shining Path may at any time try to recover a toehold there, it would be unadvisable to visit Ayacucho until at least 1995.

On the economic front, through 1994 and 1995, Peru will continue going through radical changes as it tries to institute a free market economy. Among the most significant of these changes will be the **privatization** of every state-owned company. In 1993 the government sold the national airline, **AeroPerú,** to **Aeroméxico.** Other tourism-related sales will include the state's hotel chain, **Enturperu,** which runs the Hoteles de Turistas in many cities; the railroad company, **ENAFER;** and the service concessions at the nation's airports.

In 1993 Peru experienced an airline boom. Four **new domestic airlines** serving major Peruvian cities and destinations moved into the commercial market with regularly scheduled flights: **Aero Continente, Aero Tumi, Expreso Aereo,** and **Imperial Air.** Meanwhile, with the recent sale of **AeroPerú,** the airline's service and puntuality initially declined, but promised improvement in the medium term. Peru's oldest airline, **Faucett,** expanded its routes and improved its on-time record, while the youngest of the established airlines, **Americana,** offered excellent service and punctuality in an effort to withstand the increased competition. Americana, which flies domestic routes only, is planning to go international. All these changes ensure an unsettled future for the Peruvian airline industry. While the continued predominance of Faucett and of AeroPerú is not in doubt, the other domestic airlines, especially the latest entrants, face a Darwinian struggle to survive the coming year. It is highly unlikely that Peru can support seven national airlines, so look for some to fold. Watch out for their evolving safety records as well, since the new ones were at press time too fresh to judge. One plus for visitors during the airline battle will probably be reduced fares.

As Peru continues normalizing its relations with the multilateral banks and lending institutions, money is being invested in **infrastructure improvement and development.** The government is working hard to improve the country's major highway, the Pan- American Highway, and even minor roads are being repaired. These changes will make overland travel more comfortable, but highway bandits will remain a problem, since the government has moved very slowly on reforming the national police force.

As tourism springs back to life throughout Peru, wholesale operators are offering more group tours, and individual travelers are flocking back as well. The revival of tourism may well mean **increased prices,** however, as the opportunities to bargain down the rates of hotels, tour operators, private guides, and other services shrink. At the same time, the dollar is likely to be worth more as the government continues to slowly allow the sol to devalue.

The **jungle** is the hot destination in Peru, especially Iquitos, which now has direct air service from Miami. But Madre de Dios will no doubt be competing seriously for its share of international tourists, playing a better chance to see wild animals as its trump card.

Visitors to the **Brüning Museum** in **Lambayeque** expecting to see the Moche treasures of the royal tombs of Sipán, a find that has been compared to that of the tomb of Egyptian King Tutankhamen, will be disappointed; 200 of the choicest objects will be on tour in the United States until the fall 1995. While the artifacts are on the road, the Brüning will undergo major renovations and will build a new wing to house the Sipán collection.

Uruguay Uruguay will soon have its first—and only—internationally recognized five-star hotels, the renovated **Victoria Plaza** in Montevideo and the brand-new **Conrad in Punta** del Este.

Venezuela Nineteen ninety-three was a turbulent year for Venezuela. Two coup attempts in 1992 and persistent rumors of a another coup in 1993 have left many Venezuelans feeling uneasy about their country's political and economic future. However, following early elections, the government once again enjoys wide-spread support. Partly as a result, tourism figures are up, particularly for Caracas and Margarita Island.

On the cultural front, Caracas is preparing for its biannual **International Theater Festival,** to be held in April 1994 at the Teatro Ateneo. The festival features work by up-and-coming South American playwrights in addition to performances by European and North American troupes. In May of 1994, Caracas will host its annual **Jazz Festival** in venues throughout the city.

Fodor's Choice

No two people will agree on what makes a perfect vacation, but it can be fun and helpful to know what others think. We hope you'll have a chance to experience some of Fodor's Choices yourself while visiting South America. For detailed information on individual entries, see the relevant sections of this guidebook.

Eating

Argentina Mixed grill of blood sausage, short ribs, and internal and external organs at an *asado*, a barbecue

A tender, three-inch steak grilled over charcoals at a *parilla*, or barbecue restaurant, Buenos Aires

Dulce de leche, a thick, caramel-color cream of boiled-down milk with sugar and vanilla, used as a topping or filling

Milanesa, breaded meat or chicken cutlet *Empanadas*, savories of pastry filled with chese, corn, or meat

Bolivia *Timpu*, an Andean lamb stew

Salteña, sweet pastry filled with eggs, olives, and chopped meat

Chicha, a drink made from corn mash that's chewed, spat out, and left to ferment

Brazil *Feijoada*, the national dish of stewed pork parts served over white rice, with collard greens, orange slices, and fried manioc on the side

Frango ao molho pardo, broiled chicken served in a sauce of its own blood, from Minas Gerais

Romeu e Julieta, a slice of fresh Minas cheese spread with guava jelly

Caipirinha, a drink made with *cachaça* (sugarcane liquor), limes, and sugar

Bahian specialities such as *muqueca* (seafood catch of the day cooked in a clay pot with coconut milk, lemon, palm oil, dried shrimp, chile, tomato, and spices) and *acarajá* (a spicy deep- fried bean cake filled with crunchy dried shrimp, red pepper, and vinaigrette sauce), accompanied by chilled, refreshing *agua de côco* (coconut milk)

Chile *Humitas*, ground corn seasoned and steamed in its own husk

Vaina, sweet sherry whipped with egg white and topped with a dash of cinnamon

Gazuela, a hearty vegetable soup with a piece of meat or poultry

Mariscal (raw shellfish soup) and *machas* (razor clams) *a la parmesana* at the Angelmó Market, on the coastal road near Puerto Montt

Colombia *Sancocho de sábalo,* grilled fish with coconut milk, potatoes, plantains, and yuca, a Caribbean coast specialty

Ajiaco, a Bogotá stew made from three types of potato, chicken, corn, fresh cream, and avocado

Ecuador *Humitas,* corn tamale taken with black coffee

Llapingachos, mashed cheese and potato pancakes, from the Andes

Paraguay Smoked *suribí,* a fish resembling a catfish, and grilled *dorado,* a salmon-like fish

Peru *Cebiche,* usually raw sea bass or flounder marinated in lime juice, chile, and garlic

Pisco sour, made of lemon, egg white, sugar, crushed ice, and a liquor similar to taquila

Grilled *paiche* and other Amazon River fish, served with *chonta,* a spaghetti-shape vegetable from the treetops

Venezuala *Hallaca,* a Christmas specialty made of chicken, corn, olives, and pork wrapped in banana leaves

Lodging

Argentina Alvear Palace Hotel, Buenos Aires (*Very Expensive*)

Hotel Internacional Cataratas, Iguazú National Park (*Expensive*)

Bolivia Hotel Portales, Cochabamba (*Very Expensive*)

Residential Rosario, La Paz (*Inexpensive*)

Hotel las Balsas, Puerto Perez (*Expensive*)

Hotel Real Audiencia, Sucre (*Expensive*)

Brazil
Amazon Ariaú Jungle Tower, outside Manaus (*Very Expensive*)

Tropical, Manaus (*Very Expensive*)

Bahia Praia do Forte Resort, Praia do Forte (*Very Expensive*)

Quinta Pitanga, Itaparica (*Very Expensive*)

Mucugê Hotel Village, Arraial d'Ajuda (*Moderate*)

Taperapuan Praia Hotel, Porto Seguro (*Moderate*)

Minas Gerais Pousada do Mondego, Ouro Preto (*Very Expensive*)

Solar da Ponte, Tiradentes (*Expensive*)

Rio de Janeiro Caesar Park (*Very Expensive*)

Inter-Continental Rio (*Very Expensive*)

Sheraton Rio Hotel & Towers (*Very Expensive*)

Everest Rio (*Expensive*)

Ouro Verde (*Moderate*)

São PauloCaesar Park (*Very Expensive*)

Grande Hotel Ca D'Oro (*Expensive*)

Chile Cabins, Cascada de Las Animas, Maipo Canyon (*Inexpensive*)

Plaza San Francisco Kempinski, Santiago (*Very Expensive*)

Colombia Hotel Tequendama
Bogotá (*Very Expensive*)

Las Terrazas, Bogotá (*Moderate*)

Cartagena Caribe (*Expensive*)

San Andrés Island Nirvana Inn Palace (*Expensive*)

Ecuador Hostería Cusín, Imabura (*Moderate)*

Palm Garten, Quito (*Moderate*)

Hotel La Casona, Quito (*Inexpensive*)

Paraguay Hotel Casino Yacht y Golf Club Paraguayo, Asunción (*Very Expensive*)

Centu Cué, Villa Florida, The South (*Moderate*)

Peru Machu Picchu Pueblo Hotel, Aguas Calientes (*Very*
Cuzco and Environs *Expensive*)

Hotel Alhambra III, Sacred Valley of the Incas (*Moderate*)

Lima Hotel El Olívar (*Expensive*)

Hostal Miramar Ischia (*Moderate*)

The South Hotel Mossone, Ica (*Expensive*)

Uruguay Hosteria del Lago, Montevideo (*Very Expensive*)

La Posta del Cangrejo, Punta del Este (*Very Expensive*)

Venezuela Eurobuilding, Caracas (*Expensive*)

Hotel Los Bordones, Cumaná, Caribbean Coast (*Expensive*)

Hotel Flamingo, Margarita Island, Caribbean Coast (*Very Expensive*)

Hotel Belansante, Mérida (*Expensive*)

Natural Wonders

Argentina The cymbal-banging cacaphony of the 275 cascades of Iguazú Falls, the world's most spectacular waterfall

The 30,000-year-old Perito Moreno Glacier in Glacier National Park, Patagonia

Bolivia The view of Mt. Illimani from La Paz's 13,000-foot-high El Alto airport

The semitropical valleys of Las Yungas, near La Paz

Sunset at placid Lake Titicaca, the world's highest navigable lake

Brazil The "meeting of the waters," where the Negro and Solimões rivers join to form the Amazon, near Manaus

The *pororoca*, north of Macapá

The 1,300-foot granite bolock of Sugarloaf Mountain in Rio de Janeiro

Chile Hiking up to the incandescent mouth of Villarrica Volcano, Villarrica National Park, Lakes District

Towering mountains surrounded by turquoise lakes, Torres del Paine National Park, near Punta Arenas

Colombia The rugged *Cordillera Central*, the central ridge of the Andes, which joins Bogotá with Cali

The jungle-clad slopes and deserted, palm-fringed beaches of Parque Tayrona, on the Caribbean Coast

Ecuador The caldera of Volcán Sierra Negra, Isabela, Galápagos Islands

The snow-covered dome of Volcán Cotopaxi, Cotopaxi National Park

The Avenue of the Volcanoes, the volcano-pocked stretch of Pan- American Highway between Quito and Cochabamba

Peru The walk among the treetops at the Canopy Walkway near Iquitos

The desolate, windswept desert and dunes at the Paracas National Reserve in the South

The snowcapped mountains and dizzying drop at the Colca Canyon

Venezuela Angel Falls, the world's highest waterfall

The Llanos, a 600-mile stretch of verdant, largely uninhabited grasslands

The skyline of Mérida, dominated by the glacier-encrusted peaks of the Five White Eagles

Wildlife

Argentina Whales and elephant seals at Península Valdés

The annual gathering of the Magellanic penguin clan on the beaches at Punta Tombo

Brazil Giant sea turtles emerging from the ocean at night from September to March to lay their eggs on the beach at Praia do Forte

Colombia Petrels and parrots in the jungle canopy of Parque Tayrona, the Caribbean Coast

Chile Flamingos, llama-like guanacos, and foxes in Torres del Paine National Park

Ecuador Galápagos tortoises and penguins on Santa Cruz and Isabela, Galápagos Islands

Spotting the pterodactyl-like *hoatzin* in the Amazon jungle canopy

Peru Brilliantly colored macaws and parrots at the clay licks in Tambopata and Manu National Park

Monkeys swinging through the trees, caymans dozing on the riverbanks, and giant otters cavorting in the lakes, all in Manu National Park

Pelicans, boobies, cormorants, and sea lions in raucous colonies on the Ballestas Islands, Paracas

Grazing vicuñas looking deceptively fragile in the barren Reserva Nacional de Aguadas Blanca, between Arequipa and the Colca Canyon

Venezuela Crakes, trogons, flamingos, and harpies on the Llanos plains

Ocelots and otters, monkeys and crocodiles, which you can spot while paddling upstream in the wild Amazonas territory

Adventure Treks and Trips

Bolivia Hiking Bolivia's rugged Cordillera Real mountain range on a week-long trek with the American Alpine Institute

Driving through the misty Chaparé jungle between Santa Cruz and Cochabamba

Descending into the dank, sweaty bowels of a Cerro Rico silver mine in Potosí

Brazil Sleeping in a hammock under the stars aboard a double-decker commercial boat on the Amazon River

Chile River-rafting around Pucón

The horseback journey into the canyon from San Alfonso

Ecuador One- or two-week cruises of the Galápagos Islands aboard *Andando*, a double-masted Brigantine motorsailer

Paraguay Sport fishing for the salmon-like *dorado* from a launch on the Tebicuary River, whose banks are home to monkeys, carpinchos, and the occasional alligator

Peru The four-day trek between Inca ruins on the Inca Trail from Kilómetro 88 to Machu Picchu

Flying over the Nazca lines

Venezuela Flying over Angel Falls

Trekking on the Llanos plain in search of jaguars and exotic birds

Riding the world's highest cable car in Mérida

Markets and Crafts

Argentina The Sunday flea market in the San Telmo district in Buenos Aires

Bolivia Calle Sagarnaga, La Paz's so-called Gringo Street, where a thousand voices clamor for everything from llama fetuses to coca leaves to colorful alpaca sweaters

Brazil Belém's daily Ver-o-Peso market, stocked with everything from Amazon fish and good-luck charms to aphrodisiacs and medicinal roots and herbs

Salvador's daily Mercado Modelo crafts market, peddling local foodstuffs, lace, fossils, gemstones, African print clothing, and regional musical instruments

Chile Hats, sweaters, lamps, antiques, and wicker work at the daily Crafts Village, Pueblo de la Domínica, in Santiago

Colombia Blankets, ponchos, and crafts at the Pasaje Rivas market in Bogotá

Rough emeralds being cut and polished at Sterling Joyeros in Bogotá

Ecuador Finely woven toquilla hats from the Ortega Brothers' factory in Cuenca

Inca *tupus* (brooches) and other pre-Columbian-style jewelry at the Saturday market in Otavalo

Paraguay *Ñandutí* lacework and *ao p'oí* embroidery at Ao P'oí Raity and Overall in Asunción

Paraguayan harps and guitars in Luque, outside Asunción

Peru Andean demon masks and weavings at Pisac's Sunday market in the Cuzco area

Retablos shadow boxes and handmade alpaca and llama woolens at the Indian Market in Lima

Everything you could want or need for your favorite *brujería* (witchcraft) and *curandero* (magical healer) at the market in Chiclayo on the North Coast

Uruguay The Tristan Narvaja market, Montevideo's premier Sunday attraction

Venezuela The Sunday market on the Plaza Las Heroínas in Mérida

Caracas's Plaza Morelos and its mountainous displays of trinkets, ponchos, and jewelry, and grilled meats

Museums and Works of Art

Bolivia The Museo National del Arte (National Museum of Art) in La Paz

Sucre's Museo Antropológico Charcas

Pre-Columbian gold and silver masks at the Museo Pedro Domingo, La Paz

Brazil *Balangandās,* oversize chains of silver tropical fruits once worn by slave women around the waist, at Museu Carlos Costa Pinto, Salvador, Bahia

Candomblé deity costumes and Hector Carybé's inlaid wood panels, Museu Afro-Brasileiro, Salvador, Bahia

Aleijadinho's life-size soapstone sculptures of the Old Testament prophets, Bom Jesus do Matosinho church, Congonhas do Campo, Minas Gerais

Corcovado Mountain's 100-foot-tall statue of Cristo Redentor, with outstretched arms embracing Rio de Janeiro

Chile The Huge carved stone heads known as *maoi,* some over 21 meters tall, scattered across Easter Island

Santiago's Pre-Colombian Museum, for extraordinary artwork by Latin America's original peoples

Colombia The gem-encrusted Tunja and Lechuga processional crosses at the Museo de Arte Religioso (Museum of Religious Art), Bogotá

Bogotá's phenomenal Museo de Oro (Gold Museum), with the world's largest collection of pre-Columbian gold artifacts

Ecuador The magnificently sculpted facade of La Compañía de Jesús church, Quito

Paraguay Carved wood statue of St. Paul, with Indian faces at his feet, Museo de San Ignacio, San Ignacio

Peru Inca ceramics and mummies, Museo de Historia RegionalPulpit of San Blas, Cuzco

Chancay weavings, Museo Amano, Lima

Chavín obelisks and Paracas weavings, Museo Nacional de Antropología y Arqueología, Lima

Gold treasures and the yellow feather poncho, Museo de Oro, Lima

Venus de Frías, Brüning Museum, Lambayeque, North Coast

Whistling huacos, Museo Cassinelli, Trujillo, North Coast

Paracas weavings and Nazca ceramic sculptures, Museo Regional, Ica, the South

Uruguay Montevideo's Museo del Gaucho y la Moneda (Gaucho and Coin Museum)

Venezuela Museo de Bellas Artes, Caracas

The gilded baroque altar of Caracas' Catedral Metropolitano (Metropolitan Cathedral)

Pre-Columbian Ruins

Bolivia The mysterious stones and temples at Tiahuanaco, near La Paz

Colombia La Ciudad Perdida (The Lost City), near Cartagena on the Caribbean Coast

The mammoth, mysterious megaliths of San Augustín, near Cali

Ecuador The Inca and pre-Inca ruins at Ingapirca, two hours beyond Cuenca

Peru Almost everything, but especially Machu Picchu, Tipóm's agricultural terracing, the fortresses of Pisac and Ollantaytambo, and the Korikancha

Chullpas (burial towers) at the Colla necropolis of Sillustani

Chimu city of Chán Chán, outside Trujillo

Moche tomb of the warrior priest at Sipn

Inca and pre-Inca terraces in the Colca Valley

The Nazca lines, gigantic, mysterious "drawings" in the desert

Architecture: Colonial to Modern

Argentina Walking anywhere in the San Telmo district of Buenos Aires to see the rich cache of 19th-century masonry buildings

Bolivia The lavish baroque facade of the Museo Nacional del Arte in La Paz

The weathered colonial mansions along La Paz's Calle Jaén

Brazil Teatro Amazônas, Manaus, Amazon

The gold-leaf-covered Igreja de São Francisco, Salvador, Bahia

Salvador's Largo do Pelourinho, one of the largest groupings of Brazilian colonial architecture

Oscar Niemeyer's Congressional complex and Palácio dos Arcos in Brasília

Igreja São Francisco de Assis, Aleijadinho's masterpiece, Ouro Preto, Minas Gerais

Colombia The colonial city of Mompós, reached by *chalupa* (river launch) from Magangue, on the Caribbean Coast

Cartagena's magnificent Old Town, protected by brawny stone walls and sturdy colonial fortresses

Ecuador Quito's colonial Old Town, protected by UNESCO as a World Heritage Site

Cuenca's El Museo de las Conceptas, a sober colonial mansion turned convent turned museum

Paraguay Ruins of the Jesuit mission at Trinidad, The South

Peru Cathedral, Lima

Casa Pilatos, Lima

Iglesia de San Francisco, Lima

Casa del Mayorazgo de Facala, Trujillo

Casa Urquiaga, Trujillo

Cayma church and plaza, Arequipa

Santa Catalina Convent, Arequipa

The colonial churches and Inca ruins of the Plaza de Armas, Cuzco

Uruguay The neogothic Sagrada Familia chapel, in Montevideo's El Prado district

Venezuela Parque Central, Caracas' twin 56-story towers

The 17th-century Castillo de San Antonio (Fort San Antonio), Cumaná, the Caribbean Coast

Quintessential South America

Argentina
Buenos Aires Being swept off your seat by a human wave as enthusiastic crowds cheer a goal at a Sunday soccer game, Estadio Boca

An espresso at any corner café

Dancing the tango until 3 AM at one of the city's dance halls

Bolivia Sipping a *mate de coca*, a sweet tea made from coca leaves, while bartering in a busy La Paz market

Braving throngs of ice cream-vendors and shoeshine boys on the narrow colonial streets of Sucre

Brazil
Bahia Dancing the lambada with just about the whole town at the Boca da Barra shed, Porto Seguro

Learning about your present, past and future from an African-style *búzios* (cowrie shell) reading by Mãe Edina in Salvador

Watching a *candomble* ceremony, an evening street rehearsal of the Olodum percussion group, or the bewitching *capoeira* footfight dance, Salvador

Minas Gerais A walk in the morning mist along the cobblestone streets of Ouro Preto

Rio de Janeiro Attending an all-night Carnival ball

São Paulo Grasping the immensity and power of South America's largest city from high atop the Edifício Itália

Striking workers bring traffic on Avenida Paulista to a standstill

Chile
Santiago Strolling through the General Cemetery, especially on Sundays, when people visit their dead for lengthy chats

Watching Chilean schoolchildren play hookie, young couples meet, and families enjoy the sunshine at Parque Forestal

Colombia Bartering with Highland Indians selling fruit, flowers, and livestock on the rod between Bogotá and Cali

Sipping a *jugo* (fruit juice) in a swank Zona Rosa café in Bogotá

Ecuador Savoring the motley street scene—impatient taxis swerving through crowds of Indian sellers and shoeshine boys—around Quito's La Plaza Grande

Eating *cuy* (roasted guinea pig) while watching the parade of dancers and musicians during Ambato's Fiesta de Flores y Frutas (Festival of Flowers and Fruit)

Paraguay
Asunción A glib, white-suited salesman touting miracle cures to incredulous Guaraní Indians in the Plaza de los Héroes

The South Listening to the sunset on the banks of the Tebicuary River as the evening calls of wildfowl give way to the chorus of frogs

Peru
Cuzco and Environs Statues of saints carried in procession at the Corpus Christi festival on June 2

Lima Coffee at dusk at the Café Haiti in Miraflores

Purple-clad worshippers packing the streets for the October 18 procession of the Señor de los Milagros

Vendors, street comedians, and snake-oil salesmen in the Plaza San Martín

Madre de Dios Machiguenga Indians poling slowly up and down the Manu River

Kids joyriding on mopeds down Puerto Maldonado's one paved street

North Coast Dancers at the Marinera Festival in January in Trujillo

Fishermen going to sea in rough totora rafts in Huanchaco

The South Colorfully dressed peasant drovers with herds of pack-bearing llamas along the road running through the Colca Valley

Uruguay Lunch along Montevideo's waterfront any day of the week

Greeting the sunrise from a beachfront disco in Punta del Este

Venezuela Keeping track of all the ice-cream vendors, preachers, con artists, and the simply disinterested on Caracas' Plaza Venezolano

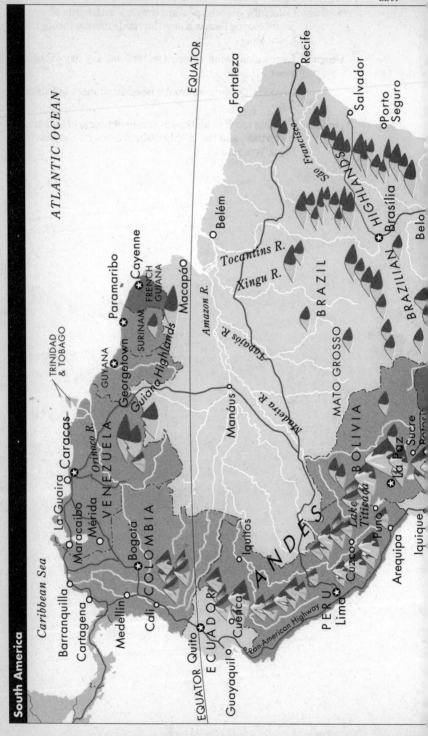

South America

ATLANTIC OCEAN

EQUATOR

Recife

Fortaleza

Salvador

Porto Seguro

São Francisco

BRAZILIAN HIGHLANDS

Brasília

Belo

Belém

Tocantins R.

Xingu R.

Amazon R.

Tapajós R.

BRAZIL

MATO GROSSO

Cayenne

FRENCH GUIANA

Macapó

Paramaribo

SURINAM

Georgetown

GUYANA

Guiana Highlands

TRINIDAD & TOBAGO

Caracas

La Guaira

Orinoco R.

VENEZUELA

Maracaibo

Mérida

Caribbean Sea

Barranquilla

Cartagena

Bogotá

COLOMBIA

Medellín

Cali

Madeira R.

Manáus

Iquitos

BOLIVIA

Sucre

Potosí

La Paz

Lake Titicaca

Cuzco

Puno

Arequipa

Iquique

ANDES

PERU

Lima

Pan-American Highway

Cuenca

Guayaquil

Quito

ECUADOR

EQUATOR

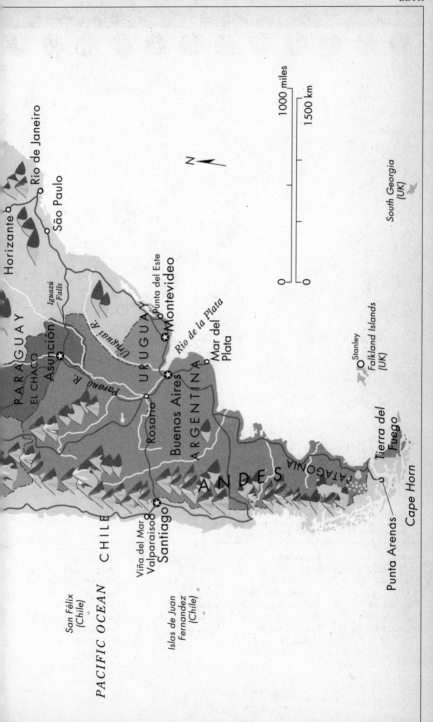

World Time Zones

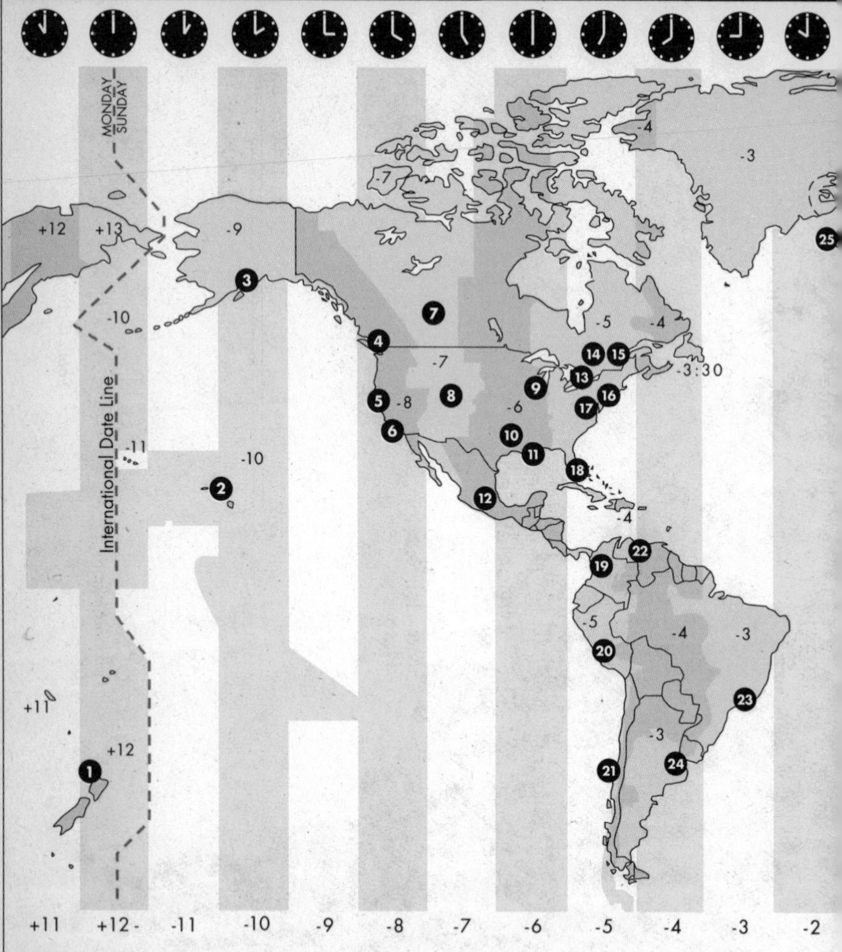

+12 +13

-9

-10

-11

+11

+12

MONDAY
SUNDAY

International Date Line

+11   +12 -   -11   -10   -9   -8   -7   -6   -5   -4   -3   -2

-4

-3

-7

-9

-4

-5   -4

-3:30

-6

-5   -4

-8

-6

-4

-5

-4   -3

-3

-3

3 Anchorage
7
4
14 **15**
13
5 **8** **9** **16**
6 **10** **17**
11 **18**
12
2
19 **22**
20
23
1 **21** **24**

Numbers below vertical bands relate each zone to Greenwich Mean Time (0 hrs.).
Local times frequently differ from these general indications,
as indicated by light-face numbers on map.

Algiers, **29**	Berlin, **34**	Delhi, **48**	Istanbul, **40**
Anchorage, **3**	Bogotá, **19**	Denver, **8**	Jerusalem, **42**
Athens, **41**	Budapest, **37**	Djakarta, **53**	Johannesburg, **44**
Auckland, **1**	Buenos Aires, **24**	Dublin, **26**	Lima, **20**
Baghdad, **46**	Caracas, **22**	Edmonton, **7**	Lisbon, **28**
Bangkok, **50**	Chicago, **9**	Hong Kong, **56**	London (Greenwich), **27**
Beijing, **54**	Copenhagen, **33**	Honolulu, **2**	Los Angeles, **6**
	Dallas, **10**		Madrid, **38**
			Manila, **57**

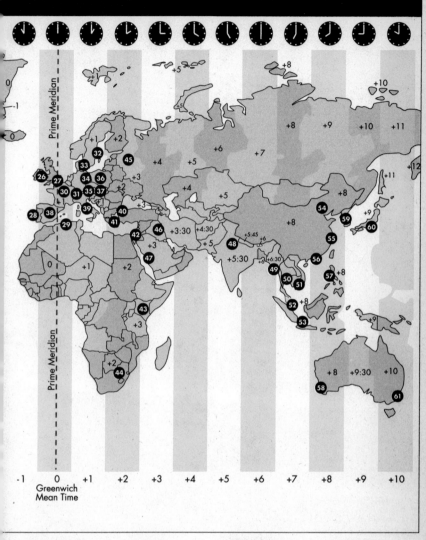

1 Essential Information

Before You Go

Government Information Offices

By Carla Hunt

Most South American countries offer very little basic travel information. There are no special travel sections in most embassies and consulates, and no travel information is available by mail. Nor are there tourist offices in Canada or the United Kingdom. Your best bets are the airlines that fly to each country and tour operators with programs to South America (*see* Airports and Airlines *and* Tours and Packages, below and in specific country chapters). At press time, the only overseas tourist information offices were the **Argentina National Tourist Council** (12 W. 56th St., New York, NY 10019, tel. 212/603–0443; 5055 Wilshire Blvd., Los Angeles, CA 90036, tel. 213/930–0681; 2655 Le Jeune Rd., Miami, FL 33134, tel. 305/442–1366) and the **Ecuador Tourism Office** (1390 Brickell Ave., Miami, FL 33131, tel. 305/577–0522 or 800/553–6673).

The U.S. Department of State's **Citizens Emergency Center** issues Consular Information Sheets, which cover crime, security, and health risks as well as embassy locations, entry requirements, currency regulations, and other routine matters. Travel Warnings, which counsel travelers to avoid a country entirely, are issued in extreme cases. For the latest information, stop in at any U.S. passport office, consulate, or embassy; call the interactive hotline (tel. 202/647–5225); or, with your PC's modem, tap into the Bureau of Consular Affairs' computer bulletin board (tel. 202/647–9225).

Tours and Packages

Should you book an independent package, an independent tour, or an escorted tour to South America, or make the arrangements yourself? There are many good reasons to prebook at least some of your travel arrangements: You will generally get a better airfare from North American tour operators specializing in South America than you can independently, you will get the travel arrangements you want with one domestic phone call rather than many letters and faxes to South America (which may not be answered), and you will have a pretty good idea of the trip cost from the outset.

Escorted Tours Escorted tours include a great deal of sightseeing, often via motorcoach. A tour director is in charge throughout the trip, and your baggage is handled, your time rigorously scheduled, and most meals and many special events planned. So escorted tours are fairly hassle-free. On the other hand, you may have limited free time, you'll be traveling with strangers, and costs are on the high side, since most tours are deluxe and all-inclusive. Airfare is usually quoted separately.

Independent Arrangements The independent arrangements allow more flexibility. They usually include a choice of deluxe or first-class hotels, locally hosted tours, and transfers to and from airports, with local people helping you with baggage and checkin–a major plus in South America. You can mix and match components as you wish. **Independent packages** include arrangements for just one destination, while **independent tours** cover one or more countries. You travel between destinations either by private car or motorcoach, and join other travelers for local sightseeing. The usual way to book independent arrangements is country by country, adding independent tours and packages together to create your vacation. Independent, in other words, means that you can design your own trip. Single-country independent tours and packages are sometimes quoted air-inclusive; more often, air travel is quoted separately, just as for inclusive tours.

Cruises Cruising is another all-inclusive way to book travel to South America. You can sign on to travel all around the continent or book single or multiple segments of the whole trip. Other cruises travel to Antarctica in season (November through February), up the Amazon and Orinoco rivers, around the Galápagos Islands, and along the coasts of Chile and Argentina. In general, cruises are most easily arranged through U.S. tour operators. Contact the **Cruise Lines International Association** (500 5th Ave., New York, NY 10036, tel. 212/921–0066) for information on cruise lines serving South America and cruise-specialist travel agencies.

Operators Several U.S. tour operators cover South America. **Abercrombie & Kent International** (1520 Kensington Rd., Oak Brook, IL 60521-2141, tel. 708/954–2944 or 800/323–7308) has escorted and independent programs to Antarctica, Argentina, Bolivia, Brazil, Chile, Ecuador, and Peru. For independent programs to Argentina, Bolivia, Brazil, Chile, Ecuador, Paraguay, Peru, Uruguay, and Venezuela, contact **Avanti Destinations** (851 S.W. 6th Ave., Portland, OR 97204, tel. 503/295–1100 or 800/422–5053); East Coast–based travelers should book through **4th Dimension Tours** (1150 N.W. 72nd Ave., Miami, FL 33126, tel. 305/477–1525 or 800/343–0020). **Collette Tours** (162 Middle St., Pawtucket, RI 02860, tel. 800/752–2655 in the Northeast or 800/832–4656 elsewhere) has escorted tours that include Argentina, Brazil, Chile, and Ecuador. **Ladatco Tours** (2220 Coral Way, Miami, FL 33145, tel. 305/854–8422 or 800/327–6162) has independent tours and packages covering Argentina, Bolivia, Chile, Ecuador, Paraguay, Peru, Uruguay, and Venezuela. Independent tours are available through **Marnella Tours** (33 Walt Whitman Rd., Huntington Station, NY 11746, tel. 516/271–6969 or 800/937–6999), covering Argentina, Bolivia, Brazil, Chile, Colombia, Ecuador, Paraguay, Peru, Uruguay, and Venezuela, while **Sun Holidays** (26 6th St., Stamford CT 06905, tel. 203/323–1166 or 800/243–2057) covers Argentina, Bolivia, Brazil, Chile, Ecuador, and Uruguay with both independent tours and packages. **Travcoa** (Box 2630, Newport Beach, CA 92660, tel. 714/476–2800 or 800/992–2003) has escorted tours including Antarctica, Bolivia, Brazil, Chile, Ecuador, Peru, and Uruguay.

Adventure Travel For complete coverage of special-interest and adventure travel vacations, *see* Chapter 2.

When to Go

There is no single best time to go. Two factors should guide your travel planning: the climate in a particular country and an event or activity that interests you.

Because of the great variety of latitudes, altitudes, and climatic zones on the continent, you may encounter many different kinds of weather in any given month. You'll find one type of climate in the highland areas of the Andes Mountains, which run north to south down the west coast of South America from

Colombia through Ecuador, Peru, Bolivia, and Argentina. These are at their most accessible and most comfortable in the dry season, May–October. July–September is the time to ski in Chile and Argentina, or to cruise south to Antarctica.

An entirely different climate reigns in the Amazon Basin, whose tropical and subtropical rain forests spread in a broad west–east band from the headwaters in Ecuador and Peru across the northern third of Brazil. May–September, the Andes' dry season, is the non-rainy season here—that is, it's simply less rainy than at any other time. Contrary to what you may expect, you may prefer the rainy season for an Amazon River trip; the waters are high then, and boats can venture farther upriver into the tributaries.

Certain ocean regions—the Atlantic coast from Brazil all the way down to the famous resort of Punta del Este in Uruguay, as well as the Caribbean shore of Venezuela—are at their hottest and most crowded during North America's winter, December–March. The sea moderates temperatures in most of South America's cities year-round, even as far south as Buenos Aires. The Pacific coast is bordered mostly by a strip of desert, whose climate is always hospitable. Southern Chile is fjord country, perfect for cruising from November through April.

May is probably the single best month to visit South America weather-wise. From then into June you can expect both good weather and off-season prices. These months, as well as September and October, are also relatively uncrowded.

Information Sources For current weather conditions for cities in the United States and abroad, plus the local time and helpful travel tips, call the **Weather Channel Connection** (tel. 900/932–8437; 95¢ per minute) from a touch-tone phone.

Festivals and Seasonal Events

Whatever the weather, it is fun to be in many countries—particularly Brazil and the Caribbean countries—during **Carnival,** the week before Ash Wednesday, which usually falls in February. In the Andean countries, the time between harvest and the next planting—that is, from June to November—sees many of the best **folkloric festivals,** usually village events. Your best bet for catching one, since dates vary from year to year and are difficult to obtain, is to ask a South America tour specialist such as those listed above what's being held here while you'll be visiting. In strongly Catholic South America, the dozens of **saints days** are marked by processions and other festivities; Corpus Christi in mid-June is particularly important, as is Easter. Keep in mind when planning your trip that airline and hotel reservations are more difficult in South America's high seasons, particularly around Easter, Christmas, and July school breaks. The following annual events are worth noting:

January **Argentina:** National Folklore Festival in Cosquin, province of Cordoba, runs for two weeks starting on the 15th, with costumes, dancing, and rodeos. **Bolivia:** The Alicitas Fair takes place in La Paz for two weeks beginning January 24. Miniatures of everything from clothing, shoes, and household items to houses and trucks are sold city-wide; locals believe that what they buy and bring home will accrue to them during the year in real possessions. **Brazil:** The Washing of Our Lord of Bonfim

Festival, in Salvador (Bahia), starts on the Thursday before the third Sunday of January and runs for 10 days. Festivities honor Oxala, god of the Afro-Brazilian can domblista cult, and are celebrated jointly by Candomblé priestesses and the local Catholic clergy. **Chile:** The Festival Foclorico (Folklore Festival) is held in Santiago during the fourth week of January.

February **Bolivia:** The Festival of the Virgin of Candalaria takes place in Copacabana on Lake Titicaca early in the month. On Carnival Sunday, La Diablada (Devil Dancers) perform in Oruro. Also not to miss is the Carnival in Tarabuco (near Sucre). **Brazil:** The Festival to Iemanja on February 2, a beautiful costumed salute to the sea goddess. Carnival in Rio (Saturday before Ash Wednesday), but also in Salvador da Bahia, and Recife (Olinda). **Colombia:** Carnival season is particularly festive in Cartagena. **Peru:** Festival of the Virgin of Candelaria in Puno starts on February 2 and lasts a week.

March–April **Argentina:** Vendimia, the wine harvest in Mendoza, takes place the first week of March. **Colombia:** Holy Week processions fill Popayan. **Ecuador:** There are processions for Palm Sunday in Cuenca (with participants bearing decorative palm boughs) and for Holy Week in Riobamba. **Uruguay:** Fiesta Gaucha brings rodeos to Montevideo during Easter week.

May–June **Argentina:** The northern city of Salta celebrates Semana Salta (Salta Week), a gaucho festival of note, in June. The gauchos are in their full cowboy regalia, barbecue perfumes the air, and hoofs pound in furious displays of horsemanship. **Bolivia and Peru:** Festivals of the Cross take place around lake Titicaca on May 3. **Ecuador:** Corpus Christi is observed in the market town of Pujuli in mid-June, while the Feast of St. John enlivens highland towns around Otavalo, particularly Oton, on June 24. **Peru:** Festival of Inti Raymi (Inca Sun Festival) takes place outside Cuzco on June 24.

July **Argentina:** Buenos Aires hosts a major livestock exhibition— great to see since the Argentines take their cows seriously.

August **Bolivia:** The Festival of the Black Virgin of Copacabana, one of several such pilgrimages to this locally favored saint, takes place on the 5th through 8th annually. **Uruguay:** Montevideo holds an annual Cattle Fair.

September **Chile:** Fiestas Patrias take place all over the country on national day, but there's extra fun, with hard-fought rodeo competitions, around Rancagua.

October **Peru:** Our Lord of the Miracles processions take place in Lima on October 18, 19, and 28. At the same time, the bullfight season is on in the capital's ring.

November **Bolivia and Peru:** The Day of the Dead is marked on November 1–2 all around Lake Titicaca on both the Bolivian and Peruvian sides, particularly in Puno. Also in Puno, on November 4–5, is the Festival of Manco Capac, a fabulous, full-dress reenactment of the founding of the Inca Empire.

December **Argentina:** December 8 is the Festival of Our Lady of Lujan, patron saint of the republic. **Chile:** The Feast of the Virgin of Andacollo, patron saint of miners, is honored in this northern town near La Serena. In Santiago during the second week of the month is the International Artisans' Fair.

What to Pack

Clothing   If you're doing business in South America, you will need the same business attire you would wear in U.S. and European cities: for men, suits and ties, and for women, suits for day wear and cocktail dresses or other suitable dinner clothes.

For sightseeing and leisure, casual clothing and good walking shoes are both desirable and appropriate, and most cities do not require very formal clothes, even for evenings. For beach vacations in the tropical Caribbean countries and Brazil, you'll need lightweight sportswear, a bathing suit, sun hat, and sun screen. Travel in tropical rain-forest areas will require long-sleeve shirts, long pants, socks, sneakers, a hat, light water-proof jacket, bathing suit, and insect repellent. In the Andean countries, dress conservatively—no short shorts or halters. If you're visiting Patagonian areas in the south or high altitudes, bring a light jacket or sweater, or plan to acquire one of the handknit sweaters or ponchos crowding the marketplaces.

If there is a general rule for dressing in South America, it's this: Dress more conservatively in countries on the west coast than those on the east. Colombia is conservative, Venezuela is not. Argentineans are very clothes conscious, but don't demand high-style fashion of you.

Miscellaneous   Take a carry-on bag packed with things you would need in case your luggage gets lost, including basic toilet items, antidiarrhea pills and other medications, a change of underwear, and an extra sweater. If you have a health problem that may require you to purchase a prescription drug, pack enough to last the duration of the trip, and take the prescription, written using the drug's generic name, since brand names vary.

Bring an extra pair of eyeglasses or contact lenses. Sunglasses are also essential. Other useful items include a screw-top water bottle that you can refill from bottled water in your hotel room, money pouch, travel flashlight and extra batteries, Swiss Army knife with attached bottle opener, medical kit, binoculars, and pocket calculator to help with currency conversions. Take more film than you ever thought you would use and extra batteries for your camera; if you are traveling in the jungle, take zip-closing plastic bags to hold your camera and keep it dry. If you are traveling with children, take books and games—hard to find in English in South America. And don't forget to pack a list of the addresses of offices that supply refunds for lost or stolen traveler's checks.

Electricity   The electrical current in Argentina, Chile, Paraguay, Peru, Uruguay, and parts of Brazil is 220 volts, 50 cycles alternating current (AC); the United States runs on 110-volt, 60-cycle AC current. Unlike wall outlets in the United States, which accept plugs with two flat prongs, outlets in many countries take Continental-type plugs with two round prongs.

Adapters,   To plug in U.S.-made appliances abroad, you'll need an adapter
Converters,   plug. To reduce the voltage entering the appliance from 220 to
Transformers   110 volts, you'll also need a converter, unless it is a dual-voltage appliance, made for travel. There are converters for high-wattage appliances (such as hair dryers), low-wattage items (such as electric toothbrushes and razors), and combination models. Hotels sometimes have outlets marked "For Shav-

ers Only" near the sink; these are 110-volt outlets for low-watt-age appliances; don't use them for a high-wattage appliance. Newer laptop computers are auto-sensing, operating equally well on 110 and 220 volts (so you need only the appropriate adapter plug). When in doubt, consult your appliance's owner's manual or the manufacturer. Or get a copy of the free brochure "Foreign Electricity is No Deep Dark Secret," published by adapter-converter manufacturer Franzus (Murtha Industrial Park, Box 142, Beacon Falls, CT 06403, tel. 203/723–6664; send a stamped, self-addressed envelope when ordering).

Luggage Regulations While present baggage limits on international flights are gen-erous, allowances on intra–South American and local flights are sometimes more limiting. If you're moving around a coun-try or visiting many destinations, travel will be easier if you take just one suitcase, preferably one you can carry.

Free baggage allowances on an airline depend on the airline, the route, and the class of your ticket. In general, on domestic flights and on international flights between the United States and foreign destinations, you are entitled to check two bags—neither exceeding 62 inches, or 158 centimeters (length + width + height), or weighing more than 70 pounds (32 kilo-grams). A third piece may be brought aboard as a carryon; its total dimensions are generally limited to less than 45 inches (114 centimeters), so it will fit easily under the seat in front of you or in the overhead compartment. There are variations, so ask in advance. The single rule, a Federal Aviation Administra-tion safety regulation that pertains to carry-on baggage on U.S. airlines, requires that carryons be properly stowed and allows the airline to limit allowances and tailor them to differ-ent aircraft and operational conditions. Charges for excess, oversize, or overweight pieces vary, so inquire before you pack.

If you are flying between two foreign destinations, note that baggage allowances may be determined not by piece but by weight, which generally allows 88 pounds (40 kilograms) of lug-gage in first class, 66 pounds (30 kilograms) in business class, and 44 pounds (20 kilograms) in economy. If your flight be-tween two cities abroad *connects* with your transatlantic or transpacific flight, the piece method applies. A one-suitcase al-lowance applies on some popular flights within South America, including Ecuador–Galápagos Islands and Lima–Cuzco.

Safeguarding Your Luggage Before leaving home, itemize your bags' contents and their worth; this list will help you estimate the extent of your loss if your bags go astray. To minimize that risk, tag them inside and out with your name, address, and phone number. (If you use your home address, cover it so that potential thieves can't see it.) At check-in, make sure that the tag attached by baggage handlers bears the correct three-letter code for your destina-tion. If your bags do not arrive with you, or if you detect dam-age, do not leave the airport until you've filed a written report with the airline.

Taking Money Abroad

Your traveler's checks and monies should be locked in a hotel safe, except for what you need to carry each day. Funds that you do carry are best tucked into a money belt or carried in the inside pockets of your clothing. Always remain alert for pick-pockets.

Traveler's Checks   Although you will want plenty of cash when visiting small cities or rural areas, traveler's checks are the best way to carry your money. The most widely recognized include **American Express, Thomas Cook,** and those issued by major commercial banks such as **Citibank** and **Bank of America.** American Express also issues *Traveler's Cheques for Two,* which can be countersigned and used by you or your traveling companion. Some checks are free; usually the issuing company or the bank at which you make your purchase charges 1% of the checks' face value as a fee.

Carry your traveler's checks in small denominations. Particularly if you are visiting several countries, this will allow you to change just the amount you need (and avoid being left with a difficult-to-reconvert surplus). Moreover, hotels—the most convenient place to change money—often do not have large amounts of currency on hand.

Finally, always record the numbers of checks as you spend them, and keep this list separate from the checks.

Currency Exchange   When you make a purchase in South America, you get a better exchange rate when you pay in traveler's checks than when you offer cash. On simple currency exchange, rates are better at banks but not significantly so—and there are lines. Take a few pesos less at a hotel, and save yourself some time. Plan ahead, however, since it is often hard to change large amounts of money at hotels on weekends, even in capital cities. If you're heading for rural areas, where you will probably not be able to change currency at all, don't leave the city without adequate amounts of local currency, in small denominations.

Since the dollar rarely loses strength against South American currencies, pay for costly items overseas, and use your credit card whenever possible—you'll come out ahead, whether the exchange rate at which your purchase is calculated is the one in effect the day the vendor's bank abroad processes the charge, or the one prevailing on the day the charge company's service center processes it at home.

To avoid lines at airport currency-exchange booths, arrive at your first destination in South America with a small amount of the local currency already in your pocket—a so-called tip pack. **Thomas Cook Currency Services** (630 5th Ave., New York, NY 10111, tel. 212/757–6915) is your best source of currency by mail, though it does not handle currency for Bolivia and Guyane and occasionally may not be able to supply what you need for some other countries.

Getting Money from Home

Cash Machines   Automated-teller machines (ATMs) are proliferating throughout South America, but only in the larger towns and cities; many ATMs are tied to international networks such as **Cirrus,** which has locations in Argentina, Bolivia, Chile, Colombia, and Venezuela, and **Plus,** which has locations in Colombia and Ecuador. You can use your bank card at ATMs away from home to withdraw money from an account and get cash advances on a credit-card account (providing your card has been programmed with a personal identification number, or PIN). Check in advance on limits on withdrawals and cash advances within specified periods. Ask whether your bank-card or credit-card PIN number will need to be reprogrammed for use in the area you'll be visiting—a possibility if the number has more than four digits. Remember that on cash advances you are charged interest from the day you get the money from ATMs as well as from tellers. And note that, although transaction fees for ATM withdrawals abroad will probably be higher than fees for withdrawals at home, Cirrus and Plus exchange rates tend to be good.

Be sure to plan ahead: Obtain ATM locations and the names of affiliated cash-machine networks before departure. For specific foreign Cirrus locations, call 800/424–7787; for foreign Plus locations, consult the Plus directory at your local bank.

American Express Cardholder Services The company's **Express Cash** system lets you withdraw cash or traveler's checks from a worldwide network of 57,000 American Express dispensers and participating bank ATMs. You must *enroll first* (call 800/227–4669 for a form and allow two weeks for processing). Withdrawals are charged not to your card but to a designated bank account. You can withdraw up to $1,000 per seven-day period on the basic card, more if your card is gold or platinum. There is a 2% fee (minimum $2.50, maximum $10) for each cash transaction, and a 1% fee for traveler's checks (except for the platinum card), which are available only from American Express dispensers.

At AmEx offices, cardholders can also cash personal checks for up to $1,000 in any seven-day period (21 days abroad); of this $200 can be in cash, more if available, with the balance paid in traveler's checks, for which all but platinum cardholders pay a 1% fee. Higher limits apply to the gold and platinum cards.

Wiring Money You don't have to be a cardholder to send or receive an **American Express MoneyGram** for up to $10,000. To send one, go to an American Express MoneyGram agent, pay up to $1,000 with a credit card and anything over that in cash, and phone a transaction reference number to your intended recipient, who needs only present identification and the reference number to the nearest MoneyGram agent to pick up the cash. There are MoneyGram agents in more than 60 countries, including all South American countries except Uruguay and Guyana; call 800/543–4080 for locations. Fees range from 5% to 10%, depending on the amount and how you pay. You can't use American Express, which is really a convenience card—only Discover, Master-Card, and Visa credit cards.

You can also use **Western Union.** To wire money, take either cash or a check to the nearest office. (Or you can call and use a credit card.) Fees are roughly 5%–10% (with $13–$25 minimums). Money sent from the United States or Canada will be available for pick up within minutes at agent locations in Chile, Colombia, Ecuador, Guyana, Peru, and Venezuela; money sent to Argentina, Bolivia, Brazil, Paraguay, and Uruguay takes two business days and must be picked up at Citibank branches, which charge an additional $25 fee for their services (in other words, you'll be out at least $38). Note that once the money is in the system it can be picked up at *any* location. You don't have to miss your train waiting for it to arrive in City A, because if there's an agent in City B, where you're headed, you can pick it up there, too. There are approximately 20,000 agents worldwide (call 800/325–6000 for locations).

Passports and Visas

Passports If your passport is lost or stolen abroad, report it immediately to the nearest embassy or consulate and to the local police. If you can provide the consular officer with the information contained in the passport, he or she will usually be able to issue you a new passport. For this reason, it is a good idea to keep a copy of the data page of your passport in a separate place, or to leave the passport number, date, and place of issuance with a relative or friend at home.

U.S. Citizens All U.S. citizens, even infants, need a valid passport to enter South American countries.

You can pick up new and renewal passport application forms at any of the 13 U.S. Passport Agency offices and at some post offices and courthouses. Although passports are usually mailed within two weeks of your application's receipt, it's best to allow three weeks for delivery in low season, five weeks or more from April through summer. Call the Department of State Office of Passport Services' information line (1425 K St. NW, Washington, DC 20522, tel. 202/647–0518) for fees, documentation requirements, and other details.

Canadian Citizens Canadian citizens need a valid passport to enter South American countries.

Passport application forms are available at 23 regional passport offices as well as post offices and travel agencies. Whether applying for a first or subsequent passport, you must apply in person. Children under 16 may be included on a parent's passport but must have their own passport to travel alone. Passports are valid for five years and are usually mailed within two weeks of an application's receipt. For fees, documentation requirements, and other information in English or French, call the passport office (tel. 514/283–2152).

U.K. Citizens Citizens of the United Kingdom need a valid passport to enter South American countries.

Applications for new and renewal passports are available from main post offices as well as at the six passport offices, located in Belfast, Glasgow, Liverpool, London, Newport, and Peterborough. You may apply in person at all passport offices, or by mail to all except the London office. Children under 16 may travel on a parent's passport when accompanying them. All passports are valid for 10 years. Allow a month for processing.

Visas **Argentina.** U.S., Canadian, and U.K. citizens do not need a visa for visits of up to 90 days.

Bolivia. U.S. and U.K. citizens need only a valid passport for stays of up to 30 days. Canadian citizens additionally require a tourist visa, available for C$25 from the Consulate of Bolivia (130 Albert St., Suite 504, Ottawa, Ont. K1P 5G4, tel. 613/236–8237). For more information in the United States, contact the Consulate of Bolivia (211 E. 43rd St., Suite 702, New York, NY 10017, tel. 212/687–0530).

Brazil. U.S. and Canadian citizens traveling as tourists are required to obtain a tourist visa, valid for 90 days from its date of issuance, before arriving in Brazil. Apply either in person or through the mail to the nearest Brazilian consulate or embassy in the United States (400 N. Michigan Ave., Room 3050, Chicago, IL 60611, tel. 312/464–0244; 1700 West Loop S, Room 1450, Houston, TX 77027, tel. 713/961–3063; 8484 Wilshire Blvd., Room 730, Beverly Hills, CA 90211, tel. 213/651–5833; 2601 S. Bay Shore Dr., Room 800, Miami, FL 33131, tel. 305/285–6200; 1306 Trade Center, New Orleans, LA 70130, tel. 504/588–9187; 630 5th Ave., Room 2720, New York, NY 10111, tel. 212/757–3080; 300 Montgomery St., Suite 1160, San Francisco, CA 94014, tel. 415/981–8170; and 3009 White Haven St. NW, Washington, DC 20008, tel. 202/745–2828) or in Canada (77 Bloor St. W, Suite 1109, Toronto, Ont. M5S 1M2, tel. 416/922–2503; 2000 Mansfield St., Suite 1700, Montreal, Que. H3A 3A5, tel. 514/499–0968; and 1140 W. Pender St., Suite 1300, Vancouver, BC V6E 4G1, tel. 604/687–4589). Submit a valid passport, photocopy of a round-trip ticket, and 2-by-2-inch passport photograph with your application. For U.S. visitors, there's a $10 fee when applying by proxy or by mail, no charge in person; Canadians pay C$64 Canadian in person, C$80 by proxy or by mail.

Chile. Travelers with U.S., Canadian, or U.K. passports do not require special visas. As you approach Santiago by plane, you'll receive a tourist card valid for 90 days. Don't lose it. You will face considerable difficulties if you cannot produce your original card upon departure.

Colombia. U.S., U.K., and Canadian citizens need only a valid passport to enter Colombia for up to 90 days; tourist visas are not required. Contact the Consulate of Colombia (10 E. 46th St., New York, NY 10017, tel. 212/949–9898).

Ecuador. Only a valid passport is required for U.S., U.K., and Canadian citizens for stays of up to 90 days. For additional information in the United States, contact the Consulate of Ecuador (800 2nd Ave., 5th floor, New York, NY 10017, tel. 212/808–0170).

Paraguay. Visitors who hold U.S., Canadian, and European passports do not need visas to enter Paraguay.

Peru. Visitors from the United States, Canada, and the United Kingdom require only a valid passport and return ticket to be issued a 60-day visa at their point of entry into Peru.

Uruguay. U.S. and U.K. citizens need only a valid passport for stays of up to 90 days in Uruguay. Canadian citizens further require a tourist visa (C$37.50), available from the Consulate of Uruguay (130 Albert St., Suite 1905, Ottawa, Ont. K1P 5G4, tel. 613/234–2937). Inquiries in the U.S. should be directed to the Consulate of Uruguay (747 3rd Ave., 21st floor, New York, NY 10017, tel. 212/753–8191).

Venezuela. U.S., U.K., and Canadian citizens who fly directly to Venezuela are issued 90-day tourist visas, free of charge, immediately upon arrival. If you arrive by car or bus, you may end up paying $3–$5 at the Venezuelan border. For additional information, contact the Consulate of Venezuela (7 E. 51st St., New York, NY 10022, tel. 212/826–1660).

Customs and Duties

Returning Home
U.S. Customs
Provided you've been out of the country for at least 48 hours and haven't already used the exemption, or any part of it, in the past 30 days, you may bring home $400 worth of foreign

goods duty-free. So can each member of your family, regardless of age; and your exemptions may be pooled, so one of you can bring in more if another brings in less. A flat 10% duty applies to the next $1,000 worth of goods; above $1,400, the rate varies with the merchandise. (If the 48-hour or 30-day limits apply, your duty-free allowance drops to $25, which may not be pooled.) Please note that these are the *general* rules, applicable to most South American countries; more generous allowances are in effect for some products from South American countries benefiting from the Generalized System of Preferences (GSP).

Travelers 21 or older may bring back 1 liter of alcohol duty-free, provided the beverage laws of the state through which they reenter the United States allow it. In addition, 100 non-Cuban cigars and 200 cigarettes are allowed, regardless of your age. Antiques and works of art more than 100 years old are duty-free.

Gifts valued at less than $50 may be mailed duty-free to state-side friends and relatives, with a limit of one package per day per addressee (do not send alcohol or tobacco products, nor perfume valued at more than $5). These gifts do not count as part of your exemption, unless you bring them home with you. Mark the package "Unsolicited Gift" and include the nature of the gift and its retail value.

For a copy of "Know Before You Go," a free brochure detailing what you may and may not bring back to the United States, rates of duty, and other pointers, contact the **U.S. Customs Service** (Box 7407, Washington, DC 20044, tel. 202/927–6724). A copy of "GSP and the Traveler" is available from the same source.

Canadian Customs Once per calendar year, when you've been out of Canada for at least seven days, you may bring in $300 worth of goods duty-free. If you've been away less than seven days but more than 48 hours, the duty-free exemption drops to $100 but can be claimed any number of times (as can a $20 duty-free exemption for absences of 24 hours or more). You cannot combine the yearly and 48-hour exemptions, use the $300 exemption only partially (to save the balance for a later trip), or pool exemptions with family members. Goods claimed under the $300 exemption may follow you by mail; those claimed under the lesser exemptions must accompany you on your return.

Alcohol and tobacco products may be included in the yearly and 48-hour exemptions but not in the 24-hour exemption. If you meet the age requirements of the province through which you reenter Canada, you may bring in, duty-free, 1.14 liters (40 imperial ounces) of wine or liquor *or* two dozen 12-ounce cans or bottles of beer or ale. If you are 16 or older, you may bring in, duty-free, 200 cigarettes, 50 cigars or cigarillos, and 400 tobacco sticks or 400 grams of manufactured tobacco. Alcohol and tobacco must accompany you on your return.

Gifts may be mailed to friends in Canada duty-free. These do not count as part of your exemption. Each gift may be worth up to of $60—label the package "Unsolicited Gift—Value under $60." There are no limits on the number of gifts that may be sent per day or per addressee, but you can't mail alcohol or tobacco.

For more information, including details of duties on items that exceed your duty-free limit, ask the Revenue Canada Customs and Excise Department (Connaught Bldg., MacKenzie Ave., Ottawa, Ont., K1A 0L5, tel. 613/957–0275) for a copy of the free brochure "I Declare/Je Déclare."

U.K. Customs   From countries outside the EC, you may import duty-free 200 cigarettes, 100 cigarillos, 50 cigars or 250 grams of tobacco; 1 liter of spirits or 2 liters of fortified or sparkling wine; 2 liters of still table wine; 60 milliliters of perfume; 250 milliliters of toilet water; plus £36 worth of other goods, including gifts and souvenirs.

For further information or a copy of "A Guide for Travellers," which details standard customs procedures as well as what you may bring into the United Kingdom from abroad, contact HM Customs and Excise (New King's Beam House, 22 Upper Ground, London SE1 9PJ, tel. 071/620–1313).

Traveling with Cameras, Camcorders, and Laptops

About Film and Don't count on buying film in South America. When available,
Cameras it is very expensive. And always check the expiration date. If your camera is new or if you haven't used it for a while, shoot and develop a few rolls of film before leaving home. Pack some lens tissue and an extra battery for your built-in light meter, and invest in an inexpensive skylight filter, to both protect your lens and provide some definition in hazy shots. Keep both camera and film in a cool, dry place when possible. If you are traveling in the Amazon region, or cruising on lakes or rivers by small craft, stash your equipment in a zip-closing plastic bag.

Films above ISO 400 are more sensitive to damage from airport security X-rays than others; very high speed films, ISO 1,000 and above, are exceedingly vulnerable. To protect your film, don't put it in checked luggage; carry it with you in a plastic bag and ask for a hand inspection. Such requests are honored at American airports, but up to the inspector abroad. Don't depend on a lead-lined bag to protect film in checked luggage— the airline may very well turn up the dosage of radiation to see what you've got in there. Airport metal detectors do not harm film, although you'll set off the alarm if you walk through one with a roll in your pocket. Call the Kodak Information Center (tel. 800/242–2424) for details.

About Camcorders Before your trip, put new or long-unused camcorders through their paces, and practice panning and zooming. Invest in a skylight filter to protect the lens, and check the lithium battery that lights up the LCD (liquid crystal display) modes. As for the rechargeable nickel-cadmium batteries that are the camera's power source, take along an extra pair, so while you're using your camcorder you'll have one battery ready and another recharging. Most newer camcorders are equipped with the battery (which generally slides or clicks onto the camera body) and, to recharge it, with what's known as a universal or worldwide AC adapter charger (or multivoltage converter) that can be used whether the voltage is 110 or 220. All that's needed is the appropriate plug.

About Videotape Unlike still-camera film, videotape is not damaged by X-rays. However, it may well be harmed by the magnetic field of a walk-through metal detector. Airport security personnel may want you to turn the camcorder on to prove that that's what it is, so make sure the battery is charged when you get to the airport. Note that while many South American countries use the same National Television System Committee (NTSC) video standard used by the United States, Bolivia, Brazil, Paraguay, Uruguay, and the Falkland Islands use PAL technology. So you will not be able to view your tapes through the local TV set or view movies bought there in your home VCR. Blank tapes bought in any South American country can be used for NTSC camcorder taping, however—although you'll probably find they cost more abroad and wish you'd brought an adequate supply along.

About Laptops Security X-rays do not harm hard- or floppy-disk storage. Most airlines allow you to use your laptop aloft but request that you turn it off during takeoff and landing so as not to interfere with navigation equipment. Make sure the battery is charged when you arrive at the airport, because you may be asked to turn on the computer at security checkpoints to prove that it is what it appears to be. If you're a heavy computer user, consider traveling with a backup battery. For international travel, register your laptop with U.S. Customs as you leave the country, providing it's manufactured abroad (U.S.-origin items cannot be registered at U.S. Customs); when you do so, you'll get a certificate, good for as long as you own the item, containing your name and address, a description of the laptop, and its serial number, that will quash any questions that may arise on your return. If your laptop is U.S.-made, call the consulate of the country you'll be visiting to find out whether it should be registered with customs in that country upon arrival. Some travelers do this as a matter of course and ask customs officers to sign a document that specifies the total configuration of the system, computer and peripherals, and its value. In addition, before leaving home, find out about repair facilities at your destination, and don't forget any transformer or adapter plug you may need (*see* Electricity, *above*).

Personal Security

Generally, most places in South America are no more dangerous than major cities in North America or the United Kingdom. By day, urban areas and the countryside should be quite safe, although it is always wise to use common sense and follow local advice on such decisions as whether or not it is safe to walk at night, and where. At all times, keep documents, money, and credit cards hidden in a waist or leg pouch or in zip pockets. Don't carry valuables swinging from your shoulder or hanging around your neck. Passports and tickets are best left in hotel safes. Wear the simplest of timepieces, and don't wear good jewelry (don't even bother taking any on your trip). Keep cameras in a secure camera bag, preferably one with a chain or wire embedded in the strap.

Staying Healthy

Travelers staying on the main tourist routes will have few worries. However, you may need various shots or pills for some areas, particularly Amazon regions and for long periods of traveling in the interior. For short stays, they probably won't be necessary.

La Turista When in South America, the most common visitor ailment is a temporary intestinal disorder that results in a day or two of stomach cramps and diarrhea, better known as "la turista."

Prevention Keeping healthy is key to enjoying South America. Hotels take pride in their drinking water, and longtime expatriate residents drink water in many major cities with no problem. However, if you've got just two weeks, you won't want to waste a minute of it in your hotel room. To be absolutely safe, be scrupulously careful about what you eat and drink all the way through your trip, on as well as off the beaten path. Avoid all tap water; for drinking and even to brush your teeth, use only bottled water or water that has been boiled at least 20 minutes. Avoid ice cubes in your drinks unless you're certain they've been made with properly purified water. Don't eat uncooked food, including salads and any fresh fruit you cannot peel. Keep away from meats that are not well-cooked as well as raw fish, food prepared with mayonnaise, and unpasteurized milk and milk products, including ice cream. Don't eat from long-standing buffets or open food stands.

Remedies Symptoms usually last only a day or two. Paregoric, a good antidiarrheal agent that dulls or eliminates abdominal cramps, generally does not require a doctor's prescription in South America. In the United States, you can purchase two drugs recommended by the National Institute for Health for mild cases over the counter: Pepto-Bismol and loperamide (Imodium). Other remedies will be recommended by city pharmacies on the continent; they are used to helping with this problem. If you come down with the malady, rest as much as possible and drink lots of fluids (such as tea without milk— chamomile is a good folk remedy). In severe cases, rehydrate yourself with an 8-ounce cup of purified water mixed with a couple of teaspoons each of salt and sugar.

Altitude Sickness "Soroche," or altitude sickness, which results in shortness of breath and headaches, may be a problem when you visit Andean countries. To remedy any discomfort, walk slowly, eat lightly, and drink plenty of liquids (but avoid alcoholic beverages). If you have high blood pressure and a history of heart trouble, check with your doctor before planning to travel to such heights as those at Cuzco in Peru and La Paz in Bolivia, both above 11,000 feet.

Other Maladies Be particularly attentive to the bug bites that you will receive, despite your best efforts; while most are harmless, those that get infected and stay that way for a long time need a doctor's attention.

According to the Centers for Disease Control (CDC) there is a limited risk in South America for cholera, malaria, hepatitis B, dengue, chagas, and yellow fever. While a few of these you could catch anywhere, most are restricted to jungle areas.

Shots, Medications, and Other Precautions If you plan to visit remote regions or stay in South America for more than six weeks, check with the CDC's **International Travelers Information Hotline** (Center for Preventive Services, Division of Quarantine, Traveler's Health Section, 1600 Clifton Rd., MSE03, Atlanta, GA 30333, tel. 404/332–4559).

The hot line recommends chloroquine (Analen) as an antimalarial agent. Mosquitoes carry malaria and dengue, for which there is no vaccine, so if you're visiting affected regions, take a mosquito net to sleep under, wear clothing that entirely covers your body, make liberal use of insect repellent containing DEET, and spray your living and sleeping areas with an insecticide that knocks out flying insects. To avoid cholera, a disease that affects impoverished neighborhoods with poor sanitation, make sure that the water you drink is pure (*see above*), and avoid raw fish. Cholera prevention inoculations have rarely proved effective.

Children traveling to South America should have current inoculations against measles, mumps, rubella, and polio. And scuba divers take note: PADI recommends that you not dive and fly within a 24-hour period.

Finding a Doctor When on the continent, there is no shortage of good doctors in urban centers.

The **International Association for Medical Assistance to Travellers** (IAMAT, 417 Center St., Lewiston, NY 14092, tel. 716/754–4883; 40 Regal Rd., Guelph, Ont. N1K 1B5; 57 Voirets, 1212 Grand-Lancy, Geneva, Switzerland) publishes a worldwide directory of English-speaking physicians whose qualifications meet IAMAT standards and who have agreed to treat members for a set fee. Membership is free.

Assistance Companies Pretrip medical referrals, emergency evacuation or repatriation, 24-hour telephone hot lines for medical consultation, dispatch of medical personnel, relay of medical records, up-front cash for emergencies, and other personal and legal assistance are among the services provided by several membership organizations specializing in medical assistance to travelers. Among them are **International SOS Assistance** (Box 11568, Philadelphia, PA 19116, tel. 215/244–1500 or 800/523–8930; Box 466, Pl. Bonaventure, Montréal, Qué. H5A 1C1, tel. 514/874–7674 or 800/363–0263), **Near Services** (450 Prairie Ave., Suite 101, Calumet City, IL 60409, tel. 708/868–6700 or 800/654–6700), and **Travel Assistance International** (1133 15th St. NW, Suite 400, Washington, DC 20005, tel. 202/331–1609 or 800/821–2828), part of Europ Assistance Worldwide Services, Inc. Because these companies will also sell you death-and-dismemberment, trip-cancellation, and other insurance coverage, there is some overlap with the travel-insurance policies discussed below, which may include the services of an assistance company among the insurance options or reimburse travelers for such services without providing them.

Insurance

For U.S. Residents Most tour operators, travel agents, and insurance agents sell specialized health-and-accident, flight, trip-cancellation, and luggage insurance as well as comprehensive policies with some or all of these features. But before you make any purchase, review your existing health and homeowner policies to find out whether they cover expenses incurred while traveling.

Health-and-Accident Insurance Supplemental health-and-accident insurance for travelers is usually a part of comprehensive policies. Specific policy provisions vary, but they tend to address three general areas, beginning with reimbursement for medical expenses caused by illness or an accident during a trip. Such policies may reimburse anywhere from $1,000 to $150,000 worth of medical expenses; dental benefits may also be included. A second common feature is the personal-accident, or death-and-dismemberment, provision, which pays a lump sum to your beneficiaries if your die or to you if you lose one or both limbs or your eyesight. This is similar to the flight insurance described below, although it is not necessarily limited to accidents involving airplanes or even other "common carriers" (buses, trains, and ships) and can be in effect 24 hours a day. The lump sum awarded can range from $15,000 to $500,000. A third area generally addressed by these policies is medical assistance (referrals, evacuation, or repatriation and other services). Some policies reimburse travelers for the cost of such services; others may automatically enroll you as a member of a particular medical-assistance company.

Flight Insurance This insurance, often bought as a last-minute impulse at the airport, pays a lump sum to a beneficiary when a plane crashes and the insured dies (and sometimes to a surviving passenger who loses eyesight or a limb); thus it supplements the airlines' own coverage as described in the limits-of-liability paragraphs on your ticket (up to $75,000 on international flights, $20,000 on domestic ones—and that is generally subject to litigation). Charging an airline ticket to a major credit card often automatically signs you up for flight insurance; in this case, the coverage may also embrace travel by bus, train, and ship.

Baggage Insurance In the event of loss, damage, or theft on international flights, airlines limit their liability to $20 per kilogram for checked baggage (roughly about $640 per 70-pound bag) and $400 per passenger for unchecked baggage. On domestic flights, the ceiling is $1,250 per passenger. Excess-valuation insurance can be bought directly from the airline at check-in but leaves your bags vulnerable on the ground.

Trip Insurance There are two sides to this coin. **Trip-cancellation-and-interruption insurance** protects you in the event you are unable to undertake or finish your trip. **Default** or **bankruptcy insurance** protects you against a supplier's failure to deliver. Consider the former if your airline ticket, cruise, or package tour does not allow changes or cancellations. The amount of coverage to buy should equal the cost of your trip should you, a traveling companion, or a family member get sick, forcing you to stay home, plus the nondiscounted one-way airline ticket you would need to buy if you had to return home early. Read the fine print carefully; pay attention to sections defining "family member" and "preexisting medical conditions." A characteristic quirk of default policies is that they often do not cover default by travel agencies or default by a tour operator, airline, or cruise line if you bought your tour and the coverage directly from the firm in question. To reduce your need for default insurance, give preference to tours packaged by members of the United States Tour Operators Association (USTOA), which maintains a fund to reimburse clients in the event of member defaults. Even better, pay for travel arrangements with a major credit card, so you can refuse to pay the bill if services have not been rendered—and let the card company fight your battles.

Comprehensive Companies supplying comprehensive policies with some or all
Policies of the above features include **Access America, Inc.,** underwritten by BCS Insurance Company (Box 11188, Richmond, VA 23230, tel. 800/284–8300); **Carefree Travel Insurance,** underwritten by The Hartford (Box 310, 120 Mineola Blvd., Mineola,

NY 11501, tel. 516/294–0220 or 800/323–3149); **Tele-Trip** (Mutual of Omaha Plaza, Box 31762, Omaha, NE 68131, tel. 800/228–9792), a subsidiary of Mutual of Omaha; **The Travelers Companies** (1 Tower Sq., Hartford, CT 06183, tel. 203/277–0111 or 800/243–3174); **Travel Guard International,** underwritten by Transamerica Occidental Life Companies (1145 Clark St., Stevens Point, WI 54481, tel. 715/345–0505 or 800/782–5151); and **Wallach and Company, Inc.** (107 W. Federal St., Box 480, Middleburg, VA 22117, tel. 703/687–3166 or 800/237–6615). These companies may also offer the above types of insurance separately.

U.K. Residents Most tour operators, travel agents, and insurance agents sell specialized policies covering accident, medical expenses, personal liability, trip cancellation, and loss or theft of personal property. Some policies include coverage for delayed departure and legal expenses, accidents, or motoring abroad. You can also purchase an annual travel-insurance policy valid for every trip you make during the year in which it's purchased (usually only trips of less than 90 days). Before you leave, make sure you will be covered if you have a preexisting medical condition or are pregnant; your insurers may not pay for routine or continuing treatment, or may require a note from your doctor certifying your fitness to travel.

For advice by phone or a free booklet, "Holiday Insurance," that sets out what to expect from a holiday-insurance policy and gives price guidelines, contact the **Association of British Insurers** (51 Gresham St., London EC2V 7HQ, tel. 071/600–3333; 30 Gordon St., Glasgow G1 3PU, tel. 041/226–3905; Scottish Provincial Bldg., Donegall Sq. W, Belfast BT1 6JE, tel. 0232/249176; call for other locations).

Car Rentals

Renting cars is not common among South American travelers. Those who do most frequently are business travelers. The reasons are clear. In cities, driving is chaotic; in the countryside, the usually rough roads and language differences are discouraging; and wherever you go, the cost of renting is steep: Rates range between $100 and $120 per day for mid-size cars, $150 per day and up for large cars, excluding taxes, which vary from country to country. Moreover, although the weekly rate is occasionally 10%–15% lower than the daily rate, the two prices are usually the same. However, this does not mean it is not possible. Many seasoned travelers like to drive in South America, and certain areas are most enjoyable when explored on your own in a car: in Venezuela, Margarita Island and the mountains Merida; in Chile, the central valley around Santiago and its nearby ski areas; in Brazil, the beach areas of Buzios and the Costa Verde (near Rio) and the nearby Belo Horizonte region.

Many major car-rental companies are represented at airports and in major cities in South America, including **Avis** (tel. 800/331–1084 or 800/879–2847 in Canada), **Budget** (tel. 800/527–0700), **Dollar** (tel. 800/800–6000), and **Hertz** (tel. 800/654–3001 or 800/263–0600 in Canada). These international operations will give you more help than local firms if you have a breakdown—though you should still give the car a once-over to check the headlights, jack, and the tires (including the spare) to make sure they're in working condition.

Requirements Your own U.S., Canadian, or British driver's license is acceptable; an International Driver's Permit, available from the American or Canadian Automobile Association, is not necessary, but may be a good idea. Minimum driving ages vary from country to country.

Extra Charges Picking up the car in one city and leaving it in another within the country will entail drop-off charges or one-way service fees. Because of the distances involved, one-way rentals are also pricey and not available between countries (except between Chile and Argentina). The cost of a collision or loss-damage waiver (*see below*) can also be high.

Cutting Costs For South America, you can't cut costs by booking before you leave home, as you can for other destinations outside the United States. Fly/drive packages are not sold in the United States, and only a few are available in Canada. Your best bet at getting a better rate is to rent on arrival, particularly from the smaller companies. (Reserve ahead only if you plan to rent during a holiday period, when vehicles may be in short supply.)

One of the few sources of savings are the companies that operate as wholesalers—companies that do not own their own fleets but rent in bulk from those that do and offer advantageous rates to their customers, such as **Auto Europe** (Box 1097, Camden, ME 04843, tel. 207/236–8235, 800/223–5555, or 800/458–9503 in Canada), which serves parts of South America. Rentals through such companies must be arranged and paid for before you leave the United States. Always ask whether the prices are guaranteed in U.S. dollars or foreign currency and if unlimited mileage is available. Find out about any required deposits, cancellation penalties, and drop-off charges, and confirm the cost of the collision damage waiver.

One last tip: Remember to fill the tank when you turn in the vehicle, to avoid being charged at what you'll swear is the most expensive pump in town.

Alternatively, consider hiring a car and driver through your hotel concierge, or make a deal with a taxi driver you use and like for some extended sightseeing at a longer-term rate. You will have to pay cash—but you'll spend less than you would have for a rental car.

Insurance and Collision Damage Waiver The standard rental contract includes liability coverage (for damage to public property, injury to pedestrians, etc.) and coverage for the car against fire, theft (not included in certain countries), and collision damage with a deductible—most commonly $2,000–$3,000, occasionally more. In the case of an accident, you are responsible for the deductible amount unless you've purchased the collision damage waiver (CDW), which costs an average $12 a day, although this varies depending on what you've rented, where, and from whom.

Because this adds up quickly, you may be inclined to say "no thanks"—and that's certainly your option, although the rental agent may not tell you so. Note before you decline that deductibles are occasionally high enough that totaling a car would make you responsible for its full value. Planning ahead will help you make the right decision. By all means, find out if your own insurance covers damage to a rental car while traveling (not simply a car to drive when yours is in for repairs). And check whether charging car rentals to any of your credit cards will get you a CDW at no charge.

Student and Youth Travel

Travel Agencies The foremost U.S. student travel agency is **Council Travel,** a subsidiary of the nonprofit Council on International Educational Exchange (CIEE). It specializes in low-cost travel arrangements, is the exclusive U.S. agent for several discount cards, and, with its sister CIEE subsidiary, **Council Charter,** is a source of airfare bargains. The Council Charter brochure and CIEE's twice-yearly *Student Travels* magazine, which details its programs, are available at the Council Travel office at CIEE headquarters (205 E. 42nd St., New York, NY 10017, tel. 212/661–1450) and at 37 branches in college towns nationwide (free in person, $1 by mail). The **Educational Travel Center** (ETC, 438 N. Francis St., Madison, WI 53703, tel. 608/256–5551) also offers low-cost rail passes, domestic and international airline tickets (mostly for flights departing from Chicago), and other budgetwise travel arrangements. Other travel agencies catering to students include **Travel Management International** (TMI, 18 Prescott St., Suite 4, Cambridge, MA 02138, tel. 617/661–8187) and **Travel Cuts** (187 College St., Toronto, Ont. M5T 1P7, tel. 416/979–2406).

Discount Cards For discounts on transportation and on museum and attractions admissions, buy the **International Student Identity Card** (ISIC) if you're a bona fide student, or the **International Youth Card** (IYC) if you're under 26. In the United States the ISIC and IYC cards cost $15 each and include basic travel accident and sickness coverage. Apply to **CIEE** (*see* address *above*, tel. 212/661–1414; the application is in *Student Travels*). In Canada the cards are available for $15 each from **Travel Cuts** (*see above*). In the United Kingdom they cost £5 and £4 respectively at student unions and student travel companies, including Council Travel's London office (28A Poland St., London W1V 3DB, tel. 071/437–7767).

Hosteling An **International Youth Hostel Federation** (IYHF) membership card is the key to more than 5,300 hostel locations in 59 countries, including Argentina, Brazil, Chile, and Colombia. The sex-segregated, dormitory-style sleeping quarters, including some for families, go for $7–$20 a night per person. Membership is available in the United States through **American Youth Hostels** (733 15th St. NW, Washington, DC 20005, tel. 202/783–6161), the American link in the worldwide chain, and costs $25 for adults 18–54, $10 for those under 18, $15 for those 55 and over, and $35 for families. Volume 2 of the two-volume *Guide to Budget Accommodation* lists hostels in South America, Asia, and Australasia as well as in Canada and the United States ($13.95 including postage). IYHF membership is available in Canada through the **Canadian Hostelling Association** (1600 James Naismith Dr., Suite 608, Gloucester, Ont. K1B 5N4, tel. 613/748–5638) for $26.75, and in the United Kingdom through the **Youth Hostel Association of England and Wales** (8 St. Stephen's Hill, St. Albans, Herts. AL1 2DY, tel. 0727/55215) for £9.

Traveling with Children

South Americans love children, and having yours along may prove to be your special ticket to meeting local people. Children are welcomed in hotels and in restaurants, especially on weekends, when South American families go out for lunch in droves. On the continent, there seems to always be someone to hold your baby or toddler.

Older children will adjust better if you have let them join in on planning and if you find time to scout your library for picture books, storybooks, and maps about places you will be going. Try to explain the concept of foreign language; some kids, who may have just learned to talk, are thrown when they cannot understand strangers and strangers cannot understand them. For children of reading age, be sure to bring their books from home; locally, literature for kids in English is hard to find. Make sure that health precautions, such as what to drink and eat, are applied to the whole family. Children should have had all their inoculations before leaving home. Not cramming too much in a day will keep the whole family healthier while on the road.

Publications
Newsletter

Family Travel Times, published 10 times a year by **Travel With Your Children** (TWYCH, 45 W. 18th St., 7th Floor Tower, New York, NY 10011, tel. 212/206–0688; annual subscription $55), covers destinations, types of vacations, and modes of travel.

Books

Traveling with Children—And Enjoying It, by Arlene K. Butler ($11.95 plus $3 shipping per book; Globe Pequot Press, Box 833, Old Saybrook, CT 06475, tel. 800/243–0495 or 800/962–0973 in CT), will help you plan your trip with children, from toddlers to teens.

Getting There
Airfares

On international flights, the fare for infants under 2 not occupying a seat is generally 10% of the accompanying adult's fare; children ages 2–11 usually pay half to two-thirds of the adult fare. On domestic flights, children under 2 not occupying a seat travel free, and older children currently travel on the "lowest applicable" adult fare.

Baggage

In general, infants paying 10% of the adult fare are allowed one carry-on bag, not to exceed 70 pounds or 45 inches (length + width + height). The adult baggage allowance applies for children paying half or more of the adult fare. Check with the airline for particulars, especially regarding flights between two foreign destinations, where allowances for infants may be less generous than those above.

Safety Seats

The FAA recommends the use of safety seats aloft and details approved models in the free leaflet **"Child/Infant Safety Seats Recommended for Use in Aircraft"** (available from the Federal Aviation Administration, APA–200, 800 Independence Ave. SW, Washington, DC 20591, tel. 202/267–3479). Airline policy varies. U.S. carriers must allow FAA-approved models, but because these seats are strapped into a regular passenger seat, they may require that parents buy a ticket even for an infant under 2 who would otherwise ride free. Foreign carriers may not allow infant seats, may charge the child's rather than the infant's fare for their use, or may require you to hold your baby during takeoff and landing, thus defeating the seat's purpose.

Facilities Aloft

Airlines do provide other facilities and services for children, such as children's meals and freestanding bassinets (to those sitting in seats on the bulkhead, where there's enough legroom to accommodate them). Make your request when reserving. The annual February/March issue of *Family Travel Times* gives details of the children's services of dozens of airlines ($10; *see above*).

Lodging Most hotels do not charge for young children sharing a room with their parents, but not all; you are apt to be asked to pay a surcharge for older children. However, you can sometimes arrange special family rates when you take two rooms. You may want to try for hotels with pools or health-club facilities, which children usually enjoy. If your children are younger, hotels with cafeteria-style restaurants will probably work better than those with only formal dining rooms and room service. If you stay in top establishments, the management will probably have a list of baby-sitters—though you can't count on their speaking good English.

Hints for Travelers with Disabilities

Although international chain hotels in large cities have some suitable rooms for travelers with disabilities and it is easy to hire private cars and drivers for excursions, South America is not very well equipped to handle travelers with disabilities. There are few ramps and curb cuts, and it takes effort and planning to negotiate cobbled city streets, get around museums and other buildings, and explore the countryside. City centers such as Rio de Janeiro, Buenos Aires, Santiago, and Caracas are the most comfortable to visit, and cruising is convenient, since cruises make it easier to cover distances and give you the option of making many special excursions.

Organizations Several organizations provide travel information for people
In the United States with disabilities, usually for a membership fee, and some publish newsletters and bulletins. Among them are the **Information Center for Individuals with Disabilities** (Fort Point Pl., 27–43 Wormwood St., Boston, MA 02210, tel. 617/727–5540 or 800/462–5015 in MA between 11 and 4, or leave message; TDD/TTY tel. 617/345–9743); **Mobility International USA** (Box 3551, Eugene, OR 97403, voice and TDD tel. 503/343–1284), the U.S. branch of an international organization based in Britain (*see below*) and present in 30 countries; **MossRehab Hospital Travel Information Service** (1200 W. Tabor Rd., Philadelphia, PA 19141, tel. 215/456–9603, TDD tel. 215/456–9602); the **Society for the Advancement of Travel for the Handicapped** (SATH, 347 5th Ave., Suite 610, New York, NY 10016, tel. 212/447–7284, fax 212/725–8253); the **Travel Industry and Disabled Exchange** (TIDE, 5435 Donna Ave., Tarzana, CA 91356, tel. 818/368–5648); and **Travelin' Talk** (Box 3534, Clarksville, TN 37043, tel. 615/552–6670).

In the United Main information sources include the **Royal Association for**
Kingdom **Disability and Rehabilitation** (RADAR, 25 Mortimer St., London W1N 8AB, tel. 071/637–5400), which publishes travel information for the disabled in Britain, and **Mobility International** (228 Borough High St., London SE1 1JX, tel. 071/403–5688), the headquarters of an international membership organization that serves as a clearinghouse of travel information for people with disabilities.

Travel Agencies **Directions Unlimited** (720 N. Bedford Rd., Bedford Hills, NY
and Tour Operators 10507, tel. 914/241–1700), a travel agency, has expertise in tours

and cruises for the disabled. **Evergreen Travel Service** (4114 198th St. SW, Suite 13, Lynnwood, WA 98036, tel. 206/776–1184 or 800/435–2288) operates Wings on Wheels Tours for those in wheelchairs, White Cane Tours for the blind, and tours for the deaf and makes group and independent arrangements for travelers with any disability. **Flying Wheels Travel** (143 W. Bridge St., Box 382, Owatonna, MN 55060, tel. 800/535–6790 or 800/722–9351 in MN), a tour operator and travel agency, arranges international tours, cruises, and independent travel itineraries for people with mobility disabilities.

Publications In addition to the fact sheets, newsletters, and books mentioned above are several free publications available from the **Consumer Information Center** (Pueblo, CO 81009): "New Horizons for the Air Traveler with a Disability," a U.S. Department of Transportation booklet describing changes resulting from the 1986 Air Carrier Access Act and those still to come from the 1990 Americans with Disabilities Act (include Department 608Y in the address), and the Airport Operators Council's *Access Travel: Airports* (Dept. 5804), which describes facilities and services for the disabled at more than 500 airports worldwide.

Twin Peaks Press (Box 129, Vancouver, WA 98666, tel. 206/694–2462 or 800/637–2256) publishes the *Directory of Travel Agencies for the Disabled* ($19.95), listing more than 370 agencies worldwide; *Travel for the Disabled* ($19.95), listing some 500 access guides and accessible places worldwide; the *Directory of Accessible Van Rentals* ($9.95) for campers and RV travelers worldwide; and *Wheelchair Vagabond* ($14.95), a collection of personal travel tips. Add $2 per book for shipping.

Hints for Older Travelers

Because South America is so interesting and varied, there is no reason that active, well-traveled senior citizens should not visit, whether on an independent (but prebooked) vacation, an escorted tour, or an adventure vacation. The continent is full of good hotels and competent ground operators who will meet your flights and organize your sightseeing. Choose travel to whatever areas when the weather is good and it's off-season.

Before you leave home, determine what medical services your health insurance will cover outside the United States; note that Medicare does not provide for payment of hospital and medical services outside the United States. If you need additional travel insurance, buy it (*see above*). Some precautions: Carry an identification card for your health-insurance policy, put an emergency stateside contact in your passport, pack medications in their original containers, and take your doctor's prescription, written generically. In case of serious legal, medical, or financial difficulty, contact your embassy or consulate.

Organizations The **American Association of Retired Persons** (AARP, 601 E St. NW, Washington, DC 20049, tel. 202/434–2277) provides independent travelers the Purchase Privilege Program, which offers discounts on hotels, car rentals, and sightseeing, and arranges group tours, cruises, and apartment living through AARP Travel Experience from American Express (400 Pinnacle Way, Suite 450, Norcross, GA 30071, tel. 800/927–0111); these can be booked through travel agents, except for the cruises, which must be booked directly (tel. 800/745–4567).

AARP membership is open to those 50 and over; annual dues are $8 per person or couple.

Two other membership organizations offer discounts on lodgings, car rentals, and other travel products, along with such nontravel perks as magazines and newsletters. The **National Council of Senior Citizens** (1331 F St. NW, Washington, DC 20004, tel. 202/347–8800) is a nonprofit advocacy group with some 5,000 local clubs across the United States; membership costs $12 per person or couple annually. **Mature Outlook** (6001 N. Clark St., Chicago, IL 60660, tel. 800/336–6330), a Sears Roebuck & Co. subsidiary with 800,000 members, charges $9.95 for an annual membership.

Note: When using any senior-citizen identification card for reduced hotel rates, mention it when booking, not when checking out. At restaurants, show your card before you're seated; discounts may be limited to certain menus, days, or hours. If you are renting a car, ask about promotional rates that might improve on your senior-citizen discount.

Educational Travel **Elderhostel** (75 Federal St., 3rd floor, Boston, MA 02110, tel. 617/426–7788) is a nonprofit organization that has offered inexpensive study programs for people 60 and older since 1975. Programs are held at more than 1,800 educational institutions in the United States, Canada, and 45 other countries; courses cover everything from marine science to Greek myths and cowboy poetry. Participants generally attend lectures in the morning and spend the afternoon sightseeing or on field trips; they live in dorms on the host campuses. Fees for two- to three-week international trips—including room, board, and transportation from the United States—range from $1,800 to $4,500.

Interhostel (University of New Hampshire, 6 Garrison Ave., Durham, NH 03824, tel. 800/733–9753), a slightly younger enterprise than Elderhostel, caters to a slightly younger clientele—that is, 50 and over—and runs programs in about 25 countries. But the idea is similar: Lectures and field trips mix with sightseeing, and participants stay in dormitories at cooperating educational institutions or in modest hotels. Programs are usually two weeks in length and cost $1,500–$2,100, not including airfare from the United States.

Tour Operators **Saga International Holidays** (222 Berkeley St., Boston, MA 02116, tel. 800/343–0273), which specializes in group travel for people over 60, offers a selection of variously priced tours and cruises covering five continents.

Arriving and Departing

From North America by Plane

Flights are either nonstop, direct, or connecting. A **nonstop** flight requires no change of plane and makes no stops. A **direct** flight stops at least once and can involve a change of plane, although the flight number remains the same; if the first leg is late, the second waits. This is not the case with a **connecting** flight, which involves a different plane and a different flight number.

Airports and Airlines The major gateway cities for flights from the United States to South America are Miami, New York, and Los Angeles. Major

U.S. carriers serving South America include **American Airlines** (tel. 800/433–7300), which flies to all countries covered in this book except Uruguay, and **United Airlines** (tel. 800/538–2929), flying to Caracas, Rio de Janeiro, São Paulo, Montevideo, Buenos Aires, and Santiago. **Continental Airlines** (tel. 800/231–0856) flies from Houston to Guayaquil and Quito.

Many South American national airlines fly directly from the United States to their home countries.

Aerolineas Argentinas (tel. 800/333–0276) flies to Buenos Aires from Los Angeles, Miami, and New York.

Aces (tel. 800/846–2237) serves Medellín and Bogotá from Miami.

AeroPeru (tel. 800/777-7717) runs between Lima and Miami.

Avensa (tel. 800/428–3672) flies to Caracas, Maracaibo, and Porlamar from Miami and New York.

Avianca (tel. 800/284–2622) provides service to Barranquilla, Bogotá, Cali, Cartagena from Los Angeles, Miami, and New York.

Ecuatoriana (tel. 800/328–2367) serves Quito and Guayaquil from Chicago, Los Angeles, and New York.

Faucett (tel. 800/334–3356) flies to Iquitos and Lima from Miami.

LAB (tel. 800/327–7407) operates between La Paz and Miami.

Ladeco (tel. 800/825–2332) has service to Santiago from New York, Baltimore, and Miami.

LanChile (tel. 800/735–5526) flies to Santiago from Miami, Los Angeles, and New York.

LAP (tel. 800/327–3551) operates between Asuncion and Miami.

Saeta (tel. 800/827–2382) serves Quito and Guayaquil from Miami and New York.

Varig (tel. 800/468–2744) has service to Rio de Janeiro and São Paulo from Chicago, Los Angeles, Miami, New York, and San Francisco, and to Manaus, Recife, Fortaleza, and Salvador from Miami.

Viasa (tel. 800/468–4272) operates to Caracas, Maracaibo, and Porlamar from Houston, Miami, and New York.

Flying Time From New York to Rio, 9 hours; 10½ hours to Buenos Aires; 5 hours to Caracas. From Miami to Rio, 7 hours; 8½ hours to Buenos Aires; 3 hours to Caracas.

Between the Airport and Center City Airport bus service is not a feature at most South American airports. Taxi fares, however, are very reasonable; if you are concerned about your city destination not being understood, write it down on a piece of paper and present it to the taxi driver.

Reconfirming Flights It is extremely important that you reconfirm your next onbound flight on arrival at each South American destination.

Cutting Flight Costs The Sunday travel section of most newspapers is a good source of deals. When booking, particularly through an unfamiliar company, call the Better Business Bureau to find out whether any complaints have been registered against the company, pay with a credit card if you can, and consider trip-cancellation and default insurance (*see* Insurance, *above*).

Promotional Airfares All the less expensive fares, called promotional or discount fares, are round-trip and involve restrictions. The exact nature of the restrictions depends on the airline, the route, and the season and on whether travel is domestic or international, but you must usually buy the ticket—commonly called an APEX (advance purchase excursion) when it's for international travel—in advance (7, 14, or 21 days are usual). You must also respect certain minimum- and maximum-stay requirements (for instance, over a Saturday night or at least 7 and no more than 30, 45, or 90 days), and you must be willing to pay penalties for changes. Airlines generally allow some changes for a fee. But the cheaper the fare, the more likely the ticket is to be nonrefundable; it would take a death in the family for the airline to give you any of your money back if you had to cancel. The lowest fares are also subject to availability; because only a certain percentage of the plane's total seats will be sold at that price, they may go quickly.

Consolidators Consolidators or bulk-fare operators—also known as bucket shops—buy blocks of seats on scheduled flights that airlines anticipate they won't be able to sell. They pay wholesale prices, add a markup, and resell the seats to travel agents or directly to the public at prices that still undercut the airline's promotional or discount fares. You pay more than on a charter but ordinarily less than for an APEX ticket, and, even when there is not much of a price difference, the ticket usually comes without the advance-purchase restriction. Moreover, although tickets are marked nonrefundable so you can't turn them in to the airline for a full-fare refund, some consolidators sometimes give you your money back. Carefully read the fine print detailing penalties for changes and cancellations. If you doubt the reliability of a company, call the airline once you've made your booking and confirm that you do, indeed, have a reservation on the flight.

The biggest U.S. consolidator, C.L. Thomson Express, sells only to travel agents. Well-established consolidators selling to the public include **UniTravel** (Box 12485, St. Louis, MO 63132, tel. 314/569–0900 or 800/325–2222); **Council Charter** (205 E. 42nd St., New York, NY 10017, tel. 212/661–0311 or 800/800–8222), a division of the Council on International Educational Exchange and a longtime charter operator now functioning more as a consolidator; and **Travac** (989 6th Ave., New York, NY 10018, tel. 212/563–3303 or 800/872–8800), also a former charterer.

Discount Travel Travel clubs offer their members unsold space on airplanes, *Clubs* cruise ships, and package tours at nearly the last minute and at well below the original cost. Suppliers thus receive some revenue for their "leftovers," and members get a bargain. Membership generally includes a regular bulletin or access to a toll-free telephone hot line giving details of available trips departing anywhere from three or four days to several months in the future. Packages tend to be more common than flights alone, so if airfares are your only interest, read the literature before joining. Reductions on hotels are also available. Clubs include **Discount Travel International** (114 Forrest Ave., Suite 203, Narberth, PA 19072, tel. 215/668–7184; $45 annually, single or family), **Moment's Notice** (425 Madison Ave., New York, NY 10017, tel. 212/486–0503; $45 annually, single or family), **Travelers Advantage** (CUC Travel Service, 49 Music Sq. W, Nashville, TN 37203, tel. 800/548–1116; $49 annually, single or family), and **Worldwide Discount Travel Club** (1674 Meridian Ave., Miami Beach, FL 33139, tel. 305/534–2082; $50 annually for family, $40 single).

Enjoying the Flight International travel between the Americas is a bit less wearing than to Europe or the Orient because there is far less jet lag. New York, for instance, is in the same time zone as Lima and there is only a three-hour time difference between Lima and Los Angeles. If you have a choice between day or night flights—and those to Rio de Janeiro and Buenos Aires always depart after dark—take the night plane if you sleep well while flying. Especially en route to the Andean countries, you will have lovely sunrises over the mountains. Southbound, the best views are usually out windows on the left side of the plane.

Because the air aloft is dry, drink plenty of beverages while on board; remember that drinking alcohol contributes to jet lag, as do heavy meals. Sleepers usually prefer window seats to curl up against; restless passengers ask to be on the aisle. Bulkhead seats, in the front row of each cabin, have more legroom, but since there's no seat ahead, trays attach awkwardly to the arms of your seat, and you must stow all possessions overhead. Bulkhead seats are usually reserved for the disabled, the elderly, and people traveling with babies.

Smoking Since February 1990, smoking has been banned on all domestic flights of less than six hours duration; the ban also applies to domestic segments of international flights aboard U.S. and foreign carriers. On U.S. carriers flying to South America and other destinations abroad, a seat in a no-smoking section must be provided for every passenger who requests one, and the section must be enlarged to accommodate such passengers if necessary as long as they have complied with the airline's deadline for check-in and seat assignment. If smoking bothers you, request a seat far from the smoking section.

Foreign airlines are exempt from these rules but do provide no-smoking sections, and some nations, including Canada as of July 1, 1993, have gone as far as to ban smoking on all domestic flights; other countries may ban smoking on flights of less than a specified duration. The International Civil Aviation Organization has set July 1, 1996, as the date to ban smoking aboard airlines worldwide, but the body has no power to enforce its decisions.

Getting Around South America

By Plane

Because distances are great between and within countries and there is little long-distance transportation overland, most visitors travel from point to point within South America by plane.

Special air-travel passes are available in the United States for travel within Argentina, Bolivia, Brazil, Chile, Colombia, Peru, and Venezuela. *See* country chapters for details.

Always reconfirm your flights, even if you have a ticket and a reservation, since departure times and days of operation may have changed and your reservations may be cancelled. Moreover, on many routes all over the continent, every flight operates full—usually of passengers with a great deal of baggage to process before departure. So always arrive at the airport well in advance of take-off to allow for the lengthy check-in. When leaving any country, you'll need to show your passport and pay departure taxes, either in the local currency or in dollars.

Smoking Both within and between countries, flights have smoking as well as no-smoking sections.

Luggage If you're arriving on an international flight to South America and connecting directly to a domestic flight, or flying between two countries on the continent, international baggage allowances apply. (*See* Luggage in What to Pack, *above*.) On flights within a single country, local baggage restrictions apply. For instance, between Lima and Cuzco and between mainland Ecuador and the Galápagos, you are limited to 44 pounds (20 kilograms).

By Car

Road conditions vary from country to country. But where the highways are paved, they are manageable.

Some commonsense rules of the road: Plan your daily driving distance conservatively. Don't drive after dark. Ask before you leave about gasoline stations. Obey speed limits (given in kilometers per hour) and traffic regulations. And above all, if you get a traffic ticket, don't argue—and plan to spend longer than you want on getting it settled.

A U.S., Canadian, or U.K. driver's license suffices for driving. Most countries use international driving signage on highways.

By Train

In most South American countries, trains do not play an important role in the transportation system. Still, there are high points.

There is no better way to see parts of South America than on some of its rail rides: in Peru, the three-hour run to Machu Picchu from Cuzco and the all-day ride from Cuzco to Puno on Lake Titicaca; in Ecuador, the dawn-to-dusk run through the Andes down the Avenue of the Volcanoes between Quito and Riobamba; in Chile, the overnight trip from Santiago to Puerto Montt; and in Argentina, the all-day or all-night ride from Buenos Aires to San Carlos de Bariloche. The latter two have sleeping and dining cars, the others few facilities at all.

Argentina's rail system, in the process of being sold to private industry, was built by the British. The most popular routes are all from Buenos Aires—the long trips to Bariloche, Tucuman, and Mendoza. Chile also has a good rail system, running south from the capital to the Lake District and beyond. One country to see at least in part by rail is Paraguay, where some lines are operated with steam locomotives dating from the 19th century.

Ticket prices are low. Usually there are two classes of travel. Make your purchase at least a day ahead, and arrive at the station well before departure time.

There are no rail passes except in Argentina (whose passes are difficult to obtain in the United States), and there is no way of reserving seats before you leave home.

By Bus

Bus service varies from country to country. Brazil, Chile, and Venezuela have relatively good service. Main routes are served by air-conditioned buses, some with toilets and movies. In Ecuador and Peru, bad roads and washed-out roads can make for interminable delays—but the views are spectacular.

However, bus service is generally reliable. And since buses are the primary means of transportation for most South Americans, traveling by bus gives you a chance to get to know the people. It also lets you see their homelands: Buses go almost anywhere there's a road, to all corners of most countries. Without doubt, the low cost of bus travel is its greatest advantage; its greatest drawback is the time you must allow, not only to cover the distances involved but also to allow for breakdowns and delays due to faulty equipment.

When traveling by bus, it is best to bring your own food and beverages, although food stops are usually made en route. Travel lightly, dress comfortably, and keep a close watch on your accompanying luggage and belongings.

Tickets are sold at city bus terminals. Note that in larger cities there may be different terminals for buses to different destinations. Come early to get a ticket, and expect to pay cash. On holidays such as Christmas, Easter, or national independence days, count on buying your ticket as far in advance as possible and arrive at the station extra early.

2 Adventure Vacations

*By Kurt Kutay
and Jenny Keller*

The New World holds the same fascination and attraction for modern-day adventure travelers as it did for early explorers. Despite the inherent difficulties, trekking in the Andes, Amazon jungle expeditions, and other off-beat travel opportunities in South America have become more available, thanks to the development of facilities in remote areas and tour services catering to the fit and adventurous. The safety record of established tour operators is excellent, although travel to remote areas in South America is subject to delays, inconveniences, and risks. Few trips to South America go entirely as planned; this is particularly true of adventure trips.

Adventure vacations are commonly split into soft and hard adventures. A hard adventure requires a substantial degree of physical participation, although you don't necessarily need technical skills or athletic abilities. In most cases previous travel experience in developing countries is recommended but not required; a doctor's approval may be needed as well. In a soft adventure the destination itself, rather than the means of travel, is often what makes it an adventure. Although a day's activity might include easy rafting or hiking, you can usually count on a hot shower and warm bed at night.

Below are the addresses of the major adventure-tour operators mentioned in this chapter.

Above the Clouds Trekking (Box 398, Worcester, MA 06102, tel. 508/799–4499 or 800/233–4499, fax 508/797–4779).
Adventure Associates (13150 Coit Rd., Suite 110, Dallas, TX 75240, tel. 214/907–0414 or 800/527–2500, fax 214/783–1286).
Adventure Center (1311 63rd St., Suite 200, Emeryville, CA 94608, tel. 510/654–1879).
Amazon Tours and Cruises (8700 W. Flagler, Suite 190, Miami, FL 33174, tel. 305/227–2266 or 800/423–2791, fax 305/227–1880).
American Alpine Institute (1212 24th St., Bellingham, WA 98225, tel. 206/671–1505).
American Wilderness Experience (Box 1486, Boulder, CO 80306, tel. 800/444–0099, fax 303/444–3999).
Andean Treks (65 Prentiss St., Cambridge, MA 02140, tel. 617/864–1422, fax 617/864–2303).
Anglers Travel Connections (3220 W. Sepulveda Blvd., Suite B, Torrance, CA 90505, tel. 213/325–9628 or 800/624–8429).
Big 5 Expeditions (110 Rte. 110, S. Huntington, NY 11746, tel. 516/424–2036 or 800/445–7002, fax 516/424–2154).
Blyth & Company (13 Hazelton Ave., Toronto, Ont. M5R 2E1, Canada, tel. 800/387–1387).
Brazil Nuts (79 Sanford St., Fairfield, CT 06430, tel. 203/259–7900 or 800/553–9959, fax 203/259–3177).
Close-Up Expeditions (1031 Ardmore Ave., Oakland, CA 94610, tel. 510/465–8955, fax 510/465–1237).
Earthquest Adventures (Box 1614, Flagstaff, AZ 86002, tel. 602/779–2585).
Earthwatch (680 Mount Auburn St., Box 403GB, Watertown, MA 02272, tel. 800/776–0188, fax 617/926–8532).
Ecotour Expeditions (Box 1066, Cambridge, MA 02238, tel. 617/876–5817 or 800/688–1822).
Elite Custom Travel (2817 Dumbarton St. NW, Washington, DC 20007, tel. 202/625–6500 or 800/662–4474, fax 202/625–2650).

Expediciones Andinas (Box 66, Riobamba, Ecuador, tel. 02/962845).

Explorandes (Bolognesi 159, Lima 18, Peru, tel. 469889, fax 454686).

Far Horizons (Box 1529, 16 Fern La., San Anselmo, CA 94960, tel. 415/457–4575, fax 415/457–4608).

Field Guides, Inc. (Box 160723, Austin, TX 78716, tel. 512/327–4953).

Fits Equestrian (685 Lateen Rd, Solvang, CA 93463, tel. 805/688–9494 or 800/666–FITS).

Focus Tours (Rua Grao Mogol 502s/223, Sion 30 330, Belo Horizonte, MG Brasil Embratur 07367–00–41–1, tel. 223–0358. U.S. address: 14821 Hillside La., Burnsville, MN 55377).

4th Dimension Tours (1150 N.W. 72nd Ave., Suite 250, Miami, FL 33126, tel. 305/477–1525 or 800/343–0020).

Frontiers (Box 959, Pearce Mill Rd., Wexford, PA 15090, tel. 412/935–1577 or 800/245–1950).

Hanns Ebensten Travel (513 Fleming St., Key West, FL 33040, tel. 305/294–8174).

Inca Floats (1311 63rd St., Emeryville, CA 94608, tel. 414/420–1550, fax 415/420–0947).

International Expeditions (1776 Independence Ct., Birmingham, AL 35216, tel. 800/633–4734).

Joseph Van Os Photo Safaris (Box 655, Vashon Island, WA 98070, tel. 206/463–5383).

La Selva (Box 635, Av. 6 de Diciembre 2816, Quito, Ecuador, tel. 02/550995 or 02/554686, fax 02/567297). U.S. Rep: Wildland Adventures (*see below*).

Lihué Expediciones (Belgrano 262, #104, San Isidro (1642), Buenos Aires, Argentina, tel. 01/747–7689, fax 01/112206).

Lost World Adventures (1189 Autumn Ridge Dr., Marietta, GA 30066, tel. 404/971–8586 or 800/999–0558, fax 404/977–3095).

Massachusetts Audubon Society (S. Great Rd., Lincoln, MA 01773, tel. 617/259–9500).

Metropolitan Touring (Box 310, Quito, Ecuador, tel. 02/560050, fax 02/564655). U.S. Rep: Adventure Associates (*see above*).

Mountain Travel-Sobek (6420 Fairmount Ave., El Cerrito, CA 94530, tel. 510/527–8100 or 800/227–2384, fax 510/525–7710).

Nature Expeditions International (Box 11496, Eugene, OR 97440, tel. 503/484–6529 or 800/869–0639).

Oceanic Society Expeditions (Fort Mason Center, Bldg. E, San Francisco, CA 94123, tel. 415/441–1106 or 800/326–7491).

Overseas Adventure Travel (345 Broadway, Cambridge, MA 02139, tel. 617/876–0533 or 800/221–0814, fax 617/876–0455).

Quest Nature Tours, represented by Worldwide Adventures, Inc. (920 Yonge St., Suite 747, Toronto, Ont. M4W 3C7, Canada, tel. 800/387–1483 or 416/963–9163 in Toronto).

Questers Tours (257 Park Ave. S, New York, NY 10010, tel. 212/673–3120 or 800/468–8668, fax 212/473–0178).

Rod and Reel Adventures (3507 Tully Rd., Modesto, CA 95356, tel. 209/524–7775 or 800/356–6982).

Safaricentre (3201 N. Sepulveda Blvd., Manhattan Beach, CA 90266, tel. 213/546–4411 or 800/223–6046).

Southwind Adventures (Box 621057, Littleton, CO 80162, tel. 303/972–0701, fax 303/972–0708).

Special Expeditions (720 5th Ave., New York, NY 10019, tel. 212/765–7740, fax 212/265–3770).

Turtle Tours (Box 1147, Dept. FG, Carefree, AZ 85377, tel. 602/488–3688).

University Research Expeditions Program (University of California, Berkeley, CA 94720, tel. 510/642–6586).
Victor Emanuel Nature Tours (Box 33008, Austin, TX 78764, tel. 512/328–5221 or 800/328–VENT).
Wilderness Travel (801 Allston Way, Berkeley, CA 94710, tel. 415/548–0420 or 800/247–6700).
Wildland Adventures (3516 NE 155th, Seattle, WA 98155, tel. 206/365–0686 or 800/345–4453, fax 206/363–6615).
Wings, Inc. (Box 31930, Tucson, AZ 85751, tel. 602/749–3175).
Woodstar Tours, Inc. (908 S. Massachusetts Ave., DeLand, FL 32724, tel. 904/736–0327).

Adventure Cruising

Spanning 4,200 miles, the Amazon River is the longest river in the world. From its source in southern Peru, the river encompasses western Brazil, eastern Peru and Ecuador, southern Colombia, and northern Bolivia. The river and its more than 1,000 tributaries provide a vast network of waterways for vessels of all sizes and classes to bring travelers into the heart of the South American continent. They comprise the last great wooded wilderness of its kind on earth, a natural laboratory with over half the world's species of birds and thousands of species of mammals and plants. Options for exploring the Amazon by boat range from a luxury cruise expedition with all the amenities to a low-budget adventure in native dugout canoes. Traditional riverboat cruises, with private or shared cabins, are also quite popular.

Brazil **Season:** Year-round.
Locations: Manaus, upper Amazon, Rio Negro, Belem.
Cost: From $2,990 for eight-day luxury cruise, $1,810 for a 10-day Ecotour Amazon River safari, and $270 for a two-night jungle-lodge package.
Tour Operators: Amazon Tours and Cruises, Ecotour Expeditions, Safaricentre, Special Expeditions.

For luxury expedition cruising, Special Expeditions is a good choice for an eight- to 15-day itinerary on the upper Amazon and Río Negro from Manaus, Brazil, to Iquitos, Peru. Their ship, the M.S. *Polaris,* comfortably accommodates up to 80 passengers. Go-everywhere Zodiac boats allow passengers easy access up twisting tributaries. A team of naturalists and specialists accompanies each expedition to provide leadership and conduct seminars. Trips depart in September and October, round-trip from Manaus.

Ecotour Expeditions offers a variety of natural-history trips on a small scale (10–15 participants). They use expedition vessels (60 feet or more in length) on the main rivers and smaller boats with outboard motors to enter the forest directly. Among the ecological zones toured is the *igapo,* or black-water flooded forest. Ecotour Expeditions, Amazon Tours and Cruises, and Safaricentre are well represented throughout the Brazilian Amazon, with options ranging from six-day, round-trip luxury cruises from Belem or Manaus, to riverboat cruises along the Río Negro, as well as lodge-based tours and private exploratory expeditions by Indian dugout canoe.

Chile **Season:** October–February.
Locations: Tierra del Fuego, Santiago.

Cost: From $2,499 including flight from Miami.
Tour Operator: 4th Dimension Tours.

An eight-day cruise through the glacier-studded waters around Tierra del Fuego, the island at the southern tip of South America, is featured on a new 10-day package. The 100-passenger *Terra Australis* provides all the comforts of an adventure ship; on-board meals include such regional specialties as king crab, oysters, Magallanes lamb, Argentine beef, and Chilean wines.

Peru   **Season:** Year-round.
Locations: Iquitos to Leticia, Pacaya-Samiria National Reserve.
Cost: From $495 for four-day cruise to $2,795 for 15-day cruise.
Tour Operators: Amazon Tours and Cruises, Oceanic Society Expeditions.

Amazon Tours and Cruises offers four-day downriver cruises from Iquitos to Tabatinga, Brazil, and to Leticia, Colombia, aboard the *Río Amazonas,* and four-day upriver cruises operating in reverse. Itineraries may be combined for a six-day round-trip cruise. The vessel has 20 air-conditioned cabins with private facilities and six non-air-conditioned cabins with shared facilities. Three-day cruises between Iquitos and Leticia aboard the *Arca* (of similar design) are also available. Among the many other options available is the *Margarita,* a handsome, two-deck wooden riverboat that departs Sundays on five-night cruises to the rain forest downriver from Iquitos, an ideal area for fishing, birding, and orchid or butterfly collecting.

Oceanic Society Expeditions penetrates the Peruvian Amazon on two eight-day expeditions (one in June, one in July), cruising the upper Amazon, Tahuayo, and Ucayali rivers aboard the *Margarita.* The destination is the Pacaya-Samiria National Reserve, the largest nature reserve in Peru. A high point is the observation of lively pink freshwater dolphins. The itinerary also includes easy nature hikes into the rain forest and a visit to an Indian village to observe traditional customs.

Amazon Jungle Camping

Because the Amazon River provides an easy and natural access to the jungle, it is a great starting point for Amazon-jungle camping excursions. Transportation is usually provided by expedition boats (thatch-roof motorboats), speedboats, and canoes. Passengers can expect to sleep on board in hammocks, at improvised campsites in the jungle, or on sleeping mats in *tambos* (thatch-roof shelters with raised flooring). Since these camping expeditions are more of the rough-and-ready nature they can be tremendously rewarding for the adventure seeker who wants to see the deep rain forest at close range and who enjoys sleeping in the jungle miles from the nearest village.

Ecuador   **Season:** May–August.
Locations: Amazon basin, the highlands.
Cost: From $2,090 for 17 days, round-trip from Quito.
Tour Operators: Wilderness Travel, Wildland Adventures.

Wilderness Travel's 17-day expedition takes you deep into the forest to meet the Cofan Indians. Daily expeditions are by dug-

2

out canoe and include hikes along jungle trails. There are eight nights of jungle camping in communal huts built on stilts; other nights are spent in hotels in the highlands.

Less demanding is La Selva's seven-day "Amazon Trek" along the Napo River. Trek through pristine jungle, sometimes on foot, sometimes in dugout canoes, and be greeted most nights by a prepitched camp and hot food. Departures are from Quito. La Selva's "Amazon Light Brigade" takes you from Quito to Coca and, over the next six days, to various camp sites along the Challuacocha River. This trip is demanding, but accommodations are luxurious and the food delicious.

Peru **Season:** June–August.
Locations: Manu National Park, Iquitos and environs.
Cost: From $1,425 for six days to $2,500 for 19 days.
Tour Operators: Amazon Tours and Cruises, Oceanic Society Expeditions, Wildland Adventures.

Located in Peru's Amazon basin, Manu National Park is the most undisturbed, biologically rich region on the continent. Protected by unnavigable rivers, impenetrable forests, and the towering Andes, this remote region is now accessible to small groups; several tour operators offer Manu as a separate itinerary or in combination with mountain trekking in the highlands. Accommodations include tent camps and jungle lodges. If you prefer a more comfortable setting, the Amazon Camp, operated by Amazon Tours and Cruises, comprises 42 screened rooms constructed entirely of native material, with thatch roofs and solid-bamboo siding, each with private facilities but no electricity.

Antarctica

Argentina **Season:** December–March.
Location: Ushuaia, Tierra del Fuego.
Cost: From $3,500 for two weeks.
Tour Operator: Blyth & Company.

Blyth & Company's nine-day treks to Antarctica include—weather permitting—daily onshore excursions to glacial bays, penguin colonies, and scientific research stations. Departures are from the Argentinian port of Ushuaia, after which you'll spend eight nights at sea aboard 50- to 75-passenger research vessels. Accommodations are in simple cabins or more expensive suites. Substantial discounts are available for those who join the tour in Buenos Aires or Ushuaia; rates from North America include airfare plus three nights in Buenos Aires and one night in Ushuaia.

Bicycling

Ecuador **Season:** February–August.
Location: Northern Ecuador highlands.
Cost: From $1,290 for eight days.
Tour Operator: Andean Treks.

This easy inn-to-inn adventure takes you bicycling and hiking on a circuit of the 15,000-foot Imbabura Volcano in northern Ecuador's scenic highlands, home to several distinct indigenous groups. With only one day of biking, this trip may be disappointing for serious mountain bike enthusiasts. On the other hand, people who want a quick getaway into the Andes can spend a week in the mountains with a naturalist guide without forsaking the comfort of modern accommodations.

Peru   **Season:** May–June, October; other departures on request.
Locations: Machu Picchu, Amazon.
Cost: From $1,750 for 16 days. Bikes available for rent.
Tour Operator: Andean Treks.

Cycle amid ancient ruins in the wondrous Sacred Valley of the Incas near Machu Picchu and down into the Amazon rain forest. Andean Treks' moderate bike adventure includes six nights' camping, one night at Machu Picchu, and a canoe expedition in Manu National Park.

Venezuela   **Season:** Year-round.
Locations: Mérida, Trans-Andean Highway, Sierra Nevada National Park.
Cost: From $890 per week. Includes hotel/inn accommodations, meals, vehicle support, guide services. Bike rental available at $50–$100 per week.
Tour Operators: Lost World Adventures, Safaricentre.

The Venezuelan Andes are crisscrossed by scenic roads and trails; you'll encounter everything from tropical cloud forest to rugged highland plains. If you want a greater challenge, high unpaved passes lead to secluded mountain lagoons and picturesque villages. Two-week tours include the Andes, Venezuela's eastern Caribbean coast, and the Gran Sabana.

Birding Tours

Argentina   **Season:** October–December.
Locations: Northern Argentina: Chaco; southern Argentina: the pampas, Patagonia.
Cost: From $2,495 to $4,250 for 17–20 days, and $4,695 for 32 days.
Tour Operators: Field Guides, Inc., Victor Emanuel Nature Tours.

Ponds, marshes, and grasslands in northern Argentina are the natural habitats of immense numbers of birds, including greater rheas, waterfowl, swans, red shoveler, and a host of others. On the Patagonian coast, most tours explore both the renowned Valdes Peninsula and Punta Tombo, home to a colony of some one million Magellanic penguins. Birding tours include the grasslands around Río Grande, the forests of the far south at Ushuaia, and the shores of the Beagle Channel. With either company you can expect comfortable, quaint accommodations with world-class ornithologists and naturalists as your guides.

Brazil   **Season:** Year-round.
Locations: Pantanal, Itatiaia National Park, Amazon basin.
Cost: From $1,000 for six days to $4,500 for 20 days.
Tour Operators: Field Guides, Inc., Turtle Tours, Victor Emanuel Nature Tours, Wings, Inc.

In southeastern Brazil, bird habitats range from coastal rain forest and wet pampas to cloud forest and plateau grassland. Such breathtaking birds as the red-billed curassow, bare-throated bellbird, and banded cotinga have their last stronghold here. Midway between Río de Janeiro and São Paulo is Brazil's second-highest mountain, in beautiful Itatiaia National Park. A family-run inn here invites longer stays for extensive birding in the area. Many companies offer tours through these regions and through Brazil's Pantanal, a vast area of seasonally flooded grassland considered by some naturalists to be the most stunning spectacle of the Americas.

Ecuador **Season:** Year-round.
Locations: Quito, Mt. Pichincha, Río Napo, Amazon, Galápagos Islands.
Cost: From $1,995 for two weeks to $4,745 for four weeks.
Tour Operators: Quest Nature Tours, Field Guides, Inc.

Ecuador's bird habitats include the steaming Amazonian rain forests in the east, the lush temperate and subtropical forests on the slopes of the Andes, and the paramo grasses and marshes above timberline. Each region is home to its own variety of birds—hummingbirds, the gigantic Andean condor, bush-tyrants, and brush finches in higher elevations and the zigzag heron, harpy eagle, Salvin's and nocturnal curassows in the jungle.

Venezuela **Season:** December–February.
Location: The Llanos.
Cost: From $2,850 for 16 days.
Tour Operators: Field Guides, Inc., Massachusetts Audubon Society, Victor Emanuel Nature Tours, Woodstar Tours.

Birds are especially abundant in Venezuela's vast expanse of savanna known as the Llanos. Among those you may see are seven species of ibis, herons, the primitive-looking hoatzin, and many raptors. Even yellow-knobbed curassows and the elegant sunbittern are easy to spot, as are scarlet macaws, noisy thorn birds, and a host of smaller birds.

Cultural Tours

Many travelers to South America are motivated by the archaeological heritage preserved here in religious sites, fortresses, terraces, and tombs. Others seek the living legacy of cultural expression found in local art and handicrafts, created by South American artists from traditions dating to the earliest human settlements in the Andes. Still others are drawn to experience the cultures of South America's rapidly vanishing indigenous tribes. Conserving these cultures is important: embedded in the fabric of so-called primitive societies are centuries-old secrets for living harmoniously with nature.

Chile and **Season:** February.
Easter Island **Locations:** Santiago, Easter Island.
Cost: From $2,295 for 12 days (Easter Island land cost only) to $3,895 for 19 days (Chile and Easter Island, land only). Approximate round-trip airfare from Miami via Santiago to Easter Island is $1,825.
Tour Operators: Far Horizons, Hanns Ebensten Travel, Nature Expeditions International.

Despite its remote location in the Pacific Ocean, 2,300 miles west of Chile, windswept Easter Island continues to draw hundreds of visitors each year to its unique open-air archaeological museum. Nearly 1,000 stone statues, or *moai*, stand gazing with brooding eyes over the island's gently rolling hills, and hundreds of perplexing petroglyphs stand out from their rock surfaces. Far Horizons' 12- or 19-day cultural discovery tour, led by archaeologist Dr. Georgia Lee, offers in-depth exploration of the island. Hanns Ebensten, who led one of the first tour groups to Easter Island some 25 years ago, offers a specialized 10-day tour during the Easter holiday, including five days on the island and three in Santiago. Nature Expeditions International has offered trips to Easter Island since its inception and now offers one of the most comprehensive explorations available, lasting anywhere from 5 to 14 days.

Ecuador **Season:** April–September.
Locations: From Quito to Cuenca, Ecuadorian Amazon.
Cost: From $1,455 for 15 days; jungle trip to Jivaro Indians from $2,575 for 16 days.
Tour Operators: Turtle Tours, Wildland Adventures.

Traveling by private vehicle from Quito to Cuenca with Wildland Adventures, you will visit several remote Indian markets and handicraft centers and explore significant archaeological ruins, including Ingapirca, the main Incan ruin in Ecuador. Between treks, accommodations are in hacienda-style inns near small towns; while trekking, large three-person tents are used. Turtle Tours, on the other hand, takes visitors by small plane, foot, and canoe into the heart of the jungle to live among the Jivaro Indians for six days. You can join your Indian hosts in fishing, jungle treks to thermal waterfalls, and canoe trips to neighboring villages. Monthly departures (except March and April) include hotels, meals, and guides.

Peru **Season:** May–October; Sipan, year-round.
Locations: Cuzco, Pitumarca, Chincheros, San Blas, Urubamba, Lima, Sipan.
Cost: $1,425–$1,925 for up to 18 days; Sipan, from $1,294 for 10 days, including airfare from Miami, lodging, and most meals.
Tour Operators: Andean Treks, Earthquest, 4th Dimension Tours, Hanns Ebensten Travel.

In Sipan, Peru, archaeologists unearthed a sealed, pre-Incan tomb in 1988 to find treasures of pure gold: ornate headdresses and masks, exquisite jewelry, and intricately sculpted figures. This priceless trove is on permanent display at the Bruning Museum in Sipan. It is also featured on a 10-day archaeological tour sponsored by 4th Dimension Tours, with departures from Lima. On Hanns Ebensten Travel's "Best of Peru," travelers explore ancient Inca sites rarely visited in the remote Vilcabamba.

With Andean Treks you can meet weavers in highland villages in Peru and Bolivia where the tradition of backstrap weaving remains strong. Both trips involve camping and hiking with some overnight stays in hotels and colonial-style haciendas. Earthquest has an 18-day tour featuring Peru's finest weavers and spinners, and for ceramics enthusiasts, a two-week tour that focuses on the traditional designs of the pre-Inca and Inca cultures.

Venezuela **Season:** Year-round.
Location: Amazonian rain forest.
Cost: $1,250 for six days and five nights, including round-trip flights from Caracas, hotel/camp accommodations, meals in Indian village, guide, and equipment.
Tour Operator: Lost World Adventures.

Previously available only to a select few explorers, anthropologists, and missionaries, the Lost World Adventures tour is still limited (six to a group) to those with serious ecological and anthropological interests. Conditions in these remote locations are extremely primitive: participants sleep in hammocks hung in rustic dwellings and eat local fish and game. Wilderness experience and a high degree of cultural sensitivity are required.

Fishing

Argentina   **Season:** December–April.
Locations: Tierra del Fuego, Patagonia.
Cost: From $3,400 for six full days fishing.
Tour Operators: Anglers Travel Connections, Frontiers.

For anglers Argentina is the southern hemisphere's Alaska, offering world-class brown- and rainbow-trout fishing on clear streams. Frontiers offers Argentine angling in three select regions: San Martin de los Andes, Esquel, and Tierra del Fuego. Anglers Travel Connections conducts expeditions to Patagonian waters, where wild browns and rainbows are found in greater numbers and in significantly larger sizes than in the United States. Group size is limited to six or eight.

Venezuela   **Season:** Year-round.
Locations: Throughout Venezuela.
Cost: $1,400–$2,600 for seven nights.
Tour Operators: Anglers Travel Connections, Rod and Reel Adventures.

In recent years Venezuela has gained a reputation for world-class bonefishing at El Gran Roque Island. Guri Lake has also established itself as the world's premier place for peacock bass, and Rio Chico offers options for tarpon and snook. Rod and Reel Adventures coordinates angling holidays to all of these destinations. Anglers Travel Connections has its own style of "exotic angling adventures," including combination fresh-and-saltwater packages for the best of both worlds, from budget to luxury; custom trips are available.

Horseback Riding

Argentina   **Season:** Year-round.
Locations: Pampas, Entre Rios region, northern Patagonia, Argentina wine country, the Andes.
Cost: From $705 for seven days to $2,040 for 18 days, including camping, meals, and accommodations in first-class hotels.
Tour Operator: Fits Equestrian.

Fits Equestrian offers a basic seven-day trip, covering traditional gaucho *estancias* (cattle ranches) in the Entre Ríos region. At the other extreme is an 18-day tough-adventure tour on which you ride 11 days on steep mountain trails through the Andes (expect few comforts on this trip).

Chile   **Season:** January–February.
Locations: Central Andes; east of Cruico, Peteroa Volcano; high Andes: near Santiago.
Cost: $2,200 for 13 days.
Tour Operator: Fits Equestrian.

Four to seven hours riding per day takes you at a leisurely pace across the Andes from west to east, all the way to the Argentina border. Only basic riding ability is required, although there is some rough terrain.

Peru **Season:** May–September.
Locations: Cuzco and Cordillera Vilcanota.
Cost: From $1,550 for 12 days.
Tour Operators: American Wilderness Experience, Wildland Adventures.

Both operators offer treks through some of the wildest country in the world—past cascading waterfalls, over 15,000-foot passes, and among remote, ancient Incan ruins. Horses carry expedition gear. Participants can hike with light day packs or ride on horseback.

Mountaineering

Argentina **Season:** December–March.
Location: Aconcagua Mountain, Patagonia.
Cost: Aconcagua, from $2,880 for 23 days; Patagonia, $1,880 for 14 days.
Tour Operators: American Alpine Institute (AAI), Andean Treks.

About 2,500 feet higher than Alaska's Mt. McKinley, Argentina's Mt. Aconcagua is the highest peak in the Western Hemisphere. When climbed by the Polish Glacier on its eastern face—the route taken by Andean Treks and the American Alpine Institute—the ascent provides high-quality ice climbing. Other routes range from grueling scrambles to severe technical challenges, making this a strenuous, high-altitude ascent for experienced mountaineers only. In Patagonia, the American Alpine Institute offers a 13-day expedition to the Fitzroy Peak area in February and a 13-day expedition to the Torres del Paine area in March.

Bolivia **Season:** April–September.
Locations: Lake Titicaca and the Bolivian altiplano, Cordillera Real range.
Cost: From $690 for seven days to $1,860 for 14 days.
Tour Operator: American Alpine Institute.

Though the Cordillera Real of Bolivia offers some of the continent's finest and most varied alpine climbing, it is probably the least known and least scaled range among comparable mountain groups. American Alpine Institute has a series of climbing programs here, ranging from sub-alpine day hikes to advanced climbs for experienced mountaineers only. Climbers are required to acclimatize for at least six days before participating in the institute's most strenuous programs, ideally spending the majority of their time between 10,000 and 12,000 feet. To round out their offerings, AAI sponsors a short expedition to the summit of 21,201-foot Nevado Illimani, the highest peak in Bolivia's Cordillera Real.

Ecuador **Season:** November–February.
Locations: Cotopaxi, Cayambe, Chimborazo, El Altar, Galápagos.
Cost: $2,060 for 15 days; from $1,390 for 10-day Antisana climb. Galápagos costs vary with boat and length of trip.

Tour Operator: American Alpine Institute.

The American Alpine Institute offers 14-day programs to three of the Andes' finest peaks: 19,348-foot Cotopaxi, 19,107-foot Cayambe, and 20,703-foot Chimborazo, the highest peak in the Cordillera Real. These itineraries can also be followed by a seven-day exploration of the Galápagos Islands by motor launch. Groups are kept small, either three to five climbers with one guide or six to 10 climbers with two guides. Climbing instruction is provided.

Peru **Season:** May.
Locations: Cordillera Vilcanota, southern Peru.
Cost: Varies with size of group.
Tour Operator: Andean Treks.

Intermediate climbers seeking high-altitude ice- and snow-climbing experience can join an Andean Treks climber's work-shop in the Vilcanota range of southern Peru. Included are expert instruction, strenuous high-altitude mountaineering, plus an attempt on 21,000-foot Nevado Ausangate, southern Peru's highest summit. The program lasts 22 days—including 15 nights camping and seven nights in three-star hotels—and begins and ends in Cuzco.

Venezuela **Season:** Year-round.
Locations: Mérida, Mucuchies, Mt. Toro, Pico Espejo, Pico Bolivar.
Cost: $690 for six days and five nights.
Tour Operator: Lost World Adventures.

For those in excellent physical condition, Lost World Adventures offers an exhilarating six-day "Ultimate Andes" trekking and climbing trip that culminates with an ascent of Pico Bolívar, Venezuela's highest peak, at 16,427 feet. Rock-climbing and mountaineering techniques are taught by experienced, English-speaking guides.

Nature Study

Argentina **Season:** October–February.
Locations: Valdes Peninsula, Iguazu Falls, Patagonia.
Cost: From $2,495 for 17-day overland safari.
Tour Operators: Elite Custom Travel, Wildland Adventures.

Argentina offers a vast array of natural-history experiences, from the tropical forests surrounding Iguazu Falls to the Antarctic environment of Tierra del Fuego, and from the Andes Mountains to the Patagonian steppe. Elite Custom Travel specializes in nature and photography travel to Argentina and excels at customizing itineraries to suit the individual traveler's interests and budget. Their most popular tour is the 16-day Patagonia Safari. Wildland Adventure's Argentina Wildlife Odyssey includes Valdes Peninsula, Patagonia, and Tierra del Fuego, plus a visit to the tropical rain forests of Iguazu Falls, for a comprehensive natural-history overview.

Brazil **Season:** Year-round.
Locations: Pantanal, Atlantic Coast, Iguaçu Falls.
Cost: From $100 per day.
Tour Operators: Brazil Nuts, Focus Tours, Questers Tours.

The Pantanal, the world's largest wetlands, lies in the center of South America. Unlike the dense rain forests of the Amazon, this marshy grassland makes an ideal place for wildlife observation; during the rainy season (October through March) flooding forces animals to congregate in high areas. Backcountry travelers in the Pantanal will see a spectacle of colorful tropical birds, caimans (alligators), anteaters, capybaras (large rodents), and possibly tracks of the elusive jaguar. Focus Tours specializes in the Pantanal and provides qualified naturalist guides who are sensitive to the environment. Their services are available only to preformed groups. Questers Tours, which works with Focus Tours in Brazil, offers several innovative, top-quality natural-history tours, one of which includes the Pantanal, Atlantic rain forests, and highland plateaus of central Brazil. Brazil Nuts has the widest range of lodge-based Pantanal safaris.

Chile Season: October–February.
Locations: Patagonia, Tierra del Fuego.
Cost: From $5,590 including flight from the United States.
Operator: Oceanic Society Expeditions.

Oceanic Society Expeditions, which specializes in marine natural-history trips, offers an in-depth, 18-day trip to the Falklands Islands, which boast some of the most ruggedly spectacular wilderness on the South American continent and an abundance of interesting wildlife. The December trip features the 4,000-foot granite towers in Paine National Park, a reserve for hundreds of graceful guanacos (cousins to the llama and alpaca). Flying inter-island in the Falklands, stops include visits to Macaroni, rockhopper, Magellanic, and gentoo penguin colonies, as well as huge seabird colonies.

Ecuador Season: Year-round.
Location: Galápagos.
Cost: From $900 to $3,000.
Tour Operators: Adventure Associates, Inca Floats, Metropolitan Touring, Wilderness Travel, Wildland Adventures.

The barren, volcanic Galápagos archipelago is habitat for some of the world's most bizarre animals and plants. Two-thirds of the resident birds and most reptiles at this showcase of evolution are found nowhere else in the world. Since the wildlife in Galápagos National Park never developed a fear of humans you can approach the animals for close-up photography and observation. One- and two-week cruise itineraries begin in Baltra or San Cristóbal. Two-week trips, such as Wilderness Travel's "Ultimate Galápagos," are conducted in vessels ranging from cruise ships holding 90 passengers to small yachts with a capacity of 12 or fewer. An advance deposit (six months to a year) should be made for the best boats, dates, and guides.

Venezuela Season: November–March.
Locations: The Llanos and Guayana Highlands.
Cost: From $1,500 to $3,000 for 15-day tour.
Tour Operators: International Expeditions, Lost World Adventures, Questers Tours, Safaricentre.

Some tours penetrate the largely uninhabited Guayana Highlands of Bolívar state, a region of mountainous tablelands, luxuriant rain forests, rivers, and spectacular waterfalls, including Angel Falls, the world's highest waterfall. Lost World Adventures offers one of the better treks in Venezuela, the "Auyan-Tepui Natural History Trek to the Guyana Highlands," a challenging ascent through the cloud forests to the top of a gigantic sandstone massif, or *tepuis*, one of many that dominate this bizarre landscape.

Overland Safaris

There is no faster way to immerse oneself in a number of cultures and landscapes than by an overland trip in special vehicles designed to cross the toughest desert, jungle, and mountain areas. On such an adventure you journey far from the beaten path to explore a South America seldom seen by the average tourist. Camping is the most common way to spend the night, though you may prefer to stay in lodges, inns, and hotels occasionally. You'll be expected to help with tenting, cooking, and with pulling the vehicle out of a ditch in more remote spots, if necessary. A camaraderie evolves on these long-distance trips that often sparks long-term friendships. Flexibility and adaptability are the key.

Season: Year-round.
Locations: Throughout South America.
Cost: From $35–$50 per day for 3–13 week itineraries.
Tour Operators: Adventure Center, Safaricentre.

Adventure Center specializes in cross-continental overland trips, covering as much of South America's culture, history, and geography as possible in one extended adventure tour. Complete itineraries run from one to three or more months, but can be broken into two- to four-week sections. Destinations range from Ecuador to the Patagonia region of Argentina, encompassing also the highlights in Peru, Bolivia, Chile, and Paraguay. You travel through mountains, steaming jungles, endangered rain forests, flat grasslands, and desert. You visit lost kingdoms and bustling modern cities and meet with gauchos, Amazon Indians, and highland peoples. Safaricentre operates shorter, but still well-rounded three-week overland adventures along the Inca Real in Peru; two-week jeep safaris in Venezuela; and three-week trips to Argentina, Bolivia, and Chile.

Photo Safaris

The tours listed below are all led by professional photographers who enhance the trip with instruction and valuable hands-on tips.

Argentina and Chile

Season: March and November.
Locations: From Iguazu Falls to Tierra del Fuego.
Cost: From $3,636 for 20 days, including accommodations, meals, transportation, guide services, and admissions within the trip.
Tour Operator: Close-Up Expeditions.

This tour focuses in on Chile and Argentina's landscapes and animals with an action-packed itinerary designed for wildlife and nature photographers. Transportation is by plane, private van, and minibus. Groups are kept small to allow for flexibility to react to changing light conditions and serendipitous events along the way. Close-Up trips can be specially designed to accommodate active seniors.

Ecuador **Season:** Year-round.
Locations: Galápagos.
Cost: From $650 for four days/three nights up to $1,355 for eight days/seven nights.
Tour Operators: Big 5 Expeditions, Joseph Van Os Photo Safaris.

The Galápagos archipelago is a paradise for wildlife photographers: There are frigate birds and blue-footed boobies, prehistoric iguanas, sea lions, fur seals, and 500-pound tortoises that seem to be suspended in time. Exceptionally rewarding for photographers is the rare opportunity to approach many of these animals closely, since they have remarkably little fear of people. Big 5 Expeditions offers nature-photography tours aboard the 90-passenger *Galapagos Explorer.* Cruises depart Wednesday and Saturday from San Cristobal Island in the Galápagos. Joseph Van Os Photo Safaris, on the other hand, offers a private photo safari to the Galápagos on board a small, deluxe yacht. Island excursions are led by an expert photographer and a local naturalist guide.

Venezuela **Season:** December–January.
Locations: The Llanos, Andes Mountains.
Cost: From $1,995 for 13 days.
Tour Operator: Joseph Van Os Photo Safaris.

During the dry season an incredible number of animals congregate along the drying lagoons and pools that punctuate the vast grassland known as the Llanos. On a Joseph Van Os Photo Safaris tour much of your stay is at a private ranch, Hato Pinero, where you can also view ocelot and red howler monkeys along with some of the ranch's estimated 75,000 spectacled caiman. The ranch is outfitted with photography blinds and vehicles especially adapted for photographing wildlife. Included in the tour is a trip into the scenic Andes Mountains to photograph villages, people, and broad vistas of the *paramo,* Venezuela's tropical alpine grassland, where some of the most unusual plants in the world grow. There is also the chance to photograph 16,000-foot Pico Bolívar from the top station of the world's highest cable car.

Scientific Research Trips

Whether your interests lie in helping to preserve the earth's dwindling resources, working on projects that will improve the lives of people in developing nations, or searching for clues to the past at archaeological sites, joining a research-expedition team contributes labor and money to the research. No prior research experience is necessary to join these trips. Instead, organizations look for people who are interested in learning, want to be part of a team, and have the flexibility and sense of humor needed to meet the challenges of a research expedition. Some programs are tax-deductible.

Brazil **Season:** January, April, June (one two-week trip offered each month).
Locations: Ilha do Cardoso tropical rain forest, near São Paulo.
Cost: From $1,545, including lodging and meals.
Tour Operator: Earthwatch.

One of the last remnants of an Atlantic coastal rain forest lies near the city of São Paulo, on Ilha do Cardoso, an island state park. In 1976 a research center was established, and it is from this base that Earthwatch teams work in shifts around the clock to assess the island's animals and plants. The work is essential for understanding how this severely threatened habitat works and how to save what is left of it in other parts of Brazil. Teams search for caiman nests and observe the animals' behavior; record the local habitat; map streams, swamps, and other topographic features; photograph animals and habitats; and enter the data into computers. Lodging is in research-station houses and dorms, which have electricity, water, and flush toilets.

Ecuador **Season:** July–August.
Locations: Napo Province, Maquipucuna Reserve.
Cost: From $1,395 for two weeks, from Quito.
Tour Operator: University Research Expeditions Program (UREP).

UREP has a 15-year history of sending research teams of University of California scientists, teachers, students, and others to investigate issues of human and environmental concern throughout the world. Current projects in South America include two environmental-studies programs in Ecuador, including workshops in the field and forest for U.S. and Ecuadorian scientists and educators. On "People of the Rain Forest: Conservation Their Way," expedition participants gather information to assist an indigenous Quichua community and a small-scale, nonintrusive ecotourism program that emphasizes traditional knowledge and resource use. Sensitivity to other cultures, ability to speak Spanish, and wilderness experience are helpful. Accommodations are rustic.

Peru **Season:** April–October.
Locations: Amazon River Basin, Inca Trail.
Cost: From $1,950 for eight-day trip, $2,890 for 15-day trip (includes airfare from Miami) for Amazon Dolphin Project; from $1,395 for 11-day Inca Trail Preservation Trek.
Tour Operators: Oceanic Society Expeditions, Wildland Adventures.

Oceanic Society Expeditions, the travel affiliate of Friends of the Earth, a conservation organization, has scheduled research trips in March, June, and July to study the botos, the largest river dolphin, native to the Amazon River basin. Participants on the "Amazon Dolphin Project" are to collect data to use in developing a long-term study focusing on the dolphins' movement patterns, social organization, and behavior in relationship to their environment. No special skills, other than knowing how to swim, are required. Headquarters is a 76-foot motor vessel with double-occupancy cabins.

Another conservation project in Peru is the "Inca Trail Preservation Trek," cosponsored by Wildland Adventures, The Earth Preservation Fund, and local Peruvian conservation organizations. The trek offers participants the opportunity to help preserve the natural and cultural heritage of Machu Picchu National Park.

Trekking

At the height of the Inca empire, the Andes were crisscrossed by a vast network of roads. They followed valleys and traced impossible pathways through narrow, precipitous terrain. Today remnants of Inca trails and footpaths used by today's indigenous people of the Andes lead adventurous hikers to ancient ruins, spectacular mountain peaks, jungle highlands, and small Indian communities. Trekking usually refers to an organized tour with experienced native guides and cooks who provide food, equipment, and camp services. Porters or pack animals carry gear, leaving trekkers the freedom of hiking with only a light day-pack. Treks are graded according to difficulty in terms of distance, terrain, and elevation. Whether you join an organized trek or arrange your own party it is recommended that you select a group with an experienced local guide when trekking through remote areas.

Argentina and Chile

Season: November–March.

Locations: Tierra del Fuego, Patagonia, Lake District.

Cost: From $1,550 for all-inclusive tour with nine days of trekking to $1,700 for 13 days.

Tour Operators: Earthquest, Lihué Expediciones, Mountain Travel-Sobek, Wildland Adventures.

Active local mountaineering clubs and well-established national parks systems in both countries are responsible for the excellent trail systems, campsites, and shelters used by trekkers in this region. Long daylight hours, lasting until 11 PM, add to the attraction of trekking here. The best trekking focuses on a magnificent area of the southern Andes shared by both countries that is generally referred to as Patagonia in Argentina and as the Lake District in Chile. Mountain Travel-Sobek and Earthquest jointly offer a 10-day trek around "The Wondrous Towers of Paine." These precipitous walls of glacier-carved peaks protrude a near-vertical 6,000 to 8,000 feet out of rolling grasslands, wild chasms, and deep azure lakes. Wildland Adventures has a "Patagonian Wildlands Safari" that combines a series of short treks in Glacier National Park, Torres del Paine, and the Fitzroy massif. Their Tierra del Fuego sail trek, dubbed "the southernmost trek in the world," follows the south Atlantic coast of Tierra del Fuego to Cape Horn. Buenos Aires–based Lihué Expediciones, one of the most respected adventure-tour companies in Argentina, has trekking programs throughout that country.

Bolivia

Season: April–September.

Location: Cordillera Real.

Cost: From $100 per day.

Tour Operators: Andean Treks, Wildland Adventures.

La Paz, the highest capital city in the world, is the base for trekking in Bolivia and the place to acclimatize before heading higher. A recommended highland-trekking itinerary combines a two-day trek over a pre-Inca road, the Takesi, with a three-day, high-elevation trek over two 16,500-foot passes to lakes and glaciers in the heart of the Cordillera Real mountain range. The trip is outfitted by Magri Turismo but can be booked through Wildland Adventures. Llamas and herders are used instead of pack horses. Andean Treks also offers several programs in Bolivia, including a llama trek in the Cordillera Real combined with visits to the Island of the Sun in Lake Titicaca.

Ecuador

Season: Year-round.

Locations: Central valley, western and eastern Cordillera ranges.

Cost: From $80 per day.
Tour Operators: Above the Clouds Trekking, Wilderness Travel, Wildland Adventures.

The Andes cross Ecuador from north to south in two ranges. Between them lies the fertile Central Valley, along what German explorer Alexander von Humboldt called "The Avenue of the Volcanoes" because the valley is edged by one of the largest concentrations of volcanoes in the world. Spectacular trekking routes, such as the Antisana Highlands Trek offered by Wildland Adventures, lead to high-elevation and glacier-clad volcanic peaks and descend to the tropical highlands of the Amazon basin. Other treks combine short hikes in the Andean foothills with visits to rural villages and little-known Indian markets, where visitors can mingle with a variety of distinctive ethnic groups.

Peru **Season:** April–October.
Locations: Cordillera Blanca, Cordillera Vilcanota, and Cordillera Vilcabamba.
Cost: From $300 for a four-day trek to $1,500 for a complete two-week itinerary.
Tour Operators: Explorandes, Mountain Travel-Sobek, Overseas Adventure Travel, Southwind Adventures, Wilderness Travel, Wildland Adventures.

The ancient Inca capital of Cuzco lies within the Cordillera Vilcabamba, where Yale archaeologist Hiram Bingham discovered the lost city of Machu Picchu, in 1911. Today the 45-kilometer (28-mile) Inca Trail affords adventurous trekkers the opportunity to reach Machu Picchu as the Incas did, by hiking along the royal road built over 500 years ago. This popular route passes through rare examples of cloud forest over a 14,000-foot pass, before descending into subtropical vegetation. Independent trekkers can join with others by booking directly with local trekking outfitters in Cuzco.

Wilderness Travel and Mountain Travel-Sobek offer the greatest diversity of trekking programs in Peru. Southwind Adventures organizes a "Highland Vistas Trek," which combines several ranges in one itinerary. Explorandes, the largest adventure-travel tour outfitter based in Peru, has the widest range of itineraries.

Water Sports

Alternately exhilarating and relaxing, white-water rafting and sea kayaking provide a pace and perspective all their own. You don't have to be an expert paddler to enjoy a river adventure, but you should know how to swim. Rivers are rated according to difficulty, and South America has some of the wildest commercially rafted rivers in the world. Generally speaking, Class III and IV rapids are rolling to rollicking and suitable for beginners. Many Class V (potentially dangerous) rapids are strictly for the experienced.

Chile **Season:** December–March.
Location: Bio-bio River, Class IV.
Cost: From $1,950 to $2,390 for 14 days, round-trip from Santiago.
Tour Operators: Mountain Travel-Sobek, Earthquest.

Since the first descent of Bio-bio, undertaken by Mountain Travel-Sobek in 1978, the river's reputation for white-water action has become known to rafters around the world. At the headwaters the gradient is gentle, as the river ripples through soft, rolling countryside. This changes abruptly, however, as metamorphic and granitic gorges pinch the river channel to create challenging and complex white-water sections. In 10 days on the river you ride nearly 100 rapids, but there are opportunities to enjoy the scenery and hot springs along the way. There's trout fishing, hiking, lounging on soft beaches, and interaction with the people who live along the river—farmers, cowboys, and Indians. Kayakers may join any of the Earthquest and Mountain Travel-Sobek raft trips on the Bio-bio. Earthquest also offers a new trip called "Sea Kayaking Archipelagic Chile" which explores the volcanoes of the Lake District and paddles along the wild Chilean coast.

Ecuador **Season:** November–April for rafting; May–August, November for riverboating.
Locations: Quijos River, Class III, IV, and V; Toachi River, Class III.
Cost: From $45 for one day; from $180 for two days/one night (one rafting); from $1,480 for 10 days aboard riverboat.
Tour Operators: Earthquest, Mountain Travel-Sobek.

Venezuela **Season:** Year-round.
Locations: Orinoco and Caroni rivers, Classes IV and V.
Cost: From $1,490 for seven days.
Tour Operator: Lost World Adventures.

Orinoco's Ature Rapids in Amazonas Territory and the Caroni River's Nekuima Canyon in the Guayana Highlands give even experienced river rafters a memorable roller-coaster ride on their giant frothy waves. Lost World Adventures' skilled river guides lead seven-day rafting expeditions along these formidable rivers. Trip cost includes four days rafting, lodge and camp accommodations, meals, guide services, and equipment.

3   Argentina

By Ed Shaw

Ed Shaw writes about travel, art, and finance for magazines and newspapers in the United States and Latin America.

Most travelers think they've stumbled on a long-lost European country when they get to Argentina. Most Argentines, too, are convinced they are more European than American. A quick look at the people walking down the avenues of any Argentine city confirms the impression. There are more Italian surnames than Spanish, and here is the largest colony of Yugoslavians outside the fractured homeland. There are millions of descendants of Jewish immigrants from Eastern Europe, and communities of British, French, and German families enjoy cultural and financial clout far beyond their insignificant numbers.

But in spite of the symbiosis with Europe, the country has had a chaotic past, politically and economically. No one can thrive on inflation—and survive hyperinflation—like an Argentine can. Traditionally a long-term bank note deposit has been measured in hours. The pitfalls of Argentine politics have been popularly portrayed in the musical *Evita*. "Truth is stranger than fiction" is a maxim confirmed by the musical chairs–like process that has gotten both civilians and soldiers into the country's precarious presidency. But President Carlos Saúl Menem's massive privatization program—sell-offs that include the national railways and Argentina's telephone system—should do much to get the economy back on track and attract outside investment.

Argentina is a me-first society that considers government a thorn in its side and whose citizens avoid paying taxes with the finesse of bullfighters. As a community, it's totally chaotic, but as individuals, Argentines are generous and delightful, full of life and eager to explain the intricacies of their complex society. They are also nonstop philosophers, anxious to justify their often enviable existence. Friendship is a time-consuming priority, and family connections are strong—children leave the nest, but not the neighborhood. Argentines work longer hours than New Yorkers—just not so efficiently—and rival Madrileños at dining until dawn.

Geographically, Argentina more closely resembles the United States than Europe. Its vast territory stretches more than 5,000 kilometers (3,000 miles) from north to south and encompasses everything from snow-covered mountains to subtropical jungle. In the north, in the sultry province of Misiones, nature is raucous and rampant; here the spectacular Iguazú Falls flow amid foliage that is rain forest–thick. In the pampas, or plains, of central Argentina, the countryside recalls the American West: Gauchos herd the cattle that provide Argentina with the beef it consumes in massive quantities. In the west, the Andean backbone Argentina shares with Chile attracts climbers to Mt. Aconagua, the Southern Hemisphere's highest peak, and draws skiiers to Bariloche and other resorts. Patagonia, in the south, is like no other place on earth. Monumental glaciers tumble into mountain lakes, depositing icebergs like meringue on Floating Island. Penguins troop along beaches like invading forces, whales hang out with several yards of their tails emerging from the sea, and at the tip of Patagonia, South America slips into Beagle Channel in Tierra del Fuego.

Staying Safe and Healthy
Crime

Women are safer in Buenos Aires than in any other major city in the world. Don't over- or under-dress, or flash jewelry in the

streets. Just act like you know what you are doing, and you
should have no problems.

Health   Drinking tap water and eating uncooked greens are safe in
Buenos Aires. There are several hundred cases of cholera registered in the northern part of Argentina each year, mostly in
the indigenous communities near the Bolivian border; your
best protection is to avoid raw seafood. Overeating and over-
drinking, a constant temptation, may cause health problems
that cannot be blamed on Argentine fare.

Essential Information

Before You Go

When to Go   If you can handle the heat, Buenos Aires can be wonderful in
summer, which peaks in January. At this time, the traditional
vacation period, Argentines are crowding inland resorts and
beaches, but Buenos Aires has no traffic, and there is always a
seat at shows and restaurants. Avoid visiting popular resort
areas in January and February and in July, when they become
overcrowded again due to school holidays.

The best time to visit Iguazú Falls is August–October, when
temperatures are lower and the spring coloring is at its bright-
est. Rain falls all year, dropping about 205 centimeters (80
inches) annually. Summer temperatures (January–February)
usually range in the high 90s to low 100s (35°C–40°C). Winter
temperatures (June–August) drop considerably.

Resort towns like Bariloche and San Martin de los Andes stay
open all year. Summer temperatures can get up into the high
70s (about 25°C), but most of the year, the range is from the
30s to the 60s (0°C–20°C).

The Patagonia coast is located on the infamous latitude that
sailors call the "Roaring Forties," with southern seas that batter Patagonia throughout the year. Thirty-mile-per-hour winds
are common, and 100-mile-an-hour gales are not unusual. Summer daytime temperatures reach the low 80s (about 28°C), but
can drop suddenly to the 50s (10°C–15°C). Winters hover near
the freezing mark.

Most travelers visit Tierra del Fuego in the summer, when temperatures range from the 40s to the 60s (5°C–20°C). Fragments
of glaciers cave into southern lakes with a rumble throughout
the thaw from October to the end of April, which is the best
time to enjoy the show.

Climate   From the northern subtropical jungles to the southern glaciers, Argentina's climate encompasses it all. Temperatures,
though, are generally slightly milder than they are in equivalent latitudes in the Northern Hemisphere, because in the
southern half the country is narrow, and the oceans moderate
temperatures.

The following are the average daily maximum and minimum
temperatures for Buenos Aires.

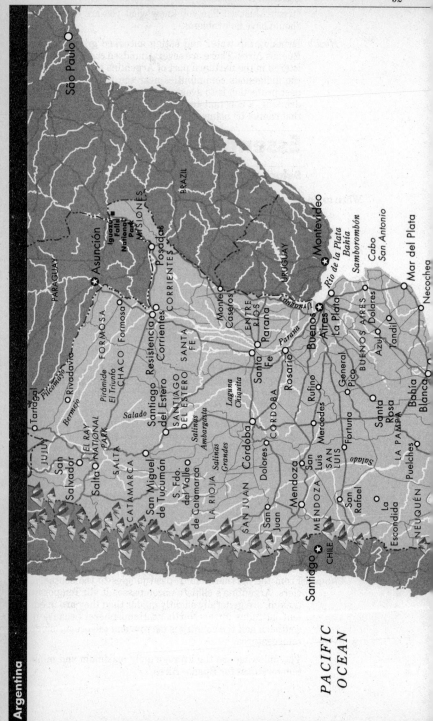

Argentina

PACIFIC OCEAN

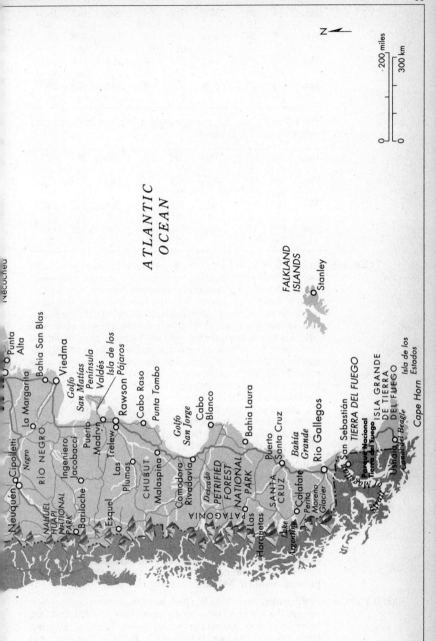

ATLANTIC
OCEAN

FALKLAND
ISLANDS

Stanley

Necochea
Punta Alta
Bahía San Blas
Viedma
Golfo San Matías
Península Valdés
Isla de los Pájaros
Rawson
Cabo Raso
Punta Tombo
Golfo San Jorge
Cabo Blanco
Bahía Laura
Puerto Santa Cruz
Bahía Grande
Río Gallegos
San Sebastián
Isla de los Estados
Cape Horn
Ushuaia
Canal del Beagle
ISLA GRANDE DE TIERRA DEL FUEGO
TIERRA DEL FUEGO
Parque Nacional Tierra del Fuego
Strait of Magellan
Perito Moreno Glacier
Lake Argentino
Calafate
El Chaltén
Los Horquetas
PETRIFIED FOREST NATIONAL PARK
Deseado
SANTA CRUZ
Comodoro Rivadavia
Malaspina
CHUBUT
Esquel
Bariloche
NAHUEL HUAPI NATIONAL PARK
Neuquén
Cipolletti
La Margarita
RÍO NEGRO
Negro
Ingeniero Jacobacci
Puerto Madryn
Trelew
Las Plumas
PATAGONIA

200 miles
300 km

Jan.	85F	29C	May	64F	18C	Sept.	64F	18C
	63	17		47	8		46	8
Feb.	83F	28C	June	57F	14C	Oct.	69F	21C
	41	5		63	17		50	10
Mar.	79F	26C	July	57F	14C	Nov.	76F	24C
	60	16		42	6		56	13
Apr.	72F	22C	Aug.	60F	16C	Dec.	82F	28C
	53	12		43	6		61	16

The following are the average daily maximum and minimum temperatures for Bariloche.

Jan.	70F	21C	May	50F	10C	Sept.	50F	10C
	46	6		36	2		34	1
Feb.	70F	21C	June	45F	7C	Oct.	52F	11C
	46	8		34	1		37	3
Mar.	64F	18C	July	43F	6C	Nov.	61F	16C
	43	6		32	0		41	5
Apr.	57F	14C	Aug.	46F	8C	Dec.	64F	18C
	39	4		32	0		45	7

Currency In March 1991, as part of the government's program to stabilize the economy, Argentina's currency was pegged to the dollar. As a result, the Argentine peso (which replaced the austral) is on a one-to-one parity with the U.S. dollar. In the past, dramatic value swings occurred during periods of hyperinflation. In fact, in a bleak, short-lived moment, a cup of coffee cost twice as much in local currency after dinner than it did for breakfast. Nevertheless, economic stability has gradually occurred in the last few years, and the currency appears to be considerably more stable as well. At press time (Summer 1993), the exchange rate was one peso to the U.S. dollar, 80 pesos to the Canadian dollar, 1.50 pesos to the pound sterling. Dollars are the most flexible form of exchange in Argentina, so residents of other countries should change their currencies to dollars before their journey. Be sure the bills are not torn or dirty; bills in poor condition won't be accepted.

You can change money at your hotel, at banks, or at *casas de cambio* (money changers), which offer small competitive variations on rates. Some display rates for all major currencies. Larger stores in downtown areas catering to foreign visitors will often accept payment by a personal check drawn on a major U.S. bank, or traveler's checks. Smaller shops and restaurants are leery of traveler's checks. The long period of price stability also has meant a boom in the acceptance of credit cards. American Express, Diners Club, MasterCard, and Visa are the most commonly accepted, although there are often good discounts to be found for using U.S. dollar bills.

What It Will Cost For decades, Argentina has had one of the most volatile economies in the world, a boom–bust seesaw driven by inflation that sometimes rose several percentage points in a day. At press time, inflation has been tamed, and indications that the trend will continue are plentiful, making it more likely that costs can be predicted with some degree of accuracy. Argentina is no longer cheap, although bargains can be discovered by those accustomed to New York and London prices. The most sumptuous dinners, particularly in French restaurants, can run as high as $100 per person with wine and tip. But a thick slab of rare, wood-grilled sirloin with salad, potatoes, a house wine, and an espresso will cost $20 at a steak houses in Buenos Aires, less in the hinterlands.

Order only national liquors in the bars or you'll pay a tremendous import premium. Shops get $75–$100 for a bottle of the all-time Latin American favorite, Chivas Regal. Simply ask for *"whiskey nacional por favor"* or *"vodka nacional."*

Sample Prices A cup of coffee in a café, $1.50; a glass of soda, $2. Taxi ride in central Buenos Aires, $2–$5. About $40 for a tango show with a couple of drinks; $80–$100 for a double room in a moderately priced, well-situated hotel, including taxes.

Customs on Arrival If you come directly to Buenos Aires by air or ship, you will find that customs officials usually wave you through without any inspection. Also, the international airports have introduced a customs system for those with "nothing to declare," which has streamlined the arrival process. Foreign bus passengers usually have their suitcases opened, along with all other passengers.

Personal clothing and effects are admitted free of duty, provided they have been used, as are personal jewelry and professional equipment, including portable computers. Travel agents or airlines can make advance arrangements for hunting equipment. Fishing gear presents no problems.

Up to 2 liters of alcoholic beverages, 400 cigarettes, and 50 cigars are admitted duty-free.

Language Argentines speak Spanish. English replaced French as the country's second language in the 1960s. Just about every high school graduate has a working knowledge of English, and most shops have English-speaking personnel. Since many Argentines are of Italian descent, Italian is understood by many *porteños* (residents of Buenos Aires).

Getting Around

By Plane All medium-size and large cities in Argentina are served by the jets of **Austral** (tel. 1/325–0777) and **Aerolineas Argentinas** (tel. 1/362–5008, or 800/333–0276 in the U.S.), which also flies the international routes. Aerolineas was privatized in late 1990 and purchased by a consortium composed of the Spanish airline Iberia, the Argentine government, and local investors. **CATA** (tel. 1/775–6800), another private service, offers a limited number of flights at competitive rates, particularly in summmer. Small remote towns in the south are visited regularly by **LADE** (tel. 1/361–0853), whose commuter-size airplanes are operated by the Argentine Air Force. Again, frequencies are greatly reduced in the winter.

Like the United States and Canada, Argentina has large, sparsely inhabited areas to cross, so many travelers find themselves taking several internal flights. The **Visit Argentina** pass is designed for them: Four coupons cost $450; each additional coupon is $120 up to a maximum of eight; all must be used within 30 days of the first flight, and you cannot stop twice in any city except to connect. The passes can be purchased only outside the country and only through Aerolineas Argentinas, upon the presentation of an international ticket. Seats are usually available on domestic flights, even in high season, except at holiday peaks. Keep in mind that Buenos Aires's domestic and international airports are 61 kilometers (38 miles) apart.

By Car The **Automovil Club Argentino** (ACA, Av. del Libertador 1850, tel. 1/802–6061 or 1/802–0522) operates filling stations, motels, and campgrounds, and provides tow trucks and a large team of motorized mechanics for unexpected breakdowns and subsequent repairs.

The club, which has several hundred thousand active members, also offers detailed maps and experts (some of whom speak English) to help plan your route. For drivers who rent a car and want to see the country, ACA provides gas coupons and can make accommodation arrangements according to a series of standard itineraries. AAA members can use the consulting services without charge, with proof of membership.

Road Conditions Superhighways do not exist in Argentina. Most roads are not divided and are not in good condition. Highways have also been privatized, so there are now more roads, even old ones, on which the driver must pay tolls. Night driving can be hazardous, as cattle often get onto the roads and trucks seldom have all their lights working.

Parking Parking has also been privatized in Buenos Aires, so ticket-happy entrepreneurs are busy putting yellow metal hobbles on the front wheels of cars that stand too long at a meter, and tow trucks haul violators off to a nearby parking lot. Fines and costs for getting towed start at $75. There are a few public underground car parks and numerous private garages. They start at $2–$3 for the first hour.

Rules of the Road Give everyone else on the road priority in Buenos Aires, especially aggressive *colectivos* (buses) and taxi drivers who think they're race-car drivers. Seat belts are required by law but are not often used. Traffic lights are not always observed. Proceed with care.

Gasoline Argentina produces and markets its own gasoline. It is sold by the liter in regular and premium octanes. At press time, a U.S. gallon cost the equivalent of $2.75 for premium and $2.40 for regular.

Car Rental All cities and most remote areas that attract tourists have rental-car agencies. When these companies have branches in other towns, arrangements can be made for a one-way dropoff. **Avis** (Maipú 944, tel. 1/311–1000), **Hertz** (Pasaje Ricardo Rojas 451, tel. 1/312–1317), and **National** (Esmeralda 1084, tel. 1/312–4318) offices in Buenos Aires can make reservations in other locations; provincial government tourist offices also have information on car-rental agencies in their areas. Car rental is expensive by U.S. standards—$95 per day for a medium-size car, $475–$600 weekly. Ask about special rates; generally a better price can be negotiated.

By Train At the moment the railway system is being privatized and most long-distance and overnight service has been suspended. Trains to Buenos Aires's suburbs run frequently, as do trains to Mar del Plata and Rosario. Up-to-date information can be obtained from **Argentine Railways** (Maipú 88, tel. 1/331–3280).

By Bus Frequent and dependable bus service links Buenos Aires with all the provinces of the country and with neighboring countries. Luxurious buses of a kind unknown in the United States, with sleeper seats similar to first-class airline seats, travel to the most remote destinations; more spartan buses cover the same routes at lower fares. Long-distance buses leave from the central terminal at the port end of **Retiro** (Av. Ramos Mejia 1680, tel. 1/311–6073 or 1/311–6088), one of the city's central train stations. There are dozens of competing bus companies that cover the country like a cobweb.

By Boat There is no internal boat travel in Argentina. Cruise ships stop in Tierra del Fuego, and hydrofoils and ferries connect Buenos Aires with nearby Uruguay (*see* Arriving and Departing in Buenos Aires, *below*).

Staying in Argentina

Telephones Pay phones can be found on the streets, in public buildings, **Local Calls** offices, airports, and other transportation terminals, and in pharmacies, bars, and restaurants. They operate on tokens called *fichas,* which can be bought at newsstands, kiosks, and in many bars and restaurants. One ficha buys two or three minutes of time, depending on whether you are calling at prime time (8 AM–8 PM) or otherwise. Phone service throughout the country can be a frustrating experience. Despite the recent privatization of ENTEL, the formerly government-run telephone monopoly, service in the city is still erratic. Phone numbers are being changed, and a common phone greeting is *equivocado* (e-kee-voh-CA-do), meaning wrong number. Often the best bet is to get operator assistance or have the operator at your hotel help put through calls. Using phones in post offices (correos) is another good option. For information dial 110, for the time 113.

Argentines, accustomed to living with frustrating infrastructure, are uncomfortable doing business by phone. The fax is now replacing the phone as the easiest form of speedy in-city communications.

International Calls International calls can be made from telephone company offices around Buenos Aires and from private companies with streetfront offices. Most hotels have direct-dial international lines in the rooms. **Telefónica de Argentina** (Av. Corrientes 707 at the corner of Maipú, tel. 1/372–7098) offers 24-hour international service.

For an international operator, dial 000. For information about international calls, dial 953–8000. AT&T, MCI, and Sprint have direct calling programs. AT&T's **USA Direct** service allows you to call collect or charge calls from abroad to your AT&T calling card. To access USA Direct, dial 011–800/200–1111. For more information, call 412/553–7458, ext. 314, collect from outside the U.S., or 800/874–4000 in the United States. MCI and Sprint's services are similar; to access MCI's **Call USA** service, dial 001–800/333–111. To use Sprint's **World Travel card,** dial 001–800/777–1111.

Mail When delivery is normal and there are no strikes or postal vacations, a letter takes 7–15 days to get from Buenos Aires to the United States; 10–15 days to the United Kingdom. An international airmail letter costs 70¢. Put postcards in envelopes and they will arrive more quickly.

Visitors can receive mail at the **Correo Central** (Central Post Office, Sarmiento 151, 1st floor, tel. 1/312–1048). Letters should be addressed to Lista/Poste Restante, Correo Central, 1000 Buenos Aires, Argentina. American Express cardholders can have mail sent to the company's Buenos Aires office: c/o American Express, Arenales 707, 1061 Buenos Aires, Argentina, tel. 1/312–0900 or 1/312–1661.

Opening and Closing Times Banking hours are 10–3. Shops in Buenos Aires are open weekdays 9–7 or 8, Saturdays 9–1. In the city's suburbs, with the exception of the large malls like Unicenter and Shopping Soleil, and most places outside the capital, shops close for a siesta break from approximately 12:30 to 3:30 or 4, when they open again until 7:30 PM. Post offices are open weekdays 8–6, Saturdays 8–1. There is 24-hour telephone and telex service at Avenida Corrientes 707.

National Holidays January 1; Maundy Thursday (optional holiday, some offices close); Good Friday; May 1 (Labor Day); May 25 (Anniversary of the 1810 Revolution); June 10 (Malvinas Day); June 20 (Flag Day); July 9 (Independence Day); August 17 (Anniversary of San Martín's Death); October 12 (Columbus Day); December 8 (Immaculate Conception); and December 25.

Dining Beef, or *bife*, as they say in Argentine Spanish, is still the staple of the country's diet. Once a major export, cattle traditionally have outnumbered people two to one in Argentina. Gauchos spent their lifetimes in the saddle eating exclusively the range-fed native cattle they raised. Some 50 million Angus, Hereford, and a dozen other breeds thrive on the pampa grasses, which are so nutritious that there is no need for grain supplements.

Nothing can duplicate the indescribable flavor of a lean, tender, 3-inch-thick steak grilled over coals of a log from the *quebracho* tree, an ax-breaking hardwood from the Chaco. Many different cuts of a steer are grilled on the *parilla* (grill) at an *asado*, as a barbecue is called here. Steaks can be accompanied by *picante* (hot) sauce, although Argentines traditionally prefer theirs straight. (Picante does not burn like Mexican chilis or Indian curries.) If you ask for *chimichurri*, chefs will serve a picante sauce prepared from garlic, olive oil, vinegar, and cilantro. *Bife de chorizo* is a basic strip sirloin, but three times the size; *bife de lomo* can be a 3-inch-high fillet. Often a half portion is more than enough. *Jugoso* means rare, but Argentines like their meat well-done, so it is hard to get a *parillero* to prepare a steak so that it is red when sliced.

Adventurous meat eaters will want to have their steak served sizzling on a miniature grill, the *parillada*, whose hot coals keep the cuts warm at the table. The mixed grill includes blood sausage, short ribs, and various internal and external organs like intestines and udder. A typical beef hors d'oeuvre consists of thin slices of *matambre*, made by laying out boiled eggs, chunks of ham, and hearts of palm on flank steak, rolling it into a loaf, soaking it in a marinade, and baking it. Beef is also traditionally served in the form of a breaded cutlet, called a *Milanesa*, often wrapped in ham and cheese with a tomato sauce. The simple version is a *Milanesa*, the kind with ham, cheese, and sauce a *Milanesa Napolitana*. Hamburgers are usually served at home or at fast-food emporiums; Argentines don't have the knack for making great burgers. Stick to steaks.

Most Argentine desserts are made with one principal ingredient: *dulce de leche*, a sticky sweet made of milk boiled with sugar, a pinch of soda, and a few drops of vanilla. The thick, brownish cream is spread on breakfast toast, baked in cakes, meringues, and tarts, and is often eaten alone by the spoonful. Mixed with bits of chocolate, it is a favorite flavor in Argentine ice-cream shops. Most Argentines travel with several pots when they go abroad.

Italian cuisines, particularly that of Naples and Sicily, are found throughout Argentina. Buenos Aires has the most concentrated immigrant influence, with Jewish delicatessens, British restaurants (especially good for high tea), and French, German, Irish, Cantonese, and Middle Eastern cuisines, to name a few. Lamb asado (*corderito al asador*), king crab (*centolla*), and hot potato salads are popular in Ushuaia, while in the Trelew–Puerto Madryn area, the favorites are Welsh high teas with seven varieties of rich cakes, and local fish—*trucha* (sea trout), *salmon* (sea salmon), *corvina* (white sea bass), and *calamares* (squid).

Given the high consumption of beef rather than fish, Argentines understandably drink *vino tinto* (red wine). For those who prefer *vino blanco* (white wine), try vintages from Mendoza and from less-known wineries farther north: La Rioja and Salta. Here the Torrontés grape thrives. The Torrontés varietal produces a dry white with an overwhelming, unforgettable bouquet that has been a consistent prizewinner in recent competitions in Germany and France.

A popular summer cooler is *clericot*, a white version of sangria, made with strawberries, peaches, oranges, or whatever fruits are in season or appeal to a particular bartender. Sangria is also available in many restaurants.

Mealtimes Breakfast is usually served until 10; lunch runs from 12:30 to 2:30; dinner is from 9 to midnight. Several restaurants in Buenos Aires and other large cities stay open all night, catering to the after-theater crowd.

Dress Jacket and tie are suggested for more formal restaurants in the evening in the top price category, but casual chic or informal dress is accepted in most restaurants.

Ratings Prices quoted here are per person and include a first course, a main course, and a dessert, without wine or tip. Highly recommended restaurants in each price category are indicated by a star ★.

Category	Cost
Expensive	over $25
Moderate	$15–$25
Inexpensive	under $15

Lodging While Argentina has very few world-class deluxe hotels, it offers far more excellent tourist-class hotels than most countries both north and south of the equator.

Hotels Amenities in most hotels are above average, with private bath, 24-hour room service, heating and air-conditioning, cable TV, dry cleaning, and restaurants.

Albergues *Albergues transitorios,* or temporary lodgings, is the euphe-
Transitorios mistic name for drive-in hotels, which generally are used for

romantic trysts; those that are legitimate motels can be found through the **Automovil Club Argentino**'s nationwide network. These motels are inexpensive and more than adequate, costing $35–$45 a night. Make reservations through the ACA (Av. del Libertador 1850, tel. 1/805–6061 or 1/802–0522).

Youth Hostels The local branch of the **Youth Hostel Association** (Talcahuano 214, 2nd floor, tel. 1/476–1001) is open weekdays 11–8; it provides details on hostels throughout the country.

Camping Campsites can be found in popular tourist destinations, including some of the beach areas. Usually they have running water, electricity, and bathroom facilities with toilets and showers. The **Automovil Club Argentino** (*see* Getting Around By Car, *above*) can provide a list of campgrounds nationwide. Provincial tourist offices in Buenos Aires have lists of campgrounds in their regions. Some have telephones so that you can make reservations.

Ratings Prices are for two people in a double room and include all taxes. Highly recommended lodgings in each price category are indicated by a star ★.

Category	Cost
Very Expensive	over $120
Expensive	$70–$120
Moderate	$50–$70
Inexpensive	$30–$50

Tipping Add 10–15% in bars and restaurants; 10% is enough if the bill runs high. Argentines round off a taxi fare, but there is no need to tip cab drivers, although a few of the cabbies who hang around hotels popular with North Americans seem to expect it. Hotel porters should be tipped at least $1. Give doormen about 50¢ and beauty- and barbershop personnel about 5%.

Buenos Aires

Buenos Aires is a sprawling megalopolis that rises from the Rio Plata and stretches more than 194 square kilometers (75 square miles) to the surrounding pampa, the famed and fertile Argentine plains. Block after block of tidy, high-rise apartment buildings interspersed with 19th-century houses continue as far as the eye can see. Dozens of suburban neighborhoods, each with its own particular character and well-groomed parks, surround the downtown area.

Unlike most South American cities, whose architectural styles reveal a strong Spanish colonial influence, Buenos Aires looks more like Paris, with wide boulevards lined with palatial mansions. It was built up into its present form at the turn of the century, when Argentine exports created a wealthy merchant class, and homes in the French classical style became a must among the elite.

The city brings Paris to mind in other ways as well: Flowers are sold at colorful corner kiosks, the smell of freshly baked bread fills the air around well-stocked bakeries, and cafés appear on every block. Porteños—as B.A. residents are called, because many of them originally arrived by boat from Europe and started out in the city's port area, called La Boca—enjoy philosophical discussions and support a larger population of psychoanalysts per capita than any other city in the world. The city's women continue to care how they look, and with the men's flashing stares or piquant compliments, they receive ample recognition for their efforts.

Buenos Aires has no Eiffel Tower, no internationally renowned museum, no must-see sights that clearly identify it as a world-class city. Rather, it provides a series of small interactions—sunlight streaking through the trees, a block or two of great window shopping, a flirtatious glance, a heartfelt chat, a juicy steak—that combine to create an accessible and vibrant urban experience.

Tourist Information

The national office of tourism is called **Secretaria de Turismo de la Nación** (Av. Santa Fe 883, tel. 1/312–5611 or 312–5621). Information kiosks run by the city, located along Calle Florida, have English-speaking personnel and city maps, but few brochures. Occasionally a copy of the useful guides *Where* or *Buenos Aires Today* can be found at downtown newsstands, but they are published sporadically and are hard to find.

Arriving and Departing

By Plane Buenos Aires is served by **American Airlines, United Airlines, Aerolineas Argentinas, Ecuatoriana, Lan Chile,** and **Varig** from the United States; by **Canadian Airlines, Aerolineas Argentinas,** and **Varig** from Canada; and by **Aerolineas Argentinas** and **British Airways** from the United Kingdom. (For more information, *see* Chapter 1, Essential Information.) Most international flights land at **Ezeiza Airport,** 34 kilometers (21 miles) and 45 minutes from downtown. Flights within Argentina depart from **Aeroparque Jorge Newbury,** which is a 15-minute cab ride from downtown.

Between the Bus ($10) or taxi limousine ($50) tickets can be purchased from
Airport and the well-marked transportation counter in the airport. **Manuel**
Downtown **Tienda León** (Carlos Pelegrini 509, tel. 1/383–4454) provides 24-hour airport bus service to all downtown hotels. For the return trip, Tienda León provides frequent van service to the airport from its office in front of the obelisk. Regular taxi service from the airport to downtown costs around $35.

By Train At press time (summer 1993) **Ferrocarriles Argentinos** (Argentine Railways) is being privatized and, for the moment, international train service has been discontinued. The city is served by six commuter rail lines: **Linea Sarmiento** (Estación Once, Bartolome Mitre 2815, tel. 1/870041), **Linea Mitre** (Estación Retiro, Av. Ramos Mejia 1398, tel. 1/312–6596), **Linea Belgrano** (Estación Retiro, Av. Ramos Mejia 1430, tel. 1/311–5287), **Linea Roca** (Estación Constitución, Av. Brasil 1138, tel. 1/230021), **Linea San Martín** (Estación Retiro, Av. Ramos Mejia 1552, tel. 1/311–8704), and **Linea Urquiza** (Estación Lacroze, Av. Federico Lacroze 4181, tel. 1/553–5213).

Bus Terminal Most long-distance and international buses arrive at and depart from the **Estación Terminal de Omnibus** (Av. Ramos Mejia

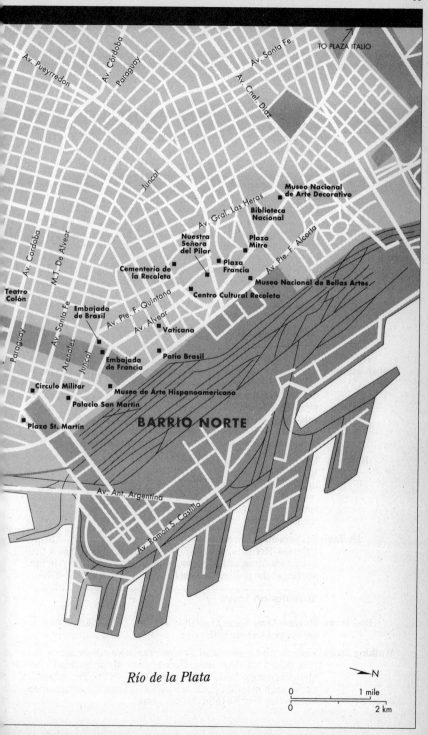

TO PLAZA ITALIO

Av. Pueyrredon

Av. Córdoba

Paraguay

Av. Santa Fe

Av. Cnel. Díaz

Juncal

Av. Gral. Las Heras

Museo Nacional
de Arte Decorativo

Biblioteca
Nacional

Nuestra
Señora
del Pilar

Plaza
Mitre

Av. Pte. F. Alcorta

Av. Córdoba

M.T. De Alvear

Cementerio de
la Recoleta

Plaza
Francia

Teatro
Colón

Av. Pte. F. Quintana

Centro Cultural Recoleta

Museo Nacional de Bellas Artes

Embajada
de Brasil

Av. Alvear

Av. Santa Fe

Vaticana

Paraguay

Arenales

Juncal

Embajada
de Francia

Patio Brasil

Círculo Militar

Museo de Arte Hispanoamericano

Palacio San Martín

BARRIO NORTE

Plaza St. Martin

Av. Ant. Argentina

Av. Ramón S. Castillo

Río de la Plata

N

0   1 mile

0   2 km

1680, tel. 1/311–6073). There are numerous types of service, from standard to deluxe, with video films, meals, rest rooms, and sleeper seats.

By Hydrofoil and Ferry Hydrofoils and ferries cross the Río de la Plata between Buenos Aires and Uruguay several times a day. Hydrofoils are run by **Aliscafos** (downtown: Av. Cordoba 787, tel. 1/322–2473; in the port: Darsena Norte, Av. Madero at Av. Cordoba, tel. 1/311–1346) and **Buquebus** (downtown: Av. Cordoba 867, tel. 1/313–9861; in the port: Av. Pédro de Mendoza 20, tel. 1/361–9186); ferries by **Ferrylineas** (downtown: Calle Florida 780, tel. 1/394–8421; in the port: Darsena Sur, Ribera Este, tel. 1/361–3140). **Buquebus** also runs Hovercraft and ferry service between Montevideo, the Uruguayan capital, and Buenos Aires.

Getting Around

By Car Porteños drive with verve and independence. For the rest of us, it's a guaranteed thrill learning how to negotiate along tremendously broad boulevards where traffic lanes are only a state of mind. A more convenient and comfortable option is to have your travel agent or hotel arrange for a car with a chauffeur, especially for a day's tour of the suburbs or nearby pampas. An approximate price is $15 per hour, but add an additional charge per kilometer if you drive outside the city limits. Small firms offering this service are **Novas Tour** (Balcarce 914, tel. 1/361–8929), **Remises Paraguay** (Paraguay 2380, tel. 1/961–3245), and **Remises Plaza de Mayo** (Azopardo 523, tel. 1/343–4735).

By Public Transportation There is no central terminal for urban buses, or *colectivos*; the routes are marked on blue signs at their stops. Buenos Aires's subway system is excellent; it is the oldest in South America, dating back to 1913, and many of the stations are decorated with original artwork showing historic scenes of the city or murals by contemporary artists. Tokens cost around 45¢ and can be used throughout the system. The subway closes between 1 and 4 AM.

By Train Commuter trains serve the northern suburbs, leaving from Retiro, the central station across from the British Clock Tower, in front of the Sheraton Hotel. The fare for an *ida y vuelta* (round-trip) ticket to Tigre on the delta is only $1.30, and you can stop at San Isidro and other fancy suburbs on the route without charge.

By Taxi In the central downtown area, fares are about $2–$4; out to the Palermo–Recoleta, about $7. It is never difficult to hail a taxi in Buenos Aires, although you might want to call a private taxi service in the predawn hours (tel. 1/972–4991 or 1/552–2939).

Orientation Tours

Bus Tours **Buenos Aires Tours** (Lavalle 1444, tel. 1/371–2304) offers an extensive bus tour of the city.

Walking Tours Visitors who understand Spanish can take advantage of the free guided walking tours offered by the **Municipalidad** (City Hall, Sarmiento 1551, 5th floor, tel. 1/476–3612). The schedule varies each month; details are available from the information booths (*see* Tourist Information, *above*).

Tours to Other Parts of Buenos Aires Province The pampas start at the edge of Buenos Aires, and a convenient way to experience gaucho life would be to join the full-day program offered Wednesday and Sunday at the **Estancia Magdalena** (Magdalena Ranch; book through City Service Travel Agency, Calle Florida 890, tel. 1/312–8416). Outings to this thoroughbred ranch include lunch with folk music entertainment and fine displays of the horses and gauchos. **La Cinacina** (in Buenos Aires, Bartolmé Mitre 734–10B, tel. 1/342–1986 during office hours; at other times, call La Cinacina restaurant, tel. 1/326–2773) runs a Tuesday and Friday tour that provides a closer look at today's pampa traditions as well as the life of the gauchos.

Exploring Buenos Aires

Buenos Aires spreads from south to north along the shores of the Río de la Plata (River Plate). La Boca (the mouth, in this case, of a small, filthy river) is the most picturesque neighborhood, now run-down and shabby but colorful, with brightly painted pressed-tin houses. South of downtown, San Telmo, a seedy sort of Greenwich Village, is the area to go to trace the city's origins in layers of 19th-century masonry buildings covered with interesting decorative details, good and bad tango bars, and tempting and tawdry antiques shops. The city grew north from there in leaps and bounds: Wide avenues, parks, and skyscrapers spill over into seemingly endless residential areas. Going north from San Telmo, the city's early 20th-century commercial center was established in a neighborhood known as Catedral al Sur, just south of the Plaza de Mayo.

The residential areas grew northward and the city's center sprang up around Plaza San Martín at the beginning of the century, finally establishing itself in Barrio Norte in the 1920s. The Barrio Norte maintains its elegant charm, although many prominent families have moved to the northern suburbs and now commute to their offices or to the theater.

San Telmo San Telmo is halfway between midtown Buenos Aires and the south end of the city, a setting similar to that of Manhattan's SoHo. Along with its neighbor, Boca, San Telmo is a self-proclaimed republic, whose folkloric traditions are preserved by a bevy of self-appointed authorities. San Telmo's main attraction is the Sunday flea market, which offers junk at outrageous prices and people-watching at its most intense. On weekdays the dozens of antiques shops are easier to browse.

Plaza Dorrego, at the corner of Calles Defensa and Humberto Primo, is the focal point of San Telmo. On weekdays it provides a peaceful haven for chess-player pensioners, with outdoor tables shaded by the plaza's stately old trees. On Sunday from 10 to 5 the plaza is alive with the bustling San Telmo Antiques Fair, a magnet for both porteño and tourist. A young couple dances frenzied tangos on one corner to the music of a tape recorder; veteran tango musicians play violin and a bandoneon—the local version of the accordian—nearby. A look up at the buildings that surround the plaza provides a sampling of all the architectural styles—leftover Spanish colonial, French classical, and lots of ornately decorated masonry done by Italian craftsmen—that have gained a significant presence in the city over the past century.

Marking the southern edge of San Telmo are the gardens of **Parque Lezama,** with its enormous magnolia, palm, cedar, and elm trees planted on the sloping hillside and winding paths that lead down to the river. The land fell into the hands of an English family in the 1840s, who sold it to George Ridgely Horne, an American businessman, who in turn sold it in 1858 to Gregorio Lezama, an entrepreneur who decorated the gardens of his luxurious estate with life-size statues and enormous urns. At the end of the last century, Lezama's widow donated the property to the city, and it has since become a popular spot for family picnics on weekends.

The Lezama homestead became the **Museo Histórico Nacional** (National Historical Museum). The official history of Argentina is on display in the stately if decaying old mansion, covering the country's past from the 16th century to the beginning of this century. Most prominently displayed are the memorabilia dedicated to General José de San Martín and his campaigns during the War of Independence in 1810. The jewel that shouldn't be missed is the collection of paintings by **Cándido Lopez,** a forceful forebear of contemporary primitive painting. Lopez, who lost an arm in the Paraguayan War of the 1870s, which Paraguay fought against Argentina and Brazil, learned to paint with his left hand and produced an exciting series of war scenes on a scale that would have captivated Cecil B. deMille. *Calle Defensa 1550, tel. 1/304–1182. Admission charged. Closed Tues.–Fri. before 4, Sun. before 3:30, and all day Sat.*

Overlooking the park, visible above the trees that line Avenida Brasil, the onion-shape domes of the small **Catedral Ruso Ortodoxo** (Russian Orthodox Cathedral) emerge. The sky-blue-domed church was hastily built in the late-1910s by the eclectic Danish architect Alejandro Cristophersen for the congregation of Russians who had settled in the city. The property, strangely, still belongs to Russia.

Continuing north from the park along **Calle Defensa,** with its neighborhood shops and tenement apartments, San Telmo offers its most distinctive flavor, that of a down-at-the-heel dowager. Halfway between what was once the colonial city and Riachuelo, the port where immigrants flocked at the end of the last century, San Telmo has changed its facades to adapt to the circumstances of the moment. Now it is a magnet for antiques shops. In the past 20 years, real-estate operators and decorators have converted the formerly derelict old houses, with large courtyards draped with ivy and wisteria, into shops, art galleries, restaurants, and bars.

Heading north, Calle Defensa leads to many of the city's important art spaces. The **Fundación San Telmo** (San Telmo Foundation) is an example of what postcolonial houses, with their enclosed courtyards adorned with flowering shrubs, were like. The foundation offers stimulating monthly shows by contemporary Argentine and international artists, and concerts. *Calle Defensa 1344, tel. 1/361–5485. Closed weekdays before 4, Sun. before 2, and in summer.*

An old cigarette factory on Calle Defensa with a classical brick facade recently became the new site of the **Museo de Arte Moderno** (Museum of Modern Art), which shows temporary exhibitions of the work of local painters and sculptors. Renovations are still underway and only part of the building is open. *Calle*

Defensa 1344, tel. 1/361–3953. Admission charged. Closed weekdays before 4, Sun. before 2.

The **antiques shop district** begins at the corner of Calle Defensa and Avenida San Juan. Old family homes have been converted into shops, or a series of them, like **Pasaje de la Defensa** (Defensa Alley), the elaborate Italianate house of the Ezeiza family, built in the 1850s, that was turned into a tenement for immigrants at the turn of the century and now houses several dozen antiques shops.

Close to the corner of the Plaza Dorrego, on Calle Humberto Primo, stands **Nuestra Señora de Belén** (Our Lady of Belén), also known as the **Parroquia de San Pedro González Telmo** (San González Telmo Parrish; Humberto Primo 340, tel. 1/361–1168). The church was abandoned halfway through its construction by the Jesuits in 1767, when the order was expelled from Argentina, and was not completed until 1858. The cloisters and the domed chapel to the left, designed by Father Andrés Blanqui in 1738, are the only visible remnants of the original construction. The Jesuits also built the adjoining cloister, which later became a hospice and then a prison for women. It is now the **Museo Penitenciario** (Penitentiary Museum; Humberto Primo 378, tel. 1/361–5803), a modest museum with a few amusing mementos of early 20th-century prison life. Behind the museum's large courtyard is the **Capilla de Nuestra Señora del Carmen,** a chapel that dates to the Jesuit period.

A few relics of the colonial period still stand on **Calle Carlos Calvo,** just off Calle Defensa. **La Casa de Esteban De Luca,** an old home turned into a restaurant, is a prime example of what a simple city dwelling looked like in the late-1700s. A glimpse at **Pasaje Giuffra,** a short alley running toward the river, offers a more complete panorama of what the city looked like two centuries ago. At Calle Defensa, just south of Avenida Independencia, the old **Cine Cecil,** once the neighborhood cinema, has been turned into a rambling antiques market similar to those on Portobello Road in London.

The **Viejo Almacén,** on Avenida Independencia, once a popular tourist night spot that featured tango shows, is another of the few remaining examples of colonial architecture. Originally an old store, as its name indicates, the building later became the English Hospital in the 1830s.

Catedral al Sur Calle Chile, a street that was originally a stream, once separated Buenos Aires's first residential community from the more rural southern suburbs. A little bridge along Calle Defensa once linked the two neighborhoods. Here the district known as **Catedral al Sur** (South of the Cathedral) starts and extends until the **Plaza de Mayo,** half a dozen blocks to the north. Once a warehouse area with easy access to the port, this district is now the city's tourist tango center, with dozens of small clubs offering lively evening entertainment.

Santo Domingo, one of the city's oldest churches, dates from the 1750s. Its austere exterior has been maintained as it was originally. The church is dedicated to Our Lady of the Rosary, in whose chapel four banners captured in 1806 from fleeing British troops—after their unsuccessful attempt to invade the then-Spanish colony—are on display, as well as two flags taken from the Spanish armies during the War of Independence. On one of the bell towers, bullet craters—testimony of the battle with British soldiers—are reminders of the conflict. The remains of General Manuel Belgrano, a hero of the War of Independence, rest in the atrium in an imposing marble coffin guarded by marble angels. *Calle Defensa 422, tel. 1/331–1668. Admission free.*

Farther along Calle Defensa, at the corner of Calle Alsina, climb the steep stairs to the **Museo de la Ciudad** (Municipal Museum; Calle Alsina 412, tel. 1/331–9855; admission charged), which displays whimsical and probing temporary exhibitions about many aspects of domestic and public life in Buenos Aires in times gone by. The **Farmacia La Estrella** (La Estrella Pharmacy), a quaint survivor from the 19th century, is on the ground floor of the building.

The **Iglesia de San Francisco,** and the smaller **Capilla San Roque** to its left, are just across Calle Defensa. This remodeled church was originally built in 1754. Its Bavarian Baroque facade was added in 1911, and the interior was lavishly refurbished after the church was looted and burned in 1955 in the turmoil just before Peron's government fell.

La Manzana de las Luces (the Block of Bright Lights), at the corner of Calles Alsina and Perú, is the name that was given to the cultural institutions that were housed in various large buildings built here in the early 19th century. Before that the block belonged to the Jesuits until they were expelled from the Spanish colonies in 1767. The bulky, neoclassical building on the site where the old San Ignacio School stood is the **Colegio Nacional,** the leading public high school.

Next to the school stands what is probably Buenos Aires's oldest church. **San Ignacio** was started in 1713 and is the only church from that era to have a Baroque facade. Behind the church, a neoclassical facade dating from 1863 hides the old colonial building that headquartered the administrators of the Jesuits' vast land holdings in northeast Argentina and Paraguay. In 1780 the city's first **Facultad de Medicina** (Medical School) was established here. In the early 19th century, the **Universidad de Buenos Aires** (the university) was here. The tunnels underneath the building, which crisscrossed the colonial town and were used by the military or by smugglers, depending on which version you believe, can still be visited. *Calle Perú 272, tel. 1/342–6973. Admission charged. Guided tours on weekends at 3:30 and 5.*

A short walk along **Diagonal Sur** (also called Avenida Roque Saenz Peña), one of two wide avenues bisecting the access streets, leads to the **Plaza de Mayo,** the city's most historic plaza, named after the Revolution of May in 1810. This two-block-long plaza has been the stage for many important events in local history, including the uprising against Spain on May 25, 1810. The tradition of staging both celebrations and protests in this central plaza continues to this day. It is here that the **Madres de la Plaza de Mayo** (Mothers of Plaza de Mayo), the mothers of young people who vanished during the military government's reign from 1976 to 1983, hold their Thursday afternoon marches, which attracted international attention in the late 1970s. The present layout dates from 1912, when the obelisk known as the **Piramide de Mayo** was placed in the center. The pyramid was erected in 1811 to celebrate the first anniversary of the Revolution of May. A bronze equestrian statue of

General Manuel Belgrano at the east end of the plaza was made in 1873. Looking west at the far end of **Avenida de Mayo,** the tall dome of the home of Argentina's parliament, the **Congreso,** on the Plaza del Congreso, is often framed against spectacular sunsets. The dozen blocks of Avenida de Mayo, built at the turn of the century in the manner of Parisian boulevards, offers many sidewalk cafés. A look at the architecture along the avenue, with whimsical towers and imposing facades, is worth the risk of tripping on the often uneven or broken sidewalk.

The **Cabildo,** located directly in front of the Casa Rosada on the Plaza de Mayo, is considered one of Argentina's national shrines. Here is where patriotic citizens gathered in May 1810 to vote against Spanish rule. The original building dates from 1725. *Calle Bolivar 65, tel. 1/343–1782. Closed Tues.–Sat. before 12:30, Sun. and holidays before 3.*

At the eastern end of the square, the **Casa de Gobierno** (Presidential Office Building), better known as the **Casa Rosada,** dominates the view toward the river. The first-floor balcony on the northern wing of this pallid pink palace is used by the country's leaders to harangue the enormous crowds that gather below. In the back, at the basement level, the thick ground-floor brick walls of the Taylor Customs House (named for the builder), the old customs house dating from the 1850s, have been partially uncovered after being buried for half a century when the Plaza Colón was built. The site can be visited from the outside or as part of a visit to the adjoining **Museo de la Casa Rosada,** a museum that features anecdotal presidential memorabilia. *Hipólito Yrigoyen 211, tel. 1/342–0421; for guided tours, tel. 1/342–0421. Admission free. Closed Wed. and Sat.*

Across Avenida Rivadavia, adding a conservative tone to the plaza's profile, is the **Banco de la Nación Argentina,** the state bank, designed in 1940 in monumental neoclassical style by architect **Alejandro Bustillo,** who designed most of the city's government buildings in the 1930s and 1940s. On the next block the **Catedral Metropolitana** hardly looks like a Latin American church. The neoclassical facade of the city's cathedral was initiated in 1822, but the building itself predates it by a century. The remains of **General José de San Martín,** known as the Argentine Liberator in the War of Independence against Spain, are buried here in a marble mausoleum carved by the French sculptor **Carrière Belleuse.** The tomb is permanently guarded by soldiers of the Grenadier Regiment, a troop created and trained by San Martín in 1811.

At the intersection of **Diagonal Norte** (also called Avenida Roque Saenz Peña), **Avenida Corrientes** and the **Avenida 9 de Julio** stands the **Obelisco,** the enormous pointed tower (67.5 meters, or 221½ feet, tall) that is one of the city's most prominent landmarks. It was built in 1936 as part of a major public works program.

Calle Florida, a pedestrians-only shopping street, runs from Diagonal Norte to the Plaza San Martín. The closer you get to the San Martín Plaza, the better the offerings. Once the shopping was Buenos Aires's best, but no longer. Now the crowd is composed of businesspeople and secretaries scurrying to work and those who prey on unsuspecting passersby, trying to lure them into nearby shops.

Lavalle, another pedestrian street, intersects Calle Florida a block north of Avenida Corrientes. Corrientes and Lavalle between Florida and Avenida 9 de Julio house cinemas and theaters. Lavalle, being narrower, becomes a solid sea of flesh when the street's dozen cinemas simultaneously change their clientele. On weekends these few blocks are packed until 3 AM, when the last moviegoers are finishing their post-show pizza.

The **Teatro Colón,** the world-famous opera house and lyric theater, has hosted the likes of María Callas, Arturo Toscanini, Igor Stravinsky, and Enrico Caruso. The Italian-style building with French decoration is the result of a joint effort by several successive turn-of-the-century architects. With a capacity of only 3,500, many of whom are season ticket holders, the lines stretch around the block when an international celebrity is starring. A fascinating guided tour of the theater and museum provides a glimpse at the building's inner workshops, which are like medieval cities in which the guilds busily ply their trades. The international season runs from April to November. *Ticket office: Cerrito 618, tel. 1/355–4146, ext. 230. Guided tours by appointment only, Mon.–Sat. hourly 10–4.*

The former headquarters of the Buenos Aires–Pacific Railway, a building designed during Buenos Aires's turn-of-the-century golden age after Milan's Gallerie Vittorio Emanuele, was refurbished in 1992 into a glossy, multilevel California-style shopping mall called **Galerías Pacífico.** In an earlier renovation a large central dome was added, and five leading Argentine artists were commissioned to paint murals.

Plaza San Martín Once a field in a muddy suburb, **Plaza San Martín** gradually evolved at the northern end of the city next to the steep riverbanks. Originally populated by vagrants and marginal members of a rough-and-tumble colonial society, the area eventually became the site of some of the most sumptuous town houses in Buenos Aires. The imposing bronze equestrian monument to General San Martín by French artist Louis Daumas that dominates the park was built in 1862. French landscape architect Charles Thays designed the park in the 19th century with a mix of traditional local and exotic imported trees that continue to add to the stately feel of the neighborhood.

On the southern side of the plaza, the **Edificio Kavanagh,** a soaring apartment tower built in the 1930s in the then-popular Rationalist style, rises in all its glory. It is still one of the few truly handsome apartment buildings in the city. Next to it, local financier Ernesto Tornquist commissioned German architect Alfred Zucker in 1908 to build the **Plaza Hotel,** a building which—like its namesake in New York City—still maintains its glow.

The city's most active art gallery, **Galeria Ruth Benzacar** (Calle Florida 1000, tel. 1/313–8480), is down a flight of stairs just where Florida ends in front of the Plaza San Martín. Ask to see the vast stock of paintings in the basement if you want a stimulating overview of contemporary Argentine art. The gallery itself is well designed and offers monthly shows of significant modern Argentine artists.

The **Círculo Militar,** a monument to the nobler historic pursuits of the Argentine armed forces, was built in 1902 as the Paz family residence by French architect Louis Sortais in the heavily ornamental French style of the period. The **Museo Nacional**

de Armas in the basement is packed with military memorabilia. *Maipú 1092, tel. 1/311–0729, ext. 130. Admission free. Closed Wed.–Fri. before 3 and Sat.–Tues.*

Across Avenida Marcelo T. de Alvear from the Círculo, behind the sixth-floor windows of the corner apartment (Maipú 994) are the rooms where Jorge Luis Borges lived and wrote many of his poems and short stories.

The **Palacio San Martín,** which was once the residence of the Anchorena family, has been the Ministry of Foreign Affairs since 1936. The ornate building, designed in 1909 by Alexander Christophersen in the grandiose French neoclassical style, is an example of the turn-of-the-century opulence in Buenos Aires that rivaled that of Manhattan.

Barrio Norte **Barrio Norte,** a residential and shopping district just north of the Plaza San Martín, is a wonderful walking area, packed with boutiques and cafés, handsome old homes, clubs, and plazas. Here many of the city's most distinguished—and wealthy—citizens live, some in palatial splendor. The not-as-affluent live in one-room boxes built in the '60s, when ceilings were reduced to less than 7 feet. It's basically a residential neighborhood, so at night the streets are quiet and uncrowded. In the morning, the only people to be seen early are hordes of uniformed kids scurrying off to school and *porteros* (janitors) hosing down the sidewalk in front of their buildings; Buenos Aires is a city of late risers.

Barrio Norte boasts one of the city's few winding streets, **Arroyo,** which has become a magnet for boutiques, galleries, and antiques shops. The **Museo de Arte Hispanoamericano Isaac Fernández Blanco** (Museum of Hispano-American Art) was built as the residence of the architect Martín Noel, who designed it in the late-18th century in an eclectic post-Spanish style. The overgrown, almost junglelike garden provides an awesome background for outdoor theatrical performances mounted here in summer. The museum has an extensive collection of colonial silver, wood carvings, and paintings, which give a hint of the wealth and quality of craftsmanship in colonial South America. *Suipacha 142, tel. 1/393–5899. Admission charged. Closed Tues–Sun. before 2 (3 in summer), Mon.*

The **Plaza Carlos Pellegrini** is surrounded by a cluster of important buildings, also formerly residences of the country's large landowning families. The **Embajada de Brasil** (Arroyo 1142) has a stately neoclassical facade, but it holds an even better treasure inside: A series of murals by Spanish artist **José Luis Sert** cover the walls and ceilings.

The **Embajada de Francia,** once the home of the Ortiz Basualdo family, was designed in the early 20th century by French architect Phillipe Pater; it is so monumental that the city decided to loop the continuation of Avenida 9 de Julio around the back of it. Across the street the **Atucha** family home and the **Jockey Club** are two more examples of neoclassical French architecture. A French Renaissance house, the **Alzaga Unzué** residence, built in the late-19th century, was saved from demolition by a group of local conservationists. The Park Hyatt Hotel rises from what was the property's garden, and the old home has been converted into suites.

Patio Bullrich, on Calle Posadas, is the most exclusive shopping center in town. The multilevel mall was once the headquarters for the Bullrich family auction house, Buenos Aires's most renowned auctioneers. The basement held hundreds of head of cattle during auctions and the upper floors were dedicated to selling paintings, furniture, and antiques, including portraits of the livestock and their owners. If you look carefully at the walls on the upper level, you'll see stucco heads of steers emerging in relief. The auction business now functions next door under the name of **Posadas** (Calle Posadas 1227, tel. 1/327–2025); its exhibits, furnishings and artworks from many important local estates, offer a penetrating look at how Argentines traditionally decorate their homes.

The five-block-long **Avenida Alvear** is a condensed version of New York's Park Avenue. At the beginning of the century it became the exclusive site for mansions in the French grand hôtel tradition. The **Vatican** has its local headquarters, the Papal See, near the corner of Calle Libertad, and the property stretches downhill to Calle Posadas, giving the papal ambassador one of the finest gardens and views in the city. On the other side of Avenida Callao are the best jewelers and the fanciest boutiques in town, along with the spectacular **Alvear Palace Hotel,** whose roof garden and lobby are famous gathering places; the lobby, set out with tables, is a great spot to stop for a cup of tea or a drink.

The **Recoleta,** at the far end of Avenida Alvear, was once notorious as a neighborhood where no one wanted to live because it bordered a cemetery. About 20 years ago a few brave restaurateurs decided to take advantage of the low rents. Now the two blocks next to the cemetery form the most fashionable dining area in the city. Several years ago part of the area was closed to traffic and streetside cafés spread into the street. Here people-watching is a highly developed art practiced predominantly by the perennially tanned and trim. This is a sight not to be missed on a sunny spring day. The **Centro Cultural Recoleta** (Recoleta Cultural Center) attracts tens of thousands of visitors on weekends to its art shows and concerts. *R.M. Ortiz 1750, tel. 1/803–9751. Admission free. Closed Tues.–Sat. before 2, Mon.*

The first buildings at the Recoleta date from the early 18th century, when Franciscan monks were given the land by the Spanish crown to develop. The friars built **Nuestra Señora del Pilar,** a rambling church and cloister complex that is a fine example of early colonial Baroque. The principal altar is made of engraved silver from Peru. Today the church is a popular place for weddings, and you can sometimes see the elegantly dressed guests mingling with the craftsmen who hold a weekend fair on the slopes of the adjoining park.

 The **Cementerio de la Recoleta** (Recoleta Cemetery), next to the church, contains the elaborate mausoleums of a *Who Was Who* of Argentine history: presidents, political leaders, soldiers, authors, ranchers. The embalmed body of Eva Duarte de Peron rests here in the Duarte family tomb, and there is a handsome statue of Luis Angel Firpo, the world heavyweight boxing champion known as the "Bull of the Pampas." To see the highlights, proceed from the entrance along the main avenue until you reach the central crossing, then turn right and continue counterclockwise through the back pathways.

The **Museo Nacional de Bellas Artes** (National Museum of Fine Arts), Buenos Aires's only major art museum, is housed in a building that was once the city's waterworks. The collection includes several major Impressionist paintings and an overview of 19th- and 20th-century Argentine art, the highlight of which is a room dedicated to the Paraguayan war scenes painted by a soldier, Cándido Lopez, whose paintings are also in the National Historical Museum (*see above*). A new wing offers a challenging selection of contemporary Argentine art. *Av. del Libertador 1473, tel. 1/803–0802 for a guided tour. Admission charged. Closed Mon.*

At the center of **Plaza Francia,** between Avenida Pueyrredon, Avenida del Libertador, and Calle Luis Agote, is a large outdoor group of statuary donated by the French government for the centennial. A large equestrian statue of General Bartolomé Mitre, a former president, dominates **Plaza Mitre,** on Avenida del Libertador between Calles Luis Agote and Aguero. The site, which was once at the edge of the river, provides a perspective on the surrounding parks.

It took three decades to build the **Biblioteca Nacional** (National Library), which finally was inaugurated in 1991. At press time the library still had no books, just a reading room with magazines. The eccentric modern building was the result of an international design competition won by Argentine architects Clorindo Testa and Francisco Bullrich. *Calle Aguero 2502, tel. 1/806–6155. Admission free. Closed Sun.*

The **Museo Nacional de Arte Decorativo** (National Museum of Decorative Arts), housed in a magnificent French classical landmark building, has a fascinating collection, mostly donated by the country's leading families. The **Museo de Arte Oriental** is also housed here on a "permanent" temporary basis. *Av. del Libertador 1902, tel. 1/801–8248. Admission charged. Closed Sat.–Tues.*

Parks and Gardens

Plaza Italia, a busy place in the Palermo district, is bordered by three important sites: the **Jardín Zoológico** (zoo; Republica de la India 2900, tel. 1/802–2174), the **Jardín Botánico** (botanical gardens; 3817 Av. Santa Fe, tel. 1/831–2915), and the **Sociedad Rural Argentina** (livestock fairgrounds; 4051 Av. Las Heras, tel. 1/804–2589), which often have exhibitions of interest to children. **Palermo Park,** which extends north parallel to the river, just beyond the zoo, is vast, with lakes, walking trails, and places to eat or have coffee. It is solid humanity on weekends, with cars parked on the grass and flying soccer balls everywhere.

Off the Beaten Track A 30-kilometer (18-mile) drive through the shady riverside suburbs of Buenos Aires is the river port town of Tigre, the embarkation point for boats plying the vast delta of the Paraná River. Most North Americans skip this day trip, but it's worth trying, especially when the weather is warm: The boat ride is pure nostalgia and a favorite local weekend escape. Of the several sightseeing possibilities, all involving boats, the most comfortable option is to tour aboard a large catamaran. In addition, the small motor launches that deliver groceries and mail and take children to school and workers to their jobs, will drop you off at the island of your choice along the delta's tentacle-like canals. The boats travel past colorfully painted houses built on stilts to survive floods. **Cities Service Travel Agency** (Calle Florida 890, tel. 1/312–8416) runs guided tours from downtown. If you prefer to go on your own, catch a Mitre commuter line train, departing every 15 minutes from Retiro Station (Av. Ramos Mejia 1398, tel. 1/312–6597). Four-hour catamaran cruises around the delta, offered by **Cruceros Catamarán** (Estación Tigre, tel. 1/749–4529; $20 per person), depart daily from a canal dock parallel to Tigre Station at 1 and 4 PM; an inexpensive lunch or snack is available on board.

Shopping

The appeal of shopping in Buenos Aires depends on the exchange rate of the moment. When the dollar is strong, it's a great place for clothing, leather goods, and furs—which boast top designs, fine materials, and good workmanship. When the peso is strong, as it has been in recent years, paintings, engravings, and wine are also possible options. In any case, just looking at Tierra del Fuego fox in the latest Yves St. Laurent styles, butter-soft leathers, evening gowns with snakeskin appliqués, French designer suits for men, cashmere sweaters, high boots and loafers, briefcases and bags, is a joy. Look for *liquidaciones* (sales) signs in the window. Argentine shops have fixed prices but often give discounts for cash.

Shopping Districts **Calle Florida,** the downtown shopping street, is a good place to look first and establish a quality standard by which you can gauge so-called bargains in factory outlets. Downtown **Avenida Santa Fe** is designed for browsing, along with the streets and avenues in the **Recoleta** neighborhood. Sensational Art Deco items can occasionally be found at **San Telmo**'s antiques shops.

For many years the city's most luxurious shopping arcade was the galleried **Patio Bullrich** (Av. del Libertador 750) near the Park Hyatt, but it has recently been eclipsed in popularity by **Alto Palermo** (corner of Av. Santa Fe and Av. Colonel Diaz; take the D subway line to Bulnes) and **Paseo Alcorta** (Salguero 3212, Palermo Chico), which opened in 1992 and has a gigantic Carrefour hypermarket. The most recent addition is **Galerías Pacífico** (Calle Florida 755). This spectacular mall—the only one downtown—is decorated with murals by several of Argentina's most important artists and has an eating area with first-rate people-watching.

Specialty Stores Furs are gorgeous and great bargains in Argentina, at times
Furs costing half the price of a coat of the same quality in the United States. The stub-tailed nutria, a cousin of the beaver, is native to Argentine rivers and lakes. Its long outer hair is waterproof and a bit harsh to the touch, but the short fur underneath is as soft as velvet. Plucked nutria, therefore, is more costly. Fox from Tierra del Fuego is a reddish color, while the Magellanic fox is a more silky, beigy gray. Minks for coats are raised on farms near Mar del Plata. **Dennis Furs** (Calle Florida 989, tel. 1/311–8920) is one of the leading fur dealers. Look also at the excellent selections at **Charles Calfun** (Calle Florida 918, tel. 1/311–1147) and at **Piel y Cuer** (M.T. de Alvear 529, tel. 1/313–7640), just off the Plaza Hotel lobby.

Jewelry Precious and semiprecious stones are priced similarly all over Latin America. What varies are the price and quality of the workmanship. Argentina has benefited from the expertise of

French, German, and Italian jewelers who brought with them a sophisticated sense of design. **H. Stern** (Sheraton, Plaza, Hyatt, and Alvear Palace hotels) is a good place to begin looking at what Argentine designers do with Brazilian stones. One semiprecious stone—known as the Rose of the Inca, or *rodocrosita*—is native only to Argentina; stones range from pink to red, with some of them as red as rubies. Sculptures of birds in flight from **Cousino** (Paraguay 631, 3rd floor, Suite A, tel. 1/312–2336, and the Sheraton Hotel) are exhibited in the National Museum of Decorative Arts. Among other top jewelers are **Guthman** (Viamonte 597, tel. 1/312–2471) and **Santarelli** (Calle Florida 688, tel. 1/393–8152).

Leather   A seasoned buyer can choose from a rainbow of pastels and vivid colors, rough suedes and others that are babyskin soft. Argentina's reputation for fine leathers is occasionally well deserved, and you can find cowhide, kidskin, pigskin, sheepskin, lizard, snake, or porcupine. For men the styles range from conservative to hip; women can find everything from bikinis to evening gowns. **Casa Lopez** (M.T. de Alvear 640 and other locations, tel. 1/311–3044) has generations of experience in dealing with travelers. **Lofty** (M.T. de Alvear 519, tel. 1/311–1424) features reversible coats of smooth suede on one side and shiny leather on the other. **Jota U Cueros** (Pasaje Tres Sargentos 439, tel. 1/311–0826) specializes in sewing any style or color to your measurements within a few hours.

For briefcases, try **Pullman** (Calle Florida 985, tel. 1/311–0799), which features the latest yuppie-lawyer styles as well as lightweight leather bags for carry-on luggage.

Shoes, boots, and saddles can be found at **Rossi y Caruso** (Av. Santa Fe 1601, tel. 1/811–1538). This London-style shop offers the best in riding equipment as well as handbags and clothing. King Juan Carlos of Spain as well as many other celebrities are clients here. Polo equipment and saddles can be found at **H. Merlo** (Juncal 743, tel. 1/327–6116), and **La Martina** (Paraguay 661, tel. 1/311–5963). For men's loafers, **Guido** (Calle Florida 704, tel. 1/802–6340) is Argentina's favorite; for men's shoes that look great and last forever, try **Lopez Taibo** (Av. Corrientes 350, tel. 1/311–2132).

Sheepskin and   Argentina has traditionally been the world's largest exporter
Knitwear   of wool. Sheepskin jackets at the **Ciudad de Cuero** (Calle Florida 940) would make the Marlboro man leap off his mount to purchase a winter's supply; **Jota U Cueros** (Pasaje Tres Sargentos 439, tel. 1/311–0826) can provide quickly made-to-order sheepskin clothing in stunning combinations of gray, black, and brown. Two legitimate factory outlets for sweaters located downtown are **IKS** (Paraguay 472, tel. 1/311–4452) and **Silvia y Mario** (M.T. de Alvear 550, tel. 1/311–4107); the latter stocks a huge selection of cashmere and very elegant, two-piece knit dresses.

Spectator Sports

Horse Racing   Historians consider the strong thoroughbreds from Argentina one of the factors that favored the British in the South African Boer War. Argentines on spending binges brought, and occasionally still bring, the best stock in the world home to breed, and swift Argentine horses are prized throughout the world. Although the past 40 years of rough economic times have handicapped the thoroughbred industry, Argentine horses still win their share of stakes races in North America and Europe. There are two main tracks in Buenos Aires; check the English-language *Buenos Aires Herald* (Azopardo 455, tel. 1/342–8476) for schedules. Generally, races take place on Wednesday and weekends at **Hipódromo de San Isidro** (Av. Márquez 504, tel. 1/743–4010) in the historic suburb of San Isidro. Closer to downtown is the dirt track at the traditional **Hipódromo Argentino** (Av. del Libertador 4499, Palermo, tel. 1/772–6022).

Polo   Argentine polo has been compared to a performance of Moscow's Bolshoi Ballet in its heyday—a strenuous display of stunning athletic showmanship. At the Canchas Nacionales in Buenos Aires, sold-out crowds of 20,000 cheer on national heroes like Gonzalo Pieres, a 10-goaler ranked tops in the world. For match information, contact the **Asociación Argentina de Polo** (H. Yrigoyen 636, 1st floor, tel. 1/343–0972). Seasons run March–May and September–December. The best teams compete in the World Championships in November, and the world polo set gathers in Buenos Aires to celebrate.

Soccer   Soccer matches are played year-round. Passions run high when Boca Juniors from the fanatic community of La Boca take on their arch-rivals, River Plate, at the **Estadio Boca.** To see another side of Argentine passion, go to a game. Try to find an Argentine to show you the ropes. Sitting among tens of thousands of roaring fans can be a disconcerting experience, especially if you get swept off your perch in the bleachers as a human wave slides five rows back and forth to cheer a goal.

Tennis   Professional tennis is played at the **Buenos Aires Lawn Tennis Club** (Av. Olleros 1510, tel. 1/772–9227). Guillermo Vilas, José Luis Clerc, and Gabriela Sabatini are products of local clubs.

Other Sports   Boxing and wrestling matches are held in **Luna Park** (Bouchard 465, tel. 1/311–1990 or 1/312–2538), an indoor arena; cricket at the suburban **Hurlingham Club** (Av. J.A. Roca 1411, tel. 1/665–0401) and other Anglo-Argentine enclaves. Check the *Herald.*

Participant Sports and Games

Chess   Pursuing a hobby is a good way to meet Argentines, especially a hobby with a universal language such as chess. It is played in the basement lounge of the **Richmond** (Calle Florida 468, tel. 1/322–1341), where you can also play billiards; upstairs at the **Confiteria Ideal** (Suipacha 384, tel. 1/294–1081); and at **Café Tortoni** (Av. de Mayo 825, tel. 1/342–4328), where dice shooters are also welcome. The newest spot for chess is in the mansion wing of the **Park Hyatt Buenos Aires** (*see* Lodging, *below*), where you can also find an elegant game of billiards.

Golf   The city has a public golf course 10 minutes from downtown: **Cancha Municipal de Golf** (Tornquist and Olleros, Palermo, tel. 1/772–7576); for practicing, try **Costa Salguero Golf Center** (Av. Costanera and Salguero, tel. 1/805–1216), a driving range with the city's best view of the river. For more information, call the **Asociación Argentina de Golf** (Argentine Golf Association, Av. Corrientes 538, tel. 1/394–2743).

Tennis There are public tennis courts at the **Buenos Aires Lawn Tennis Club** (Olleros 1510, tel. 1/772–9227), **Parque Norte** (Cantilo and Guiraldes, Costanera Norte, tel. 1/784–9653), and **Parque Jose Hernandez** (Av. Valentin Alsina 1270, Palermo, tel. 1/782–0936). Arrangements can be made through the executive offices at the **Sheraton** (San Martín 1225, tel. 1/311–6331) to play on the hotel's courts.

Squash Try the centrally located **Olimpia Cancilería** (Esmeralda 1042, tel. 1/313–7375), which also offers racquetball; **Posadas Squash Club** (Calle Posadas 1265, 7th floor, tel. 1/327–0548); or the **Tribunales Squash Courts** (Montevideo 550, tel. 1/373–8358).

Paddle Tennis The city has hundreds of courts; call for a reservation at one of the following: Ayacucho 1669, tel. 1/801–3848; Necochea 854, tel. 1/361–7277; Salguero 3450, tel. 1/802–2619; or Rio Bamba 515, tel. 1/373–2573.

Dining

Dining out is one of the Argentines' favorite pastimes, and a very time-consuming diversion, with three-course dinners lasting two or three hours. No one can linger over an espresso longer than an Argentine—and no waiter would consider rushing a client through his conversation—but then Argentine waiters enjoy the sport of conversation as much as the customers. One consequence is that the restaurant ambience, whether elegant or casual, is a delightful combination of gusto and languidness. Reservation times for second sittings tend to be elastic, as it is impossible to calculate how long any table may stay and chat.

Except in the hottest months of summer (December–February), Argentines dress up to go out. In general, reservations are not necessary, except in the fanciest establishments and on weekends. Most restaurants serve dinner from around 8:30 PM to 2 AM or later, and several are closed on holiday in January and February, when many transfer their staff to branches at the beaches. For price ratings, *see* Dining in Staying in Argentina, *above.*

Expensive **La Cabaña.** Catering to an international crowd, this classic, elegant steak house specializes in steaks, but also offers a wide selection of international cuisine. Two stuffed steers greet guests at the front door; the formal dining room within is done in dark paneling, and the tables are spaced so that you don't feel squeezed in. A *baby beef* (a gigantic steak from a young steer) and *omelette surprise* (baked Alaska) make a meal you'll never forget. *Av. Entre Rios 436, tel. 1/381–2373. Reservations advised. AE, DC, MC, V.*
Argentine
★

La Herradura. This is a suburban parrilla featuring meats prepared over charcoal embers. Favorites include grilled lamb and suckling pig, plus a wide range of imaginative salads. *Dardo Rocha 1260, San Isidro, tel. 1/798–5962. Reservations required on weekends. AE, DC, MC, V.*

British **Alexander.** It's a bit on the shabby side, but the food outclasses the environment. The rare rack of lamb melts in the mouth and is a classic choice for the city's anglophiles, especially at lunch. Dinner is less crowded. *San Martín 774, tel. 1/311–2878. Jacket and tie required. AE, DC, MC, V. Closed Sun.*

Down Town Matías. Tucked behind the Plaza Hotel on the ground floor of a modern high rise, this establishment serves such typical English fare as lamb stew and kidney pie in a chummy, publike atmosphere. *San Martín 979, tel. 1/312–9844. Reservations required. AE, DC, MC, V. Lunch only, pub closes at 10 PM; closed weekends.*

London Grill. Tasty roast beef and Yorkshire pudding, chicken pie, and steak-and-kidney pie are all served in a clublike atmosphere of paneling with the proper patina. *Reconquista 455, tel. 1/311–2223. Reservations advised. AE, DC, MC, V. Lunch only.*

French ★ **Au Bec Fin.** Delectable prawn mousse and a tartly sweet plum bavarois are the culinary stars in this baronial town house, the perfect site for a splurge or a romantic occasion. Trout stuffed with shrimp and a beef fillet with cheddar-and-mushroom sauce are two other delicious choices. *Vicente Lopez 1825, tel. 1/801–6894. Reservations required. AE, DC, MC, V. Closed Sun.*

★ **Catalinas.** Chef Ramiro Pardo gives a personal touch to a basically French menu in which seafood and game stand out. Decorated in the fashion of a countryside auberge, this restaurant offers unforgettable meals. Lobster tail on country-fresh eggs with caviar and cream, and pejerrey stuffed with king crab mousse are not to be missed. The dining room is packed wall-to-wall with businessmen at lunch, but draws a more varied crowd at night. *Reconquista 875, tel. 1/313–0182. Reservations required. AE, DC, MC, V. Closed Sat. lunch.*

La Cave de Valais. This small, cozy restaurant is one of the few places in town to try venison. There's a fixed-price menu. Or have a fondue or raclette, a Swiss melted-cheese dish. *Zapiola 1779, tel. 1/551–4435. Reservations required. AE, DC. Closed lunch and Sun.*

Hippopotamus. This trendy, ultramodern dining room attached to a high-tech nightclub serves such light but satisfying dishes as pink salmon baked in foil with an herb sauce. The view of the Recoleta Park at lunchtime is delightful. Dinner is frequented by an elegant international crowd. *R.M. Ortiz 1787, tel. 1/804–8310. Reservations required. AE, DC, MC, V. Closed Sun.*

★ **Lola.** With a full house day and night, this is the obligatory place to be seen on the city's restaurant circuit. A terrine of duck and truffles prepared in cognac, and chicken stuffed with ham, cheese, and mushrooms are good ways to test the usually brilliant chef. *R. M. Ortiz 1805, tel. 1/804–3410. Reservations required. AE, DC, MC, V.*

La Mansion. With its turn-of-the-century French decor, this fine restaurant in the mansion wing of the Park Hyatt hotel is one of the most exclusive dining experiences in Buenos Aires. Try the appetizer of smoked salmon with dill-cream sauce, or the pheasant with port wine sauce as a main course. Afternoon tea is served weekdays 4–7. *Posades 1086, tel. 1/326–3610. Reservations required. Jacket required. AE, DC, MC, V. Closed Sat. lunch; closed Sun.*

La Pergola. This restaurant in the Hotel Libertador Kempinski offers a classic French menu that is rated very highly by local connoisseurs for savor and service. Crêpes aux champignons are among the lighter options; pastas and grilled steaks are also available. *Maipú and Av. Cordoba, tel. 1/322–2095. Reservations required. AE, DC, MC, V.*

International **Blab.** A varied menu of international favorites like stuffed veal cutlets and tender fresh sole is offered at this intimately decorated basement hideaway. An upbeat luncheon spot, it's a favorite of the bankers and politicians who work nearby. *Calle Florida 325, tel. 1/394–2873. Reservations required. AE, DC, MC, V. Lunch only.*

Clark's. Sophisticated California-style food is served in an elegant, dark-wood panelled setting, with an outdoor garden for summer dining. Traditionally Clark's is one of the city's most popular spots; the chefs are ambitious and innovative but sometimes fall short. *R.M. Ortiz 1777, tel. 1/801–9502. Reservations required. AE, DC, MC, V.*

★ **Clark's.** Carlos Dumas kept the paneling of this former menswear store, added a few trophy heads, and installed what is perhaps the city's handsomest restaurant. Don't miss *lomo Clark's,* a whole beef fillet wrapped in a crisp crust. *Sarmiento 645, tel. 1/325–1960. Lunch reservations advised. AE, DC, MC, V. Closed weekends.*

Gato Dumas. The focus here is on Continental fare with an emphasis on naturally grown vegetables and herbs lovingly tended and harvested by the restaurant's rather eccentric owner, Carlos "The Cat" Dumas. A recent specialty was "Black Spaghetti Surrounded by the Cosmos." *R.M. Ortiz 1745, tel. 1/804–5828. Reservations required. AE, DC, MC, V.*

Harper's. A popular luncheon and dinner spot serves an upscale, yuppie crowd. It's a place to see a revealing cross-section of natives and to enjoy a tender steak or a good plate of pasta. *Cordero del Diablo* (a tangy lamb dish) is a traditional favorite. Paintings by local artists hang on the walls. *R.M. Ortiz 1763, tel. 1/801–7140. Reservations advised. AE, MC, V.*

Patagonia. Young chef Francis Mallman has a new spot—a small, rustic, and homey establishment where he serves such specialties as sirloin with potatoes Patagonia (prepared with cream and herbs), and tenderloin with hash browns. Mallman never disappoints his faithful clientele, so reservations are at a premium. *Salguero 3118, tel. 1/806–0608. Reservations required. AE. Closed Sun.*

Pedemonte. The traditional businessman's lunch at this establishment is a three-course, fixed-price meal well worth trying. The menu is extensive and the plates are well prepared, especially the *Pascualina de alcauciles* (artichoke pie) and the pepper steak. *Av. de Mayo 676, tel. 1/331–7179. Reservations required. AE, DC, MC, V. Closed Sun. dinner and Sat.*

★ **Plaza Hotel Grill.** This traditional gathering place for top executives and politicians offers a Continental menu and wine list that are up to the Plaza's high standards. Specialties include sole meunière, rabbit stewed in red wine, and a chestnut mousse. *Calle Florida 1005, tel. 1/311–5011. Reservations required. Jacket required. AE, DC, MC, V.*

Puerto Marisko. Fresh seafood is served in a cluttered nautical atmosphere, with fish trophies and thick ropes hanging on the walls. Fried rings of squid are a favorite starter; follow with the fresh catch of the day, flown in from Mar del Plata. Simply prepared grilled fish, prawns, and scallops are specialties. *Demaria 4658, tel. 1/773–9051. AE, DC, MC, V. Closed lunch.*

El Repecho de San Telmo. This restaurant is tucked into an small 1807 house on a plaza in the San Telmo historic district. The luxurious dining room has a colonial atmosphere, with Spanish arches, white linen tablecloths, and sterling silver utensils on the tables, and waiters in tuxedoes. Elaborate meat dishes like baby beef on creamed watercress and glazed sweet potatoes are served. *Calle Carlos Calvo 242, tel. 1/362–5473. Reservations required. AE, DC, MC, V. Closed lunch and Sun.*

★ **Tomo Uno.** Ada Cocaro has been serving up the best food in Buenos Aires for over a decade in this comfortable old town house. Try either lamb with herbs, garnished with Spanish potatoes and green salad, or trout cooked in light butter with lemon sauce and roasted almonds. *Av. Las Heras 3766, tel. 1/801–6253. Reservations required. AE, DC, MC, V. Closed Mon. lunch and Sun.*

Veracruz. This old-fashioned restaurant, which caters to a mature crowd, is representative of what dining in Buenos Aires has always been about. Carefully prepared Spanish-style seafood dishes are served by staid, seasoned waiters. Try a jam-packed *cazuela* (seafood stew with clams, shrimp, octopus, scallops, and lobster) or lobster Veracruz. *Uruguay 538, tel. 1/371–1413. Reservations advised. Jacket required. DC. Closed Feb. and Sun.*

Italian **Círcolo Italiano.** This elegant restaurant in the Barrio Norte, housed in a turn-of-the-century French mansion with high ceilings and spacious rooms, caters to the city's influential Italian community. Its varied menu offers more than just excellent pasta. Meat and fish plates are also well prepared. *Calle Libertad 1264, tel. 1/811–1767. Reservations required. Jacket and tie required. AE, DC, MC, V. Closed Sun.*

Clo-Clo. An Italian restaurant with a river view, Clo-Clo is a new addition to the waterfront. *Trucha Capri* (trout in a cream sauce with prawns) is a good way to start. *Costanera Norte and La Pampa, tel. 1/788–0487. Reservations advised. AE, DC, MC, V.*

Japanese **Kitayama.** Here, tourists mix with the city's Japanese population, who come to enjoy the well-prepared sushi, tempuras, and seafood, and to browse through the restaurant's collection of Japanese comic books. Japanese-style private dining rooms for six or more are available (with plastic backrests for less flexible patrons). *Mexico 1965, tel. 1/941–8960. Reservations advised. AE, DC, MC. Closed Sun.*

Yuki. Sashimi, yakitori, and other favorites are attractively presented in this restaurant, which caters to visitors from Japan. Private dining rooms are available. *Venezuela 2145, tel. 1/942–5853. Reservations advised. No credit cards. Closed lunch, Sun., and Dec. 15–Jan. 15.*

Moderate **A Los Amigos.** Steaks, ribs, and innards of various sorts are the
Argentine fare at this eatery at the edge of the Río de la Plata. Both outdoor and indoor dining areas offer panoramic views. *Av. Rafael Obligado/Costanera Norte, tel. 1/782–9140. Reservations advised. AE, DC, MC, V.*

La Caballeriza. This grill occupies what was once a renowned racing stable and a courtyard shaded by grapevines. The ambience, the young, enthusiastic staff, and the fine preparation and presentation combine to make the journey to the northern suburbs well worth the effort. Excellent grilled steaks are the specialty. *Dardo Rocha 1740 (take the Mitre line train from Estación de Retiro to the Acassuso station in Martinez; the restaurant is a 5–10 min. taxi ride from the station), Martinez, tel. 1/793–6085. Reservations required. No credit cards.*

★ **Dora.** This is the basic Argentine eatery at its best, the place to go for your first Argentine steak, if you like your steak thick and juicy. Walls and ceiling are hung with hams and wine bottles. The portions are generous and the quality of the food excellent. Perhaps the only restaurant in Argentina with a line at the door, it can be noisy when full, but is well worth experiencing. Try to arrive early—by 12:30 for lunch and 8:30 for dinner. *Av. Leandro N. Alem 1016, tel. 1/311–2891. No reservations. No credit cards. Closed Sun.*

Happening. This restaurant on the Costanera Norte stands out among the many eateries strung along the river beyond the city airport. Competing with the water view are good service and good food—broiled or grilled beef, pork, or fish—that goes beyond the area's usual steak-and-potato meals. Porteños gather here in hordes on weekends. *Costanera Norte, tel. 1/782–8207. AE, DC, MC, V.*

Happening II. Under the same management as the riverside Happening (*above*), this restaurant in Recoleta is all urban elegance, with a glass roof and plants. Here, too, grilled beef, pork, and fish are the specialties; especially recommended is grilled chernia, a tasty fish from the south Atlantic. *Guido 1931, tel. 1/805–2633. Reservations advised. AE, DC, MC, V.*

La Mosca Blanca. Don't let the name—The White Fly—or the crazy location put you off. Be prepared for super-huge menus, an amusingly eclectic clientele, and gigantic portions; you can split a plate with your dinner partner. Try a *milanesa rellena* (a cutlet topped with ham, cheese, and tomato) or other typical Argentine food at its tastiest—your reward for being adventurous enough to attempt to find this place. It is on the access road between the Belgrano and San Martín railway stations in Retiro. *Turn at Av. Ramos Mejia 1430, across from the Sheraton hotel, tel. 1/313–4890. Reservations required on weekends. AE, DC, MC, V. Closed Sun.*

Las Nazarenas. This popular parilla is across the street from the Sheraton in a two-story, Spanish colonial–style building with wrought-iron sconces and potted ferns. A popular lunch stop for Argentine businessmen, it features grilled steaks and brochettes. For an appetizer, try sliced *matambre* (a stuffed roll of flank steak) or thick slices of grilled provolone cheese sprinkled with oregano. *Reconquiste 1132, tel. 1/312–5559. Reservations advised. AE, DC, MC, V.*

Parilla Rosa. What is currently the city's trendiest grill on a corner in Villa Freud, the neighborhood where the city's analysts practice, serves well-prepared brochettes, *Lomo a la mostaza* (beef fillet with mustard sauce), and steaks. The plain decor is the backdrop for lots of people talking as fast as they can. *Uriburu 1488, tel. 1/806–7720. Reservations advised. AE, MC, V. Closed lunch.*

Rio Alba. This eatery serves up juicy, lean pork served with lemon slices and shoestring potatoes and an excellent variety of plates from the grill, like tuna steak. The decor is basic Argentine, with lots of stacked wine bottles, hanging hams, and sports-related memorabilia. Its location near the U.S. Embassy makes it a favorite of the American expatriate crowd, among others. It's noisy when packed. *Cerviño 4499, tel. 1/773–9508. Reservations required on weekends. AE, DC, MC, V.*

La Tranquera. This is one of the few *asado*, or grilled meat, restaurants that serves *chivito* (kid)—and it's grilled to finger-licking perfection. You can also order parilladas with the works: tripe, sweetbreads, kidneys, and sausages from the south. Banks of coals and sizzling meat on spits flank the entrance pavilion. Icy pitchers of *clerico* (white-wine sangria) are a cooling choice on summer nights. *Av. Figueroa Alcorta 6464, tel. 1/784–6119. Reservations advised. AE, DC, MC, V.*

Los Troncos. You can't miss the seedy steers at the door. An outrageously translated menu provides laughs, but the parillero masterfully grills steak and other cuts. The grilled kid is an inspiring combination of tender and crisp. *Suipacha 732, tel. 1/322–1295. Reservations advised. AE, DC, MC, V.*

Middle Eastern **Asociación Cultural Armenia.** Ex-generals and future presidents can be found enjoying extraordinary Armenian fare alongside the moguls of the city's powerful Armenian community in this rather institutional-looking club. The hummus, tabbouleh, and stuffed eggplant are authentic and well prepared. *Armenia 1366, tel. 1/771–0016. Jacket required. Reservations advised on weekends. AE, DC, V. Closed Sun.–Mon. dinner and Mon.–Sat. lunch.*

Colbeh Melahat. This cozy, delightful spot is Buenos Aires's only authentic Iranian restaurant—and well worth a journey out to the suburbs. Try *fesendjan* (duck with a grenadine sauce) or the Pakistani dishes. *Av. del Libertador 13041, Martinez, tel. 1/793–3955. Reservations required on weekends. Jacket and tie required. AE, DC, MC, V. Closed lunch and Sun.*

Asian **Cantina China.** Probably the best-known and oldest Asian restaurant in town, the Cantina has been a favorite for years. The chicken with almonds and seafood plates are good choices. The decor is pure Hong Kong: gold and red with an eclectic selection of paintings. *Maipú 967, tel. 1/312–7391. AE, DC, MC, V.*

Chinatown. In a city not noted for its Chinese cuisine, Chinatown stands out. It's in Belgrano near the train station, with the traditional red-and-black pagoda-style decor. *Av. Juramento 1656, tel. 1/786–3456. AE, DC, V.*

Midori. This sushi bar in the Caesar Park hotel serves Japanese dishes in a typically Tokyo atmosphere: brightly lit, modern, clean, and crisp. Try the teppanyaki dishes—prime cuts of meat, fish, and seafood grilled right at your table. *Calle Posadas 1232, tel. 1/814–5150. Reservations required. AE, DC, MC, V. Closed Mon.*

International **Il Barbetto.** Try *malfatti*, or chicken with polenta, in this small, cozy new restaurant. *Calle Posadas 1387, tel. 1/812–8306. Reservations advised. AE, DC, MC, V. Closed Jan. 1–Feb. 15; closed Sun.*

Club Vasco Francés. This old-fashioned racquet club with a vast dining room, recently spruced up, is one of the few places in Buenos Aires to get frogs' legs. Seafood is flown in from Spain for a homesick Basque clientele. *Moreno 1370, tel. 1/382–0244. Reservations advised. AE. Closed Sun.*

Elevage. The dining room of this restaurant in the Elevage Hotel displays a decorator's idea of British clubbiness, with a giant chandelier, fox-hunt tapestries, darkwood furniture, and lots of mirrors, but the meals can be excellent. Try chicken with tarragon sauce or *lenguado* (sole) with Roquefort sauce. *Maipú 960, tel. 1/313–2082. Reservations advised. AE, DC, MC, V.*

Friday's. Although the decor is uninspired, this small, intimate restaurant is an ideal place for a quiet tête-à-tête. Brochettes of prawns and mushrooms or tenderloin scallops with martini sauce are specialties worth a try. *San Martín 961, tel. 1/311–5433. Reservations advised. Closed Sun.*

★ **Ligure.** This longtime favorite of diplomats and other frequent visitors to Argentina offers French cuisine adapted to Argentine tastes, including unusual dishes like thistles au gratin, as well as more standard steak au poivre; the dessert pancakes are a must. The service is exemplary, not surprising since the waiters have part ownership of the restaurant. *Juncal 855, tel. 1/394–8226. AE, DC, MC, V.*

Mora X. Large and airy, this restaurant is a pleasant mix of modern architecture and decor typical of Recoleta eateries. Profiteroles with raspberry sauce make a fine finish to a delightful meal of grilled sirloin with Cheddar sauce and mushrooms, or sole with lemon sauce. The handsome wooden bar and potted plants contrast with the stark postmodern architecture. *Vicente Lopez 2152, tel. 1/803–0261. Reservations required. AE, DC, MC, V. Closed Sun.*

★ **Munich Recoleta.** This jam-packed gathering spot has been a favorite for almost 40 years. The basic fare is great steak, creamed spinach, and shoestring fried potatoes. Arrive early if you don't want to wait. *R.M. Ortiz 1879, tel. 1/804–3981. No reservations. No credit cards.*

La Terrasse. This restaurant in the Plaza Hotel offers a good variety of healthy, low-calorie dishes in a dining room that overlooks the hotel's swimming pool and the treetops in San Martín Plaza. A popular spot for stressed executives and women who exercise at the hotel's adjacent health club. *Calle Florida 1005, tel. 1/311–5011. Reservations advised. AE, DC, MC, V.*

Zum Edelweiss. This classic restaurant starts to swing after midnight, when the nearby after-theater crowd, actors included, comes to dine. The fare is German, and the people-watching superb. Goulash, sauerkraut and sausages, and steak tartare are all well prepared. *Calle Libertad 431, tel. 1/382–3351. Reservations advised. AE, DC, MC, V.*

Italian **A'Nonna Immacolata.** Amusingly, the walls of this Italian-American restaurant along the Costanera Norte are papered with out-of-circulation 1,000-peso notes. The tablecloths are pink to complement the pale orange bills. Homemade pastas, saltimbocca à la Romana, and such seafood dishes as lobster pescatore and linguini with clams are the specialties. *Av. Rafael Obligado, tel. 1/782–1757. Reservations advised. AE, DC, MC, V.*

Lucca. This small restaurant on the Recoleta specializes in ravioli. Try the *sorrentinos* (large ricotta-filled ravioli) with a creamy mushroom sauce, or the fresh, well-seasoned carpaccio. An intimate Roman feeling pervades the compact space under fresco-style scenes of old Italy. *R.M. Ortiz, tel. 1/802–0500. Reservations advised. AE, DC, MC, V. Closed Mon.*

Pizza Cero. Crisp crust and frothy mozzarella make the pizzas quite memorable at this eatery on a quiet street corner. There are tables on the sidewalk and a sparkling dining room is bathed in greenery—an upscale setting for the city's most "in" pizza parlor. *Cerviño 3701, tel. 1/803–3449. AE, DC, MC, V. Closed lunch.*

Robertino. Glorious northern Italian delectables like *cassunzei* (pasta with beets, ricotta, and egg) and fillet of veal are served in a rustic but elegant dining room in an old house. Little pots, plates, and jars hang here and there as in an old-fashioned restaurant in Tuscany. *Vicente Lopez 2158, tel. 1/803–1460. Reservations advised. AE, DC, MC, V. Closed lunch Mon.–Sat.*

Spanish **Club Español.** A down-at-heel club with a once-aristocratic dining hall, this restaurant serves earthy Spanish fare including varied fish dishes. Octopus à la Gallega is well prepared. It is busy at lunchtime but quieter for dinner. *Bernardo de Irigoyen 180, tel. 1/334–3043. Reservations required on Sat. AE, DC, MC, V. Closed Sun.*

Hispano. In a scene straight out of Madrid circa 1950, several dining rooms are filled with garrulous Galicians devouring Serrano ham and gigantic platters of paella accompanied by bottles of crisp Chablis. Rustic and bordering on chaotic at rush hour, this is the place to savor the still-predominant Spanish presence along the Avenida de Mayo in downtown Buenos Aires. *Av. Rivadavia 1199, tel. 1/382–7534. Reservations advised. No credit cards.*

Mayorazgo. Spanish fare—with an emphasis on seafood—is cooked with fresh ingredients, natural flavors, and the spirit of the Iberian peninsula. Grilled squid comes tender and tasty. *Uspallata 701, tel. 1/362–3121. Reservations required on weekends. DC, MC, V. Closed Jan., Sat. lunch, and Sun.*

Taberna Baska. Old-world decor combined with efficient service is offered in this busy, no-nonsense restaurant with dark wood paneling. A Basque clientele is drawn by such well-prepared dishes as *chiripones en su tinta* (a variety of squid in ink). *Chile 980, tel. 1/334–0903. Reservations required on weekends. AE, DC, MC, V. Closed Jan. and Mon.*

Inexpensive **El Ceibal.** The food here is from the northwest part of the country
Argentine that borders Bolivia and Chile, with Spanish-Incan dishes, such as *carbonada* (a beef stew) and *locro* (a rich, savory soup made with potatoes and corn). *Av. Las Heras 2379, tel. 1/803–6633. AE, DC, MC, V. Closed Mon.*

El Palacio de la Papa Frita. A family restaurant with good steaks and an endless general menu, this restaurant is an institution, packed at lunch and dinner, catering to the movie crowd. *Lavalle 735, tel. 1/393–5849. AE, DC, MC, V.*

La Querencia. The classic gaucho fare in this tidy little restaurant includes various types of empanadas and tamales, plus rich local soups and stews. *Two locations: Esmeralda 1392 and Junin 1304, tel. 1/822–4644. Reservations advised. No credit cards.*

International **Brizzi.** Trout mousse with a fresh salad, and sweetbreads prepared in sherry with yams are two good choices at this simple restaurant, which also offers a good brunch. *Lavalle 445, tel. 1/393–5364. No credit cards. Closed dinner.*

Sabot. In this no-frills, good-value spot, standard international fare such as steak au poivre with green peas and cream are favorites among a lunchtime banker clientele. *25 de Mayo 756, tel. 1/313–6587. Reservations advised. Closed lunch Sat. and Sun.*

Italian **Broccolino.** Pizza and pasta dishes are served efficiently on
★ red-checkered tablecloths. Families crowd the place for dinner on Sunday, the traditional maid's night off. It also bustles with tourists and nearby office workers. *Esmeralda 776, tel. 1/322–7652. No credit cards.*

Vegetarian **Yin-Yang.** A comfortable spot, Yin-Yang caters to health - conscious executives and the weight-conscious with a well-balanced menu of tasty plates of brown rice, fresh vegetables, and vegetable tarts. Nonfat pastry is a specialty. *Paraguay 858, tel. 1/311–7798. DC. Closed dinner and Sun.*

Cafés   Cafés with good locations are always busy, from the first espresso before breakfast to the last one long after dinner. Some people talk, others write, many just look at the handsome array of passersby. Some cafés offer a wider fare and are called *confiterías*. They serve open-face fillet sandwiches, grilled ham and cheese, and *triples* (three-decker clubs spread with ham, cheese, tomatoes, olives, eggs, and onion). Sandwiches can be made on *media lunas* (croissants); and salads and desserts are also available. There are about 400 cafés in midtown Buenos Aires; the average bill comes to around $10 with a small bottle of wine.

Confitería del Molino. Politicians have been gathering to argue here since the nearby Congress Building was inaugurated in 1906. *Corner Av. Rivadavia 1801, tel. 1/952–6016.*

Florida Garden. Customers line up elbow to elbow along the 20-foot bar to sip espresso and cappuccino, and drink hot chocolate—the smoothest, richest drink in the city. *Calle Florida 889, near the Plaza San Martín, no phone.*

Gran Cafe Tortoni. This is the oldest *confitería* in town, dating to 1858, and it is as popular now as it was then. Its interior is grand, with elaborate, two-story-high, tin ceilings and the faded air of a glorious past. *Near Plaza de Mayo at Av. de Mayo 829, tel. 1/342–4328.*

Ideal. This downtown Buenos Aires landmark is a turn-of-the-century tearoom with a loyal following. There is a piano player, and high teas are excellent. *Suipacha 384, near the corner of Av. Corrientes, tel. 1/294–1081.*

Lodging

One of the great pleasures of Buenos Aires is the variety of fine hotels. Several of the more expensive ones were built for the 1978 World Cup soccer matches, while others opened at the turn of the century. All listed here are in the city center. For price ratings, *see* Lodging in Staying in Argentina, *above.*

Very Expensive   **Alvear Palace.** Conceived as a luxury apartment building in
★ 1932, the building was converted to a hotel in 1991. Guest rooms are soothingly decorated in burgundy and deep blues, with large windows. The roof garden has a spectacular view of the city and the river. The location in the fashionable Recoleta section makes this hotel convenient to the museums and good restaurants. *Av. Alvear 1891, tel. 1/804–4031, fax 1/804–0034. 160 rooms with bath, 60 suites. Facilities: restaurant, traditional tearoom, coffee shop, health club, indoor pool, business center. AE, DC, MC, V.*

Caesar Park. Located opposite Patio Bullrich, the hotel is near the Recoleta and Plaza San Martín. Rooms on upper floors have a panoramic view of the river. The lavish, spacious guest rooms have tasteful fabrics and period furniture and good light. *Calle Posadas 1232, tel. 1/814–5150 or 1/814–5160, fax 1/814–5148. 273 rooms with bath, 6 suites. Facilities: 3 restaurants, café, fitness center, indoor pool. AE, DC, MC, V.*

Claridge. This stylishly appointed hotel sports a British elegance in its public rooms, with wood paneling and high ceilings, and an Anglo-Argentine clientele to match. Guest rooms are decorated in shades of blue, with dark wood furnishings with bronze fittings. It has a good location near the financial district.

Tucuman 535, tel. 1/322–7700, fax 1/322–8022. 161 rooms with bath, 6 suites. Facilities: squash courts, minigolf, small gymnasium, outdoor pool. AE, DC, MC, V.

Libertador Kempinski. Its central location in a modern 22-story building just a few blocks from the banking district makes this hotel headquarters for many businesspeople. The huge lobby area with marble floors has a bar, and the pastel-shaded deluxe rooms have walk-in closets, marble baths, and mahogany furniture. *Av. Cordoba 680, tel. 1/322–2095, fax 1/322–9703. 200 rooms with bath. Facilities: restaurant, fitness center, coffee shop, bar, indoor/outdoor pool, sauna. AE, DC, MC, V.*

Panamericano. A newish, 18-floor building has been tastefully disguised as a conservative, classic hotel, with an emphasis on good service and spotlessness. A room at the top guarantees a good night's sleep in a room with a view over the Obelisk and the Colon Theater. *Carlos Pellegrini 525, tel. 1/393–6017, fax 1/393–6570. 204 rooms with bath, 6 suites. Facilities: fitness center, pool, sauna, business center. AE, DC, V.*

Park Hyatt Buenos Aires. Argentina's first Hyatt has a strategic location at the end of Avenida 9 de Julio on the fringe of the Recoleta district. In addition to the 12-story building that houses the crisp, comfortable guest rooms and executive suites, it occupies a redecorated turn-of-the-century French town house where sumptuous suites and a gourmet restaurant cater to VIP visitors. *Posades 1086, tel. 1/326–1234, fax 1/326–3736. 166 rooms with bath, 50 suites (6 suites in La Mansion, 44 in the main hotel). Facilities: restaurant, coffee shop, bars, business center, fitness center, outdoor pool, conference rooms. AE, DC, MC, V.*

★ **Plaza Hotel.** The city's most gracious hotel is located across from the towering old trees of Plaza San Martín. Some rooms have great bay windows overlooking the park. Crystal chandeliers and deep red Persian carpets decorate the public rooms. The President entertains visiting statesmen and -women here. *Calle Florida 1005, tel. 1/311–5011, fax 313–2912. 320 rooms with bath, 10 suites. Facilities: 2 restaurants, outdoor pool, health club, shops. AE, DC, MC, V.*

Sheraton Buenos Aires Hotel and Towers. As the headquarters of Sheraton's South American division, this hotel at the bottom of Plaza San Martín has a broad range of facilities. The institutionally decorated guest rooms have views of either the River Plate or the British Clock Tower and park. It is popular with American businesspeople and tour groups. *San Martín 1225, tel. 1/311–6331, fax 1/311–6353. 694 rooms with bath, 37 suites. Facilities: restaurant, coffee shop, bar, outdoor pool, tennis courts, business services. AE, DC, MC, V.*

Expensive **Bisonte Hotel.** Located on a popular shopping street in the center of the city, the Bisonte has a sunny two-story lobby and a coffee shop overlooking a small park. Rooms are small and decor is on the stiff side. *Paraguay 1207, tel. 1/394–8041, fax 1/393–9086. 87 rooms with bath. Facilities: coffee shop, private offices available. AE, DC, MC, V.*

Bisonte Palace Hotel. Sister hotel to the Bisonte, this more brightly lit version is centrally located. Since it's on a busy corner, rooms higher up are better bets for peace and quiet. Decor is standard—modern and comfortable, and guests are well attended. *M.T. de Alvear 902, tel. 1/311–4751, fax 1/311–6476. 65 rooms with bath. Facilities: coffee shop. AE, DC, MC, V.*

Buenos Aires Bauen Hotel. With its theater, auditorium, and active entertainment program, the Bauen is a beehive of activity. It is near the intersection of two noisy avenues lined with lively restaurants and cafés, cinemas, and theaters, so avoid lower floors if you're sensitive to noise. *Av. Callao 360, tel. 1/476–1600, fax 1/372–6822. 226 rooms with bath, 28 suites. Facilities: coffee shop, convention center. AE, DC, MC, V.*

Carsson. A long mirrored corridor leads to the lobby, which is far from the sound and fury of downtown traffic, in this centrally located sleeper. An English atmosphere pervades; rooms have been redone in staid stripes of green and deep red, with Louis XIV–style furniture. *Viamonte 650, tel. 1/322–3551, fax 1/322–3551. 108 rooms with bath, 9 suites. AE, DC, MC, V.*

City. This dowager of the downtown hotels is the last one to resist renovation. With its hand-operated elevators, enormous lobby, and period paintings, it's definitely a nostalgia trip. Rooms are large and in various stages of redecoration, with plastic-covered furniture and foam paneling on doors. Not for the fussy, but a good choice for the price-conscious who want to be on the San Telmo side of town. *Calle Bolivar 160, tel. 1/342–6490, fax 1/342–6490. 400 rooms with bath, 80 suites. AE, DC, MC, V.*

De las Américas. In this hotel just off the best shopping stretch of Avenida Sante Fe, the sunken lobby is drearily decorated, but the rooms are comfortable and larger than one expects in a 10-year-old property. The clientele consists mainly of South American tour groups and visitors from the provinces, but solitary visitors who want to be in a basically residential area will also feel at home. *Calle Libertad 1020, tel. 1/393–3432, fax 1/393–0418. 150 rooms with bath, 15 suites. Facilities: coffee shop. AE, DC, MC, V.*

El Conquistador Hotel. This hotel, well-situated near Plaza San Martín, is popular with Argentine businessmen. There is a cheerful restaurant for breakfast or a snack, and the wood paneling in the public rooms lends a cozy touch. Large windows, flowered bedspreads, and light pink carpets brighten the recently redecorated guest rooms. *Suipacha 948, tel. 1/313–3012, fax 1/313–3012. 130 rooms with bath, 14 suites. Facilities: restaurant, piano bar, sauna, massage. AE, DC, MC, V.*

★ **Lancaster.** This handsome hotel was decorated by a countess with her countless antiques. Old family portraits, museum-quality landscapes, and a 200-year-old clock grace the lobby, where elegant porteños come regularly for tea or drinks. Rooms have antique mahogany furniture and views of the port. *Av. Córdoba 405, tel. 1/312–4061, fax 1/311–3021. 88 rooms with bath, 16 suites. Facilities: restaurant, bar. AE, DC, MC, V.*

Hotel Plaza Francia. This is the best located small hotel in town. The guest rooms—large and French in feel—have great views overlooking La Plaza Francia park. It's also near the Recoleta and the museums. If traffic noise bothers you, sacrifice the view for a quiet inside room. *Pasaje E. Schiaffino 2189, tel. and fax 1/804–9631. 36 rooms with bath, 14 suites. AE, DC, MC, V.*

★ **Hotel Posta Carretas.** This gem of a hotel—modern and very comfortable, with the feeling of an auberge—is tucked right in the heart of the city. Some of the brightly decorated rooms have Jacuzzis. Wood paneling abounds, creating a coziness in contrast with the bustle outside. *Esmeralda 726, tel. 1/322–8534, fax 1/313–6017. 40 rooms with bath, 11 suites. AE, DC, MC, V.*

Regente Palace. The small but pleasant rooms are decorated with black-wood furniture and bedspreads and curtains in beiges and rose. The location is convenient, near Plaza San Martín on a block with several new cafés and trendy shops. American breakfast is served in the restaurant. *Suipacha 964, tel. 1/313–6628, fax 313–7460. 150 rooms with bath, 6 suites. Facilities: restaurant, snack bar. AE, DC, MC, V.*

Hotel Salles. This quiet, centrally located establishment is the only family-oriented hotel in the heart of the theater district. Rooms are adequate, the decor businesslike and neutral; personal service is a focus. *Cerrito 208, tel. 1/382–3962, fax 1/382–0754. 90 rooms with bath, 5 suites. Facilities: coffee shop. AE, DC, MC, V.*

Moderate **Crillon.** Superbly located across from Plaza St. Martín, the
★ Crillon was built in the classic French style in 1948 and remodeled in 1992. Front rooms have beautiful views and are large and luminous. The lobby is statesmanly and sedate, which may explain why this establishment appeals to provincial governors and the well-to-do from the interior. *Av. Santa Fe 796, tel. 1/312–8181, fax 1/312–9955. 96 rooms with bath, 12 suites. Facilities: restaurant, bar, disco, conference room. AE, DC, MC, V.*

Gran Hotel Colón. Near the Obelisk, on the busy Avenida 9 de Julio, the Colón has suites with private patios, but normal rooms are shoe-box small. Everything is shiny and modern. Airport buses leave from next door, so it is convenient if you're making connections with international flights. *Carlos Pellegrini 507, tel. 1/325–1017, fax 1/325–4567. 192 rooms with bath, 10 suites. Facilities: 24-hour snack bar, beauty salon, indoor pool, sauna. AE, DC, MC, V.*

Gran Hotel Dora. A cozy lobby with a small bar greets the guest. The atmosphere is old-fashioned and the rooms are comfortably elegant, with their Louis XVI–style decor. The Dora caters to Europeans and to Argentines who want a Continental atmosphere. *Maipú 963, tel. 1/312–7391, fax 1/313–8134. 100 rooms with bath. Facilities: bar, conference rooms, snack bar. AE, DC, MC, V.*

Principado. Built for the World Cup soccer matches in 1978, this hotel has reception areas with large windows and lots of light, and two-tier Spanish colonial–style lobby with leather couches. The highlight is the friendly coffee shop. Rooms are modest but comfortable. *Paraguay 481, tel. 1/313–3022, fax 1/313–3952. 88 rooms with bath. AE, DC, MC, V.*

Inexpensive **Hotel Deauville.** The Deauville, located in the most elegant part of town, is aging gracefully, like most of its provincial clientele. The dining room is family-oriented, and the guest rooms are fairly large, with ample drawer and closet space. For the budget-conscious traveler who wants to be away from tourists, this is one of the best choices. *Talcahuano 1253, tel. 1/429481, fax 1/812–1560. 60 rooms with bath, 4 suites. Facilities: restaurant. AE, DC, MC, V.*

Gran Hotel Orly. On the river side of Calle Florida, the Orly caters to Brazilian tourists and budget visitors from the interior. Though the entrance is impressive, the comfortable rooms are small and rather plain. *Paraguay 474, tel. 1/312–5344, fax 1/312–5344. 168 rooms with bath, 8 suites. Facilities: 24-hour bar and coffee shop. AE, DC, MC, V.*

Rochester. Get an inside room at this 20-year-old hotel, which is on a busy street though convenient to movies and shops. The lobby is simple and rooms are basic. *Esmeralda 542, tel. 1/393–9589 or 1/393–9339, fax 1/322–4689. 155 rooms with bath, 20 suites. Facilities: 24-hour room service, breakfast room. AE, DC, MC, V.*

The Arts and Nightlife

Partial listings of entertainment and cultural events in English appear in the daily edition of the English-language *Buenos Aires Herald.*

The Arts Some 40 theaters are open almost constantly, ranging from
Theater those presenting Argentine dramatic works or translations of foreign plays to *revista* (revue) theaters with comics who strike out at local political mishaps, and chorus lines notable for the brevity of the costumes and the dimensions of their wearers. Publicly supported dance, mime, puppets, and theater are performed on the three stages of the municipal theater complex, **Teatro San Martín** (Av. Corrientes 1532, tel. 1/953–0111). A new entertainment center worth a visit is **La Plaza** (Av. Corrientes 1660, tel. 1/373–8781), an open-air mall with a small outdoor amphitheater and two theaters, along with shops and small restaurants with tables under the trees.

Music The season of the **National Symphony,** headquartered in the Colón Theater, runs from April to November (Cerrito 618, tel. 1/396–5414).

Opera By any standard of comparison, the **Colón Theater** (Cerrito 618, tel. 1/396–5414) is one of the world's finest opera houses. Tiered like a wedding cake, the gilt and red-velvet auditorium has unsurpassed acoustics. An ever-changing stream of imported talent bolsters the well-regarded local company. The opera season runs from April to November.

Dance The **National Ballet Company** is also headquartered at the Colón but gives open-air performances in Palermo Park in summer. Don't miss the world-class contemporary dance company that performs several times a year at the **Teatro San Martín** (Av. Corrientes 1532, tel. 1/953–0111).

Film International first-run films, the often-powerful films of Argentine directors, and Italian comedies can be found at the more than 50 theaters in the downtown area alone. Most of these are along two parallel streets, Avenida Corrientes and Lavalle. The *Herald* has daily listings. The names of the films are generally given in Spanish, but English-language films are shown undubbed, with Spanish subtitles.

Nightlife It is good to begin with a basic understanding of the Argentine idea of nightlife. A date at 7 PM is considered an afternoon coffee break. Theater performances start at 9 or 9:30, the last movie after midnight, and nightclubs don't begin filling up until 2 AM. Tango begins after midnight and never seems to stop. Porteños never go early to discos—no one you'd want to be seen with goes before 2 AM.

Tango Performance Argentine tango, that sensual dance and soulful song, is philosophizing and passion set to music. Haunting Andean pipe music from Salta–Jujuy in the north combines with flirtatious handkerchief dancing in the sentimental *zambas.* A typical tango performance in a nightclub includes a serious singer, a passionate, woeful singer, a virtuoso *bandoneon* star flashing his fingers across double sets of accordionlike buttons, and finally, the peacocklike performances of tango dancers. To watch the drama unfold, Argentines and tourists sit together in tango clubs, sipping drinks and listening to seasoned singers wade their way through the emotion-packed lyrics. Clubs can be sampled on nightclub tours of the city, available through hotels, but an easier way to slip into the feeling of tango is to attend a folkloric show, which runs about $40, including two drinks. Currently the best folkloric performance is at **Casa Blanca** (Balcarce 668, tel. 1/361–3633), President Menem's favorite spot. **Café Homero** (J.A. Cabrera 4946, tel. 1/733–1979) is a good place to start one's initiation into the rites of the tango. Highly polished **Michelangelo** (Balcarce 433, tel. 1/331–5392) combines folkloric, tango, and international music in its dinner show in a striking, remodeled old warehouse. Another way to delve deeper into the music is to visit **La Casa de Carlos Gardel** (Jean Jaures 735, tel. 1/962–4265), open only at night, where there are audiovisual displays, a tango show, and a museum of the life of tango's most famed figure. Gardel, known for his dark, Tyrone Power looks, died in a plane crash in 1935 at the age of 40. Some claim that Gardel's 1,200 recordings continue to outsell all others in Argentina.

Once you have settled into the mood of tango, head for San Telmo and try **Bar Sur** (Estados Unidos 299, tel. 1/362–6086) or any of a number of spots with more spontaneous outbursts of tango, at lower cost.

Dancing Tango is meant to be danced more than watched, and Buenos Aires has many exciting dance halls. Most don't open until 11 PM, and many open only one night a week, so the tango crowd circulates from place to place, from night to night. Most tango joints have no telephones, and opening days and times listed below regularly change. **Akarense** (Donado 1355 at Av. Los Incas; Fri. 11 PM–3 AM) draws the best dancers to its beautiful hall, where pure tango music from the 1920s to the 1960s is featured. The very special **Sin Rumbo** (Av. Constituyentes 6000 at Calle Tamborini; Sat. 11 PM–3 AM) attracts old dancers of the *milonga* (a samba-like dance that predates the tango) and features music from the '20s and '40s. **Salón Helénico** (Av. Scalabrini Ortiz 1331; Fri. and Sun. 11 PM–3 AM, preceded by tango lessons from 8 to 11) recalls larger dance halls from the '30s, with a melancholy atmosphere and bucolic Greek landscapes on the walls. The very large **Social Rivadavia** (Av. Rivadavia 6400 at Boyaca; Fri.–Sun. 11 PM–3 AM) has two dance floors, many milonga dancers, and music mainly from the '40s, but with a lot of tropical music and jazz as well. **Regine's** (Rio Bamba 416; Wed. 11 PM–3 AM) is a small place reminiscent of Fellini's *Satyricon.* **Viejo Correo** (Av. Diaz Velez 4820; Mon., Thurs., Sat. 11 PM–3 AM) has a more sophisticated atmosphere than most of the other tango spots. **La Galería del Tango Argentíno** (Av. Boedo 722; Fri., Sat., and Sun. 11 PM–3 AM) has competitions and shows and draws both older milonga dancers and young dancers. Tango fantasía, a fancy version that allows dancers to show off their abilities, is more popular here than in the other halls. **Antonio Todaro** (Estudio Superior de Arte, Av. Belgrano 2259, tel. 1/952–1109), considered the best tango teacher in town, offers formal tango instruction in his studio weekdays 11 AM–9 PM.

For international dancing that sometimes includes a tango as well, **Atalaya** on the 23rd floor of the Sheraton (tel. 1/311–6331) has an orchestra, a view of the city, and the elegant spirit to draw full crowds on weekends. **Africa** in the Alvear Palace Hotel (Av. Alvear 1885, tel. 1/804–4031) and **Mau Mau** (Arroyo 866, tel. 1/393–6131), both discos, appeal to the 25–45 crowd, while the popular **Hippopotamus** (R.M. Ortiz 1787, tel. 1/802–0500) in the Recoleta appeals to middle-aged dancers and a younger crowd, both affluent.

Buenos Aires dance clubs, like clubs everywhere, come and go, and places that are frenetically popular one month are "out" the next.

Jazz Clubs Jazz in Buenos Aires is treated seriously by audiences and played enthusiastically by musicians. In San Telmo, for local and foreign groups, try **Gazelle Jazz Club** (Estados Unidos 465, tel. 1/361–4685), or **Balcon de La Plaza** (Calle Humberto Primo 461, tel. 1/362–1144). **Café Tortoni** (Av. de Mayo 825, tel. 1/342–4328) has jazz on weekends, and **Patio Bullrich** (Av. del Liberador 750) frequently has jazz concerts in the evening. For a combination of jazz and traditional *mate* (herbal tea) drinking, try **Oliverio Mate Bar** (Paraná 328, tel. 1/542–1537).

Iguazú Falls National Park

Iguazú Falls (Cataratas de Iguazú) is one of the wildest wonders of the world, with nature on the rampage in a show of sound and fury that cannot be duplicated anywhere. The grandeur of this Cinemascope sheet of white water cascading in constant cymbal-banging cacophony makes Niagara and Victoria Falls seem sedate by comparison. Set at a bend in the Iguazú River at the border of Argentina and Brazil, it consists of some 275 separate waterfalls—in the rainy season as many as 350—that send their white cascades plunging 76 meters (250 feet) onto the rocks below. Dense, lush jungle surrounds the falls: Here the tropical sun and the omnipresent moisture set the jungle growing at a pace that produces a towering pine tree in two decades instead of the seven it takes, say, in Scandinavia. By the falls and along the roadside, rainbows and butterflies are set off against vast walls of red earth, which is so ubiquitous that eventually even peso bills long in circulation in the area turn red from the stuff.

Allow at least two full days to see this magnificent sight, and be sure to see it from both the Brazilian and Argentine sides. The Brazilians are blessed with a panoramic view that is accessible to nonwalkers, the communion with nature broken only by the sound of the gnatlike helicopters that erupt out of the lawn of the Hotel das Cataratas right in front of the falls. (Unfortunately, most of the indigenous macaws and toucans have abandoned the area to escape the whine of the helicopters' engines.) The Argentine side offers the better hiking paths, with catwalks that approach the falls, a sandy beach to relax on, and places to bathe in the froth of the Iguazú River, where you can swim right up to a cascade and feel its power. If tropical heat and humidity hamper your style, plan to visit between April and October. Be aware, however, that the river can be so high in April and May that access to certain catwalks is impossible. Whatever time of year you visit, be sure to bring rain gear (or buy it from vendors along the trails on the Brazilian side), since some of the catwalks take you right through the cascades and leave you thoroughly drenched.

Tourist Information

Contact **Centro de Visitantes** (visitors center; at the falls, tel. 0757/20180; open daily 8–6) for information and guides.

The **Oficina de Turismo** for the international zone of Iguazú is at Avenida Victoria Aguirre 396 (tel. 0757/20800) in the town of Puerto Iguazú, as is the **Intendencia del Parque,** the local park administrative offices (tel. 0757/20382; open weekdays 7–1). In Buenos Aires, contact the **Administración de Parques Nacionales** (National Park Administration, Av. Santa Fe 690, tel. 1/311–1943) or the **Casa de Misiones** (House of Misiones, Av. Santa Fe 989, tel. 1/393–1812). **Teletur** (tel. 0455/139 from Brazil, Argentina, and Paraguay; 0455/742196 from outside South America) has an information line where you can get detailed information on area excursions.

Getting There

By Plane   Argentina and Brazil each have an international airport at Iguazú. The Argentine airport is 16 kilometers (10 miles) from the town of Puerto Iguazú, Argentina; **Aerolineas Argentinas** (Av. Aguirre, Puerto Iguazú, tel. 0757/20849) and **Austral** (Av. Aguirre 429, tel. 0757/20144) fly to and from Buenos Aires in an hour and a half. An occasional Aerolineas flight goes on to São Paulo and Rio de Janeiro. The Brazilian airport is 11 kilometers (7 miles) from Foz do Iguaçu and 17 kilometers (10½ miles) from the national park. The Brazilian airlines **Varig** and **Cruzeiro** (tel. 0455/741424), **Vasp** (tel. 0455/742999), and **Transbrasil** (tel. 0455/742029) have offices in Foz do Iguacú and offer connecting flights all over Brazil. **Lineas Aéreas Paraguayas** flies between the airport on the Brazilian side and Asunción, Paraguay.

From the Airport   **Asociación de Taxis** (Av. Córdoba 370, tel. 0757/20973)
to the Falls   provides taxi service to both sides of the park. The Hotel Internacional Cataratas and the visitor center at the national park are 8 kilometers (5 miles) from the Argentine airport.

By Car   Iguazú is a two-day, 1,290-kilometer (800-mile) drive from Buenos Aires on national highways 12 and 14. The roads are paved, but often empty, and cross vast stretches of farmland. Much of the area is dedicated to rice, so the fields at the sides of the road are often covered with herons, ducks, and storks; there's even an occasional flamingo. There are a number of picturesque towns to spend the night in along the Paraná River and inland, among them San Nicolás, Rosário, Santa Fe, Goya, Corrientes, Posadas, and El Dorado.

By Train   At press time the Argentine railroads were being privatized and the **Urquiza Line** from Buenos Aires to Posadas was no longer running. If it is revived, the overnight train ride, through Entre Rios and Corrientes, will be a low-cost alternative to flying.

By Bus Buses are a comfortable way to see the often bird-filled lagoons that at times seem to swallow the highway. The trip from Buenos Aires takes 21 hours; **Expreso Singer** (Perito Moreno 150, tel. 0757/21560; in Buenos Aires, tel. 1/313–2355) provides regular service, leaving from the **Central Terminal** in Buenos Aires. Organized tours to Iguazú by bus are available at most Buenos Aires travel agencies.

Exploring Iguazú National Park

The **Cataratas de Iguazú** (Iguazú Falls) should be seen from both sides of the Iguazú River, which means that you must establish headquarters on one side of the Argentine–Brazilian border and take a taxi or one of the regularly scheduled buses across the International Bridge to the national park on the other side. At each park, well-marked trails provide access to the best views of the falls. United States, British, and Canadian citizens need a visa for visiting Brazil, which is easy and quick to get at the border after crossing the bridge. If you are staying in the town of Puerto Iguazú, there is an hourly bus service back and forth to the Argentine side of the park; the 16-kilometer (10-mile) trip takes half an hour. Taxis are available in Puerto Iguazú, at the visitor center, and at the Hotel Internacional Cataratas (*see* Dining and Lodging, *below*).

Argentine Side Since the falls themselves are mostly on the Argentine side, there is more to see and do there. There is a variety of ways to visit the falls: Just wandering along the access paths is the best way to immerse yourself. These paths are a combination of bridges, ramps, stone staircases, and wooden catwalks set in a forest of ferns, begonias, orchids, and tropical trees. The catwalks over the water put you right in the middle of the action—so be ready to get doused by the rising spray. When the river floods, many of the installations have to be replaced; the floods of 1983 swept away many of the walkways. The last major rebuilding program was undertaken when the Hollywood movie *The Mission*, starring Robert De Niro and Jeremy Irons, was filmed here.

The **Centro de Visitantes** (visitor center; at the falls, tel. 0757/20180), in what was the park's original hotel, makes a good first stop. Useful maps are posted on the walls, and friendly, multilingual rangers are happy to help you understand the layout of the park. The rangers also preside over a small zoo and museum with local fauna and exhibits related to the area's history. In an adjoining room, slide shows are offered about Argentina's national park program. On the night of a full moon, rangers lead groups from the visitor center for a night walk through the upper trails when the moon is high. The sensation of walking through the subtropical forest at night is eerie and exciting and shouldn't be missed. The roar of the falls drowns out the sounds of the jungle and what was all bright green, red, and blue in the daytime takes on luminous hues of phosphorescent whites. Check at the visitor center for details.

There is a snack bar in the visitor center with tables on the lawn, and a restaurant, **El Fortín**—across from the parking lot—where natives from Paraguay come to sing and play their soulful melodies, and then sell their traditional instruments.

Most tourists are Argentines, and it is a colorful spot for a good steak or a sandwich.

Lower Circuit   The **Circuito Inferior** (the Lower Circuit) is a loop trail that leads to the brink of several falls. To get to the trail, follow the well-marked path from the Hotel Internacional and then the main path leading from the visitor center. After a five-minute walk down an access road, you'll see signs for the circuit, indicating which sights are in each direction. Protected promontories, rimmed with wooden or metal fences, offer close-ups of the wonderful view. At times the falls arise above you, framed by primeval forest.

The approximately 1-kilometer (one-half mile) long Lower Circuit leads to the edge of the **Río Iguazú** (Iguazú River)—with the Hotel das Cataratas and the noisy helicopter launching pad almost directly above on the opposite bank, a mile downstream from where the falls take their first magnificent leap. On this route you cross the small, peripheral **Salto Alvar Núñez,** falls named for the Spanish conquistador Alvar Núñez Cabeza de Vaca, who accidentally stumbled onto the spectacle in the 16th century; the **Peñon de Bella Vista** (Rock of the Beautiful View); and the **Salto Lanusse** (Lanusse Falls), the falls farthest from the Devil's Gorge. These preliminaries get you warmed up for the main event. In the distance on the right, **Salto Dos** and **Salto Tres Mosqueteros** (Two and Three Musketeers Falls) fall obliquely, offering a head-on view to those on the Brazilian side. Wear your bathing suit on this route and take a dip in the calm pools at the trail's edge.

Halfway along this circuit you get a panoramic peek at what is to come. Through the foliage you can see the gigantic curtain of water in the distance. The trail leads along the lower side of the **Brazo San Martín,** a branch of the river that makes a wide loop to the south. This tributary pushes to get back to the river's main course, opening up dozens of minor and a few major waterfalls along a face of rock that measures almost a mile. On the back side of the circuit—that is, where the trail loops around and starts heading back to your starting point—the **Salto Ramiréz** (Ramirez Falls), the **Salto Chico** (Small Falls), and the **Salto Dos Hermanos** (Two Brothers) appear directly before you, opposite the bridge. This section of your circuit, about a half-mile long, offers the most exciting panoramic view of the Devil's Gorge, the **Salto Bossetti** (Bossetti Falls), and Salto Dos Hermanos. Two or three hours are needed to appreciate all the views along the circuit.

At the vantage point opposite the Bossetti Falls, a trail leads along the edge of the river to a small pier, where sturdy little boats will take you across a branch of the river to **Isla San Martín** (San Martín Island). The service operates all day, except when the river is too high. On the island, a steep climb up a rustic 160-step stairway leads to a circular trail that opens out onto three spectacular panoramas of the **San Martín Falls,** the Devil's Gorge, and the **Ventana Falls** (Window Falls). If you want to just sit and watch 1,700 cubic meters (1,300 cubic yards) of water splash below you every second, this is the place to do it. From the southernmost point you see **Salto Escondido** (Hidden Falls), and from the easternmost point, the panorama is breathtaking. The falls on the Brazilian side come into view: **Salto Santa María, Salto Floriano,** and **Salto Deodoro.** Few people make the effort to cross the river to San Martín Island

and do this climb, so you can often enjoy the show in solitary splendor. The island has a small beach near the point where the boats land; frustrated sunbathers stretch out on its sands to dry out from the mist and warm up after losing sun under the thick tropical greenery.

Upper Circuit The **Circuito Superior** (Upper Circuit)—not a circuit at all but a path about 700 meters (2,300 feet) long—borders the ridge on the south side of the river, along the top of the falls. The trail leads across the rapid waters of the **Brazo San Martín,** a branch of the river, as far as the **Cresta de los Saltos,** providing great views of **Dos Hermanos, Bossetti, Chico, Ramirez,** and **San Martín** falls. You can also see San Martín Island and the Brazilian side.

Devil's Gorge The Devil's Gorge is 150 meters (492 feet) wide and 750 meters (2,460 feet) long. To stand at the brink and watch the river fall off into space is an awesome sight, especially when accompanied by the sound of nature at its most outrageous.

The best viewing point is a short walk from **Puerto Canoas,** a settlement 4 kilometers (2½ miles) up the river from the visitor center. Puerto Canoas has a campsite nearby (on the banks of the Nandú River), a restaurant, and a bar. Many prefer to walk along the road that borders the river and then take the quarter-mile catwalk across the river to the top of the gorge. The hourly bus from Puerto Iguazú to the national park ends its route at Puerto Canoas, and taxis are available at the visitor center.

A Jungle Hike Mix your outings to the different panoramic points overlooking the falls with a hike in the jungle. The **Centro de Investigationes Ecológicas Subtropicales** (Center for Subtropical Ecological Investigation; tel. 0757/20180) is a five-minute walk from the visitor center on the road to Puerto Iguazú. The center maintains the **Sendero Macuco** (Macuco Trail), which extends 4 kilometers (2½ miles) into the jungle, ending at the **Arrechea Falls,** farther downriver from the main falls. The trail is very carefully marked and descriptive signs in Spanish explain the jungle's flora and fauna. The closest you'll get to a wild animal is likely to be a paw print in the dirt, though you may be lucky enough to glimpse a monkey. The foliage is dense, so the most common surprise are the jungle sounds that seem to emerge out of nowhere. You can turn back at any point, or continue on to the refreshing view of the river and the Arrechea Falls. The best time for hearing animal calls and for avoiding the heat is either early in the morning or just before sunset. The batallions of butterflies, also best seen in the early morning or late afternoon, can be marvellous, and the intricate glistening cobwebs that crisscross the trail are a treat in the dawn light.

The Jungle by Car A 29-kilometer (18-mile) circuit especially for vehicles gives a more complete overview of the jungle. Macaws, parrots, and toucans rest in the tree branches, and brightly colored butterflies flit across the road. The birds and animals come out in numbers at sunrise and sunset, and conceivably you could catch sight of a fleeing feline. Poachers from Brazil ford the river above the falls and come to hunt the little wildlife that is left in Argentina's national park. There are not enough rangers to provide adequate protection. A jeep can be hired through the visitor center to undertake this simple safari, which takes two or three hours, depending on what there is to look at.

Brazilian Side The Brazilian national park, one of the few worthy of the name in Brazil, covers 1,550 square kilometers (600 square miles) of rainforest. The central attraction is the incredible panoramic view, which can be seen starting at the Hotel das Cataratas (*see* Dining and Lodging, *below*). Well-groomed pathways lead from the terrace of the hotel directly down to the edge of the cliff overlooking the falls, and steps take you to the river itself, where a catwalk penetrates the flow. Vendors sell plastic rain-wear on the trail. A path then leads to the head of the falls, where you can take an elevator ride back up for a small fee (open daily year-round).

Just a little farther along, you can brave one of the boat rides that venture over the Devil's Gorge. These rides feature a local variation on the old jalopy sport, "chicken": The driver turns off the boat's motor and drifts downstream toward the gorge, awaiting the panic-stricken response of his passengers. No boats have ever gone over the edge—yet.

The astonishing panorama extends all along the path that leads from the hotel to the observation tower by the **Floriano Falls** and finally to the **Santa María Falls.** The path that follows the river's edge on the Brazilian side is about 2 kilometers (1 mile) long, and the paved roadway running parallel to it leading to and from the hotel can be easily negotiated with a wheelchair.

Sports and the Outdoors

Argentine Side Jungle tours and photo safaris are conducted by the Puerto Iguazú–based **Güembé Tours** (Av. Victoria Aguirre 481, tel. 0757/20413 or 0757/20510). When you book, ask for a wildlife list. Take binoculars to see distant birds, and a tape recorder if you want to remember their songs. Butterflies, parrots, woodpeckers, hummingbirds, lizards, inch-long ants, and spec-tacular spiders are usually spotted, along with toucans, the big-gest stars of the skies around Iguazú. Park ranger Daniel Somay offers personalized Jeep tours through his **Explorador Expediciones** in Puerto Iguazú (tel. 0757/20338).

Brazilian Side An obnoxiously noisy helicopter ride is operated by **Helisul Taxi Aereo** (tel. 0455/741786). The seven-minute ride starts in front of the Hotel das Cataratas. *Cost: $50 adults, $25 children under 10. Open Apr.–Oct., daily 9–5; Nov.–Mar., daily 9–7.*

Shopping

Anxious shoppers from Argentina, Brazil, and Paraguay seek-ing duty-free bargains on items like televisions, tape recorders, and camcorders descend on the border towns in great num-bers, some traveling in shopping-tour buses from the cities. Border-town shopping generally doesn't present tremendous bargains for foreigners, though; your time would be better spent in the park.

Dining and Lodging

Argentine Side
Dining and Lodging
Hotel Esturion. This hotel in Puerto Iguazú has gardens and a sweeping view of the river. *Av. Fronteras 650, Puerto Iguazú, tel. 0757/20020 or 0757/20161, or tel. 800/338–2288 for reserva-tions in the U.S., fax 0757/20414. 121 rooms with bath, 4 suites.*

Facilities: restaurant, outdoor pool, 2 tennis courts, sauna, gymnasium. AE, DC, MC, V. Expensive.

★ **Hotel Internacional Cataratas.** Half the rooms in this five-star hotel have direct views of the falls, so be sure to ask for a view when you make a reservation. Floor-to-ceiling windows provide constant views—from the lobby, restaurants, and bars—and the large lobby combines antique colonial and concrete-slab modern furniture. Guests can have breakfast or a drink on spacious balconies. The handsomely decorated main restaurant serves a memorable trout maitre d'hôtel (stuffed trout wrapped in pastry). At sunset and at dawn, an occasional parrot or toucan crosses in front of the view of the roaring waters. *Parque Nacional Iguazú, tel. 0757/20311 or 0757/20295. 152 rooms with bath. Facilities: 2 restaurants, coffee shop, nightclub, casino, outdoor pool with view of the falls, 2 tennis courts. AE, DC, MC, V. Expensive.*

Brazilian Side
Dining and Lodging

Hotel Bourbon. This large, comfortable hotel is in Foz do Iguaçú, the nearest town to the park on the Brazilian side. *Rodovía das Cataratas, km 2¹/2, tel. 0757/231313. 310 rooms with bath, 11 suites. Facilities: 3 restaurants, 1 coffee shop, 2 bars, boutiques, 2 tennis courts, outdoor pool, health club, sauna. AE, DC, MC, V. Expensive.*

★ **Hotel das Cataratas.** This handsome old building surrounded by galleries and gardens provides the more traditional comforts—large rooms, terraces, hammocks—of a colonial-style hotel. The restaurant serves a smorgasbord-style dinner featuring *feijoada*, the Brazilian national dish based on rice, beans, and pork, with a variety of tasty side dishes. *Rodovía das Cataratas, tel. 0757/232266; in São Paulo, tel. 011/231–5844. 110 rooms with bath. Facilities: 2 restaurants, coffee shop, bar, boutiques, outdoor pool, tennis courts. AE, DC, MC, V. Expensive.*

Patagonia

Patagonia, the vast territory that covers the southern half of Argentina and Chile, is a state of mind that has possessed travelers and writers since the first sailing ships touched its gale-swept shores centuries ago. Brilliantly publicized by Charles Darwin after his cruises on the *Beagle* in the 1840s, by Reverend Lucas Bridges at the turn of the century in his inspiring *Uttermost Part of the Earth,* and brought back to a human scale by British writer Bruce Chatwin's more recent *In Patagonia,* the region—like the Amazon—attracts polemic attention. Briefly an empire under the aegis of an ambitious Frenchman—even today there is an office in Paris dedicated to recovering the empire—Patagonia is too vast and complex to get to know in a single visit.

It's a land for romantic adventurers whose idea of a good time includes an ample dose of physical discomfort and unexpected challenges. You can't rent a camper and circle this vast territory in a week. Tackling Patagonia means hit-and-run plane trips into desolate, windswept airports. (It was here that Antoine de Saint-Exupéry got his start as a commercial pilot, struggling to keep his tiny aircraft and its brave passengers from blowing off the runway before takeoff.) Comfortable accommodations are available near the four major sights: Perito Moreno Glacier National Park, Tierra del Fuego, Bariloche, and Península Valdés. Getting from one place to the other, however, is still a time- and energy-consuming struggle involving dawn flights, poor connections, and unpredictable weather conditions that stymie the best-laid plans.

The Perito Moreno Glacier, in the southern Andes near the border with Chile, is one of the world's greatest natural monuments. A sight as awesome as Iguazú Falls, it's a solid translucent mass of ice that is always on the move. Visits to the glacier are basically by tour and rather brief, considering the time and energy it takes to get there. This is a one-sight attraction, worth two days to see the spectacle from land and from the water.

Tierra del Fuego, an island at the southern tip of Argentina, is the capital of Everyman's imaginary Patagonia. Yet its allure is based more on its mythic past than on reality. Darwin's Indians are long gone, and the capital town—Ushuaia, located at 55 degrees latitude south—can be called picturesque at best. It resembles an oversize mining camp awaiting the next strike. But what makes the place special is the light: At sundown, it casts the landscape in a subdued, sensual tone; everything feels closer, softer, more human in dimension despite the vastness of the setting. You can also catch record-size seagoing brown trout and put your toe in the Beagle Channel, as Magellan must have done so long ago. Perhaps the greatest lure is that the traveler setting foot in Ushuaia gets to add a notch to his own personal record book: It is the southernmost human settlement on the globe, just a proverbial stone's throw from Antarctica.

Bariloche and the Andean Lake region, for many years the queen bee of Argentine winter sports, has the best-developed tourism infrastructure, so it is the easiest place to start a tour of Patagonia. There's nowhere in South America comparable to this enclave of idyllic scenery reminiscent of Switzerland, Scandinavia, and the Rockies. Often called Brazil-oche because so many Brazilians flood in to enjoy the snow, Bariloche mixes Teutonic architecture with Italian levity.

Puerto Madryn is the gateway to some of the world's best whale watching, penguin perusal, and seal searching. The surrounding coast—especially Península Valdés—is for hard-core nature lovers. Where else these days can you make merry with a million penguins, or share the sea with a whale?

Traveling conditions in southern Argentina can be frustrating. Tourists are often seen as a cash crop to be fleeced, like the sheep whose wool used to be the region's major money-producer. Be ready for wind, but also be aware that Ushuaia is tucked into a microclimate that makes its weather about as temperate as that of North Carolina.

Perito Moreno Glacier National Park

Soon after the discovery of the Perito Moreno Glacier late in the last century, scientists crossed the Patagonian desert to hike up into the Andean foothills to study this icy wonder of the world. Last year 20,000 travelers, half of them from the Northern Hemisphere, followed in their footsteps to gaze upon the 1.5 million acres of ice, water, mountains, and virgin forest that make up Parque Nacional Los Glaciares (Glacier National

Park), nature's number-one ice show. There are two ways to see the glaciers, and both should be tried.

Getting There **Aerolineas Argentinas** and **Austral** fly from Buenos Aires to Río
By Plane Gallegos, a town 250 kilometers (150 miles) from Perito Moreno Glacier National Park. In summer **LADE,** the Air Force transport line, flies small planes from Río Gallegos to Calafate, the jumping-off point for tours to the glacier, a 50-minute flight.

By Bus **Interlagos** (Fragano 35, Oficina 5, tel. 0966/22614) runs regular bus service between Río Gallegos and Calafate. The bus leaves from the airport in Río Gallegos. In summer a bus runs from Puerto Natales, Chile, to Calafate.

By Car **Localiza** (Sarmiento 237, tel. 0902/20169), **Rent-a-car** (Av. San Martín 1504, tel. 0902/21588), and other car rental agencies operate in Río Gallegos; rates are high by U.S. standards.

Getting to the glacier can be an arduous exercise. The trip can take up to five hours across desolate plains filled with more sheep than you can count in a lifetime of sleepless nights, but is occasionally enlivened by a sighting of *ñandu* (rhea), herds of the elegant llama-like *guanaco*, silver-gray fox, and fleet-footed hares. The solitude of Patagonia pervades the landscape, and the traveler is swept along with the never-flagging wind. But the memory of the effort involved in the drive vanishes instantly when the glacier comes into view near **Calafate,** a frontier town that slows down in winter, when inclement weather makes visiting the national park more difficult. The **Oficina de Turismo** (Tourist Office) in Calafate is at Coronel Rosales 25, tel. 0902/91090; in Rio Gallegos, tel. 0966/22702.

What to See and Do As space on glacier tours is limited, reservations must be made in advance. Any travel agent can do the booking in Buenos Aires if it hasn't been arranged before the trip. Take the boat that goes across the northern branch of **Lago Argentino** (Lake Argentina) to as close to the **Glaciar Upsala** (Upsala Glacier) as it dares to get, dodging icebergs along the way. Off to the side, the **Onelli** glacier also tumbles its blocks of ice into the lake below. This trip takes 11 hours, with a two-hour lunch break at a lodge on the banks of the lake. The expedition starts with a half-hour bus ride along the side of Lago Argentino to the pier at **Puerto Bandera,** at the confluence of the lake's north and south basins. There a comfortable, enclosed motorboat carries up to 120 passengers through 15,000-year-old Lake Argentina—which has a milky, emulsive appearance—and between the multi-toned icebergs. The seven glaciers that feed the chilly lake melt, filling it with minerals ground to fine powder by the glacier's moraine—an accumulation of boulders, stones, and other debris swept along in its path. At one time the ice of the glacier measured 914 meters (3,000 feet) high; now it has shrunk considerably, and the melted ice covers almost 2,590 square kilometers (1,000 square miles). After a 2 1/2-hour cruise, the boat crisscrosses in front of the Upsala Glacier while everyone takes their fill of pictures. Then the boat docks alongside **Onelli Bay** for a bracing lunch. After lunch, passengers walk as far as they can inland, past baby icebergs fallen from the **Agassiz, Boladas, Heim,** and **Onelli** glaciers, which fill **Onelli Lake,** a small body of water that looks like an aquatic sculpture garden. Icebergs of all sizes and shapes compete for your attention, and each inspires all sorts of associations. The side of the lake is overflowing with ferns and *lenga* trees, a scraggly variety native to the region. If you are lucky, you can observe condors soaring overhead, flying from perch to perch in the towering peaks to the west. If you miss your condor here, the captain will probably point one out on the ride homeward.

Save the best for day two. A two-hour drive from Río Gallegos by bus gets you to the wooden gate of **Parque Nacional Los Glaciares** (Glacier National Park), and a few bends farther down the road, one of the sights of a lifetime zaps into view. You get out of the bus at the tip of **Península de Magallanes** and walk 46 meters (50 yards) to the guardrails, where you look across the **Canal de los Témpanos** (Iceberg Channel) at an astounding 3.2-kilometer- (2-mile-) wide wall of ice that partially disintegrates before your eyes, producing the thundering sound of crackling and splashing ice, turned up to rock-concert volume. Declared a World Heritage Site by UNESCO, the **Perito Moreno Glacier** is a 30,000-year-old elongated ice cube shaded in tones of white and a deep blue hue that is due to compression, which squeezes the oxygen out of the ice. The Perito Moreno is a river in solid form creeping down out of the Andean Cordillera like a snake in a polar-bear fur coat. To the left of the glacier, the **Brazo Rico** (Rico Branch) of the lake is divided from the main body of the lake by accumulated icebergs; once every four or five years the weight of the accumulated water is so great that it breaks through with a crash that can be heard back in Calafate, 48 kilometers (30 miles) away. No one can predict the exact time of the next crash.

After an hour's stop, the tour bus heads back to town. Most travelers bring a prepackaged picnic lunch, which your hotel can provide, to munch while waiting for the next crash. Ideally, one should visit the glacier by car and go early or late, to savor the sight before or after the tour buses have moved on. Should the lake be too rough on the day you plan your boat trip, you can try shore fishing for trout from the side of the road (your hotel can get you tackle and steer you to the best spots) or drive up into the mountains near Fitz Roy. A brief walk onto the edge of the glacier can be arranged at local travel agencies, as can fishing outings with guides.

Dining and Lodging Within sight of the glacier, an hour's drive from Calafate, is a small but elegant auberge, **Los Notros** (Arenales 1473, 1061 Buenos Aires, tel. 1/812–2166 for reservations, fax 1/814–0317). In Calafate the choice spot is **Hotel Kau-yatun** (Estancia 25 de Mayo, tel. 0902/91059), a former ranch redone in deluxe comfort. Both places offer mouth-watering, country-fresh meals.

Tierra del Fuego

Getting There
By Plane **Aerolineas Argentinas** has regular flights to Ushuaia, the capital of the newly created province of Tierra del Fuego. **LADE** flies from Calafate and Río Gallegos and other southern towns to Río Grande, Tierra del Fuego's largest city. Aerolineas's twice-weekly transpolar flight from Buenos Aires to Auckland and Sydney stops in Río Gallegos for fuel: A traveler from the other side of the world can stop over and visit Tierra del Fuego. Note: Cruises to Antarctica and the Malvinas (Falkland Islands), rarely stop at Ushuaia nowadays; they call instead at Punta Arenas in Chile.

What to See and Do When you stand on the banks of the **Canal del Beagle** (Beagle Channel) near Ushuaia, the spirit of the farthest corner of the world takes hold. The light is magical, the air exhilarating. The snowcapped mountains of Chile reflect the illumination of the setting sun back onto a stream rolling into the channel, as nearby peaks echo their image—on a windless day—in the still waters. Ushuaia itself looks like a mining town between booms. Wooden huts, precariously mounted on upright tree trunks, ready for speedy displacement to a different site, look like entrants in a contest for most original log cabin. An occasional brightly painted structure gives the chaotic urban landscape a touch of much-needed color. Town planning has never been a strong point in Ushuaia; instead, irregular rows of homes sprout with the haphazardness of mushrooms in a moist field. While staying in Ushuaia, try tidbits of *corderito* (baby lamb) right off the spit, the tasty mainstay of Patagonian cuisine, as well as *centolla,* the large crab trapped off the town's shores, and gigantic *mejillones* (mussels), often 5 inches long.

Above the city, the last mountains of the Andean Cordillera rise, and just south and west of Ushuaia they finally vanish into the often-stormy sea. Snow dots the peaks with white well into summer. Nature is the principal attraction here, with trekking, fishing, horseback riding, and sailing among the most rewarding activities. In winter, when most international tourists stay home to enjoy their own summer, the adventurous have the place to themselves for cross-country skiing and snowmobiling across the powdery dunes (*see* Sports and the Outdoors, *below*). Tourism information on Tierra del Fuego can be obtained at the **Hotel Albatros** (Av. Maipu 505, tel. and fax 0901/23340).

Most tourists stay for three nights, visiting the **Parque Nacional Tierra del Fuego** (for information contact Tierra del Fuego National Park, Av. San Martín 395, tel. 0901/21315) the first day and Estancia Harberton, the area's oldest ranch, the next. The park is 19 kilometers (12 miles) from town, tucked up against the Chilean border. **Tolkeyén** (12 de Octubre 150, Ushuaia, tel. 0901/22637) and **Rumbo Sur** (Av. San Martín 342, Ushuaia, tel. 0901/21139) offer bus tours that give an overview of the park. **Kilak Expeditions** (Kuanip 67, Ushuaia, tel. 0901/22234), **Caminante** (Deloqui 368, Ushuaia, tel. 0901/22723), and **Tiempo Libre** (Av. San Martín 154, Ushuaia, tel. 0901/21273) offer a wide variety of more adventurous tours: horseback trips; a four-night camping trip to **Lake Kami** or **Fagnano**; and 10-hour treks led by seasoned mountaineers that include a three-hour hike through forest and peat bogs with the snowcapped Andes as a constant backdrop, then a canoe trip across Lapataia Bay. Chartering a sailboat is another option; contact **Velero María Galante** (Gob. Fernández Valdéz 290, Ushuaia, tel. 0901/23711).

Estancia Harberton (Harberton Ranch) consists of 50,000 acres of coastal marshland and wooded hillsides. The property was a late-19th-century gift from the Argentine government to Reverend Thomas Bridges, officially considered the "Father of Tierra del Fuego." Today the ranch is managed by Bridges' great-grandson, Thomas Goodall, and his American wife, Natalie, a scientist who has cooperated with the National Geographic Society on conservation projects; most visitors come in organized tours, but they welcome the stray tourist who stumbles onto their spread. They serve up a solid and tasty tea in their home, the oldest building on the island.

Sports and the Outdoors Local travel agencies offer specialized tours and adventure trips (*see* What to See and Do, *above*). Fishing, trekking, hunting, mountain climbing, horseback expeditions, and sailing trips that head south toward Antarctica are all available. Sailing out to sea usually means contact with wide-eyed seals, sea elephants, and sea lions sunning on the rocks, plus gigantic albatross who fly in from Dunedin, New Zealand. **Gador Viajes** (Tucumán 941, 1049 Buenos Aires, tel. 1/322–6344 or 1/322–9806) offers carefully prepared and managed tours of the area, with connecting trips to Lago Argentino, Trelew, and Bariloche. **Zagier & Urruty** (C.C. 94 Sucursal 19B, 1419 Buenos Aires, tel. 1/572–1050, fax 1/572–5766) publishes a guide to Tierra del Fuego with an excellent map as well as an English-language adventure guide to all of Patagonia, both of which can be found in some bookstores in Buenos Aires.

Skiing Ushuaia is the cross-country skiing center of South America, thanks to enthusiastic Club Andino members who took to the sport in the 1980s and made the forested hills of a high valley about 20 minutes from town a favorite destination for traveling skiiers. From **Hosteria Tierra Major** and **Hosteria Los Cotorras,** two small inns, trails lead out through evergreen boxwood and past beaver huts. Skis, poles, and boots can be rented in town, as can windskis, snowmobiles, and Snowcats. For downhill skiers, the club has bulldozed a couple of short, flat runs directly above Ushuaia.

Bariloche and the Lake Region

Getting There The town of Bariloche is the gateway to the Andean lake region. **Aerolineas Argentinas** and **Austral** fly daily from Buenos Aires to Bariloche. **LADE** and **CATA** are less expensive but have fewer flights. The 1,935-kilometer (1,200-mile) trip takes two hours. There are several flights a week between Bariloche and Trelew and Esquel.

By Train Train service at press time (fall 1993) has been suspended pending the outcome of the privatization program. If reinstated, this 30- to 40-hour trip is a great way to experience the vastness of Argentina's plains.

By Bus **Chevallier** (Moreno 107, tel. 0944/23090; in Buenos Aires, tel. 1/313–5108) and **La Estrella** (Palacios 246, tel. 0944/22140; in Buenos Aires, tel. 1/313–2435) run comfortable and reliable overnight buses to Bariloche; the trip takes 22 hours.

By Car Driving to Bariloche from Buenos Aires is a long haul. Half the trip is over a rocky, rippling dirt road. The local roads in the lake region are dusty but passable.

What to See and Do The area around **Bariloche** is postcard-pretty: forests of evergreens; snow-capped peaks as a constant backdrop; large lakes of deep, deep blue, transparent green, or luminous gray; alpine architecture with updated postmodern details; and spring wildflowers galore. A show as impressive as the fall change of seasons in New England happens here in April, when the southern beech turns outrageous tones of yellow, red, and orange. Nature keeps tourists' cameras snapping away at the scenery.

It's a region that offers plenty for everyone: *Town and Country* magazine billed it "The Last Great Place" for its appeal to European and American jet-setters who spend a season here riding, fishing, or hunting and build beautiful homes here. The less well-heeled traveler can enjoy the same scenery and sports at one of the many inns dotted around the region. European aristocrats without their own homes have a fabulous small hotel, **El Casco** (Casilla de Correo 436, Bariloche, Neuquen, tel. 0944/61032 or 0944/61068; very expensive), where they stay while visiting the game preserves or private trout streams tucked away in indescribably beautiful foothills. If you enjoy nature in small doses, stay in town, and you'll feel the impact of consumerism at its normal touristic clip. If you can take a stronger diet of the great outdoors, then settle into one of the area's many inns. Most are sited at the edge of a lake and offer access to all the region's activities and sports. Downtown Bariloche is swamped in July, and in January and February, but the countryside is calm enough even then that it doesn't feel crowded.

Travel agents can provide details for all the excursions listed below. There are dozens of small hotels and inns in strategically scenic spots, rivers for rafting, hills to be hiked, and campgrounds (ask at the **Automovil Club Argentino,** Av. 12 de Octubre 785, Bariloche, tel. 0944/23000). This is vacationland, whether as a winter wonderland or a summer haven from the heat.

Bariloche is on the northeastern shore of **Lake Nahuel Huapí** and is blessed with a fabulous view of the Andes across the blue waters. Much of the area around Bariloche is part of the **Parque Nacional Nahuel Huapí,** which in itself offers no services to tourists. To find out what is available, go to the **Municipal Tourist Office** in the unexpectedly Germanic-looking **Centro Cívico** on the plaza (Civic Center; tel. 0944/23022). The **Club Andino** (20 de Febrero 30, tel. 0944/22286; open Mon.–Thurs. 4–10) provides information on the trail conditions, refuges, and mountain climbing. There is the small **Museo de la Patagonia** (Patagonia Museum) in the Civic Center; it offers an overview of the region's now-scarce wildlife. Handknit woolen sweaters, jams made with local berries, and locally made chocolate—items that make up 99% of what tourists take home—can be bought within a short walk of the Civic Center.

The most popular driving tour out of Bariloche is a three-hour excursion south along the lake, up into the foothills of the **Cerro Catedral** (Mt. Cathedral), whose slopes were groomed for Argentina's first ski resort earlier in the century. The chair-lift ride up the side of the gentle 2,134-meter (7,000-foot) mountain from the parking area at the base provides a bird's-eye panorama of lakes, peaks, and plains, mixed in a kaleidoscope of bright colors. The **Hotel Catedral,** just above the point where the cable car takes off, is a favorite of upscale winter-sports lovers and a good spot for a meal or tea for day-trippers. Drive back down the mountain to the lake's edge and continue east along its coast. You are now on what is called the **Circuito Chico** (Small Circuit), a 57-kilometer (35-mile), half-day tourist trail that follows the lake to the **Península San Pedro,** which juts out several miles into the lake and is the site of many spectacular homes. The more adventurous can take an unmarked dirt road off to the left before getting back to the lake; it leads to the rustic village of **Colonia Suiza,** a good spot for tea or lunch. Follow the road through the village and bear south, skirting **Lago Moreno** and **Laguna El Trebol.** Soon you'll come out on

the **Península Llao Llao** behind the **Hotel Llao Llao,** a monumental hotel recently reopened after being closed for more
than a decade. Don't worry about getting lost on the unmarked
roads: They all wind around and get you back to where you
started. And there is an Austrian- or German-run inn or restaurant at every bend where you can ask directions over hot
chocolate and strudel.

The **Circuito Grande** (Large Circuit) is a more ambitious tour,
covering 242 kilometers (150 miles) of lakes and forests, with
many spots to stop and enjoy views of lakes and mountains. It's
an all-day trip along mostly dirt roads. It first takes in the **Valle
Encantado** (Enchanted Valley), with its wall of strange rock
formations, called, for example, the Finger of God, the Siamese
Twins, and Express Train, along the valley of the **Limay River.**
The road then bears west along the **Traful River,** reaching a
large lake of the same name and later **Lago Correntoso** and the
village of **Villa La Angostura.** By now you'll be ready for a typical Bariloche tea or a cup of hot chocolate, and in La Angostura
confiterías abound. The excursion ends at the edge of Nahuel
Huapí Lake. The Large Circuit is particularly lovely in spring
and fall; during the fishing season, you can stop along the way
and try your luck in any of the lakes.

The **Circuito de los Siete Lagos** (Seven Lake Circuit) takes you
about 403 kilometers (250 miles) of fairly deserted, mostly dirt
roads through a twisting, turning chain of seven lakes: **Correntoso, Espejo** (Mirror), **Traful, Villarino, Falkner, Hermoso**
(Beautiful), and **Meliquina.** If you drive on to **San Martín de los
Andes,** at the end of **Lake Lácar,** for lunch, you can visit the
area's second city, a paradise for fishermen in summer and a
center for skiers in winter.

Another day trip is to **Isla Victoria** (Victoria Island), the home
of the **Parque Nacional Los Arrayanes** (Arrayanes National
Park). If the Llao Llao was inspired in a rapture of pure Disney,
Walt himself was inspired by the *arrayanes,* a native tree with
a cinnamon-color bark and dark green foliage, for his film
Bambi, according to local lore. In any case, on the boat ride
across the Nahuel Huapí, you'll pass the spot where Dwight D.
and Mamie Eisenhower caught the largest trout of their lives.
The day trip includes an institutional lunch at the Victoria Island Inn. Spend as much time as you can walking about the
park: The arrayanes create a mysterious, surreal atmosphere.

Skiing With about 80 kilometers (50 miles) of skiable terrain, Bariloche is the largest ski resort in Argentina. It is also the oldest:
The cable car has been carrying skiers up Cerro Catedral since
the 1950s. The resort is popular with Brazilians and with high
school students who have never seen snow. Although rain often
washes snow from the base by mid-August, Bariloche's four
bowls are superb through September. Bariloche has eight
chair-lifts, three T-bars, seven Pomas, and a cable car. Bariloche ski packages, which include a six-day pass, seven nights
in Bariloche, breakfast, and transportation to the slopes, run
$500–$900 per person for one week, depending on the accommodations you choose. The **Latin America Reservation Center**
(Box 1435, Dundee, FL 33838, tel. 800/327–3573) offers reasonable rates on a range of hotels, or ask **Aerolineas Argentinas**
(tel. 800/333–0276 in the United States, tel. 514/282–1011 in
Montreal, tel. 416/967–6043 in Quebec) for names of U.S. agencies that offer ski packages.

Fishing Driving out of Bariloche to the north, past the airport, takes you to some of South America's great fishing streams. Trout fanatics flock here from all over the world during the season (November 15–April 15). The bar and dining room at the handsome, large old **Hotel Correntoso** (Ruta 231, km 3, Villa Correntoso, tel. 0944/94426) near Villa La Angostura is the place to go to swap stories and discover where the rainbows are biting. When your neighbor mentions his recent 12-pounder, he may not be exaggerating. The Argentine record for a trout—weighing in at 35 pounds!—was a brown caught in the waters of the Nahuel Huapí in 1952. Boats are available, but the tried-and-true method is to hike the banks in search of that perfect pool along the **Chimehuin,** the **Limay,** or the **Correntoso** itself, where a legendary trophy has been seen lurking for years. An easy-to-get license allows you to catch brown trout, rainbow trout, perch, brook trout, and *salar sebago* (landlocked) salmon. Driving a bit farther gets you to another favorite fishing center, **Junin de los Andes,** a picturesque town. Here the **Malleo River** and the **Currhué, Huechulaufquen, Paimún,** and **Lácar** lakes are where you'll find the real pros. While many a fisherman releases his trophy, most hotels and inns will grill or bake your catch of the day for dinner.

Península Valdés and Trelew

Getting There **Aerolineas Argentinas** and **Austral** fly daily to the town of
By Plane Trelew from Buenos Aires. The airlines provide bus service from the airport to the town of Puerto Madryn; the 50-minute trip costs less than $10. There are also occasional flights to Trelew from Río Gallegos.

By Bus **Donotto** (tel. 0965/32434) and **La Puntual** (tel. 0965/33748) offer regular bus service from Buenos Aires to both Trelew and Puerto Madryn.

What to See and Do The coast along the Patagonian province of Chubut is a mainland Galápagos, the second most important concentration of visible marine wildlife in South America. Few sights match the annual gathering of the Magellanic penguin clan—at least a million of the elegant creatures come back to roost every August on the stark beaches at Punta Tombo. Right-whale watching is a less predictable activity, but worth the chance to feel the spray of a jet of water launched from a whale's spout an arm's length away. Birds, seals, sea elephants, and sea lions round out the menu of natural marvels at this aquatic wonderland. The **Tourist Office of Chubut Province** (tel. 0965/20121) has stands in Trelew at the bus terminal at Calles Lewis Jones and Urquiza. In Puerto Madryn the tourist office is at Avenida Roca 201 (tel. 0965/73029).

The best time to catch the migrant maritime population at home and without visitors—and in various stages of the rites of reproduction—is in October and November (in December, when vacations start, the area becomes crowded with school excursions and families).

While the action is on the coast, where whale-watching can be complemented, December to March, with swimming, diving, and deep-sea fishing, a day tour to the nearby Welsh communities is another option. In 1865, a group of Welsh nationalists settled the valley of the Chubut River to establish a community where they could keep their customs intact. Now the towns of

Gaiman, Trevelin, and Esquel still reflect their culture. While the settlers' descendents all now speak Spanish and have intermarried, they have maintained their traditions, including the recipes for their delicious cakes, which are features of their teas. Trelew (pop. 52,000) is the largest town in the community, and it is here that most travelers stay—busing or driving out to the wildlife colonies, which are all within a couple of hours' drive along good roads.

Most tourists go straight to **Punta Tombo** (120 kilometers, 75 miles, south of Trelew) after checking into their hotel in Trelew. Try to visit between August and April, since the clan breaks up and heads north to the warmer waters from May through July. In August, future parents spring-clean the burrows they've left for the winter. In September they are rapt in the rites of romantic courtship. In October—the mating season—they pair off with their permanent partner (penguin relationships last for years). In November the eggs are laid and both parents share the task of incubating them and then finding tasty tidbits of fresh fish for the newly born, who appear late in the month. In summer, the babies are protected and raised amid great spurts of activity. In February, the adults molt, which means they cannot go to sea to fish. This is a sad time, with multitudes of scraggly penguins moping about the beach like frustrated bathers grounded by a shark warning. Once the feathers grow back, the entire family heads north.

Rivaling the penguins are the whales, which are to be found north of Trelew near Puerto Madryn, in the gulfs on both sides of the **Península Valdés.** With the whales, too, timing is everything: The southern right whale—the right got its name because it was the "right" whale for commercial purposes, so persistently sought by the whalers of yore—comes to the Argentine coast at the end of winter to mate. A year later, at the same time and place, the mothers return to give birth between August and October. The whales, which weigh over 30 tons and measure up to 12 meters (40 feet) in length, thrive on krill, the abundant and nutritious shrimp-like crustaceans, collecting them like lawn mowers by cruising the surface of the sea with their mouths wide open. The tourist may get to see them leap, which they do for no apparent reason. At other times, they hang out for up to a quarter of an hour with several yards of their tail sticking up out of the water. When it isn't being chased by an aggressive killer whale, the right whale can be found basking in the waters of three bays, the **Golfo San José,** the **Caleta Valdés,** and the **Golfo Nuevo.** At Puerto Pirámides, boats and scuba-diving equipment can be rented, and tour organizers advertise "Close Encounters with Right Whales," with a money-back guarantee if you don't get within a hundred yards of one. Whale watching tours are conducted on six-passenger catamarans moving slowly through the waters; the whales often come close enough to touch! Two- to three-hour tours cost $20 per person and can be arranged through your hotel.

Another great sea sight is the southern elephant seal, which has established its northernmost mainland colony at Península Valdés. If you climb down the cliffs near the lighthouse at **Punta Delgada** in the **Reserva Faunística de Punta Norte,** you can visit an *elefantería*, a colony for elephant seals (your hotel can arrange transportation). They, too, appear in late winter to set up homes for the summer. Their mating rites are colorful and noisy. Males weigh up to 4 tons and thrive on a good fight, which can be an awesome spectacle. A colony of fur seals, called a *lobería*, can be found at Punta Norte at the northern tip of the peninsula.

The **Isla de los Pájaros,** about 37 kilometers (22 miles) from Puerto Madryn, is home to an infinite number of seabirds, such as cormorants, herons, flamingos, and gulls.

Tours to all of the areas mentioned above can be set up through **Nievemar Tours** (Italia 20, tel. 0965/34114 or 0965/35646). Remember the best time to go is in October or November—the local tourists haven't started to migrate yet.

4 Bolivia

*By Chris
Philipsborn and
Sarah Lythe*

*Chris Philipsborn is
La Paz
correspondent for*
The Economist *and
the BBC World
Service. Sarah Lythe
is a freelance writer
and researcher
living in La Paz.*

Landlocked and soft-spoken, Bolivia is perhaps the least discovered—and certainly the least talked about—country in South America. But anonymity has a few distinct advantages. Despite being larger than Texas and California combined, Bolivia has fewer people than New York City. And with most of its 6.2 million inhabitants concentrated in a handful of urban centers such as La Paz, Sucre, and Potosí, there's little to detract from Bolivia's sometimes brooding, sometimes austere, but always captivating landscapes.

Bolivia contains every type of geologically classified land—from tropical lowlands to parched desert to rugged Andes plains. Bolivia is generally considered an Andean nation, but nearly two-thirds of the country sweats it out in the steamy Amazon basin, remote, overlooked, and as inhospitable as it is soul-stirring. Here in Bolivia's last and wildest frontier, primitive tribes live as they have for centuries, unimpressed, it seems, by the displays of modern civilization. (In the Beni and Santa Cruz departments, near the border of Brazil, some tribes attack riverbank villages with bows and arrows.

Beyond these tropical lowlands, just west of Cochabamba and Santa Cruz, the Andes rise sharply to form the backbone of South America's Pacific coast. This two-prong mountain range shelters between its eastern and western peaks a rambling high-altitude plain. Known as the *altiplano*, this bleak, treeless plateau, about 85 miles wide and 520 miles long, claims 30% of Bolivia's landmass and supports more than half the country's population. For centuries, the Aymara Indians have clung to the hostile land, harvesting small crops of potatoes and beans, or fishing the deep-blue waters of Lake Titicaca, the world's highest navigable lake, which forms Bolivia's western border with Peru.

Perched on the edge of the altiplano is La Paz, the capital, overlooking the barren plateau at an altitude of 11,811 feet. If you fly into La Paz's 13,000-foot-high El Alto airstrip, the plateau breaks without warning and reveals below a deep jagged valley covered with adobe and brick homes clinging to the hillsides. At dusk, as the sun settles on the bare flatlands surrounding La Paz, a reddish glow envelops the city's greatest landmark, the 21,000-foot Mt. Illimani—a breathtaking backdrop to the world's highest capital.

From its earliest days, Bolivia's fortunes have risen and fallen with its mineral wealth. Centuries ago it was the Inca and Aymara who dug deep for precious silver. In the 17th century, Spain's colonization of South America was fueled largely by the vast amounts of silver hidden deep in the bowels of *Cerro Rico,* the "Rich Hill" that towers over Potosí, in Southern Bolivia. Cerro Rico's rich lode, first discovered in 1545, quickly brought conquerors, colonists, and prospectors to what was at the time the greatest mining operation in the New World. During the 17th and 18th centuries, Potosí, the most populous city in the Americas, was transformed with grand colonial mansions, stately baroque churches, and thick-walled fortresses. For the Spanish, *Vale un Potosí* ("worth a Potosí") became a favorite description for untold wealth.

As the silver mines in Cerro Rico were exhausted, modern Bolivia began to take shape. Spanish aristocrats fled north to Sucre, Cochabamba, and La Paz, leaving Bolivia's eastern and

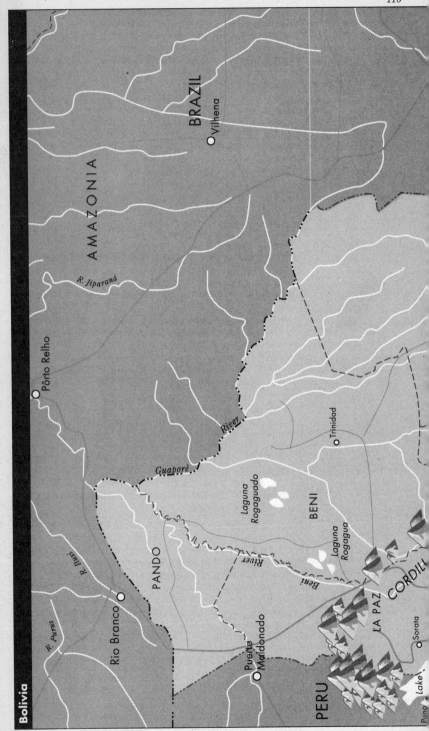

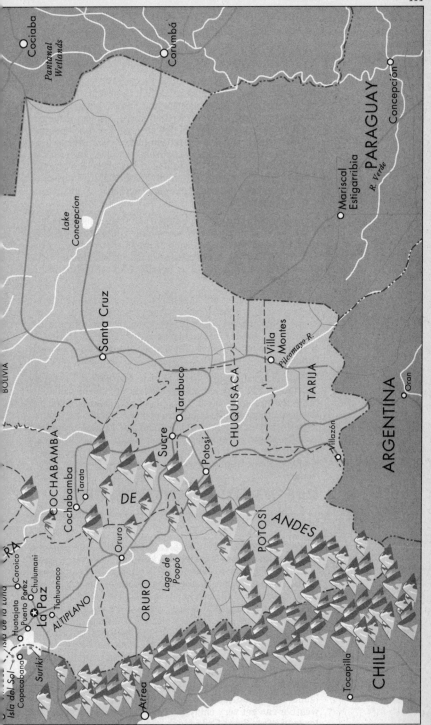

northern extremes to Aymara Indians and the Quechua-speaking Inca. Today, Bolivia remains equally divided between the Old and New World: over 50% of its 6.2 million people are direct descendants of the Aymara and Inca, while the other half is a mix of mestizo and *criollo,* people of Spanish ancestry born in the Americas.

Centuries of Spanish conquest have left their mark on Bolivia, particularly in the cities of Sucre and Potosí, where ebullient baroque cathedrals crowd both cities' narrow streets. But modern Bolivia remains a land of Indian farmers, ranchers, and artisans. On the windswept Andean plateau, you will still see Indian weavers toting their red-cheeked children and crafts to weekly markets. By the time the sun has risen, the brightly dressed Aymara are in place, ready to offer a wide variety of textiles and ponchos, not to mention vegetables, fruits, whole pigs, and medicinal herbs.

Staying Safe and Healthy Compared with its neighbors—Peru and Chile, among them—Bolivia is an island of peace and tranquility. More than a decade later, Bolivia's civilian government remains strong, bolstered by a stable economy and a controlled rate of inflation (in 1985, by comparison, Bolivia had the world's highest inflation rate, at 24,000%).

Crime In Bolivia, you are more likely to be chased by bad-tempered llamas than muggers. However, in larger cities such as La Paz, Sucre, and Santa Cruz, petty theft—from pickpocketing to bag slashing—is on the rise. Avoid displays of money and be aware of your surroundings at all times, especially on busy plazas and in markets.

Health Cholera is a growing problem in Bolivia, so avoid tap water, raw vegetables, raw fish, and washed salads. If you're headed for the Amazon region, lay in a supply of antimalarial medicine. Because of the altitude in La Paz, upon arrival you may suffer from *soroche* (dizziness); avoid alcohol and strenuous exercise at first, and get plenty of sleep. If your symptons persist, locals recommend a cup of *mate de coca,* an herbal (and completely legal) tea made from coca leaves.

Essential Information

Before You Go

When to Go Bolivia has every climate and terrain imaginable, and temperatures are determined largely by altitude. The rainy season runs from October to March and is typified by heavy downpours that, particularly in the lowlands, make many roads virtually impassable. In the highlands, though it may rain only for an hour or two, the rainy season brings dark and cloudy skies that cast a gloom over the high-altitude landscape. If you plan to travel by bus or car, come in the dry season, between April and September. No matter when you come, there are still relatively few visitors and no real tourist season as such in Bolivia.

Climate Climate varies significantly between the highlands and lowlands: In high-altitude La Paz and around Lake Titicaca, the weather can get very chilly, particularly at night, while in the lowland city of Santa Cruz and the central Chaparé, the climate is tropical—in other words, hot and humid. Cochabamba, known as the "City of Eternal Spring," enjoys temperate weather year-round.

The following are the average monthly maximum and minimum temperatures for La Paz.

Jan.	64F	18C	May	66F	19C	Sept.	62F	17C
	43	6		35	2		38	3
Feb.	64F	18C	June	60F	16C	Oct.	65F	18C
	43	6		36	2		40	4
Mar.	64F	18C	July	61F	16C	Nov.	67F	20C
	43	6		34	1		42	6
Apr.	66F	19C	Aug.	62F	17C	Dec.	64F	18C
	40	4		35	2		43	6

Festivals and Events All Bolivia celebrates *Carnaval*—a week-long binge that includes street dance and music performances, parades, and merrymaking—during the week that includes Ash Wednesday. **Good Friday** celebrations—featuring candlelight religious processions by masked supplicants—are particularly lively in La Paz and Copacabana. In early March, Tarabuco celebrates *Pujilay,* one of South America's most colorful festivals, honoring the 1816 victory by local Indians over the Spanish. *Gran Poder,* celebrated in La Paz in late May or early June, features thousands of dancers performing "La Diablada," the Dance of the Devils. During the *Fiesta San Juan,* held on June 24 in La Paz and other Andean cities, hundreds of fires are lit at dusk to fend off the cold of winter.

Currency The unit of currency is the boliviano (Bs), which can be divided into 100 centavos. Bolivianos come in bills of Bs 2, Bs 5, Bs 10, Bs 20, Bs 50, Bs 100, and Bs 200. Coins come in denominations of 5, 10, 20, and 50 centavos and 1 boliviano. At press time (Fall '93), the exchange rate was Bs 5 to the U.S. dollar and Bs. 6.1 to the pound sterling.

Credit cards are accepted in many hotels and restaurants, but never in small villages or outside major urban centers. U.S. dollars (but not British pounds) are widely accepted, though the notes must be in good condition—no torn edges. Money-changers, which can be found on the main streets of most cities, offer competitive rates and are usually reliable. However, never accept boliviano bills that are grubby, since some shopkeepers may not accept them. Traveler's checks are not usually accepted in banks, though they can be changed, at slightly inferior rates, in *casas de cambio* (exchange offices).

What It Will Cost Because the boliviano is a relatively stable currency, Bolivia remains one of the least expensive countries in South America to travel in. A basic meal at a basic restaurant should cost no more than $5, and even at the most elegant of restaurants you can eat well for under $15. Moderate hotels cost $30–$50 for a double room, often including breakfast. Luxury hotels are more pricey, at $120–$150 per night for a double.

Throughout Bolivia, a 12% value-added tax (IVA) is added to hotel and restaurant bills and to most store-bought purchases.

Sample Prices Cup of coffee or *mate de coca* (a traditional herbal tea made from coca leaves), 20¢–50¢; bottle of soda, 50¢–$1; bottle of beer, 75¢–$1.50; cross-town taxi ride, 50¢.

Customs All bags are usually checked on arrival at La Paz's El Alto airport. Visitors are allowed to import 400 cigarettes and three bottles of wine or two bottles of spirits. There is no strict limit on the amount of foreign currency you can bring into the country. For certain electronic goods—video cameras and personal computers, for example—you should carry your receipt or proof of purchase unless the item shows obvious signs of wear.

Passengers flying internationally from Santa Cruz are often asked to produce a yellow fever certificate; have yours handy, or you may be required to get an injection before being allowed to leave. Do not attempt to import or export contraband drugs of any kind; sniffer dogs patrol the airports, and penalties are severe.

Language Spanish is the main language in the cities and lowlands, and travelers find Bolivian Spanish to be one of the easiest on the continent to understand. Quetchua and Aymara are spoken by the highland peoples, who may or may not also understand Spanish. Hotel staff usually have some knowledge of English, French, or German.

Getting Around

By Plane The state-run airline, **Lloyd Aereo Boliviano** (LAB, Av. Camacho 1460, La Paz, tel. 02/371020), flies regularly from La Paz to Sucre ($48), Potosí ($52), Santa Cruz ($80), and Cochabamba ($38). **AeroSur** (Av. Camacho, La Paz, tel. 02/371822), a new private airline, tends to compliment LAB schedules and goes to a number of cities—such as Rurrenabaque and Tarija—not covered by the state airline. Most domestic flights are heavily booked, so try to reconfirm your reservation and arrive at the airport at least an hour in advance lest your seat be given to a standby passenger.

At the airport all passengers must pay a departure tax—$20 for international flights, under $5 for domestic flights—at an easily identifiable booth marked *Impuestos.*

By Train Train timetables in Bolivia are generally works of fiction, and even express trains tend to move at a snail's pace. However, first-class carriages offer a relatively high standard of service and comfort—though even in first class crowds can be a problem. Overnight *ferrobus* trains, such as the one to the Argentinean border, have reclining seats. When you purchase a ticket you will be issued a meal voucher, which can be exchanged in the dining car for a set-menu meal.

At press time, the Bolivian train network was being updated and expanded. For the moment, train service is limited to La Paz, Sucre, Potosí, and Villazon (on the Argentinean border). Trains also join Santa Cruz with Puerto Suarez, on the Brazilian border. One-way tickets between La Paz and Potosí cost $15; between La Paz and Sucre, $20.

By Bus A variety of private bus companies connect Bolivia's major cities. Because road surfaces are poor, however, bus journeys do not always make sense for travelers with limited time: The La Paz–Santa Cruz trip, for example, can take more than 24 hours. Crowds can be a problem on some routes; but if you can get a seat, it's likely to be fairly comfortable. Between La Paz and Santa Cruz expect to pay $15 one way; between La Paz and Cochabamba, $5; between La Paz and the Yungas, around $3.

By Boat Bolivia is landlocked, so the only international arrivals are from the Peruvian port of Puno, on Lake Titicaca. The rest of Bolivia is crisscrossed by navigable rivers served by supply ships, which often accept passengers for a small, negotiable fee.

By Car Bolivia's road network is virtually nonexistent, and there is just one decent paved road in the entire country, linking the cities of La Paz and Oruro. Elsewhere, you'll be constantly jolted by dirt tracks littered with potholes. During the rainy season, prepare for impassable roads and lots of mud. In rural areas you will see few private cars, and even fewer roadside facilities. Parking is a problem in larger cities, and cars left out at night often face the morning bereft of wheels and mirrors. Bolivia's drunk-driving laws are rarely enforced, so exercise caution when driving at night or on small mountain roads.

Car Rental Renting can be an expensive business in Bolivia, particularly since you really need a four-wheel-drive vehicle. The going rate for a four-by-four is $300–$375 per week, including 1,200 free kilometers (745 free miles). Compact cars cost $150–$200 per week.

In La Paz you can rent standard and four-wheel-drive vehicles from **IMBEX** (Av. Montes 522, tel. 02/379884) or **National Car Rental** (Calle Frederico Zuazo 1935, tel. 02/376581). In Cochabamba contact **Barron's Rent-a-Car** (Calle Sucre E. 0727, tel. 042/22774 or 042/23819) or **National Car Rental** (Calle Nataniel Aguirre S. 0685, tel. 042/26911 or 02/376581). In Santa Cruz contact **IMBEX** (Calle Monseñor Peña 320, tel. 03/533603).

Gasoline The national oil company, **YPFB,** maintains service stations on most major roads. Station opening times vary, though a number are open 24 hours. Away from the main roads, *gasolina* (gasoline) signs alert you to private homes where fuel is sold (make sure they filter the gasoline for impurities when they fill your tank). Unleaded gasoline is still a novelty in Bolivia.

Breakdowns There is no national roadside automobile service, though Bolivians will often stop and offer help in case of a breakdown.

Staying in Bolivia

Telephones Pay phones use 30-centavo tokens sold by people usually sitting right next to the phone booth. Many street vendors have telephones available for local calls; look for signs marked *teléfono.* Local calls also can be made from ENTEL and COTEL offices.

International Calls International calls are best made through AT&T (tel. 0800–1111) or MCI (tel. 0800–2222). Otherwise, collect and direct-dial calls can be made from ENTEL offices or by calling 35–67–00, which connects you with a Bolivian international operator, who will ask for the city and number you wish to reach, then, up to 20 minutes later, call you back after the connection has been made.

Mail Most cities and towns have at least one post office, and these are generally open weekdays 8–7:30, Saturday 9–6, and Sunday 9–noon. International airmail costs 50¢ (about 30¢ for international postcards) and generally arrives in Europe or the United States within 7–10 days.

Receiving Mail Mail can be sent in care of Post Restante, Correo Central, in the city of your choice. You will need a passport to retrieve your mail from the central post office.

Shopping Bolivia has a wealth of traditional crafts ranging from weavings and knitwear to gold and silver jewelry. Craft shops are usually grouped together (in La Paz, for instance, most can be found on Calle Sagarnaga, known locally as Calle Gringo). However, it is always worth looking for cooperative craft shops outside the capital. These sell traditional textiles made in rural areas, especially in the departments of Chuquisaca and Potosí. The traditional shawls, hats, and skirts worn by highland women are sold in local markets and certain shopping districts in La Paz, but shopkeepers sometimes refuse to sell traditional garments to foreigners. In La Paz there are black market sellers hawking electronic and other goods smuggled in from Japan via Peru.

Do not expect many shopping bargains in Bolivia. Prices are high for tourist-oriented goods, and, unusual in South America, bargaining is not very common. Many sellers will drop their prices, but only by small amounts (particularly if you look fresh off the tourist boat).

Opening and Closing Times **Banks** are open weekdays 9–11:30 and 2:30–5. **Museums** are generally open Tuesday–Friday 9–noon and 3–7. **Shops** close for lunch between 12:30 and 3, after which they open again until 8 or so. Many shops are also closed Saturday afternoon and Sunday.

National Holidays January 1; Shrove Tuesday and preceding Monday; May 1 (Good Friday); Corpus Christi; August 6 (Independence Day); November 2 (All Saints Day); December 25.

There are a number of local carnivals and feast days when shops may be closed; check with local tourist offices for more details.

Dining Lunch, the main meal of the day in Bolivia, means a set, four-course menu. The only choice you may have is between entrées, so once you sit down, simply relax and wait for your meal to arrive, course by course. Many Bolivians find it hard to digest large evening meals because of the high altitude, so dinner tends to be light and informal. To ease your transition, many restaurants offer English-language menus. In major cities such as La Paz, Sucre, Potosí, and Cochabamba, restaurants run the gamut from elegant international to basic hole-in-the-wall. In rural areas your choice is largely limited to basic Bolivian cooking in simple surroundings.

Lunch is usually served from noon to 2; dinner between 7 and 10. Informal dress is acceptable in all restaurants. Also note that some establishments add a cover charge to your bill—from 10¢ to $2 per person—whether you eat a full meal or simply stop for a cup of coffee.

Specialties Traditional Bolivian cuisine is very regional. In the highlands, where carbohydrates are the dietary mainstay, look for *chuña*, freeze-dried potatoes that accompany main dishes. Other traditional highland dishes are *timpu* (lamb stew) and *asado de llama* (llama steak). A ubiquitous traditional dish is *pique macho*, beef grilled with hot peppers, chopped tomatoes and onions, and often served with fried potatoes and gravy. Vegetarians will have a hard time of it because meat, usually grilled, figures prominently in the Bolivian diet. *Surubí*, a popular Amazon River fish, is delicious grilled or baked.

Bolivians satisfy a sweet-savory tooth with *salteña*, a sweet pastry filled with olives, eggs, and meat—usually beef or chicken. Alcohol is available in the form of local beers and Bolivian or Chilean wine. *Singani*, a refined grape alcohol, is the national liqueur. Traditional cocktails include the potent *pisco sour*, made from singani and lime juice, and *chicha*, a grain alcohol made by chewing corn, spitting out the resulting mash, and allowing it to brew.

Precautions Two percent of Bolivians fall victim to cholera each year, and tap water is the main suspect. Stay with bottled water, which is safe if not always appetizing, and avoid raw vegetables, salads, and raw fish. Food on the street should generally be avoided, unless you see it being thoroughly cooked.

Ratings Prices are per person for a four-course meal, not including alcohol and gratuities. A tip of 10% is expected unless the service is really dismal. Best bets are indicated by a star ★.

Category	La Paz	Other Areas
Very Expensive	over $15	over $5
Expensive	$10–$15	$3–$5
Moderate	$5–$10	$1–$3
Inexpensive	under $5	under $1

Lodging The Bolivian tourist board rates hotels on an escalating one- to five-star basis. There are no international chain hotels in Bolivia, which is not necessarily a bad thing since even the most expensive resorts are often family-run affairs. Some hotels have two pricing systems—one for Bolivians and one for foreigners. Still, even if you fall into the latter category, good, clean rooms can be found for $25 or less, particularly away from the cities. Do not be afraid to ask to see the room in advance—it's a common practice in Bolivia.

Ratings Prices are for two people in a double room. Best bets are indicated by a star ★.

Category	La Paz	Other Areas
Very Expensive	over $100	over $40
Expensive	$50–$100	$25–$40
Moderate	$25–$50	$10–$25
Inexpensive	under $25	under $10

Tipping Taxi drivers do not expect tips unless you hire them for the day, when a $5–$10 tip is appropriate. Waiters expect a 10% gratuity. Airport porters expect $1 per bag they handle.

La Paz

One of the most often heard comments made by visitors to the world's highest capital city is, "Why here?" La Paz, set in a lunarlike landscape of great—if rather stark—beauty, nestles in a bowl-shaped valley that ranges in altitude from 11,811 to 9,951 feet. The high elevation forces even the locals to walk slowly, and the pace of life here seems more gentle than in other South American capitals.

Though you may have to struggle to get used to La Paz's rare-fied air, you'll find certain advantages to the altitude and climate. There are none of the bugs, or mosquitoes, or stifling humidity that you encounter at lower altitudes. There is no smog; the air, though thin, is crystal clear, and the colors of the sky and landscape can be magically vibrant. (If you still find yourself suffering from the altitude, locals recommend a cup of piping hot *mate de coca*, an herbal tea made from coca leaves and sweetened with sugar.)

Nearly half of the city's million residents live in the deep jagged valleys encircling La Paz, in adobe and brick homes that cling to the hillside. In downtown La Paz, the feeling is more cosmopolitan: buses and taxis, businesspeople and Aymara Indians crowd the city's cobblestone streets. During the lunchtime ritual, when many *Paceños*, as La Paz residents are called, head home for lunch and a nap, the capital miraculously clears itself of people. As the sun fades behind the Andes, the streets of La Paz once again fill with merchants and gawkers, and with well-heeled Paceños headed for one of the city's many bars or night-clubs.

La Paz is a compact city, with the main sites gathered in and around the walkable city center. Yet while there are some excellent museums and interesting buildings, the bulk of the downtown area is burdened with undistinguished high rises. The real allure of La Paz is its stunning natural surroundings, its small side streets, and its vibrant outdoor markets, where you can buy everything from food to computers.

Tourist Information

Oficina de Turismo (Edificio Mariscal Ballicán, 18th floor, Calle Mercado, tel. 02/367441).

Arriving and Departing

By Plane All international and domestic flights to La Paz arrive at **El Alto** airport (tel. 02/810122), situated high above the city on the altiplano plain, 12 kilometers (7 miles) from downtown. From El Alto, the state-run airline, **Lloyd Aereo Boliviano** (LAB), and **Aerosur** fly regularly to Sucre, Potosí, Santa Cruz, and Cochabamba. At the airport all departing passengers must pay a tax at the booth marked *Impuestos* ($20 for international passengers, under $5 for domestic passengers).

Some La Paz hotels run their own shuttle buses to and from the airport; check with the hotel when you make your reservation. Taxis are the only real alternative. The current going rate for the 30- to 45-minute journey is around $10, but be sure to fix a price with the driver before getting in.

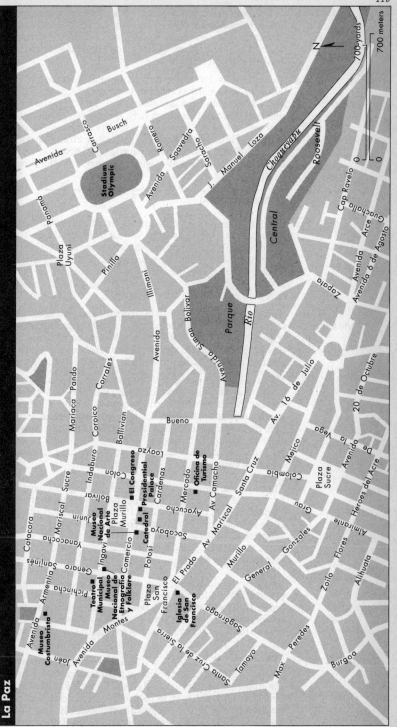

By Train La Paz is served by a single railway station, the **Estación Central de Ferrocarriles** (Plaza Kennedy, tel. 02/373069); a cab to downtown costs less than $1. The only rail destinations from La Paz are Sucre, Potosí, Villazón, and a handful of towns along the Argentinean frontier.

By Bus All buses to La Paz arrive at the **Terminal de Buses** (Av. Péru, tel. 02/367274), which is not quite centrally located but still only a $1–$2 taxi ride from downtown. You can travel almost anywhere in Bolivia by bus from here, though you should reserve your seat at least a day in advance for the numbingly long rides to Sucre, Potosí, and Santa Cruz. Contact **Flota Copacabana** (tel. 02/362803), **Trans Copacabana** (tel. 02/322888), or **Expreso Mopar** (tel. 02/340737), all of which have agents at the Terminal de Buses.

Getting Around

By Bus La Paz is served by a comprehensive network of *micros* (buses), which run daily from 6:30 AM to 10 PM. There is a flat fare of roughly 25¢ per person in the city center, payable to the driver upon entry. Slightly more expensive are *trufis,* 12-seat minivans that travel the same bus routes, only more quickly. Micros and trufis are short on comfort and sometimes rather crowded, but they are safe for tourists.

By Taxi and Colectivo Shared taxis, easily identifiable from the taxi sign lodged in the windshield, are cheap and plentiful; expect to pay under $1 for trips within the city center. Newer-looking radio taxis, identified by the illuminated sign perched on the roof, are not shared and cost slightly more.

If you are simply going down a main street, take a *colectivo,* a taxi with a green flag fixed to its front bumper and a sign in the window indicating which main streets it serves. The fare depends on your destination but is even cheaper than a shared taxi. Be prepared to share a four-seat car with up to seven occupants.

Guided Tours

The following companies offer guided, English-language walking tours of La Paz for $10–$15 per person: **Diana Tours** (Calle Sagarnaga 328, tel. 02/375374), **Plaza Tours** (Hotel Plaza, Av. 16 de Julio, tel. 02/378311), and **Tourismo Balsa** (Av. 16 de Julio 1650, tel. 02/357817).

Exploring La Paz

Crossing the downtown area is the busy main thoroughfare, called **El Prado** for half its length, after which it becomes **Avenida Mariscal Santa Cruz**. Downhill and away from the city center, the Prado splits into two major one-way streets, Avenida 6 de Agosto and Avenida Arce, which are more residential.

Downtown La Paz At the heart of downtown is **Plaza San Francisco,** where Indian sellers hawk all sorts of handicrafts and trinkets. Flanking the plaza is the impressive **Iglesia de San Francisco** (San Francisco Church), built in 1549 and considered one of the finest examples of Spanish colonial architecture in South America. The carved facade is adorned with birds of prey, ghoulish masks, pinecones, and parrots, a combination of Spanish and Indian motifs created by native artisans during the 16th and 17th centuries. Indian weddings can sometimes be seen spilling out onto the plaza on Saturdays. A warren of handicraft stalls line the church wall; most days you'll find colorful weavings and handmade Bolivian musical instruments such as the *quena, zampoña tarka, and charango. Admission free. Closed Mon.*

Adjacent to the church lies the extremely steep **Calle Sagarnaga,** unofficially known as Calle Gringo, dotted with crafts shops and street vendors selling more weavings and trinkets. The street is also lined with inexpensive pensions and hotels.

Continue along Calle Sagarnaga and turn right at **Calle Max Paredes.** In this area you will find whole streets filled with peddlers hawking traditional shawls, hats, and clothing. A number of stalls offer traditional Indian cures used by modern-day *callawayas,* the medicine men who attended the ancient Incan courts, not to mention dried llama fetuses and other ingredients used by many Bolivians in ceremonies to bless new dwellings or offices. Tucked away in alleys and courtyards are *tambanos,* where oranges, bananas, and coca leaves are sold. The latter are chewed by farmers and miners (and tourists) to ward off hunger and the effects of altitude.

Back at the Plaza San Francisco, walk down Avenida Mariscal Santa Cruz and take a left at Calle Ayacucho. Keep walking uphill until you reach **Plaza Murillo** and La Paz's principal **Catedral** (Cathedral), built in 1835 in a severe neoclassical style, with a sober facade and imposing bronze doors. *Plaza Murillo. Admission free. Closed Fri.–Mon.*

Adjacent to the cathedral is the **Presidential Palace** (closed to the public), which was guarded by tanks and machine-guntoting soldiers until 1982, when the constitutional government was restored following a coup in 1979. In front of the palace is a statue of former President Gualberto Villarroel. In 1946 a mob attacked the palace, forcibly brought Villarroel to the square, and then hanged him from a lamp post; a nearby statue commemorates the event. Diagonally across from the palace is Bolivia's congress building, **El Congreso,** which has a visitor's gallery. *Plaza Murillo. Admission free. Closed weekends.*

The **Museo Nacional del Arte** (National Museum of Art) is housed in a stunning baroque mansion commissioned by a Spanish noble in 1775. The carved facade and high walls keep the noise of Calle Comercio, a busy shopping street, at bay. Inside, a broad courtyard opens onto three stories of painting and sculpture. The first floor is devoted to contemporary Bolivian and foreign artists; the second, to the master of Andean colonial art, Melchor Perez Holguin, and his disciples; and the third, to a permanent collection of Bolivian artists. *Plaza Murillo (at Calle Comercio), tel. 02/371177. Admission charged. Closed Sun.*

From Plaza Murillo continue on Calle Comercio and turn right up Calle Genaro Sanjines. Just ahead is the **Teatro Municipal** (Municipal Theater, Calle Ingavi, tel. 02/375275), a handsome building both inside and out, which regularly stages traditional dance and music shows. Be warned: its circle seats are wooden and hard on the posterior. A few doors down, the **Museo Nacional de Etnografía y Folklore** (National Ethnographic and Folklore Museum), housed in an ornate 18th-century building, exhibits feathers, masks, and weavings. It also has permanent displays on the Ayoreos Indians, who live in the Amazon region, and the Chipayas Indians, who come from the surrounding altiplano. *Calle Ingavi 916, tel. 02/358559. Admission charged. Closed weekends.*

Calle Jaén, one of the city's few remaining colonial streets, houses four excellent museums: The **Museo Costumbrista** (Calle Jaén at Calle Sucre, tel. 02/361613), dedicated to the political and cultural history of La Paz; the **Museo de Metales Preciosos** (Museum of Precious Metals, Calle Jaén 777, tel. 02/371470), with an expansive collection of pre-Columbian gold and silver artifacts, in addition to Inca and pre-Inca ceramics; the **Museo Pedro Domingo Murillo,** (Calle Jaén 79, tel. 02/375273), with a collection of masks, herbal medicines, and weavings housed in a restored colonial mansion; and the **Museo de Litoral** (Seashore Museum Calle Jaén 789, tel. 02/371222), a repository for artifacts connected with the 1867 War of the Pacific, when Bolivia lost its Pacific ports to Chile. *Purchase a ticket ($2) for all four museums at the Museo Costumbrista. Closed Mon.*

The city's main avenue, **El Prado,** is a colorful blur of trees, flowers, and monuments. The street is often clogged with pedestrians and vendors, especially on weekends, and many of La Paz's luxury hotels are found here, rising high above the old colonial-style homes with their elaborate latticework and balustrades. Continue south down El Prado until it turns into Avenida 6 de Agosto, then turn right on Calle Guachalla, past a number of chic bars and restaurants. Just ahead is **Avenida Ecuador,** the heart of the Sopocachi district and, where it intersects Calle Guachalla, the site of a vast indoor market, worth seeing for its colorful displays of fresh produce and flowers. Vegetarians should avoid the meat stalls, which display such delicacies as freshly cut beef tongue and cow udders.

From the market, take a taxi or walk along Avenida Ecuador (which becomes a small side street) until you reach beautiful little **Monticulo Park.** Served by a small church, it has breathtaking views of 21,000-foot Mount Illimani, especially fine during a blazing altiplano sunset. Continuing along the main road, Calle Victor Sanjinez, you will soon reach **Plaza España,** a pleasant residential square.

The Lower Suburbs The **Muela del Diablo** (Devil's Molar) is a tooth-shape rock perched on the edge of a small farming village on the outskirts of La Paz. Take a taxi or *trufi* to Los Rosales and walk uphill until you reach the cemetery, then follow the path uphill all the way. You will soon see the unmistakable outline of the Muela. There are several trails you can follow; one of them encircling the rock itself and offering spectacular views of La Paz and the surrounding countryside. Keep and eye peeled for condors, which can often be seen soaring overhead.

Eucalyptus-lined **El Parque Mallasa** (Mallasa Park) has been partly appropriated La Paz's zoo, which is in the process of moving. Still, the park remains a fragrant escape for picnicking Paceños on sunny weekends. Take a taxi for under $5 from downtown and, at the front entrance, turn left and keep walking until you reach the edge of a precipice with stunning views of the river valley below and of the Devil's Molar opposite. *Admission free. Open Sunrise–Sunset.*

Shopping

In La Paz you'll find everything from roughly made silver plates to sophisticated jewelry, from woven-rope sandals to intricately designed sweaters made of the softest alpaca wool. Prices are reasonable by North American standards, although, as always, good quality does not come cheaply.

Shopping Districts **Calle Sagarnaga** is a good place to begin. The small streets leading off to the right and left harbor a variety of crafts shops, while Calle Murillo, to the left, is devoted entirely to cheap furniture. The extensive black-market area on **Avenida Buenos Aires,** which runs parallel to El Prado, is crammed with every sort of craft and contraband; some of the peasant women selling computers seem to know more about their wares than your average computer nerd. The police don't seem to mind the blossoming black market, but, as always, buyer beware.

For traditional Aymara embroidered shawls, try the market area around **Calle Santa Cruz de la Sierra** and **Calle Max Paredes.** Prices start at $15 and peak at over $200 for more intricate designs. *Polleras,* the traditional skirts worn by local Indians, are priced between $50 and $200; distinctive bowler hats up to $250. Also browse the crafts shops just past the entrance to Iglesia de San Francisco; some sell high-quality masks and weavings.

Department Stores There are two main shopping malls in the city center, both on Calle Potosí near Calle Ayacucho. The better of the two is **Shopping Norte,** with its wide selection of jeans, T-shirts, shoes, and sports equipment.

Specialty Stores For Alpaca sweaters, the rule is: You get what you pay for. High-quality hand-knit designs go for around $100, though you may cheer yourself with the fact that they can sell for three or more times that amount at home. A wide range of sweaters and cardigans can be found at **Casa Fisher** (Handal Center, Av. Mariscal Santa Cruz), **Fotrama** (Calle Colombia), and **Edificio Hoy** (Av. 6 de Agosto at Calle Guachalla). On Calle Sagarnaga, **Toshy Export** has a selection of hand-knit cardigans with ethnic designs. Just before Toshy there is an arcade with a good selection of medium-priced alpaca sweaters.

Spectator Sports

Soccer Bolivians would be lost without their weekly soccer fix; even the poorest, most remote villages have their own playing field. La Paz itself has two teams: Bolivar and The Strongest. Both strut their stuff in the **Hernando Siles** stadium (Plaza de los Monolitos, tel. 02/357342), in the Miraflores district.

Volleyball Three major teams—San Antonio, Litoral, and Universidad—compete regularly in the **Coliseo Julio Borelli** (Calle Mexico, tel. 02/320224), in the San Pedro District.

Dining

La Paz restaurants range in style from Italian and Chinese to traditional Bolivian. Plaza Abaroa and the residential Sopocachi district probably have the widest selection of restaurants in La Paz, while Calle Sagarnaga generally harbors the least expensive. Midmorning is the time when Paceños eat *sal-*

teña, a hearty beef, olive, hard-boiled egg, potato, and pea stew wrapped in dough, available from stands throughout the city for under $1. For price ranges, *see* Dining in Staying in Bolivia, *above.*

Very Expensive **Utama.** Situated on the penthouse floor of the Hotel Plaza, this rooftop restaurant is a must for its panoramic views of the city and surrounding mountains. There is a well-stocked salad bar, and the grilled entrées—generally steak and chicken accompanied with rice and beans—are passable. *Hotel Plaza, El Prado, tel. 02/378311. Reservations advised. AE, MC, V.*

La Suisse/El Gourmet. Two restaurants in one, La Suisse is a small, very comfortable eatery with a range of Swiss and German dishes; try the veal cooked with cream and mushrooms and served with lightly fried potato slivers. The more formal El Gourmet, located upstairs and open only for dinner, is better known for its meat and cheese fondues. *Av. Arce 2164, tel. 02/353150. Reservations advised. Closed Sun. AE, MC, V.*

Expensive **Chifa Emy.** As long as you remember where you are (Bolivia), you shouldn't be too disappointed with the selection of Chinese dishes at Chifa Emy, a popular meeting place for well-heeled Paceños. The atmosphere is lively and loud, no doubt fueled in part by the selection of interesting cocktails. An English-language menu will help guide you through the maze of chow meins, sweet and sours, and seafood dishes. *Calle Cordero 257, tel. 02/323725. AE, MC, V.*

Gringo Limón. Befitting its name, this relatively new restaurant is painted an unmistakably bright shade of yellow. In fine weather, the outside patio makes a pleasant backdrop for hearty dishes like *frente y costilla* (rack of beef ribs) and *pollo desnogado* (chicken in a spicy peanut sauce). A trek to the extensive salad bar is included in the price of your entrée. *Plaza Abaroa, tel. 02/355225. AE, MC, V.*

★ **Pronto.** This small but inviting basement restaurant, decorated with modern artwork and an artistic flair, is one of the few places in La Paz that serves fresh pasta: the raviolis, tortellinis, and tagliatellis are prepared fresh daily and smothered in a variety of tomato, garlic, and basil sauces. There's also a daily selection of standard Bolivian entrées. *Calle Jauregi 2248, off Calle Guachalla, tel. 02/355869. Reservations advised. AE, MC, V. Dinner only.*

Moderate **Café La Paz.** This quaint old café is a popular hangout with many La Paz politicians, journalists, and expatriates. It used to be the haunt of Nazi war criminal Klaus Barbi, until he was expelled from Bolivia in 1983. Lunch at the café is overpriced, but stop in for potent espresso, *café helados* (ice cream coffee), and elaborate pastries. *Calle Ayacucho at Av. Camacho, no phone. No credit cards. Open lunch only.*

El Refugio. Pepper steak and Lake Titicaca trout are favorites at this small, quiet restaurant a short walk from El Prado and the university. In season, indulge yourself with strawberries and cream for dessert. *Av. 20 de Octubre 2453, tel. 02/355651. MC, V. Closed Sat. lunch and Sun.*

Inexpensive **Confitería Elis.** Don't be deterred if the first floor is full; this vastly efficient restaurant has a large dining area in the basement, too. The set menu changes daily, or you can try an à la carte special, such as *pique macho*, a traditional dish of beef, hot peppers, freshly chopped tomatoes, and onions served with fried potatoes. *Av. 16 de Julio 1494, no phone. No credit cards.*

Pizzeria Morello. At Morello, possibly the best pizzeria in La Paz, you can order what's hot from the oven or design your own pizza from the voluminous list of toppings. The dining area is cramped and characterless, which may be why many Paceños avail of Morello's takeout and delivery services. *Av. Arce 2132, tel. 02/372973. No credit cards. Closed Sat. and Sun. lunch.*

Lodging

La Paz has a limited number of hotel rooms, and hotels at either end of the price spectrum are sometimes booked solid during holidays and festivals. Make reservations in advance whenever possible. Also note that the Hotel La Paz, formerly the Sheraton, was recently sold as part of the government's privatization program. It currently is being refurbished and may be open for business late in 1994.

There are inexpensive pensions and small hotels on Calle Sagarnaga, but what you save in price may not adequately compensate for the lack of facilities and cleanliness. For price ranges, *see* Lodging in Staying in Bolivia, *above.*

Very Expensive **Hotel Plaza.** La Paz's most expensive hotel, on El Prado, commands fine views of the city center and the surrounding countryside, especially from the rooftop restaurant and bar. The rooms are comfortable if without much character, and you can opt for an executive room or a suite as well as standard digs. Ask for quarters facing Mt. Illimani; not only are the views better, but street noise is less noticeable. *Av. 16 de Julio 378–300, tel. 02/378311. 175 rooms, 10 suites. Facilities: 2 restaurants, 2 bars, business facilities, sauna, pool, gift shop. AE, MC, V.*

Hotel Presidente. The most modern and perhaps most inviting of La Paz's luxury hotels, the Presidente is a short walk from Plaza San Francisco and the downtown sights. The rooms are plain but comfortable; most face the street, but at least on the upper floors, noise is not a problem. The top-floor disco gives stunning views of the city. *Calle Potosí 920, tel. 02/367193, fax 02/354013. 101 rooms, 18 suites. Facilities: 2 restaurants, 2 bars, discotheque, casino, pool, exercise room. AE, MC, V.*

Expensive **Hotel Gloria.** If you don't mind sacrificing a few creature comforts—many rooms do not have phones or televisions, and there's nothing even remotely like a sports or recreation facility—you will appreciate the Gloria's location, one block from the central San Francisco church and its rooftop restaurant. *Calle Potosí, tel. 02/370010, fax 02/370123. 79 rooms. Facilities: restaurant, bar. AE, MC, V.*

Hotel Sucre Palace. The suites are fairly charming at the centrally located Sucre (it's on the Prado). Not so the standard rooms, which are gloomy, or the public spaces, which could stand a fresh coat of paint. *Av. 16 de Julio 1636, tel. 02/363323, fax 02/392052. 137 rooms, 4 suites. Facilities: restaurant, bar. AE, MC, V.*

Moderate **El Dorado.** This is a functional but popular mid-size hotel situated in the city center just opposite the university. Street-facing rooms tend to be noisy, as do those near the elevator shaft. *Av. Villazon, tel. 02/363355 or 02/363403, fax 02/391438. 50 rooms, 2 suites. Facilities: restaurant, bar, cafeteria. AE, MC, V.*

Hotel Max Inn. The location is perhaps not all it could be (the San Pedro Jail is adjacent), but the recently built Max Inn offers comfortable quarters, and the prices are reasonable. The Plaza San Pedro itself is lively and quite pleasant. *Plaza San Pedro, tel. 02/374391, fax 02/341720. 50 rooms, 5 suites. Facilities: restaurant. MC, V.*

Inexpensive **Hostal República.** The República is a good choice for travelers on a budget. The comfortable rooms are reasonably priced, and a number overlook a small, quiet garden. Some rooms share a communal bathroom. *Calle Comercio 1455, tel. tk/357966. 35 rooms. Facilities: restaurant. No credit cards.*

★ **Residencial Rosario.** A popular option with budget-conscious tourists, the Rosario has all the hallmarks of a traveler's hotel, including, in the lobby, a useful bulletin board and a travel agency that arranges tours in Bolivia and to Machu Picchu in Peru. *Calle Illampu 704, tel. 02/326531, fax 02/375532. 40 rooms. Facilities: restaurant, travel agency. No credit cards.*

The Arts and Nightlife

The tourist office (*see* Tourist Information, *above*) can fill you in on local festivals and special events. For concert and cinema listings pick up a copy of *Ultima Hora* or *La Razón,* two Spanish-language newspapers, and the English-language *Bolivian Times.*

The Arts The **Cinemateca Boliviana** (Calle Pichincha at Calle Indabura,
Film tel. 02/325346), an art theater, regularly screens foreign and even a few Bolivian films.

Galleries The **Galleria Emusa** (Av. 16 de Julio 1607), centrally located on El Prado, hosts rotating exhibits of Bolivian sculpture and art. **Arte Unico** (Av. Arce 2895) mounts varied exhibits.

Theater The **Teatro Municipal** (Calle Genaro Sanjines, tel. 02/375275)
and Music stages folk events and traditional music and dance concerts.

Nightlife Calle Belisario Salinas boasts the city's largest selection of
Bars bars, which start to fill up around 10:30 PM. Along the avenue, look for **Panyco,** owned by a Frenchman who knows how to attract trendy Paceños with offbeat decorations and live music. Across the street and more popular with professional Bolivians, **Caras y Caretas** often features live bands. Away from Calle Belisario Salinas, the intimate **Matheus** (Calle Guachalla at Av. 6 de Agosto) has a well-stocked bar and the occasional live band. The **Hotel Plaza** and **Hotel Presidente** (*see* Lodging, *above*) have rooftop bars worth a visit if only for the stunning views.

Nightclubs **El Loro en Su Salsa** (Calle Goitia at Calle Capitán Ravelo) is a popular, lively salsa club. Trendy **Socavón** (Calle 20 de Octubre, near Calle Guachalla) draws crowds of younger Paceños and foreigners with live, dance music most nights. **New Tokio** (Av. 6 de Agosto), a smaller venue, attracts slightly more mature boppers.

Peñas Peñas are nightclubs that showcase Bolivian folkloric music and dance. The energetic live performances are popular with tourists and Paceños alike and usually include dinner in the price—from $8 to $20 per person. Popular peñas are **Casa del Corregidor** (Calle Murillo 1040, tel. 02/363633), **Peña Naira** (Calle Sagarnaga 161, tel. 02/325736), **Marka Tambo** (Calle

Jaén, tel. 02/340416), and **Los Escudos** (Av. Mariscal Santa
Cruz, Edificio Club de la Paz, tel. 02/322028).

Excursions from La Paz

Tiahuanaco   Tiahuanaco is Bolivia's most important archaeological site. Unfortunately, there is very little to see, apart from the Gate of
the Sun, an imposing stone fixture that is thought to be a solar
calendar built by a civilization that mysteriously surfaced
around 600 BC only to disappear around AD 1200. The gate is
part of an elaborate observatory and courtyard that contain
monoliths and a subterranean temple. Although the site lacks
the splendor of Peru's Machu Picchu, it does provide a glimpse
into the ancestry of the Aymara people, many of whom still live
in the area.

Getting There   Tiahuanaco is 80 kilometers (50 miles) west of La Paz and 32
kilometers (20 miles) east of Lake Titicaca. There are no guides
available at the site, so book in advance with a travel agency in
La Paz; try **Diana Tours** (Calle Sagarnaga 328, tel. 02/375374),
Tourismo Balsa (Av. 16 de Julio 1650, tel. 02/357817) or **Plaza
Tours** (Hotel Plaza, Av. 16 de Julio 1650, tel. 02/378311).

Las Yungas   Within easy reach of La Paz, **Las Yungas** (literally "The Valleys") are a semitropical paradise where the snow-covered
Andes tower above waterfalls and valleys carpeted with lush
vegetation. The drive to the Yungas is an experience in itself:
Dropping in altitude by some 3,000 meters (9,840 feet) in just
under 80 kilometers (50 miles), the poorly maintained, mostly
single-lane highway is one of the most scenic and hair-raising
in South America. And the views certainly make up for any
discomfort.

Your first glimpse of small, picturesque **Coroico** is unforgettable, particularly after three hours of tortuous hairpin bends.
Set in steep, undulating hills overrun with citrus and banana
trees, coffee plants, and coca bushes, Coroico is a resort town
for Paceños, who flock from the capital on weekends. You can
rent horses from Dany and Patricio of **Ranch Beni,** signposted
near the hospital, for around $5 per hour. You can also bargain
for jewelry and crafts at one of the shops huddled around the
main square. A 30-minute walk from Coroico on the road to
Caranavi, **El Viejo Molino** (tel. 0811/6004 or 02/361076 for reservations) is the best hotel for miles. You can linger over a
plate of grilled steak in the excellent restaurant, or ponder intense valley views from the balcony of your clean, spacious bedroom (from $50 per night). The most popular restaurant in
town is **La Casa** (Calle Kennedy, no phone), which specializes
in meat and cheese fondues for around $5 per person. La Casa
also has a handful of clean, simple rooms priced well under $5
per night.

Chulumani, in the southern Yungas, is surrounded by waterfalls and sprawling ranch properties and offers an authentic
glimpse of traditional life in the Andes. Although a bit larger
than Coroico, Chulimani is not really geared for tourists: Its
busy market offers local produce rather than crafts, and the
only hotel, the **San Bartolomé** (tel. 0811/6114), a 30-minute
walk downhill from the main square, is rustic at best (though
it does have a pool and restaurant).

Getting There   Day-tours of Coroico and Las Yungas cost $70–$80 per person, including lunch. Try the La Paz–based **Plaza Tours** (Hotel Plaza, Av. 16 de Julio, tel. 02/378311) or **Balsa Tours** (Av. 16 de Julio 1650, tel. 02/372370). From La Paz, the private bus companies **Veloz del Norte** (Av. de las Americas 283, tel. 02/311753) and **Transporte 20 de Octobre** (Calle Yanacachi 1434, tel. 02/317391) also make the three- to four-hour trek to Coroico ($8) and Chulumani ($8). If you're planning to drive yourself, get a four-wheel-drive vehicle. Remember that cars traveling downhill have the right of way, and that when traveling on the mountain passes of Las Yungas, people drive on the left-hand side of the road.

Lake Titicaca

Lake Titicaca, which at an altitude of 3,814 meters (12,506 feet) is the world's highest navigable lake, is in fact two bodies of water joined at the narrow Strait of Tiquina. The smaller section of the lake—freshwater Lago Huiñamarca—is the easiest to reach from La Paz; for a sight of the larger section—brackish Lago Chucuito—you need to include Copacabana on your itinerary. Either way, the lakes' still waters reflect an equal measure of high-altitude sun and cloudless blue sky, in addition to the palette of browns injected by the sunbaked hills encircling Lake Titicaca.

Beyond the bumpy profile of islands with names like Suriki, Sun, and Moon, each with a smattering of Inca ruins in varying states of decay, the horizon-wide panorama encompasses fishing vessels and tourist launches headed for port. On the lakeshore, the scene may include local Amayaras Indians who've come to tend to a crop of potatoes and beans, or to fish for trout in their small wooden boats.

At its largest point, Lake Titicaca measures 200 kilometers by 60 kilometers (124 miles by 37 miles). On a clear day you can see Peru, which borders the lake to the west and can be reached overland or by boat from the Bolivian port of Copacabana. Most visitors, however, are content to remain on the eastern shore, in the Bolivian villages of Puerto Perez or Huatajata, from where you can arrange boat treks to the island of Suriki. Tour operators in La Paz cover Lake Titicaca (and occasionally the islands) in a long but rewarding day. Yet with the wide selection of hotels and restaurants in the area, adventure-minded travelers should consider renting a four-wheel-drive vehicle in La Paz and striking out on their own.

Getting There

By Car   From La Paz, take El Alto Highway northwest. After the tollbooths, follow signs for Batallas, Río Seco, Huatajata, and Tiquina. The road is paved between La Paz and Tiquina, and barring heavy traffic it takes less than two hours to drive. Be very careful about leaving your car unattended, particularly in Copacabana.

By Bus   Minibuses run regularly from the gates of the Old Cemetery in La Paz to destinations along the lakeshore, including Batallas, Huatajata, and Tiquina. One-way prices to Huatajata are about $1. Private buses collect passengers from their hotel at

8 AM and charge roughly $10 round-trip to Copacabana (4 hours), $15 to Sorata (6 hours); in La Paz, contact **Combi Tours** (Calle Illampu 735, tel. 02/375378), **Diana Tours** (Calle Sagarnaga 328, tel. 02/340356), or **Turibus** (Calle Illampu, Residencia Rosario, tel. 02/325348).

By Taxi Taxis waiting outside La Paz's Hotel El Dorado will bring you to Puerto Perez or Huatajata and back for about $50 (up to four people). The fare to Copacabana is roughly $100.

By Boat There is no direct boat service between Peru and Bolivia, but you can travel by bus and catamaran or by bus and hydrofoil between La Paz and the Peruvian port of Puno, with brief stops in Copacabana. Purchase tickets for the four- to five-hour trek in La Paz from **Diana Tours** (Calle Saranaga 328, tel. 02/340356), or in Puno from **Transturin** (Jíron Libertad 176, tel. 054/35–2771).

Guided Tours

Travel agencies and the large hotels in La Paz arrange guided treks around the lake, sometimes in conjunction with a short boat tour and overnight stay, for $50–$80 per person. Contact: **Crillon Tours** (Av. Camacho 1223, tel. 02/350363), **Diana Tours** (Calle Sagarnaga 328, tel. 02/340356), **Plaza Tours** (Hotel Plaza, Av. 16 de Julio, tel. 02/378311), or **Turismo Balsa Ltd.** (Av. 16 de Julio 1650, tel. 02/357819).

Exploring Lake Titicaca

Just one hour from La Paz, after trekking through the barren landscape of the altiplano plain, you can see the smaller section of Lake Titicaca glistening in the distance. Take a left off the main road at **Batallas**—a forgettable outcrop of ramshackle houses—and, 15 minutes farther down a dusty dirt road, you'll come to the village of **Puerto Perez** (72 kilometers [42 miles] from La Paz). Nestled on the banks of Lake Titicaca, Puerto Perez, like most lakeshore villages, is barely developed: Houses are made of brick and adobe, and farm animals graze in fields nearby. There is no nightlife to speak of here, although you can linger over a potent British ale at the Britannia hotel (*see* Dining and Lodging, *below*). Another advantage to staying in Puerto Perez is location: it's one of the few villages with easy access to long, rambling walks through the small farming villages flanking Lago Huiñamarca. From Puerto Perez's lazy main square, there are also inspiring views of Titicaca's placid waters at dusk.

Back on the main road, continuing north, it's a 40-minute drive to lakeside **Huatajata,** a popular weekend escape for Paceños and a regular stop on the guided-tour circuit. Huatajata, endowed with a handful of hotels, makes a practical base for exploring the area, but it lacks lakefront walking paths; for picnics try the tree-lined waterfront at **Chúa,** the next village beyond Huatajata.

Hotels in Puerto Perez and Huatajata organize frequent trips to **Suriki,** a small, hilly island visible from the shore. When Norwegian explorer Thor Heyerdahl wanted to sail in 1970 from Morocco to South America in a reed-and-wood boat, to prove that South American cultures could have made contact with Europe long before the age of Columbus, he commissioned native craftsmen on Suriki to build his vessel, the *Ra II*. (In 1947, Heyerdahl sailed from Peru to Polynesia in the balsa wood *Kon-Tiki* to test his theory that the first Polynesians came from South America). Although the *Ra II* is on display in Oslo, Norway, several of the original builders maintain a souvenir shop and **museum** close to the main pier; Paulino Esteban, the curator, accepts small donations for entry to the museum, which is littered with newspaper clippings, photos, and diagrams of the *Ra II*. There are no hotels or restaurants on Suriki, so pack a picnic lunch and set out on one of the dirt roads that crisscross the island; at some point, they all seem to skirt the shore, offering good views of the lake. If you do not wish to join a guided tour of Suriki, fishermen in Huatajata will bring you over for a small, negotiable fee.

From Huatajata, the road continues to **Tiquina,** where you can see the handful of tiny patrol boats that make up Bolivia's navy (Bolivia was left landlocked after Chile seized 160 miles of coast in 1879). In Tiquina, vehicles are loaded precariously onto rafts and taken across the Strait of Tiquina to San Pedro. From unmemorable San Pedro it's a 90-minute drive to **Copacabana,** a pleasant, almost laid-back town fronting Lago Chucuito from the shelter of a protected bay. Copacabana is the main stopping point for those headed to Peru, and it provides easy access to the lake and surrounding countryside, as well as to the islands of the Sun and Moon. During Holy Week, throngs of young Paceños walk to Copacabana from the capital to pay homage to the miracle-working Black Virgin of Copacabana; the candlelight procession on Good Friday is especially spectacular. In town, the highlights of the **Catedral,** built between 1610 and 1619, are the majestic gilded altar and the striking sculpture of the Black Virgin carved by Tito Yupanaqui in 1592.

Isla del Sol (Island of the Sun), the nearest Bolivia gets to the Mediterranean, lies a few miles off the coast from Copacabana in the serene upper lake, Lago Chucuito. The island sees relatively few tourists and is the perfect place to savor the splendor of Lake Titicaca, particularly if you have time to get away from the main landing point and cross the island on foot—a four- to five-hour proposition. There are a number of beautiful walks along the island's shore: dirt paths crisscross the terraced terrain, leading to secluded coves and dilapidated Inca ruins. According to ancient myths, Isla del Sol is the cradle of Incan civilization, and the birthplace of the mighty sun itself. Few ruins survive today, though you will find groups of carved rocks on the island's southeast and northwest corners. Like Suriki, there are no hotels or restaurants on Isla del Sol, but you can arrange to stay overnight with locals for less than $5.

Isla de la Luna (Island of the Moon), smaller and more difficult to reach than the Isla del Sol, contains the ruins of an Inca temple and observatory. Boatmen anchored at Copacabana's beach will bring you to either island for $20–$80 depending on how long you want to remain ashore and whether you travel by sail or motor.

Sorata, roughly 45 kilometers (28 miles) north from Huatajata via the villages of Huarina and Warisata, lies in a lush mid-altitude valley—nearly 8,200 feet above sea level—at the foot of **Mt. Illampu** (21,277 feet). A lively Sunday market is held in Sorata's tree-lined square, though most visitors are drawn by various hiking opportunities: either up snowcapped Mt. Illampu, recommended only for experienced hikers, or along the **Camino del Oro** (Trail of Gold), an arduous weeklong trek through lush tropical valleys to where gold-mining coopera- tives still ply their dangerous trade. For information about these and other hikes, contact **Plaza Tours** or **Diana Tours** (*see* Guided Tours, *above*).

Dining and Lodging

With the exception of the Hotel Playa Azul, Copacabana offers a meager choice of hotels and restaurants; you're much better off in Puerto Perez or Huatajata. Throughout the region, re- servations are recommended for the Easter festivals and on weekends, when many Paceños migrate to the area. For price ranges, *see* Dining and Lodging in Staying in Bolivia, *above*.

Copacabana
Dining

Restaurant Puerta del Sol. The specialties at this locally popu- lar and sometimes boisterous eatery, located next to the Hotel Playa Azul, are fresh trout and *perreiey,* a Lake Titicaca white- fish. *Av. 6 de Agosto, no phone. No credit cards. Inexpensive.*

Dining and Lodging
★

Hotel Playa Azul. Recent renovations have given the Playa Azul a cozy dining room romantically lit with gas fires. The comfortable, simple bedrooms, most of which overlook a quiet courtyard, come equipped with private bathrooms. *Av. 6 de Agosto, tel. 08622/227 or 02/320068. 35 rooms with bath. Facili- ties: restaurant. MC, V. Expensive.*

Hotel Ambassador. The best that can be said of this clean but basic hotel is that some rooms have private toilets. The adja- cent restaurant serves typical Bolivian dishes—mostly chicken and steak accompanied by rice and beans—and fresh trout when it's available. *Plaza Sucre, tel. 02/343110 for reservations. 45 rooms, some with bath. Facilities: restaurant. No credit cards. Inexpensive.*

Huatajata
Dining and Lodging

Hotel Lake Titicaca. Coming from La Paz, you'll see this well- equipped but slightly dated complex on the lakeshore a few kilometers before Huatajata. The sweeping views of the lake almost justify the inflated prices. *Tel. 02/374877. 24 rooms with bath. Facilities: restaurant, bar, racquetball, sauna, games room, canoes and paddleboats for hire. AE, MC, V. Expensive.*

Hotel Inca Utama. This well-maintained hotel has tremendous, romance-inspiring views over the lake, perhaps best appreci- ated after a drink in the lounge or dinner in the simple, tradi- tional Bolivian restaurant. The small rooms are comfortable enough but lack real character. The hotel also arranges excur- sions to the islands. *For reservations call Crillon Tours at tel. 02/350363. 44 rooms. Facilities: restaurant, bar. AE, V. Very Ex- pensive.*

Puerto Perez
Dining and Loding
★

Hotel las Balsas. Perched on the lakeshore, Las Balsas occu- pies a corner of the main square and is within reach of walking trails to nearby farming villages. The owner, Swiss-born Jean- Jacques Valloton, maintains a respectable on-site restaurant and can arrange visits to Suriki Island. *Main square, tel. 02/357817 for reservations. 16 rooms, 2 suites. Facilities: restau- rant, bar. MC. Expensive.*

The Britannia. Englishman Tom Clough and his wife, Theresa, offer a little something for everyone: basic but comfortable bed-and-breakfast accommodation, fine bar meals, and won- derfully strong English beers. *Main square, tel. 02/813229, fax*

02/811–9121. 9 rooms, none with bath. Facilities: bar. No credit cards. Inexpensive.

Sorata
Dining and Lodging
Hotel Prefectural. Accommodations here are simple at best, and what lures most visitors are the traditional Bolivian restaurant, the outdoor garden, and the lovely views across the valley. Coming from La Paz, the hotel is on the main highway less than a kilometer from Sorata's central square. *For reservations, contact SERVITUR in La Paz (Edificio Naira, Calle Potosí, tel. 02/350559). Facilities: restaurant. No credit cards. Moderate.*

Central Bolivia

Central Bolivia stretches from Cochabamba, nestled in the eastern foothills of the Andes, to the lowland city of Santa Cruz, perched on the edge of the Amazon basin. Climates range from mild and sunny in Cochabamba to hot and humid in Santa Cruz, with heavy rainfall throughout the region between October and March.

Both Cochabamba and Santa Cruz have a good selection of tourist facilities, including hotels ranging from colonial style to ultramodern. Yet the real attraction is not so much the cities themselves—both are large urban centers, after all—but rather the surrounding landscape. Santa Cruz, easy to reach by plane, gives a strong sense of Bolivia's tropical lowlands; Cochabamba, the so-called "City of Eternal Spring," balances rugged mountain scenery with fertile valley vegetation.

The highlight, however, may be a quick trek through the Chaparé, where most of the coca used for illegal cocaine production is grown. Traveling by car or bus through the Chaparé region—in other words, traveling between Cochabamba and Santa Cruz—is an unforgettable experience: The road snakes its way through bare, arid highlands before dropping into a vast expanse of cloud and tropical rain forests shrouded in mist. There are few tourist centers in the area, but those who make it to the village of Villa Tunari may find themselves wishing to linger a while.

Tourist Information

Cochabamba: Oficina de Turismo (Plaza 14 de Septiembre, tel. 042/23364); Fremen Travel (Calle Tumusla 0245, tel. 042/47126). **Santa Cruz:** Oficina de Turismo (Immigration Ministry Building, Av. Irala, tel. 03/348644); Tajibos Tours (Tajibos Hotel, Av. San Martín 455, tel. 03/429046); Umpex Travel (Calle René Moreno 226, tel. 03/336001).

Getting There

By Plane
LAB and AeroSur fly daily from La Paz and Sucre to Cochabamba's **Aeropuerto Jorge Wilsterman** (tel. 042/21635) and Santa Cruz's **Aeropuerto Viru-Viru** (tel. 03/44411), a 16-kilometer taxi ride ($6) from downtown. Cochabamba's airport is a 10-kilometer taxi trek ($4) from downtown.

By Bus
Depending on breakdowns and the state of the road, it takes about seven hours to travel by bus between La Paz and Cochabamba; roughly 20 hours between La Paz and Santa

Cruz. One-way tickets for either trek cost less than $10. **Flota Copacabana** (tel. 02/362803) buses leave La Paz terminal at 9 and 9:30 AM for both cities. **Trans Copacabana** (tel. 02/322888) buses depart La Paz at 8:30 AM, 1:30 PM, and 10 PM. To avoid standing in the aisle for 20 hours, book tickets at least one day in advance.

By Car It takes nearly six hours to drive between La Paz and Cochabamba, even though the road is paved for three-quarters of the way. From La Paz drive in the direction of Oruro until you reach the village of Caracollo, some 190 kilometers (118 miles) south from La Paz and one of the few villages en route with a gas pump. Beyond Caracollo is a signposted, left-hand turn for Cochabamba. The drive between Cochabamba and Santa Cruz takes 10 hours on the *Nuevo Camino* (New Road) and is recommended only for four-wheel-drive vehicles. You can break the trip into almost equal parts by staying overnight in Villa Tunari.

You can rent a car for less than $40 per day in Cochabamba from **Barrons Rent-a-Car** (Calle Sucre E. 0727, tel. 042/22774 or 042/23819).

By Train There is no train service between La Paz and Cochabamba. Officials claim the Cochabamba–Santa Cruz line will open in the near future, but don't hold your breath.

Exploring Central Bolivia

Cochabamba Cochabamba, set in a lush grassy valley at an altitude of 2,571 meters (8,430 feet), is the third-largest city in Bolivia, with a population of more than 320,000. Although it is more compact than sprawling Santa Cruz, Cochabamba's sights are scattered between the apartment-lined Río Rocha (Rocha River) and, a dull 25-minute walk to the southwest, **Plaza 14 de Septiembre,** the city's tree-lined and colorful heart. Flanking the square, the **Catedral** (admission free), started in 1701 and completed in 1735, stands sentinel over the old men and streetsellers who sometimes congregate in the plaza at dusk. One block southeast from the square stands the **Temple of San Francisco,** a colonial masterpiece built in 1581 but thoroughly recast in 1782 and again in 1926. Still, it boasts elaborately carved wooden galleries and a striking gold-leaf altar. *Calle 25 de Mayo. Admission free.*

Cochabamba's excellent **Museo Arqueológico** (Museum of Archaeology) is one of the more comprehensive and interesting museums outside of La Paz; on display are pre-Columbian pottery, silver and gold work, and strikingly patterned, handwoven Indian textiles. Hour-long, English-language tours can be arranged for a small fee. *Calle 25 de Mayo 145, no phone. Admission charged. Closed Sun.*

Plaza Colón, at the eastern foot of Calle 25 de Mayo, marks the start of **El Prado** (sometimes called Avenida Ballivían), a shop- and bar-lined avenue that stretches north to the Río Rocha. Cross the river and hail a taxi for the five-minute trip to **Centro Portales.** This elegant mansion was completed in 1927 after 10 years of building by Simón Patino, a local-born tin baron who amassed one of the world's largest private fortunes. The mansion now houses a cultural center, which sponsors the occasional art exhibition, but the extensive grounds and gardens are the real reason to visit. *Av. Potosí 1450, no phone. Admission free. Closed weekends.*

To get a good view of Cochabamba, take a taxi from the city center to **Cerro Coronilla** (Coronilla Hill, also called San Sebastían Hill), on the city's outskirts, with sweeping views of surrounding hillside farms. At the top there's a monument honoring the women and children who died during Bolivia's protracted War of Independence, which ended in 1825.

Tarata and the Chaparé   **Tarata,** a tiny, well-preserved colonial village 25 kilometers (15 miles) southeast of Cochabamba, hosts a busy open-air market on Thursdays. Tarata is known throughout Bolivia for its *chorizo* (sausage), which you can buy in bulk—along with other handicrafts—on the village's flower-filled main square. For fine views of Tarata, consider the 15-minute uphill walk to **Iglesia San Pedro** (San Pedro Church) and the **Convento de San Francisco** (San Francisco Monastery). In Cochabamba, buses for Tarata depart from Avenida Barrientos, at the corner of Avenida 6 de Agosto. Alternatively, Fremen Travel (*see* Tourist Information, *above*) offers weekly tours of Tarata and the nearby village of Hayculi, famous for its pottery and ceramics.

Traveling between Cochabamba and Santa Cruz on the Nuevo Camino (New Road), you're in a section of Bolivia known as **Chaparé,** a sparsely populated region of low-lying mountains and thickening jungle. The few communities that survive here tend to earn a living through the harvesting of coca, the raw ingredient used in the production of cocaine. Locals assume that all light-skinned people are connected with the U.S. Drug Enforcement Agency. But once it's recognized that you are only passing through, people tend to be friendly. The village of **Villa Tunari** (*see* Dining and Lodging, *below*) is well equipped to deal with overnight visitors.

Santa Cruz   Santa Cruz is a lively lowland city whose sprawling industrial districts are connected by a series of *anillos,* or ring roads. Twenty years ago, oxen pulled carts through the mud streets of Santa Cruz; today, well-dressed businesspeople dodge taxis and street sellers as they maneuver between modern downtown office buildings—a sure sign that Santa Cruz and its more than 600,000 inhabitants have been dramatically transformed in recent years. Apart from its main plaza, Santa Cruz has little to offer in terms of sites, museums, or architecture. After a brief downtown tour, consider hiring a taxi to explore the handful of nearby farming villages, many of which host small produce and livestock markets on a regular basis. The going rate is about $4 per hour. Also note: Carry your passport at all times in Santa Cruz. The police have a bad reputation and may harass or even fine you for not carrying your documentation.

Santa Cruz has grown up around **Plaza 24 de Septiembre,** its busy main square, lined with modern shops—of the souvenir, clothing, and travel variety—and a few sober architectural relics from the colonial era. The colonnaded streets feeding the plaza are lined with food stands and slightly rundown electronic and curios shops that are still fun to browse. More attention-grabbing is the **Basílica Menor de San Lorenzo,** built between 1845 and 1915 on the ruins of a 17th-century cathedral. Inside the imposing but architecturally uninspired church, the **Museo Catedralicio** (Cathedral Museum) exhibits colonial-era religious objects, paintings, and sculptures. *Plaza*

24 de Septiembre. Admission free. Closed Mon., Wed., and Fri.–Sat.

The adjacent **Casa de la Cultura** hosts art exhibitions, recitals, and concerts, in addition to a permanent exhibit of local Indian crafts. *Plaza 24 de Septiembre. Admission free.*

At the **Zoologico Municipal** (City Zoo), considered one of the finest in South America, you'll see llamas and alpacas, flamingos, owls, snakes, bears, and a good collection of native species that includes jaguar, tapirs, and toucans. The animals are well cared for and displayed in settings that approach natural. Taxis will take you from the main square to the zoo for less than $5. *3ero Anillo Interno at Av. Banzer. Admission charged.*

A popular day trip from Santa Cruz is **Lomas de Arena,** a large freshwater lake surrounded by mammoth sand dunes. The white sand dunes provide the perfect desert backdrop for swimming and sunbathing, while the juxtaposition of barren desert and lowland Andean scenery, besides giving off a vaguely surreal quality, entice visitors to take long walks and hikes. Umpex Travel (*see* Tourist Information, *above*) arranges excursions from Santa Cruz to Lomas de Arena that include visits to the colonial village of El Palmar. Umpex also organizes treks to various far-flung Jesuit Missions.

Shopping

Cochabamba is well-known for its high-quality alpaca sweaters and knitwear, but don't expect prices to be much lower than in La Paz. Some of the better-quality (and more expensive) knitwear shops include **Asarti** (Calle Roche 375), **Casa Fisher** (Calle Ramorán Rivero 0204), **Fotrama** (Av. Heroínas) and **Amerindia** (Av. San Martín 6064). The local market, **La Cancha,** held Wednesdays and Saturdays on Avenida Aroma, is a good place to browse for less expensive crafts.

In **Santa Cruz,** crafts stands and shops are scattered around the main square. The goods they sell are more typical of La Paz than of the lowlands, and don't expect any real bargains. That said, **Artecampo** (Calle Monseñor Salvatierra 407) is an outstanding cooperative craftshop with a good selection of handmade hammocks, mobiles, ceramics, and intricate hand-painted woodworkings. **Areka Bambú** (Calle Murillo 334) offers fine ceramics and macramé in addition to hand-woven baskets. The main city market, **Mercado los Pozos,** held at Calle Quijarro at the corner of Avenida 6 de Agosto, features mounds of fresh local produce.

Sports and the Outdoors

Fishing In Santa Cruz, the **Club de Caza y Pesca** (Av. Argentina 317, tel. 03/35707) arranges day-long and overnight fishing trips to nearby lakes.

Horse Racing There are periodic horse races at Cochabamba's **Hipódromo** (Av. B. Galindo).

Dining and Lodging

Hotels in Cochabamba and Santa Cruz are among the best in Bolivia, and prices even in the upper categories tend to be substantially cheaper than at similar establishments in La Paz. Hotel restaurants are your best dining bet in the region, though many towns and villages have a decent selection of small, very informal eateries. For price-category definitions, *see* Dining and Lodging in Staying in Bolivia, *above.*

Cochabamba
Dining

Casa de Campo. Informal and lively, the Casa de Campo features traditional Bolivian specialties—mostly grilled meats and a perfectly fiery *picante mixto* (grilled chicken and beef tongue)—served on a shaded outdoor patio. *Av. Aniceto Padilla, tel. 042/43937. No credit cards. Moderate.*

Restaurant Gopal. Indian restaurants are a rarity in Bolivia, so don't miss the chance to indulge your palate at this even rarer breed—a *vegetarian* Indian restaurant. A good bet is the lunchtime buffet, or try one of the curried meat and vegetable entrées. *Calle España 250, no phone. No credit cards. Inexpensive.*

Dining and
Lodging
★

Hotel Portales. Cochabamba's most luxurious address features numerous recreation facilities and extremely well equipped, air-conditioned rooms, not to mention lush gardens. Plan on a short taxi ride to reach the center of town. *Av. Panda 1271, tel. 042/48507, fax 042/42071. 98 rooms, 8 suites, all with bath. Facilities: 2 restaurants, piano bar, gym, 2 pools, TV and telephone in rooms, hairdresser, shopping gallery. AE, MC, V. Very Expensive.*

Gran Hotel Cochabamba. Much at the Gran Hotel highlights its lush courtyard, where you are likely to hear soothing birdsong in the evening; in fact, most of the hotel's simple but comfortable rooms overlook the plant-filled courtyard. The adjoining Restaurant Carillon serves an excellent *pique macho* as well as *surubí*, a delicious Amazon River fish with white flesh and few bones. *Plaza Ubaldo Anze, tel. 042/43300 or 042/82551, fax 042/82558. 43 rooms, 5 suites, all with bath. Facilities: restaurant, bar, TV and telephone in rooms, tennis court, pool. AE, V. Expensive.*

Hotel Aranjuez. A short walk from the city center brings you to this intimate, elegant hotel, noted for its lovely terraces and gardens. Aranjuez's well-equipped rooms are spacious and comfortable. A live jazz band plays in the lobby bar most weekends. *Av. Buenos Aires E. 0563, tel 042/41935 or 042/80076, fax 042/40158. 30 rooms, 3 suites, most with bath. Facilities: restaurant, bar, TV, phones, minibar in rooms, pool. AE, MC, V. Moderate.*

Hotel Uni. Budget-minded travelers will appreciate the Uni's central location, one block from the main square, and its simple, clean rooms. *Calle Baptista S. 9111, tel. 042/22444. 50 rooms, all with bath. Facilities: restaurant, bar, TV and telephone in rooms. AE, MC, V. Inexpensive.*

Santa Cruz
Dining and
Lodging

La Quinta. This ideal family hotel is only 10 minutes by taxi from the city center. All but two rooms have kitchens, a dining area, a living room, and up to four bedrooms. The rooms are air-conditioned, and most have balconies. *Barrio Urbari, Calle Arumá, tel. 03/522244, fax 03/522667. 31 rooms, 2 suites, most with bath. Facilities: restaurant, bar, 3 small pools. AE, MC, V. Expensive.*

★

Gran Hotel Santa Cruz. The rooms—and even the suites—are on the small side, but the family-owned Santa Cruz offers excellent value for your money. The recently refurbished rooms feature air-conditioning and cable television, while rooms overlooking the pool have small private balconies. *Calle Pari 59, tel. 03/348811, fax 03/324194. 22 rooms, 12 suites, most with bath. Facilities: restaurant, 2 bars, cafeteria, TV in rooms, pool. AE, MC, V. Moderate.*

Hotel Colonial. It's hard to believe that the ancient-looking air conditioners and televisions at this budget hotel actually work, but they do. Even more surprising are the private shower and toilet facilities. The adjoining restaurant is open for breakfast and snacks only. *Calle Buenos Aires 57, tel. 03/327316. 21 rooms, all with bath. Facilities: restaurant, TV and telephone in rooms. AE, MC, V. Inexpensive.*

Villa Tunari
Dining and Lodging

El Puente. The secluded El Puente is situated in thick forest a few kilometers outside Villa Tunari, at the end of a rough, pebble-strewn path accessed from the Nuevo Camino. Trails cut into the undergrowth lead to a nearby river with clear, swimmable pools. The scattered cabins do not have hot water, but considering the outside temperature, this is not a serious drawback. Reservations are recommended and should be made through Fremen Travel in La Paz (Plaza Abaroa, Calle Pedro Salazar, tel. 02/327073). The on-site restaurant serves hearty, simple food. *Off Nuevo Camino, no local phone. 12 cabins. Facilities: restaurant. AE, MC, V. Inexpensive.*

Hotel las Palmas. Despite the roadside setting, the centrally located Las Palmas offers a range of modern comforts, including private showers and toilets. The hotel restaurant features a limited menu of grilled chicken and *pique macho. Nuevo Camino, tel. 0411/4103. 10 rooms, 4 cabins. Facilities: restaurant, pool, garden. No credit cards. Inexpensive.*

Sucre and Potosí

Sucre, founded in 1540 by the Spaniard Pedro de Anzurez, manages to sustain a population of over 100,000 without feeling too urban. In fact, La Ciudad Blanca (The White City)—so called because the town's houses are whitewashed every year by government edict—is a pleasant throwback to the colonial era with its many churches and grand mansions. At an altitude of only 2,751 meters (9,022 feet), Sucre is further blessed with a mild climate and offers some relief from the thin atmosphere of La Paz and Potosí. Sucre is also Bolivia's official capital and the seat of the Supreme Court: in 1776, Spain crowned Sucre capital of its eastern Andes territories, and in 1825 it was named capital of the newly created Republic of Bolivia. All government offices have since relocated to La Paz, Bolivia's *de facto* capital, but Sucre's tone remains upbeat due to its University of San Xavier, founded in 1624. On balmy evenings, students pack Sucre's trendy downtown cafés and bars.

Modern Potosí is one of Bolivia's poorest cities: The lack of road links and a depressed mining industry have taken their toll on the city and its 110,000 inhabitants. Still, Potosí retains a great deal of historic flavor, with its narrow cobblestone streets and elaborate though largely neglected colonial architecture. Towering above Potosí, *Cerro Rico* is the "rich hill" that has provided most of Bolivia's mineral wealth and is now depicted on the national flag. In the 17th century, Cerro Rico also fueled Spain's conquest of the South American continent. Despite some very sobering facts—among them, that the average life span of a miner is just 45 years—a visit to Potosí would not be complete without a trip down a working cooperative mine.

Tourist Information

Potosí: Oficina de Turismo (Cámara de Minería, 2nd floor, Calle Quijarro, tel. 062/25288); Transamazonas (Calle Quijarro 12, tel. 062/27175); Koala Tours (Calle Oruro 136, tel. 062/24708). **Sucre:** Oficina de Turismo (Calle Potosí 102 tel. 064/25983); Fremen Travel (Plaza 25 de Mayo 4, tel. 064/30351); SurAndes (Calle Nicolás Ortiz 6, tel. 064/21983).

Getting There

By Plane   **Lloyd Aereo Boliviano** (LAB) and **AeroSur** fly several times a week between La Paz and Sucre; the 45-minute flight costs about $50 each way. Both airlines also fly from La Paz to Potosí, though only AeroSur makes the 15-minute flight between Sucre and Potosí. The airport in Sucre is 20 minutes by taxi ($4) from downtown; the airport in Potosí, 15 minutes by taxi ($4).

By Bus   Buses leave La Paz daily at 6:30 PM and 8 PM for Sucre (via Potosí); the 19-hour trek costs less than $15. To reserve space on the five-hour ride between Sucre and Potosí, contact **Transmin** (tel. 064/21753) or **Andesbus** (tel. 064/30751). The former leaves Sucre at 7 AM from Calle Loa 639, the latter at 7 AM from Calle Bolívar 621. Buses for Santa Cruz and Cochabamba also depart from Sucre's **Terminal de Buses** (Calle Ostria Gutiérrez, tel. 064/22029) and Potosí's **Terminal de Buses** (Av. Universitaria, tel. 062/25422).

By Train   Trains leave La Paz every Tuesday and Saturday at 6 PM for Sucre's centrally located **Estación Ferrocariles** (Plaza 25 de Mayo, tel. 064/23449) and Potosí's **Estación Ferrocariles** (Av. Sevilla, tel. 062/31000). Each journey takes 12–14 hours and costs less than $20 each way.

By Car   From La Paz, take the main highway south to Oruro and look for signs for both Sucre (18 hours) and Potosí (12 hours) near the village of Machacamarca. The road is paved from the capital to Oruro; after that, expect dirt and many potholes.

Exploring Sucre and Potosí

Sucre   In Sucre's city center, throngs of ice-cream vendors and shoeshine boys fill the tree-lined **Plaza 25 de Mayo,** the city's social fulcrum. Waiting taxis can take you on brief city tours for less than $5 per hour, but there's little in Sucre that's not within walking distance of the main plaza. The baroque **Catedral Metropolitana,** one of three impressive monuments flanking the square, is famous for its priceless statue of the Virgin of Guadalupe, garbed in diamonds, gold, emeralds, and pearls donated during the 17th century by residents with secure mining fortunes. Next door, the **Museo de la Iglesia** (Cathedral Museum; Admission free; closed Mon.) displays colonial paintings, volumes of parchment, and religious statuary. Also on the plaza, **Casa de la Libertad** (admission free; closed weekends) is where Bolivia's Declaration of Independence was signed in 1825. Fittingly, the small museum now displays historical documents and artifacts related to Bolivia's turbulent struggle for independence.

Two blocks from the square, the mammoth 17th-century **El Templo de San Felipe Neri** (Church and Monastery of San Felipe Neri) testifies to the wealth once enjoyed by the Roman Catholic Church in Bolivia. From the church's domed roof and towers you can enjoy the grand panorama of Sucre's spire-entangled skyline. The nearby Universidad de Tourismo (Calle Nicolás Ortiz 182) arranges guided tours of the church and monastery. *Calle Nicolás Ortiz 182. Admission charged.*

From the main plaza, Calle Calvo leads past the Church of Santo Domingo to the **Museo y Convento de Santa Clara** (Museum and Convent of Santa Clara), founded in 1639, which houses a magnificently hand-painted organ dating from the 17th century along with devotional paintings and colonial statuary. Also on display are works by colonial painter Melchor Pérez Holguín and his Italian mentor, Bernardo Bitti. *Calle Calvo 212. Admission charged. Closed Sat.–Mon.*

Don't leave Sucre without visiting the impressive **Caserón de la Capellenía**, with its exhibit of modern Indian weavings. The adjacent ASUR gift shop sells a range of locally produced weavings; future plans include traditional music available on cassettes and compact disc. *Calle San Alberto 413 (near Calle Potosí). Admission free. Closed Sun.*

Beyond the textile museum, Calle San Alberto curves and joins Calle Polanco, at the end of which is **Plaza Pedro Anzures,** a beautiful residential square set atop the less-than-towering Churuquella Mountain. Still, there are good views of Sucre's tiled roofs and whitewashed homes as well as of the ragged mountains and farmland that fade into the horizon. On one corner of the sqaure, the **Museo y Convento de la Recoleta** (Museum and Convent of the Retreat), founded in 1601 by Franciscan monks, displays colonial religious works in a setting of serene courtyards and gardens. Equally noteworthy is the restored chapel and its intricately carved choir seats. *Plaza Pedro Anzures. Admission charged. Closed weekends.*

The most popular exhibit at the **Museo Antropológico Charcas** (also called the Museo de la Universidad) are mummified bodies discovered in the 1960s (museum curators believe the centuries-old mummies were entombed as human sacrifices). More tame are the galleries of colonial painting and textiles. *Calle Bolívar 698, tel. 064/23455. Admission charged. Closed Sun.*

The faded wonder **La Glorieta** (The Summerhouse) lies 6 kilometers (4 miles) southwest of Sucre on the road to Potosí. Built at the end of the 19th century by wealthy industrialist Don Francisco Argandoña, La Glorieta featured Venetian-style canals and expansive gardens crowned by an exotic residential palace built in a combination of Moorish, Spanish, and French styles. Today, the house and gardens, though still impressive, are in ruins, and you may have to show your passport to one of the army cadets from the adjacent military base. The taxi ride from town costs less than $2 per person. *Admission free. Closed weekends.*

Tarabuco, 80 kilometers (50 miles) east from Sucre along a rough and dusty road, is best seen on Sunday during its colorful crafts and produce market. Mingle with local Indians in traditional dress, and browse the stalls for handcrafted weavings and ponchos, musical instruments, and *chuspas* (bags for carrying coca leaves and money). In early March, Tarabuco hosts one of South America's liveliest traditional festivals, the **Pujllay,** celebrating the March 12, 1816, victory by local Indians over the Spanish. Buses leave year-round for Tarabuco from Calle Calvo in Sucre. Round-trip tickets cost less than $3.

Potosí   At the heart of Potosí lies the **Plaza 10 de Noviembre,** bordered by an imposing baroque **Catedral** open only on Sunday morning. More intriguing is the nearby **Casa de Monedas,** a massive block-long mint once used to forge coins with silver mined from the depths of Cerro Rico (Rich Hill), around which Potosí is built. Opened in 1572 and then rebuilt in 1753, the stone-and-brick mint contains a wide range of colonial treasures—from the 8-foot-high wheels used to produce silver ingots to galleries lined with Spanish and South American coins. Also on display are colonial statuary, furniture, and paintings, including works by Bolivia's celebrated 20th-century painter Cecilio Guzmán de Rojas. Admission is by guided tour only (at 9 and 1:30), and wandering is definitely not allowed. English-speaking guides are available for a small fee. *Plaza 10 de Noviembre, tel. 062/22777. Admission charged. Closed Sun.*

Many of Potosí's churches have erratic opening times. It is important to check with the tourist office for current schedules, or to arrange special visits to the **Iglesia San Agustín** (Calle Bolívar), the **Iglesia San Martín** (Calle Hoyos), and the **Iglesia Jerusalén** (Plaza del Estudiante). Potosí's most spectacular church is the **Iglesia San Lorenzo** (Calle Bustillos), which offers some of the finest examples of baroque carvings in South America: an elaborate combination of mythical figures and indigenous designs carved in high relief on the stone facade.

The **Convento y Museo Santa Teresa** (Convent and Museum of Saint Theresa), three blocks below the main plaza, displays a strange mix of religious artifacts. In one room there are sharp iron instruments once used to inflict pain on penitent nuns, as well as a blouse embroidered with wire mesh and prongs meant to prick the flesh. Other rooms contain works by renowned colonial painters such as Melchor Pérez Holguín. *Calle Chicas, tel. 062/23847. Admission charged. Closed weekends.*

Five thousand tunnels wend their way through the distorted mound of **Cerro Rico,** the "Rich Hill" of silver that helped to fill Spain's imperial coffers until the reserves were exhausted during the early 19th century. Today tin is the primary extract, though on the barren mountainside, independent miners still sift for silver in the remnants of ancient excavations. If you are accustomed to the altitude and not affected by confined spaces, consider a tour through one of the active cooperative mines. Along with hundreds of local miners, you will descend into the dark and humid tunnels where it's common to work almost naked because of the intense heat. Conditions are shocking in these noisy, muddy shafts, and tours are not recommended for anyone with a weak stomach. Be sure to wear the dirtiest clothes you have. Koala Tours and Transamazonas (*see* Tourist Information, *above*) organize excursions into Cerro Rico, as do the independent, English-speaking guides Raul Braulio (tel. 062/25304) and Marco Alarcón (tel. 062/26432 or 062/27677).

Potosí is surrounded by natural lagoons that are fed by hot thermal springs. Koala Tours and Transamazonas (*see* Tourist Information, *above*) arrange trips to two such lagoons, **La Laguna del Inca** and **Kari Kari,** and they can advise you regarding which of the seething pools are safe for bathing (some have strong currents and literally boiling-hot water).

Shopping

In **Sucre,** the ASUR gift shop at the **Caserón de Capellanía** (Calle San Alberto) has a good selection of local weavings, and the cooperative ensures that the majority of profits go directly to the weavers rather than middlemen. For a spot of local color, the market at Calle Ravelo and Calles Junín features produce and household items.

Despite **Potosí**'s rich mineral wealth, do not expect bargains on handcrafted silver jewelry. However, brass and low-grade silver jewelry and silver coins can be found at an outdoor market between Calle Oruro and Calle Bustillos. Another market on Calle Bolívar features fresh tropical fruits and produce, while one on the corner of Calle Sucre and Calle Modesto Omiste, four blocks from San Lorenzo Church, has locally produced crafts.

Dining and Lodging

Sucre has a good range of restaurants and cafés, though many are closed at lunchtime. The local cuisine is distinctly spicy: If you do not appreciate a little fire with your meal, avoid dishes prefaced with the word *ají* or *picante.* By no stretch of the imagination can Potosí be called a gourmet's delight: The choice of restaurants in this industrial mining town is severely limited.

Hotels in high-altitude Potosí are rarely heated, encouraging the use of thermals or pajamas on cold nights. Hotels in Sucre maintain reasonably high standards, though you may experience the occasional shortage of electricity and water. For price-category definitions, *see* Dining and Lodging in Staying in Bolivia, *above.*

Potosí **El Mesón.** With its international menu and central location op-
Dining posite the cathedral, El Mesón bills itself as Potosí's most exclusive restaurant. But beyond the linen napkins and tablecloths, you'll find walls in need of paint and a rather characterless, very quiet dining room. The menu includes traditional Potosí and international dishes, so if the lure of offal is wearing thin, consider the lasagne. *Plaza 10 de Noviembre, no phone. No credit cards. Moderate.*

Sky Room. You'll have a fine view of central Potosí from this third floor, rooftop restaurant. The menu features traditional Potosí dishes such as *pichanga,* a mixture of intestines and offal served with salad. Less adventurous diners may want to try a grilled chicken entrée. *Edificio Matilde, 3rd floor, Calle Bolívar 701, tel. 062/26345. No credit cards. Moderate.*

★ **Cherry's.** At this delightful coffee shop you can sip mugs of coffee, or mate de coca while pondering the delicious selection of cakes and strudels. *Calle Padilla 8, no phone. No credit cards. Inexpensive.*

Dining and **Hotel Claudia.** More practical than refined, the newly built
Lodging Claudia matches well-equipped rooms with other features
rarely found in Potosí: an on-site restaurant, bar, and terrace.
Breakfast is included in the room price. *Av. El Maestro 322,
tel. 062/22242, fax 062/24005. 22 rooms with bath. Facilities:
restaurant, bar, terrace, TV and phone in rooms. No credit
cards. Moderate.*

Lodging **Hostal Colonial.** This whitewahsed, vaguely colonial-looking
low rise is just two blocks from the main square. Many of the
well-equipped but undistinguished rooms overlook the hotel's
two airy courtyards. Breakfast—there is no lunch or dinner
service—is brought to your bedside or served in the dining
room. *Calle Hoyos 8, tel. 062/24265, fax 062/27146. 20 rooms with
bath. Facilities: TV and phone in rooms. MC, V. Moderate.*

Hostal Carlos V. Budget-minded travelers will appreciate this
basic but clean hotel near the main square. The bare, undeco-
rated rooms share communal showers and toilets. Breakfast is
served on the enclosed, viewless balcony. *Calle Linares 42, tel.
062/25121. 12 rooms, none with bath. No credit cards. Inexpensive.*

Sucre **El Huerto.** Vegetarians can indulge in all sorts of pastas and
Dining meat-free lasagnes at El Huerto, located near the municipal
★ park, while adventurous carnivores should try a traditional Bolivian entrée such as *picante de lengua* (spicy beef tongue). The
open-air patio is a fine place to linger over a long meal. *Ladislao
Cabrera 86, tel. 064/21538. No credit cards. Expensive.*

Arco Iris. Cheese and meat fondues draw crowds to the Swiss-
owned Arco Iris. Chocolate lovers may have difficulty waiting
until dessert to tackle the decadent chocolate mousse. *Calle
Nicolás Ortiz 42, tel. 064/22902. No credit cards. Moderate.*

Alliance Française la Taberna. The traditional French menu at
La Taberna includes hard-to-find delicacies such as coq au vin,
ratatouille, and dessert crepes. Seating is available indoors or
on the outside courtyard, where you must be prepared to deal
with wandering street vendors pushing their crafts. *Calle Aniceto Arce 35, no phone. No credit cards. Inexpensive.*

★ **Bibliocafé.** The dinner menu—mostly pastas and grilled
meats—may be small, but most people come instead for post-
dinner coffee and dessert. A divinely sweet option are crepes
stuffed with banana and smothered in chocolate sauce. *Calle
Nicolás Ortiz 30, no phone. Open dinner only. No credit cards.
Inexpensive.*

Dining and **Hotel Real Audiencia.** The newly renovated Real Audiencia
Lodging combines period looks—it's set in a converted colonial mansion—with modern fixtures and styling. The spacious rooms
feature an above-average range of amenities. From the hotel
restaurant there are good views over the city. *Calle Potosí 142,
tel. 064/30823, fax 064/32809. 22 rooms with bath. Facilities: restaurant, bar, TV and phone in rooms. V. Expensive.*

Hotel Municipal. You can expect typically comfortable and
clean—if not also characterless—rooms at this modern midrise
near the municipal pool. The main plaza with its bars and restaurants is only 10 minutes by foot, or enjoy traditional Bolivian meals in the lobby restaurant. *Av. Venezuela 1052, tel.
064/21216 or 064/25508, fax 064/24826. 39 rooms with bath. Facilities: restaurant, bar, TV and phone in rooms, garden. AE,
MC, V. Moderate.*

Hostal Sucre. The colonial-style Sucre, just two blocks from the main square, is built around two inner courtyards, keeping noise to a pleasant minimum. An on-site restaurant serves light meals and snacks. *Calle Bustillo 113, tel. and fax 064/21411. 30 rooms with bath. Facilities: restaurant, TV and phone in rooms. MC, V. Moderate.*

5 Brazil

By Edwin Taylor

A resident of Rio de Janeiro, Edwin Taylor has written extensively about Brazil since 1979. In addition to producing travel and business articles for American and European publications, he has co-authored four books about the country and is the publisher of Brasilinform, an English-language information service on Brazil.

Nowhere in South America is the catchphrase "land of contrasts" more appropriate than in Brazil. From one end to the other of this continent-size nation, you will go from tropical rain forest to urban jungle, from primitive native culture to modern high rises, from distressing poverty to embarrassing wealth.

The two extremes of national life are summed up in the frantic hedonism of Rio de Janeiro and the primeval beauty of the Amazon rain forest. Beaches, sun, and fun are the obvious calling cards of Rio, still South America's premier beach resort, although suffering from growing pains. Even crowded as it is with cars and people, Rio remains one of the world's most seductive cities, uniting the raw beauty of granite monoliths and jungle-covered mountains with white sand and blue water.

At the other extreme is the country's vast northern region, occupying 42% of the national land mass and dominated by the Amazon forest, home to one-fifth of the world's freshwater reserves and responsible for one-third of the earth's oxygen. Although gold prospectors and farmers have been making rapid inroads into the forest over the past decade, most of the destructive development in their wake has occurred on the southern and western edges, leaving the bulk of the forest relatively untouched. For travelers, the adventure remains, eased today by comfortable accommodations and pleasant river cruises. From Manaus and Belém, the two gateway cities to the region, Amazon tours spread out along the great river and its tributaries, reaching into the jungle itself.

With the largest continuous coastline of any nation in the Americas at 7,700 kilometers (4,600 miles), Brazil boasts a seemingly infinite variety of beaches. Styles range from the urban setting of Rio's Copacabana and Ipanema to isolated, unspoiled treasures along the northeastern coast. Brazil's Portuguese colonizers chose to concentrate on the coastal region, avoiding the inland areas with rare exceptions—a preference that has dictated national life to this day. In the 1960s, the government moved the capital from Rio to inland Brasília in an effort to overcome the "beach complex," but three decades later, the majority of the population remains concentrated along a narrow coastal strip.

To understand Brazil, it is necessary to always keep in mind the awesome size of this country, the fifth largest in the world. Brazil is larger than the continental United States, four times the size of Mexico, and more than twice as large as India. Occupying most of the eastern half of South America, it borders on all of the other nations of the continent, with the exception of Chile and Ecuador. Its population of 146 million is equal to that of the continent's other nations combined, making Brazil truly the colossus of South America.

In addition to size, Brazil's population stands out as one of the most heterogeneous in the world, a melting pot of races and cultures that rivals that of the United States. Beginning with its Portuguese colonizers, Brazil has attracted waves of immigrants from throughout the globe, including the forced immigration of black slaves from Africa. The result is the ethnic mix of modern-day Brazil—Italian and German communities in the south, a prosperous Japanese colony in the state of São Paulo, a thriving Afro-Brazilian culture in Bahia and the northeast, the remnants of Indian cultures in the Amazon region. But

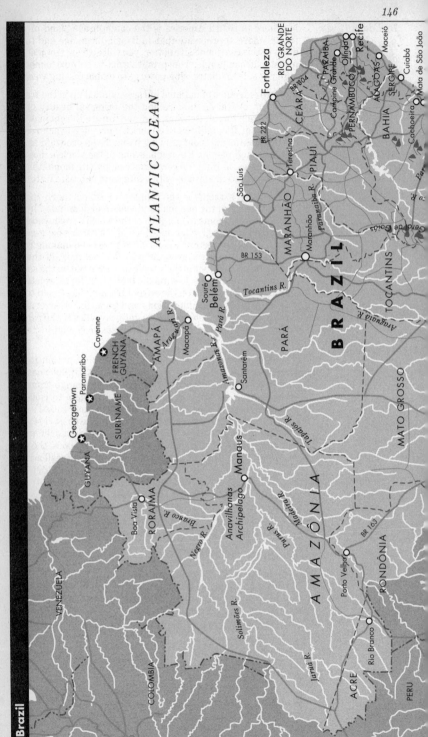

Brazil

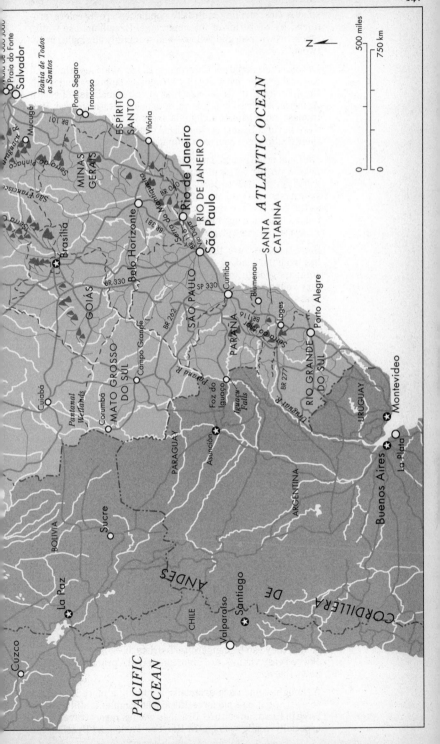

what is most striking in Brazil's population are its colors, produced by centuries of intermarriage. Brazilians are white, black, brown, red, and yellow—and seemingly all shades in between.

Despite their apparent differences, Brazil's various ethnic and cultural groups are united by a common language and a cultural heritage distinct from that of the remainder of South America. As Brazilians are quick to point out, they speak Portuguese, not Spanish, and unlike most of their neighbors, they were never a Spanish colony. This distinction, plus the size of their country, is a source of immense pride to Brazilians.

National pride reached its zenith in the 1970s, when Brazil appeared on the verge of entering the ranks of the developed world. From 1968 to 1980, Brazil's economy expanded by an average annual rate of 8.9%. During these boom years, known as the period of the Brazilian miracle, the nation completed its industrialization and emerged as the largest economy in Latin America and the world's 10th largest economic power.

Since then, however, the country's march to superpower status has been derailed by chronic economic instability marked by stagnant growth and uncontrolled inflation. Although the military relinquished control of the government in 1985 after 21 years in power, the first two civilian governments were compromised by economic problems and corruption scandals, culminating in the impeachment of President Fernando Collor de Mello in 1992. Brazil's political leaders are today attempting to restore the public's faith in the nation's still young democracy while at the same time attacking the sizable economic and social problems left over from previous governments.

Staying Safe and Healthy
Security

The rapid urbanization of Brazil over the past two decades has brought with it a growing crime problem that has been aggravated by the country's economic difficulties, in particular the most recent recession. In Rio, São Paulo, Salvador, Manaus, Belém, and major cities along the northeastern coast, tourists should take precautions to protect themselves from petty crime. Smaller cities tend to be safer, and Brasília and Belo Horizonte do not have the high crime rates of the nation's other large cities.

Most crimes involving tourists occur in public areas where there are large numbers of people, such as the beaches, crowded sidewalks, or on buses. In these settings, pickpockets, usually young children, work in groups. One or more will try to distract the victim while another grabs a wallet, bag, camera, or other target. Be particularly wary of children who suddenly thrust themselves in front of you to ask for money or to offer to shine your shoes. In such moments, it is easy for another member of the gang to strike from behind, grab whatever valuable is available, and take off to disappear in the crowd. Do not under any circumstances pursue or attempt to stop one of these robbers. Many of them are armed and although often quite young, they can be dangerous. Tourists, because they are considered easy victims, are unfortunately the primary targets of petty thieves.

Although women are gradually assuming a more important role in the nation's job force, the macho complex is still a strong force in Brazilian culture. Brazilian women rarely travel alone, especially young women. In Rio, São Paulo, and Brasília, the sight of women alone at night in restaurants or bars is more common today than in the past, but even in these cities it is liable to attract attention. In the rest of the country, women alone, depending on the time and setting, run the risk of being considered prostitutes.

Health No vaccinations are required to enter Brazil. In 1992, the Amazon region and the northeast coast were hit by an outbreak of cholera that had spread to Brazil from Peru. The disease has since reached Rio and São Paulo, but as of mid-1993, the total number of recorded cases throughout Brazil was less than 30,000 out of the nation's total population of 146 million. Nearly all of the known cases of cholera have occurred either in rural areas or urban slums where sanitary conditions are precarious. There is no effective vaccine for cholera, a disease marked by severe diarrhea and that is contracted primarily through contact with contaminated water or food. The chances of a tourist coming down with cholera are extremely limited, but to be safe, avoid consuming food or drink in locations whose health standards are questionable (*see* Precautions in Dining, *below*).

Malaria exists in regions of the Amazon, but these are isolated areas far from the routes frequented by tourists. Experienced and reliable travel operators who run Amazon trips say they have never advised tourists to concern themselves with malaria.

Essential Information

Before You Go

When to Go Throughout Brazil the high tourism season runs from November to April, although there are festivals, special events, and sporting attractions year-round. Carnival, the year's principal festival, occurs during the four days preceding Ash Wednesday, which usually falls in February but can occur in March. In 1994 Carnival will be held February 12–15; in 1995 it runs February 25–28. For top hotels in Rio and Salvador, the two leading Carnival cities, you must make reservations a year in advance. Hotel rates go up on the average 20% for Carnival, and you should also expect to pay more for taxis, up to double regular fares. Besides crowded hotels, you will find the downtown streets in Salvador packed with revelers during Carnival. In Rio, street Carnival is more sedate, but spontaneous groups of dancers parade across streets in the city's south zone on a regular basis.

Not as well known outside of Brazil but equally impressive is Rio's New Year's Eve celebration. Over a million people gather around the crescent curve of Copacabana beach for a massive fireworks display. In the hours preceding midnight, the beach is alive with the throbbing of drums as followers of Brazil's African religious cult Macumba conduct ceremonies to honor the sea goddess Iemanjá. At the stroke of midnight, the white-clad faithful rush to the water's edge and throw in their offerings to the goddess, culminating in a unique spectacle. As with Carnival, Rio's better hotels usually fill up for New Year's Eve, especially those overlooking Copacabana beach. To assure a room, book at least six months in advance.

Seasons below the Equator are the reverse of the north—summer in Brazil runs from December to March and winter from June to September. The rainy season in Brazil occurs during the summer months, but this is rarely a nuisance. Showers can be torrential but usually last no more than an hour or two, after which the sun reappears. The only area of the country with a pronounced rainy season is the Amazon. In this region, the rainy season runs from November to May and is marked by heavy downpours that usually occur twice a day.

Prices in beach resorts invariably are higher during the high season (Brazilian summer). If you are looking for a bargain, stick to the off season (from May to October). In Rio and at beach resorts along the coast, especially in the northeast, these months offer the added attraction of relief from the often oppressive summer heat, although in Rio the temperature can drop to uncomfortable levels for swimming in June through August.

Climate Rio de Janeiro is located on the Tropic of Capricorn, and its climate is just that—tropical. Summers are hot and humid, with temperatures rising as high as 105°F (40°C), although the average ranges between 84–95°F (29–35°C). In winter, temperatures stay in the 70s (20s C), occasionally dipping into the 60s (15–20°C). The same pattern holds true for all of the Brazilian coastline north of Rio, although in general temperatures are slightly higher year-round in Salvador and the coastal cities of the northeast. In the Amazon region where the equator crosses the country, temperatures in the high 80s to the 90s (30s C) are common throughout the year. São Paulo, the inland state of Minas Gerais, and Brasília, due to their higher altitude, are substantially cooler than Rio. These regions tend to have more of a change of seasons, although nowhere in Brazil, with the exception of the south, are there four distinct seasons. In the south, in São Paulo and Belo Horizonte, winter temperatures can fall to the low 40s (5–8°C). In the southern states of Santa Catarina and Rio Grande do Sul, snowfalls occur in the winter, although it is seldom more than a dusting. The following are the average daily maximum and minimum temperatures for Rio de Janeiro.

Jan.	84F	29C	May	77F	25C	Sept.	75F	24C
	69	21		66	19		66	19
Feb.	85F	29C	June	76F	24C	Oct.	77F	25C
	73	23		64	18		63	17
Mar.	83F	28C	July	75F	24C	Nov.	79F	26C
	72	22		64	18		68	20
Apr.	80F	27C	Aug.	76F	24C	Dec.	82F	28C
	69	21		64	18		71	22

The following are the average daily maximum and minimum temperatures for Salvador.

Jan.	87F	31C	May	80F	27C	Sept.	78F	26C
	76	24		70	21		69	21
Feb.	88F	31C	June	80F	27C	Oct.	80F	27C
	76	24		67	19		69	21
Mar.	87F	31C	July	78F	26C	Nov.	83F	28C
	77	25		66	19		72	22
Apr.	84F	29C	Aug.	80F	27C	Dec.	86F	30C
	73	23		67	19		77	25

Currency In August 1993, Brazil underwent a currency reform with the replacement of the cruzeiro (Cr$) with a new currency, the cruzeiro real (CR$). The reform was made necessary by Brazil's chronic high inflation, which reached $1,200 in 1992, leaving the cruzeiro increasingly worthless. Under the reform, each cruzeiro real (plural: cruzeiros reais) is worth 1,000 cruzeiros; thus, three zeroes have been removed from the old cruzeiro. The existing cruzeiro bills and coins were not removed from circulation with the reform and will continue to circulate legally for some time. This means that you will have to deal with currency marked as cruzeiros as well as the new cruzeiro real currency. (Should you come upon any bills or coins marked as cruzeiros, lop off three zeroes before you divide by the exchange rate at which you changed your currency.)

There are 100 cents (centavos) to each cruzeiro real. The lowest value of the new currency system is one cent, which is equal to 10 cruzeiros. This means that any cruzeiro bill or coin below Cr$10 is worthless and should not be accepted.

The first cruzeiro real notes, printed in the fall of 1993, will be CR$1 and CR$5. Until additional cruzeiro real bills are printed, the national mint will continue to print cruzeiro bills stamped with their value in cruzeiro reais. At press time (summer 1993), the government planned to issue the following cruzeiro bills stamped with cruzeiro real values: Cr$50,000 (CR$50), Cr$100,000 (CR$100), and Cr$500,000 (CR$500). Also, the mint was scheduled to issue cruzeiro real coins by the end of 1993 in the following denominations: CR$5 and CR$10.

Changing Money Travelers' checks (well-known names are best), dollars in cash, credit cards, and personal checks (in dollars) are all accepted by many Brazilians, albeit at slightly varying exchange rates. You would do well to take your money in some of each of these forms. Barring a wage and price freeze, the exchange rates vary daily.

In 1993, Brazil had three different exchange rates, all floating and thus subject to daily variation: the tourism rate, called *câmbio turismo* (this is lower for travelers' checks and credit cards than for cash and personal checks), the official exchange rate (*comercial*), used only for government and business transactions, and the parallel, or black market rate (*paralelo* or black). In 1993, the tourism rate averaged 13% above the official exchange rate, and the parallel rate was only slightly above the tourism rate. The three rates are published daily in local newspapers on the front page or in the financial section (look under the column labeled "Compra"), but refer to the previous day's rate (with no change over the weekend) and often are not exactly the same as those used in actual transactions. Some big cities also have special phone numbers you can call to find out the day's exchange rates. As a tourist, the rate you will most often get is the tourism exchange rate, used by hotels and credit card companies. Brazil's exchange rate system is by no means set in stone, and may change in response to the latest economic conditions.

Travelers' checks are safest, of course, especially given the dangers you may face in big cities and in the poorer parts of the country, where poverty often drives crime against tourists. These can easily be exchanged at the tourism rate for cruzeiros reais at hotels, banks, officially authorized currency exchange houses (*casas de câmbio*), travel agencies, and shops in shopping malls or catering to tourists (many smaller tradesmen are at a total loss when faced with travelers' checks or even cash dollars). The rate for travelers' checks is lower than that for cash, and hotels often change them at a rate that is lower than that available at banks or casas de câmbio. You will need your passport to change dollars at the tourist rate.

In big cities, cash dollars (viewed as desirable hard currency because the local currency loses value on a daily basis) are often accepted as payment in shops, restaurants, hotels, and even by some taxi drivers, at a rate that is slightly better than that given for travelers' checks.

Credit cards can be used to pay hotel bills, but ask first if there is a discount for cash. The economic situation is such that many hotels, restaurants, and shops have taken to cutting costs (including the percentage paid to credit card companies) by awarding discounts for cash. Local shoppers find that the cheapest form of purchase is usually by paying in monthly installments with personal predated cruzeiro real checks, but since this option is not available to visitors, you should try to bargain hard for a cash-on-the-barrel discount, paid either in dollars or local currency.

Personal checks are a good last resort for luxury items (such as jewelry) or when an unexpected expense is incurred. Some hotels will accept personal checks from guests. These are usually exchanged on presentation of a passport, at the cash tourism or parallel rate, and only if the vendor has access to a U.S. bank account (which is increasingly common).

Unless the government decrees a wage and price freeze in late 1993 or in 1994, you will have to weigh the time it takes to change money frequently against the loss you will incur by changing large amounts and carrying around a pile of cruzeiros reais that lose value on a daily basis (monthly inflation in late 1993 was over 30%).

For an average day in a Brazilian city, a good strategy is to convert up to $50 in travelers' checks into cruzeiros reais before leaving your hotel, more if you are planning on a big meal. This provides sufficient cash for the most of the day's expenses, such as taxis and small purchases and snacks, and saves the trouble of haggling over the exchange rate with taxi drivers and restaurant managers, who often try to take advantage of tourists.

What It Will Cost A decade of uncontrolled inflation at annual rates running above 1,000% has left Brazilian prices in total disarray. Some products are amazingly inexpensive, while others are so high that they defy the imagination. In general, the 1990s have seen a slight decline from the levels reached in the second half of the

1980s, but Brazil is still far from the bargain destination it once was. Prices in Brazil's largest cities, though, are well below prices for the same goods and services in comparable cities in the United States, Europe, and Asia. Top hotels in Rio and São Paulo go for over $200 a night, but quality restaurants are surprisingly moderate, seldom over $20 a person. Quality declines, often sharply, with lower prices. Outside of Brazil's two largest cities, prices for food and lodging tend to drop significantly, although Brasília is an exception to this rule. Fast-food outlets are now arriving in Brazil, led by the American McDonald's and Pizza Hut, with prices at roughly the same level as in the United States. Taxis, city buses, subways, and long-distance buses are all inexpensive. Plane fares, however, are definitely not: The round-trip airfare from Rio to São Paulo is $200, for example, and the fare from Rio to Manaus is $425 round-trip.

Sample Prices A cup of coffee in Rio de Janeiro is 15¢; bottle of beer or glass of draft, 55¢; soft drink, 50¢; fresh fruit drink, 70¢; hamburger, 80¢–$2.75; 3-mile taxi ride, $3.25.

Credit Cards In Brazil's largest cities and leading tourist centers, top restaurants, hotels, and shops accept major international credit cards. Off the beaten track, however, tourists will have great difficulty in finding establishments that accept them. Gas stations in Brazil do not take credit cards.

Customs on Arrival Former strict import controls have been substantially liberalized as part of the Brazilian government's efforts to open the nation's economy to foreign competition. In addition to personal items, visitors are now permitted to bring in duty free up to $500 worth of gifts purchased abroad. An additional $500 worth of gifts, including alcoholic beverages, may be purchased at the airport duty-free shops.

Language The language in Brazil is Portuguese, not Spanish. Although the two languages are distinct, common origins mean that several words are identical, and fluent speakers of Spanish will be able to make themselves understood. English is widely spoken among educated Brazilians and representatives of the tourist trade. In all hotels, someone on the staff will speak English, and in the better hotels, most of the staff will be at least able to answer basic questions. In restaurants, waiters will probably have only a smattering of English but maître d's will be able to speak well. Travel agencies and tour operators all employ bilingual staff. Taxi drivers, however, will rarely speak any English, and shop vendors outside of fashionable malls in large cities usually know very little. In such cities as Rio, São Paulo, Brasília, and Salvador, tourists have little difficulty in finding someone who speaks English to help them. The smaller the location, the further off the beaten track, the greater the difficulty of finding English-speaking Brazilians.

Getting Around

By Car Brazil's economic woes of the past 10 years have meant there
Road Conditions has been little money left over for highway maintenance. This fact is particularly alarming when considering that Brazil's network of federal highways was largely built between 1964 and 1976, with maintenance nearly nonexistent in the 1980s. The National Highway Department estimates that 50% of the nation's federal highways, which constitute 70% of Brazil's

total road system, are in a dangerous state of disrepair, and each year an additional 3,000 kilometers (1,800 miles) fall into this category.

The evidence of this is everywhere. Potholes, lack of signalization, and inadequate shoulders are the most obvious of the precarious driving conditions on the federal roads. Landslides after heavy rains have become increasingly frequent, often shutting down entire stretches of key highways. The greatest danger, though, is the combination of decaying roads and increasing traffic, which has produced an explosion in deadly highway accidents. Brazilian drivers also tend to be reckless and pay little attention to the speed limit or the most basic rules of safe driving. The worst offenders are bus and truck drivers. For these reasons, you should avoid driving on Brazilian highways, but if you do drive, do so with the utmost caution.

Rules of the Road Brazilians drive on the right-hand side of the road, and in general, traffic laws are the same as in the United States. The use of seat belts is mandatory. The national speed limit is 80 kph (48 mph) but is seldom observed or enforced. U.S. driver's licenses are accepted in Brazil in theory, but police, particularly highway police, have been known to invent violations in order to shake down drivers for bribes. It is therefore recommended to have an international driver's license, which is seldom challenged.

Parking Finding a parking space in most of Brazil's leading cities is a major task. This is particularly true in Rio, São Paulo, Belo Horizonte, and Salvador. The situation is somewhat better in Brasília. The best option is to find a parking garage and leave your car with the attendant. Should you find a parking space on the street, you will probably have to pay a parking fee. Because of Brazil's rampant inflation, which has made the use of coins virtually impossible, there are no parking meters. There is instead a system involving parking coupons, which are purchased either from uniformed street parking attendants or at newspaper stands. Each coupon is good for two hours. No parking zones are marked by a capital letter E that is crossed out. The E stands for *estacionamento*, which means parking. These zones are more often than not filled with cars, which are rarely bothered by the police.

Gasoline Gasoline in Brazil costs around 50¢ a liter ($1.90 a gallon). Unleaded gasoline is called *especial* and carries the same price. Brazil also has an extensive fleet of ethanol-powered cars. Ethanol fuel is sold at all gas stations, and costs 38¢ a liter ($1.45 a gallon). Although ethanol fuel is less expensive, alcohol cars get lower gas mileage, so they have no advantage over gasoline-power automobiles. Gas stations are plentiful both within cities and on major highways, and many are open 24 hours a day.

Breakdowns The **Automobile Club of Brazil** (Automóvel Club do Brasil; Rua do Passeio 90, Rio de Janeiro, RJ, tel. 021/297–4455) provides emergency assistance to motorists in cities and on highways throughout the country. The club services members of foreign automobile clubs, but will not provide assistance to nonmembers.

By Train Brazil has an outdated and insufficient rail network, the smallest of any of the world's large nations. The basic problem of Brazil's railroads is historical. Railroad construction was almost entirely overlooked during the early years of the country's development. Only in the 1930s were lines built along the coast, linking the large port cities mainly in the southeast. Inland regions, however, were largely forgotten in the initial transportation scheme. Brazil today has only some 30,000 kilometers (18,000 miles) of functioning rail lines, less than one-tenth the size of the United States' network and 20% smaller than that of Argentina, a country one-third the size of Brazil.

The failure to construct new lines, however, is only part of the problem. Nationwide, aging trains and tracks are rapidly deteriorating. Only 6,000 kilometers (3,600 miles) of the existing tracks were constructed since 1930.

Because of these continuing problems, passenger train service is spotty at best. The government-owned Federal Railway System, the only national rail network, no longer operates passenger trains between any of Brazil's leading cities. A subsidiary of the federal network, the Brazilian Urban Train Company (CBTU), is responsible for the nation's commuter trains. These trains, which are for the most part in terrible condition, carry the poor residents of the outskirts of Brazil's urban centers to work.

By Bus The nation's bus network is extensive and highly efficient, compensating for the lack of trains and the high cost of air travel. Every major city in the country can be reached by bus, and most of the small- to medium-size cities are also linked to the network. Buses are for the most part modern and comfortable, and the companies have excellent on-time records. On the well-traveled routes, service is frequent and inexpensive. Between Rio and São Paulo (6½–7 hours), for example, a bus departs every half hour costing about $10 (a night sleeper costs about $20). The sleeper is basically a regular bus with fewer seats, permitting more space for each passenger to stretch out. The seats also decline more, and these buses are air-conditioned, the only ones today that guarantee this luxury (regular buses that are labeled air conditioned often are not).

Trips to the north, northeast, and central Brazil tend to be long and tiring. The steady deterioration of the highways in recent years has also led to an increase in accidents involving buses. This is a recurring problem that is unlikely to be resolved in the short term. Lengthy bus trips anywhere in Brazil will inevitably involve travel over bad highways, an unfortunate fact of life in Brazil today.

There has been a recent spurt of robberies aboard buses traveling between Rio and São Paulo. In these cases, a member of the gang travels on board as a passenger, later pulling out a gun and forcing the driver to stop while his cohorts arrive in a car and rob the passengers.

Brazil's leading bus company is **Itapemirim** (Av. Brasil 12417, Rio de Janeiro), with countrywide operations. Tickets may be purchased only at the bus station (each city has one bus station). You cannot make reservations by phone, but you can buy a ticket at the station before the date you are traveling. This is a necessity when traveling the weekend of Carnival, over Easter, or during the holiday season at the end of the year.

By Plane There is regular jet service between all of the country's major cities and a steadily growing number of medium-size cities.

Flights can be long, lasting several hours on trips to the Amazon with stops en route. Planes tend to fill up on the weekends, so book in advance if you plan to fly anywhere on a Friday, especially to or from Brasília or Manaus.

Three major commercial airlines handle most of the domestic air traffic in Brazil: **Varig** (in Rio: tel. 021/217–4591; in New York: tel. 212/459–0210; in Toronto: tel. 416/926–7500; in London: tel. 071/629–9408), **Vasp** (in Rio: tel. 021/292–2080; in Los Angeles: tel. 213/243–9207 or 310/364–0160), and **Transbrasil** (in Rio: tel. 021/521–0300; in New York: tel. 212/944–7374).

The most widely used service is the Rio–São Paulo shuttle, the **Ponte Aérea,** which has departures every hour from 6 AM until 10:30 PM (every half hour during morning and early evening rush hours). Other shuttle services now link the cities of São Paulo, Belo Horizonte, and Brasília. The south of Brazil is served by **Rio Sul** (tel. 021/263–2797), a regional airline that connects Rio and São Paulo with the principal cities of the southern states of Paraná and Rio Grande do Sul. **Nordeste** (tel. 071/233–7880) is a small regional airline with flights connecting Salvador with Porto Seguro, in the state of Bahia, and Vitória, capital of the neighboring state of Espírito Santo.

Prices are high by American standards, and there are no promotional fares. Brazilian airlines offer discounts of 30% for a 30-day advance purchase. Senior citizens over 60 have a right to a 30% discount. **Transbrasil** offers a 50% discount for its midnight flights linking Rio with São Paulo, Brasília, and Salvador.

If you are planning to do a good deal of flying in Brazil, consider purchasing the **Brazil Air Pass,** which is sold only outside the country and is offered by Varig, Transbrasil, and Vasp. This $440 pass permits five flights within Brazil for 21 days. All major destinations are served, including São Paulo, Manaus, Brasília, Belém, Recife, and Búzios.

By Boat Some international cruise lines stop at Brazilian ports during worldwide or South American cruises. The most popular port of call is Rio during Carnival. International cruises also stop regularly at Santos, the port of the state of São Paulo, and Salvador. Some international liners include cruises along the Amazon River in their itineraries. These cruises and ports of calls, however, vary from year to year.

Check with your travel agent or contact one of the following cruise lines, which stop regularly at Brazilian ports: **Royal Viking Lines** (95 Merrick Way, Coral Gables, FL 33134, tel. 305/447–9660), **Sun Line** (1 Rockefeller Plaza, Suite 315, New York, NY 10020, tel. 212/397–6400), and **Cunard** (555 Fifth Ave., New York, NY 10017-2453, tel. 800/221–4770).

Within Brazil, passenger traffic on inland waterways is limited to the Amazon region, where river boats are the principal mode of transportation for inhabitants of the area (*see* Getting There by Boat in The Amazon, *below*).

Staying in Brazil

Embassies and **Canada:** embassy (Brasília: Av. das Nações, Q 803 lote 16, tel.
Consulates 061/321–2171); consulates (Rio de Janeiro: Rua Lauro Muller 116, room 1104, tel. 021/542–7593; São Paulo: Av. Paulista 1106, 1st floor, tel. 011/285–5099).

Great Britain: embassy (Brasília: Av. das Nações, QD 801 lote 8, tel. 061/225–2710); consulates (Rio de Janeiro: Praia do Flamengo 284, 2nd floor, tel. 021/552–1422; São Paulo: Av. Paulista 1938, 17th floor, tel. 011/287–7722).

United States: embassy (Brasília: Av. das Nações, QD 801 lote 3, tel. 061/321–7272); consulates (Rio de Janeiro: Av. Presidente Wilson 147, tel. 021/292–7117; São Paulo: Rua Padre João Manoel 933, tel 011/881–6511).

Telephones
Local Calls
All parts of Brazil are serviced by Embratel, the national telephone company. Public phones are everywhere and are called *orelhões* (big ears). These are yellow with the blue phone company logo for local calls, or solid blue for calls between cities (*interurbana*). To use the public phones, you must buy tokens, called *fichas*, at newspaper stands or phone company stations. Local fichas, which are good for three minutes, cost the equivalent of 2¢; long-distance tokens cost about 22¢ and last 18 seconds. It is wise to buy several at a time so that you can insert them in advance and avoid getting cut off. A three-minute call from Rio to São Paulo requires 10 long-distance tokens. Unused fichas are returned when you hang up. Rates double during peak hours (9 AM–noon and 2–6 PM). The lowest rates are available after 11 PM.

Although the public phones are visible on every street corner, vandalism is on the increase in Rio and São Paulo. As a result, you may have to try several of the phones before you find one that is working. Commercial establishments do not usually have public phones, although a bar, restaurant, or drugstore will probably allow you to use their private phone if you are a customer. Otherwise, you may be refused or be required to pay to use the phone. Phone company stations are found at airports, many bus stations, and in downtown neighborhoods of large cities. At these you can pay in cash after making the call. International credit cards are not accepted.

For local directory assistance, dial 102. For directory assistance in another Brazilian city, dial the area code of that city plus 102.

International Calls
For international phone calls with the assistance of the operator, dial 000111. For international information, dial 000333. To dial direct, dial 001 plus the country code, the area code of the city you are calling, and then the number. Collect international calls can be made from any public phone either by dialing 107 and then asking for any international operator, or by dialing 000107 from a blue public phone. International calls from Brazil are extremely expensive, double the international rates in the United States. Hotels also add a surcharge, increasing this cost. To pay American long-distance rates and deal with American operators, AT&T and MCI cardholders can dial direct to a U.S. operator from any phone in Brazil. To reach an AT&T operator, dial 000–8010; for MCI, call 000–8012.

Mail
Postal Rates
Post offices are called *correios,* and branches are marked by the name and a logo that looks somewhat like two interlocked fingers. Mailboxes are small yellow boxes marked "Correios" sitting atop metal pedestals on street corners. An airmail letter from Brazil to the United States and most parts of Europe, including the United Kingdom, costs approximately $1. Aerograms and postcards cost the same. Airmail takes at least five days to reach the United States from Brazil. Brazil has both

national and international express mail service, the price of which varies according to the weight of the package and the destination. International express mail companies operating out of Brazil include Federal Express and DHL. Objects of value—especially currency, checks, or credit cards—should never be sent through the mail.

Postal codes recently were converted from five to eight digits throughout Brazil. At press time (summer 1993), postal authorities were still delivering mail addressed with the old, five-digit codes.

Receiving Mail Mail can be received at Post Restante at any major post office. The address must include the code for that particular branch. American Express will hold mail for its cardholders.

Shopping
Bargaining Prices in department stores are fixed, but in smaller shops and boutiques there is usually some room for discussion. Because of Brazil's high inflation, shop owners often give discounts for cash payments; some shops refuse to accept credit cards. Shops in areas that cater to tourists invariably charge more. At outdoor antiques and art fairs, crafts markets, and food markets, bargaining is a way of life. If you wish to try your hand at haggling over prices, the Portuguese phrase for too expensive is *"Está muito caro."*

Opening and Closing Times **Banks.** Banks are open weekdays 10–4:30. Nearly all the nation's major banks have automated teller machines scattered throughout the country.

Museums and churches. Churches are typically open throughout the day, but museum hours vary considerably. Be sure to check in advance.

Post Offices. Post offices are open weekdays 8–5 and Saturday until noon.

Shops. Stores generally open at 9 and close at 6:30 during the week and at 1 PM on Saturday. Shopping malls are open 10 AM to 10 PM weekdays and until 6 PM on Saturday. All stores are closed on Sunday, although newsstands and convenience stores that stay open on Sunday are just now beginning to appear in Rio and São Paulo. The business day generally begins at 9 and ends at 6, although punctuality is not a Brazilian trait. Stores and offices may open later and frequently stay open until the last customer leaves.

Holidays and Festivals **Jan.:** In Salvador, Bahia, on the first Sunday of the month, the **Festival of the Boa Viagem,** the Good Lord Jesus of the Seafarers, is held for four days, with samba music, *capoeira* (a fight, dance, and a bit of judo rolled into one), and feasts of Bahian food. The highlight is a procession of hundreds of small vessels led by a decorated galley to the end of Boa Viagem beach. Also in Salvador, on the third Sunday of January, is the **Feast of Bonfim,** when Bahian women dressed in their traditional white hoop skirts and tunics clean the steps of the Basilica of Bonfim with perfumed water.

Feb.: In Salvador, the **Festival of Iemanjá** is held on the second Sunday of the month. The devotees of Brazil's African religious cult Candomblé begin singing the praises of the goddess of the sea at the crack of dawn along the city's beaches.

Feb.–Mar.: Always held during the four days before Ash Wednesday, **Carnival** is the biggest party of the year, featuring dancing and singing in the streets, Brazilians donning wild costumes, splashy floats in parades carrying samba dancers and musicians, and posh balls. Although Rio's version attracts the most tourists, Carnival is also spectacular in Bahia (especially in Salvador) and the northeastern cities of Recife and Olinda.

Mar.: Holy Week is celebrated in Ouro Preto, in the state of Minas Gerais. Solemn Easter celebrations in this historical city include religious rites from the 17th and 18th centuries. Also held during March is the **Formula I Grand Prix** in São Paulo.

Apr.: Good Friday (April 1, 1994), **Easter** (April 3, 1994). April 21 is **Tiradentes Day,** a national holiday in honor of the father of the 18th-century Brazilian independence movement, Joaquim José da Silva Xavier, known as Tiradentes (tooth puller) because he was a dentist. On this date, Tiradentes was executed for treason by the Portuguese crown in the city of Ouro Preto. The city itself celebrates the date over a four-day period, April 18–21, with civic ceremonies.

May: Labor Day (May 1).

June: Corpus Christi falls on June 10. **Festas Juninas** is a cycle of celebrations throughout the month honoring various saints. The festivals are particularly noteworthy in Parati, the state of Rio de Janeiro, and in several interior regions of the northeast such as Campina Grande in the state of Paraíba. **Bumba-Meu-Boi,** a festival held in São Luís (in the state of Maranho) and other cattle-raising areas, celebrates the religious legend of the slave who kills his master's ox and must resurrect it or be put to death himself. The festivities, which begin June 24 and continue well into July, include street processions and dancing. The **Amazon Folklore Festival** takes place in Manaus.

July: Bahian Independence Day (July 2).

Aug.: Brazilian Sweepstakes, Jockey Club, Rio de Janeiro (first Sunday of the month).

Sept.: Held every other year in even years in São Paulo, the **Biennial Art Exposition** is the largest art show in Latin America, lasting several months.

Oct.: In Blumenau, Santa Catarina, southern Brazil's large German colony holds a month-long beer festival called **Oktoberfest.** Not only is October 12 the saint's day of the patron saint of Brazil, **Nossa Senhora de Aparecida,** celebrated all over the country and particularly in Aparecida (in the state of São Paulo), but it's also Children's Day.

Nov.: Aleijadinho Week, in Ouro Preto, honors the great 18th-century sculptor, whose work adorns many of the city's churches. Other national holidays are **All Souls' Day** (November 2) and **Independence Day** (September 7).

Dec. 31/Jan. 1: New Year's Eve (Ano Novo) is celebrated all night on Copacabana Beach in Rio de Janeiro. Ritual music pulses as the priestesses of Brazil's African religious cult light candles and set up small shrines to Iemanjá, goddess of the sea. Dressed all in white, they set afloat boats carrying candles, white lilies, perfume, and other gifts; if the waves take a boat out to sea, the sender's wishes for the year will come true.

Dining You may be visiting Brazil, but you would hardly know it from the restaurants. Most of the finer restaurants in Rio and São

Paulo are either French or Italian. In addition, there is excellent Portuguese, Chinese, Japanese, Arab, Hungarian, and Spanish cuisine to be sampled. Traditional Brazilian food may be hard to come by, but when it is found, it can make for a delicious dining experience. A typical, low-cost Brazilian meal consists of beans, rice, french fries, and beef, chicken, or fish. Brazilians are not fond of vegetables, and salads must be ordered separately. Visitors will quickly discover that eating is a national passion, and they are often shocked by the huge portions. The number of eateries is staggering: Restaurants of all sizes and categories, snack bars, and more recently, fast-food outlets line downtown streets and fight for space in shopping malls.

Many Brazilian dishes are adaptations of Portuguese specialties. Fish stews called *caldeiradas* (tomato sauce, layered fish, and potatoes) and beef stews called *cozidos* (a wide variety of vegetables boiled with different cuts of beef and pork) are popular, as is *bacalhau*, salt cod cooked in sauces or grilled. Dried salted meats form the basis for many dishes from the interior and northeast of Brazil, and pork is used heavily in dishes from Minas Gerais. The national dish of Brazil is *feijoada*, traditionally served on Saturday at lunch. Originally a slave dish, feijoada now consists of black beans, sausage, beef, and pork. It is always served with rice, finely shredded kale, orange slices, and *farofa*, manioc flour that has been fried with onion and egg.

The cuisine of Bahia is often equated with Brazilian food as a whole, although it is actually best eaten in Salvador, where it originates. *Muqueca* is composed of many kinds of shellfish cooked quickly in a sauce of *dendé* (palm) oil, coconut milk, onions, tomatoes, and coriander. Dried shrimp, coconut milk, and cashews are the basic ingredients of *vatapá*, a fish and shrimp stew cooked with peanuts and dendé oil, and *xinxim de galinha*, a vatapá-like chicken stew that uses lime juice instead coconut milk.

From Brazil's southeast comes *churrasco*, meats marinated and grilled or roasted over charcoal. Restaurants specializing in steaks are called *churrascarias*, which are served either à la carte or *rodizio* (all you can eat) style.

You will find Brazilian desserts sweeter than you are used to. Desserts are referred to as *doces* (sweets) and are sold in street shops and restaurants. Many doces are direct descendants of the egg-based custards and puddings of Portugal and France. Coffee is served black and strong with sugar in demitasse cups and is called *cafezinho*. Coffee is taken with milk (*café com leite*) only at breakfast. The national drink is the *caipirinha*, made of crushed lime, sugar, and *pinga* or *cachaa*, strong liquors made from sugarcane. When whipped with crushed ice and fruit juices, the pinga becomes a *batida*, which sometimes contains condensed milk. Bottled mineral water is sold in two forms: with and without bubbles (*com gas* and *sem gas*, respectively). Brazil's best bottled beer is Cerpa, sold at most restaurants. In general, though, Brazilians prefer tap beer, called *chop*, which is sold by all bars and some restaurants.

Mealtimes Lunch and dinner typically are eaten later than in the United States. Lunch in a restaurant usually starts at around 1 and often lasts until 3. Dinner is always eaten after 8, in many cases not until 10.

Precautions Do not drink water anywhere unless it is bottled mineral water; nor should you drink beverages with ice made from tap water. At press time (summer 1993) cholera had reached epidemic proportions in the northeast states and was also beginning to appear in Rio. For utmost protection from cholera, a disease marked by extreme diarrhea and vomiting, and which in severe cases can lead to dehydration and death, make sure that the fresh fruit you eat is peeled and that seafood (particularly in cold seafood salads) and vegetables are thoroughly cooked. Avoid all food and beverages from street vendors. To be safe, you should avoid fruits and vegetables unless you are certain they have been properly cleaned or cooked. Currently, cholera vaccines are not recommended for travelers. For further information on cholera, contact the U.S. Department of Health and Human Services, Centers for Disease Control, tel. 404/332–4559.

Dress Informality is the rule of thumb. Only at the top restaurants do Brazilians dress up, and men seldom wear jackets and ties.

Ratings Prices are for one person and do not include alcoholic beverages and tips but do include the *couvert*, an appetizer course served in Brazilian restaurants that includes bread, butter, and, depending on the restaurant, cheese or pâté, olives, quail eggs, and sausage. Highly recommended restaurants in each category are indicated by a star ★.

Category	Rio, São Paulo	Other Areas
Very Expensive	over $30	over $25
Expensive	$20–$30	$15–$25
Moderate	$10–$20	$8–$15
Inexpensive	under $10	under $8

Lodging Top prices are not always indicators of deluxe hotels in Brazil. The best hotels are located in Rio and São Paulo, where the five-star rating given by the government tourism authority Embratur is usually reliable, although there is a tendency to elevate four-star hotels to the top rating for reasons that are not always clear. In general, the Embratur system merely takes into consideration the amenities offered by a hotel without evaluating such vital intangibles as the quality of service. Below four stars, the quality of hotels drops dramatically. Also, the quality of hotels, even the top rated, tends to fall in areas outside of Rio and São Paulo.

Although personal inspection of the premises is impossible if you are making reservations from afar, checking out the room in an inexpensive or moderate hotel before you take it is particularly important in Brazil. Reservations at expensive and deluxe establishments should be made well in advance, particularly if you're planning a trip during high season or special events. For Carnival, unless you are traveling with a tour, reservations in the best hotels must be made at least a year ahead. Unlike those in the United States, motels in Brazil do not have free parking, and are rented out for the hour, afternoon, or overnight. Though they are frequented by couples having assignations, these establishments are completely legitimate.

Ratings Prices are for a double room and include all taxes. Highly recommended lodgings in each price category are indicated by a star ★.

Category	Rio, São Paulo	Other Areas
Very Expensive	over $200	over $100
Expensive	$120–$200	$70–$100
Moderate	$70–$120	$30–$70
Inexpensive	under $70	under $30

Tipping At restaurants that levy a 10% service charge, it is customary to give the waiter a 5% tip in addition to the service charge included on the check. If there is no service charge, leave a 15% tip.

In expensive-to-deluxe-category hotels, tip porters 50¢ per bag, chambermaids 50¢ per day, $1 for room and valet service. Tips for doormen and concierge vary and depend primarily on the services provided. A good tip would be $10 or higher, average $5. For moderate and inexpensive hotels, tips tend to be minimal. At this level, salaries are so low that virtually anything is well received. If a taxi driver helps you with your luggage, a per bag charge of about 35¢ is levied in addition to the fare. In general, tip taxi drivers 10% of the fare.

At the barber shop or beauty parlor, a 10%–20% tip is expected. If a service station attendant does anything beyond filling up the gas tank, leave him a small tip of a nickel or dime. Tipping in bars and cafes follows the rules of restaurants, although at outdoor bars Brazilians rarely leave a tip if they have had no more than a soft drink or beer. In general, tip washroom attendants and shoeshine boys about one-third what you would tip at home. At airports and at train and bus stations, tip the last porter who puts your bags into the cab (50¢ a bag at airports, 25¢ a bag at bus and train stations). In large cities you will often be accosted on the street by children looking for handouts. Always carry some loose change to hand out to street beggars. No more than 25¢ is necessary.

Rio de Janeiro

By Michael Adams

Revised by Edwin Taylor

When you first arrive in Rio de Janeiro, think of the journey from airport to hotel as a brief spell of purgatory, minor dues to be paid for entry into what harried Americans will consider heaven. If you've traveled overnight, your tongue can be thick and your eyes bleary, and the initial sights that welcome you—mostly gray, nondescript industrial buildings—are unpromising. But by the time you reach Avenida Atlântica, flanked on one side by white beach and azure sea, and on the other by the pleasure-palace hotels that stand as testimony to the city's eternal lure, your heart will leap with expectation. Now you're truly in Rio, where the wicked angels and shimmering devils known as cariocas dwell.

The word *carioca* comes from the country's earliest European history, when it meant "white man's house" and was used to describe a Portuguese trading station. Today the word defines more than birthplace, race, or residence: It represents an ethos of pride, sensuality, and a passionate dedication to life. Much of the carioca verve comes from the sheer physical splendor of the city: seemingly endless beaches, sculpted promontories, and the ocean stretching to infinity.

While in Rio, prepare to have your senses engaged and your inhibitions untied. You'll be seduced by a host of images: the joyous bustle of vendors at Sunday's Hippie Fair; the tipsy babble of a sidewalk café as latecomers sip their last glass of wine under the stars; the blanket of luminescent lights beneath Sugarloaf. Borrow the carioca spirit for your stay; you may find yourself reluctant to give it back.

Tourist Information

The Rio de Janeiro city tourism department, **Riotur** (021/297-7117), is located at Rua da Assembléia 10, downtown, near Praça XV Square. In addition, Riotur has information booths at the Sugarloaf cable car station (Av. Pasteur 520, Urca, open 8–8), Marinha da Glória (Atêrro do Flamengo, Glória, tel. 021/205–6447, open 8–5), and the Rodoviária Novo Rio (the main bus depot at Av. Francisco Bicalho 1, São Cristóvão, tel. 021/291–5151, open 6 AM–midnight).

The Rio de Janeiro state tourism board, **Turisrio,** is also located downtown at Rua da Assembléia 10, 7th and 8th floors. For information call 021/252–4512 weekdays 9–6.

Brazil's national tourism board, **Embratur,** is headquartered in Rio near the Túnel Rebouças (inconveniently far from beach neighborhoods and hotels) at Rua Mariz e Barros 13, Praça da Bandeira, tel. 021/273–2212.

Arriving and Departing

By Plane All international flights, and most domestic flights, arrive and depart from the **Galeão International Airport.** The airport is approximately 45 minutes from the beach area where most of Rio's hotels are lócated and is served by most major airlines. The **Santos Dumont Airport,** located just outside downtown Rio, serves the Rio–São Paulo air shuttle and a few air-taxi firms. Santos Dumont is 20 minutes from the beaches and walking distance from downtown.

Exiting Rio's international airport can be confusing. Taxi drivers will assault you, but to be safe, stick to either the special airport taxis or to buses. Air-conditioned buses park curbside outside customs; for about $3.50 they will take you to the beaches where the majority of Rio's hotels are located. The trip takes about an hour, and drivers follow the beachfront drives, stopping at all hotels. If you are going to a hotel inland from the beach the driver will stop at the nearest corner (but remember, you'll have to handle your own luggage). Buses leave from the airport every half hour from 5:20 AM to 11 PM. Buses to the airport leave from the Hotel Nacional in São Conrado every half hour from 6:30 AM to 11 PM.

Rio de Janeiro

Guanabara Bay

Ilha das Cobras

Aeroporto Santos Dumont

Menezes Cortes Bus Terminal

Gen. Justo

Trav. A. Carlos

Av. Rio Branco

CENTRO

MÉTRO

R. Visc. do Rio Branco

R. Rep. do Paraguai

R. da Glória do Lape

MÉTRO

FLAMENGO

Praia do Flamengo

Av. Infante Dom Henrique

R. Pinheiro Machado

R. dos

Ttúnel Santo Bárbara

Av. Mem de Sá

R. Visc. de Rio Branco

Av. Presidente Vargas

R. Senador Pompeu

R. Santo Cristo

Vidal de Negreiros

Av. Rodrigues Alves

Av. Perimetral

Túnel

Itapiru

TO GALEAD INT'L AIRPORT

Av. Francisco Bicalho

Av. Eng. de Freyssinet

MÉTRO

Av. Brasil

Mons. Manuel São Gomes

Camboata

Figueiro de Melo

R. Matriz e Barros

Rodrigues

Rodrigues

Estrada do Sumaré

São Luís Gonzaga

Museu Nacional

Quinta do Boa Vista

MÉTRO

Maracanã Stadium

Av. Osvaldo Aranha

Av. Bartolomeu Cusmão

São Francisco Xavier

Av. Paulo e Sousa

Conde de Bonfim

Conde de Bonfim

Av. Maracanã

MÉTRO

Visc. de Niterói

Sugarloaf

Av. João
Luís Alves

Av. Portugal

BOTAFOGO

Praia do Diabo

Av. das Nações Unidas

São Clemente

Túnel Rebouças

Av. Princesa Isabel

R. Gustavo Sampaio

COPACABANA

ATLANTIC OCEAN

R. Voluntários da Pátria

R. Real Grandeza

R. Alvaro Ramos

R. General Polidoro

R. Clemente

R. Cupertino Durão

Av. Nossa Senhora de Copacabana

R. Santa Clara

Av. Henrique Dodsworth

R. Figueiredo Magalhães

Raul Pompéia

R. R. Guimarães

R. R. Otaviano

Parque da Catacumba

LAGOA

Estrada das Paineiras

Estrada do Redentor

Corcovado

Tijuca Forest

Av. Epitácio Pessoa

Lagoa Rodrigo de Freitas

R. Jardim Botânico

Av. Borges de Medeiros

Jardim Botânico

R. Jardim Botânico

Jockey Club

R. Mário Ribeiro

Av. Visconde de Albuquerque

LEBLON

Av. Bartolomeu Mitre

Av. Delfim Moreira

Av. Ataulfo de Paiva

R. Visconde de Pirajá

R. Prudente de Morais

Av. Vieira Souto

R. Farme de Amoedo

IPANEMA

Av. Borges de Medeiros

GÁVEA

Av. Pe. Leonel Franca

TO CONRADO,
BARRA DA TIJUCA,
PRAINHA, GRUMARI

N

KEY
••••• Cable Car

0   1 km
0   1 mile

Special airport taxis are operated by two firms, **Transcoopass** (tel. 021/270–4888) and **Cootramo** (tel. 021/270–1442), both of which have booths in the arrival area of the airport. Fares to all parts of Rio are posted at the booths, and you pay in advance in the range of $17–$20. Also trustworthy are the white radio taxis parked in the same area, which charge on the average 20% less than the special airport cabs. Avoid all yellow taxis.

If you are coming to Rio from São Paulo via the air shuttle, you will be landing at Rio's downtown Santos Dumont airport. Here the same transportation options exist as at the international airport. Again, stick to the special buses, the airport taxis, or the radio cabs, and avoid the yellow city cabs.

By Bus Regular, generally good bus service is available to and from Rio. Long-distance buses leave from the Rodoviária Novo Rio station (Avenida Francisco Bicalho 1, São Cristóvão, tel. 021/291–5151), near the port area. Any local bus marked Rodoviária will take you to the bus station. Tickets can be purchased at the depot or, for some destinations, from a travel agent. Buses also leave from the more conveniently located Menezes Cortes terminal (Rua São José 35, Centro, tel. 021/242–5414), near Praça XV downtown.

By Car Before taking the wheel into your own hands be aware that driving in Brazil is only for the brave. Travelers arriving by car from São Paulo and Brasília will enter Avenida Brasil which connects directly with the downtown area's beachside drive, Avenida Infante Dom Henrique, known popularly as the Atêrro. This expressway runs along Rio's Guanabara Bay and passes through the Copacabana Tunnel. On the far side of the tunnel is the beach neighborhood of Copacabana, site of most of Rio's hotels. The beachside street here is called Avenida Atlântica, and continues into the neighborhoods of Ipanema and Leblon along Avenidas Vieira Souto (Ipanema) and Delfim Moreira (Leblon). For travelers arriving at the Galeão Airport, take the Airport Expressway, known in Portuguese as the Linha Vermelha, to the beach area. This expressway takes you through two tunnels and into the Lagoa neighborhood. Exit on Avenida Epitacio Pessoa, the winding street that circles the lagoon. To reach Copacabana, exit again at Avenida Henrique Dodsworth (known popularly as the Corte do Cantagalo). For Ipanema and Leblon, there are several exits beginning with Rua Maria Quitéria. Some distances: Rio–São Paulo, 429 kilometers (266 miles); Rio–Brasília, 1,150 kilometers (714 miles); Rio–Belém, 3,250 kilometers (2,018 miles).

Getting Around Rio

Getting around in Rio can be a colossal headache, especially during the hot summer months. The infamous carioca traffic jam, which can occur at any time of day, leaves exasperated motorists pounding their car horns in the midst of 90° heat. Parking is another major problem. Rio has few parking garages, which results in drivers leaving their vehicles anywhere they will fit, including sidewalks.

By Bus Local buses in Rio are inexpensive and will take you anywhere you want to go, but for tourists there are definite liabilities. The principal one is the threat of being robbed. You enter a Brazilian bus at the rear and exit at the front, paying in the middle when you pass through a turnstile. Thieves strike as tourists reach for their wallets and then race to the back of the bus, jumping out the rear door. Have your fare in your hand when you go to the turnstile, and use small bills (most fares are in the range of 25¢). Also, should you be victimized, never react. Many of these thieves are armed.

Most hotels recommend that their guests avoid city buses, with two exceptions: the safer *frescão* and *jardineira* bus lines. The air-conditioned frescãos provide transportation between the beaches, downtown, and Rio's two airports. The standard fare is $3.50. These buses, which look like highway buses, stop at regular bus stops but also may be flagged down wherever you see them. Also recommended are the jardineira buses, open-sided vehicles that follow the beach drive from Copacabana to São Conrado, and also take passengers to the Barra da Tijuca neighborhood. Fares are about 35¢, and white posts along the street mark jardineira bus stops. These buses, which look like old-fashioned streetcars, were introduced specifically for tourists and have become a major hit. They offer excellent views of the scenery and drive slowly along the beach avenue, a welcome relief to anyone who has ridden the regular city buses, whose drivers are considered the city's most reckless.

By Subway Rio's subway system, called the Mêtro, operates Monday through Saturday 6 AM to 11 PM. Unfortunately, it is not yet finished. The part that is completed, though, offers the fastest and most comfortable transportation in the city. In the stations and in each car are maps showing the subway stops.

A single Mêtro ticket costs 37¢, a double costs 66¢. Combination Mêtro-bus tickets allow you to ride special buses to and from the Botafogo station: The M-21 runs to Leblon via Jardim Botânico and Jóquei, while the M-22 goes to Leblon by way of Túnel Velho, Copacabana, and Ipanema.

By Taxi Taxis are plentiful in Rio and are the most convenient mode of transportation available to tourists. Dealing with cabdrivers, however, is not always a pleasant experience. Few of them speak English, and most will attempt to increase the fare for tourists. Because of Brazil's high inflation, fares change constantly and it is impossible to keep meters adjusted. Taxis are required to post a chart noting the latest fare adjustments on the inside of the left rear window. The driver may try to tell you that the chart is out of date. Don't believe it. Also, beware of the meter itself. When the driver resets the meter he raises a flag, which will have either the number one or two on it (for digital meters the numbers one and two appear in red). Number two means 20% more but can only be used in certain circumstances: between 10 PM and 6 AM, on Sundays and holidays, during the month of December, in the neighborhoods of São Conrado and Barra da Tijuca, or when climbing steep hills. In most cases, it should be on number one. Cabbies also like to tell tourists that the number two means double the fare. Not true.

To avoid hassle, ask your hotel to call a radio cab or use one of the taxis that routinely serve hotel guests. Radio cabs charge 30% more but are honest, reliable, and usually air-conditioned. Other cabs working with the hotels will also charge more, normally a fixed fee explained before you leave.

By Car Driving in Rio is not recommended. The carioca flair for driving is usually enough to leave most tourists shaking in their shoes. In addition, there are the traffic jams and the endless confusion of the city's streets, all of which have strange-sounding Portuguese names, although not all of them have street signs. If you wish to have an automobile without the headache of having to drive it, hire a car and driver. The firm **Transcoopass** (tel. 021/270–4888) will supply both for $58 for three hours.

Orientation Tours

Bus Tours   **Gray Line** (Rio Sheraton Hotel, Avenida Niemeyer 121, Vidigal, tel. 021/274–7146) excels in transportation and in tour guides. Their guides are superb and will speak your language. The tours available include the following: Sugarloaf and the City (4 hours, $20); Corcovado and the Tijuca Forest (4 hours, $20); Rio by Night (6 hours, $50); Helicopter Ride (30 minutes, $75); Petrópolis (6 hours, $20).

Special-Interest   Peter O'Neill, a respected travel agent and longtime member
Tours   of Rio's foreign community, organizes tailor-made tours for groups. He specializes in trips for nature lovers, and has arranged visits to Rio's Tijuca Forest, the Amazon, the mineral spas in Minas Gerais, and the historical towns of Paratí and Salvador. Call **Marlin Tours** (tel. 021/255–4433).

Upon request, Carlos Roquette, a Brazilian history professor, conducts, in English and French, historical tours of Rio's neighborhoods for $20 (tel. 021/237–3031).

Boat Tours   Boat tours are available to nearby islands. The tropical-islands tours depart from the fishing village of Itacuruçá, about 90 minutes by car from Rio. Brazilian schooners, *saveiros,* are used, and the day-long trips include lunch and time for swimming at some of the beautiful deserted beaches on the 36 islands of Sepetiba Bay. The trips are offered by Rio-based operators; the two best are run by **Itacuruçá Turismo** (tel. 021/259–2599) and **Gray Line** (tel. 021/274–7146). The cost is about $36 and includes ground transportation to Itacuruçá.

Personal Guides   Personal English-speaking guides are not common in Rio. **Marlin Tours** (tel. 021/255–4433), which caters to English-speaking tourists, and **Rio Custom Tours** (tel. 021/274–3217) are the best options.

Security

Better safe than sorry should be your motto while in Rio. Although not every tourist in Rio is a crime victim, petty theft is an always-present threat, so take precautions. If you are victimized, the police emergency number is 190. Multilingual operators should be on duty.

Most crimes involving tourists occur in public areas where there are large numbers of people, particularly on beaches, crowded sidewalks, and city buses. Pickpockets, usually children, work in groups. One will distract their victim while another grabs a wallet, bag, or camera. Be particularly wary of children who suddenly thrust themselves in front of you and ask for money or offer to shine your shoes. Another member of the gang may strike from behind, grab your valuables and disappear into the crowd. Do not pursue or attempt to stop one of these robbers—many of them are armed and can be dangerous. Whenever you can, leave valuables in your hotel room or safe. Don't be ostentatious in your dress, and don't wear expensive jewelry or watches. Keep cameras out of sight in bags.

Don't walk alone at night on the beach. Be aware of Rio's hillside shantytowns, which in some cases are close to hotels and tourist attractions; don't walk in front of them. If at all possible don't take city buses except for the air-conditioned frescão buses or the open-sided jardineiras. In particular avoid the Santa Teresa streetcar, and the 553 bus around the Inter-Continental and Nacional hotels. Also, don't get involved with drugs. Penalties in Brazil for possession of drugs are severe, and dealers are the worst of the worst.

Exploring Rio

Nearly all of Rio's attractions are found in the affluent Zona Sul, the neighborhoods located on or near the beach. It is here that hotels, restaurants, shops, and nightlife are concentrated.

During the day, Rio life focuses on the beaches, the most active of which remains Copacabana. To sense the carioca spirit, spend a day on Copacabana Beach and the sidewalk cafés that populate its beachfront drive, Avenida Atlântica. Ipanema beach life is more restrained and cliquish, and thus harder for outsiders to penetrate; also, there are only three beachside bars in the entire length of Ipanema and its western extension, Leblon. The more distant southern beaches, beginning with São Conrado and extending past the Barra to Grumari, are rich in natural beauty and increasingly isolated.

Although Rio is more than 400 years old, it is in every respect a modern city. Most of the city's historic structures have fallen victim to the wrecking ball, leaving only a handful that can be visited by tourists. What's left is found in and around the downtown area in churches and other buildings scattered about the city center. Organized tours, both walking and in sightseeing buses, are highly recommended. The scattered nature of these sites, plus the sometimes undesirable nature of their surroundings, makes individual sightseeing problematic at best.

Admission to most of Rio's museums, churches, and other sites is free. If there is a fee, it is usually 5¢ or 10¢ or less.

Historical Rio If you are not on an organized tour, the best approach to visiting the historical sites is to take the subway. A half block from the Catete station is the **Catete Palace,** the former official residence of Brazil's presidents and today the **Museu da República** (Museum of the Republic) (Rua do Catete 153, tel. 021/225–4302). This elegant granite-and-marble 19th-century building became the presidential residence after the 1889 military coup that overthrew the monarchy and installed the Republic of Brazil. All of Brazil's presidents lived in the palace until 1954, when then-president Getúlio Vargas committed suicide in his palace bedroom. Today its three floors house presidential memorabilia, including period furniture and paintings, from the proclamation of the Republic in 1889 to the end of Brazil's latest military regime in 1985. One subway stop north of Catete is the Glória station and the nearby **Nossa Senhora da Glória do Outeiro** church (Praça da Glória 135, tel. 021/225–2869). This elegant 1720 church, with its bell tower and carved ceiling, is a prime example of colonial Brazilian Baroque architecture. It stands sentinel-like atop a small hill, with an unobstructed view

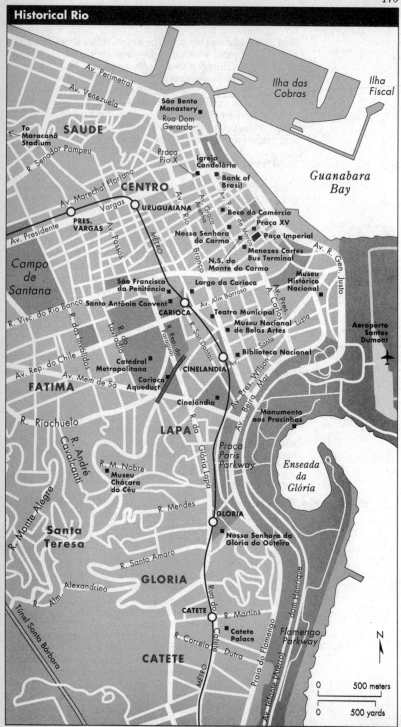

Historical Rio

Ilha das Cobras

Ilha Fiscal

Guanabara Bay

São Bento Monastery
Rua Dom Gerardo

To Maracanã Stadium

SAUDE

R. Senador Pompeu

Av. Perimetral

Av. Venezuela

Praça Pio X

Igreja Candelária

Bank of Brasil

CENTRO

Av. Marechal Floriano

URUGUAIANA

Vargas

Av. Presidente

PRES. VARGAS

Av. Passos

Beco do Comércio

Praça XV

Nossa Senhora do Carmo

Paço Imperial

Menezes Cortes Bus Terminal

N.S. do Monte do Carmo

Museu Histórico Nacional

Av. R. Gen. Justo

Campo de Santana

R. Visc. do Rio Banco

R. dos Invalidos

R. do Lavradio

R. Rep. do Chile

São Francisco da Penitência

Santo Antônio Convent

CARIOCA

Largo da Carioca

Av. Alm Barroso

Teatro Municipal

Museu Nacional de Belas Artes

Biblioteca Nacional

Aeroporto Santos Dumont

Catedral Metropolitana

Carioca Aqueduct

Av. Mem de Sá

CINELANDIA

Cinelândia

FATIMA

R. Riachuelo

LAPA

Monumento aos Pracinhas

R. André Cavalcanti

R. M. Nobre

Museu Chácara do Céu

Praça Paris Parkway

Enseada da Glória

R. Monte-Alegre

R. Mendes

GLORIA

Nossa Senhora da Glória do Outeiro

Santa Teresa

R. Santo Amaro

GLORIA

Alexandrino

Túnel Santa Bárbara

CATETE

R. Martins

Catete Palace

R. Correia Dutra

CATETE

Flamengo Parkway

N

0 500 meters

0 500 yards

of the downtown area. Each year on August 15, the church's saint's day, Glória comes into her full glory, shining in the night sky with a crown of white lights.

Directly across the freeway from the Glória church is the **Glória Marina,** and at the northern edge of the marina is the imposing **Monumento aos Pracinhas** (Monument to the Brazilian Dead of World War II), two soaring columns flanking the tomb of an unknown soldier. A small museum (open 10–6) relates the country's war effort.

Cinelândia is a downtown landmark marked by a conglomeration of movie theaters and a large open space that has become Rio's version of London's Hyde Park. Political debates and speeches are continuous here with rival groups sometimes coming to blows. On the outer edge of Cinelândia, is the **Teatro Municipal** (Municipal Theater, Praça Floriano 210, tel. 021/210–2463), a scaled-down version of the Paris Opera House. The theater is located at the beginning of **Avenida Rio Branco,** the main thoroughfare of downtown. Modeled after the Champs-Elysées, Rio Branco was constructed in 1905 with 115 classical buildings. Time and progress, however, have eliminated all but 10 of those original structures, the most impressive of which is the theater and the downstairs **Café do Teatro,** one of the city's most unusual restaurants (*see* Dining, *below*). Two blocks south of the theater is the Victorian **Biblioteca Nacional** (National Library, Av. Rio Branco 219, tel. 021/220–3040).

Next to the library is the French neoclassical **Museu Nacional de Belas Artes** (Museum of Fine Arts). The museum houses works by Brazil's leading 19th- and 20th-century artists, including canvases by the country's best-known modernist, Cândido Portinari. *Av. Rio Branco 199, tel. 021/240–0160. Admission free. Closed Mon.*

Five blocks down Avenida Rio Branco and one block west is the **Largo da Carioca,** a large public square. Atop a low hill overlooking the Largo is the **Santo Antônio Convent** (Largo da Carioca, tel. 021/262–0129). The convent was completed in 1780, but parts of its construction date from 1608, making it the oldest surviving structure in Rio. Its Baroque interior contains priceless colonial art, including wood carvings and wall paintings. The convent is currently undergoing restoration and is often closed to the public. The next-door **São Francisco da Penitência** church (Largo da Carioca 5, tel. 021/262–0197; closed for renovations) dates from 1739 and is famed for its wood sculptures and the rich gold leaf that covers its interior.

Continuing down Avenida República do Chile are two other Rio landmarks, the **Catedral Metropolitana** (Av. Rep. do Chile 245, tel. 021/240–2869) and the city's 18th-century aqueduct. The cathedral resembles an American space capsule from the early 1960s, the period when the building was designed and construction began on it. The **Carioca Aqueduct** (known to Brazilians as the **Arcos da Lapa**), is an imposing structure of 36 colossal stone arches built in 1723 to carry water from the hillside neighborhood of Santa Teresa to the downtown area. In 1896 the city transportation company took over the then-abandoned aqueduct and converted it to a viaduct, laying trolley tracks across its length. Since then, Rio's distinctive trolley cars (called *bondes* because they were financed by foreign bonds) have carried passengers between Santa Teresa and downtown. Rio's soaring crime rate has made this particular diversion virtually off-limits for tourists. The open-sided, slow-moving cars invite purse snatchers; take a taxi to Santa Teresa.

Santa Teresa, with its cobblestone streets, is Rio's most delightfully eccentric neighborhood. Gabled Victorian mansions are intermingled with alpine chalets and more prosaic dwellings, often hanging at unbelievable angles from the flower-encrusted hillside. Santa Teresa's special flavor has attracted artists and intellectuals to its eclectic slopes. Their hangout is the **Bar do Arnaudo** (Rua Almirante Alexandrino 316-B, tel. 021/252–7246), a nondescript bar and restaurant whose main appeal is as a neighborhood listening post.

One of Santa Teresa's most popular attractions is the **Museu Chácara do Céu,** an outstanding modern-art collection left by one of Rio's greatest patrons of the arts, Raymundo de Castro Maya. Included are originals by such 20th-century masters as Picasso, Braque, Dalí, Degas, Matisse, Modigliani, and Monet. It also contains works by Brazil's leading modernists, such as Portinari, Volpi, and Di Cavalcanti. The grounds of the museum offer Santa Teresa's finest views of the bay and downtown with the aqueduct in the foreground. *Rua Murtinho Nobre 345, tel. 021/224–8981. Admission free. Closed Mon.*

At the beginning of Avenida Presidente Vargas, closest to the bay, stands the solid form of the **Igreja Candelária** (Candelária church). The classic symmetry of Candelária's white dome and bell towers casts an unexpected air of sanity over the chaos of downtown traffic. Construction on the church began in 1775, and while it was formally dedicated by the emperor in 1811, work on the dome was not completed until 1877. *Praça Pio X, tel. 021/233–2324. Admission free.*

Facing the entrance of Candelária is the former headquarters of the **Bank of Brazil** (Rua Primeiro de Março 66, tel. 021/216–0237), a six-story building constructed in 1888, which has been renovated and converted into a cultural center where art exhibits are held.

Five blocks north along the bay is the **São Bento Monastery.** Its ornate interior with gold-leaf-covered wood carvings is extraordinarily rich and beautiful, and getting to it is half the fun. The monastery is located on a slight elevation that can only be reached by an elevator from a store at Rua Dom Gerardo No. 40. One flight up is the monastery and grounds. The view of Guanabara Bay from here is one of the most peaceful in Rio. *Rua Dom Gerardo 68, tel. 021/291–7122. Admission free.*

South of Candelária is **Praça XV,** the site of a number of historical buildings, including the former imperial palace. This square, known during colonial days as Largo do Paço, was the center of the imperial government that ruled Brazil for most of the 19th century. Its modern name is from the date of the declaration of the Republic of Brazil, November 15, 1889.

The dominating structure in the square is the **Paço Imperial,** one of Rio's few restored colonial buildings. This two-story structure is notable for its thick stone walls and entranceway, and courtyard paved with huge stone slabs. The paço was built in 1743, and for the next 60 years it was the headquarters for Brazil's viceroys, appointed by the Portuguese court in Lisbon.

When King João VI arrived, he converted it into his royal palace. With Brazil's declaration of independence and the founding of the Empire of Brazil, the paço became the imperial palace and was home to emperors Pedro I and II. After the monarchy was overthrown, the palace became Rio's central post office. Restoration work in the 1980s transformed it into a cultural center and concert hall. *Praça XV 48, tel. 021/232–8333. Admission free. Closed Mon.*

Facing Praça XV across Avenida Primeiro de Março are two 18th-century churches. The larger of the two, **Nossa Senhora do Carmo** (tel. 021/242–7766), was built in 1761 to serve as Rio's first metropolitan cathedral. Both of Brazil's emperors were crowned here. Next door is the smaller **Nossa Senhora do Monte do Carmo** (tel. 021/242–4828), circa 1770, noted for its Baroque facade.

Behind Avenida Primeiro de Março is a network of narrow streets and alleys highlighted by the **Beco do Comércio,** a pedestrian street flanked by restored 18th-century buildings and homes, now converted to offices. The best known is the **Telles de Menezes** building (Praça XV 34) whose famous arch, the **Arco dos Telles,** links this fascinating street with Praça XV. A popular stop here for lunch or drinks is the **English Bar** (Beco do Comércio 11, tel. 021/224–2539), where you may partake of Old World cuisine in a New World setting.

A few blocks south of Praça XV is the **Museu Histórico Nacional** (National History Museum), an intriguing collection of colonial buildings. The museum's archive includes rare documents and colonial artifacts. Much of this, however, is shut away in sections undergoing "renovations," a euphemism for a dearth of funding to prepare and maintain exhibits. In 1988 the museum unveiled the first of what is planned to be a series of modular showcases dividing Brazil's history into distinct periods. The first section, called "Brazil as a Colony," is now on permanent display. *Praça Marechal Ancora, tel. 021/220–5829. Admission free. Closed Mon.*

The Bay and Sugarloaf The vast 147-square-mile **Guanabara Bay** is where the first Portuguese explorers anchored their ships in 1500. Guanabara is an Indian name meaning "arm of the sea," and it was along the banks of this bay that the city of Rio de Janeiro took shape and grew. Virtually the only remaining evidence of the bay's historical importance are two small forts that guard its narrow entrance, Santa Cruz (17th century) and the São João (19th century).

Once the playground of Rio's wealthy, the bay-side beaches are no longer fit for bathing, and tourists should avoid any contact with them.

The principal attraction of the bay is the view it offers of Rio, best seen on day cruises. Cruises also provide a cool-off from the oppressive summer heat of the city. Boat trips are available at both ends of the fare scale. Inexpensive ferries and only slightly more expensive hydrofoils toil and scoot across the bay at regular intervals. If you are traveling in a group, you may be interested in renting a *saveiro* (schooner) with crew for a day's outing on the bay. For information on boat rentals call the **Glória Marina** (tel. 021/205–6447 or 021/285–2247).

There are 84 islands in the bay, the largest of which is **Paqueta,** once the site of holiday homes for Rio's upper class. Today Paqueta's main attraction is its slow pace of life. Cars are banned from the island, so transport is by bicycle or horse-drawn buggy (a buggy trip around the island costs $3). You can make the trip in 90 minutes by ferry or in 15 minutes by hydrofoil. Both depart from the **Estação dos Barcos** at Praça XV, downtown. *Ferries (tel. 021/231–0396) run daily 5:30 AM–11 PM. Tickets: $1.40 each way. Hydrofoils (tel. 021/231–0339) operate weekdays 10–4, weekends 8–5. Tickets: $5 each way.*

For cariocas, the only reason to visit **Niterói** across the bay is to admire the view of Rio. The best views are from Niterói's bayside beaches, beginning with **Icarai** and continuing on to **Jurujuba.** Beyond Jurujuba on the coastal highway is the **Santa Cruz Fort** (tel. 021/711–0166 or 021/711–0462), the time-honored guardian of the entrance to Guanabara Bay. In its three centuries, the well-preserved fort has also served as a military prison. Its most famous prisoner was 19th-century Italian revolutionary Giuseppe Garibaldi, who learned the art of guerrilla warfare while fighting with a separatist movement in the south of Brazil. The galleries, dungeons, and courtyards of this sprawling fort are fascinating to explore, but access is difficult since the fort is still controlled by the military. Organized sightseeing tours are the best option.

With the cable car ride to the top and the unsurpassed views on all sides, the trip to **Sugarloaf** is not to be missed. This soaring 1,300-foot granite block standing at the mouth of Guanabara Bay was originally called *pau-nd-acugua* by the Indians, meaning "high, pointed peak." To the Portuguese the Indian phrase was similar to their *pão de açucar,* or "sugarloaf," and the rock's shape reminded them of the mold used to refine sugar into the conical form known as a sugarloaf. Italian-made bubble cars holding 75 passengers each move up the mountain in two stages, the first stopping at the **Morro da Urca,** a smaller mountain (705 feet high) in front of Sugarloaf, and the second continuing on to the summit, each stage taking three minutes.

The viewpoints on Urca Mountain and Sugarloaf offer unobstructed vistas of most of the city below. Sunsets are awe inspiring, and at night the lights below are an unforgettable sight. Urca Mountain is also home to an international restaurant called **Sugarloaf** (tel. 021/541–3737).

During high season, from January to March, long lines often form for the cable car trip. For the remainder of the year, the wait is seldom more than 30 minutes. *Cable cars: Praia Vermelho. Tickets: about $5. Runs 8 AM–10 PM daily.*

Close to Sugarloaf in the Botafogo neighborhood is the **Casa Rui Barbosa,** the former home, now turned museum, of one of Brazil's most important 19th-century statesmen and politicians. This pink mansion houses memorabilia of Barbosa's life, including an extensive library, which is often consulted by scholars from Brazil and abroad. *Rua São Clemente 134, tel. 021/286–1297. Admission charged. Closed Mon.*

Corcovado and the Tijuca Forest An eternal argument among Brazilians and tourists is which view is better, that from Sugarloaf or that from its "rival," **Corcovado.** Corcovado Mountain has two advantages: at 2,300 feet it is nearly twice as high as Sugarloaf and offers an excellent view of Sugarloaf itself. Whichever you favor, don't leave Rio without making the trip up to the top of Corcovado, where the powerful image of Christ with arms outstretched crowns the summit.

The sheer 1,000-foot granite face of Corcovado (the name means "hunchback" in Portuguese and refers to the mountain's shape) has always been a difficult undertaking for climbers. A railroad was constructed in 1885, later joined by a road. It was not until 1921, the centennial of Brazil's independence from Portugal, that someone had the idea of placing a statue on top. The project was handed over to a team of French artisans headed by sculptor Paul Landowski. The idea was to build a statue of Christ with his arms apart as if he were embracing the city. It took 10 years, but finally on October 12, 1931, the **Cristo Redentor** (Christ the Redeemer) statue was inaugurated. The figure stands 100 feet tall atop a 20-foot pedestal and weighs 700 tons. A 1981 cleanup of the statue and the installation of a powerful lighting system have enhanced the forceful presence of this unique image, visible night and day from most of the city's neighborhoods.

There are two ways of reaching the top of Corcovado, either by the recently renovated cogwheel train or by the winding road that climbs the mountain. The train is the more interesting of the two, providing a close look at the thick mountain vegetation during the steep, 2.3-mile ascent, lasting around 20 minutes. The train is comfortable and the view spectacular, but as at all tourist attractions, keep your eyes on your valuables when entering and leaving the cars. If you wish to go up by the road, you will need either to rent a car, hire a taxi, or go with a sightseeing tour. Of these, a tour is the safest choice, giving you the best price (around $20), an English-speaking guide, plus the assurance that you won't be ripped off.

Should you go by train, it is likely that there will be at least a 30-minute wait at the **Cosme Velho train station.** *Train station: Rua Cosme Velho 513, tel. 021/285–2533. Trains leave every 30 min. daily 8:30–6. Late-afternoon trains are the most popular; on weekends be prepared for a long wait. Nominal fee.*

Whether you arrive by train, bus, or car, there is a formidable climb up long and steep staircases to reach the summit, where the statue and viewpoints are located (there are no elevators or ramps for wheelchairs). Once you have reached the top, all of Rio stretches out before you. The best time to visit, lines permitting, is the late afternoon shortly before sunset.

The Beach Neighborhoods Rio is home to 23 beaches, an almost continuous 45-mile stretch of white sand. You can't fit them all into one day, but try to leave time to explore the city's different beaches and their neighborhoods during your visit. (*See also* Beaches).

Flamengo and **Botafogo.** These two bay-side beaches were once the city's prime location for bathing. Pollution and population shifts have changed that, and today the two are no longer recommended for sunbathing or strolling.

During the years Rio served as Brazil's capital, Botafogo was the site of Rio's glittering embassy row. The embassies are gone now, transferred to Brasília, but the mansions that housed them remain scattered along Botafogo's tree-lined streets. The neighborhood also contains many of Rio's better small restaurants. Try the boisterous **Café Pacifico** (Rua Visconde de Silva

14, tel. 021/246–5637), Rio's only Mexican restaurant. Among the neighborhood's more interesting streets, lined with the mansions built in Botafogo's heyday, are **Mariana, Sorocaba, Matriz,** and **Visconde de Silva.**

Copacabana. Maddening traffic, unbearable noise, packed apartment blocks, and one of the world's most famous beaches—this is Copacabana, a Manhattan with bikinis. The privileged live on beachfront **Avenida Atlântica,** famed for its wide mosaic sidewalks, hotels, bars, and cafés. A walk along the classic 2-mile crescent curve of the beach is a must. On Copacabana you see the essence of Rio beach life, a cradle-to-grave lifestyle that begins with toddlers accompanying their parents to the water and ends with graying seniors walking hand in hand along the beach sidewalk. Two blocks from the beach and running parallel to it is **Avenida Nossa Senhora de Copacabana,** the neighborhood's main commercial street, whose sidewalks are always crowded with the colorful characters that give Copacabana its special flavor.

Stop in for a drink at one of Avenida Atlântica's outdoor cafés. The draft beer is cold and cheap, the view of Copacabana beach life is unmatched. Try **Lucas** (Av. Atlântica 3744, tel. 021/247–1606); **Rio-Jerez** (Av. Atlântica 3806, tel. 021/267–5644); or **Terraço Atlântico** (Av. Atlântica 3431, tel. 021/521–1296).

Ipanema. Today, Ipanema, nearby **Leblon,** and the blocks surrounding the nearby **Rodrigo de Freitas Lagoon** comprise Rio's money belt. For a close-up look at Rio's most posh apartment buildings, stroll down beachfront **Avenida Vieira Souto** and its extension **Delfim Moreira,** or take a drive around the lagoon on **Avenida Epitácio Pessoa.** The tree-lined streets between Ipanema Beach and the lagoon are among the most peaceful and attractive of the city. For sophistication, stroll down the **Rua Garcia D'Avila,** where most of Ipanema's boutiques are clustered. Other "in" addresses of Rio's trendiest neighborhoods are **Praça da Paz, Rua Vinicius de Morais, Farme de Amoedo,** and **Anibal Mendonça.**

On the beachfront, the lone watering hole in Leblon is the **Caneco 70** (Av. Delfim Moreira 1026, tel. 021/294–1180), a good stop for a beer or cooling orange juice. The upstairs tables have the best view of the beach action, while the downstairs tables have the closest view of Rio's promenading beautiful people.

Have you ever wondered if there really *was* a Girl from Ipanema? The song was inspired by schoolgirl Heloisa Pinheiro, who caught the fancy of songwriter Tom Jobim and his pal lyricist Vinicius de Morais as she walked home from school past the two bohemians sitting in their favorite bar. The two then penned one of the century's top pop classics. That was in 1962, and today the bar has been renamed **Vinicius** and is one of Ipanema's most "in" addresses for drinks and conversation. *Rua Vinicius de Morais 49-A, tel. 021/267–8787.*

São Conrado and the Southern Beaches. For a wonderful outing, take a cab from Ipanema to the fishing village of **Pedra da Guaratiba,** 45 minutes west. The drive starts out by climbing **Avenida Niemeyer** at the end of Ipanema where the imposing **Dois Irmãos Mountain** stands. The road hugs the rugged cliffs with spectacular sea views on the left before snaking down to sea level again in São Conrado, a natural amphitheater surrounded by forested mountains and the ocean.

São Conrado is a mostly residential neighborhood divided, starkly, between high- and low-income families. Wealthy cariocas live on the valley floor in plush condominiums, while the high ground has been taken over by Rio's largest shanty-town, **Rocinha,** which "houses" over 80,000 people. Called *favelas*, these hillside slums are present throughout the South Zone of Rio and are the result of the city's chronic housing problem coupled with the unwillingness of many of the city's poor to live in distant working-class neighborhoods. Most of these makeshift dwellings have electricity, and in some cases there is running water, but there is no sewage system and the slums are subject to flooding and landslides when the summer rains come. The favelas are crime centers, and tourists should consider them off-limits, though you can drive by and get an idea of how deplorable life in a shantytown is.

São Conrado is also home to more pleasant sights. Hang gliders float overhead preparing to land on the beach, while in the middle of the small valley is the exclusive Gávea Golf and Country Club. The far end of São Conrado is marked by the towering presence of **Gávea Mountain,** a huge flat-topped granite block. Next to it is **Pedra Bonita,** the mountain from which the gliders depart.

Continuing along the coast, the road becomes an elevated viaduct hanging half over the water, with views of the ocean on the left and sheer mountain cliffs on the right, where sumptuous homes hang at precarious angles. Emerging from a tunnel you enter **Barra da Tijuca,** Rio's suburbia. Condominium complexes are springing up along the beach, while inland the city's largest shopping centers and supermarkets have made the Barra their home. Drive along the beachfront avenue, **Sernambetiba.** At the end is a massive rock that marks the **Recreio dos Bandeirantes,** a small cove popular for bathing.

From here the road again climbs, following the undulating coastline to the small surfers' beach **Prainha,** and beyond that to the crown jewel of Rio's beaches, **Grumari.** From Grumari, a potholed road climbs almost straight up through the thick forest, finally emerging at the top of a hill overlooking the vast **Guaratiba flatlands.** Down the hill is the fishing village of **Pedra da Guaratiba,** site of some of Rio's finest, albeit rustic, seafood restaurants, including **Quatro Sete Meia** (*see* Dining, *below*).

Parks and Gardens

The **Flamengo Parkway,** known popularly as the **Atêrro,** or "Landfill," flanks the bay beginning in the Flamengo Beach neighborhood and ending in Glória. It was built through landfill and lovingly designed by Brazil's master landscape architect Roberto Burle Marx. Long paths used for jogging, walking, and bicycling wind through the park, and there are also public tennis and basketball courts and playgrounds for children. On weekends the freeway that runs alongside the park is closed to traffic, and the entire area becomes one enormous public park.

Quinta da Boa Vista is home to Rio's zoo and the **Museu Nacional** (National Museum), Brazil's natural history museum. The museum, a former imperial palace dating from 1803, features exhibits on Brazil's past and its flora, fauna, and minerals. The landscaped parks, pools, and marble statues on the grounds are entrancing. *Tel. 021/264–8262. Admission free.*

Next door, the **Jardim Zoológico** presents animals from Brazil's wilds in their natural habitats. *Tel. 021/254–2024. Admission charged. Closed Mon.*

Surrounding Corcovado Mountain is a dense, beautiful tropical forest called the **Tijuca Forest.** The forest was once part of a private estate belonging to a Brazilian nobleman and is studded with exotic trees, thick jungle vines, and a delightful waterfall, the **Cascatinha de Taunay.** About 200 yards beyond the waterfall is the small but distinctive **Mayrink Chapel,** with an altar painting by Brazil's most famous 20th-century artist, Cândido Portinari. Many of Rio's most breathtaking viewpoints are located along the 60 miles of narrow, winding roads that pass through this national park. The most famous are the **Dona Marta Viewpoint,** located on the way up Corcovado; the **Emperor's Table,** supposedly the site where Brazil's last emperor, Pedro II, brought his court for picnic lunches; and the **Chinese View,** farther down the road.

The **Jardim Botânico** (Botanical Garden) is one of Rio's most striking natural attractions. The 340-acre garden contains more than 5,000 species of tropical and subtropical plants and trees, including 900 varieties of palm tree. The garden was created by Portuguese King João VI in 1808, during his exile in Brazil. In 1842 the garden gained its most impressive adornment, the **Avenue of the Royal Palms,** an 800-yard-long double row of 134 soaring royal palms that graces the edge of the garden next to **Rua Jardim Botânico.** The garden makes for a marvelous afternoon stroll—especially on a hot day, when the temperature here is usually a good 10° cooler than it is on the street. *Rua Jardim Botânico 1008, tel. 021/294–6012. Admission free.*

The pleasant, statue-filled **Parque da Catacumba** is located off the western edge of Avenida Epitácio Pessoa, the road that circles the Rodrigo de Freitas Lagoon. The lagoon is also surrounded by a jogging path and has several tennis courts.

What to See and Do with Children

Hotels with pools are usually the best choice if you are traveling with children. The more activities the better, and Rio's two resort hotels, the **Sheraton Rio Hotel & Towers** and the **Inter-Continental Rio** (*see* Lodging, *below*), are popular with families because of their multiple pools, sports facilities, and varied dining and entertainment options. In addition, the Sheraton is the only hotel in Rio with a playground.

A visit to the **Barra Shopping** center (*see* Shopping, *below*) is a guaranteed hit with youngsters. The mall has a mini–amusement park with rides and all the extras, including cotton candy (*algodão doce* in Portuguese). The mall also has Rio's only bowling alley and an indoor ice-skating rink.

Boat trips in the bay (*see* The Bay and Sugarloaf, *above*) offer an exciting and time-consuming distraction. The horse-and-buggy trip around the island of **Paqueta** is particularly recommended.

During **Carnival,** many private clubs hold children's balls in the afternoon. These are delightfully tame and innocent, virtually the only balls where the primary emphasis is on wearing costumes, often elaborate ones. Ask at your hotel for help in gaining admittance to one of these balls.

Rio has a large and complete amusement park, the **Tivoli Park,** located on the banks of the lagoon. There you'll find every stomach-churning ride imaginable. *Lagoa Rodrigo de Freitas, tel. 021/274–1846. Admission charged. Closed Mon.–Wed.*

Rio's prime viewpoints, **Sugarloaf** and **Corcovado,** are fascinating for all ages. On occasion, the amphitheater atop Sugarloaf has special plays or musical shows for children, although in Portuguese. Call 021/541–3737 for information.

Rio's **zoo** (tel. 021/254–2024) is excellent entertainment for kids of all ages.

Shopping

Rio de Janeiro is one of South America's premier shopping cities. Shoppers can stroll down city streets lined with fashionable boutiques, wander through modern, air-conditioned malls, or barter with the vendors at street markets and fairs.

Shopping Districts **Ipanema** is the most fashionable shopping district in Rio, with a seemingly endless array of exclusive boutiques. Cool summer clothing in natural fibers, appropriate for the climate, is the top item here.

Many of Ipanema's shops are concentrated in arcades, the majority of which are located along Rua Visconde de Pirajá. Try **Forum de Ipanema** at number 351 near the Praça da Paz square; **Quartier de Ipanema** at number 414; the upscale **Galeria 444** at number 444; and **Vitrine de Ipanema** at number 580.

Although **Copacabana** has lost some of its former glamour, attractive shops still line Avenida Nossa Senhora de Copacabana and the side streets. Here you'll find a number of souvenir shops, bookstores, and branches of some of Rio's better stores, although for top-of-the-market jewelers, head for Avenida Atlântica.

Known in Rio as the **Hippie Fair,** the colorful handicraft street fair held every Sunday from 9 AM to 6 PM on Ipanema's Praça General Osório is popular among foreign visitors. Paintings and wood carvings, leather bags, sandals and clothing, batik fashions, jewelry, hand-printed T-shirts, rag dolls, knickknacks, and even furniture are on sale. Finely crafted items are mixed in with basic junk. One noisy, popular booth sells samba percussion instruments.

In the evenings along the median of **Avenida Atlântica,** artisans spread out their wares. Here you will find paintings, carvings, handicrafts, sequined dresses, and hammocks from the northeast. On Saturday there is an **open-air antiques fair** during daylight hours on **Praça Marechal Ancora,** downtown near **Praça XV.** Here you can purchase china and silver sets, old watches, Oriental rugs, chandeliers, rare books, all types of paintings and art objects, and even old records. The fair moves out to the **Casa Shopping Center** in Barra da Tijuca on Sunday.

The **Feira Nordestino (Northeastern Fair),** held every Sunday morning at the Campo de São Cristóvão from 6 AM to 1 PM, is a social event for northeasterners living in Rio, who gather to hear their own distinctive music, eat regional foods, and buy tools and cheap clothing. The crowded, noisy market offers a glimpse of a side of Brazil not often seen by tourists.

Department Stores **Mesbla,** Rio's largest department-store chain, focuses on mostly casual fashions for men, women, and children. But it also has a wide selection of toys, records, cosmetics, musical instruments, and sporting goods. *Main store: Rua do Passeio 42/56, Downtown, tel. 021/297–7720. Branches: Rio Sul and Barra Shopping malls.*

Due to its size, **C&A** is classified as a department store, but it sells only clothing—for men, women, and children, including accessories, shoes, and a sporting line. *Av. Nossa Senhora de Copacabana 749, Copacabana, tel. 021/325–0179. Branches: Rio Sul and Barra Shopping malls.*

Specialty Stores For collectors as well as tourists looking for distinctive gifts,
Art Brazilian art has great appeal. The following galleries can be counted on to contain a worthwhile, representative sampling.

Bonino is the most traditional, best known, and most visited of Rio's art galleries. It has been around for some 30 years and is very active, with a high turnover of shows. *Rua Barata Ribeiro 578, Copacabana, tel. 021/235–7831.*

Contorno is a more eclectic gallery, but the art it displays is certainly Brazilian. *Shopping Center da Gávea, Rua Marquês de São Vicente 52, Gávea, tel. 021/274–3832.*

Galeria de Arte Jean-Jacques specializes in paintings by Brazilian primitive artists. *Rua Figueiredo Magalhães 219, Sobreloja 201, within walking distance of the Sugarloaf cable car station, tel. 021/236–1397.*

The **Rio Design Center** contains several galleries, including **Borghese, Beco da Arte, Montesanti, Museum,** and **Way.** *Av. Ataulfo de Paiva 270, Leblon, tel. 021/274–7893.*

Women's Clothing **Krishna** (Rio Sul, tel. 021/542–2443) specializes in classic, feminine dresses and separates, many in linen and silk. Also featuring classics, **Aspargus** (Rua Carlos Goes 234, Leblon, tel. 021/239–9694; and Rua Maria Quitéria 59B, Ipanema, tel. 021/287–3994) is known for its knit fashions. **Spy & Great** (Barra Shopping, tel.021/325–5294) is known for its casual fashions.

Many boutiques carry bikinis—**Cantão** (Rio Sul, tel. 021/542–4848), has a good selection of colors and styles—but the market leader is **Bum Bum,** with stores at Rua Vinicius de Morais 130 (tel. 021/521–1229), in the Rio Sul and Barra Shopping malls.

Men's Clothing For men, classic, elegant casual fashions are the specialty at **Richard's** (Rua Maria Quitéria 95, Ipanema, tel. 021/227–8649, and in Barra Shopping, tel. 021/325–8158). Other stores carrying handsome, quality men's clothing include **Dijon** (Rua Garcia D'Avila 110, Ipanema, tel. 021/297–8849; Rua Barata Ribeiro 496-A, tel. 021/255–0239 and Av. Nossa Senhora da Copacabana 680, tel. 021/235–0260, in Copacabana); **Philippe Martin** (Barra Shopping, tel. 021/325–0846); and **Van Gogh** (Galeria 444, Rua Visconde de Pirajá 444, Ipanema, tel. 021/541–0595). Trendy, but quality, men's fashions can be found at **Mr. Wonderful** (Rua Visconde de Pirajá 503A, Ipanema, tel. 021/274–6898).

Men's, Women's, **Bee** (Rua Visconde de Pirajá 483, Ipanema, tel. 021/239–4941;
and Children's Barra Shopping mall, tel. 021/325–7181), offers original, casual
Clothing designs for men, women, and children.

Jewelry Brazil is one of the world's largest producers of gold and the
largest supplier of colored gemstones, with important deposits
of aquamarines, amethysts, diamonds, emeralds, rubellites, topazes, and tourmalines.

The top names in jewelry in Rio are **H. Stern** and **Amsterdam-
Sauer.** At the H. Stern world headquarters at Rua Visconde de
Pirajá 490 in Ipanema (tel. 021/259–7442), you can see exhibits
of rare gemstones and take a free tour demonstrating how raw
stones are transformed into sparkling jewels.

Amsterdam-Sauer (tel. 021/259–8495) and **Roditi** (tel. 021/239–
0099) have large outlets next door to H. Stern. Other reliable
jewelers are **Masson, M. Rosenmann, Maximino, Natan, Sidi,
Moreno, Gregory and Sheehan,** and **Ernani G. Walter.**

Leather Leather goods, especially shoes, are an excellent buy in Rio. At
the Rio Sul shopping center, **Germon's** (tel. 021/541–1995) and
Sagaró (tel. 021/287–3729) carry high-quality, dressy women's
shoes, and **Birello** (tel. 021/295–1898) carries both men's and
women's dress shoes. Also at the Rio Sul, **Victor Hugo** (tel.
021/275–3388) and **Santa Marinella** (tel. 021/275–9346) specialize in handbags for women. **Bottega Veneta** (tel. 021/274–8248)
and **Nazaré** (tel. 021/294–9849), both at the Shopping Center
da Gávea carry fine women's shoes and bags.

In Ipanema you will find fashionable footwear at **Mariazinha**
(tel. 021/541–6695) and **Soft Shoes** (tel. 021/247–1828), both at
the Forum de Ipanema arcade on Praça Nossa Senhora da Paz.
Nearby at Rua Visconde de Pirajá 371, **Rotstein** (tel. 021/267–
2412) and **Pucci** (tel. 021/247–7370) both have a large variety of
exclusive and casual women's shoes and bags.

With stores all over town, **Sapasso** and **Polar** are the two largest shoe-store chains, with footwear for men, women, and children. For low prices you can't beat **Formosinho** (tel.
021/287–8998) and **Dá no Pé** (tel. 021/255–2538), which sell
stock ends of export models. Formosinho, with men's and
women's shoes, has three stores along Rua Visconde de Pirajá
and one at Avenida Nossa Senhora de Copacabana 582.

The first name in leather clothing in Rio is **Frankie Amaury**
(tel. 021/294–8895), located in the Shopping Center da Gávea.

Malls Rio's shopping malls are modern and attractive, based on the
American model. Hours are generally from 9 or 10 AM to 10 PM,
Monday through Saturday.

Rio Sul (Av. Lauro Müller 116, tel. 021/295–1332) in Botafogo
has the city's best boutiques and traditional clothing stores
represented in its more than 400 shops. Adjoining the Rio Palace hotel, is the **Shopping Center Cassino Atlântico** (Av. Atlântica 4240, tel. 021/247–8709). Here you will find a concentration
of antiques stores, art galleries, and souvenir shops. The **Shopping Center da Gávea** (Rua Marquês de São Vicente 52, tel.
021/274–9896) in Gávea has a mixture of fashionable clothing
stores as well as many leather goods stores, and top art galleries, of which the best are **Ana Maria Niemeyer, Beco da Arte,
Borghese, Bronze, Paulo Klabin, Saramenha,** and **Toulouse.**
The **São Conrado Fashion Mall** (Auto-Estrada Lagoa-Barra,

tel. 021/322–0300) sells many fashionable clothes. Since the mall is within walking distance of the nearby hotels, it has unfortunately attracted the attention of petty thieves. **Barra Shopping** (Av. das Américas 4666, tel. 021/431–2161) is the largest and most complete of Rio's malls. Although it is located in Barra da Tijuca, shoppers from all over town head for this large complex.

Spectator Sports

Horse Racing Races are held year-round at Rio's **Jockey Club** (Praça Santos Dumont 31, Gávea, tel. 021/274–0055) beginning Monday and Thursday at 7 PM and weekends at noon. The big event of the year, the **Brazilian Derby,** is held the first Sunday of August.

Soccer Rio, like the rest of Brazil, is soccer mad. The top three teams are **Flamengo** (currently the best and most popular), **Fluminense,** and **Vasco da Gama.** Play between any of these three is soccer at its finest.

Even if the game doesn't turn you on, the 180,000-seat **Maracanã Stadium** (Rua Prof. Eurico Rabelo, Gate 18, tel. 021/264–9962) is impressive, and the crowd itself is half the spectacle. During the season the top game each week is played on Sunday starting around 5 PM. The easiest way to see a game is through a guided tour. Admission to the grandstand is only about 50¢, but you may not enjoy rubbing shoulders with the huge crowds and sitting on a hard concrete slab; reserved seats are around $2 and far more comfortable.

Beaches

The following is a listing of Rio's primary beaches. All are public and all, except Prainha and Grumari (the most westward), are served by buses and taxis. There are no public rest rooms or changing rooms, although you may use the rest rooms at nearby restaurants and cafés. Despite increased security (especially near the major hotels), theft is still a big problem on Rio's beaches. Don't bring any valuables with you, and try not to leave your towel or beach chair unattended.

Barra da Tijuca Rio's longest beach is the 18-kilometer (11-mile) Barra da Tijuca. Water pollution is not a problem here, and for most of its length, the Barra beach escapes the crowds that flock to Copacabana, Ipanema, and São Conrado. The exception is the first 6 kilometers (4 miles) of the beach, where the construction of apartment buildings has been concentrated. The waves here tend to be strong, so swim with caution. Entrepreneurs have begun renting surfboards and Windsurfers on the beach.

Copacabana You can swim here, although pollution levels are not always perfect and there is a strong undertow. Lifeguard stations are found once every kilometer along the beaches. At the Sugarloaf end of Copacabana is **Leme,** really no more than a natural extension of Copacabana. Here a rock formation extends into the water, forming a quiet cove less crowded than the rest of the beach and good for bathing. Avoid the opposite end near the Copacabana Fort, where an ever-present stench will extinguish forever your romantic notions of Copacabana.

Grumari What preserves this spectacular beach, the most beautiful and unspoiled of Rio, is precisely the fact that it has not yet been "discovered". Located 30 minutes from Ipanema on a road that hugs the coastline, Grumari, like Prainha, can be reached only by car. Grumari doesn't have the amenities of the other beaches—only two unimpressive snack bars—but it does have a glorious beach and quiet cove backed by low hills covered with tropical vegetation.

Ipanema The most chic of Rio's beaches, Ipanema and its extension, **Leblon** (the two are divided by a canal), are favored by affluent cariocas. Pollution levels on Leblon Beach in recent years have reached the point where bathing has occasionally been prohibited. Swimmers should also be aware that there is an undertow here. **Arpoador,** the Copacabana end of Ipanema, is good for surfing, as is the end of Leblon, next to Dois Irmãos Mountain.

Prainha The length of two football fields, this vest-pocket beach is a favorite for surfers who take charge of it on the weekends. The swimming here is good, but keep alert for flying surfboards!

Recreio dos Bandeirantes Located at the far end of the Barra beach is the Recreio, a half-mile stretch of sand anchored by a huge rock, which creates a small protected cove. Its quiet, secluded nature makes it popular with carioca families. The calm, pollution-free water, with no waves or currents, is good for bathing, but don't try to swim around the rock—it's bigger than it looks.

São Conrado São Conrado lies in a natural amphitheater surrounded on three sides by forested mountains including the imposing Gávea Mountain. Unfortunately, São Conrado is also home to Rio's largest *favela*, and sewage from the slum runs freely into the ocean at the end closest to Ipanema. Bathers should stay on the far end, near the hang-glider landing point.

Dining

The most popular Brazilian restaurants among visitors are the *churrascarias,* or steak houses, especially those serving meat *rodízio*-style. Rodízio in effect means "going around," and waiters circulate nonstop carrying skewers laden with charbroiled hunks of beef, pork, and chicken, which is sliced at each table. For a set price you get all the meat and side dishes you can eat. The traditional weekend lunch, *feijoada,* is offered by most hotel restaurants every Saturday.

Lunch is typically a full meal, as dinner is usually eaten late. If you arrive for dinner at 7, you may be the only diner in the restaurant. Popular restaurants will still be seating customers after midnight on weekends; the normal closing hour is 2 AM. Many restaurants are closed on Monday.

Many restaurants offer a special fixed-price menu, but in all instances an à la carte menu is also available. Every restaurant includes a cover charge for the bread and other appetizers placed on the table, and a 10% service charge is added to the final bill. It is customary to leave an additional 5% tip. For details and price-category definitions, *see* Dining in Staying in Brazil, *above.*

Very Expensive
French
★
Le Pré Catelan. Le Pré Catelan has a menu divided between the modern and the traditional, and is a must stop for aficionados of gracious French dining. A *menu confiance* (the chef's choice) will guide you through two starters, sherbet, main course, and dessert. Although the menu changes monthly, it is

certain to contain succulent meat dishes topped by light sauces, as well as such house classics as quail stuffed with apricots in a cinnamon sauce. *Av. Atlântica 4240 (Rio Palace hotel), Copacabana, tel. 021/521–3232. Reservations advised. Dress: neat but casual. AE, DC, MC, V. Dinner only.*

★ **Le Saint Honoré.** Le Saint Honoré offers diners excellent French cuisine and an extraordinary view of Copacabana Beach. The accent is on originality, with frequent use of Brazilian fruits and herbs to produce such gems as *les pièces du boucher marquées sauces gamay et béarnaise,* a fillet with both béarnaise and red-wine sauces. For lunch the restaurant has a special prix-fixe menu, one of Rio's great dining bargains. *Av. Atlântica 1020 (Meridien Hotel), Copacabana, tel. 021/275–9922. Reservations required. Jacket and tie advised. AE, DC, MC, V.*

★ **Monseigneur.** A pleasing mix of modern and traditional French cuisine is the calling card of this superb restaurant. The decor here matches the elegance of the meals—two striking lighted columns of translucent crystal dominate the center of the restaurant. Try the rabbit terrine with tropical raspberry jelly or the sautéed slices of salmon on a bed of vegetables and sorrel. *Av. Prefeito Mendes de Morais 222 (Inter-Continental Hotel), São Conrado, tel. 021/322–2200. Reservations required. Dress: neat but casual. AE, DC, MC, V. Dinner only.*

Troisgros. Considered by many to be Rio's finest restaurant, Troisgros has suffered slightly from the exit of its founder, distinguished French chef Claude Troisgros. The menu is famed for nouvelle cuisine relying entirely on Brazilian ingredients. Every dish, whether a crab or lobster flan or chicken, fish, or duck prepared with exotic Brazilian herbs and sauces, is pure pleasure, always exceptionally light. The dessert menu is headed by passion fruit mousse, a Troisgros classic that alone could make a trip to Rio memorable. *Rua Custódio Serrão 62, Jardim Botânico, tel. 021/226–4542. Reservations required. Dress: neat but casual. No credit cards. Dinner only; lunches can be arranged in advance for a minimum of 10 persons.*

Italian **Valentino's.** The emphasis here is on dishes mixing seafood and
★ pasta with succulent cheese sauces. Among the dishes that have earned enthusiastic praise are *nido di fettuccine con ostriche fresche al burro di salivia* (fettuccine with fresh oysters and sage butter) and lobster tail in a truffle cream sauce. Romantic piano music, subdued lighting, and Valentino's luxurious appointments all spell sophistication and a memorable dining experience. *Av. Niemeyer 121 (Rio Sheraton Hotel), Vidigal, tel. 021/274–1122. Reservations required. Jacket and tie advised. AE, DC, MC, V. Dinner only.*

Expensive **Club Gourmet.** Owner and master chef, José Hugo Celidonio,
Brazilian/French has created a unique cuisine (as yet unnamed) that includes the
★ basics of Brazilian cooking but employs European (especially French) techniques. Try the honey-glazed duck breast served with an almond and prune *farofa.* A favorite dessert is the passion fruit crepes. Guests choose one item from each of four courses, paying a set price for the meal. *Rua General Polidoro 186, Botafogo, tel. 021/295–1097. Reservations required. Dress: casual. No credit cards. Closed for lunch Sat. and dinner Sun.*

Churrascaria **Rodeio.** In this popular traditional churrascaria, dishes are
(Steak House) served à la carte rather than as an all-you-can-eat meal. As you enter the restaurant you pass by the grill, where succulent

meats sizzle over charcoal. The decor is slightly rustic, with wine bottles lining the wood-paneled walls. *Av. Alvorada 2150, Barra da Tijuca, tel. 021/325–6166. Reservations advised. Dress: casual. AE, DC, MC.*

Continental **Rio's.** Above-average international cuisine and an unbeatable view of Guanabara Bay and Sugarloaf Mountain are a winning combination here. Located flush against the bay, this is one of the few places in town with a great vista even on rainy days. At night, the view by starlight is one of the most romantic in Rio. The menu has both seafood and meat dishes, and famed flambé desserts. *Parque do Flamengo, Flamengo, tel. 021/551–1131. Reservations required. Dress: jacket and tie at lunch, neat but casual at dinner. AE, DC, MC, V.*

French **Le Bec Fin.** Le Bec Fin has maintained a menu of traditional dishes not unlike those with which it opened its doors in 1948. If you're a fan of traditional French cuisine, you'll find all of your favorites at this intimate, nine-table restaurant—steak au poivre, steak Diane, plus a few house specialties, like fresh fish stuffed with smoked salmon and topped with hollandaise sauce. *Av. Nossa Senhora de Copacabana 178, Copacabana, tel. 021/542–4097. Reservations required. Dress: casual. AE, DC, MC, V. Dinner only.*

★ **Ouro Verde.** The cuisine here is primarily French. The ample and varied menu has remained largely unchanged for two decades. The decor is traditional and elegant, with soft, green hues, exquisite table settings, and Old World chandeliers. Recommended is the *filet Muscovite,* a chateaubriand with a caviar and vodka sauce that is set ablaze at your table. *Av. Atlântica 4240 (Ouro Verde Hotel), Copacabana, tel. 021/542–1887. Reservations advised. Dress: informal. AE, DC, V.*

Italian **Alfredo.** In this Rio franchise of the famed Roman eatery, the
★ mainstay is the pasta that made the original Alfredo world famous—fettuccine Alfredo. An ample cold buffet of antipasti can start off your meal, which, may include traditional pastas served with a variety of sauces. The restaurant is located in the Inter-Continental Hotel with a view of the pool area. *Av. Prefeito Mendes de Morais 222 (Inter-Continental Hotel), São Conrado, tel. 021/322–2200. Reservations advised. Dress: informal. AE, DC, MC, V.*

Seafood **Petronius.** Although it overlooks the action-packed beachfront
★ of Ipanema, the mood is one of quiet elegance. For sheer indulgence order the imperial seafood platter, a meal for two, with lobster, shrimp, shellfish, and three types of fish fillets, all grilled and served with herb butter. *Av. Vieira Souto 460 (Caesar Park Hotel), Ipanema, tel. 021/287–3122. Reservations advised. Dress: neat but casual. AE, DC, MC, V. Dinner only.*

★ **Quatro Sete Meia.** Internationally renowned, this restaurant is located one hour by car from Copacabana, at the end of a highway that offers stunning views of the coastline. Simplicity is the soul of the village and the restaurant, whose name in Portuguese is its street number. There are only 11 tables—five indoors and six in the garden at water's edge. The menu carries seven delicious options, divided between shrimp and fish dishes, from moquecas to grilled seafood to curries. *Rua Barros de Alarcão 476, Pedra da Guaratiba, tel. 021/395–2716. Reservations required. Dress: casual. No credit cards. Lunch only Wed., Thurs.; lunch and dinner Fri.–Sun.*

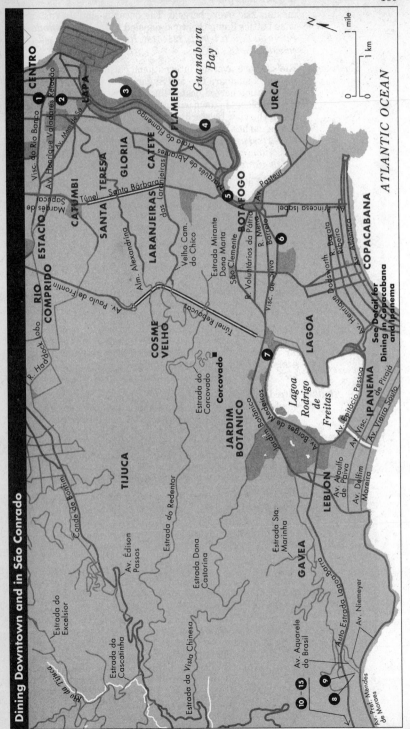

Dining Downtown and in São Conrado

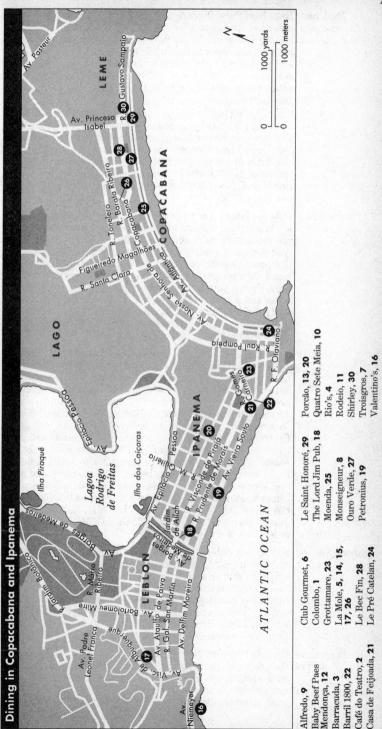

Moderate
Churrascarias
(Steak Houses)

Baby Beef Paes Mendonça. This traditional churrascaria occupies a top spot among the city's steak houses. Its huge rooms, seating a total of 600, are packed seven nights a week, an impressive testimony to the quality of the charbroiled beef, pork, and chicken served here. Portions are equally impressive. *Av. das Américas 1510, Barra da Tijuca, tel. 021/399–2187. Reservations suggested. Dress: casual. AE, D, DC, MC, V.*

★ **Porcão.** The quintessential churrascaria, rodízio-style, Porcão (literally "big pig") is everything that its name implies. Waiters fly up and down between rows of wooden tables wielding giant skewers laden with sizzling barbecued beef, pork, and chicken. This steakhouse captures the good humor of a slightly primitive form of eating. *Two locations: Rua Barão da Torre 218, Ipanema, tel. 021/521–0999; and Av. Armando Lombardi 591, Barra da Tijuca, tel. 021/399–3157. No reservations. Dress: casual. AE, DC, MC, V.*

International **Café do Teatro.** The international food, while palatable, is an afterthought at this extraordinary restaurant, which easily has the most unusual decor in Rio. Taking center stage is the Assyrian motif, replete with columns and wall mosaics that look like something out of a Cecil B. DeMille epic. The bar resembles a sarcophagus, and two sphinxes flank the sunken dining area. Even if you have no interest in eating here, stop by for a drink and a look at this spectacle, located in the basement of the Teatro Municipal. *Av. Rio Branco, Centro, tel. 021/262–4164. Reservations advised. Dress: casual. AE, DC, V. Lunch only; closed weekends.*

Seafood **Barracuda.** Hidden away inside the Glória Marina, this intimate seafood restaurant is an excellent choice for a quiet dinner away from the rush of Copacabana and Ipanema. At lunchtime it is usually crowded with downtown executives, probably eating the restaurant's famed grilled jumbo shrimp served on a skewer. *Marina da Glória, Glória, tel. 021/265–4641. Reservations required for lunch. Dress: casual. AE, DC, MC, V.*

Grottamare. This seafood establishment is popular with tourists, who make up the majority of its customers during high season. The lobster, shrimp, and octopus are excellent, but the house specialty is fish oven-baked with rosemary and other herbs, olive oil, tomatoes, and potatoes. Grottamare's own fishermen venture out daily to bring in the day's catch. *Rua Gomes Carneiro 132, Ipanema, tel. 021/287–1596. Reservations required after 9 PM. Dress: casual. AE, DC, MC, V. Dinner only Mon.–Sat.; lunch and dinner Sun.*

Spanish Seafood **Shirley.** Spanish-seafood casseroles and soups are the draw at this traditional Copacabana restaurant. Try the *zarzuela,* a seafood soup, or *cazuela,* a fish fillet served with white wine sauce. Don't be turned off by the simple decor—nothing more than a few paintings hung on wood-paneled walls: The food is terrific. There is usually a waiting line, so step up to the bar while you wait. *Rua Gustavo Sampaio 610, Leme, tel. 021/275–1398. No reservations. Dress: casual. No credit cards.*

Inexpensive
Brazilian

Casa de Feijoada. Tourists anxious to sample Brazil's national dish, *feijoada,* no longer need to wait until Saturday. Saturday comes seven days a week at this relaxed Ipanema restaurant, and *feijoada* is always on the menu. Diners may also choose from other traditional Brazilian meals. *Rua Prudente de Mo-*

rais 10, Ipanema, tel. 021/267–4994. No reservations. Dress: casual. AE, DC, MC, V.

★ **Moenda.** For Brazilian food, you can do no better than this time-honored eatery in the Hotel Trocadero. Here, while you enjoy the view of the Copacabana beachfront, waitresses in white turbans and long flowing dresses serve meals from Bahia. The emphasis is on seafood served with spicy sauces prepared with tomatoes, peanuts, and okra. Popular dishes are vatapá, moquecas, *camarão a baiana* (shrimp cooked in tomatoes and coconut oil, similar to shrimp Creole), and *caruru* (a shrimp-and-okra gumbo cooked in palm oil). *Av. Atlântica 2064 (Hotel Trocadero), Copacabana, tel. 021/257–1834. Reservations advised. Dress: casual. AE, DC, MC, V.*

British **The Lord Jim Pub.** This is a carioca version of a London pub
★ right down to the red phone box at the front door. Steak-and-kidney pie, Yorkshire pudding, fish-and-chips, and appetizing curries await those who climb up a cast-iron spiral staircase to the pub's upper two floors. The cuisine is as determinedly British as the decor, although a few asides for Americans include barbecued ribs and T-bone steaks. A special attraction is the afternoon tea, served from 4 to 6:45. *Rua Paul Redfern 63, Ipanema, tel. 021/259–3047. Reservations required for afternoon tea. Dress: casual. No credit cards.*

Cafés **Barril 1800.** Snacks and cold draft beer are the most popular items at this beachside café, an Ipanema landmark and one of only three bars along the entire length of the Ipanema–Leblon beach. The menu ranges from hamburgers and french fries to seafood (try shrimp rolled inside balls of mozzarella) and steaks of prodigious size. *Av. Vieira Souto 110, Ipanema, tel. 021/287–0085. No reservations. Dress: casual. DC, MC, V.*

Colombo. At the turn of the century this was Rio's preeminent café, home to afternoon teas for high-society senhoras and a center of political intrigue and gossip. Food here clearly loses out to ambience. The meals are adequate, although on the heavy side; portions will usually serve two. Stop in for a pastry and coffee and absorb the atmosphere and history. *Rua Gonçalves Dias 32, Centro, tel. 021/232–2300. No reservations. Dress: casual. No credit cards. Lunch only. Closed Sun.*

Italian **La Mole.** This popular chain of low-cost Italian restaurants is
★ a good bet for that day when you are not interested in spending a great deal of money for lunch or dinner. Yet for low prices (under $8 for a filet mignon), the food is surprisingly good and servings are hearty. Pasta is the main item, and lasagna, fettuccine, and gnocchi dishes are all tasty. *Five locations: Rua Dias Ferreira 147, Leblon, tel. 021/294–0699; Av. Nossa Senhora de Copacabana 552, Copacabana, tel. 021/235–3366; Praia de Botafogo 228, Botafogo, tel. 021/551–9499; Av. Armando Lombardi 175, Barra da Tijuca, tel. 021/399–0625; Barra Shopping center, Barra da Tijuca, tel. 021/325–5271. No reservations. Dress: casual. No credit cards.*

Lodging

Rio's largest concentration of hotels is in Copacabana and Ipanema. Copacabana hotels are close to the action, but the noise level in Copacabana must be the highest in the world, and few hotels in the neighborhood escape it. Ipanema is better in this respect, but hotels in São Conrado and Barra da Tijuca are the quietest, although somewhat removed from the center of things. There are at present no recommendable downtown hotels; those that exist are aging relics that most visitors will want to avoid. For business travelers there are a handful of hotels in the near downtown neighborhoods of Glória and Flamengo, but most business people will choose to travel to a beachfront hotel, several of which offer executive services.

Expect to pay a premium for a room with a view: Rooms overlooking either the beach or Rio's distinctive mountain backdrop will cost an average of $25 more per night. All hotels include breakfast in the room rate, although the quality ranges from a full buffet to a hard roll with butter.

Rio has many "motels," but be warned that they are not aimed at tourists. They attract couples looking for romance and privacy, and usually rent by the hour.

Room rates given in this guide are for high season (approximately December to April), although the days just prior to and during Carnival can see rates double, or even triple, according to what the traffic will bear. Remember that if you are traveling during Carnival or other peak periods it is important to make reservations as far in advance as possible. Rates are calculated at the official exchange rate. For details and price-category definitions, *see* Lodging *in* Staying in Brazil, *above*.

Very Expensive **Caesar Park.** Since its opening in 1978, this beachfront hotel
★ has established itself as a favorite of business travelers, celebrities, and heads of state, who appreciate its impeccable service. The lobby reflects the hushed elegance of the hotel with its marble walls, thick carpeting, and rosewood furnishings topped by fresh flowers. The rooms are decorated in soft tones of rose, beige, blue, and gray. To assist business guests, the hotel provides fax machines and microcomputers for use in guest rooms. The Caesar Park boasts Rio's finest Japanese restaurant, the Mariko, and an acclaimed Saturday *feijoada. Av. Vieira Souto 460, Ipanema, 22420, tel. 021/287-3122. 221 rooms and suites. Facilities: 3 restaurants, 3 bars, small pool, sauna, satellite TV. AE, DC, MC, V.*

★ **Inter-Continental Rio.** This member of the respected Inter-Continental chain is one of only two resort hotels in the city. It is located in the São Conrado Beach neighborhood right next door to the Gávea Golf and Country Club. Standing alone on its own slice of beachfront, the hotel gives one a pleasant feeling of isolation. Attractions include one of Rio's smartest cocktail lounges, a lively discotheque, the Monseigneur restaurant (*see* Dining *above*), a business center, and convention facilities. Every room has an original tapestry done by a Brazilian artist and a balcony overlooking the ocean. *Av. Prefeito Mendes de Morais 222, São Conrado, 22600, tel. 021/322-2200. 483 rooms and suites. Facilities: 5 restaurants, piano bar/nightclub, disco, 2 bars, 3 pools, lighted tennis courts, sauna, fully equipped exercise center, business center, travel agent, car rental agency, American Airlines ticketing office, shopping arcade, satellite TV. AE, DC, MC, V.*

★ **Meridien.** Of the leading Copacabana hotels, the 37-story Meridien is the closest to downtown, making it a favorite among business travelers. Service is efficient and the rooms are tastefully decorated in pastel tones with dark wood furniture. The hotel features a complete executive center, a VIP room for its business guests, and Le Saint Honoré restaurant (*see* Dining, *above*). *Av. Atlântica 1020, Copacabana, 22012, tel. 021/275– 9922. 443 rooms, 53 suites. Facilities: 3 restaurants, bar, pool, sauna, satellite TV. AE, DC, MC, V.*

Rio Othon Palace. The flagship of the Othon chain, Brazil's largest hotel group, this 30-story hotel is a Copacabana landmark. The high point, literally, of the hotel is its rooftop pool/bar and sun deck, offering the best view of Copacabana's distinctive black-and-white sidewalk mosaic. At night the magic of the rooftop setting is enhanced by live music at the Skylab Bar. The hotel reserves one entire floor for business guests, with access to the executive services. *Av. Atlântica 3264, Copacabana, 22070, tel. 021/521–5522. 554 rooms, 30 suites. Facilities: 2 restaurants, 2 bars, nightclub, pool, health club, sauna, satellite TV. AE, DC, MC, V.*

★ **Rio Palace.** This is recognized as the best hotel on Copacabana Beach—a case in studied elegance, from the marbled lobby to the antique Brazilian furnishings and colonial artwork that decorate the public areas and rooms. The Imperial Club offers the business traveler a range of services, including bilingual secretaries and fax and telex machines. The hotel has a fine French restaurant, Le Pré Catelan (*see* Dining, *above*), the Horse's Neck piano bar, and the Palace Club, a private night-club with live Brazilian music. The building's *H*-shape gives all rooms views of either the sea or the mountains—or both. *Av. Atlântica 4240, Copacabana, 22070, tel. 021/521–3232. 418 rooms and suites. Facilities: 2 restaurants, tearoom, 2 bars, nightclub, 2 pools, fitness center, sauna, executive center, satellite TV. AE, DC, MC, V.*

★ **Sheraton Rio Hotel & Towers.** Built so that it dominates Vidigal Beach, between Ipanema and São Conrado, this is the only hotel in Rio that is located directly on the beach. Guest rooms are decorated in soft, soothing colors, and all have beach views. Four floors (97 rooms) are reserved for business travelers, who receive special treatment. Called the Towers, this section of the hotel has its own check-in, a private lounge, a business center, a buffet breakfast, and around-the-clock butler service. The Sheraton is home to Valentino's, a favorite with Rio high society (*see* Dining, *above*), and to the lively beat of Brazilian music at the One Twenty One Lounge. *Av. Niemeyer 121, Vidigal, 22450, tel. 021/274–1122. 617 rooms, 22 suites. Facilities: 4 restaurants, bar/nightclub, bar, 3 pools, lighted tennis courts, sauna, fitness center, shops. AE, DC, MC, V.*

Expensive **Copacabana Palace.** At one time this hotel was better known than Copacabana Beach itself. Built in 1923, Copacabana Palace was the first luxury hotel in South America, and it held this singular distinction for the next 30 years. In 1990 the hotel was purchased by the British Orient Express group and is now un-dergoing a $25 million renovation. The Copa, as it is known to cariocas, will retain its timeless grace marked by high ceilings, large public areas, and long, wide corridors. The hotel's ice-cream–cake facade will remain untouched by the renovations, and the new owners are promising to maintain the sizable guest rooms, each to be individually decorated. Modern touches will be added to the restaurants, pool, lobby, and bathrooms. *Av. Atlântica 1702, Copacabana, 22021, tel. 021/255–7070. 122 rooms, 102 suites. Facilities: 2 restaurants, 2 bars, large pool, sauna, theater. AE, DC, MC, V.*

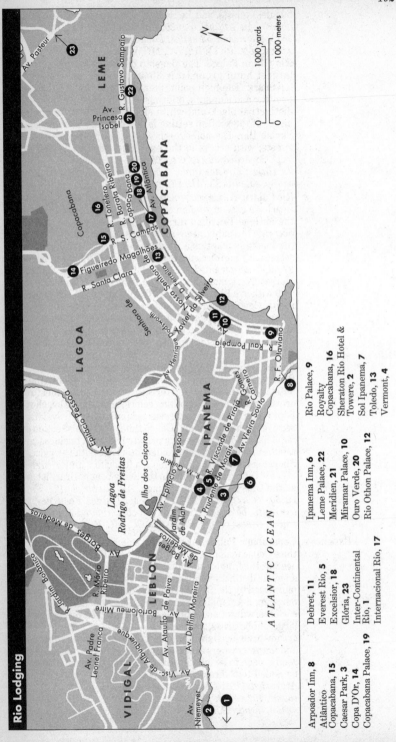

Rio Lodging

192

Arpoador Inn, **8**
Atlântico
Copacabana, **15**
Caesar Park, **3**
Copa D'Or, **14**
Copacabana Palace, **19**

Debret, **11**
Everest Rio, **5**
Excelsior, **18**
Glória, **23**
Inter-Continental
Rio, **1**
Internacional Rio, **17**

Ipanema Inn, **6**
Leme Palace, **22**
Meridien, **21**
Miramar Palace, **10**
Ouro Verde, **20**
Rio Othon Palace, **12**

Rio Palace, **9**
Royalty
Copacabana, **16**
Sheraton Rio Hotel &
Towere, **2**
Sol Ipanema, **7**
Toledo, **13**
Vermont, **4**

★ **Everest Rio.** Offering impeccable service and one of Rio's finest rooftop views (a postcard shot of Corcovado and the lagoon), this hotel is a favorite with those who know the ins and outs of Rio's hotels. Back rooms offer sea views, and front rooms above the 14th floor look out on Corcovado and the lagoon. A block away from Ipanema Beach, the hotel is in the heart of the neighborhood's premier shopping and dining area. *Rua Prudente de Morais 1117, Ipanema, 22420, tel. 021/287–8282. 159 rooms, 11 suites. Facilities: restaurant, bar, small rooftop pool. AE, DC, MC, V.*

★ **Leme Palace.** Large rooms and a quiet beachfront location have made Leme Palace the hotel of choice with frequent Rio visitors. Built in 1964, it was partially remodeled in 1987 and 1988 but still retains its original subdued, conservative air. *Av. Atlântica 656, Leme, 22010, tel. 021/275–8080. 168 rooms, 26 suites. Facilities: restaurant, bar. AE, DC, MC, V.*

Internacional Rio. Rio's newest beachfront hotel, the red frame of the Internacional has quickly become a Copacabana landmark. Swiss-owned and aimed at the business traveler, the hotel offers a rarity for Copacabana—all rooms have balconies with sea views. *Av. Atlântica 1500, Copacabana, 22010, tel. 021/295–2323. 117 rooms, 12 suites. Facilities: restaurant, 2 bars, pool, sauna, business center. AE, DC, MC, V.*

★ **Miramar Palace.** One of Rio's veteran hotels, the Miramar is a satisfying mix of the old and the new. The beachfront hotel's rooms are among the largest in Rio, and the public areas are dominated by classic touches, from the Carrara marble floor of the lobby to the spectacular glass chandeliers that light the two restaurants. The hotel's 16th-floor bar is notable for its unobstructed view of the entire sweep of Copacabana; after 6 PM live Brazilian music adds a special touch of romance to the view. *Av. Atlântica 3668, Copacabana, 22010, tel. 021/287–6348. 133 rooms, 11 suites. Facilities: restaurant, coffee shop, tearoom, 2 bars. AE, DC, MC, V.*

Moderate **Copa D'Or.** The newest and largest nonbeachfront hotel in Rio, the Copa D'Or has quickly established an excellent reputation for service and amenities. Business people are well served, due to the hotel's location on a thoroughfare to downtown. For beach goers, the hotel provides free transportation to Copacabana beach, four blocks away. *Rua Figueiredo Magalhães 875, Copacabana, 22060, tel. 021/235–6610. 195 rooms, 20 suites. Facilities: restaurant, 2 bars, pool, sauna, convention facilities. AE, DC, MC, V.*

Debret. This former apartment building scores points for combining a beachfront location with moderate prices. The decor pays tribute to Brazil's colonial past: In the lobby there are baroque statues and prints depicting colonial scenes, and in the rooms there is dark, heavy wood furniture. The hotel has a loyal following among diplomats and business people. *Av. Atlântica 3564, Copacabana, 22041, tel. 021/521–3332. 90 rooms, 10 suites. Facilities: restaurant, bar, satellite TV. AE, DC, MC, V.*

Excelsior. More than any of its contemporaries, this 1950s hotel has retained its original style and flavor. The result is a Copacabana beachfront hotel with surprising touches of refinement, such as a marble lobby with leather-upholstered sofas, and closets paneled in rich *jacarandá* (Brazilian redwood). *Av. Atlântica 1800, Copacabana, 22000, tel. 021/257–1950. 175 rooms, 13 suites. Facilities: restaurant, bar. AE, DC, MC, V.*

Glória. The grande dame of Rio's hotels, this classic was built in 1922. Frequent renovations and convenience for business travelers (it's a five-minute taxi ride from downtown) have helped it retain its popularity. The hotel responded well to its transition to catering to business people, and it provides ample convention and meeting facilities. Its major liability is its distance from the beaches, which forces guests to rely on taxis for transportation. *Rua do Russel 632, Glória, 22210, tel. 021/205–7272. 600 rooms, 33 suites. Facilities: 4 restaurants, 3 bars, 2 pools, sauna, exercise room. AE, DC, MC, V.*

★ **Ouro Verde.** One of only a handful of Rio hotels aimed at the "discriminating traveler," this has been a preferred lodging for visiting business people for three decades. The hotel is famed for its efficient, personalized service. Tasteful Brazilian colonial decor and dark wood furniture are right in step with the hotel's emphasis on quality and graciousness. All front rooms face the beach, and back rooms from the 6th to 12th floors have a view of Corcovado. A lively alfresco bar plus one of Rio's finest restaurants, the namesake Ouro Verde, attract patrons into the morning hours (*see* Dining, *above*). *Av. Atlântica 1456, Copacabana, 22041, tel. 021/542–1887. 61 rooms, 5 suites. Facilities: restaurant, bar, reading room. AE, DC, MC, V.*

Royalty Copacabana. Opened in 1987, this hotel's moderate price has made it one of the best bargains in Rio and has caught the attention of travelers who want to escape the hectic pace of the beachfront Avenida Atlântica. The hotel's location, three blocks from the beach, is convenient for beach goers yet removed enough to satisfy those looking for peace and quiet—a rarity in Copacabana. The back rooms from the third floor up are the quietest, and all have mountain views; front rooms have sea views. *Rua Tonelero 154, Copacabana, 22030, tel. 021/235–5699. 130 rooms, 13 suites. Facilities: restaurant, bar, small rooftop pool, exercise room, sauna, satellite TV. AE, DC, MC, V.*

Sol Ipanema. Another of Rio's crop of tall, slender hotels, this one anchors the eastern end of Ipanema Beach. Guest rooms have motel-style beige carpets and drapes and light-colored furniture. The front rooms have panoramic views of the beachfront, while the back rooms, from the 8th floor up, have views of the lagoon and Corcovado. *Av. Vieira Souto 320, Ipanema, 22420, tel. 021/267–0095. 66 rooms, 12 suites. Facilities: restaurant, bar, small rooftop pool, satellite TV. AE, DC, MC, V.*

Inexpensive **Arpoador Inn.** This pocket-size hotel occupies one of Rio's more
★ privileged locations, a stretch of beach known as Arpoador at the Copacabana end of Ipanema. Here surfers ride the waves and pedestrians rule the roadway—a traffic-free street that gives the hotel's guests direct access to the beach. Simple but comfortable, the hotel is reasonably priced considering the location. At sunset the view from the rocks that mark the end of the beach is considered one of the most beautiful in Rio. Both sights are visible from the hotel's back rooms. Avoid the front rooms, which face a noisy street. *Rua Francisco Otaviano 177, Ipanema, 22080, tel. 021/247–6090. 46 rooms, 2 suites. Facilities: restaurant, bar. AE, MC, V.*

Atlântico Copacabana. One of Rio's newer hotels, this was built in 1986. The large lobby with its marble walls, red carpeting, black leather furniture, and mirrors will look modern to some, pretentious to others. Guest rooms are slightly larger than the average for Rio hotels. The Atlântico is located four blocks from the beach in a residential area. *Rua Siqueira Campos 90,*

Copacabana, 20000, tel. 021/257–1880. 97 rooms, 18 suites. Facilities: restaurant, 3 bars, small rooftop pool, sauna. AE, DC, MC, V.

★ **Ipanema Inn.** This small, no-frills hotel was built for tourists who want to stay in Ipanema but have no interest in paying the high prices of a beachfront hotel. To that end, it has been a complete success. Just a half block from the beach, it is convenient not only for sun and water worshipers but also for those seeking to explore Ipanema's varied nightlife. *Rua Maria Quitéria 27, Ipanema, 22410, tel. 021/287–6092. 56 rooms. Facilities: bar. AE, MC, V.*

Toledo. This unpretentious hotel goes the extra mile to make the best of what it has. There are few amenities, but service is friendly and efficient. Its main plus is its location on a quiet back street of Copacabana, one block from the beach. The back rooms from the 9th to the 14th floors have sea views. *Rua Domingos Ferreira 71, Copacabana, 22050, tel. 021/257–1990. 87 rooms, 8 suites. Facilities: coffee shop, bar. DC, MC, V.*

Vermont. Newly renovated, this hotel is clean, reliable, and situated just two blocks from the beach—a good choice for budget travelers. The hotel's only drawback is its location on the main street of Ipanema, which means incessant noise during the day, although it tends to quiet down at night after the shops close. *Rua Visconde de Pirajá 254, Ipanema, 22410, tel. 021/521–0057. 54 rooms. Facilities: bar. No credit cards.*

The Arts and Nightlife

The Arts

By Dwight V. Gast

Revised by Edwin Taylor

There are many performing-arts options in Rio, including theater, music, dance, and film. The city's main venue is the recently renovated **Teatro Municipal.** Dance, opera, and theatre events are scheduled year-round, although the season officially runs from April to December. For current listings for this and other venues, pick up a copy of the bilingual *Este Mês no Rio/This Month in Rio* or similar publications available at most hotels. Also check the entertainment sections of the Portuguese-language newspapers *Jornal do Brasil* and *O Globo* (which are generally easy to understand even for those who don't speak Portuguese).

Tickets are inexpensive by international standards and may be purchased at the theater or concert hall box offices. Dress is informal but upscale at most cultural events in Rio, and the conservative upper crust still likes to dress up for the Teatro Municipal. No matter what you wear, though, remember not to put on valuable jewelry and to carry minimal cash.

Dance In addition to the Teatro Municipal's own ballet company and the international ballet festival held in the theater during April and May, dance in Rio takes many other forms. Check local listings under "Dança" for information on these venues.

Casa Laura Alvim (Av. Vieira Souto 176, Ipanema, tel. 021/247–6946); **Teatro João Caetano** (Praça Tiradentes, Centro, tel. 021/221–0305); **Teatro Municipal** (Praça Floriano, Centro, tel. 021/210–2463); **Teatro Nacional** (Hotel Nacional, Av. Niemeyer 769, São Conrado, tel. 021/322–1000); **Teatro Nelson Rodrigues** (Av. Chile 230, Centro, tel. 021/262–0942); **Teatro Villa Lobos** (Av. Princesa Isabel 440, Leme, tel. 021/275–6695).

Film Original-language films are screened in small *cineclubes,* or state-of-the-art movie theaters. Cinelândia, the area where many of Rio's theaters are concentrated, is dangerous at night. The following are the most comfortable first-run movie theaters; check local listings under "Cinema" for current programs. All movies are shown in their original language with Portuguese subtitles.

Art Casa Shopping I, II, & III (Casa Shopping, Barra da Tijuca, tel. 021/325–0746); **Art Fashion Mall I, II, III, & IV** (São Conrado Fashion Mall, São Conrado, tel. 021/322–1258); **Barra I, II, & III** (Barra Shopping, Barra da Tijuca, tel. 021/325–6487); **Condor Copacabana** (Rua Figueiredo Magalhães 286, Copacabana, tel. 021/255–2610); **Largo do Machado I & II** (Largo do Machado 29, Flamengo, tel. 021/205–6842); **Mêtro Boavista** (Rua do Passeio 62, Centro, tel. 021/240–1291); **Ricamar** (Av. Nossa Senhora de Copacabana 360, Copacabana, tel. 021/237–9932); **Roxy** (Av. Nossa Senhora de Copacabana 945, Copacabana, tel. 021/236–6245); **São Luiz I & II** (Rua do Catete 307, Catete, tel. 021/285–2296); **Veneza** (Av. Pasteur 184, Botafogo, tel. 021/295–8349).

Music While the proliferation of Brazilian popular music (known in Portuguese as *música popular brasileira,* or MPB) may overshadow classical music (called *música erudita*) in the city, Rio has a number of orchestras. The Orquestra Sinfônica Brasileira and the Orquestra do Teatro Municipal are the most prominent. The following are the most patronized, most reliable places to hear classical music in Rio. For current information check the "Música Erudita" listings in local periodicals.

Sala Cecilia Meireles (Largo da Lapa 47, Centro, tel. 021/232–4779) is a center for classical music; **Teatro Dulcina** (Rua Alcindo Guanabara 17, Centro, tel. 021/240–4879) is a small theater that features classical opera and concerts; **Teatro João Caetano** (Praça Tiradentes, Centro, tel. 021/221–0305) offers variety shows featuring comedy, music, and dance nightly; **Teatro Municipal** (Praça Floriano, Centro, tel. 021/210–2463) presents a variety of arts—ballet, concerts, and theater, to name a few; **Teatro Paço Imperial** (Praça XV, Centro, tel. 021/232–7762), like the Teatro Municipal, features a varied schedule of theatrical, musical, and dance performances.

Opera The **Teatro Municipal's** (Praça Floriano, Centro, tel. 021/210–2463) opera company puts on superb productions and often attracts international divas as guest artists. Also try the **Teatro João Caetano** (Praça Tiradentes, Centro, tel. 021/221–0305), and check listings under "Opera" in local periodicals.

Theater The following theaters are among the most active in the city, but there are dozens more, so check local listings under "Teatro" for current programs.

Casa Laura Alvim (Av. Vieira Souto 176, Ipanema, tel. 021/247–6946); **Teatro Cândido Mendes** (Rua Joana Angélica 63, Ipanema, tel. 021/267–7098); **Teatro Copacabana Palace** (Av. Nossa Senhora de Copacabana 327, Copacabana, tel. 021/257–0881); **Teatro Ipanema** (Rua Prudente de Morais 824, Ipanema, tel. 021/247–9794); **Teatro João Caetano** (Praça Tiradentes, Centro, tel. 021/221–0305); **Teatro Municipal** (Praça Floriano, Centro, tel. 021/210–2463); **Teatro Villa Lobos** (Av. Princesa Isabel 440, Leme, tel. 021/275–6695).

Nightlife Apart from Rio's beaches, the city's biggest year-round draw for natives and visitors alike is its nightlife. Options range from samba shows shamelessly aimed at the tourist, to sultry dance halls called *forrós*, which originated in Brazil's northeast during World War II when American GIs stationed at refueling stops opened up their clubs "for all." Musically, you'll find night spots featuring the sounds of big band, rock, and everything in between. One of the happiest mediums is MPB, the generic term for current Brazilian sounds ranging from pop to jazz. Nightlife establishments often keep unusual schedules. Always call ahead to make sure they are open.

Bars and Lounges These establishments often ask a nominal cover in the form of either a drink minimum or music charge, and, as opposed to nightclubs, usually admit single patrons with no fuss. Don't overlook the hotel bars and lounges, which are often as popular with locals as they are with hotel guests.

Banana Café (Rua Barão da Torre 368, Ipanema, tel. 021/521–1047) is one of the city's most popular bar/restaurants. Owner Ricardo Amaral is an international socialite and draws a chic crowd to this laid-back night spot.

Biblo's Bar (Av. Epitácio Pessoa 1484, Lagoa, tel. 021/521–2645), with its magnificent nighttime views of Corcovado, houses a discotheque and is attached to the French restaurant Rive Gauche. The biggest draw is its piano bar, which offers a program of jazz and MPB in an intimate candlelit setting.

Chico's Bar (Av. Epitácio Pessoa 1560, Lagoa, tel. 021/287–3514) is owned by Rio night-spot entrepreneur Chico Recarey. Both the bar and the adjoining restaurant, Castelo da Lagoa, are big with affluent cariocas, both singles and couples.

Horse's Neck (Av. Atlântica 4270, Copacabana, tel. 021/521–3232) is an option for guests at the Rio Palace hotel, where it is located, or for anyone who wants to admire the sweeping crescent of Copacabana.

Jazzmania (Av. Rainha Elizabeth 769, Ipanema, tel. 021/227–2447) is Rio's number one-jazz club and the only place in town that offers jazz exclusively.

La Tour (Rua Santa Luzia 651, Centro, tel. 021/240–5493), a revolving eatery set atop a downtown office building, offers a grand view of the downtown historical area, the bay, and virtually all of the city's leading landmarks. The food is always bad; step up to the bar and sip a drink while the restaurant revolves.

Le Rond-Point (Av. Atlântica 1020, Copacabana, tel. 021/275–9922), with its red-leather banquettes just off the lobby of the Meridien hotel, gets a mixed crowd to listen to *le jazz hot,* Brazilian-style.

Mistura Fina (Av. Borges de Medeiros 3207, Lagoa, tel. 021/266–5844), also houses a restaurant and outdoor café. A guitarist or pianist is featured until 10 PM, when a livelier band takes over until 2 AM.

One Twenty One Lounge (Sheraton Rio Hotel, Av. Niemeyer 121, Vidigal, tel. 021/274–1122) is among the most pleasant of the city's hotel lounges.

People (Av. Bartolomeu Mitre 370, Leblon, tel. 021/294–0547) has a musical-instrument decor and is the most popular place in the city for listening to MPB and meeting people.

Skylab Bar (Av. Atlântica 3264, Copacabana, tel. 021/521–5522), true to its name, occupies the top floor of the Rio Othon Palace hotel, with views of the ocean and hills on either side.

Cabaret Variety is the byword of the cabaret scene in Rio, which provides visual and sensual stimulation to suit all tastes.

Frank's (Av. Princesa Isabel 185, Copacabana, tel. 021/275–9398) is one of the most established of many dark little clubs devoted to burlesque, striptease, and sex shows along Avenida Princesa Isabel near the Meridien hotel.

Oba-Oba (Rua Humaitá 110, Botafogo, tel. 021/286–9848) is a private-house-turned-club where Oswaldo Sargentelli, known locally as Mr. Samba, emcees one of Rio's two remaining grand-scale samba shows.

Plataforma I (Rua Adalberto Ferreira 32, Leblon, tel. 021/274–4022) holds the older and more spectacular of Rio's two samba shows, with elaborate costumes and a greater variety of Brazilian musical numbers. Each night's performance begins at 10.

Teatro Alaska (Galeria Alaska, Copacabana, tel. 021/247–9842) puts on a tired transvestite show in its slightly seedy space in Galeria Alaska. The club is located in the main drag of Rio's gay and lesbian scene, and the area gets somewhat rough at times.

Dance Clubs In addition to discos, there are a number of places in Rio that offer Brazilian rhythms for dancing to live music. Samba clubs specialize in the beat of the country's best-known dance. *Gafieiras* are old-fashioned ballroom dance halls, usually patronized by an equally old-fashioned clientele. *Forrós* are much funkier, and feature the rhythms of Brazil's northeast.

Asa Branca (Av. Mem de Sá 17, Lapa, tel. 021/252–4428) is Chico Recarey's large and glamorous nightclub, where the decor combines modern, geometric designs with old-fashioned fixtures. Big bands and popular Brazilian musicians keep the crowd moving until the wee hours.

Elite (Rua Frei Caneca 4, Centro, tel. 021/232–3217) is an unpretentious gafieira in a tough part of town (take a taxi here). Once inside and up the rickety stairs, however, you'll find an oasis for respectable if not necessarily affluent couples—usually middle-aged—who take their ballroom dancing seriously.

Sôbre as Ondas (Av. Atlântica 3432, Copacabana, tel. 021/521–1296) overlooks Copacabana Beach. Here you can dance to live music, usually MPB or samba, and dine at the Terraço Atlântico restaurant downstairs.

Vogue (Rua Cupertino Durão 173, Leblon, tel. 021/274–4145), in addition to dancing, has a busy bar/restaurant/*karaokê* club that keeps its chic young patrons busy.

Discos Rio's discotheques (*danceterias* in Portuguese) offer flashing lights, loud music, and exclusive memberships. Staying at one of Rio's better hotels guarantees admission to the most selective places; ask the concierge to call ahead for you. Otherwise, try to arrange to go with a member.

Biblo's Bar (Av. Epitácio Pessoa 1484, Lagoa, tel. 021/521–2645) is one of Rio's most active places for live music and disco dancing; it is especially popular with singles.

Caligula (Rua Prudente de Morais 129, Ipanema, tel. 021/287–1369) is decorated in the glamorous decadence of the late Roman Empire, with both live and taped music providing the entertainment.

Help (Av. Atlântica 3432, Copacabana, tel. 021/521–1296) is Rio's largest and noisiest disco. It attracts a huge, mixed crowd of tourists, single men, and single women, many looking to offer some "help" of their own, for a price.

Hippopotamus (Rua Barão da Torre 354, Ipanema, tel. 021/247–0351) is the most exclusive and expensive of Rio's discos, requiring membership (available to guests of the better hotels) and a stiff cover (about $30 per person) to get in. The disco is often closed for private parties, so be sure to call.

Zoom (Largo de São Conrado 20, São Conrado, tel. 021/322–4179), is a glitzy mecca for reggae, rock, and café music. Its elaborate light show, six bars, and casual atmosphere attract a young crowd, usually couples.

Nightclubs The following nightclubs serve food, but because their main attraction is usually music, it's best to eat elsewhere earlier if you're looking for serious dining. Remember that many clubs have a policy of admitting couples only; singles should have their hotel check to make sure they'll be admitted.

Asa Branca (Av. Mem de Sá 17, Lapa, tel. 021/252–4428) is considered by many to be a dance hall, but owner Chico Recarey made certain from the beginning that his hall would be the most glamorous in Rio. The house band plays until show time, when a major Brazilian talent usually takes over.

Canecão (Av. Venceslau Braz 215, Botafogo, tel. 021/295–3044) is the city's largest nightclub. It can seat nearly 2,500 people at the tiny tables in its cavernous space, making it the logical place for some of the biggest names on the international music scene to hold their concerts.

Circo Voador (Arcos da Lapa, Lapa, tel. 021/221–0405) presents top MPB artists in a circus-tent setting, and after the concert you can stay and dance. There is limited seating, so be sure to reserve in advance or you may wind up sitting on the dance floor.

Scala (Av. Afrânio de Melo Franco 292, Leblon, tel. 021/239–4448), Chico Recarey's flagship nightclub, recently changed its "gringo show" offerings to include well-known Brazilian musicians.

For Singles Besides such gathering places as **Chico's Bar** or **Biblo's Bar** and other discos, plain but pleasant bars called *choperias* attract an unattached crowd. An ice-cold *chope*, or Brazilian draft beer is the order of the day.

Alberico's (Av. Vieira Souto 236, Ipanema, tel. 021/267–3793) is a choperia packed on weekends, especially the tables facing Ipanema Beach.

Barril 1800 (Av. Vieira Souto 110, Ipanema, tel. 021/287–0085) is an unpretentious and popular beachfront meeting place before an evening at the nearby club Jazzmania (*see above*).

The Lord Jim Pub (Rua Paul Redfern 63, Ipanema, tel. 021/259–3047), attracts a lively crowd of English-speakers. Chope is served in beer mugs and if drinks turn to dinner there is a full menu of pub-style specialties (*see* Dining, *above*).

Lucas (Av. Atlântica 3744, Copacabana, tel. 021/247–1606), ranks as Copacabana's most popular beachfront gathering spot. Draft beer has been served here for more than 40 years.

Vinicius (Rua Vinicius de Morais 39, Ipanema, tel. 021/267–5757) is where Vinicius de Morais, author of "The Girl from Ipanema," used to sit and longingly watch the song's heroine head for the beach.

São Paulo

By Julia Michaels

After 12 years in smoggy São Paulo, former Christian Science Monitor *correspondent Julia Michaels boasts amazing pulmonary defenses, but these did not prevent the theft of her laptop from a hotel room while she reviewed Salvador's beaches and churches for Fodor's. The robbery did contribute to a Brazil-located novel she is writing.*

Crowded buses grind through the streets spouting black smoke, endless stands of skyscrapers block the horizon, and the din of traffic and construction deafens the ear. But native *Paulistanos* love this megalopolis of 17 million, though during Brazil's postwar industrialization it grew too fast for urban planners to keep up with. São Paulo now sprawls across 7,951 square kilometers (3,070 square miles), only 1,502 square kilometers (580 square miles) of which, double the size of New York City, make up the city proper.

The draw is the dynamism of the immigrants who have been coming since the start of the century, from Italy, Portugal, Spain, Germany, Japan, and from other regions of Brazil, to put their talents and energy to work here. That energy has turned São Paulo from a sleepy Jesuit mission post into the financial hub of Latin America, home of the Third World's largest industrial park, and capital of the Brazilian state of the same name accounting for half of the country's $450 billion gross national product. And as crime and pollution have increasingly beset Rio de Janeiro, São Paulo has aggressively moved in to take over that city's role as Brazil's cultural center.

Ultimately, the immigrants, their offspring, their varied lifestyles, and the overall fast-paced urban culture they have generated are the focus of the visitor's interest. Even as the smog reddens the eyes, there is much to learn here about a city committed to making dreams come true.

Staying Safe Security is a concern in São Paulo, much as it would be in any large American city. The local tourist police caution travelers to be alert and watch belongings carefully at all times, especially at tourist attractions. Wearing shorts, expensive running shoes, or flashy accessories will bring unwanted attention, they add. Be aware of a local scam in which one man throws a dark liquid on a tourist's back and another offers to help clean up while the first *really* cleans up!

Tourist Information

The **Secretaria de Esportes e Turismo do Estado de São Paulo,** or SEST (Praça Antônio Prado 9, tel. 011/229–3011; open weekdays 9–5:30) provides maps and information about tourist attractions in the city and excursions in the rest of the state of São Paulo. SEST also has booths at Guarulhos–Cumbica airport, in the arrivals terminal (tel. 011/945–2380; open daily 9 AM–10 PM).

The city-operated **Anhembi Turismo e Eventos da Cidade de São Paulo** (Anhembi Convention Center, Avenida Olavo Fontoura, 1209, tel. 011/267–0702; open weekdays 9–6) has four branch locations, all open daily 9–6: on the Praça da República, facing Rua Sete de Abril (tel. 011/231–2922); Avenida São Luís in front of the Praça Dom José Gaspar (tel. 011/257–3422); Avenida Paulista, across from the Museu de Arte de São Paulo (tel. 011/231–2922); and in front of the Shopping Iguatemi, on Avenida Brigadeiro Faria Lima (tel. 011/211–1277). Others were expected to open in late 1993 and early 1994.

The **Delegacia de Turismo,** or tourist police, has offices at Avenida São Luís 115 (tel. 011/254–3561 or 011/214–0209) and Rua XV de Novembro 347, mezzanine (tel. 011/37–8332 or 011/37–5642). Both are open weekdays 8–8.

The small red English-language *Pocket Guide/The Best of São Paulo,* which lists addresses and telephone numbers of museums, theaters, restaurants, art galleries, shops, and other places of interest to visitors, is sold at newsstands and bookstores.

Arriving and Departing

By Plane   São Paulo's international airport, **Cumbica** (tel. 011/945–2111), also known as **Guarulhos,** is located in the industrial suburb of Guarulhos, 30 kilometers (19 miles) from downtown and a 45-minute drive away. All international flights land there, as well as domestic flights of the large airlines. The airlines using Cumbica are American, United, Varig, Vasp, Canadian, British Airways, Transbrasil, and charter flights by Tower Airlines and World Airlines. The smaller **Congonhas** Airport (tel. 011/536–3555, ext. 195) serves the smaller regional airlines and the **Ponte Aérea,** the Rio–São Paulo shuttle. Congonhas is 14 kilometers (9 miles) from the city center, about a 15-minute drive, but the city's unpredictable traffic can double this time. In the winter, both airports are sometimes fogged in during the early morning, and flights are rerouted to the **Viracopos Airport** (tel. 0192/47–0909), in the city of Campinas; airlines transfer passengers by bus (an hour's ride) to their original destination in São Paulo.

EMTU executivo buses (tel. 011/945–2505), fancy green-stripe vehicles, shuttle between Cumbica and Congonhas, and also link the international airport with the Tietê bus terminal and the downtown Praça da República. The bus to São Paulo costs less than $5 and runs every half-hour to an hour from about 6 AM to 11 PM or midnight, depending on the departure point. Municipal buses, with "CMTC" painted on the sides, stop at the airport and go downtown by various routes, such as via Avenida Paulista to the Praça da Sé and Tietê bus station. The sleek blue and white, air-conditioned **Guarucoop radio taxis** (tel. 011/940–7070) will convey you from Cumbica to downtown for around $15; regular, or **comum,** taxis, charge the same amount from this airport. The radio taxi fare from Congonhas to downtown is around $10, and around $7 in a regular taxi. At press time, the new **Fleet Car Shuttle** (counter at Cumbica Airport's arrivals terminal 1, tel. 011/945–3030; open daily 6 AM–midnight) was starting operation, serving groups of up to 10 people and stopping at one destination of choice only. For one downtown stop, for example, the company charges a flat rate of about $35 per carload.

If you want to skip the traffic from Congonhas Airport, try an **IRC** helicoptor (tel. 011/61–9459 or 011/61–6830), which does short hops for about $700 an hour. The company plans an airport-to-airport shuttle service for 1994, charging $100 for the transfer.

By Car   The main highway linking São Paulo and Rio de Janeiro is the Via Dutra (BR 116 North). The modern Rodovia dos Trabalhdores (SP 70) charges small tolls, runs parallel to the Dutra for about a quarter of the trip beginning at São Paulo,

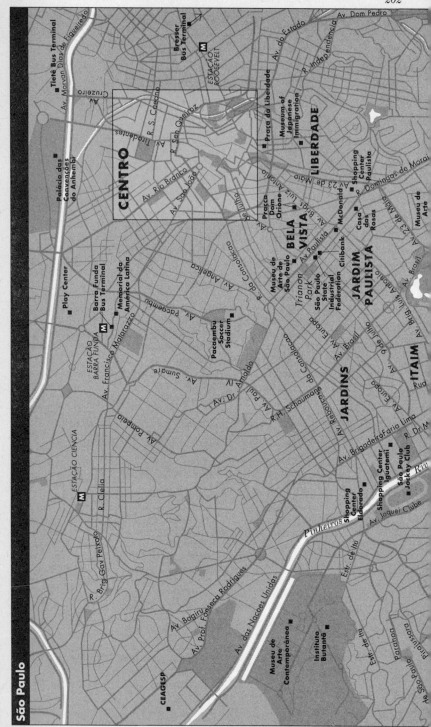

São Paulo

CENTRO

LIBERDADE
- Praça da Liberdade
- Museum of Japanese Immigration
- Shopping Center Paulista

BELA VISTA
- Praça Dom Orione
- McDonald
- Casa das Rosas
- Museu de Arte
- Museu de Arte de São Paulo
- Trianon Park
- São Paulo State Industrial Federation
- Citibank

JARDIM PAULISTA

JARDINS
- Pacaembu Soccer Stadium

ITAIM

- Tietê Bus Terminal
- Bresser Bus Terminal
- ESTAÇÃO ROOSEVELT
- Palácio das Convenções do Anhembi
- Play Center
- Barra Funda Bus Terminal
- ESTAÇÃO BARRA FUNDA
- Memorial da América Latina
- ESTAÇÃO CIÊNCIA
- Shopping Center Eldorado
- Shopping Center Iguatemi
- São Paulo Jockey Club
- CEAGESP
- Museu de Arte Contemporânea
- Instituto Butantã

Av. Dom Pedro
Av. do Estado
R. Independencia
Av. Morvan Dias de Figueiredo
Av. Cruzeiro
R. S. Caetano
Av. Tiradentes
R. Sen Queiroz
Av. Rio Branco
Av. São João
Av. Brig. Luiz Antonio
Av. 23 de Maio
R. Domingos de Morai
Av. Ipiranga
9 de Julho
Av. Paulista
Av. Angélica
R. da Consolação
Av. Pacaembu
Av. Sumaré
Av. Dr.
Av. Pompeia
Av. Francisco Matarazzo
R. Clelia
R. Brig. Gav Peixoto
R.H. Schaumann
Av. Rebouças
Av. Brasil
Av. Europa
Av. 9 de julho
Av. Brasil
Av. Dr. Arnaldo
Av. Paul IV
Av. da Consolação
Av. Brigadeiro Faria Lima
R. Dr M
Av. Joquei Clube
Pinheiros
Estr. de Ihu
Estr. de Ihu
Av. Bagiru
Av. Prof. Fonseca Rodrigues
Av. das Nações Unidas
Paraná
Piraquissu

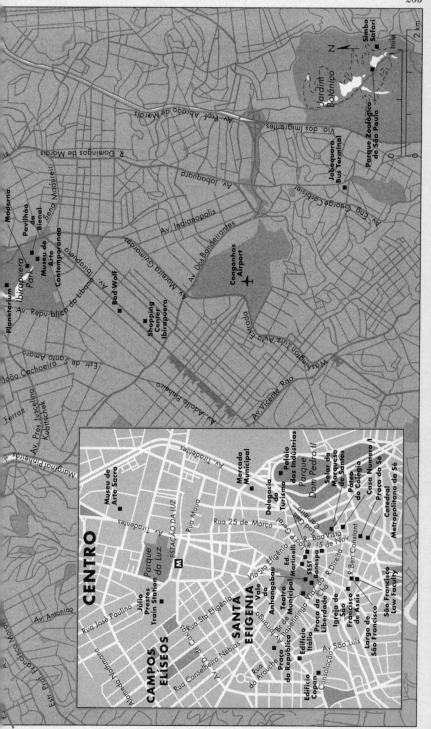

N

2 km

1 mile

0

Simba Safari

Jardim Botânico

Parque Zoológico de São Paulo

Parque Zoológico de São Paulo

Via dos Imigrantes

Av. Prof. Abrão de Morais

R. Domingos de Morais

Jabaquara Bus Terminal

Av. Eng. George Corbisier

Av. Jabaquara

Moderna

Pavilhão da Bienal

Sena Madureira

Av. Indianópolis

Museu de Arte Contemporânea

Ibirapuera Park

Av. Ibirapuera

Av. Morelia Guimarães

Av. Dos Bandeirantes

Congonhas Airport

Planetarium

Bad Wolf

Av. República do Líbano

Shopping Center Ibirapuera

Washington Luiz Auto Estrada

Estr. de Santa Amaro

Av. Adolfo Pinheiro

Av. Vicente Rao

João Cachoeiro

Ferraz

Av. Pres. Juscelino Kubitschek

Marginal Pinheiros

Av. Antônico

Estr. Prof. Francisco Morat

Al. Prof. Francisco Morat

CENTRO

Museu de Arte Sacra

Av. Tiradentes

Mercado Municipal

Delegacia do Turismo

Palácio das Indústrias

Parque Dom Pedro II

Solar da Marquesa de Santos

Casa Numero I

Pátio do Colégio

Praça da Sé

Catedral Metropolitana da Sé

Rua Mauá

Rua 25 de Março

R. Boa Vista

Rua Cnel Gen

ESTAÇÃO DA LUZ

Parque da Luz

M

Rua Tiradentes

R. 15 de Nov

R. Direita

Júlio Prestes Train Station

Rua José Paulino

Rua Sta Efigênia

Via Sta Efigênia

Ed. Martinelli

SEST

Bonespa

R. Ben Constant

Igreja de São Francisco de Assis

São Francisco Law Faculty

SANTA EFIGENIA

Vale do Anhangabaú

Teatro Municipal

Praça da Liberdade

Largo de São Francisco

Av. São Luís

Praça da República

Av. Ipiranga

Av. Cásper Líbero

Edifício Itália

Rua Consalheiro Nébias

Alameda Nothmann

Rua do Arouche

Edifício Copan

Consolação

CAMPOS ELÍSEOS

and is an excellent alternate route, but the rest of the trip must be done on the obsolete, dangerous Dutra, which is traveled largely by trucks; the entire trip takes five hours. If you have the time, you might consider taking the much longer, spectacular coastal corniche-type road, the Rio–Santos highway (SP 55 and BR 101), a trip that can be easily made in two days, with a midway stopover at the Portuguese colonial city of Parati in the state of Rio de Janeiro.

Other main highways are the Castelo Branco (SP 280), which links the southwestern part of the state to the city; the Via Anhanguera (SP 330), which originates in the state's rich northern agricultural region, passing through the university town of Campinas; SP 310, which also runs from the farming heartland; BR 116 South, which comes up from Curitiba; plus the Via Anchieta (SP 150) and the Rodovia Imigrantes (SP 160), parallel roads that run to the coast, each operating one way on weekends and holidays.

Train Station At press time there was no train service between Rio and São Paulo. Most travel to the interior is done by bus or automobile. The principal train station is the **Estação da Luz** (Praça da Luz 1, tel. 011/991–3062), near São Paulo's liveliest and cheapest shopping district, 25 de Março, which connects the city to small towns in the interior of the state and to some metropolitan suburbs. The west zone's **Estação Barra Funda** (Av. Marquês de São Vicente, tel. 011/66–1677) serves towns in the western part of the state. The **Estação Júlio Prestes** (Praça Júlio Prestes 148, tel. 011/223–7211), in the downtown Campos Eliseos neighborhood, operates trains to the southeast and some surburban trains; and the **Estação Roosevelt** (Praça Agente Cícero, tel. 011/292–5417) serves the suburbs only.

Bus Station There are four bus stations (information for all stations: tel. 011/235–0322) in São Paulo. The main station, serving all Brazilian state capitals (except Belo Horizonte), other important cities, plus Paraguay, Argentina, Uruguay, and Chile, is the **Tietê** bus terminal (Av. Cruzeiro do Sul), in the north zone, on the Marginal Tietê beltway. Service to Rio is every half-hour on the half hour. The others are the **Bresser** terminal (Rua do Hipódromo), in the east zone district of Brás, with service to the south of Minas Gerais state and Belo Horizonte; **Jabaquara** terminal (Rua Jequitibas) in the south zone near Congonhas airport, with buses to and from coastal towns; and the **Barra Funda** terminal (Rua Mário de Andrade 664), located in the west zone near the Latin America Memorial. All stations have or are close to metrô stops.

Getting Around São Paulo

Your choice of transportation will depend largely on the weather and the state of air pollution during your stay. During the winter, taxi and metrô are the best ways to see the sights while avoiding rain and/or the dirty air caused by thermal inversions. In the summer, walking is fine for downtown sights and for shopping in the Jardins district, as long as you carry an umbrella for the inevitable heavy but short-lived summer rains. Details on the bus and subway systems can be found in a book of street maps, the *Guia São Paulo*, available at newsstands and bookstores. Driving is not recommended in São Paulo, because of inadequate roadways and traffic control, the generally poor level of driving, and the antiquated vehicles that often break down; the city's 4.5 million vehicles frequently clog main arteries.

By Public Transportation Safe, quick, comfortable, and clean, the **metrô,** or subway (information tel. 011/284–8877), is by far the best means of transportation, but unfortunately it leaves out a large portion of the city's southern districts. There are three lines: the blue North–South, the orange East–West, and the new green Vila Prudente–Vila Madalena line, which runs under Avenida Paulista to the Clínicas hospital. The blue and orange lines run daily 5 AM–midnight and cross at the downtown Praça da Sé. At press time, the third line ran daily 6 AM–8:30 PM, but was scheduled to expand its hours to 5 AM–midnight in late 1993. Magnetic tickets are sold for less than 50¢ in the metrô stations, with a discount for round-trips; they are inserted into a turnstile at the platform entrance and returned only if there is unused mileage. Transfers within the subway system are free, and for bus–subway trips (one bus only), a *bilhete integração* can be purchased on buses or at subway ticket windows for under $1, with a round-trip discount. Multiples of 10 tickets can also be purchased at a discount. Ticket sellers do not have to make change for large bills. Maps of the metrô system are available from the Departamento de Marketing Institucional (Avenida Paulista 1842, 19th Floor, tel. 011/283–4933).

Ample bus service (CMTC information tel. 133) complements the metrô, but regular buses (white with a red horizontal stripe on the sides) are overcrowded at rush hour and when it rains. Bus stops are clearly marked, but routes are spelled out only on the bus itself. The fare is about 40¢. For bus numbers and names, routes, and schedules for CMTC buses, purchase the *Guia São Paulo Ruas,* published by *Quatro Rodas* magazine. Passengers enter at the front and exit the back, after paying the fare to the *cobrador* seated on a platform at the back of the bus. Often the cobrador has no change, and gives out *vale transporte* slips, or bus fare vouchers, instead. The green and gray **CMTC executivo** buses (information tel. 158), whose numbers all end in the letter *E,* are more spacious and cost less than $1, paid on entry to the driver, but at press time the city was considering discontinuing their use. There are also many *clandestino* (unlicensed, privately run buses) traversing the city; most of them are quite battered, and some are painted to look like the CMTC buses. (Last year the city planned to regulate these buses and have them painted white with blue stripes.) They charge the same fares as the CMTC, or less.

By Taxi Owner-driven taxis are the best maintained, and these unbattered vehicles are the ones to look for among São Paulo's gray-blue **comum** fleet, in order to avoid breakdowns and trips that never emerge from second gear. Fares are calculated from the number of UTs (units) shown on the meter, using a chart pasted in the back window. Each UT is about 35¢, and each ride begins with four UTs already on the meter; additional UTs are accumulated with each kilometer (half-mile), and also while the cab is not in motion, on the basis of 27 clicks of one-second duration. Radio taxis are very reliable and quick. **Radio Taxi São Paulo** (tel. 011/251–1733) is the most popular, and accepts credit cards for a small percentage over the meter.

Orientation Tours

Walking Tours There are no regularly scheduled guided walking tours offered in São Paulo, but you can design your own with the aid of information provided by SEST or Anhembi booths around the city (*see* Tourist Information, *above*). You can hire a bilingual guide through a travel agency or hotel concierge to accompany you for about $15 an hour (minimum of four hours). The best areas to explore on foot are the Japanese neighborhood of Liberdade, the Italo-Portuguese Bexiga-Bela Vista quarter, the pedestrian-only streets of the old financial district, downtown (with great attention to security), and for shopping, the boutique-packed, hilly Jardins neighborhood.

Bus Tours The least expensive alternative on wheels are the 12 different half-day bus tours offered every Sunday by the municipal tourism board, Anhembi Turismo e Eventos da Cidade de São Paulo. Seven Circuíto Turístico Cultural (Cultural Tourist Circuit) tours cover a variety of museums, parks, shopping locales, monuments, outdoor fairs, and historic buildings. Another five tours comprise the Circuíto Ecológico, or Ecological Circuit; these cover parks and ecological preserves, the zoo and botanical gardens, plus the Interlagos automobile race track, where the São Paulo Formula One race takes place every March. The Circuito tours all depart from the Anhembi booth at the Praça da República. Tickets, which can be purchased at the booth on weekends from 9 to 3, cost less than $1 for adults, with discounts for children under 10, students, and senior citizens. For more information, call 011/267–2122, ext. 640, or 011/267–0702.

Local travel agencies with downtown offices, such as **Gol Tour Viagens e Turismo** (Av. São Luís 187, basement, shop no. 12, tel. 011/256–2388) and **Opcional Tour and Guide Viagens e Turismo** (Av. Ipiranga 345, 14th floor, office 1401, tel. 011/259–1007), offer a variety of guided automobile tours for small groups, and are willing to create tours to meet specific interests. Typical tours are a half-day city tour costing about $35 a person (group rate); a visit to the zoo and the Simba Safari, where jungle animals can be seen from the safety of a car, for $35–$40 a person; a São Paulo night tour that includes a samba show, dinner, and drinks, for $85 a person; and, for $60–$70, day-long excursions to the Guarujá beach resort, a coffee farm, an ecological farm preserve, or the Portuguese colonial city of Embu, site of a Sunday arts and crafts fair (*see* Excursions from São Paulo, *below*).

Exploring São Paulo

The city's enormous energy has dispersed over time, as its sources have changed and developed. The largely pedestrian-only hilltop and valley area centering on the downtown **Vale do Anhangabaú** was where São Paulo's first inhabitants, Jesuit missionaries and treasure-hunting pioneers, lived. Later it became a financial and cultural center, and it is still home to the stock exchange and many banks. Decadent from the mid-1970s to the start of this decade, the district is now the focus of a municipal bid to revitalize the downtown. The **Bela Vista** and **Bexiga** neighborhoods abutting downtown house most of the city's theaters and bars. As coffee became the focus of Paulista wealth in the late 19th century, many families built whimsical-looking mansions on the ridge-top **Avenida Paulista,** homes that beginning in the post–World War II industrial boom gave way to skyscraper bank headquarters. Many of the city's best hotels are located near this avenue, which Paulistanos often compare to New York's Fifth Avenue. The next growth spurt came in the 1970s, when real estate firms, advertising agencies, fancy restaurants, and other companies went west and literally downhill to a former swamp, to take up residence in the tall buildings of **Avenida Brigadeiro Faria Lima,** near the stylish homes of the **Jardins** neighborhood and the Iguatemi Shopping Center (Brazil's first mall), just off the banks of the **Pinheiros River.** At press time, despite the recession, large-scale office construction of many corporate headquarters was continuing just south of this area, between the **Marginal Pinheiros** beltway and the **Avenida Engenheiro Luís Carlos Berrini,** not far from the luxurious Shopping Center Morumbi, with many high-income apartment buildings going up just across the river from this district.

Downtown   If you are willing to brave what many Paulistanos believe is the most dangerous part of the city (*see* Staying Safe and Healthy, *above*), this is the the place to start, devoting at least a half day to the area, on foot and by subway. Begin by taking in the overpowering view of the world's third-largest city from its highest building, the **Edifício Itália.** To do so, you'll have to patronize the bar or dining room of the **Terraço Itália** restaurant, located on its 41th floor; the restaurant is expensive and not one of the city's best. Afternoon tea or a drink is the quickest, least expensive option. *Av. Ipiranga 344, 41st fl. tel. 011/257–6566. Tea 3–5:30, $6. Bar opens 6 PM, minimum around $10. Reservations recommended.*

A few doors up to the left is the serpentine apartment and office building designed by renowned Brazilian architect Oscar Niemeyer, the **Edifício Copan.** Walk back down Avenida Ipiranga, cross Avenida São Luís, and cross Ipiranga itself to the **Praça da República,** the large central square where a huge arts and crafts, food, hobby, and semiprecious stones fair is held every Sunday, sometimes with live music. Some artisans display their work here all week long, so it's worth a peek anytime.

Now cross back over Ipiranga and walk down the pedestrian-only **Rua Barão de Itapetininga,** packed during the week with dawdling messenger boys, street vendors and entertainers, and men bearing sandwich boards advertising jobs. The neo-Baroque **Teatro Municipal,** inspired by the Opéra de Paris and built between 1903 and 1911 with Art Nouveau elements, lies at the end of this street on the **Praça Ramos de Azevedo,** facing the **Mappin** department store, once the purlieu of high-class ladies who purchased only European imports. Unfortunately, the theater's fully restored auditorium, full of gold leaf, moss-green velvet, marble, and mirrors, is only open to those attending cultural events (*see* The Arts and Nightlife, *below*), but it is sometimes possible to walk in for a quick view of the vestibule.

Now cross the square eastward to walk over the Art Deco **Viaduto do Chá,** into the heart of São Paulo. *Chá* means tea, and the bridge is so named because tea was once grown in the **Vale do Anhangabaú** it crosses. Keeping pace with the city's haphazard development, the Anhangabaú later became a city park, then a noisy and dirty thoroughfare, and in 1992, with the completion of two vehicular-traffic tunnels, was turned back into breathable people space. Frequented by office workers, the area is also the site of outdoor concerts and large political rallies. Stopping for a moment on the viaduct, look north at the crowded **Viaduto Santa Ifigênia,** whose metal structure was imported from Belgium at the start of this century. Turn right onto Rua Libero Badaró at the end of the Viaduto do Chá. This street leads into the Largo São Francisco, home to the **São Francisco Law Faculty,** one of Brazil's first educational institutions, founded in 1824. Nearby is the Baroque **Igreja de São Francisco de Assis** (Saint Francis of Assisi Church). The church actually consists of two churches by the same name, one run by Catholic clergy, and one by lay brothers. One of the city's best-preserved Portuguese colonial buildings, the complex was built from 1647 to 1790. *Largo São Francisco 133, tel. 011/36–0081. Admission free. Lay brothers' church closed weekdays 11:30–1, weekends after 10 AM.*

A short walk from here up Rua Benjamin Constant is the **Praça da Sé,** the city's most central spot and the location of the **Catedral Metropolitana da Sé** (Praça da Sé, tel. 011/37–6832; admission free; crypt closed Thurs.–Sun. before 2:30 and Mon.–Wed.), the Metropolitan Holy See Cathedral, a fairly ugly neo-Gothic structure with a crypt, completed in 1954.

The huge, busy square, under which the city's two major metrô lines cross, is where migrants from Brazil's poor northeast region often go to enjoy their typical music and to sell and buy products from that region, such as medicinal herbs, sold in sacks spread out on the ground. It is also the central hangout for São Paulo's street children and the focus of periodic (and controversial) police sweeps to get them off the street. The square and most of the historic area and financial district to its north have been set aside for pedestrians, official vehicles, and public transportation only, although at press time the city was considering reopening some parts to private cars.

Moving north out of the square on the Rua Roberto Simonsen, you will come across **Casa Numero 1,** at Rua Roberto Simonsen 136B, sole intact survivor of a wave of European-style chalets that swept São Paulo in the 1880s and now home of the city archives, open only for historical research. Next door is the **Solar da Marquesa de Santos** (Rua Roberto Simonsen 136A, tel. 011/36–2218; admission free; closed Mon.), the only late-18th-century residence remaining in the city. From 1834 to 1867, this home belonged to the Marchioness of Santos, the mistress of Emperor Pedro II and a hostess to much of Brazilian aristocracy of her day. A little farther up the street and around the corner to the right is the **Pátio do Colégio,** a complex of white-walled buildings on the site of the first Jesuit mission in the city, founded by Father José de Anchieta in 1554 to convert the local Indians. The complex houses a museum (Casa de Anchieta, Pátio do Colégio, s/n, tel. 011/239–5722; admission charged; closed Tues.–Sun. until 1 and Mon.) that displays rustic Portuguese colonial furniture, a model of the early city, and a piece of the mud and wattle wall from the original mission; and a **chapel** (Capela de Anchieta, Pátio do Colégio 84, tel. 011/35–6899; admission free; closed Sun. after 11:30 and Sat.).

Now walk north down Rua Boa Vista and take a left onto Rua Direita, then the first right onto Rua 15 de Novembro. No. 275, on the left, houses **BOVESPA,** the São Paulo Stock Exchange, Brazil's busiest and a hub for new foreign investment attracted here especially by the government's efforts to privatize state-owned companies. Those who leave an ID with the guard at the front desk can go up to the mezzanine gallery to watch the hurly-burly and consult a computer terminal for the latest stock quotes. BOVESPA has plans to put an English-language terminal in the gallery, but at press time there was no set installation date. BOVESPA offers personalized tours in English to representatives of foreign investment institutions, but these must be set up in advance; direct requests to the Superintendência Executiva de Desenvolvimento, fax 011/239–4981. *Rua 15 de Novembro 275, tel. 011/258–7222, ext. 516. Admission free. Gallery closed weekdays 1–3 and weekends.*

Near the end of Rua 15 de Novembro, at Rua João Brícola 24, stands the 36-floor **Banespa building** (tel. 011/259–7722), built in 1947 and modeled after New York's Empire State Building. If you couldn't fit tea or drinks at the top of the Edifício Itália into your downtown walking tour (*see above*), here's a second, no-frills chance for a panoramic look at the city. A radio traffic reporter squints through the smog every morning from this tower. To the north, you will note the whimsy of the penthouse residence on the 30-floor **Edifício Martinelli** (Rua Líbero Badaró 504, tel. 011/35–1664), the city's first skyscraper, built in 1929 by Italian immigrant-turned-count Giuseppe Martinelli. This rooftop is open weekdays 9–4 to visitors by permission of the building administrator, located on the ground floor. Just leave a photo ID at the front desk and ride the elevator to the 34th floor, then walk up two more flights. The deck is open to the public weekdays 10:30–4.

If you're up for a last thrill from this megalopolis that draws buyers, sellers, watchers, and doers from all over the continent, top off your downtown walking tour with a foray into the crush of the crowds on the **Ladeira General Carneiro, Rua 25 de Março,** and the **Ladeira Porto Geral.** *Ladeira* means incline, and from the first one listed here you will get a quick view of the **Palácio das Indústrias** (Industrial Palace), an eclectic-style convention and exhibition center with two red towers built in 1924, last year reinaugurated as São Paulo's **city hall.** Ladeira Porto Geral, named for a port on the Tamanduateí River now shrunk into the confines of a concrete canal, is the street of Carnival costume shops; you'll find sequins, towering feather headdresses, and masks galore there year-round. Finally, Rua 25 de Março, precinct of the city's Lebanese immigrants and their offspring, is a wholesale and retail shopping district stuffed with textiles, clothing, carpets, toys, birthday party materials—you name it. Not far to the north of this area is the **Mercado Municipal** (Municipal Market), fruit of São Paulo's coffee wealth, built in 1933 and still functioning, with beautiful stained-glass windows depicting harvest and cattle-raising activities.

Campo Elíseos A short metrô ride from the central downtown area to the Santa Cecília stop is a district that until recently was a virtual slum, studded with decrepit relics of the era when coffee was king and the railroads were the route to its rule. Now the **Campos Elíseos** neighborhood, adjacent to both the Júlio Prestes and Luz railroad stations, is undergoing slow but sure renovation. Perhaps in the not-too-distant future, Paulistanos will get their first taste of U.S.-style gentrification. The governor's seat was originally at **Palácio Campos Elíseos** (Av. Rio Branco

1269, tel. 011/220–0033; admission free; closed Wed.–Sun. until 2 and Mon. and Tues.), but in 1965, the official residence moved to a new mansion in Morumbi. Built between 1896 and 1899 in a combination of Italian Renaissance and French Baroque revival styles, the Palácio has become a rather elegant state secretariat of science, technology, and economic development. With an eye toward the area's rebirth, at press time the secretariat had begun to hold art exhibitions in the palace. The district also has several restored turn-of-the-century mansions, along streets that are amazingly still tree-lined (and in some cases named after the affluent families who once lived here), such as **Alameda Nothmann** and **Rua Conselheiro Nébias.** Nearby is the **Júlio Prestes train station,** built between 1926 and 1937, with its two huge stained-glass windows depicting the role of train travel in the Brazilian economy. At press time, the station was under restoration, with a slated 1994 completion date. And just around the corner from that station is another, the **Estação da Luz,** inaugurated in 1901 and built of iron and red brick shipped mostly from England. To the west of the station is **Rua José Paulino,** once a redoubt of Jewish Brazilians in the textiles business, now given over to Koreans who have continued in the neighborhood tradition.

Paulista   In the 1960s, São Paulo builders began directing their energies toward a wide ridge-top avenue about five minutes' drive from downtown and lined with the eclectic-style turn-of-the-century mansions of the coffee barons. Avenida Paulista quickly became the showplace of São Paulo, and perhaps even Brazil's most important street, with its myriad bank headquarters and other business institutions. An imposing long and straight shot, the avenue has also increasingly lent itself to protest marches, which often finish down in the Anhangabaú. The avenue is also part of the annual Saint Sylvester footrace, which takes place on New Year's Eve.

As historic preservation came late to São Paulo, only a handful of the old mansions remain; one of them, totally restored, now houses a McDonald's, at No. 709. Another, the Casa das Rosas (No. 35), was recently preserved as part of a new building project on a lot adjacent to it.

Avenida Paulista's other attractions include the Tenente Siqueira Campos Park, better known as the **Trianon Park** (Rua Peixoto Gomide 949, tel. 011/289–2169; admission free), a rare remaining patch of the Atlantic forest that once lined most of eastern Brazil; the **Museu de Arte de São Paulo,** known as **MASP** (*see* Museums, *below*), at No. 1578; the sloping grilled facade of the **São Paulo State Industrial Federation** (FIESP), one of the country's most important business groups, at No. 1313; and the postmodern **Citibank** headquarters, at No. 1111, whose pink-marble and blue-glass facade spills down to the street in a curve like a waterfall.

Little Tokyo   At the beginning of the century, a group of Japanese arrived to work as contract farm laborers in the state of São Paulo. In the next five decades, over a quarter of a million of their countrymen followed, forming the largest Japanese colony outside Japan. Distinguished today by a large number of college graduates and successful businesspeople, professionals, and politicians, the colony made important contributions to Brazilian agriculture and the seafood industry. The Liberdade neighborhood, which is located south of Praça da Se behind the cathedral, and whose entrance is marked by a series of red porticoes, is home for many first-, second-, and third-generation Japanese-Brazilians. Here, clustered around Avenida Liberdade, you will find shops selling everything from imported bubble gum with miniature robots in the box, to Kabuki face paint. It's also the setting for some of the city's finest sushi bars and Japanese restaurants, plus a growing number of Korean and Chinese dining spots. On Sunday morning the **Praça Liberdade,** by the Liberdade metrô station, hosts a sprawling Oriental food and crafts fair, where the free and easy Brazilian ethnic mix is in plain view; you'll see, for example, black Brazilians dressed in colorful kimonos hawking grilled shrimp on a stick. Liberdade also hosts several ethnic celebrations, such as the April Hanamatsuri, commemorating Buddha's birth, and the July Feast of Stars.

Just a 10-minute walk from the Liberdade metrô station, you will find the intriguing **Museum of Japanese Immigration** (Rua São Joaquim 381, tel. 011/279–5465; admission charged; closed Tues.–Sun. morning and Mon.), with two floors of exhibits about the immigrants' culture and farm life and their contributions to Brazilian horticulture, such as the persimmon, azalea, and tangerine.

Museums A city that has long been on the go, São Paulo has allocated relatively little space or funds for the arts. Its museums do house some treasures, but because they often operate on a shoestring, they can be disappointing for those expecting exhibits on a par with those of the great First-World institutions.

A striking low rise elevated on two massive concrete pillars 78 meters (256 feet) apart, the **Museu de Arte de São Paulo (MASP)** is the city's premier fine-arts museum. The highlights are a few dazzling, world-famous works by Bosch, Rembrandt, Poussin, Van Gogh, Renoir, and Degas, suspended from the ceiling in glass "sandwiches." The huge open area underneath the building is often used for cultural events, and is the scene of a Sunday antiques fair (*see* Shopping, *below*). *Av. Paulista 1578, tel. 011/251–5644. Admission charged. Closed Tues.–Sun. until 2 PM and Mon.*

Designed by Oscar Niemeyer, the **Museu de Arte Moderna** (Museum of Modern Art) houses 2,600 paintings, sculptures, works on paper, and objects centering on the Brazilian modernist movement, which began in the 1920s. The museum often holds shows of up-and-coming local artists. *Ibirapuera Park, tel. 011/549–9688. Admission charged. Closed weekday mornings and Mon.*

Located on the campus of the University of São Paulo, the **Museu de Arte Contemporânea** (Museum of Contemporary Art) consists of the main building and an annex. Together they contain almost 5,000 works by foreign and Brazilian artists, including Modigliani, Picasso, Chagall, Matisse, Miró, Di Cavalcanti, Anita Malfatti, João Câmara, and Wesley Duke Lee. *Main building: Rua da Reitoria 109, tel. 011/211–0011, ext. 3538. Admission free. Closed Tues.–Sat. mornings and Mon. Annex: Rua da Reitoria 160, tel. 011/211–0111, ext. 3033. Admission free. Same hours as main building.*

The **Fundação Maria Luiza e Oscar Americano,** a private wooded estate, is an especially pleasant place to spend an afternoon. The collection includes Portuguese colonial, imperial, and modern furniture, sacred art, silver, porcelain, engravings, personal objects of the Brazilian royal family, paintings, tapestries, and sculpture. The foundation holds Sunday concerts, and afternoon tea is served until 6. *Av. Morumbi 3700, tel. 011/842–0077. Admission charged. Closed weekday mornings until 11 and Mon.*

In addition to displaying a permanent exhibition of Latin American handicrafts, the **Memorial da América Latina,** a new state-run complex designed by Oscar Niemeyer, holds a series of Latin American art shows throughout the year. *Rua Mário de Andrade 644, tel. 011/823–9611. Admission free. Closed Mon. except during concerts.*

In 1888, a Brazilian scientist, with the aid of the São Paulo state government, turned a farmhouse into a center for the production of snake serum. Today, the **Instituto Butantã** is the largest snake farm in South America, with a collection of over 70,000 snakes, spiders, scorpions, and lizards. The institute extracts venom and processes it into serum available to victims of poisonous bites throughout Latin America. Unfortunately, the institute has suffered from underfunding and is somewhat run-down. Far behind modern museum technology, exhibits are not as accessible to children as they could be. *Av. Vital Brasil 1500, tel. 011/813–7222. Admission charged. Closed Mon.*

Parks and Gardens

Only 15 minutes by taxi from downtown, **Ibirapuera Park** is São Paulo's answer to New York's Central Park, although it's slightly less than half the size and gets infinitely more crowded on sunny weekends. The park's 395 acres contain jogging and bicycle paths, a lake, and rolling lawns, as well as 10 exhibition halls. The **Japanese Pavilion** is an exact replica of the Katura Imperial Palace in Kyoto, Japan. The internationally renowned Biennial Art Show is held here, in the **Pereira Pavilion,** in even-numbered years (*see* The Arts and Nightlife, *below*). In addition to being the setting for several museums (*see* Museums, *above*) and many fairs and other special events, the park is also home to São Paulo's **planetarium,** extremely popular among Paulistanos; there are special shows for children over seven on weekends 4–6, and for children aged 5–10 Sunday at 10:30. *Ibirapuera Park, Av. Pedro Álvares Cabral, s/n, tel. 011/575–5511. Planetarium: tel. 011/575–5206. Admission charged. Closed weekdays and weekend mornings.*

Among the world's 10 best zoos, the sprawling **Parque Zoológico de São Paulo** (Av. Miguel Stéfano 4241, tel. 011/267–0811; admission charged) is a must, even if you don't have children in tow as an excuse for a visit. Its 200 acres include a lake with small islands where monkeys live in houses on stilts, plus more than 2,000 animal species, many of which are endangered. The animals are housed not in cages but in large open areas separated from visitors by ditches. The simian, reptile, and bird sections are especially good. Next door to the zoo are the botanical gardens, **Jardim Botánico** (Av. Miguel Stéfano 3031/3687, tel. 011/577–3055; admission charged; closed Mon. and Tues.), an immense nursery of about 3,000 plants belonging to more than 340 native species. There is also a hothouse of Atlantic forest species, an orchidarium, and a collection of aquatic plants.

São Paulo for Free—Or Almost

Free city-sponsored concerts often attract large crowds to
public spaces such as the open area under the **Museu de Arte
de São Paulo** and the new pedestrian-only **Anhangabaú Valley**
area. Visiting international orchestras often are invited to play
for Sunday morning concertgoers in **Ibirapuera Park;** local musicians also frequently perform there. Free state-sponsored
concerts take place at the **Memorial da América Latina** (Rua
Mário de Andrade 644, tel. 011/823–9611; closed Mon. except
during concerts). Weekend antiques and arts and crafts fairs
are held in various locales around the city (*see* Shopping,
below). **Senac** (tel. 011/256–5522), a retailing trade guild and
school, organizes many free courses and cultural events at several locations. The best source of information on low-cost (and
other) events is the *Veja São Paulo* magazine, which comes as
an insert in the Sunday newsweekly, *Veja.*

What to See and Do with Children

Many local families spend leisure time at one of the many malls
that have **mini-amusement parks,** such as **Iguatemi** or **Morumbi shopping centers;** the latter also has an ice-skating rink
with skates to rent. The *Veja São Paulo* magazine in the
newsweekly *Veja* has a special listing of events for children.

Exclusively child-centered fun can be had at **Simba Safari** (Av.
do Cursino 6338, tel. 011/946–6249; admission charged; closed
Mon.), a minijungle near the zoo, with lions, camels, monkeys,
and tigers roaming free while visitors drive through. The management provides transportation for a per-person fee. The
most traditional venue for kids is **Playcenter** (Rua Dr. Rubens
Meirelles 380, tel. 011/824–9666; admission charged; closed
Mon. and Tues.), a dizzyingly huge and often crowded amusement park on the banks of the Tietê River, about 10 minutes
by car from downtown. Near the Pinheiros River, the **Eldorado
Shopping Center** has the **Parque da Mônica** (Av. Rebouças
3970, tel. 011/816–7766; admission charged; closed Mon. except
holidays), an amusement park with a theater and cinema built
around the theme of the popular Brazilian cartoon character
Mônica. For older children who know how to swim, one of the
best attractions is **The Waves** (Av. Guido Caloi 25, tel. 011/521–
8666; admission charged; closed Fri. morning and Mon.–
Thurs.), an aquatic park with heated swimming pools, artificial
waves, and mammoth slides. Bring your own towels and
shower accessories, or purchase them at the gift shop. Kids
over five love to split their eardrums—but not, it's hoped, their
bones—at **Bad Wolf** (Av. Ibijaú 353, tel. 011/241–9811; admission charged; closed Tues.–Sun. mornings and Mon.), a rocking
roller rink near Ibirapuera Park that rents both traditional and
Rollerblade-style skates. São Paulo also has an interactive children's science museum, the **Estação Ciência** (Rua Guaicurus
1274, tel. 011/263–7022; admission free; closed weekend and
holiday mornings and Mon.), a 10-minute drive from downtown; your kids will probably go for the live reptiles and spiders. Sunday is the best day for avoiding crowds of
school-children.

Shopping

People come from all over Brazil and even from neighboring countries to shop in São Paulo, where boutiques and shopping malls help shoppers forget the city's lack of beauty and the extreme poverty of many of its residents. Department stores do exist, but they generally lack the glitz of their U.S. counterparts; well-to-do Brazilians prefer the personal attention they get in smaller stores. Price and quality vary dramatically, according to the country's ever-fluctuating economy. Most stores either tack on a hefty surcharge for credit cards or give discounts for cash. São Paulo street shops are open weekdays from about 9 to 6:30, closing Saturday around 1. Some that participate in a marketing gambit called Shop Tur are open on Sunday. For a list of the participants and their Sunday hours, call 011/210–4000 or 011/813–3311. Shopping malls open weekdays 10–10 and Saturday 9 AM–10 PM; they open Sundays preceding gift-giving holidays.

Shopping Districts The **Jardins** neighborhood, centering on **Rua Augusta** (a cross street of Avenida Paulista) and **Rua Oscar Freire,** is the most traditional and chic shopping area. Double-parked Mercedes Benzes, BMWs, and Mitsubishis point the way to the city's fanciest clothing and leather goods boutiques, jewelers, gift shops, antiques stores, art galleries, restaurants, bars, and beauty salons. Most of the same boutiques can be found at upscale shopping malls. **Downtown,** the **Rua do Arouche** is another shopping venue, especially for leather goods. The area surrounding **Rua João Cachoeira,** in the **Itaim** neighborhood, has evolved from a neighborhood of small clothing factories into a wholesale and retail clothing sales district. Nearby is **Rua Dr. Mário Ferraz,** stuffed with elegant clothing, gift, and home decoration stores.

Shopping Malls São Paulo has seen a crush of malls since 1980, largely in response to safety considerations. As in the United States, a "mall culture" has come into being, but ubiquitous security guards are quick to snuff out any teenage (or other) misbehavior. The city's oldest and most sophisticated mall, **Shopping Center Iguatemi** (Av. Brigadeiro Faria Lima 1191, tel. 011/210–1333), has a recent addition, replete with the latest in fashion and fast food. Just to the south, in the city's fastest-growing area, is a top competitor: **Shopping Center Morumbi** (Av. Roque Petroni Jr. 1089, tel. 011/553–2444), with just about the same boutiques, record stores, bookstores, and restaurants, plus a department store at either end. Both malls, as well as most others, have several movie theaters that usually show U.S.-made films in English with Portuguese subtitles. Other large malls convenient to hotels include **Shopping Center Ibirapuera** (Av. Ibirapuera 3103, tel. 011/543–0011), **Eldorado Shopping Center** (Av. Rebouças 3970, tel. 011/815–7066), **Shopping Center Paulista** (Rua 13 de Maio 1947, tel. 011/288–8666), and **Shopping Jardim Sul** (Av. Giovanni Gronchi 5819, tel. 011/855–1000).

Outdoor Markets Almost every neighborhood has a weekly outdoor food market (days are listed in local newspapers) featuring loudmouthed hawkers, exotic scents, and piles of colorful fruit, vegetables, herbs, fish, dried meats, and chicken. **CEAGESP,** an agricultural clearing house located where the Pinheiros and Tietê beltways and rivers meet, houses a flower market selling both dried and fresh varieties at wholesale prices. It's open to the public Tuesday and Friday 6 AM–noon. A fruit and vegetable market located there is closed mornings except for Saturday. CEAGESP's restaurant (Av. Dr. Gastão Vidigal 1946, tel. 011/260–3366), with its famed onion soup, is a favorite pit stop for wintertime all-night revelers.

On Sunday the open space under the **Museu de Arte de São Paulo** shelters the city's best **antiques fair** (Av. Paulista 1578, tel. 011/251–5644), competing with a similar fair on Sunday afternoon in the **Shopping Center Iguatemi**'s parking lot (Av. Brigadeiro Faria Lima 1191, tel. 011/210–1333). The city's best **arts and crafts fair,** featuring gemstones, embroidery, leather goods, toys, clothing, paintings, musical instruments, and jewelry, takes place Sunday morning at the downtown **Praça da República;** many booths move over to the nearby **Praça da Liberdade** neighborhood in the afternoon, joining Japanese-style ceramics, wooden sandals, cooking utensils, food, and miniature bonsai trees. There is also a **flea market** on Sunday at the Praça Dom Orione, in the Italian **Bela Vista** neighborhood.

Specialty Stores Most of the stall owners at the Sunday Museu de Arte de São
Antiques Paulo antiques fair also have shops, and they hand out their business cards so you can browse throughout the week at your leisure. There are many stores specializing in high-priced **European antiques** in the **Jardins,** on and around **Rua da Consolaçao,** but nearby **Paulo Vasconcelos** (Alameda Gabriel Monteiro da Silva 1881, tel. 011/852–2444) sells 18th- and 19th-century Brazilian furniture, plus folk art. You can find Brazilian antiques at reasonable prices at **Patrimônio** (Alameda Ministro Rocha Azevedo 1068, tel. 011/64–1750), as well as some Indian artifacts and modern furnishings crafted from iron. **Arte e Companhia** (Rua Oscar Freire 146, tel. 011/64–1574) is a group of three dealers selling local, Latin American, and European antiques, such as lamps, silver, and decorative birds. And **Renato Magalhães Gouvêa Escritório de Arte** (Av. Europa 68, tel. 011/853–2569) offers a potpourri of antiques and modern furnishings and art, both European and Brazilian. A slew of lower-priced antique furniture stores line **Rua Cardeal Arcoverde** in **Pinheiros,** and there are also some shops selling smaller items on **Rua Tabapuã,** in **Itaim.**

Art If naïf art is your thing, the **Jacques Ardies** gallery (Rua do Livramento 221, tel. 011/884–2916) is a must. **Camargo Vilaça** (Rua Fradique Coutinho 1500, tel. 011/210–7390) specializes in up-and-coming Brazilian artists. Trendsetting mainstream galleries include the **Galeria São Paulo** (Rua Estados Unidos 1456, tel. 011/852–8855) and **Mônica Filgueiras de Almeida** (Rua Haddock Lobo 1568, tel. 011/282–5292).

Clothing Much of Brazil's best **women's designer clothing** can be found in **Jardins** boutiques and shopping-mall branch stores, such as **Maria Bonita** (Rua Oscar Freire 702, tel. 011/852–6433; also at Shopping Center Iguatemi), **Reinaldo Lourenço** (Rua Bela Cintra 2173, tel. 011/853–8150), and **G** (Rua Oscar Freire 978, tel. 011/852–3346; also at Shopping Center Iguatemi). **Huis Clos** (Rua Dr. Mário Ferraz 538, tel. 011/820–2396) is another top store, in the Itaim neighborhood. Another option for those who, like some Brazilian first ladies, enjoy ultrapersonalized attention and privacy, are the "closed" (no storefront) designer-label boutiques of the **Vila Nova Conceição** neighborhood, such as **Daslu** (Rua Domingos Leme 284, tel. 011/822–

7461), **Claudete e Deca** (Rua Brás Cardoso 201, tel. 011/532–1855), and **Bebé** (Rua Lourenço de Almeida 811, tel. 011/531–0190). For **children's outfits**, try **Giovanna Baby** (Shopping Center Iguatemi, tel. 011/814–8463). While men's clothing generally doesn't meet European or U.S. standards, the best sportswear is found under a trendy Rio de Janeiro label, **Richard's**, at stores of the same name (Alameda Franca 1185, tel. 011/282–5399; also at Shopping Center Iguatemi). And at the **Vila Romana factory store** (Via Anhanguera, km. 17.5, tel. 011/706–2211, open Sun.), a 40-minute car ride from downtown, you can't beat the prices for suits, blazers, jeans, and even some women's wear such as silk blouses.

Gems and Jewelry Aside from the mainstream **Natan, H. Stern,** and **Amsterdam Sauer** stores in the shopping malls, there are many smaller, innovative (and sometimes cheaper) jewelry designers, such as **Sérgio Penteado** (Rua Moacir Piza 84, tel. 011/851–0487), an architect with a penchant for silver and gold jewelry with whimsical moving parts and Brazilian stones; **Antônio Bernardo** (Rua Bela Cintra 2063, tel. 011/883–5034), whose exclusive modern and classical designs utilize only precious stones; and **Francesca Romana** (Rua Carlos Steinenn 50, tel. 011/884–4691), who crafts inexpensive but great-looking Italian-style pieces out of gold-plated metal and Brazilian semiprecious stones. If you are short on shopping time, **Christina Kursell** (tel. 011/492–3673) will visit you with her collection of Brazilian stones set mostly in gold; her artisans can inexpensively copy any piece from a photograph. The work usually takes two or three days. For creative costume jewelry, try **Bella Golzer** (Rua Bela Cintra 1833, tel. 011/853–8094) or **Serpui Marie** (Alameda Lorena 1742, casa 1, tel. 011/280–1677).

Handicrafts São Paulo showcases handicrafts from just about all over Brazil at its weekly outdoor fairs (*see* Outdoor Markets, *above*). In addition, you will find upscale handiwork inspired by abstract native motifs at **Arte Nativa Aplicada** (Rua Dr. Mário Ferraz 351, tel. 011/829–6511), embroidered home furnishings at **Dentelles** (Rua Augusta 2483, tel. 011/853–9566), and Indian tribal work at the government-run **Art Índia** (Rua Augusta 1371, store No. 119, tel. 011/283–2102) and the **Casa do Amazonas** (Galeria Metropôle, Av. São Luís 187, store No. 187, tel. 011/258–9727).

Housewares Pewter is a specialty here, made from tin mined in Minas Gerais. The place to buy stunning reproductions of 17th- and 18th-century pewter goblets, dishes, and other shipboard wares is the **John Somers** store (Shopping Center Morumbi, tel. 011/61–2945).

Leather Goods **Santa Marinella** sells gorgeous Italian-style shoes and bags (Shopping Center Iguatemi, tel. 011/814–2481). For a more modern look, try **Franziska Hübener** (Shopping Center Iguatemi, tel. 011/814–3575). There are many leather shops in the Jardins area.

Spectator Sports

Basketball The clubs are amateur and privately sponsored; many of their players have made a name at the Olympics. For information on venues and schedules, contact the **Federação Paulista de Basquete** (tel. 011/251–1466). The best women's team is Ponte

Preta, boasting Brazil's top player, Hortensia; the best men's club is All Star de Franca.

Car Racing São Paulo hosts the **Formula One** race every March, bringing this city of 4.5 million cars to heights of spontaneous combustion, especially when Brazilian Ayrton Senna wins. For ticket information contact the Confederação Brasileira de Automobilismo (Rua da Glória 290, 8th floor, Rio de Janeiro, RJ 20241–180, tel. 021/221–4895, fax 021/242–4494).

Soccer Brazil's only professional sport, this is also São Paulo's favorite. Each of the city's five clubs (São Paulo, Palmeiras, Portuguesa, Corinthians, and Juventus) has its own stadium, but the major ones are São Paulo's **Morumbi** (Praça Roberto Gomes Pedrosa, tel. 011/842–3377) and the municipally run **Pacaembu** (Praça Charles Miller, tel. 011/256–9111). Covered seats offer the best protection against rowdy spectators.

Tennis International tournaments are held in the region sporadically. For information, contact the **Paulista Tennis Federation** (tel. 011/549–7955).

Thoroughbred Races are held at the **São Paulo Jockey Club** (Av. Lineu de Paulo
Horse Racing Machado, tel. 011/016–4011) weeknights 7:30–11:30 except Tuesday, and weekends 2–6. Card-carrying members of other jockey clubs gain entry to the best seats and the club's elegant restaurant.

Volleyball These clubs are amateur and privately sponsored, and some players have gained world renown. The best clubs are the women's São Caetano and Vila São José clubs, and the men's União Suzano Pirelli and Banespa. For information, contact the **Federação Paulista de Voleibol** (tel. 011/887–2833).

Beaches

São Paulo rests on an elevated plateau only 64.5 kilometers (40 miles) from the coastline, so a quick getaway from smog and gray buildings to warmer weather and blue ocean is just a matter of facing traffic on the parallel Imigrantes (BR 160) or Anchieta (BR 150) highways, each of which becomes one way on weekends and holidays. Buses run down to the coast from the Jabaquara terminal near the Congonhas Airport, and there are once-daily trains to the Santos port from the Estação da Luz.

Just after the Cubatão industrial park, once known as "Death Valley" because of its pollution (which has lessened in the last decade), comes the port of **Santos;** once a fashionable seaside port, it turned seedy long ago but is trying to clean up its beaches. To the north, by ferry or roadway, is **Guarujá,** a very popular resort where the summer social scene pretty much drowns out the crash and roar of the waves. Guarujá has numerous hotels, restaurants, nightclubs, bars, and good beach facilities. The cleanest and best beaches, however, are farther north, past Bertioga, about 2½ hours away from São Paulo by car (longer by bus or on holidays or hot summer weekends), where the mountains hug numerous small sandy coves, such as **Juquey, Barra do Sahy,** and **Maresias.** Some of these beaches are untouched, but many are sadly succumbing to the inevitable condominium encroachment. Still, on summer weekdays when school is in session, the region is gloriously deserted. Farther north still lies the huge, pristine island of **Ilha Bela,** where many Paulistanos brave terrorist mosquitoes to commune with nature and Neptune.

Dining

This is the focus of social life in São Paulo, centering on the Jardins district; there are, however, a great variety of ever-changing eateries in other parts of the city. The latest food trend—besides fast food—is Italy's *nuova cucina*. The city's immigrant groups are extremely well represented, with many German, Lebanese, Japanese, Spanish, Italian, and Portuguese restaurants, plus top-quality French and Indian spots. There are uncountable *churrascarias* (traditional barbecue restaurants), a favorite among Paulistanos; some of the best ones are up and down Rua Haddock Lobo, in the Jardins. As in other Brazilian cities, many restaurants serve the national rice, beans, and pork dish, *feijoada*, on Wednesday and Saturday; top restaurants do it up in fancy buffet style, with each type of pork meat presented separately. Lebanese immigrants have contributed a wonderful sandwich to the city's menu, the *beirute*, a Middle Eastern version of a submarine sandwich, served hot in toasted Syrian bread and sprinkled with oregano.

Restaurants in São Paulo frequently change their credit card policies, sometimes adding a surcharge for their use or not accepting them at all. No restaurant requires jacket and tie, but those in the Moderate to Very Expensive categories expect patrons to look sportily elegant (no shorts or muddy or torn jeans). *Veja São Paulo*, inserted in the newsweekly *Veja*, is an excellent source of restaurant listings, especially new establishments.

For details and price-category definitions, *see* Dining in Staying in Brazil, *above*.

Very Expensive **Ca D'Oro.** Located in the hotel of the same name (*see* Lodging, ★ *below*), this is a longtime northern Italian favorite among Brazilian bigwigs, many of whom have their own regular tables in the Old World–style chandeliered dining room. Quail, osso buco, and veal and raisin ravioli are winners, but the most famous specialty is the Piedmontese *gran bollito misto*, a variety of steamed meats and vegetables served from a wheeled cart, accompanied by three sauces. *Rua Augusta 129, tel. 011/256–8011. Reservations advised for good tables. AE, DC, MC, V.*

Fasano. Both the decor and the northern Italian cuisine here are impressive; the former boasts marble, mahogany, and a skylight; the latter, innovative salmon in a yogurt and rosemary sauce, and risotto with arugula pesto and giant shrimp. The traditional *tiramisú* makes a great finish. *Rua Haddock Lobo 1644, tel. 011/852–4000. Reservations advised. AE, DC, V. Closed Sat. lunch and Sun. dinner.*

★ **Freddy.** You'll leave behind the grunge and noise of São Paulo's streets when you walk through the doors of this long-lived eatery with the feel of an upscale Parisian bistro. Try the house duck with Madeira sauce and apple puree, pheasant with herb sauce, hearty *cassoulet* (a casserole of white beans, lamb, preserved duck, and garlic sausage), or the fish quenelles. *Praça Don Gastão Liberal Pinto 111, tel. 011/829–0977. Reservations advised. AE, DC, MC, V.*

Govinda. Authentic Indian cuisine is served in a spacious skylit dining room in a former aluminum factory, where ceiling fans whir in summer and three fireplaces plus assorted coal stoves roar in winter; additional heat comes from the chili (you can specify your chili tolerance). The house curry, a subtle blend of 16 spices, seasons dishes such as the clay oven-baked *tandoori* chicken, lamb curry in yogurt, and curried filet mignon with apples and mushrooms. Live sitar music is played Friday and Saturday. *Rua Princesa Isabel 379, tel. 011/531–0269. Reservations advised. AE, DC. Closed Sun. dinner.*

Laurent. Famous for his alchemy of Brazilian ingredients with French nouvelle cuisine, chef Laurent Suaudeau recently relocated this Rio de Janeiro restaurant to a São Paulo apartment hotel, where the decor is modern with classical French touches, such as 18th- and 19th-century art reproductions. Specialties include broccoli crêpes with cashew curry, and codfish tart rolled in spinach leaves, with basil, tomato, and soya. *Alameda Jaú 1606, tel. 011/853–5573. Reservations advised. AE. Closed Sun.*

La Vecchia Cucina. Chef Sergio Arno changed the face of the city's Italian restaurants with his *nuova cucina*, exemplified by such dishes as frog risotto, duck ravioli with watercress sauce, and apple crêpes. Well-to-do patrons feast in an ochre-color dining room decorated with Italian engravings and huge sprays of fresh flowers, or in the glassed-in garden gazebo. *Rua Pedroso Alvarenga 1088, tel. 011/282–5222. Reservations advised. AE, DC. Closed Sat. lunch and Sun.*

Massimo. Just off Avenida Paulista, this is the city's prime spot for heavyweight lunchtime dealmaking over refined Italian pleasures, including gnocchi with shrimp, tomato, and pesto sauce, or leg of lamb with leeks. Owner Massimo Ferrari, a tubby man in shirtsleeves and suspenders, keeps the best tables on standby for the nation's VIPs. *Alameda Santos 1826, tel. 011/284–0311. Reservations advised for good tables. No credit cards.*

Expensive   **Alfama dos Marinheiros.** This Portuguese restaurant serves Continental cuisine plus the traditional codfish 20 different ways, amid blue Portuguese tiles, paintings of famous personages from the old country, and upstairs, candlelight. The most popular dish is codfish *Vila Real*, baked with olive oil, potatoes, tomatoes, and onions. *Rua Pamplona 1285, tel. 011/884–9203. No credit cards. Closed Sun.–Tues.*

Bolinha. This is the place to have *feijoada*, served daily for the last 47 years. Although it's not the city's best, it's fun to nip a preprandial *caipirinha* at one of the sidewalk tables while you take in the crowded Saturday street scene, where almost every other store nearby is an imported-car dealership, and new car owners seem to adore driving back and forth. *Av. Cidade Jardin 53, tel. 011/852–9526. AE, DC, MC, V.*

Esplanada Grill. A beautiful-people hangout (especially at the bar), this is one of three top churrascarias located on the same street. The thin-sliced *picanha* steak (similar to rumpsteak) is excellent, and great with the house salad (prepared with hearts of palm and shredded fried potatoes), onion rings, and creamed spinach. The restaurant's rendition of the traditional *pão de queijo* (hot cheese-bread balls) is just right. *Rua Haddock Lobo 1682, tel. 011/881–3199. Reservations advised. V.*

★ **La Casserole.** Located downtown facing a little flower market, this charming bistro has been around for generations. Surrounded by cozy wood-paneled walls decorated with eclectic posters, you can dine on such delights as *gigot d'agneau aux*

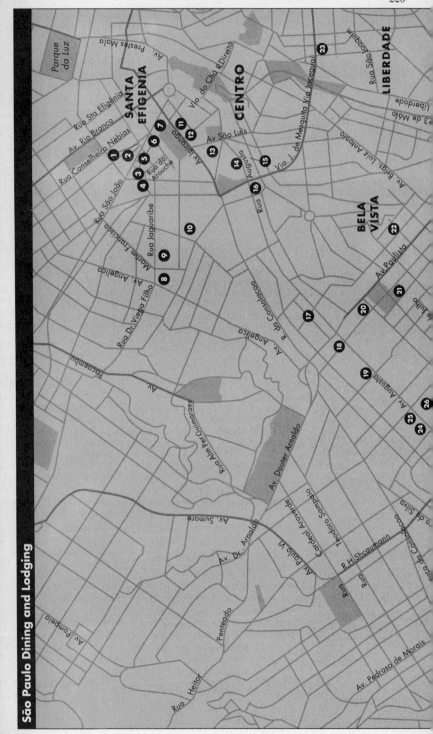

São Paulo Dining and Lodging

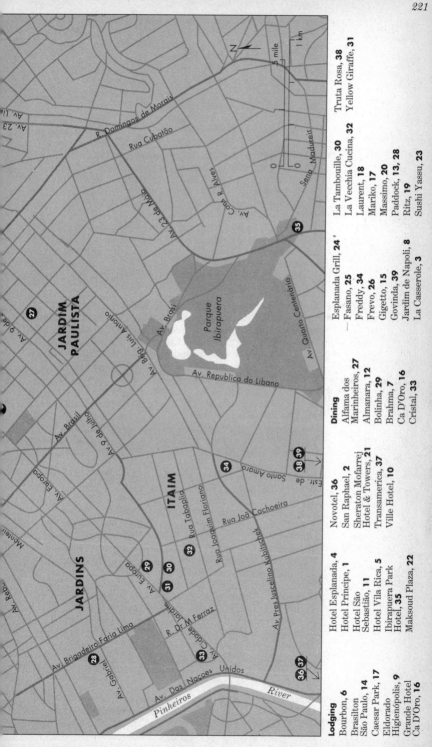

Lodging
Bourbon, 6
Brasilton
São Paulo, 14
Caesar Park, 17
Eldorado
Higienópolis, 9
Grande Hotel
Ca D'Oro, 16
Hotel Esplanada, 4
Hotel Príncipe, 1
Hotel São
Sebastião, 11
Hotel Vila Rica, 5
Ibirapuera Park
Hotel, 35
Maksoud Plaza, 22
Novotel, 36
San Raphael, 2
Sheraton Mofarrej
Hotel & Towers, 21
Transamerica, 37
Ville Hotel, 10

Dining
Alfama dos
Marinheiros, 27
Almanara, 12
Bolinha, 29
Brahma, 7
Ca D'Oro, 16
Cristal, 33
Esplanada Grill, 24
Fasano, 25
Freddy, 34
Frevo, 26
Gigetto, 15
Govinda, 39
Jardim de Napoli, 8
La Casserole, 3
La Tambouille, 30
La Vecchia Cucina, 32
Laurent, 18
Mariko, 17
Massimo, 20
Paddock, 13, 28
Ritz, 19
Sushi Yassu, 23
Truta Rosa, 38
Yellow Giraffe, 31

soissons (roast leg of lamb in its own juices, served with white beans) and cherry strudel. *Largo do Arouche 346, tel. 011/220–6283. Reservations advised. AE, DC, MC, V. Closed Sat. lunch and Mon.*

La Tambouille. A favorite among advertising executives and their clients, this Italo-French restaurant with a partly enclosed garden is a place to be seen. The food is also worth a visit, with delightful seafood lasagna, filet mignon stuffed with Parma ham and *funghi secchi* (dried mushrooms), and *marrons glacés* crêpes with ice cream. *Av. Nove de Julho 5925, tel. 011/883–6276. Reservations advised. AE, DC, MC, V.*

★ **Mariko.** Perched atop the Japanese-owned Caesar Park hotel (*see* Lodging, *below*), this restaurant caters to demanding Japanese business executives and boasts a view of the city. Everything from sushi to tempura is top quality; the grilled whole anchovy is superb. *Rua Augusta 1508, tel. 011/285–6622. Reservations advised. AE, DC, MC, V.*

Paddock. A traditional spot for relaxed business lunches, this restaurant in two locations is equally professional with its Continental cuisine. Try lamb with mint sauce or the poached haddock. *Av. São Luís 258, tel. 011/257–4768; Av. Brigadeiro Faria Lima 1541, store No. 109, tel. 011/814–3582. Reservations advised. AE, DC, MC, V. Closed Sun.*

Moderate **Brahma.** Located downtown at an intersection made famous
★ by a popular Brazilian song, this longtime favorite was recently renovated, in step with the center city's revitalization. The menu includes Brazilian and Continental dishes, with specialties such as chicken pie, roast duck with red cabbage, and apple strudel. *Av. São João 677, tel. 011/223–6720. AE, DC, MC, V. Closed Sun.*

★ **Jardim de Napoli.** This neighborhood restaurant is so good it draws outsiders. No matter where you've come from, you'll have to wait patiently in line to feast on meatballs stuffed with mozzarella cheese in Parmesan sauce, linguine with mushrooms and cream sauce, and other Italian specialties. *Rua Dr. Martinico Prado 463, tel. 011/66–3022. No credit cards. Closed Mon.*

Sushi Yassu. At one of the best Japanese restaurants in Liberdade (Little Tokyo), you'll dine on sushi, sashimi, tempura, yakisoba, or grilled fish, made with the freshest ingredients. *Rua Tomás Gonzaga 98, tel. 011/279–6622. AE. Closed Mon.*

Truta Rosa. Homegrown trout, prepared in an endless variety of ways, is making this small new restaurant with a huge fish-shape window a hit. You'll cross a metal bridge over a small lagoon to reach the dining room, where sashimi and quenelles are reeling in the customers. *Av. Vereador José Diniz 318, tel. 011/247–8629. Reservations advised. AE. Closed Sun. dinner and Mon.*

Yellow Giraffe. The fashionable atmosphere here—clean Italian modern decor, beautiful people eyeing each other, and valet parking—lends refinement to the lowly beirute, São Paulo's answer to the hero sandwich. Other great eats include grilled chicken and mashed sweet potatoes, "garnished" with a breaded, deep-fried whole banana. *Rua Amauri 356, tel. 011/853–2438. No credit cards.*

Inexpensive **Almanara.** Part of a chain of Lebanese semi-fast-food outlets that began at this downtown location, Almanara is perfect for a quick lunch of *hummus* (chick-pea spread), *tabbouleh* (salad with cracked wheat, tomato, parsley, mint, and lemon juice), grilled chicken, and rice. There is also a full-blown restaurant on the premises serving Lebanese specialties *rodízio*-style (you get a taste of everything until you can ingest no more). *Rua Dr. Basílio da Gama 70, tel. 011/257–7580. AE, DC, MC, V.*

Cristal. This Jardins pizzeria with the ovens in an atrium and modern art on the walls serves the thin-crust variety to upper-crust families and singles. Toppings on the personal pizzas include *portuguesa*, with ham, onion, hard-boiled egg, cheese, and olives; and *marguerita*, with cheese, basil, and tomatoes. *Rua Professor Artur Ramos 551, tel. 011/816–6227. No reservations. V.*

★ **Frevo.** Paulistanos of all ilks and ages flock to this Jardins luncheonette near the U.S. Consulate for its beirute sandwiches, draft beer, and fruit juices in flavors like *acerola* (Antilles cherry), passionfruit, and papaya. *Rua Oscar Freire 603, tel. 011/282–3434. No credit cards.*

★ **Gigetto.** This often-packed cantina stays open late for the after-theater crowd, both spectators and performers. Try the tender deep-fried squid or the *cappelletti* pasta in cream sauce with peas, ham, and mushrooms. *Rua Avanhandava 63, tel. 011/256–9804. AE, DC, MC, V.*

Ritz. The fare is basic but the look is artsy at this Jardins eatery, popular nights among gays. Go for the chicken pie, *penne mediteránneo* (tubular pasta with buffalo mozzarella, black olives, fresh tomatoes, and basil), and hot apple pie with ice cream. *Alameda Franca 1088, tel. 011/280–6808. No credit cards.*

Lodging

São Paulo's hotels are almost exclusively geared to the business traveler, both homegrown and foreign. For this reason, most are located in and around downtown and the Avenida Paulista area, with a few new ones springing up near the up-and-coming Marginal Pinheiros neighborhoods. Because of the size of the city and its frequent traffic jams, your choice should depend a great deal on the activities you are planning to undertake. Less expensive hotels are mostly found right in the city center, which can be dangerous for tourists, especially at night (the Largo do Arouche area, however, is fairly safe and quiet at night, and there are many good hotels there). For longer stays, the city offers many *apart-hotels,* which usually have small in-room kitchenettes but also house a fairly good restaurant at street level. The **Grande Hotel Ca D'Oro** (*see below*), a top European-style hotel, caters to families who are moving to or leaving São Paulo, having recently renovated to offer no fewer than 60 suites. There are two youth hostels charging about $4 a night; contact the **Associação Paulista de Albergues da Juventude** (Rua Jandaia 154, São Paulo, 01320-040, tel. 011/35–3077). Many hotels offer discounts of 20%–40% for cash payment or on weekends, and all include breakfast in the room rate. São Paulo hosts many international conferences, training courses, and business meetings, filling up hotels, so it is wise to make reservations well ahead of your arrival.

For details and price-category definitions, *see* Lodging in Staying in Brazil, *above.*

Very Expensive **Caesar Park.** Halfway between downtown and Avenida
★ Paulista, appointed with myriad mirrors, granite floors, and
Chinese rugs, this hotel caters to demanding business travelers, especially Japanese executives. Rooms are done in beige
or blue, with mahogany furniture and reproductions of 19th-
century Brazilian genre scenes by French artist Jean-Baptiste
Debret; some of the city's best sushi can be had at the top-floor
restaurant, Mariko (*see* Dining, *above*). *Rua Augusta 1508, tel.
011/253–6622, toll free within Brazil tel. 0800–111164, fax
011/288–6146. 177 rooms. Facilities: 3 restaurants, pub, beauty
salon, health club, outdoor pool. AE, DC, MC, V.*

★ **Maksoud Plaza.** Ronald Reagan *almost* stayed overnight here
on a 1982 presidential visit, but the Secret Service thought the
soaring atrium lobby, with its panoramic elevators, fountains,
greenery, artwork, and shops, presented too much of a security
risk! The staff provides highly professional service, the hotel's
six restaurants are very good, and the in-house theater and
Maksoud 150 Nightclub offer some of the city's best entertainment. *Alameda Campinas 1250, tel. 011/251–2233, fax 011/253–
4544. 420 rooms. Facilities: 6 restaurants, 3 bars, business
center, nightclub, theater, health club, heated indoor pool. AE,
DC, MC, V.*

Sheraton Mofarrej Hotel & Towers. Located just behind Avenida Paulista, next to the Trianon Park, this hotel features a
subdued lobby done in glass, with dark granite floors, plants,
a bar, and an art gallery. Guest rooms are decorated in brown,
ocher, and orange tones, and four floors boast butler service
plus other extras; rooms on the west side overlook the park.
*Alameda Santos 1437, tel. 011/284–5544, fax 011/289–8670. Fa-
cilities: 2 restaurants, 2 bars, business center, 2 pools (indoor
and outdoor). AE, DC, MC, V.*

Transamerica. Located on the Marginal Pinheiros beltway directly across the Pinheiros River from the Centro Empresarial
office complex, where many U.S. companies are housed, this
hotel can be a highly comfortable and convenient choice, and is
a prime convention venue. The skylit lobby is decorated with
granite, marble, Persian carpets, palm trees, leather sofas, and
oversize modern paintings; the spacious rooms have no special
charm, but their pastel colors, wood furnishings, and beige carpeting create a relaxing ambience for the business traveler. *Av.
das Nações Unidas 18591, tel. 011/523–4511, toll free within Brazil tel. 0800–126060, fax 011/523–8700. 211 rooms. Facilities: restaurant, 2 bars, fitness center, business center, pool, 5 tennis
courts, 1 squash court, jogging area, 9-hole golf course. AE, DC,
MC, V.*

Expensive **Brasilton São Paulo.** The smaller of two Hiltons in downtown
São Paulo, this one attracts many foreign musicians performing in the concert halls nearby. There's a cozy bar with a good
lunch buffet in the understated lobby, decorated with traver-
tine marble floors and wood paneling. Rooms are done in blue,
maroon, and brown with wood details, and bathrooms have
granite sinks. *Rua Martins Fontes 330, tel. 011/258–5811, fax
011/258–5812. 250 rooms. Facilities: 3 restaurants, bar, pool,
sauna. AE, DC, MC, V.*

Eldorado Higienópolis. Set in one of the city's oldest residential
neighborhoods, only a five-minute taxi ride from downtown,
this hotel possesses a large pool and a lobby dressed in traver-
tine marble with a pink granite floor. The green-carpeted
rooms have print bedspreads, beige walls, and wooden furni-

ture; the noise level is lowest in the back rooms or in the front above the fifth floor. *Rua Marquês de Itu 836, tel. 011/222–3422, fax 011/222–7194. 155 rooms. Facilities: 2 restaurants, bar, pool. AE, DC, MC, V.*

★ **Grande Hotel Ca D'Oro.** Owned and run by a Northern Italian family for over 40 years, this Old World–style hotel near downtown boasts bar-side fireplaces, lots of wood and Persian carpeting, a great variety of room decor (all along classic European lines), ultrapersonalized service, and one of the city's best restaurants (*see* Dining, *above*). All these amenities attract Brazilian bigwigs, expatriate families arriving and departing São Paulo, and guests who have been returning for decades. *Rua Augusta 129, tel. 011/256–8011, fax 011/231–0359. 290 rooms. Facilities: 2 restaurants, bar, fitness center, sauna, 2 pools (1 heated indoor). AE, DC, MC, V.*

Novotel. This French-chain hotel is a bit run-down, but was undergoing gradual renovation at press time. One of the few accommodations in the Morumbi neighborhood (and less expensive than the nearby Transamerica), Novotel has rooms that sport stucco walls and a basic brown decor; the lobby is somewhat dark, with maroon leather armchairs and matching carpeting, but it gives onto a pleasant patio and pool area. *Rua Ministro Nelson Hungria 450, tel. 011/844–6211, fax 011/844–5262. 190 rooms. Facilities: restaurant, bar, pool. AE, DC, MC, V.*

Moderate **Bourbon.** Both furnishings and guests are well cared for in this
★ small hotel near the Largo do Arouche, one of the few downtown districts that has retained the city's erstwhile charm. A black- and brass-accented basement bar features live piano music; the lobby has print upholstered sofas, an abstract handcrafted black and white wall hanging, and granite flooring, while the rooms are decorated in beige and blue, with marvelously large and sunlit bathrooms. *Av. Vieira de Carvalho 99, tel. 011/223–2244, fax 011/221–4076. 122 rooms. Facilities: restaurant, bar, sauna. AE, DC, MC, V.*

Hotel Vila Rica. Also in the Largo do Arouche vicinity, this hotel is smaller, less grand, and less expensive than the Bourbon. The lobby and guest rooms are decorated in Brazilian colonial style, with details in carved wood and stone; back rooms are less noisy. *Av. Vieira de Carvalho 167, tel. and fax 011/220–7111. 60 rooms. Facilities: restaurant, bar. AE, DC, MC, V.*

Ibirapuera Park Hotel. A short cab ride from Congonhas Airport, this hotel with excellent sports facilities and five minutes from Ibirapuera Park is an ideal choice for visitors addicted to exercise. The rooms and lobby are unpretentious, done in shades of brown, with lots of granite, wood, and leather. *Rua Sena Madureira 1355, tel. 011/572–0111, fax 011/572–3499. 79 rooms. Facilities: restaurant, bar, fitness room, sauna, outdoor pool, 2 tennis courts. AE, DC, MC, V.*

San Raphael. Right on the charming Largo do Arouche, with its flower market, great restaurants, and cafés, this recently refurbished hotel has a tastefully decorated lobby, with lots of oil paintings and watercolors. Rooms have small balconies, with furnishings in beige leather, Formica, marble, and tiles. *Largo do Arouche 150, tel. 011/220–6633, fax 011/221–3202. 219 rooms. Facilities: restaurant, bar. AE, DC, MC, V.*

Inexpensive **Hotel Esplanada.** It's old and worse for wear, but it's clean and in a safe neighborhood, with a great bakery and a movie theater next door. Many business travelers on a budget stay at this downtown hotel, which costs only about $20 a night, breakfast included. *Largo do Arouche 414, tel. 011/220–5711. 52 rooms. AE, DC, MC, V.*

Hotel Príncipe. This is a simple, clean hotel with attentive staff, near the central Praça da República. The decor is somewhat helter-skelter, with a mosaic stone floor in the lobby, old wallpaper and modern tile decorations in the corridors, and orange and brown room furnishings. *Av. São João 1072, tel. 011/221–8155, fax 011/222–6079. 84 rooms. Facilities: restaurant, bar. AE, DC, MC, V.*

★ **Hotel São Sebastião.** This rock-bottom option, popular among European backpackers, costs only $16 a night, breakfast included. The plain but tasteful accommodations, reminiscent of a Continental pension, are housed in the oldest building on a central, pedestrian-only street, which means it's quiet at night. *Rua Sete de Abril 364, tel. 011/257–4988 or 011/255–1594. 50 rooms. No credit cards.*

★ **Ville Hotel.** Located in the lively Higienópolis neighborhood of apartment buildings, bars, and bookstores abutting Mackenzie University, this recently opened hotel is well worth the $44 a night. The small lobby features a black and pink granite floor, recessed lighting, and black leather sofas; rooms are done in pastel colors with brown carpeting. *Rua Dona Veridiana 643, tel. and fax 011/255–1216. 54 rooms. Facilities: restaurant, pool, sauna, exercise room. AE, DC, MC, V.*

The Arts and Nightlife

São Paulo presents a growing challenge to Rio de Janeiro's traditional position as the country's cultural center. The world's top orchestras, opera and dance companies, and other troupes always include the city in their South American tours, often performing for vast open-air audiences in Ibirapuera Park during their stays. A local cultural organization, the **Mozarteum Brasileiro Associação Cultural** (Av. Brigadeiro Faria Lima 1664, 10th floor, tel. 011/815–6377), sponsors a lively April–October season of classical music concerts at the Teatro Municipal, including performances by visiting musicians. Local orchestras include the São Paulo State Symphony and the Municipal Symphony Orchestra, both suffering the debilitating effects of inadequate funding. Two municipally sponsored chorales often band together to produce operas, increasingly in conjunction with foreign companies. In the realm of contemporary arts expression, São Paulo boasts a world-class dance company, the **Ballet Stagium** (tel. 011/852–3451), and contemporary music ensemble, **Grupo Novo Horizante** (tel. 011/256–9766), neither of which have permanent homes.

The city hosts several arts festivals, the most significant being the internationally renowned biennial art exhibition known as the **São Paulo Biennial,** held every even year from mid-October to mid-December in Ibirapuera Park. In 1994 the event will take place October 12–December 11. For more information contact the Fundação Bienal (Parque Ibirapuera, Portão 3, em frente ao Detran, 04098-900, tel. 011/572–7722, fax 011/549–0230).

Other festivals include the **Carlton Dance Festival,** held annually in June and July, and the annual three-day **Free Jazz Festival** in August, both organized by Dueto Produções e Publicidade Ltda. (att: Monique Gardenberg, Rua Lauro Muller 116, Sala 4203, Rio de Janeiro, RJ 22290-160; tel. 021/542–3938 or 021/541–3743). An international film festival, **Mostra Internacional de Cinema** (Alameda Lorena 937, cj. 303, 01424-001, tel. 011/883–5137 or 011/64–5819), is held in October.

Although it often rains in São Paulo just prior to Lent, the city's colorful **Carnival** celebration, centering on a dancing downtown parade, is a viable alternative for those unable to travel to Rio de Janeiro or Salvador. The samba schools (groups that participate in the parade) rehearse throughout the year Wednesday–Friday evenings and Sunday, and hold samba parties on Saturday night. For more information, call Anhembi at 011/267–0702.

Sunday to Sunday listings of entertainment and cultural events appear in the *Veja São Paulo* insert of the newsweekly *Veja.* The arts sections of the dailies *Folha de São Paulo* and *O Estado de São Paulo* also carry arts listings and reviews. The monthly booklet **"São Paulo Este Mes,"** distributed in hotels and for sale at some newsstands, has current nightlife listings.

The Arts São Paulo's theater district in the bohemian **Bela Vista** neigh-
Theater borhood, also known as **Bexiga,** boasts dozens of theaters dedicated mostly to plays, especially comedies, in Portuguese. The **São Paulo Hilton, Transamerica, Maksoud,** and **Holiday Inn Crowne Plaza** hotels have in-house theaters featuring plays and musical events; the one at the Holiday Inn is a venue for "fringe" performances. In addition to these and the theater district per se, top venues include the **Teatro Artur Rubinstein** at the Hebraica Club (Rua Hungria 1000, tel. 011/814–4433) for plays and concerts; the **Teatro da Cultura Artística** (Rua Nestor Pestana 196, tel. 011/258–3616) for dance, musicals, and plays; the new **Teatro Faculdade Armando Álvares Penteado** (FAAP) theater (Rua Alagoas 903, tel. 011/824–0233) for old movies, concerts, and plays; the **SESC Anchieta** (Rua Dr. Vila Nova 245, tel. 011/256–2322) for dance and classical theater with a contemporary twist; and the Catholic University's **Tuca** (Rua Monte Alegre 1024, tel. 011/65–0111) for counterculture concerts and theater. Half-price tickets are available for students only, except during sporadic promotional events.

Tickets are sold at the various theater box offices and are also available at **special booths** in the **Shopping Center Morumbi** (Av. Roque Petroni Jr. 1098, top floor, no phone; open weekdays 10–8, Sat. 10–6); **Shopping Center Ibirapuera** (Av. Ibirapuera 3103, top floor, tel. 011/61–0194; open weekdays 10–8, Sat. 10–6); and **Shopping Center Iguatemi** (Av. Brigadeiro Faria Lima 1191, top floor, tel. 011/212–7623; open weekdays 10–10, Sat. 10–4). Some theaters will deliver tickets for a surcharge, as will **Lucas Shows** (tel. 011/858–5783).

Music São Paulo's most serious music, ballet, and opera are performed in the intimate gilt and moss-green velvet surroundings of the turn-of-the-century **Teatro Municipal** (Praça Ramos de Azevedo, s/n, tel. 011/223–3022) and the **Teatro da Cultura Artística** (Rua Nestor Pestana 196, tel. 011/258–3616), with its fine acoustics. Chamber music is performed at the new **Sala São Paulo Luiz** (Av. Juscelino Kubitschek 1830, tel.

011/534–4556). Popular, jazz, and rock music concerts are held in the deluxe club atmosphere of the **Olympia** (Rua Clélia 1517, tel. 011/252–6255); at the fully carpeted **Palace** (Av. dos Jamaris 213, tel. 011/531–4900); **Sesc-Pompéia** (Rua Clélia 93, tel. 011/864–8544), a converted, exposed-brick factory; and the newly renovated **Teatro Hall** (Rua Rui Barbosa 672, tel. 011/284–0290), as well as at top discotheques and clubs (*see* Nightlife, *below*).

Film It is wise to call ahead for confirmation because theaters often change their programming without notice. Only foreign children's movies are dubbed; the rest carry subtitles with the original dialogue intact. European and other non-American foreign films are shown mostly at the **Belas Artes** movie theater complex (Rua da Consolação 2423, tel. 011/258–4092 or 011/259–6341). The **Museu da Imagem e do Som** (Museum of Image and Sound) hosts special free film festivals (Av. Europa 158, tel. 011/852–9197).

Nightlife **Resumo da Opera** (Eldorado Shopping Center, Av. Rebouças
Discos and 3970, tel. 011/211–2411), sister club of a Rio spot of the same
Dance Clubs name, is a wild place for the young set, with quick-change-artist DJs, a slide down to the dance floor, and decor inspired by the musical *Phantom of the Opera*. Located in the Jardins, **Columbia** (Rua Estados Unidos 1570, tel. 011/282–8086 and 011/64–3380) is one of the city's hottest clubs, attuned to the latest fads and fashions; the best night to go is Tuesday. Not far away is the **Victoria Pub** (Alameda Lorena 1604, tel. 011/881–3822), dedicated to classic rock. **Star Dust** (Rua Franz Schubert 135, tel. 011/210–5283) is just one in a row of clubs on the same street, specializing in flashbacks for the over-40 crowd. **Palladium** (Eldorado Shopping Center, Av. Rebouças 3970, tel. 011/813–9045) offers a little of everything, including samba, rock, *axé* (Bahian music with a fast-paced rhythm), boleros, and popular Brazilian music. Named after the Mrs. Kravitz character in the TV sitcom "Bewitched," **Sra. Kravitz** (Rua Fortunato 34, tel. 011/220–6220) attracts an eclectic crowd, including transvestites and yuppies; the DJ is into striptease. In a shed that houses a children's drama school by day, the Bohemian **Teatro Vento Forte** (Rua Brigadeiro Haroldo Veloso 150, tel. 011/820–3095) does Brazilian music every which way, Saturday only, bringing in college students and soap opera stars. And **Caipirasso** (Av. Marquês de São Vicente 319, tel. 011/67–2328) rounds up crowds with Brazilian country music and a mechanical bull.

Jazz Clubs The **Café Piu Piu** (Rua Treze de Maio 134, tel. 011/258–8066), in the bohemian Bexiga district, is best known for jazz, but also hosts groups that play rock, bossa nova, and the tango. **The Blue Note** (Av. São Gabriel 558, tel. 011/884–9356) is a venue for traditional jazz and blues. And **Sanja Jazz Bar** (Rua Frei Caneca 304, tel. 011/255–2942) is an old town house in Bexiga dedicated to live jazz.

Brazilian Music Popularly known as MPB (Música Popular Brasileira) clubs,
Clubs these clubs play quiet, largely acoustic instrumental and vocal music in the style of Milton Nascimento, Chico Buarque, and Gilberto Gil, with an emphasis on the samba and bossa nova. **Café Soçaite** (Rua Treze de Maio 46, tel. 011/259–6562) is one of the most popular spots for Brazilian music, especially with singles, playing all kinds of local sounds. **Bar da Virada** (Rua Simão Álvares 575, tel. 011/210–0635) is a traditional

address for samba and popular music from the 1960s. **Café Paris** (Rua Waldemar Ferreira 55, tel. 011/813–5158) is known for its bossa nova and other Brazilian pop music.

For Singles   *Correio Elegante* (or elegant mail, notes delivered from table to table by messenger) is the latest way to make a match at **Clyde's** (Rua da Mata 70, tel. 011/883–0300), where there's a bar, restaurant, and live music; and at **Zeibar's Paulista** (Av. Paulista 2678, tel. 011/257–1019 and 011/256–0040), which also has live music. **Supremo** (Rua Oscar Freire 950, tel. 011/881–2250) is a lively, beautiful-people corner bar in the Jardins.

Gay Clubs   One of the best discos for Saturday night dancing is **Gents Theater House** (Avenida Ibirapuera 1911, tel. 011/572–8227), frequented by men of all ages. There are three different bars, a stage for shows, and a big screen with music videos. Another popular spot is **Nostromundo** (Rua da Consolação 2554, tel. 011/257–4481), one of the oldest gay discos in São Paulo, featuring transvestite shows and a wild "anything goes" atmosphere.

Women's Clubs   The **Clube das Mulheres** (Rua Padre João Manuel 199, tel. 011/85–21450; shows Tues. and Thurs. only) features spicy striptease acts by male dancers, who, in the best belly dancer tradition, expect cash donations from the audience.

Excursions from São Paulo

Embu   Only 27 kilometers (17 miles) southwest of the city, this is a Portuguese colonial town of whitewashed houses, old churches, a museum and an apiary, woodcarvers' studios, and antiques shops. A huge handicrafts fair is held here every Saturday and Sunday, the latter day being the best for shopping. Sightseeing information is available at the municipal tourism board, the **Secretaria do Turismo** (Praça 22 de Abril 139, Embu, tel. 011/494–5333).

Getting There   To make the half-hour drive, take Avenida Prof. Francisco Morato to the Rodovia Régis Bittencourt, then follow the signs for Embu. The **Soamin** bus company (tel. 011/495–2520) has service to Embu every half-hour, with buses departing from any one of several locations around the city.

Itu   This Portuguese colonial town 90 kilometers (55 miles) northwest of São Paulo is famous for its 18th-century churches (Igreja do Bom Jesus and Nossa Senhora da Candelária), loads of antiques stores, and a tendency to exaggerate; after a television comedian from Itu made his career in the 1960s with a routine about how things in his town were bigger than anywhere else, the local chamber of commerce decided to capitalize on the idea and built an oversize traffic light and pay phone. The gimmick still pays off at local stores, where giant hats, pencils, and other gargantuan items are sold. Tourist information is available at the **Secretaria de Cultura** (Rua Paula Souza 664, Itu, tel. 011/299–8974).

Getting There   To make the 50-minute drive to Itu, take the Rodovia Castello Branco to SP 312 (Rodovia do Açucar) west, which runs right through town. The **Viação Vale do Tietê** bus company (tel. 011/299–8974) has buses to Itu every hour from the Tietê bus station.

Minas Gerais: Belo Horizonte and the Historical Cities

By Edwin Taylor

Brazil's mountainous central region is dominated by the state of Minas Gerais, which means "general mines" in Portuguese. The name refers to its great mineral wealth, typified by its once vast reserves of gold, which in the 18th century provoked a gold rush that for a time made Minas Gerais, particularly Ouro Preto, the de facto capital of the Portuguese colony. The legacy of that period of gold, diamond, and semiprecious stone trading is preserved in the so-called historical cities scattered throughout the mountains, with their abundance of Baroque churches and artwork.

Exploration of Minas Gerais began in the 17th century, when bands of adventurers from the coastal areas came in search of Indian slaves and gold. The explorers found a black stone near the town of Vila Rica that was later verified to be gold (the black coloring was the result of the iron oxide in the soil of Minas). Vila Rica thus came to be called Ouro Preto (black gold), and at the beginning of the 18th century, Brazil's first gold rush began. The population of the region quickly mushroomed. Along with the wealth seekers came Jesuit priests, and by the middle of the century the colonial cities of Minas were gleaming with new churches built in the Baroque style of Europe.

By the end of the 18th century, the gold began to run out, and Ouro Preto's population and importance decreased. The Baroque period itself came to an end at the start of the 19th century, when the Portuguese royal family, in flight from the conquering army of Napoleon Bonaparte, arrived in Brazil, bringing with them architects and sculptors with different ideas and artistic styles.

Today, Minas Gerais is Brazil's second most industrialized state, after São Paulo. The iron that darkened the gold of Ouro Preto is today an important source of income for Minas, which has evolved into one of the world's leading producers of iron ore. The steel industry followed, and today the capital, Belo Horizonte, is home to a Fiat auto production plant and other large industrial facilities. Minas is also a major coffee producer.

The state, however, has paid a price for its development: The once heavily wooded mountains of Minas are now for the most part stripped bare. For visitors, though, the principal attractions remain—magnificent Baroque churches that contain prized sculptural masterpieces, and cities whose hilly cobblestone streets lined with whitewashed buildings retain the atmosphere of 18th-century towns.

The region is famous for its Easter and Corpus Christi celebrations. In Ouro Preto the residents of the city gather the night before Easter Sunday along the route of the Easter religious procession and decorate the street with flowers and colored sawdust. Using these elements, they design intricate patterns as well as portraits of Christ and the saints. The result is an immense multicolored carpet over which the procession passes on Easter morning. Tourists gather on the city's streets

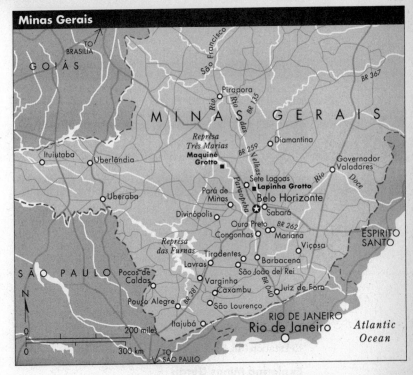

the night before to watch and also to help out in the preparation of this "magic carpet." Similar processions are held in Tiradentes, Sabará, and Diamantina on Corpus Christi. Diamantina is also known for its lively Carnival celebration.

Tourist Information

Turminas (Av. Bias Fortes 50, Belo Horizonte, tel. 031/212–2134; open weekdays 12:30–6:30), the Minas Gerais state tourism authority, can supply information on the historical cities and other attractions in the state. For information on **Belo Horizonte:** Belotur, the city tourism authority (Rua Tupis 149, 17th floor, tel. 031/222–5500; Mercado das Flores, Av. Afonso Pena and Rua da Bahia, tel. 031/222–4336; at the bus station, tel. 031/201–8111; or at Confins airport, tel. 031/689–2140; all open weekdays 8 AM–8 PM, weekends 8–4). **Diamantina:** Casa da Cultura (Praça Antônio Eulálio 53, tel. 038/931–2137; open weekdays 8 AM–8 PM, weekends 8–5). **Mariana:** Associação de Guias (Praça Tancredo Neves, tel. 031/557–1122; open weekdays 8–5). **Ouro Preto:** Associação de Guias (Praça Tiradentes 41, tel. 031/551–2655; open weekdays 8 AM–8 PM, weekends 8–5). **São João del Rei:** Terminal Turístico (Praça Dr. Antônio Viegas, tel. 032/371–3522; open weekdays 8–5). **Tiradentes:** Secretária de Turismo (Rua Resende Costa 71, tel. 032/355–1212; open weekdays 8–5:30, weekends 8–5).

Getting There

By Plane Belo Horizonte is the hub for tours to the state's colonial cities. The city has two airports, **Tancredo Neves,** or **Confins** (tel. 031/689–2700), 39 kilometers (24 miles) from downtown, which serves international flights, and **Pampulha** (tel. 031/441–2000), 9 kilometers (5 miles) from downtown, which serves domestic airlines, primarily shuttle flights from Rio and São Paulo. Between them the two airports connect Belo Horizonte with every major city in Brazil. Varig, Transbrasil, and Vasp airlines fly to both airports.

By Car Highway BR 040 connects Belo Horizonte with Rio; Highway BR 381 links the city with São Paulo. Belo Horizonte is connected with all of the historical cities by well-maintained roads. Trips to the historical cities may be made only by car or bus.

By Bus There is frequent bus service connecting Belo Horizonte with Rio and São Paulo. There are also buses plying the roads between Belo Horizonte and the historical cities. All of the historical cities have local bus service. For information on buses call 031/201–8111 in Belo Horizonte and 031/862–1603 in Ouro Preto.

By Train A restored 19th-century train makes the 13-kilometer (8-mile), 30-minute journey between the cities of Tiradentes and São Joã del Rei. The train operates only Friday through Sunday and on holidays. It departs Tiradentes (Praça da Estação, tel. 032/355–1269) at 1 and 5 PM and returns from the São João del Rei station (tel. 032/371–2888) at 10 AM and 2:15 PM.

Exploring Minas Gerais

Belo Horizonte Brazil's third-largest city, with a population of almost 2.4 million, Belo Horizonte is the capital of Minas Gerais, a state as renowned for its conservative traditions as for its gold, gemstones, and iron ore. Tradition is all-important in Minas: In terms of family values and politics, Mineiros are considered the most conservative of Brazilians. A jumping-off point for trips to the surrounding historical region, Belo Horizonte itself offers little of historical value. It is, in fact, relatively young; it was founded in 1897.

The **Parque Municipal** is located in the heart of the business district and close to several hotels. With its tree-lined walks, small lakes, and rustic bridges, the well-maintained park is an example of the passion for orderliness that is a characteristic of Mineiros. This same trait has helped make Belo Horizonte one of the cleanest and safest of Brazil's leading cities. Located within the park is the **Palácio das Artes** (Av. Afonso Pena 1537, tel. 031/201–8900; admission free), a cultural center containing a library, art gallery, theater, and the **Centro de Artesenato Mineiro,** with examples of contemporary Minas Gerais handicrafts, including works of soapstone and wood, Minas pottery, and tapestries, all for sale.

Ironically, while tourists come to Belo to visit the nearby historical region, one of the principal attractions of the city is the Pampulha neighborhood, famed for its examples of modern Brazilian architecture. Foremost among these is the **Chapel of São Francisco,** completed in 1943 and considered one of the most important works of Brazil's famed architect Oscar Niemeyer. Inside the small but distinctive chapel with its undulating roof, a Niemeyer signature, are frescoes painted by one of

Brazil's most important 20th-century painters, Cândido Portinari. The Cubist works depict Saint Francis and the Stations of the Cross. To reach the chapel, take a taxi or a bus that goes north on Avenida Presidente Antonio Carlos. The chapel is located on the edge of an artificial lake a half hour from downtown. *Av. Otacílio Negrão de Lima, km 12, tel. 061/441–2628. Admission free.*

The Historical Cities With the possible exception of Salvador, there is no better preserved example of colonial Brazil than in the mountains of Minas Gerais. Unlike Bahia, however, Minas was blessed with the presence of an artistic genius. Working in cedarwood and soapstone, O Aleijadinho carved the passion of his religious beliefs in sculptures that grace churches throughout the region. His given name was Antônio Francisco Lisboa, and he was born in 1738 in what is today the city of Ouro Preto, then called Vila Rica, the mulatto son of a Portuguese architect and a former slave. Nicknamed O Aleijadinho, "the little cripple," he was left deformed as an adult by an illness that has been variously described as leprosy or syphilis, but is generally assumed to have been arthritis.

Disabled as he was, the use of his hands hindered, Aleijadinho could not have chosen a more demanding profession than that of sculptor. Yet little does one perceive in the delicately expressive features of his figures the pain and effort in their creation; legend has it that in the advanced stages of his disease, the artist had to strap his hammer and chisel to his wrists with leather thongs so he could work. Beginning in the 1760s and continuing practically until his death in 1814, Aleijadinho traveled back and forth between the cities and towns of Minas, sculpting and overseeing the construction of the region's churches, in the process leaving for posterity an artistic heritage unmatched anywhere in Brazil.

Just east of Belo Horizonte, 19 kilometers (12 miles) east on Highway BR 383, about a half-hour ride from the town center, is the city of **Sabará**. This former colonial town is today a sprawling suburb of 90,000 whose historical buildings are scattered about, requiring tourists either to join a tour or drive. Here the enormous wealth of Minas Gerais during the gold rush days can best be appreciated. The interiors of the Baroque churches of Sabará are rich in gold leaf paneling, such as the ornate **Nossa Senhora da Conceição** (Praça Getúlio Vargas, tel. 031/671–1724; admission charged; closed Tues. before noon and Mon.), completed in 1710. The simple exterior of this small church gives no indication as to the wealth inside, typified by its luxurious gold altar. Even more impressive, however, is the interior of the narrow **Nossa Senhora de Ó church** (Largo do Ó, no phone; closed Tues. before noon and Mon.), another explosion of gold leaf; it dates from 1720. Both churches contain paintings with Oriental themes that are said to have been executed by 23 Chinese artists brought from the Portuguese colony of Macao, on the coast of China.

In the main square of Sabará, the Praça Melo Viana, sits the unfinished **Senhora do Rosário dos Pretos** (1767), built, like its counterpart in Ouro Preto, by former slaves. In Sabará, however, they ran out of gold before the project could be completed. Examples of Aleijadinho's work can be found in the nearby church of **Nossa Senhora do Carmo** (Rua do Carmo, tel.

031/671–1523; admission charged; closed Tues.–Sat. before noon, Sun. before 1, and Mon.), where he designed the pulpits, choir loft, and doorway. This is one of several Minas churches on which Aleijadinho and the painter Manuel da Costa Ataíde, a contemporary of Aleijadinho and a brilliant artist in his own right, collaborated.

The best place to see Aleijadinho's artistry is **Ouro Preto,** the former gold rush capital, which has been preserved not only as a national monument but as a World Heritage site. Located 97 kilometers (60 miles) southeast of Belo Horizonte (south on Highway BR 040 and then east on BR 356), at an elevation of 3,200 feet, Ouro Preto is a city of narrow cobblestone streets and alleys built on a series of steep hills. The surrounding mountains, the geometric rows of whitewashed buildings, the red-tile roofs that climb the hillsides, the morning mist and evening fog that drift over the city all give Ouro Preto a strongly evocative air, as if at any moment it could be transported back two centuries.

The true treasures of Ouro Preto, however, are its 13 colonial churches, representing the supreme achievement of Mineiro Baroque architecture. Typically, the Minas Baroque style is marked by elaborately carved doorways with strongly curving lines and soapstone sculptures. Most distinctive, though, are the interiors, richly painted and decorated lavishly with cedarwood and soapstone sculptures. In many of the churches, the interior style is unabashedly Rococo, with an often ostentatious use of gold leaf, a byproduct of the gold boom that brought wealth to this region.

All of the churches are located within walking distance of each other and are relatively close to the central square, the Praça Tiradentes. The city's professional tour guides have formed an association, the **Associação de Guias** (Praça Tiradentes 41, tel. 031/551–2655; open 8–6). The association's well-informed and courteous guides provide general information on the city and conduct walking tours of the historical area. Tours are available in English and typically last six to seven hours. Be prepared for some stiff hiking up and down Ouro Preto's numerous hills.

Two blocks east of the Praça Tiradentes is the distinctive twin-towered **Igreja São Francisco de Assis** (Largo de Coimbra, no phone; admission charged; closed Tues.–Sun. 11:45–1:30 and Mon.), Aleijadinho's masterpiece, which was completed in 1810. In addition to designing the church, Aleijadinho was responsible for the wood and soapstone sculptures on the portal, high altar and side altars, pulpits, and cross arch. The panel on the nave ceiling representing the Virgin's glorification was painted by Manuel da Costa Ataíde. Cherubic faces, garlands of tropical fruits, and allegorical characters decorate the main altar, still covered with their original paint.

Three blocks south is the **Igreja de Nossa Senhora das Mercêse Perdões** (Rua das Mercês, parish tel. 031/551–3282; admission charged; closed Tues.–Sun. after 2 and Mon.), built from 1740 to 1773. The church contains etchings done by Aleijadinho as studies for his sculptures. Three blocks east is the **Igreja da Nossa Senhora da Conceição** (Praça Antônio Dias, tel. 031/551–3282; admission charged; church and museum closed Mon.–Sat. 11:30–1 and Sun. before noon), a lavishly gilded church completed in 1760 that contains the tomb of Aleijadinho as well as a museum dedicated to the artist.

The **Igreja Nossa Senhora do Carmo,** on the west side of the Praça Tiradentes, contains major works by Aleijadinho and Ataíde. The church was originally designed by Aleijadinho's father, himself an architect, but was later modified by the son, who added more Baroque elements, including characteristic soapstone sculptures of angels above the entrance. The church was completed in 1776. *Parish tel. 031/551–1209. Admission charged. Closed Tues.–Sun. before 11 and Mon.*

Next door to the church is the **Museu de Arte Sacra do Carmo,** a museum dedicated to religious art, with wood carvings of saints by Aleijadinho and other 18th-century art. *Rua Brigadeiro Mosqueiro, tel. 031/551–1383. Admission charged. Church and museum closed Tues.–Sun. 11–1 and Mon.*

Three blocks west of Carmo is the **Nossa Senhora do Pilar** church (Praça Mons. Castilho Barbosa, tel. 031/551–1209; admission charged; closed Tues.–Sun. before noon and Mon.), built in 1733 and the most richly decorated of Ouro Preto's churches; the gold leaf that seems to cover every surface is said to have consumed 182 kilograms (400 pounds) of gold. Other prominent churches are the 1771 **Nossa Senhora das Mercês e Misericórdia** (Rua Padre Rolim, parish tel. 031/551–1209; admission charged; closed Fri.–Sun. before noon and Mon.–Thurs.), containing soapstone sculptures by Aleijadinho; the 1785 **Basílica do Senhor Bom Jesus de Matosinhos** (Rua Alvarenga, 1½ km (1 mi) from Tiradentes, parish tel. 031/551–1209; admission charged), the most distant of the churches, which at press time (summer 1993) was closed for restoration; and the 1745 **Igreja de Santa Efigênia** (Id. de Santa Efigênia, parish tel. 031/551–3282; admission charged; closed Tues.–Sun. after noon and Mon.), containing cedar sculptures by Francisco Xavier de Brito, Aleijadinho's teacher.

One of the smaller but more intriguing churches is the domed **Igreja Nossa Senhora do Rosário dos Pretos** (1785), built by slaves, some of whom who bought their freedom with the gold they found in Ouro Preto. According to legend, the interior of the church is bare because the slaves ran out of gold after erecting the church's Baroque structure. *Largo do Rosário, parish tel. 031/551–1209. Admission charged. Closed Tues.–Sun. before noon and Mon.*

In its heyday, Ouro Preto was not simply a city of gold and churches. It was also one of the most progressive cities in Brazil and birthplace of the colony's first stirrings of independence. A movement called the Inconfidência Mineira was organized to overthrow the Portuguese rulers and establish an independent Brazilian republic. It was to have been led by a resident of Ouro Preto, Joaquim José da Silva Xavier, a dentist known as Tiradentes, or "tooth puller." But the Minas rebellion never got off the ground. In 1789, word of Tiradentes' intentions reached the capital of Rio de Janeiro and the leader of the rebels was hanged and quartered, his followers either imprisoned or exiled. Artifacts of this turbulent era, such as clothing, toys, slaves' manacles, firearms, books, and gravestones, as well as works by Aleijadinho and Ataíde, can be seen at the **Museu da Inconfidência,** housed in a former 18th-century prison on Praça Tiradentes, in the city center. *Praça Tiraden-*

tes 139, tel. 031/551–1121. Admission charged. Closed Tues.–
Sun. before noon and Mon.

Among the city's other attractions is the **Casa dos Contos** (Rua
São José 12, tel. 031/551–1444; admission charged; closed daily
before 1), the colonial coinage house, which contains the foun-
dry used to mint the gold coins of the gold rush period plus
examples of the coins and period furniture. The former opera
house, built between 1746 and 1769, is now the **Teatro Municipal** (Rua Brigadeiro Mosqueira; admission charged; closed
daily before noon). The theater still presents shows and plays,
thus making it the oldest municipal theater still in operation in
Latin America. There is no regular schedule for performances,
however; check with the Associação de Guias to see if a play is
being performed. The **Museu de Mineralogia e das Pedras**
(Praça Tiradentes 20, tel. 031/551–1666; admission charged;
closed weekdays before noon, weekends before 1), housed opposite the Museu da Inconfidência in the former governor's
palace, contains an excellent collection of precious gems, gold,
and crystals.

Eleven kilometers (7 miles) east of Ouro Preto along Highway
BR 365 is the colonial mining city of **Mariana,** the oldest city in
Minas Gerais (founded in 1696) and the birthplace of Aleijadinho's favorite painter, Ataíde. Mariana, like Ouro Preto, has
preserved much of the appearance of an 18th-century gold
mining town. Its three principal churches all showcase examples of the art of Ataíde, who intertwined sensual romanticism
with religious themes. The faces of Ataíde's saints and other
figures often have mulatto features, reflecting the composition
of the area's population at the time.

The **Catedral Basílica da Sé** (Praça Cláudio Manoel, tel.
031/557–1237; admission charged; closed Mon.), completed in
1760, contains paintings by Ataíde, although it is probably better known for its 1701 German organ, transported by mule
from Rio de Janeiro in 1720. Behind the cathedral is the **Museu
de Arte Sacra** (Rua Frei Durão 49, tel. 031/557–1237; admission
charged; open Tues.–Sun. noon–1 and Mon.), which claims to
have the largest collection of Baroque painting and sculpture
in the state, including wood and soapstone works of Aleijadinho
and paintings of Ataíde.

Nearby is the **Nossa Senhora do Carmo Church** (Praça Minas
Gerais, tel. 031/557–1635), with works by Ataíde, which at press
time was closed for restoration work. The artist is buried at the
rear of the church. Next door is the 1793 **São Francisco de Assis
Church** (Praça Minas Gerais, no phone, admission charged),
featuring soapstone pulpits and altars by Aleijadinho. The
church's most impressive work, however, is a series of ceiling
panels in the sacristy painted by Ataíde, which depict in somber tones the passion and death of Saint Francis. Considered
by many to be the artist's masterpiece, the wooden panels have
unfortunately been damaged by termites and water.

To see Aleijadinho's crowning effort, head directly south of
Belo Horizonte to the small gold-rush town of **Congonhas do
Campo,** some 77 kilometers (48 miles) away. Dominating Congonhas is the hilltop pilgrimage church of **Bom Jesus do Matosinho** (Praça da Basílica, tel. 031/731–1590; admission
charged; closed Mon.), built in 1757, the focus of great processions during Holy Week and the major reason for coming here.

At the entrance to the churchyard, you'll see the artist's 12 life-size Old Testament prophets carved in soapstone, a towering achievement and one of the greatest works of art anywhere of the Baroque period. Every facial expression seems marked with the sculptor's own pain during his final years. Leading up to the church on the sloping hillside are six chapels, each containing a scene representing a Station of the Cross. Each of the 66 figures in this remarkable procession was carved in cedar by Aleijadinho and painted by Ataíde.

Continuing south on Highway BR 040, then west on BR 265 for a total of 129 kilometers (80 miles), brings you to **Tiradentes,** the birthplace of the eponymous martyr (the town was formerly called São José del Rei). Tiradentes can also be reached from Rio by BR 040, a 388-kilometer (230-mile) trip. Life in this tiny village—nine streets with eight churches!—moves slowly, and one can easily believe that time here has stopped in the 18th century. This quality has recently attracted wealthy residents of Rio, São Paulo, and Belo Horizonte, who have sparked a local real estate boom by buying up 18th-century properties as weekend getaways.

The charming town's principal attraction is the **Igreja de Santo Antônio,** built in 1710 and containing some of the best-preserved gilded carvings—of saints, cherubs, and biblical scenes—in the historical cities. The church's soapstone frontispiece was sculpted by Aleijadinho, and the church also boasts a sundial created by the artist. *Rua da Câmara, no phone. Admission charged.*

Continue 13 kilometers (8 miles) southwest to **São João del Rei,** the second largest of the historical cities, with a population of 80,000. On weekends the trip between the two can be made aboard a restored 19th-century train (*see* Getting There by Train, *above*). The Victorian **train station** at São João is a treat in itself, containing a **railway museum and roundhouse** with a collection of locomotives dating back to the 19th century. *Av. Hermílio Alves 366, tel. 032/371–2888. Museum: admission charged. Closed daily 11:30–1.*

Although far more modern in appearance than the other colonial cities, São João del Rei has preserved three superb Baroque churches. The three are within walking distance of each other in the downtown area, close to the train station. The church of **Nossa Senhora do Carmo** (Largo do Carmo, no phone; admission charged), built in 1734, was designed by Aleijadinho, and its interior contains several sculptures by the master. The **Catedral Nossa Senhora do Pilar** (Rua Getúlio Vargas, tel. 032/371–2568), constructed in 1721, is known for its seven richly decorated altars; at press time it was closed for restoration. One of Aleijadinho's most brilliant designs, the twin-towered church of **São Francisco de Assis** (Praça Frei Orlando, tel. 032/371–3966; admission charged; closed daily noon–1:30) is notable for its elegant symmetry. The church also contains two of his sculptures, including the Crucifix on the altar, in which rubies represent the blood of Christ.

Seeing the lone historical city of **Diamantina,** 290 kilometers (180 miles) north of Belo Horizonte, requires an overnight trip. Diamantina took its name from the diamonds that were extracted in great quantities from its soil in the 18th century. Perhaps because of its remote setting in the barren mountains close to the semi-arid Sertão area, Diamantina is considered the best-preserved colonial town in Minas, although its churches lack the grandeur of those in some of the other towns. Its white-walled homes and churches stand in pristine contrast to the iron red of the surrounding mountains. As in the other historical cities of Minas, the principal attraction in Diamantina is the simple pleasure of walking along the clean-swept cobblestone streets surrounded by colonial houses. Note the covered overhanging roofs with their elaborate brackets.

The city was the home of two legendary figures of the colonial period: diamond merchant João Fernandes and his slave mistress Xica da Silva, today a popular figure in Brazilian folklore. According to legend, Xica had never seen the ocean, so her lover built her an artificial lake and then added a boat. In Diamantina you may visit the **home of Xica da Silva** (Praça Lobo Mesquita 266; no phone), whose highlights are its colonial furniture and Xica's private chapel. You may see the house by guided tour only; contact the Casa da Cultura (Praça Antonio Eulalio 53, tel. 038/931–2137). On the same square is the **Igreja Nossa Senhora de Carmo** (Rua do Carmo; no phone; by guided tour only; contact the Casa da Cultura [*see above*]), 1751, a gift from Fernandes to his mistress. Supposedly Xica ordered that the bell tower be built onto the back of the building so that the ringing would not disturb her.

On Rua da Glória, a covered wooden foot bridge connects the second stories of two buildings that once served as the head-quarters of the colonial governors. The **Museu de Diamante** (Rua Direta 14, tel. 038/931–1382; admission free; open Tues.–Sat. before noon, Sun. after noon, and Mon.), the city's diamond museum, is housed in a 1789 building and displays equipment used in the colonial-period diamond mines. A few blocks away is the **birthplace of Juscelino Kubitschek** (Rua São Francisco 241, no phone; admission free; open Tues.–Fri. before noon, weekends after noon, and Mon.), one of Brazil's most important 20th-century presidents and the man who built Brasília.

At night, Diamantina enjoys a special distinction. The city is famed as Brazil's center of serenading, although the art form has never had the popularity in Brazil that it enjoys in the rest of Latin America. Still, on weekend nights and often during the week, the city's romantics gather in a downtown alley known as **Beco do Mota,** the former red-light district and now home to several popular bars frequented by students and young professionals. Strolling guitar players also gather on Rua Direita and Rua Quitanda.

What to See and Do with Children

On the road from Ouro Preto to Mariana is the **Minas de Passagem** (tel. 031/557–1340; admission charged), a former gold mine that can be visited on a guided tour. For amateur spelunkers, the mountains of Minas Gerais are replete with **caves** to be explored. The largest and most popular cavern is the **Maquiné Grotto** (nearby tel. 031/931–1313; admission charged), 113 kilometers, or 70 miles, northwest of Belo Horizonte near the town of Cordisburgo, where six large chambers are open to visitors but must be seen as part of a guided tour. Closer to Belo, only 48 kilometers (30 miles) away near the city of Lagoa Santa and located 12 kilometers (7 miles) from Confins airport on the road leading from the airport, is the **Lapinha Grotto** (no phone; admission charged), which also must be seen with a guided tour.

Shopping

Gems are the obvious focus in an area still famous for its mines. The state is particularly well-known for the quality of its topazes. Gemstones should be purchased only from reputable dealers. They include the **Gem Center** (Av. Afonso Pena 1901, 5th floor, Belo Horizonte, tel. 031/222–8189), **Hans Stern** (Trevo Nova Lima Shopping Center, BR 040, Belvedere Ioja 105-106, Belo Horizonte, tel.031/286–1568), **Amsterdam Sauer** (in the Othon Palace Hotel, Av. Afonso Pena 1050, Belo Horizonte, tel. 031/273–3844; Praça Tiradentes 69, Ouro Preto, tel. 031/551–3383), and **Manoel Bernardes** (Trevo Nova Lima Shopping Center, BR 040, Nivel BL, Ioja 29-30, Belo Horizonte, tel. 031/286–2492; Rua Espírito Santo 835, third floor, Belo Horizonte, tel. 031/201–3822; Rua Conde de Bobadela 48, Ouro Preto, tel. 031/551–2487).

Regional arts and crafts are sold throughout Minas. Hand-carved **wood and soapstone figures** and objects, such as crucifixes and ashtrays, are sold by street vendors in all the historical cities. Other typical handicrafts include pottery and tapestries, in particular the hand-woven *arraiol* tapestries for which the area around Diamantina is famous. In Belo Horizonte, the **Centro de Artesenato Mineiro** (Av. Afonso Pena 1537, tel. 031/201–8900), in the Palace of the Arts, offers for sale a wide range of regional crafts. A large **outdoor crafts market** is held on Thursday evenings and Sunday mornings on Praça da Liberdade. In Ouro Preto, an **outdoor fair** is held daily in the Largo do Coimbra, and there are stores around the central Praça Tiradentes and along nearby streets where gemstones and soapstone carvings are sold. Another crafts center is Tiradentes, where some 20 shops line Rua Direita in the town center.

Sports and the Outdoors

The two most popular wilderness areas for hiking are the **Serra do Cipó National Park** (96 kilometers, or 60 miles, northeast of Belo Horizonte on BR 367), with waterfalls, lakes, and two canyons; and the mountainous area just south of Diamantina, famed for its waterfalls. At both areas, facilities are poor and the park rangers are not very helpful. Thus, unless you have been there before and know your way around, you should hire a guide or visit the areas as part of an organized tour.

The best source of information about hiking in the region is the **Associação de Guias** (Praça Tiradentes 41, tel. 031/551–2655) in Ouro Preto. The association also organizes hiking tours and rents sports equipment.

Spectator Sports

Soccer   Belo Horizonte's **Mineirão Stadium** (Av. Antônio Abrão Carão 1001, Pampulha, tel. 031/441–6133) is the third-largest stadium in Brazil and the home field for the city's two professional soccer teams, Atletico Mineiro and Cruzeiro.

Dining and Lodging

Dining options are admittedly limited in the historical cities, but you will find several excellent restaurants offering typical Minas Gerais food in Ouro Preto, Tiradentes, São João del Rei, and Diamantina.

The mainstay of Mineiro cuisine is *tutu,* a tasty mash of black beans and manioc meal served with meat dishes. Another bracing favorite is *feijão tropeiro,* a combination of brown beans, bacon, and manioc meal. Among meat dishes, pork is the most common, in particular the famed Minas pork sausage (*lingüiça*) and pork tenderloin (*lombo*). The most typical chicken dish is *frango ao molho pardo,* broiled chicken served in a sauce made with its own blood.

Accommodations vary dramatically in the colonial cities, although in general, hotels tend to be small and unpretentious. Some of the cities—including Congonhas do Campo, Mariana, and Sabará—have virtually no accommodations. In recent years a number of small, intimate hotels that capture the colonial spirit of the area have been built; all of these are located in Ouro Preto and Tiradentes. In Ouro Preto, some families rent rooms in their homes, usually only during Carnival and Easter, when the city's hotel rooms fill up. For a list of rooms to rent, contact the **Associação de Guias de Turismo** (Praça Tiradentes 41, tel. 031/551–2655). The association also provides information on areas where camping is permitted.

For details and price-category definitions, *see* Dining and Lodging in Staying in Brazil.

Belo Horizonte **Casa do Baile.** Considered the best restaurant in the stylish
Dining Pampulha neighborhood, the emphasis here is on international
★ cuisine, but there is also a healthy selection of regional cuisine. An excellent view of Pampulha Lake and live music contribute to the romantic atmosphere. *Av. Octacílio Negrão de Lima 751, tel. 031/443–3486. Reservations recommended. AE, DC, MC, V. Closed Sat. Very Expensive.*

L'Apogee. This self-described traditional French restaurant actually has a wide-ranging menu that even includes Italian cuisine. Meat and fish dishes and some pasta dishes are served. *Rua Antônio be Albuquerque 729, tel. 031/227–5133. Reservations required. AE, DC, MC, V. Closed Sun. and Mon. Very Expensive.*

★ **Chez Dadette.** Although most of Belo's better restaurants specialize in traditional Minas Gerais cuisine, this establishment in the Santo Agostinho neighborhood, near downtown, is a delightful exception to the rule. The cooking is classic French, with such specialties as steak au poivre, and the quality surprisingly high for what Paulistanos and Cariocas consider to be "the provinces." *Rua Coelho de Souza 70, tel. 031/275–1400. AE, DC, MC, V. Closed Sun. Expensive.*

Brock's Steak House. A wide variety of cuts of beef and pork are offered at this restaurant in the Mangabeiras neighborhood, in a colonial-style dining room with Portuguese blue tiles on the walls. Customers may choose from 20 types of potato dishes, ranging from baked to soufflé, and nine kinds of sauces, including béarnaise and mustard. *Av. Afonso Pena 4276, tel. 031/223–7686. No credit cards. Moderate.*

Casa dos Contos. The menu at this gathering place for local journalists, artists, and intellectuals is unpretentious and varied, ranging from fish and pasta to traditional Minas cuisine. In keeping with its bohemian clientele, Casa dos Contos serves well past midnight. *Rua Rio Grande do Norte 1065, tel. 031/222–1070. AE, DC, MC, V. Moderate.*

★ **Chico Mineiro.** Dining Minas Gerais–style means ample portions of hearty dishes such as tutu mineira, the local equivalent of meat and potatoes. Nowhere is it better prepared than at this traditional restaurant in the Savassi neighborhood, home to Belo's liveliest nightspots. *Rua Alagoas 626, tel. 031/261–3237. AE, DC, MC, V. Inexpensive.*

Dona Lucinha II. Traditional Minas dishes are offered in this cafeteria-style eatery in the Savassi neighborhood, a prime example of a recent fad for "self-service" among Minas restaurants. *Rua Sergipe 811, tel. 031/226–5930. AE, DC. Inexpensive.*

Lodging **Brasilton Contagem.** This modern, motel-style hotel in the
★ Contagem industrial district belongs to the Hilton chain and is popular among business travelers. Guest rooms face a central courtyard with a pool and tropical gardens, creating an atmosphere of total relaxation. *Hwy. BR-381, km 3.65, tel. 031/396–1100, fax 031/396–1144. 144 rooms. Facilities: restaurant, bar, outdoor pool. AE, DC, MC, V. Expensive.*

Othon Palace. The acknowledged top downtown hotel, the Othon is reliable but undistinguished and in need of renovation. The hotel overlooks the trees and lakes of the downtown Municipal Park. *Av. Afonso Pena 1050, tel. 031/273–3844, fax 031/212–2318. 302 rooms. Facilities: restaurant, bar, outdoor pool. AE, DC, MC, V. Expensive.*

★ **Real Palace.** Recently renovated, this downtown hotel close to the Municipal Park has ample, comfortable rooms decorated in pastel colors, with views of the park and the distant mountains. *Rua Espírito Santo 901, tel. 031/213–1211, fax 031/273–2643. 256 rooms. Facilities: restaurant, bar, outdoor pool. AE, DC, MC, V. Expensive.*

★ **Terminal Center Hotel.** This new downtown hotel is next door to the bus station serving the historical cities. Spacious rooms and efficient service make this an excellent value. *Av. Amazonas 1445, tel. 031/291–0022, fax 031/275–3955. 120 rooms. Facilities: restaurant, bar, outdoor pool, travel agency. AE, DC, MC, V. Moderate.*

Wembley Palace. This traditional, aging high-rise downtown hotel offers clean rooms, reliable service, and a central location. *Rua Espírito Santo 201, tel. 031/201–6966, fax 031/244–9946. 105 rooms. Facilities: restaurant, bar. AE, DC, MC, V. Moderate.*

Amazonas. This downtown hotel is clean, simply furnished, and reasonably priced. There's an excellent restaurant on the 11th floor. *Av. Amazonas 120, tel. 031/201–4644, fax 031/202–4236. 76 rooms. Facilities: restaurant, bar. AE, DC, MC, V. Inexpensive.*

Palmeiras da Liberdade. This new, comfortable, and inexpensive hotel is in the chic Savassi neighborhood. *Rua Sergipe 893, tel., fax 031/261–7422. 62 rooms. Facilities: restaurant, bar. AE, DC, MC, V. Inexpensive.*

Diamantina **Cantina do Marinho.** This well-respected establishment spe-
Dining cializes in Mineiro cuisine. Favorites are pork steak with tutu and pork tenderloin with feijão tropeiro. *Beco do Mota 27, tel. 038/931–1686. No credit cards. Inexpensive–Moderate.*

Lodging **Tijuco.** Virtually the only option in Diamantina, this small inn is located in the heart of the historical center of the city. *Rua Macau do Meio 211, tel. 038/931–1022, fax 038/931–2283. 26 rooms. Facilities: restaurant. AE, DC, V. Inexpensive.*

Ouro Preto **Casa Grande.** This colonial-style restaurant on the central
Dining square provides a view of the 18th-century buildings that line
★ the square. Among the regional dishes served are *lomo tutu á mineiro* (pork tenderloin served with beans, cabbage, and hard-boiled egg), *frango al molho pardo* (chicken in brown sauce), and, for dessert, *dôce de leite comqueijo* (fresh white cheese with carmelized milk). *Praça Tiradentes 84, tel. 031/551–2976. AE, DC, MC, V. Moderate.*

★ **Casa do Ouvidor.** This walk-up over a jewelry store in the heart of the historical district has garnered several awards for regional dishes such as tutu mineiro and lingüiça. It's a favorite stop for tours, but don't be discouraged—it's worth going here at odd hours. *Rua Conde de Bobadela 42, tel. 031/551–2141. AE, DC, MC, V. Inexpensive–Moderate.*

Taverna do Chafariz. Regional cuisine is served cafeteria-style in this informal eatery near the colonial coinage house. *Rua São José 167, tel. 031/551–2828. No credit cards. Inexpensive.*

Lodging **Pousada do Mondego.** This converted house dating from 1747
★ and furnished with period antiques is located next door to the church of São Francisco de Assis. In addition to the colonial ambience, the small and intimate *pousada* (inn) provides highly personalized and professional service. Advance reservations are a must. *Largo de Coimbra 38, tel. 031/551–2040, reservations (Rio) tel. 021/287–3122, ext. 601, fax 031/551–3094. 23 rooms. Facilities: restaurant, bar, art gallery, guided tours available. AE, DC, MC, V. Very Expensive.*

Estrada das Minas Gerais. Cozy and spacious rooms plus delightful chalets with fireplaces are the calling cards of this roadside hotel located at the entrance to Ouro Preto on the highway from Belo Horizonte. Be sure to book ahead. *Rodovia dos Inconfidentes, km 87, tel. 031/551–2122, fax 031/551-2709. 30 rooms, 12 chalets. Facilities: art gallery, crafts shop, outdoor pool. AE, DC, MC, V. Expensive.*

Grande Hotel. Immense by Ouro Preto standards—35 rooms—it's the city's largest hotel. It's also the premier modernist structure in town—a curving two-story building on concrete pillars—designed by world-acclaimed architect Oscar Niemeyer, but cultural purists consider it an eyesore. *Rua Senador Rocha Lagoa 164, tel., fax 031/551–1488. 35 rooms. Facilities: restaurant, bar. AE, DC, MC, V. Moderate.*

Colonial. This is a good example of the small, no-frills inns that can be found in most of the historical cities. What you'll get is a very basic, clean room for a low price. *Rua Camilo Veloso 26, tel. 031/551–3133, fax 031/551-3361. 18 rooms. No credit cards. Inexpensive.*

São João del Rei **Cantina do Italo.** One of the few restaurants in the region that
Dining serve nonregional cuisine, this Italian cantina, with the requisite chianti bottles hanging from the walls, offers a generous range of pasta dishes. *Rua Min. Gabriel Passos 317, tel. 032/371–2862. DC, MC, V. Moderate.*

Rex. This downtown restaurant is one of the city's best options for regional cooking. Specialties include pork tenderloin accompanied by either tutu or feijão tropeiro. *Rua Artur Benardes 137, tel. 032/371–1449. No credit cards. Moderate.*

Lodging **Porto Real.** This small hotel on the city's main street is a good option if you want to stay in São João del Rei and make day trips to the nearby mountain towns. *Av. Eduardo Magalhães 254, tel., fax 032/371–1201. 30 rooms. Facilities: restaurant, bar, pool. AE, DC, MC, V. Moderate.*

Tiradentes **Casa dos Cantos.** One of the region's more unusual eateries,
Dining this Tiradentes restaurant has two tables and three fixed
★ meals—fish broiled in an herb sauce, chicken curry, and roast beef. All three are excellent, but the main reason for the line at the door is dessert—mint mousse covered with chocolate sauce. *Rua da Cadeia 37. No phones. No credit cards. Moderate.*
Canto do Chafariz. This center of regional cuisine is rated tops for its tutu. *Largo do Chafariz 37, tel. 032/355–1377. No reservations accepted. No credit cards. Closed Mon. Inexpensive–Moderate.*

★ **Estalagem.** Another Tiradentes favorite, the Estalagem draws raves for its feija[t]o tropeiro. *Rua Min. Gabriel Passos 280, tel. 032/355–1144. No credit cards. Closed Mon. Inexpensive–Moderate.*

Lodging **Solar da Ponte.** Long included among Brazil's finest small ho-
★ tels, the Solar has the spirit of a house in the country, complete with sprawling lawns and gardens. In every respect, from the design of the comfortable beds to the choice of ceramic tableware, the hotel is a faithful example of regional style. The breakfast and afternoon tea, included in the room rate, are special treats. *Praça das Mercês, tel. 032/355–1255 or 021/287–3122, ext. 601, for reservations in Rio. 12 rooms. Facilities: bar, pool. Expensive.*

★ **Pousada Richard Rothe.** This inn, named after a German antiques dealer who used to live in the town, is extravagantly decorated with antiques such as Louis XV armchairs in the living area and French tapestries on the walls of the guest rooms. It is located in the historic center of Tiradentes. *Rua Pedro Toledo 124, tel. 032/355–1333. 6 rooms. No credit cards. No children under 12. Moderate.*

The Arts and Nightlife

The center of cultural life in Belo Horizonte is the downtown **Palácio das Artes** (Rua Afonso Pena 1537, tel. 031/201–8900), where ballet companies and symphony orchestras sporadically perform. The box office is only open when performances are coming up. The principal venue for performances in Ouro Preto is the **Teatro Municipal** (Rua Brigadeiro Mosquerira).

Mineiros are conservative by nature, and nightlife, especially in the colonial cities, is extremely limited. The action in Belo Horizonte is concentrated in the Savassi neighborhood, where there are many outdoor bars as well as a handful of clubs with live Brazilian music. One popular night spot is **Era Uma Vez um Chalezinho** (Rua Paraíba 1455, tel. 031/221–2170), where you can dip into an excellent fondue while listening to live music. Another traditional bar is the **Cervejaria Brasil** (Rua Aimorés 78, tel. 031/225–1099), Belo's late-night hangout for artists and intellectuals. For homesick cowboys, there is nothing better than **Casa de Chopp Cowboy,** (Av. Getúlio Vargas 489, tel. 031/227–7029) Belo's only country and western bar.

Salvador

By Julia Michaels

Misery and mystery live side by side in Brazil's first capital, founded in 1549 to protect the nascent Portuguese colony against Dutch invaders. Built on a bluff, Salvador, capital of the state of Bahia, overlooks the astonishing Bahia de Todos os Santos (All Saints' Bay), one of the world's widest, covering 1,036 square kilometers (400 square miles). The Portuguese court moved the capital to Rio de Janeiro in 1763, and ever since, Salvador's strategic and shipping importance—and its great wealth, originally deriving from sugar and tobacco— have been in decline, giving rise to widespread poverty and crime. Happily, however, the city's decadence has also preserved the music, art, dance, religions, cuisine, folkways, and festivals of the thousands of African slaves settled there by the Portuguese.

It is this legacy that captivates visitors to Salvador, where at least 70% of the 2.5 million population is black. African rhythms roll forth everywhere, from buses and construction sites to the giant drums of musicians such as the Olodum percussion group, which has recorded with Paul Simon. The scents of coriander, coconut, and palm oil waft around corners that also play afternoon host to white-turbaned women cooking and selling deep-fried spicy shrimp bean cakes. Baroque church interiors covered with gold leaf hark back to the riches of the Portuguese colonial era, when slaves masked their religious beliefs under a thin veneer of Catholicism. And partly thanks to modern-day church acceptance of those beliefs, Salvador has become the fount of Candomblé, a religion based on personal dialogue with the *orixás,* a family of African deities closely linked to nature.

The influence of Salvador's African heritage on Brazilian music has turned this city into one of the most stirring places in the world to spend Carnival, the bacchanalian last fling that precedes Lent (and only one of more than 20 marvelous processions and festivals punctuating the local calendar). As Bahia's distinctive *axé* music has gained popularity around the country, the city has begun to compete with Rio de Janeiro's more traditional celebration. Salvador's Carnival means dancing night after night in the street to the ear-splitting, bone-rattling music of bands perched atop special sound trucks called *trios elétricos.* It means watching the parades of outlandish Carnival associations, such as the Filhos de Gandhi, or Sons of Gandhi (founded by striking stevedores in 1949), men dressed in white tunics and turbans that are the relics of ancient Muslim conversions in Africa. This movable feast formally lasts a week in February or March but begins in spirit at New Year's and continues even into Lent in small towns outside Salvador, with street festivals called *micaretas.*

Bahia is the largest state in Brazil's poor Northeast. Although the inland areas suffer periodically from severe drought, the coast, including Salvador, has a healthier economic outlook, being the country's most popular travel destination. Current governor Antônio Carlos Magalhães spent $10 million in 1993 to restore Salvador's historic district, while private investors have focused on developing southern Bahia's pristine beaches.

Brazil's economic problems have also led to a constant scarcity of resources needed to provide top-quality travel services. Travelers ideally should speak at least some Spanish if they know no Portuguese and be prepared for delays and mix-ups; Bahians pride themselves on a laid-back approach to life.

Staying Safe Bahia's extreme poverty and growing tourism dollars together have made security a major travel consideration. It is advisable to leave valuables at home. The Salvador tourist police suggest that travelers not change dollars with strangers on the street and that they photocopy passports, leaving originals at the hotel. However, even hotel safes and rooms may not be totally secure. Saturday afternoon and Sunday are the days with the least police presence in historic areas.

Tourist Information

The main office of the state tourist board, **Bahiatursa** (Centro de Convenções, Jardim Armação s/n, 41750–270, tel. 071/370–8400; open weekdays 7 AM–7 PM) is located far from tourist attractions, but there are branches at the airport (Aeroporto Internacional 2 de Julho s/n, tel. 071/204–1244; open daily 8:30–10); bus station (Avenida Antonio Carlos Mahalhães s/n, Terminal Rodoviário, tel. 071/358–0871); downtown historical center (Terreiro de Jesus s/n, tel. 071/321–0388; open daily 8–6); in the Upper City (Porto da Barra s/n, tel. 071/247–3195; open daily 8–6); and at the Mercado Modelo crafts market (Praça Visconde de Cairú s/n, tel. 071/241–0240; open daily 8–6). **Emtursa,** the municipal tourist board, has offices at Largo do Pelourinho 12 (tel. 071/243–6555 or 071/243–5738; open weekdays 8–6) and Travessa da Ajuda 2, 2 andar (tel. 071/321–4346 or 071/321–9307; open weekdays 8 AM–9 PM). Dial 131 for **Disque Turismo,** a phone hot line offering spotty multilingual information on special events and tourist attractions. The *Bahia Tourist Guide* is available in bookstores and at newsstands, and Bahiatursa periodically publishes a leaflet with updated basic tourist information, available at hotel reception desks. The office of the **Delegacia de Proteção ao Turista** (tel. 071/320–4103), the tourist police, is located down the steps at the back of the Belvedere at the Praça da Sé. This office deals as best it can with tourist-related crime after the fact, on a shoestring budget; there are also military police foot patrols wearing armbands identifying them as **policia turística** officers, who speak rudimentary second languages.

Arriving and Departing

By Plane The **2 de Julho Airport** (tel. 071/377–2016), located 37 kilometers (23 miles) outside the city, has scheduled flights by Brazilian airlines Varig, Vasp, and Transbrasil. The only international carriers serving the airport are Lufthansa, Trans Europa, and Aeroflot. Travelers are advised to avoid taking *comum* (regular) taxis at the airport, as drivers often jack up the fare by refusing or "forgetting" to turn on the meter. Prepaid *cooperativa* (co-op) taxis, white with a broad blue stripe, are preferred, and cost $15–$20 for the 20- to 30-minute drive downtown. The **Ônibus Executivo,** an air-conditioned bus, runs daily from 6 AM to 9 PM at no set intervals, costs about 70¢, and takes about an hour to reach downtown, stopping at hotels along the way. Drivers don't speak English, but will stop at a specific hotel if shown a written address. Several companies operate these buses, the largest being **Transportes Ondina** (Av. Vasco da Gama 347, tel. 071/245–6366). The municipal **Circular** bus line, operated by both Transportes Ondina and **Transportes Rio Vermelho** (Av. Dorival Caymmi 18270, tel. 071/377–2587), costs about a quarter and runs along the beaches to downtown, ending up at São Joaquim, where ferries depart for Itaparica Island.

By Car Coming from Rio de Janeiro, Salvador can be approached by two highways, BR 101 and BR 116. Drivers on BR 101 should leave the highway at the city of Santo Antônio/Nazaré and follow the signs for Itaparica, 61 kilometers (38 miles) away. At Itaparica, either take the 45-minute ferryboat ride to Salvador, or continue on until BR 101 connects with BR 324. Heading north on BR 116, exit at the city of Feira de Santana, 107 kilometers (67 miles) from Salvador, for BR 324, which approaches the city from the north. Follow the signs marked Iguatemi/Centro for downtown and nearby destinations. Coming from Brasília, take BR 20 north, BR 242 east, then from Ponte Paraguaçu take BR 116 north to the city of Feira de Santana, where you can pick up BR 324 south into Salvador.

Bus Station **Terminal Rodoviário** (Av. Antônio Carlos Magalhães, Iguatemi, tel. 071/358–6633).

Getting Around Salvador

The Baroque churches, museums, Portuguese colonial houses, and narrow, cobbled streets are best seen on foot with a Bahiatursa-accredited personal guide (*see* Guided Tours, *below*). To get around the rest of the city, use the inexpensive comum taxis (white with a red and blue stripe), which can be hailed on the street or called by phone (Ligue Taxi, tel. 071/358–0733). Both these and the more expensive and usually air-conditioned **especial** taxis, which can be called by telephone (Coometas, tel. 071/244–4500; Contas, tel. 071/245–6311), line up in front of the top hotels. They charge on the basis of a unit registered on the meter that must be converted into Brazilian currency using a chart posted in the window. Tipping isn't expected. If you bargain, a comum taxi can be hired for the day for as little as $30.

Buses are crowded, dirty, and dangerous, but service most of the city and cost a pittance (20¢ for adults and nothing for children who can squeeze under the turnstile); the fancier **executivo** buses (70¢ for adults, free for children under five) serve tourist areas more completely but have been subject to a spate of robberies. The glass-sided green, yellow, and orange **Jardineira** bus (marked "Praça da Sé"), running from the downtown Praça da Sé to the Stella Mares beach, along the beachfront **Orla Maritima** series of avenues, is fine for getting to the beach. (Note that some hotels also provide this service.) Due to a lack of parking, rental cars are impractical for sightseeing in the Upper City (although the government plans to build more parking areas), but are handy for visiting outlying beaches and some far-flung attractions. Itaparica and the other harbor islands can be reached by taking a ferry, a launch, hiring a motorized schooner, or joining a harbor schooner excursion, all departing from the docks behind the Mercado Modelo.

To get from the Upper to the Lower City, or vice versa, it's fun to travel in the room-size Lacerda Elevator (*see* Exploring Salvador, *below*), or the more utilitarian funicular railway that runs from behind the Cathedral down to the city's commercial district.

Guided Tours

Orientation Tours Group tours provide some initial orientation, but are fairly cursory, with guides often speaking minimal English; these larger groups are also targeted by hordes of street vendors at almost every stop of the way. Several travel agencies offer half-day minibus orientation tours with hotel pickup and drop-off for about $15. Agencies also offer "By Night" packages, which include dinner and an Afro-Brazilian music and dance show, for $35; and day-long harbor tours on motorized schooners, costing $25 (*see* Boat Tours, *below*). A private beach tour including the Lagôa de Abaeté can be arranged as well, with a car and guide provided for about $20 a head (minimum 2 people). Reservations for all tours can be made through your hotel. The leading agencies offering these tours are **L.R. Turismo** (Av. Otávio Mangabeira 2365, tel. 071/248–3333), **Crismota Turismo** (in Salvador Praia Hotel, Av. Presidente Vargas 2338, tel. 071/247–9888), **Globe Turismo** (Rua Dra. Praguer Fróes 97, tel. 071/245–9611), **Lilás Viagens e Turismo Ltda.** (Av. Tancredo Neves 274, Bloco B, Centro Empresarial Iguatemi II, tel. 071/358–7133 or 071/358–9254). Crismota Turismo also offers 15-minute helicopter flyovers costing $60 per person with a four-passenger minimum.

Private Guides Bahiatursa guides, hired through your hotel, a travel agency, or a Bahiatursa kiosk, carry credentials you can ask to check. For about $25 a head per couple per day (or $50 per single or $70 for a small group), the guide will provide a car, hotel pickup, and lunch; his presence also enhances security. Beware of guides who pick up tourists at church entrances, and overcharge for telling tall tales.

Walking Tours The most complete and personalized English-language walking tours are offered by **Tatu Tours** (Ed. Victoria Center, Sala 1108, Av. Centenário No. 2883, tel. and fax 071/237–7562), which also operates special-interest tours and excursions to locations outside Salvador (*see* Excursions from Salvador, *below*).

Boat Tours The same tour agencies that organize bus tours (*see* Orientation Tours, *above*) also offer full-day harbor excursions on motorized schooners. For $25, you get hotel pickup and drop-off, a 90-minute stop at the beach and drinks and appetizers on one of the 38 islands in All Saints' Bay, plus a stop for lunch (included in the price) on the largest island, Itaparica.

Exploring Salvador

Salvador sprang up on a cliff overlooking All Saints' Bay, and today occupies a triangle sided by the bay and the ocean, coming to a point at the **Farol da Barra** (Barra Lighthouse). The original city is today called the **Cidade Histórica** (Historical City), the site of the oldest government, ecclesiastical, and residential buildings, dating as far back as the 16th century. Over the years, the city spread down the cliff, and in the space between the dropoff and the bay, a commercial district grew up;

today this area is also the site of the fully enclosed handicrafts market, the Mercado Modelo, and the port, from which harbor excursions depart. Sleepy **Itaparica Island,** the largest of the harbor's 38 islands, is across the water. The city also grew sideways; to the northwest around the bay lies the **Itapagipe Peninsula,** site of the Nossa Senhora do Bomfin church and the Monserrat Fort, as well as the city's outdoor fruit and vegetable market, factories, and poorer neighborhoods. The beaches and better residential neighborhoods and hotels begin close to the Barra Lighthouse and north of it on the ocean side. Up on the cliff, south toward the mouth of the bay from the historical city, there are numerous old mansions, churches, some hotels, the city's main shopping street, **Avenida Sete de Setembro,** and the **Campo Grande,** the square where Carnival begins. To the east lie a series of hills and valleys crowded with many poor districts, beyond which lie the better oceanside neighborhoods. The tree-lined Avenida Sete de Setembro contines south through the **Vitória** neighborhood and down past the Iate Club (Yacht Club) to the **Barra** neighborhood, a mix of beach, yuppie bars, good cheap restaurants, low-life cafés, and moderately priced hotels. Here the city comes to a point at the Barra lighthouse before running up east and north again on the oceanside leg of the triangle. The next beaches, **Ondina** and **Rio Vermelho,** are home to Salvador's most expensive resort hotels; the latter neighborhood is quite Bohemian, with some of the city's best bars and music. Going north along the so-called **Orla Marítima** (a series of connecting avenues running along the coast), there are many restaurants, the cleanest beaches, and, at the city's northernmost point, the mysterious **Lagôa de Abaeté,** a deep, black freshwater lagoon.

Upper City The **Terreiro de Jesus,** a large square with three churches and a small handicrafts fair, opens the way to exotic, historic Salvador. Where nobles once strolled under imperial palm trees, protected by their slaves, visitors will see men practicing *capoeira,* a stylized, dancelike foot-fight with African origins, to the thwang of the *berimbau,* a rudimentary but mesmerizing bow-shape musical instrument. Walk east down the Ladeira do Cruzeiro de São Francisco to enter the most famous of the city's 176 churches, the 18th-century Baroque **Igreja de São Francisco** (Church of St. Francis), and its still-active monastery. Listen for the sound of African drums in the square outside as you appreciate the ceiling painted by José Joaquim da Rocha, a mulatto who founded Brazil's first art school, in 1774. The ornately carved cedarwood and rosewood interior virtually writhes with images of mermaids, acanthus leaves, and caryatids, bathed in shimmering gold leaf. Guides will tell you that there is as much as a ton of gold here, but restoration experts say there is actually much less, as the leaf used is just a step up from a powder. A super Sunday morning alternative to crowded beaches is mass here (9–11, 11–11:45); stay until the end, when the electric lights go off, to catch the wondrous subtlety of gold leaf under natural light. On Tuesday at 6:30 PM there is a blessing of the church, followed by an open street rehearsal by the Afro-Brazilian Olodum percussion group. *Praça Padre Anchieta, tel. 071/243–2367. Admission free. Closed Mon.–Sat. 11:30–2, Sun. after 11:45.*

Next door is the **Igreja da Ordem Terceira de São Francisco** (Praça Anchieta s/n, tel. 071/242–7046; admission free), whose 18th-century Spanish Plateresque sandstone facade (unique in all Brazil, it was carved to resemble the Spanish silver altars hammered into wooden molds) was hidden for decades under a thick coat of plaster, until, the story goes, a drunk electrician went wild with a hammer in the 1930s. Walk back up toward the Terreiro de Jesus, past the coffin shops. At the top left corner where the Terreiro begins is **Simon** jewelers (Rua Ignácio Accioli, tel. 071/242–5218; closed Sun. afternoon), whose obliging owners will allow you the use of their bathroom and give you a free glass of cold water or a coffee. This is one of Salvador's top jewelry manufacturers, with a window onto the room where goldsmiths work.

Moving into the square itself, turn right and see the **Igreja São Domingos de Gusmão da Ordem Terceira** (Church of the Third Order of Saint Dominick), which was begun in 1723. The lay clergy of this Baroque church were restoring it at press time, hoping to open a museum in a side chapel to display their fascinating collection of carved processional saints and other sacred objects. Such sculptures often had hollow interiors used to smuggle gold into Portugal to avoid government taxes. You will see Oriental features and details in the church decoration, evidence of long-ago connections with Portugal's Asian colonies of Goa and Macao. Upstairs are two impressive rooms used for the lay brothers' meetings and receptions, with carved wooden furniture. *Terreiro de Jesus, tel. 071/242–4185. Admission free. Closed Mon.–Sat. noon–2, Sun. after 9:30 mass.*

Directly at the other end of the Terreiro is the 17th-century **Catedral Basílica,** where an Oriental influence also is seen: Note the intricate ivory and tortoise shell inlay from Goa on the Japiassu family altar, third on the right as you enter; the Asian facial features and clothing of the figures in the transept altars; and the 16th-century tiles from Macao in the sacristy. A Jesuit who lived in China painted the ceiling over the cathedral entrance. *Terreiro de Jesus. Tel. 071/321–4573. Admission free. Closed Mon.–Sun. 11–3:30. Mass Tues.–Sat. at 5.*

Also on the square, just to the left of the cathedral, is a building that housed Brazil's first medical school, today home of the **Museu Afro-Brasileiro.** This rich collection of African costumes, masks, musical instruments, tools, and statues plumbs much that drives contemporary Bahian culture. Don't miss the stunning series of wooden panels—inlaid with silver, gold, shells, copper, and brass—by the Argentine-born artist Carybé. The museum also sells literature on African culture. *Terreiro de Jesus, tel. 071/321–0383. Admission charged. Closed weekends.*

Turning left as you exit the museum, go left again onto Rua Alfredo de Brito, once a high-class address, later a slum, and recently restored to pastel cleanliness. On the right you'll find the **Casa Santa Barbara** (tel. 071/244–0458; closed Sat. afternoon and Sun.), selling Bahian clothing and lacework of top quality, albeit at prices a bit higher than elsewhere. A bit farther down the street on the left is a garden on the grounds of the former medical school, featuring a cacau tree, native to Brazil and southern Bahia's top source of income. Walk a bit more to No. 20, on the left, housing several shops, the Hotel Pelourinho, and the site of a house where Bahian writer Jorge Amado, author of *Dona Flor and Her Two Husbands,* lived and wrote in his student days. Cut through the shopping gallery to a courtyard and up some stairs to the left for a panoramic view of the city shoreline and the bay, and you'll understand why the Portuguese felt so well protected here. Downstairs is a café.

Rua Alfredo de Brito leads into the famed triangular **Largo do Pelourinho** (little pillory), named for the pillory where slaves were punished, now the setting for one of the largest groupings of Brazilian colonial architecture. Down to the right stands the Baroque **Igreja de Nossa Senhora do Rosário dos Pretos,** built by and for slaves between 1704 and 1796. Guides tend to skip over this church, but it's worth a look at the side altars, to see statues of some of the few black saints of the Catholic church. Each has a fascinating story. A fellow at the entrance organizes groups to watch candomblé ceremonies (*see* Off the Beaten Track, *below*). *Ladeira do Pelourinho s/n, tel. 071/312–6280. Admission free. Closed weekend afternoons.*

Walk up the hill past ancient pastel-color houses growing beards of ferns on cornices, and African handicrafts shops and art galleries to the **Igreja e Museu do Convento do Carmo.** The 17th-century church is famous for its restored French organ and carved cedarwood figure of Christ, the latter kept in the sacristy. Studded with tiny Indian rubies to represent blood, the figure was once carried through the streets in a silver-handled litter during Holy Week, but is now too fragile to be removed. Although at press time the museum was closed, with only part of its collection (religious art objects, paintings, and furniture) on view at the monastery next door, it was expected to be open by 1994, at which time the monastery may return to its previous function as a hotel (*see* Lodging, *below*). The monastery, which was occupied by the Dutch when they invaded in 1624, features a small church built in 1580 and a chapel with blue Portuguese tiles that recount the story of the Jesuit order. *Largo do Carmo, s/n, tel. 071/242–2042. Admission free. Church: Open daily for mass only, 7 AM, but accessible from museum. Museum closed Mon.–Sat. noon–2, Sun. afternoon.*

Mercado Modelo Besides walking or taking a taxi, you can travel between the Upper City (Ciudade Altá) and Lower City (Ciudade Baixa) aboard the popular **Lacerda Elevator,** which costs about 2¢ and covers 72 meters (236 feet) in a minute. The elevator runs between the Praça Municipal in the Upper City and Praça Cairú and the Mercado Modelo, Salvador's main handicrafts market. Built in 1872, the elevator ran on steam until its 1930 restoration. Bahians joke that the elevator is the only way to "go up" in life.

Exiting the elevator at the Lower City, cross the Praça Visconde de Cairú to get to the market building. Outside, you'll hear the nasal-voiced *repentistas,* regional folksingers who make up songs on the spot. Notice the blue Portuguese tiles on a Gothic-style windowed building, once a sort of chamber of commerce, now a supermarket. The **Mercado Modelo** (closed Sun. afternoon) may not be the cheapest place to buy handicrafts—and you do have to bargain—but it must be experienced. This enclosed market assaults the senses, with its *cachaça* (Brazilian firewater made from sugarcane), cashew nuts, pepper sauces, cigars, the dried shrimp that are an integral part of Bahian cooking, manioc flour, leather goods, hammocks, lace goods, musical instruments, African sculptures, fossils, and gems. Be sure to visit **Didara** (upstairs, stall 9–10) for striking African print clothing by Goya, a local designer. The upper floor also has a restaurant with a gorgeous view of

the bay. At the rear of the market outside, boys practice capoeira and sell monkeys; across the way are moored the harbor
excursion boats.

Itapagipe A 20-minute taxi ride from the market, around the bay to the
Peninsula northwest, brings you to the Itapagipe Peninsula and the **Igreja
Nosso Senhor do Bonfim,** Salvador's most important church. A
procession of black women dressed in petticoat-puffed Em-
pire-waist white dresses, turbans, and ritual necklaces comes
here the Thursday before the third Sunday in January to wash
the steps with holy flower water. Built in the 1750s, the simple
church is filled with *ex-votos*—wax, wooden, and plaster replicas of body parts—objects of devoted prayer and believe to be
capable of miraculous cures. Many figures in Catholicism have
a counterpart deity in Candomblé; Nosso Senhor do Bonfim's
is Oxalá, the father of all the gods and goddesses. Thus the
seemingly bizarre mixture of figurines found in the shops opposite the church: St. George and the Dragon, devils, Indians,
monks, sailors, warriors plus ex-votos that include house keys
and Volkswagen Beetles for the devotees of consumerism.
*Praça do Senhor do Bonfim, Alto do Bonfim, Itapagipe, tel.
071/312–0196. Admission free. Closed Tues.–Sun. noon–2:30
and Mon.*

Here or in the square facing the church you will be accosted by
someone selling a printed ribbon, willing to tie it around your
wrist with three knots (and sell 20 more to take home to
friends), each good for one wish if you wear the ribbon until it
falls off and throw it into the ocean. Each color stands for a
paired Catholic saint and Candomblé deity.

A five-minute drive from the church is the dazzling white **Mont
Serrat Fort,** built in 1500 and named for the shrine of the Black
Virgin at Montserrat, near Barcelona. Still used by the Brazilian military, the fort is not open to the public. There is a church
by the same name nearby, rarely open, with a renowned carving of Saint Peter.

Other Museums Housed in a former Carmelite monastery near the Upper City,
the **Museu de Arte Sacra** (Sacred Art Museum) and its adjoining **Igreja de Santa Teresa** (Church of Saint Teresa) are two of
the city's best-cared-for repositories of religious objects. An
in-house restoration team has worked miracles that bring alive
Bahia's 1549–1763 golden age as Brazil's capital city and main
colonial port. See the silver altar in the church, moved there
from the demolished Sé church, and the blue-and-yellow-tiled
sacristy replete with a bay view. *Rua do Sodré 276, tel. 071/243–
6310. Admission charged. Closed weekday mornings and weekends.*

Up the cliff from the Sacred Art Museum, in the Vitória district, is the **Museu Carlos Costa Pinto,** fruit of one wealthy couple's fascination with art and antiques, a rare example of
private support for the arts in Brazil. Among the museum's
3,000 objects fashioned around the world over the last three
centuries is Costa Pinto's collection of oversize gold and silver
jewelry worn by favored slave women. Here are some prime
examples of the *balangandã,* a chain of large silver tropical
fruits worn by slave women around the waist, said alternately
to be good-luck charms or symbols of the owner's wish for freedom. The balangandã usually includes a *figa,* a closed fist with
thumb sticking out the top, supposedly used among slaves as

an invitation to sex and at the very least a fertility symbol. Many jewelry and crafts stores sell replicas of these charms. *Av. Sete de Setembro 2490, tel. 071/247–6081. Admission charged. Closed Wed.–Mon. until 2:30 PM and Tues.*

A mid-16th-century waterfront mill set between the Upper and Lower Cities houses the **Museu de Arte Moderna da Bahia** (Bahian Museum of Modern Art), with its permanent collection of artwork by some of Brazil's top modern painters, including Cândido Portinari, Alfredo Volpi, Siron Franco, and Hector Carybé. The museum building is part of a complex that includes the **Solar da Unhão,** a former sugar mill/residential complex dating from the 18th century. The slave quarters is now a restaurant where Salvador's best Afro-Brazilian dinner show takes place (*see* The Arts and Nightlife, *below*). At press time the church in the courtyard was due to open shortly as a small theater. *Avenida Contorno, s/n, tel. 071/243–6174. Museum: Admission free. Closed Tues.–Sun. until 1:30 and Mon.*

Off the Beaten Track

Salvadorans are willing and eager to share their African practices and rituals with visitors. These include the **Candomblé temple ceremony,** performed nightly except during Lent, in which believers sacrifice animals and become possessed by the gods; a **reading of the *búzios*** (small brown shells, thrown like jacks into a circle of beads; the pattern they form tells about your life) by a *pãe de santo* or *mãe de santo* (Candomblé priest or priestess); and a **capoeira exhibition.** You can make an appointment and arrange to see these performances through hotels or tour agencies.

Candomblé temples, usually located in poor neighborhoods at the city's edge, do not allow photographs or video or sound recordings. Visitors should not wear black (white is preferable) or revealing clothing. The ceremony is long and repetitive, there is no air-conditioning and sometimes not even chairs; men and women are separated.

Don't select your mãe de santo for the shell reading through an advertisement or sign, as many of them are best not at fortune-telling but at saying "one hundred dollars" in every language under the sun. One of the most authentic is Mãe Edina (tel. 071/241–8154; cost approximately $10). Make an appointment yourself, or contact Tatu tours (Ed. Victoria Center, Sala 108, Avenida Centernário No. 2883, tel. and fax 071/237–7562) to provide a car and interpreter for the 10-minute ride from downtown.

Capoeira practice takes place Tuesday, Thursday, and Saturday night at 7 at the 17th-century **Forte Santo Antônio Além do Carmo,** just a bit north of the Carmo museum and monastery, in the Upper City, a 5- to 10-minute taxi ride from downtown. There are two schools practicing here; the more traditional is the **Grupo de Capoeira Angola,** run upstairs by Mestre (Master) Morães. Weekday nights are classes and the real show happens on Saturday; the schools charge no admission but accept donations. Take a taxi and have the driver wait while you watch this hypnotic African sport accompanied by the berimbau.

Just off the Avenida Sete de Setembro, a five-minute taxi ride south from the historical Upper City, lies the **Largo da Piedade,** worth a visit for a look at some very impressive, well-hidden residents: the yard-long chameleon lizards that inhabit the square's flame trees! Not far away is **Praça Campo Grande** (also known as Praça Dois de Julho), where the crowd first gathers for the Carnival procession to **Praça Castro Alves,** the square named for the abolitionist and Bahia's foremost 19th-century poet (said to have had 54 wives, he died of tuberculosis at age 24), where over a million people cram in to dance to those bands perched atop special sound trucks called trios elétricos.

Shopping

In addition to the overwhelming variety and quantity of goods at the **Mercado Modelo** (*see* Exploring Salvador, *above*), Salvador has several state-run **handicrafts** stores, with lower prices and smaller selections. The best are the **Instituto Mauá** (Praça Azevedo Fernandes 2, tel. 071/235–5440; closed weekend afternoons) and **Artesanato Fieb-Sesi** (Rua Borges dos Reis 9, tel. 071/245–3543; closed weekend afternoons). Here you will find woven and lace goods, musical instruments, sandals, and pottery.

For **paintings,** especially *art naïf,* visit the many galleries in the Upper City in and around the **Largo do Pelourinho.** Top local artists (many of whom use only first names or nicknames) include Totonho, Calixto, Raimundo Santos, Joailton, Nadinho, and Nonato, for art naïf; and Maria Adair, Carybé, Mário Cravo, and Jota Cunha.

Two big shopping malls boast Brazil's top boutiques, cinemas, and restaurants. **Shopping Center Iguatemi** (Av. Antônio Carlos Magalhães 148) is the older and more traditional of the two, located near the bus station, while **Shopping Barra,** in the Barra neighborhood back from the beach (Av. Centenário 2992), is newer and glitzier. The top hotels provide free transportation to it. Both the Iguatemi and Barra malls have boutiques selling locally manufactured clothing as well as franchise outlets or branch stores of Rio, São Paulo, and Minas retailers. The city's most traditional shopping area for a variety of everyday goods, with lower prices than in the malls, is **Avenida Sete de Setembro.**

Spectator Sports

Soccer **Bahia** (tel. 071/230–4227) and **Vitória** (tel. 071/231–1055) are the two best local teams, and they play year-round (except at Christmastime) Wednesday night and Sunday at 5 PM at the **Estádio da Fonte Nova** (Av. Vale do Nazaré, Dique do Tororó, tel. 071/243–3322, ext. 237), formally known as the Estádio Governador Otávio Mangabeira. Tickets are sold at the stadium one day in advance. Avoid sitting behind the goals, where the roughhousing is worst. The best seats are in the *arquibancada superior* (high bleachers).

Beaches

At most local beaches the food and drink kiosks provide chairs and umbrellas free of charge; you pay only for what you consume. Some also offer rudimentary bathroom, changing, and shower facilities free of charge for patrons. Aside from these, there are no functioning bathrooms on the beaches, but some have public showers that run on one-minute tokens costing less than 25¢.

Do not sit directly on the sand, as it's likely to have fungi that cause skin diseases. And don't leave belongings unattended. Beaches are wall-to-wall people on the weekends, but if you don't mind a crowd it's fun to soak up both sun and beach culture, which includes sand sports, firewater drinks, spicy seafood snacks (don't miss the *acarajé*, a deep-fried beancake with dried shrimp and sauce) at sandside kiosks, live music, and the briefest of swimwear.

As a rule, the farther away from the port, the better the beach. Some Salvadorans, especially singles, swear by the urban beaches **Porto da Barra** and **Farol da Barra,** which boast a colorful fauna including workers who live nearby and tourists staying at neighboring hotels. Petty thievery is a problem here. There are no bathrooms or kiosks, but you can rent a beach chair for about $1. The corner of Porto da Barra closest to the Grande Hotel da Barra is a gay hangout. Toward the other end, around the corner from the lighthouse, lie the hotel districts of **Ondina** and **Rio Vermelho,** where the beaches intermittently suffer pollution problems.

Leaving the more built-up areas of the city behind, the first truly safe (healthwise) beach is the wide oceanside **Piatã** (20 km, or 9 mi north of downtown), whose calm waters and golden sand attract many families with children. The Jardineira bus stops at all the beaches along the coast, from downtown north as far as the **Stella Maris** beach (28 km, or 13 mi from downtown), which is popular with surfers. A more comfortable Ônibus Executivo (marked "Roteiro das Praias") runs from Praça da Sé to Flamengo beach, stopping at all the same stops. The kiosks at Stella Maris are famous, especially the Padang Padang, with beach dancing on weekends, and Kajila, with its delicious appetizers and live music in the evenings.

Other popular beaches include:

Barra do Jacuípe A river runs down to the ocean at this long, wide, pristine beach lined with coconut palms, about 40 kilometers (25 miles) north of Salvador. There are beachfront snack bars and, if you like it so much you decide to stay overnight, you can check in at an inn beside the surf. The Santa Maria/Catuense bus company (tel. 071/359–3474) operates six buses (marked "Praia do Forte") daily stopping at this beach.

Guarajuba With palm trees and calm waters banked by a reef, this is the nicest beach of them all, though it's 60 kilometers (38 miles) north of Salvador. The bus to Barra do Jacuipe (*see above*) continues on to Guarajuba. There are snack kiosks, fishing boats, surfing, dune buggies, and even a children's playground.

Itapuã Frequented by artist types who live nearby, this beach is the farthest away along the city beachfront and polluted at some points, but one of the best for atmosphere. At around K and J streets, there are food kiosks, music bars, and amusement park rides, too. The beach is served by the Executivo and Jardineira buses, which leave from Praça da Sé.

Jaguaribe This is the "in crowd" hangout, frequented by singles on Saturday and good for surfing, windsurfing, and sailing. There are the ubiquitous snack bars, of course. The Executivo and Jardineira buses stop at Jaguaribe.

Dining

Seafood is the thing in Bahia, in great variety and quantity, prepared either Bahian style or using more traditional Continental recipes. A happy mix of African and native ingredients has come down the centuries from the hands and hearts of slave women, and then maids, working in Bahian kitchens. The basic raw materials are coconut milk, lemon, coriander, tomato, palm oil (*dendé*), onions, dried shrimp, salt, and hot chili peppers. The ubiquitous *muqueca*, which has all these ingredients plus the seafood catch of the day, is cooked quickly in individual portions (though big enough for two) in a clay pot over a high flame. Other main dishes include *vatapá*, a fish pudding made of bread, ginger, peanuts, cashews, and olive oil; *caruru*, okra mashed with ginger, dried shrimp, and palm oil; *ximxim de galinha*, chicken with peanuts and coconut; and *efo*, a bitter chicory-like vegetable cooked with dried shrimp. Most restaurants serve hot pepper sauce on the side, as well as *farofa*, seasoned manioc meal that does a delicious job of soaking up sauces. Palm oil is high in cholesterol and hard to digest; you can order these dishes without it. And if you've had enough of Bahian food, most restaurants are happy to prepare a simpler fish or shrimp dish even if it's not on the menu.

Batida, a strong drink made from *cachaça* (sugarcane liquor) and fruit juice, prepares the way for Bahia's spicy, heavy food, which also goes well with beer or white wine.

Bahian desserts are very sweet, providing relieving contrast with the spicy food they follow. They are usually made from some combination of sugar, coconut, fruit, eggs, or milk. *Cocada* is shredded coconut caked with sugar; *quindim* is a little tart made from egg yolks and coconut; *doce de banana* (or any other fruit) is banana cooked in sugar; *ambrosia* is a lumpy milk and sugar pudding.

You can easily find restaurants serving Bahian specialties in Barra, a yuppie neighborhood full of bars and sidewalk cafés. There are also many good spots in Bohemian Rio Vermelho, near the Meridien hotel, and a slew of newer places along the beachfront drive beginning around Jardim de Alah. At press time, many new restaurants were opening up in and around the restored Pelourinho area in the Upper City. It is wise to order meat only in *churrascaria* (barbecue) restaurants, avoiding it in seafood places. Some restaurants give discounts for cash.

For details and price-category definitions, *see* Dining in Staying in Brazil, *above*.

Very Expensive **St. Honoré.** You can feast here on a dazzling nighttime view of the bay, live piano music, and classical French food cooked by a disciple of French chef Paul Bocuse in this candlelit restaurant on the 23rd floor of the Le Meridien hotel. Specialties include raw marinated salmon for starters, shrimp with *tagliarini* noodles and basil, and lastly, a piece of St.-Honoré (caramelized cream-puff cake with whipped cream) off the dessert cart. *Rua Fonte do Boi 216, tel. 071/248–8011. Reservations required on weekends and holidays. AE, DC, MC, V.*

Expensive **Bargaço.** Typical Bahian food is served in this oversize, brightly lit shed a 20-minute drive along the beach from downtown, once a must in Salvador that now caters mostly to tour groups. Starters such as *pata de caranguejo* (vinegared crab claw) are hearty and plentiful, but they may do more than take the edge off your appetite for the requisite *muqueca de camarão* (shrimp) or *muqueca de siri mole* (soft-shell crab); try the *cocada baiana* (sugar-caked coconut) for dessert, if you have room. *Rua P, Lote 1819, Quadra 43, Jardim Armação, Boca do Rio, tel. 071/231–5141 or 071/231–3900. Reservations advised during high season. No credit cards.*

★ **Casa da Gamboa.** A longtime favorite of Bahian writer Jorge Amado, this small Portuguese colonial house close to downtown boasts excellent Bahian cooking and, from some of its 14 tables, a stirring view of All Saints' Bay. *Casquinha de siri* (breaded crab in the shell) comes as a complimentary starter; then try the *muqueca de ouro*, a Bahian bouillabaisse, or the *peixe com risoto de ostras* (grilled fish with oyster risotto), followed by the very good traditional desserts. *Rua Newton Prado 51, Gamboa de Cima, tel. 071/321–9776. Reservations required. No credit cards. Closed Sun., Dec. 24–25.*

Phelippe Camarão. Named for a shipwreck off the Brazilian coast and decorated with nautical treasures, this dining spot draws many local advertising executives, journalists, and artists just for its outstanding lemon pie. Its lovely outdoor terrace with view is the perfect place to top off a day at the beach, over such tropicalized Continental fare as *núvola de caranguejo* (crab pudding); a house salad of vegetables, fruit, and shrimp; or the Chateaubriand, served with noodles and vegetables. *Rua Alexandre Gusmão 104, Rio Vermelho, tel. 071/237–4404 or 071/235–1596. Reservations required. AE, D, MC.*

Moderate **Baby Beef Martinez.** Those seeking a break from Bahian cooking will welcome top-quality beef served attentively in comfortable air-conditioned surroundings (*see* Lodging, *below*). While the Chateaubriand comes with Argentine-style puffed potatoes, the *bisteca Martinez* steak is served with garlic sauce and rice with minced meat; *feijoada* is on the menu Wednesday and Saturday. *Ondina Apart Hotel, Av. Oceania 2400, tel. 071/203–8314. AE, DC, MC, V.*

Frutos do Mar. This plain, traditional seafood spot in the hopping Barra neighborhood is a favorite among cash-conscious locals for its shrimp muquecas and *ensopados* (catch-of-the-day stews resembling bouillabaisse), which come with a typical, sweet-flavored bean called *feijão de leite*. *Rua Marquês de Leão 415, Barra, tel. 071/245–6479 or 071/254–6322. AE, DC, MC, V.*

Iate Clube da Bahia. From your captain's chair in this informal air-conditioned yacht club restaurant, set on the cliff between Barra and the Vitória neighborhood, you get a spectacular view of boats bobbing in the bay and honest Continental and Bahian cooking, such as double gratinéed fish and muquecas. *Av. Sete de Setembro 3252, Barra, tel. 071/336–9011. Reservations advised on weekends. AE, DC, MC, V. Closed Mon.*

Iemanjá. Probably the best value for regional cooking, here's a place with a bubbly, underwater atmosphere, replete with aquamarine sea-goddess murals and aquariums. The service is somewhat slow and there's no air-conditioning, but most patrons don't seem to mind, concentrating instead on plowing through mountainous portions of muqueca or ensopado. *Av. Otávio Mangabeira 929, tel. 071/231–5770. No credit cards.*

★ **Quinta Pitanga.** For its Magic Realism paintings and decor, its ever-evolving menu, and the personalized attention of American owner-artist Jimmy Valkus and partner/chef Jacinto Batista, this restaurant in an inn set in a fruit grove (*see* Lodging, *below*) is a must even though a meal means a ferry ride over the bay to the island of Itaparica (*see* Excursions from Salvador, *below*). Favorites, sometimes served buffet style, are chili-style feijoada, baked stuffed fish, stir-fried soft-shell crab, and curried chicken with peanuts presented in a pineapple half; sweet finishes include a torte of *pitanga* (a berrylike fruit) and passion fruit mousse. *No street address, Itaparica, tel. 071/831–1554. Reservations required. Dress: casual, neater at night. No credit cards. Owner stops seating for dinner between 8 and 10.*

Inexpensive **Arroz de Hauçá.** Two unemployed brothers convinced their family's 70-year-old cook to go public, and turned their plant-filled house into a restaurant that put the home-cooked dish it's named for on the map of Bahian cuisine. This hefty plate of rice in coconut milk with a circle of fried jerked beef and onions in the middle, the rice covered with a sauce of shrimp paste and onions, is the star here, but you can also find the usual Bahian specialties on the menu, and the management doesn't frown on sharing dishes. *Rua Sabino Silva 598, Jardim Apipema, tel. 071/247–3508. Reservations advised on weekends. AE, MC, DC, V.*

Extudo. Young professionals and singles jam-pack this bar and restaurant near Le Meridien hotel just about every night. Bahian and international dishes include *camarão comodoro*, shrimp and prunes gratinéed in a creamy tomato sauce; *Finnegan's*, steak with black pepper sauce; and *frango flambado*, flambéed chicken. *Rua Lídio Mesquita 4, Rio Vermelho, tel. 071/237–4669. No credit cards. Closed Mon.*

Galletu's. This simple whitewashed veranda overlooking the main drag in Barra puts a grill of cooked food right on the table, with piping, succulent meat, sausage, or chicken served with potato salad and fried polenta. Cars race by and the waves crash against the sand across the street below as the evening gears up in this neighborhood full of nighttime fun. *Av. Oceanica 693, Barra, tel. 071/245–5391. AE, DC, MC, V.*

Lodging

Because of Brazil's shaky economic situation, even the best hotels are a bit run-down, with most of the rest downright shabby. As the government awards stars according to local criteria, many guests are surprised to find that a Salvador five-star property is far below U.S. or European standards. No hotel combines a great beach setting with convenience to historic areas, so you will have to decide which has greater priority. There are few hotels in the **Upper City** historical district overlooking the bay, but this may change as its renaissance takes root. At press time the Carmo monastery in the Upper City, which once functioned as an unusual hotel, was negotiating with hotel operators on a possible reopening. Going south into the Vitória neighborhood along **Avenida Sete de Setembro,** there are many inexpensive hotels, convenient both to the Barra area beaches and to historical sights. Just around the corner from the bay is the yuppie Barra neighborhood, with many less expensive hotels, and cafés, bars, restaurants, and clubs within walking distance. The city's resort hotel district lies further north, somewhat isolated from the rest of the city, a 10-minute taxi ride from downtown and historical areas, on and around the Ondina and Rio Vermelho beaches (*see* Beaches, *above*). If you decide to stay outside the city itself, consider Praia do Forte, where, aside from the Praia do Forte Resort Hotel (*see below*), there are many smaller hotels and inns to choose from.

At peak season (December–March and the month of July), especially during Carnival, the rates are higher and reservations must be made months in advance. Many hotels give discounts of up to 30% for cash payment. All rates include Continental breakfast.

For details and price-category definitions, *see* Lodging in Staying in Brazil, *above*.

Very Expensive   **Bahia Othon.** A short drive from most historic sights, nightlife, restaurants, and in-town beaches, this busy modern business and tourist hotel offers an ocean view from all rooms, whose ceramic-tile floors and wood furniture are a bit worn. Top local entertainers often perform at the hotel's outdoor park, and during the high season, the staff organizes poolside activities, plus trips to better beaches. *Av. Presidente Vargas 2456, tel. 071/247–1044 or toll-free 800–4877, fax 071/245–4877. 300 rooms, 25 suites. Facilities: restaurant, coffee shop, bar, disco, health club, pool, sauna, concierge floor with free happy hour and breakfast room. AE, DC, MC, V.*

Hotel Sofitel Quatro Rodas. Located just beyond the city's northern perimeter, this resort and convention hotel near good beaches is a world unto itself, decorated with local art and oversize, old-fashioned farm implements. The green-and-blue–accented rooms all have a view of the spacious grounds and the ocean beyond. *Rua da Pasárgada, s/n, Farol de Itapuan, tel. 071/249–9611, fax 071/249–6946. 194 rooms, 9 suites. Facilities: 2 restaurants, bar, beauty salon, masseuse, gallery, boutiques, crafts demonstrations, 2 pools, 3 tennis courts, 9-hole golf course, all-purpose sports fields, pedal boats, free minibus to downtown. AE, DC, MC, V.*

★ **Praia do Forte Resort Hotel.** A 90-minute drive north of Salvador, this beachfront complex is not only a complete resort but is also right next door to the Tamar sea turtle preservation project and an artsy fishing village (*see* Excursions from Salvador, *below*). Public areas are decorated in deluxe Robinson Crusoe style, using natural materials, while rooms are like hideaways, with verandas, hammocks, and ceiling fans. *Rua do Farol s/n, Praia do Forte, Mata de São João, tel. 071/832–2333, fax 071/832–2100. 132 rooms, 4 suites. Facilities: 2 restaurants, 3 bars, disco, health club, 4 pools, 2 tennis courts, windsurfing, sailboats, kayaks, snorkeling, bird-watching, supervised children's activities. Price includes breakfast and dinner. AE, DC, MC, V.*

★ **Quinta Pitanga.** This boarding school and Catholic retreat turned country inn on the island of Itaparica, owned and decorated in Magic Realist style by American artist Jimmy Valkus, is a favorite among filmmakers and other jet-setters looking to escape the "real" world. Valkus and partner-chef Jacinto Batista have developed a superb menu for the inn's restaurant (*see* Dining, *above*), and all meals are included in the price of lodging. *No street address, Itaparica, tel. and fax 071/831–1554. 7 rooms, 6 with bath. Facilities: restaurant, masseuse, beach,* *free transport to mainland. No credit cards. No children under 12* .

Tropical Hotel da Bahia. Owned by Varig Airlines and often included in package deals, this centrally located hotel is a bit tattered, but quite practical for those whose priority is Salvador's history and culture, not beachcombing. Some rooms overlook the square where Carnival begins; the Concha Acústica do Teatro Castro Alves, site of many big musical shows, is within walking distance, and performers there often stay at the hotel. *Praça Dois de Julho 2, Campo Grande, tel. 071/321–9922 or 071/321–3699, fax 071/321–9725. 282 rooms, 10 suites. Facilities: restaurant, coffee shop, bar, disco, 2 pools, masseuse, sauna, free beach shuttle, games room. AE, DC, MC, V.*

Expensive **Ondina Apart Hotel Residência.** Located in the resort hotel district a short drive from the sights, nightlife, and restaurants, this recently opened apartment-hotel complex on the beach has simple, modern furniture and kitchenettes. Many businesspeople and families opt for this hotel when they are staying in Salvador for an extended period. *Av. Presidente Vargas 2400, Ondina, tel. 071/203–8000, fax 071/247–9434. 100 suites. Facilities: restaurant, coffee shop, bar, disco, 2 pools, health club, 2 tennis courts. AE, DC, MC, V.*

Praiamar. Practically across the street from the best downtown beaches, this hotel could use a renovation, and its furniture is mismatched, but it functions efficiently, has a big pool, and is close to a bus stop for lines going almost everywhere. *Av. Sete de Setembro 3577, Porto da Barra, tel. 071/247–7011, fax 071/247–7973. 170 rooms, 10 suites. Facilities: restaurant, bar, pool. AE, DC, MC, V.*

Moderate **Grande Hotel da Barra.** This older hotel with a 1980 addition, located by the best downtown beaches and convenient to the historical center, has comfortable, well-maintained rooms with such decorative touches as pink-and-green-flower bedspreads, latticework screens, and lots of wood carvings. The front rooms sport verandas, and guest rooms in the "new" section have ocean views; all rooms come equipped with a VCR. *Av. Sete de Setembro 3564, Porto da Barra, tel. 071/336–6011, fax 071/247–6223. 112 rooms, 5 suites. Facilities: restaurant, bar, beauty salon, in-house video movies, sauna, pool. AE, DC, MC, V.*

Hotel Bahia do Sol. This hotel's low rates and prime location, close to museums and historical sights, may make up for its battered wooden furniture. Front rooms have a partial ocean view, but those in the back are less noisy. *Av. Sete de Setembro 2009, Vitória, tel. 071/336–7211, fax 071/336–7776. 86 rooms, 4 suites. Facilities: restaurant, bar. AE, DC, MC, V.*

Inexpensive **Hotel Bella Barra.** Owned by a Chinese family with a restaurant next door, this hotel is right in the middle of one of the city's liveliest districts, both night and day. The rooms and furniture are rickety, but plain and clean, with less noise in side rooms and an ocean view from the front quarters. *Rua Afonso Celso 439, Barra, tel. 071/237–8401, fax 071/235–2313. 21 rooms. AE, DC, MC, V.*

Hotel Vila Romana. Located on a quiet street minutes from the beach and not far from many upscale bars and cafés, this Bahian version of a Roman *palazzo* that's seen better days is favored by many Italian visitors, who don't seem to mind the rudimentary plumbing. Try for one of the back rooms, which are better ventilated. *Rua Prof. Leme de Brito 14, Barra, tel.*

071/336–6522, fax 071/247–6748. 46 rooms, 3 suites. Facilities: restaurant, bar, pool. AE, DC, MC, V.

The Arts and Nightlife

The Arts Considered by many artists as a laboratory for the creation of new rhythms and dance steps, Salvador has a lively performing arts scene. Some of the most electric local performers are Daniela Mercury, Gerónimo, Chiclete com Banana, Roberto Mendes, and Margareth Menezes.

Afro-Brazilian percussion groups begin "rehearsing"—actually, these are creative jam sessions that are worth visiting any time—for Carnival around midyear (*see* Off the Beaten Track, *above*). Olodum, Salvador's most innovative percussion group, has its own venue, the **Casa do Olodum** (Rua Gregório de Matos 22, Pelourinho, tel. 071/321–5010); see the events calendar published by Bahiatursa or local newspapers for performance schedules and locations of others, such as the more traditional black drumming group Ilê Aiyé, or Araketu.

Festin Bahia is a three-day international music festival held every August or September, featuring foreign and local performers; past participants have included Maxi Priest, Youssoun D'our, China Head, Carlinhos Brown, Pepeu Gomes, and Olodum. Many of the events, which mainly take place at the Centro de Convenções, in Jardim Armação, are free, but those that do require tickets cost $6. Tickets go on sale a month before the festival begins and are available through a U.S. travel agency representing **DL Turismo** (Rua Dra. Praguer Froes 102, Barra, Salvador, 40130–020). Contact DL Turismo for details.

New musicians can be discovered at the **Teatro ACBEU** (Av. Sete de Setembro 1883, tel. 071/247–4395 and 071/336–4411), where both contemporary and classics are represented in music, dance, and theater performed by both Brazilian and international talent. Theater and music are performed at the **Teatro Maria Bethânia** (Largo da Mariquita, tel. 071/247–6413), and all kinds of music are heard at the **Concha Acústica do Teatro Castro Alves** (Ladeira da Fonte, s/n, tel. 071/247–6414), a bandshell. At press time the **Teatro Castro Alves** (Ladeira da Fonte, s/n, tel. 071/247–6414), a top venue for theater, music, and dance, was closed for renovation, but it was slated to open some time in late 1993 or early 1994. Small theater groups perform at the German–Brazilian Cultural Institute's **Teatro ICBA** (Av. Sete de Setembro 1809, tel. 071/237–0120), which also screens German films. You can see theatrical, ballet, and musical performances at the **Teatro Iemanjá** (Jardim Armacão, s/n, Centro de Convenções), and the **Casa do Comércio** offers music and some theater (Av. Tancredo Neves 1109, tel. 071/371–8700).

Nightlife The after-hours scene is changing in Salvador as the historical district makes a comeback, with new bars and night spots expected to open there. At press time, activity centered on the neighborhoods of Barra and Rio Vermelho, catering to yuppies and bohemian types, respectively, and both areas are quite near to most hotels. Two top members-only nightclubs catering to older, moneyed couples who like to dance are located in hotels and are open to hotel guests: Le Zodiac, at the Hotel Le Meridien (Rua Fonte do Boi 216, tel. 071/248–8011), and the

Hippopotamus, at the Bahia Othon (Av. Presidente Vargas 2456, tel. 071/247–1044). Another upper-class favorite is **Bual'Amour** (Rua do Corsário, s/n, tel. 071/231–9775). **Mobi Dick** (Av. Presidente Vargas 3719, tel. 071/235–1596) draws a younger, dating crowd.

Some of the most popular bars in Barra are **Berro D'água** (Rua Barão de Sergi 27, no phone), with a relaxed atmosphere, attracting a more intellectual set; and **Tiffany's** (Rua Barão de Sergi 37, tel. 071/247–4025) and **Le Privê** (Av. Sete de Setembro 3554, no phone), both catering to yuppie sophisticates. In Rio Vermelho the top spots are **Extudo** (Rua Lídio Mesquita 4, tel. 071/237–4669; *see* Dining, *above*), **Opus 65** (Rua do Meio 65, tel. 071/248–0185), and **Off the Wall** (Rua da Paciência 30, tel. 071/235–0385). At press time, the watering holes in the Upper City's historic district included the somewhat grungy but well-located **Cantina da Lua** (Terreiro de Jesus 2, tel. 071/321–0331) and the tranquil **Casa do Benin** (Rua Padre Agostinho 17, tel. 071/321–6835), with an indoor waterfall and also a restaurant.

Many visitors enjoy the Afro-Brazilian dinner shows at the **Solar Do Unhão** (Av. do Contorno, s/n, tel. 071/321–5588; Mon.–Sat. at 8 PM), and the **Moenda** (Jardim Armação, Rua P, Quadra 28, Lote 21, tel. 071/231–7915 or 071/230–6786; daily at 8 PM). Both serve buffets that are best forgone in favor of an early dinner elsewhere or ordering from the à la carte menu.

Excursions from Salvador

Cachoeira This riverside Portuguese colonial town 121 kilometers (70 miles) west of Salvador is the site of some of Brazil's most authentic Afro-Brazilian rituals and festivals. Every August 14–16, the **Irmandade da Boa Morte** (Sisterhood of the Good Death, once a slave women's secret society) holds a syncretized Candomblé/Catholic festival honoring the spirits of the dead, featuring a solemn procession and a spinning samba street dance. Other special events in Cachoeira include a feast marking the town's anniversary (March 13), and the typical Saint John's feast (June 23–24) commemorating the harvest season, with children dressing up as hillbillies. However, an excursion to Cachoeira is worthwhile any time of the year, to visit the sisterhood's small museum (Largo D'Ajuda s/n, tel. 075/725–1343 [private phone of Dona Anália, one of the sisters]; admission voluntary; closed weekdays 1–3 and weekends) and meet these elderly but energetic women, to walk through the colorful country market, and to see the architecture preserved from an age when Cachoeira shipped tons of tobacco and sugar downriver to Salvador. You can stay overnight or have lunch at a 17th-century former Carmelite monastery, **Pousada Convento do Carmo** (Praça da Aclamação, s/n, tel. 075/725–1716).

Getting There The Camurujipe bus company has hourly bus service from Salvador's bus terminal, Terminal Rodoviário, from 5:30 AM to 7 PM. You can also get there by a combination of boat and bus: A boat leaving weekdays at 2:30 PM from the **Terminal Marítimo** (behind the Mercado Modelo, Av. França s/n, tel. 071/243–0741) to Maragojipe takes three hours; you then board a bus (Via Azul and Camurujipe companies) for the bumpy half-hour ride to Cachoeira. If you're going by car, drive north out of Salvador on BR 324 for about 55 kilometers (34 miles), then west on BR 420 through the town of Santo Amaro. The trip takes 1½ hours.

Tatu Tours (Ed. Victoria Center, Sala 1108, Av. Centenário 2883, tel. and fax 071/237–7562) offers a two-day trip that includes a ferry ride upriver, and tours of a cigar factory, cacau farm, and manioc flour mill.

Itaparica Originally settled because of its ample supply of fresh water, Brazil's largest maritime island doesn't boast notable beaches, but there are some very good restaurants (*see* Dining, *above*), set in quiet shady cobbled streets lined with pastel-color colonial homes. The Club Mediterranée is also here, open only to guests. As the complete schooner tour can be tiresome, one super option is to take it one way, get off at Itaparica, skip the cattle-call lunch, take a taxi to a good restaurant, enjoy a postprandial afternoon stroll, and ride the ferry back to Salvador.

Getting There Although harbor tours stop here for lunch (*see* Guided Tours, *above*), you may want to make a more leisurely visit to this bucolic retreat, taking a launch or the ferry from the docks behind the Mercado Modelo. Launches cost less than $1 and leave every 45 minutes from 7 AM to 6 PM from **Terminal Turístico Marítimo** (Av. França s/n, tel. 071/243–0741). The ferry takes passengers and cars and leaves every half hour between 6 AM and 10:30 PM from the **Terminal Ferry-Boat** (Terminal Marítimo, Av. Oscar Ponte 1051, São Joaquim, tel. 071/321–7100). The fare is less than $1 for passengers, under $5 for cars, and takes 45 minutes to cross the bay. Reservations are accepted for small cars.

Lagoa de Abaeté This mystical freshwater lagoon lies inland from Itapuã Beach, at the end of the string of beaches stretching north from Salvador, about a half-hour drive from downtown. Set in lush greenery, its black depths provide a startling contrast with the fine white sand of its shores. No one knows the source of these waters, where Bahian women wash their clothes every morning. At press time, the state government was building a small shopping mall to house the crafts kiosks that have long lined the lagoon; it is hoped that the commercialism won't spoil the atmosphere.

Getting There City buses going to the lagoon leave from Campo Grande or Estação da Lapa and cost less than 50¢. If you are driving, take the Orla Maritima beach drive north out of the city until Itapuan. At the Largo da Sereia (a square with a mermaid statue), follow signs for the lagoon. Tour operators include the lagoon on their beach tours, which cost about $25.

Praia do Forte For those seeking a little R and R, this beach resort and ecological preserve 70 kilometers (44 miles) north of Salvador might well be a destination in itself, functioning as a base for day visits to Salvador (*see* Lodging, *above*). This is the site of the **Projeto Tamar,** an ecological project set up to protect the giant sea turtles that emerge at night from September to March to lay their eggs along Brazil's northeastern coastline. Other attractions are the 600-hectare **Reserva Sapiranga,** which preserves a remnant of the forest that once lined most of the Brazilian coast until Portuguese colonization, with a great diversity of flora and fauna (including monkey families that eat from visitors' hands); the ruins of the Portuguese Garcia D'Avila family's **stone castle and chapel,** dating from 1600; a **fishing village** full of great snack bars and restaurants; the **Pojuca River falls and rapids;** and the **Timeantube Lake,** with over 50 bird species.

Odara Turismo is the main tour operator at Praia do Forte, offering half- and full-day jeep tours for $20–$66. *In Praia do Forte Resort Hotel, Av. do Farol s/n, Mata de São João. Mailing address: Visconde do Rosário 114, sobreloja 103, Comércio, Salvador, Bahia, 40015. Tel. 071/876–1080, fax 071/876–1018.*

Getting There   **Santa Mana Catuense** (tel. 071/359–3474) has hourly bus service from Salvador's main bus terminal starting at 7:30 AM, with the last bus returning to the city at 5:30 PM; tickets cost under $2. By car, take the Estrada do Côco north and follow signs for Praia do Forte; there is a short stretch of unpaved road at the end.

Porto Seguro and Environs

By Julia Michaels   The entire southern coastal area of Bahia has much to offer, including the Abrolhos archipelago marine preserve and the cacau capital of Ilhéus, where Bahian writer Jorge Amado was born and where he set one of his most famous novels, *Gabriela, Clove and Cinnamon.* The hub of this region, however, is quickly becoming Porto Seguro, which means "safe port" in Portuguese.

Here, 713 kilometers (442 miles) south of Salvador, is where Portuguese explorer Pedro Álvares Cabral in the year 1500 discovered Brazil and named it after the *pau Brasil* (brazilwood) that is native to the region. Almost 500 years later, as Bahia's transportation infrastructure improves and Rio de Janeiro's appeal dims, modern-day travelers are rediscovering Porto Seguro, with its stunning beaches, exciting nightlife, outstanding restaurants, and timeless fishing villages.

Besides miles of clear water, coral reefs, and coconut palms, the region offers a bewitching mix of sophistication and simplicity. Europeans and Brazilians from other parts of the country have abandoned the big-city rat race to move here, bringing with them such cosmopolitan delights as sushi and Polynesian-style sportswear. But even as they and others help to improve the tourism infrastructure, much of the region remains lost in time. Fishing communities, home to artists and hippies, are connected by dirt roads, and center on tiny 17th-century churches and main squares where donkeys are tied to shade trees and chickens peck the dust. The Pataxó Indian tribe of about 3,000 also lives here, moving back and forth among the towns to sell their simple handicrafts.

Tourist Information

Portur (Praça António Carlos Magalhães s/n, Porto Seguro, Bahia, tel. 073/288–2126; open weekdays 8–noon, 2–6) has information on hotels, restaurants, beaches, excursions, shopping, car rentals, foreign exchange, and campgrounds for Porto Seguro and nearby towns. **Bahiatursa** (Centro de Convenções, Jardim Armação s/n, Salvador, Bahia 41750–270, tel. 071/370–8400), in Salvador, also can provide information about the region.

Getting There

By Plane At press time, only two carriers were flying directly into the Porto Seguro Airport: **Rio Sul** (tel. 073/288–2327), with daily flights from São Paulo and Rio de Janeiro; and **Nordeste** (tel. 073/288–1888), which flies weekdays from Salvador. **Tam** runs charter weekend flights from São Paulo; reservations must be made through the Turnac travel agency (Rua Barão de Itapetininga, 93, 10th floor, São Paulo, tel. 011/231–2044) in São Paulo.

By Car From either north or south, take BR 101 to Eunápolis, which is linked to Porto Seguro by BR 367.

By Bus The **São Geraldo bus company** (Porto Seguro: tel. 073/288–1198; São Paulo: 011/290–8344; Rio: 021/263–7618) serves Porto Seguro from São Paulo and Rio de Janeiro; **Águia Branca** (Porto Seguro: tel. 073/288–1039; Salvador: 071/358–4704, 071/358–1153, or 071/358–4973) also connects with Salvador. Local bus service is provided by **Espresso Brasileiro** (tel. 073/288–1048). There are two lines, one from Porto Seguro to Cabrália and back, and one that only goes as far as Taperapuan and back to Porto Seguro.

Exploring Porto Seguro and Environs

The attractions in this area are spread apart, so it's advisable to rent a car (Localiza National, Av. dos Navegantes 580, tel. 073/288–2662). Alternatively, you can hire a taxi (Chametaxi, tel. 073/288–2046; ask for Marco, who speaks some English and charges about $50 for a full day for four people, or $20 for a three-hour orientation tour) or take a bus or boat tour (Grou Turismo, Av. 22 de Abril 1077, tel. 073/288–2714; either costs just over $10 a person). Public buses do run down Porto Seguro's main drag, but are not convenient for late nights out.

Porto Seguro Perched on a bluff overlooking Praia do Cruzeiro, the tiny **Upper City** (Ciudade Alta) is composed of the ruins of a 16th-century Jesuit school, some small pastel-color colonial houses, and several simple churches washed in the blinding sun mirrored on the sea below. To the left of the Igreja da Matriz (Mother Church), facing the cross erected in 1503 to mark Portugal's possession of Brazil, is the **former jail and city hall,** now the offices of the local tourism board, Portur (*see* Tourist Information, *above*).

Bounded by Avenidas Getúlio Vargas, 22 de Abril, and dos Navegantes, the **Lower City** (Ciudade Baixa) is full of hotels, inns, shops, cafés, and restaurants, a great place for strolling day or night. Aptly named for the firewater drinks you can buy there at night, the **Passarela do Álcool** (Alcohol Way), an oceanside promenade (*see* Nightlife, *below*) right around the corner from a nightly handicrafts fair also has booths selling fruit. Brazil's first or second mass—no one is quite sure—was said in 1500 at **Coroa Vermelha** beach, a 15-minute drive north of town. The Pataxó Indians sell their handicrafts at booths surrounding a giant cross marking the spot. Ten minutes' drive farther north is the fishing town of **Santa Cruz de Cabrália,** with its own 17th-century historical area and a reef-protected beach.

Coroa Alta, a coral atoll full of natural pools at low tide, lies 4 kilometers (2½ miles) off the coast at Cabrália, and can only be reached by boat. Excursions are easily arranged through hotel reception desks or local travel agencies.

Arraial d'Ajuda *Arraial* means pilgrim campsite, and this town, an eight-minute ferry ride across the Buranhém River from Porto Seguro, centers on one that is now a main square of grass and dirt, populated by burros, goats, and chickens. Pilgrims are still drawn by the town's **miraculous spring,** now housed in a tiny chapel. Sophisticated restaurants, boutiques, and cafés turn up on the side streets, while a walk on **Broadway** reveals simple outdoor cafés and restaurants. The blue and white **Igreja Nossa Senhora d'Ajuda** (Our Lady of Help Church), built by Jesuits in 1549, has an ocean view in the back.

Trancoso, a fishing town that became a hippie hideout in the 1970s, lies 20 kilometers (13 miles) south down a dirt road. On the way, stop 5 kilometers (3 miles) outside of Trancoso at the **Mirante de Taipe** to see the majestic purple clay cliffs above **Lagoa Azul** (Blue Lagoon). There is a road down to Taipe beach; the lagoon lies a kilometer (half-mile) walk north, where bathers spread the soothing white clay on their skin. Up a short trail and back from the beach is a grove with a waterfall (dry when rainfall has been low). Trancoso has its own beaches (one for nude bathing) and a huge arraial, bordered by hotels, inns, galleries, bars, and the Igreja de São João (Saint John's Church), a country church built in 1580; ask for the key to it at Silvana & Cia., a café on the campsite.

Shopping

The nightly **feira hippie** (hippie fair) in Porto Seguro's Lower City showcases a variety of handicrafts, including Pataxó Indian artifacts, at low prices. At stall No. 22, Vera de Moura sells stunning tropical-color batik prints of parrots, flowers, and fruit. For local fashion, there is also the **Mini-Shopping** mall (Av. dos Navegantes 69, no phone) of boutiques, selling mostly T-shirts and souvenirs. For every imaginable kind of locally produced *cachaça* (sugarcane-based brandy), complete with bawdy labels in Portuguese, try **Cachaçaria Colonia Brasil II** (Av. Getúlio Vargas 528, no phone). In Arraial d'Ajuda, the **Beco das Cores** minimall (Rua Assis Chateaubriand, altura No. 60, no phone), open till midnight, has 10 stores that sell sportswear and resort wear (even Polynesian imports!), and a food court featuring a range of fast-food outlets.

Beaches and Water Sports

Porto Segurans have invented a unique, all-around beach entertainment center, a must-see even if you'd rather be alone with the coral and the coconuts. Called *barracas* (kiosks), as they are elsewhere in Bahia, these are different. They offer not only restaurants, snack bars, ice-cream stands, and boutiques, but inflatable boat rides, live music shows, even bank branches, nude sunbathing areas set away from the restaurant and bar crowds, and dance lessons. There are chairs on the sand, or chairs and shaded tables on a wooden platform, where you can sit for free and pay only for what you consume. They usually serve fried snacks and seafood, plus regional dishes (enough for two), soft drinks, alcoholic beverages, and fruit juices.

Thousands cram into these places at Carnival time. The two hottest locales are at Taperapuan beach, a 15-minute drive north from town: **Barramares** (BR 367, km 70.02, tel. 073/288–2980) and **Virasol** (BR 367, km 69, no phone).

Equipment for snorkeling, windsurfing, and canoeing can be rented from the **Club Mistral** (in Hotel Porto Bello, BR 367, km 6.5, Praia de Itaperapuã, tel. 073/288–2320). **Porto Mar Nautica** (Rua 2 de Julho 178, tel. 073/288–2606), rents diving equipment and organizes diving trips with experienced instructors to the coral reefs.

Other, less crowded, clean beaches can be found up and down the entire 89 kilometers (56 miles) of coastline (except right in town), especially from Mucugê to Trancoso.

Dining and Lodging

The region's beaches, shopping, nightlife, historic sights, and fishing villages are strung out over a wide area. If you're into the social scene, day or night, stay in Porto Seguro itself. Taperapuan beach is best if you want to hang out on the beach, while the Lower City in Porto Seguro itself is where the action is at night. If you prefer wide empty spaces and artsy sophistication, stay across the Buranhém River, in Arraial d'Ajuda or Trancoso, linked to Porto Seguro by ferry service.

For details and price-category definitions, *see* Dining and Lodging in Staying in Brazil, *above*.

Arraial D'Ajuda
Dining

Bistro Mucugê. In this tiny tropical bistro in the Mucugê Hotel Village (*see* Lodging, *below*), recorded jazz music accompanies ★ such imaginative fare as seafood in a béchamel sauce with Brazilian *catupiry* cheese, whipped up by Cícero, who doubles as the house architect. *Sítio Mucugê, Arraial d'Ajuda, tel. 073/875–1238 or 073/875–1212. Reservations required even for hotel guests. No credit cards. Moderate.*

★ **Le Bateau Ivre.** The French, Vietnamese, and typical Bahian cooking here makes the most of the local seafood, served at 14 tables on a wood and thatch beach deck. *Estrada d'Ajuda, s/n, 250 m from the ferry landing, tel. 073/875–1247. Reservations advised in high season. No credit cards. Closed Mon. Moderate.*

Restaurante Rosa dos Ventos. Continental recipes with an emphasis on Austrian desserts, a surprising treat in this locale, are the fare at this seven-table restaurant, which also features recorded classical music and candlelight at night. *Alameda dos Flamboyans, s/n, tel. 073/875–1271. Reservations advised during high season. No credit cards. Moderate.*

La Vie en Rose. Off the main square, this rustic spot has its own wood-burning pizza oven, and also serves French food, with unexpected delights such as profiteroles for dessert. *Praça São Brás, s/n, no phone. V. Closed Sun. Inexpensive.*

Lodging

Hotel Paradise. Although it's the fanciest hotel in the region, located just beyond the ferry landing, it could use a bit of redecorating in the lobby. Still, the guest rooms, which face the river or the ocean, are fine, done in wood, polished granite, and tile floors, with big bathroom mirrors and verandas. *Ponta do Apaga Fogo, tel. 073/875–1010, fax 073/875–1016. 168 rooms, 4 suites. Facilities: restaurant, bar, 2 tennis courts, sauna, pool, reef-protected beach, kayaks, basketball court. AE, D, MC, V. Very Expensive.*

★ **Hotel Pousada das Brisas.** A honeymooner's paradise, this inn amid breeze-rustled palm fronds affords breathtaking hilltop views of the ocean. Bungalows are rustic, with brick walls, a small veranda, and mosquito netting hanging from the ceiling over the beds. *No street address, tel. 073/875–1033, fax 073/875–1147. 10 bungalows, 4 duplex suites. Facilities: bar, coffee shop, pool, jeep tours. No credit cards. Moderate.*

★ **Mucugê Hotel Village.** Robert De Niro has hidden away in one of these beachside bungalows of brick, wood, and tile, camouflaged by Atlantic forest vegetation covering 100 hectares. An in-house travel agency arranges excursions and boat, motorcycle, and dune buggy rentals, and nearby tennis courts are available to guests. *Sítio Mucugê, Arraial d'Ajuda, tel. and fax 073/875–1238 or 073/875–1212 and 073/875–1875. 8 3-person bungalows, 2 larger bungalows. Facilities: 2 restaurants, pizzeria, pool, sauna, horseback riding. AE, DC, MC, V (30% surcharge with credit card). Moderate.*

Pousada Berro D'água. This beachfront inn has thatch-roofed bungalows, woodblock-frame beds, and wooden ceilings; some are air-conditioned. *Estrada D'Ajuda, km 1, tel. and fax 073/875–1073. 15 rooms, 4 duplex suites. Facilities: restaurant, pool, beach. No credit cards. Moderate.*

Pousada Araçaipe. These bungalows are quite simple, in brick and wood, with hammocks and Indian print fabric adorning the walls for an exotic, tentlike look, and rudimentary bathrooms. *Estrada d'Ajuda, km 17, tel. 073/875–1028. 5 bungalows. Facilities: beach, kayaks, catamarans. No credit cards. Inexpensive.*

Porto Seguro Dining

Sambuca. Locals flock to this authentic Roman-style pizzeria. Try the *caprichosa* pizza with mozzarella cheese, hearts of palm, ham, and mushrooms. *Praça dos Pataxós, 216, tel. 073/288–2366. No credit cards. Inexpensive.*

Bar e Restaurante do Japonês. This sushi bar above a grocery store serves both Japanese (cooked and raw) and Chinese specialties, plus breakfast. *Praça dos Pataxós 38, tel. 073/288–2592. AE, DC, MC, V. Moderate.*

Korea Tropical. After their textile business burned down in São Paulo, the Korean owners turned to cooking. They've met with great success, serving up Korean, Japanese, Chinese and Bahian fare, with an emphasis on seafood. Specialties include *lagosta tropical* (lobster with fruit); and lighter (less palm oil) moquecas. *Av. Portugal, 258, tel. 073/288–1607. No credit cards. Moderate.*

★ **Restaurante Grelhados.** Under a bamboo roof, shrimp, fish, and meat come to your table already cooked; food stays hot on wrought-iron grills. The concept is simple, the results delicious. *Av. 22 de Abril, 212, tel. 073/288–1177. No credit cards. Moderate.*

Corais do Porto. This restaurant with a beachside deck serves Italian and Bahian food, everything from snacks to full dinners. Arrive hungry—most dishes are big enough for two. *Praia de Taperapuan, km 69, tel. 073/288–2859. No credit cards. Inexpensive.*

Lodging

Porto Bello Praia Hotel. This efficiently run hotel across from Taperapuan beach is decorated with lots of wicker, ceramics, plants, and woven rugs, with blue slate floors and candy-stripe bed linens in the guest rooms. Great Brazilian country-style breakfast, with eggs, fruit, cheese, cereals, etc. *BR Mar 367, km 68.5, tel. 073/288–2329, fax 073/288–2911. 51 rooms, 1 suite.*

Facilities: restaurant, 2 bars, health club, sauna, 2 pools, games room, soccer field, video room. AE, DC, MC, V (lodging only). Discount with cash payment. Very Expensive.

Porto Seguro Praia Hotel. Owned by the town's mayor (a big-time cacau farmer), this large hotel (spread out over 50,000 square meters) with a country-club atmosphere is frequented by bus tour groups and is right across the street from Taperapuan beach. *BR 367, km 65, tel. 073/288–2321, fax 073/288–2069. 120 rooms, 6 suites. Facilities: restaurant, barbecue pit, bar, tennis court, health club, sauna, 2 pools, games room. Very Expensive.*

★ **Hotel Adriático.** This comfortable, homey in-town hotel sports an atrium pool with batik wall hangings and bamboo furniture. Each guest room, with high, sloping ceiling, blue slate floors, and clean white linens, has its own private veranda. *Av. 22 de Abril, 1075, tel. 073/288–1188, fax 073/288–2879. 37 rooms, 2 suites. Facilities: sauna, pool, games room. AE, DC, MC, V. Moderate.*

Pousada Aconchêgo. It's easy to forget that this inn is located downtown, with its garden of coconut palms and caged parrots. The bungalow guest rooms have hammocks and handwoven bedspreads. *Av. 22 de Abril 435, tel. 073/288–2522, fax 073/288–2207. 15 bungalows. Facilities: coffee shop, sauna, pool, games room. AE, DC, MC, V. Moderate.*

★ **Taperapuan Praia Hotel.** These two-story thatched bungalows 5 kilometers (2 miles) from town are perfect for families. All have hammocks, lace curtains, and porches; the front ones offer an ocean view. *BR 367, km 67.6, tel. 073/288–2449, fax 073/288–2597. 8 bungalows, 4 duplex suites. Facilities: restaurant, pool, fitness machines, volleyball court, kayaks. V. Moderate.*

Santa Cruz de Cabrália
Lodging

Bahia Cabrália Hotel. This is one of the few hotels in the area with its own beach—and it has a natural-reef pool. The Bahia Cabrália boasts lobby art by local wood sculptor Antônio Carlos Portela de Carvalho and spacious guest rooms. *Rua Sidrack de Carvalho 141, tel. and fax 073/282–1176 or 073/282–1145. 78 rooms, 6 suites. Facilities: restaurant, bar, health club, 2 saunas, 2 pools, games room, volleyball court. AE, DC, MC, V. Discount with cash payment. Expensive.*

Trancoso
Dining and Lodging

Pousada e Restaurante Capim Santo. The bungalow units here have loft beds, two doors for cross-ventilation, and ceiling fans. Originally specializing in health food, the restaurant (Expensive, closed Sun.) has expanded its menu from whole (unpolished) rice and fish to include such varied fare as lobster mousse, Argentine beef, and homemade ice cream, served both outside and inside at picnic tables. *Praça São João, s/n, tel. and fax 073/868–1122. 9 bungalows. No credit cards. Moderate.*

Lodging

Hotel da Praça. Set in a garden, these bungalows have brick floors, tile roofs, and a veranda where you can hang a hammock and relax. *Arraial de Trancoso, tel. and fax 073/868–1177. 8 bungalows, 3 suites. No credit cards. Moderate.*

Pousada Hibisco. The edges are literally smoother in these rustic ochre-wall bungalows, as the Argentinian owner is a carpenter and made all the furniture himself. The rooms are 400 meters from the beach. *Rua Bom Jesus s/n, Ladeira de Trancoso (mailing address: Caixa Postal 133, Porto Seguro 45820), tel. 073/868–1129. 8 bungalows. Facilities: volleyball court, games room. No credit cards. Inexpensive.*

Nightlife

Evening entertainment—dining, drinking, and dancing—centers on Arraial d'Ajuda and Porto Seguro's Lower City, where the sensual *lambada* dance was born. **Broadway** is the main drag in the former; in the latter, it's the **Passarela do Álcool,** with its myriad square wooden tables set outside and booths overflowing with fruit.

The Passarela is a great place to stoke up (try a *guaraxaxá,* a deadly mixture of energizing guaraná powder and cachaça) for the **Boca da Barra** (Praia do Cruzeiro, no phone), a thatch-roof, barnlike structure open to the beach on one side, where every night people of all ages, colors, shapes, and sizes dance the lambada, sometimes till dawn. Periodically, the best dancers lead line dances, teach steps, and give out prizes. Classes are held between 5:30 and 9, with dancing thereafter. Entrance is free except for the bleacher area, where the cover charge is about 50¢.

The Amazon

By Edwin Taylor

For both outsiders and inhabitants of the Amazon, there is a mystical attraction to this legendary region and its two great constants, the river and the jungle. A flight over the jungle is an unforgettable experience; the jungle seems to go on forever, an endless green carpet sliced by the curving contours of the area's 1,000 rivers and broken only occasionally by a clearing.

From the sky, it is easy to believe that the Brazilian Amazon is the largest tropical rain forest in the world, larger than all of Western Europe and accounting for 60% of the nation's total territory—and yet it is inhabited by only 16 million people, the population of metropolitan New York. The rain forest is home to more than 35,000 plant species, a number that is constantly being upgraded.

The region's life centers on its rivers, the largest and most important of which is the Amazon itself, the second-longest river in the world at 6,290 kilometers (3,900 miles). Of the Amazon's hundreds of tributaries, 17 are more than 1,600 kilometers (1,000 miles) long. It is along these rivers that Amazon society has developed. Although in recent years there has been an increasing urbanization of the region, 45% of its residents still live in rural areas, many of them in frontier settlements along the river banks.

Whatever class of boat you take, a trip along the Amazon River or one of its principal tributaries—especially the 1,700-kilometer (1,020-mile) journey between the region's two major cities, Belém and Manaus—is unmatched anywhere in the world. In some spots the Amazon is so wide that neither bank is visible, giving the impression of traversing an inland sea. At night, the only light that can be seen is that of the moon and stars, reinforcing the sense of being in one of the world's greatest wilderness areas.

By day, each sighting is an adventure in itself: Indians fishing in canoes, wooden huts on the banks of the river, small river settlements, frontier homesteads, and extraordinary flora, with trees ranging from 15 to 45 meters (50–150 feet) in height.

(Spotting wildlife on the banks of the rivers, however, is a rare occurrence. The density of the vegetation makes such sightings, with the exception of birds, extremely difficult.) More direct contact with the river's inhabitants, both human and animal, occurs on the narrower waterways that you can tour on day trips, which typically include a visit to the home of a river dweller.

The vast size of the Amazon region has always been its principal source of security. In the past decade, however, civilization has been gnawing away at the edges of this great forest. Settlers from Brazil's festering urban centers have been pouring into the western Amazon, slashing and burning the forest and setting up small homesteads. At the same time, major gold discoveries throughout the southern Amazon have lured thousands of prospectors into the region. In the southeastern Amazon, a series of major development projects are underway, most of them designed to exploit the region's untapped mineral wealth, including the world's richest iron ore deposits.

All of this activity in one of the world's most ecologically sensitive regions has attracted the ire of conservationists, who view plans to develop the Amazon as a threat to humanity. Thus far, however, the Brazilian government has adopted the view that the fate of the region is a purely domestic matter and has rejected outside pressures to curtail development.

Getting There

By Plane The **International Airport Eduardo Gomes** (Av. Santos Dumont, tel. 092/621–1210) in Manaus, 17 kilometers (10 miles) from downtown, is served by Varig flights from Miami and Los Angeles. Varig also operates weekly flights from Miami to Belém's **International Airport Val de Cans** (tel. 091/233–4122), 11 kilometers (6 miles) from downtown. There are daily flights on the major domestic carriers to both airports from Rio, São Paulo, and Brasília as well as daily flights between Manaus, Belém, and Santarém.

By Boat A growing number of oceangoing cruise ships now make calls at Belém, continuing upriver to Manaus. The most important cruise lines stopping at the two cities are **Marquest, Ocean Cruise Lines, Princess, Seabourn, Special Expeditions,** and **Sun Line. Crystal Cruises** goes to Belém but not to Manaus.

Many visitors to the region prefer to experience firsthand the Amazon's primary mode of transportation, the riverboat. Riverboats travel throughout the region, on all of the Amazon's leading tributaries, connecting Belém with Manaus and numerous river towns in between, which tend to be austere in their accommodations. Although the region encompasses hundreds of navigable rivers, local commerce—and boats specifically designed for tourists—follow a few well-beaten paths, mainly the Amazon, Negro, Solimões, Madeira, Pará, and Tapajós rivers.

First-time visitors to the Amazon can gain a sensation of river life in a few hours on a "tourist boat" on the Negro River in Manaus, the Pará in Belém, or the Tapajós and Amazon in Santarém (halfway between Belém and Manaus). Longer tourist boat trips on the Negro departing from Manaus—which last three to five days, or even longer if you choose to take a customized private expedition—have become increasingly popular in recent years because they explore the upper reaches of the Negro, where the river is narrower and river life is easier to observe. These boats do not travel at top speed and sail close to the banks to allow a better look at the jungle. Tourist boats are more comfortable than riverboats, with an open upper deck that permits the best vantage points for observing the river and forest, and meals are included in the fare. The better tours have an expert on the region on board, usually an ecologist or a botanist, who is fluent in English. Passengers can either sleep out on deck in hammocks they must purchase themselves (don't worry about mosquitos; the humic acid in the Negro River serves as a natural insect repellent) or in cabins, which usually have air-conditioning or a fan. While the cabins may seem like a more attractive option, keep in mind that one of the jungle's primary attractions is its night sounds. With air-conditioning you may sleep better, but you will miss part of the show.

The major trips, however, are reserved for commercial boats on the Amazon and Madeira rivers and are recommended only if you have the time and the willingness to rough it. The most exciting of these is a cruise on the mighty Amazon itself, between Belém and Manaus with a stop in Santarém. The voyage lasts between four and seven days, depending on the direction of sail and the type of vessel. The level of comfort on different kinds of boats can vary dramatically.

Those for whom comfort takes a back seat to adventure may want to consider a trip aboard a standard double-decker boat that carries both freight and passengers. (Keep in mind, however, that while romantic in appearance, these aging boats have shown themselves in recent years to be increasingly unreliable—major accidents have occurred on the average of once every two years.) Usually only one kind of accommodation is available, and the ships tend to be overcrowded. Conditions are primitive: Passengers sleep out on deck in hammocks, and the sanitary conditions are the worst imaginable. Food is served, but the quality is deplorable. Experienced Brazilian travelers bring their own food and bottled water on board, together with gas-powered stoves, plates, cups, and cutlery; fresh fruit may be purchased at the various stops along the way.

Although some of the riverboats have first-class cabins in addition to the third-class hammock space, those that do usually have very few of them. In some cases it is necessary to bribe the captain to get one. The cabins are seldom air-conditioned. Fares can vary widely, but hammock space generally costs between $50 and $100 for a trip between Belém and Manaus; a cabin averages about $200.

Several private companies operate riverboats along the region's extensive river system. Among those offering service between Belém and Manaus are **Antonio Rocha** (Travessa Almirante Vandercopa 561, Belém, tel. 091/224–3969) and **Alves é Rodrigues** (Eco de Curro 73, Sala 2, Belém, tel. 091/225–1691), both of which operate boats that have first-class (cabins) as well as third-class (hammock) accommodations. In 1993 the government-owned **Enasa** line suspended their operations. A luxury catamaran service operated by Enasa between Manaus and Belém was suspended in 1992 but resumed on a trial basis in the second half of 1993, run by a private tour operator, **Sand-**

piper Turismo (Av. Rio Branco 277, Gr. 1601, Rio de Janeiro, tel. 021/262–2892).

For Amazon riverboat schedules and information about individual boats and their facilities, contact the **Paratur** office in **Belém** (Praça Kennedy, tel. 091/223–6198) and **Emamtur,** the Amazon Tourism Authority, in **Manaus** (Av. Tarumã 379, tel. 092/234–5503).

By Bus Land transportation in the Amazon is mostly limited to the area south of the Amazon River. There are highways linking southern and southeastern Brazil with Belém and another major Amazon city, Porto Velho. The most famous of these is the Belém–Brasília Highway, the 2,118-kilometer (1,300-mile) stretch of roadway made famous by the movie *Bye Bye Brazil.* The 45-hour jaunt through the center of the country is hot (buses are not air-conditioned) and dusty, and road maintenance is poor. The road is subject to frequent closings due to mud slides and washouts. Bus companies plying this route on a daily basis are **Transbrasiliana** (tel. 061/233–7572) and **Rapido Marajó** (tel. 061/233–7572); the bus station in Belém is about 15 minutes from downtown (Praça do Operário, tel. 091/228–0500).

From Belém it is also possible to travel by bus to Santarém via the city of Marabá, south of Belém. The trip, however, is not recommended because of the poor state of the roads, some of which are remnants of the Transamazon Highway, a classic Amazon boondoggle built in the 1970s in an attempt to provide an east–west link running south of the Amazon River. Today most of the highway has been reclaimed by rain forest. In theory, the bus trip to Santarém, with a stopover in Marabá, takes 50 hours, but due to such common problems as blowouts and rainstorms, it can last three to four days. There are no highways connecting either Belém or Santarám with Manaus. From Manaus, the only land connection south is Highway BR 319, which runs 900 kilometers (540 miles) southwest of Porto Velho. The highway, however, is closed more often than it is open, and there is no bus traffic at present.

The Amazon Delta: Belém, Marajó, and Macapá

Tourist **Paratur** (tel. 091/224–9633 or 091/223–2130, open weekdays 8–6, Sat.
Information 8–noon), the tourist authority for the state of Pará, has an office in Belém at Praça Kennedy on the waterfront.

Exploring the **Belém** is a fast-growing river port of 1.2 million located on the
Amazon Delta southern bank of the Amazon River 145 kilometers (90 miles) from the sea. Like the upriver city of Manaus, Belém has ridden the Amazon booms and busts, at times bursting with energy and opulence, then slumping into relative obscurity. Founded in 1616 as a trading center and defense against European invaders, the city had its first taste of prosperity with the Amazon rubber boom at the start of this century. Wood and mining operations have since provided the impetus for the city's growth.

In the past 10 years, Belém has enjoyed a rapid expansion, pushed in large part by major development projects in the surrounding area, including the construction of the Tucurui hydroelectric dam, the second-largest in Brazil, and the development of the Carajás iron ore mining region. All of this is evident in the architecture of the increasingly cosmopolitan city, where modern high rises are gradually replacing the colonial structures. Still surviving are several distinctive turn-of-the-century buildings, located along the downtown tree-lined streets and around the Praça Frei Caetano Brandão, an area known as the **Old City.** Here you will find the **Catedral da Sé** (Praça Frei Caetano Brandão, tel. 091/223–2362; admission free; closed Tues.–Sun. before 1 PM and Mon.), completed in 1771, known for its Carrara marble interior. On the other side of the square, with an excellent view of the Pará River (a tributary of the Amazon), is the city's fort, **Forte do Castelo,** constructed in 1878 and today housing a restaurant whose tables are set out on a part of the ramparts (*see* Dining, *below*). Other venerable buildings in the Old City are the 17th-century **Nossa Senhora das Mercés Igreja** (Largo das Mercés, tel. 091/224–2402; free admission; closed Tues.–Sun. before 11 AM and Mon.), the city's oldest church, and the **Nossa Senhora do Carmo Igreja** (Praça do Carmo, tel. 091/241–1100; free admission; closed Mon.), built between 1626 and 1766.

In the port area next door to the fort is one of Belém's primary attractions, the daily market known as **Ver-o-Peso** (literally, "see the weight," a colonial-era sales pitch). The market is a hypnotic confusion of colors and voices, with vendors hawking regional fruits, "miracle" roots from the jungle, alligator teeth, and good-luck charms for the body and soul. There are jars filled with animal eyes, tails, and even heads, plus an endless variety of herbs, each with its own legendary power. A regional oddity are the sex organs of the river dolphin, supposedly unmatched cures for romantic problems. Here you will get a close-up look at the fish of the Amazon, including the *pirarucú,* the river's most colorful species; the *mero,* which can weigh more than 91 kilos (200 pounds); and the silver-scale *piratema.*

In the Nazaré neighborhood, east of the Old City, is the **Basilica de Nazaré** (Praça Justo Chermont, tel. 091/241–3402; free admission; closed Sun. before noon), built in 1908 and financed with the wealth of the rubber boom. The basilica's ornate interior is replete with Carrara marble and gold. On the second Sunday in October, a religious procession carries a replica of the basilica's image of the Virgin to the cathedral. Known as the **Cirio,** it is one of the Amazon's most impressive public festivals, attracting hundreds of thousands of worshipers.

Close to the basilica is the **Praça da República,** dominated by the municipal theater, the **Teatro da Paz** (tel. 091/224–7355; admission charged; closed weekdays noon–2 and weekends). The neoclassical-style theater, completed in 1874, is the third oldest in Brazil.

Belém is home to one of Brazil's most unusual museums, the **Museu Emílio Goeldi** (Av. Magalhães Barata 376, tel. 091/224–9233; admission charged; closed Fri. noon–5 and Mon.). The museum contains an extensive collection of Indian artifacts, including samples of the distinctive and beautiful pottery of the Marajó Indians, known as *marajoara.* Attached to the museum complex is a small zoo with native animals and a jungle park, an area of virgin rain forest containing reflection pools with giant Victoria Régia water lilies.

River excursions, which range from trips of a few hours to half- and all-day tours and often include jungle stops, depart daily from the port area as well as from the docks of the Novotel Hotel (Av. Eng. Azarias Neto 17). One of the better operators is **Ciatur** (tel. 091/223–0787), which offers half-day trips and a short hike through the jungle. Half- and full-day tours include meals.

North of Belém is the island of **Marajó,** which, with an area larger than Denmark, claims to be the largest river island in the world. The island is famed for its vast herds of water buffalo and its unspoiled nature. Sparsely populated, Marajó is one of the few accessible sites in the Amazon that give a true feeling of isolation from the civilized world. In addition to abundant wildlife, the island also possesses excellent beaches.

Marajó can be reached from Belém by boat (a five-hour trip) or plane (30 minutes). If you travel by boat, however, you will have to spend at least one night on the island before returning. The flight from Belém offers an incomparable view of the meeting of the waters of the Amazon and Tocantins rivers with the ocean. Boats (tel.091/223–3011) leave from Belém to Souré, the island's main city, on Wednesday and Friday at 8 PM and Saturday at 2 PM, with return trips leaving Thursday at 5 PM and Sunday at 5 PM and midnight. **Taba** (tel. 091/241–1770) has flights to Souré departing from Belém's international airport on Monday, Wednesday, and Friday.

Many tourists opt to visit the island as part of a tour from Belém, by far the easiest way, since there are very few buses or taxis. A typical tour includes a visit to a buffalo ranch, canoeing on inland waterways, and demonstrations of a local dance, the *carimbo,* performed to music combining African and Indian rhythms. Some tours stay overnight at a ranch, also featuring four-wheel-drive trips into the backlands, horseback riding, and bird-watching. Tour operators conducting trips to Marajó from Belém include **Gran Pará** (Hilton International Belém, Av. Presidente Vargas 882, tel. 091/224–2111), **Lisotur** (Av. Braz de Aguiar 612, tel. 091/241–2000), and **Mururé** (Av. Presidente Vargas 132, tel. 091/241–0891). While on the island, sample the distinctive local cuisine, with such delicacies as water buffalo steak and desserts made with water buffalo milk.

To the north of Marajó is the state of **Amapá** and its capital, **Macapá,** a city of 150,000 on the northern channel of the Amazon delta that is beginning to shed its frontier image. The city, one of only five in the world that sit directly on the equator, is 40 minutes' flying time from Belém (there are scheduled flights on Varig and Vasp airlines). Boats also link the two cities, but service is irregular. Usually there is a boat at least once a week in each direction; the trip takes one to two days, depending on the boat. For information, call the **Capitania dos Portos** (Av. FAB 427, tel. 096/222–0415). For tourist information on Amapá, contact the state tourism authority in downtown Macapá, **Coordenaria Estadual de Indústria, Comércio e Turismo** (Rua Raimundo Alvarce da Costa 18, tel. 096/223–4135).

Like Belém, Macapá was an Amazon outpost built by the Portuguese to develop the region and protect Brazil from her European enemies. The fort constructed for this end, **Fortaleza de São José de Macapá** (Av. Amazônas, next to Novotel Macapá, no phone; free admission) was the largest in Brazil. Completed in 1764, the fort was built of stones brought from

Portugal as ship ballast. Its well-preserved ruins are today one of Macapá's top attractions.

The main lure here, however, is nature, in the form of the **pororoca,** an extraordinary phenomenon that occurs daily from January to May, when the Amazon delta is in flood stage and the incoming ocean tide crashes against the outflowing waters of the Araguari River 200 kilometers (120 miles) north of Macapá. The violent meeting produces churning waters and waves that reach 5 meters (15 feet) in height. And for nearly an hour before the final clashing of the waters, the air is filled with what sounds like a continuous crack of thunder, gradually building in intensity until, at the end, the rushing ocean waves sweep into the forest along the river banks. The mouth of the Araguari can be reached by boat, although the round-trip excursion takes 15 hours. It is also possible to arrange flights to the site of this phenomenon. For information on river and air transportation, call the **Martinica Tourism Agency** (tel. 096/222–3569).

Shopping Belém's main shopping area is **Avenida Presidente Vargas,** which runs along one side of Praça da República. Here you will find numerous shops selling regional crafts, such as **Artinida** (Av. Presidente Vargas 762, Loja 6, tel. 091/223–6248), which specializes in Indian handicrafts. **Paratur** (Praça Kennedy, tel. 091/224–9633) operates a handicrafts center. In all of these shops you will find examples of the region's two unique styles of pottery: *marajoara,* distinguished by its intricate, hand-painted geometrical designs, and *tapajônica,* marked by well-defined human and animal figures. In addition, Belém's shops sell various handmade objects of wood, straw, and leather. Indian crafts include straw wristbands and headdresses decorated with parrot feathers. On the island of Marajó there are some shops in Souré that sell handmade leather goods. In Macapá there is a recently opened regional handicrafts center, the **Núcleo Artesenal** (Av. Eng. Azarias Noto, tel. 096/222–2313).

Beaches A string of 18 beaches lined with hotels, bars, and restaurants is located along the Pará River's **Mosqueiro Island,** a one-hour drive from Belém. Several of the beaches—Farol, Grande, Chapé, Virado, São Francisco, and Baía do Sol—have spectacular views of the island's jungle, just a stone's throw away. Closer to the city are the beaches on the island of **Oureiro,** linked to the mainland by ferry.

Dining In general, dining in the Amazon is as different as everything else in the region. Besides water buffalo steak, you will have the opportunity to try armadillo, wild Amazon duck, piranha, and other river fish with such exotic Indian names as *tucunaré, pirarucú, tambaquí, curimatá, jaraquí,* and *pacú.* Although it's against the law, alligator and turtle are also found on menus. Watch out for the *pimenta-de-cheiro,* a local hot pepper whose potency can burn your fingers just touching it. For dessert, try some of the region's tropical fruits, such as *cupuaçu, graviola, taperebá, pupunha, biribá, bacabá, abio,* and *açaí.* Belém's Cerpa beer is excellent, mild and tasty.

For details and price-category definitions, *see* Dining in Staying in Brazil, *above.*

Belém **O Teatro.** This restaurant in the Hilton International Belém (*see* Lodging, *below*) offers an excellent sampling of Amazon cuisine in a small and intimate setting. River fish prepared with regional herbs and sauces is the specialty. *Av. Presidente Vargas 882, tel. 091/223–6500. AE, DC, MC, V. Expensive.*

★ **Círculo Militar.** The combination of good regional food and excellent location—on the ramparts of Forte do Castelo, overlooking the river—makes this the city's most appealing restaurant for visitors. Try the *filhote salgado,* sautéed river fish in a spicy coconut milk sauce. *Praça Frei Caetano Brandão, tel. 091/223–4374. AE, DC, MC, V. Moderate.*

Lá em Casa. This downtown restaurant is famous for Amazon specialties, including the premier dish of Belém, *pato no tucupi,* duck in a yellow herb sauce made from the juice of the manioc root and served with kale. *Av. Governador José Malcher 247, tel. 091/223–1212. AE, DC, MC, V. Moderate.*

Miako. This rooftop Japanese restaurant close to the Hilton offers a wide variety of fish and meat dishes. At night a refreshing breeze blows off the river, making for comfortable outdoor dining. *Rua 1 de Março 76, tel. 091/223–4485. AE, DC, MC, V. Moderate.*

Macapá **O Boscão.** This downtown eatery is considered the city's best choice for river fish. *Rua Hamilton Silva 997, no phone. No credit cards. Moderate.*

Marajó **Marojoara.** The top choice on the island of Marajó, this Souré restaurant, located in the hotel of the same name (*see* Lodging, *below*), specializes in grilled water buffalo steak. *Pousada Marajoara, 4 Rua, Souré, tel. 091/741–1287. No credit cards. Moderate.*

Lodging Belém is quickly emerging as the business and financial center of the Amazon region, and the city's better hotels are geared toward business travelers. In Macapá and Marajó, on the other hand, accommodations are aimed mostly at tourists.

For details and price-category definitions, *see* Lodging in Staying in Brazil, *above.*

Belém **Hilton International Belém.** Easily the top hotel in Belém, the
★ Hilton offers reliability and comfort and is especially popular among business travelers, with an excellent location in the downtown commercial center, close to the Old City. *Av. Presidente Vargas 882, Praça da Republica, tel. 091/223–6500, fax 091/225–2942. 361 rooms. Facilities: 2 restaurants, 2 bars, pool, sauna. AE, DC, MC, V. Expensive.*

Equatorial Palace. Generally considered to be the city's number-two hotel in terms of amenities and quality of service, the Equatorial is located near downtown in the Nazaré neighborhood, within walking distance of the Old City and the port area. *Av. Braz de Aguiar 612, tel. 091/241–2000, fax 091/223–5222. 211 rooms. Facilities: restaurant, bar, pool. AE, DC, MC, V. Moderate.*

Vanja. This downtown hotel is a favorite of backpackers and other bargain hunters. The rooms are clean and comfortable and an outstanding value for the money. *Tr. Benjamin Constant 1164, tel. 091/222–6688 or 091/222–6709. 154 rooms. Facilities: restaurant, bar, pool. AE, DC, MC, V. Inexpensive.*

Macapá **Novotel.** The newest and best hotel in Macapá, the Novotel is located downtown on the riverfront. Although the decor is undistinguished, the hotel is immaculate, and all the guest rooms are air-conditioned. *Av. Eng. Azarias Neto 17, tel.*

096/222–1144, fax 096/231–1115. 76 rooms. Facilities: restaurant, bar, pool, tennis court. AE, DC, MC, V. Moderate.

Amapaense Palace. This Amazon veteran offers no frills but is clean and has air-conditioning (although you should check first to make sure yours is working). *Av. Tiradentes, tel. 096/222–3366. 44 rooms. No credit cards. Inexpensive.*

Marajó **Pousada Marajoara.** On the island of Marajó, visitors on their own who wish to stay the night have few options. Located on the river in the island's main city, Souré, this lodging is the best choice, with clean rooms that are air-conditioned, always an important consideration in the Amazon region. *Quarta Rua, Souré, tel. 091/741–1287. 14 rooms. Facilities: restaurant, bar. No credit cards. Inexpensive.*

Buffalo Ranches For an unusual but memorable experience on Marajó, visitors should seek out one of several buffalo ranches that offer accommodations. You do not need to be part of a tour to stay at these ranches. The top ranches, accessible only by plane, are **Fazenda Bom Jardim** (tel. 091/224–3233, fax 091/241–5531) and **Fazenda Jilva** (tel. 091/225–3728), both of which charge $1,100 for two people for a three-day, two-night stay including meals. In the moderate price range are **Fazenda Marçal** (tel. 091/223–3177) and **Fazenda Carmo Camará** (tel. 091/223–5330).

Santarém

Tourist Information The closest tourist information office is in Belém. The leading travel agencies in Santarém are **Amazônia** (tel. 091/522–3325), **Lago Verde** (tel. 091/522–1645), and **Tapan** (tel. 091/522–1946).

Exploring Santarém Located halfway between Belém and Manaus, this laid-back port of 242,000, rich in history and legend, is a traditional stopping point for Amazon boats. The trip from Belém usually lasts two days, and boat trips to Manaus can run from two to five days, depending on the vessel.

Founded in 1661, Santarém has weathered all the various booms of the region—first wood, then rubber, and today mineral wealth have been the lures for thousands of would-be magnates hoping to carve their fortunes out of the jungle. Many have left behind them decaying monuments to their frustrated dreams.

The most noteworthy of these is **Fordlândia,** an Amazon boondoggle envisioned by Henry Ford, who in a period of 20 years starting in 1927, poured $80 million into a vast rubber plantation to supply him with the raw material for the tires of his cars. The scheme, however, failed, primarily due to the workers succumbing to malaria and yellow fever and to Ford's eventual loss of enthusiasm for the enormous undertaking. Today, the rusted remains of trucks and electric generators together with abandoned American-style bungalows can be seen in the jungle some 40 miles outside the city.

The principal attraction of Santarém, however, is the river. The city is located on the Tapajós River about 3.2 kilometers (2 miles) from its confluence with the Amazon. Local tour operators such as Amazônia and Lago Verde offer two standard all-day **river cruises** on specially outfitted boats. One trip takes passengers to the rivers' meeting point, continuing on the Amazon to **Pouso das Garças,** a beautiful region of small rivers, lakes, and forest marked by the presence of hundreds of snow-white egrets. Another boat trip follows the Tapajós to **Alter do Chão,** a picturesque Amazon village located in an *enseada* (inlet) of Lago Verde and renowned for its white, sandy beaches.

Dining For details and price-category definitions, *see* Dining in Staying in Brazil, *above.*

Tropical. This restaurant of the Hotel Tropical Santarém (*see* Lodging, *below*) is known for the high quality of its fish dishes, in particular *pirarucú tropical* and *caldeirada,* a type of fish stew. *Av. Mendonça Furtado 4120, tel. 091/522–1533. AE, DC, MC, V. Moderate.*

Storil. This establishment near the Santarém Palace Hotel offers excellent river fish dinners, including filet of pirarucú, and tucunaré prepared in a corn sauce. *Rua Turiano Meira 115, tel. 091/522–3159. No credit cards. Inexpensive–Moderate.*

Lodging For details and price-category definitions, *see* Lodging in Staying in Brazil, *above.*

★ **Tropical Hotel Santarém.** This riverfront hotel, the city's top accommodation, offers river tours that depart from the hotel's docks. Although not as deluxe as its upriver sister hotel, the Tropical Manaus, the Sentarém version is still one of the region's finer hotels, with sprawling grounds and comfortable rooms, all with river views. *Av. Mendonça Furtado 4120, tel. 091/522–1533, fax 091/522–2631. 122 rooms. Facilities: restaurant, bar, pool, river tours. AE, DC, MC, V. Moderate.*

Santarém Palace. Compared with the Tropical, the city's other hotels come out decidedly on the short end. The best among this rather nondescript grouping is this traditional downtown hotel. *Av. Rui Barbosa 726, tel. 091/522–5285. 47 rooms. Facilities: restaurant. No credit cards. Inexpensive.*

Manaus

Tourist Information The Amazon Tourism Authority, **Emamtur** (Av. Tarumã 379, tel. 092/234–5503) is open weekdays 7:30–6. Emamtur operates information desks at the airport (tel. 092/621–1210; open 24 hours a day) and at the Canto da Cultura (corner of Av. Eduardo Ribeiro and José Clemente, tel. 092/232–1646; open weekdays 8–6, Sat. 8–1), near the Opera House, and has a 24-hour telephone service, Disk-Tur (tel. 092/232–1646).

Exploring Manaus Manaus is an urban oasis in the midst of the rain forest, a sprawling, hilly city of more than 1 million built on the banks of the Negro River in the densest part of the jungle. The capital of the state of Amazônas, the city has long flirted with prosperity, first at the turn of the century, when for 25 years the Amazon rubber boom turned Manaus into the rubber capital of the world, supplying 90% of the globe's rubber. The immense wealth that resulted was monopolized by a handful of Amazon rubber barons, never numbering more than 100, who lived in Manaus and dominated the region like feudal lords.

The rubber boom ended abruptly in the 1920s with the appearance of competition from Malaysia, but the vestiges of this opulent era still remain in Manaus. Foremost among these is the city's symbol, the Opera House, **Teatro Amazônas,** which was completed in 1896 after 15 years of labor. This grandiose theater was restored to its former splendor in 1990, when a major renovation, the third in its history, was completed. The

Italian Renaissance–style interior provides a clear idea of the wealth and ostentation that marked the Amazon rubber boom: marble doorways from Italy, wrought-iron banisters from England, crystal chandeliers from France, and striking panels of French tiles and Italian frescoes depicting Amazon legends. One-hour tours are conducted daily between 10 and 5. *Praça São Sebastião, tel. 092/234–2776. Admission charged. Closed Mon.*

Another classic rubber-era structure is the yellow **Alfândega,** the Customs House, built by the British in 1902 of Scottish bricks imported as ship ballast and erected alongside the floating dock that was built at the same time to accommodate the annual 12-meter (40-foot) rise and fall of the river. The Customs House is now the home of the regional office of the Brazilian tax department and is not open to the public. Also located in the port area is the 1882 municipal market building, the **Mercado Adolfo Lisboa,** a wrought-iron copy of the market (destroyed) in Les Halles in Paris; the ironwork is said to have been designed in Paris by Gustave Eiffel. Vendors at the market sell Amazon food products and handicrafts.

The city's newest attraction is the **Museu de Ciências Naturais de Amazônia,** a natural history museum of the region that displays collections of insects, butterflies, and Amazon river fish in large tanks. The museum is on the outskirts of the city in the suburb of Aleixo. *Cachoeira Grande, tel. 092/244–2799. Free admission. Closed Mon.*

River and Jungle Excursions River and jungle tours from Manaus vary from a few hours to several days. The most common is a tourist boat trip, lasting six–eight hours, to the point just east of the city where the Negro and Solimões rivers join to form the Amazon. Here, about 15 kilometers (9 miles) from Manaus, you can see the black waters of the Negro flowing beside the muddy brown Solimões for 18 kilometers (11 miles) without mixing before merging into one as the Amazon River. All of these "Meeting of the Waters" tours include side trips, usually motorboat rides through narrow Amazon streams or bayous, providing a close-up view of the remarkable Amazon vegetation. (These motorboat trips cannot be made during the low-water season, October to January.) Many of these tours also stop at the **Parque Ecológico do Januauary,** where you can see a number of Amazon birds, and within it the **Lago de Janaury,** a lake filled with giant Victoria Regia water lilies. Among the operators that offer these tours are **Amazon Explorers** (Rua Nhamunda 21, Praça da Afilhadora, tel. 092/232–3511, 092/232–3319, or 092/232–3433), **Anavilhanas** (Rua Coração de Jesus 11, tel. 092/671–1411), and **Fontur** (in Tropical Hotel, Estrada da Ponte Negra s/n, tel. 092/568–5000). Tours leave from the downtown harbor area.

Overnight boat trips that bring you into contact with the rain forest are also popular excursions from Manaus. A typical excursion of this sort follows the Negro River, exploring flooded woodlands and narrow waterways and stopping for a hike on a jungle trail. At night, guides take you by canoe on an alligator "hunt." The guides shine flashlights into the eyes of the alligators, momentarily transfixing them, after which they are grabbed and held for photographs and then released.

Similar tours of up to five days are offered, as well as customized private expeditions. The longer trips have become increasingly popular because they explore the upper reaches of the Negro, where the river is narrower and therefore life along the banks is easier to observe. These trips usually make stops at river settlements, with visits to the homes of typical Amazon families. They also offer jungle treks, bathing at river beaches, and piranha fishing, and invariably enter the **Anavilhanas.** The world's largest freshwater archipelago, it contains some 350 islands with exuberant Amazon flora. Due to the dense vegetation, however, do not expect to spot much wildlife other than birds and, in the narrow channels or onshore, monkeys.

What to See and Do with Children Easily the best museum in the Amazon region is the Indian Museum, **Museu do Índio** (Rua Duque de Caxias 356, Manaus, tel. 092/234–1422; admission charged; closed weekdays 11:30–2, Sat. afternoon, and Sun.), which displays handicrafts, weapons, ceramics, ritual masks, and clothing of the tribes of the upper Amazon.

Manaus has a zoo, the **Mini-Zoo do CIGS** (Estrada de Ponta Negra 750, tel. 092/625–2044; admission charged; closed Mon.) run by the Brazilian army's jungle survival training school; some 300 animals native to the Amazon can be seen.

Located a half-hour boat ride from the Tropical Hotel along the Tarumã bayou is the **Tarumã Ecological Park** (tel. 092/234–0939; admission charged), containing a monkey jungle, waterfalls, and a large collection of Amazon birds. The park offers half- and full-day tours with professional guides.

Shopping Although Manaus is a free-trade zone, visitors who are not from South America will find little of interest in the dozens of shops scattered throughout the downtown district, most of which offer duty-free electronics imports at prices higher than in their countries of origin. Regional crafts include straw baskets, hats, and other articles; fantastical necklaces and headpieces made from iridescent bird feathers; and jewelry made out of seeds. These and other handicrafts are sold at the **Casa de Beija-Flor** (Rua Quintino Bocaiúva, tel. 092/234–2700); the shop at the **Museu do Índio** (Rua Duque de Caxias 356, tel. 092/234–1422); the **Mercado Adolfo Lisboa; Artíndia** (Praça Adalberto Vale 2, tel. 092/232–4890); and the **Artesenal Centro,** or Handicraft Center (Rua Recife 1999, tel. 092/236–1241).

Sports and the Outdoors *Fishing* Most river trips of two days or longer include some fishing, usually for piranha; equipment is supplied by the boat operators. For more extensive fishing expeditions, contact **Amazon Explorers** (tel. 092/232–3511), **Anavilhanas** (tel. 092/671–1411), or the **Tropical Hotel** (tel. 092/238–5757).

Beaches Manaus's popular **Ponta Negra** beach, known to locals as the Copacabana of the Amazon, is a sandy stretch along the river. Don't worry about piranhas; there is no danger here.

Dining River fish is the obvious specialty here, and which is the city's best fish restaurant is hotly debated. There is no clear winner, and factors such as the quality of the view often tip the balance. Other than fish, the city's restaurants offer few specialties, and the quality of food in general ranges from average to poor. For details and price-category definitions, *see* Dining in Staying in Brazil, *above.*

★ **Tarumã.** Always a reliable choice for good regional cuisine, this restaurant in the Tropical Hotel (*see* Lodging, *below*) has a varied menu of international fare in addition to serving the traditional river fish. The hotel is a 20-minute taxi ride from downtown, but the ride is pleasant, with good views of the river. *Estrada da Ponta Negra, tel. 092/658–5000. Reservations recommended. AE, DC, MC, V. Closed for lunch. Very Expensive.*

★ **La Barca.** One of Manaus's most popular eateries, this fish restaurant is noted for its huge variety of preparations, such as *pirraucú,* a stew of shrimp, river fish, and vegetables in a tomato and manioc broth. Meals are accompanied by live music. *Rua Recife 684, tel. 092/236–8544. AE, MC, V. Expensive.*

Panorama. Fish servings are large here, although their preparation tends to be slightly unimaginative, with an overreliance on tomato and onion sauces. Patrons, though, swear by the restaurant, mainly because of its view of the Rio Negro. *Boulevard Rio Negro 199, tel. 092/624–4626. MC, V. Moderate.*

Caçarola. Simple and unpretentious, this fish restaurant has won a large following in recent years for its creative cuisine, a rarity in Manaus, where most restaurants tend to use the same sauces and preparation. You will have to take a taxi to reach the restaurant, but the effort is worthwhile. *Av. Maués 188-A, tel. 092/233–3021. No credit cards. Inexpensive.*

Lodging The recent surge of international interest in ecological tourism to the area, plus the city's free-trade zone, has created a soaring demand for hotel rooms, the supply of which remains woefully inadequate. This problem is especially acute at the so-called jungle lodges, the hotels that are the most sought after by international travelers (*see* Jungle Lodges, *below*). For details and price-category definitions, *see* Lodging in Staying in Brazil, *above.*

★ **Tropical.** The only major resort hotel in the Amazon region and considered the region's best hotel, this sprawling complex 20 kilometers (12 miles) from downtown has a privileged location overlooking the Negro River and verdant gardens all around. It also has its own dock from which river tours depart daily. *Praia de Ponta Negra, tel. 092/658–5000, fax 092/238–5221. 606 rooms. Facilities: 2 restaurants, bar, pools, tennis courts, zoo. AE, DC, MC, V. Very Expensive.*

Amazonas. Located in the center of Manaus, the Amazonas is the city's oldest and most traditional hotel, frequented by many tour groups. The hotel, however, is showing its age, and you may not enjoy musty corridors in the middle of the Amazon. *Praça Adalberto Valle, tel. 092/622–2233, fax 092/622–2064. 182 rooms. Facilities: restaurant, bar, pool. AE, DC, MC, V. Expensive.*

Lord. Another downtown hotel in the heart of the free-trade zone, this hotel is better preserved than the Amazonas and less expensive. The staff is particularly helpful and efficient. *Rua Marcílio Dias 217, tel. 092/622–2844. 102 rooms. Facilities: restaurant, bar. AE, DC, MC, V. Moderate.*

Sombra Palace. Like several small downtown hotels that have been built in the last 15 years, this establishment, Manaus's newest hotel, is aimed primarily at Brazilian tourists visiting Manaus to shop in the free-trade zone. *Av. 7 de Setembro 1325, tel. 092/234–8777, fax 092/234–3395. 43 rooms. Facilities: restaurant. DC, MC, V. Inexpensive.*

Jungle Lodges In recent years, the demand for "authentic" Amazon experiences has resulted in the construction of several jungle lodges, actually small hotels located within the rain forest. These lodges, all in the Expensive or Very Expensive price categories, typically offer jungle treks, alligator "hunts," (*see* River and Jungle Excursions, *above*), canoe trips, fishing, and swimming plus the obvious attraction of staying amid the jungle. Many of the lodges are located near the Negro River. The best lodges are **Acajatuba Jungle Lodge** (mailing address: Rua Dr. Alminio 30, Centro, Manaus, 69005-200, tel. and fax 092/233–7642), four hours by boat from Manaus; **Amazon Lodge** (mailing address: Rua Leonardo Melcher 734, Centro, Manaus, 69010-170, tel. 092/622–4144, fax 092/622–1420), three hours by boat from Manaus; **Lago Salvador Lodge** (mailing address: Estrada da Ponta Negra s/n, Centro, Manaus 69037-060, tel. 092/658–5000, fax 092/656–5026), 40 minutes' boat ride from Manaus; and **Pousada das Guanavenas** (mailing address: Av. Constantino Nery 2486, Bairro Flores, Manaus 69050-002, tel. 092/656–3656, fax 092/656–5027), on the Urubu River, six hours from Manaus by car and boat. Accommodations are limited, so if you wish to stay at one of these lodges, you must make reservations well in advance.

The most renowned of the jungle lodges is the **Ariaú Jungle Tower.** This remarkable compound, located three hours by boat from Manaus on the Ariaú River near the Anavilhanas Archipelago, actually has three four-story wooden towers with thatched roofs, supported on stilts. Its most popular accommodation, especially sought after by honeymooners, is the Tarzan House, a tree house built 100 feet off the ground amid the treetops. As with most jungle lodges, the primitive surroundings are not repeated in the interiors, where electric generators and indoor plumbing ensure basic comforts. The complex also contains a 130-foot-high observation tower. *Mailing address: Rua Silva Ramos 41, Centro, Manaus 69010-180, tel. 092/234–7308, fax 092/233–5616. 92 rooms. Facilities: restaurant, pool, jungle and river excursions, heliport, dock. AE, DC, MC, V. Very Expensive.*

Brasília

By Edwin Taylor **Getting There**

Brazil's capital, Brasília, is located 726 kilometers (450 miles) northwest of Belo Horizonte and 960 kilometers (595 miles) from Rio, in the middle of a plateau that dominates the central region of Brazil.

By Plane The city can be reached by air from all of Brazil's major cities. **Brasília International Airport,** 12 kilometers (7 miles) from downtown, is served by all of Brazil's domestic carriers as well as international flights of **Varig** airlines.

By Bus Bus service is available from all of Brazil's major cities. Daily service links the capital with Rio, São Paulo, Belo Horizonte, and Salvador. **Real** (tel. 061/361–4555) provides service between the city and São Paulo, a 14-hour ride. **Itapermirim** (tel. 061/233–7766) provides service from Belo Horizonte (11 hours) and Rio de Janeiro (17 hours); **Paraíso** (tel. 061/233–7656) serves Brasília from Salvador (24 hours).

By Car Highway 040 connects the city with Rio and Belo Horizonte; Highway 050 connects it with São Paulo. Get a recent, reliable road map before attempting to drive from Salvador.

Exploring Brasília

Completed in 1960 in an astonishing three years' time, Brasília is one of the world's unique cities. The Brazilian government, headed by President Juscelino Kubitschek, looking to develop the isolated interior of the country, chose an all-star Brazilian design team: urban planner Lúcio Costa, landscape architect Burle Marx, and architect Oscar Niemeyer. Commonly described as a monument to the future, to its many critics, however, Brasília is a city trapped in a 1950s vision of the future, a brave new world that is overly functional, cold, impersonal, and lost in the middle of Brazil.

Conceived as a unified design, the city embodies some of the major trends of post–World War II design. Whether you view this homage to the glass box as the International Style at its purest and most refined, or at its most banal and monotonous, Brasília is a rare reflection of a single moment in the history of architecture.

In recent years, however, this image has begun to change as the city has acquired a certain sense of maturity. Although it remains an urban island in the heart of Brazil's hinterlands, Brasília is a far more hospitable setting for working and raising families than Brazil's coastal cities. The preponderance of well-paid (by Brazilian standards) civil servants has given Brasília the highest standard of living of any Brazilian city, and while crime problems are beginning to appear, the city is considerably safer than the nation's other urban centers. Traffic also flows smoothly in the city, which was built for the car, with ample freeways. Since space was abundant, large areas were reserved for parks and public squares. Homes and apartments also tend to devote large spaces to gardens and lawns. As a result, Brasília has more green space per inhabitant than any other city in Brazil.

Brasília's principal problems today originate in the surrounding suburbs, once home to the construction workers who were brought in from other states to build the capital. In contrast to the orderly efficiency of the city proper, these so-called satellite cities have developed into urban jungles similar to São Paulo and Rio and are growing at a far faster rate than the capital. Today Brasília itself accounts for only 22% of the total population of the federal district, with the other 78% living in the impoverished cities.

Most visitors find that half a day is more than enough to see the high points of the city. The best option is to take a three-hour city tour or hire a taxi. Because the distances between sights are great, walking is not practical except in the area around the Congress building. Tourist information is available from the city's official tourism authority, **Detur** (Setor de Divulgação Sul, Centro de Convenções, 3rd floor, SDC Eixo Monumental, tel. 061/321–3318; open weekdays 1–7). Recommended travel agencies that offer city tours include **Bradesco** (at the airport, tel. 061/225–1511), **Presmic** (in the Hotel Nacional, Bloco A, Lojas 35, tel. 061/225–5515), and **Buriti** (CLS 402, Bloco A, Lojas 27/33, tel. 061/225–2686).

A tour of the city's architectural attractions is a must in Brasília. For the most part, the government buildings and monuments still preserve a daring, futuristic air 30 years after they were designed. You will quickly discover, however, that the buildings are essentially works of sculpture, marked by impressive exterior forms and generally unimpressive and often deteriorating interiors.

The highway from the airport passes beside the residential buildings of this planned city. The six-story, glass-encased buildings are set at right angles to each other in so-called **super blocks,** designed to be complete living units containing, in addition to apartments, shopping areas, supermarkets, schools, and playgrounds. Although at first criticized as artificial living environments, the super blocks have withstood the test of time. Today the residents praise them for their orderliness, especially when compared to the urban chaos of Rio and São Paulo.

To understand the layout of Brasília, head for the **Torre de Televisão Divertão Cultural,** or Television Tower (Eixo Monumental Oeste, no phone; free admission; closed daily after 8 PM). From its observation deck you can easily see Costa's master plan: a residential arc bisected by the **Eixo Monumental** (Monumental Axis), with the government buildings clustered east of the arc along the 8-kilometer- (5-mile-) long axis. Farther east is a lake, **Lago do Paranoá,** echoing the curve of the arc.

It was in the creation of the government ensemble, a five-minute drive from the Television Tower, that Niemeyer concentrated his major efforts in Brasília. The long, symmetrical mall, the **Esplanada dos Ministérios,** is flanked by 16 identical glass-sheathed rectangular high rises split into two parallel rows separated by a grassy promenade. The **Catedral Metropolitano Nossa Senhora Aparecida** (Esplanada des Ministéries s/n, Eixo Monumental, tel. 061/224–4073; free admission) on the south side takes its inspiration from Jesus' crown of thorns. The high rises, which are not unlike a series of dominoes, terminate in a cluster of major buildings on the triangular **Praça dos Tres Poderes** (Plaza of the Three Powers). On the north side of the plaza is the **Palácio de Justiça** (tel. 061/226–8015; admission free; closed to public weekdays 11:30–5 and weekends), a low concrete box sheathed in marble and surrounded by a phalanx of soaring white marble columns and arches. Facing it across the wide plaza is the presidential palace, the **Palácio do Planalto** (tel. 061/311–1241), another slab of a building, with curved abstract columns and glass walls; note the abstract figures of *The Warriors,* a sculpture by Bruno Giorgi, nearby. (The building is closed to visitors, but the changing of the palace guard can be seen Tuesday at 8:30 and Friday at 5:30.) The apex of the mall is the highly photogenic symbol of the city, the **Congressional complex** (Chamber of Deputies: tel. 061/311–5107; Senate: 061/311–4141; admission free; closed weekends and Jan. and July), a low, horizontal platform flanked by a shallow dome (the Senate chamber), a saucerlike inverted dome (the Chamber of Deputies), and 25-story twin glass-wrapped towers. Niemeyer's masterpiece here, however, is generally considered to be the **Palácio dos Arcos** (the Foreign Ministry building, or Itamarity), on the south side of the plaza, which seems to float, suspended by its elegant concrete arches above a surrounding reflecting pool. Unlike his other creations, all faced with marble, this building is exposed concrete, a square pavilion set within a frame of landscaped pools. The interior is exceptionally opulent, a luxurious mix of polished marble, mirrors, deep carpets, tapestries, and fine furniture. The plaza also contains the **Museu Histórico de Brasília** (admission charged; closed Sat.–Mon.), commemorating the founding of the city, famed for the oversize bust of the city's founder, ex-president Juscelino Kubitschek, that protrudes from its walls.

East of the plaza is the center of Brasília's social life, the manmade **Paranoá Lake.** Since its contruction, the lake has become landocked Brasília's answer to Rio's Copacabana beach. Private social clubs, foreign embassies, and the residences of the city's powerbrokers, including ministers and other high government officials, line the winding contour of the lake. On the east side of the lake is the **Palácio da Alvorada,** official residence of the president, although only one of Brazil's last five presidents has lived there (at press time the current president, Itamar Franco, was planning to move in). The simple, boxlike form is enhanced by a screen of decorative, tapering columns. The building is not open to the public.

According to legend, a 19th-century Catholic priest had a vision that one day on the central plateau of Brazil a city on a lake would rise and become the promised land. Since its inception, mystics have considered Brasília the city envisioned by the priest, winning it the sobriquet "Capital of the Third Millenium" and turning it into one of Latin America's leading centers of spiritualism and religious cults. The most unusual cult is the **Valley of the Dawn,** a commune of some 3,000 persons located 50 kilometers (30 miles) south of the city, where every Sunday followers dressed in long flowing robes gather in an outdoor arena containing oversize statues, ponds, fountains, and astrological symbols—easily one of Brazil's more unusual sights. The rituals (held at noon, 2:30, and 6:30; admission charged) are open to the public. Another popular mystical site is the pyramid-shape temple of the **Legião da Boa Vontade** (beside the Television Tower, SGAS 915, Lote 75-76; admission free; open 24 hours a day), a nondenominational meditation center. The temple is famous for its "energy," which supposedly is transmitted to worshipers, who lift their hands toward the top of the pyramid. Both of these sites, as well as others in the city and surrounding area, are included in the so-called **"mystical tours"** offered by several travel agencies in the area. These tours are by far the best way to visit the sites, which are widely scattered.

6 Chile

By Lake Sagaris

*Lake Sagaris is a
Canadian poet and
journalist who has
lived in and covered
Chile for 13 years.
Her latest book is*
Medusa's Children:
A Journey from
Newfoundland to
Chiloé *(Cocteau
Press, Canada).*

"I live now in a country as soft/ as the autumnal flesh of grapes," begins "Country," a poem by the Chilean poet and Nobel Prize winner Pablo Neruda. With his odes to artichokes, birds, hope, Valparaíso, fish soup, socks, and September, he sang Chile into being and taught us to inhale its sharp salt air or the dry winy bouquet of its Andean mountains before we hold them to our lips and drink them down.

Chile is as luminous and pungent, as rustic and urban, as any of Neruda's poems about it. It combines the world's driest desert, a pie slice of Antarctica, the "navel of the universe" (Easter Island), Robinson Crusoe's former haunts, a sophisticated urban landscape, and a temperate southern jungle, all in one slim extension of land squeezed between the Pacific Ocean and the Andes, with a vast and varied human geography to match. In some places the 200-mile territorial limit is wider than the country itself, making Chile as much ocean as earth.

From 1973 to 1990, Chile was virtually synonymous with the name of General Augusto Pinochet, who, with U.S. support, led a coup against the elected socialist government in September 1973. His regime's reputation for human rights violations and violent social conflict discouraged many visitors, but the advent of a civilian, elected government in March 1990 brought improvements. Today the country enjoys considerable social harmony and the most advanced economy in South America.

The first traveler to reach Chile barely gave it a glance: Hernando de Magallanes left his name and little else behind when he journeyed up the southwestern coast in 1520. Later, Pedro de Valdivia traveled south along the Camino del Inca (the Incas' Road) with a motley assortment of adventurers and a sole woman, his lover, Inés de Suárez; they founded Santiago in 1541. For the next 300 years, Chile's original inhabitants, especially the southern Mapuche, successfully defended against Spanish encroachment a sizable territory and their way of life. Chilean independence from Spain, after a war that lasted from 1810 to 1818, marked the beginning of the end of the Mapuche's independence. Their last great rebellion failed in 1881, and soon after, Chilean governments started shipping in German, Swiss, and other European colonists to fill their "empty" lands.

Today's Chileans are a mixture of European and native gene pools, with the lightest hair, skin, and eyes to be found at the top of a hierarchically organized society. Native peoples include about half a million Mapuche living in the region around Temuco; Aymara, who live in Chile's difficult north, in the world's driest desert; and Polynesians, who still form the majority of the population of Rapa Nui (Easter Island).

Santiago is virtually the center of Chile's world, in spite of recent attempts to decentralize. With one-third of Chile's national population, art galleries of all shapes and sizes, world-class hotels, and some of the best theater and music in Latin America, Santiago has blossomed since the lifting of curfews and vehicular restrictions, and it offers a varied nightlife whose truly Chilean pastimes, people, and places are easily accessible to international tourists as well.

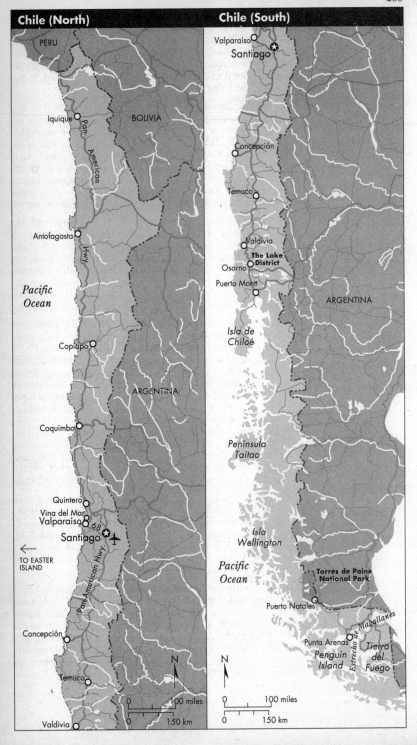

Chile (North)

Chile (South)

PERU

BOLIVIA

Iquique

Pan-American

Antofagasta

Hwy

Pacific Ocean

Copiapo

ARGENTINA

Coquimbo

Quintero

Vina del Mar
Valparaíso   68

Santiago

← TO EASTER ISLAND

Pan-American Hwy

Concepción

Temuco

Valdivia

0   100 miles
0   150 km

N

Valparaíso   Santiago

Concepción

Temuco

Valdivia
The Lake District

Osorno

Puerto Montt

ARGENTINA

Isla de Chiloé

Península Taitao

Isla Wellington

Pacific Ocean

Torres de Paine National Park

Puerto Natales

Punta Arenas
Penguin Island

Estrecho de Magallanes

Tierra del Fuego

N

0   100 miles
0   150 km

Staying Safe and Healthy

Personal Security Santiago's city center and most areas frequented by tourists are generally pretty safe, provided you dress down, don't wear flashy jewelry, and don't ever handle money in public. It's a good idea to keep your money in a pocket rather than a wallet, which is easier to steal. On buses and in crowded areas, hold purses or handbags close to the body; thieves use knives to slice the bottom of a bag and catch the contents as they fall out. The poor residential areas of Santiago, known as *poblaciones*, which ring most neighborhoods and commercial centers, have an interesting history and informed, opinionated people, but you need a knowledgeable guide to visit them safely. Chilean men are more subtle in their machismo than men in other South American countries, but it's still a strong aspect of the culture, and foreign women are considered fair game. Men are apt to misinterpret a casual, informal attitude and take advantage.

Health Chile is one of the safer countries you can travel in from a health point of view. Almost all drinking water receives proper treatment and is unlikely to produce health problems. The cholera epidemic that swept the continent in the early 1990s has been effectively controlled here. Restaurants are not allowed to serve raw salads and seafood, which represent the prime sources of the bacteria that produce not only cholera but also typhoid fever, hepatitis, and gastroenteritis in general. Avoid raw vegetables unless you know they've been thoroughly washed and disinfected. Be wary of strawberries and other unpeeled ground fruits and vegetables for the same reason, because many farm fields are irrigated with barely treated sewage. When purchasing ice cream, pastries, and other sweet items, buy in locales with proper refrigeration. Avoid luncheon meats, except good-quality ham, because these are a prime source of bacterial infections, especially in summer. Mineral water is good and comes in carbonated and noncarbonated incarnations, but you'll probably do all right with tap water.

Essential Information

Before You Go

When to Go Chile's seasons are the reverse of North America's—that is, June–August is Chile's winter. Tourism peaks during the hot summer months of January and February, except in Santiago, which tends to empty during that period. Though prices are at their highest, summer is a good time to visit if you're interested in lying on the beach or enjoying concerts, folklore festivals, and outdoor theater. A second tourist season occurs in the Chilean winter, as skiers descend onto Chile's mountaintops for some of the world's best skiing, available at the height of northern summers. Winter smog is a good reason for staying away from Santiago during July and August, unless you're coming for a ski holiday and won't be spending much time in the city. In spring Santiago blooms, and the fragrance of the flowers will distract even the most avid workaholic; in summer it empties as most *Santiaguinos* head for the coast, but theater, film, and music festivals make it worth braving the heat.

Climate Chile's climate is agreeable and varied given the country's enormous length. The north enjoys the extremes of desert weather, with hot, dry days and freezing nights, except on the coast, where the ocean moderates, providing a mild climate year-round. Santiago has hot summers, cool springs and falls, and very gray, smoggy winters. Farther south, in the Lake District, you should be prepared for hot days, cold nights, and rainstorms. And even farther south, in Punta Arenas, summer temperatures are seldom higher than 20°C (68°F), and you'll contend with snow and icy winds in winter.

The following are the average daily maximum and minimum temperatures for Santiago.

Jan.	85F	29C	May	65F	18C	Sept.	66F	19C
	53	12		41	5		42	6
Feb.	84F	29C	June	58F	14C	Oct.	72F	22C
	52	11		37	3		45	7
Mar.	80F	27C	July	59F	15C	Nov.	78F	26C
	49	9		37	3		48	9
Apr.	74F	23C	Aug.	62F	17C	Dec.	83F	28C
	54	7		39	4		51	11

The following are the average daily maximum and minimum temperatures for Punta Arenas.

Jan.	58F	14C	May	45F	7C	Sept.	46F	8C
	45	7		35	2		35	2
Feb.	58F	14C	June	41F	5C	Oct.	51F	11C
	44	7		33	1		38	3
Mar.	54F	12C	July	40F	4C	Nov.	54F	12C
	41	5		31	0		40	4
Apr.	50F	10C	Aug.	42F	6C	Dec.	57F	14C
	39	4		33	1		43	6

Currency Exchange rates fluctuate constantly, but at press time (Summer 1993) they were approximately 310 pesos to the Canadian dollar, 390 pesos to the U.S. dollar, and 590 pesos to the pound sterling. Shop around for a good exchange rate. Chilean coins come in units of 1, 10, 50, and 100 pesos; bills are issued in 500, 1,000, 5,000, and 10,000 pesos.

What It Will Cost Chile is more expensive than most visitors expect, but less so than for travelers to most North American or European regions. Inflation has been low, around 12% in 1993. There are plenty of less costly alternatives to the top international hotels. In most small towns, dozens of residents provide bed-and-breakfast-type accommodations in their home at quite inexpensive rates. Accommodations and food in and around Punta Arenas are generally very expensive.

There's an 18% value-added tax (VAT, called IVA here) added to the cost of most goods and services in Chile; often you won't notice because it's included in the price quoted. When it's not, the seller gives you the price, plus IVA. At many hotels you may receive an exemption from the IVA if you pay in American dollars or traveler's checks; some also offer this service if you use an American Express credit card.

Sample Prices A cup of coffee in a restaurant usually costs about 50¢, espresso usually less than $1. Coffee fanatics beware: The brew served is invariably instant. Ask for espresso, cappuccino, or cortado if you want "real" coffee. A steak or a ham-and-cheese sandwich (*barros luco*) will cost about $2.50. Add a cold draft beer for under $1.

Customs on Arrival You may bring into Chile up to 400 cigarettes, 400 grams of tobacco, 50 cigars, two open bottles of perfume, 2 liters of alcoholic beverages, and gifts. Visitors are seldom questioned when they depart, but by regulation you're allowed to leave with handicrafts and souvenirs worth not more than $500. You will be charged a $12.50 airport tax upon leaving.

Language Chile's official language is Spanish, and you'd be wise to learn at least a few words and carry a good phrase book. Many taxi drivers and hotel and restaurant reception staff speak English, as do many store salespeople. But you'll miss some of the best parts of Chile if you go only where English is spoken.

Getting Around

By Plane Flying around Chile is fast and comfortable. Excellent-value air travel packages are available, but only for purchase outside Chile. Both of Chile's main airlines, **Ladeco** (in the United States, tel. 800/328–1003; in Canada, tel. 800/423–7492; in Chile, tel. 2/698–1258) and **Lan Chile** (in the United States, tel. 800/735–5526; in Canada, tel. 800/535–9526; in Chile, tel. 2/632–3211) offer "Visit Chile" passes, valid for 21 days, which allow you to fly to several northern or southern cities for around $300 ($1,080 if you include Easter Island). The advantage of flying is that you avoid the dangers of the Chilean highway; the disadvantage is that you miss the landscape. You can compensate for this by renting a car and exploring locally.

By Train Good train service is a thing of the past in Chile; the only real advantage of trains now is they allow travelers to avoid the Pan-American Highway. Accommodations include sleeper cars, salón, economy, and, for some destinations, first and second classes. There are daily departures from Santiago for most places in southern Chile; there is no northbound service from Santiago. Delays are frequent, and there are occasional accidents. Reservations are recommended; make them at the train station itself (tel. 2/689–5401), in the city center (tel. 2/632–2802), or in the Escuela Militar metro station (tel. 2/228–2983).

By Bus Bus travel in Chile is relatively cheap and safe, provided you use one of the better lines. Luxury bus travel between cities costs about one-third the plane fare but is more comfortable, with wide, reclining seats with footrests, drinks, music, movies, and meals or snacks. Intercity bus service is a comfortable, safe, and reasonably priced alternative for getting around Chile. The cheaper the fare, the less comfortable (and often less safe) the service.

Cruz del Sur (tel. 2/779–3852 or 2/696–9324), **TurBus** (tel. 2/779–9233, 2/776–3133, or 2/776–3690), and **Varmontt** (tel. 2/232–1116 or 2/231–3505) offer luxury as well as regular service to many points between Santiago and Puerto Montt and beyond, at reasonable prices. You can often negotiate a cheaper fare with roaming vendors during a stroll through the relevant bus terminal. Most individual bus companies are difficult to phone; your best bet is to check schedules and purchase tickets personally. Buses can fill quickly on holiday weekends and over Christmas and Easter, so plan accordingly.

Travel Southward **Terminal Alameda** (Av. Libertador Bernardo O'Higgins 3724) handles traffic for Pullman del Sur (tel. 2/776–2426) and Tur Bus (tel. 2/776–3133) buses. **Terminal los Héroes** (Roberto Pretot 21, tel. 2/696–9087) handles Cruz del Sur (tel. 2/696-9324); and **Terminal Santiago** (Av. Libertador Bernardo O'Higgins 3848, tel. 2/779-1385) handles another 20 or so bus companies. **Varmontt** has its own premises (Av. 11 de Setiembre 2212, Local 111, tel. 2/231–3505).

Travel Northward **Terminal de Buses Norte** (Amuntegui 920, tel. 2/671–2141) handles 16 bus companies; **Terminal los Héroes** (Roberto Pretot 21, tel. 2/696–9087) handles Flota Barrios (tel. 2/699–0230); and **Terminal Torres de Tajamar** (Av. Providencia 1072) handles three other lines.

By Car Your own driver's license or an International Driving Permit makes it legal for you to drive, but your stay in Chile will probably be more pleasant if you avoid using a car or if you use one with great prudence.

Road Conditions Chilean drivers are wild and reckless and tend to make up the rules as they go along. Roads are hopelessly overcrowded, especially in Santiago, and parking is a problem in most major cities. The main highway is the Panamericana (Pan-American Highway), which begins on the Chile-Peru border and extends south through Santiago and on to Puerto Montt and beyond. Foreign insurance may cover the basic costs of an accident, but if you're in an accident that kills or cripples someone, you can be sued, and a Chilean court may award damages far beyond your ability to pay. Local insurance is provided by rental car agencies. A good alternative is to travel by plane, train, or bus to the main city of your destination and rent a vehicle for local excursions only. Speed limits are usually 100 kph (62 mph) on highways and 50 kph (31 mph) in cities but are often disregarded by other drivers. It is a poor idea to emulate those drivers, because many roads can be in such bad condition that driving even under the legal speed limit may be hazardous, even on the Pan-American Highway.

Gasoline Gasoline prices range from 41¢/liter for 84 octane to 44¢/liter for 93 and unleaded and 33¢/liter for diesel. Prices increase the farther away you travel from Santiago. There are plenty of gas stations on main routes, but make sure your tank is full before you head out into a national park or some other less-populated area.

If you're traveling by car, you may want to take advantage of an excellent train service that carries you and your vehicle between Santiago and southern Chile. Round-trip prices from Santiago to Temuco are $168 to transport your car ($185 in the peak season of January and February), plus $122 for a private cabin for two or $50 for two coach seats. The trip must be booked well in advance, particularly if you intend to travel during the peak season; tickets must be paid for when you make a reservation (tel. 2/689–5401).

Staying in Chile

Telephones *Local Calls* There are two kinds of phones for local calls. The large yellow phones require a 50-peso piece; you then dial in the usual way and will have three minutes to complete your call before a tone warns you to insert another 50 pesos or be cut off. The large metallic phones are called "intelligent," which means you can insert varying amounts of money and make several calls in succession, provided you don't hang up in between: there's a special button to push that cuts off one call and starts another. The intelligent phone also includes English-language instructions. Most city areas have standing phone booths, but they are also found at restaurants and even newsstands, many of which provide such public telephone service. You may have to wait several seconds after picking up the receiver before a steady humming sound signals you may dial. After dialing, you'll hear a characteristic beep-beep repeatedly as your call goes through; then there's a pause, followed by a long tone signaling that the other phone is ringing. A busy sound is similar but repeats itself with no pause in-between.

International Calls To call internationally, direct from a private phone, you first dial 00, then wait for the international system tone; you then dial the country code, the specific area or city code, and the phone number. Reduced rates to most places apply after 6 PM and on Sunday and holidays. Most hotels charge extra for long-distance calls made from your room. You may find it less expensive to use a phone center; they are centrally located in all major towns and cities.

For long-distance operator service, the national number is 108 and the international 182. Dial 183 for general information in English or Spanish on international phone calls. AT&T, MCI, and Sprint have direct calling programs. AT&T's **USADirect** service allows you to call collect or charge calls from abroad to your AT&T calling card. To access USADirect, dial 00–00312; service is not available from pay phones. For more information, call 412/553–7458, ext. 314, collect from outside the United States, or 800/874–4000 in the United States. MCI and Sprint's services are similar; to access MCI's **Call USA** service, dial 00–0316. To use Sprint's **World Travel card**, dial 00*0317.

Mail Postage on regular letters and postcards to Canada and the
Postal Rates United States costs about 66¢. The postage to Britain is about 80¢.

Shopping Chile is one of only two countries in the world that produces lapis lazuli, so it's worth checking out the workshops and stores along Bellavista Avenue in Santiago. Handicrafts include warm sweaters that are hand dyed, spun, and knitted in southern Chile (it's cheaper to purchase them there) and ponchos, whose designs vary according to the region; the best ones are by the Mapuche artisans in and around Temuco and by the Chilote women on the islands of Chiloé, off the coast from Puerto Montt. Thick wool blankets are woven in Chiloé but are heavy to carry, as are the figures of reddish clay from Pomaire and the famous black clay of Quinchamalí, available at most crafts fairs. Santiago artisans are increasingly sophisticated, and you can find at crafts fairs earrings, rings, and necklaces to please virtually every taste. Several towns specialize in wicker, particularly Chimbarongo (about an hour's drive from Santiago) and Chiloé, where baskets and woven effigies of that island's mythical figures abound.

Opening and Banking hours are weekdays 9–2, with no exceptions. Stores
Closing Times generally open weekdays 10–7 and on Saturday to 2. In small towns, stores close for lunch between about 1 and 3 or 4. Museum hours tend to coincide with shopping hours; most museums are closed on Monday, as are theaters and many restaurants.

National Holidays January 1 (New Year's Day); second Friday in April (Good Friday); May 21 (Day of Naval Glories); June 10 (Corpus Christi); June 29 (Feast of St. Peter and St. Paul); September 11 (Anniversary of Coup); September 18 and 19 (Independence Celebrations); October 12; December 8 (Day of the Virgin); December 25 (Christmas).

Dining Santiago has the widest selection of restaurants and prices, but many of the local spots can provide meals as carefully prepared and as delicious. Several of the larger hotels in isolated cities or resorts have good chefs. *Fuente de soda* (soda fountain) is the most common classification for Chilean restaurants and, while they may be a good place for a soft drink, a cup of tea, or a light breakfast, you should be cautious about eating much else, because the hygiene may not be the best.

Pisco sours (lemon, egg white, sugar, and a Chilean liquor, similar to tequila, called *pisco*) are a refreshing start to an evening meal, as is the more gentle *vaina* (sherry or some other sweet wine, whipped with egg white and topped with a dash of cinnamon). Chilean wine is known around the world and is good and cheap, so make the best of it! Chilean food is simple, focusing on a main meat, fish, or shellfish dish, preceded by a salad and followed by a sweet desert. The food is seldom spicy, but watch for the delicious but hot red sauce *ají*, and *pebre*, a sauce made of fresh parsley, fresh coriander, onions, and sometimes tomatoes, using ají as a base.

Many simple country dishes are among the best offerings of Chilean cuisine. *Gazuela*, a superb soup that includes a piece of meat (beef, pork, chicken, or turkey, usually with bone), varied vegetables, and a thick, rich broth, is a full meal in itself. If your stomach's been rough, a rich chicken *gazuela* is just the thing. In the summer, *porotos granados*, a thick bean, corn, and squash soup, is the rage with Chileans, as are *humitas*, ground corn seasoned and steamed in its own husk, and *pastel de choclo*, a corn pastry roll that usually contains minced beef, a piece of chicken, and seasonings. An *ensalada chilena* of tomatoes and onions is delicious if well prepared (the onions must be soaked in brine beforehand to reduce their acid flavor). Empanadas (pastry folded around a beef, shellfish, or cheese filling) are the Chilean answer to hamburgers, but as with hamburgers themselves, it's hard to find a good one.

Raw shellfish is a health hazard, but cooked with cheese or white wine, lemon, and fresh coriander, it's an excellent doorway to Chilean cuisine. Chile enjoys a variety of fine fish: the conger eel, *corvina* (corbina), and other species are all worth tasting, as is the humble *merluza* (hake), which makes a delicious, cheap lunch; the *centolla* crab, caught off the coast of Patagonia; and *machas* clams, similar to razor clams but unique to Chile.

Pork is another Chilean specialty, especially in *arrollados* (a stuffed pork roll encased in pork rind), *costillares* (ribs, often covered in ají), *lomo* (roast pork loin), and *pernil* (the whole leg, so make sure you're hungry).

Some Spanish-inspired dishes like *guatitas* (intestines) send Chileans into transports, as do blood sausage, *chunchules* (a spicy stew of beef or pork intestines) and other odds and ends of edible beasts. If you order a *parillada* (a barbecue at your table), check on the cuts being served so as to avoid those that are too peculiar for your taste.

Fixed-price menus are uncommon, but some restaurants use them. There is no system of government classification of restaurants, although in theory they're all subject to the same standards. Your own eyes and nose are your best guides.

Mealtimes Chileans usually eat a light breakfast, a hot and hefty lunch, evening tea, and a late dinner. Many households settle for a filling *once* (pronounced ON-say), an afternoon tea with bread, cheese, ham, and pastries, and skip the late dinner.

Ratings Prices are per person and include a first course, main course, and dessert, but not wine. Highly recommended restaurants are indicated by a star ★.

Category	Cost
Expensive	$25–$35
Moderate	$15–$25
Inexpensive	under $15

Lodging Santiago is slowly getting over a shortage of high-quality hotels, with new ones opening throughout the city. Smaller towns and cities usually have at least one large hotel that serves as a local landmark. But don't forget the *residenciales*, especially if you're trying to stretch your budget. These accommodations are either modest, no-frills hotels or private homes, usually with a separate bathroom and a Continental-style breakfast. "Apart Hotels" provide apartments by the day or week. For a night's adventure, you and a partner could also try out a lovers' hotel (some call themselves "motels"); they offer hot tubs, private videos, and drinks, and some of the more sophisticated also have special theme rooms.

Hotel prices sometimes include the 18% VAT and sometimes don't. If you pay in cash or traveler's checks in U.S. dollars and if the hotel has an "export billing number" you do not have to pay it. Prices are generally lower in the off-season (in Santiago, January and February, when tourism is at its height in most other regions). Showers are common; full tubs are not.

Ratings Prices are for double rooms and include all taxes. Highly recommended hotels are indicated by a star ★.

Category	Cost
Very Expensive	over $200
Expensive	$125–$200
Moderate	$75–$125
Inexpensive	under $75

Tipping The usual tip in restaurants is 10%, more if you really liked the service. City taxi drivers don't usually expect a tip, because most own their cabs. If you hire a taxi to take you around a city, you should consider a good tip.

Guided Tours Literally dozens of tour groups will guide you in Chile. **Altué Expediciones** (Encomenderos 83, tel. 2/232–1103) offers adventure trips such as rafting on wild rivers and hiking to the mouths of volcanoes. **Turismo Cocha** (Agustinas 1173, tel. 2/698–3341) and **Chilean Travel Services** (Agustinas 1291, 5th floor, Office F, tel. 2/696–7820) handle tours of both Santiago and the rest of Chile. A smaller agency offering individualized tours, both guided and group, is the reliable and imaginative **Rigtur** (Ahumada 312, Office 606, tel. 2/698–5766 or 2/698–7535).

Santiago

A curious mixture of modern skyscrapers, 19th-century European architecture, and Spanish colonial adobe bungalows, Santiago's architecture reflects the fact that the city is really a universe composed of multiple, separate worlds. The population is over 4 million; nevertheless, residents are always likely to bump into an acquaintance along the city center's overcrowded streets and bustling walkways, since they're concentrated in a small area around the Ahumada and Huérfanos pedestrian malls. The Paseo Ahumada stretches northward from the Alameda (Avenida Libertador Bernardo O'Higgins) to the Plaza de Armas and is bisected about halfway along by Paseo Huérfanos. Modern stores and banks in skyscrapers and 19th-century buildings stretch out for blocks around the Plaza de Armas, full of colorful gardens and fountains. The parks, the food, and a more relaxed attitude toward time exercise a magnetic attraction on visitors, along with dancing and nightlife, which begins at 10 PM and goes on most of the night.

Tourist Information

SERNATUR, the National Tourist Service (Providencia 1550, Santiago, tel. 562/236–1416) is on Providencia Street between the metro stops Manuel Montt and Pedro de Valdivia.

Arriving and Departing

By Plane Chile's national airport is about 30 minutes' drive west of Santiago. It is hopelessly out of date and undergoing major renovation; the first phase is scheduled for completion in early 1994. You can get from the airport to Santiago by taxi for under $20, or via **Buses Tour Express** (tel. 2/671–7380) for $1.60; or you can rent a car in the airport from **Avis** (tel. 2/601–9050), **Budget** (tel. 2/601–9421), or **Hertz** (tel. 2/601–9262). There is no subway connection.

By Car If you're coming into Santiago from the north, you'll probably arrive via the Panamericana (Pan-American Highway), Highway 5; from Viña or Valparaíso, Highway 68; from the south, the Panamericana Sur, Highway 5; from the Andes (Argentina), Highway 57. Route 78 brings you into Santiago from San Antonio and other coastal towns.

By Train The train station is **Estación Central** (Central Station) on Alameda (Av. Bernardo O'Higgins) at Exposición Street. It has its own metro stop of the same name.

By Bus The **Terminal Norte** (Amunátegui 920, 2/671–2141) handles northern and northeastern (coastal) service. **Terminal Santi-**

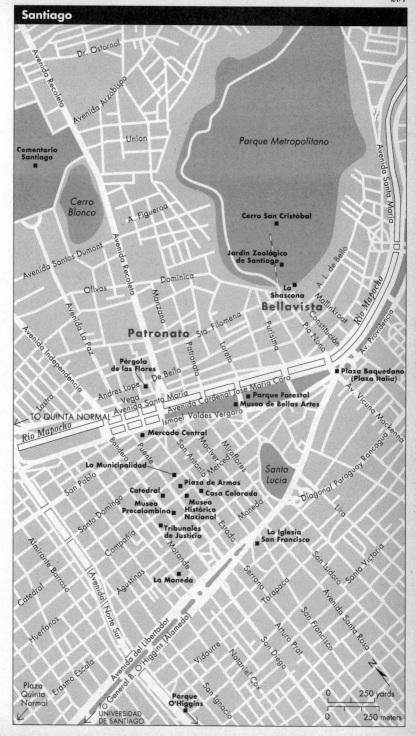

Santiago

Parque Metropolitano

Cementario Santiago

Cerro Blonco

Cerro San Cristóbal

Jardin Zoológico de Santiago

La Chascona

Bellavista

Union

Dr. Ostornol

Avenida Recoleta

Avenida Arzobispo

A. Figueroa

Patronato

Avenida Santos Dumont

Olivos

Dominica

Avenida La Paz

Avenida Independencia

Avenida Recoleta

Manzano

Sta. Filomena

Loreto

Purisima

Pio Nono

Constitución

Mallinkroat

A. L. de Bello

Rio Mapocho

Av. Providencia

Pérgola de las Flores

Andres Lope

De Bello

Patronato

Vega

Avenida Santa Maria

Avenida Cardenal Jose Maria Caro

Parque Forestal

Museo de Bellas Artes

Plaza Baquedano (Plaza Italia)

Av. Vicuna Mackenna

Lastra

TO QUINTA NORMAL

Rio Mapocho

Ismael Valdes Vergara

Mercado Central

Bandera

Puente

Maciver

Miraflores

Merced

Santa Lucia

Diagonal Paraguay Rancagua

Litra

San Antonio

La Municipalidad

Catedral

Museo Precolombino

Plaza de Armas

Casa Colorada

Museo Histórico Nacional

Tribunales de Justicia

Estado

Moneda

La Iglesia San Francisco

San Pablo

Santo Domingo

Compania

Morande

Agustinas

La Moneda

Serrano

Tarapaca

San Isidoro

Santa Victoria

Avenida Santa Rosa

San Francisco

Almirante Barroso

Avenida Norte Sur

Huerfanos

Catedral

Erasmo Escala

Avenida del Libertador

Avenida General B. O'Higgins (Alameda)

Vidaurre

Nataniel Cox

San Diego

Arturo Prat

San Ignacio

Plaza Quinta Normal

TO UNIVERSIDAD DE SANTIAGO

Parque O'Higgins

N

0 250 yards
0 250 meters

ago (Av. Libertador Bernardo O'Higgins 3848, tel. 2/779–1385) handles southern and coastal traffic. **Terminal Los Héroes** (Roberto Pretot 21, tel. 2/696–9076, 2/696–9080, or 2/696–9082) handles some northern and southern traffic. **Terminal Alameda** (Av. Libertador Bernardo O'Higgins 3750, tel. 2/776–3690) handles some coastal and southern traffic. (*See* Essential Information, *above,* for phone numbers of individual lines.)

Getting Around

Much of Santiago is best explored on foot, using the metro and an occasional taxi to manage larger distances. However, a combination of the metro and taxis is probably the quickest and most comfortable, and most economical, way of getting around. The metro is best for reaching downtown, or anywhere along its east-west axis. You'll probably want the rented car or taxi to get to the *barrio alto* (upper-class neighborhoods) or take a general tour of the city. Most individual taxi drivers are willing to be hired for the day; to increase your bargaining power, head for the taxi stand at Huérfanos and MacIver streets in the heart of downtown, where you can talk to more than one driver. You can catch buses to the Maipo Canyon, about an hour's drive south of the city, in the Parque Bernardo O'Higgins.

By Car   Drivers in Santiago don't respect traffic signs, lights, or lines on the road, and rush hour means wall-to-wall cars lined up along major and minor thoroughfares. However, a rented car or taxi is still your best bet for an overview of the city or for enjoying short drives into the surrounding countryside. Between May and August, roads, underpasses, and parks flood whenever it rains and can become very dangerous, especially for drivers who don't know their way around the city. Avoid driving if it's been raining for several hours.

By Public   Santiago's metro is modern, comfortable, cheap, and safe;
Transportation   make it the backbone of your explorations. Every station has a clear map of the north–south (the secondary route) and east–west (the main route) lines, with adjoining roads. The University of Chile stop on the east–west line is the main station for the city center; the Escuela Militar is the upper-class end of the city; and Pudahuel is the poorer, less developed area. Buy tickets in the glass booths at the stations; a "carnet" of 10 tickets good on both metro lines is cheapest, about $2.50. Main line tickets can be used on the secondary lines as well, but the cheaper, north–south tickets can't be used on the main line.

Buses have improved but are still fast, reckless, and unreliable; bus drivers almost invariably say they go where you want to go, whether they do or not. Bus fare is usually 100–110 pesos (about 30¢), paid upon boarding, and drivers can usually change up to a 1,000-peso bill.

By Taxi   Taxi drivers aren't as honest as they used to be, but taxis, especially when combined with the metro for large distances, are a reasonable alternative for most transportation needs. You can flag one down on most city streets; the average ride costs around $10 (more for designated airport taxis). Radio-dispatched cabs (**Alfa**, tel. 2/773–7228 or 2/773–7634 or **Andes Pacífico**, tel. 2/225–364, 2/204–0104, or 9/221–3891) are slightly more expensive but will pick you up at your door.

Guided Tours

SERNATUR maintains a register of experienced individual tour guides who for a half-day fee (around $25 per group) will take you on a personalized tour of Santiago and the surrounding area. These guides can greatly enrich visits to Santiago's less documented museums, for example, by providing background knowledge that is not generally available to the public. **Lizzie Wagner** (tel. 2/220–4500) offers an excellent private tour of the Natural History Museum as well as of the Central Market, some noteworthy Santiago architecture, and the Cousiño Palace.

Exploring Santiago

Downtown *Santiaguinos* orient themselves along an east–west axis, with the Cordillera (the Andes mountain range) to the east and the coastal mountains on the west. Santiago itself nestles in the valley between them and is cut approximately in half north–south by the Mapocho River. The Avenida Libertador Bernardo O'Higgins, better known as the Alameda, is laid out over what was once the southern arm of the Mapocho River, from east to west. In Plaza Baquedano, also known as Plaza Italia, the Alameda becomes Providencia, an upscale shopping district; farther east and northward it's called Apoquindo; and yet farther along it turns into Las Condes and is the address of some of the city's fanciest houses.

The city center nestles just to the south of the Mapocho, radiating out on a grid pattern from the central square known as the Plaza de Armas (Weapons Square). The Central Market is on the river's south side, about three blocks north of the plaza; the Vega, a cheaper, more colorful version of the market, is across the river. The General Cemetery is about five minutes' drive north from the Vega, and the Bellavista area, full of restaurants, theaters, and art galleries, is about five minutes' drive east of the Vega. The Parque O'Higgins is about 20 minutes' drive south of downtown, or about 10 minutes via the north–south metro line.

If you really want to get to know Santiago, start at the city's heart, the central square known as the **Plaza de Armas,** between Estado, Catedral, and Compañía streets, four blocks north of the Universidad de Chile metro station. Flanked by **La Municipalidad** (City Hall), the **Museo Histórico Nacional** (National History Museum), **la Catedral,** and a motley assortment of commercial arcades, the square is a genuine center for activities, top among them loafing and people-watching. The distinctive fountains and gardens, constantly being replanted, reveal Chileans' pride of place. The *pelusas* (street children) who hang out at the square, the photographers with their old-fashioned box cameras who make a living taking people's pictures, the street vendors hawking toys, candies, and the latest peculiar knickknack, and the elderly and unemployed sunning themselves on the benches display a cross section of Chileans, many of whom will be willing to squeeze out a few words of English in order to talk to a foreign guest.

If you're going to visit only one museum in Santiago, it should be the **Museo Precolombino** (Pre-Columbian Museum), located about three blocks west of the Plaza de Armas, in the city center. It contains a well-endowed collection of artifacts of Central and South America's original peoples housed in a beautifully restored colonial building that once served as the Royal Customs House. The permanent collection includes textiles and ceramics from what is now Mexico southward, including Chile. As in most Chilean museums, there isn't a lot of information with the displays so you might want to call upon a local guide with expertise in the museum's area (*see* Guided Tours, *above*). *361 Bandera, tel. 2/695–3851. Admission charged. Closed Mon.*

Just across the street from the Pre-Columbian Museum are Chile's lordly **Tribunales de Justicia** (Tribunals of Justice), the site of many a human rights demonstration during the military government and even today. If you continue southward on Bandera Street for three blocks, then follow Moneda Street westward one block, you'll find yourself at **La Moneda** (literally, "the coin," so-called because the structure was originally built as the national mint), designed by the Italian architect Joaquín Toesca in 1799. The traditional Spanish colonial–style palace complex, with offices and galleries built around spacious cement courtyards, one planted with orange trees, has housed Chilean presidents since the 19th century but was bombed during the 1973 military coup and then restored and occupied by General Pinochet.

Just south of the square and a block east on Merced Street you'll find the **Casa Colorada** (Reddish House), a red-washed, colonial-style building that now houses the modest but informative Santiago Museum, an excellent place to learn some of Santiago's and Chile's long history if you can read Spanish. *Merced 860, tel. 2/633–0723. Admission charged. Closed Mon.*

The **National History Museum,** on the square, is remarkable mostly for the quality of a recent restoration performed on the building itself, which dates to 1804. As a source of information about Chilean history it's extremely poor, for example, marking 300 years of native resistance to Spanish and Chilean invasions with a pen-and-ink sketch entitled "La Pacificación de la Araucanía" ("The Pacification of the Araucanian Territories") and reducing most major historical events to the uniform worn by such-and-such a general or the bed that X slept in every night. *Plaza de Armas, tel. 2/638–1411. Admission charged; free on Sun. Closed Mon.*

The central market area, three blocks north of the museum, offers a smelly, colorful, intriguing glimpse of everyday life in Santiago. The **Mercado Central** (Central Market) itself was prefabricated in England and erected in Chile between 1868 and 1872. It has the lofty wrought-iron ceiling of a Victorian train station and soars above a matchless selection of Chilean fruits and vegetables along with many rare delicacies that can be purchased only in this market, including exotic mushrooms and piñones, Chile's giant pine nuts from the monkey puzzle tree. The **pescadería** (fish market), just to the east in an adjoining building, provides a complete introduction to Chile's varied and marvelous sea creatures. Depending on the season, you might see the delicate beak of *picorocos,* the world's only edible barnacle; the orange stars of sea urchins in their prickly shells; or shadowy pails full of succulent bullfrogs. You can find a cheap, filling meal at most of the stands along the south end of the whole market. You can expect to be served a clandestine glass of wine with your meal if you ask, although most stands don't have a liquor license.

Santiago's green and grassy **Parque Forestal** (Forest Park) starts near the market and runs parallel to the Mapocho River for several blocks. A stroll under Oriental banana and other imported and Chilean trees takes you past a children's playing area to the park's pointed tip, distinguished by the Wagnerian-scale ship of German immigrants that forms the **Fuente Alemana** (German Fountain) in Plaza Baquedano. Along the way you'll pass the **Museo de Bellos Artes** (Fine Arts Museum; Calles José Miguel de la Barra and Loreto, tel. 2/633–0655), with paintings, drawings, and sculpture by 16th- to 20th-century Chilean and European artists. Closed during the time of the military regime but reopened in 1990, the museum has worked hard to reach international standards of quality.

Across the river from the central market, you'll find the **Pérgola de las Flores** (Trellis of Flowers), the source of the complex wreaths and flower arrangements made mostly for visitors to the two cemeteries in the area. Right next door is the **Vega,** a low-ceilinged collection of stands where many Santiaguinos buy their fruits and vegetables and where the vendors joke congenially with their customers and each other.

Just across Recoleta Avenue, east of the Vega, is Santiago's **Patronato** area, with bargains in clothes, sheets, and towels. Once the exclusive preserve of Chileans of Arab origin, this traditional textile neighborhood is now home to more and more Korean-owned shops. If you continue eastward along Antonia López de Bello, you'll pass the storefront shops in old Arab-style mansions built by families that made their fortune in textiles, and you'll eventually reach the trendy **Bellavista** neighborhood, where the streets are lined with acacia trees, small cafés, and one-story adobe homes painted in pinks, aquamarines, and blues. This is a good place to stop for lunch. The heart of Bellavista is at Pío Nono and Antonia López de Bello streets; one of its main attractions is the **Parque Metropolitano** (Metropolitan Park), located at the north end of Pío Nono Street, which covers the entirety of Santiago's highest hill, **Cerro San Cristóbal** (St. Christopher Hill; tel. 2/777–6666 for park administration). If you turn left at Pío Nono Street and walk two blocks northward along a paved road, then up a steep but well-cleared path, you'll reach the entrance to the hill. You can walk up (it's a steep but enjoyable one-hour climb) or take the funicular or an open bus to the summit, which is crowned by a huge white statue of the Virgin Mary and a fabulous view of the entire city. Halfway up the hill is the **Jardín Zoológico de Santiago** (Santiago Zoo), a good place to see examples of many Chilean species you might not otherwise encounter, some nearly extinct. Be careful: Some of the cages aren't properly protected and the animals can bite.

At the foot of the hill, just a block east along Constitución and then left on Fernando Márquez de la Plata Street, you'll find the house Pablo Neruda designed, **La Chascona** (Woman with Tousled Hair, named for Mathilde Urratia, the lover with whom he lived out his final years; tel. 2/777–8741). Visits, by appointment only, are like stepping into the extraordinary mind of the poet who has been called an "organic architect": winding this way and that around the hillside is a path through the garden, leading to a library stuffed with books, a bedroom in a tower, and a secret passsageway—all filled with the collections of butterflies, books, seashells, bowsprits, wineglasses, and other odd objects that inspired Neruda's poetry. *Fernando Márquez de la Plata 192, tel. 2/777–8741. Admission charged. Closed Sun. and Mon.*

It may be unusual as far as tourist attractions go, but the **Cementerio General,** Santiago's general cemetery, at the end of Avenida la Paz (Peace Avenue), a short taxi ride northwest from the Cerro San Cristóbal or downtown, is a fine source of insights into traditional Chilean society. You pass through the lofty stone arches of the main entrance and find yourself among marble mausoleums, the squat mansions belonging to Chile's wealthy families. The cemetery has well-maintained gardens, neat roads and walkways, stained-glass windows, and religious icons. The 8- or 10-story "niches" farther along—literally concrete shelves housing thousands of coffins—resemble middle-class apartment buildings; their inhabitants lie here until the "rent" runs out and they're evicted.

Parks and Gardens

On the south side of the city is the large **Parque Bernardo O'Higgins,** at the southern line subway stop by the same name. The park, named for Chile's national liberator, who led rebel troops to victory against the Spanish, thus creating an independent Chile in 1818, has an open area, complete with paved marching grounds for military parades, swimming pools, and lots of space to fly kites. Street vendors sell kites and thread outside the park year-round; high winds make September and early October the prime kite-flying season.

To the west of the city center is another park, the **Quinta Normal,** founded in 1830 to reproduce foreign plant species. It's a popular place for a stroll or picnic and has a small pond with rowboats that can be rented. The park also contains the **Museo Nacional de Historia Natural** (National Natural History Museum), with displays on Chilean animal life, and the **Museo de Ciencia, Tecnología, Ferroviario e Infantil** (Museum of Science and Technology, Railway Museum, and Children's Museum). The Children's Museum caters primarily to prearranged tours by groups of local schoolchildren. The main entrance to the park is at Avenida Matucana, near Agustinas. *Natural History Museum, tel. 2/681–4095; Science and Technology and Railway Museum, tel. 2/681–6022; Children's Museum, tel. 2/681–8800. Admission charged at all. Closed Mon.*

What to See and Do with Children

In addition to the zoo and the parks and museums listed in Parks and Gardens, *above,* Santiago has several permanent fairs. The main attractions of **Mundo Mágico** (Magic World), about 20 minutes west of the city center, near the Pajaritos metro station, are games and a train ride around a miniature map of Chile that includes lakes, hills, and ocean along with architectural landmarks such as the Municipal Theater. *Av. Gen. Oscar Bonilla 6100, tel. 2/779–0150. Admission charged. Closed Mar.–Dec.*

Fantasilandia (Fantasyland) in the Parque O'Higgins includes a roller coaster, pirate ship, haunted house, huge slide, and other rides. *Av. Beaucheff 938, tel. 2/689–3035. Admission charged. Closed weekdays Mar.–Nov.; Mon. Dec.–Feb.*

Shopping

If you want to put in a day of shopping, your best bet is to visit Providencia's exclusive boutiques and comfortable department stores, especially **Falabella** (Nueva de Lyon 064, tel. 2/233–7171) and **Almacenes París** (Av. 11 de Setiembre 2221, tel. 2/233–5045) along Providencia Street, which is the continuation of the Avenida Libertador Bernardo O'Higgins east of Plaza Baquedano. If you'd like to see a good selection in a relatively short time, take a taxi to the **Parque Arauco** (Av. Kennedy 5413, tel. 2/242–0600) or **Apumanque** (Av. Manquehue Sur 31, tel. 2/246–0169) shopping centers in the Barrio Alto. Both have an excellent selection of stores specializing in clothing, particularly for women, and each center also has a reasonably good bookstore with some books in English, a leather goods store, and a store offering Chilean handicrafts. For an opportunity to buy hand-crafted articles more directly, check with SERNATUR to learn where local crafts fairs are currently operating. There's a **permanent crafts fair** in Bellavista in the evenings, in the Domingo Gómez Park near the Law School on Pío Nono, just across the river from Plaza Baquedano. More vendors gather during the weekend to display their handicrafts.

The **Pueblo de los Artesanos,** is a crafts "village" with a wonderful display of cockatoos, exotic chickens, and other live birds. It's a nice place to visit, especially on weekends, when traveling musicians and performers add live entertainment to an already interesting mix of handicrafts and antiques. *Los Graneros del Alba, Av. Apoquindo 8600, beside the Church los Domínicos. Closed Mon.*

Spectator Sports

Horse Racing Horse racing is popular at every level of society, and there are two large hippodromes in Santiago, the **Club Hípico** (Blanco Encalada 2540, tel. 2/683–6535) and the **Hipódromo Chile** (Hipódromo Chile 1715, tel. 2/736–9276).

Soccer Chile's most popular and most absorbing spectator sport is soccer, but a close second is watching on the news and on the sidelines the endless battles and bickering that go on among owners, players, and trainers whenever things aren't going well. The venue is the **Estadio Nacional** (Av. Grecia 2001, tel. 2/238–8102); the season is March through December; and matches are on weekends and some Wednesdays.

Dining

In the past five years, restaurants have blossomed in Santiago, particularly in the Bellavista neighborhood. Many specialize in "international cuisine," a term that can mean just about anything, from lasagna to sushi to fiery Szechuan beef. Ethnic restaurants in general are not necessarily very good: Chile hasn't had the kind of immigration that has produced the excellent Chinese and other restaurants of Canada and the United States. In addition to good Chilean restaurants, however, there are several restaurants that serve above-average Italian, Argentine, Spanish, and Peruvian fare. Prices vary enough between dishes that depending on what you order, your meal may move the restaurant up or down a category. Beware: most restaurants are closed on Sunday. For details and price-category definitions, *see* Dining in Staying in Chile, *above*.

Expensive **Balthazar.** Nouvelle cuisine with a Chilean twist is served in
★ this carefully restored old adobe stable. In the center of the small dining room, a rough-hewn wooden trestle table groans with exquisite, inventive salads and hors d'oeuvres that borrow from Indonesian, Japanese, Chinese, Arab, and other cuisines, available as a buffet. The scallops and the stuffed trout with olive sauce are simply spectacular. *Av. las Condes 10690, tel. 2/215–1090. Reservations advised. AE, DC, MC, V. Closed Sun.*

Bristol. This restaurant in the Hotel Plaza San Francisco Kempinski attracts a crowd of government ministers, businesspeople, and well-heeled Santiago visitors. Many dishes apply the techniques of French cooking to Chilean ingredients, but the Bristol's most extraordinary culinary hit is a buffet-style offering of hors d'oeuvres and desserts, served with fresh fruit and excellent cheeses. *Alameda (Av. Bernardo O'Higgins) 816, tel. 2/639–3832. Reservations advised. AE, DC, MC, V.*

Enoteca. This restaurant high up on the San Cristóbal Hill is definitely one to visit at night. It includes Chile's own wine museum, where you can visit and taste before settling down to a well-prepared meal of international cuisine. Specialties include poached salmon with smoked salmon sauce, and sole stuffed with mushrooms. It's hard to find, so take a taxi. *Parque Metropolitano, tel. 2/232–1758. Reservations required on weekends. AE, DC, MC, V.*

Giratorio. International cuisine is served in a revolving restaurant on the top floor of a building in Providencia. It's worth trying not only for the view but also for the fresh, well-prepared, and extremely tasty fish and meat dishes, such as *filet panorama* (beef fillet stuffed with ham and cheese in a mushroom and wine sauce). *11 de Setiembre 2250, 16th floor, tel. 2/232–1827. Reservations suggested. AE, DC, MC, V. Closed New Year's Day.*

Moderate **Aquí Está Coco.** The best fish and shellfish in Santiago is served
★ up in comfortable surroundings decorated with a nautical theme; the walls are covered with flotsam and jetsam from Chilean beaches. Ask your waiter what's best each day. This is a good place to try Chile's famous *machas*, here served *á la parmesana*, and *corvina*, one of Chile's tastiest fish, offered with a choice of various butters and sauces. *La Concepción 236, Providencia, tel. 2/205–5985 or 2/251–5751. Reservations required on weekends. AE, DC, MC, V. Closed Sun.*

★ **Da Carla.** The chef and owner, Carla, arrived from Italy 30 years ago, and she's now as much of an institution as the restaurant itself. The walls are covered with plaques, posters, pictures, and large wooden ladles and spoons. The lasagna and spaghetti dishes are fine, and the hors d'oeuvres served buffet-style, ranging from stuffed mushrooms to *vitello tonatto* (veal with tuna sauce), are extraordinary. *MacIver 577, tel. 2/633–3739. Reservations suggested on weekends. AE, DC, M, V. Closed Sun.*

El Otro Sitio. This two-story Peruvian restaurant in the heart of Barrio Bellavista has an enticing wood-trimmed bar, but the food is even better than the drink. The restaurant's specialty is *ceviche,* a cold shellfish soup steeped in lemon, white wine, and seasonings. The recipe has been modified to kill cholera-causing bacteria (ingredients are briefly boiled before marinating), so you can indulge safely. Both seafood and meat dishes, especially the filet mignon, are delicious. *Antonia López de Bello 53, tel. 2/777–3059. Reservations required on weekends. AE, DC, MC, V. Closed Sun.*

★ **La Esquina al Jerez.** This noisy establishment with hams hanging from the rafters specializes in food from the *madre patria* (mother country), as many Chileans refer to Spain. The mixed shellfish hors d'oeuvres are tasty and a bit on the hot side. If you want to try *callos* (beef stomach lining, boiled and then sautéed in oil with chorizo, red pepper, garlic, and red wine), a Spanish delicacy, this is the place to do it; the filet mignon seasoned with mountain herbs similar to sage and thyme is a delight for the less daring. *Mallinkrodt 102, Barrio Bellavista, tel. 2/735–4122. Reservations required on weekends. AE, DC, M, V. Closed Sun.*

Inexpensive **Don Peyo.** For first-rate Chilean food at reasonable prices, Don
★ Peyo's is hard to beat. The hand-kneaded country bread, hot sauce, and garlic and avocado spreads in themselves warrant a visit, but the beef dishes, especially the *plateada,* a Chilean version of roast beef, are what first put this restaurant on the map. A mixed group of working- and middle-class Chileans enjoy a night out here amid the rustic decor and woven straw chairs. *Av. Grecia 448 and Lo Encalada 465, Nuñoa, tel. 2/274–0764. Reservations suggested on weekends, or arrive early, around 8 PM. DC, MC, V. Closed Sun.*

El Vegetariano. This large, economical vegetarian restaurant in the heart of downtown Santiago is the perfect place to stop for a pick-me-up, a light lunch, a rich *once* (Chile's afternoon tea), or fresh yogurt and fruit desserts. The country pancakes with a light, spicy tomato sauce and a spinach stuffing are good, especially on a cold day. Cold dishes include mixed salads with avocado, several kinds of cheese, and miniature onion quiches. *Huérfanos 827, Local 18, downtown, tel. 2/639–7063. AE, DC, MC, V. Closes 4:30 PM Sat. Closed Sun.*

★ **El Venezia.** Long before the Bellavista neighborhood became fashionable, there was the Venezia, a tacky, bare-bones sort of restaurant where TV stars and publicists rub elbows with the people of the street. The beer is icy, the waiters are *simpáticos,* and the food is abundant and well prepared. There's no fish on Monday, but *congrío frito* (fried conger eel, really a fried fish), available the rest of the week, is delicious, as are the pork ribs (*costillar de chancho*), the filet mignon, and the roast or stewed chicken. *Pío Nono 200, tel. 2/737–0900. AE, DC, MC, V.*

Mercado Central. For a delicious and reenergizing cold or hot fish soup, try one of the stands in the fish market beside Santiago's Central Market. Santiaguinos traditionally come here for a good belt of breakfast after spending the night painting the town, especially New Year's dawn. *Take Puente St. north from the Plaza de Armas, then San Pablo, 21 de Mayo until you almost reach the river.*

Lodging

In Santiago, accommodations range from five-star international hotels to comfortable, inexpensive *residenciales,* the Chilean equivalent of bed-and-breakfasts. With 19 new hotels, the city is slowly overcoming a chronic shortage of rooms, but it's still wise to reserve well in advance, especially for the peak seasons (Jan.–Feb. and July–Aug.). For details and price-category definitions, *see* Lodging in Staying in Chile, *above*.

Very Expensive **Carrera.** Recent renovations have kept Santiago's oldest hotel traditional in atmosphere yet have added up-to-date amenities, including many for businesspeople. The flavor is distinctly English, with chintz bedspreads, hunting prints, and floral upholstery on the comfortable armchairs. Try for a room on the plaza; interior rooms tend to be dark. *Teatinos 180, behind the Moneda, tel. 2/698–2011, fax 2/672–1083. 325 rooms with bath, 30 suites. Facilities: 2 restaurants, bar, health club, outdoor pool, in-room VCRs, executive floor with private bar and butler, business services, kitchenettes, meeting rooms, children's room. AE, DC, MC, V.*

Hyatt Regency. Located far from downtown in the wealthy residential area known as Las Condes, the Hyatt Regency compensates by offering its own transportation services, air that's slightly less smoggy, and first-class accommodations. The building is an architectural wonder, with rooms curving around a 24-story central shaft completely lined with windows; each room has an excellent view and many have terraces. The health club is large and its windows overlook a kidney-shape pool complete with waterfall. *Av. Kennedy 4601, Las Condes, tel. 2/218–1234, fax 2/218–2513. 310 rooms with bath, 10 suites with Jacuzzis. Facilities: 2 restaurants, tearoom, bar, health club, outdoor pool, in-room VCRs, stereo equipment, business services, baby-sitting, shopping arcade, 4-story executive suites with private dining and games areas. AE, DC, MC, V.*

★ **Plaza San Francisco Kempinski.** One of Santiago's newer offerings, this executive-oriented hotel includes a first-rate restaurant (*see* Dining, *above*). The restaurant, with its heavy wooden trim, richly colored wallpapers, and bronze lamps, has a slightly nautical feeling. Artwork is modern and sophisticated, a tribute to the owners' private collection, and there's an art gallery in the basement. The cozy rooms have large beds, custom antique-style furniture, and marble-trimmed bathrooms. *Alameda (Av. Bernardo O'Higgins) 816, tel. 2/639–3832, fax 2/639–7826. 160 rooms with bath, 20 suites. Facilities: restaurant, bar, health club, indoor pool, in-room VCRs, fax connection in room, business services. AE, DC, MC, V.*

Moderate **Acacias of Vitacura.** The rooms are modest, with thick gray
★ carpets, textured wallpaper, and printed bedcovers in quiet colors, but the owner's eclectic collection of old carriages and Oriental handicrafts gives this hotel personality, as does its extraordinary location in the midst of a lush garden and towering eucalyptus and acacia trees, some over 100 years old. The hotel is quite a distance from the city center (about 30 minutes by bus), in the wealthy shopping and residential area of Vitacura, in the northwest section of Santiago. *El Manantial 1781, tel. 2/211–8601, fax 2/229–0575. 36 rooms with bath, 3 suites. Facilities: dining area, outdoor pool, outdoor concerts in the woods. AE, DC, MC, V.*

Foresta. This seven-story hotel just across the street from Santa Lucía Hill, on the edge of Santiago's city center, feels like an elegant old home. Guest rooms have flowered wallpaper and antique furnishings, accented by bronze and marble. Rooms on the upper floors overlooking the hill are best. The building was remodeled in 1993 and includes a rooftop restaurant and bar and at street level, a popular piano bar. *Victoria Subercaseaux 353, tel. and fax 2/639–6261. 35 rooms with bath, 4 with Jacuzzis; 8 suites. Facilities: restaurant, 2 bars. AE, DC, MC, V.*

Hostal del Parque. This nine-story hotel near the Parque Forestal not far from downtown has won an excellent reputation for personalized service. Rooms are comfortable and large, and all are equipped with stove, refrigerator, kitchen sink, and hot plate. *Merced 294, tel. 2/639–2694, fax 2/639–2712. 29 rooms with bath, 13 suites, 2 luxury suites with large fireplaces. Facilities: restaurant, bar. AE, DC, MC, V.*

Inexpensive   **Apart-hotel Marqués del Forestal.** An excellent alternative for families or groups, the Marqués offers small apartments for four people for under $50. Rooms are furnished simply in pinks and browns, with sofa beds and double beds and kitchenettes. It's near the Central Market area and overlooks the Parque Forestal. *Ismael Valdés Vergara 740, tel. 2/633–3462, fax 2/639–4157. 14 apartments with shower. Facilities: small bar, telephones, kitchenettes. AE, DC, MC, V.*

Hotel Principado. Rooms at this hotel a block from Plaza Baquedano overlook a busy street but are generally not noisy; some have rounded corners and leafy views and all have kitchenettes. *Arturo Burhle 015 (off Vicuña Mackenna), tel. 2/635–3879, fax 2/222–6065. 24 rooms. Facilities: common lounge area, direct-dial telephones. AE, DC, MC, V.*

Residencial Londres. An older-style house in the picturesque Londres/París neighborhood, right across the road from the city center and just behind the San Francisco Church. Rooms are bare-bones but comfortable, and hosts are friendly and helpful to visitors. *Londres 54, tel. 2/638–2215. 25 rooms. No credit cards.*

The Arts and Nightlife

The Arts   Provided you understand Spanish, you can enjoy Chilean theater, which is among the best in Latin America. Long-respected ICTUS performs in the **Teatro la Comedia** (Merced 349, tel. 2/391–1523); **Teatro la Feria** (Crucero Exeter 0250, tel. 2/737–7371) mounts Chilean versions of English comedies; and **El Conventillo** (Bellavista 173, tel. 2/777–4164) produces a mixed offering of Latin American humor and drama. Good Chilean music is harder to find these days, but the **Teatro Municipal** (San Antonio at Agustinas, tel. 2/633–2549), Santiago's 19th-century theater, presents excellent classical concerts and ballet by national and international groups throughout its season (Mar.–Dec.).

Nightlife   After years of curfews during the military government, Santiago is slowly developing an active nightlife, with good food, music, theater, dancing, and comedy as the main activities.

There are good restaurants for late-night dining throughout most of the city, particularly in Bellavista, Providencia, and Las Condes. Several have floor shows, including **Los Adobes de Argomedo** (Argomedo 411). **La Candela** (Purísima 129) offers Chilean folk music hosted by Charo Cofré, with homemade *empanadas* and other Chilean delicacies. A block away on Purísima near Antonia López de Bello is the **Café Libro** (Book Café), always packed with young people. Dancing is best at *salsotecas,* which play music that combines the sensuous, cheerful rhythms of such Latin American performers as Rubén Blades and Juan Luís Guerra with the catchy, socially critical lyrics of salsa. Discotheques, many of which are in Bellavista around Pío Nono and Antonia López de Bello, include **La Punta** and **La Nota Falsa.** Just a block from Pío Nono on Antonia López de Bello is the Camilo Mori Square, with an imposing Elizabethan-style residence that locals call "El Castillo" (the Castle). While young couples enjoy the square, a quiet bar across the road provides refuge for more monied lovers. In Apoquindo, the discotheque **Gente** (Av. Apoquindo 4900) continues to attract large crowds, while the "dancing bar" **Nerón** (Antonia López de Bello near Pío Nono) offers an interesting mixture of music and drink. If you understand Spanish, look out for Chile's best, most intelligent humorist, **Coco Legrand,** who has his own theater (Providencia 1176, tel. 2/235–1822).

Excursion to Maipo Canyon

Santiago offers many interesting excursions, most of which can be taken by bus. The most diversified is a visit to the Cajón del Maipo, or Maipo Canyon, deep in the Andes, an outing that can include visits to interesting mountain villages whose low adobe houses line the road, a soak in a natural hot spring, and a drive through the stark but majestic landscape. As you drive along the Maipo River you'll see massive mountains of sedimentary rock, heaved up and thrown sideways, as if ready for a geology lesson. On a sunny day, colors are subtle but glowing, ranging from oranges and reds to ochers, buffs, beiges, and elusive greens and browns. At the far end of the canyon, if you reach it, you'll find yourself in an austere moonscape of blue and gray rocks, with the mountains themselves displaying shades of violet and purple. You can spend an hour, an afternoon, or several days on this excursion.

Getting There You may rent a car, hire a taxi for the day (about $50), or simply take one of the buses that travel daily from the **Parque O'Higgins** up into the canyon as far as its main town, **San José de Maipo,** or beyond. A car gives you maximum flexibility, but driving along the narrow mountain road can be demanding, especially if there's a lot of traffic.

By Car From Plaza Baquedano, turn south on Ramón Carnícer (one block east of Vicuña MacKenna) to Grecia, and left (east) on Grecia to Avenida José Alessandri, turn right and continue southward to the Rotonda Departamental, a large roundabout. There you can take Camino Las Vizcachas, following it south into the canyon as far as you choose to go.

By Bus Bus service is cheap (around $1) and frequent, with buses running about every half hour, depending on the season. Take the Santiago metro southern line to the Parque O'Higgins stop, turn left on leaving the station, and enter the park through the main gates. This area, with adobe restaurants and museums, is called the Pueblito, and it is where you catch the bus. Within half an hour you'll have started the climb through the canyon; sit on the right side of the bus for a good view of the river itself. Buses go as far as the Baños Morales, 92 kilometers (57 miles) from the Pueblito, approximately a 1 1/2-hour ride.

Exploring Maipo The narrow road winds its way up into the Andes mountain
Canyon range along the route of the Maipo River, which supplies most of Santiago's drinking water. As you drive along you'll pass

through a series of small towns, any of which is worth stopping at for a visit. Most have small cafés offering basic Chilean meals at reasonable prices. **Las Vertientes** (the Slopes) has a nice outdoor swimming pool. Farther up the canyon, near the village of **El Manzano,** is a picnic area where you can barbecue a good piece of beef (*asado*, as the Chileans call it) and spend the day enjoying the sun and fresh air. Groceries are available in any of the small towns; restaurants and cafés may prepare sandwiches or snacks for your picnic, but you're better off buying lunch supplies in Santiago.

The canyon's main town, **San José de Maipo,** an hour's journey from the Pueblito, is a nice place to stop for refreshment, stretch your legs, and generally get a sense of small-town mountain life. Five kilometers (3 miles) farther along is **San Alfonso,** a small but extraordinary village where the traditional landowning family went hippie, producing fantastic houses that look like they've been stolen from a fairy tale. One of their creations, the **Cascada de las Animas** (Waterfall of the Spirits; Orrego Luco Norte 054, 20 piso, Providencia, Santiago, tel. 2/232–7214, fax 2/232–7214) in San Alfonso, off to the right of the highway and straddling the Maipo River, has a circular outdoor swimming pool, and a jealously protected wildland park, plus lovely cabins that can be rented at reasonable prices (you must book well ahead in the busy season). The family also organizes daily and overnight trips on horseback high up into the Andes. The guides are excellent. You can have a filling lunch of hot Chilean dishes—pork, fillet, pot roast—or typical summer foods like *porotos granodos* (beans and squash) or *pastel de choclo* (corn and chicken mixture)—at the **Hostería los Ciervos** (Av. Argentina 711, San Alfonso; no tel.) and spend a satisfying afternoon strolling around the area. There are nine simple guest rooms, plus a small outdoor pool for guests.

If you really want to make a day of it, don't settle for the lesser temptations of the low-level mountain villages: Instead, pass them by and push on up the canyon, past San Alfonso and El Volcán, and take the gravel road into the mountains. The landscape becomes harsher and more majestic as green slopes give way to drier and barer mountain cliffs. Here you'll see layer on layer of sedimentary rock, packed with fossils from the time when this whole area was under the ocean. There are hot springs at **Baños Morales,** but if you're driving and have the time, take the right fork onward and upward to **Lo Valdés,** stopping for refreshment or a filling lunch or tea at the **Refugio Alemán.** You can quit here or carry on another 11 kilometers (7 miles) along the difficult road through an impressive, rocky moonscape of mauves, grays, and steely blues to the **Baños de Colina** hot springs. These huge natural bowls scooped out of the mountain edge, overflowing with hot water, are well worth the trip. Here you can slip into a bathing suit, changing in your vehicle, and choose the pool with the temperature most to your liking. Let your body float gently in the mineral-rich waters, and enjoy the view down the valley as your fellow soakers give each other medical advice, trade salt and lemons to suck on, and chat about the medicinal properties of these waters.

On your way back to Santiago, the Café Vienés in **Guayacán,** clearly visible from the highway, is a good place to stop for a strong espresso or cappuccino and delicious pastries or kuchen.

Easter Island

Getting There

The only way to reach Easter Island, which lies 3,700 kilometers (2,300 miles) west of Chile, is by plane. The airport is a few minutes southwest of the island's only town, Hanga Roa. Service is via **LanChile** (tel. 2/632–3211 in Santiago, 800/735–5526 in the United States). Round-trip fare from Santiago is about $800; if you buy a Visit Chile pass before leaving home (*see* Getting Around in Essential Information, *above*), you can include a visit to Easter Island at a more moderate price.

Exploring Easter Island

Easter Island is perhaps one of the world's most persistent mysteries, only 130 square kilometers (50 square miles) in size, with a mixed European-Chilean-Polynesian population that recalls its own history in a series of often contradictory stories. The landscape itself, formed by the action of a now-dormant volcano, is characterized by the idyllic palm-lined beaches of golden sand and low rocky mountains typical of most South Pacific islands. One small town on the southwest tip of this inverted triangle, Hanga Roa, houses the island's 2,500 permanent residents, and rough dirt roads trace the footsteps of the ancient and modern peoples who have used, and often abused, the island in their quest for their future. Huge stone statues known as *moai* are scattered all over the island, attesting to the skills of the crafts-people who carved, moved, and erected these imposing creatures, some over 21 meters (57 feet) tall. Count on spending at least 1½–2 days here (4–5 days to see the entire island without feeling rushed).

You can rent a Jeep from **Gas,** the local gas station a few doors down from Hotel Hotu Matua (Av. Pont, tel. 2/23242), from **Viajes Kia Koe** (Policarpo, tel. 2/23282), or from **Hertz** (Av. Constanera 1469, tel. 2/236–1323 in Santiago); count on spending about $80 per day for a jeep, or $60 per day for a motorcycle. You can rent boats or arrange for a skin-diving tour in the *caleta* (fishing village) near Hanga Roa, or you can rent a horse to explore the island, without guides, for less than $20 a day near the Hotu Matua Hotel (Av. Point, tel. 2/635–3275, or via operator #108, tel. 242, on the island itself).

Take the day trip to **Orongo,** a small village to the south of Hanga Roa that has been re-created by Chile's National Parks division to provide insight into the mysteries of a culture that left 150 carvings behind on cliffs. Nearby is the **Rano Kau Volcano,** a ceremonial crater a mile wide that is decorated with characteristic petroglyphs. Bring solid, comfortable walking shoes appropriate for stony roads and some climbing, along with a light rain jacket and a flashlight for exploring caves. It's also worth driving across to the northeast shore of the island for a day at Anakena Beach, where natural caves that you can explore on your own once sheltered the island's earliest residents.

Conflicting theories battle to explain how Easter Island was first settled. Anthropologist Thor Heyerdahl argued that similarities between customs in parts of Peru and Easter Island indicate that native peoples from the South American mainland first settled the island. However, the dominant theory is that the island was first occupied by a thriving Polynesian culture that at its height had a population of 15,000 and developed a sophisticated system of beliefs expressed by the island's massive stone *moai.* Archaeologists believe the island's population experienced a crisis toward the end of the 16th century, possibly due to overpopulation, and after a lengthy period of violent conflicts, a new culture developed.

In 1870 a ship raced westward and claimed the island for Chile, before France could do so, and in 1888 Easter Island formally became part of Chile. The owners of a private sheep ranch ran the island as their own, shutting inhabitants up in the main town of Hanga Roa, until 1952. Today the main activities of the town's 2,500 inhabitants, 75% of whom are of native origin, include servicing a growing tourism industry and conducting scientific excavations and studies, along with more traditional pursuits such as agriculture, fishing, and handicrafts produced in the form of wood carvings of ancient figures, necklaces, and other pieces worked in shells and coral.

In the town of **Hanga Roa** itself, it's well worth visiting the **church,** where traditional Catholic figures are rendered by island carvers with surprising results. The noon service on Sunday is usually in the island's Rapa Nui language, and the songs have a distinctly Polynesian rhythm and flavor. There's also a modest **museum** with shells, carvings, and other interesting pieces on view just outside town near the **Tahai** archaeological site, which is on the coast. A pleasant half-day walk along the dirt road to Tahai will take you through a coastal landscape dotted with buried and broken moai, past the **plaza** that once served as a ceremonial meeting place, near which religious and social leaders built their boat-shape residences, or **hare paenga** (meaning "the foundations of one who remains visible").

Valparaíso and Viña del Mar

Twin cities could hardly be more different than these two are, side by side on the Chile's Pacific coast, just over an hour and a half's drive from Santiago. Valparaíso (population 285,000) is a working port, complete with naval installations, sailors' bars, and bordellos, along with the winding, hilly streets and colorful houses that have made it a classic setting for travel posters. Viña del Mar (literally, "the Sea's Vineyard") with a population of 300,000, is an international showcase, with beautifully kept gardens, expensive hotels, stylish restaurants, and a luxury casino. There is cheap, regular bus service between the two. If you want to lie on the beach, arrange to stay overnight in Viña. It's lively, crowded, fashionable, and somewhat expensive, with plenty of nightlife in its central cafés. But if you want to watch the workings of a busy international port, check out Valparaíso; there are plenty of good walks, most of which converge upon Plaza la Victoria (Victoria Square).

Tourist Information

SERNATUR, Av. Valparaíso 507, Office 305, Viña del Mar, tel. 32/882285, fax 32/684117.

Getting There

By Car Take Route 68 westward from Santiago to Valparaíso and Viña.

By Bus There's excellent, continual bus service between Santiago and Valparaíso/Viña. Take the metro to the Universidad de Santiago station, southside exit, and check out the **Terminal Alameda** (Av. Libertador Bernardo O'Higgins 3724) or the main **Terminal Santiago** (Av. Libertador Bernardo O'Higgins 3848, tel. 2/779–1385) just a block westward for regular service.

Guided Tours

Contact **Chilean Travel Services** (Agustinas 1291, 5th floor, Office F, tel. 2/696–7820 or 2/696–7193), **Gray Line** (Agustinas 1173, tel. 2/696–0518), or **Turismo Cocha** (Agustinas 1173, tel. 2/698–3341) in Santiago, or **Trans Tourcargo** (Diego Portales 325, tel. 32/664459) in Viña del Mar.

Exploring Valparaíso and Viña del Mar

The most pleasant way to see ships loading and unloading their cargo at the port is to take an hour-long motorboat tour around the harbor from the **Muelle Prat** (Prat Dock) in Valparaíso, which costs about $2. The dock, which has permanent crafts kiosks, is between the historic buildings of the Dirección Nacional de Aduana (National Customs House) and the Estación Puerto del Ferrocarril (Port Railway Station).

Five miles west of the dock in Valparaíso is the 19th-century customs building and next to it the **Ascensor Artillería,** a cable car that will pull you uphill to the **Paseo 21 de Mayo,** a wide cliff's-edge balcony surrounded by well-tended gardens and tall, old trees, from which you can survey the port and a goodly portion of Valparaíso. Here you are in the **Cerro Playa Ancha** (Wide Beach Hill), one of Valparaíso's nicest neighborhoods. Near the top of the cable car is a large neoclassical mansion that until recently housed the Naval School and continues to belong to the navy. Avid picture takers should be careful, because much of Valparaíso Harbor is considered part of the naval base, and photography is prohibited. In this same building is the **Museo Naval y Marítimo** (Naval and Maritime Museum), which offers historical information on the port and displays of the ships and forts that once defended it. *Subida Astillera, tel. 32/281845. Admission charged. Closed Mon.*

Take the cable car back down the hill, then head down the first street on your right, Bustamante Street. Here, in Valparaíso's oldest neighborhood, you'll see the **Plaza y Iglesia de la Matriz** (Plaza and Church of la Matriz), built in 1842, which contains a 17th-century carving of Jesus on the cross donated by the king and queen of Spain.

If you'd like to see a sampling of the sort of wall murals that have made several Latin American artists famous, head down Bustamante Street to **Plaza Victoria** (Victory Square) to visit

Valparaíso's **Museo a Cielo Abierto** (Open-Air Museum). Start from the Plaza Victoria and follow along Molina Street to Aldunate Street, then right one block to Huito, toward the hill, where there's a long, long stairway and the first of 17 murals painted by Chile's most important painters. As the name suggests, the exposition takes the form of colorful murals painted on the walls that line the many stairs, walkways, and streets leading up and down Valparaíso's crowded hillsides. An easier route is to take the **Ascensor Espíritu Santo** (Holy Spirit Elevator; admission charged, open daily 7 AM–11 PM), from Calle Aldunate, near the bottom of the hill, up and then walk down through the museum.

You can have an excellent breakfast, light lunch, or delicious afternoon tea at the Vitamin Service, one of the few spots in Valparaíso that serves fresh-squeezed orange juice, along with hot espresso, just half a block from **Plaza Victoria** along Pedro Montt Street.

Viña del Mar's **Central Square,** with majestic palms and the possibility of a short tour in a horse-drawn buggy ($3–$4 for a 15-minute tour), is worth a visit. A stroll through the adjoining shopping areas will take you though glittering stores and all kinds of cafés and ice-cream parlors.

Viña has one of Chile's best botanical gardens, the **Quinta Vergara,** which includes its own palace, **Museo de Bellas Artes** (Fine Arts Museum), a fine arts school, and a large, open-air theater famous for an international music festival held every February. *Park open daily 7:30–6 and until 8 in Jan.–Feb. Fine Arts Museum: Errazuriz 563, tel. 32/680618. Admission charged. Closed Mon.*

What to See and Do with Children

Try the boat trip around Valparaíso Harbor (*see* Exploring Valparaíso and Viña del Mar, *above*). If you're traveling by car or hire a taxi for a drive up the coast, northward from Viña, you'll find interesting beaches and rocky islands where you'll see seals, cormorants, pelicans, and other marine animals. Most children can't resist the sandy beaches, although you must be very careful of the water itself. Strong currents and undertow and sudden large waves make close supervision vital.

Shopping

The **Feria Internacional de Artesanía** (International Crafts Fair) sets up in Viña's Central Square from mid-January through early February. Outdoor stalls feature weaving, leathercrafts, jewelry, paintings, ceramics, and toys. For more information, contact UNEMUS (tel. 32/233387).

Sports and the Outdoors

Golf can be played at the **Granadillas Country Club** (tel. 032/689527). Shipowners and operators at the Prat Dock in Valparaíso rent out their boats or take passengers on ocean excursions. **Empresa de San Juan** (Golfo de Corcovado 580, Canal Beagle, Viña del Mar; tel. 032/852937) and **Lobo de Mar** in the nearby town of Quinteros (Arturo Prat 2070, Quinteros, tel.

032/931040) offer boat trips; fishing for tuna, corvina, sea bass, and conger eel; skin diving; and scuba diving.

Beaches

Follow Viña's Avenida Pedro Montt until you reach a large, solar-powered clock, consisting of continually replanted flowers and two large working hands. Just across from the clock you'll find **Playa Los Marineros** (Los Marineros Beach). This is followed by a long stretch of coastline belonging to the navy (off-limits to the public) that ends at **Playa Las Salinas** (Las Salinas Beach), a sheltered area packed with sun-loving crowds in summer. Quieter seaside areas lie to the north: **Concón,** 8 kilometers (5 miles) up the coast; **Quintero,** 18 kilometers (11 miles); **Maitencillo,** 65 kilometers (40 miles); and **Papudo,** 88 kilometers (55 miles).

Pollution is a problem around Viña and up the coast, in addition to strong currents, undertow, and sudden, large waves. A red flag indicates you should definitely not bathe at a specific beach, although you'll probably see people in the water anyway.

Dining

For price-category definitions, see Dining in Staying in Chile, *above.*

★ **Cap Ducal.** This ship-shaped restaurant rises out of the sea and affords excellent views of the shore and out toward the horizon. The creative kitchen specializes in European-style cooking, along with its own inventions, including a popular eel stew and grilled fish in a spicy herb sauce. *Av. Marina 51, Viña del Mar, tel. 32/626655. Reservations recommended on weekends. AE, MC, V. Expensive.*

Bar Inglés. The "English Bar" boasts the longest bar in Chile and incorporates Dutch lamps and American oak furnishings as part of its effort to imitate an English country pub. The specialty is international cooking, particularly hot and cold soups, shellfish baked with cheese or sautéed with garlic or dipped in mayonnaise (Tues.–Sat. only), and beef, along with imaginative vegetable dishes such as an artichoke, mushroom, and asparagus combination. *Cochrane 851, Valparaíso, tel. 32/214625. Reservations recommended, particularly for lunch. No credit cards. Closed Sun. and holidays. Moderate.*

★ **Bote Salvavidas.** This restaurant at the end of Prat Dock in Valparaíso offers the best view of the harbor and specializes in seafood. Its Greek-style fish dishes, such as tuna wrapped around fresh sage then wrapped in a thin slice of ham and sautéed, are popular specialties, served in a simple dining room filled with plants. *Muelle Prat, Valparaíso, tel. 32/251477. Reservations recommended on weekends. AE. Moderate.*

Mastrantonio. This moderately priced Italian restaurant near the casino in Viña has a reputation for great food. It specializes in fish and pasta dishes—try the lasagna and canellone romagni, stuffed with chicken, almonds, asparagus, and ham—beef, and fish. It's decorated in Italy's national colors (red, white, and green). *San Martín 410, Viña del Mar, tel. 32/977010. Reservations required on weekends. AE, D, MC, V. Moderate.*

Lodging

For price-category definitions, *see* Lodging in Essential Information, *above*.

Hotel Miramar. This 40-year-old fixture is Viña's only five-star hotel. It's right on the sea's edge, with a gorgeous terrace restaurant from which you can devour your food and the horizon to your heart's content—a view that's also available from most of the public rooms and some guest rooms. The rooms are decorated in pastels and floral patterns and are hung with landscape paintings, some by Chilean artists. *Av. Marina, Caleta Abarca, tel. 32/626677, in Santiago 2/671–3165. 120 rooms with bath, 12 suites. Facilities: 2 restaurants, 2 bars, outdoor pool, gym, 2 saunas. AE, DC, MC, V. Expensive.*
Apart Hotel Sahara. Each room in this comfortable small hotel has thick, dark carpeting and cream-colored walls and opens onto its own small, semiprivate garden. *Alberto Blest Gana 397, Viña del Mar, tel. 32/685161. 14 rooms, all with bath. No credit cards. Moderate.*

The Arts and Nightlife

Viña's artistic activities and nightlife vary considerably according to the season, with the most glittering attractions concentrated in the summer months, January and February. Check the newspapers (including Santiago's) for listings.

The **Casino** (Av. San Martín 199, Viñā del Mar tel. 32/689200) has a restaurant, dancing, a cabaret, and, of course, games (roulette, blackjack). It's open nightly until the wee hours; formal dress is required in the game rooms.

The Lake District

If you've never flirted with a volcano, Chile's Lake District is the place to start. As you travel along the roads lined with fields of grazing cattle herds or through dense forests of eucalyptus, pine, and the more exotic of Chile's native species, the broad, snowcapped shoulders of volcanoes emerge, towering over the landscape, then mysteriously disappear, only to materialize again, peeping through trees or rising massively over lake-lined valleys. The sometimes difficult journey along narrow mountain roads that wind through breathtaking passes is almost inevitably rewarded by a clear mountain lake, vibrant and blue, and often there are hot springs to soak out stiff muscles and renew tired travelers. Your best route is to start in the south; the weather, the scenery, and the variety improve as you move north from Puerto Montt to Temuco, a distance of about 340 kilometers (212 miles).

Getting There

By Plane LanChile and Ladeco have flights to the main cities within the Lake District, particularly **Puerto Montt** (Lan Chile, tel. 065/253141; Ladeco, tel. 065/252090), **Valdivia** (Lan Chile, tel. 063/213042; Ladeco, tel. 063/213392), and **Temuco** (Lan Chile, tel. 045/211339; Ladeco, tel. 045/214325).

The Lake District

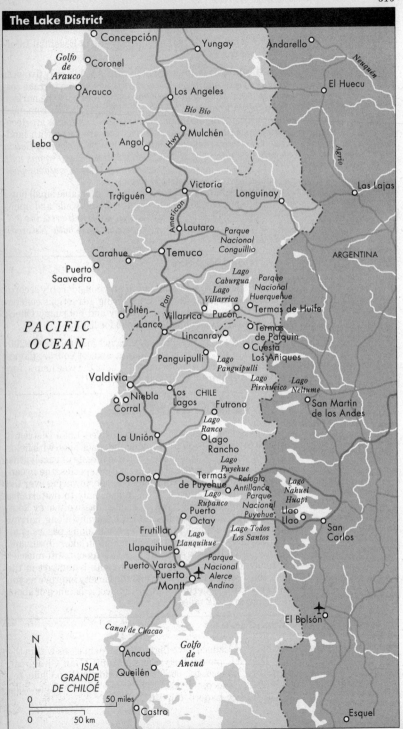

Concepción
Yungay
Andarello
Golfo de Arauco
Coronel
El Huecu
Arauco
Los Angeles
Bío Bío
Neuquén
Leba
Angol
Mulchén
Hwy
Victoria
Longuinay
Las Lajas
Troiguén
American
Lautaro
Parque Nacional Conguillio
ARGENTINA
Carahue
Temuco
Puerto Saavedra
Lago Caburgua
Parque Nacional Huerquehue
Pan
Lago Villarrica
Termas de Huife
Toltén
Villarrica
Pucón
Lanco
Lincanray
Termas de Palguín
Panguipulli
Cuesta Los Añiques
Lago Panguipulli
Valdivia
Lago Pirehueico
Lago Neltume
Niebla
Los Lagos
CHILE
San Martín de los Andes
Corral
Futrono
La Unión
Lago Ranco
Lago Rancho
PACIFIC OCEAN
Lago Puyehue
Osorno
Termas de Puyehue
Refugio Antillanca
Lago Nahuel Huapi
Lago Rupanco
Parque Nacional Puyehue
Llao Llao
Puerto Octay
San Carlos
Frutillar
Lago Todos Los Santos
Llanquihue
Lago Llanquihue
Puerto Varas
Parque Nacional Alerce Andino
Puerto Montt
El Bolsón
Canal de Chacao
N
Golfo de Ancud
Ancud
Queilén
ISLA GRANDE DE CHILOÉ
0   50 miles
0   50 km
Castro
Esquel

By Car You will see a lot more of the region if you have the use of a vehicle, so it's well worth renting a car, at least for part of your visit. To avoid traveling along the Pan-American Highway, however, choose an alternative form of traveling south (*see* Getting Around, *above*), then rent a vehicle in one of the major cities for exploring the entire region. There's far less traffic, even on the Pan-American Highway itself, once you're this far south, and the driving is much easier, at least in terms of other drivers. Since many of the mountain roads you must follow are gravel at best, a four-wheel-drive vehicle is ideal, if you feel comfortable driving one; if not, most new cars will serve just as well, at least on the main routes. Rentals are available through **Automóvil Club** (Puerto Montt, tel. 065/254776; Temuco, tel. 045/213949), **Autovald** (Puerto Montt, tel. 065/256355), **Avis** (Temuco, tel. 045/211515), **First** (Temuco, tel. 045/233890; Valdivia, tel. 063/215973), **Hertz** (Temuco, tel. 045/235385; Valdivia, tel. 063/218316), and **Turismo Safari Tehuel'che** (Puerto Montt, tel. 065/250412), as well as a few local travel agencies; several of the latter include a return service.

By Train Chile's **State Railway Company** (Santiago, tel. 2/689–5401, 2/632–2802, or 2/228–2983; Temuco, tel. 045/233522; Valdivia, tel. 063/214978; Puerto Montt, 065/254908) has frequent service southward from Santiago, usually several times a day, particularly in the peak period during the summer. The journey to Temuco, at the northern limit of the Lake District, takes about 11½ hours; to Puerto Montt, at the southernmost end of the line, is a 20-hour trip. If you prefer to rent a vehicle in Santiago, you can use the auto-train service from there to Temuco or Puerto Montt, but it's probably cheaper to rent a car in Temuco or Puerto Montt.

By Bus There are two levels of service within the region: regular intercity buses provided by companies based primarily in Santiago and local buses that bump between Lake District cities and the small towns that adjoin them; both services are reasonably priced. Both Puerto Montt and Valdivia have their own bus terminals, where most bus companies' offices are concentrated. Puerto Montt's is on Avenida Diego Portales (no phone); each bus line has its own phone number, listed in the local phone book's yellow pages. **Cruz del Sur** (tel. 065/254731 in Puerto Montt, 2/696–9324 in Santiago) is one of the largest and most popular. Other companies operating from Santiago include **Tur Bus** (tel. 2/776–3690), **Buses Pullman del Sur** (tel. 2/696–9797), and **Varmontt** (tel. 2/232–1116). Valdivia's bus terminal is on Anfión Muñoz 360 (tel. 063/212212). In Temuco, there's no central bus terminal, but several are close together along Vicuña MacKenna (**Cruz del Sur,** Vicuña MacKenna 671, tel. 045/210701; **Buses JAC,** Vicuña MacKenna 798, tel. 045/210313).

Osorno, Puerto Montt, and Puerto Octay

Tourist Information Contact **SERNATUR** in Puerto Montt (Edificio Intendencia, 2nd floor, tel. 065/254580).

Exploring the Area Unlike in Chile's fertile Central Valley region between Santiago and Temuco, weather can become a major factor in your seeing and enjoying Puerto Montt and the surrounding area. The summer (December–early March) offers the most likelihood of sunshine, although if you're prepared for rain, it probably won't bother you.

Puerto Montt For most of Chile's history, Puerto Montt has been the end of the line, whether you were traveling by railway, dirt road, or highway. Today the Austral Highway carries on southward, but for most intents and purposes, Puerto Montt remains the last significant outpost of civilization, a small provincial city that is the hub of local fishing, textile, and tourist activity.

Start with a drive around Puerto Montt, a local supply center full of low clapboard and wooden houses perched on hills above the ocean, with four- to six-story office buildings and stores, most built earlier this century. If it's a warm, sunny day, head east along the shoreline to **Pelluco** or one of the other beaches (*see* Beaches, *below*). If you're more interested in getting to know the area generally, drive along the shoreline through the city for a good view of the surrounding hillsides and the relatively protected stretch of ocean where the city is located. Driving from east to west, you'll pass the yacht club and the main docking area.

The **Museo Juan Pablo II** (Juan Pablo II Regional Museum), just east of the bus terminal, has a good collection of crafts and relics from one of Chile's strongest regional cultures, that of the archipelago of Chiloé. Historical photos give a sense of the area's slow and often difficult growth and the impact of the 1960 earthquake, which virtually destroyed the port. *On the Costandera (Coast Road) by the bus terminal, no phone. Admission charged.*

The **Caleta Angelmó** (Angelmó Fishing Cove), along the Coast Road, provides a good view of Tenglo Island, which protects a busy port serving small fishing boats, large ferries, and cruisers carrying travelers and cargo southward through the straits and fjords that form much of Chile's shoreline. On weekdays you'll notice the water traffic from many of the outlying islands—small launches and fishing boats that arrive early in the morning and leave in the afternoon. The **market** in Angelmó offers one of the most varied selections of seafood in all of Chile (*see* Dining, *below*).

An excellent selection of handicrafts sold at the best prices in Chile can be found nearby at the **Feria Artesanal** (Crafts Fair of Angelmó). Baskets, Chilote ponchos, mythical Chilote figures woven from different kinds of grasses and straws, and warm sweaters of raw, hand-spun, and hand-dyed wool are all offered. Most of the people selling here are intermediaries, and many of the styles have been adapted to buyers' tastes, but if you look carefully you'll also see the less commercial, more authentic offerings. Dickering over prices is expected. *On the Coast Road near the Angelmó Fishing Cove.*

Heading north from Puerto Montt, **Puerto Varas,** on Lake Llanquihue, with a spectacular view of the Osorno and Calbuco volcanoes, is worth a stay of several days, or at least a day trip. **Puerto Octay,** beyond Puerto Varas, offers a comfortable hotel with reasonably priced cabins, a restaurant, and a full view of the Osorno Volcano. The building is said to be the first summer home erected in southern Chile, in the '30s or '40s; windows line the restaurant's walls and you can dine on salmon fished fresh from the lake.

What to See and Do with Children You can arrange a boat ride through the Port Authority in Angelmó or by talking directly with the owner or captain of one of the boats. **Montonave Maité,** based in Calbuco (Av. los Héroes, tel. 0659/588; closed Apr.–Aug.), offers excursions along the channel around Angelmó (two hours) or all the way to the small port and fishing village of Calbuco (three hours). You can spend the day there, then return by the same boat or take a bus back along the main road to Puerto Montt for a different view.

Sports and the Outdoors
Fishing Trout (brown, rainbow, steelhead, and sea), salmon (ketta, coho, chinook, salar, sakura, and king), perch, and smelt are among the popular sportfish in Chile; many areas within the Lake District were first developed as fishing resorts. However, the restocking programs were suspended and good fishing is now harder to find. In order to fish the rivers and lakes of Chile, you must get a permit from the National Fisheries Service, known as **SERNAP** (tel. 800/320032). The permit is personal and valid throughout Chile; if you're fishing on private property and the landowner is nearby, be sure to get his or her permission. SERNAP is a good source of information on what's biting and where; also check with local tourist offices. **SERNATUR** publishes a brochure in English called "Lakes and Fishing," which provides location-specific details of the fishing rules, creel limits, and the like. For information on fishing tours, *see* Chapter 2, Adventure Travel.

Hiking and Backpacking Southern Chile has several of the country's most beautiful national parks, including **Conguillío,** near Melipeuco, and **Villarrica,** near the town of Villarrica, and **Huerquehue,** near Pucón. All provide sites for camping, as well as well-marked hiking trails of differing degrees of difficulty. All provide necessary information at their ranger stations, but not all have telephones. Contact the national forestry service, **CONAF** (tel. 45/236312 or 45/44126), which administers the parks, or **SERNATUR** in Santiago (tel. 2/236–1417) or in the town nearest the park.

Beaches and Water Sports The entire Lake District is full of beaches offering every kind of water sport and comfort imaginable, except perhaps solitude. **Licanray** and **Lake Villarrica** offer the most in the way of waterskiing, motorboat rental, and more sophisticated water sports. **Lake Tinquilco** in Huerquehue National Park is more isolated and quieter. You can rent a rowboat and tow a fishing line through the depths. The beaches along **Lake Panguipulli** are clean and comfortable. There is some current concern about possible pollution of Lake Villarrica, but nearby **Lake Caburgua** remains crystalline and is slightly warmer for swimming, thanks to volcanic activity in the surrounding region.

For ocean beaches, Puerto Montt and the coast west of Valdivia represent the best choices. Puerto Montt's main beach is 3 kilometers (2 miles) east of town along the shoreline, in the village of **Pelluco,** which offers several restaurants specializing in seafood and a scenic lookout point. If your idea of a good beach is something a little more peaceful and solitary, head west past Angelmó on the road to Chinquihue, and choose from beaches at camping sites at El Ciervo (tel. 65/255271), 1 kilometer (1/2 mile) west of Puerto Montt; Paredes (tel. 65/258394), 6 kilometers (3 1/2 miles) west; and Chinquihue (no phone), 10 kilometers

(6 miles) west. Be careful: Many beaches have been polluted in recent years from developing industry in the region.

Dining For price ranges, see Dining in Staying in Chile, *above.*

★ **Café Central.** This old-style café in the heart of Puerto Montt has been remodeled but retains the spirit of the 1920s and 1930s. It's a good place for a filling afternoon tea, with its menu of creamy coffees, ice cream, sandwiches, and pastries. *Rancagua 117, Puerto Montt, tel. 065/254721. No credit cards. Moderate.*

Angelmó Market. A wide selection of small and medium-size kitchens offer *mariscal* (raw shellfish soup) and *caldillo* (hot soup), as well as *machas* (razor clams), *ostiones* (scallops), and *almejas* (clams) *à la parmesana.* There are tables and counters for each kitchen at this enclosed market. *At Angelmó Fishing Cove, about 7 km (4.3 mi) west of Puerto Montt along the Coastal Road. No credit cards. Inexpensive–Moderate.*

Cafe Restaurant Vicorella. This two-story café provides a warm, comfortable refuge and an inexpensive hot meal when the weather proves unfriendly. You can order a steak and mashed potatoes, or try one of the daily specials. *Av. Antonio Varas 515, Puerto Montt, tel. 065/253759. No credit cards. Closed Sun. Inexpensive–Moderate.*

Lodging For price ranges, *see* Lodging in Staying in Chile, *above.*

Viento Sur. One of Puerto Montt's newer establishments, Viento Sur sits on its hill like a castle, giving a majestic view of the city and the sea. Rooms are comfortably furnished with generous use of native Chilean woods. *Ejército 200, Puerto Montt, tel. 065/258700, fax 065/258700. 27 rooms, 21 with bath, 6 with shower; 2 suites with Jacuzzis. Facilities: Universal gym, saunas. AE, MC, V. Moderate–Expensive.*

Hotel O'Grimm. This three-year-old, four-story hotel in the center of Puerto Montt offers rooms in pastel grays, roses, greens, and golds. *Guillermo Gallardo 211, Puerto Montt, tel. 065/252845, fax 065/258600. Facilities: 27 rooms, all with bath; 1 suite. AE, DC, MC, V. Moderate.*

Hotel Puerto Montt. This hotel, formerly called Residencial los Chilcos, is known for its attentive service and comfortable family atmosphere. Guest rooms are decorated in cheerful yellows and creams. *St. Teresa 665, Puerto Montt, tel. 065/257410. 15 rooms, 1 with bath, 14 with showers. No credit cards. Moderate.*

Don Luis Gran Hotel. The rooms are comfortable, clean, and modern, and there's a small salon for breakfast, which is included in the rate. *Urmeneta and Quillota, Puerto Montt, tel. 065/259001. 60 rooms, 12 with bath, 48 with showers. AE, DC, MC, V. Inexpensive.*

Spas The **Termas de Puyehue** hot springs are part of a resort center in Puyehue National Park that offers skiing, indoor thermal baths, meeting facilities, horseback riding, and sportfishing. *Termas de Puyehue Hotel, on Lake Puyehue, tel. 064/232157 or 2/231–3417 in Santiago.*

Campgrounds Campgrounds around Puerto Montt all charge around $10 per vehicle per night, but offer various comfort levels and views. **Chinquihue** (on the Coast Road, 7 km, or 4 mi, west of Angelmó Fishing Cove, tel. 065/255498) has a restaurant, bathrooms, showers, and attractive views of the beach. **El Ciervo** (on the Coast Road, 1 km, or 1/2 mi, west of Angelmó, tel. 65/255271) offers 20 sites with electrical hookup, general lighting, hot showers, and boat rental. **Los Alamos** (on the Coast Road, 11 km, or 6 mi, west of Angelmó, tel. 065/254067) has fine views of the Reloncaví Strait and Tenglo Island and offers electricity, roofed sites, general lighting, water, bathrooms, hot showers, a dock and launching area, a play area and sports field, and boat rentals. **Paredes** (on the Coast Road, 6 km, or 3½ mi, west of Angelmó, tel. 65/258394) is short on shade but has a pretty beach, hot showers, a soccer field, and playground.

RVs are virtually nonexistent in Chile. Camping equipment is available from major department stores, but it's not cheap; you're better off bringing your own. For renting camping equipment, contact **Aire Libre** (tel. 2/233–3100) and **Industrias Jesus Yarur y Hijo** (tel. 2/672–3696) in Santiago.

The Arts and Nightlife The town of Frutillar, 25 kilometers (15 miles) south of Puerto Octay, hosts the **Semanas Musicales de Frutillar** (tel. 2/222-5116), a series of classical concerts in an idyllic outdoor setting, each January and February.

A small **casino** in the Gran Hotel de Puerto Varas, open year-round, offers late-night bingo games popular with locals and tourists. *Klenner 351, Puerto Varas, tel. 065/232282. Closed Mon.*

The Valdivia–Seven Lakes Area

Tourist Information SERNATUR (Prat 555, Valdivia, tel. 063/213596).

Exploring the Area Valdivia is one of Chile's oldest and most beautiful cities, with a style combining the architecture of wooden houses covered with shakes and Germanic style brought by settlers in the late 1800s. It's also an excellent base for day trips throughout the area or a good starting point for a journey northeast into the Andes, the longest mountain range in South America, and the Seven Lakes Area, a region full of roses, volcanoes, and natural hot springs in rural and wild settings. The city's character has been profoundly influenced by the well-to-do German settlers who colonized the area. Located between two rivers and near the coast, it offers fine evening walks along the waterfront and restaurants that serve fresh fish and seafood and tasty küchen. The region has many cattle ranches and farms, and native communities make a hardscrabble subsistence on the less fertile grounds.

For a historic overview of the region, start with a visit to the **Museo Histórico de Valdivia,** on the campus of the Austral University. The museum's valuable collection focuses on the German immigrants and the city's colonial period, during which it was settled by the Spanish, burned by the native Mapuche people, and invaded by Dutch corsairs. *Isla Teja, tel. 063/212872. Admission charged. Closed Mon. in winter.*

The **Botanic Gardens,** also on the university campus, is a fine place to walk whatever the weather, although it's particularly enjoyable in spring and summer. *Isla Teja, tel. 063/216964. Admission free.*

The **Seven Lakes** region north of the city in the southern Andes is one of the loveliest, least spoiled areas of the Lake District. Towering volcanoes shoot off wisps of vapor during the day and glow orange through the clear nights. The ideal way to travel is by car, spending the night in a local hotel or residential or camping out. Wherever you sleep, step out at night to enjoy the southern sky, full of stars and constellations unfamiliar to those who live north of the equator.

Panguipulli, a small town that sits comfortably on the shore of Lake Panguipulli, is a pleasant place to stop for lunch or a picnic and swim on the beach. In spring and summer, the roads, houses, public squares, and private gardens seem to stagger under a display of roses of all sizes, scents, and colors.

The resort town of **Licanray** (lee-can-rye), on Lake Calafquén, has modern hotels and hostels, supermarkets, dance halls, restaurants, and some of the best beaches among the southern lakes. You can rent rowboats and sailboats along the shore. From Licanray you can return to Valdivia or carry on northward to the Temuco–Villarrica–Pucón area (*see below*).

What to See and Do with Children Several companies in Valdivia offer boat rides along the rivers, among them **Lancha Ainlebu** (tel. 063/215889), **Motonave Calle Calle** (tel. 063/212464), and **Motonave Neptuno** (tel. 063/215889). Check the boat for life jackets and an inflatable raft; there have been some serious boating accidents. Most of the companies are located on Avenida Prat along the Calle Calle River.

Sports and the Outdoors *See* Sports and the Outdoors in Osorno–Puerto Montt–Puerto Octay, *above.*

Beaches The ocean beaches, 43 kilometers (27 miles) from Valdivia, make a good day trip from the city. The road is paved as far as **Niebla**; from there drive along ocean cliffs toward **Los Molinos** beach or **San Ignacio** beach or past the villages of Loncollén and Calfuco to the village and beach of **Curiñanco.**

Dining For price ranges, *see* Dining in Staying in Chile, *above.*

★ **Camino de Luna Restaurant.** This unusual restaurant floats in the river, near the Pedro de Valdivia bridge in Valdivia. It specializes in beef and seafood; the *congrio calle calle* (a fishlike conger eel served with a cheese-and-tomato sauce) is particularly good. Most tables are by the windows and offer views of the river, Teja Island, and Valdivia. *Costanera s/n (no number), Valdivia, tel. 063/213788. Reservations recommended Jan.–Feb. AE, DC, MC, V. Expensive.*

Castillo de Alba. This large, comfortable restaurant in the Hotel Villa de Río offers a fine view of the Calle Calle River. Specialties include venison marinated in wine with a ham and mushroom sauce and duck in a sauce made with local berries. *Av. España 1025, Valdivia, tel. 063/216292. AE, DC, MC, V. Expensive.*

★ **Café Haussmann.** Valdivia was the center of German and Swiss immigration at the turn of the century, and this is one place to enjoy the fruits of that exchange: excellent *crudos* (steak tartare) and German-style sandwiches, with delicious kuchen for dessert. *Libertador B. O'Higgins 394, Valdivia, tel. 063/213878. No credit cards. Moderate.*

Centro Español. For Spanish cooking, this is the best place in Valdivia. Try the paella, a filling dish that blends chicken, pork, shellfish, and saffron rice. *Camilo Henríquez 436, Valdivia, tel. 063/213540. Reservations recommended on weekends. AE, DC, MC, V. Closed weekends Apr.–Oct. Moderate.*

Café Paula. This is part of a chain that is famous for ice cream and pastries, but in Valdivia the café also offers sandwiches and

So, you're getting away from it all.

Just make sure you can get back.

AT&T Access Numbers
Dial the number of the country you're in to reach AT&T.

ANGUILLA	1-800-872-2881	**COLOMBIA**	**980-11-0010**	JAMAICA††	0-800-872-2881
ANTIGUA (Public Card Phones)	#1	*COSTA RICA	114	MEXICO◇◇◇	95-800-462-4240
ARGENTINA◆	001-800-200-1111	**CURACAO**	**001-800-872-2881**	MONTSERRAT†	1-800-872-2881
BAHAMAS	**1-800-872-2881**	DOMINICA	1-800-872-2881	**NICARAGUA**	**174**
BELIZE◆	555	DOMINICAN REP.††	1-800-872-2881	PANAMA◆	109
BERMUDA†	1-800-872-2881	ECUADOR†	119	PARAGUAY†	0081-800
*BOLIVIA	0-800-1111	*EL SALVADOR	190	PERU†	191
BONAIRE	**001-800-872-2881**	GRENADA†	872	ST. KITTS/NEVIS	1-800-872-2881
BRAZIL	**000-8010**	*GUATEMALA	190	**ST. MAARTEN**	**001-800-872-2881**
BRITISH VIRGIN IS.	1-800-872-2881	***GUYANA††**	**165**	**SURINAME**	**156**
CAYMAN ISLANDS	1-800-872-2881	HAITI†	001-800-972-2883	URUGUAY	00-0410
CHILE	**00◇-0312**	HONDURAS†	123	*VENEZUELA†	80-011-120

Countries in bold face permit country-to-country calling in addition to calls to the U.S. *Public phones require deposit of coin or phone card. †May not be available from every phone. ††Collect calling only. ◆ Not available from public phones. ◇ Await second dial tone. ◇◇◇ When calling from public phones, use phones marked "Ladatel." ©1993 AT&T.

Here's a travel tip that will make it easy to call back to the States. Dial the access number for the country you're visiting and connect right to AT&T **USADirect®** Service. It's the quick way to get English-speaking operators and can minimize hotel surcharges.

If all the countries you're visiting aren't listed above, call **1 800 241-5555** before you leave for a free wallet card with all AT&T access numbers. International calling made easy—it's all part of **The i Plan.℠**

THE i PLAN™

AT&T

All The Best Trips Start with Fodor's

Fodor's Affordables
Titles in the series: Caribbean, Europe, Florida, France, Germany, Great Britain, Italy, London, Paris.

"Travelers with champagne tastes and beer budgets will welcome this series from Fodor's." — *Hartford Courant*

"These books succeed admirably; easy to follow and use, full of cost-related information, practical advice, and recommendations...maps are clear and easy to use." — *Travel Books Worldwide*

The Berkeley Guides
Titles in the series: California, Central America, Eastern Europe, France, Germany, Great Britain & Ireland, Mexico, The Pacific Northwest, San Francisco.

The best choice for budget travelers, from the Associated Students at the University of California at Berkeley.

"Berkeley's scribes put the funk back in travel." — *Time*

"Hip, blunt and lively." — *Atlanta Journal Constitution*

"Fresh, funny and funky as well as useful." — *The Boston Globe*

Fodor's Bed & Breakfast and Country Inn Guides
Titles in the series: California, Canada, England & Wales, Mid-Atlantic, New England, The Pacific Northwest, The South, The Upper Great Lakes Region, The West Coast.

"In addition to information on each establishment, the books add notes on things to see and do in the vicinity. That alone propels these books to the top of the heap."— *San Diego Union-Tribune*

Exploring Guides
Titles in the series: Australia, California, Caribbean, Florida, France, Germany, Great Britain, Ireland, Italy, London, New York City, Paris, Rome, Singapore & Malaysia, Spain, Thailand.

"Authoritatively written and superbly presented, and makes worthy reading before, during or after a trip. " — *The Philadelphia Inquirer*

"A handsome new series of guides, complete with lots of color photos, geared to the independent traveler." — *The Boston Globe*

Visit your local bookstore or call 1-800-533-6478 24 hours a day.

Fodor's The name that means smart travel.

full meals. *Vicente Pérez 633, Valdivia, tel. 063/212328. DC, MC, V. Inexpensive.*

Lodging For price ranges, *see* Lodging in Staying in Chile, *above.*

★ **Hotel Pedro de Valdivia.** This hotel, a four-star-rated property with SERNATUR, is large, old, and elegant, with a pleasant view of the green gardens of Valdivia. *Carampagne 190, Valdivia, tel. 063/212931; in Santiago, 2/695–1151. 77 rooms with bath. Facilities: restaurant, bar, outdoor pool, meeting rooms, access to golf and tennis clubs. AE, DC, MC, V. Expensive.*

Hotel Isla Teja. This hotel on Teja Island (in the middle of Valdivia between three rivers), very near Austral University and its famous botanical gardens, has the air of a university residence. Rooms are comfortable and modern. *Las Encinas 220, Valdivia, tel. 063/215014. 96 rooms, 32 with bath. Facilities: restaurant. AE, DC, MC, V. Moderate.*

Hotel Termas de Liquiñe. The hot springs are the main attraction, but you can also rent a cabin for the night. *Casilla 202, Liquiñe, tel.: ask for operator's assistance, or ask for help at your hotel or local tourist office. 13 cabins, all with spring-fed thermal bath. No credit cards. Moderate.*

Campgrounds Most of the camping around Valdivia is located along the rivers and is relatively expensive. **Isla Teja** (Los Cipreses, Valdivia, tel. 063/213584) on Teja Island, with an attractive view of the river, has campsites with electricity and hot showers. **La Playa** (3 km, or 2 mi, from Licanray on the road to Coñaripe, no tel.) offers grassy sites with cold showers near the Lake District's main resort and has an attractive, quiet beach.

Temuco, Villarrica, and Pucón

Tourist Information SERNATUR (Bulnes 586, Temuco, tel. 045/211969).

Exploring the Area Both Pucón and Villarrica are small, rural supply centers most of the year, but during the summer holiday and winter skiing seasons they become trendy resorts crowded with wealthy, fashionable Chileans who come to enjoy their luxurious vacation homes, stroll along the main strips, and flock to the major night spots.

Villarrica National Park, between Villarrica and Pucón, offers skiing, good hiking, and hot springs. **Huerquehue National Park** is accessible only during the summer unless you're an expert driver with a four-wheel-drive vehicle. However, it's well worth a visit for the two-hour hike from the ranger station near the entrance up into the high Andes through groves of araucaria pine to three startling lagoons with panoramic views of the whole area, including the distant Villarrica volcano. Contact SERNATUR in Temuco (*see above*), CONAF (tel. 45/236312 or 45/441261), or the rangers in the parks themselves for trail information.

Temuco, about 200 kilometers (124 miles) northwest of Villarrica, is home to a large population of Mapuche, one of Latin America's most long-lived groups of native people. The **Museo Araucano** (Araucanian Museum) covers some aspects of Mapuche history along with a general history of the area. Although much official rhetoric tries to reduce the colonization of this area to a process called the "Pacification of the Araucania," which took place in the 1880s, in reality the Mapuche successfully fought off the Spanish and defended a huge tract of territory for the better part of three centuries before finally facing defeat in the shape of the Chilean army, fresh from war with Peru and Bolivia. A smaller museum over the library in Villarrica has a number of fascinating relics on display, but with little explanation. *Av. Alemania 084, tel. 045/212208. Admission charged. Closed Mon. in winter.*

Shopping Handicrafts are the main offering of this region, but you have to shop carefully to avoid overpriced, cheaply made souvenirs. The best traditional work is to be found in the baskets, ponchos, and woven blankets created by the Mapuche artisans, who sell on the main streets of Pucón and Villarrica, in seasonal (usually summer) crafts fairs, and outside the **main market** (Manuel Rodríguez 960, tel. 045/210964) in Temuco.

Sports and the Outdoors Pucón is the major departure point for adventure sports in the region, and there's plenty to choose from: rafting down rivers, skiing, hiking up to the volcano's incandescent mouth, biking.

Biking Dozens of shops along the main road in Pucón offer mountain bike rentals during the summer.

Hiking and Backpacking Both Huerquehue and Villarrica parks have well-marked hiking trails that zigzag past open fields and massive Chilean oak trees, with views of lakes and volcanoes occasionally appearing as you walk uphill. Try the visitor centers in the parks or SERNATUR in Temuco (*see* Tourist Information, *above*) or CONAF (tel. 45/236312 or 45/441261) for more information.

Rafting Pucón is the center for rafting expeditions in the Lake District. **Altué Expediciones** has a Santiago office (Encomenderos 83, tel. 2/232–1103). Other small companies offer similar services during the summer season in Pucón. They usually set up shop along the main street, complete with photographic displays and other information on prices and services.

Ski Areas The popular Villarrica–Pucón skiing area is in Villarrica National Park, in the lap of the Villarrica volcano. Villarrica is one of the best-equipped ski areas in southern Chile, with 15 runs, three rope tows, and three double-chair tows.

Dining Establishments come and go frequently in this region, and many close up after the peak summer and winter seasons. A stroll through the towns should reveal other dining choices. For price ranges, *see* Dining in Staying in Chile, *above*.

★ **La Estancia.** This restaurant offers good southern beef in the form of steaks, roasts, and barbecues in a traditional country atmosphere. Cured hams hang from the ceiling, and the walls are decorated with reindeer heads. *Rudecindo Ortega 02340-A Interior, tel. 045/220287. Reservations recommended on weekends. MC, V. Closed Sun. dinner. Expensive.*

Café 2001. For a thick, filling sandwich and an espresso or cappuccino made from freshly ground beans, topped off with a freshly baked kuchen, this is the place to stop in Villarrica. Pull up around a table up front, or slip into one of the quieter booths by the fireplace in the back. The sandwich known as the "Lomito Completo," with a slice of pork, avocado, sauerkraut, tomato, and mayonnaise, is one of the best in the south. *Camilio Henríquez 379, Villarrica, tel. 045/441241. MC, V. Moderate.*

Grill de la Piscina Municipal. During the summer, this spot at the municipal swimming pool is an excellent place to stop for lunch, especially if you're traveling with children. You can savor a good meal and the pleasant view while they enjoy the water. *Municipal Pool, Av. Estadio 01080, Temuco, tel. 045/240649. No credit cards. Closed Apr.–Nov. 14. Moderate.*

Club Alemán. Temuco's German club is open to the public year-round. The spacious restaurant overlooks a lush Valdivian garden; the green walls feature murals of German landscapes and folk figures. In the summer there are tables outside. Specialties include roast pork, lemon-marinated *tártaros* (minced beef on toast), goulash, and meatballs. *Senador Estzbañez 772, Temuco, tel. 045/240034. No reservations. No credit cards. Closed New Year's Day. Inexpensive.*

Temuco Market. In the central market around the produce stalls are small stands and kitchens offering such typical Chilean meals as gazuelas (meat or poultry soups), fried fish, winter fish soup, and other seasonal fare such as empanadas and pastel de choclo. *Manuel Rodríguez 960, Temuco, tel. 045/210964. Inexpensive.*

Lodging   For price ranges, *see* Lodging in Staying in Chile, *above.*

Gran Hotel Pucón. Burned down and rebuilt a few years ago, this imposing building sprawls along one end of the Lake Villarrica, providing access to the beach and a good view of the lake. *Clemente Holtzapfel 190, Pucón, tel. 045/441001; in Santiago, tel. 2/232–6008. 143 rooms, 135 with bath, 10 with shower. Facilities: dining room, bar, 4 saunas, heated pool, tennis courts, gymnasium, weight room. AE, DC, MC, V. Expensive.*

Hotel Nueva la Frontera. This elegant modern hotel on Temuco's central square has rooms that are comfortable, light, and airy, especially if you can arrange for a view of the plaza. *Bulnes 726, Temuco, tel. 045/210718; in Santiago, tel. 2/232–6008. 65 rooms with bath. Facilities: restaurant, bar, sauna, meeting rooms, heated pool. AE, DC, MC, V. Expensive.*

Hotel Gudenschwager. Once a fishing lodge, this attractive three-story building, covered with the wooden shakes typical of southern Chile, has a view of a corner of the lake and a comfortable country atmosphere. *Pedro de Valdivia 12, Pucón, tel. 045/441156. 30 rooms, most with bath. Facilities: restaurant. MC, V. Closed Apr.–Aug. Moderate.*

Hospedaje. Miguel Castro and Nelly Epul offer comfortable bed-and-breakfast–style accommodations in their home in Villarrica, with freshly baked bread and homemade jams included with breakfast. *General Korner 442, Villarrica, tel. 045/411235. 4 rooms with shared bath. No credit cards. Inexpensive.*

Campgrounds   The **Volcán Villarrica–Sector Rucapillán** camping area is located in the lap of the Villarrica Volcano in the midst of a wood of coigüe, Chile's massive red oaks. For more information, contact SERNATUR in Temuco (tel. 045/211969).

Spas   **Termas de Huife** (Casilla 18, Pucón, tel. 045/442333; in Santiago, tel. 2/233–2288) offers thermal baths and two hot pools made of natural stones beside an icy mountain stream. For an additional fee, you can enjoy an individual bath, massage, or both. The resort includes a small hotel with luxury apartments (Termas de Huife, tel. 2/204–1222). Just past the spa, there's a country house where for a modest fee you can relax in hot pools in a more natural setting. **Termas de Palguín** hot springs are near the Villarrica National Park, amid *mañio, tepa,* and other native trees, on the property of a comfortable hotel of the same name (Casilla 1-D, Pucón, Temuco, tel. 045/233021), where you can stay overnight or simply enjoy afternoon tea after a pleasant stroll and a hot bath in the pools.

Punta Arenas

The saying that "history is written by the conquerors" was never more true than in Punta Arenas, where the main streets and even the cemetery bear the names of the Yugoslav, Portuguese, and English settlers who colonized the area. They founded the enormous sheep ranches for which the region became famous, exploited the gold during a short-lived rush at the turn of the century, and directly and indirectly contributed to the genocide of the region's native people through policies that included the hiring of headhunters, paid a pound sterling for every ear and testicle they brought in. Out of six different native groups, only one woman survived.

Punta Arenas is 3,141 kilometers (1,960 miles) from Santiago and light-years away in attitude, too. It's the main city in a region with a fascinating history peopled by some of the world's most unusual indigenous groups and rapacious settlers from around the globe—daring explorers and pirates. Today's residents share this extraordinary natural landscape with flamingos, the llamalike guanacos, and other wildlife.

Punta Arenas looks like it's about to be swept into the Strait of Magellan, and on a windy day it feels that way, too. The houses are mostly made of sheets of tin with colorful tin roofs, best appreciated when seen from above. Although the general view of the city may not be particularly attractive, look for details: the pink-and-white house on a corner, the bow window full of plants, a garden overflowing with flowers.

In general, tourist services in the entire region are expensive, although you'll find exceptions. If you make the effort to come south, bring extra funds so you can really travel and enjoy some of the once-in-a-lifetime experiences that the region offers, particularly the journey by car or bus through Patagonia to the Torres del Paine National Park; the boat trip north from Puerto Natales, the closest supply center to the park, to the glaciers; an excursion by car and boat to Penguin Island, in the Strait of Magellan; and the day trips to historic sites. You'll probably want to spend a day or so visiting Punta Arenas itself, particularly the museums, which offer valuable background information on this extraordinary area. Tour offices conduct excursions to the old Fort Bulnes and Hunger Port region south of the city, where the original settlers attempted to establish a foothold in this windswept region. Punta Arenas is also South America's major jumping-off point for cruises and flights to Antarctica (*see* Chapter 2, Adventure Travel).

The island of Tierra del Fuego, to the south of Punta Arenas, is an open area crisscrossed with the sheep ranches that brought the region wealth and led to the final destruction of several native groups for whom this was a last refuge.

Tourist Information

SERNATUR (Waldo Seguel 689, Punta Arenas, tel. 061/223798).

Arriving and Departing

By Plane Both **LanChile** and **Ladeco** have regular flights; if you don't
have a Visit Chile pass (*see* Getting Around in Essential Information, *above*), try for a reduced fare seat. These must be
booked at least two to three months in advance, especially if
you plan to travel during the peak season in January and February, when the weather in Punta Arenas is at its best. Your
best bet is to use a travel agency such as **Rigtur** (Ahumada 312,
Office 606, in Santiago, tel. 2/698–5766 or 2/698–7535), since
travel agents can work the occasional miracle of getting
cheaper seats at the last minute.

By Car It's an exhausting four-to-five-day drive to Punta Arenas from
Santiago. The prettiest route is via the Pan-American Highway
south as far as Osorno, then eastward through the mountains
via Paso Puyehue to Bariloche, Argentina. From there drive
south through the Argentine National Parks (Nahuel Huapi,
Los Alerces) to the town of Comdoro Rivadavia (1,200 km, or
750 mi, from Osorno) on Argentina's Atlantic coast. At Comodoro Rivadavia, drive south to Río Gallegos (1,916 km, or 1,200
mi, from Osorno) and on to Punta Arenas. Some sections of the
route are unpaved. Punta Arenas is about 2,230 km (1,400 mi)
from Osorno.

By Bus **Bus Norte** (tel. 2/779–5433) and **Turibus** (tel. 2/776–3848), both
departing from the Terminal Santiago (Av. Libertador Ber-
nardo O'Higgins 3848, tel. 2/779–1385) in Santiago, provide bus
service to and from Punta Arenas.

By Boat **Navimag** (tel. 2/696–3211, fax 2/633–1871) offers luxury
cruises from Puerto Montt down Chile's west coast as far as
the Strait of Magellan.

Getting Around

Punta Arenas is a small, walkable city, with most of its main
attractions concentrated around the central square. Tourist
agencies and even cafés offer day trips to Penguin Island and
Fort Bulnes, and there is regular bus service to Puerto Natales
and the Torres de Paine National Park, so you can get to most
places whether you've got a vehicle or not. To really explore
the surrounding region, however, you may find a car worth the
expense.

Exploring Punta Arenas

The best place to start a walking tour of Punta Arenas is from
the central square, where you'll see the famous statue of a
Selk'nam Indian whose toe you must touch if you want to return. Climb Calle Fagnano about four blocks to reach the
Mirador Cerro La Cruz (Hill of the Cross Lookout). From
there you have a truly breathtaking view of the city's colorful
roofs, orderly streets, and the Strait of Magellan. From there
walk back one block to Avenida España and turn left, walking
six blocks through a primarily residential area to reach Avenida Colón, which has a narrow park running down the middle
of the street. You can follow Colón all the way down to the
oceanfront and enjoy a windy, invigorating walk along the edge
of the strait westward, back toward the city and the port. If
your tastes run toward a more urban experience, follow Bories

or 21 de Mayo back along store- and restaurant-lined streets toward the city center.

From the central square, take Calle 21 de Mayo to Avenida Bulnes, where you'll find the best museum in the region, **Museo Salesiano de Mayorino Borgatello** (Mayorino Borgatello Museum, commonly referred to as the Salesianos), operated by the Salesian religious order, which came to Punta Arenas in the 19th century, ostensibly to bring God to the native people and help them integrate into Chilean society. The adventurous Italian clergy, most of whom spoke no Spanish, proved to be daring explorers; they traveled throughout the region, collecting artifacts as well as native survivors, who were "relocated" to a camp on Dawson Island, across the Magellan Strait, where they died by the hundreds. (The island was used as a prison camp by the military government after the 1973 coup.) The museum contains an extraordinary collection of everything from skulls and native crafts to stuffed animals (some with sensational birth defects, like a two-headed lamb). *Av. Bulnes 398, tel. 061/241096. Admission charged. Closed Mon.*

If you're interested in how Punta Arenas's European settlers lived, visit the **Museo Regional** (Regional Museum), located in the central square in the former mansion of the powerful Braun-Menéndez family. From the Mayorino Borgatello Museum, walk two or three blocks toward the water until you reach Hernando de Magallanes. With its lavish, marble-floored salons restored and filled with plush European-style furnishings, it provides an intriguing view of a wealthy provincial family's pretensions at the beginning of this century. The wall separating the main bedroom from the men-only games room carries two telling paintings: on the games room side, where women were never allowed, is a painting of a sexy young woman in a low-cut dress; on the bedroom side, an oil painting extolls the virtues of the Virgin Mary. *Hernando de Magallanes 949, tel. 061/244216. Admission by donation. Closed Mon.*

The **Club de la Unión** (Union Club), also in the central square, is in the former mansion of Sara Braun, the wealthy and powerful resident who also donated the main gate to the **cemetery** (Av. Bulnes and Calle Angamos) on the condition that she be the only person ever to use it! The city accepted, so when visitors enter the cemetery, it is through a side gate rather than the main entrance, which has not been opened since Braun's funeral. Huge yew trees carved into giant humps edge the cemetery paths; the niches lined with the photographs of the dead citizens of Punta Arenas are particularly intriguing.

Off the Beaten Track

Penguin Island, a half-day drive from Punta Arenas followed by a boat trip, provides an extraordinary opportunity for visitors to see penguins in their natural habitat. The island is a reserve where penguins are free to reproduce and raise their young with full protection from hunters. Trips to the island usually last all day, and are offered by Café Garogha (*see* Dining, *below*), **Turismo Comapa** (Independencia 840, Punta Arenas, tel. 61/224256, fax 61/225804), and **Traveltur Turismo** (in Punta Arenas, tel. and fax 61/211107).

Dining

The limitations of dining in a small provincial city are compensated for in Punta Arenas by the delights of fresh seafood, especially salmon, crab, and scallops, along with the local staple, lamb, whose flavor is slightly stronger than in other regions in Chile. Watch out for warnings of red tide, which makes shellfish toxic, but health authorities are strict about monitoring toxic levels, so you're unlikely to have problems. For price-category definitions, *see* Dining in Staying in Chile, *above.*

Los Navegantes. This restaurant in the Hotel los Navegantes (*see* Lodging, *below*) serves delicious grilled salmon and roast lamb, with shellfish appetizers, in a simple but comfortable dining room with a bright garden at one end. *José Menéndez 647, tel. 61/244677. Reservations advised. AE, DC, MC, V. Expensive.*

Café Garogha. This tearoom and bar offers cable television, good espresso, fresh pastries, moderately priced sandwiches, and more expensive salmon and crab dinners. The proprietors also offer tours to Penguin Island and Fort Bulnes. *Bories 817, tel. 61/241782. No reservations. DC, MC, V. Moderate.*

★ **Carioca.** The decor is simple, with paneling of rough-hewn logs and tables and chairs imprinted with Coca-Cola logos, but the sandwiches are unbeatable, especially the "Carioca" itself, a hamburger with cheese, bacon, tomato, avocado, egg, and green beans for less than $4. This place is popular with students and pensioners, who sit nursing a beer through hours of conversation. *Calles José Menéndez and Chiloé, no phone. No reservations. DC, MC, V. Inexpensive.*

El Rinconcito. Given its location across from the railyards down by the port, this hole-in-the-wall with a six-stool counter is for the adventurous, but the fresh raw shellfish soup, served with green and white onions, *ají* (chilis), oil, wine, and lemon, doesn't get any better, or any cheaper. *Take Independencia (it turns into Brasilera) until it ends near the port, and turn right on Costanera until you pass a doorway in the wall on your right. No reservations. No credit cards. Inexpensive.*

Lodging

Hotels are springing up throughout Punta Arenas, so you may want to either wander around a bit before you choose or simply book into one place the first night and then move. For price-category definitions, *see* Lodging in Staying in Chile, *above.*

Cabo de Hornos. The Cabo de Hornos, Punta Arenas's only five-star hotel, occupies a massive eight-story building along the central square. It has seen better days: Lobby decor dates back to the '60s, and its carpets are stained. The saunas have been turned into meeting rooms, and the guest rooms, decorated in beige and browns, are clean and comfortable but nothing special. End rooms on upper floors have spectacular views of the Strait of Magellan: others overlook the square itself. *Plaza Muñoz Gamero 1025, tel. 61/242134. 103 rooms, 10 suites. Facilities: restaurant and tearoom, bar. AE, DC, MC, V. Expensive.*

★ **José Nogueira.** The management of Punta Arenas's new hotel is looking for a five-star designation, and it probably deserves one. The place is delightfully comfortable and beautifully designed: Public rooms are decorated with richly textured striped wallpaper, pillars of polished wood, marble floors, and lots of bronze details. Guest rooms are high ceilinged if on the small side, with thick carpets, antique-style wood furniture, and ceramic-tiled bathrooms. The suites have Jacuzzis. *Bories 959, tel. 61/248840, fax 61/248832. 23 rooms, 2 suites. Facilities: restaurant, bar. AE, DC, MC, V. Expensive.*

Los Navegantes. This comfortable, unpretentious hotel has an excellent restaurant and spacious double rooms with gray-and-pink carpets and colorful paisley bedspreads. The price includes a substantial, American-style breakfast and transportation from the airport. *José Menéndez 647, tel. 61/244677. 52 rooms, 4 suites. Facilities: restaurant, cable TV, minibar. AE, DC, MC, V. Moderate.*

★ **Hostal Carpa Manzano.** This new and comfortable establishment is decorated in warm pastel colors, with wicker furniture and low poster beds. It's centrally located and has a friendly, helpful proprietor. *Lautaro Navarro 336, tel. 61/242296, fax 61/248864. 7 rooms with bath; more rooms are planned. DC, MC, V. Inexpensive.*

Hotel Condor de Plata. The idiosyncrotic decor includes scale models and photographs of old-fashioned airplanes that once traveled to the Magellan region. Rooms are small, carpeted, and colored in neutral browns and beiges. *Av. Colón 556, tel. 61/247987, fax 61/241149. 14 rooms with bath. Facilities: cafeteria, cable TV. DC, MC, V. Inexpensive.*

★ **Hostal de la Avenida.** The rooms of this comfortable, homey *residencial* all overlook a garden that is lovingly tended by its owner, a local of Yugoslav origin. *Av. Colón 534, tel. 61/247532. 6 rooms with showers only. Facilities: snack bar. No credit cards. Inexpensive.*

Excursions from Punta Arenas

Torres del Paine National Park offers a once-in-a-lifetime experience that you should definitely not miss. The spectacular towering mountains that give the park its name are surrounded by sparkling turquoise lakes, some touched by the icy-blue sculptures of icebergs and glaciers. You'll see much of the typical wildlife of the region, including foxes, flamingos, guanacos, a woolly, graceful version of the llama, and *ñandús,* (Chilean ostriches) along with a wide variety of birds, wildflowers, and berries.

The best way to visit the park, which is 400 kilometers (250 miles) from Punta Arenas along a road that is gravel for the last 145 kilometers (90 miles), is to rent a car and then camp for several nights. If you're not a camper, stay in the **Hostería Pehoe** (tel. 61/241373, fax 61/248052; closed May–mid-Sept.), on a small island. Its somewhat cramped (and expensive at $100 a night) rooms have great views and the service is marvelous. Book well in advance.

Arka Patagonia (tel. 61/241504) and **Andes Patagónicos Expeditions** (Blanco Encalada 226, Puerto Natales, tel. 61/411594) offer one-day package tours to the park, which may or may not include transportation from Punta Arenas to Puerto Natales, the main town on the way to Paine. These tours are thorough but exhausting. You might want to spend the extra money and stay overnight, then catch the next day's tour back to Puerto

Natales. Arka also organizes adventure tours and scientific expeditions.

Puerto Natales is bursting with hotels; among the newer offerings are the **Hotel Glaciares** (Eberhard 104, tel. 61/411452) and the **Lady Florence Dixie** (Bulnes 659, tel. 61/411158, fax 61/411943), a welcoming inexpensive hotel that has peach-colored rooms with TV and telephones and breakfast included. If you stop overnight, try **Don Alvarito's** restaurant (Blanco Encalada 915, tel. 61/411187) for carefully prepared scallops and filet mignon in simple, tasty sauces.

Plan to spend an extra day in **Puerto Natales** and take the day-long boat ride to the glaciers on the **21 de Mayo Cutter** (Eberhard 560, Puerto Natales, tel. 61/411978; $32). Arrange a bag or box lunch and take warm clothes. The trip takes you through canals lined with sheer rock walls, past a cormorant nesting area and a seal colony, and on to the glaciers, one of which you can visit on foot. On your way back to port, you can sip on a *pisco* or whiskey chilled with glacier ice.

Getting There **Buses Fernández** (tel. 61/2423313, fax 61/225984) and **Buses Victoria Sur** (tel. 61/241213) offer daily bus service between Punta Arenas and Puerto Natales; be sure to book and arrive early or you may not get on. **Bus Turismo Carahue** (Bories 370, Puntas Arenas, tel. 61/411339) and **Turismo Michay** (Baquedano 388, Puerto Natales, tel. 61/411149) have daily bus service to the park.

7 Colombia

By Tom Quinn
and Philip Eade

Tom Quinn is a
freelance writer for
Time magazine
living in Bogotá.
London-based
Philip Eade is an
itinerant writer,
barrister, and
amateur painter,
not to mention an
author of Fodor's
Costa Rica, Belize,
Guatemala.

Colombia, land of emeralds and coffee, is blessed with more than its fair share of natural splendors. It faces two oceans, the Atlantic and the Pacific, and its fertile soils and varied climates are home to more plant and animal species than almost anywhere else on the planet. In Colombia, it's possible to jump on a plane and, less than an hour later, find yourself awed by a different dramatic landscape—be it the cobblestone streets of a weathered colonial port, the stalls of a crowded market where Indian sellers still speak the tongues of the ancient Chibcha and Inca, or a cluster of snow-covered volcanoes rising sharply from the steamy coastal plain.

Bogotá, Colombia's sprawling capital, stands on a vast plateau in the eastern Andes, commanding views over an olio of farms, suburban apartments, and shantytown ghettoes. Poverty and drug-related violence are facts of life in Bogotá, but there are sides to this city of 6 million rarely covered in the international press: elegant shopping streets, grand high-rise office towers, and chic La Zona Rosa nightclubs where young and stylish Bogataños gather to watch the sunrise. Bogotá's other surprise is La Candeleria, the colonial old city, with its narrow streets and thick-walled mansions.

The western half of Colombia, traversed by the central ridge of the Andes, the *Cordillera Central,* is where the majority of the country's 33 million people live. As you begin your ascent of the mighty Andes, subtropical valleys give way to rigid, fern-carpeted mountains where ever-present mists are brightened only by the votive candles placed by truck drivers in roadside shrines. Heading west from Bogotá, you pass quiet Indian villages hugging the hillsides before reaching Medellín, home to the notorious Medellín drug cartel. Despite its reputation, Medellín is safe and strikingly beautiful, surrounded by velvety green hills and miles of lush farmland. Continuing south, the Pan-American Highway meanders through dramatic mountain landscapes before making its descent into Cali and colonial Popayán, famous across the continent for its Holy Week festival.

If you feel like lounging in the sun, Colombia boasts some of the best beaches on the continent. In particular, the resort islands of San Andrés and Providencia, separated from the mainland by more than 400 miles of Pacific Ocean, are where Colombians escape to sunbathe, swim, and shop in the shadow of palm trees and thatched waterfront bars. Back on the mainland, Cartagena, widely revered as the most striking colonial city in South America, makes an excellent base for forays along the Caribbean Coast.

Before the arrival of the Spanish, Colombia was sparsely inhabited by indigenous Indian tribes. In the high basins of the Andes, the most powerful of these tribes was the Chibcha, masterful goldsmiths who, with their tradition of anointing a chief each year by rolling him in gold dust, likely sparked the El Dorado myth. The Chibchas had given up this custom long before the first Europeans landed on Colombian shores, but the legend lingered and drove a host of New World adventurers in search of gilded cities paved with gold.

The Spanish settled parts of Panama as early as 1510. But it was not until Rodrigo de Bastidas founded the Colombian port of Santa Marta, in 1525, that a permanent settlement was es-

Colombia

334

SAN ANDRÉS AND
PROVINDENCIA ISLANDS

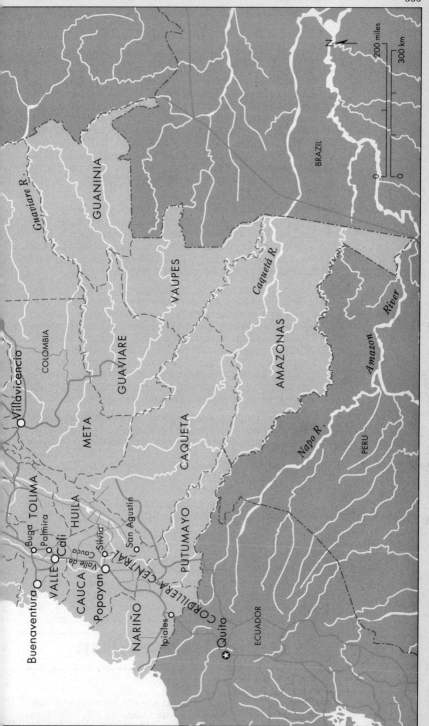

tablished. Explorers like Gonzalo Jiménez de Quesada were soon driving deep inland, plundering and pillaging as they went. Quesada reached Bogotá in 1535 and, after quickly dispatching the local Chibcha Indians, decided he had found a striking location for his Spanish settlement.

Despite their near extinction, Colombia's Indian cultures have left a lasting mark on the country. The extraordinary carved stones at San Agustín, in southwestern Colombia, speak of Indian empires once rich in gold, emeralds, and the technological skills necessary to erect massive temples to long-forgotten gods. In the Andes and on the coastal plains, you'll find modern descendants of these lost tribes living a simple, traditional life that hasn't changed all that much since Columbus presumptuously claimed Colombia in the name of King Ferdinand of Spain.

Staying Safe and Healthy Although its reputation has been marred by the Medillín and Cartagena drug cartels, Colombia is hardly a war zone. To be sure, you will encounter machine-gun-toting soldiers in many cities and military checkpoints on otherwise peaceful mountain roads. But there is a fairly well-established "gringo trail," and thousands of people visit each year without mishap.

Crime Violence from the drug cartels and guerrilla groups are a fact of life in Colombia, but travelers who observe the same precautions they would take in, say, a big city back home are unlikely to run into problems. Certain land journeys are best not undertaken at night, or avoided altogether, because of the risk of ambush by guerrillas (the road from Bucaramanga to Santa Marta, for example, should be avoided). Have nothing to do with drug dealers, especially since many of them freelance as police informers. Possession of cocaine or marijuana can lead to a long jail sentence—not a pleasant thought in Colombia.

In many of the large cities, especially the downtown area of Bogotá, do not be taken in by plainclothes "policemen" demanding to register your money—they are almost certainly thieves. Nor should you change money on the black market or get involved in any dubious transactions aimed at getting a better rate of exchange. Don't accept gifts of food, drink, cigarettes or chewing gum from strangers, especially on bus journeys; there have been reports of travelers being drugged and relieved of their valuables in this way.

Health Water in Bogotá and Medellín is heavily chlorinated and safe enough to drink, but rely on bottled or bagged water in other parts of the country. Also avoid eating unpeeled fruit, uncooked vegetables, salads, and ice cubes. You don't need to bring stacks of medical supplies with you: Colombia's pharmacies are well stocked. Some people experience dizziness and headaches upon arrival in Bogotá because of the thin mountain air. Take it easy and be careful with alcohol until you acclimatize.

Essential Information

Before You Go

When to Go December, January, and February are the best—in other words, the driest—months to visit Colombia. Yet, Colombians themselves tend to travel during these sometimes hot and humid months, when tourist prices peak and some nontourist businesses close. Visiting during one of the country's festivals adds an exciting cultural edge to your trip, but expect inflated prices and often overwhelming crowds. **Holy Week,** during March or April, in the colonial towns of Popayán and Mompós and the week-long **Carnival** in Barranquilla, held the week before Ash Wednesday, are famous throughout South America. Other popular festivals include Cali's *feria* (December 25-January 1), the **flower festival** in Medellín (late May or early June), the **Folklore Festival** in Ibagué (usually the last week in June), and Cartagena's *Reinado* (early November), featuring beauty contests and a full week of merrymaking.

Climate   Although Colombia is perceived as a steamy tropical country, climate is very much a matter of altitude. Temperatures range from an average of 82°F (28°C) along the Caribbean Coast to a chilly 54°F (12°C) in Bogotá, which, like Medellín, is perched in the Andes mountains.

Seasons as such do not exist in Colombia, but rainfall and brisk winterlike weather is common October–November and April–June. Rainfall is rarely excessive and only a problem if you plan to travel off the beaten track on Colombia's rough-paved mountain roads. The dry season usually runs December–March in mountainous areas, mid-December–April and July–September in low-lying coastal regions.

The following are the average monthly maximum and minimum temperatures for Bogotá.

Jan.	67F	19C	May	66F	19C	Sept.	66F	19C
	48	9		51	10		49	9
Feb.	68F	20C	June	65F	18C	Oct.	66F	19C
	49	9		51	10		50	10
Mar.	67F	19C	July	64F	18C	Nov.	66F	19C
	50	10		50	10		50	10
Apr.	67F	19C	Aug.	65F	18C	Dec.	66F	19C
	51	10		50	10		49	9

Currency   Colombia's monetary unit is the peso, which has lost so much value it is no longer divided into centavos. Peso bills are circulated in the following denominations: 100, 200, 500, 1,000, 5,000, and 10,000. Peso coins come in denominations of 5, 10, 20, 50, and 100.

At press time (fall 1993) the official exchange rate was 840 pesos to the U.S. dollar and 1,250 pesos to the pound sterling. To squeeze the most out of your dollars and pounds, whenever possible use your credit card for cash advances: In Colombia, credit cards give the most stable and highest rate of exchange. Either way, keep your exchange receipts. Upon departure you can convert unused pesos back into U.S. dollars (up to $60).

Credit cards and traveler's checks are accepted in resorts and in a large number of shops and restaurants in major cities. U.S., British, and Canadian currency can be exchanged for a small fee in many hotels, banks, and travel agencies.

What It Will Cost   Colombia is one of the few countries in South America where inflation remains relatively stable. Bogotá, Cali, Cartagena, and San Andrés are the most expensive destinations; but, even then, you can find first-class accommodations for less than $50 per night. The least expensive areas are coastal and mountain villages, where you may have difficulty parting with more than $2 for a meal and $5 for accommodation. Throughout Colombia hotels add 15% to your bill, and there is a 14% value-added tax (IVA) on most anything you might want to buy.

Sample Prices Cup of coffee, 25¢; bottle of beer, 75¢; bottle of wine in a restaurant, $10–$15; bottle of wine in store, $4–$6; 1-mile taxi ride, $2; city bus ride, 50¢; theater or cinema ticket, $2.

Customs On arrival the duty-free allowance per person is 200 cigarettes, 50 cigars, up to 250 grams of tobacco, and two bottles of either wine or spirits. You can also bring into the country electronic equipment such as a video camera as long as it bears clear signs of use. There is no limit on the amount of money tourists can bring in and out of the country. On departure, gold and platinum articles and emeralds require proof of purchase.

Language The official language is Spanish, though you will probably encounter more than one of the roughly 90 Indian languages spoken in Colombia. English is widely understood on San Andrés and Providencia islands and commonly spoken in resort hotels and restaurants in the major cities.

Getting Around

By Car Driving in Colombia is recommended only for confident, experienced drivers. Roads are narrow, winding, not always signposted, and often in poor condition, with unpredictable surfaces. During the rainy season roads can turn to mud or wash out completely. Even in good weather, maniac truck and bus drivers—combined with the likelihood of encountering stray animals—make negotiating the highways extremely difficult. Nighttime driving is especially dangerous since many vehicles lack headlights. Tolls (up to $1, payable only in pesos) are common; motorcycles are usually exempt. In town leave your car in an attended parking lot, especially at night.

Car Rental Car rentals in Colombia cost $130–$150 per week including mileage. Even if you pay in pesos—dollars are not usually accepted—a credit card may be needed in addition to your passport or driver's license as proof of identity. The main international car-rental companies in Bogotá are **Avis** (El Dorado airport, tel. 1/266–2147; Calle 99 No. 11–26, tel. 1/610–4455), **Hertz** (El Dorado airport, tel. 1/413–9302; Av. 15 No. 107–24, tel. 1/214–4228 or 1/214–9745), or **National** (Calle 100 No. 14–46, tel. 1/612–5635 or 1/620–0055).

Fuel Gasoline comes in two grades: *premium* (95 octane), available only in large cities for about 80¢ per U.S. gallon; and *corriente* (84 octane), sometimes called *regular*, which costs around 65¢ per U.S. gallon and is available throughout the country. Most towns hugging a highway tend to have at least one working pump, though the towns themselves are few and far between.

Rules of the Road National driver's licenses are accepted but must be accompanied by an official translation—a lot of bureaucratic bother that can be avoided by getting an international license before you leave home. Police checkpoints are common and you should make sure your documents are always at hand. There is an automatic fine for running out of gasoline on the road.

Breakdowns In an emergency contact the **Policía Vial** (tel. 1/247–1151), who have a mobile workshop for fixing breakdowns. Otherwise, when hiring a car it is a good idea to affiliate yourself with the **Automóvil Club de Colombia** (Av. Caracas 14 No. 46–72, Bogotá, tel. 1/288–1900), who will tow your car to a mechanic if they cannot fix it themselves. American Automobile Association (AAA) members can contact the local representatives, Allen and Mary Lowrie, for maps and driving hints (Carrera 7 No. 19–29, 3rd floor, Bogotá, tel. 1/243–2546 or 1/243–2457).

By Plane Faced with almost insurmountable natural barriers, Colombia has developed one of the best air transportation systems in the world. Avianca, the oldest airline in the Americas and the second-oldest in the world, operates daily flights between Colombia's major cities. The airline also offers a *Conozca Colombia* ("Know Colombia") air pass that permits travel to as many as 10 cities in 30 days as long as you don't stop in the same city twice except for connections. The air pass, which can only be purchased outside Colombia, costs $250 if San Andrés Island and Leticia are not included, $365 if they are.

There are daily flights to Bogotá, Barranquilla, Medellín, and San Andrés Island with **Avianca** (Carrera 7 No. 13–36, Bogotá, tel. 1/266–9700). Other airlines offering domestic service are **SAM** (Carrera 13 No. 28–01, office 401, Bogotá, tel. 1/266–9600), **Aces** (Carrera 10 No. 27–51, office 201, Bogotá, tel. 1/413–8648), **Intercontinental de Aviación** (Carrera 10 No. 28–31, Bogotá, tel. 1/387–9777 or 1/288–7266), and **AIRES** (Av. 13 No. 56–79, Bogotá, tel. 1/413–9517).

By Bus Colombia has an extensive bus network that connects the major cities with even the smallest mountain villages. There are two classes to choose from: the very standard *corriente, sencillo,* or *ordinario* service; and a first-class service variously called *pullman, metropolitano, de lujo,* or *directo.* There are also deluxe air-conditioned buses known as *thermo* or *climatizado,* but these are common mainly on routes between Bogotá, Medellín, and the Caribbean Coast. Standard bus service costs $1.50–$2 per 100 kilometers (62 miles), and the ancient vehicles (which probably should have been scrapped decades ago) tend to be very crowded. First-class and deluxe coaches can be quite comfortable with reclining seats and respectable toilets; the average cost is $2–$5 per 100 kilometers (62 miles). On longer journeys buses stop for meals, but not necessarily at mealtimes and not for very long.

By Train The Colombian railway company, **Ferrocariles Nacionales de Colombia,** finally went bust in April of 1993, signaling the end of passenger rail travel in Colombia.

Staying in Colombia

Telephones Colombia's telephone service is reasonably efficient, though direct dialing is still not available from many places in the Andes and along the coast. Public telephones, which are common in large cities but scarce everywhere else, accept 5-, 10-, 20-, and 50-peso coins. For intercity calls use the blue-and-yellow or red long distance booths marked *larga distancia* (which only accept 20-peso coins). If you cannot find one, or if you do not have access to a private or hotel telephone, go to the local Telecom office—there is one in most towns. When dialing long distance from within Colombia, dial 9, the area code, and then the number.

International Calls Unless you have access to a private phone, credit card and collect calls can only be made by dialing AT&T toll-free at tel. 980/11–00–11 or 980/11–00–10. Sprint and MCI services will not be in place until the end of 1994. Direct-dial international calls are best made from a Telecom office, where you must leave a deposit of roughly $25; or from your hotel at a *substantially* higher rate (the average rate per minute to the United States is $6; from a hotel, about $10).

Mail All international airmail is handled by Avianca, Colombia's largest airline. Airmail post offices are normally located next to those of the airline and open weekdays 7:30 AM–8 PM, Saturday 8–5. Airmail service costs less than 50¢ to the United States and is relatively reliable; most letters reach their intended international destination in 10–14 days.

Receiving Mail Avianca holds letters for up to 30 days, and you will need your passport to reclaim them from the poste restante desk. Letters should be sent to Post Restante, Correo Aéreo Avianca, followed by the city and province name.

Shopping Colombia is a shopper's paradise, both for the high-quality locally manufactured clothes, and for the range of indigenous handicrafts. In all of the major cities there are good department stores and boutiques to tempt you. In rural areas, village markets and shops stock a full range of Colombian handicrafts. Among the best buys are natural wool *ruanas* (ponchos) woven by the Indians in the south, embroidered blouses from Cali, and replica pre-Columbian jewelry in Bogotá. Antiques are also sold in shops throughout Colombia. Colonial objects can be taken out of the country without hindrance, but exporting pre-Columbian artifacts is against the law.

Opening and Closing Times Standard hours at **banks** are weekdays 8–11:30 and 2–4 (until 4:30 on Friday). In Bogotá many banks are open weekdays 9–3 only. On the last working day of the month banks are open only in the morning, though in Bogotá they stay open until noon.

There are no standardized opening hours for **shops** and stores, though a majority close daily for lunch between 12:30 and 2 PM. Many are also closed on Sunday.

Museums have similar hours to shops but tend to be closed on Monday rather than Sunday.

National Holidays Jan. 1 (Circumcision of our Lord); Jan. 10 (Epiphany); Mar. 21 (St. Joseph's Day); Mar. 31 (Viernes Santo [Holy Thursday]); April 1 (Good Friday); May 1 (Labor Day); May 16 (Ascension Day); June 6 (Corpus Christi); June 13 (Sacred Heart); July 4 (Saints Peter and Paul's Day); July 20 (Independence Day); Aug. 7 (Battle of Boyacá); Aug. 15 (Assumption); Oct. 17 (Discovery of America); Nov. 7 (All Saints' Day); Nov. 14 (Independence of Cartagena); Dec. 8 (Immaculate Conception); Dec. 25 (Christmas Day).

Dining Colombian cuisine is a fusion of Spanish, Indian, and African culinary traditions. It is varied and regional by nature, but unfortunately the same cannot be said of the standard *almuerzo,* or lunch, offered day after day by a majority of restaurants throughout the country. It starts with soup and is followed by a main dish, or *bandeja,* consisting of a piece of chicken or fish garnished with *fríjoles* (beans), vegetables, and rice. The only good news is the price: $1–$3.

Colombians do not necessarily drink alcoholic beverages with dinner, although they are fond of imported Chilean wines and two reasonable national offerings: *Santo Tomás,* a full-bodied red wine, and the Chianti-like *Vino Moriles.*

The best restaurants in Bogotá and Medellín can certainly compete with those in Rio de Janeiro or Buenos Aires, and in such establishments a jacket and tie for men and smart dress for women is the norm; everywhere else informal dress is appropriate.

Mealtimes Restaurants serve lunch between 12:30 and 2:30. In the provinces people tend to have their evening meal just after sundown, but in Bogotá hours are much more Spanish: you may find yourself sitting down to an "early" dinner at 9.

Specialties On the Caribbean Coast try *cazuela de mariscos,* a seafood soup traditionally made with shrimp, squid, crab, lobster, and red snapper. Also popular is *sancocho de sábalo,* fresh fish prepared in coconut milk with strips of potato, plantain banana, and yucca. On San Andrés and Providencia islands the local favorite is *rendón,* a fish-and-snail soup slowly cooked in coconut milk with yucca, plantain, breadfruit, and dumplings. In the Andes, and particularly in Bogotá, *ajiaco*—a thick soup prepared from three types of potato, chicken, corn, capers, fresh cream, and avocado—is among the most typical dishes. So, too, are tamales, which consist of chicken, corn, and potatoes rolled in a maize dough and wrapped in banana leaves.

Colombians are fond of bread, particularly dinner rolls and muffins: be sure to try *mogollas,* whole-wheat muffins with raisin-flavored centers; *roscones,* sugar-sprinkled buns filled with guava jelly; and *almojábanas,* corn muffins enriched with cottage cheese. Popular desserts include *obleas,* giant wafers spread with sugar and milk paste, and *empanadas,* pastries filled with spices, chopped meat, and rice or potato.

Ratings Prices are per person and include an appetizer, main course, and dessert. Wine and gratuities are not included. Highly recommended restaurants are indicated by a star ★.

Category	Cost
Very Expensive	over $25
Expensive	$15–$25
Moderate	$7–$15
Inexpensive	under $7

Lodging Colombia's resort hotels are of a very high standard, though on the coast and in the capital, and particularly in Medellín, resorts are sometimes completely booked for conventions. Away from the resorts quality is more variable. Nevertheless, in most areas you'll find moderately priced pensions equipped with private bathrooms. (Hot water, however, may only be available at certain hours of the day.) The local tourist office can normally book visitors into the better hotels and provide recommendations regarding the rest.

Ratings Prices are for two people in a double room, based on high-season rates but not including 15% tax. Highly recommended lodgings are indicated by a star ★.

Category	Cost
Very Expensive	over $80
Expensive	$65–$80
Moderate	$40–$65
Inexpensive	under $40

Tipping Taxi drivers do not expect tips. Porters at airports and hotels are usually given 300 pesos for each piece of luggage. In many restaurants, bars, and cafés, a 10% service charge is automatically added to the bill; if not, a 10% tip is common. Hotel maids or clerks are seldom tipped.

Bogotá

Bogotá is a city of many faces—a city of ostentatious wealth and shocking poverty, and the home of a people as heterogenous as the country itself. On the one hand there is ultramodern Bogotá, a city of futuristic glass towers and elegant shopping centers that never sleeps. Then there is historical Bogotá, a treasure trove of colonial mansions grandly conceived by the Spanish and built by Indian slaves with plundered gold. Finally, there is Bogotá the sprawling metropolis, a city of nearly six million people that has grown twentyfold in the past 50 years. This immense conurbation suffers the typical growing pains of a modern South American city, and a few uniquely its own: a collapsed transport system, chronic air pollution, squalid shantytowns, and a scurrilous drug trade responsible for the recent spate of political bombings.

Spanish conquistadors built their chain of cities in South America in magnificent locations, and Bogotá, which stands on a high plane in the eastern Andes, is no exception. During his disastrous search for the legendary El Dorado, Gonzalo Jiménez de Quesada, the Spanish explorer on whom Cervantes reputedly modelled Don Quixote, was struck by the area's natural splendor and its potential for colonization. Though it is a mere 1,288 kilometers (800 miles) from the equator, Bogota's 2,593-meter (8,500-foot) altitude lends it a refreshing, bracing climate. Jiménez de Quesada failed to find the elusive City of Gold, but he did discover one of South America's most advanced pre-Colombian tribes, the Chibcha, master goldsmiths whose exquisitely wrought articles most likely sparked the El Dorado myth. Despite their skill as goldsmiths, the Chibchas were no match for the Spaniards: On August 6, 1538, Quesada christened his new conquest Santa Fe de Bogotá, in honor of the razed Chibcha village of Bacatá.

Bogotá rapidly established itself as an important administrative center and during 1740 was crowned the capital of New Granada, an area comprising modern day Colombia, Venezuela, Panama, and Ecuador. The city's status meant it was not long before grand civic and religious buildings began to spring up, often with the handcarved ceilings and sculpted doorways

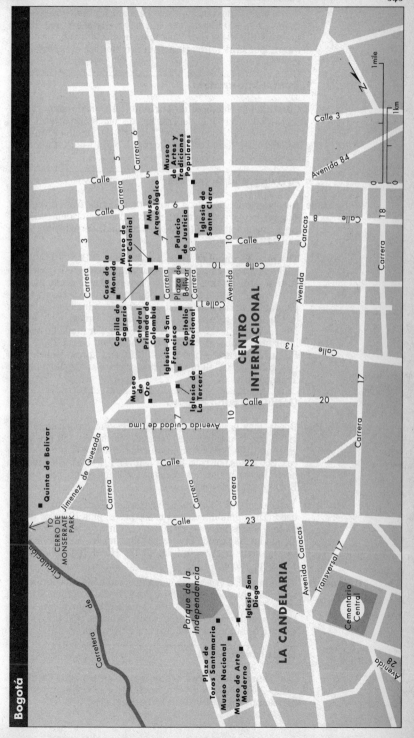

Bogotá

Calle 3

Avenida 84

1 mile

1 km

Calle 18

Carrera 6

Museo de Artes y Tradiciones Populares

Calle 5

Calle

Carrera

Museo Arqueológico

Carrera 3

Palacio de Justicia

Iglesia de Santa Clara

Calle 6

Calle 8

Calle

Casa de la Moneda

Museo de Arte Colonial

Calle 10

Calle 9

Carrera Caracas

Carrera

Capilla de Sagrario

Carrera

Plaza de Bolívar

Avenida Caracas

Calle

Catedral Primada de Colombia

Carrera

Calle 10

Avenida

Iglesia de San Francisco

Calle 11

CENTRO INTERNACIONAL

Capitolio Nacional

Museo de Oro

Iglesia de La Tercera

Calle 13

Carrera 7

Avenida Ciudad de Lima

Calle 17

Carrera 3

Calle 10

Calle

Quinta de Bolívar

Carrera

Calle 20

Jimenez de Quesada

TO CERRO DE MONSERRATE PARK

Calle 22

Carrera

Circulación

Carrera

Calle 23

Carrera

Avenida Caracas

Carretera de

Parque de la Independencia

Iglesia San Diego

Transversal 17

LA CANDELARIA

Cementario Central

Plaza de Toros Santamaria

Museo Nacional

Museo de Arte Moderno

Avenida 28

that were the hallmark of New Granada architecture. Nevertheless, by 1900 Bogotá was still only a city of 100,000. It was not until the 1940s that rapid industrialization and the consequent peasant migration spurred Bogotá's exponential growth.

Tourist Information

Corporacion Nacional de Turismo (El Dorado airport, tel. 1/413–9500; Terminal de Transportes bus station, tel. 1/295–1100; Calle 28 No. 13a–15, tel. 1/281–4341). **Oficina Municipal de Turismo** (Plaza Bolívar, Carrera 8 No. 10–65, 1st floor, tel. 1/283–5554).

Arriving and Departing

By Plane **Aeropuerto El Dorado,** a 20-minute taxi ride from downtown Bogotá, is served by some foreign and all major domestic carriers, including **Avianca**, **Intercontinental de Aviación**, **Aces**, and **AIRES**.

By Bus The new **Terminal de Transportes** (Calle 33B No. 69–13, tel. 1/295–1100) is served by all major bus companies. To reach the station catch any bus traveling Carrera 13 with a sign marked TERMINAL, or take a taxi from downtown for less than $4. Dependable carriers for coastal destinations include **Copetrán** (Calle 33B No. 69–13, tel. 1/263–2102) and **Omega** (Carrera 17 No. 15–71, tel. 1/341–4056 or 1/341–8618). For Medellín and the interior regions contact **Flota Magdalena** (tel. 1/295–1100), **Flota La Macarena** (tel. 1/295–0539), or **Expreso Bolivariano** (tel. 1/295–1200), all of which have agents at the Terminal de Transportes.

Getting Around Bogotá

By Bus Buses, mainly noisy, ancient, and driven at top speed, are divided into two categories: *busetas,* which cost 150 pesos per ride, and the larger and more comfortable *ejecutivos,* which cost 250 pesos per ride. Buses 7, 13, and 15 cross the city from north to south along carreras of the same numbers (calles in Bogotá run east–west).

By Taxi Taxis are required by law to have meters—make sure they are used. The minimum charge is 500 pesos, plus 10 pesos per 90 meters. Fares increase by 30% after dark; a list of surcharges should be displayed. Taxis with bilingual drivers can be hired by the hour or for a full day at the Hotel Tequendama (*see* Lodging, *below*).

By Colectivo This service, a cross between a taxi and a bus, is operated by surprisingly modern minibuses that, because of their size, are often able to get through traffic jams better than buses. Colectivos, which travel the same routes as buses, cost the same as ejecutivos but are a good deal more cramped.

Orientation Tours

The **Tierra Mar y Aire** travel agency (Carrera 7 No. 35–20, tel. 1/288–2088 or 1/288–1888 offers bus tours of the city, both by day and by night, for about $10 per person.

Exploring Bogotá

Bogotá's oldest meighborhood and a favorite with foreign visitors, the La Candelaria district, at the foot of Monserrate Peak, is packed with colonial churches and museums. To the north is the seedy downtown area, which nevertheless boasts a handful of fairly decent bars and restaurants. Farther uptown and marked by towering office buildings is the Centro Internacional, the financial heart of the city. This modern development, built largely in the 1970s and showing its age now, is fringed by the Parque de la Independencia, a welcome area of green in Bogotá's urban landscape. The city becomes very much smarter after Calle 72 (Av. Chile); and 10 blocks later you come to the leafy Zona Rosa, a popular boutique- and tavern-filled district.

La Candelaria   **La Candelaria** is where you will find the city's largest concentration of colonial mansions and churches. **La Plaza del Chorro del Quevedo,** an attractive little square surrounded by low whitewashed colonial buildings, is where Quesada and his soldiers celebrated the founding of Bogotá on August 6, 1538. In the center of the square stands a small fountain that recalls the "Chorro del Quevedo," the mythical brook where the conquistadors quenched their thirst and that today has been prosaically confined to subterranean drainage pipes.

From here it is only a short walk to **Plaza de Bolívar,** the most important historical point in the city. It was here that the formal founding of Bogotá took place in the presence of Spanish potentates. Dominating the square is the graceful **Catedral Primada de Colombia** (Primate Cathedral of Colombia), with its elegant French Baroque facade built from locally mined sandstone. Begun in 1565, it was not completed until nearly three centurues later due to a series of misfortunes—including the disastrous earthquake of 1785. The large windows give the immense interior a light and airy feel, even on one of Bogotá's many gray days. The ornate altar with gold leaf over heavily carved wood contrasts with the lack of ornamentation elsewhere. In one of the side chapels lies Quesada's tomb. *Admission free. Closed Sun.*

Next door to the cathedral is one of the most important examples of religious architecture in Colombia, the late 17th-century **Capilla del Sagrario.** The exquisite canopied altar, a smaller version of that found at St. Peter's in Rome, would be reason enough for a visit. But the chapel also houses a splendid collection of paintings, including works by the Taller de Figueroa and Gregorio Vasquez. *Admission free. Closed weekends.*

At the square's southern end is the grand 19th-century **Capitolio Nacional,** where the national Congress sits. Behind this is the **Palacio de Nariño,** the Colombian "White House," rebuilt in 1949 following its destruction during a popular uprising in the capital. Each day at 5 PM the guard is changed with great pomp and ceremony. On the palace's northern side is the **Palacio de Justicia,** being rebuilt following its taking by guerrillas in November 1985.

Just around the corner look for the **Luis Angel Arango cultural center.** Of its several museums, the most interesting is the **Museo de Arte Religioso,** with rotating displays of colonial church art. Don't miss its two spectacular gold processional crosses, the Tunja and the Lechuga; the latter is encrusted with 1,600 emeralds. *Calle 12 No. 4–31, tel. 1/247–7200. Admission free. Closed weekends.*

The **Casa de la Moneda,** Colombia's former national mint, has a vast collection of coins; novelties include coins whose gold content was secretly reduced by the king of Spain, some made by revolutionaries from empty cartridges, and some made for use exclusively in Colombia's former leper colonies. *Calle 11 No. 4–16, tel. 1/243–7200. Admission free. Closed weekends.*

The **Museo Arqueológico** (Museum of Archaeology) occupies a magnificent mansion that once belonged to the Marquís of San Jorge, a colonial viceroy famous for his cruelty; on display today is a large collection of pre-Columbian ceramics. *Carrera 6 No. 7–43, tel. 1/282–0940. Admission charged. Closed Mon.*

The **Museo de Artes y Tradiciones Populares** (Museum of Art and Crafts) is housed in a former Augustinian cloister that dates back to 1583, making it one of the oldest surviving buildings in Bogotá. This is a good place to see a range of contemporary crafts made by Indian artisans from across the country. There is also a crafts shop and a good restaurant specializing in traditional Andes cooking. *Carrera 8 No. 7–21, tel. 1/284–5319 or 1/284–5418. Admission charged. Closed Sun. and Mon.*

The simple, unadorned facade of the 17th-century **Iglesia de Santa Clara** gives no hint of the dazzling frescoes and wall reliefs—the work of nuns who were once cloistered here—that bathe the interior walls. Also inside is a small museum with paintings and sculpture by various 17th-century artists. *Calle 9 at Carrera 8, tel. 1/282–8197. Admission free. To arrange English-language tours, call 1/341–6017 or 1/284–1373. Closed weekday afternoons and weekends.*

Between Plaza de Bolívar and the encroaching mountains, a network of narrow streets contains Bogotá's finest colonial mansions—thick-walled, refined, and austere, with heavily carved doorways, tiled roofs, and wide eaves. A good example south of the plaza is the **Museo de Arte Colonial** (Museum of Colonial Art), housed in a grand 17th-century Andalusian-style mansion. On display inside is a substantial collection of colonial art, including paintings by Vasquez and Figueroa, plus 17th- and 18th-century furniture and precious metalwork. *Carrera 6 No. 9–77, tel. 1/241–6017. Admission charged. Closed Mon.*

North of the plaza on Carrera 7 are two equally imposing colonial monuments. The first you'll encounter is the 16th-century **Iglesia de San Francisco** (Av. Jiménez at Carrera 7), famous for its fabulous Mudéjar interior, carved with intricate linear designs borrowed from the Islamic tradition. Also note the huge gilded altar, shaped like an amphitheater with shell-top niches. A short walk away is the equally elaborate **Iglesia de La Tercera** (Carrera 7 at Calle 16). The natural mahogany carvings on the altar, lauded as the most beautiful in Bogotá, are said to have so used up artist Pablo Caballero's artistic capacities that he died a madman.

Bogotá's phenomenal **Museo de Oro** (Gold Museum) contains the most comprehensive collection of pre-Columbian gold artifacts anywhere in the world. The collection consists of more than 36,000 pieces (by weight alone worth $200 million) culled over the centuries—often by force—from indigenous pre-Colombian cultures, including the Muisca, Nariño, Calima, and Sinú. Don't make the mistake of thinking of these treasures as primitive—they represent virtually all the techniques of modern gold making. Most of the gold, as well as one of the largest uncut emeralds in the world, are stored in a strong room on the top floor. Tours in English are given daily at 10:15 AM and 12:15 PM. *Calle 16 at Carrera 6A, tel. 1/281–3065. Admission charged. Closed Mon.*

Centro Internacional The **Iglesia San Diego,** a simple double-naved church built by Franciscan monks at the beginning of the 17th century, once stood on a quiet hacienda on the outskirts of colonial Bogotá; today trees and pastureland have been replaced with the towering offices of Bogotá's "little Manhattan," the Centro Internacional. Nonetheless, the church houses a very beautiful statue of the Virgin of the Fields, with a crown made of intricate filigree work in gold and silver. *Carrera 7 at Calle 26, tel. 1/241–2476. Admission free. Closed Sat.*

Nestled at the foot of Cerro Monserrate (*see* Excursions from Bogotá, *below*) is **Quinta de Bolívar,** the charming rustic country house where Bolívar, the Creole general who drove the Spanish from the northern half of the continent, passed the last years of his life with his mistress, Mañuela Saenz. Built in 1800, it was donated to Bolívar in 1820 in gratitude for his services to the fledgling republic. The house has a distinct Spanish flavor and is set in a lovely garden. *Calle 20 No. 3–23 este, tel. 1/284–6819. Admission charged. Closed Mon.*

Plaza de Toros Santamaría is Bogotá's bullring, designed by the Spaniard Lazcano in traditional Andalusian style. The best time to visit is in the morning, when you often can see young matadors polishing their skills. The main season only runs January through February, but small fights with local *toreros* (bullfighters) are held throughout the year. On the grounds, the **Museo Taurino** has exhibits devoted to bullfighting. *Carrera 7 at Calle 26. Admission free. Closed Mon.–Sat. afternoons and Sun.*

The **Museo de Arte Moderno** (Museum of Modern Art), housed in a beautifully designed building whose large windows give it a marvelous sense of spaciousness, has a strong permanent collection of contemporary Colombian painters as well as rotating exhibitions of national and international art. The museum bookshop stocks a wide range of (rather pricey) English-language titles on Colombian and international painters. *Calle 26 No. 6–05, tel. 1/283–8545. Admission charged. Closed Mon.*

The striking **Museo Nacional** (National Museum), designed by English architect Thomas Reed, housed a prison until its conversion in 1946; some parts of the museum, particularly the narrow galleries on the top floor, still have a sinister feel. On display is a mixed bag of pre-Columbian to contemporary art. The highlight is probably the third-floor collection of works by well-known 19th- and 20th-century Colombian artists—including Enrique Grau, Alejandro Obregón, Fernando Botero, and Andrés Santamaría, among others. *Carrera 7 No. 28–66, tel. 1/234–2129. Admission charged. Closed Mon.*

Shopping

Bogotá's shops and markets stock all types of leather and pure wool goods appropriate for life on the high plains. Handwoven *ruanas* (ponchos) are particularly popular; the oil in the wool makes them almost impervious to rain. Colombian artisans also have a way with straw: *Toquilla*, a tough native fiber, is used to make a dizzying variety of hats, shoes, handbags, and even umbrellas. The massive **Unicentro Shopping Center** (Av. 15 No. 123–30, tel. 1/213–8800) in Bogotá's affluent northern quarter is one of the largest in South America and has a vast selection of crafts and specialty shops. There is a good selection of fashionable but relatively expensive clothing at boutiques in the Zona Rosa, roughly between Calles 81 and 84 and Carreras 11 and 15.

Antiques Antiques shops are mainly found in the districts of Chapinero and Chicó, in the north of the city; one of the best is **Medina's** (Carrera 7 at Calle 50). On Plaza de Bolívar, **Cancino Sisters** (Calle 76 No. 2–65, tel. 1/212–7945) is a good place not just for Colombian antiques but also for pieces originally brought from Europe by aristocratic Colombian families. Another good bet is **Jaime Botero's** (Calle 10 No. 2–57), housed in the 17th-century La Toma de Agua building.

Emeralds Seventy percent of the world's emerald supply is mined in Colombia, but unless you know how to spot a fake you should buy only from reputable dealers, who provide certificates of authenticity. Try **Kawai** (Carrera 9 No. 99–02–P8, tel. 1/618–3070), **W.K. Bronkie** (Carrera 9 No. 74–08, office 1203, tel. 1/211–4621), or **Stern** (Tequendama Hotel, tel. 1/282–3562). **Sterling Joyeros** (Calle 11 No. 68B–43, tel. 1/262–6700) offers factory tours that give you a chance to see stones being cut, polished, and mounted.

Handicrafts Located in the cloister of Las Aquas, **Artesanías de Colombia** (Carrera 3 No. 18–60, tel. 1/284–3095) stocks an excellent variety of high-quality handmade crafts—from straw umbrellas to handwoven ponchos. Also try **El Cacique** (Carrera 7 No. 3–40) and the shop at the **Museo de Artes y Tradiciones Populares** (Carrera 8 No. 7–21).

Markets In the warren of stalls at the **Pasaje Rivas** market (Carrera 10 at Calle 10) look for bargain-priced ponchos, blankets, leatherware, and crafts. The **Mercado de Pulgas,** which sprawls northward along Carrera 3 from Calle 19, is a good place for bargain hunting on Sunday. Consider taking a taxi from downtown, and don't linger long after dark: The surrounding neighborhood has an unsavory reputation.

Pottery Pre-Columbian pottery can be found in several shops in the Centro Internacional; try **Precolombianos San Diego** (Carrera 10 No. 27–51, int. 167) or **Galeria Cano** (Carrera 13 No. 27–98, int. 1–19).

Spectator Sports

Bullfighting Bullfights are held every weekend in January and February and at least once a month the rest of the year at the **Plaza de Santamaría,** near Parque de la Independencia.

Horse Racing There is horse racing every weekend and on public holidays at the **Hipódromo los Andes,** on Autopista Norte, and at **Hipódromo del Techo,** on Bogotá's southwest fringe. Races generally start at 2 PM.

Soccer Soccer or "futbol" matches are held on most Sundays at 3:45 PM and Wednesdays at 8 PM at the **Estadio Municipal** (Municipal Stadium), near the Hipódromo del Techo; and at the **El Campín** stadium. Tickets can be bought from Cigarrería Bucana (Calle 18 No. 5–92). There is no need to book in advance except when there's a match between the two most poular local teams—Santa Fe and Millionarios.

Dining

The Bogotá yellow pages lists more than 1,000 restaurants, and the best offer first-class service and outstanding Colombian cuisine. Bogotá's most traditional recipes aim to fill the belly and ward off the cold. Probably the most common dish on local menus is *ajiaco,* a thick soup with chicken and several types of potato, garnished with fresh coriander, capers, and sour cream. Another popular broth is *puchero,* with chicken, pork, beef, potato, yucca, cabbage, corn, and plantain, accompanied by rice and avocado. Bogotaños like to start the day off with *chocolate santafeño,* a steaming cup of chocolate accompanied by a slab of cheese—you are meant to melt the cheese in the chocolate.

Bogotaños have lunch between noon and 2. Restaurants open for dinner around 7 and the more expensive ones stay open until after midnight. For price categories, *see* Dining in Staying in Colombia, *above.*

Very Expensive **Casa Medina.** Chef Ernest Reuter prepares outstanding
★ French cuisine that's unrivaled anywhere in Colombia. Try the medallions of trout bathed in fennel and onion or the excellent coquilles St. Jacques with asparagus. Each of the elegant dining rooms evokes a different European country, strewn as they are with antique heirlooms brought over from the Old World by aristocratic Bogotáno families. *Carrera 7 No. 69A–22, tel. 1/217–0288. Reservations advised. AE, MC, V. Closed Sun.*

La Fragata. With its slowly revolving dining room, this is probably the most striking of the capital's Fragata ("frigate") chain-restaurants. And believe it or not, the dimly lit and dark oak wood interior successfully conveys the atmosphere of a 19th-century sailing ship. The seafood, lobster, crab, red snapper, and locally caught rainbow trout are satisfying but slightly overshadowed by the service and presentation. *Calle 100 No. 8A–55, 12th floor; tel. 1/222–8806. Reservations advised. AE, MC, V. Closed Sun.*

Expensive **Carbón de Palo.** This is Bogotá's premier grilled meat restau-
★ rant and a favorite meeting place of senior politicians and plutocrats. Huge cooked-to-order beefsteaks (chicken or pork if you prefer) and excellent salads are served up with great aplomb in a delightful indoor patio full of hanging plants. On weekends, musicians serenade guests with traditional Colombian *rancheros* country music. *Av. 19 No. 106–12, tel. 1/214–0450. Reservations advised. AE, MC, V.*

Harry's Cantina. This stylish restaurant and bar, in the heart of the glitzy Zona Rosa, is definitely the "in" place to eat and drink in Bogotá. Glitterati come here as much to see and be seen as for any other reason, although Harry's selection of

Mexican food is wide—and the enchiladas and tacos are particularly good. Don't miss the potent *feijoa* margarita, made with tequila and fresh Colombian fruit. *Carrera 12A No. 33–11, tel. 1/610–6548. Reservations advised. AE, MC, V.*

Moderate **Andrés Carne de Res.** This is a popular restaurant among Bogotaños who enjoy hearty Colombian fare in a rural, relaxed setting. The atmosphere is bohemian, with fittings ranging from auto parts (the ashtrays) to valuable Vasquez statues. Try a succulent steak or braised chicken accompanied by potatoes, fried yucca, and *patacon* (fried plaintain). *Calle 114A No. 19–44, on the road to Chia, tel. 1/215–8284. Reservations advised. AE, MC, V.*

Crepes and Waffles. Smartly dressed waiters rush to serve you a tasty selection of stuffed pancakes and waffles. With its wide variety of ice creams and junior menu, this eatery is also a good place for families. *Carrera 11 No. 85–79, tel. 1/610–5298. AE, MC, V.*

Inexpensive **El Patio.** None of the cutlery or plates match and the small dining room is a little cramped, but that simply adds to the charm of this eccentric Italian restaurant in the bohemian La Macarena neighborhood, a couple of blocks up from the bullring. Try one of the masterful salads, or the veal Parmesan. *Carrera 4A No. 27–86, tel. 1/282–6141. No credit cards. Closed Sun.*

★ **Intermezzo.** Based in a fine old brick home in the distinguished Chapinero neighborhood, Intermezzo has a graceful dining room and a pleasant adjoining sunroom that's perfect for relaxed lunches. Chef and co-owner Luis Alberto Gonzalez has traveled the world picking up culinary cues from the French, Germans, Swiss, Italians, and North Americans. The cooking is essentially "nouveau," heavy on the vegetables, light on the oils. Particularly worthwhile is the *Schnecken mit Krauterbutter,* imported snails prepared in a delicate herb-butter sauce. *Calle 69 No. 10–85, tel. 1/248–9845. No credit cards.*

Lodging

The standard of accommodation in Bogotá is quite high: Private bathrooms are standard features, and all but the very cheapest hotels have hot water. Bogotá's better hotels are in the leafy, very wealthy northern districts—undoubtedly one of the most pleasant parts of the city and also the safest (there are security guards quite literally on every corner). If you want to soak up the color of the bustling downtown area, look into the handful of picturesque places to stay in the historic La Candelaria neighborhood. No matter where you stay, avoid walking unescorted at night. For price categories, *see* Lodging in Staying in Colombia, *above.*

Very Expensive **Bogotá Royal.** Besides offering spacious rooms with good views, cable TV, and excellent room service, the Royal is strategically located in Bogotá's World Trade Center on the tree-lined Avenida 100, a short taxi ride from both the airport and downtown. *Av. 100 No. 8A–01, tel. 1/218–9911. 144 rooms with bath. Facilities: restaurant, 3 bars, gym with sauna. AE, MC, V.*

★ **Hotel Tequendama.** This is one of Bogotá's oldest and most refined luxury hotels, boasting a gym and casino as well as an impressive complex of boutiques and shops on the ground floor. Its central location—just five minutes by taxi from the Centro

Internacional—makes it a popular choice with business travelers. Its large rooms lack real character but have impressive views over the city. *Carrera 10 No. 26–21, tel. 1/286–1111. 800 rooms with bath. Facilities: 24-hr room service, 2 restaurants, 2 bars, sauna, gym, florist, hair salon. AE, MC, V.*

Expensive **Hotel Charleston.** Just east of downtown is the very elegant and well-maintained Charleston, one of the few hotels in Bogotá where spacious suite accommodations are not exorbitantly priced. Plan on a short taxi ride to downtown sites. *Carrera 13, No. 85–42, tel. 1/257–1100, fax 1/236–7981. Facilities: restaurant, bar. AE, MC, V.*

Los Urapanes. At this intimate hotel in the heart of Zona Rosa, guests stay in modestly sized but luxurious suites with full room service and a minibar. The adjoining restaurant is popular for its exquisitely presented Colombian and international cuisine. *Carrera 13 No. 83–19, tel. 1/218–1188. 32 rooms with bath. Facilities: room service, restaurant, bar, minibar in each room, parking. AE, MC, V.*

Moderate **El Presidente.** You'll find the friendly El Presidente in a quiet, residential quarter just north of downtown; you'll need a taxi to reach La Candeleria and the bars and restaurants in Zona Rosa. Most suites and doubles have private bathrooms. *Calle 23, No. 9–45, tel. 1/284–1100. 160 rooms. Facilities: restaurant, bar. MC, V.*

★ **Las Terrazas.** Despite its downtown location, this small hotel has an almost rustic charm about it, partly because it is built into the hillside overlooking the city. The scrupulously clean rooms come in various sizes and have good views over downtown. A respectable adjoining restaurant serves Bogotá specialties as well as standard international fare. *Calle 54 No. 2–12, tel. 1/255–5777. 33 rooms with bath. Facilities: restaurant, TV in rooms, room service, parking. MC, V.*

Inexpensive **Hosteria de la Candelaria.** This small, friendly hotel occupies a 1920s mansion in the heart of the historic Candelaria district. The comfortably sized rooms are strewn with colonial antiques—the owners also run a small antiques business, so if anything takes your fancy you may be able to strike a deal. *Calle 9 No. 3–11, tel. 1/342–1727. 14 rooms with bath. Facilities: restaurant, 24-hr reception. No credit cards.*

The Arts and Nightlife

Bogotá's reputation for random violence and muggings has not put a damper on its ebullient nighttime scene, which often lasts well beyond sunrise. People start the evening off at the cinema or theater and continue on to one of the many restaurants or bars in the Zona Rosa and La Calera districts, which are full of security guards and quite safe. Less so is the lively, bohemian downtown district, La Macarena, though you still should not have any problem if you travel by taxi and don't wander alone and aimlessly.

The Arts Bogotá has a lively and well developed theater scene, *Theaters* though you must understand Spanish to appreciate it. Among the better-known theaters are **Teatro la Candelaria** (Calle 12 No. 2–59, tel. 1/281–4814), which earned itself international fame for its recent production of the play *Guadalupe Años Sin Cuenta*, about Colombia's bloody political turmoil in the 1950s;

Teatro Popular de Bogotá (Carrera 5 No. 14–71, tel. 1/242–8406); and **Teatro Nacional** (Calle 71 No. 10–25, tel. 1/211–9119), which puts on musicals and popular comedies.

Nightlife Bogotá's two main partying areas are the Zona Rosa, between Calles 81 and 84 and Carreras 11 and 15, and La Calera in the affluent northern part of the city, shortly before it becomes almost entirely residential. Downtown at the intersection of Carrera 5 and Calle 27 there's also a handful of popular salsa bars.

Bars and Bogotá's top night spot is **Bahia** (Via La Calera KM 4, tel.
Nightclubs 1/610–0208), a large and beautifully designed club spread over two floors. The view of Bogotá stretching away to the horizon from Calera Hill is reason enough for the trip. **Coconuts** (Calle 82 No. 12–50, tel. 1/257–2006) is really a restaurant in nightclub clothing, though the huge patio that overlooks the street is a popular spot for drinks and chitchat. **Charlotte's** (Calle 82 No. 12–51, tel. 1/257–3508) is a popular Zona Rosa nightclub, complete with an outdoor dancefloor and blazing log fires to keep you warm.

Excursions from Bogotá

Cerro de You can get a good overview of the city from the top of **Mon-**
Monserrate **serrate Peak,** which looms menacingly over the downtown area. Although dense smog often obscures the skyline, the view of chaotic Bogotá stretching to the horizon is still breathtaking. The panorama extends from the Río Bogotá to the colonial city, whose red Spanish tiles make it easy to spot.

Getting There A cable car (*teleférico*) runs from Monserrate Station near Quinta de Bolivia to the top of the peak weekdays 9–6 and Sundays 6–6. The only other alternative is making the hour-long walk up the winding footpath that parallels the cable car route; however, as weekday robberies are all to common, attempt this only on Sunday when the path is busy.

Tunja Tunja, the capital of Boyacá province, was founded in 1539 by Captain Gonzalo Suárez Rendón. Although modern Tunja is infested with industry and shantytowns, the historic center retains some of its original colonial character, with its stately churches and pre-Republic mansions. Of the latter you can tour **Casa del Fundador Suarez Rendón** (Plaza Bolívar), with a small museum devoted to Tunja's founder, and **Casa de Don Juan de Vargas** (Calle 20 near Carrera 8, closed Mon.), which exhibits colonial artworks and paintings. Don Juan was a scribe and his large library of art books was probably the inspiration for much of the imagery of the ceiling frescoes.

Getting There Tunja lies 137 kilometers (85 miles) northeast of Bogotá on the road to Cúcuta, near the Venezuelan border. Buses depart regularly from Bogotá's Terminal de Transporte, and the three- to four-hour bus ride costs under $4 each way.

Western Colombia

West of Bogotá the Pan-American Highway drops sharply into the stifling heat of the *Tierras Calientes,* or hotlands, of the Magdalena Valley. Continuing southwest along the highway, the landscape becomes rigid and mountainous as you approach the central ridge of the Andes, the *Cordillera Central.* The whole area is wonderfully fertile; the province of Antioquia, in particular, lies like a gigantic garden around its capital, Medellín. This sprawling though somewhat isolated city is lodged in a narrow valley and encircled by lush and thickly wooded hills—hardly what you would expect from Colombia's second-largest and perhaps most notorious city in terms of its industrial heritage and modern drug trade.

The fertile *Valle de Cauca* (Cauca Valley), dominated by its young and lively capital, Cali, is the center of Colombian agriculture, though colonial architecture and Indian markets are what draw the bulk of visitors to the region. Farther south, the Pan-American Highway climbs toward the colonial village of Popayán and, even farther south, on to the Ecuadorian border. Western Colombia, and the southwest in particular, is a treasure house of indigenous culture; with just a little effort—and a sense of adventure—you can visit the enigmatic carved stones of San Agustín and primitive Guambiano and Paez Indian villages near Popayán.

Getting There

By Plane Medellín's **Jose Maria Córdoba** airport, 38 kilometers (24 miles) southeast of the city, is served by **Avianca, Aces,** and **Sam.** The flight from Bogotá takes 45 minutes and costs $100; the flight from Cali lasts one hour and costs $80. Between the airport and downtown Medellín expect to pay $7 for a taxi, $3 for a *colectivo* bus.

Most domestic carriers offer regular connections between Bogotá and Cali's **Aeropuerto de Palmaseca** (tel. 4/255–6707), 20 kilometers (12 miles) northeast of the city. The only international carrier based in Cali, **Avianca**, has daily flights to New York, Miami, and Panama. Taxis from the airport to the city cost around $6; minibuses that connect the airport and bus terminal depart every 10 minutes and cost less than $1.

By Car A paved, two-lane highway opened just a few years agao, connecting Bogotá and Medellín via Manizales and Honda. The 560-kilometer (347-mile) journey takes about nine hours and passes through some beautiful cattle country in the Magdalena Valley. Although this is one of Colombia's major cocaine routes, the road is generally well-patrolled and safe, and there are police controls around Honda. Watch out for landslides in wet weather, and expect detours and potholes on the Medellín–Honda leg.

Also fully paved but in poor condition is the highway between Bogotá and Cali. The 680-kilometer (422-mile) journey takes around 10 hours, and, being one of Colombia's major routes, is relatively safe. South of Armenia the Cali road joins with the Pan-American Highway and climbs the spectacular Quíndio Pass (3,352 meters/10,990 feet) before diverging west toward the coast at Palmira.

By Bus Medellín's long-distance bus station, **Terminal de Transporte Moriano Espina Pérez,** is 3 kilometers (2 miles) northwest of the city center and has a cafeteria and information desk. Cali's bus terminal is at Calle 30n No. 2a–29. Plan on a nine- to 12-hour trek between Bogotá and Medellín, 10–13 hours between Bogotá and Cali, and 11–13 hours between Cali and Medellín.

Medellín

<table>
<tr>
<td>**Tourist Information**</td>
<td>**Oficina de Turismo** (Calle 57 No. 45–129, tel. 4/254–0800). **Turantioquia** (Carrera 48 No. 58–11, tel. 4/254–3864) stocks maps and organizes a nighttime bus tour of the city on Friday.</td>
</tr>
<tr>
<td>**Exploring Medellín**</td>
<td>**Medellín,** the capital of Antioquia Province, stands neck and neck with Cali as Colombia's second-largest city, with a population of more than 2 million; it is also the country's main industrial beehive. But don't expect a sooty city full of smoking chimneys. Medellín is set in a lush sylvan valley at an altitude of 1,488 meters (4,880 feet), and the deep-green mountains that rise sharply all around provide an attractive backdrop to the glass-and-concrete towers of its elegant financial district.</td>
</tr>
</table>

A dynamic industrial and commercial center, Medellíin is lauded as Latin America's "Convention Center." It has three respected universities and a large student population, not to mention a sober hardworking middle class. It is also home to the notorious Medellín cocaine cartel. Though the security forces have dealt important blows to the drug mafia, it is no less violent or unpredictable. Visitors are unlikely to have any problems, but you should be cautious about wandering around Medellín after dark and stick to central areas of the city.

The best views of Medellín are from the top of **Cerro Nutibara** (Nutibara Hill), a smallish peak overlooking downtown, best reached by taxi (under $2) from anywhere in the city center. At the very top is **Pueblito Paisa,** a reconstructed traditional Antioquian village complete with a church, town hall, barbershop, school, and village store. Surrounding the pueblito is the **Parque de las Esculturas,** a maze of paths dotted with modern and traditional sculptures by Colombian and other Latin American artists. There is also an open-air theater, used mainly for rock concerts on Saturday night.

At the heart of downtown Medellín lies **Parque Bolívar,** a surprisingly generous open space for such a central area of the city. In the evenings, the park is popular among young people, who congregate on the steps of the Romantic-style **Catedral de Villanueva,** whose ornate coffee-color facade dominates the park and is one of Medellín's most striking buildings. Designed by Frenchman Charles Carré and begun in 1875, it is the largest cathedral in South America and the third-largest brick building in the world. *Admission free. Closed Mon.*

Three blocks south of Parque Bolívar lies the elegant **Parque Berrío.** Be sure to look for the huge female torso by Colombia's most famous sculptor, Fernando Botero, which stands to the left of the Banco de la Republica building. On the other side of the bank stands a bronze fountain and a marble monument dedicated to Atanasio Girardot, an 18th-century freedom fighter who helped gain Colombia its independence.

Just two blocks from the park you can admire the fine 18th-century facade of the **Ermita de la Veracruz.** The cool interior of the church, while a little disappointing, is nonetheless a pleasant place to escape from Medellín's noisy streets. *Calle 51 No. 52–58. Admission free.*

In the old mint building opposite the main post office is the **Museo de Antioquia,** which contains the world's largest collection of paintings and sculptures by sculptor Fernando Botero and other well-known Colombian artists. *Carrera 52A No. 51A–29, tel. 4/251–3636. Admission charged. Closed Mon., Tues., and Sat.*

The **Museo El Castillo,** located in the nearby suburb of El Poblado, is considered the most elegant palace in Medellín. This 1930s gothic-style structure, whose beautiful French-style gardens comprise sweeping lawns and exuberant flower gardens, was once the home of one of Medellín's most powerful families. Their original belongings are on display along with furniture and art collected from around the world. *Calle 9 Sur No. 32–260, tel. 4/268–6040. Admission free.*

For a gastronomic tour of Antioquia, come to Medellín's **Parque de las Delicias** (Delicacies Park) on the first Saturday of each month, when a wealth of small stalls do a brisk business in everything from *obleas* (thin jam-filled waffles) to *lechona* (roast stuffed pork). *Carrera 73 and Av. 39D.*

The **Jardín Botánico Joaquín Antonio Uribe,** in the suburbs 10 minutes north of Parque Bolívar by taxi, boasts more than 500 native plant species, an aviary with strikingly colored tropical birds, and a massive greenhouse teeming with orchids. *Carrera 52 No. 73–298, tel. 4/244–0722. Admission charged.*

Eighty kilometers (50 miles) northwest of the city is the historic town of **Santa Fé de Antioquia,** founded in 1541 and the former capital of the region. The town is a colonial masterpiece with an extremely well-preserved downtown district brimming with cobbled streets and old whitewashed houses. Santa Fé is also well known for its *orfebrería* (goldwork). Visit the workshops clustered on Carrera 10 between the cathedral and the Bogotá River. There are daily buses from Medellín's Terminal de Transporte, or take a taxi (up to four people) for around $50.

Shopping Medellín's **Centro Commercial San Diego** shopping mall (Calle 12 No. 30–5), near the Inter-Continental Hotel, offers a good selection of crafts, jewelry, and clothing shops. Both **El Arhuaco** (Calle 56A No. 49–80) and **La Piel** (Calle 53 No. 49–131) stock a wide range of high-quality Antioquian crafts. However, the most comprehensive selection of handmade Antioquian crafts is available at an open-air crafts market held on the first Saturday of each month at the Plaza Bolívar.

Dining Traditional Antioquian cooking means hearty peasant fare—plenty of meat, beans, rice, and potatoes. But Medellín is full of quality restaurants where you'll find a wide range of foreign as well as traditional Colombian cuisines. For price ranges, *see* Dining in Staying in Colombia, *above.*

Las Cuatro Estaciones. Medellín's most popular restaurant balances first-rate food and service with decor that might easily be mistaken for tacky. Choose one of four thematic dining rooms—one is decorated in a Colombian style, others in European, Asian, and Spanish styles—or simply close your eyes and concentrate on the meal at hand. The house specialty is seafood, and the Spanish rice-and-seafood dish paella regularly draws crowds of devoted locals. On the last Tuesday of each month there's an amusing medieval banquet. *Calle 17 No. 43–79, El Poblado, Medellín, tel. 4/266–7120. MC, V. Expensive.*

La Mesa del Rey. This friendly and informal ranch-style eatery is the place to sample hearty Antioquian dishes. You sit at wooden benches, and servers in traditional Colombian dress bring on the food—try the *bandeja paisa*, a sampler of steak, beans, pork, and avocado; or a platter of pork loin strips and sirloin steak. *Pueblito Paisa, Cerro Nutibara, Medellín, tel. 4/235-7740. MC, V. Moderate.*

★ **La Aguacatala.** Housed in a colonial-style mansion in the leafy hills of the exclusive El Poblado district, this charming roadside tavern offers a good selection of local dishes, including excellent chicken and *fríjoles* (beans) served by staff dressed in traditional Antioquian peasant garb. *Carrera 43A No. 7 Sur-130, Medellín, tel. 4/246-6093. MC, V. Inexpensive.*

Lodging Medellín's better hotels are in the wealthy El Poblado district to the east of the city center. Downtown, and just a stone's throw away from most of the city's monuments, there are some quite respectable places to stay—but you should avoid walking around here late at night. For price ranges, *see* Lodging in Staying in Colombia, *above.*

Hotel Nutibara. The Nutibara is not laid out on such a grand scale as the Inter-Continental, but nevertheless it is a luxurious and well-maintained complex, housed in a stylish 1930s-era building replete with a casino and heated indoor pool. Although the Nutibara is conveniently situated in the heart of downtown and is only a short taxi ride from Medellín's restaurants and bars, the immediate surrounding area is not particularly safe at night and should be avoided. *Calle 52A No. 50-46, Medellín, tel. 4/511-5111, fax 4/231-3716. 90 rooms with bath. Facilities: restaurant, café, bar, pool, whirlpool, discotheque. AE, MC, V. Very Expensive.*

Inter-Continental. This spacious modern hotel just outside Medellín has spectacular views of the city. The services are what you would expect from an international chain, with several good restaurants, a disco and casino, as well as a large outdoor swimming pool. The hotel is about 20 minutes by taxi ($6) from the city center and 35 minutes from the airport. *Variante Las Palmas, tel. 4/266-0680, fax 4/268-2986. 300 rooms with bath. Facilities: 3 restaurants, café, disco, bar, swimming pool, gym, massage, Turkish bath, children's facilities, tennis, basketball and volleyball courts. AE, MC, V. Very Expensive.*

Veracruz. With many of the facilities of the five-star internationals, the Veracruz is nevertheless a good deal less expensive. Rooms in the newly built "diplomatic" wing are slightly more expensive than in the older part of the hotel and a little more spacious and luxurious. There is a small pool on the 11th floor with a panoramic view over the city. The Veracruz's restaurant is one of the best in Medellín. *Carrera 50 No. 54-18, Medellín, tel. 4/511-5511, fax 4/231-0542. 60 rooms. Facilities: restaurant, café, bar, sauna, Turkish bath, pool. AE, MC, V. Expensive.*

Ambassador. Located in an uninspiring 1970s tower block, the four-star Ambassador is a good example of how Medellín's poor reputation has kept lodging prices in check. All rooms have a private bathroom and cable TV, and the hotel facilities are excellent even by international standards. The lobby restaurant also has a first-rate reputation. *Carrera 50 No. 54-50, Medellín, tel. 4/511-5311, fax 4/231-5312. 45 rooms. Facilities: restaurant, pool, bar, sauna, Turkish bath, restaurant, swimming pool, bar, restaurant, travel agency, beauty salon. AE, MC, V. Moderate.*

Mariscal Robledo. Housed in a lovely colonial-style mansion in the heart of La Pintada's old quarter, this roomy hotel has a beautiful pool on a quiet patio surrounded by trees. *La Pintada,* *tel. 4/826–1111. 35 rooms, some with bath. Facilities: pool, TV, bar, breakfast and lunch included. MC, V. Inexpensive.*

Cali and Valle de Cauca

Tourist Information

Cali: Corporacion Regional de Turismo del Valle de Cauca (Calle 16N No. 4N–20, tel. 23/67–56–12); Comité Proturismo del Valle (Av. 2N No. 9N–09, tel. 23/68–69–72).

Exploring Cali and Valle de Cauca

Cali is the economic center of Valle Province, responsible for a hefty portion of the country's sugar, coffee, and maize exports. Cali itself lies at the southern end of Cauca Valley at an elevation of over 900 meters (3,000 feet), contributing to the city's springlike temperatures and the lush tropical vegetation that encroaches upon its shantytown outskirts. Despite vertiginous expansion in the 20th century (the city has grown fourfold in the past 40 years), Cali is better planned than most Colombian industrial centers. Cali has few historical monuments, but its tree-lined avenues and lazy open-air cafés attract small throngs of foreigners, particularly during the Christmas–New Year *feria,* when the city unapologetically devotes itself to merrymaking.

At the heart of Cali is the quiet **Plaza de Caycedo,** guarded by rows of tall palms and a statue of Joaquín Caicedo y Cuero, an 18th-century freedom fighter who liberated Cali from the Spanish. The plaza is skirted by the neoclassical **Catedral** (admission free; closed Mon.), with its massive limestone walls, marble columns, and brilliantly gilded main altar. Across from the cathedral is the Republican-period **Palacio Municipal** (City Hall), with minutely carved doors set within equally ornate arches. A first-floor **museum** has a small exhibition of 300 years of sugar growing and processing, for which Cali and Valle de Cauca are famous. *Plaza de Caycedo. Admission charged. Closed Mon.*

One block beyond is the 18th-century church and monastery of **San Francisco** (admission free), a post-colonial redbrick structure that's undistinguished except for its domed bell tower, which is lavished with dazzling multicolored mosaics. A few doors down, the **Torre Mudéjar** (Moorish Tower), a curious brick bell tower that looks like an Islamic temple, is considered one of the finest examples of Spanish-Moorish art in South America. *Carrera 6 at Calle 10. Admission free. Closed Mon.*

A short walk away is Cali's oldest church, **La Merced,** built in 1680 on the site where the city's founders celebrated their first mass in 1536. The adjoining convent houses two museums: the **Museo de Arte Colonial,** featuring the country's most complete collection of Vazquez y Ceballos religious paintings, and the **Museo Arqueológico,** which displays pre-Columbian pottery and a scale-model reproduction of Cali and its aboriginal inhabitants. *Carrera 4 at Calle 7. Admission charged. Closed Sun. and Mon.*

Avenida Colombia runs mostly parallel to the languid Río Cali and is lined with colossal palm trees and flower-filled parks. Looming over the avenue is the imposing **Iglesia de la Ermita,** a striking white-and-red neogothic creation, built between 1930 and 1948. Its rococo towers have been locally dubbed "la torta matrimonial" for their resemblance to wedding-cake spires. *Av. Colombia at Calle 13. Admission free. Open only for mass.*

There are spectacular views from the stubby range of mountains overlooking Cali. A popular scenic overlook is **Alto de los Cristales** (1,421 meters/4,660 feet), atop which is a monumental statue of Christ visible from miles around. You can take Bus No. 3 to Bellavista and then scramble uphill to the top, or take a taxi from downtown for around $5.

At **Cañasgordas,** a colonial hacienda set in the countryside an hour's drive from Cali, relics of Cali's last royal sheriff are preserved. Visitors can still see the high canopied beds reached by ladders and an intriguing Moorish system of rainwater canals that supplies both water and a primitive form of air-conditioning. Cañasgordas was also the setting for Eustaquio Palacios's film, *El Alférez Real. Via Tulua. Admission charged. Closed Mon.*

In **Palmira,** a beautifully preserved Colonial village 42 kilometers (26 miles) northwest of Cali, you can hire a horse-drawn carriage for a tour of the town's compact center. Palmira is dominated by the soaring 85-meter- (279-foot-) tall tower of its 17th-century **cathedral.** On Palmira's outskirts look for the 18th-century **Hacienda de la Concepción,** one of the most beautiful country houses in Valle Province, built by a sugar baron who had an eye for colonial furnishings and rich detailing. Spanish-language tours are given every hour or so. *Via Palmira. Admission charged. Closed Mon.*

Buga, 50 kilometers (31 miles) beyond Palmira, is chockablock with preserved 17th- and 18th-century buildings due to its status as a National Monument. Of particular note are the **Iglesia de San Francisco,** the **Catedral de San Pedro,** and the **Basilica del Señor de los Milagros,** all within four blocks of Buga's peaceful main square.

Founded in 1537 by Sebastian de Belalcázar, **Popayán** quickly became an important administrative center of the Viceroyalty of New Granada due to its location on the Cartagena–Quito gold route. Testimony to that importance are the many colonial buildings the town boasts. A catastrophic earthquake on Good Friday, 1983, left the town nearly in ruins, but since then Popayán and its colonial treasures have been painstakingly rebuilt. In fact, the best way to appreciate this historical town is on foot, wandering its narrow streets or lingering in a plaza outside one of its lavish, embellished churches. The most popular time to visit is during Holy Week, when penitents parade the cramped streets by candlelight, shouldering heavy platforms crowned with freakish statues and religious icons.

Fifty kilometers (31 miles) northeast of Popayán, the village of **Silvia,** really an isolated cluster of adobe houses, is home to the Gaumbiano Indians, a fiercely proud people who have managed to preserve many of their centuries-old ancestral customs, among them their love for black bowler hats and bright purple skirts that are worn by both women and men. The best day to visit is Tuesday, market day, when the central square is crammed with local products such as corn, Andean tubers, and heavy wool ponchos.

Dedicated hikers will want to visit **Puracé National Park,** 60 kilometers (37 miles) east of Popayán and spread over one of

Colombia's most spectacular mountain regions. The park ranges in altitude from 2,500 meters (8,202 feet) to almost 4,800 meters (15,748 feet) and is the source of Colombia's largest rivers—the Magdalena, Cauca, and Caqueta. The park also nurtures an extraordinary variety of wildlife that includes the Andean condor, the rare spectacled bear, the puma, and the tapir.

San Agustín, nearly 50 kilometers (31 miles) southeast and a four-hour drive from Popayán, is where mysterious, heroic-size statues are strewn across what must once have been the sacred grounds of a forgotten empire. These stubby graystone statues look more like the megaliths of Chile's Easter Island than anything else you'll find in Colombia—hence the surrounding mystery. Some archaeologists have linked these larger-than-life stone figures to the Maya, but it's likely they are the work of a pre-Columbian tribe that was decimated by disease and simply vanished shortly after the arrival of Europeans on the continent.

The closest airport to San Augustín is in the village of **Pitalito,** where you can rent a car ($30–$50) or taxi ($25 for the day) to bring you to the site. The nearby Los Balcones hotel (*see* Dining and Lodging, *below*) rents horses and guides for daytime treks through San Augustín. Ask your guide to detour to El Estrecho, a tight deep gorge through which the Río Magdalena rushes, crashing against the huge boulders that clog the chute. *Park admission charged.*

Shopping   The region's handicrafts reflect the different races who conquered and colonized southwestern Colombia. Descendants of the black slaves brought to work on sugarcane plantations still handcarve elaborate bowls and cutlery from Pacific Forest wood, while a Spanish influence is seen in the fine embroidered blouses and dresses offered in street markets. The indigenous Guambiano Indians from Silvia are better known for their handwoven ponchos and *chumbes,* long multicolored woolen strips used for belts.

In Cali try the narrow streets surrounding the main square, where you'll find a decent selection of crafts shops. One of Cali's best handicrafts shops is **Artesanías Pancandé** (Av. 6AN No. 17AN–53). In Popayán there's a cluster of handicrafts stores near Ermita church, three blocks below the main square.

Dining   For price ranges, *see* Dining in Essential Information, *above*.

Cali Viejo. This old stately manor is in the hills high above Cali, and the shady veranda makes a pleasant spot to sample some typical Cali dishes. Try *sancocho de gallina,* a local version of chicken soup; and Cali *tamales,* hand-rolled corn dough filled with pork and vegetables and wrapped in a banana leaf. *Casona Vieja del Bosque Municipal, Cali, tel. 23/52–38–12. MC, V. Expensive.*

Don Carlos. This dimly lit and somewhat formal restaurant is considered one of the best in southwestern Colombia, and it is a popular meeting place with elite Caleños. The specialty is seafood, from fried snapper to fish stew, impeccably presented. *Carrera 1 No. 7–53, Cali, tel. 23/51–11–32. MC, V. Moderate.*

El Orquideal. Set in a parklike area full of huge trees and lush tropical vegetation, and with a play area for children, the Orquideal consists of several large thatched huts where diners eat in the shade of thick reed thatch. The menu includes Colombian and international dishes, from *primo lomo* (strip steak) and catfish medallions to simple pasta, and the service is quick and efficient. *Carretera El Aguacatal, Cali, tel. 23/80-86–62 or 23/80–98–00. MC, V. Moderate.*

El Simonetta. A stone's throw from the Hotel Inter-Continental, this stylish and airy restaurant, decorated in elegant shades of red and white, serves what many consider to be the finest Italian cuisine in Cali. The tagliatelle is superb, and there is a reasonable range of Italian wines to chose from. *Diagonal 27 No. 27–117, Cali, tel. 23/81–87–01. MC, V. Moderate.*

Lodging For price ranges, *see* Lodging in Essential Information, *above.*

★ **Inter-Continental.** The main lobby is grand and sprawling, which simply highlight the deficiencies of the rather small and plain rooms. Still, the Inter-Continental is endowed with excellent facilities—including poolside and rooftop restaurants—and is probably Cali's most luxurious offering. It is also the social center of the city: When national and international artists come to Cali they invariably stay and perform here. *Av. Colombia No. 2–72, Cali, tel. 23/82–32–25, fax 23/83–49–02. 375 rooms, most with bath. Facilities: room service, restaurant, bar, swimming pool, sauna, whirlpool, tennis courts. AE, MC, V. Very Expensive.*

Hotel Dann. Located in an attractive residential quarter near the banks of the Río Cali, this luxury hotel offers excellent secretarial services for business travelers, and large air-conditioned rooms—each with a good view of the city—equipped with TVs and minibars. On balmy days cool off in the hotel's vast swimming pool. *Av. Colombia 1–40, Cali, tel. 23/82–28–66 or 23/82–32–30, fax 23/83–01–29. 90 rooms, most with bath. Facilities: restaurant, bar, laundry service, swimming pool. MC, V. Expensive.*

Don Jaime. This intimate 30-room hotel provides more personalized attention than its larger corporate rivals without sacrificing any of the competition's luxuries. A popular feature is Don Jaime's pleasant café which overlooks the elegant Avenida 6. The hotel restaurant, too, is among the best in Cali. *Av. 6 No. 15N–25, Cali, tel. 23/67–28–28 or 23/67–82–87, fax 23/68–70–98. 30 rooms, most with bath. Facilities: restaurant, bar, room service, cable TV, air-conditioning. MC, V. Expensive.*

Hotel Monasterio. Housed in a renovated 17th-century convent in downtown Popayán, the Monasterio is well-kept and stylish, with high ceilings and colonial-style furnishings. The plumbing works best on the first two floors, which face a central courtyard. The on-site restaurant and bar are popular gathering spots during Holy Week, when reservations are imperative. *Calle 4 (between Carreras 9 and 10), Popayán, tel. 28/32–98–76. 48 rooms. Facilities: restaurant, bar, pool. MC, V. Moderate.*

Hotel Osoguaico. If you want to sleep near the ruins at San Augustín, or if you simply crave a hearty lunch or dinner, keep an eye out for this basic hotel a few kilometers from the entrance to the archaeological site. The rooms themselves are very simple but clean. *Via San Augustín, San Augustín, tel. 88/37–30–01. 16 rooms. Facilities: restaurant, horse rental, guided tours of ruins. MC. Moderate.*

The Caribbean Coast

A world away and lost to another time, it seems, is Colombia's sultry Caribbean Coast, a self-contained region linked to Bogotá and the interior only by the national flag, the milky Magdalena River, and a couple of snaking highways. Exotic and handsome, the local *costeño* people, a blend of mestizo, Negro, mulatto, and zambo, project an air of gaiety unheard of in the capital, driven by Cuban funk and the accordion-heavy *vallenato* music, a regional specialty. Remarkably, perhaps, despite the strength-sapping heat and persistent Carnival-like atmosphere, the Caribbean Coast has nurtured Colombia's best-known writers and artists, including novelist Gabriel García Márques and painter Alejandro Obregón.

The appeal of the region lies in its diversity. Toward the western end of the 1,600-kilometer (992-mile) Caribbean shoreline, the city of Cartagena ranks as the most striking colonial relic in South America. And just offshore, the delicate Rosario Islands are ideal for snorkeling and diving. Heading east by car or bus, you pass mangrove-encircled lagoons before reaching the dramatic, snowcapped Sierra Nevada mountains, whose rain-forested slopes harbor the mysterious Ciudad Perdida (Lost City) and magnificent Parque Tayrona, one of Colombia's finest national parks. The nearby port of Santa Marta is where drug traffickers discreetly load cocaine aboard U.S.-bound banana boats—and it goes without saying that inquisitiveness in this feral, fascinating city is extremely unwise.

The resort islands of San Andrés and Providencia lie 645 kilometers (400 miles) northwest off the coast, though frequent air service and San Andrés' duty-free status mean neither island has been overlooked by tourists. Despite its somewhat remote location, San Andrés, in particular, is where Colombians and a few foreigners gather to dive and snorkel in between bouts of sunbathing and shopping.

Tourist Information

Cartagena: Oficina de Turismo (Crespo Airport, tel. 53/65–55–00; Casa del Marqués Valdehoyos, Calle de la Factoría No. 36–57, tel. 53/64–70–15). **San Andrés:** Oficina de Turismo (Sesquicentenario Airport, tel. 811/6110; Av. Colombia, tel. 811/4230); Islatur (Hotel Cacique Toné, Av. Colombia, tel. 811/24251). **Santa Marta:** Oficina de Turismo (Convento del Santo Domingo, Cra. 2 No. 16–44, tel. 54/21–24–25); Inderena (Cra. 1 No. 22–79, tel. 54/23–63–65).

Getting There

By Plane There are daily flights between Bogotá and Cartagena's **Crespo** international airport (tel. 53/65–55–00), 3 kilometers (2 miles) east of downtown; and between Bogotá and Santa Marta's **Simón Bolívar airport** (tel. 54/23–73–74), 20 kilometers (12 miles) and an $8 taxi ride from the city center. Carriers include **Avianca, Aces,** and **Intercontinental** (Cartagena, tel. 953/66–29–95). **American Airlines** offers less frequent international service to Santa Marta.

San Andrés' **Sesquicentenario** airport (tel. 811/6110), a short taxi ride from the island village of El Centro, is regularly serviced by **Avianca**, **Aces**, **Intercontinental**, and **Sam**. The 90-minute flight from Bogotá costs $125 each way; the one-hour flight from Cartagena about $90 each way. Sam also links San Andrés with Providencia Island three times daily for less than $40 round-trip.

By Bus **Expresso Brasilia** (Cartagena, tel. 53/66–16–92; Santa Marta, tel. 54/23–40–88) regularly connects Bogotá with Cartagena (24 hours) and Santa Marta (20 hours). Its air-conditioned buses also travel six times daily between Cartagena and Mengangue. **La Costeña** (Cartagena, tel. 53/66–40–58; Santa Marta, tel. 54/23–42–73) departs every 20 minutes or so between 6 AM and 4 PM on the five-hour trip between Cartagena and Santa Marta, with stops in Barranquilla.

By Car Panama is inaccesible from the Caribbean Coast. Traveling from Bogotá and the interior of Colombia is laborious but manageable; the drive between Bogotá and Cartegena, for example, takes 20 hours on the Pan-American Highway.

By Boat Buses from Cartagena stop in Magangue, where you can catch a *chalupa* (river launch) to Mompós. The boat trip takes two–three hours and the last launch leaves at 4 PM.

Guided Tours

In Cartagena, **Tesoro Tours** (Av. San Martín No. 6–129, Bocagrande, tel. 53/65–47–13) arranges city tours for $10 per person. Tours to the coral-encircled **Islas del Rosario** depart daily at 8 AM from the Muelle de los Pegasos and return by 4 PM; book through **Raphael Pérez** (tel. 53/66–21–98), **Media Maranja** (tel. 53/66–17–06), or **Caliente Tours** (tel. 53/65–53–46).

From Santa Marta, **TMA** (Calle 15, No. 2–60, Edif. Bolívar, tel. 54/23–41–90) offers a range of city tours plus treks to Pueblito, Ciudad Perdida, and Parque Tayrona. A more informal and flexible option is **Ecotours** (tel. 54/20–16–72), run by Eduardo Buscamente—look for him at the Frutera Tropical, next door to Santa Marta's Hostal PanAmerican.

Exploring the Caribbean Coast

Plan for a decent chunk of time in Cartagena, which is a convenient base for excursions to the enchanting colonial river port of Mompós. Santa Marta is a good base from which to explore Parque Tayrona's stunning tropical coastline. Treks to Ciudad Perdida (the Lost City) also set out from Santa Marta. Barranquilla deserves a visit only during its Ash Wednesday carnival.

Cartagena With its barrel-tile rooftops and wooden balconies, modern Cartagena often looks more Spanish than Spain, but the feeling is tropical, Creole, and altogether more exotic. When founded in 1533 by Pedro de Heredia, Cartagena was the only port on mainland South America. Gold and silver, mined in the interior and looted from Indians, passed through here on the way to Spain, making Cartagena an obvious target for pirates. The most destructive of these was Sir Francis Drake, who in 1586 torched 200 houses, destroyed the cathedral, and made off to England with more than 100,000 gold ducats. Cartagena's magnificent walls and countless fortresses grew in response to these raids, helping to protect the most important African slave market in the New World (the Spaniards forbade Indian slavery).

The ocher-painted **Casa de Marqués Valdehoyos,** although scantily furnished, exudes a powerful whiff of well-to-do colonial life (the sturdy mansion and its shady courtyards were built with the marqués's slave-trade fortune). Also note: The tourist office inside provides useful maps. *Calle Factoría No. 36–57, tel. 53/64–70–15. Admission free.*

Walk two blocks south to **Plaza Santo Domingo.** The eponymous church looming over the plaza is the city's oldest; begun in 1539, it has a simple whitewashed interior, bare limestone pillars, memorial floor slabs, a raised choir, and an adjacent cloistered seminary. Local lore tells how the bell tower's twisted profile is the work of the Devil, who, dispirited at having failed to destroy it, threw himself into the plaza's well. The Dalmania Café alongside the seminary is a good spot for breakfast or a cooling *jugo* (fruit juice). *Admission free.*

Continue straight for one block, past pricey antiques stores, and turn left down Calle Inquisición to **Plaza Bolívar.** To your left stands the whitewashed **Palacio de la Inquisición** (Palace of the Inquisition) with its grand limestone baroque doorway. In its heyday, this headquarters of repressive political and spiritual cleansing had jurisdiction over Colombia, Ecuador, Venezuela, Central America, and the Caribbean. The ground-floor rooms contain implements of torture—racks and thumbscrews, to name but a few—and architectonic models of bygone Cartagena. *Plaza Bolívar. Admission charged.*

Directly opposite is the **Museo del Oro y Arquelogíca** (Gold and Archaeological Museum), which houses an interesting assortment of gold ornaments and pottery culled from the Zinús, an indigenous tribe who lived in the region 2,000 years ago. *Admission charged. Closed weekends.*

Two blocks south lies the 17th-century convent of **San Pedro Claver,** named after a Spanish monk who devotedly ministered to black slaves until his death here in 1654 (in 1888 he became the New World's first saint). You can visit Pedro Claver's dim, cell-like bedroom and the infirmary where he died from Parkinson's disease. His body rests in a glass coffin beneath the altar of the adjoining church. *Admission charged.*

Five minutes by taxi or 15 on foot from the center rises the impregnable **Castillo de San Felipe de Barajas.** Designed by Antonio de Arévalo in 1639, the fort's steep-angled redbrick and concrete battlements were so arranged to destroy each other if the castle were to fall into the wrong hands—it never did. A lengthy series of tunnels, minimally lit today to allow for spooky exploration, still connect vital points of the fort. *Admission charged. Closed Mon.*

For a spectacular view of Cartagena, take a cab up to **Cerro de la Popa,** a 152-meter (500-foot) hill crowned by the **Convento de Nuestra Señora de la Candelaria,** a monastery founded in 1608 and fortified two centuries later. *Cerro de la Popa. Admission charged.*

Finally, one late afternoon, find your way to **Plaza Fernandez de Madrid,** a garden square that marks the beginning of the old city's **Barrio San Diego.** The streets of this seldom-visited yet enchanting barrio are lined with squat colonial mansions, brightly painted in white, ochre, and electric blue. Cascades of geraniums flow over balconies and open doorways reveal hidden, luxuriant courtyards. Zigzagging right then left toward the sea, you arrive at the **Bóvedas,** an arcaded row of 18th-century strong rooms, now occupied by crafts shops. Then, as the setting sun reddens the Caribbean, take a stroll along the nearby city walls.

Mompós Founded in 1537 on the eastern branch of the Magdalena river, Mompós was a key trading link between the Caribbean and the interior for more than two centuries. However, in the 18th century the direction of the Magdalena's flow shifted toward the western branch, leaving Mompós stranded on what has become an unnavigable channel. Although the commercial vibrancy of the town quickly dissipated, its fine colonial architecture remains: Mompós' parallel streets, curved so as to thwart cannonball volleys, are lined with squat mansions guarded by intricate iron grilles, and several fine churches.

Simón Bolívar once stayed in Mompós at the **Casa Bolivariana.** The town's impression on the liberator was obviously profound for he reputedly said: "While to Caracas I owe my life, to Mompós I owe my glory." The house contains several of the liberator's effects and a collection of pre-Columbian gold. *Calle Media. Admission charged. Closed Sun.*

One block farther is the **Casa de Cultura** (Calle Media; admission charged; closed weekends), with its small Mompós history museum. Continue three blocks and turn left to find the **Iglesia de Santa Bárbara,** the most interesting of the town's various churches because of its Moorish bell tower. Mompós is also noted for its handworked filigree jewelry, probably the finest to be found anywhere in Colombia.

Barranquilla The Caribbean Coast's largest industrial center, set at the mouth of the muddy Río Magdalena, is also Colombia's fourth-largest city, home to the country's largest soccer stadium, the Metropolitana, and to its most modern—and hideous—cathedral. There's no doubt about it: Barranquilla is a bizarre mix of well-to-do grid development in the west and filthy, seedy urban sprawl elsewhere. The only time really worth visiting is during the four days leading up to Ash Wednesday, when its dusty streets are overcome by flower-covered floats, costumed dancers, and crazed drunks swilling *aguardiente* (fire water).

The road onward to Santa Marta traverses the Magdalena River via a white girder bridge and runs along a narrow sand bank known as **Isla de Salamanca** (Salamanca Island). The construction of this highway badly upset the area's delicate ecological balance, which hinged upon a precise interchange of fresh and salt water. Mangroves once flourished here; today there's nothing but an eerie expanse of dead tree trunks protruding from bare mud. Farther along on the right side of the road you pass **Ciénaga Grande,** a large lagoon rich in birdlife and home to fishing villages built entirely atop stilts. As the road bends, the wooded foothills of the Sierra Nevada loom to the right, heralding your arrival in Santa Marta.

Santa Marta   Santa Marta, founded in 1525, lies at the foot of the snowcapped Sierra Nevada, the highest coastal range of mountains in the world. Although Santa Marta is the oldest surviving Hispanic town in Colombia, modern industry and architecture largely obscure its colonial look. Today the city's 200,000 inhabitants rely heavily on the natural deep-water port where banana boats lie anchored in thick clusters. Most of the cargo, of course, is legitimate, but Santa Marta also handles more contraband than any other port in Colombia. In the 1970s, that meant mostly Sierra Nevada–cultivated marijuana; in the 1990s, U.S.-solicited cocaine reigns supreme. Santa Marta is mostly nonchalant and friendly, but don't go looking for trouble: There are those here who carry weapons as a matter of course.

The **tourist office,** which provides maps and can recommend a guide, is housed along with other municipal offices in the 18th-century **Convento Santo Domingo** at Cra. 2 No. 16–44.

Two blocks farther along Cra. 2 and across the main square the **Museo Arqueológico Tayrona,** housed in a handsome erstwhile customs house, has a small collection of Tayrona gold and pottery and a model of the Lost City (Ciudad Perdida), well worth a look *before* you set out. *Calle 14 at Cra. 2. Admission free. Closed weekends.*

On the seafront, flag down a taxi or any bus marked MAMATOCO and ask to be let off at the **Quinta de San Pedro Alejandrino,** 20 minutes away. This pleasant honey-color hacienda is where a sick Simón Bolívar died in 1830, ironically enough as a guest of a Spanish royalist. On the grounds are a huge gleaming monument to the liberator and a helpful pictorial history of his life. *Manmatoco. Admission charged. Closed Tues. June–Sept.*

Again from Santa Marta's seafront, you can catch a taxi or *colectivo* (minibus) to **Taganga,** a small fishing village nestled in the next bay north—an easy 15-minute drive over tawny, brush-covered hillside. From the beach in Taganga you can hire boats to take you to Playa Grande across the bay, or make the 20-minute walk to "Big Beach" along the marked coastal path.

Parque Tayrona   **Parque Tayrona** (Tayrona National Park), 38 kilometers (22 miles) east of Santa Marta, is a tropical treasure trove of steep jungle-clad slopes, ancient ruins, deserted palm-fringed beaches, and coral reefs, all approached from the Santa Marta–Riohacha highway. (A taxi to Tayrona from Santa Marta costs less than $20 round-trip.) Inside the park, the western bays of **Concha** and **Negangue,** reached via paved but unsignposted roads, are both good snorkeling spots; at Neguangue, have a boat take you for a dive in the coral, then dine at one of the beachfront restaurants.

The eastern sector of the park around Cañaveral is far more lush than the west, and the final few kilometers to the beach at **Cañaveral** weave through damp jungle before arriving at a parking lot and restaurant. Get your bearings from the spectacular *mirador* (viewpoint), a 10-minute walk east, then descend to the beach to inspect the giant sculptured monoliths, which lend something of a Planet-of-the-Apes look to the scenery.

At **Arrecifes,** a 45-minute walk west of the parking lot along a slippery jungle trail, a cluster of simple bars and restaurants nourishes the hippies who inhabit the string of nearby beautiful beaches. Note that swimming here and at Cañaveral is extremely dangerous due to riptides, and, yes, sharks.

Pueblito, an ancient Tayrona village that's currently being excavated, is a two-hour uphill hike from Arrecifes; the path is lined with a few basic camping areas. From Pueblito on a clear day you can glimpse the snowbound Sierra Nevada in the distance.

Stay overnight in Parque Tayrona in either one of Cañaveral's "Eco-habs," circular thatched huts (under $10 per person) with paneled interiors, firm beds, cotton sheets, and balconies with 360° views; or rent a hammock at Arrecifes for about $1 and pray you don't fall victim to a falling coconut. Eco-habs should be reserved in Santa Marta through Inderena (*see* Tourist Information, *above*). *Park admission charged.*

La Ciudad Perdida Stumbled upon by *guaqueros,* or treasure hunters, in 1975, **La Ciudad Perdida** (the Lost City) is one of the largest pre-Columbian citadels ever discovered in the Americas. Founded sometime between AD 500 and 700, it is anchored at an altitude of 1,200 meters (3,937 feet) on the rugged northern slopes of the Sierra Nevada and can only be reached by means of a six-day guided trek or a three-hour helicopter ride, both of which can be arranged from Santa Marta (*see* Guided Tours, *above*). The mortarless buildings and terraces linked by steep stairways are sacred to the Kogui Indians who still inhabit the region; not surprisingly, they take unkindly to loudmouthed, litter-spilling tourists. Still, with much time and energy the trek to La Ciudad Perdida is unforgettable.

San Andrés and Providencia Islands On his fourth voyage to the New World, Christopher Columbus became the first European to set foot on San Andrés and Providencia islands, which lie 645 kilometers (400 miles) off Colombia's Caribbean coast. The uninhabited islands were later settled by English pilgrims (who landed in their vessel, the *Seaflower,* at the same time pilgrims landed at Plymouth Rock) and then by Jamaican cotton growers. Centuries of intermingling have produced a "native" population that speaks an English patois, although with the recent influx of mainlanders, Spanish is also prevelant.

San Andrés's duty-free status is responsible for the cluster of bland boutiques and shops in the concrete jungle of **El Centro,** the island's commercial center. While the prices are not very attractive to U.S. and European visitors, the surrounding coral cays and reefs certainly are. Diving is a big draw on San Andrés, as is angling for sailfish, bonita, and marlin.

San Andrés is only 13 kilometers (8 miles) long, and the best way to see the island is to rent a bicycle or motor scooter from one of the many shops along Avenida Colombia in El Centro and complete a circuit of the coastal road. **Cueva Morgan,** a small beachfront settlement, is where the pirate Henry Morgan (who also, conveniently, was England's lieutenant governor of Jamaica) reputedly stashed his loot after pillaging coastal Cuba and Panama in the 1670s. Beach bums should head for **Johnny Cay** or **San Luis,** the island's two most popular strands.

Volcanic in origin and ringed by coral cays, **Providencia Island** has rugged hills, abundant fresh water, and far less development than neighboring San Andrés, 90 kilometers (56 miles) southeast. The pace of life on Providencia is decidedly laid-back, even jolly; islanders gather on the beach at sunset to drink and chat, and most people are happily tucked into bed by 11 PM.

In **Aquadulce,** the island's largest town, you can hire bicycles and motor scooters, or join a boat tour of the surrounding islets. The best beaches are in Manzanillo and South West Bay; Crab Cay is best for snorkeling. Choose a clear day to hike up the 305-meter (1,000-foot) summit of **El Pico,** which gives superb views of the island's turquoise seashore and necklace of coral; it's a 90-minute trek each way from Casa Baja.

Shopping

In **Cartagena** the best place to hunt for handicrafts and hats, hammocks and leather, are the shops and arcades in the **Bóvedas,** in Barrio San Diego. The thing to buy in **Mompós** is filigree gold jewelry. In **Santa Marta,** Almacenes Tipicos El Tiburón (Cra. 2A No. 18–05) and Artesanias Park (Cra. 1 No. 18–65) have wide selections of hats, leather, and handicrafts.

Sports and the Outdoors

Fishing In Cartagena, the **Club de Pesca** in Manga (Calle 24 at Cra. 17, tel. 53/66–46–47) will take you sportfishing for marlin and sail-fish for around $75 per person.

Hiking The **Sierra Nevada** has some outstanding hiking and climbing that includes Pueblito, Ciudad Perdida, and the 5,770-meter-(18,930-foot-) high summit of Picó Colón. The latter two require guides, most conveniently arranged in Cartagena or Santa Marta (*see* Tourist Information, *above*).

Snorkeling In **Cartagena,** the **Caribe Dive Shop** (tel. 53/65–08–13) at the
and Diving Caribe Hotel (*see* Dining and Lodging, *below*) organizes snorkeling treks to the Islas del Rosario archipelago; and diving trips to underwater wrecks. The dive shop also organizes introductory dives for beginners. **Parque Tayrona** has various good snorkeling spots that can be explored with Ecotours (*see* Guided Tours, *above*). On **San Andrés,** you can organize a diving trip or rent snorkeling gear from **Aquamarina** (Av. Colombia, next to El Aquamarina hotel, tel. 811/26649).

Beaches

Cartagena's tourist-oriented beaches are on the **Bocagrande** peninsula, although they are becoming ever narrower as the none-too-clear sea washes away the brownish sand. Still, the beaches are plied by vendors of *gaseosas,* ice cream, and sunglasses while *vallenato* musicians stroll tirelessly along the strand. For peace and quiet, white sand, and palm trees, your best bet is **Playa Blanca,** reached by boat from Cartagena's Muelle del Pescadores.

The beaches at Santa Marta and Taganga are dirty; but just south is **El Rodadero,** a white-sand beach with excellent lodging facilities (*see* Dining and Lodging, *below*). Farther north are the spectacular and deserted white-sand strands on the outskirts of **Parque Tayrona.** Bathing here is extremely dangerous, however, due to riptides and sharks. Drownings are *very* common.

Dining and Lodging

Seafood is the regional specialty, as is *arroz con coco* (rice cooked in coconut milk) and *sancocho* (a tasty broth with fish, potatoes, yucca, and green bananas). *Jugos* (fruit juices) are an excellent companion to *carimañolas* (stuffed yucca), *butifarras* (small meatballs), *arepas de huevo* (egg-filled pancakes), and, February through April, *huevos de iguana* (iguana eggs), which are threaded together like rosaries. Upper-end restaurants are restricted to Cartagena and the region's resorts.

Lacking rivers, San Andrés' big snag is the absence of fresh water; a desalination plant is planned but persistently postponed, and all but the most expensive hotels have saltwater showers.

Hotel reservations should be made well in advance for Holy Week and throughout June and December, when prices are typically inflated by 15%. For price ranges, *see* Dining and Lodging in Staying in Colombia, *above.*

Barranquilla **El Prado.** This is an elegant colonial-style hotel where the
Dining and chessboard-tiled lobby complements the carpeted and tastefu-
Lodging lly furnished bedrooms. Along with its sports facilities, El
★ Prado is justly revered for its Principe Eduardo restaurant, offering a mixed bag of international dishes. *Cra. 54 No. 70–10, tel. 58/34–00–20, fax 58/45–00–19. 280 rooms with bath. Facilities: restaurant, bars, sauna, gym, massage, whirlpool, clay tennis courts. AE, DC, MC, V. Very Expensive.*
Majestic. Refurbished in 1993, the Majestic now boasts carpeted bedrooms with firm beds, TVs, and air-conditioning. The airy neoclassical lobby leads to an ornately plastered dining room reminiscent of Versailles; a Moorish reception room; and a verdant courtyard equipped with a pool and bar. *Cra. 53 No. 54–41, tel. 58/32–01–50, fax 58/41–37–33. 46 rooms with bath. Facilities: restaurant, bar, pool, parking; air-conditioning and TV in rooms. AE, DC, MC, V. Moderate.*

Cartagena **Classic de Andrei.** Swirling iron grilles, white classical columns,
Dining and patterned hardwood decorate this popular upmarket res-
★ taurant. The setting—vaguely *belle époque*—is well suited to the top-notch Mediterranean cuisine; try the *trucha corcega* (trout with prosciutto, tomatoes, and tarragon) or, a unique offering, an order of sushi. *Calle de Las Damas at Calle Ricaurte, tel. 53/64–26–63. Reservations advised. AE, DC, MC, V. Closed Sat. lunch and Sun. Expensive.*
Club de Pesca. Time slips gently by in this 18th-century fortress that overlooks the adjacent marina. Diners linger on a terrace shaded by a giant rubber tree, treated to delicate specialties such as lemon-and-soy snapper garnished with tahini and mint. *Fuerte de San Sebastián del Pastelillo, Manga, tel. 53/66–12–39. AE, DC, MC, V. Expensive.*
Paco's. Heavy beams, rough terra-cotta walls, chunky wooden benches, and weekend tunes from an aging Cuban band are the hallmarks of this downtown eatery, a favorite with journalists and politicians. Drop by for a drink and tapas, or try the more substantial *langostinos a la sifú* (prawns fried in batter). *Plaza Santo Domingo, tel. 53/64–42–94. Reservations advised for dinner. AE, DC, MC, V. Moderate–Expensive.*

El Ancora Café. With his tables spilling across the lively harborside sidewalk, Frederico Bega serves *costeño* recipes against an interior backdrop of designer peeling plaster. Go for the *langostinos en salsa de tamarindo y coco* (prawns in tamarind and coconut sauce). Live Cuban music daily competes with neighbouring vallenato bands. *Calle del Arsenal 9A–47, tel. 53/64–82–36. Reservations advised. AE, DC, MC, V. Moderate.*

Lodging **Hilton.** Every room in this blandly modern Y-shape block at the far tip of El Laguito has a sea-facing balcony, but the best overlook the pool. Leafy gardens lead directly onto a beach lined with palms, magnolias, and thatched oyster bars. Children under 12 stay free. *Av. Almirante Brión, tel. 53/65–06–66, fax 53/65–22–11. 289 rooms, 5 suites, all with bath. Facilities: restaurant, bar, sauna, massage, gym, pool, tennis, parking. AE, DC, MC, V. Very Expensive.*

★ **Caribe.** The oldest hotel on the Bocagrande peninsula has retained its colonial mood despite recent expansion. The pastel bedrooms in the refurbished old building have heaps more charm than those in the modern wings, though no rooms have balconies. Giant rubber trees shade a large pool at the rear, while out front only a narrow lane separates the hotel from the beach. *Cra. 1a No. 2–87, Bocagrande, tel. 53/65–01–55, fax 53/65–09–73. 372 rooms with bath. Facilities: restaurant, bars, sauna, massage, gym, pool, tennis, parking. AE, DC, MC, V. Expensive.*

Casa Grande. An original Bocagrande beachfront house, now dwarfed by surrounding skyscrapers, Casa Grande takes first prize for intimacy. The rooms vary in style and price—those located off the back garden have fans attached to their sloping wooden ceilings and are good value; but choose for yourself on arrival. *Cra. 1 No. 9–128, tel. 53/65–39–43, fax 53/65–68–06. 26 rooms with bath. Facilities: restaurant, bar. AE, DC, MC, V. Moderate.*

Hostal Santo Domingo. Well located in the walled city and close to the sea and sights, this colonial minimansion contains simple whitewashed rooms with fans, very basic bathrooms, and windows overlooking a leafy courtyard. *Calle Santo Domingo No. 33–46, tel. 53/64–22–68. 10 rooms with bath. No credit cards. Inexpensive.*

Islas del Rosario **La Isleta.** This is a unique lodging and living experience that you can have all to yourself: a private tropical island with wooden houses scattered across two rustic and wooded hectares. The caretakers will cook for you, but pack in any luxuries. Transportation is available to the island, which sleeps 20 or so; the price is about $100 per day for the entire facility. *Contact María Trujillo at A.C.T., Calle 71 No. 13–86, office 201, Bogotá, tel. 1/211–2338, fax 1/211–9623; or the Hernandez family, Calle 74A No. 4–23, Bogotá, tel. 1/310–4986. AE, DC, MC, V. Very Expensive.*

Mompós **Hostal Doña Manuela.** The airy colonial-style rooms in this
Dining and Lodging beautiful old *casona* (house) lead off a wide veranda that overlooks a patio and pool—indispensable features due to the sweltering summertime heat. *Calle Real del Medio No. 17–41, tel. 528/55620. 28 rooms with bath. Facilities: restaurant, bar, pool. DC, MC, V. Inexpensive.*

El Rodadero **Irotama.** This fully equipped resort features *cabañas*—some
Lodging indigenous in design, others plain suburban—sprinkled among landscaped jungle that fronts a long stretch of secluded beach.

Despite its location, 7 kilometers (4 miles) south of El Rodadero, the Irotama is your best bet around here. *Via Cienaga at km 15, tel. 54/21–80–21, fax 54/21–80–77. 155 rooms with bath. Facilities: 3 restaurants, 3 bars, disco, pool, gym, sauna, massage, whirlpool, tennis, water sports. AE, DC, MC, V. Very Expensive.*

Providencia Island
Dining and Lodging

Cabañas El Paraiso. On the beach in Aquadulce, these wooden cabins have clean and simple fan-ventilated rooms with ocean views and fresh-water showers. Adjoining the complex is a no-frills but dependable restaurant. Cabaña reservations are booked through Islatur on San Andrés (*see* Tourist Information, *above*). *Aguadulce, Apto. 958, tel. 811/48036. 15 rooms with bath. Facilities: restaurant. No credit cards. Inexpensive.*

San Andrés Island
Lodging

Maryland. Somewhat overpriced but one of the few hotels at press time with fresh water, the Maryland has small chintzy rooms that open onto a seafront balcony—the architectural norm around here. The airport is nearby. *Av. Colombia 9–38, Apdo. 1197, tel. and fax 811/24825. 65 rooms with bath. Facilities: restaurant, bar, pool, whirlpool. AE, DC, MC, V. Very Expensive.*

★ **Nirvana Inn Palace.** Midway along the coast, this secluded series of white villas has airy and eccentric rooms—saltwater sinks are perched on coral pilings, and the wood ceilings have a definite slope. There's no beach, but the surrounding garden is lush and the jagged shore ideal for snorkeling; the hotel rents diving gear, as well as cars and motor scooters. *Km. 14, Apdo. 1290, tel. 811/27013, fax 811/27928. 22 rooms with bath. Facilities: restaurant, bar, pool, garden. AE, DC, MC, V. Expensive.*

El Aquarium. Large fan-ventilated suites occupy 13 diminutive islands at the fringe of the sea; insist on a sea view. Fresh-water showers are planned for the near future. *Av. Colombia 1–19, Punta Hansa, tel. 811/23120, fax 811/26938. 135 rooms with bath. Facilities: 3 restaurants, bar, saltwater pool. AE, DC, MC, V. Moderate.*

Santa Marta
Lodging

Hostal PanAmerican Miramar. Despite its concrete-block appearance, this friendly hotel offers efficient service and huge, bright, airy bedrooms. Insist on a sea-facing room with a balcony; air-conditioning is available for a small charge but scarcely needed with the sea breeze. *Cra. 1a No. 18–23, tel. 54/21–47–51. 43 rooms with bath. Facilities: TV and phones in rooms. AE, DC, MC, V. Inexpensive.*

Sol Hotel Inn. Rooms here are slightly small and lack TVs, but most have sea-facing balconies, comfortable beds, and powerful fans. The hotel also offers inexpensive daily minibus service to Tayrona National Park. *Cra. 1 No. 20–23, tel. 54/21–11–31. 32 rooms with bath. DC, MC, V. Inexpensive.*

8 Ecuador

By Jane Onstott

Jane Onstott, a frequent visitor to and one-time resident of Quito, is a freelance writer based in San Diego.

Sandwiched between Peru and Colombia, tiny Ecuador could easily be overlooked, or worse, dismissed as a mere stepping stone to the more adventurous Galápagos Islands. But mainland Ecuador—and not just the Galápagos archipelago—is an adventurer's paradise. To the delight of fishermen, Antarctic upwellings along the coast attract striped marlin, Pacific sailfish, and big-eye tuna. For birders, Ecuador nurtures more than 1,500 indigenous and migratory species—from toucans and tangers to macaws and parrots—that can be spotted in a variety of habitats, including the rain forest's five-story-high jungle canopy.

Traversing the entire country from north to south, the rugged Andes embrace a series of fertile, high-altitude valleys that, despite their isolation, are easily traversed on the Pan-American Highway. The Andes' snowcapped volcanoes are an irresistible challenge to intrepid hikers, but most visitors find it equally impossible to resist repeated forays into Andean crafts markets. On market day, highland Indians dressed in wool ponchos or embroidered skirts woven with a dozen different colors sell small mountains of hand-wrought crafts, textiles, and locally grown produce. In Otavalo, one of Ecuador's largest and most prosperous market villages, you can barter for rugs, sweaters, and brilliantly colored weavings, not to mention squealing pigs, candied apples, and medicinal herbs.

Most travelers to Ecuador begin or end their trip in the highlands, with a visit to Quito, which, at 2,907 meters (9,530 feet) above sea level, is South America's second-highest capital city. Quito is a pleasant mixture of sights modern and colonial: You'll find art galleries and stylish cafés in the New City and an historic Old City with striking colonial architecture that's protected by UNESCO.

West of Quito towers the now-dormant Pichincha volcano, beyond which the Andes plummet to the coast. Despite its fantastic scenery, Ecuador's Pacific coast is largely undeveloped. Business-oriented Guayaquil, South America's busiest port, is a staid and downtrodden jumping-off point for the Galápagos Islands, and there are few sights here to attract more than a trickle of backpack-carrying tourists.

More impressive is Ecuador's upper Amazon Basin, the *Oriente,* which comprises about one-third of the country's landmass but only 4% of its population. Raids and skirmishes with Peru have reduced Ecuador's portion of the Oriente by half over the years—a fact that Ecuadorian mapmakers have yet to accept. However, this has not hindered the flow of adventure-minded travelers: there are simply too many rivers and canals to traverse, too many species of wildlife and little-known Indian cultures to discover deep within Ecuador's majestic rain forest.

Ecuador's most touristed treasure is the Galápagos Islands, separated from the mainland by 600 miles of Pacific Ocean. This barren, volcanic archipelago is inhabited not only by giant tortoises and spiny marine iguanas, but also by modern Robinson Crusoes who have traded creature comforts for an island existence in shorts and sandals. Tour the islands by boat for a few days, all the while spying on piles of colorful reptiles basking in the sun, and you, too, may understand why locals will-

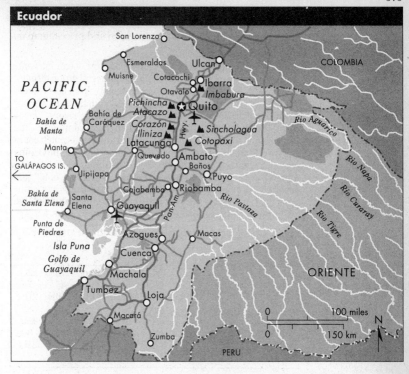

ingly accept a lack of "civilization" in exchange for life in Darwin's "living laboratory of evolution."

Staying Safe and Healthy

Crime Political turmoil and violence are not a part of the Ecuadorian landscape. In the Galápagos, the most serious threat you'll face is sunburn—do not underestimate the intensity of the equatorial sun. And remember to pack your seasickness pills if you're planning a ship-based tour of the archipelago. In Quito and throughout the country, pickpockets and purse slashers are a growing problem. Leave your valuable jewelry at home, keep a good grip on cameras and daypacks, and avoid displaying cash. In Quito, you should use extra caution on and around Plaza de San Francisco and on the stairs leading to El Panecillo.

Health Cholera and dysentery are not serious problems in Ecuador, but drink bottled water whenever possible and avoid the typical culprits—ice, washed vegetables and fruits, and uncooked meats. Pack a supply of malaria pills if you're travelling to the rain-forest regions east of the Andes or to the northern coast around Esmeraldas.

Essential Information

Before You Go

When to Go You may want to plan your trip around one of the country's many festivals or, if snorkeling or diving in the Galapagos is on your itinerary, during the hotter, albeit rainy, winter months.

The high season revolves around holidays, especially Christmas, New Year's, Carnival, and Easter week. During these peak periods hotel rooms become scarce and prices jump noticeably higher.

Climate Ecuador's climate is strongly influenced by ocean currents, trade winds, and altitude, which makes generalization difficult. One constant is the rainy season, which lasts from late November to May and occasionally precipitates landslides, power outages, or road closure because of overflowing rivers. On the coast, the rainy season is uncomfortably hot and muggy, especially in Guayaquil; the rest of the year the coast is much cooler and drier than might be expected on the equator. In the Galápagos, the weather is generally hot and humid from January through April, with frequent afternoon showers. Cooler temperatures prevail the rest of the year, creating the *garua*, a fine, light mist. The seas are roughest in September and October, when many Galápagos tour boats head for dry docks.

The following are the average daily maximum and minimum temperatures for Quito.

Jan.	69F	20C	May	69F	20C	Sept.	72F	22C
	46	8		47	8		45	7
Feb.	69F	20C	June	70F	21C	Oct.	70F	21C
	47	8		46	8		46	8
Mar.	69F	20C	July	71F	22C	Nov.	70F	21C
	47	8		44	7		46	8
Apr.	69F	20C	Aug.	71F	22C	Dec.	70F	21C
	47	8		44	7		46	8

Festivals and Events **Galápagos Days,** celebrating the islands' statehood, is held February 12–18 and features parades and all-out revelry throughout the country. During **Carnival** (Mon. and Tues. before Lent) Ambato celebrates the **Festival of Fruits and Flowers** with huge parades and dances, while those in the rest of the country dowse each other (and the tourists!) with buckets of water, water balloons, and squirt guns. Carnival motivates festivities in Cotopaxi Province—local dances and fairs are held in Saquisilí, Pujilí, Latacunga, and Salcedo. **Holy Week** (March '94) is celebrated throughout the country with colorful religious processions. **Corpus Cristi,** approximately two months after Easter, is celebrated in many mountain towns with fireworks, bands, and dances. Otavaleños give thanks to Mother Earth for her bounty during the **Festival of Yamor,** celebrated the first two weeks in September. September 24 in Latacunga is the **Fiesta de la Mamá Negra,** honoring Our Lady of Mercy with lively processions and dancers in disguise. Quito's **Las Fiestas de Quito** is vigorously celebrated Dec. 1–6 with bullfights, exhibitions, and outdoor concerts.

Currency Ecuador's currency, the *sucre,* is named for its revered liberator, Field Marshal Antonio José de Sucre. Bills come in denominations of 5, 10, 20, 50, 100, 500, 1,000, 5,000, and 10,000 sucres. Coins are rarely used, but you may receive a 10- or 50-sucre coin in change from time to time. While U.S. dollars are easily exchanged in Quito and Guayaquil (and are accepted in payment at larger hotels and restaurants and by dollar-wise locals), you should carry sucres when traveling to smaller towns and the Galápagos Islands.

At press time (fall '93), the exchange rate was 1,950 sucres to the U.S. dollar and 2,900 sucre to the pound sterling. Prices, unless otherwise noted, are listed in U.S. dollars.

What It Will Cost Many items—from taxi fare and domestic air travel to ceramic tea sets—are extremely reasonable in price. You can gorge yourself at even the most elegant restaurants and still struggle to spend $15 for dinner. Accommodations ranging from comfortable and clean to downright charming cost $10–$30 per person, though international chain hotels charge $70–$200 per night for a more generic double room. Tourist facilities sometimes are scarce outside the major cities, but when you do find them they inevitably will fall into the "bargain" category.

All hotels and many restaurants add a 20% tax to your bill. Some include this government tax when quoting prices, others do not, so be sure to inquire.

Sample Prices A 750-ml bottle of beer at a restaurant, $1; bottle of wine, $4.50; 1-mile taxi ride, 50¢; city bus ride, 50¢; a newspaper and shoeshine (including tip), 50¢.

Customs *On Arrival* You can import one liter of spirits, 300 cigarettes or 50 cigars, and reasonable amounts of perfumes, gifts, and personal effects. Do not bring firearms, ammunition, drugs, fresh or dried meats, or plants and vegetables into the country.

On Departure There is a $25 airport departure tax, which can be paid in U.S. dollars or sucres at the airport.

Language Ecuador's two official languages are Spanish and Quechua, the language introduced by the Inca and still spoken by indigenous peoples in both the highlands and the Oriente. English is the lingua franca of tourism, and you will find many young Ecuadorians in travel-related fields who speak excellent English. In rural areas you may have to struggle along in Spanish.

Getting Around

By Car *Car Rental* Car rental offices outside Quito, Guayaquil, and Cuenca are virtually nonexistent. In Quito, the most reliable agency is **Budget** (Av. Colón at Av. Amazonas, tel. 02/237026; at the airport, tel. 02/459052), which offers a three-day rental with free mileage. Other Quito-based agencies include **Avis** (Av. Colón at Av. 10 de Agosto, tel. 02/550238; at the airport, tel. 02/440270) and **Hertz** (Calle Santa María 517 at Av. Amazonas, tel. 02/545117; at airport tel. 02/440270). If you rent a car, make sure to check your headlight alignment, tires, spare tire, and jack. The average rental rate per week is $175–$250, including mileage.

Road Conditions The Pan-American Highway runs the length of the country, entering from Colombia in the north, passing through Quito and the major cities of the Andes, and continuing south into Peru. The highway is usually in fair condition except during the rainy season, when potholes form. On the narrow mountain roads, bus drivers are notorious for passing on curves and other dangerous maneuvers. The coast road is incomplete in some areas, requiring inland detours. Road signage is poor, especially outside the major cities.

Breakdowns No emergency roadside service exists, although passing motorists will frequently stop to help a disabled vehicle.

Gasoline Regular gasoline is called *extra* and costs about 80¢ per U.S. gallon; higher octane *super* is used by later-model cars and costs roughly $1 per U.S. gallon.

By Train Ecuador's railroad network presently operates in chunks and slices, and by no means services the entire country. Only three lines exist, and at press time regular service was disrupted on two of the three. The Ibarra–San Lorenzo line, for instance, is being constantly repaired, and the normal schedule of one train per day is regularly canceled. The famous Alausí–Guayaquil line currently runs only as far as Chunchi (about half the distance to Guayaquil), and only through the tour operator Metropolitan Touring. There is no train service between Alausí and Cuenca, although Metropolitan Touring's *autoferro* (a bus converted to ride the rails) makes the trip as part of a three-night adventure from Quito. Service on the Quito–Riobamba–Alausí line is scheduled to resume after years of neglect, but don't pin your hopes on it. In any case, trains are extremely inexpensive but also quite crowded with farmers, their produce, and sometimes even small farm animals.

By Plane Ecuador's three principal carriers are **Saeta** (Calle Santa Maria at Av. Amazonas, Quito, tel. 02/502706), **SAN** (Av. Colón 535, at Av. 6 de Diciembre, Quito, tel. 02/561995), and **TAME** (Av. Colón 1001, at Calle Rábida, Quito tel. 02/554905). All three fly regularly between Quito and Guayaquil ($30), Guayaquil and Cuenca ($22), and Quito or Guayaquil and the Galápagos Islands ($330–$375). Saeta and SAN also fly internationally from Miami and New York to the Galápagos Islands and Quito's **Aeropuerto Mariscal Sucre** (tel. 02/440083 or 02/241580). Other carriers offering service from Quito include **American Airlines** (Av. Amazonas 367, at Calle Robles, Quito, tel. 02/561144), **Continental** (Av. Amazonas at Av. Naciones Unidas, Quito, tel. 02/461489), and **Ecuatoriana** (Av. Colón at Calle Reina Victoria, Quito, tel. 02/563003).

By Bus Buses run frequently and are extremely cheap: the two-hour Quito–Otavalo bus ride costs $1, the 10-hour Quito–Guayaquil about $5. Sadly, pickpocketing and bag slashing are on the rise, so keep all valuables under close supervision. Private bus companies, such as **Reytur** (Calle Gangotena 158, Quito, tel. 02/565299 or 02/546674) and **Reina del Camino** (Av. Amazonas 351, Quito, tel. 02/572673), offer first-class service both to destinations within Ecuador and to Colombia and Peru. First-class buses traveling within Ecuador usually are equipped with toilets, and many provide a light snack service.

Staying in Ecuador

Telephones Coin-operated pay phones have become nearly obsolete since Ecuadorian coins have all but lost their value. If you do find a pay phone, you will need either a 1-sucre coin or, more commonly, a 1-sucre token purchased at a newsstand or nearby shop. Some stores sell local calls just as they sell candy bars, at about 15¢ for a brief call; look for a sign in the window announcing *teléfono* or *llamadas*. Another alternative is **IETEL**, Ecuador's communications agency. Offices are located in every major and minor city and some villages, and most are open daily 8 AM–9:30 PM.

International Calls To make collect or credit-card calls, dial 119 (free) to reach an English-speaking AT&T operator. Direct-dial calls made from hotels are subject to a 20% surcharge. You can call direct or collect from any IETEL office. Dialing from the United States, Ecuador's country code is 593. When calling from abroad, drop the "0" preceding all area codes.

Mail International first-class mail costs about 30¢. The casualty rate for letters and postcards is surprisingly low, and you can expect most letters to reach international destinations within two weeks. Post offices throughout the country keep fairly standard hours: weekdays 9–5.

Shopping Browsing and bartering at one of Ecuador's Indian and crafts markets is a must for all but the most black-hearted shopping haters. Weekly markets are a tradition in the Andes region, where local Indians wearing colorful regional dress arrive from the countryside on foot, horse, burro, and fancy new pickup trucks. Bargaining is an indispensable yet polite ritual. Mild curiosity, with a slightly shocked look when the price is offered, begins the process. A counteroffer of half the asking price is usual, and the norm is to agree on a price of about 75% the original asking price. Greater discounts should be expected when several items are purchased.

Opening and Closing Times **Banks.** Banks are open weekdays only 9–1:30; exchange houses, which are much more efficient and less crowded, often open in the afternoon from 3 to 6.

Shops. Traditional shop hours are 9–1 and 3 or 4 to 6. Tourist-related shops generally do not close for lunch, but many are closed Saturday afternoon and Sunday.

National Holidays January 1; Easter; May 1 (Labor Day); May 24 (Battle of Pichincha); July 24 (Simón Bolívar's birthday); August 10 (Independence Day); October 9 (Independence of Guayaquil); October 12 (Columbus Day); Nov. 2 (All Soul's Day); Nov. 3 (Independence of Cuenca); Dec. 25.

Dining In the major cities you can enjoy international and traditional Ecuadorian dishes at pleasingly low prices, although wines and most hard liquors are imported and can double the tab. The main meal of the day is lunch, *el almuerzo,* which features soup, a meat or fish plate accompanied by rice and fried potatoes, and a small salad (time to relax or sleep after such a large meal is essential). Seafood is a mainstay on the coast, though even Andean menus feature fresh fish and seafood.

Most Very Expensive and Expensive restaurants do not require coat and tie; however, Ecuadorians spending that amount on dinner *do* dress up, and you may feel uncomfortably shabby, or be spurned by your waiter, if you do not follow suit.

Mealtimes Cafeterias and inexpensive restaurants often are open throughout the day. Better restaurants open for lunch between noon and 4 PM, and reopen for dinner at 7 PM. Many restaurants are closed early on Saturday and all day Sunday.

Specialties For the adventurous carnivore, there are succulent suckling piglets and guinea pig, often roasted—teeth, paws, and all—over a charcoal fire. *Seco de chivo* is a traditional goat stew. *Humitas* are sweet corn tamales eaten by tradition-minded Ecuadorians only in the late afternoon, with black coffee. Other Andean favorites include *llapingachos,* mashed cheese and potato pancakes; and *locro de queso,* a milk-based soup containing corn, potatoes, and a garnish of fresh avocado. An Ecuadorian favorite is ceviche, fish or seafood marinated in lime juice and seasoned with onion, tomato, chili peppers, and cilantro and often served with popcorn. Because of the distant threat of cholera, ceviche has recently declined in popularity, at least among tourists. Typical coastal cuisine is based around *arroz con menestra*, huge portions of white rice served with either beans or lentils, and *patacones*, green bananas fried in oil, smashed, and refried.

Ratings   Highly recommended restaurants in each price category are indicated by a star ★.

Category	Cost*
Very Expensive	over $20
Expensive	$12–$20
Moderate	$5–$12
Inexpensive	under $5

per person, excluding tax, alcohol, and service

Lodging   A wide variety of accommodations is available in Ecuador, and the most money does not always buy the most charm. The larger high-rise hotels offer services such as on-site restaurants and bars, saunas, gyms, and business centers, but the staffs can be impersonal and sometimes downright cold. For less money you often can find restored colonial and republican-era homes furnished in antiques, with more ambience and more personalized service. In rural and jungle regions accommodations range from rustic to *really* rustic: Expect cold-water showers and sometimes pit toilets. Basic accommodations are also the norm in the Galápagos Islands, although cruise ships are generally equipped with hot-water showers.

Ratings   Highly recommended lodgings in each price category are indicated by a star ★.

Category	Cost*
Very Expensive	over $130
Expensive	$80–$130
Moderate	$25–$80
Inexpensive	under $25

Prices are for two people in a double room, based on high-season rates.

Tipping   A tip of 5%–10% is appropriate for waiters, although you are not expected to tip if the service is poor. Taxi drivers are not tipped. Porters and bellhops receive the equivalent of 25¢ per bag. Naturalists and other expert guides expect $5–$10 per person per day; drivers about $2 per person per day.

Quito

Quito, South America's second-highest capital city, at an altitude of 2,821 meters (9,250 feet), is scenically situated in a long

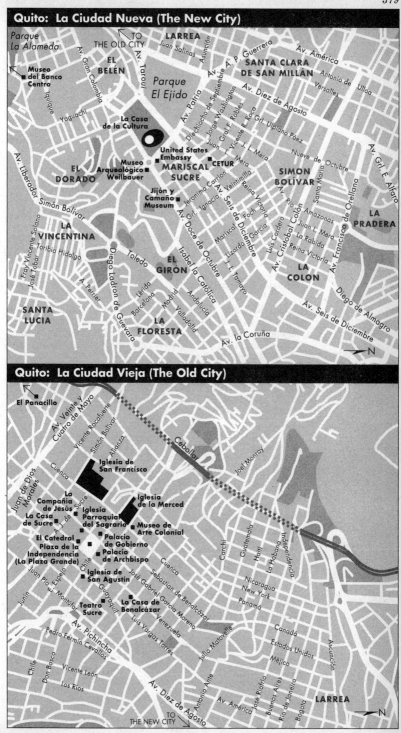

Quito: La Ciudad Nueva (The New City)

Parque
La Alameda

TO
THE OLD CITY

LARREA

Juan Salinas

Asunción

Guerrero

Av. América

Museo
del Banco
Centro

Av. Gran Colombia

EL
BELÉN

Av. Patria

Av. Tarqui

SANTA CLARA
DE SAN MILLÁN

Antonio de Ulloa

Versalles

Iquique

Yoguachi

Parque
El Ejido

Av. Patria

Dieciocho de Septiembre

A. P. Aguirre

Av. Diez de Agosto

La Casa
de la Cultura

Jorge Washington

Grl. F. Robles

Grl. Ulpiano Páez

Nueve de Octubre

Av. Grl. E. Alfaro

Av. Liberador Simón Bolívar

EL
DORADO

Museo
Arqueológico
Weilbauer

United States
Embassy

MARISCAL
SUCRE

CETUR

Juan

Vicente R. Roca

J. L. Mera

Mera

SIMON
BOLÍVAR

LA
PRADERA

Jijón y
Camaño
Museum

Jerónimo Carrión

Av. Grl. Ignacio de Veintimilla

Reina Victoria

Foch

Amazonas

Juan L. Mera

Av. Francisco de Orellana

LA
VINCENTINA

Fray Vicente Solano

Simón Bolívar

Toribio Hidalgo

José Tobar

A. Pettier

Diego Ladrón de Guevara

Toledo

Av. Doce de Octubre

Isabel la Católica

Mariscal Sucre

Lizardo García

J. L. Tamayo

Luis Cordero

Av. Cristóbal Colón

La Rábida

Reina Victoria

LA
COLON

Diego de Almagro

SANTA
LUCIA

Lérido

Barcelona

EL
GIRÓN

Madrid

Andalucía

Valladolid

Av. Seis de Diciembre

N

LA
FLORESTA

Av. la Coruña

Quito: La Ciudad Vieja (The Old City)

El Panecillo

Av. Veinte y
Cuatro de Mayo

Vicente Rocafuerte

Simón Bolívar

Alianza

Cebollar

Joel Monroy

Juan de Dios Morales

Cuenca

Iglesia de
San Francisco

La
Compañía
de Jesús

Sucre

A. J. de Sucre

Iglesia
Parroquial
del Sagrario

Iglesia
de la Merced

La Casa
de Sucre

Museo de
Arte Colonial

Carchi

Guatemala

Haití

La Habana

Independencia

El Catedral
Plaza de la
Independencia
(La Plaza Grande)

Palacio
de Gobierno

Palacio
de Archbispo

Cuenca

Sebastián de Benalcázar

Nicaragua

New York

Panamá

Juan Pío

Espejo

Montúfar

Iglesia de
San Agustín

José Gabriel García Moreno

Junín

Chile

Guayaquil

Teatro
Sucre

La Casa de
Benalcázar

Luis Vargas Torres

Venezuela

Canadá

Estados Unidos

Ascunción

Av. Pichincha

Pedro Fermín Cevallos

Julio Matovelle

Antonio Ante

Av. América

José Riofrío

Buenos Aires

Río de Janeiro

Bogotá

Méjico

Don Bosco

Vicente León

Los Ríos

Av. Diez de Agosto

TO
THE NEW CITY

LARREA

N

and narrow valley at the foot of the slumbering Pichincha volcano. Ecuador's sprawling capital lies only 15 miles south of the equator, but because of its altitude it has a mild, springlike climate all year: Lush green fields and snowcapped volcano cones surround Quito, providing the sort of photogenic backdrop you might not expect to find in a city of 1.5 million people. *Quiteños* are fond of saying that their city gives you four seasons in one day—cool mornings, warm days with frequent, brief showers, and nights often cold.

Quito's other surprise is its Old City, a bastion of colonial mansions, cathedrals, and crowded cobblestone streets, preserved and vibrant. UNESCO has declared the Old City a World Heritage Site, banning both the destruction of colonial buildings and the construction of any new buildings, leaving the colonial sector one of the best preserved in South America. After a morning in the hectic Old City, the relative tranquility of the New City, with its outdoor cafés, galleries, and smart shops, is a welcome change of pace. More than a simple stopping-off point on the way to the Galápagos Islands, Quito is an engaging city, and an excellent base for short excursions into the nearby Central Highland and Imbabura regions.

Tourist Information

CETUR (Calle Reina Victoria 514, near Calle Roca, tel. 02/527074), in the New City, provides maps and brochures and is open weekdays 8:30–4:30. CETUR also maintains a small information booth in the New City at Avenida Amazonas and Jorge Washington.

LibriMundi (Calle Juan León Mera 851, tel. 02/234791) carries maps and tourism-related publications. For members, the **South American Explorers Club** (Calle Toldedo 1254, at Calle Cordero, tel. 02/566076) has an information board and travel library.

Arriving and Departing

By Plane Quito's international **Aeropuerto Mariscal Sucre** (tel. 02/440083 or 02/241580), located 6 miles north of the city center, is regularly served by **American Airlines, Continental, Ecuatoriana**, and **Saeta**. Ecuador's three major domestic carriers, **SAN, TAME**, and **Saeta**, each fly daily from Quito to Guayaquil (30 minutes) and Cuenca (40 minutes) for less than $30 one-way.

Taxis within Quito use meters, but those leaving the airport are exempt. Agree on a price before entering a cab. Unless you look particularly green, expect to pay about $3 to the Old City and $3.50 to the New City.

By Car Quito is on the Pan-American Highway, an easy four-hour drive (269 kilometers/167 miles) from Tulcan, on the Colombian border.

By Train The only dependable train service from Quito is operated by Metropolitan Touring (tel. 02/464780, in U.S. tel. 800/527–2500). Their multiday treks by train and *autoferro* (buses converted to ride the rails) join Quito with Riobamba and Cuenca and cost $200–$450 per person.

Getting Around Quito

It's roughly 3 kilometers (2 miles) from the center of the Old City to the beginning of the New City at Avenida Amazonas. Sights within the Old City are easy to explore on foot, but the New City—apart from the Mariscal, Colón, and La Floresta districts—is larger and best conquered by cab.

By Bus   Commuters pack Quito's buses—which are inexpensive (less than 20¢) and run frequently during the day—like sardines during the morning and afternoon rush, when it's best to walk or hail a taxi. To alight make your way to the front or back and shout *"baja!"*

By Taxi   Taxis are extremely cheap and therefore an ideal form of transportation. Meters are used, but make sure the driver resets it when you get in. Agree on a price beforehand if the driver says his meter is not working. Standard crosstown fare is under $5, much less if you stay within the Old or New City, and tipping is not common. Fares increase by 25%–50% after dark.

Orientation Tours

Guided, English-language tours cost $10–$25 per person and cover Quito's principal sights in around three hours. Contact **Kleinturs** (Av. de los Shyris 1000, at Calle Holanda, tel. 02/430345); **Metropolitan Touring** (Av. República del Salvador 9–70, tel. 02/464780, fax 02/564655); or **TurisMundial** (Av. Amazonas 657, at Calle Ramírez Dávalos, tel. 02/546511).

Exploring Quito

The Old City   The oldest part of Quito was founded in 1534 by the Spanish explorer Sebastian Benalcazar, on the site of the ancient Indian town of Shyris (prior to that it belonged to the Quitus Indians, the town's namesakes). The original colonial town was bordered by its four most important monasteries: San Francisco, La Merced, San Agustín, and Santo Domingo. Today, informal markets and street vendors still crowd the Old City's cobbled plazas and walkways.

At the southern foot of the Old City sits **El Panecillo**, "the bread roll," a rounded hill that affords a marvelous view of the city and surrounding countryside. At the top stands the monumental cast-aluminum statue of the city's protectress, the Virgin of Quito—a copy of Bernardo de Legarda's famous 18th-century sculpture *Virgin of the Apocalypse of the Immaculate Conception,* on display in the Church of San Francisco. Although a long flight of stairs at the foot of Calle García Moreno climbs to the top of El Panecillo, muggers sometimes lie in wait for tourists here, and most people opt for a taxi (around $3 round-trip).

On Quito's main square, called **La Plaza Grande** or **Plaza de la Independencia,** the white neoclassical **Palacio de Gobierno** (Government Palace), built in the 19th century, is where shoeshine boys and merchants gather throughout the day. The guards usually let visitors enter to see the handsome mural in the palace's inner courtyard; it was painted in 1960 by the aged, prolific, and very popular Ecuadorian painter Oswaldo Guayasamín.

El Catedral (The Cathedral), flanking the square on the south, houses the tomb of Quito's liberator Mariscal Antonio José de Sucre. The exceptional sculpting abilities of Manuel Chili "Caspicara" can be appreciated in the 18th-century tableau *The Holy Shroud*, which hangs behind the choir, and in the intricate designs of the rococo Chapel of St. Ann, in the right nave. *Plaza de la Independencia. Admission free.*

Adjoining the cathedral is the elegant **La Iglesia Parroquial del Sagrario** (Parish Church of Sagrario), noted for its flamboyant 17th-century facade punctuated with carved masks and grotesque faces—a fine example of indigenous motifs being interwoven with classical European design. *Main entrance at Calle García Moreno and Calle Espejo.*

One block south, **La Compañía de Jesús** (Church of the Company of Jesus), with its magnificently sculpted stone facade, is considered one of the most beautiful religious structures in the Americas. The high central nave and the delicacy of its Arabic-inspired, gilded plasterwork give it a sumptuous, almost sinfully rich appearance. Indeed, almost $1^{1}/_2$ tons of gold were poured into the ceilings, walls, pulpits, and altars during its 170 years of construction, between 1605 and 1775. At the center of the main altar is a statue of the Quiteña saint, Mariana de Jesús; her remains lie at the foot of the altar. *Calle García Moreno at Calle Sucre. Admission free.*

La Iglesia de San Francisco (Church of St. Francis) is named for the patron saint of both Quito and the order that established the church in 1536, the Franciscans. The twin towers, destroyed by an eruption of Pichincha volcano in 1582, were rebuilt at half their original size, contributing to the facade's less than impressive appearance. The church interior, however, is extraordinary; it preserves the first New World example of walls, columns, and ceilings entirely covered with sculpted, gilded, and painted wood (the style was later copied not only in Quito but throughout the continent). **El Convento de San Francisco,** the museum at the north end of the complex, is temporarily closed for renovations, but with some luck you may entice one of the monks to show you the church brewery, where homemade ale was brewed until the 1970s. Also on display is Bernardo de Legardo's famed 18th-century sculpture *Virgin of the Apocolypse of the Immaculate Conception. Plaza San Francisco, tel. 02/211124. Admission free (donation encouraged).*

Recent restorations at **La Iglesia San Agustín** (Church of St. Augustine) highlight its stunning caissoned ceilings, patterned in precise geometric and floral designs. Crowding the side naves is a series of paintings of St. Augustine. The gilded, polychrome wooden crucifix on the main altar is an impressive example of School of Quito art. *Calle Chile at Calle Guayaquil. Admission free.*

A few blocks west, the rather sober Spanish baroque facade of **La Iglesia de la Merced** (Church of Mercy) belies an interior of surprising light and beauty. The polychrome image of the Virgin of Mercy, which occupies a central niche by the main altar, was sculpted to honor a virgin who supposedly intervenes to save Quito from earthquakes and volcanic eruptions. **El Convento de la Merced** (Convent of Mercy), adjoining the church and shown by appointment only, houses a rich collection of colonial paintings and sculptures, and a vast library that includes *La Celda del Provinvial* (the Provincial's Cell), whose walls are covered with exquisite paintings of the 12 apostles. *Calle Chile at Calle Cuenca. Admission free.*

La Casa de Sucre, the home of Field Marshal Antonio José de Sucre, displays 19th-century furniture and clothing, as well as photographs, historical documents, and letters. The house, from the kitchen to the adjoining stables, has been entirely restored, and to many it may be more interesting than the hodge-podge memorabilia within. *Calle Venezuela 573, at Calle Sucre, tel. 02/512860. Admission charged. Closed Sun. and Mon.*

La Casa de Benalcázar is the restored home of Quito's founder, lieutenant and governor Sebastián de Benalcázar, who took possession of Quito on December 6, 1534. There is little in the way of historical displays or original furnishings inside, though concerts and other performances are sometimes held here in the evenings; check the newspaper or inquire at the site. *Calle Esmeraldas at Calle Venezuela, tel. 02/514511. Admission free. Closed weekends.*

The **Museo de Arte Colonial** (Museum of Colonial Art) displays an excellent collection of paintings and sculptures from the 16th to the 18th centuries. The museum is located in a restored 17th-century colonial mansion, and the pieces, which include a collection of colonial furniture and works by Miguel de Santiago, Samaniego, Rodríguez, and anonymous members of the School of Quito, are spread over two floors. *Calle Cuenca at Calle Mejia, tel. 02/212297. Admission charged.*

The New City The triangular **Parque La Alameda,** at the southern extreme of the New City, is a sanctuary of shady trees where old men sit gabbing on bright-painted benches. A few blocks north is the much larger **Parque El Ejido,** where couples stroll in the sunshine and theater groups sometimes hold impromptu performances. On Saturday mornings there also are open-air art exhibitions.

On the east edge of Parque El Ejido, **La Casa de la Cultura** (House of Culture) is the new home of the **Museo del Banco Central** (Central Bank Museum). Ground-floor exhibits concentrate on pre-Columbian archaeology, while upstairs there's an excellent collection of colonial religious art and two additional floors of contemporary Ecuadorian works. *Av. Patria at Av. 6 de Diciembre. Admission charged. Closed Mon.*

Also housed inside La Casa de la Cultura, **El Museo de Arte Moderno** (Museum of Modern Art) exhibits contemporary Ecuadorian and indigenous art, as well as religious and children's art and a collection of pre-Columbian and colonial musical instruments. *Tel. 02/527440 (ext. 47). Admission charged. Closed Sun. and Mon.*

Across the street, the **Museo Arqueológico Weilbauer** (Weilbauer Archaeology Museum) offers free English-language tours of its extensive collection of pre-Columbian ceramics. *Calle Patria at Av. 12 de Octubre, tel. 02/230577. Admission free. Closed weekends.*

The nearby **Jijón y Camaño Museum,** in the Catholic University, has an extensive collection of colonial art, with paintings and sculptures from some of the masters of the School of Quito.

There also is a small collection of Ecuadorian and Peruvian archaeological finds, historical documents, and military uniforms. *Av. 12 de Octubre at Calle Roca, tel. 02/521834. Admission charged. Closed weekends.*

Oswaldo Guayasamín, one of Ecuador's most famous living artists, has a **workshop** and **museum** in the New City, in the residential neighborhood of Bellavista. On display are pre-Columbian ceramics and colonial sculptures and paintings, as well as a permanent exhibit of Guayasamín's paintings. In the gift shop, jewelry designed by Guayasamín's daughter are sold, as well as other handicrafts. *Calle José Bosmediano 543, tel. 02/242779 or 02/244373. Admission free. Closed Sun.*

Shopping

Quito's specialty and crafts stores are reasonably priced and sometimes rival the outlying Indian markets for bargains. In Quito look for giant, brightly painted balsa-wood birds made in the Amazon region, and statues carved of cedar from highland villages. Handknit wool and cotton sweaters, shawls, and tapestries vary in quality and price, as do items made of leather. The New City's Mariscal district, between Avenidas Amazonas, 6 de Diciembre, Patria, and Colón, is tightly packed with all sorts of boutiques and crafts stands. Stores throughout Quito are generally closed Saturday afternoon and all day Sunday.

Markets You can lose yourself among the stalls at **Santa Clara market,** in the New City at the corner of Calle Versalles and Calle Marchena. At this traditional neighborhood market a blind man plays the accordion for small change; fruits are piled high in pleasing geometrical arrangements; and bundles of dried and fresh herbs, grains, and groceries are bartered for in a time-honored ritual. Another daily **market** is held in the Old City two blocks south of Plaza San Francisco. There are no handicrafts or antiques here, only fruits and vegetables and household goods. Watch your pockets carefully in the crowded downtown marketplaces.

Specialty Stores **Casa Indo Andina** (Calle Roca 606, at Juan León Mera) sells original and reproduced religious art and silver-gilded wood frames. The alabaster votive figures, when buried under your home, are supposed to bring good luck. **Olga Fisch's Folklore** (Av. Colón 260) is one of Quito's more expensive boutiques, specializing in handwoven rugs and tapestries. In addition to its regional handicrafts, **La Bodega** (Calle Juan León Mera 614) has an expansive collection of handknit wool and cotton sweaters; so, too, does **Centro Artesenal** (Calle Juan León Mera 804). **Galería Latina** (Calle Juan León Mera 833) offers an enormous variety of sterling silver jewelry, woven rugs, ceramic figures, and antiques.

Spectator Sports

Soccer Games are held during the season (Mar.–Dec.) at 10 AM on Saturday and 3 PM on Sunday at the **Estadio Olímpico "Atahualpa"** (tel. 02/247510), located at Avenida 6 de Diciembre and Avenida Naciones Unidas. Tickets, which cost $2.50–$10, must be purchased at the stadium, though try asking your hotel concierge first.

Bullfighting The only regularly scheduled bullfights are held during the weeklong Fiestas de Quito, in early December. Hotels will sometimes purchase tickets for guests with advance reservations. The bullring is located at Avenida Amazonas and Calle Juan de Azcara.

Dining

Quito's better restaurants are found in the New City. Formal attire is required only at the most expensive establishments, though well-dressed Quiteños frequent the moderate and even inexpensive options. Most restaurants close daily between 3 and 7 PM, and many also are closed on Sunday. For price ranges *see* Dining in Staying in Ecuador, *above.*

Very Expensive **El Arlequín.** The atmosphere at this popular New City restaurant is elegant but not overly formal, and diners can comfortably chat above the sound of the classical guitarist who plays most evenings. The smattering of European dishes is supplemented by Ecuadorian specialties such as roast pig with rosemary, and fresh crab basted in a spicy cream and wine sauce. *Av. Orellana 155 (at Av. 12 de Octubre), tel. 02/509875. Reservations recommended. DC, MC, V. Sat. dinner only; closed Sun.*
★
La Querencia. There are excellent views of Quito from the dining room, and the serene outdoor garden is the perfect place to linger over a meal. La Querencia is best known for its superb Ecuadorian dishes; try the lamb stewed with fruit, or king prawns served *au flambée* in cognac. *Av. Eloy Alfaro 2530 (at Calle Catalina Aldaz), tel. 02/461664. AE, DC, MC, V. Sun. lunch only.*

Expensive **Paella Valenciana.** This restored, two-story Republican-era home is popular with Quiteños for a relaxed business lunch or informal dinner. Paella, the restaurant's namesake, is excellent, and there is a large menu of Spanish-style seafood such as octopus in vinaigrette and deep fried squid. *Calle Almagro (at Av. Republica), tel. 02/239681. AE, DC, MC, V. Sun. lunch only.*

★ **La Taberna Piedmonte.** Locals and resident diplomats have been coming to this superb Italian eatery for years, to indulge in *rosette de margro,* a homemade spinach pasta oven-baked with herbs; or *pizza iola,* a fillet of beef topped with cheese, vegetables, and fresh herbs. From the intimate dining room, the view of Quito at night is breathtaking. *Calle C.J. Arosemena Tola 173 (at Av. Eloy Alfaro), tel. 02/433607 or 02/433608. Reservations recommended. DC, MC, V. Closed Sun.*

Trattoria del Veneziano. Arches divide the stylish, dark beamed house into more intimate spaces, and the open fireplace adds more than charm on chilly evenings. For under $5 you can sample the fabulous antipasto buffet, which can provide a meal in itself. For an entrée try the gnocchi or *spaghetti al Hilton* (pasta with prawns and cream). *Calle Roca 562 (at Calle Juan León Mera), tel. 02/523085. AE, DC, V. Sun. lunch only; closed Mon.*

Moderate **Adam's Rib.** The owner, an expatriate from New York, orchestrates the presentation of delicious barbecued ribs, fried chicken, hamburgers, and crispy onion rings for crowds of locals and visiting Americans. The fireplace brings cheer to an otherwise unremarkable environment; there is a small bar and a billiards table in an adjoining room. *Calle Juan León Mera 442, tel. 02/563196. MC, V. Closed Sat.*

La Ronda. During the day businesspeople gather for traditional Ecuadorian meals such as seafood casserole, Galápagos lobster, or *mote pillo,* a traditional peasant dish of corn, cheese, avocado, and scrambled egg. Sunday brunch is extensive, inexpensive, and features live Ecuadorian music. *Calle Belo Horizonte 400 (at Calle Almagro), tel. 02/540459 or 02/545176. AE, DC, MC, V.*

Wonder Bar. Most come for the enormous servings of *ceviche* (white fish marinated in lime juice, onions, and cilantro), though you will find the ancient movie theater it is housed in to be a welcome respite from the bustling crowds of the Old City. *Cine Bolívar, between Calles Guayaquil and Espejo, tel. 02/215778. No credit cards.*

Inexpensive **La Canoa Manabita.** Virtually unknown to tourists despite its location in the Mariscal district, this no-frills eatery serves exquisite renditions of coastal Ecuadorian dishes: try the *viche,* a hearty fish soup with corn, peanuts, and bananas; or fried fish served with rice, lentils, and *patacones* (fried green bananas). *Calle Calama 231 (at Calle Almagro), no phone. No credit cards. Closed Mon.*

Lodging

Most hotel rooms in Quito have neither air-conditioning nor heating, nor are these ambience controls missed in Quito's moderate climate. For price ranges *see* Lodging in Staying in Ecuador, *above.*

Very Expensive **Hotel Colón Internacional.** Located in the New City across from the Parque El Ejido, this large modern hotel has numerous shops and on-site services. The rooms, in which the color brown prevails, are rather nondescript but clean. The lower floors are noisy because of street traffic. *Av. Amazonas (at Av. Patria), tel. 02/560666, fax 02/563903, in U.S. tel. 800/327–9854. 415 rooms. Facilities: 2 restaurants, 2 coffee shops, casino, gymnasium, sauna, barber shop, travel agency, bookshop. AE, DC, MC, V.*

★ **Hotel Oro Verde.** Quito's most luxurious high-rise hotel is only a 10-minute walk from the New City and its restaurants, and within a 15-minute taxi ride of the Old City. The rooms are modern and comfortable, with sea-green carpets, floral spreads, and modern, attractive screen prints. High tea, served in the hotel café between 4 and 6:30 PM, is currently in vogue with well-to-do Quiteños. *Av. 12 de Octubre 1820 (at Calle Cordero), tel. 02/568079 or 02/569189, fax 02/569189, in U.S. tel. 800/223–6800. 193 rooms, 48 suites. Facilities: 3 restaurants, bar, indoor/outdoor pool, casino, gymnasium, sauna, steam room, squash and racquetball courts. AE, DC, MC, V.*

Expensive **Alameda Real.** Situated in the heart of the New City, this modern high-rise hotel offers spacious, comfortable suites at reasonable prices, though they're incongruously decorated in forest green, brown, and mauve. Delicious breakfast buffets are served at the 24-hour coffee shop. *Calle Roca 653 (at Av. Amazonas), tel. 02/562345 or 02/564217, fax 02/565759, in U.S. tel. 800/327–3573. 130 suites, 22 rooms. Facilities: Restaurant, bar, coffee shop, barber shop, beauty salon. AE, DC, MC, V.*

Hotel Quito. Only a 15-minute walk from the center of the New City, this high-rise hotel overlooks both the valley of Guápulo and Quito itself, with exceptional views around sunset. Ask for one of the recently renovated rooms as some of the older ones are a bit shabby. *Av. González Suárez 2500, Box 2201, tel. 02/230300 or 02/544600, fax 02/567284, in U.S. tel. 800/528–1234. 230 rooms. Facilities: rooftop restaurant and bar, coffee shop, casino, sauna, pool. AE, DC, MC, V.*

Moderate **Apart–Hotel Antinea.** Each of the seven apartments in this charming new inn has its own kitchenette, well stocked with all necessary cooking and serving utensils. A mixture of French and Flemish architecture, the inn has whitewashed brick walls and rough-hewn, exposed wood beams, and several pleasant patios. *Calle Juan Rodríguez 175 (at Calle Almagro), tel. 02/506839 or 02/506838, fax 02/504404. 7 apartments. Facilities: garage, laundry. AE, MC, V.*

Hostal Los Alpes. This intimate colonial inn, located in a quiet residential neighborhood near the New City's Casa de la Cultura, has been designated a World Heritage Site by UNESCO. There are several cozy sitting rooms with fireplaces, and a sunny, cactus-filled reading room on the second floor. *Calle Tamayo 233 (at Calle Jorge Washington), tel. 02/561110 or 02/561128. 25 rooms. Facilities: restaurant. AE, MC, V.*

★ **Palm Garten.** Turn-of-the-century, wood-framed mirrors and French Provincial furniture characterize this 100-year-old mansion, recently converted into a luxurious bed-and-breakfast inn. The Attic Room is cozy with its sloping ceiling and antiques, while the Wiesbaden Room has its own fireplace. Continental breakfast is included and served in an intimate dining room. *Av. 9 de Octubre 923 (at Calle Cordero), tel. 02/523960, fax 02/568944. 16 rooms. MC, V.*

Inexpensive **Ambassador.** Centrally located in the New City near plenty of bars and restaurants, the Ambassador is clean, cheerful, and surprisingly inexpensive. The recently restored, two-story lobby is attractive while the rooms themselves are comfortable and spacious. *Av. 9 de Octubre (at Av. Colón), tel. 02/561777 or 02/562054. 30 rooms. Facilities: restaurant, bar. AE, DC, MC, V.*

Hotel La Casona. This is the most charming hotel in the Old City—a lovely, restored colonial-style house with red tile floors and decorative white plaster ceilings. The rooms are small but have firm beds and colonial-style furnishings. *Calle Manabí 255 (near Calle Flores), tel. 02/514764. 23 rooms. Facilities: cafeteria. MC, V.*

The Arts and Nightlife

Quito's arts and nightlife are quiet by most standards, but the situation is not hopeless. Check the local papers, *El Comercio* and *Hoy*, and the monthly booklet *Qué Hacer* (sold in bookstores and at newsstands) for information about theater, concerts, clubs, gallery openings, and art expositions.

The Arts The **National Folkloric Ballet "Jacchigua"** performs Wednes-
Ballet day at 8 PM in the Old Town's **Teatro Sucre** (Sucre Theater, Calle Flores at Calle Manabí, tel. 02/216644). Tickets cost $14–$20 and can be purchased in advance at the theater or through Metropolitan Touring (tel. 02/464780).

Concerts Classical and folkloric concerts sometimes are held at the **Conservatorio Nacional de la Música** (National Conservatory of Music, Av. Madrid 1159, tel. 02/564790) and at the **Corporación Financiera Nacional** (National Financial Corporation, Calle Juan León Mera, behind Hotel Colón, tel. 02/561026).

Film Cinemas in Quito often show American films in English with Spanish subtitles; try the cinema at **La Casa de la Cultura** (Av. Patria at Av. 12 de Octubre, tel. 02/565808).

Nightlife Quito is not known for its wild nightlife, but there are plenty of discotheques (for the MTV generation), *salsatecas* (for lovers of salsa music), and *peñas*, where you can hear traditional Ecuadorian music and drink leisurely with locals. Bars usually open in the late afternoon, discos and peñas around 10 PM. Cover charges for the latter two range from free to $10.

Bars and **La Puerta de Alcalá** (Calle Lizardo Garcia at Calle Juan León
Cafés Mera, no phone) serves traditional Spanish tapas and good *tinto* (red wine). It's a bar for conversation and a bite to eat, not for wild flirting. At **Ghoz** (Calle La Niña 425, at Calle Reina Victoria, tel. 02/239826) you can play darts, pool, or board games while listening to Ghoz's high-decibel rock and salsa music. **El Pobre Diablo** (Calle Santa María 338, at Calle Juan León Mera, tel. 02/231982) is a gathering place for local artists and young intellectuals. The stylish **Bangalo Tea House and Bar** (Calle Carrion 185, at Calle Tamayo, tel. 02/520499) features a blazing fireplace and nonstop Brazilian music. Upstairs you can relax with coffee, imported tea, and Brazilian pastries.

Discotheques Rock and salsa are featured at **Blues** (Calle La Granja 132, at Av. Amazonas), a popular and noisy, Western-style discotheque. Locals have been coming to **Salsateca Serseribó** (Calle Veintimilla, at Av. 12 de Octubre) for years to dance cumbia, son, salsa, and merengue.

Peñas **Ñuncanchi Peña** (Av. Universitaria 496, at Calle Armero, tel. 02/540967) is one of Quito's well-established, not-too-rowdy, late-night peñas. Other established peñas in the New City are **Nuestra America** (Calle Iñaquito 149, at Av. Amazonas, tel. 02/444356) and **La Taberna Quiteña** (Av. Amazonas 259, at Calle Calama, tel. 02/230009). In the Old City try **La Taberna Quito Colonial** (Calle Manabí at Calle Vargas, tel. 02/213012).

Excursions from Quito

Papallacta Hot It's a stunning drive over the eastern range of the Andes to the
Springs small village of **Papallacta,** where a mile beyond there is a set of eminently swimmable natural springs, one hot and one cold. It's a beautiful setting, and on a clear day you can see the snow-capped peak of Antisana. It costs a few hundred sucres to enter the site, which also has a café and changing facilities.

Getting There If you travel by bus to Papallacta, 60 kilometers (37 miles) southeast of Quito, you may have to pay the entire Quito–Tena fare. For $35–$40 you can hire a taxi to bring you to the springs, wait for an hour or so, and then return you to Quito.

Guápulo The village of **Guápulo,** nestled in a secluded valley below the Hotel Quito, grew up around its impressive 17th-century church, **El Santuario de Guápulo** (Guápulo Sanctuary). The church contains pieces by some of Quito's most exceptional sculptors and painters: The paintings in the central nave are the work of Miguel de Santiago, while the side altar and pulpit—completed in 1716 and considered a masterpiece of colonial art—were carved by Juan Bautista Menacho. Guápulo itself, its narrow cobblestone lanes lined with traditional two-story, white-and-blue-trimmed houses, is a preserved pocket of colonial architecture only 10 minutes by foot from Quito's New City. If you visit in early September, you can help celebrate Guápulo's annual festival, with food and drink and marching bands.

Getting There Walk downhill to Guápulo via the steep staircase directly behind the Hotel Quito, and return with a taxi for less than $1.

La Mitad del Mundo La Mitad del Mundo (Equatorial Monument) marks the spot that the French Geodesic Mission determined to be the exact latitudinal center of the earth in 1736. Nowadays people enjoy straddling the equatorial line (latitude 0° 00' 00") or leaping back and forth between the northern and southern hemispheres, even though the monument itself—a 33-foot-tall trapezoidal stone—is not particularly attractive. Inside the monument an **ethnographic museum** (closed Mon.) has displays on Ecuador's diverse cultural groups.

Getting There Buses depart daily from the Old City at the intersection of Calle Mejía and Calle José López; the 60-minute ride costs around $1.50. A taxi will take up to four persons for $20, including the wait while you visit the monument and museum. Most Quito-based tour operators offer half-day tours for $10–$20 per person.

Mindo Just 81 kilometers (50 miles) west of Quito lies the 19,000-hectare **Mindo-Nambillo Protected Forest,** which extends from the small village of Mindo to the slopes of Pichincha. The forest is largely subtropical and ranges in altitude from 4,000 to 15,000 feet above sea level. The reserve harbors at least 300 species of birds, including the quetzal, cock-of-the-rock, numerous tanager and hummingbird species, falcons, woodpeckers, and toucans. Walking trails cut a rough course through thick, canopied vegetation, and dedicated hikers will be rewarded with good views of the park's many waterfalls. There are two basic huts for overnight stays, one about an hour's hike from Mindo. Both facilities are administered by **Amigos de la Naturaleza** (tel. 02/455344), a local ecotourism group. Mindo itself is just beginning to be developed for tourism, and its services are still rudimentary; there are no restaurants in town and only two very basic hotels.

Getting There The road to Mindo and the reserve is not a good one, and even in a four-wheel-drive vehicle it takes three hours in good weather (the road is often impassable during the rainy season). Consider booking through a Quito-based tour operator such as **Metropolitan Touring** (tel. 02/464780) or Amigos de la Naturaleza (*see above*).

Pasochoa **Pasochoa Protected Forest** is administered by **Fundación Natura** (tel. 02/447341 or 02/447342), a private conservation organization, with the goal of preserving the remaining 988 acres of high Andean forests that once covered the region. Nearly 100 species of birds have been identified here, including hummingbirds, honeycreepers, and tanagers. Camping is permitted within the park, and there are picnic areas with spigots and latrines. Fires are not permitted and you should bring all of your own supplies. There are many walking trails, from short loops to all-day hikes; the trail to the summit (13,800 ft.) is popular but rigorous, and you should bring drinking water and snacks. Guides can be hired through Fundación Natura. The park fee is $7 for day use and $12 for overnight camping.

Getting There There are no direct buses to Pasochoa; in fact, the closest you can get by bus is about 7 kilometers (4¹/₂ miles) away. It's best to hire a taxi for the day—the going rate is around $30.

Imbabura

When the Spaniards conquered the territory north of Quito—called Imbabura after the 15,190-foot volcano of the same name—they introduced sheep to the indigenous Otavalo Indians. Over time the mountain-dwelling Otavaleños became expert wool weavers and dyers; even today you can still find Indian weavers who painstakingly collect and prepare their own natural dyes, despite the increasing popularity of modern synthetic colors. Traditional dying methods may be declining, yet the Otavaleños themselves proudly retain many of the old customs, including their manner of dress. The women are striking in their embroidered white ruffle-and-lace blouses, straight blue wraparound skirts, black or blue headcloths, and row upon row of beaded gold necklaces. The men, extremely handsome with their beige felt hats and long braided hair, are most often seen in Western attire, although some of the older men still wear the traditional calf-length white pants, white shirt, and dark blue poncho.

Many small weaving villages dot the green and gold valleys of Imbabura, and artisans make the trek to Otavalo—the largest and most prosperous of these crafts towns—for its fabulously colorful market. Otavalo's *Plaza de Ponchos* (Poncho Plaza) fills up each Saturday with merchants selling weavings, rugs, ponchos, colorful cotton and wool sweaters, jewelry, and antiques. Locals shop for *alpargates* (rope-soled sandals), medicinal herbs, squealing pigs, cackling hens, and colossal guinea pigs. Smaller villages like Cotacachi (famous for its leather) and San Antonio de Ibarra (famous for its woodworks) host their own colorful markets, though neither are as lively as the Saturday market in Otavalo.

Visitor Information

CETUR (Calle Colón 7–43, at Calle Olmedo, Ibarra, tel. 02/955355 or 02/955711; closed weekends).

Guided Tours

One- and two-day tours are available through most operators in Quito. These typically include sightseeing in Otavalo followed by weaving demonstrations in a nearby Indian village. **Metropolitan Touring** (Av. República del Salvador 9–70, Quito, tel. 02/464780, fax 02/564655) has daily departures from Quito. More extensive and economical are **Zulaytur's** (Calle Sucre at Calle Colón, 2nd floor, Otavalo, tel. 02/921176, fax 02/920461) day-long treks, which depart from Otavalo.

Getting There

By Car and Taxi Otavalo is just off the Pan-American Highway, 113 kilometers (70 miles) north of Quito. For around $70, taxis that carry up to four passengers can be hired in Quito for a day-long trip to Otavalo and any surrounding village—perhaps Ibarra or Cotacachi. A taxi ride between Otavalo and Ibarra costs about $6.

By Bus From Quito's Terminal Terrestre buses depart every 30 minutes for Ibarra (2½ hours) and Otavalo (2 hours); round-trip fare costs under $5. **Transportes Otavalo** (tel. 02/570271) deposits passengers in Otavalo's center; **Flota Imbabura** (tel. 02/572657) has direct service to Ibarra, but for Otavalo they drop you a half-mile outside of town.

Exploring Imbabura

Otavalo is situated in the rugged lake district nearly 12,602 meters (8,530 feet) above sea level. Days in this high-altitude valley—a mosaic of tiny gardens, lakes, and fields—are often sunny and warm. Over the picturebook landscape rise the craggy peaks of three now-extinct volcanoes—Imbabura, Cotacachi, and Cayambe, Ecuador's third-tallest mountain. Local Indians trudge along the road carrying huge burdens or prodding their laden burros to do the same; come Thursday or Friday, there is a good chance they're headed for Otavalo's famous Saturday market, held at the **Plaza de Ponchos**. Although tourist-oriented, the market is still a remarkable event—beautiful and self-assured Otavaleñas crowd the warren of stalls and stands surrounding the plaza, selling piles of woolen and cotton sweaters; traditional and modern ponchos; tapestries, rugs, and wall hangings; antiques; and sterling silver and *alpaca* (Nickle silver) jewelry imbedded with Andean jade, lapis lazuli, and other semiprecious stones.

Near the corner of Calles Modesto Jaramillo and García Moreno locals shop for embroidered blouses, alpargates, and herbs for curing ailments and attracting lovers. The produce market held simultaneously on **Plaza 24 de Mayo** does an equally brisk business; so, too, does the animal market on **Plaza San Juan,** where Indians and mestizos bargain for cows, pigs, and other livestock. The animal market begins at 5:30 AM, and most sellers are packing to go by 11 AM. The Plaza de Ponchos market doesn't reach full swing until 7 or 8 AM and lasts all day; a smaller version of the Saturday crafts market is held every day of the week.

Easily accessible from Otavalo is deep blue **Lago San Pablo** (San Pablo Lake), 8 kilometers (5 miles) southeast. From the lakeshore you have an unobstructed view of Volcán Imbabura (4,633 meters/15,190 feet), which dominates the landscape. The lake can be reached via paths behind Otavalo's defunct train station, or take a taxi for less than $10.

Cotacachi, 15 kilometers (9 miles) north of Otavalo, is a famous leather town, proffering jackets, skirts, shoes, purses, and luggage of respectable quality. Stores tend to offer identical designs at near-identical prices, but dedicated shoppers may find bargains lurking in one of the many cramped shops along the main street. Although most people pass quickly through

Cotacachi, it is a pleasant, lived-in sort of town where around the small main plaza children play and old men sit gossiping.

Nearly 18 kilometers (11 miles) west is mile-wide **Laguna de Cuicocha,** a near-circular lake cradled in a crater on the lower flanks of an extinct volcano. Marked hiking trails meander along the crater's rim, giving good views of the volcanoes Imbabura, Cayambe, and Chile. There are also good views of Cuicocha's two vegetation-covered volcanic islands, which are part of an ecological reserve and closed to the public. The nearby **Restaurant Muelle Bar** (tel. 02/951965) has a fantastic view of the lake but keeps unpredictable hours. Motorboats anchored by the Muelle Bar can sometimes be hired for brief tours.

Ibarra, capital of Imbabura province and roughly 25 kilometers (16 miles) north of Otavalo, is a pleasant colonial city, but most tourists go directly to **San Antonio de Ibarra,** located on the Pan-American Highway a few miles before the capital. San Antonio is the "Cotacachi of woodcarvings"—stores surrounding its central plaza sell variations on identical woodworking themes. A favorite design is the "cringing beggar," carved of cedar or walnut; nearly as popular are religious statuary costing anywhere from a few to several hundred dollars.

Sports and the Outdoors

Bicycling **Adventura Flying Dutchman** (Casilla 314, Sucursal 12 de Octubre, Quito, tel. 02/449568) organizes day and overnight bicycle treks in the Imbabura region.

Boating Motorized boats (with pilots) can sometimes be rented inexpensively on Laguna de Cuicocha at the Restaurant Muelle Bar. The Hostería Puerto Lago (*see* Dining and Lodging, *below*) rents paddleboats, rowboats, and motorboats.

Horseback Riding **IntiExpress** (Calle Sucre 11–06, Otavalo, tel. 02/290737) arranges single and multiday horseback treks to local Indian villages and to natural mineral springs. Horses can also be rented by the guests of Hostería Puerto Lago, Hostería La Mirage, and Hostería Cusín (*see* Dining and Lodging, *below*).

Dining and Lodging

Lodging reservations are advised on weekend nights, when tourists fill the region's hotels and hosterías in anticipation of Otavalo's Saturday market. There are few dependably good restaurants in the area, but hosterías typically serve simple, wholesome meals. Hosterías usually serve nonguests, although some require advance reservations. For price ranges, *see* Dining and Lodging in Staying in Ecuador, *above*.

Cotacachi **Hostería La Mirage.** While some hosterías evoke words like
Dining and Lodging *rustic* and *bucolic*, La Mirage brings to mind the words *elegant*
★ and *sophisticated*. A profusion of antiques add to the refined atmosphere, as do the inn's many windows, which provide views across five acres of landscaped gardens and, beyond, of Volcán Imbabura itself. The rooms and suites are tastefully decorated and equipped with comfortable four-poster beds. *Av. 10 de Agosto, tel. 02/915237, fax 02/915065. 16 rooms. Facilities: restaurant, cafeteria, bar, swimming pool, sauna, steam room, tennis court, horse rental. DC, MC, V. Expensive.*

Ibarra
Dining and Lodging

Hostería Chorlaví. Wide, shaded verandahs, thick white-washed walls, and spacious antiques-furnished rooms make this inn a favorite weekend retreat for Ecuadorians and tourists. The restaurant emphasizes fresh fish and typical Andean dishes, all served on a flower-filled patio serenaded by folkloric groups on weekend afternoons. *Pan-American Highway, 2 km (1¼ mi) south of Ibarra, tel. 02/955777 or 02/955775, fax 02/956311. 42 rooms. Facilities: restaurant; tennis, squash, basketball, and volleyball courts; heated pool, sauna, steam room, whirlpool. DC, MC, V. Moderate.*

San Pablo Lake
Dining and Lodging
★

Hostería Cusín. The quiet hacienda, draped in a thick carpet of flowers and foliage, was built in 1602 and, after centuries as a working farm, converted to a comfortable country inn. You can rent a horse or mountain bike and, after a day of rambling through the farm-dotted countryside, mingle with fellow travelers in the congenial fireside bar. *Lago San Pablo, tel. 02/504167 or 02/440672, reservations in U.S. tel. or fax 212/988–4552. 25 rooms. Facilities: restaurant, bar, games room, horses, mountain bikes. MC, V. Moderate.*

Hostería Puerto Lago. A panorama of volcanic peaks forms the backdrop of this lakeside country inn, just a few miles southeast of Otavalo. In the downstairs restaurant, women in traditional Indian dress serve up the locally famous and quite outstanding panfried trout, served head and all. *Pan-American Hwy., 5½ km (3 mi) from Otavalo, tel. 02/920920, fax 02/920900. 19 rooms. Facilities: restaurant, cafeteria, bar, satellite TV; paddleboat, Jetski, and horse rental. AE, V. Moderate.*

Otavalo
Dining

S.I.S.A. Here is a relaxed café where potent espresso, pastries, and fresh juices are supplemented by hamburgers and thick, hearty sandwiches. Unobtrusive renovations will soon clear the way for an adjoining restaurant and tea shop. *Abdón Calderón 409 (near Calle Sucre), no phone. No credit cards. Inexpensive.*

Dining and Lodging

Ali Shungu. The American owners of this squeaky-clean hotel go out of their way to make guests feel at home: The terracotta-tile bedrooms are supremely comfortable, and there's plenty of steaming hot water for showers. Dinner usually means a selection of wholesome international dishes such as vegetarian lasagna or deep-dish chicken pie served with organically grown vegetables. *Calle Quito (at Calle Quiroga), tel. 02/920750. 20 rooms. Facilities: restaurant, gardens. V. Moderate.*

The Arts and Nightlife

Many of the *hosterías* (*see* Dining and Lodging, *above*) present local bands on Friday and Saturday nights. The music is traditional Andean, the crowds a mix of Ecuadorian and foreign tourists. During the week things are very quiet in the Imbabura region (some would say downright dull). In Otavalo, S.I.S.A. (*see* Dining and Lodging, *above*) presents occasional art exhibits and live music and dance demonstrations. Their plans for the future include a movie theater. Otavalo also has a reasonable selection of peñas—dance and music clubs where you'll see traditional Andean musicians perform in a less antiseptic venue than that served up at the hosterías. Two reliable

peñas are **Amauta** (Calle Modesto Jaramillo 664, at Calle Sa-
lina, tel. 02/920967; open Fri. and Sat. after 8 PM) and **Tuparina
El Encuentro** (Calle Morales at Calle 31 de Octubre, tel.
02/920680; open Thurs.–Sat. after 9 PM). Both have a small
cover charge.

Central Highlands

South of Quito the Andes rise sharply on either side of the Pan-
American Highway, creating a narrow corridor of fertile, high-
elevation valleys that are home to nearly half of Ecuador's
population. Located along this 175-kilometer (109-mile)
stretch between Quito and Riobamba are seven of Ecuador's
10 tallest volcanoes. Alexander von Humboldt, the German scientist who explored the area in 1802, was so impressed that he
coined a sobriquet still used today: the Avenue of the Volcanoes.

Among the Central Highlands' most accessible destinations
are Latacunga, Ambato, and Baños. All three can be covered
on a guided tour from Quito, but consider renting a car in order
to explore the handful of small market villages—Saquisilí and
Pujilí, among them—near Latacunga. Die-hard cyclists should
contemplate the 65-kilometer (40-mile) downhill trek from
Baños to Puyo (you and your cycle can return to Baños by bus).
Riobamba, the pleasant yet somnolent capital of Chimborazo
province, makes a good ending point for the Central Highlands
tour as it is connected by rail with Cuenca and Guayaquil; both
rail routes pass through some of the country's most spectacular scenery, and both descend the infamous *Nariz del Diablo*
(Devil's Nose)—a 305-meter (1,000-foot) drop that the narrow-
gauge train negotiates via an ingenious system of hairpin
turns, span-bridges, and tunnels.

Tourist Information

CETUR provides the usual maps and brochures at the following locations: **Ambato** (Calle Guayaquil, next to Hotel Ambato;
closed weekends); **Baños** (Parque Central; closed Sun. and
Mon.); **Riobamba** (Calle Tarqui 2248, at Primera Constituy-
ente; closed Sun. and Mon.).

Guided Tours

Reliable tour operators that offer day and overnight excursions to the *ferias* (markets) in Central Highlands include: **TurisMundial** (Box 1210, Av. Amazonas 657, Quito, tel. 02/546511),
Nuevo Mundo (Box 402-A, Av. Amazonas 2468, Quito, tel.
02/552839, fax 02/565261), and **Metropolitan Touring** (Av.
República Salvador 9–70, Quito, tel. 02/464780, fax 02/564655).

Getting There

By Car   Latacunga lies just off the Pan-American Highway, 89 kilometers (55 miles) south of Quito. The nearby villages of Pujilí and
Saquisilí are accessed via unpaved but hard-packed roads.
Baños is 23 kilometers (14 miles) east of Ambato on the road
to Puyo. Riobamba is nestled along the Pan-American Highway 188 kilometers (117 miles) south of Quito.

By Bus Buses traveling between Quito and Ambato or Riobamba will drop you along the Pan-American Highway, near Latacunga, after a scenic two-hour trip. From Quito there are frequent buses to Ambato (three hours) and Riobamba (four hours); it is another hour east from Ambato to Baños. Packed local buses connect Latacunga with Pujilí, Saquisilí, and San Miguel de Salcedo.

By Train At press time there was no regular rail service between Quito and Riobamba, although local officials contend the service will resume at any moment. Until it does, your only reliable option is Metropolitan Touring (*see above*), which offers a two-day trek by *autoferro* (a bus converted to ride the rails) that includes one night at a hostería plus a visit to an Indian market. The trip costs $200–$450 and can be booked through Metropolitan Touring and most Quito-based tour operators. Metropolitan Touring also offers the only reliable rail service between Riobamba, Guayaquil, and Cuenca.

Exploring the Central Highlands

Latacunga, the capital of Cotopaxi province, has been rebuilt three times following massive eruptions of Volcán Cotopaxi, whose perfect snow-covered cone dominates the city. Latacunga's main plaza, **Parque Vicente León,** is large, green, and peaceful, with giant topiary trees carefully trimmed in an assortment of geometric shapes. At the Saturday market held on **Plaza San Sebastián,** most of the goods for sale are geared for locals—fruits and vegetables, plasticware, and medicinal herbs. Still, you may find *shigras,* the colorful, handwoven hemp bags used by local Indians. On nonmarket days stroll the quiet streets for views of Latacunga's remaining colonial architecture.

In the tiny mountain village of **Pujilí,** 10 kilometers (6 miles) west of Latacunga, colorful markets are held on Sunday and, with much less ado, on Wednesday. Few tourists find their way to Pujilí, and its markets have a definite authentic feel: Local Indians wearing bright turquoise ponchos and porkpie hats fill the plaza and line the streets, buying, selling, and trading pottery, cheap costume jewelry, and produce. In **Saquisilí,** 13 kilometers (8 miles) north, throngs of Indians fill all eight of the village's dusty plazas during the Thursday market, where you can pick through heaps of traditional wares—including grotesque, painted wooden masks of animals and devils. Taxis will make the short, bumpy journey between Latacunga, Pujilí, and Saquisilí for less than $15 each way.

Ambato, with a population of 125,000, assaults the senses as only a large and noisy city can. The city's market is more practical than picturesque, as vendors laden with produce and domestic goods mob the streets rather than a particular plaza. A good time to visit Ambato is during La Fiesta de Flores y Frutas (Festival of Fruits and Flowers), which coincides with the pre-Lent Carnival in February. Most of the fruits and flowers are found on floats parading through the streets; there are also crafts fairs, dances, bullfights, and concerts. For culture vultures there is the off-beat Museo de Ciencias Naturales (Natural Science Museum), with an assortment of ragged stuffed animals and black-and-white photographs of turn-of-the-century Ecuador. *Calle Sucre 839, tel. 02/821958. Admission charged. Closed weekends.*

Baños, 23 kilometers (14 miles) east of Ambato on the road to Puyo, is a tourist town, no doubt about it. Quiteños have been soaking in the curative thermal springs here for decades, if not centuries, and the locals are well used to outsiders. Despite the tourists, Baños retains its enormous appeal, largely because of its superb location, nestled by a river at the foot of Volcán Tungurahua. (Many species of birds and butterflies inhabit this thickly vegetated subtropical valley.) In town, the twin spires of **La Iglesia de la Virgen del Agua Santa** rise above the tree-lined plaza. The church, whose newly painted black and white facade is slightly startling, was built to honor Baños's miracle-working Virgin; the huge paintings inside are testimonials from her many exultant beneficiaries.

There are several thermal springs in town, but the best is a series of pools called **El Salado** (The Salty), 2 kilometers (1 mile) outside town on Via al Salado, off the main road to Ambato. Its six man-made pools overflow with brownish mineral water of various temperature and are adjoined by a refreshing, fast-moving stream. *Admission charged.*

Three of Ecuador's most formidable peaks—Chimborazo, Altar, and Tungurahua—are visible from **Riobamba,** a pleasant high-altitude town with wide tree-lined streets and some well-preserved colonial architecture. There are good buys at the tourist-oriented Saturday market held in the Parque de la Concepción (Calle Orozco at Calle Colón); look for embroidered belts, Otavalan sweaters and weavings, *shigra* bags, and locally produced clothing and jewelry. Across the street from the market, the **Museo de Arte Religioso** (Museum of Religious Art), housed in the beautifully restored church **La Concepción,** has an impressive collection of colonial art. *Calle Argentinos, tel. 02/952212. Admission charged. Closed Sun. and Mon.*

Sports and the Outdoors

Biking   In Baños, **Karsson Cafe Bar** (Calle Eloy Alfaro at Calle Oriente) rents 18-speed mountain bikes by the day ($9) or hour ($1). A popular route is the five-hour, 65-kilometer (40-mile) downhill ride to Puyo, which winds its way through subtropical jungle and past thundering waterfalls. You can board a bus in Puyo, bike and all, for the return trip to Baños.

Aventura Flying Dutchman (Casilla 314, Sucursal 12 de Octubre, Quito, tel. 02/449568) organizes day and overnight bike treks from Quito along the Avenue of the Volcanoes. Helmets, knee and elbow pads, plus transportation, are provided.

Hiking   The area's most challenging climb is Volcán Tungurahua (5,019 meters/16,457 feet), Ecuador's 10th-highest peak. It is not a technically difficult mountain to climb, but hidden grottos make it extremely dangerous without an experienced guide. William Naverete, owner of Baños' El Higueron (*see* Dining and Lodging, *below*), can suggest experienced local guides and offer advice for less ambitious hikes. In Ambato, **Surtrek** (Box 865, tel. 02/846964, fax 02/844512) arranges guided climbing treks throughout the region.

Horseback Riding   **Caballo Negro** (Calle Halsans 1–31, Baños, tel. 02/740609) offers 3½-hour guided horseback treks into the Baños countryside for $15 per person (minimum three people). Two- and three-day horseback camping trips also can be arranged.

Dining and Lodging

Hosterías with comfortable, homespun rooms are common throughout the region. These rustic country inns also serve dependably hearty meals. For price ranges, *see* Dining and Lodging in Essential Information, *above*. Highly recommended restaurants and hotels are indicated by a star ★.

Latacunga
Dining and Lodging
★

La Ciénega. The hacienda, converted to a country inn in 1982, is over 300 years old and has been owned by the descendents of the marquis de Maenza since colonial days. The country-style furnishings in the main salon are elegant, though the room decorations are more functional than inspired. The lovely ornamental gardens behind the hotel give way to open fields; in the distance, the huge cone of Cotopaxi can be seen. The restaurant serves respectable Ecuadorian cuisine, including *llapingachos* (potato pancakes) and *locro de queso*, a typical Andean soup of potatoes and cheese. *Lasso, 20 km (13 mi) north of Latacunga, tel. 02/549126 or 02/541337, fax 02/549126. 6 suites, 22 rooms. Facilities: restaurant, horseback riding. DC. Moderate.*

Rumipamba de las Rosas. This rustic but comfortable hostería, located 10 kilometers (6 miles) south of Latacunga in San Miguel de Salcedo, is an ideal spot to sleep or dine when traveling the Avenue of the Volcanoes. Sunday lunch includes barbecue-grilled meats and live folkloric music. *Pan-American Hwy., San Miguel de Salcedo, tel. 02/800520 or 02/800550 (ext. 128). 35 rooms. Facilities: restaurant, bar, swimming pool. DC. Moderate.*

Baños
Dining and Lodging

Hotel Sangay. Numerous recreational facilities partly make up for the small plain rooms that characterize this family-oriented hotel, as do the 26 attractive and spacious on-site cabins. The Sangay's second-story bar gives good views of the Waterfall of the Virgin, just across the road. *Plazoleta Ayora 101, Baños, tel. 02/740490, fax 02/740056. 51 rooms. Facilities: restaurant, bar, heated pool, tennis court, squash court, two hot tubs. Nonguests pay $4 for use of sports facilities. DC. Moderate.*

Casa Nahuazo. Located near the El Salado hot springs, this bed-and-breakfast inn is owned and operated by two Peace Corps volunteers who never went home. There is a large communal living room and lovely views of the surrounding mountains. The restaurant serves three eclectic, international-style meals a day; nonguests can eat here by reservation. *Via al Salado, Casilla 1922, Baños, tel. 02/740315. 6 rooms. No credit cards. Inexpensive.*

Dining

El Higuerón. Sandwiches and snacks are served seven days a week in this brand-new restaurant, owned by William Navarete, one of the best authorities in Baños on climbing. *Calle 12 de Noviembre 270 (at Calle Luís A. Martínez), no phone. No credit cards. Inexpensive.*

★ **Le Petit Restaurant.** It's the food and not the simple, unassuming decor that draws locals and tourists alike to this boisterous, popular restaurant. The large menu features a mixture of French, Ecuadorian, and international dishes, all served in hearty portions—definitely Baños's most sophisticated cuisine. *Calle Eloy Alfaro 246 (at Calle Montalvo), tel. 02/740936. Closed Mon. No credit cards. Moderate.*

Ambato
Dining and Lodging

Hotel Villa Hilda. Serving guests in Ambato for 63 years, the Hilda has small apartments with kitchens (although little in the way of kitchen equipment) in addition to its standard rooms. The on-site restaurant, which has gold and red flocked wallpaper and parquet flooring, serves respectable Ecuadorian and international food. *Av. Miraflores, Casilla 120, tel. 02/820700 or 02/824065, fax 02/845571. 60 rooms. Facilities: restaurant, heated pool. AE, DC, MC. Moderate.*

Riobamba
Dining and Lodging
★

Hostería El Troje. Some of the world's most cozy, soft, and delicious beds make this Riobamba's premier sleeping stopover. Every room has a fireplace and a supply of wood, and there is plenty of steaming hot water in the bathrooms. The restaurant serves delicious breakfasts and traditional Ecuadorian dinners. *Box 50, Riobamba, 4 1/2 km southeast of town on the minor road to Chambo, tel. 02/960826 or 02/965073. 33 rooms. Facilities: restaurant, bar; playground, tennis and basketball courts, heated indoor pool. AE, DC, MC, V. Moderate.*

Cuenca

For centuries Cuenca was isolated from the more worldly cities of Quito and Guayaquil; in fact, paved roads between them were not laid until the 1960s. Cuenca may be Ecuador's third-largest city, but isolation has saved it from the sobering effects of industry and mass tourism, while simultaneously helping to preserve its cobblestone streets and colonial architecture. Running along Cuenca's southwestern edge, the pensive Tomebamba River forms a peaceful backdrop to the town's brightly painted colonial mansions, most of which display iron-grilled balconies virtually overcome with potted plants and fresh flowers. Adding to Cuenca's charm are its 52 churches and cathedrals, not to mention the fact that it is surrounded by velvety hills and some of Ecuador's most stunning countryside.

On market days—Thursday and Sunday—thousands of townspeople and Otavalo Indians throng Cuenca's open-air plazas to buy, sell or trade almost everything imaginable. Around these plazas old men sit gossiping at all hours, oblivious to the call of lanky shoeshine boys, while cars and taxis trundle by in a relaxed manner unthinkable in Quito or Guayaquil. Another fixture in Cuenca are *Cholas Cuencanas,* the female descendants of mixed Spanish and Cañari Indian couples, famed for their beauty and afforded a higher social status partly because of it. On market day, Cholas Cuencanas sport their finest straw hats and their most colorful *polleras,* wide, gathered wool skirts woven with a dozen vivid colors. (A crowd of cheerfully gossiping Cuencanas resembles a field of brilliant blossoms—in violet, emerald green, rose red, and marigold.)

Tourist Information

CETUR (Calle Hermano Miguel 6–86, at Calle Presidente Córdoba, tel. 07/822058; closed weekends).

Getting There

By Plane Cuenca's **Aeropuerto Mariscal Lamar** (Av. España) is 2 kilometers (1 mile) from the city center, just past the bus terminal. A cab from the airport to downtown costs around $3. **SAN** (tel. 07/804033) and **TAME** (tel. 07/800193) each fly twice daily between Quito and Cuenca; the 40-minute flight costs $28 each way. Weekdays only, TAME makes the 30-minute flight between Guayaquil and Cuenca ($22 each way).

By Car Cuenca is 472 kilometers (293 miles) south of Quito via the Pan-American Highway. The drive from Quito (eight hours) and Guayaquil (four hours) both have fantastic scenery: The former takes you along the Avenue of the Volcanoes, while the latter climbs through sub-tropical lowlands before beginning a dizzying mountain ascent—2,532 meters (8,300 feet) in just over 240 kilometers (150 miles).

By Bus From Cuenca's **Terminal Terrestre** (Av. España), 1½ kilometers (1 mile) from the town center, there are daily departures to Quito (10 hours) and Guayaquil (5–6 hours), both priced under $5.

By Train Cuenca's train station is at the end of Avenida Huayna Capac on the southeastern edge of town. The Cuenca–Riobamba line (via the ruins at Ingapirca) is incredibly scenic; the highlight is probably the infamous *Nariz del Diablo* (Devil's Nose), a 1,000-foot drop traversed by a precarious but ingenious system of hairpin turns and bridges.

At press time, rail service between Cuenca and Riobamba was extremely erratic. The only reliable—albeit pricy—option is **Metropolitan Touring** (Av. República del Salvador 9–70, Quito, tel. 02/464780, in U.S. tel. 800/527–2500), which joins Riobamba and Cuenca by *autoferro* (a bus converted to ride the rails). The journey costs $200–$450 per person and includes an overnight stay at a hostería plus a visit to an Indian market.

Getting Around

Cuenca's center is small and extremely easy to negotiate on foot. Most of its churches, museums, and shops are within a six-block radius of the main plaza, Parque Calderón. Taxis do not use meters, so agree on a price beforehand.

Exploring Cuenca

In the heart of Cuenca's compact center lies the tree- and flower-filled **Parque Calderón,** where old gentlemen read the paper on bright red benches and shoeshine boys ply their trade. The periwinkle blue domes of Cuenca's **Catedral de la Inmaculada,** also known as the New Cathedral, unhurriedly built between 1886 and 1967, dominate the park below. Inside, what little light enters through the miniature stained-glass windows becomes diffused and golden, casting a pale glow over thick walls of brick. The heavy atmosphere is lightened somewhat by pillars of Ecuadorian marble and Italian marble floors. Opposite sits the small, unimposing **El Sagrario** (also called the Old Cathedral), begun in 1557, the year the city was founded. At press time, the Old Cathedral was closed to the public and the New Cathedral had irregular hours; plan your visit to co-incide with a Sunday or holiday service.

One block west of Parque Calderón are the twin-spire church and nunnery of **Carmen de la Asunción.** The stone carvings surrounding the doorway are a good example of Spanish Ba-roque design, while the church interior is typically ostenta-tious—especially noteworthy is the gold-covered pulpit encrusted with mirrors. The flower market held on the square outside is in full bloom on Saturday only, though a few vendors still sell on a daily basis. *Calle Mariscal Sucre (at Calle Padre Aguirre). Open sporadically and for Sun. and holiday services.*

One block south, vendors occupy a maze of stalls at **Plaza de San Francisco,** hawking a variety of shoes and sweaters, lip-stick, shampoo, and low-quality bric-a-brac. Under the north-ern colonnade, Otavalo Indians sell their more attractive handmade wares, mainly colorful handwoven ponchos and handknit sweaters, and woven wall hangings. Across the plaza is the tan and white **Iglesia de San Francisco,** built in the 1920s and famous for its intricately carved, gold-drenched main altar. It, too, is often closed, so try to visit on Sunday. Among Cuenca's other attractive churches are the blue-spired **Iglesia San Alfonso** (Calle Simón Bolívar at Calle Presidente Borrero) and the twin-towered **Iglesia de Santo Domingo** (Av. Gran Co-lombia at Calle Padre Aguirre).

In the 16th century one of Cuenca's leading citizens donated her house to the Catholic church, whereafter it became the cloistered convent of the Order of the Immaculate Conception. Four centuries later, this spacious and well-preserved edifice houses **El Museo de las Conceptas,** containing an impressive collection of religious art from the 16th to 19th centuries. *Calle Hermano Miguel 6–33 (at Calle Presidente Córdova), tel. 07/830625. Admission charged. Closed Sun.*

The **Museum of Modern Art** always has several interesting, well-presented exhibitions of local artists, though its perma-nent collection consists mainly of dark, bleak paintings by anonymous colonial masters. *Calle Mariscal Sucre (at Calle Coronel Talbot), tel. 07/831027. Admission free. Closed Sun.*

The **Central Bank** is just inaugurating its new concrete-and-glass headquarters, which will eventually house an ethnog-raphic and archaeological museum with revolving exhibits of precolonial art. Near the river behind the museum there is a small archaeological site under excavation. *Calle Larga (at Calle Hauyna-Capac). Admission charged. Closed weekends.*

Shopping

Cuenca is among Ecuador's leaders in cottage industries, pro-ducing fine ceramics, textiles, and weavings. Among its most important products is the Panama hat, whose name sticks in the collective craw of proud *Cuencanos*. (These finely made straw hats—also known as "toquilla" hats—are named for the country to which they were first exported en masse, hence the "Panama" sobriquet.)

Antiques Several high-quality antiques stores lurk on President Cór-dova street: Try **El Anticuario** (Calle Presidente Córdova 6–25), with a large collection of old-fashioned irons, furniture, and religious icons, or **Galerías Inti Nan** (Presidente Córdova 6–14), which has a limited but precious collection of antiques and, upstairs, a soon-to-open archaeology museum.

Ceramics **Artesa** (two locations: Calle Luis Cordero 6–96 and Av. Gran Colombia at Calle Luis Cordero) is Cuenca's leading producer of utilitarian and decorative ceramicware.

Handicrafts **Kinara** (Calle Mariscal Sucre 7–70, at Calle Luis Cordero) stocks stylish gold and silver jewelry, women's hats, and jackets and shawls featuring traditional *ikat* weaving. **Señor Ortega** (Calle Vega Muñoz at Calle Padre Aguirre) is one of Cuenca's premier Panama hatmakers. If you don't see what you want at the store, ask for a tour of the factory where the hats are made.

Dining

Cuenca suffers a dearth of restaurants and bars—Cuencanos are a stay-at-home lot and tourism is still relatively new. Most family-owned restaurants—but not necessarily hotel restaurants—are closed Sunday. For price categories, *see* Dining in Essential Information, *above.* Highly recommended restaurants are indicated by a star ★.

Expensive **Villa Rosa.** Cuenca's newest international restaurant is per-
★ fectly ensconced in a meticulously restored republican-era house, with thick white walls and marble floors. Soft music floats through severally tastefully decorated salons to the upper balcony, where an open fireplace blazes. Try the grilled trout with almonds and, for dessert, the fruit-and-chocolate fondue. *Av. Gran Colombia 12–22, tel. 07/837944. Reservations recommended. AE, DC, MC, V. Closed Sun. and Mon.*

Moderate **La Ruota.** The elegant black-and-white interior of this popular Italian restaurant belies very reasonable prices for a wide range of pizzas and fresh pastas. *Av. Gran Colombia 21–156 (at Calle Unidad Nacional), tel. 07/842351. MC, V. Closed Mon.*

Los Capulíes. This blue and white, glass-domed restaurant is a good place to sample traditional Ecuadorian cuisine. The *plato típico* (sampler plate) consists of *llapingachos* (potato pancakes), grilled pork, *mote pillo* (hominy with green onions and scrambled eggs), blood sausage, and *empanadas* (meat turnovers). A variety of live music is presented Thursday to Saturday after 8:30 PM. *Calle Borrero at Calle Córdova, tel. 07/831120. AE, DC, MC, V. Closed Sun.*

Inexpensive **Govindas.** The menu is limited but the vegetarian food is wholesome and very inexpensive: For less than $1 you get soup, rice, salad, the veggie stew of the day, juice, and dessert. *Calle Padre Aguirre 8–15 (at Calle Mariscal Sucre), no phone. No credit cards. Closed Sun.*

Napolitana. The ambience is clean, bright, and casual; the framed posters and elaborate graffiti on the walls add to the informal charm. Pizza is the norm, but there is a healthy selection of pastas and soups. Live bands often perform on weekend evenings. *Calle Benigno Malo 4–104 (at Calle Larga), tel. 07/821093. DC, V.*

Lodging

Deluxe hotels are noticeably absent in Cuenca, though several moderately priced establishments offer friendly, reliable service in elegant surroundings. The listings below are all within walking distance of the city center. For price ranges, *see* Lodging in Essential Information, *above*. Highly recommended hotels are indicated by a star ★.

Expensive **Hotel Dorado.** This modern high-rise exudes no special warmth. The standard rooms are rather plain, so consider a small splurge for one of the substantially more cheerful suites; many of these have excellent views. *Av. Gran Colombia 7–87 (at Calle Luis Cordero), tel. 07/831390, fax 07/831663, in U.S. tel. 800/327–3573. 88 rooms, 4 suites. Facilities: 2 restaurants, disco, gift shop, sauna. AE, DC, MC, V.*

Moderate **Hotel Crespo.** This intimate hotel overlooking the Tomebamba ★ River on the southeastern edge of town combines comfort with a friendly, unpretentious setting. About a third of the rooms and the restaurant have good views of the river. Numerous sitting and reading rooms give the Crespo a familiar, homey atmosphere. *Calle Larga 9–73 (at Calle Luis Cordero), tel. 07/827857, fax 07/835387. 31 rooms. Facilities: restaurant, bar, parking garage. AE, DC, MC, V.*

Hotel El Conquistador. This five-story hotel has amenities not frequently found in Cuenca's other budget-friendly hotels, such as bathtubs, hair dryers, and panoramic views of the city. An enormous breakfast buffet with eggs and potatoes, cereals, fruits, and juices is included in the price. *Av. Gran Colombia 6–65 (at Calle Presidente Borrero), tel. 07/831788, fax 07/831291. 44 rooms. Facilities: restaurant, bar, disco, satellite TV, airport shuttle. AE, DC, MC, V.*

Inexpensive **Residencial Siberia.** Simple and unassuming, the Siberia is still one of Cuenca's best budget hotels, largely because of its central location between Calle Larga and Parque Calderón. A jungle of green potted plants nearly makes up for mismatched furniture and the small rooms. *Calle Luis Cordero 4–22, tel. 07/840672. 24 rooms. Facilities: restaurant, parking, cooking facilities. No credit cards.*

The Arts and Nightlife

Cuenca is not about nightlife. Locals usually stay home during the week and sally forth on Friday and Saturday nights to have dinner and drinks, maybe to see a movie or a play.

The Arts Theater is sometimes performed at **La Casa de la Cultura** (Calle Luis Cordero 7–50). For information regarding current cultural events, look in the daily newspaper, *El Mercurio*, or contact **La Fundación Paul Rivet** (Calle Luis Cordero 9–32, tel. 07/835655), which distributes a monthly newsletter of cultural events. **La Casa de la Cultura** also shows movies most nights at 9 PM.

Nightlife **La Cantina** (Calle Presidente Borrero at Calle Córdova) is one of Cuenca's most attractive and lively bars and a popular local hangout on weekend nights. The nearby and popular **Pub Piccadilly** (Calle Presidente Borrero) serves cakes and tea during the afternoon, appetizers and cocktails in the evenings.

Excursions from Cuenca

Mirador de Turi For a fantastic view of Cuenca by night or day, hike or take a taxi to the *mirador* (lookout) at the tiny village of **Turi,** where there is also a photogenic mural-covered church. If you walk along Turi's main street you will soon find yourself in green, sometimes burnt-brown hills where stucco and adobe farmhouses punctuate cornfields and potato patches.

Getting There Either hike south (and uphill) for several miles along Avenida Fray Vicente Solano, or take a taxi for less than $2 each way.

Ingapirca Long before the Inca invasion of Ecuador in the latter half of the 15th century, the fierce and industrious Cañari people ruled *Guapondélig* ("Plain as Wide and Beautiful as the Sky"), their name for the fertile highlands surrounding Cuenca. Yet while **Ingapirca** was an important religious and political center to the Cañari, the site is better remembered for its Inca ruins; after the Incan King Tupac-Yupanqui conquered the Cañari he added his own temples and monuments to the site (Ingapirca literally means "Wall of the Incas"). The mortarless stone-built structures are thought to be Cañari temples to the moon, while the elliptical building at the center is acknowledged to be the conquering Incas' vast temple to the sun. An on-site museum displays archaeological drawings penned by German explorer Baron von Humboldt, one of the first white men to visit Ingapirca, as well as Inca, Cañari, and pre-Cañari ceramics. *Admission to archeological site and museum: $4. Open daily. Museum closed Sun.–Mon.*

Getting There Guided tours can be arranged through CETUR (*see* Tourist Information, *above*) and most Cuenca-based operators for $30–$40 per person, including lunch. Try to find a tour that stops in either Azogues, the center of Ecuador's Panama hat industry and the site of a colorful Saturday market, or in tiny Cañar, which has a small Sunday market.

Guayaquil

Guayaquil, the capital of Guayas province, is South America's busiest Pacific port and Ecuador's largest city, with a population of 1.5 million people. Such statistics do not bode well for visitors: Guayaquil may lie on the heavily wooded banks of the Guayas River, but the city itself is unattractive and dirty, infiltrated by industry. Oil and sugar refineries line the crowded riverbank, while ramshackle factories infest the city's impoverished working-class quarters. Even in first-class hotels guests are sometimes subject to shortages of water and electricity. Crime, too, is a serious and growing problem.

There is little to draw tourists to this business-oriented city, and most visitors to Guayaquil are usually just passing through. Those stopping in Guayaquil en route to the Galápagos need not even leave the airport. During the hot and stifling rainy season, usually December to April, Guayaquil becomes particularly unbearable, and Guayaquileños head en masse for the beach cities of Playas and Salinas. Here the blue waters of the Pacific Ocean teem with black, blue, and striped marlin, sailfish, albacore, wahoo, and dolphin, providing a year-round lure for sport fishermen.

Tourist Information

CETUR (Calle Aguirre 104, at Malecón, tel. 04/328312; closed weekends).

Getting There

By Car From Riobamba drive southwest through Cajabamba and El Truinfo. From Quito (416 kilometers/259 miles) drive west along a narrow paved road over the Cordillera mountains, descending through stunning subtropical landscapes to Santo Domingo de los Colorados on the way to Quevedo and Babahoyo.

By Bus Guayaquil is eight–nine hours by bus from Quito, around five hours from Cuenca. Both treks cost under $5.

By Plane Guayaquil's domestic and international airport, **Aeropuerto Simón Bolívar** (Av. de las Américas, tel. 04/319958), is 6 kilometers (4 miles) north of the city center; taxis to downtown cost under $3. From Guayaquil, **TAME** (tel. 04/329855) and **SAN** (tel. 04/303128 or 04/302277) fly daily to Quito ($30), and TAME has one flight per day to Cuenca ($25). For the Galápagos, SAN flies five times a week to San Cristóbal Island while TAME flies daily to Baltras, both for $320–$350 round-trip.

By Train At press time, all rail service from Guayaquil was temporarily suspended; contact CETUR (*see* Tourist Information, *above*) for the latest details. If and when service resumes, Guayaquil's **Estación Durán** (tel. 04/332576), across the river in the suburb of Durán, will once again be joined with Cuenca (five hours) and Alausí (four hours). Taxi fare from downtown to the station costs less than $2.

Getting Around

The most pleasant sector for strolling in Guayaquil is Urdesa; the adjacent neighborhoods of La Garzota and Nueva Kennedy also have numerous bars, cafés, and restaurants. El Parque Centenario lies at the heart of the city, and Avenida 9 de Octubre—the main financial and shopping street—runs roughly west–east on either side. Taxis throughout the city are inexpensive, but most do not use meters; be prepared to haggle a bit.

Exploring Guayaquil

A walk along the **Malecón,** Guayaquil's waterfront promenade, is pleasant around sunset; small fishing trawlers and the occasional native dugout add a dash of life to this otherwise busy commercial waterway. Overlooking the river at the foot of Avenida 9 de Octubre, the impressive stone monument **La Rotunda** commemorates the historic meeting in 1822 between Ecuador's venerated liberator, Simón Bolívar, and Argentine general San Martín, who liberated Chile and Peru.

The **El Pedregal** social club welcomes any and all to its riverside water park, where you can swim, play tennis and volleyball (sports equipment not provided), or snack in a café or food stand. Future plans include a wave machine and water slide. Admission includes the 20-minute riverboat ride to and from El Pedregal's dock, located across from the Ramada Inn at Malecón and Calle Imbabura. *For information contact Corturis at Calle Córdova 709, tel. 04/397401 or 04/397444. Admission charged. Closed weekdays.*

Both the **Nahim Isaias Museum** (Calle Clemente Ballén at Calle Pichincha, tel. 04/329099) and the **Central Bank Anthropology Museum** (Calle J. Antepara at Av. 9 de Octubre, tel. 04/327482 or 04/329785) present rotating archaeological exhibits in addition to their extensive displays of colonial and 19th-century South American art. The latter also displays contemporary Ecuadorian art. Call in advance, however, as both museums keep irregular hours and are often closed during the rainy season.

Dining

The majority of Guayaquil's restaurants are clustered in the Urdesa, La Garzota, and Nueva Kennedy districts, north of downtown. Many close daily between 4:30 and 7:30 PM. For price ranges, *see* Dining in Staying in Ecuador, *above.* Highly recommended restaurants are indicated by a star ★.

Expensive **Paper Moon.** This lilac and white restaurant is nestled in the rich hills of the Urdesa district. Thursday to Saturday the menu features traditional Ecuadorian dishes—mainly barbecued and grilled meats. At other times you can indulge in a wider range of dishes such as grilled suckling pig or trout with almonds. *Av. Séptima 302 (at Calle Las Lomas), tel 04/386702. DC, MC, V. Sun. lunch only.*

★ **Trattoria da Enrico.** Tiny shuttered windows set into thick whitewashed walls, plus a profusion of plants, reflect this restaurant's Mediterranean influence. After a prosciutto and melon appetizer, try a fresh homemade pasta, or chicken with sour cream, vodka, and mushroom sauce. *Calle Bálsamos 504 (at Calle Ebanos), tel. 04/387079. DC, MC, V. Closed Tues.*

Moderate **El Cangrejo Criollo.** The atmosphere is casual and maritime at this popular La Garzota district eatery. Waiters dress in swashbuckling attire and serve up steaming plates of local crab, shrimp in coconut sauce, and other fresh-caught seafood. *Av. Principal La Garzota, tel. 04/232018. DC, MC, V.*

La Parrillada del Ñato. Local families and a sprinkling of tourists fill this enormous, pleasantly informal restaurant seven days a week. South American barbecue is the house specialty, from suckling pig and pork ribs to chicken and beef. Pizzas also appear on the menu. *Av. V.E. Estrada 1219 (at Calle Costanera), tel. 04/387098. AE, DC, MC, V.*

Lodging

For price ranges, *see* Lodging in Staying in Ecuador, *above.*

Very Expensive **Gran Hotel Guayaquil.** Sea-green carpets contrast nicely with coral and white walls in this modern, well-furnished high rise. Suites contain all necessary kitchen accoutrements as well as refrigerator, stove, and a spacious sitting room. *Calle Boyaca (at Av. 10 de Agosto), tel. 04/329690, fax 04/327251, in U.S. tel. 800/223–6764. 180 rooms. Facilities: 4 restaurants, sauna, steam room, gym, swimming pool, car rental. AE, DC, MC, V.*

Expensive **Ramada Inn.** Businesspeople will appreciate not only the location, across from the Guayas River near the financial district, but also the hotel's secretarial and business services. (There are even plans to install fax machines in every room.) Tourists will appreciate the river views and excellent on-site restaurants, which serve delicious *comida criolla,* traditional coastal dishes. *Malecón Simón Bolívar, Box 10964, tel. 02/312200 or 02/311888, fax 02/322036, in U.S. tel. 800/334–3782. Facilities: 2 restaurants, 2 bars, pool, sauna, steam room, casino, business center. AE, DC, MC, V.*

Uni Hotel. This clean and modern downtown high rise features bathroom phones and fine views of the adjacent Parque Seminario. The building's first four floors house a shopping center. *Calle Clemente Ballén 406, tel. 04/327100 or 04/324046, fax 04/328352, in U.S. tel. 800/223–5652. 110 rooms, 36 suites. Facilities: 2 restaurants, 2 bars, gym, sauna, casino. AE, DC, MC, V.*

Moderate   **Hotel Del Rey.** This pleasant midsize hotel is located in the geographic center of Guayaquil, about a 10-minute taxi ride from the financial district. The well-kept rooms are on the small side, but this is one of the few moderately priced hotels in town with exercise facilities. *Calle Aguirre (at Calle Andrés Marín), tel. 04/369595 or 04/373951, fax 04/374351. 44 rooms. Facilities: restaurant, bar, gym, sauna. DC, MC, V.*

Inexpensive   **Hotel Velez.** The very plain but well-kept Velez has few amenities aside from rooms with firm beds and ceiling fans. The clientele largely consists of small businessmen and budget-minded foreigners. *Calle Velez 1021 (at Av. Quito), tel. 04/525430 or 04/526292. 30 rooms. Facilities: cafeteria. No credit cards.*

Excursions from Guayaquil

Salinas   *Guayaquileños* flock to **Salinas**'s long, if sometimes dirty, sand beach on holidays and during the hot and humid rainy season (during the off-season many restaurants and hotels close). For tourists, sea fishing is the main draw here. The continental shelf drops sharply to the ocean floor just 19 kilometers (12 miles) offshore, providing a fertile feeding ground for Pacific sailfish, swordfish, amberjack, tuna, sailfish, grouper, and shark, as well as striped, blue, and black marlin. The biggest catches are made November through May, but fishing continues year-round. **PescaTours** (Guayaquil, tel. 04/443365, fax 04/443142; Salinas, tel. 04/772391) organizes day-long charters for two to six people for around $250.

Getting There   Taxis will bring you from Guayaquil to Salinas for less than $10 each way.

The Galápagos Islands

It is possible that indigenous coastal Indians were the first to discover the remote Galápagos Islands—the chain of rocky, highly active volcanic islands that lie roughly 966 kilometers (600 miles) off the coast of Ecuador; at least some think this is the explanation for legends among Ecuador's coastal peoples referring to "a land of fire across the sea." Less dramatic, perhaps, and certainly better documented, was the arrival of Fray Tomás de Berlanga, the Bishop of Panama, in 1535. His ship was becalmed on a fact-finding mission to Peru and eventually drifted on strong currents to the Galápagos. Berlanga's dutiful report to the King of Spain may have put the *Insulae de los Galopegos* on the map, but seafaring men found the black volcanic islands inhospitable, lonesome, and lacking a regular source of fresh water. Centuries later, English pirates used the

The Galápagos

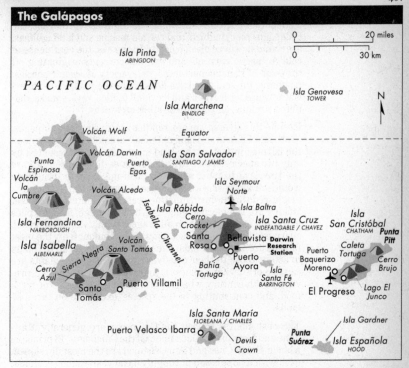

0   20 miles
0   30 km

PACIFIC OCEAN

Isla Pinta
ABINGDON

Isla Genovesa
TOWER

Isla Marchena
BINDLOE

N

Volcán Wolf   Equator

Volcán Darwin   Isla San Salvador
SANTIAGO / JAMES

Punta   Puerto
Espinosa   Egas
Volcán
la
Cumbre

Volcán Alcedo   Isla Seymour
Norte

Isla Baltra

Isla Rábida

Isla Fernandina
NARBOROUGH

Cerro
Crocket

Isla Santa Cruz
INDEFATIGABLE / CHAVEZ

Isla
San Cristóbal
CHATHAM   Punta
Pitt

Isla Isabella
ALBEMARLE

Volcán
Santo Tomás

Santa
Rosa

Bellavista   Darwin
Research
Station

Puerto
Baquerizo
Moreno

Caleta
Tortuga

Cerro
Brujo

Cerro
Azul

Sierra Negra

Bahía
Tortuga

Puerto
Ayora

Isla
Santa Fé
BARRINGTON

Santo
Tomás

Puerto Villamil

El Progreso

Lago El
Junco

Isla Santa María
FLOREANA / CHARLES

Isla Gardner

Puerto Velasco Ibarra

Punta
Suárez

Isla Española
HOOD

Devils
Crown

Isabella Channel

remote Galápagos as a covert base for plundering the Ecuadorian and Peruvian coast. Many of the islands received their English names—some of which are still in use—during the patriotic tenure of these scurrilous buccaneers.

The Galápagos' most famous visitor was Charles Darwin, in 1835. A dropout theology student with no formal scientific training, Darwin nonetheless visited the islands in the capacity of resident naturalist aboard the sailing vessel H.M.S. *Beagle* during its five-year, around-the-world scientific mission. Darwin stayed just five weeks and visited only a handful of islands, but his findings contributed enormously to his theories of evolution and adaptive radiation eventually published in 1859 in his revolutionary work, *On the Origin of Species by Means of Natural Selection.*

Despite the interest generated by Darwin's publications, the islands attracted mainly adventure seekers and solitaries until well into the 20th century. Tourism began in a limited fashion after the Ecuadorian government declared the islands a National Park in 1959. Four decades later, the Galápagos must cope with more than 80,000 yearly visitors, and some ecologists are concerned that the steadily increasing numbers will prove destructive to this unique, irreplaceable environment.

Carried by winds and ocean currents, everything from seeds and plants to birds and reptiles miraculously have made their way to these remote volcanic islands. Over the course of thousands of years many have evolved in response to the Galápagos's harsh environment and are now classified as distinct species—an integral aspect of Darwin's theory of natural selection. Some species, including the flightless cormorant, the Galápagos mockingbird, and certain marine and land iguanas, are found nowhere else on earth. In the sea, the confluence of cold Antarctic currents and warmer currents originating off the coast of Panama nurtures a rich variety of oceanic species: penguins, fur seals, and sea lions share the multicolor underwater world with green and hawkbill turtles, rays, sharks, dolphins, urchins, and countless other creatures.

Despite this diversity of life, reptiles are king in the Galápagos. (Both amphibians and land mammals are noticeably absent on the islands; in fact, native land mammals are represented by only two species of rice rat.) The most easily seen reptiles are the tiny lava lizards: males do push-ups both to intimidate would-be aggressors and impress females, who develop a bright red throat during mating season. Definitely the oddest looking are the marine iguanas, who lie in huge, friendly piles in the sun and resemble small dragons with their spiny crests, sharp front claws, and thick scaly hides. Undoubtedly the most famous are the giant Galápagos tortoises, which can weigh up to 550 pounds. To their disadvantage, these gentle giants are capable of surviving almost a year without food or water, providing 19th-century whalers with a delicious source of fresh food, and contributing to the species' extinction on three islands.

The best months to visit the Galápagos are generally May–June and November–December. Of the Galápagos' 13 principal islands, Santa Cruz and San Cristóbal are the most developed, each with a population of roughly 6,000 year-round residents. However, only Santa Cruz has much allure for visitors, with its dozen or so hotels and restaurants, boutiques, and even discotheques. The Archipelago's four populated islands can be visited on a limited basis without guides, but the vast majority of islands can be visited only with a guide licensed through the Galápagos National Park Service. Visitors commonly book their own airfare and prearrange a one- to two-week ship-based package that includes guided visits to islands such as Hood and Isabela. Cruises of 10 days or longer generally are needed to reach the more remote northern islands or to climb either of Isabela's two accessible volcanic craters.

Tourist Information

There are no telephone lines to the Galápagos Islands, so hotel and tour reservations are typically booked through agencies in Quito, Guayaquil, or the United States. Island and interisland calls are possible, and local telephone numbers are not preceded by an area code. **CETUR** (Av. Charles Darwin, Santa Cruz Island, tel. 174) offers limited information about tours and guides. A few doors down, both **Armadores de Turismo** (no phone) and **Coltur** (tel. 177) arrange single and multiday tours.

Island Tours

Three classes of boat offer tours of the Galápagos: luxury, tourist, and economy. Economy vessels (usually converted fishing trawlers) can be booked from the islands for day tours costing $35–$75 per person, but such boats are often poorly maintained and accompanied by auxiliary guides who need a refresher course in English. Luxury and tourist class vessels generally offer three-, four-, and seven-night tours for $100–$275 per day. You dine and sleep on board, and most of the sailing is done at night to maximize time spent touring the islands. These vessels employ naturalist guides knowledgeable in biology and related sciences, and who speak at least two languages. At least once a day you will have an opportunity to swim or snorkel. (For information about special-interest tours, *see* Chapter 2.)

Cruise Ships   There are three cruise ships currently operating in the Galápagos, all of which can be booked through **Metropolitan Touring** (Av. República Salvador 9–70, Quito, tel. 02/464780, fax 02/564655; in U.S. tel. 800/527–2500, fax 214/783–1286). The *Santa Cruz,* which departs from Baltra, and the *Galápagos Explorer,* which departs from San Cristóbal Island, both carry up to 90 passengers and have comfortable dining rooms and bars (the latter also has a swimming pool). The *Galápagos Explorer* has a reputation as the "party" boat and seems to attract more Ecuadorian nationals; the *Santa Cruz* has a slightly more academic bent. The most luxurious—and expensive—option is the 38-passenger *Isabela II,* equipped with a whirlpool, sauna, and exercise room. It is based in Baltra and can be booked only for seven-night itineraries.

Private Vessels   Luxurious three- to 12-person yachts can be booked FIT (for individual travelers) or, more commonly, as charters for private groups. You may save money by booking directly with operators within Ecuador; contact **Angermeyer's Enchanted Excursions** (Calle Foch 769, at Av. Amazonas, Quito, tel. 02/569960, fax 02/569956) or **Quasar Naútica** (Box 17-01-0069, Quito, tel. 02/446996, fax 02/446997; in U.S. tel. 800/247–2925, fax 813/637–9876).

Land Based   Those who do not relish three–seven nights aboard a ship should consider Metropolitan Touring's land-and-sea Delfin package. The three-, four-, or seven-night itineraries combine lodging at the comfortable Hotel Delfin, on Santa Cruz, with daily island excursion on the newly refurbished, 36-passenger *Delfin II.* However, all but the most queasy landlubber should seriously consider a ship-based package, which allows you to see more of the islands and their wildlife.

Getting There

By Plane   **TAME** flies once daily between Quito, Guayaquil, and Baltra,
Santa Cruz   a tiny island just north of Santa Cruz. The flight takes roughly three hours and costs $350–$400 round-trip. To reach Puerto Ayora, on Santa Cruz, follow the crowds to the ferry and, once across the channel, hop on any bus for the trek across the island.

San Cristóbal   **SAN** has one flight per day, five days a week, from Quito and Guayaquil to San Cristóbal Island. If you fly round-trip internationally with **Saeta** you can arrange a free stopover on San Cristóbal Island (30 days maximum).

By Boat   There are no scheduled sailings between mainland Ecuador and the Galápagos Islands (the crossing takes three days in good weather). Passage can sometimes be booked on supply boats for around $100 each way; contact the Port Captain in Puerto Ayora, Santa Cruz Island, for details.

Getting Around

Limited interisland transportation is available by boat with the municipal agency **INGALA** (no phone), located on Santa Cruz Island on the road to Bellavista. Currently there is one trip per week from Santa Cruz to Floreana and Isabela Islands ($20 one-way); and two boats per week between Santa Cruz and San Cristóbal. The latter five-hour trip costs less than $15.

Exploring the Galápagos Islands

Santa Cruz Overlooking Academy Bay on the island's southern shore is **Puerto Ayora,** a relatively developed town equipped with hotels, souvenir shops, restaurants, and even a few discotheques. Follow the main road east to the **Charles Darwin Research Station** and its Van Straelen visitor center, which has an informative exhibit explaining the basics of Galápagos geology, weather patterns, volcanology, and ecology. Self-guided trails lead to the station's tortoise pens, where several different populations can be viewed. *Tel. 189. Admission charged. Closed Sun.*

Tortuga Bay, 3 kilometers (2 miles) southwest of Puerto Ayora, boasts a long white-sand beach where marine iguanas sometimes bask in large piles. There are no facilities along the water, but walking from town (take the road to Bellavista and turn left just past the bank) you will pass a soda and beer stand at the top of a lava-rock staircase.

Near the small village of **Bellavista** you can explore amazing underground lava tubes. **Los túneles,** as they are known on the island, were created when flowing lava cooled more quickly on the surface, forming crusts that ensconced a labyrinth of tall, empty chambers. The underground tunnels are nearly a mile long, and you can easily walk upright as you grope through the caverns with the aid of a flashlight. To reach the tunnels from Puerto Ayora go north on the road to Bellavista; turn right (east) at the crossroad and walk about a mile until you find a farm with a sign announcing LOS TÚNELES. A small entrance fee is collected by the farm owners, who also provide flashlights.

The road to **Santa Rosa,** 13 kilometers (8 miles) beyond Bellavista, is lined with giant elephant grass, avocado and papaya trees, and boughs of yellow trumpet vines, in marked contrast to the dry, cactus-spotted lowlands. About 2 kilometers (1 mile) beyond Santa Rosa look for a pair of giant sinkholes called **Los Gemelos,** one on either side of the road.

The unattended **National Park Tortoise Reserve** is one of the few places in the archipelago where you can view bales of giant Galápagos turtles in the wild. An unmarked track leads to the reserve from Santa Rosa. Along the way keep alert for Galápagos hawks, Darwin finches, and short-eared owls. In Santa Rosa, a small restaurant across from the church sometimes rents horses, which you are allowed to ride inside the tortoise reserve.

San Cristóbal **Puerto Baquerizo Moreno** is the capital of Galápagos Province and the largest town on San Cristóbal, though with only a few hotels and restaurants it is less tourist-oriented than Puerto Ayora. Still, Puerto Moreno's harbor provides anchorage for numerous tour boats, and there is some good hiking in the area. Two kilometers (1 mile) east of the port is **Frigatebird Hill,** where both great and magnificent frigate birds—two species of black seabirds famed for their courtship displays—make their nests. On a clear day there are sweeping views of Bahía Wreck bay.

El Progreso, one of San Cristóbal's first colonies, is a small village about 8 kilometers (5 miles) east of Puerto Moreno at the end of one of the island's few roads (weary buses connect the two towns twice daily). You can rent a jeep in town and explore the shores of **Laguna el Junco,** one of the archipelago's few permanent freshwater lakes, 10 kilometers (6 miles) east.

Punta Pitt, at the northeastern tip of the island, is the only place in the Galápagos where you can view three species of boobies—masked, blue-footed, and red-footed—nesting together, as well as frigate birds, storm petrels, and swallow-tailed gulls. The site is accessible by motor launch from Puerto Moreno; inquire at your hotel for details.

Isabela   Although **Isabela** is the largest island in the archipelago, no tour boats are based here and its infrastructure is extremely limited. Its few hotels are very basic, with intermittent hot water, and there are only two restaurants. Sleepy **Puerto Villamil,** founded in 1897 as a center for extracting lime, is the focus of the island's scant tourist trade. Nearby there are several lagoons where flamingos and migrant birds can be viewed up close, and sand-and-lava beaches with large populations of herons, egrets, and other birds.

Isabela's active volcano, **Volcán Sierra Niegra** (1,389 meters/4,488 feet), can be climbed with local guides based in Puerto Villamil or Santo Tomás, a rural village 18 kilometers (11 miles) northwest. From Santo Tomas you can also hire horses for the 9-kilometer (5½-mile) trek to the volcano's rim. The view from here is awe-inspiring: The volcano's caldera—roughly 10 kilometers (6 miles) in diameter—is the largest in the Galápagos and the second-largest in the world. A more ambitious climb, requiring adequate planning and equipment, is **Volcán Alcedo** (3,600 feet). The site can only be reached by boat, after which a 10-kilometer (6-mile) trail climbs over rough terrain. Your rewards: stunning vistas and the opportunity to view the archipelago's largest population of Galápagos tortoises.

Dining and Lodging

Island restaurants maintain reasonably high standards, but lodgings can be quite rustic. Many hotels have only cold running water, and rooms often lack electrical outlets (which shouldn't be a serious problem since electricity is shut off nightly between midnight and 7 AM). For price categories, *see* Dining and Lodging in Staying in Ecuador, *above.*

Santa Cruz   **Hotel Galápagos.** This casual and comfortable hotel, drenched
Dining and Lodging   in bougainvillea and other flowering plants, is halfway between Puerto Ayora and the Darwin Research Station—a relatively short walk to either. The rustic rooms have cement floors covered by palm frond mats; some have ocean views. The restaurant serves healthy but uninspired meals; the seaside lounge has hammocks, bookshelves, and a self-serve bar. *Av. Charles Darwin, Puerto Ayora, no phone (for reservations tel. 02/545777*

or fax 02/502449). 18 rooms. Facilities: restaurant, bar, hot show-ers. Meals for nonguests by previous arrangement only. MC, V. Very Expensive.

Gran Hotel Fiesta. This brand-new complex has six small, three-person cabins, each with a separate dining room and small refrigerator. Like most hotels here, hot water is unheard of. Its location near Las Ninfas lagoon means bugs may be a serious problem during the rainy season. At press-time the on-site restaurant was not yet completed. *Las Ninfas, Puerto Ayora, no phone (for reservations tel. 02/530449). Facilities: res-taurant. No credit cards. Moderate.*

Dining **Bambú Bar.** Fresh juices, salads, empanadas, and homemade cakes are served in the lush garden of this elegant two-story house. Bambú is known for its coffees, mixed drinks, and the congeniality of its owners. *Av. Charles Darwin, Puerto Ayora. No credit cards. Closed Sun. Moderate.*

★ **Four Lanterns.** The Italian proprietress of this popular restau-rant takes pride in her culinary creations: The lasagna, gnoc-chi, cannelloni, and pizza are all homemade and excellent. An accepted piece of local wisdom: Everyone eventually ends up at the Four Lanterns. *Av. Charles Darwin, Puerto Ayora, no phone. No credit cards. No lunch. Moderate.*

Henri's Snack Bar. The best thing about this cheerful, orange and white bar-cum-restaurant is the *roeschti*, a giant Galápa-gos version of the Swiss potato pancake. Henri also serves burgers and sandwiches plus a rotating "meal of the day." The bar is a popular spot for sipping beer and gossiping. *Av. Charles Darwin, Puerto Ayoro, no phone. No credit cards. Closed Sun. Moderate.*

Narwahl. Located in the lush highlands of Santa Cruz, with a gorgeous view of the island on a clear day, this hide-away eatery features set meals that include a welcome cocktail, soup or salad, and a dependably good entrée of chicken, fish, or beef (vegetarian entrées are available with advance notification). *Road to Santa Rosa, no phone. Reservations required; make arrangements at Henri's Snack Bar or the Coltur tourist desk. No credit cards. Moderate.*

San Cristóbal **Gran Hotel San Cristóbal.** Although it is expensive and not par-*Dining and Lodging* ticularly attractive, this is the best hotel in town. Air-condition-ing and hot water showers help to make up for the lack of charm. *Playa Man, tel. 179. Facilities: restaurant, hot water. Expensive.*

9 Paraguay

By Richard Jarvie

Richard Jarvie has worked as a foreign correspondent in South America for 15 years. He was chief correspondent for Reuters news agency in Brazil and later moved to a similar position in Argentina where part of his duties included extensive coverage of events in Paraguay.

Viewed by even seasoned travelers as a curious footnote to South America's more glamorous regions, Paraguay remains a largely unknown quantity. Isolated by its landlocked position and by more than three decades of authoritarian rule under General Alfredo Stroessner, toppled in a 1989 coup, the country was left behind by the rapid economic progress experienced by neighboring Brazil and Argentina.

At the same time, this isolation also means that Paraguay has not entered the rat race, and many visitors comment on the easy pace of life and the charm of the people, with their Old World courtesies and generous hospitality. And while tourism here is undeveloped, the up side is the lack of crowds and a freedom to explore both the countryside and places of interest, which include restored Jesuit missions and, in the capital, Asunción, fine examples of both Spanish colonial and 19th-century architecture, without the controls and restrictions common in Europe and North America.

Museums are run down, maintained more by enthusiasm than government funds. The highway system is primitive and good hotels few and far between. But the advantages to this less-than-perfect infrastructure are enormous. Visitors to a Jesuit ruin can find themselves totally alone and, without a hawker in sight, allow the overwhelming tranquillity of the site to transport them back to the time when missionaries worked the fields alongside their Guaraní Indian converts.

With little effort nature lovers can explore the subtropical jungle of the northeast, home to parrots, macaws, and toucans as well as the fast-disappearing jaguar, or observe varied and abundant birdlife in the swamps of the Paraná plateau or on the sun-scorched plains of the Chaco, where kites, vultures, and eagles soar. Rivers that teem with salmonlike *dorado* and giant *surubí* catfish offer some of the best fishing in the world. Anglers can test their skills as clouds of snowy egrets take flight and monkeys swing through riverside trees.

More than one-quarter of Paraguay's 4.5 million people live in Asunción and most of the rest in or around the numerous small towns to the east. West of the capital and the Paraguay River (which bisects much of the country) is the Chaco plain, an arrid scrubland covering half of Paraguay and one of the most sparsely populated spots on earth, with less than one inhabitant for each of its 250,000 square kilometers (97,500 square miles).

Spanish and Guaraní are the official languages, reflecting a society in which around 80% of the population is of *mestizo*—mixed Spanish and Indian—stock. Some say that while Spanish is the language of business, the soft-toned Guaraní is the language of love.

Paraguay has a fairly large and influential German community—one reason for the high quality of the local beer—while more recently Koreans have taken over many of the shops in Asunción, Ciudad del Este, and Encarnación, where they sell a wide range of imported goods.

In stark contrast to the otherwise untamed quality of the Chaco are the Mennonite settlements. Starting in 1927, when the first Mennonites arrived from Canada, 1 million hectares

415

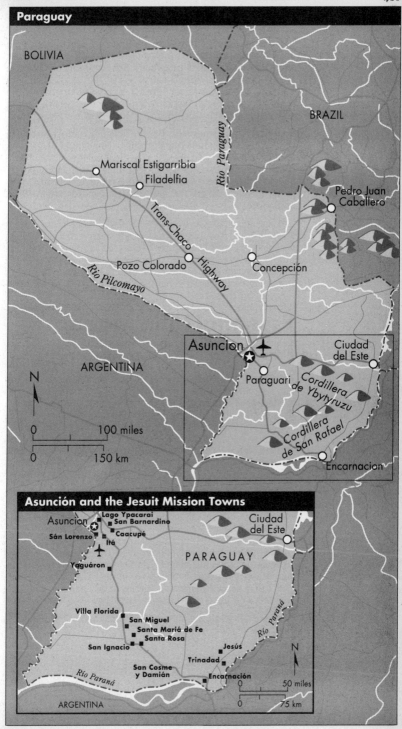

of inhospitable scrub were turned into fertile farmland, supplying more than half of Paraguay's dairy produce.

Agriculture, particularly cotton and soybeans, and cattle breeding are the driving forces of the Paraguayan economy, while industry is still in its infancy. After an economic boom in the 1970s, fueled by the construction of the Itaipú Dam with Brazil, Paraguay's economic growth has slowed to a trickle, the most important factor being the success or failure of the cotton and soybean harvests.

Paraguay is a partner with Brazil, Uruguay, and Argentina in the Mercosur Common Market, due to come into full effect on January 1, 1995. Opinions as to the benefits are mixed. While the market's promoters say integration will give Paraguay access to new markets, enabling industry and agriculture to expand, opponents argue the local economy could drown in a flood of imports.

But Paraguay faces an even greater challenge. Although press and individual freedoms have been fully restored, and free elections have been held, vestiges of the past continue in the form of widespread corruption and smuggling as beneficiaries of the old system refuse to yield to the new. It remains to be seen if Paraguay's still fragile democracy can withstand and eventually destroy these forces.

Essential Information

Before You Go

When to Go Although Paraguay has no high or low tourist seasons, visitors should make advance reservations for accommodations in Asunción, where space in high-quality hotels is limited. Since the opening up of both the country and the economy in 1989, the stream of businesspeople looking for opportunities in Paraguay has increased dramatically. This, coupled with frequent conferences and congresses linked to the country's move from isolation to integration, means that rooms in all price categories can be scarce.

Climate Rain falls throughout the year in Asunción and the southeast, frequently in the form of torrential cloudbursts that can turn streets into torrents of muddy red water, bringing traffic to a standstill. The wettest months are December through April, the driest June, July, and August. Temperatures are high most of the year, and visitors should make sure that guest rooms have air-conditioning or fans. In the summer months (November–March), the heat is usually so intense that it is advisable not to plan activities between midday and 4 PM. Remember, the siesta is a national institution in Paraguay!

The following are the average daily maximum and minimum temperatures for Asunción.

Jan.	93F	34C	May	77F	25C	Sept.	80F	27C
	72	22		55	14		60	16
Feb.	93F	34C	June	72F	22C	Oct.	84F	29C
	72	22		55	13		62	17
Mar.	91F	33C	July	75F	24C	Nov.	88F	31C
	70	21		57	14		66	19
Apr.	82F	28C	Aug.	77F	25C	Dec.	91F	33C
	64	18		57	14		70	21

Currency The unit of currency in Paraguay is the guaraní (G). There are bills of 500, 1,000, 5,000, 10,000, and 50,000 guaraníes, with coins in units of 10, 50, and 100 guaraníes. At press time (summer 1993) the exchange rate was around 1,731 guaraníes to the U.S. dollar and 2,616 guaraníes to the pound sterling. The value of the guaraní against the U.S. dollar falls at a rate that roughly offsets inflation, meaning that prices remain constant in dollar terms.

Changing Money It is most convenient to change money either at the *casas de cambio* (exchange houses) or at major hotels, which offer a slightly lower rate than casas de cambio. Banks, which in South America are highly bureaucratic, have longer procedures, probably more form filling, and more lines in which to wait. Their tourist exchange rates are normally less competitive than the casas de cambio. (The bank at the Asunción airport, however, changes money at competitive rates.) There are several casas de cambio along Calle Palma and around the main square in Asunción that accept both cash and traveler's checks; no commission is charged. Visitors should shop around for the most competitive rates. U.S. dollars are easiest to change. Rates for other currencies might not reflect their true international value. Money changers also operate in the streets, but because their rates are generally no better than in the casas de cambio, it is probably not worth the risk of counting and showing money in public.

As it is virtually impossible to change guaraníes outside the country, visitors should exchange them before leaving Paraguay. The constant devaluation of the currency means it is not worth saving for a future visit.

Credit Cards Most hotels and restaurants in the main cities accept credit cards. American Express, MasterCard, and Visa are the most widely accepted, although the majority of more expensive establishments also take Diners Club. Some department stores accept the major cards, but smaller shops generally expect payment in cash. Small stores selling electronics and other imported items sometimes impose a surcharge on credit card sales, or will limit the degree to which you can bargain. These stores also accept payment in U.S. dollars. Outside major cities businesses rarely accept payment by credit card or in U.S. dollars, so be prepared to pay for everything in guaraníes.

What It Will Cost Unlike neighboring Brazil and Argentina, Paraguay has not experienced hyperinflation. Although prices rise faster than in Europe and the United States, the constant devaluation of the guaraní means that the costs for foreign visitors remain about the same. With the exception of car rentals, the country is remarkably good value. Prices run as low as $15 for an non-air-conditioned double room in an budget hotel and up to $150 or more in a luxury establishment. In between there are numerous options, but high-quality accommodations in a well-situated hotel with private bathroom and air conditioning can easily be found in the $50–$100 per night range for two people, including breakfast. Gourmet meals with imported wines can be enjoyed at surprisingly low prices—$30 per person, including tip—while a three-course meal without alcoholic beverages in a good restaurant runs around $10 a head. Long-distance buses and internal flights are inexpensive, and cab fares are much cheaper than in the United States or Europe. Gasoline is around $1 a gallon. Most museums are free, but contributions are welcome, especially in churches. The budget-conscious traveler touring South America might consider taking care of shoe and luggage repairs, laundry, and dry cleaning while in Paraguay, where such services cost only a fraction of what they do in, for example, Argentina.

Taxes A 10% value-added tax known as IVA was introduced in 1992, and is charged on all goods and services. Although it is incorporated into most prices, including restaurant and bar bills, it is added to hotel bills. Guests checking out of hotels should ensure that the tax has been charged only on accommodation and services such as laundry; it should not be added to restaurant and bar bills charged to the room.

Sample Prices In Asunción, a cup of espresso coffee costs around 40¢; a pint of beer in a bar, $1.20; hamburger and french fries, $2; ham and cheese sandwich, $1.25; ice-cream cone, 35¢; local bus ride, 10¢; and 1-mile taxi ride, 80¢.

Embassies and Consulates **British Embassy** (Presidente Franco 706, Piso 4, Asunción, tel. 021/444–472; open 8 AM–1 PM).

Canadian Consulate (Benjamin Constant and Colón, Asunción, tel. 021/449–505; open 8–11:30 AM).

United States Embassy (Av. Mariscal López 1776, Asunción, tel. 021/213–715; open 8–11:30 AM).

Customs on Arrival Visitors may bring into the country any items considered to be for personal use plus one liter of spirits or two bottles of wine, and 400 cigarettes. Pets must have a valid health certificate. If arriving from a non-bordering country the certificate should be validated at a Paraguayan consulate in the country of issue. Sums of over $10,000 or its equivalent per person may not be taken in or out of Paraguay.

Language In the more expensive hotels the reception staff speaks English. Few of the restaurant staff speak English, although many menus are in several languages. Outside the main cities it is unusual to find anyone who speaks anything but Spanish or the native Guaraní language. There are some immigrant communities where German is spoken; some Mennonites speak Platdeutsche, a German dialect.

Getting Around

By Car Paraguay has few paved roads and only a few, either in or on the approaches to the main cities, have more than one lane in each direction. Two main roads leave Asunción to the east, one cutting south to Encarnación and the other heading to Ciudad del Este and Iguazú Falls. To the northwest is the Trans-Chaco highway, which when completed will link Paraguay with Bolivia. At press time (spring 1993) the road was paved as far as Mariscal Estigarribia, some 600 kilometers (372 miles) from

Asunción. The main highways and some bridges have tolls, approximately 60¢ per car.

The dirt roads crisscrossing most of the country can be uncomfortable, dangerously riddled with potholes, ruts, and puddles, and liable to closure because of flooding. Beware of wild animals, cattle, and horses that wander onto the highways, particularly at night. On weekends and around public holidays, access roads in and out of the capital can be blocked as the city's residents spend their leisure time in the countryside.

In Paraguay the same street can be called a different name depending on the section of that street, frequently causing the street numbers to run out of sequence. Therefore, addresses often are given as the intersection of two streets, for example, "Ayolas y Brasil" or "Ayolas con Brasil" (*y* means "and" and *con* means "with"). The word *calle* (street) is hardly ever used before the name of a street.

Rules of the Road Visitors' home driver's licenses are accepted by the local authorities. The speed limit throughout the country outside the cities is 80 kph, although this is widely disregarded in isolated areas. The speed limit in urban areas is 40 kph. Paraguayans drive on the right, and seat belts are not obligatory. Care should be taken at intersections in Asunción, as drivers rarely offer to give way.

Road maps can be obtained from the **Instituto Geográfico Militar** (Artigas y Perú, Asunción).

Gasoline Distances between gas stations can be long, so drivers should top off their tanks regularly. Stations are normally open until midnight. Two grades of gasoline, sold by the liter, are available: normal and super.

Car Rentals In Asunción: **Budget** (Av. Mariscal López 2801, tel. 021/661–200); **Hertz** (airport: tel. 021/206–196 or 021/206–199; downtown: Av. Eusebio Ayala, km 4.5, tel. 021/605–708 or 021/503–921); **National** (Yegros 501, tel. 021/491–848, 021/492–157, or 021/491–379); **Touring Cars** (airport: tel. 021/206–195, ext. 24; downtown: Iturbe 682, tel. 021/447–945).

By Bus Paraguay has an extensive privately owned bus network, which serves as the basic form of transport for the mass of the population. Buses are inexpensive, fast, and reliable. Long-distance buses, some air-conditioned and with reclining seats (and some showing videos!), race between the major centers, while bone-shaking local buses, known as *colectivos*, rattle between villages and along city streets. The 370-kilometer (230-mile) journey from Asunción to Encarnación takes about five hours by bus and costs $7.35; the 330-kilometer (205-mile) trip from Asunción to Ciudad del Este also takes five hours and costs $7.05. For the names and telephone numbers of the companies serving each route, call Asunción's main bus terminal (tel. 021/551–732).

By Train There are only two train services in Paraguay: one connecting the capital with Ypacaraí (*see* Excursion from Asunción, *below*), and the other between Asunción and Encarnación. Every Friday the train for Encarnación leaves at 6 PM. The trip takes 15½ hours and costs $3.80 for pullman class, $3.23 for tourist class. At its final destination it connects with an Argentine train to Buenos Aires. The journey is uncomfortable, but at only $3, a cheap one. For more information, contact the Asunción train station (Mexico y Eligio Ayala, tel. 021/44–316).

By Plane American Airlines, Líneas Aéreas Parguayas (LAP), Aerolíneas Agrentinas, Varig, Pluna, Ladeco, Iberia, and Lloyd Aéreo Boliviano (LAB) have flights to Asunción. **LATN** (Linéas Aéreas de Transporte Nacional, Brasil y Meriscal Estigarribia, tel. 021/212–277) and **TAM** (Transportes Aéreas Militares, Oliva 467, tel. 021/447–315), an airline run by the Paraguayan armed forces that civilians can use, provide almost daily service between Asunción and the major cities in the interior. Fares are reasonable. The one-hour flight to Ciudad del Este from Asunción costs $36, while the nearly two-hour flight to Pedro Juan Caballero, on the northeastern border with Brazil, costs $49. Visitors planning to go to the northeast jungle, including the Cerro Corá National Park, should consider going by plane, as the overland journey is arduous. Two air taxis operate out of Asunción: **Paraguayo SRL** (Próceres de Mayo 783, tel. 021/206–300) and **C Ruben Viveros** (Manuel Dominguez 2795, tel. 021/23–297).

By Boat Passenger boats run up the Paraguay River to northern ports. The scenery along the river is interesting for its birdlife and the possibility of sighting monkeys, *carpinchos*, tapirs, and alligators. Some of the ships go as far as the Pantanal wetlands in the Brazilian state of Mato Grosso, one of the world's greatest nature reserves, teeming with birdlife, alligators, jaguars, and piranhas. Air-conditioned cabins with full board are available at a reasonable price. For schedules and reservations contact the travel agency **Chacotur** (Montevideo 1447, tel. 021/440–448). **Flota Mercantil del Estado** (tel. 021/490–086), the state-owned shipping fleet, has a boat leaving every Tuesday for Concepción. The boat also makes a weekly three-day trip to Corumbá in Brazil. Tickets are available at the line's booking office at Estrella 672 in Asunción.

Staying in Paraguay

Telephones Pay phones are few and far between, taking tokens called *fichas* (approximately 20¢), which can be purchased at tobacco kiosks, bars, and post offices. Phone service, run by ANTEL, is improving rapidly, with direct dialing to most main cities in and outside Paraguay. Long-distance and international calls (*see below*) cannot be made from public phones other than those in ANTEL telephone offices or in some roadside service stations that have operators in attendance. Hotels normally add a surcharge to telephone calls made from guest rooms.

The peak period is weekdays 8–5 except public holidays. The cost of a three-minute local call is 9¢; calls to the United States cost $2.85 per minute during peak hours, $2.53 off-peak. For operator assistance for local calls, dial 010; for information dial 12.

International Calls International calls can be made directly by dialing 002 followed by the country code and local number. Lines can become congested at peak hours. For international operator assistance dial 0010.

Mail Airmail letters and postcards to North America and Europe
Postal Rates cost about 25¢ and take about a week to arrive. Hotels generally sell stamps. Documents and anything else of value (or valu-

able-looking) should be sent by courier service provided by **DHL International** (Haedo 105, Asunción, tel. 021/496–683) or **World Courier** (Haedo 179, 14th floor, Asunción, tel. 021/448–683).

Receiving Mail Travelers who want to receive mail but don't know where they will be staying can have it sent to Dirección Nacional de Correo, Poste Restante, Alberdi 130, Asunción, where it will be held for collection on production of identity. American Express (tel. 021/442–506) will hold members' mail for free at their office at Yegros 690, Asunción. There are no postal codes in Paraguay.

Shopping International visitors cannot get refunds on the value-added tax. Prices in department stores, general stores, and supermarkets are fixed, but in handicrafts stores and stalls and stores selling electronic goods, watches, and other luxury goods, substantial reductions can be won by hard bargaining. Always shop around. Try offering street vendors approximately half the asking price and others around two-thirds. You know that your final offer is too low if the seller lets you walk away.

Opening and Closing Times Siestas, generally between noon and 3:30, are taken to beat the heat. Everything except restaurants, cafés, and some supermarkets and department stores closes during this period.

Banks. Banks are open weekdays 9–12:30. The bank at the Asunción airport is open daily 9–6. Exchange houses (*casas de cambio*) are open weekdays 8–12:30 and 3:30–7.

Museums. Opening times vary, but most are open weekdays 8–noon and 4–6 and Saturday morning.

Offices. Public offices operate weekdays 7 AM–1 PM (post offices are open 7–noon and 2:30–7:30), while private businesses start between 7:30 and 8, work until midday, and reopen from 3 to 6.

Stores. Most stores open weekdays at around 7:30 AM, close for the siesta between 12:30 and 3:30, and then reopen until around 7. Butcher shops, grocery stores, bakeries, and other food shops open between 7 and 8, closing at noon and reopening from around 3 until between 7 and 8 PM. Department stores are open weekdays 8–7:30.

National Fesivals and Holdiays **Jan.:** New Year's Day (Jan. 1).

Feb.: Day of San Blas (Feb. 3), Patron Saint of Paraguay. The town of Itá celebrates with folk dancing, popular music, and horseracing.

Mar.: Heroes Day (Mar. 1) commemorates the death of President Mariscal Francisco Solan López and others who died in the major Paraguayan wars: the War of the Triple Alliance (1865–1870) against Brazil, Uruguay, and Argentina, in which 80% of Paraguay's menfolk perished and half of her territory was lost; and in the Chaco War (1929–1935) against Bolivia.

Mar./Apr.: Maundy Thursday (in 1994, March 31), Good Friday (April 1), Easter (April 3).

May: Labor Day (May 1), Independence Day (May 15). The latter celebrates the declaration of independence from Spain in 1811.

June: Armistice of Chaco War (June 12).

Aug.: Founding of Asunción (Aug. 15).

Dec.: Day of the Virgin of Caacupé (Dec. 8), Christmas Day (Dec. 25). On December 8 the town of Caacupé attracts large numbers of pilgrims who worship the statue of the Virgin, which is paraded through the streets, followed by folk dancing and music.

Dining Asunción has plenty of excellent restaurants, bars, and cafés, but outside the capital and other major cities the choices drop dramatically. Visitors traveling along the highways will find a few good roadside restaurants serving grilled meat, fish, and fast food. Paraguayan portions tend to be generous; don't hesitate to ask to share a dish.

Mealtimes Paraguayans start the day early, and mealtimes are correspondingly earlier than in many other parts of Latin America. Lunch begins at 11:30, but 12:30 is more typical. Some restaurants stop serving lunch as early as 2. Dinner is often available at 7 PM, with restaurants staying open until 11; more sophisticated dining spots open at 8 PM and serve until shortly after midnight. At weekends and on special occasions dinner hours are extended until much later. Café hours are generally 7 AM–10 PM.

Precautions Although tap water is safe to drink in Asunción, it's advisable to drink bottled water everywhere. *Agua con gas* and *agua sin gas* are the respective terms for water with and without carbonation.

Typical Dishes The *parrillada*, or mixed grill—barbecued meats, assorted sausages including blood sausages, and organ meats—served in large portions at restaurants called *parrillas* (grills), is a staple of Paraguayan dining. Beef is the mainstay, but pork, chicken, and fish are also common. The usual accompaniments are salad (Paraguay's tomatoes are said to be the best in the region) and boiled manioc, a white, fibrous root with a bland taste. Hearts of palm are considered a delicacy and served with salad at most good restaurants. *Sopa paraguaya*, a kind of cornbread made with cornmeal, *queso fresco* (a type of cheese), eggs, and onions, or *chipá-guazú*, similar but substituting roughly ground corn for cornmeal, may also accompany meat dishes. *Chipá*, a type of bread made from corn flour, ground manioc, and sometimes cheese, is sold in bakeries, on the street, and alongside roads, and is best eaten hot. *Puchero* is a meat, sausage, vegetable, and chick-pea stew, eaten in the cooler months. *Bori-bori* is a hearty soup with bits of meat, vegetables, and balls molded from cheese and corn.

Paraguay's rivers abound with edible fish, the favorites being *surubí*, a giant fastwater catfish, and *dorado*, a ferocious, salmonlike predator. These are prepared in a variety of ways, but to appreciate the full flavor, try *milanesa de surubí* (battered and deep-fried fillets) and plain grilled dorado. The soup made from the fish's head and other leftovers is delicious.

Typical desserts include *dulce de leche*, a mixture of milk and sugar heated until it turns into a thick, light brown sauce; papaya preserved in syrup; and fresh fruit such as pineapple, banana, mango, and melon.

Cafés and bars usually sell a limited menu of quickly prepared, mostly fried or grilled foods. Popular is *milanesa*, thin slices of beef, chicken breast, pork, or fish that are batter fried. Other favorite snacks are the *empanada*, an envelope of pastry filled with beef, pork, chicken, corn, or cheese; *croquetas*, minced meat or poultry fashioned into a sausage shape, rolled in breadcrumbs, then deep fried; and the *mixto*, a sandwich of ham and cheese. Many cafés have a dish of the day—*plato del día*—on the menu. Pasta dishes are also common.

Few Paraguayans are seen without their *guampa*, a drinking vessel made of cow's horn, metal, or wood, from which they sip *tereré*, a cold infusion made from *yerba mate* tea. Mate is drunk hot throughout the southern cone, but the cold version, often mixed with medicinal herbs, is unique to Paraguay. Paraguayan beers, which are Pilsner in style, are good; the Baviera brand is especially recommended. Beer on tap is known as *chopp* (pronounced "shop"). The local wine is not recommended. Taking tea is a tradition among society women, who can be seen at the tables of the top hotels in Asunción. Baby showers and women's wedding-eve parties often take the form of teas. Espresso or, in cheaper bars and restaurants, filter coffee is served demitasse except at breakfast.

Dress   Although jackets and ties are worn to business lunches, the general rule is smart casual attire in most restaurants. Some of the most deluxe establishments turn away people wearing jeans or running shoes.

Ratings   The 10% value-added tax (IVA) is included in the menu price. Make sure that you are not charged the tax when you are dining at a restaurant in your hotel and charge the meal to your room bill. Service charges are not added to the bill; leave a tip of 5%–10%, depending on the quality of the restaurant or bar and the level of service.

Prices below are per person and are for a three-course meal with coffee and 10% IVA, but not including alcoholic beverages or tip. Highly recommended restaurants are indicated by a star ★.

Category	Cost
Very Expensive	over $25
Expensive	$15–$25
Moderate	$7–$15
Inexpensive	under $7

Lodging   Aside from the first-class hotels in Asunción, Encarnación, and Ciudad del Este, the visitor to Paraguay must be content with basic, although generally clean, accommodations. Whenever possible, try to plan overnight stays where there are recommended hotels, as many towns offer only primitive lodgings, most frequently with shared bathrooms. With the exception of San Bernardino and other resorts around Lake Ypacaraí, where many Asunceños spend the summer and weekends, rates do not vary according to season. Room rates usually include breakfast, which most often consists of a buffet of juice, fresh fruit, breads and croissants, ham, and cheese. You will generally be charged extra for eggs. In some budget hotels, showers are heated by electric heaters incorporated into the shower head. On no account should the apparatus be touched if it is not working; the wiring could be live and highly dangerous, especially if the floor is wet.

For a list of all hotels operating in Paraguay, including rates, contact the **Dirección Nacional de Turismo** (Palma 468, tel. 021/441–530), the government tourist department.

Camping There are a number of campsites along the highways running from Asunción to Ciudad del Este and Encarnación, around the shores of Lake Ypacaraí, and in national parks. Facilities range from bathrooms to swimming pools and electrical hookups. For locations of campsites contact the Dirección Nacional de Turismo (*see above*). In Asunción, camping is permitted in the Botanical Gardens. In isolated areas campers should take precautions against poisonous snakes, zipping up flaps when the tent is left unattended, checking out the tent before entering, and shaking out sleeping bags, blankets, and other bedding. Never put on clothes or shoes without first inspecting them.

Ratings Prices below are for two people in a double room with breakfast and excluding 10% IVA. Highly recommended hotels are indicated by a star ★.

Category	Cost
Very Expensive	over $120
Expensive	$70–$120
Moderate	$35–$70
Inexpensive	under $35

Tipping Service charges are not added to restaurant bills; an appropriate tip is 5%–10% of the bill, more if the service is exceptionally good. The same rule applies to the smarter bars, but in cheaper, less fashionable places, round up the bill to the nearest thousand guaraníes. Taxi fares are rounded up to the nearest 500 G. Hotel and airport porters should receive around 50¢ per bag; a doorman should get the same for hailing a taxi. Leave the chambermaid $1.50 per day and $5–$10 after a week's stay. Shoeshine boys are paid 30¢–50¢, but they will try to charge you extra. Gas-station attendants are tipped up to 30¢ for filling the tank, cleaning the windshield, and checking tires and oil. Cinema and theater ushers are given about 10¢. Checkroom and rest-room attendants should be given 10¢–30¢. Give hairdressers and barbers around 10% of the bill.

Asunción

Like most Latin American cities, Asunción suffers from haphazard development and inadequate infrastructure. During office hours the city center is packed. Street vendors crowd sidewalks, and traffic hurtles by. Drivers play a dangerous game of chicken at every intersection. Crossing the street becomes a terrifying experience as buses bear down on pedestrians with seemingly murderous intent.

But take a step back and you will see another side of the city, once the colonial capital of southern South America. On the drive from the airport, the taxi whisks by remnants of Asunción's prosperous past, the magnificent mansions lining Avenida Mariscal López. A glimpse through an open doorway reveals a peaceful patio reminiscent of those in southern Spain, while above the neon signs of a hamburger bar the delicately decorated facade and balconies of a Belle Époque building have survived the vagaries of fashion. Alongside the money changers and peddlers of fake Rolex watches, Indian women offer bundles of herbs and roots, their centuries-old remedies for every bodily ailment. Contrasting with the hustle and bustle of the commercial center 100 yards away, the pristine columnated Government and Legislative palaces overlook the Bay of Asunción as cool river breezes rustle through jacaranda and flame trees in the nearby park.

During the day rich and poor rub shoulders, air-conditioned limousines jostling at crossroads with overpacked buses. At nighttime the wealthy drive home to their elegant suburban mansions while street vendors lug their unsold wares back to the reclaimed swampland of La Chacarita shantytown just below the Legislative Palace. Yet despite the chasm between the classes, visitors need not be concerned with theft and violence. Rich or poor, the Asunceño is invariably courteous and helpful.

Tourist Information

The helpful staff at the reception desk of **Direccion Nacional de Turismo** (Palma 468, ground fl., tel. 021/491–230) provides information and pamphlets about Paraguay weekdays 7 AM–7 PM and Saturday 7–noon. More detailed information can be obtained from the offices upstairs, open weekdays 7–1. **Lions Tour,** a travel agency (*see* Orientation Tours, *below*) operates a desk at the airport that can help visitors with transport and hotel and tour bookings throughout the country. The desk is open when international flights arrive. Most hotels provide pamphlets and maps, give advice, arrange tours, and hire cars.

Arriving and Departing

By Plane Several international airlines, most of them South American (*see* Arriving and Departing in Essential Information, *above*), serve the **Silvio Pettirossi International Airport,** which is 15 kilometers (9 miles) from the city center. The most practical means of getting into town, taxis charge a fixed rate to downtown, which at press time was about $12; for the current rate check at the transport information desk. The desk will arrange for an *omnibus special* whenever there are six or more passengers. This bus costs $3 and will take passengers to any address in central Assunción. **Local bus no. 30,** which leaves not from the airport grounds but from the toll booths on the road into the airport (about 200 yards from the terminal), departs for downtown Asunción every 15 minutes; the fare is 25¢. Some hotels provide minivan service for passengers with hotel reservations; the minivans meet each international flight.

By Car There are only three major entrances to Asunción. Access from the eastern cities of Encarnación or Ciudad del Este can either be through Luque, feeding into the city center via Avenida Mariscal López or Aviadores del Chaco (which branches off Mariscal López), or by a more direct route, via Avenida Pettirossi. The former is recommended because Pettirossi, which passes through suburban shopping areas, frequently becomes jammed with heavy, chaotic traffic. The remaining access is from the Trans-Chaco Highway (Route 9), which runs through Presidente Hayes, joins with the road from the frontier post of Puerto Falcon (across from the Argentine border town of Clorinda), and then crosses the Puente Remanso bridge spanning the Paraguay River 20 kilometers (12 miles) from Asunción. Turning right, the route is still called the Trans-Chaco Highway and runs into Avenida Primer Presidente. Turn right for a few hundred yards and left onto General Artigas. The route is clearly signposted. Heading out of Asunción, one can take Avenida Pettirossi and then the left fork into Avenida Eusebio Ayala, which then becomes Route 1.

Train Station Trains are irregular, slow, and infrequent and not recommended as an efficient form of travel in Paraguay, although the short trip to Lake Ypacaraí is worthwhile for the experience of being pulled along by a wood-burning steam engine (*see* Excursion from Asunción, *below*). Even if you're not taking a train, the colonnaded train station (Mexico y Av. Aligio Ayala, tel. 021/447–316), on Plaza Uruguaya, is worth a visit.

Bus Station All intercity services leave from **Terminal de Omnibus Asunción** (España and Fernando de la Mora, tel. 021/551–732). Many bus companies have information and ticket offices on Plaza Uruguaya, in the city center. The main companies are **Tres Fronteras** (tel. 021/60733), **Pluma** (tel. 021/60343), and **Rápido Yguazú** (tel. 021/62462).

Getting Around Asunción

All attractions in the center of Asunción can be seen on foot easily and safely; the city does not suffer from the violent street crime common in other South American capitals. Unless you plan to travel out of town, avoid renting a car—driving in Asunción can be nerve-racking.

By Public Transportation Local buses are crammed and uncomfortable. During business hours, old yellow **tramcars** trundle through downtown along Palma from the Plaza Uruguaya to Colón, running approximately every half hour. The fare is about 15¢.

By Taxi Taxis, all metered, are inexpensive and can range from a modern Mercedes to a rattly Volkswagen Beetle. They can be hailed in the street and found at the more than 70 taxi stands dotting the city. They also wait outside the main hotels. (Some hotels have their own limousine service.) Beware at night, when taxi drivers frequently do not put on their meters and then charge an outrageous fare at the end of the ride. Longer taxi rides that involve waiting time can be bargained. At night it can be difficult to find a taxi, so ask the hotel or restaurant to call a radio cab.

Orientation Tours

Lions Tour (Alberdi 454, 1st floor, tel. 021/490–278 or 021/490–591), **VIP's Tour** (Mexico 782, tel. 021/497–117), and **Agen Par** (Montevideo 419, tel. 021/441–687 or 021/444–539) can all arrange guided tours of the city's major sights and parks for between $10 and $20 a person, depending on the number of people.

Exploring Asunción

The city is built on a rise overlooking a large bay formed form the Paraguay River to the northeast. The downtown area runs southwest from the bay for about 10 blocks to Teniente Fariña and from Estados Unidos in the southeast for 17 blocks to Colón. Most hotels, restaurants, shops, and offices are to be found in this rectangle. Asunción's streets follow a grid; downtown they are narrow and generally have one-way traffic. Three downtown squares—Plaza de los Héroes, Plaza de la Independencia, and Plaza Uruguay—provide cool resting places under the shade of jacaranda trees.

Downtown   Just about everything worth seeing in Asunción is in the city center, within a few blocks of the **Plaza de los Héroes,** the central square. The plaza is a fine place to rest in the shade and observe Paraguayan life. Indians wander by, selling feather headdresses and bows and arrows, artisans put their wares on display, and traveling salesmen hawk anything from patented cures to miracle knife-sharpeners. You can also climb onto a high chair for a shoe shine, or have a photo taken by an old box camera. On public holidays the square is often the scene of live music and folk-dance performances.

In the corner of the square stands the pink-domed **Panteón Nacional de los Héroes.** Modeled after Les Invalides in Paris, this columnated mausoleum bears homage to the heroes who died in the War of the Triple Alliance and the Chaco War. The Panteón, guarded around the clock by two grenadiers, houses the remains of President Carlos Antonio López (who, during his administration, from 1841 until his death in 1862, was responsible for many of the public buildings in Asunción) and his son, Mariscal Francisco Solano López, the most venerated hero of the War of the Triple Alliance. Paraguay's commander in the Chaco War, José Felix Estigarribia, is also buried here, along with the remains of two unknown soldiers. *Plaza de los Héroes, no phone. Admission free.*

Two blocks away is the **Casa de la Independencia,** a late-18th-century house with typical whitewashed walls, brick floors, and a shady patio. Now a museum displaying colonial and 19th-century furniture and religious artifacts, some dating to the early 17th century, the building was the meeting place for revolutionaries plotting independence from Spain, which was declared in 1811. *14 de Mayo and Presidente Franco, no phone. Admission free. Closed Mon.–Fri. 11:30–3, Sat. after 11:30, and Sun.*

One block farther down on 14 de Mayo, at the intersection with El Paraguayo Independiente, is **Casa de la Cultura.** Once the military college, this museum houses documents, artifacts, and trophies from the War of the Triple Alliance and the Chaco War. *14 de Mayo y El Paraguayo Independiente, no phone. Admission free. Closed weekdays 12:30–3, weekends noon–4.*

Most of the important public buildings can be seen along **El Paraguayo Independiente.** Chief among these is the neoclassical, horseshoe-shaped **Palacio de Gobierno** (El Paraguayo Independiente y Ayolas), or Government Palace, an elegant building overlooking the bay, with verandas and wide spiral staircases. It is not open to the public. Nearby, on **Plaza de la Constitución,** is the **Palacio Legislativo** (Plaza de la Independencia, tel. 021/441-077 or 021/441-078; admission free;

closed weekday afternoons and weekends), or Congress. The upper floor was added in 1857, destroying the symmetry of the original single-story Jesuit building. Debates of both senators and deputies are open to the public. On the southeast corner of the square is the **Catedral Metropolitana** (Plaza Independencia, tel. 021/449–512; free admission), which dates back to 1687. Inside is an enormous gilded altar and many 18th- and 19th-century religious statues and paintings.

Behind the cathedral toward the river is **La Chacarita,** a shantytown that, now with running water and its own school, is steadily establishing itself as a permanent community. It's well worth a visit for those whose only exposure to life in Asunción has been in luxury hotels and restaurants and gleaming high rises. In the narrow, unpaved streets that wind between rickety tin, wood, and bare brick huts, barefoot, near-naked children play while chickens peck amongst the garbage. The area is slowly becoming urbanized with the installation of electricity and a sewage system.

Two blocks from the Palacio Legislativo, the **Museum of Fine Arts** (Mariscal Estigarribia y Iturbe, tel. 021/447–716; admission free; closed weekday afternoons and weekends) houses a collection of paintings and sculpture by both Paraguayan and foreign artists. Estigarribia runs into the **Plaza Uruguaya,** a shady square where locals meet to share *tereré* tea. On one side is a covered book market and on the other the colonnaded **railway station,** built in 1861. In one corner of the terminal you can see a pristine old steam locomotive, the *Sapucaí,* no longer in use.

Other Attractions A 15-minute taxi or bus ride from the center will take you to the **Parque y Museo de Historia Natural.** Although poorly maintained, these botanical gardens have an enormous array of plants and a small zoo. There is also an 18-hole golf course and campsite. The grounds and fine example of a Paraguayan country house, typically surrounded by verandas, once belonged to President Francisco Solano López. The residence now houses the museum displaying exhibits of Paraguayan wildlife, ethnology, and history. *Gral Artigas y Primer Presidente, tel. 021/25–680. Admission free. Museum closed weekdays 11–2:30 and weekends.*

Even if you don't stay or eat there, don't miss taking a peek inside the **Gran Hotel del Paraguay** (Calle de la Residenta 902, tel. 021/200–051), about 20 blocks from downtown. The former home of Madame Lynch, the Irish mistress of Solano López, the well-preserved mansion, surrounded by verandas, is set amid lush tropical gardens and boasts a fine collection of 19th-century furniture and paintings.

Mansions reflecting Paraguay's wealthy past can be seen along the tree-lined **Mariscal López** and **España** avenues, which lead into the city from the southeast.

The **Mercado 4,** on Avenida Pettirossi, is a throbbing, crowded street market that overflows onto several blocks, its stalls laden with produce, cheap clothing, hammocks, and live poultry. An early start is advised, not only because the market starts up before dawn but also because the heat and crowds can be suffocating. The market is closed on Sunday.

Shopping

The best shopping in Asunción falls into two distinct and very different categories of objects: handicrafts and electronics. Prices for both are among the lowest in South America, and hard bargaining can make them even cheaper.

The best-known local craft is the delicate *ñandutí*, a type of spiderweb lacework. Designs represent plants, animals, or scenes from local legends, and, although traditionally made with white silk or cotton thread, colored threads are now worked in. Both this and *ao p'oí*, a type of embroidery, are incorporated into tablecloths and place mats.

The best shops for lacework are **Ao P'oí Raity** (F.R. Moreno 155, tel. 021/494–457) and **Overall** (Mariscal Estigarribia 399, tel. 021/448–657).

Woodcarvings, intricately decorated gourds, and figurines, including nativity figures, are all attractive and reasonably priced. **Arte Popular** (Ayolas 360, tel. 021/492–548) carries a wide selection of these items as well as ceramics, filigree jewelry, and lacework. Leatherware, in the form of suitcases, tote bags, knapsacks, and briefcases, is more rustic than that sold in Argentina, but is long-lasting and only a fraction of the price. For leather goods try **Casa Vera** (Mariscal Estigarribia 470, tel. 021/445–868). Plain white or colorful woven hammocks are another good buy.

All of the above are sold in the rectangle of streets bordered by Palma, Estrella, Colón, and the Plaza de los Héroes. Bargains can be found on the sidewalks, but for top-quality goods stick to the specialty stores.

In the same area are hundreds of small stores selling imported watches, electronics, cameras, pens, and athletic shoes. Largely run by Koreans, many of these shops sell the same items, and competition is keen. Watch out for fake perfumes and whiskeys. The phony Rolex, Cartier, and Gucci watches are so obvious that even the vendors don't pretend they are genuine.

Paraguayan harps, guitars, and fine silver filigree jewelry can be bought in the town of **Luque,** near the international airport. **Constancio Sanabria** (Av. Aviadores del Chaco 2852, tel. 021/662–408 or 021/609–657) is highly recommended for musical instruments.

Spectator Sports

Soccer Soccer is Paraguay's main sport. The most important teams are **Cerro Porteño** and **Olimpia**. Matches are played on Sunday throughout the year, with the best first-division games held at the **Defensores del Chaco** stadium in the suburb of **Sajonia**. Local newspapers publish the most current information on game schedules and how to get tickets.

Tennis Tennis tournaments between different South American teams, including zone matches of the Davis Cup, are held at the **Yacht y Golf Club Paraguayo** (Av. del Yacht 11, Lambaré, tel. 021/36–117).

Dining

For its small size, Asunción offers a surprising variety of top-class restaurants serving international and Paraguayan cuisine. The more expensive dining spots tend to have international menus, some offering nouvelle cuisine. The ethnic cuisine available reflects the range of immigrant groups that have settled here: Korean, Japanese, and German. A number of economical lunchtime eateries scattered throughout the city center serve fast foods such as steaks, french fries, and some local specialties. Locals particularly favor **Bar Asunción** (Estrella and 14 de Mayo), **San Roque** (Ayala and Tacuari), **Le Grand** (Oliva between Alberdi and 14 de Mayo), **Bar San Miguel** (Espana and Padre Cardoso), and **Bar Carioca** (Independencia 1793). For details and price-category definitions, *see* Dining in Staying in Paraguay, *above*.

Very Expensive **Akari.** The high percentage of Japanese among the clientele
★ vouchsafes the quality of the food at this Japanese restaurant in the Hotel Cecilia (*see* Lodging, *below*). With less than a dozen tables, you have the option of eating at the center-of-the-room sushi bar, where you can observe the chef's skills at close range. *Estados Unidos 341, tel. 021/210–365, 021/210–366, 021/210–367, 021/210–033, or 021/210–034. Reservations advised. AE, DC, MC, V. Closed Sun.*

La Cascada. The sound of the waterfall that tumbles through the Hotel Excelsior's foyer (*see* Lodging, *below*) into the luxurious, lower-level dining room helps soothe nerves frayed by the patchy service. The food, international dishes with an emphasis on local fish, is good—the surubi in shrimp sauce is particularly tasty—but overpriced in comparison to the many excellent alternatives in downtown Asunción. *Chile 980, tel. 021/495–632 through 021/495–639. AE, DC, MC, V.*

Expensive **Il Capo.** Just opposite La Pérgola Jardin (*see below*), this small, 15-table Italian eatery is simply decorated with whitewashed and brick walls, wooden beams, and tile floors. The excellent main courses include the homemade pasta, such as *lasagne con camarones* (lasagne with shrimp), and *melanzana alla parmegiana* (gratinéed eggplant with tomato and herb sauce) as main courses; the Italian wine list is reasonably priced. *Peru 291, tel. 021/213–022. Reservations advised. AE, DC, MC, V.*

★ **La Hosteria del Caballito Blanco.** Wild boar and deer trophies, wooden chairs with heart-shaped backs, and red checkered tablecloths create a rustic look at this traditional German restaurant, where the portions are so huge that they almost beg to be shared. The extensive menu features several types of sausage and plenty of pork, including *kassler* (smoked chops) and *eisbein* (knuckles). *Alberdi 631, tel. 021/444–560. AE, DC, MC, V.*

La Pérgola Jardin. Smokey floor-to-ceiling mirrors, modern black lacquer furniture, lots of plants, and live sax and piano make this restaurant one of Asunción's most sophisticated dining spots. The service is efficient and friendly, and the menu, which changes weekly, is international with nouvelle tendencies (warning—the hot *pan de queso*, small cheese-flavored rolls that come in the bread basket, are irresistible). *Peru 240, tel. 021/210–219, 021/214–014, or 021/214-015. Reservations advised on weekends. AE, DC, MC, V.*

La Preferida. Rub shoulders with politicians and diplomats at this restaurant in the Hotel Cecilia (*see* Lodging, *below*), where the Austrian owners give off an air of friendly efficiency in the two dining areas (one no-smoking at peak hours), set with crisp, no-nonsense white linen tablecloths and classic silver and glassware. Among the specialties on the menu, which includes a variety of dorado and surubí dishes, are surubí *ahumado* (smoked) as a starter; the mild *curry de surubí*; and *lomo de cerdo a la pimienta*, peppered pork tenderloin (ask for it if it's not on the menu). *25 de Mayo 1005, tel. 021/210–365, 021/210–366, 021/210–367, 021/210–033, or 021/210–034. Reservations advised. AE, DC, MC, V. Closed Sun.*

★ **Talleyrand.** Located downtown near the Hotel Cecilia, this recently renovated restaurant under the direction of Georgy Sander, one of the new wave of talented Argentine chefs, serves up seasonal dishes that range from lamb with duck pâté wrapped in pastry to venison, nutria, and alligator. Although Sander succeeds in blending traditional French cuisine with a touch of the latest European trends, the oversize, nouvelle-cuisine-style china clashes somewhat with the soft green color scheme and hunting prints that lend the dining rooms a refined Continental ambience. *Estigarribia 932. tel. 021/41163 or 021/445–246. Reservations advised, especially Fri. and Sat. AE, DC, MC, V. Closed Sun.*

Moderate
★ **Churrasquaria Acuarela.** A 10-minute taxi ride from the city center, this enormous, 1,300-seat Brazilian *rodizio*-style restaurant must be the best value in town, charging around $7 for all you can eat. The bill of fare consists of a variety of sausages, chicken, pork, and beef cut to order, all straight off the barbecue, with a buffet laden with salads, vegetables, and desserts; for something different, ask for *cupim*, a cut of meat taken from the hump of the Brahma-like cattle bred in Paraguay and Brazil. *Mariscal López y Teniente Zotti, tel. 021/601–750. DC, MC, V.*

★ **La Paraguayita.** At this, the best of a host of grills on Avenida Brasilia, you'll sit out on the terrace beneath jacaranda trees while the waiters bring huge portions of perfectly done beef and pork cooked over white-hot coals and served with the wonderful Paraguayan cornbreads, *sopa paraguaya* and *chipaguazú*. The *chorizo* sausages make a good starter, especially when dunked in the *salsa criollo* sauce of onion, tomato, garlic, pepper, and vinegar. *Brasilia y Siria, tel. 021/704–497. DC, MC, V.*

Oliver's. One block from the Plaza de los Héroes, this favorite lunchtime meeting place for executives, decked out in fashionable pinks and grays, has a buffet at midday and in the evenings. Patrons can choose from a range of all-you-can-eat hot dishes such as goulash and pasta with mushrooms and cream sauce, and cold cuts, or they can order chateaubriand Oliver and other Continental dishes from an à la carte menu. *Azara 128, tel. 021/494–931 or 021/494–932. Reservations advised. AE, DC, MC, V. Open 7 AM–midnight.*

Inexpensive
Bar Asunción. Open 24 hours a day, this no-nonsense eatery with plastic tables and chairs is in the heart of the commercial center. Grilled steak and chicken, *milanesas* of beef, chicken, and surubí, and the empanadas are recommended. *Estrella y 14 de Mayo, no phone. No credit cards. Closed Sun. and bank holidays.*

★ **Le Grand.** Located in an old, high-ceilinged building, this favorite lunchtime haunt of office workers, who come for specialties such as *puchero* and *milanesa de surubí*, is decorated with brightly colored tablecloths and wood chairs. In the evening diners are serenaded with live Latin popular music. *Oliva between Alberdi and 14 de Mayo, no phone. No credit cards. Closed Sun.*

Tio Lucas. Glossy cream and black decor with matching Thonet bentwood chairs give this corner bar and restaurant specializing in pizza a crisp, modern look. *25 de Mayo y Yegros, no phone. No credit cards. Closed Sun. and bank holidays.*

Lodging

Accommodations in Asunción are limited to hotels, which vary from modest, no-nonsense establishments costing under $15 a night to the luxury Yacht y Golf Club Paraguayo resort (*see below*), which charges about $200 a night. Most hotels are situated downtown, where only the most expensive have swimming pools. Air-conditioned rooms, generally available at all but the cheapest hotels, are recommended in the summer months, but ceiling fans are adequate in the winter. For details and price-category definitions, *see* Lodging in Staying in Paraguay, *above*.

Very Expensive **Hotel Casino Yacht y Golf Club Paraguayo.** Considered one of
★ South America's finest hotels, this resort 13 kilometers (8 miles) southeast of Asunción is set on the riverbank in the midst of a 200-acre residential and leisure development, where amenities include jet skiing, windsurfing, sailing, fishing, golf, tennis, and squash. Some of the rooms, which are decorated with modern wood furniture, give onto verdant patios where hummingbirds nest among the foliage. *Av. del Yacht 11, Lambaré; mailing address: Casilla Correo 1795, Asunción; tel. 021/36–117 or 021/37–161, fax 021/36–120 or 021/36–133. 128 rooms, 5 suites. Facilities: 3 restaurants, bar, casino, health club, outdoor pool, 18 tennis courts (10 lighted), 2 squash courts, 18-hole golf course, free transportation to city center and airport. AE, D, DC, MC, V.*

Hotel Excelsior. Elegantly decorated with Regency-style striped wallpaper, antique and reproduction dark-wood furniture, and Oriental carpets, the Excelsior is the most luxurious hotel in downtown Asunción, despite the fact that some of the guest rooms are starting to show signs of wear and tear. It has a pleasant pool area with a grill and snack bar, and a basement-level discotheque. *Chile 980, tel. 021/495–632 through 021/495–639, 021/496–743, 021/496–744, or 021/496–745, fax 021/496–748. 160 rooms. Facilities: 2 restaurants, bar, health club, outdoor pool, disco, beauty salon, free transport to airport. AE, D, DC, MC, V.*

Expensive **Guaraní.** Set right on the Plaza de los Héroes, the Guaraní has
★ recently undergone a much-needed renovation, with the guest rooms now furnished with modern wood furniture and pastel carpets and curtains, the reception and lounge areas filled with modern black leather seating. The service, fortunately, has not changed—it's as friendly and efficient as ever. *Oliva y Independencia Nacional, tel. 021/491–131. 168 rooms, 28 suites. Facilities: 2 restaurants, bar, casino, health club, outdoor pool. AE, D, DC, MC, V.*

Hotel Cecilia. Priding itself on personalized attention, the Cecilia has established a devoted clientele. The double rooms are large though slightly austere, with nondescript modern decor; the single rooms are small and the air conditioners perilously close to the bed, blasting the sleeping guest with an icy wind. *Estados Unidos 341, 021/210–365, 021/210–366, 021/210–367, 021/210–033, or 021/210–034, fax 021/441–637. Facilities: 2 restaurants, bar, outdoor pool, parking. AE, D, DC, MC, V.*

Moderate **Chaco.** This comfortable but rather unremarkably decorated hotel can be recommended for its large carpeted rooms, good breakfasts, and friendly service. There is a small rooftop swimming pool. *Caballero 285, tel. 021/492–066. 73 rooms. Facilities: restaurant, bar, pool, free parking. AE, D, DC, MC, V.*

Continental. Added in a recent renovation, lacquer furniture and abstract paintings give the former Husa Hotel a modern look. Some of the guest rooms have a view of the bay. *Estrella y 15 de Agosto, tel. 021/493–760, fax 021/496–176. 66 rooms, 12 suites. Facilities: restaurant, bar, health club, sauna, outdoor pool. AE, D, DC, MC, V.*

Gran Hotel Armele. All guest rooms at this hotel in the main shopping district have air-conditioning and some have balconies overlooking the bay. The decor is modern, but a bit tatty. *Colón y Palma, tel. 021/444–455, fax 021/445–903. 240 rooms. Facilities: restaurant. D, MC, V.*

Internacional de Asunción. Built in 1987, this centrally located hotel has a pleasant reception area, with abundant plants and floral arrangements and a bar at the rear. Many of the rooms, which are redecorated every year, have views of the bay. *Ayolas 520, tel. 021/494–114, fax 021/494–383. 100 rooms. Facilities: outdoor pool, health club, sauna. AE, D, DC, MC, V.*

★ **Presidente.** A total renovation—a swimming pool is in the planning stages—plus an efficient new management have won high praise for this hotel a block from the Plaza de los Héroes. The reception and lounge areas are crammed with plants, a theme repeated in the floral bedspreads and curtains; some of the rooms have bay views. *Azara 128, tel. 021/494–931 or 021/494–932, fax 021/444–057. 54 rooms, 5 suites. Facilities: restaurant. AE, D, DC, MC, V.*

Renacimiento. Little remains of the original interior of this converted Belle Époque building on the Plaza de los Héroes, and the heavy wooden furniture coupled with low ceilings make the rooms and hallways seem cramped. Still, the location is unbeatable, and guests get to use the pool and gardens of a mansion owned by the hotel just 2 kilometers (1 mile) away. *Chile 388, tel. 021/445–165, fax 021/496–500. 48 rooms, 9 suites. Facilities: sauna, parking, use of private house with garden and pool. AE, D, MC, V.*

Inexpensive **Asunción Palace.** Built 150 years ago in the beaux arts style as a private residence and now a national monument, the hotel is, for all its charm, noisy and rather shabby. All the sparsely furnished rooms have air-conditioning and private bathrooms, making it a good value. *Colón 415, tel. 021/492–152, fax 021/492–153. 41 rooms. Facilities: restaurant. AE.*

Senorial del Paraguay. This hotel with Spanish colonial–style decor (whitewashed walls, heavy wood furniture, dark-wood window frames and doors) is an option for those who are willing to give up convenience—the property is a 10-minute bus ride (No. 12) from the city center—for a setting among the elegant mansions of Avenida Mariscal López. Amenities such as a swimming pool and lush gardens must be weighed against the rather offhand, sometimes uncooperative management. *Av. Mariscal López 474, tel. 021/24–304. 38 rooms. Facilities: outdoor pool, parking. AE.*

★ **Stella D'Italia.** A bit run-down and austere but good value, this hotel conveniently situated in the heart of the city has a friendly staff and air-conditioning and showers in all the rooms. *Cerro Corá 933, tel. 021/448–731. 25 rooms. No credit cards.*

The Arts and Nightlife

The Arts Chief among Paraguay's outstanding contributions to the arts are its harp music—classical, contemporary classical, and Latin American popular—and folk dancing. Traditional dances include the polka, imported from northern Europe; the *chamamé*, danced with partners holding each other to the accompaniment of lively accordian music; and *la danza de las botellas*, literally dance of the bottles, a mixture of grace and balance in which the female dancer moves in time to the music while stacking six empty wine bottles on top of her head. Both the harp music and dances can be enjoyed at the shows put on at the **Jardín de la Cerveza** (Mariscal Estigarribia 932, tel. 021/600–752) and **Ygazú** (Choferes del Chaco 1334, tel. 021/601–008). Although both clubs prefer that you dine as you watch the performance, buying a meal is not mandatory, and, given the mixed quality of the food, you might do better eating elsewhere.

The standards of local modern dance and theater groups and orchestras is not high. Visiting international performers usually can be seen at the **Teatro Municipal** (Presidente Franco y Chile, tel. 021/445–169).

Nightlife Asunción does not have an exciting and varied nightlife. International disco music is featured at **Chaco's Pub** (Republica Argentina 1035, tel. 021/660–821) and **Thunder,** at the Hotel Excelsior (Chile 980, tel. 021/495–632). Dress at both is smart casual; tennis shoes, jeans, polo shirts, and T-shirts are not permitted. The bars at the Guaraní and Excelsior hotels are favorite preprandial watering holes.

You can try your luck at roulette, baccarat, and blackjack at casinos in the following hotels: **Hotel Casino Yacht y Golf Club Paraguayo** (Av. del Yacht 11, Lambaré, tel. 021/36–117 or 021/37–161), **Guaraní** (Oliva y Independencia Nacional, tel. 021/491–131), and **Itá Enramada** (Cacique Lambere y Ribera Rio Paraguay, tel. 021/333–041). The casinos are open to anyone over 21. Minimum stakes are around 20¢ in the Guaraní and 60¢ in the classier Yacht y Golf Club Paraguayo.

Excursion from Asunción

A day trip to the popular holiday resort of **San Bernardino,** on the shores of **Lake Ypacaraí,** takes you through **Itaguá,** where *ñandutí* lacework is made (*see* Shopping, *above*) and a wide variety of handicrafts are sold. The town is also interesting for its large plaza skirted by dwellings with typical Jesuit-style layout.

From December through March, San Bernardino is packed with middle- and upper-class weekenders and families who take up residence for the season. They come for the clear, dark blue waters ringed in places by thick semitropical undergrowth, the excellent water-sports facilities—boats and jet-ski and Windsurfing equipment can be rented at one of several clean, white-sand public beaches near the cloverleaf or the Condovac Hotel or the Hotel Casino San Bernardino (*see below*)—and the good restaurants. The resort town of **Areguá** is a quieter alternative to San Bernardino, also set on the lake.

Looping back toward Asunción, the road passes through the religious center of **Caacupé,** where every December 8 the Day of Our Lady of the Miracles is celebrated. The basilica there of the same name was consecrated by the Pope in 1988.

Dining **Hotel Casino San Bernardino.** Diners enjoy a spectacular view of the lake from this spacious, rather starkly decorated restaurant. Recommended are the *lomito bonne femme* (medaillon of beef in a wine sauce) and *surubí a la Fiorentina* (catfish in a white sauce served with *acelga,* Swiss-chard-like beet leaves). *Ruta General Morínigo, km 47, tel. 0512/2391. AE, MC, V. Closed weekdays Apr.–Nov. except on public holidays. Moderate.*
Hotel del Lago. This hotel has a charming, small restaurant decorated with rustic colonial-style furniture and a fine view of the lake. The menu offers a wide range of pastas, but the forté is the roast meats, beef or pork, cooked in a wood-fired oven and served with sopa paraguaya. *Caballero y Teniente Weiler, tel. 0512/2201. DC, MC, V. Inexpensive.*

Getting There This circuitous route is best done by car. A travel agency can provide a car and driver for between $35 and $50 per person, depending on the number of passengers. Leave the center of Asunción by Avenida Silvio Pettirossi and, where the road ends, take the left fork along Avenida Eusebio Ayala. This avenue becomes Route 1. Pass through San Lorenzo and follow the signs to Route 2, which should be followed to Ipacaraí, 35 kilometers (22 miles) from Asunción, where a turnoff to the left skirts the lake to San Bernardino.

A wood-fired steam train leaves the central station of Asunción for Ypacaraí at 12:15 PM every day except Sundays and public holidays. The journey, which takes around two hours, is recommended more for the experience than as an efficient mode of transport. You are advised to buy a one-way ticket (30¢ for adults, 15¢ for children under 12), as the return trip to Asunción departs at 4 AM; you can take a local bus back to the city.

Southern Paraguay and the Jesuit Ruins

The 405-kilometer (253-mile) drive from Asunción to Jesús takes in seven 17th-century Jesuit missions and affords the visitor glimpses of Paraguayan rural life amidst a variety of landscapes. The missions date back to 1609, when the newly formed Society of Jesus was granted permission to organize the nomadic Guaraní Indians, threatened by slave traders from Brazil, into stable, self-sufficient communities based on agriculture and Christianity. Each mission, called a *reducción* (literally, reduction) had a population of around 3,000 Indians under the charge of two or three priests who taught agricultural and other practical skills such as stonemasonry and metalwork. The reduction was based around a large, central plaza with a church, adjacent bell tower, priests' living quarters, and usually a school. The Indians' houses were built in rows spreading back from the central square. The main buildings were most often constructed of red sandstone blocks, with terracotta-tile, semicircular cantilevered roofs that formed wide verandas.

The Guaraní not only embraced Christianity but also proved to be sensitive artists and particularly fine musicians, performing mainly in church choirs and orchestras and able to adapt the complex European Baroque counterpoint to their own traditional musical styles. The Guaraní also excelled at woodcarving and showed skill in pottery and calligraphy. The experiment, however, became so successful that the Spanish monarchs, jealous of their power, banned the Jesuits from the South American continent in 1766. The 100,000 Guaraní soon returned to their old way of life and the missions fell into disrepair.

Tourist Information

Tourist information about southern Paraguay is available from the **Secretaría Regional de Turismo** (Monseñor Wiessen y Mariscal Estigarribia, Encarnación, tel. 071/5326). The office is open weekdays 8–noon.

Getting There

By Car Take Route 1 to Encarnación, a 370-kilometer (230-mile) drive from Asunción. From Encarnación Route 6 goes northeast to Ciudad del Este, 280 kilometers (175 miles) away, on the border with Brazil and Argentina near Iguazú Falls. All of the missions are on or just off Route 1 or Route 6. A bridge links Encarnación with the Argentine town of Posadas.

By Train The train from Asunción, pulled by a turn-of-the-century English-made steam locomotive, departs from the railway station in Asunción on Friday at 6 PM, arriving in Encarnación at 9 AM. The return train leaves Encarnación Wednesday at 2 PM, arriving at 7 AM the next day. Pullman class costs $3.80, tourist class $3.23.

By Bus There is frequent bus service between Asunción and Encarnación (Lomas Valentinas 1031). The five-hour trip costs $7.35. Bus companies operating this route are **Rapido Iguazú** (tel. 021/551–601) and **La Encarnaceña** (tel. 071/3448). The latter runs local bus service to the ruins at Trinidad and Jesús. Travelers can get off the buses along Route 1 to visit the Jesuit missions and then flag down the next bus, which will stop as long as it is not filled. Both companies also have service between Encarnación and Ciudad del Este. The one-way fare for the three-hour trip is $5.40.

Exploring Southern Paraguay and the Jesuit Ruins

Although some Asunción tour operators offer a one-day marathon of the region, visitors starting from Asunción should allow nearly two days for the round-trip, staying overnight in either Villa Florida or Encarnación. Travelers with more time can continue on to Ciudad del Este and Iguazú Falls (*see* Chapter

5, Brazil), returning to Asunción via Route 2, a 327-kilometer
(204-mile) journey. Restaurants and cafés in southern Paraguay are few and far between, but bottled drinks can be bought
at the many *despensas,* small roadside general stores, found
alongside the highway.

Leave Asunción from the southeastern part of the city on
Route 1, going through San Lorenzo. The road then splits, one
branch going east to Ciudad del Este (Route 2) and the falls,
the other southeast to Encarnación. Continue on Route 1 heading southeast. As you approach the town of **Itá** there is a state-
run handicraft exhibition on the right side of the road with local
ceramics and hammocks for sale. After Itá the countryside
opens up into fruit orchards, sugarcane fields, and maize plantations bordering the road. **Yaguarón,** 11 kilometers (7 miles)
farther on, was the center of the Franciscan missions and
boasts a fine church built between 1640 and 1720 and sub-
sequently restored. The interior is notable for its brightly colored wood sculptures by Indian artists.

Over the next 130 kilometers (80 miles) along Route 1 to Villa
Florida, the geography changes as the fertile, hilly land becomes rolling grasslands dotted with white Brahma-like
Nelore cattle. Cowboys wearing wide-brimmed hats sit astride
sheepskin saddles and tend the herds, while sheep and goats
graze outside tiny cottages with exuberant hibiscus- and bou-
gainvillea-filled gardens.

Villa Florida is a popular tourist spot on the **Tebicuary River,**
once the western border of the Jesuit mission area and now an
attraction for its many fine sandy beaches. Anglers know it as
a prime spot for catching *dorado* and *surubí* (*see* Sports and
the Outdoors, *below*). The town is not particularly pretty, but
there are magnificent sunsets over the water.

Continuing on Route 1, you will pass through **San Miguel,**
where handwoven woolen blankets, rugs, and ponchos for sale
are hung outside the houses. A few miles farther on is the Jesuit
town of San Juan Batista. The first mission, however, is found
at **San Ignacio,** where the **Museo de San Ignacio** (no address or
phone; admission free; closed daily noon–3) houses a fine collection of Guaraní wood carvings such as gilded pulpits, door
panels, and statues, and other period artifacts. A highlight is a
statue of St. Paul signalling new lands to be evangelized; at his
feet are carved a number of faces, most with Guaraní features.
The building itself, with its thick adobe walls, is believed to be
the oldest in Paraguay, dating back to 1609.

About 12 kilometers (8 miles) farther, take a left onto a dirt
road leading to **Santa María de Fe,** where nearly 7,000 Indians
lived during the early 18th century. The original church was
destroyed by fire. In the museum are displayed some 70
Guaraní carvings and statues; the latter represent the life of
Christ. The nativity scene is particularly fine. (To gain admission to the museum, find the priest or one of his helpers to let
you in.) Some of the original Indian houses in the compound
have been restored.

Back on Route 1, the main attraction in **Santa Rosa** is the red
sandstone bell tower, built in 1698 and still in use. Inside you
can see frescoes, part of the old altar, and a group of carvings
representing the Annunciation, considered to be among the
finest of their kind. The vegetation becomes denser as the road

nears the Paraná Valley. Just before Coronel Bogado, a 25-kilometer (15-mile) paved highway runs to the village of **San Cosme y Damián,** near the banks of the Paraná River. Follow the signs along a dirt track to the red sandstone mission buildings, still functioning as a school. The church was recently restored and many of the original Indian houses are still in use.

The main road continues to the border city of **Encarnación,** about an hour's drive away, which is of little interest to the visitor except as a place to eat and spend the night. Linked by bridge to the Argentine town of Posadas, its muddy streets are lined with shops selling cheap imported goods. The lower part of town, once a thriving river port, was due to be flooded in late 1993 by the lake formed by the Yacyretá Dam. Outside of the city, the **Tirol de Paraguay** attracts guests for its spa waters (*see* Dining and Lodging, *below*).

The hotel is just 8 kilometers (5 miles) from **Trinidad,** reached by taking a well-marked turnoff from Route 6. Here are the biggest and most impressive Jesuit ruins, most of which have been, or are in the process of being, restored. The reduction stands on a slight rise in an open field, enabling its size to be appreciated. Built between 1712 and 1764 of red sandstone, much of it was destroyed by the official put in charge after the expulsion of the Jesuits. (He ripped out stones to build his own residence, causing the structure to collapse.) Although the church is open to the elements, many of its walls and arches are intact. Note the elaborately carved doors and wall friezes depicting angels playing the clavichord, harp, and other musical instruments, all known to the Indians. The pulpit is made from thousands of pieces of stone and depicts the Evangelists. The only building with a roof is the sacristy, with intricate relief work above the main entrance. Also surviving are the school and cloister foundations as well as a sandstone tower.

The Jesuits were expelled from South America before they could finish the church they were building on a hilltop at **Jesús,** 10 kilometers (6 miles) from Trinidad, which is reached from a turnoff from Route 6. The architecture is distinguished from the other missions by its Moorish-style arches.

Sports and the Outdoors

Fishing Paraguayans claim to have some of the best fishing in the world. Anglers come chiefly to catch *dorado,* spectacular fighters that leap high into the air when hooked, and *surubí,* giant fastwater catfish that take off like an express train if caught. Dorado generally run between 4 and 12 kilos (9 and 27 lbs), although they have been known to weigh up to 18 kilos (40 lbs). Surubí that weigh as much as 20 kilos (44 lbs) are not uncommon, while monsters of over 40 kilos (90 lbs) are occasionally caught.

There are two spots where the angler can test his skills against these fish. The two best spots are **Ayolas,** on the Paraná River, about 350 kilometers (220 miles) from Asunción, and **Villa Florida,** on the Tebicuary River. In Ayolas, the **Hotel Nacional de Turismo** (Av. Costanera, tel. 072/2272) can arrange for boat charters, guides, and bait. Anglers should take their own medium-weight rod, line, and lures suitable for trolling, spinning, and live-baiting.

Similar arrangements can be made in Villa Florida, which is 160 kilometers (100 miles) from the capital, through the **Hotel Nacional de Turismo** (Rte. 1, km 161, tel. 083/207) or **Hotel Centu Cué** (Rte. 1, km 163; Desví, km 7, tel. 083/219). Seven kilometers (4 miles) from the highway, Centu Cué is slap-bang on top of one of the river's best fishing spots.

Dining and Lodging

Restaurants and hotels are few and far between in southern Paraguay, as many of the villages are just a few hundred yards long and consist of little more than a handful of houses, a couple of general stores, a bakery, and, sometimes, a gas station. For details and price-category definitions, *see* Dining and Lodging in Staying in Paraguay, *above.*

Encarnación
Dining and Lodging

Cristal. Situated downtown and four blocks from the bus terminal, this nine-story hotel built in 1988 has guest rooms furnished with modern wood furniture, green carpets and drapes, and abstract paintings. The restaurant, which has a busy lunchtime trade from local businesspeople, offers international cuisine and local fish specialties. *Mariscal Estigarrabia 1157, tel. 071/2371. 75 rooms. Facilities: restaurant, outdoor pool, parking. No credit cards. Moderate.*

Novotel. Located 3 kilometers (2 miles) from the town center, the hotel is set back from the main highway amid spacious gardens. The decor throughout is modern, with beige and white the predominant shades. The restaurant's menu divides between international cuisine and Paraguayan dishes such as local fish, milanesas, sopa paraguaya, and cassava. *Rte. 1, km 361, Villa Quiteria, tel. 071/4131, fax 071/4224. 102 bedrooms, 4 suites. Facilities: restaurant, bar, pool, lighted tennis court, volleyball court, soccer pitch. AE, DC, MC, V. Moderate.*

Tirol de Paraguay. With spectacular views of verdant, rolling countryside, the Tirol is built on a hillside 18 kilometers (11 miles) from Encarnación, on Route 6 running to Trinidad and Ciudad del Este. The guest rooms, which have either ceiling fans or air-conditioning, are in single-story bungalows set around four swimming pools fed by natural springs said to have therapeutic qualities. Rates include all meals. *Rte. 6, Capitán Miranda, tel. 071/2388, fax 071/5555. 56 rooms. Facilities: 4 outdoor pools fed by natural springs. V. Moderate.*

Villa Florida
Dining and Lodging

Centu Cué. A group of bungalows scattered along the banks of the Tebicuary River comprise this isolated lodge frequented mainly by anglers and wildlife observers. Seven kilometers (4 miles) from the junction with Route 1, it is an ideal spot from which to fish in or explore one of South America's most beautiful rivers. At the simply furnished riverside restaurant, festooned with mounted heads of enormous fish and photos of fishermen with their catch, what else would one eat but dorado or surubí, grilled or in a casserole, caught only a few yards from the table? *Rte. 1, km 163, Desvío, 7 km, tel. 083/219. 24 rooms. Facilities: restaurant, outdoor pool, private beach, horseback riding. Reservations advised. No credit cards. Moderate.*

Hotel Nacional de Turismo. In this one-story building built around a central courtyard, the rooms, sparsely decorated in Spanish colonial style with heavy wood furniture, all open onto a shady veranda. The high-ceilinged restaurant, which maintains the hotel's colonial style, offers a wide variety of grilled meats and poultry, but a must is the milanesa made with freshly caught surubí; the chef is highly obliging, and with reasonable notice, will prepare special orders. *Rte. 1, km 161, tel. 083/207. 20 rooms, 1 suite. Facilities: restaurant, cafeteria, outdoor pool. Reservations advised. AE, DC, MC, V. Moderate.*

10 Peru

By Corinne
Schmidt-Lynch
and Nicolás Lynch

Corinne
Schmidt-Lynch has
lived in Peru since
1986, working first
as a U.S. diplomat
and later as a
freelance writer.
Her articles have
appeared in the
Washington Post,
The Times, the
Orion Nature
Quarterly, and other
English-language
publications, as well
as in Sí magazine
and other Peruvian
periodicals. Nicolás
Lynch is a
Peruvian journalist
whose articles have
appeared in Sí
magazine and
other Peruvian
publications.

The "land of the Incas," Peru is a nation of extraordinary beauty and myriad attractions, both geographic and archaeological. Although the majestic Andes mountain chain is perhaps the best known of these, Peru's sights are in fact scattered among markedly different regions, each with its own character.

The Costa, the arid desert coast, is the setting for the Nazca lines, a mystery etched in the sand centuries before the Inca civilization appeared. To the north of Lima, ruins of vast ancient cities and adobe pyramids linger like echoes of the sophisticated Moche and Chimú societies that thrived in the desert oases as early as 200 BC. In the Sierra is the monumental city of Cuzco, once the capital of the Tawantinsuyo (the name of the Inca empire in the Incas' native tongue, Quechua), later a Spanish colonial city, and today a mestizo (mixed-blood) city, where Spanish and Indian heritages jostle for space. Spanish culture maintains a tighter hold in the colonial city of Arequipa, while the incomparable, nearby Colca Valley, the deepest canyon on earth, is crisscrossed with Inca and pre-Inca agricultural terraces.

In the highland jungles, which Peruvians call the Ceja de Selva (eyebrow of the jungle), is the famous "lost city of the Incas," Machu Picchu. Its vertiginous setting and stunning architecture make it a centerpiece of humanity's archaeological record and one of the true wonders of the world.

In Peru's Amazon basin, known as the Selva (jungle), lies the tropical rain forest and the gateway city of Iquitos. The region's marvels include the Canopy Walkway in the northeast, which takes the visitor among the treetops of one of the world's last frontiers. Farther south are the jungles of the department of Madre de Dios (aptly named Mother of God): remote, nearly untouched, but accessible to the adventurous.

Although Peru is considered an Andean nation, it is in fact 57% jungle. Its vast and still largely pristine Amazon basin rain forests end only 250 kilometers (155 miles) from the coast. From there, the Andes mountains pierce the heavens, forming an impenetrable barrier of snowcapped peaks, high plateaus, and intermontane valleys. Beyond them to the west, an utterly barren strip of coastal desert stretches north–south for 2,000 kilometers (1,240 miles), broken by dozens of fertile but narrow river valleys.

Since time immemorial the Peruvian people have shown a fierce determination to tame the land around them. That ancestral desire to conquer nature left its mark in the agricultural terraces that still lace the highlands and in the elaborate irrigation systems that watered the desert a thousand years ago. Today, for this nation of 22 million, that determination has become the fight for survival. For the past three generations, millions of campesinos (peasants) have left the countryside for the cities, principally on the coast, in the hope of building a better life. Their faces are the new landscape of cities such as Lima, Trujillo, Cuzco, and Arequipa. In an unfamiliar urban environment, the campesinos transform rocky hillsides and sand dunes into neighborhoods where they build their homes and struggle to make a place for themselves, working in small factories and workshops and as street vendors. Through this struggle, the majority of Peruvians, long without a political, social, and economic voice in society, are recovering their rights and becoming citizens of a new Peru.

Unfortunately, Peru has not enjoyed the vigorous industrialization process that would have rewarded its migrating campesinos with the jobs and comforts associated with modern urban life. The resulting deep economic crisis, poverty, and frustration of people's expectations is an explosive mix that has erupted into political violence over the past 14 years, at its most intense at the end of the 1980s and the beginning of the 1990s. Particularly brutal among the rebel groups is the Shining Path, a Marxist-Leninist-Maoist political party that launched its "people's war" in 1980, practicing violence against anyone who questions their authority; more than 27,000 people have died since the group took up arms. At press time, following the capture of the organization's top leaders, the situation was more tranquil and terrorism had begun to subside.

Peru's present political situation is still fraught with uncertainty, however. Although democracy had been nominally restored with the election of a constituent congress in early 1993, its freedom to exercise its constitutional responsibilities was limited. At press time (summer 1993), there was, however, freedom of the press.

As a nation and a people, Peru has a strong character, not unlike the national drink, *pisco*, a heady grape brandy distilled in the coastal valleys south of Lima. As pronounced as it is, however, the Peruvian personality is heterogeneous, perhaps the product of such markedly different terrains and climates. The people of the Andes, often called Serranos, tend to be introverted, especially in dealings with outsiders, with a sharp sense of identity and a melancholic side best expressed in their haunting music. Quite the opposite are the friendly and lighter-hearted inhabitants of the Costa and Selva. The Costeño is quick with a joke, but like his beloved cuisine, *comida criolla* (literally, Creole food), there is a piquant, teasing side to his nature that sometimes stings. Perhaps the easiest-going people in Peru are those of the jungle, whose friendliness is matched only by the fabulous richness of the natural life around them.

Staying Safe and Healthy
Terrorism

Although guerrilla violence has plagued Peru, the two major terrorist groups, the Shining Path and the Tupac Amaru Revolutionary Movement (MRTA)—while no friends of foreigners—have not targeted foreign tourists, and attacks on them are extremely rare.

Political violence in Peru has not taken the form of a conventional war, and tends to be quite localized. Being in the wrong place at the wrong time can be dangerous in Peru, as it can be in New York or Los Angeles, but skipping Manu National Park because of reports of violence some 200 miles away in Ayacucho is like avoiding the Delaware Water Gap because of muggings in the South Bronx.

Wherever you travel in Peru, your best safeguard is to use a reputable travel agency. Their knowledge and experience will keep you out of unsafe areas, and can also help you avoid some of the headaches of traveling in a country where underdevelopment still means too much bureaucracy and too little logical organization. Some Lima-based agencies, such **Lima Tours** (Belén 1040, Box 4340, Lima 1, Peru, tel. 014/27–6489), have offices throughout the country.

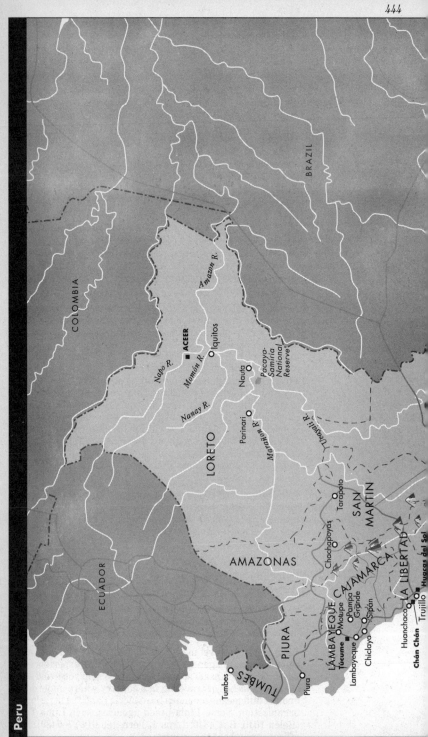

BRAZIL

COLOMBIA

Napo R.

Amazon R.

■ ACER

○ Iquitos

Momón R.

○ Nauta

Pacaya-
Samiria
National
Reserve

Nanay R.

○ Parinari

Marañón R.

Ucayali R.

LORETO

○ Tarapoto

SAN
MARTIN

○ Chachapoyas

AMAZONAS

ECUADOR

CAJAMARCA

○ Molupe

LAMBAYEQUE

○ Pampa
Grande

○ Sipán

Túcume ■

LA LIBERTAD

Huacas del Sol ■

Huanchaco ○

Chán Chán ■ Trujillo ○

○ Lambayeque

○ Chiclayo

PIURA

○ Tumbes

TUMBES

○ Piura

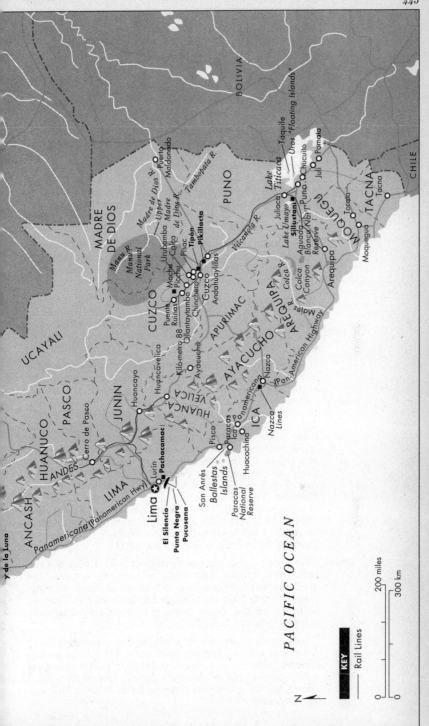

In general, air travel is safe everywhere, while long-distance overland travel is safe only in certain areas and during the daytime. Some jungle areas and much of the central and south-central highlands can be dangerous. Do not under any circumstances travel overland from Cuzco to Lima via Nazca, as the trip takes you through two of the departments where the Shining Path is strongest, Apurímac and Ayacucho. The Shining Path sometimes stops buses traveling that route and has killed foreign tourists it has found on board.

With the possible exception of the department of Puno, the regions covered in this chapter were at press time safe for travelers. Puno has seen terrorist activity in remote rural areas, and small bombs occasionally have exploded in the city of Puno, although not in areas frequented by tourists. The presence of a maximum security prison holding top Shining Path leaders just outside the city could heighten terrorist activity there. We recommend you explore only the areas around Lake Titicaca that are covered below.

After the September 1992 capture of the Shining Path's top leaders, violence in Lima and around country had diminished significantly. At press time, violence in Lima centered in the impoverished shantytowns ringing the city.

You should avoid the following departments, which the Peruvian government has declared "emergency zones": Apurímac, Ayacucho, Huancavelica, Junín, Pasco, Ucayali, Huánuco, and San Martín. In the latter two departments, under no circumstances should you visit the drug-ridden Huallaga Valley.

If you want more specific information about terrorist activity in Peru, or want to travel to areas of Peru not covered below, contact the **South American Explorer's Club** (in the U.S.: 126 Indian Creek Rd., Ithaca, NY 14850, tel. 800/274–0568; in Peru: República de Portugal 146, Breña, Lima, tel. 014/31–4480). This member-supported, nonprofit organization offers guidebooks, maps, and constantly updated tips on how and where to travel. Although some of its services are available to the general public, it offers special privileges to members. For additional updates, contact the **Peruvian Consulate** (215 Lexington Ave., New York, NY 10016, tel. 212/481–7410) or the **Peruvian Embassy** (1700 Massachusetts Ave., Washington, DC 20036, tel. 202/833–9860). The **Citizens' Emergency Center** (tel. 202/647–5225) at the U.S. State Department Bureau of Consular Affairs publishes travel advisories available by fax *see* Government Information Offices in Chapter 1).

Crime   Crime has become common throughout Peru. Urban bus and train stations, some train routes, and markets are often the scenes of purse and camera snatching and backpack slashing. Some tourists have been mugged at knifepoint in Cuzco at night. In addition, buses traveling by night are occasionally stopped by armed bandits.

You can protect yourself by traveling by day, not wearing flashy jewelry or watches, avoiding dark and empty streets, leaving your valuables in a safe deposit box at your hotel, and keeping a firm grip on your belongings. A favorite diversionary tactic among thieves is to squirt you with liquid, so don't be fooled into loosening your hold.

Health Before coming to Peru, all travelers should receive a typhoid vaccination, which consists of two injections given four weeks apart. The injections can be painful and cause a fever, so don't leave them until the last minute. Also make sure that as an adult you have had a polio booster, and that you have had a tetanus-diphtheria booster within the past 10 years. Hepatitis A is common in Peru, and although hepatitis B is found in both Lima and in the jungle, it is rarer than hepatitis A. Immune serum globulin, for hepatitis A, is usually recommended. Travelers who only visit Lima and vicinity, the coastal area south of Lima, or Lake Titicaca, Cuzco, or Machu Picchu are not at risk of contracting yellow fever. If you intend to travel in the jungle, however, you do need a yellow fever vaccination. Another threat in the jungle is malaria, for which you should take antimalarial tablets starting two weeks before and continuing six weeks after your visit.

In 1991, an epidemic of cholera, a potentially deadly illness causing severe diarrhea and vomiting, swept Peru. Tap water may be risky, so stick to bottled water and beverages. Anything raw merits caution, including *cebiche* (*see* Dining, *below*) sold on the street or at piers, although cebiche in a good restaurant should be safe. Cebiche made from deep-sea fish such as *corvina*, *cojinova*, or *lenguado* is unlikely to have cholera. In restaurants, avoid salads and fruits that you can't peel. In Lima you can buy solutions, such as Zonalin, for disinfecting fresh fruit and vegetables.

Soroche (altitude sickness) hits most visitors to sky-high cities such as Cuzco and Puno, but with care its symptoms remain mild. Headache, shortness of breath, and insomnia are common. When visiting areas at least 3,000 meters (10,000 feet) above sea level, always rest a few hours before going out to explore, and take it easy on your first day. Avoid heavy foods, alcohol, and cigarettes, and drink plenty of liquids. To fight soroche, Peruvians swear by *mate de coca*, a tea made of coca leaf.

Essential Information

Before You Go

When to Go The tourist season in Peru runs from May through September, corresponding to the dry season in the Sierra (highlands) and Selva (jungle). The best time to visit Peru is May through July, when the cool, misty weather is just beginning in the Costa (coast), and the highlands are dressed in bright green and topped with crystalline blue skies. June brings major festivals such as Inti Raymi, the Inca festival of the sun, and Corpus Christi to Cuzco. Other important festival months are February, which means Carnival throughout Peru and the Virgen de la Candelaria (Candlemas) celebrations in Puno, and October, when chanting, purple-clad devotees of the Lord of the Miracles fill the streets of Lima.

Climate The complication is that when it's dry in the Sierra and the Selva, it's wet on the Costa, and vice versa. The Selva is hot and humid yearround, with endless rain between January and April. *Friajes* (cold fronts) from Patagonia occasionally sweep through the southern rain forests of Madre de Dios, but the average daily minimum and maximum temperatures in the Selva are 20°C (69°F) and 32°C (90°F), respectively.

In the Sierra, expect rain between October and April, and especially January through March. The rest of the year, the weather is dry and the temperature fickle. The sun can be hot, but in the shade you'll find it refreshingly cool. Nights are chilly and the temperature may drop to freezing. Temperatures during Cuzco's dry months average 0°C (32°F)–22°C (71°F).

It never rains in the coastal desert, but a dank, heavy fog called the *garua* coats Lima June through December. Outside Lima, coastal weather is clearer and warm.

The following are average daily maximum and minimum temperatures for Lima.

Jan.	27C	81F	May	25C	77F	Sept.	19C	66F
	21	70		19	66		15	59
Feb.	28C	82F	June	23C	73F	Oct.	21C	70F
	21	70		17	63		16	61
Mar.	29C	84F	July	18C	64F	Nov.	23C	73F
	23	73		15	59		17	63
Apr.	27C	81F	Aug.	18C	64F	Dec.	24C	75F
	22	72		15	59		18	64

Currency Peru's national currency is the nuevo sol (S/.), or new sun, divided into 100 cents (céntimos). Bills are issued in denominations of 5, 10, 20, 50, and 100 soles. Coins are 1 céntimo and 5, 10, 20, and 50 céntimos, and 1 sol. Be careful not to confuse the 1-sol coin with the older and now worthless 1-inti coin.

At press time (fall 1993), the exchange rate was S/. 2.05 to the U.S. dollar, and S/. 3.11 to the pound sterling. The Peruvian currency is volatile, however, and the Peruvian economy is dollarized—that is, when the number of soles per dollar increases, so do the prices in soles (though prices in dollars may remain unchanged). Therefore, all prices listed in this chapter are given in dollars, a more stable indicator.

Changing Money Although the *cambistas* (freelance money changers) waving pocket calculators on the city streets may offer a slightly better exchange rate than the banks, they often stiff their clients. Exchanging money at your hotel may be convenient, but the rates can be as much as 5% below that offered at banks. (The exchange rate at the different banks is the same, so there is no advantage to shopping around.) Money can also be changed at *casas de cambio* (exchange houses). Neither banks nor casas de cambio charge commissions.

Traveler's checks are accepted at casas de cambio, banks, and big hotels. The rate is usually the same as for cash, but many banks have a ceiling on how much they will exchange at one time. Stores, smaller hotels, and restaurants rarely accept traveler's checks.

Credit Cards Major credit cards, especially Visa, are accepted in most tourist-oriented hotels, restaurants, and shops.

What It Will Cost Peru is currently in the throes of an economic restructuring that has made it one of the more expensive countries in South America. Monthly inflation persists at 2%–5%, and the dollar is undervalued but slowly rising. An 18% sales tax, known as *impuesto general a las ventas,* or IGV, is levied on everything except items bought at open-air markets and from street vendors. It is usually included in the advertised price of merchandise, but this is often not the case with food and drink. It's advisable to check before ordering. Many hotels and restaurants also impose a 10%–13% service charge. If you avoid top-flight tourist hotels and restaurants, you will find food and lodging in Peru to be reasonably priced. Restaurants and hotels outside the capital city are likely to be less expensive, except in Cuzco, where prices are comparable to those in Lima. In the jungle, food is only slightly less expensive than in Lima, but accommodations are generally moderate. Small restaurants tend to be the least expensive; eateries serving ethnic food such as French, Italian, Japanese, and Argentine are apt to be pricey. The cost of transportation is high; at press time gasoline cost between $1.60 and $1.90 per gallon. Airport taxes are approximately $18 for international and domestic flights. State-owned attractions usually charge only a nominal entrance fee, except in Cuzco and environs, where admission prices are quite hefty by Peruvian standards.

Sample Prices For Lima: cup of coffee, 95¢; bottle of beer, $1.20; pisco sour, $2–$5; glass of wine, $1.90; soft drink, 85¢; chicken and avocado sandwich, $2.70; 1-mile taxi ride, $1.35.

Customs on Arrival You may bring duty-free into Peru $1,000 worth of personal goods and gifts; everything thereafter is taxed at a flat rate of 25%. You may also bring a total of three liters of liquor; jewelry or perfume worth less than $300; and 20 packs of cigarettes or 50 cigars. If after arrival you pass through the "nothing to declare" line and a red light flashes, your baggage will be examined and any taxable items you failed to declare will be confiscated.

Language Spanish is Peru's national language, and native languages also enjoy official status. Many Peruvians speak Quechua, the language of the Incas, as their native tongue, but most speak Spanish as well. Other native languages include the Tiahuanaco language, Aymara, spoken around Lake Titicaca, and several linguistic groups in the jungle. Wealthier Peruvians and those working with tourists often speak English, but they are the exception. If you speak any Spanish at all, by all means use it. Your hosts will appreciate the effort, and any laughter that greets your words will be good-natured rather than mocking.

A word on spelling: Since the Incas had no writing system, Quechua developed as an oral language. With European colonization, words and place names were transcribed to conform to Spanish pronunciations. Eventually, the whole language was transcribed, and in many cases words lost their correct pronunciations. During the past 30 years, however, national pride and a new sensitivity to the country's indigenous roots have led Peruvians to try to recover consistent, linguistically correct transcriptions of Quechua words. As you travel, you may come across different spellings and pronunciations of the same name. An example is the city non–Latin Americans know as Cuzco. The city government uses "Qosqo" as the official spelling, though most Peruvians still use the "Cusco" spelling. To avoid confusion the Cuzco spelling is used below. You should be aware, however, that Peruvians may prefer the Quechuan pronunciations and linguistically correct transcriptions.

Getting Around

By Car
Road Conditions

The major highways in Peru are the Panamericana (Pan-American Highway), which runs along the entire coast of Peru, and the Carreterra Central, which runs from Lima to Huancayo and from there to the central jungle. Most highways have no names or numbers; they are referred to by destination, e.g., "the highway to Arequipa."

Although highway conditions have improved somewhat due to foreign loans, even the Panamericana still has rough stretches (rutted areas, blocked by sand dunes, etc.). Security on some highways is also a serious problem (*see* Staying Safe and Healthy, *above*). Signs outside Lima are relatively rare, except at major turnoffs, and lighting is nonexistent. In Lima, vehicular chaos quite literally rules, while traffic in other major cities is only slightly better.

Since taxis and public transportation are inexpensive, driving is not recommended. If you do drive, remember that most Peruvians see traffic laws as suggestions rather than a command. Outside of cities, don't drive at night, fill your gasoline tank whenever possible, make sure your spare tire is in good repair, and carry planks to help you out of soft spots on or off the road. You can purchase good maps from the **Touring and Automobile Club of Peru** (Av. César Vallejo 699, Lince, tel. 014/40–3270). Members of the American Automobile Association and affiliates can get these maps at members' prices.

Rules of the Road

You can drive in Peru with a foreign license for up to six months, after which you will need an international driver's license. Driving is on the right, with passing on the left. Speed limits are 25–35 kilometers (15–20 miles) per hour in residential areas and 85–100 kilometers (50–60 miles) per hour on highways. Traffic tickets range from a minimum of $4 to a maximum of $40. The police and military routinely do vehicle spot checks, sometimes for reasons of security, and drivers with their documents in order (driver's license, car registration, and for foreigners, valid passport) are waved on. If, however, the officer wants a bribe, he will look for the slightest violation, and you should be prepared either to argue hard or to come up with $3 or so. Peruvian law makes it a crime to drive while intoxicated, although many Peruvians ignore that prohibition. If you are caught driving while under the influence, you will either pay a hefty bribe or spend the night in jail.

Parking

Parking lots costing about a dollar an hour are common and provide the best security. Parking on the street costs between 30¢ and 50¢; you should tip someone to watch over your car.

Gasoline

Gasoline costs between $1.60 and $1.90. Gas stations on the highway are widely spaced, and most gas stations close after 11 PM.

Breakdowns

The **Touring and Automobile Club of Peru** (emergency tel. 014/40–3270 or 014/22–5957) will provide emergency road service for members of the Automobile Club of America and affiliates upon presentation of their membership cards.

Car Rentals

In Lima: **Avis,** Sheraton Hotel, Paseo de la República 170, tel. 014/33–5959; airport, tel. 014/52–4774; **Budget,** La Paz 522, Miraflores, tel. 014/44–0760; airport, tel. 014/52–8706; **First Rent A Car,** La Paz 745, Miraflores, tel. 014/46–2100; **Hertz,** Rivera

Navarrete 550, San Isidro, tel. 014/42–4475; airport, tel.
014/51–8189; **National,** Diez Canseco 319, Miraflores, tel.
014/44–2333; airport, tel. 014/52–3426.

By Train Train travel in Peru is limited to six lines, operated by
ENAFER (tel. 014/27–6620), the government-owned railway
company. For security reasons, only two routes are recommended: Arequipa–Juliaca–Puno–Juliaca–Cuzco and Cuzco–
Machu Picchu–Quillabamba. Tickets can be purchased either
at train stations or through travel agencies, and top-class tickets should be bought in advance.

Except on the Cuzco–Machu Picchu tourist train, railway
travel in Peru tends to be somewhat slow and theft is very common. Food and drinks are often not available on board, and
although vendors clamber aboard at every stop or will sell you
food from the station platform, you are advised to bring some
food and bottled water with you. If you are traveling via Puno
or La Oroya, bring a blanket, sleeping bag, or very warm
clothes, as it can get very cold at high altitudes.

By Plane Flying is the easiest, fastest, and safest way to get around Peru.
Faucett (tel. 014/64–3363; in U.S. outside Florida toll-free tel.
800/334–3356, in Florida 305/591–0610) offers a "Visit Peru"
pass, which can only be purchased outside Peru through Faucett or a travel agency. The pass, which costs $250, allows un-
limited plane travel in Peru within a 60-day period. For the
visitor who prefers to skip Lima and focus on the jungle and
Cuzco, Faucett offers direct Miami–Iquitos and Iquitos–Cuzco
flights. Cuzco is also a connecting point for flights into the jungle of Madre de Dios.

In addition to Faucett, **AeroPerú** (tel. 014/47–8900) and **Americana** (tel. 014/47–1919) have regularly scheduled flights to
major cities and towns in Peru. **Aero Continente** (tel. 014/42–
8760 or 014/42–8770), **Air Imperial** (tel. 014/76–4542 or 014/76–
0775), **Expresso Aereo** (tel. 014/45–2545 or 014/45–2745), and
Aero Tumi (tel. 014/41–2930) are new airlines that fly to the
major cities, but at press time (summer 1993), their schedules
changed frequently and their safety records were not yet established. **Aerotransporte S.A.,** or ATSA (tel. 014/51–5712 or
014/52–9230) provides charters to most of the country. A number of smaller regional airlines, such as **Aerocondor** (tel.
014/42–5663 or 014/41–1354), offer "taxi" service to smaller cities, especially in the jungle. **AeroChasqui** (tel. 014/45–7468)
serves the highlands and jungle. Airplane taxis, small planes
that depart when there are sufficient numbers of passengers,
include **Aerotaxis Carlos Palacín** (tel. 014/41–1354) and **Taxi
Aereo Selva** (tel. 014/51–2044), both of which fly throughout the
jungle.

By Bus The intercity bus system in Peru is extensive, and fares are
usually very cheap. Beware, however, of the informal, "pirate"
bus lines, whose safety records are abysmal. Some of the better
lines include **Ormeño** (tel. 014/27–5679), **Cruz del Sur** (tel.
014/23–1570), and **Tepsa** (tel. 014/27–6272). All three offer regular and first-class service. The regular second-class buses
(*servicio normal*) tend to be overcrowded and uncomfortable,
while the more expensive first-class service is safer, more comfortable, and much more likely to arrive on schedule. For
longer bus trips, you may wish to bring bottled water, snacks,
and toilet paper, and if you are traveling into the Sierra, take

on board warm clothing or a blanket. You can buy bus tickets through a travel agent. Whenever possible, travel and arrive at your destination during daytime. For caveats on where not to travel by bus, *see* Staying Safe and Healthy, *above*.

Colectivos An alternative form of public transportation are the *colectivos*, small vans or large cars that cover the same routes as the buses. They charge about twice as much as buses, but are usually much faster. The catch is that they don't leave until they fill up. Colectivos are organized by *comités* (a group of drivers who cover a given route) and usually cover specific regions. You will find them listed in the yellow pages of the telephone directory under "Transportes Terrestres," or ask at your hotel desk for a *comité* that will take you where you want to go.

By Boat Passenger boats are the most important means of transportation in the jungle. Special Expeditions, Marquest, and Tara Tours all operate Amazon cruises from Brazil to Iquitos. If you visit a jungle lodge, your hosts will probably pick you up in an outboard-powered canoe. Larger boats make 4- to 10-day cruises on the Amazon from Iquitos. In smaller towns throughout the jungle, you can arrange private river excursions by hiring a *peke-peke*, a wood longboat with a small motor that may or may not have a roof and which is slower and cheaper than a boat with an outboard motor. On Lake Titicaca, small boats offer taxi service to the Uros floating islands and the larger island of Taquile.

Staying in Peru

Embassies and Consulates In Lima:

Canada: Embassy and consulate: Libertad 130, Miraflores, tel. 014/44–4015.

United Kingdom: Embassy and consulate: Edificio El Pacifico, Avenida Arequipa (5th block), Plaza Washington. Embassy: tel. 014/33–4738 or 014/33–4839; consulate: tel. 014/35–5032.

United States: Embassy: Garcilaso de la Vega 1400, tel. 014/33–8000; consulate: Grimaldo del Solar 346, Miraflores, tel. 014/44–3621.

Telephones
Local Calls Peru does not have a "telephone culture," and many attractions, especially churches, either do not have telephones or their staffs are not accustomed to answering tourists' questions on the telephone. Thus, if you call a church, for example, you may get a quizzical or rude response.

To make local calls from pay phones, which are not very plentiful and are often broken, purchase a grooved token called a *ficha*. They are available from candy sellers and newspaper kiosks for 20¢. Local calls cost about 20¢ for the first three minutes. To call another area in Peru, first dial 0 and then the area code.

International Calls International calls are easy to make from Lima and the coast, at times difficult in the highlands, and sometimes impossible in the jungle. Hotels add hefty surcharges to international calls made from guest rooms, so you may want to call from the telephone company's calling centers (in Lima there are a handful of pay phones from which you can make international calls). In Lima, the **Companía Peruana de Teléfonos (CPT)** has calling centers in most districts. Outside Lima, **ENTEL-Peru** runs the phone network. Calls to the United States cost $2.30 per minute. To dial direct, dial 00, then 1 for the United States and Canada, 44 for the United Kingdom.

Operators To make an operator-assisted international call dial 108. For information inside Peru, dial 103.

Mail Airmail letters and postcards sent within the Americas cost 51¢
Postal Rates for less than 20 grams; outside the hemisphere, they cost 57¢. Airmail packages sent within the Americas cost $24 for up to 3 kilograms, $39 elsewhere. Packages sent second class cost one-third to one-half less. Bring packages to the post office unsealed, and be prepared to wrap them in white burlap and sew them shut after showing the contents to postal workers. Mail theft is occasionally a problem.

Receiving Mail If you don't know where you will be staying in advance, you can have mail sent to you (mark the letters "poste restante") to the following addresses: A/C Correo Central, Pasaje Piura, Lima 1, Peru; Correo de Miraflores, Avenida Petit Thouars 5201, Lima 18. If you or the sender are American Express cardholders, you can receive mail at their offices at Belén 1040, Lima. Thomas Cook (Comandante Espinar 331, Miraflores) will also hold mail.

Note that except in Lima, Peru does not have postal codes.

Shopping Large stores have fixed prices, but those devoted mostly to the
Bargaining tourist trade are willing to bargain. In markets and handicrafts stores and with street vendors, bargaining is expected.

Opening and **Banks.** Most banks are open weekdays 9–4. Some banks are
Closing Times open on Saturday morning.

Museums and churches. Most museums are open Monday–Saturday 9–6. Some close at lunchtime, usually between 1 and 3 PM or 4 PM. Church hours are more irregular. Some are open to visitors only in the early morning, while others have opening hours similar to those of museums, except that they are also open Sunday.

Shops. Stores are generally open Monday–Saturday 10–8. Many smaller stores close for two hours at lunchtime and on Saturday are open in the morning only.

National Holidays January 1; Easter (holiday begins midday on Maundy Thursday and continues through Easter Monday); May 1 (Labor Day); June 29 (St. Peter and St. Paul); July 28 (Independence Day); August 30 (St. Rosa of Lima); October 8 (commemorates the Battle of Angamos, a battle with Chile in the War of the Pacific, 1879–81); Nov. 1 (All Saints' Day); December 8 (Immaculate Conception); Dec. 25.

Festivals In addition to the major public holidays listed above, the Peruvian calendar is a patchwork quilt of religious and secular festivals. The following dates are for 1994:

Jan. 6: **Festival of the Magi,** in Puno, Cuzco, and nearby Ollantaytambo. Dancing and parades take place.
Jan. 23–29: **National Festival and Competition of La Marinera,** Trujillo. The finest artists perform the most spectacular and seductive of the coastal *criollo* dances.
Feb. 2–6: **Virgen de la Candelaria (Candlemas),** Puno. Parades and traditional dances are held. Nearby Acora holds a traditional dance festival during the same week.

Feb. 9–16: **Carnival,** celebrated throughout Peru. In Lima and many other cities, the party has degenerated into a water fight—people throw buckets of water and water balloons—but Carnival in Puno remains a colorful affair with parades and dancing in the streets. Peru's most famous Carnival is held in Cajamarca.

Mar. 4–15: **Vendimia Festival,** Ica. This is a celebration of the region's vineyards, with wine tastings and dances.

Mar. 31–Apr. 4: **Holy Week.** On Good Friday there's a procession in Puno, while on Easter Monday a Cuzco procession honors the Lord of the Earthquakes.

June 2: **Corpus Christi,** Cuzco. Statues of saints from all of Cuzco's churches are taken in procession to the cathedral.

June 24: **Inti Raymi,** Cuzco. The Inca's winter solstice is commemorated with music, dancing, and a special procession.

June 29: **St. Peter and St. Paul Day,** also called Pope's Day, is celebrated in honor of the pope.

Aug. 30: **St. Rosa of Lima,** Lima; **Day of the Campesino,** Arequipa, featuring a parade.

Oct. 2–9: **Spring Festival,** Trujillo, features dancing, parades, and exhibitions of the stunning Peruvian Paso dressage horses.

Oct. 18: **Lord of the Miracles,** celebrated with processions in many cities, but the biggest is in Lima. Throughout October devotees wear purple.

Nov. 1–2. **All Saints' and All Souls' Days,** throughout Peru. People carry food, drink, and flowers to the local cemetery.

Nov. 4–5. **Puno Days.** November 5 commemorates the legendary emergence of Manco Capac and Mama Occlo, founders of the Inca empire, from Lake Titicaca. The highlight is a stupendous procession with masked dancers.

Dining The cost and quality of dining out in Peru can vary widely, but a modest restaurant that looks clean may serve as splendid a meal as one with snazzier decor. Most smaller restaurants offer a lunchtime *menú,* a prix-fixe meal that consists of an appetizer, main dish, dessert, and beverage and costs $1–$4. Peru is also full of cafés, many with a selection of delicious pastries. Food at bars is usually limited to snacks and sandwiches.

Mealtimes Top-notch restaurants offer lunch and dinner, but most Peruvians think of lunch as the main meal of the day, and many restaurants open only for lunch. Served between 1 and 3, lunch is traditionally followed by a siesta, though the custom is dying out. Dinner can be anything from a light snack to another full meal. Peruvians tend to dine late, between 7 and 11 PM. Cafés are open from 10 AM to 10 PM or later; bars open at around 6 PM, but become lively at 10 or 11.

Dress Peruvians dress quite informally when they dine out, and often a sports jacket is sufficient for men, even at very expensive restaurants. A smart pair of slacks or skirt is always appropriate for women. Shorts are frowned upon everywhere except at the beach, and T-shirts should be worn only in very modest restaurants.

Typical Dishes Breakfast for the urban Peruvian usually is Continental, but sometimes includes eggs or oatmeal with cinnamon, along with fruit and juice. Highlanders might have soup or stew for breakfast, and in the jungle, it might consist of fried manioc or bananas.

On the coast, fresh seafood is reasonably priced and prepared in a hundred ways. The most famous is *cebiche,* a cold stew of raw fish or seafood marinated in lemon juice and smothered with onions and hot peppers. Other favorite fish dishes are *a la chorillana* (fried with tomatoes and onions) and *a lo macho* (drenched in a spicy seafood sauce.) *Corvina* (sea bass) is the most highly prized deep-sea fish in Peru, with a delicate flavor; other excellent seafood include *cojinova* (a white fish that is somewhat fishier-tasting than corvina), *lenguado* (flounder), *pulpo* (octopus), *conchitas* (scallops), and *calamares* (squid).

Chicken is a staple, and you can find anything from simple grilled chicken (*a la brasa*) to *ají de gallina,* shredded chicken cooked in a creamy piquant sauce. In the Sierra, try *cuy,* guinea pig. Typical meat dishes include *anticuchos* (kebabs of marinated beef heart) and *lomo saltado,* a Chinese-Peruvian hybrid of stir-fried beef, onions, tomatoes, hot peppers, and potatoes served over rice. The best ethnic cooking in Peru is Chinese, known as *chifa.*

Comida criolla is the favored fare along the coast. It is generally heavily spiced with hot peppers, usually includes onions, and may use fish, chicken, or meat. It is often fried, although stews and rice simmered with chicken or duck (*arroz con pollo, arroz con pato*) are also staples.

Peru gave the world the potato, and dozens of varieties are grown here. Among the tastier potato recipes are *papa a la huancaina* (potato in spicy cheese sauce), *ocopa* (potato in a spicy peanut sauce), and *carapulcra* (a stew of dried potatoes served over rice). Peru has wonderful fruit, such as the *chirimoya* (custard apple) and *tuna* (cactus fruit).

Don't forget to try Peru's national drink, the *pisco* sour, made from distilled grape liquor. Don't let its icy sweetness deceive you—it packs quite a kick. Peruvian beers are excellent, and each region boasts its own. In Lima, try Condor, which has a rich, heavy flavor, and Pilsen Callao, somewhat lighter. In Cuzco, look for the rich, dark Cusqueña. Arequipeña, available in Arequipa, is similar. Peruvian wines, such as Occucaje or Tacama, are quite good; Tacama's Blanco de Blancos is considered to be the best in the country.

Ratings Meals are subject to an 18% sales tax, which is added to the bill. Better restaurants also add a 13% service charge to the check. Prices below are per person and include appetizer, main course, and dessert, but exclude alcoholic beverages, tax, service charge, and tip. Highly recommended restaurants are indicated by a star ★.

Category	Lima	Other Areas
Very Expensive	over $35	above $20
Expensive	$15–$35	$10–$20
Moderate	$6–$15	$5–$10
Inexpensive	under $6	under $5

Lodging Accommodations in Peru range from bare-bones rooms with shared bathrooms to luxury hotels. They come with names such as *hostal, pensión, residencial,* and *hotel,* and though the implication is that the latter is more upscale, this is not always the case. Televisions in rooms are very rare and are found only in the best hotels—and not always there. Moderate and more expensive hotels tend to have telephones in the guest rooms, but be sure to ask. The slump in tourism to Peru has made it easier to find accommodations, and in places such as Cuzco you can bargain down your room rate. If you're planning on visiting during a festival, it's best to reserve in advance.

A state-owned chain, **Enturperu** (Javier Prado Oeste 1358, San Isidro, Lima 27, reservation tel. 014/42–8626) operates *hoteles de turistas* in major cities throughout Peru except Cuzco, Machu Picchu, and Madre de Dios. Their hotels, always the biggest in town, range from decent to excellent. Be sure to ask for a discount when making a reservation through Enturperu in Lima; you can get a better discount if you prepay in Lima. For hoteles de turistas in Cuzco, Machu Picchu, and Madre de Dios, contact **Emturin** in Cuzco (Portal Belén 115, Plaza de Armas, tel. 084/22–3339, 084/23–6062, or 084/23–7364).

Camping Camping in Peru is limited to some beaches (where Peruvians camp in large groups for protection), and as part of mountain and jungle treks. The only legal campsites are located in some national parks, such as Manu National Park (*see below*). Camping is for all practical purposes the only way to hike the Inca Trail.

Ratings Hotels usually charge an 18% tax, and occasionally service charges of up to 13%. Prices below are for a double room and include tax and service charge. A Continental breakfast is often but not always included in the room rate; the most expensive hotels are least likely to include breakfast. Highly recommended hotels are indicated by a star ★.

Category	Lima	Other Areas
Very Expensive	over $120	over $70
Expensive	$70–$120	$45–$70
Moderate	$35–$70	$20–$45
Inexpensive	under $35	under $20

Tipping If a 13% service charge has been included, only a nominal tip is expected (2%–5% of the pre-tax bill), otherwise 5%–10% in most restaurants is sufficient. Porters in hotels and airports expect 50¢–$1 per bag. There is no need to tip taxi drivers. At bars, tip 20–50 céntimos for a beer, more for a mixed drink. Bathroom attendants get 20 céntimos, gas station attendants 50 céntimos for extra services such as adding air to your tires or oil. Tour guides and tour bus drivers should get 5–10 soles each per day.

Lima

Lima, Peru's "City of Kings," provokes very different, and often extreme, responses from visitors. With more than 6 million people, one-third of the nation's population, it is a city to love or hate, a microcosm of all of Peru's ills and much of its appeal in a few square miles of seaside desert. Founded in 1535

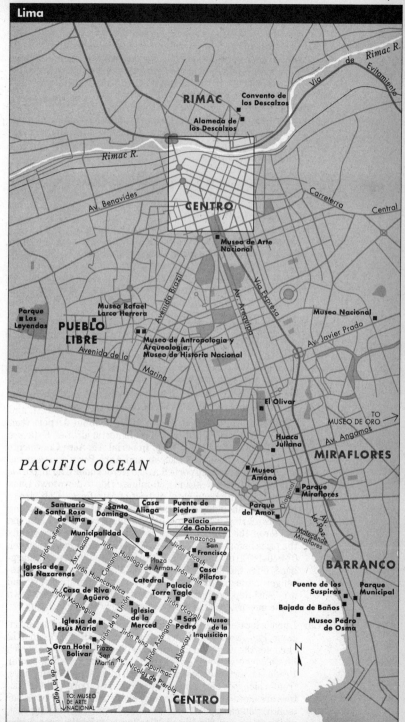

Lima

by Francisco Pizarro on the site of a small native city, for 300 years Lima was the capital of Spain's South American empire. Its vice-regal history lingers on in its sophistication, the decaying beauty of its boulevards, and the liveliness of its intellectual life. Over the past 30 years, Lima has lost its elite character as Peru's rural population, recognizing that the bulk of the country's resources is concentrated in the capital, has migrated here in hopes of finding jobs, homes, and education. Today Lima's streets are packed with these immigrants, most of them wretchedly poor. Some are beggars, often refugees from the political violence in the highlands and recognizable by their native dress—a felt hat and broad, petticoated skirt called a *pollera.* Others are reduced to trying to sell something—anything—to anyone who will buy. The press of *ambulantes* (street vendors) vigorously hawking their wares can be overwhelming.

Tourist Information

Oficina de Información Turística (Jirón de Unión 1066, tel. 014/32–3559; open weekdays 8 AM–8 PM, Sat. 9–1); **American-Peruvian Chamber of Commerce** (Ricardo Palma 836, Miraflores, tel. 014/47–9349). The daily newspaper *El Comercio* carries the most complete listing of activities in Lima. An English-language monthly, the *Lima Times,* is available at kiosks and at the publication's office (Pasaje Los Pinos 156, office B–6, Miraflores, tel. 014/45–3761; open weekdays 9–5), which also has a selection of English-language books on Peru for sale. "The Peru Guide," an advertising monthly with tourist information about Peru, is available for free at most major hotels.

Arriving and Departing

By Plane International carriers that include **American, Faucett,** and **AeroPerú** serve **Jorge Chavez International Airport** (tel. 014/52–9570), as do the Peruvian domestic airlines **Expresso Aereo, Americana, Aero Tumi, Imperial Air, Aero Continente** and domestic flights on Faucett and Aero Perú, and regional airlines like **Aerotransporte S.A.** and **Aerocondor.** The airport is 10 kilometers (6 miles) and a 30-minute ride to downtown Lima or the residential and hotel district of Miraflores. Cab fare to either area should be approximately $15, although bargaining hard can bring it down to $10. Sharing a taxi is common and will lower the fare. There are no meters, so make sure you fix the price before you get in. **Transhotel** (Ricardo Palma 280, tel. 014/46–9872) operates a shuttle to and from the airport, charging $10 for the first passenger and $2 for each additional passenger in the group. The shuttle's hours of operation vary, and it is most dependable as a means of transportation from town to the airport, especially to catch an early morning flight.

By Car Lima is located on the transcontinental Carreterra Panamericana (Pan-American Highway). Panamericana Norte (north) becomes the ring road known as the Via de Evitamiento, which hits a large and well-marked cloverleaf at Avenida Javier Prado. Javier Prado leading west will take you into San Isidro, from which it is easy and safe to get to Miraflores, where visitors are more likely to be staying. From the Panamericana Sur (south) you can get off onto Avenida Benavides heading east, which takes you directly to Miraflores, or, again, onto Javier

Prado. If madness possesses you to drive into the center of Lima, go past the Javier Prado cloverleaf to Evitamiento. Once you cross the Rimac River, you will be north of the center, and there are several bridges (Ricardo Palma, Santa Rosa) crossing back down into the center.

Bus Station **Ormeño** (Javier Prado Este 1059 or Av. Carlos Zavala 177, tel. 014/28–3650); **Cruz del Sur** (Jirón Quilca 531, tel. 014/27–1311); and **Tepsa** (Paseo de la República 129, tel. 014/27–6271).

Getting Around Lima

Lima is divided into neighborhoods, each with its own distinct flavor. The most important for visitors are **Lima** (also known as **Centro**), **Miraflores**, and **Barranco**. Walking is your best bet within a given neighborhood, but you will need to take a taxi or bus between neighborhoods.

By Car Avoid driving in Lima if you can. Many roads are in pitiful condition, while drivers are rude, reckless, and anarchic. If you must drive, park in a lot to protect the car against theft, or hire a child offering *"cuidar su carro"* (to look after your car). Pay him S/. 0.50–S/. 1 when you return and find your car intact.

By Public Buses and their smaller cousins, the schoolbus-size *micros,* and **Transportation** the van-size *combis* offer frequent service, are inexpensive (S/. 0.40 or S/. 0.50; there are no free transfers), and stop at almost every corner. You must flag them down, but it is often difficult to know where they are going. If you're not sure, ask before you board.

By Taxi Cabs are plentiful and cheap. You will find taxi stands with big black *remisse* taxis beside most of the luxury hotels; these are the most expensive because they are generally larger and well cared for. On the street, cabs come in all makes, models, and stages of decay. You can recognize them by the plastic "TAXI" sign on the windshields. If the car looks decrepit, don't get in; another cab is sure to come by soon. There are no meters. Always ask the fare before you get in, and offer 10%–25% less. Some local radio cab companies are **Taxi Fono** (tel. 014/22–6565 and 014/40–0714), **Taxi Red** (tel. 014/55–5551), and **Taxi Metro** (tel. 014/37–3689). Radio taxi fares are not negotiable.

Orientation Tours

Lima Tours (Belén 1040, tel. 014/27–6624) arranges bus tours of the city that include access to some of Lima's finest colonial mansions.

Exploring Lima

Old and new blend and sometimes clash in Lima. The old—gracious but occasionally run-down colonial and republican-era streets, mansions, and churches—is concentrated in the chaotic downtown area, the Centro, where you'll also see skyscrapers and dreadful government buildings constructed in the 1960s and 1970s. The Centro is home to hundreds of thousands of street vendors and to unmanageable traffic. Other neighborhoods, like Miraflores, offer shopping, good eating, and a chance to relax and people-watch. Here, luxury high rises and fancy stores filled with glittering imported items contrast with the grimy street children begging for tips and tidbits from patrons at the sidewalk cafés. Museums exploring the country's long history are scattered throughout metropolitan Lima.

From downtown Lima, the main roads lead like spokes of a wheel to its most important districts, leading through working-class neighborhoods like Breña, Rimac, and La Victoria to the huge shantytowns ringing the city and to upscale seafront residential neighborhoods like Miraflores and San Isidro. There are also posh neighborhoods like La Molina in the foothills of the Andes, where Lima's wealthiest live among watered lawns and behind guarded gates and high walls. From central Lima west to the sea, the city is flat, but the Peruvian coast is so narrow that the barren Andean piedmont juts spiky hills into the sky just 10 minutes east of the city center. Most of the city's parks begin on the downtown's western fringe, becoming more frequent as you near the sea.

Visitors should plan on spending a day or two seeing the Centro, with an additional one to two days devoted to the other museums, depending on their level of interest in archaeology, textiles, gold, etc. Take time to wander through Barranco, once a seaside vacation spot for the people who lived in downtown Lima. The café scene, which attracts artists and intellectuals, is lively here.

Centro Many of Lima's most interesting historical sites are contained in the **Centro,** within walking distance of the **Plaza de Armas.** Around the broad, open plaza are the buildings that formed the nucleus of power in Spanish colonial Peru. The **Palacio de Gobierno,** the official residence of the president, which also houses his offices and those of his staff, was completed in 1938 to monumental proportions. It is located on the north side of the square, on the site of Francisco Pizarro's palace, where he was murdered in 1541. An equestrian statue of the conquistador watches over the palace from across the street. The changing of the palace guard takes place daily at noon. Free tours are available through prearrangement with the public relations office (tel. 014/28–7444).

On the east side of the plaza stands the **cathedral** (tel. 014/32–3360; admission charged), completed in the 17th century and rebuilt after the 1746 earthquake nearly destroyed it. In addition to impressive Baroque decoration, especially the intricately carved choir stalls, the cathedral houses a museum of religious art and artifacts, whose highlight is a coffin said to hold the remains of Pizarro. Across the plaza stands the 20th-century neocolonial **Municipalidad** (tel. 014/27–6080; admission free), City Hall. Beside it, one block off the plaza, the late-16th-century church of **Santo Domingo** (first block of Jirón Camaná, tel. 014/27–6793; admission charged), holds the tombs of two venerated Peruvian saints, Santa Rosa de Lima and the black San Martín de Porres. One block west is the **Casa Aliaga** (Jirón de la Unión 224, tel. 014/27–6624; admission charged), which can be seen by appointment through the administration or travel agencies. Said to be the oldest colonial mansion in South America, the house has been owned and occupied by the Aliaga family since Pizarro granted the land to Jerónimo de Aliaga in 1535. Its elaborate rooms are decorated with colonial furnishings.

Behind the palace stands one of Lima's most interesting churches, **San Francisco,** completed in 1674. Note the beautiful *mudejar* decoration (a hybrid of Muslim and Spanish styles) on its vaulting and columns, Sevillian tiles, and paneled ceilings. The adjoining monastery's immense library contains thousands of antique texts, some dating back to the 17th century. You can visit the church's vast catacombs, with the remains of some 70,000 dead, discovered only in 1951. The monastery can be seen only on a guided tour, which takes place daily at 12:45 and 5:45. *Ancash 471, tel. 014/27–1381. Admission charged.*

Just across the street is a beautifully restored colonial mansion called **Casa Pilatos** (Ancash 390, tel. 014/28–7990; admission free; closed weekends), which now houses the National Cultural Institute. The Institute sponsors exhibitions on Peruvian culture, both ancient and modern. One of the more gruesome aspects of Peru's history is explored in the **Museo de la Inquisición** (Junín 548, tel. 014/28–7980; admission free; closed Sun.), located three blocks away in the building that was the Spanish Inquisition's headquarters in South America from 1570 to 1820. You can visit the original dungeons, torture chambers, and stomach-churning, life-size exhibits illustrating the Inquisition's methods of extracting information from the accused.

Nearby is Lima's most splendid colonial mansion, the **Palacio Torre Tagle** (Ucayali 363, tel. 014/27–3860; free admission; closed weekends), built in 1735. Because the Foreign Ministry has offices here, visits by the public are limited to the patio and courtyard, but even that peek reveals tiled ceilings, carved columns, and a 16th-century carriage complete with portable commode. Catty-corner across the street stands one of the finest examples of early colonial religious architecture in Peru, **San Pedro** (corner of Ucayali and Azángaro, tel. 014/24–7260; admission free), a Jesuit church built in 1638. Richly decorated with gilded altars and Moorish-style wood carvings in the choir and vestry, the church is covered throughout its interior with glazed, decorated tiles.

Once the most fashionable boulevard in Lima and now for pedestrians only, **Jirón de la Unión** runs between the Plaza de Armas and the more modern **Plaza San Martín.** Persistent vendors and pickpockets (skilled but not violent) abound here; still, the walk affords a colorful foray into modern Lima. Halfway between the two plazas is the **Iglesia de la Merced** (corner of Unión and Miro Quesada, tel. 014/27–8199; admission free), with a colonial facade and peaceful cloisters. Hernando Pizarro, Francisco's brother, started its construction in 1535. Facing the bustling Plaza San Martín are elegant buildings such as the **Gran Hotel Bolívar,** a pleasant place to stop for tea or a sandwich, and the exclusive **Club Nacional,** both dating from the 1920s. The plaza itself is a stage for a wild variety of street performers, from magicians and comedians to hawkers of modern-day snake medicine.

West of Jirón de la Unión is the **Iglesia de Jesús María** (corner of Camaná and Moquegua, tel. 014/27–6809; admission free), a simple church dating to 1659 that became a Capuchin monastery in the 18th century. The nearby **Casa de Riva Agüero** (Camaná 549, tel. 014/27–7678; admission free, by appointment weekdays; closed weekends) is a typical colonial mansion, with ornately carved wooden terraces overlooking courtyards, and balconies with celosías, intricate wood screens through which the ladies could watch passersby unobserved. An interesting museum of folk art is located on the patio. Within the small, simple 17th-century church **Santuario de Santa Rosa de Lima** (first block of Av. Tacna, tel. 014/28–7725; admission free) is the tiny adobe cell that was Santa Rosa's hermitage, keeping alive the memory of the first saint in the Western Hemisphere. The church also houses the **Museo Etnográfico,** with ethnographic exhibits detailing the lives of Peru's jungle peoples. Three blocks away, the **Iglesia de las Nazarenas** (corner of Tacna and Huancavelica, no phone; admission free) is an 18th-century church that has become the repository of the icon of the **Señor de los Milagros,** the patron of Lima's most passionate and important religious festival. In the mid-1600s, a black freeman living on this site painted a mural of Christ on the wall of his hut. When an earthquake in 1655 destroyed most of the surrounding shantytown, the wall with the mural remained standing, and the miraculous mural became the patron icon of Lima. Every year, on October 18, 19, 28, and November 1, purple-robed devotees carry an oil copy of the mural, resplendent in a gold frame atop a silver litter, through the streets of Lima.

Near the "entrance" to the Centro, where the expressway to Miraflores and Barranco begins, the **Museo de Arte Nacional** chronicles four centuries of Peruvian art and design. Highlights are 2,000-year-old weavings from Paracas and paintings from the Cuzco School. *Colón 124, tel. 014/23–4732. Admission charged. Closed daily 12:30–1:30.*

Rimac An extension of the colonial center, the district of **Rimac** has declined into a somewhat rough neighborhood, especially at night. Set just across the often arid Rimac River from the Palacio de Gobierno, Rimac is linked to the center by the 17th-century **Puente de Piedra,** whose builders strengthened their mortar with thousands of egg whites. A few blocks from the bridge, the **Alameda de los Descalzos,** a tree-lined courtship walk, is graced by 12 marble statues representing the signs of the zodiac.

This sadly deteriorated lovers' lane ends at the **Convento de los Descalzos,** a 16th-century Franciscan monastery. The monastery has four main cloisters and two lavish chapels, one with a Baroque altar gleaming with gold leaf. The kitchen still contains antique winemaking equipment, and the monastery has a fine collection of colonial paintings. *Alameda de los Descalzos, Rimac, tel. 014/81–0441. Admission charged. Closed Tues. and weekends.*

Miraflores An upscale residential district, the seaside suburb of Miraflores is an attractive place for strolling and window shopping among chic fashion boutiques, art galleries, and crafts shops. Some of Lima's swankiest hotels and restaurants are located here. Oddly enough, this posh neighborhood is also the setting for an enormous pre-Inca *huaca* (ruin of a religious site), the **Huaca Juliana.** *Corner of Larco Herrera and Elías Aguirre, Miraflores. Admission charged. Closed Mon.*

One of Lima's finest small museums, the **Museo Amano,** seven blocks away, displays a private collection of weavings by the Chancay culture (a small, central coastal state around present-day Lima dating from AD 1000–1500) and pre-Columbian ceramics. You must call ahead to arrange a tour. *Retiro 160, tel. 014/41–2909. Admission free. Closed weekends.*

The heart of Miraflores is a roughly triangular area around the **Parque Miraflores,** which lies between Larco and Diagonal avenues. The park is the site of a daily arts and crafts fair; there are also frequent open-air concerts. If you continue down either Larco or Diagonal, you will come to the **Malecón,** a clifftop road that looks out over the Pacific. Turning left or right, you'll pass small parks and the houses and apartments of the well-to-do. It's especially lovely during a summer sunset. One park along this street is the offbeat **Parque del Amor,** with a huge statue of two lovers in the grass, which celebrates the time-honored Peruvian tradition of courting in parks.

Barranco A sort of *Limeño* artists' quarter with galleries, cafés, and lots of nightclubs, this funky seafront district has a charming *malecón* (a coastal road) and winding, tree-lined streets. Above the Bajada de Baños, a cobblestone street lined with wonderful old houses and leading down to the ocean, is Lima's own "Bridge of Sighs," the **Puente de los Suspiros.** The **Museo Pedro de Osma,** a few blocks south along the seafront, has a fine collection of colonial paintings, sculpture, and silver. *Malecón Pedro de Osma 501, tel. 014/67–0141. Admission charged. By appointment only; closed weekends.*

Barranco's **Parque Municipal,** one block from the Puente de los Suspiros, is one of the best places in Lima to just sit and watch Peruvians at their best—relaxing with friends, their children playing about them. Surrounding the park and on Barranco's lanes are several trendy bars and cafés (*see* The Arts and Nightlife, *below*).

Other Attractions The **Museo Nacional de Antropología y Arqueología,** in the district of Pueblo Libre (about 8 kilometers [5 miles] northwest of Miraflores), houses the nation's most extensive collection of pre-Columbian artifacts, intelligently labeled and arranged around two colonial-style courtyards. Beginning with 8,000-year-old stone tools, Peru's precolonial history comes to life through such highlights as the granite obelisks of the Chavín culture, the weavings of Paracas, and the ceramics of civilizations such as the Nazca, Moche, Chimú, and Inca. Next door is the **Museo de Historia Nacional,** a collection of period clothing, furniture, and other items mainly dating from the War of Independence. *Plaza Bolívar, Pueblo Libre, tel. 014/63–5070. Admission charged.*

Another museum in Pueblo Libre, the **Museo Rafael Larco Herrera,** has an enormous collection of ceramics, including the largest gathering of erotic pre-Columbian ceramics in Peru. Peru's ancient artists were surprisingly explicit and uninhibited. *Bolívar 1515, Pueblo Libre, tel. 014/61–1312. Admission charged. Closed Sun.*

Although hit by economic hard times, the **Museo Nacional,** in San Borja, 6 kilometers (4 miles) northeast of Miraflores, still provides an impressive exploration of Peru's many civilizations through special exhibitions and scale and life-size models and diagrams. *Av. Javier Prado Este 2466, San Borja, tel. 014/37–7822. Admission charged.*

Far out of downtown Lima, in a basement vault, the **Museo de Oro** (Gold Museum) possesses one of Peru's biggest collections of pre-Columbian gold jewelry and artifacts. There are other fascinating items as well, including a brilliant Nazca poncho of yellow feathers made for a child, a skull with a full set of pink quartz teeth, and an extensive collection of military artifacts, uniforms, and weapons from around the world. *Alonso de Molina 1100, Monterrico, tel. 014/35–2917. Admission charged.*

Parks and Gardens

Lima sits in a desert where it never rains, so its many parks tend to look a bit wilted. The most interesting one is also a zoo, the **Parque Las Leyendas.** Although the administration eventually caved in to popular demand and bought an elephant and other animals not native to Peru, the zoo was designed to present the wildlife of Peru's three great regions, the Costa (coast), Sierra (highlands), and Selva (jungle). Don't expect a first-world zoo with animal-friendly enclosures. *Av. La Marina, block 24, tel. 014/52–6913. Admission charged. Closed Mon.*

One of Lima's prettiest public parks is the ancient olive grove, **El Olívar,** in San Isidro, adjacent to Miraflores. Now sprinkled with houses, the park has brick pathways and park benches among the nobly gnarled old olive trees.

Shopping

Most visitors to Lima will be interested in Peru's special handicrafts. Textiles are often in the form of handwoven wall hangings in earth tones of Andean genre scenes, or brightly colored folk designs in geometric shapes or of stylized animals or other pre-Columbian motifs. You can also buy vests, tote bags, and camera straps in similar designs. Clothing made of alpaca and sheep wool, usually sweaters, are attractive, as are carved gourds, silver and gold items and jewelry (especially of pre-Columbian motifs), and ceramics.

Shopping Districts On **Avenida La Paz** in **Miraflores,** crafts, jewelry, and antiques stores abound. Also on La Paz are two small shopping arcades with a wide variety of sweaters and handicrafts: **El Alamo** (5th block, no phone) and **El Suche** (6th block, no phone). A similar arcade in downtown Lima is called **1900** (Belén 1030, no phone).

Several large markets known collectively as the **Mercado Indio** are located between the 6th and 10th blocks of Avenida La Marina, running from Lima to the airport. All sell only crafts: woolen and alpaca clothing, carved wood objects, tooled leather cushions and stools, and silver jewelry and curios. Shop carefully—plan on spending a few hours rooting around—and don't be afraid to bargain. Similar, albeit more expensive, crafts are sold at another, smaller **Mercado Indio** in Miraflores, in the 52nd block of Avenida Petit Thouars.

Specialty Stores Most handicraft stores sell alpaca wool clothes. Two stores that
Clothing specialize in these products are **La Casa de la Alpaca** (La Paz 679, Miraflores, no phone) and **Alpaca 111** (Camino Real Shopping Center, Camino Real, level A, shop 32, San Isidro, no phone).

Fabric **Silvania Prints** (Nicolás de Piérola 714, no phone; in the Miraflores César's Hotel, corner of La Paz and Diez Canseco, tel. 014/44–1212; Conquistadores 905, San Isidro, no phone) sells colorful, original Peruvian designs handprinted on pima cotton.

You can buy clothing, scarves, purses, and other accessories, or fabric by the meter.

Handicrafts Some of the better shops for traditional Peruvian arts and crafts are **Artesanías del Perú** (Av. Jorge Basadre 610, San Isidro, tel. 014/40–1925), **Antisuyo** (Tacna 460, Miraflores, tel. 014/47–2557), **Kuntur Huasi** (Ocharán 182, below 2nd block of Benavides, Miraflores, no phone), and **Las Pallas** (Cajamarca 212, parallel to 6th block of Av. Grau, Barranco, no phone).

Jewelry In Lima, the Brazilian firm of **H. Stern Jewelers** specializes in gold and silver jewelry with Peruvian designs. They have stores in the Lima Sheraton Hotel (Paseo de la República 170, tel. 014/33–3320), Miraflores César's Hotel (corner of La Paz and Diez Canseco, tel. 014/44–1212), and the Museo de Oro (Alonso de Molina 1100, Monterrico, tel. 014/37–7691). **Joyería y Bisutería** sells silver jewelry in colonial-inspired designs in its stores at the Centro Comercial Pharmax (Salaverry, 31st block, San Isidro, tel. 014/61–9987) and El Suche (Av. La Paz 646, store 21, no phone).

Spectator Sports

Soccer Peru's leading teams are **Alianza, Universitario, Sport Boys,** and **Cristal.** Their most important games are played at the **Estadio Nacional** (Paseo de la República, Lima, tel. 014/33–4192), pretty much year-round.

Bullfighting Bullfighting in Peru is Spanish style (that is, the bull is killed) and is quite popular. The season is in late October and November, and the spectacle takes place at the **Plaza de Acho** in **Rimac** (Cajamarca, block 5, Rimac, tel. 014/82–3360).

Beaches

Whatever you do, and no matter how many local people you see doing it, do *not* swim at the beaches in Lima itself. The Peruvian Ministry of Health and the municipality of Lima regularly warn people that the beaches are highly contaminated. The beaches south of the city, however, are not polluted (*see* Excursions from Lima, *below*).

Dining

Lima's glory days live on in its extraordinary cuisine, as well as in the cosmopolitan breadth of its restaurants. Whether you want *comida criolla* (heavily spiced meat, fish, or poultry dishes, often with onions and prepared fried, as stews, or simmered with rice), the fresh bounty of the Pacific Ocean, or something more ethnic—*chifa*, or Chinese, is a favorite here—Lima won't disappoint you. For the freshest and least expensive seafood, look for *cebicherías.* These informal eateries, which usually serve only lunch, have, in addition to cebiche, fish prepared in a variety of ways: *a lo macho* (in a spicy seafood sauce), *a la chorillana* (fried with hot peppers, tomatoes, and onions), *al vapor* (steamed), or in a stew (*sudado*). You'll also find seafood such as octopus or squid deep fried. Typical snacks include *empanadas* (meat or cheese pastries) and *papas rellenas* (mashed potatoes rolled into a ball and filled with a spicy mixture of ground beef, onions, and raisins). For details and price-category definitions, *see* Dining in Staying in Peru, *above.*

Very Expensive **La Costa Verde.** One of several luxurious seafront restaurants in Lima, the Costa Verde has a rustic-chic dining room with polished wood columns, leading out to a glassed-in terrace with bamboo furniture and palm-leaf umbrellas. *Barranquito Beach, Barranco, tel. 014/77–2424. AE, DC, MC, V.*

★ **La Rosa Nautica.** This is Lima's loveliest restaurant, set in a Victorian-style pink and green rotunda at the end of a pier perched over the Pacific Ocean. The emphasis is, of course, on seafood, such as scallops grilled with Parmesan cheese, and *corvina* or *lenguado* fish with seafood sauce; for dessert, try the crêpes Suchard, wrapped around ice cream and topped with hot fudge sauce. *Espigón 4, Costa Verde, Miraflores, tel. 014/47–0057. AE, DC, MC, V.*

Expensive **Crillón Sky Room.** At this penthouse restaurant in the Hotel Crillón in downtown Lima, you'll dine on a varied menu of both criollo and international dishes while you take in the panoramic view, accompanied by live music. Both Peruvians and tourists come here to enjoy favorites such as *tacu tacu* (fried rice and beans), and grilled fish and meat. *Hotel Crillón, Colmena 589, tel. 014/28–3290. AE, DC, MC, V.*

★ **El Mono Verde.** Lima's newest criollo restaurant, set in a former home in downtown Miraflores, is named after the Nazca line drawing of a monkey, a spectacular painting of which hangs in one of the dining rooms. Try a pisco sour before moving on to the *seco de cabrito* (goat stew). *La Paz 651, Miraflores, tel. 014/44–0518. AE, DC, MC, V.*

El Otro Sitio. A mixture of folk-music bar and criollo restaurant, this establishment with stucco walls and exposed wooden beams, just off Barranco's "Bridge of Sighs," features live music evenings and a criollo buffet in addition to the à la carte menu. Buffet dishes might include *carapulcra* (a stew of dried potatoes) *arroz conpollo* (rice with chicken), and *cebiche. Sucre 317, Barranco, tel. 014/77–2413. AE, DC, MC, V.*

El Rincón Gaucho. Nestled on a hillside above the ocean, this steak house, which serves tender Argentine beef, has rough-hewn wood ceilings and other rustic touches, such as cowhides hangings on the walls. Your best bet is the *parillada*—the order for two will feed three or four people—mixed grill consisting of steaks, beef-heart kebabs, kidney, liver, pork chops, chicken legs, and blood pudding. *Parque Salazar, Miraflores, tel. 014/47–4778. AE, DC, MC, V.*

La Trattoria. This small restaurant, with cozy tables set around a polished bar, serves some of the best Italian food in Lima, especially the tomato and mozzarella salad and any of the pasta dishes. Be prepared to wait (unless you arrive early, say, at 7 PM)—it's wildly popular with upper-class Peruvians and resident foreigners. *Bonilla 106, Miraflores, tel. 014/46–7002. AE, MC, V.*

Las 13 Monedas. Housed in a beautifully furnished downtown mansion, this restaurant serves excellent *comida criolla* as well as international dishes. *Jirón Ancash 536, tel. 014/27–6547. AE, DC, MC, V.*

★ **Los Cebiches.** In a rustic ambience of dark stained-wood paneling, you'll dine on some of Lima's most delicious seafood. *Benavides 1597, Miraflores, tel. 014/17–5401. AE, DC, MC, V.*

★ **Lung Fung.** With interior Chinese gardens complete with tiny bridges and ponds, this is one of Lima's most spectacular *chifas* (Chinese restaurants), located about 8 kilometers (5 miles) from downtown. Try the *kam-lu wantan* (fried wontons with shrimp and sweet and sour sauce). *Av. República de Panamá 3165, San Isidro, tel. 014/41–8817. AE, DC, MC, V.*

Mi Casa. You'll dine on sushi and sashimi in intimate individual rooms set around a patio garden. Don't forget to take off your shoes. *Augusto Tamayo 150, San Isidro, tel. 014/40–3780. AE, DC, MC, V.*

Moderate **El Suizo.** A popular lunchtime spot, this casual beachfront res-
★ taurant with patio tables serves fish and seafood, including excellent cebiche. *La Herradura, Chorrillos, no phone. Lunch only. AE, V.*

La Dolce Vita. The decor in this Miraflores mansion is odd—the huge room is divided by heavy linen panels suspended from the cathedral ceiling—but the Italian food is great. One specialty is pasta with white sauce and artichokes or nuts. *Calle Esperanza 240, Miraflores, no phone. AE, DC, MC, V.*

L' Eau Vive. Dine in an old downtown colonial mansion on international dishes cooked by friendly French nuns. *Ucayali 370, tel. 014/27–5712. AE, DC.*

★ **Maury.** The Hotel Maury is a Lima landmark (*see* Lodging, *below*), and its restaurant is known for the city's best pisco sours and some of the finest comida criolla. It's a snapshot of 1920s Lima, with salmon-color walls, chandeliers, velvet curtains, and massive bronze-plated mirrors. *Hotel Maury, Ucayali 201, tel. 014/27–6210. AE, DC, MC, V.*

Shanghai. Big and breezy, decorated with plants and a fish tank, the Shanghai offers both typical Peruvian Chinese cuisine and spicy Szechuan dishes served by an efficient staff. *Av. San Luis 1988, San Borja, tel. 014/35–9132. DC, MC.*

Inexpensive **Bircher-Benner.** Set in a colonial-style house amid gardens on a quiet street in Miraflores, this vegetarian restaurant offers a wide variety of meatless international and Creole dishes. The salads are excellent, as is the soy-protein *cau-cau*. *Schell 598, tel. 014/44–4250. AE, V.*

★ **Cebichería Barranco.** Set on a patio with a roof of woven cane matting, this is a typical Limeño cebichería, always packed with locals at lunchtime. The *cebiche mixto* (fish and shellfish) is great; the daring might try *cebiche de conchas negras* (with black scallops). *Corner of Av. Panamá and Deportes, Barranco, no phone. No credit cards. Lunch only.*

Chifa Kun Fa. Serving excellent Chinese-Peruvian food in intimate private rooms separated by Chinese screens, this chifa is popular with locals and up to foreign standards of cleanliness. *San Martín 459, Miraflores, no phone. No credit cards.*

Las Tejas. This cozy little basement restaurant in Miraflores offers comida criolla in a colonial setting, with tiled floors and tables and whitewashed walls. The anticuchos, papas rellenas, and *picarones* (deep-fried doughnuts made from sweet-potato flour and drenched in molasses) are recommended. *Diez Canseco 340, tel. 014/44–4360. AE, DC, MC, V.*

Cafés Cafés play an important role in Lima's social and intellectual life, especially among the middle-class 30–50s set. The biggest café action is between 5 and 7 PM and after 10.

Haiti. A Lima landmark, this sidewalk café is a favorite hangout for Lima's artists and intellectuals. Stick to the sandwiches, coffee, and beer. *Diagonal 160, Miraflores, tel. 014/47–5052. AE, V.*

La Tiendecita Blanca. A European-style café with excellent pastries, a baby grand piano for ambience, and shelves chock full of delicacies and confections, the Tiendecita attracts foreigners as well as locals. *Larco 111, Miraflores, tel. 014/45–9797. D, MC.*

★ **Las Mesitas.** An old-fashioned *Limeño* café with wrought-iron and marble tables, this romantic spot a half block north of the Parque Munipal in Barranco is a magnet for fans of traditional sweets. The *mazamorra morada*, a sweet pudding of cornmeal and candied fruit, is heavenly. *Av. Grau 372, no phone. No credit cards.*

Lodging

Hotels are concentrated in downtown Lima and in Miraflores (on Avenidas La Paz and Alcanfores). There are a variety of price ranges in each area. Hotels through the moderate price range are probably comparable with those in the rest of South America. The cheap ones are awfully basic. Prices do not tend to vary by season, but it is useful to make reservations for the smaller hotels. People who want to concentrate on the Centro can stay there, although even in Miraflores you're within easy reach (10–20 minutes by cab when it's not rush hour). Miraflores has lots of shops and eateries, and you can stroll there at night with little fear of being mugged. Don't attempt to bargain hotel rates, except in some of the older downtown hotels. Most Lima hotels do not include breakfast; those that do serve a Continental breakfast. For details and price categories, *see* Lodging in Staying in Peru, *above.*

Very Expensive **Hotel El Condado.** The most aggressively neocolonial of Lima's luxury hotels, this hotel is located on a pedestrian-only, cobblestone shopping street. Rooms have full-size colonial-style mirrors and paintings, and some have private saunas and whirlpool tubs. *Alcanfores 465, Miraflores, tel. 014/44–3614. 74 rooms. Facilities: restaurant, bar, coffee shop, sauna. AE, DC, MC, V.*

★ **Hotel Las Américas.** Lima's newest deluxe hotel has a rather impersonal lobby and a shopping arcade up a long curving ramp. Rooms have modern furniture and paintings and miniature cactus gardens. *Benavides 415, Miraflores, tel. 014/45–9494. 151 rooms. Facilities: restaurant, coffee shop, bar, pool, whirlpool tub, parking. AE, DC, MC, V.*

Hotel Sheraton. Located at the edge of downtown Lima, the Sheraton is another big and somewhat cold luxury hotel; its guest rooms could be in a Sheraton anywhere in the world. The staff is attentive, but sometimes communication snags between departments can slow down the service. *Paseo de la República 170, Lima, tel. 014/33–3320. 490 rooms. Facilities: restaurant, coffee shop, bar, sauna, parking. AE, DC, MC, V.*

Miraflores César's Hotel. The César exudes neocolonial elegance, with carved headboards, exposed beams, and highland handicrafts. The bar is decorated as a railroad car, complete with a minilocomotive. *La Paz and Diez Canseco, Miraflores, tel. 014/44–1212. 150 rooms. Facilities: 2 restaurants, coffee shop, bar, health club, sauna, indoor pool, parking. AE, DC, MC, V.*

Expensive ★ **Hotel El Olívar.** Amid the greenery of San Isidro's olive grove—a great place for a morning jog—this new hotel has a glistening lobby full of plants and deep-green tile floors. Rooms in pastel mauves have paisley spreads and wood accents; some have their own saunas and whirlpool tubs. *Pancho Fierro 194, El Olívar, San Isidro, tel. 014/41–1454. 67 rooms. Facilities: restaurant, coffee shop, bar, pool, parking. AE, DC, MC, V.*

★ **Hotel María Angola.** Smallish and friendly, this modern hotel has a formal, colonial-style lobby that contrasts with comfortable, modern rooms done in stucco with bedspreads of swirling earth tones. Some of the rooms have saunas and whirlpool tubs. *La Paz 610, Miraflores, tel. 014/44–1280. 54 rooms. Facilities: restaurant, bar, casino, rooftop indoor pool. AE, DC, MC, V.*

Moderate **Gran Hotel Bolívar.** A Lima landmark, this decades-old institution on the Plaza San Martín has declined somewhat in terms of service, and its rooms are a little worn. The public rooms, however, retain their grandeur, and the stained-glass dome over the rotunda lobby is still magnificent. *Plaza San Martín, tel. 014/27–2305. 290 rooms. Facilities: restaurant, bar. AE, DC, MC, V.*

Hostal La Castellana. A favorite with foreign visitors, this neo-colonial hotel is built around a sunlit courtyard. Rooms have whitewashed walls, wooden shuttered windows, and industrial carpeting. Reservations should be made at least a month in advance. *Grimaldo del Solar 222, Miraflores, tel. 014/44–4662. 29 rooms. Facilities: restaurant. AE, DC, MC, V.*

★ **Hostal Miramar Ischia.** Set on a quiet street on a cliff above the Pacific Ocean, this discreet hotel offers stunning views, Spanish-tiled and parquet floors, and meals cooked by the Italian-Peruvian couple who own the establishment. Reserve a month in advance. *Malecón Cisneros 1244, Miraflores, tel. 014/46–6969. 17 rooms. Facilities: restaurant, bar. AE, DC, MC, V.*

Hotel José Antonio. Modest rates don't mean modest comfort in this business hotel in Miraflores. The bright rooms, some with ocean views and whirlpool tubs, are decorated with Peruvian weavings and plush carpets, while the restaurant and bar, blending lattice-work and leather seating, are elegant but cozy. *28 de Julio 398, Miraflores, tel. 014/45–6870. 80 rooms. Facilities: restaurant, bar. AE, DC, MC, V.*

Inexpensive **Hostal El Patio.** This family-oriented, rather ramshackle home (no sign outside), popular among foreigners in town to adopt Peruvian children, allows guests to use a common kitchen. Rooms have beamed ceilings, colonial mirrors, and bare tile floors. *Diez Canseco 341B, Miraflores, tel. 014/44–2107. 8 rooms, 7 with bath. No credit cards.*

Hostal Señorial. A former home located on a quiet street near downtown Miraflores, this hotel is family run and has an informal atmosphere, colonial paintings, and tile floors. Rooms have French doors leading to a dove-filled garden. *José González 567, Miraflores, tel. 014/45–9724. 30 rooms. Facilities: bar. AE, DC, MC, V.*

Hostal Torreblanca. Indoor–outdoor carpeting and bamboo headboards decorate the guest rooms at this homey but slightly run-down hotel set above a park near the sea, 15 blocks from downtown Miraflores. *Av. Pardo 1453, Miraflores, tel. 014/47–9998. 15 rooms. Facilities: restaurant, bar. AE, DC, MC, V.*

Hotel Maury. A model of down-at-the-heels charm, the Maury still gives a feel for the Lima that once was. The wood-and-tile bar, with bullfight posters and marble-topped coffee tables (*see* Dining, *above*), is particularly atmospheric. Rooms are clean but worn, with linoleum floors. *Ucayali 201, Lima, tel. 014/27–6210. 76 rooms. Facilities: restaurant, bar. AE, DC, MC, V.*

The Arts and Nightlife

The Arts   Lima does not often attract the top-notch musicians and the-atrical performances that, say, Buenos Aires or Mexico City can garner. There are, however, a number of venues where you can catch performances of classical and popular, including Latin American, music. The **Centro Cultural Juan Parra del Riego** (Av. Pedro de Osma 135, Barranco, tel. 014/67–3718) fea-tures Peruvian and Latin American music. The **Santa Ursula Auditorium** (Av. Santo Toribio, San Isidro, tel. 014/40–7474 or 014/40–4582) often hosts classical music concerts by interna-tional performers; the shows are usually sponsored by the **So-ciedad Filarmónica** (Porta 170, office 301, Miraflores, tel. 014/45–7395). The **Instituto Cultural Peruano Norteamericano** (corner of Av. Angamos and Av. Arequipa, Miraflores, tel. 014/46–6315) offers programs of classical and folk music nearly every week.

Miraflores is full of **art galleries** showing the work of Peruvian and occasionally foreign artists. The **Miraflores Municipal Gal-lery** (corner of Av. Larco and Diez Canseco, Miraflores, tel. 014/44–0540, ext. 16) sponsors a wide variety of exhibitions fea-turing sculpture, photography, and paintings, as does the **Alli-ance Française** (Av. Arequipa 4595, Miraflores, tel. 014/45–2186 or 014/46–0481). Two private galleries with works for sale are **Formas** (Av. Larco 743, office 605, Miraflores, tel. 014/44–0770) and **Trapecio** (Av. Larco 743, Miraflores, tel. 014/44–0842).

Nightlife   The most popular nightlife in Lima is at the *peñas*, bars offer-ing creole music (romantic ballads and waltzes that combine native Peruvian, black, and Spanish influences) or folk music, and occasionally jazz. This scene centers on Barranco, espe-cially around the municipal square. Most peñas exact a cover charge and open between 9 and 10 PM, staying open until the wee hours of the morning.

Criollo Peñas   **El Buho Pub** (Sucre 315, Barranco, no phone) attracts a lot of tourists for its *criollo* waltzes and ballads. **Los Balcones** (Av. Grau, in front of the Parque Municipal, Barranco, no phone) specializes in *música negra*, the black variant of *música criolla*. **Sachún** (Av. del Ejército 657, Miraflores, tel. 014/41–0123) is one of middle-class Lima's favorite spots for dancing and drinking.

Folk-Music Peñas   **La Estación de Barranco** (Pedro de Osma 112, Barranco, tel. 014/67–8804), located in an old train station, is frequented by locals and tourists alike, as is **Hatuchay** (Trujillo 228, Rimac, tel. 014/27–2827), where the patrons often dance with the per-formers. Call a cab to get back to your hotel, because the neigh-borhood is a bit rough. **La Taberna 1900** (Av. Grau 268, Barranco, no phone) tends to attract a younger crowd.

Nightclubs   **La Casona de Barranco** (Av. Grau 329, Barranco, no phone) of-fers jazz and contemporary music in a relaxed setting. **Satchmo Jazz Bar** (La Paz 538, Miraflores tel. 014/44–1753) is a posh nightclub featuring Peruvian and international performers; reservations are advisable.

Excursions from Lima

Beaches The coast south of Lima is strung with beaches, a bit dry and arid by foreign standards, but often backed with massive, glistening sand dunes. The ocean is rough and cold, and lifeguards, as well as amenities such as bathrooms and changing rooms, are nonexistent. You will, however, find kiosks serving cold drinks and fresh seafood at most beaches. Two of the most popular beaches are **El Silencio,** 42 kilometers (26 miles) from Lima, and **Punta Negra,** 50 kilometers (31 miles) away. Continuing south, you'll come upon **Pucusana,** a charming cliff-top fishing village 60 kilometers (37 miles) from Lima.

Getting There The beaches are all off the Panamericana (Pan-American Highway) leading out of Lima, with the exits well marked.

Pachacamac Thirty-one kilometers (19 miles) south of Lima, in the Lurín Valley, the imposing ruins of **Pachacamac** are all that remain of this ancient center of a powerful religious order linked to the Chincha culture. Although conquered by the Incas, so great was the mystique of Pachacamac that it continued to draw pilgrims throughout the Inca rule. The Spaniards were less broad-minded; they sacked the temple in 1533. The Temple of Virgins has been rebuilt.

Getting There Take the Lurín exit off the Panamericana heading south out of Lima.

The North Coast

Long before the Inca empire raised its stone marvels in the southern Andes, civilizations flourished in the fertile river valleys striping the deserts of Peru's northern coast. A thousand years ago, the Moche, Lambayeque (Sicán), and Chimú societies built their cities and pyramids of adobe brick, leaving behind the massive and enigmatic ruins that today dot the northern deserts. Their sophisticated canal and aqueduct systems irrigated more land than is cultivated even today. The Spaniards who settled these lands built their own cities—Trujillo, Chiclayo, and Lambayeque, among others—neglecting the spectacular agricultural and architectural achievements of earlier days. Although voracious looters, or *huaqueros,* have stolen many of the gold, silver, and ceramic treasures left in the ruins, modern archaeologists sifting through the sand still occasionally make miraculous finds. The tomb of the Lord of Sipán, discovered intact in 1987, is the most famous example.

Getting There

By Plane **Faucett, Aero Continente, Aero Tumi, Imperial Air, Expresso Aereo, Americana,** and **AeroPerú** have flights from Lima to both the Trujillo (tel. 044/23–2301) and Chiclayo (tel. 074/22–9059) airports.

By Car The major highway serving the north coast is the Panamericana and is the only route from Lima.

By Bus **Ormeño** (Javier Prado Este 1059 or Av. Carlos Zavala 177, Lima, tel. 014/27–5679), **Cruz del Sur** (Jirón Quilca 531, tel.

014/23–1570), and **Tepsa** (Paseo de la República 129, Lima, tel. 014/27–6272) have bus service from Lima to Trujillo and Chiclayo. **Expreso de Chiclayo** (Av. Grau 653, Lima, tel. 014/28–9273) has service from Lima to Chiclayo. **Emtrafesa** (Calle Miraflores 127, Trujillo, tel. 044/24–3981; corner of Colón and Bolognesi, Chiclayo, tel. 074/23–4291) provides bus service between Trujillo and Chiclayo, a three- to four-hour trip.

Trujillo

Tourist Information The **Touring and Automobile Club** (Av. Argentina 258, Urbanización El Recreo, tel. 044/23–2635; open daily 8:30–12:30 and 3–6). **Tourist police** (Municipalidad, Plaza de Armas, tel. 044/24–1936; open daily 8–1 and 3–6).

Exploring Trujillo Hiring a driver and guide through a reputable travel agency such as **Trujillo Tours** (Diego de Almagro 301, Trujillo, tel. 044/23–3091) is the best way to see the ruins outside the city; some of the sites are isolated and one can easily get lost on the unnamed little back roads leading to them. You can also hire taxis for about $6 per hour.

A splendid Spanish colonial city, **Trujillo** offers visitors a chance to see some of the best of both pre-Columbian and post-Conquest Peruvian architecture. Although monument-building city-states existed in the environs of present-day Trujillo more than a thousand years before Christ, the first such city-state to spread its influence over much of the north coast was Moche, between AD 100 and 700. The Moche, sometimes referred to as the Mochica, built their capital city and two enormous adobe pyramids—the **Huaca del Sol** (Pyramid of the Sun) and the **Huaca de la Luna** (Pyramid of the Moon), both constructed around AD 100—about 10 kilometers (6 miles) southeast of modern Trujillo. To get there, head south from Trujillo on the Panamericana; the ruins are across the Moche River in the Campiña de Moche.

The Huaca del Sol, the larger of the two, is today only half as big as it once was, but still stands over 40 meters (130 feet) high and measures 340 by 160 meters (1,105 by 520 feet). At least 140 million adobe bricks went into building this, the largest extant adobe brick structure in the New World. Today, scattered around the pyramid's base, you can see examples of "signature bricks," with distinctive hand, finger, and foot marks that identify the community whose tribute labor produced the bricks for their Moche lords. Archaeologists believe that the pyramid served as an imperial palace and mausoleum, a center of political and religious power. Once the stronghold of untold treasures, it has been stripped clean over the centuries by huaqueros. So great were its riches that in 1610 the Spaniards diverted the Moche River to wash away the pyramid's base and lay bare the bounty within. Southward across a 500-meter- (1,625-foot-) wide plain that once held a bustling royal city stands the smaller Huaca de la Luna. The huaca is decorated with painted anthropomorphic and zoomorphic reliefs. If you visit on a weekday with a guide, you may be allowed to observe archaeologists at work preserving one of the faded but still colorful reliefs. *No phone. Admission free.*

Three hundred years after the Moche civilization faded, a new empire, the Chimú, arose in its place. Although much less famous than the Inca empire, which in 1470 conquered it, the

Chimú empire, called Chimor, was the second largest in pre-Columbian South American history. It stretched along 1,000 kilometers (620 miles) of Pacific coastline, from Chillón, just north of present-day Lima, to Tumbes, on the border with Ecuador. Its capital, **Chán Chán,** a sprawling adobe-brick city whose ruins lie 5 kilometers (3 miles) west of Trujillo, has been called the largest mud city in the world.

Chán Chán once held boulevards, aqueducts, gardens, and palaces, and some 10,000 dwellings. Within the city were nine royal compounds, one of which, the **Tschudi compound** (named for a 19th-century Swiss explorer of the ruins), has been partially restored and opened to the public. Each compound was built by a Chimú ruler, who upon his death was buried in the compound, which his family and retainers maintained. Although wind, huaqueros, and the occasional rain storm have damaged the city, its size—20 square kilometers (8 square miles)—still impresses, and the walls are studded with adobe friezes. If you have not come with a guide, it's best to hire one at the entrance to the site for a few dollars; the ruins are largely unlabeled, and tourists accompanied by a guide are less likely to be victims of crime. The ticket for Chán Chán covers the entrance fees for the Huaca El Dragón and Huaca La Esmeralda (*see below*). *Carreterra Huanchaco, no phone. Admission charged.*

Two kilometers (1¼ miles) west of Trujillo, at the Avenida Mansiche turnoff from the Panamericana Norte (north), stands the Chimú pyramid **Huaca Esmeralda** (no phone, admission charged). Like other huacas on the north coast, this ancient temple mound served as a religious ceremonial center and burial site for the priest-kings. The highlights of the ruins are the two stepped platforms and unrestored friezes of the fish, seabirds, waves, and fishing nets that were central to the life of the Chimú.

Jarringly out of place in an urban setting north of Trujillo's center, the restored—some say overrestored—**Huaca El Dragón** (Temple of the Dragon), also known as the **Huaca Arco Iris** (Rainbow Temple), is an early Chimú walled temple pyramid decorated with the repeating figure of a mythical creature that looks like a cross between a giant serpent or dragon and a rainbow. After the National Cultural Institute restored the ruin in 1962, only half of the original huaca remained, and the contrast between the fresh-looking but crudely reconstructed friezes and the eroded but delicately intricate originals, some bearing traces of the original yellow paint, is glaring. *Panamericana Norte, La Esperanza district. No phone. Admission charged.*

Also north of the city, the privately owned **Museo Cassinelli** is located in, of all places, the basement of a gas station in the northern sector of the city. Among the most spectacular objects in the 2,800-piece collection, which covers pre-Columbian ceramics dating from 1200 BC through the Inca period, are the realistic Moche portrait vases, surprisingly sensitive renderings of individuals. The Moche ceramics also show a degree of humor, as in a charming *Potato Face*, which gives human features to the Andean tuber. The Moche and other ancient Peruvian ceramicists were famous for their erotic art, which the museum keeps in closed cabinets that the staff opens for adults. Although the collection is overcrowded on wooden shelves and interpretive materials are practically nonexistent, the museum's informality does give the visitor the opportunity to handle the objects. *Nicolás de Piérola 601, tel. 044/23–2312. Admission charged. Closed weekends.*

In 1534, the Spaniards founded the city of Trujillo, naming it in honor of *conquistador* Francisco Pizarro's birthplace in Spain. Today a lively metropolis that vies with Arequipa for the title of Peru's Second City, Trujillo still maintains much of its colonial charm. Even a piece of the 10-meter- (30-foot-) high wall dating from 1685–87 that surrounded the city remains standing, at the corner of Estete and España. The heart of Trujillo is the broad **Plaza de Armas,** fronted by the city's 17th-century cathedral and surrounded by the *casonas* (colonial mansions) that are Trujillo's architectural glory.

Like most of the restored casonas in Trujillo, **Casa Urquiaga** (Pizarro 446, tel. 044/25–6517; admission free; closed weekends) was saved by a bank whose offices now occupy part of the building. You can visit this early 19th-century mansion on the Plaza de Armas, with its Baroque patio and fine collection of furniture, mirrors, paintings, and pre-Columbian ceramics. A block away stands the **Casa del Mayorazgo de Facala** (Pizarro 314 Banco Wiese, tel. 044/25–6600; admission free; closed Sun.), built in 1709. Constructed of thick adobe and covered with white stucco, this is a classic example of Trujillo colonial architecture. Its open courtyard is surrounded by cedar columns and houses a colonial carriage. Notable features inside the house are the Moorish-style carved wood ceiling and the upstairs balcony with its *celosías,* the Moorish wooden screens that allowed modest Spanish ladies to enjoy unseen a view of the street life below. Trujillo declared its independence from Spain on December 29, 1820, in the nearby **Casa de la Emancipación** (Pizarro 610, tel. 044/24–6061; admission free; closed weekends), which has an interesting scale model of colonial, walled Trujillo.

Shopping Throughout Trujillo you may be approached by vendors offering *huacos,* usually hollow ceramic figurines, vases, or bowls. It is illegal to export genuine pre-Columbian artifacts, but anything offered you is probably not authentic. Stands at the Huaca del Dragón and Chán Chán offer imitations; for these and handicrafts, try the **Liga de Artesanos** (Artisans' League) store at Colón 423 (no phone).

Beaches Although there are two popular swimming beaches near Trujillo, the water is cold year-round. **Huanchaco,** 11 kilometers (7 miles) northwest of Trujillo via the Carreterra Huanchaco, is a fishing village with a long beach lined with seafood kiosks (we recommend you don't partake). The fishermen here still fish aboard *caballitos de totora* (little reed horses). For a few soles, fishermen will take you out to ride the waves on one of these arc-shape rafts, whose earliest representations appear on Moche and Chimú ceramics.

Dining and Lodging Trujillanos are big on fish dishes, like their compatriots to the south. Cebiches of fish or shellfish are extremely popular, as is *causa,* a cold casserole of mashed potatoes molded around a filling of fish, hot peppers *(ají),* and onions and topped with olives and slices of hard-boiled egg. Roast or stewed kid *(cabrito al horno* and *seco de cabrito)* and *shámbar,* a bean stew, are two other local specialties. Restaurants in Trujillo tend to be casual and unpretentious, making up for their lack of decorative pizazz with outstanding seafood and *comida criolla*. Many also make a fair stab at Italian recipes. Bringing picnic food bought in Trujillo for trips to isolated sites like Chán Chán is a good idea. Buy fresh food in the market in the sixth block of Gamarra; other foodstuffs are available in the many *bodegas* (the word here means a mom-and-pop grocery, not a wine cellar) in downtown Trujillo.

If you are planning to visit Trujillo in January and October during the local festivals (*see* The Arts and Nightlife, *below*), be sure to make hotel reservations at least a month in advance. For details and price-category definitions, *see* Dining and Lodging in Staying in Peru, *above*.

Dining **Las Bóvedas.** This quiet, elegant restaurant in the Hotel de
★ Turistas (*see* Lodging, *below*) has a vaulted brick ceiling—a *bóveda* is a vaulted chamber—and arched, plant-filled wall niches. The house specialty is a local delicacy, *shámbar Trujillano*, a thick soup made with beans, split peas, wheat grains, bacon, and pork and garnished with semipopped corn (*canchita*) and ground hot pepper sauce. *Independencia 485, tel. 044/23-2741. AE, DC, MC, V. Expensive.*

★ **De Marco.** Set right on the street, this noisy but cheery spot, popular with locals and tourists for its excellent *comida criolla*, has paneled walls decorated with original local art. Try the *tacu tacu*, a typical coastal dish of rice and beans, with the seco de cabrito. *Pizarro 725, no phone. MC, V. Moderate.*

El Mochica. Set in an old *casona*, in a long, open hall with whitewashed walls and chandeliers, this seafood restaurant has a down-at-the-heels flair. A typical meal starts with an industrial-size portion of spicy, fresh *cebiche de lenguado*, followed by a *picante* (seafood sauce served over rice) of shrimp (*camarones*) or other shellfish (*mariscos*). *Bolívar cuadra 4, no phone. No credit cards. Lunch only. Moderate.*

Romano. This small streetside restaurant has a café atmosphere, serves good Italian classics such as spaghetti Bolognese, lasagne, and fetuccine Alfredo, and is justly famed for its cakes and pies. They might include the mouth-watering lemon meringue pie, chirimoya meringue pie topped with chocolate shavings, or a thick, almost fudge-moist chocolate cake. *Pizarro 747, no phone. MC, V. Moderate.*

Lodging **Hotel de Turistas.** This half-century-old hotel on the Plaza de
★ Armas has been splendidly renovated to blend modern comfort and colonial elegance; the patio pool, surrounded by a hummingbird-filled garden, is especially delightful. Rooms, some with *celosías* (carved wood screens or shutters), are decorated with modern paintings interpreting pre-Columbian designs, locally tooled leather and wood, and wrought-iron wall lamps. *Independencia 485, tel. 044/23-2741, fax 044/23-5641. 75 rooms. Facilities: restaurant, café, bar, sauna, outdoor pool. AE, DC, MC, V. Expensive.*

Hotel Los Jardines. Located about 10 minutes by taxi from the Plaza de Armas, this "garden hotel" in the northern district of Los Jardines lives up to its name: Each room is a simple, uncarpeted bungalow with a big picture window looking out on gardens and trees. *Av. América Norte 1245, tel. 044/24-5337, fax 044/25-4721. 60 rooms. Facilities: restaurant, bar, pool, tennis court, soccer field. AE, DC, V. Moderate.*

Hotel Continental. The rooms are simple and clean at this hotel built above a shopping arcade and located 1½ blocks from the Plaza de Armas and across the street from the Central Market. The rooms on the seventh floor have a good view of the city. *Gamarra 663, tel. 044/24–1607, fax 044/24–9881. 51 rooms. AE, DC, MC, V. Inexpensive.*

Hotel Opt-Gar. The style is vinyl-and-Formica-meet-Moche at this safe, conveniently located downtown hotel, where huacos are scattered like knickknacks throughout the lobby and other public spaces. The rooms are clean and wallpapered. *Grau 595, tel. 044/24–2192, in Lima tel. 014/49–8717. 66 rooms. Facilities: restaurant. DC, MC, V. Inexpensive.*

The Arts and Nightlife

The Arts Trujillo has two important annual festivals. The four-day **National Marinera Competition,** in January, celebrates a romantic local dance performed to the accompaniment of guitars and the *cajón,* a boxlike wood percussion instrument. The 10-day **Festival de la Primavera** (Spring Festival) in October includes dance performances, art shows, and much more. For details about the National Marinera Competition, contact the Club Libertad (San Martín 299, Trujillo, tel. 044/24–4941, 044/24–5131, or 044/25–6982); for the Festival de la Primavera, contact the Club de Leones (Estete 411, Trujillo, tel. 044/23–4501 or 044/25–2835). Local newspapers such as *La Industria* have listings of cultural events at venues like the **Instituto Cultural Peruano Norteamericano** (corner of Húsares de Junín and Venezuela, tel. 044/23–2512) and the **Alianza Francesa** (San Martín 858, tel. 044/23–2012).

Nightlife The **Pussy Cat,** also known as Billy Bob's (Piérola 716, tel. 044/23–3592), is a friendly cocktail lounge with a disco. The area around the Central Market, on the sixth block of Gamarra, is full of movie theaters.

Chiclayo

Tourist Information **Tourist police** (Saenz Peña 836, tel. 074/23–8112; open Mon.–Sat. 8–6). **Touring and Automobile Club** (Calle Marte 120, Urbanización Santa Elena, tel. 074/23–1821; open weekdays 9–5, Sat. 8–1).

Exploring Chiclayo A lively commercial center, Chiclayo is both prosperous and easygoing, two qualities not often found in combination. It is not as big as Trujillo, 219 kilometers (131 miles) to the south, nor does it have as much preserved colonial architecture. Still, Chiclayo has enjoyed a minor tourism boom since the 1987 discovery of the unlooted tomb of the Lord of Sipán. **Indiana Tours** in **Chiclayo** (Callao 121, tel. 074/24–0833) can provide private guides for the ruins outside the city.

The Moche and Chimú both had major administrative and religious centers in the area around Chiclayo, as did a third culture, the Lambayeque (Sicán), which flourished from about AD 700 until Chimor conquered it around 1370. The Moche **tomb of the Lord of Sipán,** saved from huaqueros in 1987 by renowned Peruvian archaeologist Walter Alva in a dramatic last-minute rescue, stands in the **Huaca Rajada** (no phone; admission charged) a pyramid near the town of **Sipán,** about 35 kilometers (21 miles) south of Chiclayo. The trip takes you through the fertile valley of Chancay, past sugar plantations, to a huge, fissured mud hill that is actually the **Huaca Rajada.** The smaller hill beside it is part of the pyramid, once connected to the bigger one by a platform. The three major tombs found in the smaller mound date from about AD 290 and earlier, and together form one of the most complete archaeological finds ever made in the Western Hemisphere. The most extravagant funerary objects were found in the tomb of the so-called Lord of Sipán, now filled with replicas placed exactly where they were discovered. Among the highlights (the originals normally are on view in the Museo Brüning in Lambayeque [*see below*], but are currently touring the United States through April 1995 to raise money for a new wing) are exquisitely worked gold and silver necklaces, masks, nose ornaments, pectorals, armor, and other objects. A small museum next to the tomb has excellent interpretive displays that describe in Spanish the discovery of the complex and the Moche culture. The dig at the complex is ongoing, and there are reports that excavation may begin on another, perhaps major, tomb some time in 1994.

About 15 minutes' drive east from Sipán is the 8th-century Moche capital, **Pampa Grande** (no phone; free admission), a 6-square-kilometer (2.3-square-mile) archaeological complex that contains one of the largest pyramids ever built in the Andes, the 55-meter- (178-foot-) high **Huaca Fortaleza.** Pampa Grande marked the final years of the Moche empire, and for reasons no one knows, the city was put to the torch and abandoned near the beginning of the 9th century.

With the decline of the Moche civilization, legend has it that a lord called Naymlap arrived in the Lambayeque Valley, accompanied by his wife and retinue and a fleet of balsa boats. Naymlap and his 12 sons founded the Lambayeque dynasty, whose cities included the immense pyramid complex of **Túcume,** some 35 kilometers (21 miles) northwest of Chiclayo. Here, from the heights of the natural rock hill **El Purgatorio,** you can see 26 giant adobe pyramids and dozens of smaller ones spread across a desert sprinkled with hardy little *algarrobo* trees. Norwegian explorer Thor Heyerdahl, of *Kon-Tiki* fame, has built a home here and is leading excavations of the pyramids. *No phone. Admission charged.*

These and other pre-Inca cultures, including the Cupisnique, Chavín, Moche, Chimú, and Sicán, are explored at the **Museo Brüning,** in the town of Lambayeque, 12 kilometers (7 miles) north of Chiclayo. Directed by archaeologist Walter Alva, it is one of the finest archaeological collections in Peru. Among the highlights are the Sipán treasures, traveling in the United States through 1995; a group of ceramic frogs dating from 1200 BC; a small gold statue of a woman known as the *Venus de Frías,* 100 BC–AD 300; and the Moche and Sicán ceramics. The museum has excellent interpretive displays, but since the legends are in Spanish, you may wish to go with a guide. *Av. Huamachuco s/n, tel. 074/28–2110. Admission charged. Closed weekend and holiday afternoons.*

Shopping Chiclayo's market, on Avenida Balta, is justly famed for its colorful mix of fresh food and live animals, handicrafts such as ceramics and weavings, and herbalists' stalls selling a wide variety of herbs and charms from local *curanderos* (folk healers). If the subject interests you, ask at one of the stalls for an evening session with a local shaman.

Dining and Lodging Chiclayo is most famous for a pastry called the "king kong" (sometimes bastardized into *kinkón*), a large, round, crumbly cookie with *manjar blanco* in the center, a very sweet filling made of sweetened or condensed milk and cinnamon boiled down until it is very thick and caramel colored. Another local specialty is *pescado seco* (dried fish, often a ray), used in stews or fried.

For details and price-category definitions, *see* Dining and Lodging in Staying in Peru, *above.* Highly recommended restaurants and hotels are indicated by a star ★.

Dining **Restaurante Típico Fiestas.** The decor is rather flashy and garish at this restaurant in the Tres de Octubre district, but the main attraction is the chef, whose showcases of *comida norteña* (typical food of northern Peru) in Lima have earned him cudos. Everything served is outstanding, especially the shellfish, cebiche, and tacu tacu. *Salaverry 1820, tel. 074/22–8441. V. Lunch only. Expensive.*

Las Tinajas. A woven cane roof, wicker chairs, and ceiling fans give this simple restaurant a tropical flair. The seafood here is top-notch. *Elías Aguirre 952, no phone. No credit cards. Lunch only. Moderate.*

La Terraza. Chiclayo's version of penthouse dining, this fourth-floor restaurant has plush blue velour and steel chairs and a panoramic view of the city. The food is regional, with an emphasis on seafood and comida criolla. *Elías Aguirre 635, no phone. AE, DC, MC, V. Moderate.*

Lodging **Hotel de Turistas.** Chiclayo's biggest hotel is a bit run-down and quite noisy, thanks to traffic nearby. Some rooms, decorated in a melange of dark wood and green vinyl, have a balcony overlooking the pool. *Federico Villareal 135, tel. 074/23–4911. 128 rooms. Facilities: restaurant, bar, disco, pool. AE, DC, MC, V. Moderate.*

Inca Hotel. Although the hallways look somewhat grimy, the rooms are clean, with indoor-outdoor carpeting and ceiling fans. The rooms not facing the street have less light but are quieter. *Luis Gonzales 622, tel. 074/23–5931, fax 074/22–7651. 69 rooms. Facilities: restaurant. AE, DC, MC, V. Inexpensive.*

Dining and Lodging ★ **Garza Hotel.** A pleasant poolside patio and bar, cable TV in each room—a rarity in Peru—and very friendly staff make this modern, centrally located establishment the nicest hotel in Chiclayo. The resident restaurant (Moderate), attractive with its stucco walls, fireplace, and brass chandelier, serves excellent regional cuisine. *Bolognesi 756, tel. 074/22–8171. 71 rooms. Facilities: restaurant, pool. AE, DC, MC, V. Moderate.*

The Arts and Nightlife
The Arts The little town of **Monsefu,** 12 kilometers (7 miles) south of Chiclayo on the Panamericana, has an annual crafts fair July 27–29 known as the **FEXTICUM,** with woven textiles (especially in cotton), ponchos, and blankets, woven straw objects, and ceramics. You can join in the the general merriment fueled by *chicha* (maize beer) and see marinera performances as well as prancing *caballo de paso* horses. On August 5, a festival known as **Cruz de Chalpón,** or **Cruz de Motupe,** takes place in the town of **Motupe,** some 80 kilometers (48 miles) northwest of Chiclayo on the Panamericana, drawing thousands of religious pilgrims. For more information about both events, contact the Oficina Regional de Turismo (Elías Aguirre 830, Office 202, Chiclayo, tel. 074/22–7776).

Nightlife   There are a few peñas (bars with live Peruvian music) in town where you can listen to criollo ballads. These simple but friendly watering holes include **Brisas del Mar** (Elías Aguirre, no phone) and **Los Hermanos Balcázar** (Lora y Cordero 1150, no phone).

The South

Southern Peru is more Spanish than other regions in the country, a dry land of dusty coast and rocky hills garlanded with unexpectedly verdant oases. Although earlier civilizations have left traces such as the mysterious Nazca lines, European culture is firmly entrenched in the plazas and convents of Arequipa and other cities and in the vineyards of Ica. The animals common to all of Peru's desert coast are concentrated and protected in the Paracas National Reserve, Peru's mainland version of the Galápagos Islands.

Getting There

Peru's coastal south can be explored by land or by air, but combining both means of transportation is the most efficient way to see the region.

By Plane   **Faucett, Aero Continente, Expresso Aereo, Imperial Air, Americana,** and **AeroPerú** have flights from Lima to the **Arequipa** airport, **Rodríguez Ballón,** 7 kilometers (4 miles) from town. They also fly to Arequipa three to four times a week from Juliaca, near Puno, and have direct service from Cuzco. **Aerocondor** offers flights in smaller passenger planes from Lima to **Ica** and **Nazca,** as well as between both. The airline also conducts overflights of the Nazca lines, with planes departing from and returning to Lima, Ica, or Nazca itself.

By Car   Depending on your appreciation for desert scenery, the trip south from Lima via the Panamericana (Pan-American Highway) may strike you as starkly beautiful or grimly monotonous. Repairs on the highway are underway, but at press time road conditions between Nazca and Arequipa were still atrocious. The government plans to complete road repairs as far as Arequipa by mid-1994. In any case, the trip from Lima to Nazca is probably the easiest driving trip in Peru for foreigners to make on their own.

By Bus   **Ormeño** (Javier Prado Este 1059, Lima, or Av. Carlos Zavala 177, Lima, tel. 014/27–5679), **Cruz del Sur** (Jirón Quilca 531, Lima, tel. 014/23–1570), and **Tepsa** (Paseo de la República 129, Lima, tel. 014/27–6272) all have daily service from Lima to Pisco, Ica, Nazca, and Arequipa.

By Train   Twice a week, **ENAFER** runs a night train (10 hours) between Arequipa (corner Tacna and Huáscar, tel. 054/21–5350) and Puno. Make sure you request the safer, more comfortable Pullman class, which costs about $20. For current schedule information call ENAFER in Lima (014/28–9440 or 014/27–1824).

By Guided Tour   Most Lima travel agencies offer minivan tours of Paracas, Ica, and Nazca. Some include Arequipa on the overland tour, but ask carefully about the condition of the Panamericana before going. Operators offering overland trips from Lima to southern Peru include **Lima Tours** (Box 25349, Lima, tel. 014/27–

6624), **Explorandes** (Tudela y Varela 450, San Isidro, tel. 014/42–1738), and **Hirca Travel** (Bellavista 518, Miraflores, tel. 014/47–5583). Trips last an average of three–seven days.

Paracas

Tourist Information For information on the reserve, contact the Dirección de Areas Protegidas y Fauna Silvestre, **INRENA** (Pettirojos 355, Urb. El Palomar, San Isidro, Lima, tel. 014/41–0425).

Exploring Paracas The nearest town to the Paracas National Reserve is **Pisco,** 15 kilometers (9 miles) away, a small town with good restaurants and a main square crowded with ancient ficus trees. Local buses shuttle back and forth between the Pisco market and the office at the reserve.

The **Paracas National Reserve** (no phone; admission charged), 255 kilometers (158 miles) south of Lima, lies on a desolate, sand-swept peninsula and includes a cluster of offshore islands. Humans have lived here for thousands of years, and the Paracas culture, which produced some of the most exquisite woven textiles in pre-Columbian America, thrived here from about 500 BC to AD 200. And as inhospitable as the landscape looks—a hybrid of Saudi Arabia and the moon—the reserve encompasses two fishing villages and a small port, Puerto General San Martín. The peninsula has stunning beaches (*see* Beaches, *below*) and is home to lizards, sea lions, flamingos, pelicans, and other sea birds—the reserve has one of the highest concentrations of marine birds in the world—as well as the occasional condor.

You can explore the peninsula in a day, but if you want to see the islands and spend some time on the beach, allot two days. Although many visitors walk and bicycle alone on the peninsula, there have been reports of assaults on lone hikers. At the park office, you will find maps and a museum (no phone) devoted to natural history and archaeology. The finest examples of Paracas textiles, however, are in the Museo Histórico Regional in Ica and the Museo de Arqueología y Antropología in Lima. It's an easy hike past the office and museum to the **Mirador de Lobos,** a cliff overlooking a raucous sea lion colony. Just before the cliff, there are beaches that can be reached on foot. Don't swim alone, though—there are no lifeguards on duty. You can also walk in to the flamingo colonies (best seen in June and July) on the north side of the peninsula.

Just offshore lie the **Ballestas Islands,** which are also part of the reserve. Here seals and sea lions stake a noisy claim to the beaches below rocky outcrops, white with the guano (bird droppings) of thousands of sea birds. Pelicans, boobies, terns, cormorants, and even the small Peruvian penguin vie for nesting space on the rocks in a flapping, rowdy mass of feathers. You can visit the islands on a five-hour boat tour. Purchase your tickets in Pisco from a kiosk on the Plaza de Armas, or at the Hotel Paracas (Ribera del Mar, tel. 034/22–1736), whose 3¹/₂-hour cruise is the most reliable. To be safe, take a cruise leaving before 9:30 AM; as the day wears on, the winds get high and the sea very choppy.

What to See and Do with Children Because of the abundance of squawking, barking crowds of animals, including doe-eyed baby seals, the Ballestas boat trip is a favorite with children (as long as they don't suffer from seasickness!). The Hotel Paracas (Ribera del Mar, Pisco, tel. 034/22–1736) rents out paddleboats and has a miniature golf course.

Shopping Although it's illegal to export whole Paracas weavings, you can purchase small boxes whose lids are topped with squares of original ancient textiles. However, you should be aware that by buying these trinkets, you are encouraging the destruction of the weavings.

Sports and the Outdoors
Cycling Because the roads there are fairly well maintained and free of traffic, the Paracas National Reserve is one of the few spots along the Peruvian coast that are suitable for bike riding. You can get a map of the reserve in the park office, but you will have to bring your own bicycle, as there are no rental shops in Paracas or Pisco.

Fishing The Hotel Paracas (Ribera del Mar, Pisco, tel. 034/22–1736) can arrange for fishing trips in the Paracas Bay, where you will most likely catch mackerel. They will provide transportation but do not have tackle for rent. You do not need a fishing license.

Beaches The Paracas National Reserve has lovely, if isolated, beaches. None of the beaches have lifeguards, and only strong swimmers should swim outside the sheltered bays. There are jellyfish in these waters. The beaches are usually deserted—do not go alone—and conditions are completely rustic. Get a map from the park office before you try **La Mina** or **Yumajque,** or the longer, straighter beach at **Arquillo.**

Dining and Lodging In the fishing village of **San Andrés,** halfway between Pisco and Paracas, the seafront is lined with simple restaurants serving some of the freshest seafood in Peru. Flounder, sea bass, and mackerel abound, as do shellfish such as oysters and scallops. Of course, there's the omnipresent cebiche. These eateries are very basic and often fly-ridden, but the food is outstanding.

For details and price-category definitions, *see* Dining and Lodging in Staying in Peru, *above.*

Dining **As de Oro.** Always crowded with locals, this is one of Pisco's finest restaurants. The fluorescent lighting and plastic tablecloths don't detract from the superb seafood; try the miraculously greaseless *pejerrey,* boneless strips of mackerel dipped in batter and fried. *Plaza de Armas, Pisco. No phone. No credit cards. Moderate. Closed Mon.*

Lodging **Hotel Paracas.** This popular resort located near the entrance of the Paracas National Reserve has flower-bedecked bungalows with terraces overlooking the bay. Its only drawbacks are a sporadic odor from a nearby fishmeal factory and reports of occasional thefts from the rooms. The restaurant is excellent but expensive. *Ribera del Mar, tel. 034/22–1736, fax 034/22–5379; in Lima tel. 014/46–5079, fax 014/47–6548. 105 rooms. Facilities: restaurant, bar, outdoor pool, tennis, miniature golf, paddleboats. AE, DC, MC, V. Expensive.*
Hostal El Mirador. Cement walls and linoleum floors give this place little charm, but the rooms are fairly clean and the setting overlooking the Bay of Paracas is lovely. *Beside entrance to Paracas National Reserve. No phone. 30 rooms. Facilities: restaurant. No credit cards. Moderate.*

Ica

<table>
<tr>
<td>Tourist
Information</td>
<td>Oficina Regional de Turismo (Jirón Cajamarca 179, tel. 034/23–1225; closed weekends). Touring and Automobile Club of Peru (Av. J.M. Manzanilla 523, tel. 034/23–5061; closed weekends).</td>
</tr>
<tr>
<td>Exploring Ica</td>
<td>Ica, a colonial town 93 kilometers (56 miles) south of Pisco, with one of the most pleasant climates in Peru—hot, dry days and cool nights—is in the heart of Peruvian wine country and the center of pisco (Peruvian grape brandy) production. Ica Travel (Av. La Angostura 400, tel. 034/23–4979) offers tours of the city and can also arrange trips to Paracas and to the Nazca lines.</td>
</tr>
</table>

A visit to the region's *bodegas* (wineries) will provide a glimpse of old Peru, when the area was famous for its gracious lifestyle amidst the desert and for its high-stepping *caballo de paso* horses. Although Chilean and Argentine wines generally outstrip Peruvian wines in terms of quality and price, some of the finer Peruvian labels hold their own in competition, and Peruvians disparage Chile's attempts at producing pisco. The bodega that is most convenient to visit is the **Bodega Vista Alegre** (La Tinguiña, km 2, tel. 034/23–1432), about 3 kilometers (2 miles) outside of town. Eight kilometers (5 miles) beyond it is the **Bodega Tacama** (La Tinguiña, km 10, no phone), which produces some of Peru's finest wines; try the *Blanco de Blancos.* To make an appointment for a visit, contact the Tacama offices in Lima (Omega 251, Callao, tel. 014/64–3544). At both bodegas, you'll see wine presses and cellars and can taste samples.

Another of Ica's outstanding attractions is the **Museo Regional,** one of the best museums outside Lima. Covering a thousand years of pre-Columbian history, this small museum possesses some splendid Paracas textiles, still colorful despite the passage of centuries. From the Nazca culture, which flourished in the Nazca, Pisco, and Ica valleys around AD 500, a remarkable ceramic sculpture shows a pregnant princess pointing at her belly—and in profile shows the fetus in her womb. Many ancient Peruvian civilizations carried out cosmetic cranial deformations, the products of which are on display; perhaps the resulting headaches were what led the Paracas and other ancient societies to practice skull trepanations and simple brain surgery. That medical handiwork can also be seen. *Av. Ayabaca s/n, tel. 034/23–4383. Admission charged. Closed Sun. after 1.*

A 10-minute drive southwest from downtown Ica will take you to the oasis of **Huacachina,** a green gem nestled amidst towering fawn-colored sand dunes. In the 1920s, wealthy Peruvians flocked to this resort beneath the palm trees crowding the shores of the lagoon. After decades of decline, the resort is on the upswing. Daytrippers should enjoy the lagoon from the old promenade around the shore; the lagoon's soft, sandy bottom makes swimming hazardous.

<table>
<tr>
<td>What to See and
Do with Children</td>
<td>The Las Dunas Hotel (Av. La Angostura 400, tel. 034/23–1031) is one of the few resorts in Peru that has special activities for children, including a skateboard rink and rentals. The hotel also supplies baby-sitters and cradles for hire (see Dining and Lodging, below).</td>
</tr>
</table>

Shopping For wines or pisco, buy either in the bodegas themselves, where the wines are slightly discounted, or in the liquor stores concentrated around the Plaza de Armas. Look for Tacama's *Blanco de Blancos* and Occucaje's rich red *Fond du Cave.*

Dining and Lodging Some of the best dining in Ica is at the Las Dunas and Mossone hotels (*see* Dining and Lodging, *below*). Ica is an important pecan-growing region, and pecans are reasonably priced in the stores around the Plaza de Armas, Ica's main square. Dried fruits and nuts in a sugary sweet coating, called *tejas,* are another favorate local snack. If you are planning to visit Ica during the **Vendimia,** the wine harvest festival in March, be sure to reserve a hotel room at least a month in advance. One treat only available during the festival is *cachina,* a partially fermented wine. For details and price-category definitions, *see* Dining and Lodging in Staying in Peru, *above.*

Dining **Pizzería Venezia.** There's a lot more than just pizza here, served by a friendly staff. The spaghetti Bolognese and grilled steak and chicken are recommended. *Lima 243, no phone. No credit cards. Moderate.*

Dining and Lodging **Hotel Las Dunas.** A resort hidden amid sand dunes, this colonial-style complex is a favorite getaway spot for Lima families.
★ Spacious rooms with balconies are set in clusters of white-washed buildings among palm-lined canals and lush lawns. At the restaurant, you can dine poolside or in a gazebo-like structure on dishes such as flounder with a seafood sauce and a spicy *lomo saltado* of steak, tomatoes, potatoes, and onions. Flights over the Nazca lines leave from the hotel's airstrip. *Av. La Angostura 400, tel. 034/23–1031, fax 034/23–1007; in Lima, tel. 014/42–3090, fax 014/42–4180. 106 rooms. Facilities: restaurant (Expensive), bar, cafeteria, disco, sauna, exercise room, games room, pools, lighted tennis court, 8-hole golf course, horseback riding. AE, DC, MC, V. Very Expensive.*

★ **Hotel Mossone.** Set in a hundred-year-old mansion that was a plush resort hotel in the 1920s, the Mossone, fully restored in 1989, is a soothing trip back in time. The rooms, with their parquet floors and bright floral cotton upholstery and bedspreads, are built around an interior garden patio, and dining is on a veranda overlooking the Huacachina lagoon. Come for lunch or dinner if you can't spend the night; the comida criolla is excellent, especially the *papa a la huancaina* (potatoes in a spicy cheese sauce). *Balneario de Huacachina, tel. 034/23–1651, fax 034/23–6137. 43 rooms. Facilities: restaurant (Moderate), bar, pool. AE, DC, MC, V. Expensive.*

Lodging **Hostal El Carmelo.** At this colonial-style, slate-roof hotel, the rooms are laid out in several buildings around a flower-filled courtyard, where an inviting garden house has wicker furniture and a 19th-century wine press. The hotel is 5 kilometers (3 miles) from downtown Ica. *Panamericana, km 301, tel. 034/23–2191, fax 034/23–2191. 32 rooms. Facilities: restaurant, bar, games room, pool. DC, V. Moderate.*

Hostal Silmar. Located in downtown Ica a block from the Plaza de Armas, this budget hotel has clean, comfortable, and carpeted rooms. Some of them have TVs and phones—quite posh for the money. *Castrovirreyna 110, tel. 034/23–5089. 14 rooms. No credit cards. Inexpensive.*

The Arts The **Vendimia,** or wine festival, held here in early March, consists of a series of celebrations that include wine tasting, displays of the high-stepping Peruvian horse called the *caballo de paso,* and a fair in the city stadium. During the **festivals of the Señor de Luren** (Holy Week and the third Monday of October), there are torch-lighted all-night processions.

Nazca

Tourist Information Information about the area is available from **Alegría Tours** (Lima 168, Nazca, tel. 034/22–2150).

Exploring Nazca Nazca, 141 kilometers (85 miles) south of Ica, is the site of one of the world's great archaeological mysteries, the geoglyphs known as the **Nazca lines,** drawn on the rock-strewn **Pampa de San José** 20 kilometers (12 miles) north of the city. Ranging from straight lines to geometric forms to stylized human and animal shapes, these giant markings—the straight lines vary in length from .5 to 8 kilometers (.3 to 5 miles)—have stirred the popular imagination for decades. Although theories about their origin include extraterrestrial intervention, two main schools of thought prevail in the archaeological community. One, propounded by German mathametician Maria Reiche, who has dedicated her life to studying and preserving the lines, suggests that they were part of an immense astronomical calendar noting the rainy season in the highlands (where Nazca's water supply originates) and seasonal changes in the region's climate. The other theory suggests that the lines were physically and ritually related to the flow of water from the mountains to and across the Nazca plain. What is clear, however, is that between 1900 BC and AD 660, the people of the Nazca culture etched the lines through the desert's dark surface layer into underlying, lighter-color soil and then outlined them with stones. The most famous drawings are in the shapes of animals, such as the 46-meter- (150-foot-) long spider and 25-meter-(80-foot-) long fish.

The best way to see the lines is from the air, in one of the many small planes that offer overflights. **Aerocondor** (in Ica, tel. 034/293) and **Montecarlo** (in Ica, tel. 034/100) offer 45-minute overflights from the Nazca airport for $55 per person. You can also charter a plane at the Hotel Las Dunas in Ica (*see* Dining and Lodging in Ica, *above*).

Dining and Lodging For details and price-category definitions, *see* Dining and Lodging in Staying in Peru, *above*.

Dining **La Taberna.** With a ceiling fan over the bar and live music most Saturdays, this popular *restaurante criollo* is so laid-back that many guests sign their names on the walls. *Lima 321, no phone. No credit cards. Inexpensive.*

Lodging **Hotel de Turistas.** The guest rooms at this hotel, one of the best ★ in the state-owned chain, are laid out around a courtyard oasis and decorated with wrought-iron headboards and charcoal drawings; many rooms have a sun porch beside a sunken garden. Meals are served on a tiled walkway beside the courtyard, and an added treat are the evening lectures that hotel residents Maria Reiche and her sister, Renata, often give here. *Jirón Bolognesi, tel. (Lima) 014/46–8626. 34 rooms. Facilities: restaurant, bar, pool, tennis court. AE, DC, MC, V. Expensive.*
Hotel de la Borda. Surrounded by cotton fields in an 80-year-old hacienda, this somewhat isolated, run-down hotel 1½ kilometers (1 mile) from Nazca offers a taste of coastal farm life.

Rooms with wrought-iron chandeliers and massive antique wardrobes are set around a huge garden. *Panamericana Sur, km 447, no phone. 39 rooms. Facilities: restaurant, pool. DC, MC, V. Moderate.*

Maison Suisse. Conveniently located in front of the airport, this hotel has gardens and comfortable, carpeted rooms with somewhat old-fashioned wood furniture. *Panamericana Sur, km 445, tel. 034/232. 32 rooms. Facilities: restaurant, pool. V. Moderate.*

Arequipa

Tourist Information

Dirección Departamental de Turismo (La Merced 117, tel. 054/23–3017). **Touring and Automobile Club of Peru** (Goyeneche 313, tel. 054/21–5640). **Tourism Police** (Jerusalén 317, tel. 054/22–6549). Every hotel has a list of the members of the **Asociación de Guías de Turismo,** a local, autonomous organization of professional guides; you also can obtain the list from association member Melchior Delgado (tel. 054/21–8951). **Lima Tours Arequipa** (Santa Catalina 120, tel. 054/22–4210) offers an excellent orientation tour of the city as well as other services.

Exploring Arequipa

Perhaps the proudest and most Spanish of Peruvian cities, the "city of the volcanoes" is located in the department of the same name, which has been dubbed the "Independent Republic of Arequipa." Arequipeños love their city and are highly resentful of the notion that Peruvian life begins and ends in Lima.

Founded in 1540 by the Spaniards in the shadow of the snow-capped El Misti volcano, Arequipa is today a thriving city of 1 million that has somehow managed to preserve the best of its traditions, embodied by its broad, colonial Plaza de Armas. Situated at 2,300 meters (7,500 feet) above sea level, Arequipa enjoys constant sunshine, warm days (averaging 23°C, or 73°F), and comfortable nights (14°C, or 57°F).

Arequipeños also call their home "the white city," because of the grayish-white local volcanic rock, *sillar,* used to build most of its colonial buildings and churches. The crowning glory of Arequipa's architecture is the **Santa Catalina Convent,** a miniature walled town founded in 1579 in what is now downtown Arequipa, a few blocks from the Plaza de Armas. At press time, 20 nuns and 3 novices still lived there; at the Dominican convent's height, there were 400 women residents, including nuns and their slaves and servants. Once inside its high walls, the nuns never again left the two-hectare convent, which had its own cemetery. This city of women was a faithful reflection of the highly stratified Peruvian society of the time. Novices had to pay to join the convent, and nuns were separated according to how much they had paid: the higher the "contribution," the more luxurious the cell. Once inside, they—or their slaves—continued to buy and prepare their own food in the tiny kitchens each cell included. The convent's residents took up communal life in 1871. You should hire a guide at the entrance (plan on tipping about $2.50), but leave some time to wander through the twisting streets on your own. *Corner Santa Catalina and Ugarte, no phone. Admission charged.*

Another religious center well worth visiting is the Franciscan **La Recoleta Monastery,** located just across the Chili River from the city's colonial center. Founded in 1648, the monastery houses a huge and ancient library, a museum of the Amazon, a colonial art collection, and, of course, cloisters and cells. Hire a guide to make sure you don't miss the library (tip about $2). *Calle Recoleta, tel. 054/223–058. Admission charged.*

The colonial aristocracy left its mark in the fine mansions of downtown Arequipa, many of which you may enter through a high, arched portal. Tall gateways were a 17th-century status symbol, designed to allow the passage of an armored knight on horseback bearing an upright lance. Two particularly striking mansions are open to the public. **Casa Ricketts** (Calle San Francisco 108, tel. 054/21–5060; admission free; closed weekends), a block from the Plaza de Armas, once the archbishop's palace, is named after an important Peruvian family. Today it houses a small museum displaying colonial paintings, books, costumes, and furniture. **Casa del Moral** (corner of Moral and Bolívar, 054/21–3171; admission free; closed weekends), a block from Santa Catalina, has a stunning sillar portal carved in a *mestizo* design (or Baroque mestizo, a style blending indigenous and Spanish motifs) combining puma heads with snakes emerging from their mouths and a Spanish coat of arms.

Arequipa has two charming colonial suburbs. **Yanahuara,** within walking distance of the city center and home to many *picantería* restaurants (*see* Dining and Lodging, *below*), has an overlook with a stunning view of the city and El Misti. Uphill from Yanahuara is **Cayma,** whose 16th-century church is an outstanding example of local colonial architecture. Built of sillar and decorated with mestizo ornamentation, the church, like most of those in Arequipa, avoids the cluttered ostentation typical of colonial churches in other Peruvian cities.

Shopping The Plaza San Francisco is the site of a year-round handicrafts fair, open daily until about 7 PM. Arequipa is particularly known for its leatherwork and alpaca textiles. Jewelry and knickknacks made out of Arequipa agate and handicrafts are sold at boutiques behind the cathedral, on the narrow, pedestrians-only Pasaje Catedral.

Dining and Lodging Arequipa's cuisine is something special among the comida criolla of Peru. Perhaps the most famous dish is *rocoto relleno*—a very hot pepper, large and red, stuffed with a mixture of meat, onions, and raisins, and baked. The dish may bring tears to your eyes. *Comida arequipeña,* however, is not always spicy. There are also rich, succulent stews, like *adobo,* a beef stew that is particularly popular as a cure for hangovers! Don't forget to at least sample the *cuy,* guinea pig, an Andean staple. You'll find comida Arequipeña served at *picanterías,* casual restaurants open only for lunch. For details and price-category definitions, *see* Dining and Lodging in Staying in Peru, *above.*

Dining **La Posada del Puente.** Leather-shaded hanging lamps and
★ ocher walls, daytime views of the Chili River and the El Misti volcano, and evening dining by candlelight make this Arequipa's most delightful restaurant. Their pastas, including that old standby fettucine Alfredo, are excellent. *Av. Bolognesi 101, tel. 054/21–7444. AE, DC, MC, V. Moderate–Expensive.*

El Café. This clean, well-lighted eatery, very modern with its mirrored walls, is extremely popular with Arequipeños. Try their sandwiches and *lomo saltado;* the fresh fruit juices are especially good. *San Francisco 125. No phone. MC, V. Moderate.*

Pizzería San Antonio. A curving white bar, white barstools, and bright yellow walls give this attractive little pizza-only restaurant a quirky flair. *Jerusalén and Santa Marta. No phone. No credit cards. Moderate.*

Sol de Mayo. Live music and alfresco dining in a garden drenched with roses and bougainvillea are the hallmarks of this picantería. The *chupe*, a thick, rich chowder of corn and shrimp, is excellent. If you're up for a light dessert, ask for the local variety of papaya (or have it as juice)—it has a sweet flavor quite distinct from the jungle variety. *Jerusalén 207, Yanahuara, no phone. No credit cards. Lunch only. Inexpensive.*

Lodging **Hotel Portal.** The location of this friendly hotel, next to the cathedral, on the Plaza de Armas, couldn't be better. The guest rooms have whitewashed brick walls and colonial-style furniture, and the bar's terrace overlooks the square. *Portal de Flores 116, tel. 054/21–5530, fax 054/23–4374. 58 rooms. Facilities: restaurant, bar, indoor pool. AE, DC, MC, V. Expensive.*

★ **La Posada del Puente.** Set amid gardens and patios, this charming hotel is about 10 minutes from the Plaza de Armas. The whitewashed rooms, decorated in pastel colors, have small terraces with wicker furniture overlooking the Chili River. *Av. Bolognesi 101, tel. 054/21–7444, fax 054/21–9360. 22 rooms. Facilities: restaurant, bar. AE, DC, MC, V. Expensive.*

★ **El Conquistador.** Housed in a restored colonial mansion with sillar walls and a cobblestone courtyard, this hotel also has a modern section with rooms overlooking a garden. All the rooms have modern furniture and brown-striped bedspreads. *Calle Mercaderes 409, tel. 054/21–2916, fax 054/21–8987. 27 rooms. Facilities: cafeteria. AE, DC, MC, V. Moderate.*

Hotel Maisón Plaza. At this small hostelry in a colonial building on the Plaza de Armas, the parquet-floor rooms are clean but somewhat dark. The obvious lure is a super location at budget prices. *Portal San Agustín, tel. 054/21–8931. 9 rooms. Facilities: restaurant. No credit cards. Inexpensive.*

La Casa de Mi Abuela. A ramshackle complex of houses turned into a hotel, "my grandmother's house" has lovely gardens and homey, wood-paneled rooms with worn easy chairs. The hotel is six blocks from the Plaza de Armas. *Jerusalén 606, tel. 054/24–1206, fax 054/24–2761. 20 rooms, some with small kitchen. Facilities: cafeteria, playground. No credit cards. Inexpensive.*

The Arts and Nightlife
The Arts The **Teatro Municipal** (Calle Mercaderes 224, tel. 054/21–3388) and **Instituto Cultural Peruano Norteamericano** (Melgar 109, tel. 054/24–2493) often host evening concerts of traditional and classical music.

Nightlife **El Sillar** (corner of Alvarez Thomas and Santo Domingo, no phone) is a peña set in the La Compañía church cloister; the music is mostly Andean. Another crowded and friendly little peña is the **Bar Romie** (Plaza San Francisco, no phone).

Colca Canyon

Tourist Information There is no tourist information office in the Colca Canyon. For information on the Reserva Nacional de Aguada Blanca, contact the Instituto Nacional de Recursos Naturales, Dirección de Areas Protegidas, in Lima (tel. 014/41–0425, fax 014/41–4606).

Exploring Colca Canyon About 150 kilometers (93 miles) of rough driving from Arequipa brings you to the magnificent Colca Canyon, slicing a green and fertile trough through the region's rocky, barren mountains. Said to be twice as deep as the Grand Canyon and reputed to be the deepest canyon in the world, the Colca is a rare blend of natural and man-made beauty. Surrounded by snowcapped mountains and home to immense Andean condors, which visitors may see from the **Cruz del Condor** overlook in mid-canyon, the Colca is also the site of one of the most extensive pre-Columbian agricultural terracing networks in Peru. The vast complex of terraces is, in its way, as impressive as Machu Picchu—especially since, 450 years after the Spanish conquest, they are still in use (the crops are the indigenous, high-protein grains *quinoa* and *kiwicha*, and corn). In the canyon's unspoiled Andean villages, people of the Collaguas and Cabana tribes still wear their traditional costumes and embroidered hats. The road from Arequipa to the Colca takes you through the **Reserva Nacional de Aguada Blanca,** where herds of graceful, long-necked vicuñas graze.

It *is* possible to go on a guided tour from Arequipa for the day, with about 10 grueling hours on the road and only about two hours in the canyon itself. With all there is to see, however, a day trip seems almost criminal (in fact, the government's Ministry of Industry and Tourism has tried to ban day trips to the Colca). **Transcontinental Tours** (Santa Catalina 213, Arequipa, tel. 054/23–5999 or 054/23–5799) conducts overnight trips and will arrange lodging; and if you insist, other agencies will do the same. Don't let them convince you, as they often try, that "a day trip is more than enough." It's not, not if you travel overland. An alternative is to charter a flight from the airport at Arequipa through **AQP** (tel. 054/24–2030, fax 054/25–6068), a local charter airline. The flight lasts about a half hour, and the cost varies according to the number of passengers on board.

Sports and the Outdoors

Hiking and Backpacking The Colca Valley offers spectacular scenery for hiking, especially around **Misma Mountain,** the source of the Amazon. **Transcontinental Tours** (Santa Catalina 213, Arequipa, tel. 054/23–5999 or 054/23–5799) can arrange treks on foot or horseback; or contact Alejandro Rebaza at **TMR** (Coop. Lambramani C-4, Arequipa, tel. 054/24–1498) for guided hikes and trail riding. You can also get information on hiking and climbing around Arequipa from the **Club Andinismo de Arequipa** (Santo Domingo 416, Arequipa, no phone), and information and equipment at **Turandes** (Calle Mercaderes 130, Arequipa).

Rafting The **Majes River,** which runs through the Colca Valley, is too rough for rafting in the central part of the valley. Between January and March, however, the river above Chivay offers excellent conditions. **Transcontinental Tours** (*see* Hiking and Backpacking, *above*) can outfit these trips. Below the Colca Canyon, toward Camaná, the conditions are once again superb for rafting. **Majes Tours** (Villa Flórida B-7, Cerro Colorado, Arequipa, tel. 054/25–5819) outfits trips down this segment of the river and offers accommodations at a rustic lodge on the riverfront in Ongoro.

Dining and Lodging For details and price-category definitions, *see* Dining and Lodging in Staying in Peru, *above*.

★ **El Parador del Colca.** With finely finished adobe rooms, each with its own wood stove and glassed-in porch looking out on the Colca, the hotel is part of a working farm that raises alpacas and ancient crops such as quinoa. *Hacienda Curiña, Chivay, Colca Valley, tel. (in Arequipa) 054/23–5999. 6 rooms. Facilities: restaurant. AE, MC, V. Moderate–Expensive.*

La Posada del Inca. This new budget hotel in Chivay is very basic. The rooms are airy, some with views of the mountains and the valley. *Chivay, Colca Valley, no phone. 10 rooms. Facilities: restaurant. No credit cards. Inexpensive.*

Puno and Lake Titicaca

Legend has it that Manco Capac and Mama Ocllo, founders of the Inca empire, emerged from the waters of Lake Titicaca. Indeed, as one watches the mysterious play of light on the water, and the shadows on the mountains up here on the rooftop of the world, the myths seem to become tangible. This is the *altiplano* of Peru, the high plains where the earth has been raised so close to the sky that the atmosphere takes on a luminous quality.

Divided by the border between Peru and Bolivia, Lake Titicaca draws visitors both for its magnificent scenery and the vivid Quechua and Aymara native cultures that still thrive on its shores. Surrounded by high, barren mountains, the lake is truly an inland sea, whose opposite shores are often beyond view. Some 3,850 meters (12,500 feet) above sea level, Lake Titicaca is the largest lake in South America (8,288 square kilometers, or 3,200 square miles) and the highest navigable lake (260 meters, or 900 feet deep) in the world. The Bay of Puno, separated from the lake proper by the two jutting peninsulas of Capaschica and Chucuito, is relatively small and is home to both the floating Uros Islands and to surface plants that blossom thanks to water pollution, while the lakeshores are lush with *totora* reeds, so valuable as building materials, cattle fodder, and even, in times of famine, food for humans.

Puno, the capital of the department of the same name, is a drab and unpretentious little town. In February and November, however, Puno is dressed with colorful and timeless pageantry as Inca legends live on in the phantasmagorical masks and dances of the town festivals.

Staying Safe and Healthy

Because it is one of Peru's poorest departments, Puno has long drawn the attention of the Shining Path. But thanks largely to the democratizing influence of peasant unions, progressive Catholic priests, and political parties, the terrorists have never been able to make Puno a stronghold. Nevertheless, they make periodic incursions into the department's highlands, above Lake Titicaca. We strongly recommend you limit your visit to the town of Puno and the "low-lying" areas (in relative terms!) that hug the shores of Lake Titicaca, where terrorist activity is almost nonexistent. Using the services of a reputable travel agency to plan your trip is also a sensible security measure. Don't forget, too, that at 3,810 meters (12,500 feet) above sea level, Puno will be a challenge to your cardiorespiratory system, so take it easy your first full day there (*see* Staying Safe and Healthy in Essential Information, *above*).

Tourist Information

Touring and Automobile Club of Peru (Arequipa 457, Puno, tel. 054/35–1544).

Getting There

By Plane **Faucett, Americana, Aero Tumi, Expresso Aereo,** and **AeroPerú** have flights three to four times weekly from Lima to the **Aeropuerto Manco Capac** (tel. 054/32–1821) at **Juliaca,** a commercial and industrial center 50 kilometers (31 miles) north of Puno, with stops at Arequipa. If your trip has been arranged through a travel agency (a good one is **Turpuno,** Lambayeque 175, Puno, tel. 054/35–2001), you will be met at the airport. Alternatively, you can take a taxi to Puno, which costs about $5.

By Train An ENAFER train runs directly between Arequipa and Puno (Av. La Torre 224, tel. 054/35–1041) twice weekly. The trip takes eight hours. The train between Puno and Cuzco takes 12 hours and requires a change of trains in Juliaca, where you must wait for two hours. (Watch your belongings carefully during the layover—Juliaca's train station is notorious for its thieves.) Never travel in first or second class, as thievery in both is rampant. On the Arequipa train, travel Pullman, and on the Cuzco train travel in the *coche de turismo.* Both classes use locked and guarded cars. Food is available on board, but is expensive. Be sure to bring bottled water.

By Boat There is currently no direct service across Lake Titicaca between Bolivia and Puno. You can, however, go by bus and catamaran or by bus and hydrofoil from Puno to La Paz, Bolivia. Both trips from Puno start with a three-hour bus ride to Copacabana, where passengers have lunch. The hovercraft takes two and a half hours to cross the lake to Huatajata, Bolivia; the catamaran takes six hours to Huatajata. Passengers continue by bus to La Paz. You can buy combined tickets for the bus/catamaran trip from **Transturin** (in Puno, Jirón Libertad 176, tel. 054/35–2771; in Cuzco, Portal de Panes 109, Office 1, Plaza de Armas, tel. 084/22–2332) or from a travel agency. **Crillón Tours,** based in La Paz, runs the bus/hydrofoil trip. Although the company does not have an office in Puno, it does have a representative there, Señor Zárate (tel. 054/35–3850). Arrangements in La Paz for both the bus/catamaran and bus/hydrofoil trips to Puno can be made through **Diana Tours** (Calle Saranaga 328, tel. 02/340356).

Exploring Lake Titicaca

There is little to see in Puno itself (get around Puno by bicycle-powered taxi; the average fare is about 25¢), and for most mainland excursions you will need a car. You can sign on for a tour with a travel agency, or hire a car and driver on your own on Calle Tacna for about $35 a day; you will also find *colectivos* bound for Sillustani (*see below*) on this street. You can also hire a guide directly. One who is multilingual and highly recommended is Alcides Huanca (Jirón Lambayeque 175, Puno, no phone).

The Lakeshore High on a hauntingly beautiful peninsula in Lake Umayo, about 30 kilometers (19 miles) northwest of Puno, is the necropolis of **Sillustani** (no phone; admission charged). Twenty-eight *chullpas,* stone burial towers, represent a city of the dead that predated and coincided with the Inca empire. This was the land of the Aymara-speaking Colla people, and the precision of their masonry rivals that of the Incas. Most of the chullpas date from the 14th and 15th centuries, but some were erected as early as AD 900. The tallest chullpa, known as the Lizard because of a carving on one of its massive stones, has a circumference of 8.5 meters (28 feet) and is 12 meters (39 feet) high. Sillustani's mystique is heightened by the view it affords over Lake Umayo and its mesa-shape island, El Sombrero, and by the utter silence that prevails, broken only by the wind over the water and the cries of lake birds. On your way back to Puno, keep an eye out for shepherds watching over their sheep and alpacas. If you look closely at their fields you will see that the earth is often wrinkled in *waru warus,* rows of raised beds of earth interspersed with small canals, a pre-Columbian system used to irrigate and protect crops from the altiplano's frequent frosts.

Strung like a necklace along Titicaca's shore southeast of Puno are three fascinating towns. **Chucuito,** 20 kilometers (12 miles) from Puno, is surrounded by hillsides crisscrossed with agricultural terraces. Be sure to take a look at the stone sundial gracing its main plaza, as well as at the local lakefront cottage industry, that of making reed boats for use on Titicaca. Sixty kilometers (37 miles) farther down the highway is the town of **Juli,** considered a sort of altiplano Rome because of its disproportionate number of churches. The village, which may have been an important Aymara religious center (whose hold over popular devotion the Spanish Jesuits wanted to transfer to Catholicism), became a Jesuit base in the altiplano. Four churches dominate: **La Asunción** (apply to guard at San Juan for entry [*see below*], no phone; admission free; closed afternoons daily), which boasts lovely murals and a large courtyard; **San Juan de Letran,** (Plaza de Armas, no phone; admission charged; closed afternoons daily), now a museum that displays 17th-century paintings chronicling the lives of John the Baptist and Saint Teresa, among other artworks; **San Pedro** (no phone; admission free; closed afternoons daily), still a functioning parish church, with gilded wood screens; and **Santa Cruz** (no phone), in sad disrepair and at press time closed to the public. Continuing another 20 kilometers (12 miles) on, you'll come to **Pomata.** The mestizo Baroque carvings and alabaster windows of the church of **Santiago Apostle** (no phone; admission free; irregular hours) are spectacular.

Lake Titicaca The most famous excursion from Puno is a trip to the **Uros "floating islands,"** 8–24 kilometers (5–15 miles) offshore. These man-made islands of woven totora reed afford a fascinating look at a form of human habitation evolved over centuries. At the same time, the visit is a bit sad, with lots of runny-nosed children begging for a handout (if you don't want to give money, bring fresh fruit or candy) and adults trying to sell you miniature reed boats. You can walk around the springy, moist islands, hire an islander to take you for a ride in one of their reed boats, see the islanders—Uro Indians who have intermarried with the Aymara—weaving and drying fish in the sun, and marvel at the microwave telephone station on **Huacavacani,** the largest island in this 50-island archipelago. The excursion, which lasts three–four hours, can be arranged through **Turpuno** (Lambayeque 175, tel. 054/35–1431), **Solmar Tours** (Libertad 244, tel. 054/35–16541 or 054/35–2586), **Royal Tours** (Teodora Valcarcel 147, tel. 054/35–2423), and other travel agencies; buying a boat ticket yourself at the Puno dock is slightly cheaper.

Taquile, a natural island in the lake, 35 kilometers (22 miles) from Puno, has only recently been discovered by tourists. Unlike the floating islands, which are in the Bay of Puno, Taquile is in Lake Titicaca proper, and is surrounded by a vast, ocean-like panorama. The proud, Quechua-speaking people of this terraced green island, whose hills are topped with Inca and Tiahuanaco ruins, still wear traditional dress and have successfully maintained the strong community ties and cooperative lifestyle of their ancestors. The people on the island weave some of Peru's loveliest textiles, which are difficult to find anywhere else. Unlike the Uro islanders, the residents on Taquile do not beg, but you may wish to bring small gifts such as fruit, candy, pencils, and pads. A boat that can hold up to 10 people leaves the Puno dock every morning between 8 and 9 and leaves the island to return to Puno at 2. Unfortunately, since Taquile is a 3½-hour boat ride from Puno, the boat schedule leaves very little time to explore the island, so an overnight stay is highly recommended. There are no hotels on the island—the Taquile community refused to allow any—but upon your arrival you can request that a family put you up. The overnight stay costs about $4. Nights can be cold and the blankets inadequate, so you may wish to bring a sleeping bag. You should bring your own water or water purification tablets.

Shopping

You will find model reed boats, small stone carvings, and sheep, llama, and alpaca wool articles, among other local crafts, at the public market in **Puno,** near the train station on Calle Cahuide. A small shop in the **Hostal Los Uros** (Jirón Teodoro Valcárcel 135, tel. 054/35–2141) offers fine-quality handmade alpaca sweaters. Just down the road, at No. 164, **Aresanías Puno** (tel. 054/35–1291) sells woolen items and stone carvings. On the island of **Taquile,** there is a cooperative store on the main square where you can buy weavings and the elegantly embroidered clothing the people themselves wear. Near Sillustani, the village of **Atuncolla** has a typical country fair every Thursday morning, where the *campesinos* of the district gather to buy and barter animals, food, and manufactured goods.

Sports and the Outdoors

Hiking and Backpacking Due to the possibility of terrorist attacks, hiking on the mainland is not recommended (*see* Staying Safe and Healthy, *above*), but there are interesting hikes to hilltop Inca and pre-Inca Tiahuanaco ruins on the island of Taquile. The island people can give you directions. One safe hike out of Puno is up the road to Juliaca (the continuation of Avenida La Torre). After about 2 kilometers (1 mile) you will find a dirt road leading to your right, with a sign to Huerta Huaraya, a peasant community on the lakefront. The walk there is an easy and beautiful one that takes about an hour.

Fishing Lake Titicaca has been stocked with trout, and also has native fish, such as *pejerrey* (freshwater mackerel). There are no tackle shops in Puno, but if you've brought your own fishing gear, you might consider hiring a boatman at the Puno dock.

Dining and Lodging

Dining choices in Puno are fairly limited, with a lot of modest restaurants in town, and more elegant, more expensive dining in the Hotel Isla Esteves (*see* Lodging, *below*). There's not much variety—mostly Peruvian cuisine, grilled chicken or meats, and the one true local specialty—fish from the lake. The two favorites are *trucha*, trout, and *pejerrey.* Both are delicious and usually grilled or fried.

It's not advisable to stay in a hotel in one of the small towns outside of Puno, more because they are generally run-down and unpleasant than for security reasons. The high season, when prices can rise as much as 30%, is during local festivals in February and November. It's a good idea to reserve at least a month in advance if you're visiting then. Puno's hotels are not adequately heated, so be sure to ask for an electric space heater when you register. For details and price-category definitions, *see* Dining and Lodging in Staying in Peru, *above.*

Dining **Pizzería Europa.** The decor is simple, the clay ovens are right in front of your table, and the pizza is surprisingly good. The more exotic toppings include *aceitunas* (olives) and *a la Hawaiana* (Hawaiian style, with ham and pineapple). *Alfonso Ugarte 112, tel. 054/35-3023. No credit cards. Moderate.*

Don Piero. This offbeat, slightly seedy spot has parquet floors, hunting trophies on the walls, plastic tablecloths, and a life-size cutout of Marilyn Monroe to welcome guests at the door. The fresh fish—try the pejerrey—is a house specialty. *Lima 364, tel. 054/51-3187. V. Inexpensive.*

Dining and Lodging **Hotel Sillustani.** On a quiet street in downtown Puno, this hotel looks out over rooftops and hillsides. The rooms, set around an interior courtyard with a three-story-high cathedral ceiling, have orange bedspreads, flowered wallpaper, and stiff leather chairs. *Lambayeque 175, tel. 054/35-2641, fax 054/35-1431. 22 rooms. Facilities: restaurant, bar. AE, MC, V. Moderate.*

Lodging **Hotel Isla Esteves.** One of the jewels in the government's Hotel
★ de Turistas chain, this massive hotel set on an island connected to Puno by a causeway is decorated with local masks and weavings; the excellent restaurant has a view directly out over the lake. Guest rooms have modern Formica-top dressers and metal wall lamps, but if your room looks out on the lake, the hypnotizing view will make you forget the undistinguished furnishings. *Isla Esteves, 5 km (3 mi) from Puno, tel. 054/35-2271, fax 054/35-3860. 126 rooms. Facilities: restaurant, bar, discotheque, games room. AE, DC, MC, V. Very Expensive.*

Hostal Italia. This hotel with an interior garden and rooftop sun terrace has a restaurant (Moderate) that's considered one of the best in Puno. The rooms are simple but comfortable, with parquet floors and wood furniture; those on the fourth floor have a view of the lake. *Teodoro Valcarcel 122, tel. 054/35-2521, fax 054/35-2131. 30 rooms. Facilities: restaurant. V. Inexpensive.*

The Arts and Nightlife

Folk music and dancing are popular in Puno, especially at festival time (*see* Festivals in Staying in Peru, *above*). The hotel reception staff will know if any groups are giving concerts. Performances are often held at the **Club Samana** (Jirón Puno 334, no phone), which has a rustic thatched roof and wooden benches. A folk music show is held nightly at the **Hotel Ferrocarril** (Av. La Torre 185, tel. 054/35–1752); the cement floor is unromantic, but the music is good. The **Hotel Isla Esteves** (tel. 054/35–2271) has a disco, open to the public, with pop, salsa, and folk music.

Cuzco and Environs

Cuzco (Cusco) is a grandiose city, not so much for its size or population but for the monumental character of which its people are so proud. A cultural melting pot, Cuzco has existed for nine centuries: first as the capital of the Inca empire, then as a city conquered by the colonial Spanish, and finally as home to the mestizo culture of today. The signs of these successive groups are evident at every step, in nearly every building of Cuzco's historic center. (The presence not far from Cuzco of Pikillacta, a pre-Inca city of the Wari culture, which existed AD 600–1000, is an indication that this territory, like most of Peru, was the site of sophisticated civilizations long before the Incas appeared upon the scene. Cuzco itself was the site of an unrecorded town before the Incas arrived there, which according to official Inca history occurred around AD 1100.) Cuzco is also a gateway to other historical areas and monuments, such as Machu Picchu, the famed Inca city and a UNESCO World Heritage site; the fortress at Sacsayhuaman, on a hill overlooking Cuzco; the Inca Trail, connecting Cuzco with Machu Picchu; and the Sacred Valley of Urubamba, an Inca breadbasket for centuries, still marked with the footprints of its imperial past.

The Incas called Cuzco "the navel of the world," and the city and its surroundings certainly remain the focus of tourism in Peru. A visit is almost obligatory, and we highly recommend that you resist travel agents who will try to sell you a two- or three-day package to the area. You should plan on staying a minimum of five days.

An explanation: The name "Inca" originally applied only to the royal family, in particular the emperors, though today it is used to describe the people as a whole. Thus, we may speak of the Incas as well as of the Inca (Emperor) Pachacuti. The language of the Incas was Quechua, and their name for their empire was the Tawantinsuyo.

Tourist Information

Emturin (Portal Belén 115, Plaza de Armas, tel. 084/23–7364, 084/22–3339, or 084/23–6062) provides information about Cuzco and surroundings and makes reservations for the Hoteles de Turistas in Machu Picchu (*see* Dining and Lodging, *below*) and Puerto Maldonado. The **Oficina de Información Turística** (tel. 084/22–2159), located at the airport, and the **Asociación de Agencias de Turismo** (Av. Sol, Pasaje Grace, Edificio

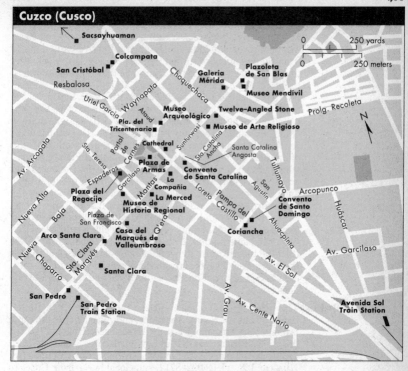

Cuzco (Cusco)

San Jorge, Oficina 5, tel. 084/22–2580) also offer information about the city. To visit the region's 14 most important historical sites (not including Machu Picchu), you must purchase a *boleto turístico*, a combined ticket available at the sites it covers. The **Oficina del Boleto Turístico** (Av. Sol 103, Office 102, tel. 084/22–6919) sells the ticket, good for five days' unlimited use. At the **Korikancha, Santa Catalina,** and the **cathedral,** you can purchase the same combined ticket, valid for 10 days, for the same price ($10, $5 for students with an international student ID), but you must specifically request it.

Recommended Reading To better understand and appreciate Cuzco, two books are indispensable: Peter Frost's *Exploring Cusco* and John Hemming's *The Conquest of the Incas*. Both are available at bookstores in Cuzco.

Arriving and Departing

By Plane **Faucett, Aero Tumi, Expresso Aereo, Aero Continente, Aero-Perú,** and **Americana** have flights to Cuzco's **Aeropuerto Velasco Astete** (tel. 084/22–2601) from Lima, as well as service from Arequipa, Tacna, Puerto Maldonado, Juliaca, and other major cities and towns in Peru. Faucett offers direct service from Cuzco to Iquitos, whence there are direct flights to Miami. The airport is 3 kilometers (2 miles) from the city.

By Car Although one can drive from Lima to Cuzco, the poor road conditions and security problems make it highly inadvisable (*see* Staying Safe and Healthy in Essential Information, *above*).

By Train There are trains twice a week between Cuzco and Puno, with connections to Arequipa. Always travel in what is known as the Turismo, or Pullman class, rather than first or second class, where thieves abound. The Puno train arrives and departs from the Avenida Sol station (tel. 084/22–2441). The only way to get to Machu Picchu is by train. The tourist train, known as the *autovagón,* leaves Cuzco daily at 6:30 AM from the San Pedro station (tel. 084/23–8722 or 084/22–1931), in front of the main city market, arriving at Machu Picchu at 9:30. The first train stop in the area of Machu Picchu, which has signs that say "Machu Picchu," is actually Aguas Calientes, the small town at the foot of the mountain where the ruins are located. Don't get off here! A few minutes later, the train stops at Puente Ruinas, where you should disembark and get on line for the buses that transport visitors to the ruins. The autovagón is comfortable and reliable, with few breakdowns and accidents. Because the San Pedro station is riddled with thieves, it's advisable to purchase the $70 round-trip ticket outside the station, from a travel agent. Local trains to Machu Picchu leave twice daily from the same station. Although they cost considerably less than the tourist train, they take longer and the risk of theft is much greater. (The local trains do, however, stop at Kilómetro 88, where Inca Trail hikers begin their trek; the tourist train does not.)

By Bus The bus trip from Lima to Cuzco takes three days. Do not travel by bus via Nazca, Apurímac, and Ayacucho, as the route is dangerous. **Ormeño** (Plaza de Armas or Av. Huascar 128, tel. 084/22–8712) and **Cruz del Sur** (Av. Pachacutec 510, tel. 084/22–1909) have bus service to Lima via Arequipa. **San Cristobál** (Av. Huascar 128, tel. 084/22–8712) runs local buses from Cuzco to the Sacred Valley.

Exploring Cuzco and Environs

In compact downtown Cuzco, the best way to get around is on foot. If you are in good health and the idea appeals to you, you can even walk to Sacsayhuaman, on the northern outskirts of Cuzco—it's about a ¹/₂-hour walk, 10 minutes by car. To visit areas such as Pikillacta, Chinchero, or the Sacred Valley, however, you must go by car. For about $40 a day, you can hire a taxi, either on the street or by phone (try **Radio Car Alpha,** tel. 084/22–2222). Recommended travel agencies that offer tours of Cuzco and the surrounding area are **Milla Turismo** (Av. Pardo 675, tel. 084/23–1710) and **Lima Tours** (Portal de Harinas 177, Plaza de Armas, tel. 084/22–8431).

Historic Center Most of Cuzco's main attractions lie within its historic center, whose heart is the **Plaza de Armas.** One of Cuzco's most imposing sights, the plaza is a direct descendant of imperial Cuzco's central square, which the Incas called the Huacaypata and which extended beyond the area covered by the present-day square to as far as the Plaza del Regocijo. In the plaza's eastern corner, you can still see remnants of an Inca wall, part of the **Acllahuasi,** or House of the Chosen Women. The palace of the great Inca Pachacuti, who turned the Inca kingdom into an empire, once stood on what is now the western corner of the plaza, and the **cathedral** (no phone; admission charged; closed daily noon–3) sits on the northeast side, where the palace of the Inca Wirachocha is believed to have been located. The Baroque church, whose construction began in 1550 and ended a century later, is considered to be one of the most splendid Spanish colonial churches in the Americas. Within its high walls are some of the best examples of the Cuzco School of painting (which added Andean motifs to its basically European style), including one of the Last Supper with a local specialty, *cuy* (stuffed guinea pig), as the main dish. Other highlights included a massive, solid silver altar and the enormous 1659 Maria Angola bell, the largest bell in South America, which hangs in one of the towers. The cedar choir has carved rows of saints, popes, and bishops, all in stunning detail down to their delicately articulated hands.

Nearly rivaling the cathedral in stature is the church of **La Compañía** (no phone; free admission; closed daily noon–2:30), on the corner diagonally across the plaza. Named for the Company of Jesus, the powerful Jesuit order that built it, the church was finished in the late 17th century. Note the outstanding carved facade and, inside, the Cuzco School paintings of the life of Saint Ignatius of Loyola.

As you face the cathedral, you will see to the right a steep, narrow street, Triunfo, now rebaptized with its original Quechua name of Sunturwasi. One block up on the right, where the street changes names to Hatunrumiyoc, stands what is believed to have been the **Palace of the Inca Roca**, who lived in the 13th or 14th century. Halfway along the palace's side wall, nestled amid other stones in perfect harmony, is the famous **12-angled stone,** an example of the Incas' masterful masonry. Today, the colonial building that rests on the Inca foundations is home to the **Museo de Arte Religioso** (Museum of Religious Art). A highlight of the collection is a 17th-century series of paintings depicting the city's Corpus Christi procession. *Corner of Hatunrumiyoc and Herejes, tel. 084/22–2781. Admission charged. Closed Mon.–Sat. noon–3, Sun. 9–3.*

The street continues up a steep, cobblestone hill known as the Cuesta de San Blas, the entry into the traditional artists' quarter of **San Blas.** Recently restored, this area of whitewashed adobe homes with bright blue doors shines anew. The Cuesta de San Blas is sprinkled with galleries selling paintings done in the Cuzco School religious style of the 16th through 18th centuries. Continue on the same street for one block to reach the **Plazoleta de San Blas,** with a simple adobe church (no phone; admission charged; closed daily until 3) that houses one of the jewels of colonial art in the Americas—the **Pulpit of San Blas,** an intricately carved 17th-century wooden pulpit dominated by the figure of Christ triumphant. Also on the square, the **Museo Mendívil** (no phone; admission free) is set in the home of one of Peru's most famous 20th-century religious artists, Hilario Mendívil. A gallery of sculptures of the Virgin, all with the elongated necks that are the artist's trademark, are on display. The work of contemporary ceramicist Edilberto Mérida is displayed a few blocks away at the **Galería Mérida** (Carmen Alto 133, tel. 084/22–1714 or 084/22–7737; admission free), which is also the artist's home.

Starting again from the Plaza de Armas, left of the cathedral, the street named Cuesta del Almirante will take you to a beautiful colonial mansion, the **Palacio del Almirante,** which today houses Cuzco's **Museo Arqueológico.** Among the displays of pre-Inca and Inca objects is a collection of Wari turquoise figures from Pikillata. *Corner of Ataud and Córdoba de Tucumán,* *tel. 084/22–3245. Admission charged. Closed weekdays noon–3 and weekends.*

The **Plazuela del Tricentenario,** in front of the mansion, has a modern fountain to whose left is a 200-meter- (656-foot-) long walkway with a fine view of the Plaza de Armas and central Cuzco.

Once again starting from the Plaza de Armas, follow Santa Catalina Angosta street along the Inca wall of the Acllahuasi to the **Convento de Santa Catalina** (Santa Catalina Angosta, no phone; museum: admission charged, closed Mon.–Sat. noon–3 and Sun.). Still an active convent, Santa Catalina has a church with high and low choirs and a museum displaying religious art.

A few blocks away stands one of the most splendid examples of Inca architecture, the Temple of the Sun, with a colonial church superimposed on it. Called **Coricancha,** it was built to honor the Tawantinsuyo's most important divinity and served as the central seat of government and repository of the realm's gold treasure (terraces facing the temple were once filled with life-size gold and silver statues of plants and animals). In the 16th century, above its looted ruins, the Spanish constructed the **convent of Santo Domingo** using stones from the temple. An ingenious restoration to recover both buildings after the 1953 earthquake allows visitors the chance to see how this convent was built on and around the walls and chambers of the temple. In the Inca structures left exposed, one can admire the fine-fitting, mortarless masonry, earthquake-proof trapezoidal doorways, curved retaining wall, and exquisite carving that exemplify the Incas' artistic and engineering skills. *Pampa del Castillo and Santo Domingo. Admission charged. Closed daily noon–3.*

West of the Plaza de Armas, along the Calle del Medio, is the Plaza Regocijo, and beyond it the **Casa de Garcilaso,** the colonial childhood home of Inca Garcilaso de la Vega, the illegitimate son of one of Pizarro's captains and an Inca princess and the famous chronicler of the Conquest. The mansion, with its cobblestone courtyard, now houses the **Museo de Historia Regional,** which displays a collection of Cuzco School paintings and Inca artifacts including mummies, ceramics, and metal objects. *Corner of Heladeros and Garcilaso, tel. 084/22–3245. Admission charged. Closed Mon.–Sat. noon–3, Sun. until 3.*

Walk down Heladeros to Mantas street to reach the church and monastery of **La Merced,** rebuilt in the 17th century. The monastery's cloister, surrounded by two stories of portals and graced with a colonial fountain, gardens, and benches, is decorated with a spectacular series of murals depicting the life of the founder of the Mercedarian order, St. Peter of Nolasco. A small but impressive museum of the convent's treasures displays, among other objects, the **Custodia,** a solid gold monstrance encrusted with hundreds of precious stones. *Calle Mantas. Admission charged. Church open daily 7–8 AM and 6–8 PM. Museum closed Mon.–Sat. noon–2, Sun.*

Follow Mantas to Calle Marquez to the **plaza and church of San Francisco** (no phone). The plaza, though unimpressive, has an intriguing garden of native plants; at press time the church, which has two sepulchres with arrangements of bones and skulls, some pinned to the wall to spell out morbid sayings, was closed for restoration. From here, through the attractive **Arco Santa Clara,** a colonial archway, Cuzco's public market area begins. Ahead are the churches of **Santa Clara** (Calle Santa Clara; admission free; open daily 6–7 AM), the oldest cloistered convent in Peru, whose altar is decorated with thousands of mirrors, and **San Pedro** (corner Santa Clara and Chaparro, no phone; admission free, closed Mon.–Sat. noon–2 and Sun.), built with stones from nearby Inca ruins. The market, though colorful, is rife with thieves and muggers, and particularly dangerous for tourists.

For the energetic, the 15-minute walk to **Colcampata** offers a tour through colonial neighborhoods to the heights above the city. Following Procuradores from the Plaza de Armas to Waynapata and then Resbalosa, you will come to a steep cobblestone staircase with a wonderful view of La Compañía on the Plaza de Armas. Continuing to climb, you will come upon the church of **San Cristóbal,** which is of little intrinsic interest but affords another magnificent panorama of the city. The church stands atop Colcampata, believed to have been the palace of the first Inca, Manco Capac. The Inca wall to the right of the church has 11 niches where perhaps soldiers once stood guard. Continuing up the road, take the lane on the left; it leads to a post-Conquest Inca gateway beside a magnificent Spanish mansion.

Northern Outskirts Dominating a hilltop 2 kilometers (1 mile) north of the city is the massive complex of **Sacsayhuaman,** perhaps the most important Inca monument after Machu Picchu. Built of stones of astonishing size and weight—the largest is 361 tons—the center seems to have served both religious and military ends, with zigwag walls and crossfire parapets that allowed defenders to rain weapons' fire down on attackers from two sides. Today only ruins remain of the original fortress city, which the Spaniards tore down after crushing Manco Inca's rebellion in 1536 and then sacked for years as a source of construction materials for the new Spanish city at Cuzco. Sacsayhuaman is a half hour's walk past Colcampata toward the right. *No phone. Admission charged.*

There are other, smaller archaeological sites around Sacsayhuaman. Two kilometers (1 mile) away, **Qenco** (no phone; admission charged) is a huaca with a small amphitheater, where the mummies of nobles and priests were kept and brought out on sunny days for ritualistic worship. Continue 6 kilometers (4 miles) to reach **Puka Pukara** (no phone; admission charged), which some archaeologists believe was a fort and others claim was an inn and storage place used by the Inca nobility. Nearby **Tambomachay** (no phone; admission charged) is a huaca built on a natural spring. Perhaps a place where water, which the Incas considered a source of life, was worshipped, the huaca is almost certain to have been the scene of sacred ablutions and purifying ceremonies.

Valley of Cuzco Along the highway running southeast of Cuzco to Sicuani are a number of lesser-known pre-Columbian sites. Despite the fact that they are easy to visit in one day by car, you may find that you have these magnificent ruins all to yourself, for they are off the traditional two-day Cuzco-Machu Picchu tourist circuit, though no less worth visiting for that.

Tipón (no phone; free admission), 23 kilometers (14 miles) southeast of Cuzco, one of the best surviving examples of Inca land and water management, consists of a series of finely constructed terraces crisscrossed by aqueducts and irrigation channels edging up a narrow pass in the mountains. One theory is that the Incas used Tipón as a kind of agricultural station for developing special crop strains. Unfortunately, the very rough dirt track leading to the complex is in wretched condition. If you visit, either walk up (about two hours each way) or go in a four-wheel drive vehicle (about 45 minutes to the site and 30 minutes back). **Peruvian Andean Treks** (Av. Pardo 705, Cuzco, tel. 084/22–5701) conducts four-wheel-drive tours of the area out of Cuzco.

Nine kilometers (5 miles) down the highway from the Tipón turnoff stand the haunting ruins of **Pikillacta** (no phone; admission charged), a vast city from the pre-Inca Wari culture, which existed between AD 600 and 1000. Like other Andean cultures, the Wari empire (which at its height stretched from near Cajamarca to the border of the Tiahuanaco empire based around Lake Titicaca) had a genius for farming in a harsh environment and built sophisticated urban centers such as Pikillacta. Wari's capital was located at Ayacucho, but little is known about their empire. The rough ruins, once enclosed by a defensive wall whose remains are still evident, confirm the Incas' superiority in architecture and masonry. They are spread over several acres, and include many two-story buildings. At the thatch-roofed excavation sites you can see uncovered walls that show that the city's stones were once covered with plaster and white-washed. Across the road lies a beautiful lagoon, **Lago de Lucre.** Continuing 8 kilometers (5 miles) along the same highway, you'll come to the small town of **Andahuaylillas,** whose main attraction is a small 16th-century church (admission charged) on the plaza. The contrast between the simple exterior and the rich, expressive colonial Baroque art inside is particularly notable. The gilt that once covered the church walls is still evident.

Sacred Valley of the Incas In the time of the Tawantinsuyo, this area's pleasant climate, fertile soil, and proximity to Cuzco made it a favorite with the Inca nobles, many of whom are believed to have had private country homes here. Today Inca remains dot the length of the valley, which is filled with Inca agricultural terraces and dominated by the archaeological remains of Pisac and Ollantaytambo.

Although many travel agencies offer one-day tours of the valley, a two- or three-day trip is recommended. This will give you time not only to see the archaeological sites but to enjoy the relaxation for which the valley has been famous since Inca times. Perhaps the best center of operations for a visit of this kind is Urubamba or neighboring Yucay, home to a magnificent hotel, the Alhambra III (*see* Dining and Lodging, *below*). Both towns are located at mid-valley and have unparalleled views.

The **Sacred Valley of the Incas** is north of Cuzco along the Urubamba River, and is traditionally held to begin at Pisac, about 30 kilometers (18 miles) northeast of Cuzco. The valley "ends" 60 kilometers (36 miles) west of Pisac at Ollantaytambo, where the cliffs around the Urubamba River grow closer together, the valley narrows, and the agriculturally rich flood-plain thins to a gorge as the river begins its abrupt descent toward the Amazon basin. (Machu Picchu itself, farther down-river, is located among the cloud forests on the Andean slopes above the Amazon jungle.)

At the southeastern extreme of the valley is **Huambutío,** set amid rugged sandstone cliffs and a launching point for raft trips on the Urubamba River (*see* Sports and the Outdoors, *below*). The road from Cuzco meets the valley at a better-known point, **Pisac.** Pisac has two parts: its colonial town, which holds a popular market on Sunday (*see* Shopping, *below*), and the Inca ruins up on a hill. From the market you can rent a horse to ride up to the ruins, or you can drive up the winding but well-maintained road. Archaeologists think there was a fortress here to defend the empire from the fierce Antis (jungle peoples). The terraces and irrigation systems also support the theory that it was a refuge in times of siege. The fortress is a masterpiece of Inca engineering, with narrow trails winding tortuously among and through solid rock. Another Sunday attraction in town takes place in Pisac's simple stone church (no phone; free admission), where a Quechua mass is held, with the local Indian *varayocs* (mayors) wearing full ceremonial regalia in attendance.

From Pisac, the valley road passes through the quiet colonial towns of **Calca, Yucay,** and **Urubamba,** and 60 kilometers (37 miles) from Pisac ends at **Ollantaytambo** (no phone; admission charged), one of the best-preserved Inca sites. The fortress of Ollantaytambo, a formidable stone structure climbing up massive terraces to the top of a peak, was the valley's main defense against the Antis and was the site of the Incas' greatest victory against the Spanish during the wars of Conquest. Below the fortress lies a complete Inca town, also called Ollantaytambo, still inhabited and with its original architectecture and layout preserved.

To return to Cuzco, take the road from Urubamba climbing the valley wall to the town of **Chinchero.** Another Inca town, apparently once one of the valley's major cities, Chinchero has a colonial church that was built on top of the remains of an Inca palace (admission charged), and immense agricultural terraces. The town has a colorful Sunday market frequented by both tourists and locals.

Machu Picchu This mystical city, a three-hour train ride from Cuzco, is the most important archaeological site in South America, and its beauty is so spectacular that the disappointed visitor is rare indeed. Its attraction lies in the exquisite architecture and the formidable scenery that surrounds it, in the synergism between the Incas' massive stone structures, the steep sugar-loaf hills around them, and the winding Urubamba River far below.

Ever since American explorer Hiram Bingham "discovered" the city in 1911, debates over Machu Picchu's original function have raged. What *is* clear is that it was an Inca religious center and small city of some two hundred homes and one thousand residents, with agricultural terraces to supply the population's needs and a strategic setting that looked over but could not be seen from the valley floor. Nobody knows exactly when Machu Picchu was built, but one theory suggests that it was a country estate of Pachacuti, which means its golden age was in the mid-15th century. Macchu Picchu's belated discovery has led some academics to conclude that the Incas abandoned Machu Picchu before the Spanish Conquest. Whatever the reason, this "lost city of the Incas" was overlooked by the ravaging *conquistadores* and thus survived untouched until the beginning of this century.

Machu Picchu deserves a two-day visit, and there are hotels in the area for every budget (*see* Dining and Lodging, *below*). Because the last bus to the local train station leaves the ruins at 2 PM, a day-tripper will have only about three hours at the main complex, with little opportunity to linger and absorb the mysterious, time-laden atmosphere. If you stay overnight, you'll not only be able to wander the ruins after most of the tourists have gone, you'll have time for a soak in the thermal baths in the village of Aguas Calientes below, a welcome relief after a day of hard climbing. To enter the ruins after hours—they close at 5 PM—you must get permission from the Instituto Nacional de Cultura, Colegio San Bernardo s/n, Cuzco, tel. 084/22–3831.

After you enter through the terraces at the agricultural sector of the ruins, you will come to a series of 16 small ritual baths linked to the Inca worship of water, and beyond them the round **Temple of the Sun.** The temple was apparently an astronomical observatory, and the straight edge of the rock in its center is aligned with the window to point to the rising sun on the morning of the summer solstice. Ancient stone staircases slice through the ruins, leading to places like the ridge where you will find the **Temple of the Three Windows.** There are few better examples of the Inca love affair with stone—one entire wall is built from a single massive rock with trapezoidal windows cut into it. Beside this temple stands the **Principal Temple,** so dubbed because its masonry is among the best in Machu Picchu. Past the temple is a hillock leading to the famous **Intihuatana,** the **Hitching Post of the Sun.** Every important Inca center had one of these vertical stone columns (known to archaelogists as gnomons), but their precise use is still a mystery. Across and around a grassy plaza are many more buildings and huts.

There are several trails to surrounding ruins. **Intipunku,** the Sun Gate, is a small ruin in a pass through which you can see the sun rise at different times of the year. It is also the gateway to the Inca Trail (*see* Sports and the Outdoors, *below*). It's a 45-minute walk southeast of the main complex. A two- or three-hour hike beyond it along the Inca Trail will bring you to the ruins of **Huiñay Huayna,** a complex that climbs a steep mountain slope and includes an interesting set of ritual baths.

A 30-minute walk along a narrow path from the cemetery at Machu Picchu brings you to yet another example of the Incas' ingenuity and engineering skills, the **Inca Bridge,** built rock by rock up a hair-raising stone escarpment. The trail up the sugarloaf hill in front of Machu Picchu, **Huayna Picchu,** offers another exhilarating, if challenging, hike. The climb, much of it straight up, follows an ancient Inca path that is still in good condition. Along the way, as well as at the summit, are scattered Inca ruins. The walk up and back takes about two hours—that is, unless you stay on the summit to enjoy the sun and drink in the marvelous view of Machu Picchu. You will have to sign in at a park kiosk before beginning the climb. Use insect repellent; the gnats are ferocious.

Shopping

Cuzco is full of opportunities to shop for both traditional crafts and artwork and more modern handmade items, especially clothing made of alpaca, llama, or sheep's wool. Vendors will approach you relentlessly on the **Plaza de Armas,** and if you keep your eyes open and bargain hard, you may find attractive sweaters. A better bet, with less of a hard sell, are two enclosed handicraft markets, the **Feria Inca** (corner of San Andres and Q'era) and **Yachay Wasi** (Triunfo 376). **Taller Maxi** (Triunfo 393, no phone) sells dolls in historical and local costumes (you can also have them custom made), *retablos* (dioramas) showing Cuzco's most popular sites, and alpaca jackets decorated with local weavings. A nonprofit cooperative store, **Antisuyo** (Portal de Carnes 216, Plaza de Armas, no phone), sells high-quality handicrafts from all over Peru. Religious art, including icons and elaborately costumed statues of the Virgin Mary, by a famous family of local artists is represented at the shop at the **Museo Mendívil** (Plaza San Blas, no phone). Also in San Blas, the **Galería Mérida** (Carmen Alto 133, tel. 084/22–1714 or 084/22–7737) sells the much imitated ceramics of Edilberto Mérida.

In the **Sacred Valley of the Incas,** both **Pisac** and **Chinchero** hold Sunday markets that sell, in addition to foodstuffs and household goods, a wide variety of handicrafts, including woolens, weavings, ceramics, and painted leather masks, mostly of feline demons worn to scare away other evil spirits. Pisac has a smaller market on Thursdays.

Sports and the Outdoors

Fishing The rainbow trout in the Vilcanota and Urubamba rivers make the towns of **Urubamba** and **Yucay** popular fishing spots. There are no tackle shops, however; most locals just use hand lines—very successfully!

Hiking and Backpacking The most famous hiking trail in Peru is the **Inca Trail.** The Incas traveled their empire via a system of carefully built and well-maintained paths, many of them paved with stone. The Inca Trail, a 50-kilometer- (31-mile-) long section of the road that probably went from Cuzco to Machu Picchu, connects the Sacred Valley and Machu Picchu. Hiram Bingham came upon the trail in 1915, although later research has shown that the trail was partially used during the colonial and early republican eras, and was, of course, well-known to the people of the area. The trail begins at a place known as **Kilómetro 88** (where you sign in and pay a $7.50 fee), at the **Corihuayrachina** stop on the local train from Cuzco to Machu Picchu, and ends at the fabled ruins themselves. Still largely paved with stones, the Inca Trail is the toughest but most beautiful way to get to Machu Picchu. Unique in the world, the walk takes visitors past a series of ruins and through stunning scenery that starts in the thin air of the highlands and ends in Machu Picchu's cloud forests.

Some recommended tour operators in Cuzco offering guided treks along the trail are **Milla Turismo** (Av. Pardo 675, tel. 084/23–1710), **Explorandes** (Pasaje Grace, Edificio San Jorge, tel. 084/23–8380, fax 084/23–3784; in Lima, Tudela y Varela 450, San Isidro, tel. 014/42–1738, fax 014/42–3114), **Hirca Travel** (Pasaje Grace, Edificio San Jorge, tel. 084/23–8380, fax 084/23–

3784; in Lima, Bellavista 518, tel. 014/47–5583, fax 014/47–5583), and **Peruvian Andean Treks** (Av. Pardo 705, tel. 084/22–5701).

Should you choose to make the trek without a guide, do not go with fewer than four people; there have been armed thefts on the trail, although they are not common. The hike usually takes three–five days. The best months in terms of weather are May–September (July is the coldest month), with chance of rain increasing in April and October and becoming a certainty the rest of the year. Even if you intend to hire porters, you should be in good shape to do the hike, since the trail is often steep and climbs to over 3,700 meters (12,000 feet); you must be in excellent shape if you will be carrying your own pack. If you've never backpacked, try a short trip near home—if you decide you hate backpacking in the middle of your trip, there's no solution except to continue or hike back the way you came. This is a rustic trail, with no comfort stations along the way (bring toilet paper and be prepared to bury it after use).

The trail is occasionally narrow and hair-raising, so you need a cool head for heights. Make sure you have a waterproof tent with fly, sleeping bag, raingear, and clothing necessary to confront cold, rainy weather. You should wear sturdy hiking boots and bring mosquito repellent, sunblock, a hat, a gas stove (no campfires are allowed), all the food you need, water and water purification tablets, matches, a flashlight, a towel, and plastic bags. There are seven well-spaced, designated campsites along the trail, and you should camp only in them, certainly never among the ruins. At Wiñay-Wayna, 7 kilometers (4 miles) from Machu Picchu, there is a badly maintained hotel where you can rent a bed for the night.

A sine qua non companion for the trip is Peter Frost's book *Exploring Cusco,* which includes maps, detailed descriptions, and heartening comments for those long, steep hauls. The best source for other maps is at the **South American Explorers Club** (*see* Staying Safe and Healthy, *above*).

There are many other magnificent hikes around Cuzco, including ones into the **Cordillera Vilcabamba,** the last stronghold of the Incas, and the snowcapped **Cordillera Vilcanota.** Consult a travel agency in Cuzco for conducted hikes to these areas.

Whitewater Rafting The Cuzco region offers some of the best rafting in Peru, east of the highlands where the rivers rapidly drop toward the Amazon basin. Many adventure travel agencies (*see* Hiking and Backpacking, *above*) in Cuzco offer rafting trips on the Vilcanota River, which is known as the Urubamba River after it passes Huambutío.

Dining and Lodging

Cuzco has an enormous variety of restaurants fit for every taste and price range. There are excellent restaurants with international menus, especially Italian, while other eateries serve local delicacies that include *cuy* (guinea pig), often served in a hot sauce, and *chicharrón,* fried pork or chicken. Accommodations are just as varied, and bargaining is expected. Although Cuzco is cold, most hotels provide enough extra blankets, and the most expensive hotels have central heating. If you visit Cuzco during June, it's a good idea to reserve a hotel room at least a month in advance, since June brings both Corpus Christi and the Inti Raymi festivals. Prices are likely to be higher in June as well.

For details and price-range categories, *see* Dining and Lodging in Staying in Peru, *above.*

Cuzco
Dining

El Truco. Big and a bit cold-looking—and cold!—with colonial paintings and high ceilings, El Truco offers local specialties such as chicharrón and a nightly show of folk music and dancing. The restaurant is a block from the Plaza de Armas. *Plaza Regocijo 261, no phone. AE, DC, MC, V. Expensive.*

★ **La Retama.** Exposed Inca stone walls, a cartwheel chandelier, and a nightly folk music show make for a charming ambience. The local dishes as well as the international fare are outstanding; try the trout in fennel cream sauce. *Pampa del Castillo 315, tel. 084/22–5911. AE, DC, MC, V. Expensive.*

★ **Mesón de Espaderos.** You'll be drinking in history as you dine on a rustic, second-floor terrace above the Plaza de Armas. The steaks and *parilladas* (mixed grill) are the best in Cuzco; the parillada for one person is more than enough for two. *Espaderos 105, no phone. AE, DC, MC, V. Expensive.*

El Paititi. Set on the Plaza de Armas, this tourist-oriented restaurant has good fish, especially the grilled or fried trout, and local food (try the spicy *aji de gallina* [chicken], served over rice), live folk-music shows nightly, and a free pisco sour for all diners. *Portal de Carrizos 270, no phone. AE, DC, MC, V. Moderate.*

Tratorria Adriano. Solid Italian fare, relying on pasta with the traditional red and white sauces, is served at this cozy eatery with a carved wood ceiling. It's a great spot for people-watching while dining next to the big picture windows. *Mantas 105, no phone. AE, DC, MC, V. Moderate.*

Café Varayoc. Perfect for a midday snack, this café with exposed wooden beams and whitewashed walls serves good pastries and huge glass mugs of coca tea with fresh leaves floating in them. *Corner of Espaderos and Plaza Regocijos, no phone. No credit cards. Inexpensive.*

★ **Chez Maggy.** If you're cold and tired, you can warm up in front of the open brick ovens that produce the café's great pizzas and calzones. The atmosphere is casual and friendly; everyone shares two long wooden tables. *Procuradores 375, no phone. No credit cards. Inexpensive.*

El Ayllu. This café on the Plaza de Armas serves hearty breakfasts accompanied by a big glass mug of *cafe con leche* (steamed milk with coffee), and mouth-watering pastries, including a scrumptious apple strudel. *Portal de Carnes 208, Plaza de Armas, no phone. No credit cards. Inexpensive.*

Govinda. This vegetarian restaurant run by Peruvian Hare Krishnas has appropriately austere benches and Hindu decoration and background music. The breakfast of juice, yogurt, fresh fruit, and granola is especially good. *Espaderos between the Plazas de Armas and Regocijo, no phone. No credit cards. Inexpensive.*

Quinta Eulalia. Set on the patio and courtyard terrace of a somewhat decrepit mansion, this is where Cusqueños go for local cooking. *Seco de cabrito* (goat stew), pork chicharrón, and *choclo* (an ear of corn served with fresh, salty cheese) are some of the dishes of choice. *Choquechaca 384, no phone. No credit cards. Lunch only. Inexpensive.*

Lodging
★ **Hotel El Dorado.** The El Dorado has successfully avoided the whitewashed neocolonial style that makes most of Peru's hotels look alike. Rooms have vaulted brick ceilings, curving walls, alpaca-skin bedcovers, and gas lanterns remade into lamps. *Av. Sol 295, tel. 084/23–1232, fax 084/24–0993. 79 rooms. Facilities: restaurant, bar, indoor pool, sauna. AE, DC, MC, V. Very Expensive.*

Hotel Libertador. Guests are greeted with a *mate de coca* (coca tea) by the fireplace before going to their rooms, which have whitewashed walls, colonial decorations, and views of patio gardens. A welcome—and unusual—amenity is the central heating. *San Agustín 400, tel. 084/23–2601, fax 084/23–3152. 130 rooms. Facilities: restaurant, café, bar. AE, DC, MC, V. Very Expensive.*

Hotel Royal Inka II. The guest rooms at this modern hotel are clean and spacious, each with its own heater and attractive wood frame windows. *Santa Teresa 335, tel. 084/22–2284, fax 084/23–4221. 45 rooms. Facilities: restaurant, bar, sauna, hot tub. AE, DC, MC, V. Expensive.*

Hotel Savoy. Located about 10 blocks from Cuzco's colonial center, the Savoy is a large hotel with shops on the first floor and richly carved wooden appointments in the rooms. *Av. Sol 567, tel. 084/22–4322, fax 084/22–1100. 139 rooms. Facilities: restaurant, bar. AE, DC, MC, V. Expensive.*

★ **Hostal Colonial Palace.** Built inside the 17th-century Santa Teresa convent, about a block from the Casa del Marqués de Valleumbroso, this hotel has simply furnished rooms, with either French doors or picture windows, laid out around a lovely brownstone patio. Space heaters are available. *Q'era 270, tel. 084/23–2151. 45 rooms, 35 with bath. Facilities: restaurant. AE, MC, V. Moderate.*

Hotel Royal Inka I. At the older sister of the Inka II (*see above*), guests can use all the facilities at the newer hotel, one block away. The style here is colonial, with rooms centered around a flagstone patio. *Plaza Regocijo 229, tel. 084/2284. 36 rooms. AE, DC, MC, V. Moderate.*

Hostal Corihuasi. Up a long, steep cobblestone street from the Plaza de Armas, the Corihuasi occupies a ramshackle 17th-century mansion. Rooms have a rustic look, with wooden floors and sloping ceilings; some overlook the city, and others are grouped around a flower-filled courtyard. *Uriel Garcia (Suecia) 561, tel. 084/23–2233. 15 rooms. V. (June–Oct. only). Inexpensive.*

★ **Hostal Loreto.** Built in a colonial building with an attractive sunlit courtyard, this tiny hostel's glory are four rooms with an original Inca wall. *Loreto 115, tel. 084/22–6352. 9 rooms. No credit cards. Inexpensive.*

Machu Picchu
Dining and Lodging
Hotel de Turistas de Machu Picchu. The decoration of the neocolonial rooms—earth-tone carpets and bedspreads—is beside the point. The charm here is sleeping at the foot of the ruins, then waking up and seeing the sun rise over Machu Picchu; you'll have the run of the ruins when the busloads of tourists have gone. The restaurant (Expensive) makes an attempt at elegance, with candlelight and white linens, and has an international menu, with standbys such as pepper steak with a creamy black pepper sauce, and grilled chicken. You must make your hotel reservation at the Emturin office in Cuzco or through a travel agency before leaving for Machu Picchu. *No phone. Reservations: Emturin, Portal Belén 115, tel. 084/23–*

6062, 084/22–3339, or 084/23–7364, fax 084/22–3339. 32 rooms. Facilities: restaurant, bar. AE, DC, MC, V. Very Expensive.

★ **Machu Picchu Pueblo Hotel.** In this semitropical garden paradise near the town of Aguas Calientes—1½ kilometers (1 mile) from Puente Ruinas, from which you catch a bus to take you on the 30-minute zigzag climb to the ruins—cathedral ceilings, exposed beams, flagstone floors, cartwheel headboards, and fireplaces in the stone bungalows create an atmosphere of rustic elegance. The dining (Expensive) is first rate (try the *crema de choclo,* corn chowder) and the staff friendly. There is an 8% surcharge at the hotel when you pay by credit card. *Aguas Calientes. In Cuzco: Procuradores 48, tel. 084/23–2161, fax 084/22–3769; in Lima: Andalucía 174, Miraflores, tel. 014/46–7775, fax 014/45–5598. 26 rooms. Facilities: restaurant, bar. AE (accepted at hotel and in Cuzco), MC, V (accepted in Cuzco only). Very Expensive.*

Sacred Valley of the Incas
Dining and Lodging
★

Hotel Alhambra III. Located in the heart of the Sacred Valley, this 300-year-old former convent with a church and museum (with extensive pre-Inca and Inca ceramics; open to nonguests) is built around gardens and cobblestone walkways. The colonial-style guest rooms, with brick-tile floors, unstained wood ceilings and closets, and carved wood headboards have balconies overlooking the gardens or the terraced hillsides of the valley. The daily luncheon buffet (Inexpensive) is excellent, as is the restaurant (Moderate–Expensive), where *sopa a la criolla* (soup with beef, noodles, and chile), choclo, pork chicharrón, grilled chicken, and *crema volteada* (similar to flan) are some typical dishes on the menu. *Plaza Manco II, Yucay. Cuzco 084/22–4076, fax 084/23–8121. 65 rooms. Facilities: restaurant, bar, games room. AE, V. Moderate.*

Hostal Naranjachayoc. This country house 21 kilometers (13 miles) from Ollantaytambo boasts verdant gardens and comfortable rooms with slightly worn colonial-style furniture and wood floors. The fixed-price lunch includes dishes such as spicy *rocoto relleno* (stuffed chile peppers). *Via Cuzco, km 69, Urubamba, no phone. 18 rooms, 12 with bath. Facilities: restaurant, swimming pool. No credit cards. Inexpensive.*

Nightlife

Cuzco is full of bars and discos where you can listen to live folk music or recorded pop dance tunes. **El Muki** (Santa Catalina Angosta 114, no phone) is like a crowded little cave, popular with the younger crowd. A favorite gringo bar, **Kamikaze** (above the Café Varayoc, Plaza Regocijo, no phone), plays disco and has live folk music. The clientele is both local and foreign at **Qhatuchy** (Portal de Confituras 233, Plaza de Armas, no phone), which features live folk music. Several restaurants have shows featuring local folk dancing and music, among them **El Truco, La Retama,** and **El Paititi** (*see* Dining and Lodging, *above*). For a beer and a game of darts, try **Cross Keys** (Portal de Confiturías 233, Plaza de Armas, 2nd floor, no phone), a British-style pub.

Madre de Dios

The department of Madre de Dios is like nowhere else in Peru—a seemingly paradisiacal appendage that has somehow been spared many of the country's most tragic ills. Its national parks, reserves, and other undeveloped areas, among the most biologically diverse in the world—the department is said to have some 15,000 plant species, 1,000 bird species, and 200 mammal species—offer the visitor the rare opportunity to see large mammals as well as birds. Small wonder that Madre de Dios has garnered the attention of conservationists around the world. Groups such as the Nature Conservancy and Conservation International view this region as one of the world's arks, a place where the rain forest has a chance for survival.

There are two regions in Madre de Dios that are of special interest to visitors. The area around the city of Puerto Maldonado, including the Tambopata–Candamo Reserve, is easily accessible, has lodges set amid primary (unlogged) rain forest, and excellent birding. Manu National Park, more difficult to reach, provides truly unparalleled occasions for observing wildlife in one of the largest areas of virgin rain forest in the New World. Puerto Maldonado and Manu are best visited between May and October, the dry months; the lodges, however, are open all year-round. For more information about Madre de Dios and the southern Peruvian rain forest, contact the Asociación para la Conservación de la Selva Sur, the Conservation Association of the Southern Rain Forest (Att: José Palomino, Las Galerias Los Ruiseñores, Oficina 305, Plaza de Armas Cuzco, tel. and fax 084/24–0911).

Staying Healthy During the dry season, especially July, sudden cold fronts (*friajes*) bring rain and cold weather to Madre de Dios, be prepared for the worst. Temperatures can drop from 32°C (90°F) to 10°C (50°F) overnight, so bring at least one jacket or warm sweater. No matter when you travel, bring a rain jacket or poncho and perhaps rain pants, since rain may come at any time, with or without *friajes*.

Puerto Maldonado

Getting There Although there is a long, rough jungle road leading to Puerto Maldonado from Cuzco—a grueling two–three-day truck ride—for practical purposes the only way to reach the area is by plane. **Faucett, AeroPerú, Americana,** and **Aero Tumi,** have flights several times a week to **Aeropuerto Padre Aldamiz** (tel. 084/57–5133), 5 kilometers (3 miles) from Puerto Maldonado, starting in Lima and stopping in Cuzco.

What to See and Do Puerto Maldonado lies at the meeting point of the Madre de Dios and Tambopata rivers. It is a rough-and-tumble town whose main attraction is the **municipal market,** where you can buy freshly harvested *castañas* (Brazil nuts) very cheaply. (Buying them also gives local people an economic incentive to protect the rain forest, and the majestic, indigenous castaña trees.) Maldonado is a convenient jumping-off point for visiting the rain forest, which you can do in one of two ways. The safest and most comfortable way is to spend a few days in one of the area's jungle lodges (*see below*), which provide rustic but more than adequate accommodations. Packages include transportation and meals. The more adventurous traveler may choose to hire a private guide in Puerto Maldonado. Guides usually provide camping equipment and handle details like stocking up on food and hiring a boat. Two guides based in Maldonado can be recommended: Victor Yohamona (contact him at Hotel de Turistas, Av. León Velarde, tel. 084/57–1029, or at his home on Calle Cajamarca) and Orlando Carlton James (Cambridge Language Center, Calle Loreto 658, tel. 084/57–1857, or in Cuzco 084/22–6671).

Up the Tambopata River from Maldonado is the **Tambopata-Candamo Reserve**, a 3.8-million-acre "reserved zone" in which only environment-friendly activities such as ecotourism, rubber cultivation, and Brazil-nut harvesting are permitted. The area holds world records in the number of bird and butterfly species recorded by scientists, and is the site of a *colpa* (clay lick) visited daily by hundreds of parrots and macaws.

Jungle Lodges For details and price-category definitions, *see* Lodging in Staying in Peru, *above*.

Cuzco Amazónico. A 45-minute boat ride downriver from Puerto Maldonado on the Madre de Dios River, this is the most comfortable of the jungle lodges. Its private bungalows are set amid trees beside the river, each with mosquito netting, bathrooms with flush toilets and showers, and porch hammocks. Because it is relatively close to Puerto Maldonado, large mammals are rare, but visitors often see smaller ones, such as anteaters and agoutis. Opportunities for wildlife viewing include a day trip to **Lago Sandoval,** where birds abound and the occasional giant Amazon river otter may be seen (note that seeing an otter here is a very rare treat). The lodge's typical jungle dinner—fried bananas, *pacamoto* (fish or chicken cooked inside bamboo over coals), and fresh papaya for dessert—is very good. *Reservations: Andalucía 174, Miraflores, Lima, tel. 014/62–775, fax 014/45–5598; Procuradores 48, Cuzco, tel. 084/23–2161. 44 bungalows. AE, MC, V. Expensive–Very Expensive.*

Explorer's Inn. About three hours up the Tambopata River from Puerto Maldonado, it is possible to see monkeys in the surrounding forest here. In addition to four-bedroom bungalows, each room with private flush toilets and showers, it has a small library, specimen collection, and interpretive displays about the rain forest. The lodge always has foreign and Peruvian researchers on hand who also serve as guides for the nature walks. Wildlife viewing includes a night trip on the Tambopata River, with a slight chance to see small caimans (the big ones flee deeper into the forest, away from contact with humans). If you are planning to stay at the inn during the rainy season, coordinate your visit well in advance; the staff will not run boats to the inn for just one passenger. *Reservations: Peruvian Safaris, Garcilaso de la Vega 1334, Lima, tel. 014/31–6330, fax 014/32–8866; Peruvian Safaris, Plateros 329, Cuzco, tel. 084/23–6919. 30 rooms. AE, MC, V. Expensive–Very Expensive.*

Tambopata Jungle Lodge. A little farther up the Tambopata River from the Explorer's Inn (*see above*), a 3½-hour ride from Puerto Maldonado, this lodge offers a chance for observing birds, butterflies, and some mammals on two–five-night excursions that include visits to the colpa and oxbow lakes. There are four bungalows with two double rooms each, and two bungalows with two quadruple rooms each; every room has a private bathroom and mosquito netting. *Reservations: Peruvian Andean Treks, Av. Pardo 705, Cuzco, tel. 084/22–5701, fax 084/23–8911. 32 beds. AE, MC, V. Expensive.*

Tambopata Research Center. Eight hours up the Tambopata River from Puerto Maldonado, this lodge has the most pristine setting of any of the lodges in the area and thus offers the best chance to see wildlife, including monkeys and the hundreds of macaws and parrots that put on a colorful show each morning at the nearby colpa. It is, however, the most primitive of the lodges, consisting of a raised, roofed platform where guests sleep dormitory-style on mattresses, each with mosquito netting; an open dining area, and latrines and showers. The lodge houses a unique research project on macaws that allows visitors to interact with wild but hand-reared the birds. *Reservations: Rainforest Expeditions, Calle Galeón 120, Chacarilla del Estanque, San Borja, Lima, tel. 014/35–3510, fax 014/47–2497. Expensive.*

Manu National Park

Getting There To reach Manu, you must leave from Cuzco either by road or by plane. The overland trip, on a road called the Carreterra a Shintuya, takes 12 hours over rugged terrain, plunging spectacularly from the highland *páramo* down into the cloud forests at Atalaya. Here or at Shintuya, further downriver, you take a boat along the Alto Madre de Dios River deep into the rain forest and Manu National Park. A more expensive alternative is to charter a plane from Cuzco on **Aerosur** (tel. 084/22–4638) to the gravel airstrip at Boca Manu, the visitors entrance to the park. From here you must travel by river into the park. (Be sure to hire a boat with a 55-horsepower outboard motor, not the much slower *peke-peke* boat.)

What to See and Do This national park the size of the state of Massachusetts encompasses more than 4.5 million acres of pristine wilderness, ranging in altitude from 3,650 meters (almost 12,000 feet) down through cloud forest and into a seemingly endless lowland tropical rain forest at 300 meters (less than 1,000 feet). Not surprisingly, this geographical variety shelters a stunning biodiversity, and the park's untouched state has left its animal inhabitants remarkably unafraid of human beings. Most visitors see myriad bird species (there are more bird species here than in the United States and Canada combined), including macaws, toucans, roseate spoonbills, and 5-foot-tall wood storks. The park is home to 13 species of monkey, who watch visitors with more curiosity than fear. White caimans sun themselves lazily on sandy river banks while the larger black ones lurk in the *cochas*, or oxbow lakes. Visitors may catch a glimpse of giant river otters and elusive big cats such as jaguars and ocelots.

To enter the park, you need permission from the park authorities. Entry costs $25. We recommend that you travel with a reputable tour operator or guide (*see below*), who will take care of getting you the proper authorization. If you wish to travel alone, you must send a written request to the Dirección de Areas Protegidas y Fauna Silvestre, INRENA, either in Lima (Pettirojos 355, Urb. El Palomar, San Isidro, tel. 014/41–0425, fax 014/41–4606) or Cuzco (Urbanización Mariscal Gamarra 4-C, Cuzco, Apartado 1057, tel. 084/22–3633, no fax). These offices also can supply information about the park.

There is only one lodge inside the park, **Manu Lodge.** Set deep in the park on a 2-kilometer- (1-mile-) long oxbow lake called Cocha Juarez, the lodge is a rustic building with a two-story dining area. Lodge guests have access to three habitats: the cochas, the river, and a trail network spanning 10 square kilometers (4 square miles) of rain forest. The lodge also has tree-climbing equipment to lift visitors up onto canopy platforms for viewing the wildlife that lives in the treetops. **Manu Nature Tours** (Av. Sol 582, Cuzco, tel. 084/22–4384, fax 084/23–4793), which owns the lodge, offers two basic programs. One lasts eight days and takes guests into the park by land and river and out by river and charter plane. Mountain biking and whitewater rafting on the Quosñipata River, in the park's highland region, is an additional option. The second, more expensive, program lasts four days and uses charter flights to enter and leave the park.

A number of agencies conduct camping trips in the park, and the visitor may wish to combine a lodge visit with some camping. Agencies usually provide all equipment (unless you specifically request a very low-budget version of the trek) and food, but you must bring your own sleeping bag. Beware of freelance guides for hire in Cuzco and Boca Manu. Although most offer relatively cheap rates and are familiar with the area, their respect for its wildlife may be questionable. For instance, although it is forbidden to camp on beaches where birds and turtles nest, let alone raid the nests, travelers with freelance guides have returned with tales of scrambled turtle eggs for breakfast. One of the most experienced guide services, the Cuzco-based **Manu Expeditions** (Procuradores 50, tel. 084/22–6671, fax 084/23–3784) offers camping trips lasting five–nine days inside the park. Another reliable agency, **Hirca** (Bellavista 518, Miraflores, tel. and fax 014/47–5583; Pasaje Grace, Edificio San Jorge, Cuzco, tel. 084/23–8380, fax 084/23–3784) operates five- and nine-day full-service treks into Manu.

Iquitos and Environs

Getting There

By Plane The easiest, if not the only, way to reach Iquitos is by plane. Perhaps the most convenient route is from Miami, on **Faucett**'s weekly direct flight to the city. There are also daily flights from Lima to Iquitos airport (tel. 094/23–2401) on **AeroPerú, Americana, Imperial Air, Aero Continente, Aero Tumi, Expresso Aereo,** and **Faucett.** The Brazilian carrier **Cruzeiro do Sul** (*see* Chapter 5) serves Iquitos from Manaus.

What to See and Do

Iquitos lies on the Amazon River at the center of Peru's northwestern jungle, one of the most biologically diverse rain forests in the world. It is a somewhat seedy city, and serves mainly as a jumping-off point from which to reach the jungle. Iquitos enjoyed its greatest importance as a port around the turn of the century, during the rubber boom. A smaller oil boom during the 1970s gave it a modern burst of growth. Today, with a population of roughly 280,000, it is still the biggest city in the Peruvian jungle and, though mainly a local port, it is navigable for oceangoing ships coming from the Atlantic Ocean. About 50 kilometers (31 miles) from Iquitos, the jungle can more precisely be called primary rain forest, where there has been no regular logging or farming, only hunting and gathering. Sadly, even this light touch of man's hand has had an effect, and hunting has all but eliminated large animals from accessible areas around Iquitos. However, visitors are likely to see birds, all kinds of insects, the occasional monkey, the lovely little freshwater dolphins of the Amazon, and, very rarely, caimans. There are three possible ways to visit the rain forest: an inland tour with a strong ecological component; a river cruise along the Amazon River (which usually includes guided overland hikes); and a stay at a relaxing resort lodge. Rates for jungle cruises usually include meals; meals and river transportation at lodges are generally included in the lodge rates. For information about Iquitos and exploring the nearby jungle, contact the municipality's information office at the Plaza de Armas (tel. 094/23–2401; open weekdays 8–noon).

Environmental Lodges Perhaps the best tour operator in Iquitos is **Explorama Tours** (Av. de la Marina 350, Box 446, Iquitos, tel. 094/23–5471, fax 094/23–4968; in the U.S. tel. 800/223–6764), which owns four lodges and is one of the sponsors of the spectacular **Canopy Walkway** (*see below*). All arrangements for stays at the lodges, which are in the Very Expensive price category (*see* Lodging in Staying in Peru, *above*), must be made through the Explorama office in Iquitos. **Explorama Inn** is Explorama's facility closest to the city, only 40 kilometers (24 miles) away. The most resort-like of the company's properties, with palm-thatched cottages that have private bathrooms, fans, running water, and electricity, it offers guided tours around the area. **Explorama Lodge**, 80 kilometers (50 miles) and three hours' cruise down the Amazon from Iquitos in an area called Yanamono, is built jungle style. Its palm-thatched buildings have private rooms and shared toilet and shower facilities, a dining area, and a bar, but no electricity or running water. Nearby is primary rain forest with more than 2,000 plant species as well as hundreds of different species of birds and insects. The lodge conducts tours on foot and by boat. Deeper in the rain forest, the **Explornapo Camp** is 70 kilometers (43 miles) up the Napo River, 3½ hours by boat from the Yanamono area. Located in the middle of a reserve run by Explorama, this is literally a camp where you sleep on a mattress on a roofed platform. The camp conducts guided nature walks in the forest. A half hour's walk from the camp is **ACEER**, the Amazon Center for Environmental Education and Research, an educational and research post open to scientists and visitors. (You must make arrangements through Explorama Tours to stay at the center.) With basic facilities similar to those of the Explorama Lodge, ACEER features the most important attraction in the Iquitos region, the **Canopy Walkway**, the only such facility in the Americas. Imagine a suspended bridge strung between immense primeval trees. Imagine being eye to eye with tropical woodpeckers. Imagine wandering along a walkway 34 meters (110 feet) above the ground with the jungle at your feet, and you have imagined the Canopy Walkway.

Other lodges include the **Anaconda Lara Lodge** (Expensive), which is only operational when visitors make advance reservations. The lodge, located west of Iquitos up the Amazon River on the Momón River tributary, has a 2,000-acre reserve but not much primary rain forest. The operator, **Anaconda Lara** (Pevas 216–220, Iquitos, tel. 094/23–9147, fax 094/23–2978) also organizes camping expeditions to the **Pacaya–Samiria National Reserve,** located 150 kilometers (93 miles) up the Amazon from Iquitos, between the Marañon and Ucayali rivers, and camping to other places in the Amazon rain forest. **Paseos Amazónicos** (Putumayo 132, Iquitos, tel. 094/23–3110; in Lima tel. 014/46–3838, fax 014/46–7946) runs the **Sinchicuyu Lodge** (Expensive), 26 kilometers (16 miles) down the Amazon River on Sinchicuyu Creek. The lodge has little primary rain forest to boast of, but organizes butterfly- and orchid-watching expeditions.

Cruises While cruising the Amazon, you may see freshwater dolphins, wildfowl, parrots, and, very rarely, small monkeys. **Amazon Camp Tourist Services** (Requena 336, Iquitos, tel. 094/23–3931, fax 094/23–1265; in the U.S., 8700 W. Flagler St., Suite 190, Miami, FL 33174, tel. 305/227–2266 or 800/423–2791, fax 305/227–1880) deals exclusively in river cruises (Very Expensive), its boats holding 7, 10, 16, and 26 cabins. The longest and most comprehensive cruise is a six-day round-trip run on the Amazon River between Iquitos and Leticia, Colombia. Passengers depart twice weekly in comfortable river boats with private cabins, some of them air-conditioned. Rooms may be furnished with Amazon mahogany and have private or shared bathrooms. The boats stop at various points for guided nature tours. The agency also arranges shorter cruises on smaller boats that are usually group chartered. These travel upriver to Nauta, where the Ucayali and Marañon rivers join to form the Amazon, and where some of the most beautiful women in Peru are said to live. All boats have a restaurant, bar, and sun deck.

Resorts A part of the Acosta hotel chain in Iquitos, **Las Colinas de Zungarococha Lodge** is located on the Zungarococha Lake along the Nanay River, 1½ hours upriver from Iquitos and 45 minutes away by car. This comfortable resort has almost all the facilities of a city hotel, including private, motel-like rooms with bathrooms in palm-thatched bungalows, as well as a small zoo. Although the restaurant serves local specialties such as *paiche* fish and hearts of palm, the focus is on international cuisine. *Hostal Acosta, Próspero 652, Iquitos, tel. 094/23–2131, fax 094/23–2499; in Lima, Ricardo Rivera Navarrete 645–E, tel. 014/42–4515. 14 rooms. Facilities: restaurant, bar, zoo, swimming lake. AE, DC, MC, V. Expensive.*

11 Uruguay

By Parker Pascua

Freelance writer Parker Pascua was attached to the U.S. embassy in Chile in the 1970s; today, after a three-year stint at the embassy in Montevideo, she's living and looking for adventure in northen China.

The second-smallest country in South America, Uruguay might be described as a lonely city buffeted by the sea, surrounded by vast amounts of farmland and *gently* rolling hills (nothing in the country is over 2,000 feet tall). In sparsely developed Uruguay, all roads lead to the capital, Montevideo, which has the country's largest university, half the newspapers (with 90% of the circulation), half the doctors, and almost half the population. Montevideo's only cosmopolitan rival is Punta del Este, one of a handful of Atlantic Ocean resorts popular with well-heeled Brazilians and Argentines who can afford the region's high-priced variety of fun (mornings and afternoons at Gucci, evenings at heady bars and discos).

Uruguay has long been considered the most European of South American countries. Its population is almost all of European descent—largely Spanish, Portuguese, and Italian—and the influence of these cultures is readily apparent in Uruguay's architecture and outlook. Even the country's "traditional cuisine" brings to mind pasta, paella, and slabs of succulent steak.

Uruguay's original inhabitants, the seminomadic Charrúas Indians, were driven out first by the Portuguese, who settled the town of Colonia in 1680, and by the Spanish, who in 1726 established a fortress in Montevideo. In 1811, José Gervasio Artigas, captain of the Spanish forces in Uruguay, mobilized Creoles and natives to fight against the heavy-handed influence of Buenos Aires. Though Artigas's bid for Uruguayan independence was unsuccessful, Uruguay finally became an autonomous atate in 1825. On July 18, 1830—a date that gives the name to many a street in Uruguay—the country's first constitution was framed.

Following a period of civil war, José Batlle y Ordóñez was elected president in 1903. Under his guidance, Uruguay became the first Latin American country to grant voting rights to women and the first country to sever relations between church and state—a striking maneuver considering the Catholic Church's strong influence on the continent. Since then, except for a brief period from 1973 (when the military staged a coup) until 1985 (when free elections were once again held), Uruguay has been one of the strongest democracies in South America.

With the continent's highest literacy rate (94%), Uruguay rightfully takes pride in its great number of outstanding artists. Local theaters and galleries are full of works by masters such as José Belloni (1880–1965), the internationally famed sculptor; Joacquín Torres-García (1874–1949), the founder of Uruguay's Constructivist movement; and Pedro Figari (1861–1938) and Pedro Blanes Viale (1879–1926), both of whom influenced a generation of Uruguayan painters. As in Argentina, the legendary *gaucho* is Uruguay's most potent cultural fixture, and it is difficult to pass a day without some reference to these cowboys who once roamed the country singing their melancholy ballads. (Remnants of the gaucho lifestyle may still be seen on active ranches, or *estancias*, throughout the country.)

Uruguay attracts internationally known artists who perform during the Montevideo opera season or cavort in the resort city of Punta del Este during the Southern Hemisphere summer. Montevideo's lively *Carnaval*, the annual celebration that marks the beginning of Lent, attracts its fair share of cele-

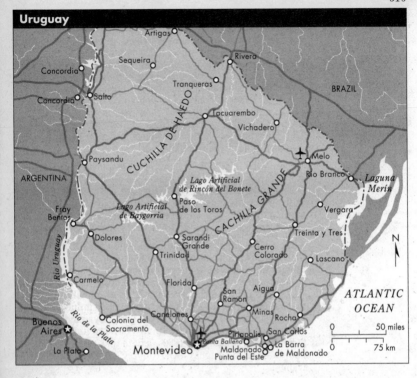

brants and performers from across the continent, though you will probably want to plan your trip around the week-long festival if large crowds, strained facilities, and high prices are not on your itinerary.

Staying Safe and Healthy
Crime Pickpockets rather than guerrillas are your biggest threat in Uruguay. Street crime has risen dramatically in recent years, particularly in Montevideo, so keep a vigilant eye on your purse or wallet. Crime at the swank Punta del Este resorts is not a serious problem.

Health Cholera is almost unheard of in Uruguay, so you can eat fresh fruit and salads with cautious abandon. You should avoid tap water, however, because many pipes are made of lead. (Bottled water is cheap and easy to come by.) Until you become accustomed to Uruguayan food and drinking water, La Tourista will likely cause problems for your digestive system.

Essential Information

Before You Go

When to Go The finest weather falls between mid-October and late-March, when the temperature is pleasantly warm, the whole country is in bloom, and prices will not yet have inflated with the annual influx of Argentines and jet-setters. However, unless you are prepared to tangle with the tsunami of tourists that overwhelms Punta del Este in January and February, late spring

(Oct.–Dec.) is the most appealing season to lounge on the beach in Punta.

Climate Uruguay's climate has four distinct but mild seasons. Summer (Jan.–Mar.) can be hot and humid, with temperatures as high as 90°F. Fall (Apr.–June) is marked by warm days and evenings cool enough for a light sweater. Winter (July–Sept.) is cold and rainy with average temperatures generally below 50°F. Although it seldom reaches the freezing point here, the wind off the water can provide a chill factor that feels like Chicago in late November. Spring (Oct.–Dec.) is much like the fall, except that the trees will be sprouting, rather than dropping, their leaves.

The following are average daily maximum and minimum temperatures for Montevideo.

Jan.	83F	28C	May	64F	18C	Sept.	63F	17C
	62	17		48	9		46	8
Feb.	82F	28C	June	59F	15C	Oct.	68F	20C
	61	16		43	6		49	10
Mar.	78F	25C	July	58F	14C	Nov.	74F	23C
	59	15		43	6		54	12
Apr.	71F	22C	Aug.	59F	15C	Dec.	79F	21C
	53	12		43	6		59	15

Festivals and Events A time of parades, dancing in the streets, and general all-hours revelry, **Carnaval** is the citywide celebration that overtakes Montevideo each year during the week that includes Ash Wednesday. **Semana de Criolla**, celebrated during the week preceding Easter Sunday at the Prado and Parque Roosevelt in Carrasco, a suburb of Montevideo, provides an excellent opportunity to observe traditional *gauchos* activities.

Currency On March 1, 1993, the Uruguayan government changed the monetary system from Pesos Nuevos (N$) to Pesos Uruguayos. The latter is officially designated UYP$, but more often you will see prices listed with a simple dollar sign ($). New bills will be issued in denominations of $1, $5, $10, $20, $50, $100, and $200 (there are no plans for coins), but it is anyone's guess when the new currency will be printed. For the moment, Peso Nuevo coins and bills are still in use and are convertible to Pesos Uruguayos by dropping the last three zeros on a given bill (N$1,000 = $1). Prices everywhere are quoted in Pesos Uruguayos even though you pay with Pesos Nuevos.

At press time (fall '93), the exchange rate was 4.12 Pesos Uruguayos to the U.S. dollar and 6.10 to the pound sterling. Both rates escalate almost daily to keep pace with Uruguay's inflation. In this chapter all prices are listed in U.S. dollars unless otherwise noted.

What It Will Cost Once one of the best bargain spots in the Southern Hemisphere, Uruguay can no longer boast about its low prices. The inflation rate rises daily; many services, especially those catering to tourists, now quote prices exclusively in U.S. dollars. Although you will need to keep some pesos for taxis and small purchases, it is best to convert dollars to pesos only as needed. You can also save a substantial amount by visiting in the low season: Prices on everything from hotels to meals can literally double during January and February, particularly in Punta del Este. Throughout the country a value-added tax (called IVA) of 12% is added to hotel and restaurant bills. Almost all other goods and services carry a 22% IVA charge.

Sample Prices Cup of coffee, 75¢; bottle of beer, $1; bottle of wine, $3.50; bus ride, should you be enough of a gambler to hazard it, 25¢; crosstown taxi ride, $3.

Customs on Arrival You may bring up to 400 cigarettes, 50 cigars or 500 grams of loose tobacco, 2 liters of alcoholic beverages, and 5 kilos of foodstuffs into Uruguay. There is no limit on the amount of currency you can bring into the country.

Language Spanish is the official language of Uruguay, though some descendants of early Italian and British settlers speak the language of their forefathers. Many Uruguayans speak at least a little English.

Getting Around

By Car Special rates or package deals are virtually nonexistent in Uru-
Car Rental guay, and rental rates are higher than in the United States because of the value-added tax (IVA). For an economy-size car, expect to pay around $45 per day, plus 22¢ per kilometer; upwards of $385 per week with unlimited mileage. In Montevideo, contact **Avis** (Rambla República de México 6333, tel. 2/608129; Carrasco Airport, tel. 2/617005); **Budget** (Calle Mercedes 935, tel. 2/916363); or **National** (Calle Cuidadela 1397, tel. 2/900035, fax 2/923516).

Gas Stations Shell, Esso, Texaco, and ANCAP (the national petroleum company) service stations throughout Uruguay are open Monday–Saturday until 9 PM or so. The ANCAP station at Carrasco Airport is open daily 6 AM–11 PM.

Breakdowns For roadside assistance, contact the **Automóvil Club Uruguayo** (Montevideo, Libertador 1532, tel. 2/911251; Punta del Este, 3 de Febrero y Roosevelt, tel. 42/20156). They will help even if you are not a member, but expect to pay $25 to enroll on the spot.

By Train Passenger train service was discontinued in 1988. Limited service between Montevideo and Cannelones is scheduled to resume by 1994, but few are placing hefty bets on it.

By Bus You can go almost anywhere in Uruguay by bus. Some buses border on the luxurious, with air-conditioning, video players, rest rooms, and snack service. Departures are frequent and fares low—Montevideo to Punta del Este, for example, costs $16 round-trip. Most bus companies are based in Montevideo and depart from its Plaza Cagancha terminal. Dependable carriers include: **COT** (Plaza Cagancha, tel. 2/963197); **ONDA** (Plaza Cagancha, tel. 2/912333); and **TTL** (Plaza Cagancha, tel. 2/915482).

By Plane All international commercial flights land at Montevideo's **Carrasco International Airport,** about 24 kilometers (15 miles) east of downtown. Uruguay's national airline, **PLUNA** (Calle Colonia 1021, Montevideo, tel. 2/980606 or 2/921414), flies daily to Uruguay from major cities throughout South America. A small airport in Punta del Este is used for commuter flights to and from Buenos Aires.

Staying in Uruguay

Telephones Public telephones are well-located, plentiful, and usually in working order. Tokens, called *fichas,* are used in place of coins and entitle you to three minutes of conversation. One peso buys two fichas, which are sold at kiosks and small stores near public phones. Most establishments will allow the use of their phone, at no charge, for local calls.

International Calls To contact an English-speaking AT&T operator directly from Uruguay, call 000410. You'll need one ficha if you are dialing from a pay phone. International calls can also be made—for a much higher price—through **ANTEL,** the national telecommunications company, which offers direct-dial services. In Montevideo there are ANTEL *telecentro* offices at Calle Fernández Crespo 1534 (9 AM–11 PM), Calle San José 1102 (24 hrs), and Calle Rincón 501 (9 AM–5 PM).

Mail Do not depend on Uruguay's postal system for anything more critical than a postcard to a friend, especially since it costs nearly $1 to send a standard-size piece of international mail. Anything sensitive should be sent via **Federal Express** (Juncal 1351, Montevideo, tel. 2/956627) or **DHL** (Zabala 1377, Montevideo, tel. 2/960217).

Opening and Closing Times **Banks.** In Montevideo, banks are open weekdays 1–4 PM. In outlying areas banks are usually open during the morning only.

Casas de Cambio. Money exchangers are open during regular business hours (9–5:30). A few are open Saturdays and Sunday mornings.

Shops. Many shops stay open throughout the day (9–6), especially in Montevideo and Punta del Este, where shops may also remain open until late in the evening. In smaller cities, it is common practice for shops to close at midday for an hour or two.

National Holidays January 1; January 6 (Three Kings' Day); March 31 (Maundy Thursday); April 1 (Good Friday); April 19 (Disembarkation of the 33 Exiles); May 1 (Labor Day); May 18 (Battle of Las Piedras); June 19 (Artigas's Birthday); July 18 (Constitution Day); August 25 (Independence Day); October 12 (Columbus Day); November 2 (All Souls' Day); December 25 (Christmas Day).

Dining Except in coastal fishing villages, beef is the staple of the Uruguayan diet. It is cheap, abundant, and often grilled in a style known as *parilla,* descended directly from the gauchos (a meal in a *parillada,* a Uruguayan steak house, is not to be missed). Beef is also made into sausage (*chorizo, salchica*), or combined with ham, cheese, and peppers to make *matambre.* Seafood can be delicious but expensive; popular among Uruguayans are *raya a la manteca negra* (ray in blackened butter), *lenguado* (flounder), *merluza* (hake), and *calamare* (squid). If you are not up to a full meal, try Uruguay's national sandwich, the *chivito,* a steak sandwich smothered with all varieties of sauces and condiments; a popular version is "a la Canadiensa," with cheese and Canadian bacon. Uruguayan wines under the Santa Rosa and Calvinor labels, a step up from table wine, are available in most restaurants.

Formal dress is rarely, if ever, required. All eateries, from the humblest to the most elegant, will bill you for the *cubierto* (cover charge), even if you have nothing more than a cup of coffee. The cubierto may be as little as 50¢ or as much as $2 or more per person.

Mealtimes Lunch is served between noon and 3; restaurants begin to fill around 12:30 and are packed by 1:30. Dinner is served late: many restaurants do not even open until 8 PM and are rarely crowded before 10 PM. Most pubs and *confiterías* (cafés) are open all day.

Precautions Tap water is claimed to be potable throughout Uruguay. However, many of the pipes are lead based, and almost everyone drinks locally bottled mineral water (*agua mineral*), which is available with or without carbonation (*con gas* or *sin gas*, respectively).

Ratings Highly recommended restaurants are indicated by a star ★.

Category	Cost* Montevideo	Punta del Este
Very Expensive	over $40	over $60
Expensive	$25–$40	$40–$60
Moderate	$10–$25	$25–$40
Inexpensive	under $10	under $25

*per person during high season for a 3-course meal, excluding alcohol, tip, cubierto (cover charge), and 12% IVA tax

Lodging Uruguay has no five-star hotels, but its resorts are generally clean, comfortable, and well equipped to deal with foreign travelers. Many quote rates that include one or two meals a day, so be sure to ask when making a reservation. Summer in Uruguay can be onerous without air conditioning, and many hotels are not yet equipped with that luxury; be sure to inquire. You can save up to 30% in the same hotel by requesting a *habitacion turística*, usually a bit plainer, smaller, and without a view, but with the same standards of cleanliness and service.

Hosterias are country inns that not only offer modest rooms, but are open for tea and dinner as well. Menus tend to be limited, though the food served is unfailingly hearty. Outside the cities hosterias are likely to be charming, but rustic. *Estancias* (ranches) offer a superb opportunity to see Uruguay as it once was. Many of these working country ranches have added horseback riding, nature tours (Uruguay is in the migration path of four major bird groups), and other delights to their overnight packages. Because of the range of activities, accommodations, and pricing, *estancia* visits are best booked through a travel agent after your arrival.

Ratings All prices are for two people in a double room based on high season rates and including breakfast and 12% IVA. Highly recommended hotels are indicated by a star ★.

Category	Montevideo	Punta del Este
Very Expensive	over $100	over $225
Expensive	$80–$100	$150–$225
Moderate	$50–$80	$90–$150
Inexpensive	under $50	under $90

Tipping In restaurants a flat 10% tip is considered adequate. For any other services, a tip of UYP$1 is the norm. For taxis, round off the fare to the next highest peso.

Montevideo

Montevideo, Uruguay's capital and only major city, has its share of glitzy shopping avenues and modern mid-rise office buildings. But few visitors come here specifically in search of big city pleasures; Buenos Aires, after all, is where Montevideans themselves go when they need a dose of urban stimulation. Montevideo, a city of 1.5 million, can be underwhelming if you let it, so turn your attention to the simpler things: walking down a quiet lane under a canopy of lavender-flowered jacaranda trees, or wandering through a warren of vendors hawking crafts and caramelized peanuts. In Montevideo, your best memories are apt to be the result of serendipity.

Legend has it that Montevideo gained its name when a Portuguese explorer first laid eyes on the 435-foot-tall El Cerro at the mouth of its harbor and uttered the words *"monte video"* (I see a hill). Built along the eastern bank of the Rio de la Plata (Plate River), Montevideo does take full advantage of its scenic locale. When the weather is good, La Rambla, a waterfront avenue that links *Ciudad Vieja* (Old City) with the eastern suburbs, is packed with fishermen, ice-cream vendors, sun worshippers, and fashionably dressed grandmothers. Around sunset, volleyball and soccer matches smooth the way for hand-in-hand strolls and music—perhaps from a street musician playing tangos on his accordion.

Tourist Information

Ministerio de Turismo (Av. Lavalleja 1409, 4th floor, tel. 2/904148), with additional offices at Carrasco Airport and Plaza Cagancha, has city maps and other basic information. **Viajes Y Turismo** (Convención 1343, 4th floor, tel. 2/925556) can arrange everything from city tours to departing flights. **Walk Over** (Plaza Independencia 811, 2nd floor, tel. 2/907620 or 2/900626) organizes city tours and excursions.

Arriving and Departing

By Plane Uruguay's principal airport, **Carrasco International Airport** (tel. 2/601272), is 24 kilometers (15 miles) east of Montevideo and regularly served by **PLUNA** (Calle Colonia 1021, Montevideo, tel. 2/980606 or 2/921414) and **United Airlines** (Calle Colonia 981, 15th floor, tel. 2/924630). Getting from the airport to your hotel is as easy as hailing a cab ($5 to downtown).

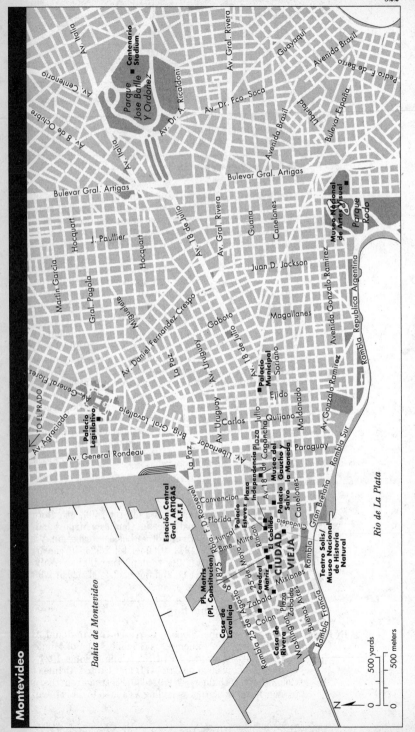

522

Montevideo

Bahía de Montevideo

Río de La Plata

Parque Jose Batlle Y Ordoñez

Centenario Stadium

Av. Ilalii
Av. Centenario
Av. 8 de Octubre
Av. Ilalii
Av. Dr. A. Ricaldoni
Av. Dr. Fco. Soca

Bulevar Gral. Artigas

Guayaquil
Av. Gral. Rivera
Avenida Brasil
Pedro F. de Berro

Bulevar Gral. Artigas

Museo Nacional de Artes Visual
Parque Rodo

Hocquart
J. Paullier
Martin Garcia
Gral. Pagola
Hocquart
Migueléte
Av. Daniel Fernandez Crespo
Av. 18 de Julio
Av. Gral. Rivera
La Paz
Av. Uruguay
Guana
Canelones
Juan D. Jackson
Gaboto
Magallanes
Av. 18 de Julio
Soriano
Ejido

Avenida Gonzalo Ramirez
Rambla Republica Argentina

Av. General Flores
TO EL PRADO
Av. Agraciada
Palacio Legislativo
Av. General Rondeau
Brig. Gral. Lavalleja
Av. Libertador
La Paz
Av. Uruguay
Carlos
Julio
18 de Cagancha
Quijano
Maldonado
Paraguay
Palacio Municipal
Av. Gonzalo Ramirez
Rambla Sur

Estación Central Gral. ARTIGAS A.F.E.
Convencion
Rbla. F. D. Roosevelt
Florida
Bme. Mitreon
Juncal
Rincón
Independencia Plaza
Av. 18
Palacio Estevez Plaza
Museo del Gaucho Y la Moneda
Palacio Salvo
Canelones
Ciudadela
Gran Bretaña

Pza. Matriz (Pl. Constitucion)
Rambla 25 de Agosto
Zabala
Colon
Casa de Lavalleja
Catedral Matriz
El Cabildo
Misiones
CIUDAD VIEJA
Buenos Aires
Rambla
Casa de Rivera Plaza
Washington Zabala
Rambla Francia

Teatro Solis/ Museo Nacional de Historic Natural

500 yards
500 meters

N

0
500 yards
0
500 meters

By Car Coming from Brazil take Route 1 west, which eventually becomes La Rambla, Montevideo's riverside thoroughfare; turn north on Calle Ciudadela to reach Plaza Independencia. Route 1 also connects Montevideo with Colonia.

By Ferry **Buquebus** (Calle Rio Negro 1400, tel. 2/601272) recently began hydrofoil service between Montevideo and Buenos Aires. Fares are reasonable (from $75 round-trip), and the trip, including boarding and customs at either end, takes roughly 3½ hours.

By Bus Most buses depart from the crowded terminal at Plaza Cagancha (a new terminal being built on Bulevar Artigas is expected to open by early 1995). From Montevideo, **CITA** (Plaza Independencia 826, tel. 2/910100) and **COIT** (Calle Paraguay 1473, tel. 2/916619 or 2/908906) offer frequent bus service to most parts of the country.

Getting Around Montevideo

If you're not on an accompanied tour, it is best to explore Montevideo on foot during daylight hours only—the Old City and especially downtown are unsavory after dark.

By Bus Montevideo's public buses crisscross the entire city during daylight hours, but they are only for the adventurous. If an overcrowded, rickety bus actually deigns to stop, board at the rear with exact change (one peso).

By Taxi All cabs have meters and the initial fare is roughly 65¢ at flag fall and 20¢ per ⅕ kilometer. You can hail taxis on the street; or, to practice your Spanish, call **Radio Taxi** (tel. 2/20391) or **TeleTaxi** (tel. 2/812416).

Orientation Tours

Walking Tours Contact **Viajes Y Turismo** (Convención 1343, 4th floor, tel. 2/925556) or **Walk Over** (Plaza Independencia 811, 2nd floor, tel. 2/907620 or 2/900626).

Bus Tours **Viajes Buemes** (Calle Colonia 979, tel. 2/921050) organizes half-day, English-language bus tours. Passengers are collected from the major hotels starting at 9 AM. On Friday and Saturday nights the "Montevideo by Night" tour includes an abbreviated city tour, dinner and a tango show at the Columbia Palace hotel, and a casino visit.

Exploring Montevideo

Modern Montevideo expanded outward from the peninsular Ciudad Vieja (Old City), which is still noted for its narrow streets and elegant colonial architecture. The El Prado district, an exclusive enclave a few miles north of the city center, also retains the look and attitude of colonial Montevideo with its lavish mansions and grand parks. Bear in mind that these magnificent mansions were once summer homes for aristocratic Uruguayans who spent most of the year elsewhere, and you have some idea of the wealth this small country once enjoyed.

Ciudad Vieja **Plaza Independencia** marks the eastern border of the Old City and is where modern mid-rises begin to outnumber the city's colonial and republican artifacts. Portions of the plaza were once occupied by the *Cuidadela* (Citadel), a military fortification built originally by the Spanish but deemed militarily useless and destroyed in 1833. In the center of the square stands a 30-ton statue of General Gervasio Artigas, the "father" of Uruguay and the founder of its 19th-century independence movement. At the base of the monument, two flights of polished granite stairs lead to the tomb where Artigas' remains are interred; a spotlight at night ensures that the general's urn is never in the dark.

When it was built in 1927, the 26-story **Palacio Salvo,** on the east side of Plaza Independencia, was the tallest building in South America; today this commercial office block is still the tallest building in Montevideo. The **Palacio Estevez** on the south side of the plaza was acquired by the government in 1878 and used by the president on occasion for ceremonial purposes.

The **Teatro Solís,** a short walk west, was completed in 1856 and named in honor of the discoverer of the Rio de la Plata, Juan B. Solis. Famed for its acoustics, it is still the most important theater in Montevideo and the site of numerous national and international cultural events. Sharing the building is the **Museo Nacional de Historia Natural** (National Museum of Natural History), with rotating history exhibits in addition to a few antiques and republican-era paintings. *Calle Buenos Aires 652, tel. 2/960908. Admission free. Call for hours.*

A few blocks west in the center of the Old City is **Plaza Matriz** (officially Plaza Constitución, but nobody calls it that). The cantilevered fountain in the center of the square was installed in 1871 to commemorate the inauguration of the city's water system. Facing the plaza is the modest **El Cabildo,** the old city hall where the Uruguayan constitution was signed in 1830. This two-story colonial edifice now houses an impressive collection of paintings, antique furnishings, and costumes, plus rotating history exhibits. English-speaking guides are available. *Av. Juan Carlos Gómez at Calle Sarandí, tel. 2/982826. Admission free. Closed Mon.*

On the opposite side of the square sits the oldest public building in Montevideo, **Catedral Matriz,** its distinctive pair of dome-capped bell towers guarding the plaza like sentinels. Except for small touches in its stained glass and domed sanctuary, the cathedral is most notable as the final resting place of Uruguay's most important political and military figures. *Calle Sarandí at Calle Ituzaingó. Admission free.*

Calle Rincón marks the commercial and financial heart of the old city; banks with names both familiar and obscure are cheek by jowl with art galleries and antiques dealers. At the corner of Calles Rincón and Misiones looms the **Casa de Rivera,** once the home of General Fructuso Rivera, Uruguay's first president. Acquired by the government in 1942, it currently houses a branch of the National History Museum. Exhibits inside document the development of Uruguay from the colonial period through the 1930s. *Calle Rincón, tel. 2/951051. Admission free. Call ahead for hours.*

Casa de Lavalleja was built during the early 18th century and later became the home of General Juan A. Lavalleja, who distinguished himself in Uruguay's war for independence from Brazil (1825–28). Donated to the state in 1940 and incorporated into the National History Museum system, this pristine colonial home now displays period manuscripts and historical memorabilia. *Calle Zabala 1469, no phone. Admission free. Closed Mon.*

The **Palacio Taranco,** built in 1908 atop the rubble of Uruguay's first theater, is representative of the French-inspired architectural styles favored in turn-of-the-century Montevideo. Today it has been converted into a cultural center filled with period furniture, statuary, draperies, clocks, and portrait paintings. *Calle 25 de Mayo 376, tel. tk/911101. Admission free. Call for hours.*

El Prado The El Prado district lies roughly 6 kilometers (4 miles) north of Plaza Independencia and the Old City; you could make the very long uphill walk along **Avenida Agraciada**—a busy commercial street loaded with every sort of shop—but most prefer to take a taxi straight to the diminutive **Sagrada Familia** (Sacred Family) chapel. Too tiny to need flying buttresses, this ornate gothic gem is complete in all other respects; a troop of gargoyles peers down at you, and the finely wrought stained glass windows become radiant when backlit by the sun. Like many churches in secular Uruguay, Sagrada Familia is open only on Saturday afternoons and Sunday mornings; the grounds, however, are always open. *Calle Luis Alberto de Herrera 4246, tel. 2/236824. Admission free.*

Calle Luis Alberto de Herrera cuts to the heart of the district, past numerous 18th- and 19th-century mansions. In many instances, estate grounds have been sold off and used for the later—and frankly bland—constructions that now occupy portions of this stretch. Breaking the tedium is the **Museo de Bellas Artes** (Museum of Fine Arts, known locally as the Blanes Museum), housed in an elegant colonial mansion that once belonged to Uruguay's foremost 19th-century painter, Juan Manuel Blanes. Although he was entirely self-taught and did not begin painting until he was in his 50s, his realistic portrayals of gauchos and the Uruguayan countryside compose the core of the museum's otherwise bland collection. *Av. Millán 4014, tel. 2/362248. Admission charged. Closed Mon.*

Enter the vast **Parque El Prado,** the district's namesake, at Rambla Costanera and work your way toward Avenida Buschantal. This street meanders past the park's famous rose garden and into a neighborhood of imposing colonial mansions. Near the intersection of Calle Ruiz and Avenida 19 de Abril, look for some of El Prado's most splendid colonial homes; many have been immaculately restored, and several house private international foundations. Avenida 19 de Abril eventually leads to Avenida Agraciada and the **Palacio Suarez** (Av. Agraciada 3423), the president of Uruguay's official residence. The magnificent complex is closed to the public but can still be appreciated from the street.

Avenida 18 de Julio Montevideo's main street has a little bit of everything—shops and museums, cafés and plazas, bustling markets and chrome-and-steel financial towers. Housed in a lush 19th-century rococo mansion near Calle Julio Herrera y Obes, the **Museo del Gaucho y la Moneda** (Gaucho and Coin Museum) displays ancient South American and European coins on the first floor and, on other floors, paraphernalia associated with Uruguay's "cowboys," the gauchos. From traditional gaucho garb to the detailed silverwork on the cups used for *maté* (an indigenous herb from which tea is brewed), this is one of the city's best museums. English tours are available with two-day advance notice. *Av. 18 de Julio 998, tel. 2/908764. Admission free. Closed Mon.*

In its basement, the **Palacio Municipal** (City Hall) houses the **Biblioteca de Historia del Arte** (Library of Art History) and the **Museo de Historia del Arte** (Museum of Art History). Bypass the library's large academic holding and spend some time browsing the museum's small collection of pre-Columbian and colonial artifacts. At the Calle Soriano entrance you can take an elevator to the building's 26th-floor observation deck for a panoramic view of the city. *Calle Ejido 1326, tel. 2/989252, ext. 500. Admission free. Closed Sat. and Sun.*

Other Attractions Almost 50 different types of native marble were used in the construction of the **Palacio Legislativo** (Legislative Palace), the seat of Uruguay's bicameral legislature. Free Spanish-language tours are available when the congress is in session; passes are available inside at the information desk. *Av. Agraciada at Av. Flores, tel. 2/201324. Admission free. Closed weekends.*

Parque Rodo has a little something for everyone—two amusement parks, a number of decent eateries, and the **Museo Nacional de Artes Visuales** (National Museum of Visual Arts), which recently hosted exhibits from as far afield as China and Poland. Between December 5 and January 6, Parque Rodo is also the site of Montevideo's best *feria artensal* (crafts fair). *Av. T. Girabaldi, tel. 2/716124. Admission free. Closed Mon.*

Shopping

There is only one major shopping mall in Montevideo, appropriately called the **Shopping Center** even by locals ("el Shopping" in vernacular). Two others are due to be completed by the end of 1993: the Portales de Carrasco (Avs. Bolivia and Italia), in the suburb of Carrasco; and the Punta Carretas Shopping Center (Calles Ellauri and Solano). The latter should be especially interesting since it will be housed in a former prison. Weekend *ferias* (open-air markets) are probably the best forum for leisurely browsing among a warren of crafts stalls. In Montevideo shops are generally open weekdays 9–6 and Saturday 9–noon.

Specialty Stores Calle Tristan Narvaja north of Avenida 18 de Julio is packed
Antiques with antiques dealers; try **El Rincón** (Calle Tristan Narvaja 1747, tel. 2/402283). In the Old City, Calle Bartolome Mitre and Calle Rincón are also lined with antiques stores.

Gemstones and **Cabildo Piedras** (Calle Sarandí 610) specializes in amethyst and
Jewelry topaz jewelry, agate slices, and elaborate key rings. **La Limeña** (Calle Sarandí 556) has good prices on unset stones.

Handicrafts **Manos de Uruguay** (Calle Reconquista 602) has a wide selection of woolen wear and locally produced ceramics. **Ema Camuso** (Av. 8 de Octubre 2574) offers a sophisticated line of handknit sweaters popular with style-conscious Montevideans. The **Louvre** (Calle Sarandí 652), an antiques store, is the only source for handmade and painted trinket boxes—the perfect *recuerdos* (souvenir).

Leather Shops near Plaza Independencia specialize in hand tailored nutria coats and jackets; the **Montevideo Leather Factory** (Plaza Independencia 832, 2nd floor) has a particularly good selection. Also try **Piel Afrikana** (Calle San Jose 901) or **Casa Mario** (Calle Piedras 641). Custom-made boots are available from **Damino Botas** (Calle Rivera 2747).

Ferias *Ferias* (open-air markets) are a way of life in Montevideo. Government regulations dictate that all ferias must close in the early afternoon, so plan to begin your visit around 10 AM. **Feria Tristan Narvaja** was started more than 50 years ago by Italian immigrants and nowadays is Montevideo's premier Sunday attraction. It not only spreads across both sides and down the middle of Calle Tristan Narvaja but also over most cross-streets. The Saturday morning feria at **Plaza Biarritz** in Pocitos, a nearby suburb, features foodstuffs, *artesania* (crafts), clothing, and some antiques. At **Plaza Cagancha,** between Avenida 18 de Julio and Calle Rondeau, there is a daily crafts market—a good place to find offbeat souvenirs.

Dining

Even the toniest restaurant in Montevideo is brightly lighted; you may dine by candlelight while all the house lights blaze full bore. Unfortunately, the food may or may not provide a distraction from the blinding light: menus do not vary all that much in Montevideo. For a light meal try one of the city's ubiquitous *parilladas,* informal and often family-operated steak houses. For price ranges, *see* Dining in Staying in Uruguay, *above.*

Very Expensive **Bungalo Suizo.** This small restaurant makes you feel like you are dining at the informal but refined home of a good friend. The split-level dining area is subdued and intimate, with private tables tucked into quiet corners. Fondue is the specialty of the house, supplemented by various cuts of beef. *Calle Sol 150, tel. 2/611073. Reservations recommended. MC, V. Dinner only, closed Sun.*

Doña Flor. Housed in a renovated turn-of-the-century home in Punta Carretas, a nearby suburb of Montevideo (take a cab for less than $5), this quiet, elegant restaurant offers a diverse menu heavily indebted to the French (the pâté is rich as butter and twice as smooth). The house specialty is green lasagna with salmon. *Bulevar Artigas 1034, tel. 2/785751. Reservations required for lunch. AE, D, MC, V. Closed Sun. and Mon., Christmas–Easter.*

★ **L'Hippocampe.** This casually sophisticated, art-deco restaurant, overlooking the river from the Rambla, has quickly established a reputation for excellent food and service. Any of the fresh fish dishes is a sure winner, as is the pork in plum sauce. It is also impossible not to be tempted by the decadent dessert table. *Rambla O'Higgins 5303, tel. 2/97767. Reservations recommended. MC, V. Closed Sun.*

Expensive **Meson Viejo Sancho.** What draws the posttheater crowds to this friendly but essentially nondescript downtown restaurant are gargantuan portions of smoked pork chops and *papas suiza* (fried potatoes). *Calle San José 1229, tel. 2/904063. Reservations recommended. No credit cards. Closed Sun.*

Shang Hai. Popular with Montevideo's growing Asian community, this informal Chinese restaurant is an unexpected find close to the business district. Recommended are the kung pao dishes and steamed dumplings. Uruguayans appear allergic to spicy foods; just say *"bien picante"* for extra oomph. *Calle San José 1216, tel. 2/793799. AE, MC, V.*

Moderate **El Buzon.** This unassuming restaurant-cum-bar serves excellent pastas and *parilla* (grilled beef). For dessert try the Massini—whipped cream sandwiched between extra-thin slices of caramelized sponge cake. *Calle Hocquard 1801, tel. 2/297643. MC, V. Closed Sun. dinner.*

★ **Seaport.** Mildly rowdy but always fun, the Seaport is popular with an eclectic mix of college students and diplomats. The food—almost all of which comes fresh from the ocean—is superb, particularly the *calamares a la Romana* (breaded squid); and the portions are enough for two. *Calle Berro 1088, tel. 2/793799. Reservations advised on weekends. MC, V. Dinner only, closed Christmas–Easter.*

Inexpensive **La Pasiva.** This popular *chopperia* (beerhouse) has three locations in the Old City. None of them accept credit cards, but all stay open late and serve ice-cold beer and uncomplicated bar food; try the *chivitos* (sandwiches). *Calle Sarandí at Calle J.C. Gomez; Calle Rinconada de Plaza Independencia; Av. 18 de Julio at Calle Ejido. No credit cards.*

Rio Alegre. Carmen, the proprietor of this intimate but lively restaurant, will stuff you full of homemade *chorizo* (sausage) and grilled provolone sprinkled with oregano. For a main course, *asado de tira* (short ribs) or *filete a la pimienta* (pepper steak) are good choices. *Puerto del Mercado, locale 033, tel. 2/956504. No credit cards. Closed Sun.*

Lodging

Many downtown hotels are grouped around Plaza Bolívar and Plaza Libertad. In the weeks before and after Carnaval in February, hotel rooms become scarce; be sure to book well in advance and be prepared to pay handsomely for even low-end rooms. For price ranges, *see* Lodging in Staying in Uruguay, *above.*

Very Expensive **Hosteria del Lago.** Set among 10,000 square meters of parkland ★ in Carrasco, 12 kilometers (7 miles) from downtown, this white stucco, Spanish colonial hotel offers a relaxed atmosphere, private lakefront beach, and a friendly multilingual staff. The suite-size rooms are split level and fully carpeted; all have views of the lake. *Av. Arizona 9635, tel. 2/612210. 70 rooms. Facilities: restaurant, airport transportation, 24-hr room service, outdoor pool, tennis court, horseback riding, children's playground. AE, D, MC, V.*

Victoria Plaza. Although the venerable grande dame of Montevideo is undergoing major renovations (due for completion in late 1994), parts of the hotel remain open for business, with noise and dust barely evident. The Vic Plaza's new wing will be a luxurious glass and brick contemporary, and it's slated to be Uruguay's only internationally recognized five-star hotel. The "old" Vic is as comfortable as ever and still dominates the rococo kitsch of Plaza Independencia. *Plaza Independencia 759, tel. 2/920237, fax 2/921628. 642 rooms. Facilities: 2 restaurants, coffee shop, bar, 24-hr room service, airport transportation, pool, solarium, squash courts, health club, parking. AE, D, MC, V.*

Expensive **Balmoral.** Despite ongoing renovations, the lobby and accommodations are a pleasant surprise—contemporary, bright, large, and quiet (double-paned windows nearly eliminate city noise). A gracious multilingual staff and convenient downtown location make the Balmoral a favorite with business travelers. *Plaza Libertad 1126, tel. 2/922393, fax 2/922288. 75 rooms. Facilities: restaurant, 2 bars, 24-hr room service, sauna. AE, D, MC, V.*

Moderate **Ermitage.** This unprepossessing, sandstone-fronted building
★ overlooks Plaza Tomas Gomensoro and the beach. The Ermitage has developed a loyal core of long-term residential guests, giving it a pleasant homey feeling; patrons visit over a drink or sit and play cards in the huge wood-paneled lobby. Rooms are furnished with 1920s furniture and light fixtures, reminiscent of kinder and gentler times. *Calle Juan Benito Blanco 783, tel. 2/704021 or 2/717447, fax 2/704312. 90 rooms. Facilities: restaurant. AE, D, MC, V.*

Oxford. Glass walls, broad windows, and mirrors that date from a recent renovation give the small lobby an open but intimate feel, much like the hotel itself. The rooms are immaculately clean, the staff friendly and heroically helpful. Despite its downtown location, street noise is not a problem. *Calle Paraguay 1286, tel. 2/920046, fax 2/923792. 66 rooms. Facilities: bar. AE, D, MC, V.*

Inexpensive **Lancaster.** Hidden away in a corner of Plaza Cagancha, near the bus terminal, the Lancaster might be past its glory days, but no one has told either the staff or loyal patrons. The rooms are sunny and large, with full-length French doors that open over the plaza. *Plaza Cagancha 1334, tel. 2/920029 or 2/921054, fax 2/981117. 78 rooms. Facilities: cafeteria, bar. AE, D, MC, V.*

El Palacio. El Palacio is a no-frills sort of place, yet it is also comfortable and extremely well located. The rooms are all furnished with antiques, and each has its own balcony overlooking the Old City. *Calle Bartolome Mitre 1364, tel. 2/963612. 14 rooms. No credit cards.*

The Arts and Nightlife

Montevideo has all kinds of nightlife if you know where to find it. There are quiet late-night bars as well as hip-hopping discos and folk music shows, plus a thriving theater scene. The entertainment and cultural pages of local papers are the best sources of information; particularly useful is the *Guía del Ocio*, a magazine inserted into the Friday edition of *El Pais*.

The Arts Both **Teatro Solis** (Calle Buenos Aires 678, tel. 2/959770) and **S.O.D.R.E.,** the Servicio Oficial de Difusió Radio Elétrica (Av. 18 de Julio 930, tel. 2/912850) host symphonies, ballet, and opera between May and November. A number of binational centers such as the **Alliance Française** (Calle Soriano 1176, tel. 2/908084), the **Instituto Goethe** (Goethe Institute, Calle Canellones 1524, tel. 2/493499), and the U.S.-sponsored **Alianza Artigas-Washington** (Calle Paraguay 1217, tel. 2/902721) host plays and concerts by foreign talent.

Nightlife With few exceptions bars and clubs come to life around 1 AM and do not close until it is time for breakfast. Although you need reservations for most tango shows, they are not blatantly geared for tourists.

Discos Popular with the MTV generation are **Zum Zum** (Rambla Aremnia 1647) and **New York** (Calle Mar Artico 1227). You can dance to live Top-40 music at **Clave de Fu** (Av. 26 Marzo 1125). The retro set flocks to **Aguellos Años** (Calle Beyrouth 1405), which features music from the '50s and '60s.

Tango Shows The weekend shows at **La Vieja Cumparista** (Calle Carlos Gardel 1181, tel. 2/916245) feature a tango and *candombe*—dance and music associated with Carnaval. **Tanguieria del 40** (Hotel Columbia, Rambla República de Francia 473, tel. 2/955451) has dinner tango shows Monday–Saturday.

Pubs **Flanagan's** (Calle Cavia 3082) is popular with young Montevidean professionals. **Riff Gallery Pub** (Bulevar España 2511) is the only bar in the city devoted to jazz, with live shows on Thursday and Saturday.

Excursions from Montevideo

Colonia del Sacramento Originally a Portuguese settlement founded during the 17th century, Colonia del Sacramento is the small but lovely *barrio historico* (historic district) of greater Colonia. The city's tourist office (Av. General Flores 499) stocks maps, but everything here is within walking distance. Start at the municipal museum, housed in the two-story **Casa de Brown** (Calle San Francisco), with a collection of colonial artifacts and documents. The city's oldest church, **La Vieja Iglesia** (Calle 18 de Julio), dates from 1680. The impressive **Callejon de Susperos** (Street of Sighs) is lined with single-story colonial homes over which the bougainvillea grows with abandon.

Getting There Colonia is 242 kilometers (150 miles) west of Montevideo and serviced daily by bus from Montevideo; contact COT or ONDA. The three-hour ride costs less than $15. Full-day tours with an English-speaking guide are offered by **J.P. Santos Travel Agency** (Calle Colonia 951, Montevideo, tel. 2/920397).

Piriápolis **Piriápolis** was first established as a private residence by an Argentine developer more than a century ago; nowadays it is a laid-back beachfront enclave that lacks the sophistication—and the extortionate prices—of nearby Punta del Este. Piriápolis has plenty of stores and restaurants, a casino, and the grand Hotel Argentino, built in the old European tradition with spas and thermal pools (and an ice-skating rink!). **Punta Fría** and **Playa Grande** are the town's best beaches, with white sand and large summertime crowds. The tourist office (Rambla de los Argentinos 1348) can provide you with hotel listings and maps.

Getting There COT and ONDA together travel five times daily between Montevideo and Piriápolis, with ongoing service to Punta del Este. The trip takes about 1½ hours and costs $8.

Punta del Este

Despite being a mere two hours down the pike from Montevideo, Uruguay's highly touted Punta del Este is definitely a world apart. Punta del Este (shortened to "Punta" by locals) and the handful of surrounding beachfront communities are famous as jet-set resorts and sites of countless international festivals and conferences—the sort of places where lounging on white sand and browsing designer boutiques constitute the day's most demanding actitivities.

Punta is not for everyone: The resort's colonial architecture has been largely replaced with highrise hotels and apartments, and those striking mansions you see hidden among tall pines on the beach house well-to-do Argentines, Brazilians, and Europeans, not museums. Still, Punta is justly revered for its long stretches of white sand beach and elegant shopping avenues. For thousands of younger South Americans it is also *the* place (excluding Rio, of course) to let your hair down and watch the sunrise from the balcony of an all-night disco.

Punta is underwhelming in the low season—the buildings are shuttered against the elements, their tenants gone elsewhere. On January 1 the city comes alive, lured out of dormancy by the smell of tourist dollars. Plan on a visit in either December or March (except during Holy Week, when prices skyrocket). During these two months the weather is superb, with an average daily temperature of 75°F, and the beaches are not unbearably crowded.

Tourist Information

Liga de Fomento (two locations: Rambla Artigas and Calle Angostura, tel. 42/44069; Parque Artigas, tel. 42/40514). Travel agencies on Calle Gorlero can assist with hotel bookings, onward travel plans, and excursions.

Getting There

Consider a package tour from Montevideo regardless of the length of your stay. There is much to see and do in nearby Punta Ballena and La Barra, and travel plans will be more difficult, not to mention costly, to arrange once you're in Punta. In Montevideo contact **Viajes y Turismo** (Convención 1343, 4th floor, tel. 2/925556).

By Plane There is no air service between Montevideo and Punta. However, **PLUNA** (tel. 42/41840) and **Aerolineas Argentinas** (tel. 42/43802) fly regularly between Buenos Aires and the **Aeropuerto de Punta del Este** (Camino El Jaquel, tel. 42/81808), on the northern edge of the city. The flight takes 30 minutes and costs about $60 each way.

By Bus The following companies offer daily service between Montevideo and Punta del Este's **Terminal Playa Brava** (Rambla Artigas and Calle Inzaurraga): **Buquebus** (tel. 42/84995), **COT** (tel. 42/83557), and **ONDA** (tel. 42/86801).

By Car From Montevideo follow Interbalnearia (Rte. 1) east to the Route 93 turnoff. The road is well maintained and marked.

Exploring Punta del Este

Punta del Este, which also lends its name to the broader region encompassing Punta Ballena and La Barra de Maldonado, has long been a favorite spot for sunseekers escaping the Northern Hemisphere winter. In Punta proper—the peninsular resort bounded by Playa Mansa (Mansa Beach) and Playa Brava (Brava Beach)—beach bumming is the prime activity. In fact, if you are not into eating, drinking, and worshipping the sun, about the only other attractions are the gypsies hustling tourists on Calle Gorlero, and the artisans' *feria* (market) at Plaza Artigas. This colorful crafts market is held at the intersection of El Ramanso and El Corral and is open weekends 5 PM–midnight; between Christmas and Holy Week, it's open daily 6 PM–1 AM.

Punta is circumnavigated by **Rambla Artigas,** the main coastal road that leads past residential neighborhoods and pristine stretches of beach. **Calle Gorlero,** Punta's main commercial strip, runs north–south through the heart of the peninsula and is fronted with cafés, restaurants, and elegant shopping boutiques bearing names such as Yves St. Laurent and Gucci.

La Barra de Moldonado, a small resort less than 5 kilometers (3 miles) from Punta, has the area's best beaches. Gaily painted buildings give La Barra a carnival-like atmosphere, and you'll find a handful of antiques dealers, surf shops, and pubs that are worth an afternoon's diversion. Once you move off Calle No. 7 (also called Del Encuentro), La Barra's principal thoroughfare, there's nothing notable except the ocean. From Punta you can walk along the beach and cross over to La Barra on a cement camelback bridge.

Punta Ballena, 10 kilometers (6 miles) west of Punta, is built on a bluff overlooking the ocean and is almost impossible to see from the main road—no cause for complaint for the resort's wealthy patrons. The main draw here is **Casa Ballena,** an exclusive artists' community perched at the tip of a rocky point with tremendous views of the Atlantic. Casa Ballena is a showpiece that fits no known architectural definition: Entirely of white stucco and adorned with strange projections and even stranger appurtenances, it can best be described as Dali meets Disney. Inside is an art gallery with a warren of rooms showcasing Picasso-derivative art, a restaurant, and an aloof hotel.

Inland, the **Arboretum Lussich** is a huge parkland that perfumes the air with the scent of eucalyptus. Farther up the same road is the **Country Cook,** an expanding American-owned shopping and amusement center with an "Old West" theme. The small main street, complete with raised wooden sidewalks, is lined with shops selling dried flowers and homemade bread and jams. There is also an excellent Americana restaurant that Marshall Dillon would have felt right at home in (*see* Dining and Lodging, *below*). *Camino Lussich and La Pataia, tel. 42/22973. Open Christmas–1st week in Mar., daily 1 PM–3 AM.*

Sports and the Outdoors

Equipment rental, especially for water sports, is not an idea whose time has come in Punta del Este, even in spite of the many surf shops that have sprung up over the last few years. Also note that anything other than a beach in Punta del Este is accessible to members only; leave your golf clubs and tennis racquets at home.

Golf Two golf clubs are ostensibly open one day per week to nonmembers. Greens fees average $50 for 18 holes. Contact Punta's **Club de Golf** (tel. 42/82127) or Punta Ballena's **Club de Lago** (tel. 42/78423).

Horseback Riding Mosey over to **Country Cook** (*see above*), the Old West–themed park on the distant outskirts of Punta, for an afternoon of trail riding.

Dining and Lodging

Restaurants come and go with seasonal regularity in Punta del Este. The better restaurants reopen from year to year, often transferring their operations to Montevideo during the low season and returning to Punta around Christmastime. Year-round options—none of them spectacular—are generally located along Punta's Calle Gorlero; they tend to be moderately priced and serve meat rather than seafood. For price ranges, *see* Dining in Essential Information, *above*.

There are more hotels in and around Punta del Este than you can possibly imagine, running the architectural gamut from wonderfully modern to bland ho-hum. Except during the high season many rooms are empty and often stay that way for months at a time; but during January and February, Punta teems with sunbathers and pleasure seekers, and rooms are extremely difficult to come by, so book well in advance. For price ranges, *see* Lodging in Staying in Uruguay, *above*.

Maldonado
Lodging
★

La Posta del Cangrejo. From its stylish lobby to its relaxed lounge and restaurant, this hotel takes an informal approach to luxury. The Mediterranean styling—red tile floors and white stucco walls—complements the impeccably decorated guest rooms; each is furnished with hand-stenciled antiques and canopied beds and has views of either the beach or the small country garden. The staff is warm, accommodating, and inordinately fond of their hotel. The adjoining seafood restaurant is equally outstanding. *La Barra de Maldonado, tel. 42/70021 or 42/70271, fax 42/70173. 29 rooms. Facilities: restaurant, bar, pool. AE, D, MC, V. Very Expensive.*

Punta del Este
Dining
★

La Bourgogne. A shaded terra-cotta terrace gives way to an arch-windowed breezeway, while the intimate reception area opens onto a large split-level dining room where antique sideboards serve as "stations." The food, served by impeccably clad waiters who go about their business with cordial authority, is prepared with only the finest and freshest of ingredients; the breads are baked on the premises (an adjoining bakery sells them by the loaf) and the herbs and berries are grown in the backyard garden. Start your meal with the gourmet salad, then try the plaice with pink peppercorns. All of the desserts are sublime, and the sampler is a good way to try them all. *Av. del Mar and Calle P. Sierra, tel. 42/82007. Reservations required. No credit cards. Open Christmas–Holy Week. Very Expensive.*

Blue Cheese. This restaurant on the Rambla is appropriately painted blue and white and set well back from the road, allowing a great deal of outdoor seating. Since it has the best selection of salads in town, you don't notice the rather ordinary decor. *Rambla de Circumvalación (at Calle 23), tel. 42/40354. Reservations advised. No credit cards. Expensive.*

Yacht Club Uruguayo. Long a favorite with locals, this small and unassuming eatery has a great view of the Isla de Lobos across the water. The menu includes a little bit of everything, but the specialty of the house is seafood; perennial favorites are *brotola a la Roquefort* (baked hake) and *pulpo Provençal,* likely the most tender octopus you have ever eaten. *Rambla*

Artigas (between Calles 6 and 8), tel. 42/41056. No reservations accepted. AE, D, MC, V. Moderate.

Restaurante Ciclista. This no-frills restaurant serves perhaps the best inexpensive meals in Punta. The *tortilla de papas* (potato pancake) is extremely hearty, as are the pastas. The homemade soups are another popular lure. *Calle 20 (at Calle 27), tel. 42/40007. AE, D, MC, V. Inexpensive.*

Lodging **L'Auberge.** The L'Auberge's small lobby is full to bursting with antiques and cozy sofas, and there's an 18th-century crenellated water tower rising out of its double-winged chalet. Guest quarters are not quite as elegant as the lobby leads you to expect, although some have working fireplaces. *Barrio Parque del Golf, tel. 42/82601, fax 42/83408. 30 rooms. Facilities: restaurant, bar. AE, D, MC, V. Very Expensive.*

★ **Palace Hotel.** The Palace occupies a central position on the Gorlero shopping avenue inside one of Punta's oldest structures—a three-story Spanish colonial masterpiece complete with an airy interior courtyard. The restaurant boasts one of the largest wine cellars in the country. *Calle Gorlero (at Calle 11), tel. 42/41919 or 42/41418, fax 42/44695. 44 rooms. Facilities: restaurant, bar. AE, D, MC, V. Moderate.*

Hotel Salzberg. This charming hotel is so new you can almost smell the plaster. A white stucco, three-story chalet, it was built with polished slate floors and exposed beams. Its rooms are blessed with ceiling fans, modern bathrooms, and fine views framed by flower-filled window boxes. *Calle Pedragosa Sierra and El Havre, tel. 42/88851. 14 rooms. Facilities: cafeteria, bar. No credit cards. Inexpensive.*

The Arts and Nightlife

The very name Punta del Este is synonymous with high-paced evenings in bars and nightclubs that start as late as 1 AM and only reach a fever pitch around sunrise. Nine out of 10 are open during the high season only, and nearly the same proportion have a cover charge—sometimes as much as $30 per person.

Discos Hop in a cab and head for **Las Grutas** (Rambla Artigas), near Puenta Ballena. This disco cannot be seen from the road, but the cabbie knows the route across the dunes to the entrance. The club itself is inside a grotto and has a clear acrylic floor under which the tide rolls in and out. In La Barra, **Space** occupies an enormous warehouse bursting with five different bars. It does not have an address, but your cabbie will undoubtedly know where to go.

12 Venezuela

By George Soules

George Soules, a long-time resident of Caracas, is the managing editor of Business Venezuela. Before relocating to Venezuela, he was a freelance writer for the Washington Post and the Washington Times.

Venezuela's lure has always been its rich array of natural wonders: sparkling beaches, broad sweeping plains, tropical rain forests, plus the world's tallest waterfall. And with 39 national parks covering more than 15% of the country's landmass, it's not difficult to find your way into the Venezuelan outback, far off the beaten track. Venezuela's second-largest reserve, Canaima, is bigger than Belgium and encompasses hundreds of square miles of unexplored, pristine jungle. In the Llanos, a vast grassy plain in southwestern Venezuela that's home to millions of birds and animals, the landscape is impeccably wild, inspirational, and anything but trammelled.

In Caracas, the stylish, very cosmopolitan, always ebullient capital, things are a bit different. Taxis cut corners as if there were no mañana. At a sidewalk *arepera*, where Caraqueños gather for thick black coffee and the latest gossip, the Portuguese proprietor serves Italian espresso to Argentinean businessmen and visiting French students. The red-tile roofs of colonial Caracas have all but disappeared in the march of apartment blocks and office towers. But modern Caracas still dazzles with its shopping avenues and neon-lit discos. In this bustling city of 4 million, the pulse of Latin rhythms, salsa and merengue, fuel a society caught up in the endless search for the good life.

Just beyond Caracas, along Venezuela's 2,785-kilometer (1,730-mile) seacoast, the feeling is more unhurried than hectic, more Caribbean than South American. At the western end of the 564-kilometer (350-mile) Route of the Sun, the modern four-lane highway that joins Caracas with Cumaná, the Andes plunge sharply into the sea, leaving behind a series of half-moon coves and cliffs. Heading east by car or bus, you pass sweeping white-sand beaches shaded by palms and mangroves before reaching the dramatic, water-bound jungle of Amacuro Delta. After the stifling heat of the interior, the coast's year-round mild climate may inspire thoughts of early retirement, or at least of lounging on a breezy beach, hypnotized by the heavy beat of reggae and salsa music streaming from an ocean-front bar. Just offshore is Margarita Island, Venezuela's most prized Caribbean resort, an island paradise comprising shady beaches, mangrove-lined lagoons, and some of the country's most high-style shopping streets.

In the west, where subtropical jungle gives way to rugged mountain slopes carpeted with coffee and wheat, the Andes rise sharply before curving south into Colombia. On the barren, treeless *páramo*, the high-altitude plain perched between two arms of the Andes, weatherbeaten Indians wrest a hard living from the stone-pocked land, plowing hillsides where even oxen walk precariously. In markets throughout the region, women weave sweaters, woolen blankets, and *ruanas* (ponchos); along the roadside, red-cheeked children hold up flowers and chubby puppies for sale. In Mérida, the capital of Mérida State and only a few hours' drive from the Colombian frontier, the world's longest and highest cable car makes scaling the Andes swift and unforgettable.

Staying Safe and Healthy Blessed with vast reserves of oil, Venezuela rode a tidal wave of prosperity in the 1970s. But dramatic devaluation of the bolivar in 1983 led to massive inflation and unemployment. Venezuela's standard of living is still the highest in South America. And while the country's reputation continues to suffer from

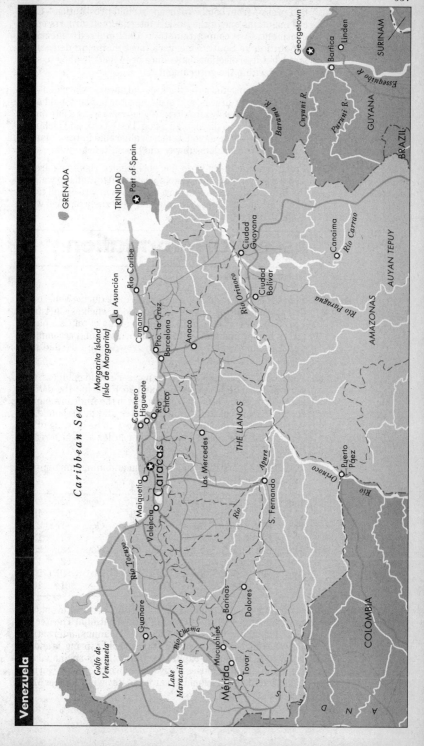

Venezuela

bad press—from bombs to drugs to child prostitution—Caracas maintains one of the busiest international airports on the continent. Two coup attempts in 1992 marred Venezuela's reputation as South America's most enduring democratic state, but free elections have since been held, leading to some reforms within the government.

Crime Unsavory shantytowns—which should always be avoided—encircle modern Caracas, and even downtown, you should avoid wandering aimlessly after 9 PM. If you're planning a late dinner or an evening at a disco, take a taxi. Petty theft and pickpocketing are on the rise; you're most vulnerable in busy marketplaces and in crowded subway and bus stations.

Health Fresh fruit and salads do not pose health risks in Caracas. Avoid washed fruits and vegetables, raw fish, and tap water in the interior because of cholera epidemics in Brazil and traces of cholera in Venezuela. Throughout Venezuela, bottled water is cheap and readily available.

Essential Information

Before You Go

When to Go Plan to visit between November and April, during Venezuela's dry season. During peak holiday periods, such as Christmas, Carnival in February, and Easter, an influx of tourists pushes prices higher and makes it more difficult to find accommodations. During winter (Nov.–Mar.) crowds are rare and hotel prices drop significantly.

Climate Venezuela's weather is prized for its year-round mildness; temperatures range between 65°F and 75°F during the day and rarely drop below 55°F at night except in the Andean mountain regions. Some coastal areas are hotter and more humid, but you can usually depend on a cool breeze to be blowing off the ocean. This is a country where you can leave your sweaters behind.

The following are the daily maximum and minimum temperatures for Caracas.

Jan.	79F	26C	May	81F	27C	Sept.	82F	28C
	60	16		66	19		64	18
Feb.	80F	27C	June	80F	27C	Oct.	81F	27C
	62	17		65	18		64	18
Mar.	81F	27C	July	80F	27C	Nov.	82F	28C
	62	17		65	18		62	17
Apr.	80F	27C	Aug.	84F	29C	Dec.	80F	27C
	64	18		65	18		61	16

Festivals and Events Venezuela hosts a number of important cultural events, the most famous of which is Caracas's **International Theater Festival**, held every two years (April '94). An annual international **jazz festival**, held at alternating times during spring, is another cultural fixture in the capital. El Hatillo hosts an annual classical and popular music festival in November. The German-colonized town of Colonia Tovar hosts its own **Chamber Music Festival** in March.

During **Carnaval,** held in the week that includes Ash Wednesday, the entire country goes on a Mardi Gras–like binge. In Caracas, nearly everyone vacates the city and heads for the beach.

Currency   Except at a tourist center like Margarita Island, where the U.S. dollar can be openly negotiated, the bolívar is the official unit of currency. Bolívars (Bs) can be divided into *céntimos* and come in bills of Bs 5, Bs 10, Bs 20, Bs 50, Bs 100, Bs 500, and Bs 1,000. Coins include the Bs 1, Bs 2, and Bs 5, as well as smaller denominations, which are about to vanish. At press time (Fall '93), the exchange rate was Bs 100 to the U.S. dollar and Bs 145 to the pound sterling—and devaluating roughly at a rate of Bs 25 per year.

Although you can exchange money at most banks, it is best to seek out a *casa de cambio,* or exchange house, which offer better rates (and not-quite-so-long lines). Unlike the banks, many casas de cambio are open on Saturday. Hotels typically change money at a rate roughly 10% lower than banks and exchange houses. Before trekking to outlying areas, you would be wise to cash at least Bs 8,000–Bs 10,000.

Credit cards and traveler's checks are generally accepted in hotels, restaurants, and some shops in major cities and resorts, though much less often in outlying areas.

What It Will Cost   Travelers holding U.S. and strong West European currencies should find hotels and transportation relatively inexpensive, although plane fares have risen dramatically in recent years. The best hotels cost up to $150 per double, the less accommodating and spartan as little as $15. Going to the theater can cost as little as $3 and up to $60 for special shows or featured artists. Movies are still a bargain at $1.50. Nightlife ranges greatly in price; some of the best clubs charge upward of $5 for a hard-liquor drink. You will find the best prices and bargains outside the major cities and resorts.

At hotels, foreigners must pay a 10% "tourist tax." Venezuela does not have a sales tax yet, but restaurants inevitably add 10% to the bill for service; you are expected to tip another 10%.

Sample Prices   Cup of coffee, 25¢–$1.80; soft drink, 25¢–40¢; bottle of beer, 60¢–$2.50; bottle of wine, $4 at a liquor store; crosstown taxi ride, $3.

Customs on Arrival   Persons entering Venezuela may bring in duty-free up to 400 cigarettes and 50 cigars, 2 liters of liquor, and new goods such as video cameras and electronics up to $1,500 in value if declared and accompanied by receipts. Plants, fresh fruit, and pork are prohibited.

Language   Spanish is the offical language in Venezuela. The Guajiro Indians in the Amazonas speak a dialect of their own, but you are unlikely to meet a local who does not speak at least some Spanish. Outside resort areas you will find few Venezuelans proficient in English. Some European immigrants still speak their native Italian and Portuguese.

Getting Around

By Car   Venezuela has an excellent highway and road network, although signage and road surfaces are not always reliable. Travel by day whenever possible; driving at night can be unsafe due to poor lighting and the sometimes erratic behavior of truck and bus drivers. City traffic is aggressive: watch out for drivers who disregard red lights with seeming malice aforethought.

Car Rental The major rental companies are well represented in Venezuela, as are a few local, lesser-known agencies. Fees are rising swiftly with inflation; at the moment, the cheapest rental costs $40 per day including 150 free kilometers (93 free miles); dole out an additional 30¢ per kilometer after that. Make sure to obtain liability and collision insurance.

In Caracas, contact **Avis** (tel. 02/261–5556 or 02/261–1477, fax 02/261–5697), **Budget** (tel. 02/283–4333, fax 02/283–7504), **Dollar Rent-A-Car** (tel. 02/751–2741, fax 02/751–9395), **Hertz** (tel. 02/952–5511, fax 02/952–1846), or **National Rent-A-Car** (tel. 02/239–3645, fax 02/239–4119).

On Margarita Island, contact **Avis** (tel. 095/69–12–23, fax 095/61–89–20), **Budget** (tel. 095/69–10–47, fax 095/61–42–98), **Hertz** (tel. 095/69–72–37), or **National Rent-A-Car** (tel. 095/69–11–71).

Gasoline Leaded-gas prices are among the cheapest in the world: less than 5¢ per liter of 93-octane petrol (unleaded gas is not available in Venezuela). The national oil company, Petroleos de Venezuela (PDVSA), operates some 24-hour stations on main highways.

Breakdowns The major rental agencies will tow your car in an emergency, and along the main highways you will find tow trucks and *auxilios viales*, roadside service phones, at regular intervals. Towing services can be found under *grúas* in the phone book.

By Bus Almost all of Venezuela can be traversed by bus, the least expensive and often most agreeable way of seeing the country. Some lines now offer *servicio especial* (special service) buses—equipped with air-conditioning and videotape players—from the border town of San Cristóbal to Caracas, and from the capital to Mérida and Valencia.

Making sense of Caracas's busy **Nuevo Circo** bus terminal is not easy; public buses crowd under signs marked with the city of destination, leaving the station in a plume of fumes as soon as they are filled. A better bet are the private carriers, usually referred to as *rápidos* (expresses), which in Caracas also depart from the Nuevo Circo terminal. Private companies typically accept advance reservations and offer creature comforts such as numbered seats, air-conditioning, toilets, and on-board attendants. Two dependable carriers are **Rodovías de Venezuela** (Nuevo Circo, tel. 02/572–3746) and **Rápido Guyana** (Nuevo Circo, tel. 02/541–4894).

By Plane Venezuela is served by its own international carriers—**Aeropostal** (Torre Este, floor 46, Parque Central, tel. 02/573–6511), **Avensa** (Torre El Chorro, floor 12, tel. 02/561–3366, tel. 800/428–3672 in U.S.), and **Viasa** (Torre Viasa, Los Cabos, Plaza Morelos, tel. 02/572–9522, tel. 800/327–5454 in U.S.)—as well as by a number of strictly domestic regional carriers, including **Aerotuy** (Av. Abraham Lincoln, Bulevar de Sabana Grande 174, Ed. Gran Sabana, tel. 02/71–73–75 or 02/71–63–97), **Air Valencia** (J.D. Valencia, tel. 041/32–07–05), and **Cave** (Av. Principal del Bosque, Ed. Pinchincha, Chacaíto, tel. 02/951–1974). Domestic plane service is good, and locals gen-

erally prefer it to travelling by bus or car. This means long lines
during peak holiday periods. Despite inflation, prices are still
very moderate: a one-way ticket between Caracas and Mérida,
for example, costs less than $50.

By Train **Ferrocarriles de Venezuela,** the national rail company, operates
the one and only passenger line in Venezuela: between Puerto
Cabello and Barquisimeto, in the northern foothills of the
Andes, for less than $5.

Staying in Venezuela

Telephones The national phone company, CANTV, was recently purchased
by a U.S.-led consortium, and improvements are under way; in
the meantime, expect raspy connections, crossed lines, and excessive busy signals. Local calls cost Bs 1.30 per minute. Public
pay phones accept coins, but phone cards, available at kiosks
marked *tarjeta intelligente* (smart card) in denominations of Bs
250, Bs 500, Bs 1,000, and Bs 2,000, are more convenient. To
speak with a directory operator dial 103.

International Calls International calls are best made from a CANTV office, where
you can pay with a credit card. International calls are ex-
tremely expensive: The average international rate per minute
is $1.80 to the United States and $12 to Europe. Hotels typically add 40% to the CANTV rate, so avoid calling from your
room. To place an international collect call—another expensive
pursuit—dial 122 to reach an English-speaking operator.

Mail The state-owned postal service, **Ipostel,** is slow and not very
reliable. It costs Bs 24 to send a letter domestically and Bs 80
internationally. One of the main Ipostel offices in Caracas is
located in the Edificio Sur Centro Simón Bolívar, near the
Capitolio Metro stop; it's open weekdays 8–6, Saturday 8–2.

Shopping Bargaining is not common in city stores or shops, although it
is acceptable at outdoor and flea markets and sometimes in
smaller towns and villages. Mammoth and modern shopping
malls are a fixture of Caracas, as are designer boutiques bran-
dishing fashionable names like Christian Dior and Yves St.
Laurent. More pleasing—and a better bargain by far—are outdoor markets, packed with everything from fruits and plasticware to leather and handicrafts.

Opening Hours **Banks** are open weekdays 8:30–11:30 and 2–4:30. Watch for
special bank holidays—which are numerous—when all
branches are closed. Most **museums** are open 9–noon and 2–5.
Shops open weekdays 9–1 and 3–7:30; on Saturday, they tend
to stay open all day, from 9 to 7. On Sunday, most shops are
closed.

National Holidays January 1; Carnaval; April 19 (Proclamation of Independence
Day); Easter Thursday and Good Friday; May 1 (Labor Day);
June 24 (Battle of Carabobo); July 5 (Independence Day); July
24 (Simón Bolívar's birthday); December 17 (death of Simón
Bolívar); December 24–25.

Dining In larger cities you will find a wide range of international cuisine that includes Italian, French, Spanish, Arab, and Chinese,
and Venezuela's own criollo (Creole), which combines Spanish
and Caribbean influences with the local favorites—plates of
meat, chicken, and fish sided with rice. *Parrilleras,* restaurants
that specialize in criollo or Argentine-style grilled meats, offer

the chance to watch your meal cooked on a tableside charcoal grill. Menus in *tascas*—Spanish-style restaurants with bars—tend to offer some variation on hearty *hervidos* (soups) and *pabellón*, a popular bean, rice, and grilled meat platter.

Some restaurants offer a prix-fixe meal at lunchtime known as the *menu ejecutivo*. This includes a *primero* (appetizer of soup or salad); a *segundo*, the main course; and *postre* (dessert). Espresso or *guayoyo*, a lighter, American-style coffee, is included.

Throughout Venezuela, restaurants typically add a 10% surcharge to your bill.

Specialties Simple but popular chicken dishes include *milanesa de pollo* (chicken cutlet), *pollo guisado* (stewed chicken), and *pollo a la canasta*, which means nothing more than chicken served with fries. *Hallaca*, a traditional Christmas dish, is a tamalelike combination of chicken, corn, olives, and pork, all wrapped in banana leaves. Fish entrées can be excellent in Venezuela, particularly along the coast; topping the fish list are *filete de mero* (grouper), *filete de pargo* (red snapper), and the legendary *paella*, in which yellow rice comes crowned with mussels, clams, chicken, and shrimp. A *parilla de mariscos* typically includes grilled fish, shrimp, mussels, and clams and is the ideal sampler plate.

Venezuela's version of cornbread, *arepa*, automatically accompanies your meal in most restaurants. Desserts are neither good nor very popular. Beer, whiskey, and rum are the favored libations among locals. Wines tend to be expensive and suffer variations in quality, though certain Chilean and Argentine vintages—try *Valdivieso*, *Concha de Toro*, and *Valmont*—are dependably adequate.

Mealtimes Lunch, the main meal of the day, begins at noon and lasts until about 2:30. Dinner is taken between 7 and 10 PM, and don't count on being served much past 10:30 PM.

Precautions Tap water is reportedly safe, but most foreigners wisely stick with the bottled variety, which is cheap and readily available. Salads and fresh fruit, however, are not a health hazard. Street stands are popular in the interior, but because of cholera epidemics in Brazil and traces of cholera in Venezuela, you should avoid them.

Ratings Prices are per person for a three-course meal, excluding alcohol, tax, and tip. Best bets are indicated by a star ★.

Category	Caracas and Margarita Island	Other Areas
Very Expensive	over $30	over $25
Expensive	$25–$30	$15–$25
Moderate	$15–$25	$8–$15
Inexpensive	under $15	under $8

Lodging Luxury hotels, common in large cities and resort areas, are rated within Venezuela on a scale of one to five stars; a five-star rating, however, is not always indicative of superior quality. Still, most five-star hotels are reasonably modern and feature such facilities as car rental offices, swimming pools and tennis courts, souvenir shops, clothing and jewelry boutiques, restaurants, bars, and discos. Three- and four-star hotels usually offer a smattering of these. Water shortages and cutoffs are common even in the big cities, though resort hotels often have their own auxiliary supplies and thus are immune to the problem.

Beach resorts commonly have apartments for rent on a short-term basis; check listings in the classified sections of the English-language *Daily Journal* or the Spanish-language *Universal* and *Nacional* newspapers. Most rents are listed in U.S. dollars but are not particularly cheap. In fact, budget accommodation is difficult to come by except in smaller towns and villages, where local inquiries must be made. When available, a private room in a house will cost upwards of $10 per night.

Posadas, the local version of pensions, are found mostly in beach areas and the Andes and typically offer accommodation plus meals. Luxury hotels rarely include breakfast—or any meal for that matter—when quoting room rates. Also note: room prices jump 10%–20% during holiday periods, particularly during Christmas and Carnaval.

For a $2 fee, prepaid reservations for more than 300 hotels in Venezuela can be booked through **Fairmont Reserv-Hotel** (tel. 02/782–8433, fax 02/782–4407).

Ratings Prices are for two people in a double room, based on high-season rates and excluding tax. Highly recommended lodgings are indicated by a star ★.

Category	Caracas and Margarita Island	Other Areas
Very Expensive	over $150	over $100
Expensive	$75–$150	$50–$100
Moderate	$25–$75	$20–$50
Inexpensive	under $25	under $20

Tipping It is cutomary to tip hotel porters, hairdressers, and guides from Bs 20 up to 10%. Taxi drivers do not expect a tip unless they carry suitcases. At restaurants, a 10% gratuity (in addition to the 10% surcharge) is generally expected.

Caracas

When pundits say that Caracas is the Miami of South America, they are only partly right. Venezuela's capital city is indeed served by a network of modern freeways that look not a little like parking lots at rush hour. It does have nearby beaches and a generally frenetic nightlife. And it certainly caters to the jet set with glitzy shopping avenues and beachfront country clubs. But Caracas is hardly a second-rate Miami; in this fast-paced city of 4 million, the feeling is tropical, high-styled, and altogether more exotic.

The hub of Venezuelan business, government, culture, and the arts, Caracas spills out over a long, narrow valley in the Avila Mountains. The city was founded by the Spaniard Diego de

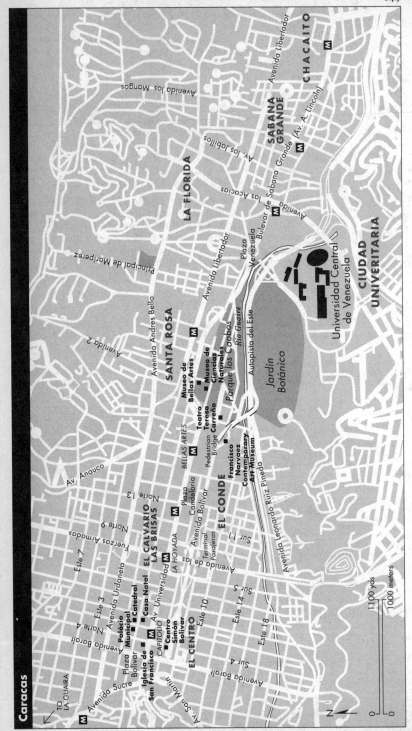

544

Caracas

TO
LA GUAIRA

CHACAITO

Avenida Libertador

SABANA
GRANDE
(Av. A. Lincoln)

Av. los Jabillos

Avenida las Acacias

Bulevar de Sabana Grande

LA FLORIDA

Avenida los Mangos

Principal de Maripérez

Avenida Libertador

Plaza
Venezuela

Río Guaire

Avenida Andres Bello

Avenida 2

SANTA ROSA

Museo de
Bellas Artes

Museo de
Ciencias
Naturales

Teatro
Teresa
Carreño

Pedestrian
Bridge

BELLAS ARTES

Parque los Caobos

Autopista del Este

Jardín
Botánico

CIUDAD
UNIVERITARIA

Universidad Central
de Venezuela

Av. Anauco

Plaza
Candelaria

Avenida Bolívar

EL CONDE

Francisco
Narváez

Contemporary
Art Museum

Fuerzas Armadas

Norte 9

Norte 13

EL CALVARIO
LAS BRISAS

Av. Universidad

LA HOYADA

Terminal
de las
Pasajeras

Avenida Leonardo Ruiz Pineda

Este 7

Este 3

Norte 4

Avenida Urdaneta

Avenida Baralt

Avenida Sucre

Palácio
Municipal

Catedral

Iglesia de
San Francisco

Plaza
Bolívar

Casa Natal

Centro
Simón
Bolívar

CAPITOLIO

EL CENTRO

Sur 4

Este 10

Sur 11

Sur 5

Este 14

Este 18

Avenida Baralt

Av. San Martín

N

1100 yds

1000 meters

0

0

Losada in AD 1567, but today you have to look hard to find traces of the red-tile colonial homes that were once its trademark. Influenced by styles and tastes imported during Venezuela's 1970s "oil rush," modern Caracas is as swank and cosmopolitan as it is rough-and-tumble: an unwieldy hodgepodge in which high-rise financial towers seem as natural and inevitable as the shantylike dwellings that crowd the hills above downtown.

The city's bustling commercial life is ubiquitous. In the downtown El Centro district, street vendors with wares laid out on blankets compete with ambulatory salespeople pitching pens, watches, and sunglasses. On the other side of town, in the posh El Rosal district, stockbrokers clutching cellular phones pause to flirt with Caraqueñas on their way to lunch. At nighttime, these same denizens are likely to meet up in a fashionable discotheque or pub and dance until 4 AM.

Caracas is a sprawling city of 4 million people, but it can be explored comfortably in the space of a few days. Worldly museums and cultural centers, spry bars, and refined dining establishments are all interconnected by the city's clean and efficient subway system, which opened in 1983 after much ado. The weather, too, facilitates exploring: at 1,000 meters (3,000 feet) above sea level, Caracas has one of the world's most comfortable climates, with an average daily temperature of 75°F. However, Caracas is not immune to crime: visitors should not go out unescorted after 9 PM, and taxis are recommended as the safest means of transportation after dark.

Tourist Information

Corporturismo has two offices: at Parque Central (Torre Oeste, 36th floor, tel. 02/507–8829 or 02/507–8612, fax 02/574–8810) and the Simón Bolívar International Airport (tel. 031/55–11–11 or 031/55–14–10). **American Express** (Torre Consolidado, Av. Blandín, Edificio "Anexo," tel. 02/260–2451). **Thomas Cook Travel Agency** (Edificio Adriático de Seguros, Av. Francisco de Miranda, piso 6, Oficina 62, tel. 02/31–35–77 or 02/32–48–46).

Arriving and Departing

By Plane The **Simón Bolívar International Airport** (tel. 031/55–11–11 or 031/55–14–10), located near Caracas in the coastal suburb of Maiquetía, is served by all major domestic and some foreign carriers. Upon landing, visitors are issued their mandatory tourist visa (free), valid for a stay of up to three months. Cab fare for the 30- to 45-minute trip to downtown Caracas costs about $18; pay in advance inside the airport at the window marked *Ticket de Taxi*, then present the receipt to any of the drivers outside. Otherwise, climb aboard any public bus parked directly outside the domestic terminal; for $1.50 these shuttle passengers to various downtown destinations, including the Gato Negro Metro stop, with a final stop at Parque Central, located near the Caracas Hilton and Bellas Artes Metro stop.

By Bus Most public and private buses depart from the hectic **Nuevo Circo** terminal (tel. 02/545–2060 or 02/545–2356) near the La Hoyada Metro stop. It is crowded and difficult to negotiate, but until the new station at La Bandera is completed, Nuevo Circo offers the only means, besides flying, of moving onward from Caracas. Dependable bus carriers with agents at Nuevo Circo include **Expresos del Oriente** (tel. 02/462–5371), **Expresos de la Costa** (tel. 02/545–3835), and **Expresos Alianza** (tel. 02/62–05–46).

By Train Caracas is not served by passenger trains.

Getting Around Caracas

Downtown Caracas covers a large area; but with a sturdy pair of shoes it can be explored reasonably well on foot. For outlying sights take a taxi or the subway. It is not recommended to venture too far by foot after nightfall.

By Metro Caracas's excellent and very safe Metro system traverses the city from east (Propatria) to west (Palo Verde) with a connecting north–south line from El Capitolio to Zoológico. The most important downtown stops are Bellas Artes, La Hoyada, and El Capitolio. Metro fares are Bs 13 (for rides of three stops or fewer) and Bs 16. Tickets can be purchased in all stations; the orange-color *Multiabono* card ($2) is valid for 10 rides, as is the *Multi-integrado* card ($2.50), which further allows you to ride city buses for free. The Metro operates daily 5 AM–11 PM.

By Bus Public buses connect all parts of the city and cost less than 50¢; they are also unbelievably crowded, slow, and sweaty. *Por puesto* buses run throughout the night but are best avoided after 9 PM or so. The main terminal is at Nuevo Circo, near the La Hoyada Metro stop.

By Taxi Crowded taxis cut corners and seemingly defy the laws of physics as they maneuver through downtown traffic. Legitimate taxis have secured signs on the roof; *pirata* (pirate) versions have portable signs. Negotiate price with the driver before getting in, as meters are often ignored or simply "broken." Fares jump up to 50% at night and on weekends.

Orientation Tours

Larger hotels sometimes organize guided tours of the city; contact the concierge or one of the local tourist offices.

Exploring Caracas

Caracas can be divided into four principal areas: the downtown El Centro district and its monument-packed Plaza Bolívar; Parque Central and the surrounding Bellas Artes cultural district; Las Mercedes and the Bulevar Sabana Grande, with its sundry boutiques and restaurants; and the residential, very wealthy suburbs of Altamira and La Castellana. These far-flung districts are all connected with El Centro by subway. Taxis, too, are extremely cheap and convenient. Also note: Few museums, cathedrals, and government buildings in Caracas charge admission fees.

El Centro Take the Metro to El Capitolio to reach the historic heart of Caracas, **El Centro,** founded in 1567 by Diego de Losada (who named the original settlement Santiago de León de Caracas). From street level it's a short walk to **Plaza Bolívar,** a pleasant shady square with wooden benches, flocks of pigeons, and an imposing equestrian statue of the plaza's namesake, Simón Bolívar, dubbed "El Libertador" in 1813 for his leadership in the struggle against Spanish rule in South America.

Facing the plaza, the former **Corte Suprema** (Supreme Court) now houses government offices. Next door and sharing the same stately neo-Gothic facade is the **Palacio de las Academias** (Palace of the Academies), home of the Academies of History, Language, and Science. Excepting a pair of flower-filled central courtyards that date from the colonial era, there is little to see inside. The adjoining, attention-grabbing **Panteón Nacional** (National Cemetary; admission free; open daily) is the city's most striking monument, with its tall, slender twin towers and pale pink-and-green color scheme. Inside are the remains of 138 Venezuelan political and historical figures, including those of Simón Bolívar.

The handsome **Catedral Metropolitana de Caracas** (Metropolitan Cathedral of Caracas, Plaza Bolívar, tel. 02/862–1518; closed Mon.), completed in 1674, is the only church in Caracas to retain unaltered its original colonial facade, which is characterized by graceful scroll designs. The highlight inside is the main altar, a magnificent Baroque creation gilded with more than 300 pounds of gold leaf. The adjacent art deco–style **Gobernación** (Government Palace, tel. 02/81–11–11, admission free), built in 1935, houses political offices and a ground-floor salon with rotating exhibits of international and Venezuelan art.

The **Palácio Municipal** (City Hall), on the south side of Plaza Bolívar, is considered the cradle of Venezuelan nationhood: on July 5, 1811, the National Congress met inside and approved the Declaration of Independence. Nowadays, the City Hall hosts the **Museo de Caracas,** which exhibits a permanent collection of works by noted Venezuelan painter Emilio Boggio (1857–1920); scale-model miniatures by Raúl Santana, depicting every imaginable aspect of Venezuela's early culture; and Ruth Neumann's scale models of Plaza Bolívar at different points in its history. *Plaza Bolívar, tel. 02/545–6706. Admission free. Closed Sun.*

The original plans for **Iglesia de San Francisco** (San Francisco Church) were drawn up in 1593, but the present church owes a heavy debt to President Guzmán Blanco, who ordered extensive renovations in 1887. According to Blanco's wishes, the church now meshes with the baroque flair of the capital. Inside, 10 dazzling gilded altars vie with colonial icons and statuary for the attention of serious supplicants. *Av. Bolsa at Av. San Francisco, tel. 02/41–57–07. Admission free.*

Venezuela's congress is housed in **El Capitolio Nacional** (National Capitol, Av. Bolsa at Av. San Francisco, tel. 02/483–3644; closed Mon.), formerly the 17th-century convent of the Sisters of the Conception. In 1874, President Guzmán Blanco ordered the disbanding of all convents, razed the building, and began constructing the Federal and Legislative palaces. The latter, home to the Senate and Chamber of Deputies, was completed in just 114 days. Sessions of congress can be observed Tuesday–Thursday between 10 and noon (men must wear jacket and tie). The adjacent Federal Palace contains the **Salón Elíptico** (Elliptical Meeting Hall), divided into three sections—the Yellow, Blue, and Red Rooms—in honor of the Venezuelan flag. The massive dome capping the Blue Room contains a mural of the 1821 Battle of Carabobo (a decisive battle in Venezuela's War of Independence against Spain) painted by Martín Tovar y Tovar. Also on display is the chest holding Venezuela's Declaration of Independence.

South of tree-lined **Plaza Venezolano,** where singing evangelists and ice-cream vendors compete for the attention of passersby, the **Museo Bolívar** (Av. San Jacinto at Av. Norte, tel. 02/45–98–28; admission charged; closed Mon.) features documents and historical paraphernalia related to Simón Bolívar and Venezuela's War of Independence against Spain. Joined to the museum but with a different stone-carved facade, **Casa Natal** (tel. 02/541–2563; admission charged; closed Mon.) is the birthplace of Simón Bolívar, born July 24, 1783. Although this 17th-century colonial mansion contains a number of artifacts from the Bolívar family, more attention is given to the monumental paintings of Tito Salas, with themes focusing on various aspects of Bolívar's early life (including his trip to Paris in 1804, where he witnessed the coronation of Napoléon).

To the south, it is hard to miss the twin-towered **Centro Simón Bolívar,** sometimes referred to as Torres de el Silencio, comprising office buildings, apartments, a mammoth shopping center, and two 30-floor towers—the tallest structures in South America when they were built in 1958.

Bellas Artes Take the Metro to the Bellas Artes stop; impossible to miss from street level are the twin 56-story towers which anchor the sprawling **Parque Central,** a complex designed to house 10,000 people within its two towers and seven condominium buildings. Besides shops and restaurants there are schools, a swimming pool, the Anauco Hilton, the Sofía Imber Contemporary Art Museum, and a tourist office.

East of the Anauco Hilton, look for the outstanding **Museo de Arte Contemporaneo de Sofía Imber** (Sofía Imber Contemporary Art Museum), built in the 1970s on the heels of Venezuela's "oil rush." Displays include sculpture by Fernando Botero and Henry Moore, as well as a permanent Pablo Picasso exhibition. *Parque Central, tel. 02/573–7289 or 02/573–8289. Admission charged. Closed Sun. and Mon.*

Just eastward, a pedestrian bridge spans a perpetually congested highway and leads to the impressive **Teresa Carreño Complejo Cultural** (Teresa Carreño Cultural Complex), where world-class ballet, opera, and classical concerts are regularly presented at the **Teatro Teresa Carreño** (Plaza Los Cabos, tel. 02/574–9122). Hanging from the theater roof is the kinetic sculpture, *Yellow Pendants,* by Venezuelan artist Jesús Soto. Adjacent to the Teresa Carreño complex is the Teatro Ateneo, home of a popular movie theater, a bookstore, and the biannual International Theater Festival.

A short stroll north brings you through an open-air market filled with artisans and food stalls, part of **Plaza Morelos** and the main entrance to **Parque Los Caobos,** tree lined and lazy. One side of the plaza is taken up by the **Museo de Ciencias Naturales** (Museum of Natural Sciences), with displays of stuffed wildlife, insects, minerals, and pre-Columbian ceramics. *Plaza Morelos, tel. 02/571–0464. Admission free. Closed Mon.*

The **Museo de Bellas Artes,** on the opposite side of Plaza Morelos, harbors two exceptional museums: the National Art Gallery, which provides a forum for renowned Venezuelan artists

such as Armando Reveron and Alejandro Otero, and the newer
Fine Arts Museum, with a hodgepodge but excellent collection
of Goya etchings, Chinese ceramics, and diverse Egyptian
pieces, plus rotating exhibitions of modern international
works. *Plaza Morelos, tel. 02/571–3697. Admission charged.
Closed Mon.*

At the eastern end of Parque Los Caobos lies the circular **Plaza
Venezuela,** with its great fountain and blazon of lights. It is a
popular spot for throngs of students from the adjacent 60,000-
student **Universidad Central de Venezuela,** designed by architect Carlos Raúl Villanueva. Campus hallmarks include
stained-glass windows by Ferdinand Léger, murals by Léger
and Mateo Manaure, and sculptures by Jean Arp, Henry
Laurens, and Alexander Calder.

Sabana Grande and   The **Bulevar de Sabana Grande** (sometimes called Avenida
Las Mercedes   Abraham Lincoln) is a festive promenade where visitors and
Caraqueños converge on weekends to sip a *marrón grande*
(double espresso) at the famous Gran Café, to browse among
the troop of street vendors, or to take in the fleeting panorama
of street musicians, mime groups, comics, and flame swallow-
ers performing for rapt crowds. Sabana Grande is flanked by
two important avenues—Avenida Casanova and Avenida Francisco Solano—both lined with numerous restaurants and affordable hotels.

The far eastern end of Bulevar Sabana Grande is anchored by
the **Central Commercial Chacaíto,** a gargantuan shopping
complex that looms impressively over the lively Chacaíto district. The nearby Chacaíto Metro stop opens onto a relaxed
square, Plaza Chacaíto, fronted by fast-food eateries and cafés;
most days an inexpensive clothing bazaar is held on the southern corner.

East of Chacaíto is the lively **El Rosal** district, noted for its
covey of night spots along Avenida Tamanaco. From here hop
in a cab for **Las Mercedes,** considered one of Caracas's chicest
districts with discotheques, boutiques and art galleries, auto
dealerships, and innumerable restaurants strewn throughout
the side streets. The main strip, Avenida Principal de las Mercedes, is worth experiencing simply to marvel at—or decry—
the extent to which U.S. mass-merchandising has infiltrated
Venezuelan culture. Appropriately, at the end of the avenue is
the large Paseo de las Mercedes shopping mall.

Altamira and   These very safe and decidedly upscale neighborhoods cater to
La Castellana   young and style-conscious Caraqueños and to the city's upper
classes. The districts can be reached by subway (Altamira
stop), or you can walk from Chacaíto along Avenida Francisco
Miranda.

Elegant restaurants line La Castellana's main thoroughfare,
Avenida Principal de la Castellana, which eventually funnels
onto the district's main square, Plaza La Castellana. Here you
will find the headquarters of Banco Consolidado and the **Centro
Cultural del Banco Consolidado,** which houses a visual arts museum with rotating displays of international art as well as a
small collection of precious gems, jewels, and medals belonging
to Simon Bolívar. *Av. Urdaneta, tel. 02/82–98–21. Admission
free. Closed Sat. and Sun.*

Shopping

Thanks partly to a still lingering "macho" culture and partly to U.S. influence, Caraqueños are a style-conscious breed. Western-style clothing, appliances, and gadgets are much sought after by this consumer culture, which partly explains the city's numerous ultramodern shopping centers. In Caracas, leather goods, shoes, handbags, and luggage are the best bargains, sometimes also jewelry. Browsing is a pleasure, because Venezuelans typically scorn the high-pressure sale. Although a fading art, bartering is still acceptable, especially in smaller establishments and on the street.

Shopping Centers A popular area for browsing and bargain hunting is Chacaíto; try the shops surrounding its Metro stop and the district's famed multistory mall, **Central Comercial Chacaíto** (Chuao, tel. 02/959–2169). With its behemoth **Paseo de las Mercedes** (Las Mercedes, tel. 02/91–72–42) shopping complex, Las Mercedes district is another good bet, even though its main strip, Avenida Principal de las Mercedes, has an overwhelming but essentially bland collection of chintzy boutiques and neon-lit trinket shops. The **Central Comercial Ciudad Tamanaco (CCCT,** Chacaíto, tel. 02/71–74–35), east of Las Mercedes in the suburb of Chuao, packs in thousands of shoppers each day with its upstairs cinemas, fast-food restaurants, and swank boutiques.

Markets The best bargains for trinkets and artwork are had on the streets, in Sabana Grande, at Plaza Morelos, and in La Hoyada near the Nuevo Circo bus terminal. The Plaza Las Americas is a good venue for handicrafts shopping, but it's located a little off the beaten track in El Cafetal district; take a taxi.

Specialty Stores Two reputable gem dealers inside the CCCT shopping center
Gems and Gold in Chuao are **Muzo Gemologists** (3rd floor, tel. 02/261–4017) and **Diamoro** (3rd floor, tel. 02/955–0988), both with displays of gemstones, crystals, and rough stones. **H. Stern,** one of South America's largest gem dealers, sells all grades of gems at outlets in the Hotel Tamanaco (tel. 02/92–73–13) and the Hilton (tel. 02/571–0520).

Handicrafts and **Artesanía Amazonas** (Calle Paris at Calle New York), just off
Tapestries the Paseo Las Mercedes, stocks handwoven baskets, carved icons and statuary, hand-crafted jewelry, and other crafts. Also in Las Mercedes, **Pablo's** (Av. Rio de Janeiro) is the place to come for hammocks and handwoven ponchos. **Artesanía Venezuela** (Calle de Sabana Grande) has a large selection of jewelry, ponchos, and textiles.

Spectator Sports

Soccer is the traditional favorite, but basketball and baseball are the current rage in Venezuela. (Baseball has been popular ever since Pete Rose and, later, Daryl Strawberry played during the off-season in Caracas's winter league.) The **Universidad Central** stadium (Ciudad Universitaria, tel. 02/572–2211) is the most accessible venue for either baseball or soccer, depending on the season.

Boxing Professional pugilism is big in Venezuela, with regularly scheduled fights held most Sundays (Nov.–Apr.) at the **Parque Miranda** stadium (Metro stop: Parque del Este, tel. 02/989–1127).

Bullfighting It is more popular by far in Mexico City and other South American capitals, but bullfighting has its devoted adherents in Caracas; during the season (Nov.–Apr.) bullfights are held at the **Nuevo Circo** arena (tel. 02/915–2213).

Horse Racing The sport's popularity is evidenced by the number of betting booths in Caracas, as well as all the radios and televisions tuned in to **La Rinconada** racetrack (tel. 02/606–6111), in the suburb of El Valle. To take part in the fun and wagers, take a taxi ($5 from downtown) any Saturday or Sunday between noon and 6 PM; admission fees to the track are less than $1.

Dining

Eating out in Caracas is considered a pleasure and a necessity; Caraqueños who otherwise earn meager wages spend heavily at *tascas,* bar-restaurants that are quite common in Caracas. The capital also has a surprisingly diverse mix of high-quality and affordable Spanish, French, Middle Eastern, and local criollo restaurants. For price ranges, *see* Dining in Staying in Venezuela, *above.*

Very Expensive **Primi.** This sophisticated international dining spot features one of the best wine lists in the capital. The variable menu bears Italian and California nouvelle cuisine influences; try the Caesar salad, with Yaracuy mushrooms, or the fettuccine with artichoke stuffed with smoked salmon, corn, and cheese. *Av. Principal de la Castellana No. 93 (at Calle José Feliz Rivas), tel. 02/31–06–14. Reservations advised. MC, V. Closed Sat. and Sun. lunch.*

Expensive **Al Vecchio Mullino.** This is one of the better Italian restaurants in Sabana Grande district, evidenced by the large lunchtime crowds. Vegetarians may appreciate the antipasto and variety of pasta dishes; carnivores will enjoy the entrecôte in Carrozza sauce. *Av. Francisco Solano López at Los Jabillos, tel. 02/71–26–97. AE, D, MC, V.*

La Estancia. A traditional Spanish-style restaurant where black-and-white photographs of famous bullfighters don't seem too out of place. Despite the obvious Spanish influences, criollo dishes are the house specialty; start with the lobster bisque and move on to the *parrillas* (criollo-style grill) or to the rabbit or chicken basted in orange sauce. *Av. Principal de la Castellana, Esquina Urdaneta, tel. 02/261–2363. Reservations advised. AE, MC, V.*

★ **Samui.** The very chic Samui in La Floresta district is one of the only authentic Thai restaurant in South America. After all, the owners do grow their own vegetables and they spice the varied dishes to perfection. Coveted entrées include *pra lad prik* (red snapper basted in garlic), and the dessert menu, weighted heavily with crème brûlée and chocolate mousse, is outstanding. *Av. Andrés Bello at Av. Francisco Miranda la Transversal, tel. 02/285–4600 or 02/283–4146. Reservations advised. MC, V. Closed Sun.*

Moderate **El Palmar.** Caracas is not known for its Chinese food, but you do have a few reasonably authentic choices in the Bello Monte district, where critics favor El Palmar. The decor is less striking than it is functional, but the service and the menu—particularly the justly acclaimed lacquered duck—are classically Chinese. *Plaza Lincoln, tel. 02/751–4442. AE, D, MC, V.*

La Layalina. There are two fine Arab restaurants next door to one another in El Bosque district, though La Layalina has the better menu and service. In addition to traditional Middle Eastern dishes such as shish kebab, La Layalina is noted for its tomato-and-beet Fatouch salad, not to mention its regular belly dance evenings. *Av. Principal del Bosque at Av. Santa Clara, tel. 02/731–1651. AE, D, MC, V.*

Inexpensive **El Tizón.** The most popular Mexican restaurant in Caracas is located in the basement of the Centro Comercial Bello Campo and features a range of Peruvian specialties, such as *chupes de camarones* (shrimp soup) and the popular Peruvian drink *pisco* sour. Mexican favorites such as ceviche and margaritas also seem to placate the sometimes large crowds. *Centro Comercial Bello Campo, tel. 02/31–67–15. Reservations advised. AE, D, MC, V. Closed Sun.*

★ **Le Coq d'Or.** Tucked away between Bulevar de Sabana Grande and Avenida Francisco Solano is this attractive teakwood-decorated French restaurant, probably the best in Caracas for the money. The varied but dependable menu is often anchored by vol-au-vent and *caracoles de Bogoña* (escargot). *Calle Los Mangos At Av. Las Delicias, tel. 02/761–0891. AE. Closed Mon.*

Lodging

Many of Caracas's best hotels are located a few kilometers north of downtown in the refined Bellas Artes and Altamira districts—a short but inevitable taxi ride away from Caracas's restaurants and nightclubs. Although security-minded visitors may feel more comfortable in established hotels like the Hilton, Caracas does offer a variety of alternative lodging options that are easier on the budget and often more interesting in terms of that amorphous quality called character. The Sabana Grande district is considered especially desirable for more adventurous travelers; you can pick and choose from the many budget-priced pensions crowding the lively Avenida Casanova and Avenida Francisco Solano. Another well-known area for hotels is the aptly named Calle de los Hoteles, an extension of Avenida Las Acacias that runs perpendicular to Avenida Casanova. For price ranges, *see* Lodging in Staying in Venezuela, *above*.

Very Expensive **Hilton.** In the high-cultured Bellas Artes district, this mammoth complex has long been the primary destination of international businesspeople. The rooms suffer from a bland "international style" of decoration, but along with its convenient location, the hotel has excellent sport facilities. *Av. México, near Bellas Artes Metro stop, tel. 02/571–2322, fax 02/575–0024. 824 rooms, 36 suites, all with bath. Facilities: restaurant, bar, pool, gym, sauna, tennis court. AE, D, MC, V.*

Expensive **Eurobuilding.** Business travelers are especially fond of this
★ modern high-rise hotel situated in the Chuao business district near the opulent CCCT shopping center. Glass-enclosed elevators carry you from the lobby, the site of numerous concerts and nightlife activities, up to spacious double rooms and suites, many with good views of the Ávila Mountains. The Eurobuilding's restaurant, Cassandra, is heralded as one of the best hotel eateries in South America. *Av. de la Guairita, Chuao, tel. 02/959–1133 or 800/325–3876 in the U.S., fax 02/92–20–69. 450 rooms, 180 suites, all with bath. Facilities: restaurant, bar, gym, sauna, pool. AE, D, MC, V.*

Tamanaco InterContinental. Caracas has long prided itself on the Tamanaco, which offers a unique combination of business and recreation facilities and is set on a hillside overlooking lively Las Mercedes district. Ponder the spectacular views from your well-equipped room, or drink and dance overlooking the swimming pool in the popular Bar Cacique. *Av. Principal de las Mercedes, tel. 02/208–7111 or 800/327–0200 in the U.S., fax 02/208–7116. 600 rooms, all with bath. Facilities: 3 restaurants, 3 bars, satellite TV and minibar in rooms, bank, travel agency, pool, health club, 3 tennis courts, jogging path. AE, D, MC, V.*

Moderate   **El Conde.** Despite its age, this newly remodeled 1950s mid-rise matches a convenient downtown location—near Plaza Bolívar and El Capitolio Metro stop—with comfortable rooms and good facilities, including the Italian restaurant Il Coratino and an all-hour tasca. *Esquina El Conde, tel. 02/81–11–71, fax 02/862–0928. 133 rooms, most with bath. Facilities: 2 restaurants, bar, gym, conference rooms. AE, D, MC, V.*

Lincoln Suites. The well-appointed Lincoln Suites straddles the busy Bulevar de Sabana Grande, Caracas's principal pedestrian and commercial artery. The bright and comfortable rooms, mostly suites and spacious doubles, come equipped with minibars and televisions, but you'll probably spend more time in the popular local watering hole Michael's Bar, in the lobby. *Av. Francisco Solano López at Av. Los Jabillos, tel. 02/762–8575 or 02/762–8578, fax 02/762–8579. 100 rooms, 28 suites, most with bath. Facilities: restaurant, bar. AE, D, MC, V.*

Inexpensive   **Hotel Luna.** This modest hotel in the Sabana Grande district has compact, clean rooms and a friendly, multilingual staff. The two luxurious suites have a living room, refrigerator, and television. *Av. Casanova at Calle El Colegio, tel. 02/762–5851, fax 02/762–5850. 63 rooms, including 2 suites. Facilities: restaurant, bar. AE, D, MC, V.*

Savoy. A Sabana Grande budget hotel where service and style are not sacrificed for price. After tackling the nearby restaurants, bars, and shops, you can relax in the Savoy's small patio restaurant or retire to your comfortable, quiet room. *Av. Francisco Solano López (near Chacaito Metro stop), tel. 02/762–1971 or 02/762–1979, fax 02/762–2792. 95 rooms with bath. Facilities: restaurant. AE, D, MC, V.*

The Arts and Nightlife

Mention a night on the town to a local and the first suggestion will likely be—dancing. Unlike their North American counterparts, Caraqueños start dancing the salsa and merengue at a tender age. The proliferation of discotheques and music venues testifies to this abiding passion, although professional theater as well as classical and popular music concerts are popular nighttime diversions. For current listings, pick up a copy of the English-language newspaper *Daily Journal,* available at most newsstands.

The Arts   The Venezuelan Symphony Orchestra regularly plays at the
Music   **Teatro Teresa Carreño** (opposite Caracas Hilton, tel. 02/574–9122). The adjacent **Teatro Ateneo** (Plaza Morelos, tel. 02/573–4622) hosts chamber music and operatic concerts between September and April. On the campus of Universidad Central, **Aula Magna** (tel. 02/61–98–11, ext. 2505) features 11 AM Sunday concerts by the Venezuelan Symphony Orchestra (except Aug.

and Sept.) as well as acoustic "clouds" by Alexander Calder, who helped design the Aula Magna.

Theater The **Teatro Municipal** (Esq. Municipal, tel. 02/41–53–85) and **Teatro Nacional** (Av. Lacuna, tel. 02/482–5424) feature active programs of dance, music, and cultural events. Traveling by taxi is a good idea since neither theater is in the best neighborhood.

Nightlife Although Caracas is a casual sort of town, jackets are typically required of men at discos and private clubs; ties, however, are optional.

Discos **El Sarao** (Centro Commercial Bello Campo, tel. 02/31–25–03) features live merengue, salsa, and *tambores* (drum) bands nightly. In Las Mercedes district, there's dancing on two levels at **Hollywood Dance Bar & Grill** (Calle Madrid at Calle Veracruz, tel. 02/91–32–57), where couples rather than singles are the preferred clientele. For salsa in Sabana Grande, **El Maní Es Así** (Calle El Christo at Av. Francisco Solano López, tel. 02/61–70–78) is a must; on weekends the dance floor is packed with all-age celebrants, though during the week you're more likely to see a Brando or Bogart film playing on its large-screen televisions. The most popular Brazilian nightclub in Caracas is **Aquarela Brasilera** (Calle Humboldt, La Chaguarmos, tel. 02/661–5897), which features live Brazilian music nightly and occasionally belly dancing.

Bars In Las Mercedes, **Weekends** (Av. San Juan Bosco at La Segunda Transversal, tel. 02/261–3839) is a popular sports bar with live music and Tex-Mex food. In El Rosal district, **Juan Sebastian Bar** (Av. Venezuela, tel. 02/951–0595) features live jazz most nights.

Excursions from Caracas

La Guaira and Macuto These lively beach resorts are a good bet for visitors who need an escape from urban Caracas without the hassle and expense of renting a car. Both are located in El Litoral district, a 30- to 45-minute trek by subway and bus from downtown Caracas, and both offer sunbathing and the opportunity to indulge in fresh fish at any of a dozen oceanfront reataurants. For sunbathing, the beach facing Macuto's Sheraton hotel is particularly popular.

Getting There Take the subway to Gato Negro, and at street level climb aboard any of the vans or buses marked LA GUAIRA or MACUTO. By car follow signs to the airport and La Guaira and then continue east along the same highway.

Colonia Tovar Colonia Tovar, roughly 145 kilometers (90 miles) from Caracas, was colonized by German immigrants in 1843 and today remains as authentically German as anything you'll find in the Black Forest. Some of the townsfolk are naturally blond, and given the cooler climate and chalet accommodations, one quickly forgets that this high-altitude (1,787 meters/5,860-feet) and sometimes-breezy mountain retreat is located in a steamy tropical country. The real joy is to hike in the hills surrounding Tovar, or to spend an evening in one of the village's jovial chalets, chomping on sausage and other hearty German foods.

Getting There Check with your hotel or the tourist office for information about frequent full-day tours to Colonia Tovar. There is no direct public transportaion to the village, though you can take a public bus as far as Junquito and then hire a cab for the 40-minute drive ($15).

Choroní Choroní is a quiet and undisturbed coastal town, a veritable beach bum's paradise with freshwater bathing, nearby camping, and lots of friendly foreign slackers who gratefully have managed to "misplace" their air ticket home. At night, the fun switches to the adjoining village of Puerto Colombia and its central square. This is where the *tambores* takes place, in the form of heavy African percussion that inspires both locals and tourists to enter into small circles and gyrate wildly, all with the help of a spirited local libation. Drum music and dancing take place most weekends, though the Feast of San Juan Bautista (June 23) draws the largest crowds. You could visit Choroní and Puerto Colombia in one very tiring day, but if you're intrigued by the tambores and decide to stay the night, a room at the relaxed **La Parchita** hotel (El Malecón, tel. 043/832560), with an adjoining vegetarian restaurant, costs around $15. More pampering is **Cotoperix** (El Malecón, tel. 02/951–6226, fax 02/951–7741), which charges $35 for a double.

Getting There Choroní is located in Pittier National Park, and whether by car or bus, the drive from Caracas is a hair-raising experience. By car follow the main highway out of Caracas west to Maracay, then take the *carrelera* (secondary road) from Maracay to Choroní. Buses leave regularly from Caracas's Nuevo Circo terminal for Maracay, where you can then find a bus to Choroní.

The Caribbean Coast and Margarita Island

The Route of the Sun is what Venezuelans call the 563-kilometer (350-mile) stretch of highway that parallels the coast from Caracas to Puerto La Cruz and Cumaná. Fueled by a surge of tourism in the 1980s, major resorts and condominiums have blossomed along the sweeping sandy shores of Higuerote and Puerto La Cruz, contributing to weekend bottlenecks along the arterial Autopista del Oriente (Eastern Highway). Still, the coast comprises unspoiled lagoons and rugged peninsulas, as well as many isolated beaches scarcely touched by tourism.

Though you may not realize it yet, your ultimate destination may be Margarita Island, reached by plane from Caracas or by ferry from Puerto La Cruz or Cumaná. Margarita is Venezuela's legendary island paradise, prized for its untamed beaches and relaxed, picturesque towns. Margarita is no quaint little island, nor is it especially inexpensive; a recent building boom has produced plenty of high-rise hotels and upscale shopping centers. But it has its charms, chief among them palm-lined beaches and friendly locals who don't seem too impressed by tourists—which is probably for the best.

Tourist Information

Barcelona: CORANZTUR (Calle Freites 2–45, tel. 081/77–71–10). **Puerto La Cruz:** CORANZTUR (Paseo Colón at Calle Maneiro, tel. 081/68–81–70). **Cumaná:** Información Turístico (Calle Sucre, tel. 093/24449). **Margarita Island:** DTNA (Aeropuerto del Caribe, tel. 095/69–14–38; Av. Santiago Mariño, Edificio Don Ramón, Porlamar, tel. 095/61–30–65, fax 095/01–19–54).

Getting There

By Bus and Por Puesto There are daily buses—some with air-conditioning and snack service—from the Nuevo Circo terminal in Caracas to Barcelona, Puerto La Cruz, and Cumaná; one-way fare for each is less than $8. Advance reservations are a must and should be made as soon as possible; contact **Expresos CaMarGui** (Nuevo Circo, tel. 02/541–0364) or **Unión Conductores de Margarita** (Nuevo Circo, tel. 02/541–0035), both of which also offer bus-ferry packages to Margarita Island (12 hours) for less than $10.

Another option is *por puesto* taxis, buses, and limousines. These carry three to 15 people and travel set routes between Nuevo Circo terminal and the Caribbean Coast. Drivers shout the names of cities they serve and leave the terminal once their vehicle is full. Por puestos do not accept reservations, and the rates are fixed; expect to pay $10 between Carcas and Puerto La Cruz.

By Car The often congested Autopista del Oriente (Hwy. 9) joins Caracas with Barcelona, Puerto La Cruz, and Cumaná; the highway has all roadside services as it is the major artery for coastal cities.

By Plane **Avensa** and **Aerotuy** fly daily to Barcelona from the Simón Bolívar International Airport in the Caracas suburb of Maiquetía. Most major domestic carriers have daily service from Maiquetía, Cumaná, Valencia, and Maracaibo to Margarita Island's **Aeropuerto Internacional del Caribe** (tel. 095/69–14–38), 29 kilometers (18 miles) south of Porlamar. No matter where you're flying from, a one-way ticket costs less than $40. **Viasa** flies directly from New York to Margarita Island, while **Aeropostal** stops on its Trinidad run. Airport taxis to Porlamar ($10) are scarce, but inside the terminal are dozens of car rental agencies.

By Ferry **Conferry** (Av. La Acacias at Av. Casanova, Caracas, tel. 02/781–6688 or 02/782–8544) shuttles passengers and up to 150 cars six times daily from Puerto La Cruz (Terminal Los Cocos, tel. 081/67–78–47) to Punta de Piedras, 25 kilometers (16 miles) west of Porlamar. It also offers twice daily service from Cumaná (Terminal Puerto Sucre, tel. 093/31–14–62). **Naviarca** (tel. 093/26230) carries up to 60 cars on its daily ferry from Cumaná to Punta de Piedras.

Purchase tickets at least two hours in advance for all ferries, particularly on weekends and holidays. The crossings take two to four hours and cost about $29 per car and $15 per passenger.

Exploring the Caribbean Coast and Margarita Island

Higerote, a haggard-looking town perched on the coast 130 kilometers (80 miles) from Caracas, is jammed with sun worshippers on weekends—mainly Caraqueños who reserved space months ago in one of the sleek resorts that line the long stretch of beach. The silt-filled waters offshore manage to attract thousands of swimmers and *guacuco,* a type of clam whose empty shells form huge mounds on the sand (locals gather live clams and cook them right on the beach).

Carenero, 8 kilometers (4 miles) north of Higerote, is where more affluent Venezuelans go for their holidays. This small resort town does not have a swimmable beach, but from Carenero's Embarcadero Nena Mar, found at the end of a kilometer-long, marked dirt road, there are daily ferries ($2 per person) to **Buche Island** and its tidy beach. **Chirimena,** 4 kilometers (2¹/2 miles) beyond Carenero, has the best beach around—a wide swath of white sand tucked into a crescent-shape cove. There is a paved parking lot here, plus stands offering light snacks and refreshments.

Río Chico, 37 kilometers (23 miles) southeast of Higerote, shares that town's dog-eared appearance, so head straight for **Playa Colada,** Río Chico's well-kept beach, lined with palm-thatched restaurants, lively bars, and umbrella-shaded tables. Join the hoard of sunbathers here, or follow the signs to **Parque Nacional Laguna de Tacarigue,** about 18 kilometers (11 miles) northeast. At the park's entrance is a fishing dock with an open-sided, very rustic bar where you can drink and dance with local beach goers. In the late afternoon, the surrounding mangrove forest comes alive as thousands of white herons and scarlet ibises return home and settle down for the night. From the dock, shuttle boats bring guests to Club Miami (*see* Dining and Lodging, *below*), which is visible on the lagoon's outer banks.

From Río Chico rejoin Highway 9 at El Guapo and continue past Clarines to **Puerto Píritu,** a sleepy village located at the edge of the sea. The streets here are lined with preserved colonial mansions fronting wooden grills, carved eaves, and somber color schemes. The highlight, though, is Píritu's beach: For nearly 2 kilometers (1 mile), the bright blue Caribbean laps a wide ribbon of clean white sand. Restaurants, bars, and hotels are clustered at regular intervals along Píritu's shoreline drive, Boulevard Fernández Padilla.

Barcelona, the capital of Anzótegui State, is 41 kilometers (25 miles) east of Puerto Píritu and the site of the region's largest airport. On the corner of Plaza Boyacá, the city's tree-lined main square, it's hard to miss **Iglesia de San Cristóbal,** a stunning two-story church built in 1748. Even more impressive is the adjacent **Palacio del Gobierno** (Palace of the Government), built in 1671 and home today to the **Museo de la Tradición,** with rotating exhibits of colonial and religious art. *Plaza Boyacá, tel. 081/77–34–81. Admission free. Open daily.*

Puerto La Cruz, the region's main tourist hub, is heavily industrialized, but its port and marinas are attractive. Visitors flock to the maze of shops on the waterfront **Paseo Colón,** a busy thoroughfare that links downtown with a sandy public beach—a seashell hunter's delight. During the day, the beach and its casual restaurants and bars are packed; at night, the crowds move to bars and discos in town. The ferry terminal for Margarita Island is at the western end of Paseo Colón; at the eastern end you'll find boats that shuttle beach goers between Puerto La Cruz and many of the small islands visible in the bay. Expect to pay $5 for round-trip service.

From Puerto La Cruz, follow signs for Guanta and Cumaná; along the way, in the tiny village of Chorrerón, you'll see a sign for **Parque La Sirena** (the entrance is 3 kilometers [2 miles] off the main highway), a small national park nestled in a valley and divided by a slow-moving river. La Sirena doesn't fall into the wildly stunning category, but there are two photogenic waterfalls, popular swimming holes, and a few marked hiking trails in addition to picnic tables, changing rooms, and a snack bar. *Tel. 081/67–44–32. Admission charged. Closed Mon.*

Beyond Guanta, Highway 9 curves and climbs high above Santa Fe Bay, giving good views of the palm-lined coast. As you make your descent, signs direct you to two popular beaches: **Playa Arapito** and **Playa Colorado,** both with smooth sand, paved parking lots, and refreshment stands.

Seven kilometers (4 miles) beyond Santa Fe is the turnoff for **Mochima,** the launching point for boat trips to the tranquil beaches of **Parque Mochima,** which encompasses hundreds of small islands and sand spits just offshore. Contract a *peñero* (boatman) to bring you to any of the nearby beaches, where you can spend a relaxing morning or afternoon bathing and eating fresh fish. The going round-trip rate is $5–$8 per person.

Cumaná is the capital of Sucre State and the oldest European settlement in Venezuela, dating from 1521. Most of Cumaná's colonial mansions and buildings are withing walking distance of the central Plaza Bolívar. One block south, the **Ateneo de Cumaná** (Calle Antonio, tel. 093/31–12–84) hosts dance and opera evenings in addition to periodic exhibits of contemporary and colonial art. **Casa Natal Blanco** (Calle Sucre; admission charged), the birthplace of one of Venezuela's greatest literary figures, André Eloy Blanco (1896–1955), displays personal paraphernalia and some of the author's first edition works. Overlooking Cumaná from its hilltop perch, **Castillo de San Antonio de la Eminencia** (admission free; open daily) is one of two forts commissioned in the 1680s to protect what at the time was the world's largest salt deposit. The four-point fort was built entirely of coral and outfitted with 16 guns, much like its companion, **Castillo de Santiago de Araya** (admission free; open daily), located on the rugged, treeless Araya Peninsula. Car and passenger ferries leave daily from Cumaná's harbor for the Araya Peninsula; the crossing takes 90 minutes.

It's estimated that **Cueva del Guácharo,** Venezuela's largest cave, has at least 10,204 meters (33,456 feet) of subterranean passageways. At the cave's entrance there's an information center—with a snack bar and rest rooms—where you can ponder a handful of displays and charts before plunging into the dank, eerie caverns. You are led in groups of 10 by a guide toting a single kerosene lantern so as not to upset the light-sensitive guácharos—nocturnal, fruit-eating birds that nest inside the cave. Visitors are not allowed to bring anything inside—no purses, flashlights, food, cameras, and the like. To reach the cave from Cumaná, take Highway 9 south toward Caripe for about 65 kilometers (40 miles) and follow the signs. *Parque Nacional El Guácharo, tel. 081/78–44–45. Admission charged. Open daily.*

Margarita Island   **Isla de Margarita,** along with the smaller islands of **Cubagua** and **Coche** and the 50 or so islets of Los Roques Archipelago, have long been a favorite sea-and-sun playground for Venezuelans. Margarita Island, in particular, has become the focus of vigorous hotel and resort development to accommodate the growing number of international tourists. Margarita is divided into two sections, connected by a narrow sandspit, and the bulk of its 200,000 residents live on the more developed eastern half. Cars are the most convenient way of getting around and can be rented at the airport; however, taxis and por puesto buses connect Margarita's larger towns with one another and with the beach.

Porlamar, founded in 1536, is the commercial heart of Margarita Island; its streets have been packed with shops and hotels ever since the area was granted free-port status by the government in 1973. (In fact, moonlighting Caraqueños sometimes come to Margarita looking for clothes and gadgets to sell back on the mainland.) There are relatively few historic sights in Porlamar—perhaps the reason why the most popular pastimes here are shopping, sunbathing, and eating. For the first, try the maze of shops huddled between the pedestrian-only Boulevard Guevara and Boulevard Gómez, or try the local market near Plaza Bolívar.

A few blocks east of shady Plaza Bolívar is the **Museo de Arte Contemporáneo Francisco Narváez,** named after the native Margariteño sculptor whose works also can be viewed on the grounds of the Hotel Bella Vista (*see* Lodging, *below*). In the museum you'll find a permanent collection of Narváez's works, plus a rotating exhibit of national and international art. *Calle Igualdad at Calle Fraternidad, tel. 095/61–86–68. Admission free. Closed Mon.*

From Porlamar follow the road 2.5 kilometers (1½ miles) north to **El Valle,** Margarita's first capital, founded in 1529. Today it is a center for souvenirs and crafts, from hammocks to rag dolls. A point of pilgrimage for islanders—especially on September 8, the Virgin of El Valle's feast day—is the **Santuario de la Virgin del Valle,** a pink twin-towered edifice on El Valle's main plaza. Adjacent to the church, a small **museum** (admission charged; closed Mon.) contains the thousands of tokens, jewelry, and holy medals left by supplicants.

North of El Valle lies mountainous **El Copey National Park,** giving striking views of the island (provided the national guard lets you in). The mountain road slowly descends to **La Asunción,** the modern capital of Margarita Island. Built in 1580, the **Catedral Nuestra Señora** (Church of Our Lady) stands prominently on La Asunción's main plaza and is one of the earliest examples of colonial architecture in Venezuela. Of particular note is it square, three-tier tower—the country's only surviving example of a colonial church tower. Adjacent to the church, the **Museo Nueva Cádiz** (tel. 095/41980; admission charged; closed Mon.) contains a hodge-podge collection of wooden model ships, religious statuary, and seashells. Overlooking the main square, the **Castillo de Santa Rosa** (admission free; open daily) is a handsomely restored fort originally built in 1681. Those who make the short but arduous uphill trek (there's a path visible from the main square) will be rewarded with panoramic views of the island.

The coastal village of **Pampatar,** 10 kilometers (6 miles) north of Porlamar, is a popular anchoring spot for yachts. Strategically placed above the harbor is the impressive **Castillo de San Carlos de Borromeo,** a brawny fort built wholly of coral rock between 1664 and 1684. It's undergoing renovations and is closed indefinitely, but the adjacent 17th-century church, **Igle-**

sia Santísimo Cristo, it worth the short trek from town. Its most notable feature is a flat-faced bell tower accessed by an outside staircase—a feature found throughout Margarita Island but rarely elsewhere in Venezuela. In Pampatar proper, take a quick peak at the replica of Christopher Columbus's ship, the *Santa Ana*, before trying your best to feel like a kid again at the waterfront **Magic Isle** amusement park, somewhat downtrodden in appearance but popular for its Ferris wheel and rather tame roller coaster.

If you rent a car you can circle Margarita Island, making side trips to beaches at **Guacuco** and **El Tirano.** Near Margarita's northern tip, **Playa El Agua** is rightly famous for its fine sands, coconut palms, and quiet restaurants. Nonbeach options include **Parque Nacional Laguna de la Restinga,** a mangrove-lined nature reserve that's 36 kilometers (22 miles) west of Porlamar and reached via the road to Boca del Río. For less than $1 per person, boatmen will give you a tour of the park's lagoons or bring you straight to a 23-kilometer- (14-mile-) long, shadeless beach, where you'll find palm-thatched restaurants and a few crafts stands. Boatmen leave from El Indio dock behind the park-information center. *Tel. 095/42995. Park admission free. Open daily.*

Shopping

In **Puerto La Cruz,** shops along **Paseo Colón** cater to tourists with trinket and crafts stands, as do the street sellers hawking jewelry and beach items—sandals, glasses, and sunscreen—at reaonable prices. Foreigners may not find the selection or prices very enticing on **Margarita Island,** but **Porlamar,** in particular, offers a good selection of local crafts *and* designer clothing and electronic goods. Shops are concentrated around Porlamar's Plaza Bolívar, east along Calle Igualdad to the intersection of Avenida Santiago Marino, and up to Avenida 4 de Mayo, where serious, expensive shopping begins.

Sports and the Outdoors

For a small fee, resort hotels sometimes allow nonguests to use tennis courts, weight rooms, and spa facilities.

Boating and Water Sports In El Morro, near Puerto La Cruz, **Odisea** (Hotel Doral Beach, tel. 081/81–22–22) rents sailboats, Windsurfers, and pedalboats. In Puerto La Cruz, you can rent sailboats from **Amerinda Tours** (Hotel Caribbean Inn, tel. 081/67–06–93). On Margarita Island, windsurfing rentals cost $15 per day at **Wind Surf Paradise** (Playa El Yaque, 21 km [13 mi] south of Porlamar, tel. 095/98–67–23).

Diving and Snorkeling In Puerta La Cruz, the **Tecnisub Diving Center** (the Marina, tel. 081/66–90–81) offers diving and snorkeling lessons in addition to organized ocean dives for experienced—and certified—divers.

Fishing Boatmen throughout the region will take you surf or lagoon fishing in their small, wooden, open-top peñeros. Prices will reflect your ability to bargain; the going rate is about $5 per person, including basic equipment, for a half-day excursion. **Amerinda Tours** (*see above*) charters deep-sea boats for serious anglers. **Cuante Agencia de Viaje y Turismo** (tel. 081/776–3304) charges $100 per person per day to fish and camp overnight on an island; the price includes boat transfers, all meals and accommodations, and fishing gear.

Dining and Lodging

Hotels on the Caribbean Coast will add 10% to your bill unless you have a Venezuelan passport. Reservations are a must on holidays and summer weekends. For price categories, *see* Dining and Lodging in Staying in Venezuela, *above.*

Cumaná
Dining and Lodging
★

Hotel Los Bordones. Cumaná's best address is this fairly modern four-star hotel, situated on the outskirts of town, with two restaurants, a vast swimming pool, and—best of all—access to a nearly secluded beach just a pebble's throw away. An on-site travel office can arrange snorkeling and windsurfing jaunts. Polinesa, the popular on-site restaurant, is considered the best in town for fresh seafood. *Av. Universidad, tel. 093/65–37–83 or 093/65–36–44. 114 rooms with bath, 3 suites. Facilities: 2 restaurants, pool, 2 tennis courts. AE, D, MC, V. Expensive.*

Gran Hotel. This plain and functional hotel is located in the center of town, opposite the entrance to the Universidad del Oriente. Most rooms are equipped with private bathrooms, air-conditioning, and televisions. The hotel restaurant is quite respectable. *Av. Universidad, tel. 093/65–37–11 or 093/65–38–11. 50 rooms. Facilities: restaurant, TV and air-conditioning in most rooms. AE, D, MC, V. Moderate.*

Puerto La Cruz
Dining
★

Casa Pueblo. An authentic colonial hacienda, where the comfortable, even romantic dining area is superbly complemented by a mile-long menu, printed in English, German, and Spanish. The house specialty is grilled fish, prepared from whatever is fresh. If you're an early riser, don't miss the hearty egg-and-steak breakfasts starting at 7 AM. *Calle Carabobo (between Paseo Colón and Calle Bolívar), tel. 081/22018. AE, D, MC, V. Moderate.*

Da Luigi Bar & Restaurant. Italian fare and ambience right on the Paseo Colón, all managed by extremely attentive waiters. The antipastos are top rate, as are the classic Roman entrées like spaghetti á la Vongole and escallopini al vino. *Paseo Colón 117 at Calle Boyacá, tel. 081/21694. AE, D, MC, V. Inexpensive– Moderate.*

Lodging
★

Hotel Rasil. This relatively new high rise at the end of Paseo Colón combines the amenities of a chain hotel—including shops and a pool with an overlooking bar—with the informal charm of a small pension. Most rooms have ocean views and whirlpool bathtubs. *Paseo Colón at Calle Monagas, tel. 081/67–24–22, fax 081/67–31–21. 350 rooms, 34 suites. Facilities: restaurant, bar, pool, disco; cable TV in most rooms. AE, D, MC, V. Expensive.*

Hotel Caribe Mar. This relatively new offering behind the Hotel Rasil features comfortable singles and suites—most with sea views—at lower-than-average rates. *Calle Ricaurte No. 14, tel. 081/67–32–91 or 081/67–49–73, fax 081/67–20–96. 74 rooms, 16 suites, all with bath. Facilities: restaurant, bar, air-conditioning in rooms. AE, D, MC, V. Moderate–Expensive.*

Hotel Gaeta. A prime reason to stay here is location, on the Paseo Colón a short walk from Puerto La Cruz's restaurants and shops. Most of the Gaeta's simple, clean rooms have balconies, and the beach is only a stone's throw away. If the main hotel is full, try the affiliated Hotel Gaeta City, only five blocks farther along Calle Maneiro. *Paseo Colón at Calle Maneiro, tel.*

081/69–16–16. 50 rooms. Facilities: restaurant, bar, air-conditioning in rooms. AE, MC, V. Moderate.

Margarita Island
Dining

Martín Pescador. This casual but busy restaurant is as popular with foreigners as it is with local families. Besides a good selection of Italian wine, the menu features Italian standards supplemented with fresh fish entrées (mostly red snapper or sea bass). For dessert, try the *Marquesa de Chocolate*, a decadent chocolate mousse layer cake. *Av. 4 de Mayo, Porlamar, tel. 095/61–66–97. AE, V. Moderate–Expensive.*

El Pirata. Overlooking the main highway opposite the CANTV telephone office is this attractive, Spanish-style open-air restaurant. Linger over a beer at the long bar, or try one of the many fish or grilled meat offerings; the house specialty, Chateaubriand steak, is the best on the island. *Pampatar, no phone. No credit cards. Closed Wed. Moderate.*

★ **Bahia.** The elegant dining area with large bay windows affords a striking view of the beach—part of the reason for Bahia's genuine popularity among locals. The international-style cuisine comes with a decidedly Spanish flavor; wade into an appetizer of octopus before moving on to the jumbo shrimp bathed in cream and topped with cheese. *Av. Raúl Leoni, on the road to El Morro beach, Porlamar, tel. 095/61–41–56. AE, MC, V. Moderate.*

Lodging
★

Hotel Flamingo. This luxurious six-story complex a few hundred meters north of Pampatar is one of the island's major lodging institutions. A glass elevator climbs to stylish rooms with views over the sea and, in many instances, the island itself. Sumptuous breakfast and dinner buffets are served on a deck overlooking the nearby beach and tennis courts. *Calle El Cristo, Sector La Caranta, Pampatar, tel. 095/62–48–22, fax 095/62–26–72; in the U.S., tel. 800/221–5333, fax 305/599–1946. 160 rooms with bath. Facilities: restaurant, bar, pool, shops, 2 tennis courts. MC, V. Very Expensive.*

Bella Vista. Despite obvious signs of wear and tear, the waterfront Bella Vista is one of Porlamar's major landmarks and located in the heart of the downtown shopping district. The lobby restaurant has a solid reputation for its fresh seafood and good selection of imported wines. *Calle Igualdad, Porlamar, tel. 095/61–72–22 or 095/61–41–57 for reservations, fax 095/61–25–57. 231 rooms with bath. Facilities: restaurant, tennis courts, pool. AE, MC, V. Expensive.*

Margarita International Resort. Suites come with two bedrooms, a living room, and kitchen facilities—reason enough why this well-equipped complex is a favorite with Venezuelan and foreign families. *Av. Bolívar, Porlamar, tel. 095/61–16–67, fax 095/61–42–21; in Caracas, tel. 02/959–3402, fax 02/959–3392. 230 rooms. Facilities: 2 restaurants, pool, gym, 2 tennis courts, shops. AE, DC, MC, V. Moderate.*

Hotel Colibri. This is a safe, centrally located budget option where bland motel-style rooms are softened by the pleasant lobby restaurant—a good spot for breakfast before trekking to the beaches. A new bar and pool area are scheduled for completion by the summer of '94. *Av. Santiago Mariño, Porlamar, tel. 095/61–63–46 or 095/61–21–95, fax 095/61–21–95. 70 rooms. Facilities: restaurant. No credit cards. Inexpensive.*

Nightlife

You won't have to look far to find bars and discos in **Puerto La Cruz**: All of them are located on either Paseo Colón or on adjacent side streets. A new and popular addition to the nightlife scene is **Harry's Pub** (Calle Bolívar No. 53, tel. 081/61–35–24), a dark but friendly watering hole with an interesting mix of young locals and seasoned wayfarers.

Many night spots on **Margarita Island** are tucked behind Avenida Santiago Mariño in **Porlamar.** Also try the sophisticated **Mosquito Coast Bar & Grill** (Paseo Guaranguao, tel. 095/61–35–24), a moderately priced bar and disco located behind the Bella Vista hotel—and very popular with Venezuela's young and beautiful set. With its low lights and sultry looks, **Piano Blanco** (Calle Jesús María Patiño, tel. 095/61–69–02), also in Porlamar, is popular for tranquil jazz and unhurried drinking.

Mérida and the Andes

As you leave behind the subtropical lowlands and begin your ascent of the Andes, which rise directly south of Lake Maracaibo, the changes are swift and unmistakable. In the foothills, thatched farms give way to tile-roofed hamlets clinging to hillsides; at 10,000 feet, the rugged mountain landscape includes stone-strewn fields sprouting wheat and coffee. Colder and higher still, the *Transandina* (Trans-Andes) road winds its way through Jají, Mérida, and San Cristóbal, looping in hairpin bends and finally climbing to the fog-bound Paso del Aguila, a forbidding mountain pass at an altitude of 13,146 feet. Just south of San Cristóbal, the Pan-American Highway swerves south on its long trek through Colombia.

Mérida, the capital of Mérida State, lies in the heart of the Andes. Sprawling in a high-altitude valley that's embraced by two arms of the mountain chain, Mérida's striking skyline is unequivocally defined by the peaks of the Five White Eagles (as Merideños call them)—La Caron, La Concha, La Columna, El Toro, and El León, each encrusted with glaciers and towering more than 4,575 meters (15,000 feet) above the distant sea. Given its proximity to these eminently climbable peaks, Mérida is a mecca for Andes-bound travelers.

Tourist Informaiton

Mérida: Corporación Meridona de Turismo (Cormetur) (Av. 1 at Av. 2, tel. 074/529566 or 074/526972, fax 074/523067).

Getting There

By Plane Mérida's **Carnavali Airport** (tel. 074/636163), five minutes by taxi from the city center, is served once daily by **Aeropostal** and twice daily by **Avensa.** One-way tickets from Caracas cost less than $15.

By Car From Caracas take Highway 51 west to Valencia. From here, the road to Barinas keeps to low-lying valleys and the plains; from Barinas, begin your ascent over the Andes via Barinitas and the Transandina highway. Another option from Valencia is the high-altitude Pan-American Highway via Barquisimeto,

Carora, and Sabana de Mendoza. Either way, the journey takes about 12 hours.

By Bus There are morning and evening departures to Mérida's **Antonio Paredes** bus terminal (tel. 074/661193) from Caracas's Nuevo Circo terminal. The 10- to 13-hour trip costs less than $9. Purchase your ticket at least a day in advance at Nuevo Circo terminal from one of the following operators: **Expreso Alianza** (tel. 02/541–1975) or **Expreso Mérida** (tel. 02/541–1975).

Exploring Mérida and the Andes

Mérida Founded in 1558, Mérida has grown up around the **Plaza Bolívar,** a pleasant and popular open-air venue for the troop of Indian artisans who regularly sell handmade crafts here. Fronting the plaza is Mérida's **Catedral Metropolitana** (Metropolitan Cathedral), considered one of the most striking in Venezuela. Begun in 1787 by Fray Juan Manuel António Ramos, the soberly colored Metropolitan bares its embellished baroque facade, carved with intricate zoomorphic and geometric designs, to the amber hills surrounding Mérida. *Plaza Bolívar. Admission free.*

At the opposite end of the square, the **Casa de Cultura Juan Felix Sánchez** hosts dynamic exhibitions of paintings, sculpture, ceramics, and woodworks by regional artists. Nearby is the Bulevar Paseo Libertador, where local painters sometimes gather to work and compare notes. *Plaza Bolívar, tel. 074/526101. Admission free. Closed Mon.*

Mérida's **Museo de Arte Colonial** (Colonial Art Museum) has a valuable collection of artifacts culled from the 16th to 19th centuries. *Av. 4, between Calles 18 and 19, tel. 074/527860. Admission free. Closed Sat.–Mon.*

Nearby, the **Museo Arqueológico** (Archaeological Museum) displays pre-Columbian art and ceramics. Opened in 1976, the museum has the region's finest collection of anthropomorphic figurines, ceramics, and tools from the prehispanic cultures that once dominated the Andes. *Av. 3, Edificio Rectorado, tel. 074/402344. Admission charged. Closed Mon.*

Los Chorros de Milla, one of Mérida's 20-some parks, features indigenous Venezuelan fauna as well as tigers and other animals kept on display in cages. Yet the real attraction are the **Andean Falls,** a pleasant set of falls that make the steep walk through the park more agreeable. *Av. Chorros de Milla. Admission charged. Closed Mon.*

On **Parque Reloj de Beethoven,** there's a well-known clock that ushers in the hour with music from the great German composer. More intriguing is the adjacent **Museo de Arte Moderno** (Modern Art Museum), with an excellent permanent collection of works by some of Venezuela's most heralded contemporary painters. *Parque Reloj de Beethoven, tel. 074/440819. Admission free. Closed Mon.*

Plaza Las Heroínas is where children gather in the late afternoon, and, as evening falls and the fog rolls in, where young lovers huddle together on benches. On Sunday it hosts an informal crafts market. More to the point, the plaza contains the substation of Mérida's **Teleférico,** the longest mountain cable car in the world and one of the town's most popular attractions. Built in the 1960s by French engineers, the Teléferico ascends in four breathtaking stages to Pico Espejo (4,768 meters/ 15,633 feet), which is nearly 900 feet taller than Switzerland's Matterhorn. Unfortunately, the last leg is not currently in operation due to a recent accident (don't fret: U.S. engineers have since pronounced the other three legs completely safe). The first car heads up around 7 AM, the last around 3 PM. It is best to take an early morning trip, because going in the afternoon only makes it harder to find a seat at the crowded mountaintop cantina. Purchase tickets early for the 90-minute trip from the Teléferico office on Calle 25. *Tel. 074/525080. Admission charged. Teléferico closed Mon.*

From Lomas Redonda station, currently the highest point served by the Teléferico, you can hire guides, mules, and horses for the four- to five-hour descent to **Los Nevados,** a secluded mountain village that was once a garrison for Spanish conquistadors. The first leg of the journey involves a sharp ascent through the Bosque de los Coloraditos, named for the flowering coloradito tree—one of the few species hearty enough to survive at this altitude. Soon you begin the descent to Los Nevados, along a boulder-strewn path best negotiated on donkey or mule rather than on foot. Bone weary and winded, you finally come upon the red-tile outline of Los Nevados, where you can find unpretentious accommodations in local *posadas* (pensions) with open-air courtyards surrounded by small but functional rooms.

The Southern Andes **Jají,** 22 miles west of Mérida on the Azulita Road, sparkles with whitewash, fountains, and flowers. Founded in the late 16th-century, Jají and its colonial buildings have been restored by the government as a tourist attraction. The highlights consist of the town's church, the main square, and a few surrounding homes. If you're in the area in late September, Jají celebrates the Feast of St. Michael Archangel on the 24th with music, dance, and much fanfare.

Bailadores, 92 kilometers (54 miles) south from Mérida, boasts the **Parque de la India Curú,** named for the Indian princess Curú, wife of chief Toquizán, who ruled these parts prior to Columbus's arrival. The park has a large waterfall and several scenic, undemanding walking trails. *Admission charged. Closed Mon.* Three kilometers (2 miles) east of Bailadores, **Parque Paez** (sometimes called Parque La Cascada) has picnic areas and pools as well as small falls that can be viewed up close with complete safety. *Admission free.*

Six hours and 300 kilometers (176 miles) beyond Bailadores lies **San Cristóbal,** capital of Táchira State and only 43 kilometers (27 miles) from the Colombian border. Every January its San Sebastian Fair draws thousands of cattle sellers, horse racers, and bullfight fans. The rest of the year, its old city provides only a minimal level of excitement. Yet even if you do not make it all the way to San Cristóbal, the mountain views from the highway are dazzling: lovely **La Negra Paramo,** a wild and desolate region where the Mocoties River has its source, may alone be worth the trip.

The Northern Andes From Mérida, take the Vía al Paramo 14 kilometers (9 miles) northeast to **Tabay,** where Alexis Montilla has created unique, 18-acre **Los Aleros,** a detailed miniature village museum peopled with Andeans in colonial dress. Montilla takes sightseers on an ancient bus through his make-believe town, while locals dressed as farmers, highwaymen, or herb collectors re-create a typical colonial scene. *Tel. 074/440430 for information. Admission charged.*

East of Mérida and Tabay, the highland road brings you to the Mucuchíes region, the "land of water" in Indian dialect, where the starkly beautiful landscape—scrub-filled fields and barren hillsides—includes half a dozen lakes. **San Rafael de Mucuchíes,** 52 kilometers (30 miles) east of Mérida and at an altitude of 5,140 meters (16,962 feet), is where Simón Bolívar persuaded his ragtag army to begin their ascent of the Andes and initiate the liberation of Colombia. To appreciate how daunting a proposition this must have been to Bolívar's poorly clothed, barely fed troops, spend an afternoon walking the switchback trails in the hills encircling San Rafael, which give good views over the severe mountainous landscape. From San Rafael you can rent horses and mules for the one- to two-hour trek to Lagunas Say-Say and Montón, two isolated but locally popular trout-stocked lagoons.

The road north to **Apartaderos** passes through more barren, austere mountain terrain; this is the Andean *páramo,* or steppe, an arid region above the timberline where only moss and shrublike *frailejones* grow. At the junction of the Apartaderos and Santo Domingo roads, you can rent horses or mules and trek to some of the nearby trout lagoons—Laguna de los Patos, Laguna Negra, and La Canoa, among them. Catches in these lakes are reported at more than 15 pounds. Local guides can be found in **Santo Domingo** and **Los Frailes,** or contact **Montaña Tours** (*see* Fishing in Sports and the Outdoors, *below*).

Those headed to Trujillo State by car should not miss the **Pico Aguila,** a 4,270-meter- (14,000-foot-) high pass that connects Apartaderos with Jají and Valera. Venezuela's highest roadway, Pico Aguila also marks the spot where Bolívar and his army actually crossed the Andes in 1813 on their way to fight the Spanish in Colombia. The crossing, commanding a dizzying view over the mountains, is commemorated by a statue, the *El Aguila Desplegada,* depicting a condor clutching between its beak and talons a medallion engraved with Bolívar's image. On cold and bracing days, a small stand sells hot chocolate and coffee near the statue overlook.

Shopping

On Sunday **Mérida**'s Plaza Las Heroínas overflows with handmade crafts and locally produced weavings. Farther south, along Avenida Las Americas, is a smaller market with produce, housewares, and a handful of crafts stalls. In **Jají, Complejo Turístico de Antier** is a co-op selling high-quality arts and crafts from around Venezuela. Some 30 kilometers (19 miles) beyond Jají, in **Azulita,** painters and artisans sell their exquisitely crafted wares along the roadside.

Sports and the Outdoors

Biking   **Montaña Tours** (Apartado Postal 645, tel. and fax 074/66–14–48) arranges multiday treks to El Tisure, the secluded village of Los Nevados, and along Pico Aguila, Venezuela's highest roadway. Bilingual guides, food, and bicycling equipment are provided. Montaña Tours' U.S. representative, Lost World Adventures (tel. 404/971–8586, fax 404/977–3095), can prebook hiking treks throughout the region.

Fishing Around Mérida, the Andes Mountains are liberally sprinkled with small lakes and lagoons regularly stocked with rainbow and brown trout. In remote reaches, hooking a 15-pound trout is not unheard of. Jeeps, horses, and mules can be rented for the sometimes arduous trek into the heart of the mountains; in Mérida, **Montaña Tours** (*see above*) offers guided fishing trips during season (March 30–September 30).

Hiking Mérida is the base for three- to seven-day treks (Grade I–4) in the Andes. Operators typically provide bilingual guides and all necessary equipment, as well as transportation to and from the sights and food and accommodations along the way. Contact **Alpi Tour** (Av. Sucre, Centro Parque Boyaca, piso 1, Oficina 2, Caracas, tel. 02/284–1433, fax 02/285–6067), **Montaña Tours** (*see above*), or **Paramo Tours** (Calle 23, Edificio EDC, piso 2, Local 2–1, tel. 074/52–52–79 or 074/52–13–70, fax 074/52–52–58).

Dining and Lodging

Although lodgings are difficult to find in Mérida during the high season (book in advance whenever possible), room rates are generally reasonable. In the Andes you can expect simple, unpretentious *hosterías* offering clean rooms and attached restaurants. Outside Mérida, hosterías are often the best (and only) dining option. For price categories, *see* Dining and Lodging in Staying in Venezuela, *above*.

Mérida **Mira Me Lindo.** This relaxed, intimate restaurant inside the
Dining Chama Hotel is noted for its succulent Basque cuisine: specialties include peppers stuffed with fish, *pargo a la champagne* (snapper in champagne), and *muslo de pollo al ron* (chicken drumstick in rum). *Calle 29 at Av. 4, tel. 074/52–10–11. AE, D, MC, V. Moderate–Expensive.*

Marisquería Tu y Yo. This colorful bar-cum-restaurant is a fine place to swill beer and enjoy plates of fresh fish while conversing with locals. At "You and I," informal is the key word. *Av. 4 Bolívar 28–70, tel. 074/52–91–38. AE, D, MC, V. Inexpensive.*

Tasca y Marisquería Vargas. Mérida's best fish eatery is popular with local families who don't mind the modern, rather dull setting. The fresh fish specialties, particularly the trout, are excellent: try *trucha* (trout) *al ajillo* (with garlic) or *a la plancha* (grilled with butter). There's also a good wine list. *Av. Don Tulio Febres 30–71 (at Calle 31), tel. 074/52–27–69. AE, D, MC, V. Inexpensive.*

Lodging **El Tisure.** Mérida's newest hotel is only a five-minute walk north of Plaza Bolívar and features well-equipped, very neat and clean rooms overlooking a quiet square. This is the only hotel in town with central air-conditioning. *Av. 4 Bolívar 17–47, tel. 074/52–07–44 or 074/52–17–44, fax 074/52–08–27. 33 rooms. Facilities: restaurant, bar, TV in rooms. AE, D, MC, V. Expensive.*

★ **Hotel Belensate.** The Belensate is situated in La Punta, a quiet residential quarter on the western outskirts of Mérida (but still only a short walk from Plaza Bolívar). Its somewhat out-of-the-way location complements its mountain chalet flavor: spacious rooms and private cabins are well equipped and overlook a lush garden. La Nonna, the on-site restaurant, is a local favorite. *Urbanización La Hacienda, tel. 074/66–37–22, fax 074/66–12–55 or 074/66–28–23. 56 rooms, 7 cabins. Facilities: restaurant, bar, garden. AE, D, MC, V. Expensive.*

Caribay. The centrally located Caribay features a helpful bilingual staff and modern, functional rooms. An on-site travel agency can help arrange tours in the Andes. *Av. 2, tel. 074/63-64–51, fax 074/63–71–41. 80 rooms. Facilities: restaurant, bar, disco, travel agency. AE, D, MC, V. Moderate.*

Hotel Teleférico. This popular but basic budget option is housed in a blandly modern, four-story block near the cable car station. Stay here if price counts more than comfort. *Plaza de las Heroínas, tel. 074/52–73–70. 18 rooms. Facilities: restaurant. AE, D, MC, V. Inexpensive.*

Apartederos
Dining and Lodging
★

Los Frailes. The "Friars" inn occupies a 17th-century monastery on the road between Apartederos and Santo Domingo. From the top of the adjoining bell tower, once the monks' cells, you can see the rugged outline of Pico Agilar in the distance. On chilly nights, warm yourself by the fire in the rumpus room, or retire to the comfort of your heated bedroom. The staff can arrange fishing or horseback trips to nearby lakes and lagoons. *70 km (44 mi) south from Mérida on road to Varina, tel. 074/63–77–37; for reservations tel. 02/564–0098, fax 02/564–7936. 48 rooms. Facilities: restaurant, bar, heaters and private bath in rooms. AE, D, MC, V. Expensive.*

San Rafael Mucuchíes
Dining and Lodging

Los Andes. This central townhouse has been attractively converted into a five-room inn with two shared bathrooms. The rooms have few amenities but are otherwise clean and cozy. The adjacent restaurant is a local favorite. *Calle Independencia 42, tel. 074/81–151. 5 rooms. Facilities: restaurant. No credit cards. Inexpensive.*

Jají
Dining and Lodging

Posada de Jají. This is the most comfortable and intimate of the handful of inns that crowd Jají's main square. The attached restaurant features Andean cuisine and semiregular folk music. *Plaza Bolívar, no phone. 4 rooms. Facilities: restaurant. No credit cards. Inexpensive.*

San Cristóbal
Dining and Lodging

El Tamá. The 10-story El Tamá, situated in residential Los Pirineos district, is a typically characterless but well-equipped resort. After trekking through the rugged Andes, however, you will think it quite luxurious. *Calle 23, tel. 076/55–43–35. 112 rooms. Facilities: restaurant, bar, pool, car rental. MC, V. Moderate.*

The Arts and Nightlife

The Arts Toward the end of January, **La Feria de San Sebastián** (Festival of San Sebastian) is a four-day explosion of bullfights, song and music processions, and markets in San Cristóbal. In February, Mérida celebrates its **Feria del Sol** (Festival of the Sun) with bullfights and open-air salsa and merengue performances.

Nightlife In the Andes, hotels and inns are often the only choice for after-dark excitement; many have informal bars and regularly host live folkloric bands, particularly on weekends. In Mérida, the disco **Birosca Tasca** (Calle 24 at Av. 2) swings into the wee hours with live salsa, rock, and Brazilian music.

Elsewhere in Venezuela

The Llanos

Getting There Aeropostal and Avensa fly daily to San Fernando de Apure, Barinas, Guanare, and Acarigua. Round-trip tickets cost roughly $150–$200. Many ranches arrange transportation for prebooked guests.

What to See and Do Besides the Andes, Venezuela's most noticeable physical feature are the Llanos, a 600-mile stretch of grassy plains that extend from the Orinoco River Delta westward into Colombia. Endlessly crisscrossed by streams and raging rivers, the Llanos nurture one of the most diverse groupings of wildlife in the Western Hemisphere. One of the many *hatos* (ranches) in the region, Hato Piñero (which banned hunting in 1950), has catalogued no fewer than 300 species of birds, 20 of reptiles, and 50 of mammals (including the ubiquitous capybara, the world's largest rodent). In the region's nature reserves and national parks, look forward to up-close encounters with otters and ocelots, jaguars, monkeys, crocodiles, and *caribes* (piranhas), not to mention pink flamingos, crakes, trogons, harpy eagles, and most any exotic bird you can imagine.

The Llanos constitute almost a third of Venezuela's landmass but less than 9% of its population, partly because the plains are mercilessly sunbeaten during summer and flooded by rain-swollen rivers from June to September. Between December and April as rivers dry to a trickle, cows and other animals die of thirst while millions of wading birds compete for the fish trapped in shrinking ponds. When thunderclaps announce the first rains, green grass carpets the plains, and hungry animals return to the task of grazing.

During the dry season the Llanos flatlands become a natural destination for birders and nature enthusiasts. More and more ranches, however, are remolding and upgrading their facilities to attract visitors with broader interests—be it horseback riding, Jeep treks through the plains, or evenings of local *joropo* music. Ranch accommodations typically consist of small, private lodges equipped with televisions, sometimes also with air-conditioning, swimming pools, and recreation facilities. Lodges are often grouped around communal dining areas, where guests and *llanero* ranchers share meals. Three- to seven-day packages cost upwards of $150 per person per day, which includes transfers to and from the airport, three meals a day, and daytime treks with experienced guides.

The best-known ranches are Hato Piñero, Hato El Frío, and Hato El Cedral. All three can be booked through **Alpi Tours** (tel. 02/284–1433, fax 02/285–6067), **Lost World Adventures** (in the U.S., tel. 404/971–8586 or 800/999–0558, fax 404/977–3095), and **Turven Tour Express** (tel. 02/951–1787, fax 02/951–1176).

Angel Falls

Getting There Avensa and Aerotuy regularly fly to Canaima from Ciudad Bolívar ($70 each way) and from the Caracas suburb of Maiquetía ($150 each way). Weather permitting, all flights to Canaima include a flyover of Angel Falls.

What to See and Do The Guayana Highlands in Bolívar State overwhelm mere mortals with their intense, dizzying beauty. At sunrise, fog and clouds rise from the grassy savanna and wrap around the flat mesas, or *tepuis,* which tower over the surrounding troop of waterfalls and lagoons. The area is known as **La Gran Sabana** (Great Savanna), and much of it forms **Canaima National Park,** the world's third largest with over 11,500 square miles of undisturbed—and in some cases, largely unexplored—mountainbound grassland.

The highlight in Canaima is undoubtedly **Angel Falls,** the world's tallest waterfall. The drop from Auyantepui (Devil's Mountain) to the turgid lagoon below is 980 meters (3,212 feet)—more than twice the height of the Empire State Building. The falls were discovered in 1937 by a U.S. pilot, Jimmy Angel, who landed on Auyantepui's vast mesa top in search of gold. After abandoning his wounded plane, Angel braved the rough terrain and eventually came across the falls later named in his honor.

The airline Avensa manages the popular **Canaima Camp** (tel. 02/562–3022 or 800/428–3672 in the U.S., fax 02/562–3475), perched on a lagoon at the base of Salto Hacha (Hacha Falls). The 160-person facility is often booked on weekends and holidays, and ticketed Avensa passengers have preference for overnight stays. Aerotuy operates a smaller overnight camp at **Kavac Falls,** while "Jungle Rudy" Truffino maintains the intimate **Ucaima Camp** (tel. 02/661–9153, fax 02/661–1980) upriver from Hacha Falls. The airlines and Jungle Rudy each arrange daylong hikes to Angel Falls and tamer Kavac Falls for $100–$150 per person; two- to three-night treks cost $200–$300. The price for overnight accommodations at each camp is roughly the same: $55–$85 per person, per night.

Amazonas Territory

Getting There **Avensa** and **Aeropostal** fly daily from Caracas's Simón Bolívar International Airport (via San Fernando de Apure) to Puerto Ayacucho ($70–$100 one way), the region's main and only tourist hub. **Aerotuy** flies once weekly to Puerto Ayacucho from Ciudad Bolívar (via Ciacara). From Ciudad Bolívar, Ciudad Guayana, and Cabruta, ferries bring cars ($50–$65) and passengers ($10–$15) up the Orinoco River to Puerto Ayacucho; the uneventful trek can take up to three days when the river swells, and meals are not provided.

What to See and Do Although the Amazon is normally associated with the wilds of Brazil, Venezuela's vastly exotic Amazonas region has recently become the target of trekkers in pursuit of serious adventure. Venezuela's Amazonas basin includes the headwaters of the Orinoco River, not to mention a seemingly endless carpet of thick jungle and more than 2,000 largely unexplored river tributaries. A dozen different Indian tribes, each with its own language and culture, make the forests and rivers their home. You may not come into direct contact with a tribe like the Makiritare (masters of river navigation and the art of hollowing dugout canoes from tree trunks) or the Yanomami (who live in the deepest depths of the jungle), but their presence adds a sort of *Heart of Darkness* edge to your journey—whether you trek through the jungle by Jeep or ply the Orinoco in a thatched river boat.

The Amazonas occupies one-fifth of Venezuela's landmass but has scarcely 85,000 inhabitants and less than 220 miles of roads. Needless to say, the Amazonas region is still little known away from the rivers that afford access to it. For this reason, most tours begin and end in Puerto Ayacucho, a small outpost perched on the banks of the Orinoco only a few miles from the Colombian frontier. From the docks in Puerto Ayacucho, launches cross over to Colombia and return again for less than $5, affording the opportunity to experience Amazonas river trekking in a single day. **Selva Tours** (tel. 048/22–122) arranges one- to four-day river treks as well as overnight stays at jungle lodges near San Juan de Manapiare. **Expediciones Aguas Bravas** (tel. 02/284–7735) offers a thrilling river raft and rapid-shooting trek on the Orinoco, while **Alechiven** (tel. 041/21–18–28) runs river tours from Puerto Ayacucho to San Simón de Cucuy.

Yutajé Camp in the Manapiare Valley, just east of Puerto Ayacucho, appeals to families who prefer bed, bath, cabins, and sit-down meals. Built and run year-round by José Raggi, the camp has a 5,000-foot airstrip and accommodations for about 30. During the day you'll probably find yourself trekking through the jungle in search of howler monkeys, or floating down a river in search of waterfalls and swimmable lagoons. **Alpi Tours** (tel. 02/283–1433, fax 02/285–6067) flies groups from Caracas to Yutajé for about $450 per person; the price includes three days, two nights, and full meals.

Spanish Vocabulary

Words and Phrases

	English	Spanish	Pronunciation
Basics	Yes/no	Sí/no	see/no
	Please	Por favor	pore fah-**vore**
	May I?	¿Me permite?	may pair-**mee**-tay
	Thank you (very much)	(Muchas) gracias	(**moo**-chas) **grah**-see-as
	You're welcome	De nada	day **nah**-dah
	Excuse me	Con permiso	con pair-**mee**-so
	Pardon me	¿Perdón?	pair-**dohn**
	Could you tell me?	¿Podría decirme?	po-**dree**-ah deh-**seer**-meh
	I'm sorry	Lo siento	lo see-**en**-to
	Good morning!	¡Buenos días!	**bway**-nohs **dee**-ahs
	Good afternoon!	¡Buenas tardes!	**bway**-nahs **tar**-dess
	Good evening!	¡Buenas noches!	**bway**-nahs **no**-chess
	Goodbye!	¡Adiós!/¡Hasta luego!	ah-dee-**ohss**/**ah**-stah-**lwe**-go
	Mr./Mrs.	Señor/Señora	sen-**yor**/sen-**yohr**-ah
	Miss	Señorita	sen-yo-**ree**-tah
	Pleased to meet you	Mucho gusto	**moo**-cho **goose**-to
	How are you?	¿Cómo está usted?	**ko**-mo es-**tah** oo-**sted**
	Very well, thank you.	Muy bien, gracias.	**moo**-ee bee-**en**, **grah**-see-as
	And you?	¿Y usted?	ee oos-**ted**
	Hello (on the telephone)	Diga	**dee**-gah
Numbers	1	un, uno	oon, **oo**-no
	2	dos	dos
	3	tres	tress
	4	cuatro	**kwah**-tro
	5	cinco	**sink**-oh
	6	seis	saice
	7	siete	see-**et**-eh
	8	ocho	**o**-cho
	9	nueve	new-**eh**-vey
	10	diez	dee-**es**
	11	once	**ohn**-seh
	12	doce	**doh**-seh
	13	trece	**treh**-seh
	14	catorce	ka-**tohr**-seh
	15	quince	**keen**-seh
	16	dieciséis	dee-**es**-ee-**saice**
	17	diecisiete	dee-**es**-ee-see-**et**-eh
	18	dieciocho	dee-**es**-ee-**o**-cho
	19	diecinueve	**dee-es**-ee-new-**ev**-ah
	20	veinte	**vain**-teh
	21	veinte y uno/veintiuno	**vain**-te-oo-noh
	30	treinta	**train**-tah

32	treinta y dos	train-tay-**dohs**
40	cuarenta	kwah-**ren**-tah
43	cuarenta y tres	kwah-**ren**-tay-**tress**
50	cincuenta	seen-**kwen**-tah
54	cincuenta y cuatro	seen-**kwen**-tay **kwah**-tro
60	sesenta	sess-**en**-tah
65	sesenta y cinco	sess-**en**-tay **seen**-ko
70	setenta	set-**en**-tah
76	setenta y seis	set-**en**-tay **saice**
80	ochenta	oh-**chen**-tah
87	ochenta y siete	oh-**chen**-tay see-**yet**-eh
90	noventa	no-**ven**-tah
98	noventa y ocho	no-**ven**-tah-**o**-choh
100	cien	see-**en**
101	ciento uno	see-en-toh **oo**-noh
200	doscientos	doh-see-**en**-tohss
500	quinientos	keen-**yen**-tohss
700	setecientos	set-eh-see-**en**-tohss
900	novecientos	no-veh-see-**en**-tohss
1,000	mil	meel
2,000	dos mil	dohs meel
1,000,000	un millón	oon meel-**yohn**

Colors	black	negro	**neh**-groh
	blue	azul	ah-**sool**
	brown	café	kah-**feh**
	green	verde	**ver**-deh
	pink	rosa	**ro**-sah
	purple	morado	mo-**rah**-doh
	orange	naranja	na-**rahn**-hah
	red	rojo	**roh**-hoh
	white	blanco	**blahn**-koh
	yellow	amarillo	ah-mah-**ree**-yoh

Days of the Week	Sunday	domingo	doe-**meen**-goh
	Monday	lunes	**loo**-ness
	Tuesday	martes	**mahr**-tess
	Wednesday	miércoles	me-**air**-koh-less
	Thursday	jueves	hoo-**ev**-ess
	Friday	viernes	vee-**air**-ness
	Saturday	sábado	**sah**-bah-doh

Months	January	enero	eh-**neh**-roh
	February	febrero	feh-**breh**-roh
	March	marzo	**mahr**-soh
	April	abril	ah-**breel**
	May	mayo	**my**-oh
	June	junio	**hoo**-nee-oh
	July	julio	**hoo**-lee-yoh
	August	agosto	ah-**ghost**-toh
	September	septiembre	sep-tee-**em**-breh
	October	octubre	oak-**too**-breh
	November	noviembre	no-vee-**em**-breh
	December	diciembre	dee-see-**em**-breh

Useful phrases	Do you speak English?	¿Habla usted inglés?	**ah**-blah oos-**ted** in-**glehs**

I don't speak Spanish	No hablo español	no **ah**-bloh es-pahn-**yol**
I don't understand (you)	No entiendo	no en-tee-**en**-doh
I understand (you)	Entiendo	en-tee-**en**-doh
I don't know	No sé	no seh
I am American/ British	Soy americano (americana)/ inglés(a)	soy ah-meh-ree-**kah**-no (ah-meh-ree-**kah**-nah)/ in-**glehs**/(ah)
What's your name?	¿Cómo se llama usted?	**koh**-mo seh **yah**-mah oos-**ted**?
My name is . . .	Me llamo . . .	may **yah**-moh
What time is it?	¿Qué hora es?	keh **o**-rah es?
It is one, two, three . . . o'clock.	Es la una. . . . Son las dos, tres	es la **oo**-nah/sohn lahs dohs, tress
Yes, please/No, thank you	Sí, por favor/No, gracias	**see** pohr fah-**vor**/no **grah**-see-us
How?	¿Cómo?	**koh**-mo?
When?	¿Cuándo?	**kwahn**-doh?
This/Next week	Esta semana/ la semana que entra	**es**-teh seh-**mah**-nah/lah seh-**mah**-nah keh **en**-trah
This/Next month	Este mes/el próximo mes	**es**-teh mehs/el **proke**-see-mo mehs
This/Next year	Este año/el año que viene	**es**-teh **ahn**-yo/el **ahn**-yo keh vee-**yen**-ay
Yesterday/today/ tomorrow	Ayer/hoy/mañana	ah-**yehr**/oy/mahn-**yah**-nah
This morning/ afternoon	Esta mañana/ tarde	**es**-tah mahn-**yah**-nah/**tar**-deh
Tonight	Esta noche	**es**-tah **no**-cheh
What?	¿Qué?	keh?
What is it?	¿Qué es esto?	keh es **es**-toh
Why?	¿Por qué?	pore **keh**
Who?	¿Quién?	kee-**yen**
Where is . . . ? the train station?	¿Dónde está . . . ? la estación del tren?	**dohn**-deh es-**tah** la es-tah-see-**on** del **train**
the subway station?	la estación del Tren subterráneo?	la es-ta-see-**on** del trehn soob-tair-**ron**-a-o
the bus stop?	la parada del autobus?	la pah-**rah**-dah del oh-toh-**boos**
the post office?	la oficina de correos?	la oh-fee-**see**-nah deh koh-**reh**-os
the bank?	el banco?	el **bahn**-koh
the . . . hotel?	el hotel . . . ?	el oh-**tel**
the store?	la tienda . . . ?	la tee-**en**-dah
the cashier?	la caja?	la **kah**-hah
the . . . museum?	el museo . . . ?	el moo-**seh**-oh
the hospital?	el hospital?	el ohss-pee-**tal**
the elevator?	el ascensor?	el ah-**sen**-sohr
the bathroom?	el baño?	el **bahn**-yoh

Here/there	Aquí/allá	ah-**key**/ah-**yah**
Open/closed	Abierto/cerrado	ah-bee-**er**-toh/ ser-**ah**-doh
Left/right	Izquierda/derecha	iss-key-**er**-dah/ dare-**eh**-chah
Straight ahead	Derecho	dare-**eh**-choh
Is it near/far?	¿Está cerca/lejos?	es-**tah sehr**-kah/ **leh**-hoss
I'd like . . .	Quisiera . . .	kee-see-ehr-ah
a room	un cuarto/una habitación	oon **kwahr**-toh/ **oo**-nah ah-bee-tah-see-**on**
the key	la llave	lah **yah**-veh
a newspaper	un periódico	oon pehr-ee-**oh**-dee-koh
a stamp	un sello de correo	oon **seh**-yo deh koh-**reh**-oh
I'd like to buy . . .	Quisiera comprar . . .	kee-see-**ehr**-ah kohm-**prahr**
cigarette	cigarrillo	ce-ga-**ree**-yoh
matches	cerillos	ser-**ee**-ohs
a dictionary	un diccionario	oon deek-see-oh-**nah**-ree-oh
soap	jabón	hah-**bohn**
sunglasses	gafas de sol	**ga**-fahs deh sohl
suntan lotion	loción bronceadora	loh-see-**ohn** brohn-seh-ah-**do**-rah
a map	un mapa	oon **mah**-pah
a magazine	una revista	**oon**-ah reh-**veess**-tah
paper	papel	pah-**pel**
envelopes	sobres	**so**-brehs
a postcard	una tarjeta postal	**oon**-ah tar-**het**-ah post-**ahl**
How much is it?	¿Cuánto cuesta?	**kwahn**-toh **kwes**-tah
It's expensive/ cheap	Está caro/barato	es-**tah kah**-roh/ bah-**rah**-toh
A little/a lot	Un poquito/ mucho . . .	oon poh-**kee**-toh/ **moo**-choh
More/less	Más/menos	mahss/**men**-ohss
Enough/too much/too little	Suficiente/ demasiado/ muy poco	soo-fee-see-**en**-teh/ deh-mah-see-**ah**-doh/**moo**-ee **poh**-koh
Telephone	Teléfono	tel-**ef**-oh-no
Telegram	Telegrama	teh-leh-**grah**-mah
I am ill	Estoy enfermo(a)	es-**toy en-fehr**-moh(mah)
Please call a doctor	Por favor llame a un medico	pohr fah-**vor ya**-meh ah oon **med**-ee-koh
Help!	¡Auxilio! ¡Ayuda! ¡Socorro!	owk-**see**-lee-oh/ ah-**yoo**-dah/ soh-**kohr**-roh
Fire!	¡Incendio!	en-**sen**-dee-oo

	Caution!/Look out!	¡Cuidado!	kwee-**dah**-doh
On the Road	Avenue	Avenida	ah-ven-**ee**-dah
	Broad, tree-lined boulevard	Bulevar	boo-leh-**var**
	Fertile plain	Vega	**veh**-gah
	Highway	Carretera	car-reh-**ter**-ah
	Mountain pass, port	Puerto	poo-**ehr**-toh
	Street	Calle	**cah**-yeh
	Waterfront promenade	Rambla	**rahm**-blah
	Wharf	Embarcadero	em-bar-cah-**deh**-ro
In Town	Cathedral	Catedral	cah-teh-**dral**
	Church	Templo/Iglesia	**tem**-plo/ee-**glehs**-see-ah
	City hall	Casa de gobierno	kah-sah deh go-bee-**ehr**-no
	Door, gate	Puerta portón	poo-**ehr**-tah por-**ton**
	Entrance/exit	Entrada/salida	en-**trah**-dah/sah-**lee**-dah
	Inn, rustic bar, or restaurant	Taverna	tah-**vehr**-nah
	Main square	Plaza principal	plah-thah prin-see-**pahl**
	Market	Mercado	mer-**kah**-doh
	Neighborhood	Barrio	**bahr**-ree-o
	Traffic circle	Glorieta	glor-ee-**eh**-tah
	Wine cellar, wine bar, or wine shop	Bodega	boh-**deh**-gah
Dining Out	A bottle of ...	Una botella de ...	**oo**-nah bo-**teh**-yah deh
	A cup of ...	Una taza de ...	**oo**-nah **tah**-thah deh
	A glass of ...	Un vaso de ...	oon **vah**-so deh
	Ashtray	Un cenicero	oon sen-ee-**seh**-roh
	Bill/check	La cuenta	lah **kwen**-tah
	Bread	El pan	el pahn
	Breakfast	El desayuno	el deh-sah-**yoon**-oh
	Butter	La mantequilla	lah man-teh-**key**-yah
	Cheers!	¡Salud!	sah-**lood**
	Cocktail	Un aperitivo	oon ah-pehr-ee-**tee**-voh
	Dinner	La cena	lah **seh**-nah
	Dish	Un plato	oon **plah**-toh
	Menu of the day	Menú del día	meh-**noo** del **dee**-ah
	Enjoy!	¡Buen provecho!	bwehn pro-**veh**-cho
	Fixed-price menu	Menú fijo o turistico	meh-**noo fee**-hoh oh too-**ree**-stee-coh
	Fork	El tenedor	el ten-eh-**dor**
	Is the tip included?	¿Está incluida la propina?	es-**tah** in-cloo-**ee**-dah lah pro-**pee**-nah
	Knife	El cuchillo	el koo-**chee**-yo
	Large portion of savory snacks	Raciónes	rah-see-**oh**-nehs
	Lunch	La comida	lah koh-**mee**-dah
	Menu	La carta, el menú	lah **cart**-ah, el meh-**noo**
	Napkin	La servilleta	lah sehr-vee-**yet**-ah

Pepper	La pimienta	lah pee-me-**en**-tah
Please give me	Por favor déme	pore fah-**vor deh**-meh
Salt	La sal	lah sahl
Savory snacks	Tapas	**tah**-pahs
Spoon	Una cuchara	**oo**-nah koo-**chah**-rah
Sugar	El azúcar	el ah-**thu**-kar
Waiter!/Waitress!	¡Por favor Señor/Señorita!	pohr fah-**vor** sen-**yor**/sen-yor-**ee**-tah

Portuguese Vocabulary

Words and Phrases

	English	Portuguese	Pronunciation
Basics	Yes/no	Sim/Não	**see**ing/nown
	Please	Por favor	pohr fah-**vohr**
	May I?	Posso?	**poh**-sso
	Thank you (very much)	(Muito) obrigado	(**moo**yn-too) o-bree **gah**-doh
	You're welcome	De nada	day **nah**-dah
	Excuse me	Com licença	con lee-**ssehn**-ssah
	Pardon me/what did you say?	Desculpe/O que disse?	des-**kool**-peh/ o.k. **dih**-say?
	Could you tell me?	Poderia me dizer?	po-day-**ree**-ah mee dee-**zehrr**?
	I'm sorry	Sinto muito	**seen**-too **moo**yn-too
	Good morning!	Bom dia!	bohn **dee**-ah
	Good afternoon!	Boa tarde!	**boh**-ah **tahr**-dee
	Good evening!	Boa noite!	**boh**-ah **noh**ee-tee
	Goodbye!	Adeus!/Até logo!	ah-**deh**oos/ah-**teh loh**-go
	Mr./Mrs.	Senhor/Senhora	sen-**yor**/sen-**yohr**-ah
	Miss	Senhorita	sen-yo-**ri**-tah
	Pleased to meet you	Muito prazer	**moo**yn-too prah-**zehr**
	How are you?	Como vai?	**koh**-mo **vah**-ee
	Very well, thank you	Muito bem, obrigado	**moo**yn-too **beh**-in o-bree-**gah**-doh
	And you?	E o(a) Senhor(a)?	eh oh sen-**yor**(**yohr**-ah)
	Hello (on the telephone)	Alô	ah-**low**
Numbers	1	um	oom
	2	dois	**doh**ees
	3	tres	**treh**ys
	4	quatro	**kwa**-troh
	5	cinco	**seen**-koh
	6	seis	**seh**ys
	7	sete	**seh**-tee
	8	oito	**ohee**-too
	9	nove	**noh**-vee
	10	dez	**deh**-ees
	11	onze	**ohn**-zee
	12	doze	**doh**-zee
	13	treze	**treh**-zee
	14	quatorze	kwa-**tohr**-zee
	15	quinze	**keen**-zee
	16	dezesseis	deh-zeh-**seh**ys
	17	dezessete	deh-zeh-**seh**-tee
	18	dezoito	deh-**zoh**ee-toh
	19	dezenove	deh-zeh-**noh**-vee
	20	vinte	**veen**-tee
	21	vinte e um	**veen**-tee eh **oom**

30	trinta	**treen**-tah
32	trinta e dois	**treen**-ta eh **doh**ees
40	quarenta	kwa-**rehn**-ta
43	quarenta e tres	kwa-**rehn**-ta e **treh**ys
50	cinquenta	seen-**kwehn**-tah
54	cinquenta e quatro	seen-**kwehn**-tah e **kwa**-troh
60	sessenta	seh-**sehn**-tah
65	sessenta e cinco	seh-**sehn**-tah e **seen**-ko
70	setenta	seh-**tehn**-tah
76	setenta e seis	seh-**tehn**-ta e **seh**ys
80	oitenta	ohee-**tehn**-ta
87	oitenta e sete	ohee-**tehn**-ta e **seh**-tee
90	noventa	noh-**vehn**-ta
98	noventa e oito	noh-**vehn**-ta e **oh**ee-too
100	cem	**seh**-ing
101	cento e um	**sehn**-too e **oom**
200	duzentos	doo-**zehn**-tohss
500	quinhentos	key-**nyehn**-tohss
700	setecentos	seh-teh-**sehn**-tohss
900	novecentos	noh-veh-**sehn**-tohss
1,000	mil	meel
2,000	dois mil	**doh**ees meel
1,000,000	um milhão	oom mee-lee-**ahon**

Colors	black	preto	**preh**-toh
	blue	azul	a-**zool**
	brown	marrom	mah-**hohm**
	green	verde	**vehr**-deh
	pink	rosa	**roh**-zah
	purple	roxo	**roh**-choh
	orange	laranja	lah-**rahn**-jah
	red	vermelho	vehr-**meh**-lyoh
	white	branco	**brahn**-coh
	yellow	amarelo	ah-mah-**reh**-loh

Days of the Week	Sunday	Domingo	doh-**meehn**-goh
	Monday	Segunda-feira	seh-**goon**-dah **fey**-rah
	Tuesday	Terça-feira	**tehr**-sah **fey**-rah
	Wednesday	Quarta-feira	**kwahr**-tah **fey**-rah
	Thursday	Quinta-feira	**keen**-tah **fey**-rah
	Friday	Sexta-feira	**sehss**-tah **fey**-rah
	Saturday	Sábado	**sah**-bah-doh

Months	January	Janeiro	jah-**ney**-roh
	February	Fevereiro	feh-veh-**rey**-roh
	March	Março	**mahr**-soh
	April	Abril	ah-**breel**
	May	Maio	**my**-oh
	June	Junho	gyoo-**nyoh**
	July	Julho	gyoo-**lyoh**
	August	Agosto	ah-**ghost**-toh
	September	Setembro	seh-**tehm**-broh
	October	Outubro	owe-**too**-broh
	November	Novembro	noh-**vehm**-broh
	December	Dezembro	deh-**zehm**-broh

Useful Phrases

Do you speak English?	O Senhor fala inglês?	oh sen-**yor fah**-lah een-**glehs**?
I don't speak Portuguese.	Não falo portugues.	nown **fah**-loh pohr-too -**ghehs**
I don't understand (you)	Não lhe entendo	nown ly**eh** ehn-**tehn**-doh
I understand (you)	Eu entendo	**eh**-oo ehn-**tehn**-doh
I don't know	Não sei	nown say
I am American/ British	Sou americano/ inglês	sow a-meh-ree-**cah**-noh /een-**glehs**
What's your name?	Como se chama?	**koh**-moh seh **shah**-mah
My name is . . .	Meu nome é . .	mehw **noh**-meh eh
What time is it?	Que horas são?	keh **oh**-rahss **sa**-ohn
It is one, two, three . . . o'clock	São uma,duas, tres . . . . horas	**sa**-ohn **oo**mah, **doo**-ahss, **treh**ys **oh**-rahss
Yes, please/No, thank you	Sim por favor/ Não obrigado	seing pohr fah-**vohr**/ nown o-bree-**gah**-doh
How?	Como?	**koh**-moh
When?	Quando?	**kwahn**-doh
This/Next week	Esta/Próxima semana	**ehss**-tah/**proh**-see-mah seh-**mah**-nah
This/Next month	Este/Próximo mes	**ehss**-teh/**proh**-see-moh mehz
This/Next year	Este/Próximo ano	**ehss**-teh/**proh**-see-moh **ah**-noh
Yesterday/today /tomorrow	Ontem/hoje amanhã	**ohn**-tehn/**oh**-jeh ah-mah-**nyan**
This morning/ afternoon	Esta manhã/ tarde	**ehss**-tah mah-**nyan** / **tahr**-deh
Tonight	Hoje a noite	**oh**-jeh ah **noh**ee-tee
What?	O que?	oh **keh**
What is it?	O que é isso?	oh **keh** eh **ee**-soh
Why?	Por que?	pohr-**keh**
Who?	Quem?	**keh**-in
Where is . . . ?	Onde é . . . ?	**ohn**-deh eh
the train station?	a estação de trem?	ah es-tah-**sah**-on deh train
the subway station?	a estação de metrô?	ah es-tah-**sah**-on deh meh-**tro**
the bus stop?	a parada do ônibus?	ah pah-**rah**-dah doh **oh**-nee-boos
the post office?	o correio?	oh coh-**hay**-yoh
the bank?	o banco?	oh **bahn**-koh
the . . . . hotel?	o hotel . . . . . ?	oh oh-**tell**
the cashier?	o caixa?	oh **kahy**-shah
the . . . . museum?	o museo . . . . ?	oh moo-**zeh**-oh
the hospital?	o hospital?	oh ohss-pee-**tal**
the elevator?	o elevador?	oh eh-leh-vah-**dohr**
the bathroom?	o banheiro?	oh bahn-**yey**-roh
. . . . . beach?	a praia de . . . . ?	ah **prah**y-yah deh

Here/there	Aqui/ali	ah-**kee** / ah-**lee**
Open/closed	Aberto/fechado	ah-**behr**-toh/feh-**shah**--doh
Left/right	Esquerda / direita	ehs-**kehr**-dah / dee-**ray**-tah
Straight ahead	Em frente	ehyn **frehn**-teh
Is it near/far?	É perto/ longe?	eh **pehr**-toh/**lohn**-jeh
I'd like to buy...	Gostaria de comprar...	gohs-tah-**ree**-ah deh cohm-**prahr** ....
a bathing suit	um maiô	oom mahy-**owe**
a dictionary	um dicionário	oom dee-seeoh-**nah**--reeoh
a hat	um chapéu	oom shah-**peh**oo
a magazine	uma revista	**oo**mah heh-**vees**-tah
a map	um mapa	oom **mah**-pah
a postcard	cartão postal	kahr-**town** pohs-**tahl**
sunglasses	óulos escuros	ah-koo-loss ehs-**koo**-rohs
suntan lotion	um óleo de bronzear	oom **oh**-lyoh deh brohn-zeh-**ahr**
a ticket	um bilhete	oom bee-ly**eh**-teh
cigarettes	cigarros	see-**gah**-hose
envelopes	envelopes	eyn-veh-**loh**-pehs
matches	fósforos	**fohs**-foh-rohss
paper	papel	pah-**pehl**
sandals	sandália	sahn-**dah**-leeah
soap	sabonete	sah-bow-**neh**-teh
How much is it?	Quanto custa?	**kwahn**-too **koos**-tah
It's expensive/ cheap	Está caro/ barato	ehss-**tah kah**-roh / bah-**rah**-toh
A little/a lot	Um pouco/muito	oom **pohw**-koh/**mooyn**--too
More/less	Mais/menos	**mah**-ees /**meh**-nohss
Enough/too much/too little	Suficiente/ demais/ muito pouco	soo-fee-see-**ehn**-teh/ deh-**mah**-ees / **mooyn**-toh **pohw**-koh
Telephone	Telefone	teh-leh-**foh**-neh
Telegram	Telegrama	teh-leh-**grah**-mah
I am ill.	Estou doente.	ehss-**tow** doh-**ehn**-teh
Please call a doctor.	Por favor chame um médico.	pohr fah-**vohr shah**-meh oom **meh**-dee-koh
Help! Help me!	Socorro! Me ajude!	soh-**koh**-ho mee ah-**jyew**-deh
Fire!	Incêndio!	een-**sehn**-deeoh
Caution!/Look out!/ Be careful!	Cuidado!	kooy-**dah**-doh

On the Road

Avenue	Avenida	ah-veh-**nee**-dah
Highway	Estrada	ehss-**trah**-dah
Port	Porto	**pohr**-toh
Service station	Posto de gasolina	**pohs**-toh deh gah-zoh-**lee**-nah
Street	Rua	**who**-ah

	Toll	Pedagio	peh-**dah**-jyoh
	Waterfront promenade	Beiramar/ orla	behy-rah-**mahrr**/ **ohr**-lah
	Wharf	Cais	**kah**-ees
In Town	Block	Quarteirão	kwahr-tehy-**rah**-on
	Cathedral	Catedral	kah-teh-**drahl**
	Church/temple	Igreja	ee-**greh**-jyah
	City hall	Prefeitura	preh-fehy-**too**-rah
	Door/gate	Porta/portão	**pohr**-tah/porh-**tah**-on
	Entrance/exit	Entrada/ saída	ehn-**trah**-dah/ sah-**ee**-dah
	Market	Mercado/feira	mehr-**kah**-doh/**fey**-rah
	Neighborhood	Bairro	**buy**-ho
	Rustic bar	Lanchonete	lahn-shoh-**neh**-teh
	Shop	Loja	**loh**-jyah
	Square	Praça	**prah**-ssah
Dining Out	A bottle of. . .	Uma garrafa de. .	**oo**mah gah-**hah**-fah deh
	A cup of. . .	Uma xícara de. . .	**oo**mah **shee**-kah-rah deh
	A glass of. . .	Um copo de. . .	oom **koh**-poh deh
	Ashtray	Um cinzeiro	oom seen-**zehy**-roh
	Bill/check	A conta	ah **kohn**-tah
	Bread	Pão	**pah**-on
	Breakfast	Café da manhã	kah-**feh** dah mah-**nyan**
	Butter	A manteiga	ah mahn-**tehy**-gah
	Cheers!	Saúde!	sah-**oo**-deh
	Cocktail	Um aperitivo	oom ah-peh-ree-**tee**-voh
	Dinner	O jantar	oh **jyahn**-tahr
	Dish	Um prato	oom **prah**-toh
	Enjoy!	Bom apetite!	bohm ah-peh-**tee**-teh
	Fork	Garfo	**gahr**-foh
	Fruit	Fruta	**froo**-tah
	Is the tip included?	A gorjeta esta incluída?	ah gohr-**jyeh**-tah ehss-**tah** een-clue-**ee**-dah
	Juice	Um suco	oom **soo**-koh
	Knife	Uma faca	**oo**mah **fah**-kah
	Lunch	O almoço	oh ahl-**moh**-ssoh
	Menu	Menu / cardápio	me-**noo** / kahr-**dah**-peeoh
	Mineral water	Água mineral	**ah**-gooah mee-neh-**rahl**
	Napkin	Guardanapo	gooahr-dah-**nah**-poh
	Nonsmoking	Não fumante	nown foo-**mahn**-teh
	Pepper	Pimenta	pee-**mehn**-tah
	Please give me	Por favor me dê	pohr fah-**vohr** mee **deh**
	Salt	Sal	sahl
	Smoking	Fumante	foo-**mahn**-teh
	Spoon	Uma colher	**oo**mah koh-ly**ehr**
	Sugar	Açúcar	ah-**soo**-kahr
	Waiter!	Garçon!	gahr-**sohn**
	Water	Água	**ah**-gooah
	Wine	Vinho	**vee**-nyoh

Index

WHEREVER YOU TRAVEL, *H*ELP IS NEVER FAR AWAY.

From planning your trip to providing travel assistance along the way, American Express® Travel Service Offices* are always there to help.

ARGENTINA	**ECUADOR**
BOLIVIA	**PARAGUAY**
BRAZIL	**PERU**
CHILE	**URUGUAY**
COLOMBIA	**VENEZUELA**

American Express Travel Service Offices are found in central locations throughout South America.